This volume employs competent scholars to write about noteworthy apologists throughout the history of the church's intellectual engagement with the unbelieving world. Apologists shouldn't defend the faith in a historical vacuum since we ought to stand on the shoulders of giants. This is the most thorough history of its kind that I know of and will repay careful study for the defense of the faith given once and for all to the saints.

> DOUGLAS GROOTHUIS, professor of philosophy
> at Denver Seminary, author of *Christian Apologetics:*
> *A Comprehensive Case for Biblical Faith*

This book contains richly developed surveys of the apologetic arguments and approaches of a wide array of the Christian faith's greatest and most influential advocates over the centuries. Though the book is easily readable, it is extraordinarily informative—like the best apologetic works themselves! I learned so much from reading this book, even with regard to authors whose writings I know. Highly recommended to every Christian and especially to clergy and scholars, for whom the task of Christian apologetics is an urgent call.

> MATTHEW LEVERING, James N. and Mary D. Perry
> Jr. Chair of Theology at Mundelein Seminary

This is a most valuable guide to the history of Christian apologetics throughout the ages. Expert authors provide readable summaries that will be useful both to those being introduced to the subject and to those who wish to review the wide range of options.

> GEORGE MARSDEN, author of *Jonathan Edwards:*
> *A Life* and *C. S. Lewis's* Mere Christianity: *A Biography*

The History of Apologetics is a must-have for the shelves of any serious student of apologetics. With an impressive list of contributors, it provides a comprehensive yet detailed survey of various approaches to the defense of the Christian faith from patristic to modern times. Of particular value is the diversity of approaches represented by the apologists included, with notable entries among the more modern figures including John Henry Newman, G. K. Chesterton, Dorothy L. Sayers, and C. S. Lewis. This provides substantial content for approaches to defending the faith that engage with cultural issues and draw on imagination and the arts as a methodology. The result is a volume that genuinely presents the historical and ecumenical richness of apologetics as a discipline and will serve as a valuable foundation for working apologists.

> HOLLY ORDWAY, Word on Fire Institute Fellow of Faith and
> Culture, author of *Apologetics and the Christian Imagination*

THE HISTORY

of

APOLOGETICS

THE HISTORY

of

APOLOGETICS

ED. BY:

BENJAMIN K. FORREST

JOSHUA D. CHATRAW

ALISTER E. MCGRATH

Editorial Advisory Board:

James K. Dew Jr.

William Edgar

Chad Meister

ZONDERVAN ACADEMIC

The History of Apologetics
Copyright © 2020 by Benjamin K. Forrest, Joshua D. Chatraw, and Alister E. McGrath

Requests for information should be addressed to:
Zondervan, *3900 Sparks Dr. SE, Grand Rapids, Michigan 49546*

ISBN 978-0-310-55941-2 (hardcover)

ISBN 978-0-310-55955-9 (ebook)

Cover design: Claudine Mansour Design
Cover photos: © Alexander Spatari / Getty Images; © vivoo / Shutterstock
Interior design: Kait Lamphere

Printed in the United States of America

20 21 22 23 24 25 26 27 28 29 30 /TRM/ 15 14 13 12 11 10 9 8 7 6 5 4 3

To Graham and Hudson: you were named after men who faithfully proclaimed the glory, grace, and mercy of God. Your mother and I pray that you will do the same with your lives and throughout your lives.

BKF

To Mark Allen, a skilled teacher, a wise leader, a faithful friend

JDC

In memory of Michael Green, an inspirational evangelist, apologist, and friend

AEM

CONTENTS

PART ONE:
Patristic Apologists

PART TWO:
Medieval Apologists

PART SEVEN:
Contemporary Apologists

ACKNOWLEDGMENTS

Ben, Josh, and Alister would first like to thank James K. Dew Jr., William Edgar, and Chad Meister for their early assistance with this book. They quickly saw the potential and agreed to lend their expertise and a collegial hand.

Second, we want to thank the Zondervan team. They are wonderful to work with, and they have encouraged each of us greatly through their partnership. Ryan Pazdur, Josh Kessler, Jesse Hillman, Sarah Gombis, and Stan Gundry—thank you! One individual deserves particular praise and appreciation, and that is Kim Tanner. Her keen attention to detail and her encyclopedic understanding of technological and footnote formatting are second to none.

In addition to these, there are countless others behind the scenes who have assisted in various ways—some of whom are Jack Carson, Jordyn Ginn, and Joshua Erb.

We also must thank our contributing authors, without whom this book would never have been possible! Their years of study and dedication to research has born this text, and we hope that the final project is honoring to their work. Thank you—to each of you—for responding to our initial inquiry and invitation. It has been a pleasure to work with you.

From Ben: I want to thank my wife, Lerisa, for her support through yet another editing project. She is an excellent wife, and the heart of this husband trusts her! Toward the end of this project, she took on more than her fair share, and she did so with grace. I also want to thank Reagan, Hudson, and Graham for their unconditional love. It is a joy to be your dad, and I hope the legacy of this book brings fruit to your own life and ministry as you too faithfully proclaim the mysteries of the gospel (Eph 6:19).

From Josh: It doesn't take long for people who know the Chatraws to realize that my wife, Tracy, is the pillar of our household. I write books. She keeps us on the right story. Tracy, I can't imagine my life without you. I'll be forever grateful and always in love with you. Thank you to my kids, Addison and Hudson. Your playfulness and curiosity inspire me! Finally, I'm grateful for the many friends who have encouraged me to keep writing and tell me when my ideas stink and when (occasionally) they think I'm on to something. I've dedicated this book to Mark Allen because he has been this kind of friend, sharing the journey with me, rejoicing when I rejoice and weeping when I weep.

From Alister: With thanks to the witness and ministry of the great apologists of the past and present, who have inspired this volume and its authors.

Lastly, we want to thank our Lord and Savior, who has called us and equipped us to give a reason for the joy we have in Christ. We are blessed and honored by this calling of making him known among the nations.

CONTRIBUTOR BIOS

BRUCE RILEY ASHFORD (PhD, Southeastern Baptist Theological Seminary) is Provost and Professor of Theology & Culture at Southeastern Baptist Theological Seminary. He is the author or coauthor of *Letters to an American Christian* (B&H, 2018), *One Nation Under God: A Christian Hope for American Politics* (B&H, 2015), and *Every Square Inch: An Introduction to Cultural Engagement for Christians* (Lexham, 2015). He is a Senior Fellow in Public Theology at the Kirby Laing Institute for Christian Ethics (Cambridge, UK), a participant in colloquia for the Institute on Religion & Public Life (New York, NY), and a Research Fellow at the Ethics and Religious Liberty Commission (Nashville, TN).

DAVID BAGGETT (PhD, Wayne State University) is Professor of Philosophy and Apologetics at Houston Baptist University. He's authored or edited over a dozen books, including *Good God: The Theistic Foundations of Morality* (Oxford, 2011) and *The Morals of the Story: Good News about a Good God* (IVP Academic, 2018), which he coauthored with his wife.

BRYAN BAISE (PhD, Southern Baptist Theological Seminary) is Assistant Professor of Philosophy and Apologetics at Boyce College.

W. DAVID BECK (PhD, Boston University) is Professor of Philosophy at Liberty University. His research interests include philosophy of religion, and he has published numerous items specifically on the existence of God and the cosmological argument.

FRANCIS J. BECKWITH (PhD, Fordham University) is Professor of Philosophy and Church-State Studies at Baylor University. Among his over one dozen books are *Never Doubt Thomas: The Catholic Aquinas as Evangelical and Protestant* (Baylor University Press, 2019) and *Taking Rites Seriously: Law, Politics, & The Reasonableness of Faith* (Cambridge University Press, 2015), winner of the

American Academy of Religion's 2016 Book Award for Excellence in the Study of Religion in the category of Constructive-Reflective Studies.

JAMES BEILBY (PhD, Marquette University) is Professor of Biblical and Theological Studies at Bethel University. In his research he has explored the intersection of theology, philosophy, and apologetics.

BYARD BENNETT (PhD, University of Toronto) is Professor Emeritus of Historical and Philosophical Theology at Grand Rapids Theological Seminary/ Cornerstone University. His publications have focused on Greek Christian philosophical texts of the patristic, Byzantine, and post-Byzantine periods.

GERALD BRAY (DLitt, University of Paris-Sorbonne) is Research Professor of Divinity at Beeson Divinity School and Director of Research for the Latimer Trust, London. He edited *Galatians, Ephesians*, the first volume of the Reformation Commentary on Scripture (IVP). His systematic theology *God is Love* was released by Crossway (2012), and his historical theology *God has Spoken* was published in 2014.

RONNIE P. CAMPBELL JR. (PhD, Liberty University) is Associate Professor of Theology at Liberty University. His publications include *Natural Theology: Five Views* (Baker Academic, forthcoming) and *Worldviews and the Problem of Evil* (Lexham, 2019).

TREVOR CASTOR (PhD, Australian College of Theology) is Professor of Muslim and Intercultural Studies at Columbia International University. Before his appointment at CIU, he was a missionary in South Asia working with Muslim populations.

JOSHUA D. CHATRAW (PhD, Southeastern Baptist Theological Seminary) serves as the Theologian-in-Residence at Holy Trinity Anglican Church and the Executive Director for the Center for Public Christianity, Raleigh, North Carolina. His recent books include *Apologetics at the Cross* (w/ Mark Allen, Zondervan, 2018), *Cultural Engagement* (w/ Karen Swallow Prior, Zondervan, 2019), and *Telling a Better Story* (Zondervan, 2020).

STEVEN B. COWAN (PhD, University of Arkansas) is Professor of Philosophy and Religion at Lincoln Memorial University. He has authored or edited several books, including *Five Views on Apologetics* (Zondervan, 2000), *The Love of Wisdom: A Christian Introduction to Philosophy* (w/ James Spiegel, B&H, 2009), and *Idealism and Christian Philosophy* (w/ James Spiegel, Bloomsbury, 2016).

MICHAEL R. DEVITO (MA, Houston Baptist University; MSc, University of Edinburgh) is pursuing doctoral work in the UK in philosophy and theology. His research interests are the philosophy of religion, epistemology, and apologetics. Prior to his academic career, DeVito spent nine seasons in the NFL with the New York Jets and the Kansas City Chiefs.

JAMES K. DEW JR. (PhD, Southeastern Baptist Theological Seminary; PhD, University of Birmingham) is President of New Orleans Baptist Theological Seminary. His publications include *Natural Theology: Five Views* (Baker Academic, forthcoming), *Inroduction to Philosophy* (Baker Academic, 2019), *God and the Problem of Evil: Five Views* (IVP, 2017), *God and Evil* (IVP, 2013).

WILLIAM EDGAR (ThD, University of Geneva) is Professor of Apologetics at Westminster Theological Seminary. He came to faith in Christ through the ministry of Francis Schaeffer while at L'Abri in Switzerland. He is also Associate Professor at the Faculté Jean Calvin.

SHAWN FLOYD (PhD, St. Louis University) is Professor of Philosophy at Malone University in Canton, Ohio. His work has been published in various philosophical and ethics journals. His research and teaching interests include Thomas Aquinas, Aristotle, the Stoics, Dante, and Nietzsche. He is currently writing a book on the subject of love and obligation.

D. G. HART (PhD, Johns Hopkins) has served as Director of the Institute for the Study of American Evangelicals at Wheaton College and Academic Dean and Professor of Church History at Westminster Seminary in California. He is currently Visiting Professor of History at Hillsdale College. He is author of *Defending the Faith: J. Gresham Machen and the Crisis of Conservative Protestantism in Modern America* (P&R, 2003).

STEVEN A. HEIN (PhD, St. Louis University) taught Theology and Apologetics at Concordia University, Chicago, and at the International Institute for Apologetics and Human Rights, Strasbourg, France. He has also taught Theology and Christian Apologetics at Patrick Henry College and Colorado Christian University. He currently serves on the DMin faculty at the Institute of Lutheran Theology and as Director of the Christian Institute for Christian Studies, where he teaches advanced pastoral theological education in West Africa. He has written many scholarly articles and is author of *Christian Life: Cross or Glory?* (NRP, 2015). His doctoral research focused on the apologetic mission of Edward John Carnell.

DANIEL J. JANOSIK (PhD, London School of Theology) is Adjunct Professor of Apologetics and Intercultural Studies at Columbia International University. His dissertation research was titled *John of Damascus: First Apologist to the Muslims* (Pickwick, 2018).

KRISH KANDIAH (PhD, Kings College, London) is the Founding Director of Home for Good, a young charity seeking to make a real difference in the lives of vulnerable children. Together with his wife, Miriam, he coauthored a catalytic book *Home for Good*, which blends the story of God's adoption of us and how to tackle the most pressing social challenges of our times. Krish has authored ten books. His dissertation was titled *Toward a Theology of Evangelism for Late-Modern Cultures: A Critical Dialogue with Lesslie Newbigin's Doctrine of Revelation*. He holds degrees in Chemistry, Missiology, and Theology, and faculty positions at Regent College, Vancouver, and Regents Park College, Oxford University.

CHRISTIAN KETTERING (PhD candidate, North-West University) is an instructor of ethics at Liberty University. His research has focused on Kierkegaard's ethical theology. He has also contributed multiple book reviews for the Kierkegaard Research Series by Ashgate.

MATTHEW D. KIRKPATRICK (DPhil, University of Oxford) is Tutor in Ethics and Doctrine at Wycliffe Hall. His research has focused on analyzing the thoughts of Søren Kierkegaard and Dietrich Bonhoeffer.

BRYAN M. LITFIN (PhD, University of Virginia) is Professor of Theology at Moody Bible Institute in Chicago. He is author of *After Acts: Exploring the Lives and Legends of the Apostles* (Moody, 2015), *Early Christian Martyr Stories: An Evangelical Introduction* (Baker, 2014), and *Getting to Know the Church Fathers* (Brazos, 2007).

R. KEITH LOFTIN (PhD, University of Aberdeen) is Associate Professor of Philosophy and Humanities, as well as Associate Dean at Scarborough College. His publications include *Christian Physicalism? Philosophical Theological Criticisms* (w/ Joshua R. Farris, Lexington Press, 2017) and *Stand Firm: Apologetics and the Brilliance of the Gospel* (w/ Paul M. Gould and Travis Dickinson, B&H, 2018).

EDWARD N. MARTIN (PhD, Purdue University) is Professor of Philosophy and Department Co-Chair at Liberty University.

MICHAEL J. MCCLYMOND (PhD, University of Chicago) is Professor of Modern Christianity at Saint Louis University. His book *Encounters with God: An Approach to the Theology of Jonathan Edwards* (Oxford University Press, 1998) received the 1999 Brewer Prize from the American Society of Church History as the best first book in the history of Christianity. His book cowritten with Gerald R. McDermott is *The Theology of Jonathan Edwards* (Oxford University Press, 2012). This work received the Book of the Year Award in Theology/Ethics from *Christianity Today*.

ALISTER E. MCGRATH (DPhil, DD, DLitt, University of Oxford) is the Andreas Idreos Professor of Science and Religion, University of Oxford; Director, Ian Ramsey Centre for Science and Religion; and Gresham Professor of Divinity.

TYLER DALTON MCNABB (PhD, University of Glasgow) is a Postdoctoral Fellow at the University of Macau. His research interests are in the area of Reformed epistemology, and he has published academic articles in *Religious Studies*, *The Heythrop Journal*, *International Journal of Philosophy and Theology*, and *Philosophia Christi*.

DAVID MCNAUGHTON (BPhil, University of Oxford) is retired and lives in Edinburgh. He is an Emeritus Professor of both Florida State and Keele Universities. He has written extensively on moral philosophy and is the editor of *Joseph Butler: Fifteen Sermons and Other Writings on Ethics* (Oxford, 2017) and is currently editing a companion volume of Butler's *Analogy of Religion* (Oxford, forthcoming).

CHAD MEISTER (PhD, Marquette University) is Professor of Philosophy and Theology at Bethel College. His publications include *Contemporary Philosophical Theology* (Routledge), *Christian Thought: A Historical Introduction* (Routledge), and *The Cambridge Companion to Christian Philosophical Theology* (Cambridge University Press). He is also general coeditor of the book series *Cambridge Studies in Religion, Philosophy, and Society*.

JONATHAN MORGAN (PhD, Marquette University) is Associate Professor of Theology at Indiana Wesleyan University and an ordained minister in the Wesleyan Church. His research is in historical theology with publications focusing on early Christian soteriology and biblical interpretation.

MATTHEW NG (MD, University of Virginia; PhD ABD Southeastern Baptist Theological Seminary) is a primary care physician pursuing doctoral studies in theology, ethics, and culture. His current research focuses on Charles Taylor, missional neo-Calvinism, and the political thought of Richard John Neuhaus.

MICHAEL O. OBANLA (PhD, Liberty University) is an Instructor of Ethics and Interdisciplinary Studies at Liberty University. His research has focused on A. E. Taylor's moral philosophy.

K. SCOTT OLIPHINT (PhD, Westminister Theological Seminary) is Professor of Apologetics and Systematic Theology at Westminster Theological Seminary. His research interests include Cornelius Van Til's apologetics, the relationship between Christian apologetics and philosophy, and the doctrine of God.

AMY ORR-EWING (DPhil, University of Oxford) is Director of The Oxford Centre for Christian Apologetics and Senior Vice President of RZIM. Her dissertation focused on the apologetics of Dorothy Sayers, and she has published several books on Christian apologetics, including *Why Trust the Bible?* She travels widely and lectures and speaks around the world.

CRAIG A. PARTON (MA, Simon Greenleaf School of Law, JD, University of California, Hastings College of the Law) is a Partner at Price, Postel, & Parma LLP in Santa Barbara, California, where he serves as Chairman of the Litigation Department. He is also the United States Director of the International Academy of Apologetics and Human Rights, which is based in Strasbourg, France. He teaches in the areas of theology, law, and human rights for two weeks each summer in Strasbourg at the annual session of this seminar. While at the Simon Greenleaf School of Law, he studied apologetics under John Warwick

Montgomery. He is the author of three books on apologetics and has contributed to a number of anthologies devoted to the subject.

GREG PETERS (PhD, University of St. Michael's College, Toronto) is Professor of Medieval and Spiritual Theology in the Torrey Honors Institute at Biola University and the Servants of Christ Research Professor of Monastic Studies and Ascetical Theology at Nashotah House Theological Seminary. He is author of *The Monkhood of All Believers: The Monastic Foundation of Christian Spirituality* (Baker, 2018), *The Story of Monasticism: Retrieving an Ancient Tradition for Contemporary Spirituality* (Baker, 2015), *Reforming the Monastery: Protestant Theologies of the Religious Life* (Cascade, 2014), and *Peter of Damascus: Byzantine Monk and Spiritual Theologian* (Pontifical Institute of Mediaeval Studies, 2011).

STEPHEN O. PRESLEY (PhD, University of St. Andrews) is Associate Professor of Church History and Director of Research Doctoral Studies at Southwestern Seminary. He is also the Director of the Southwestern Center for Early Christian Studies and the author of *The Intertextual Reception of Genesis 1–3 in Irenaeus of Lyons* (Brill, 2015), as well as many other articles and essays in early Christian studies.

KIM RIDDLEBARGER (PhD, Fuller Theological Seminary) is Senior Pastor of Christ Reformed Church in Anaheim, California, and author of *The Lion of Princeton: B.B. Warfield as Apologist and Theologian* (Lexham, 2015).

BENJAMIN C. F. SHAW (PhD, Liberty University) is a researcher and apologist. His doctoral work focused on the minimal facts argument.

W. BRIAN SHELTON (PhD, Saint Louis University) is Adjunct Professor of Theology at Asbury University. He has published principally on early Christianity in the West, including *Martyrdom from Exegesis in Hippolytus: An Early Church Presbyter's Commentary on Daniel* (Paternoster, 2008) and "Irenaeus" in *Shapers of Christian Orthodoxy* (IVP, 2010).

CORNELIU C. SIMUȚ (PhD, Aberdeen, the UK; ThD, University of Tilburg, the Netherlands; Dr Habil, the Reformed Theological University of Debrecen, Hungary; DD, University of Pretoria, South Africa) is Professor of Historical and Systematic Theology at Emanuel University of Oradea, Romania, and Senior Vice-Chancellor Postdoctoral Research Fellow, University of Pretoria, South Africa, as well as a Research Supervisor at Union School of Theology, formerly Wales Evangelical School of Theology, the United Kingdom. He is also the Editor-in-Chief of *Perichoresis*, the theological journal of Emanuel University, published by Emanuel University Press in conjunction with De Gruyter Open and occasionally the Refo500 Foundation.

EDWARD L. SMITHER (PhD, University of Wales-Trinity St. David; PhD, University of Pretoria) is Dean and Professor of Intercultural Studies at Columbia

International University and the author of *Augustine as Mentor: A Model for Preparing Spiritual Leaders, Brazilian Evangelical Missions in the Arab World* and translator of François Decret's *Early Christianity in North Africa.*

JORDAN L. STEFFANIAK (PhD ABD, Southeastern Baptist Theological Seminary) is a doctoral student studying theology and philosophy.

CHARLES TALIAFERRO (PhD, Brown University) is Professor of Philosophy and Department Chair at St. Olaf College. He is the author, coauthor, or editor of over twenty books.

A. CHADWICK THORNHILL (PhD, Liberty University) is Associate Professor of Apologetics and Biblical Studies and Director of Graduate Biblical and Theological Studies Programs at the John W. Rawlings School of Divinity at Liberty University. His publications include *The Chosen People* (IVP, 2015), *Greek for Everyone* (Baker, 2016), and *Divine Impassibility* (IVP, 2019).

SEAN A. TURCHIN (PhD, University of Edinburgh) is Associate Professor of Philosophy at Liberty University and Department Chair in the College of Arts and Sciences. His research focuses on the affinity between the thoughts of Karl Barth and Søren Kierkegaard. He has published several articles on Barth and Kierkegaard and has recently contributed to several volumes on Kierkegaard's thought published by Ashgate.

JO VITALE (DPhil, University of Oxford) is Dean of Studies at the Zacharias Institute and an itinerant speaker for Ravi Zacharias International Ministries. Her research interests include questions on biblical reliability, challenges to the character of God (sexism, war, slavery, and judgment in the Bible), and the uniqueness of Jesus.

VINCE VITALE (DPhil, University of Oxford) is a speaker and author who serves as Ravi Zacharias International Ministries's Regional Director for the Americas and Director of the Zacharias Institute. His research on the problem of evil will be published as *Non-Identity Theodicy* (Oxford University Press, forthcoming). He has also published several books in Christian apologetics, including *Why Suffering?* (w/ Ravi Zacharias, FaithWords, 2014) and *Jesus Among Secular Gods* (w/ Ravi Zacharias, FaithWords, 2017).

ROBERT A. WEATHERS (PhD, Southwestern Baptist Theological Seminary) is Assistant Professor of Philosophy and Instructional Mentor at Liberty University. He is also senior Pastor of First Baptist, Shallotte, North Carolina.

GREG WELTY (DPhil, University of Oxford) is Professor of Philosophy at Southeastern Baptist Theological Seminary and Program Coordinator for the MA in Apologetics and Christian Philosophy. He received his doctorate under Richard Swinburne. He is the author of *Why Is There Evil in the World* (Christian Focus, 2018), coeditor of *Calvinism & Molinism: A Conversation*

(Wipf & Stock, 2019), and coeditor of the apologetics series *The Big Ten* (Christian Focus).

RALPH C. WOOD (PhD, University of Chicago) is University Professor of Theology and Literature at Baylor University. He is an editorial board member for *VII: An Anglo-American Literary Review*, which is devoted to the works of G. K. Chesterton, C. S. Lewis, J. R. R. Tolkien, George MacDonald, Dorothy Sayers, Owen Barfield, and Charles Williams.

INTRODUCTION

Culture is never stagnant, changing and adapting as ideas evolve, and this means that all apologetics is contextual. Apologetics is a response to culture and its *critiques of* or *questions for* Christianity and is always done in conversation with culture and the people that define it. Even the biblical admonition from Peter to be ever ready to give an answer for the hope that we have (1 Pet 3:15) was contextually laden.[1] Like Peter, the great apologists of the Christian church engage the conversations around them and within their cultures. Some of these conversations may address antagonistic objections to Christianity, while others speak to more passive concerns raised within the body of Christ as believers seek to faithfully carry out their calling in culture. Between these poles of the apologetic endeavor, we witness a myriad of apologetic interactions—faithful men and women engaging their culture with the truth claims of the gospel. This reality sets the context for how we, as the editors of the volume you are reading, have approached this "retelling" of the history of apologetics.

CHOOSING THE APOLOGISTS

Over the course of the next forty-four chapters, we present a snapshot of Christianity's most influential apologists. In putting together the list of apologists to be covered, we sought to be comprehensive and broad, while giving each era a set of voices to tell their unique portion of the story. In the selection process, the three editors of this project leaned heavily on our editorial advisory board (James K. Dew Jr., William Edgar, and Chad Meister), who provided excellent advice

---

1. See Joshua D. Chatraw and Mark D. Allen, *Apologetics at the Cross: An Introduction for Christian Witness* (Grand Rapids, MI: Zondervan, 2018), 15–24.

for how to make this list a useful summary of apologetic history. Certainly, we could have included many more apologists, but at some point, the limitations of printing a book become a reality and cuts have to be made. For instance, we have chosen to focus predominantly on Western apologists, while still trying to recognize those who have been most influential from the eastern tradition. If we have failed in giving due recognition to a particular segment of history, we hope that this will spur additional research into the wonderful legacy we have in the history of apologetics.

EDITORIAL METHODS FOR THE HISTORY OF APOLOGETICS

Organizing an edited volume with contributions from authors of varied backgrounds and skill sets has been incredibly encouraging and enjoyable. Yet we knew going into this project that each author would bring their own voice and style to their contribution, and for the sake of future readers, we wanted the result to be useful and usable. Thus, while allowing for authorial voice, we also introduced a loose, editorial structure through the book so that readers can seamlessly move from one chapter to the next without a jarring reorientation in style. We hope this editorial decision makes the book immanently more readable, but it is also rooted in our belief that apologetics is *always* contextual. The structure of each chapter highlights this by presenting the history of apologetics through a focus on the biographical and the methodological. Each chapter revolves around four or five different headings, starting with a short biographical introduction, which provides the context for that apologist's engagement with his or her culture. From there, the author traces the key theological contours and contexts of that time and place. This theological context frames the *Sitz im Leben* from which each apologetic approach flows. The "Apologetic Response" section offers contextual analysis, as the author explores how the apologist responded to the cultural questions of their day. Following this exploration, the author moves from response to method by examining how the apologist methodized the philosophical, theological, biblical, and practical tasks of doing apologetics. And finally, each chapter concludes with reflections on the contributions of this apologist to the field as a whole.

READING WELL

Our aim in this volume is to retell the history of apologetics by connecting the practice of apologetics to the people who practiced it and their unique theological and cultural contexts. It is our hope that readers will better understand how apologetics has been done in the past, that they might strengthen their own "feeble arms and weak knees" (Heb 12:12) for the apologetic tasks we face today. The charge to each apologist is akin to the prophecy given to Malachi (1:1), weighty because it is truth from the Lord and weighty because of the character of the message, which contains both grace and condemnation. Our hope is that in reading these snapshots of past apologists you will be encouraged (cf. Heb 11) to run with endurance the race that is set before you (Heb 12:1)—just as these faithful men and women ran the race set before them.

Soli Deo Gloria!

Benjamin K. Forrest
Joshua D. Chatraw
Alister E. McGrath

Part One

PATRISTIC APOLOGISTS

The patristic period is usually taken as the formative phase of the early church between the final works of the New Testament and the Council of Chalcedon (451). This was a remarkably creative and important stage in the consolidation of Christianity in the Mediterranean world, as leading Christian thinkers set out to consolidate the core ideas of their faith, as set out in the New Testament, leading to the formulation of definitive statements about the identity and significance of Jesus Christ and the distinctively Christian understanding of God. The period saw an emerging consensus on the sources of theology, particularly through the fixing of the canon of Scripture.

Yet the early church faced other challenges during this period, most notably the need to respond to growing hostility toward Christianity on the part of other religious and philosophical movements in the Greco-Roman world. While theological clarification was of major importance in protecting the church's identity, the early Christian communities also faced challenges from Judaism and traditional Roman religion, whose members came to regard Christianity as a threat. **Justin Martyr** wrote a particularly significant apologetic work responding to Jewish criticisms of Christianity. His *Dialogue with Trypho* argued that Christianity was the fulfillment of Jewish life and thought. Christianity was the true philosophy and would displace its pagan rivals.

The rise of Gnosticism in the second century posed a particularly significant challenge to Christianity. Although our knowledge of the origins and distinct ideas of this movement is not as comprehensive as we might hope, it clearly posed a significant threat to the church by proposing alternative ideas of salvation that were verbally similar to those of the gospel or by interpreting the New Testament in decidedly non-Christian ways. **Irenaeus of Lyons** was one of the most effective critics of Gnosticism. His apologetic strategy incorporated a powerful critique of Gnosticism's internal coherence and historic roots, along with a lucid account of core Christian beliefs that emphasized their interconnectedness and superiority over those of their pagan rivals.

As Rome's political and military power began to decline in the late second century, many blamed the rise of Christianity for weakening the hold of traditional Roman religion. Christians came to be referred to as "atheists," in that they did not conform to the polytheism of Roman civil religion. Several late second-century Christian apologists responded to this criticism, most notably **Athenagoras of Athens**, who argued that Christian monotheism was to be preferred to pagan polytheism. Athenagoras countered the criticism that Christianity subverted imperial cultural norms by showing that pagan poets and philosophers were themselves monotheists, whether implicitly or explicitly. This concern about Christianity causing the decline of traditional Roman religion, on which the stability of the Roman Empire depended, peaked in the Latin west around 248, marking the one thousandth anniversary of the founding of Rome.

By this time, a significant apologetic tradition had been established within the western Latin-speaking church. One of the most important of the early Latin apologists was **Tertullian of Carthage**, a third-century orator generally thought to have been based in the great Roman North-African city of Carthage. Tertullian debated the fundamental truths of faith with a number of significant cultural groups, including secular philosophy, Gnosticism, and Judaism.

The Greek-speaking eastern church also developed a distinct apologetic approach, particularly in the great city of Alexandria. One of the most important early contributions to this approach came from the third-century theologian **Origen**, who responded to the philosopher Celsus's charge that Christianity was fundamentally irrational. Yet Celsus's criticism of Christianity went further than this. Christianity was a religious innovation that was leading people to abandon their traditional religion. Origen's rebuttal of Celsus, usually known by its Latin title *Contra Celsum*, is widely agreed to be one of the most important works of early Christian apologetics, showing that a Christian philosopher was able to hold his own against an educated pagan critic. This work represents a detailed rebuttal of Celsus's philosophical, moral, and religious criticisms of Christianity, demonstrating a remarkable confidence in the intellectual and moral credentials of the gospel. Although Origen perhaps leans on Plato too much for comfort at points, his response to Celsus opened the way to others developing similar apologetic approaches.

Origen's approach was further developed in the fourth century by other Alexandrian writers, as well as writers based in the region of Cappadocia, such as Gregory of Nyssa. **Athanasius of Alexandria**, one of the most important apologists of the fourth century, placed considerable emphasis on the internal coherency and consistency of the Christian faith, pointing out how Arius's reduced Christology could easily be shown to be incoherent. More importantly, Athanasius's treatises *De Incarnatione* and *Contra Gentes* (which many consider to be a "double treatise") include significant apologetic elements—such as an appeal to history—that could function as the basis of a defense of the Christian faith to either a Jewish or Greco-Roman audience.

Although the conversion of Constantine in or around 312 led to Christianity becoming culturally acceptable and eventually politically dominant in the second half of the fourth century, later patristic theologians rightly saw that cultural acceptability did not necessarily secure rational acceptance of the gospel. This is evident in the writings of the greatest apologist of the Latin west, **Augustine of Hippo**, whose conversion to Christianity in August 386 is widely regarded as a landmark in the development of western Christianity.

Augustine's contribution to apologetics was significant at several levels, including the philosophical defense of the rationality of the Christian faith, the appeal to divine illumination in securing human knowledge, and the importance of the subjective world of memory and feeling in matters of faith. Augustine's substantial theological output laid a robust conceptual foundation for apologetics, as he recognized the role of divine grace and illumination in conversion while at the same time highlighting the importance of human agency in the apologetic task.

Perhaps most importantly, Augustine recognized the vulnerability of the western Roman Empire and strategized about how Christianity could engage a possible postimperial scenario. It was a wise move. During the second half of the fifth century, the central Roman state collapsed. The scene was set for the rise of Christianity in western Europe, with Augustine widely recognized as one of the most important resources for Christianity's theological and apologetic foundations.

JUSTIN MARTYR

Prophetic Revelation as the
True Philosophy

GERALD BRAY

Justin Martyr (ca. 100–164/7) is the earliest
postbiblical writer to have left us writings
in defense of Christianity. He is particularly
interesting in that he addressed both Jews
and gentiles, which allows us to see how one early Christian approached these
very different audiences. He paid for his beliefs with his life and remains an
inspiration to all who would follow Jesus and preach his gospel to a hostile and
uncomprehending world.

HISTORICAL BACKGROUND

Justin was born sometime around AD 100 in the city of Flavia Neapolis, which
Emperor Vespasian had founded in AD 72 near the site of ancient Shechem in
Samaria. He described both his father, Priscus, and his grandfather Bacchius
as "natives" of the city, but it seems probable that his grandfather emigrated
there from elsewhere, possibly being one of the original inhabitants.[1] The fact
that Justin later addressed both the emperor and the Roman senate suggests
that he was a Roman citizen, though he does not tell us this in his writings.
He had considerable knowledge, not only of Jews but also of Samaritans, who
were the largest population group in his homeland. He even said that Simon
Magus, who was of Samaritan origin, belonged to the same nation as he did,
though what he meant by "nation" is not clear.[2] Justin was certainly educated in
Greek, but he may have known Aramaic and Latin as well. In his adult years he
moved from his home to Rome, perhaps to escape the Jewish revolt under Bar
Kokhba, and it was on that journey that he became a Christian.[3] In Rome he
established a school that attracted some brilliant pupils, including the Syrian,

---

1. Justin Martyr, *First Apology*, 1.
2. Justin Martyr, *Second Apology*, 15.
3. Simon bar Kokhba led a revolt of Palestinian Jews against the Romans and ruled Palestine from
AD 132–135 before he was crushed.

Tatian.[4] Justin was in the capital when the heretic Marcion was teaching there, but although Justin mentions him in passing, Marcion's errors were not the focus of his writing.

In his youth Justin had received a Greek education, which awakened in him a desire to discover the truth that the philosophers purported to make the focal point of their lives. In his later years he realized that philosophy was a noble endeavor that had gone wrong, as he eventually explained in his *Dialogue with Trypho*:

> Philosophy is, in fact, the greatest possession, and most honorable before God, to whom it leads us and alone commends us; and these are truly holy men who have bestowed attention on philosophy. What philosophy is, however, and the reason why it has been sent down to men, have escaped the observation of most; for there would be neither Platonists, nor Stoics, nor Peripatetics, nor Theoretics, nor Pythagoreans, this knowledge being one. I wish to tell you why it has become many-headed.[5]

Justin believed that the great philosophers had gone in search of the truth but had discovered only elements of it that they expressed in different ways. Their followers had merely repeated their words and turned them into new dogmas that they came to regard as mutually incompatible. In his own search for enlightenment, Justin had begun with the Stoics, but when he discovered that Stoicism made no claim to know the divine, he abandoned them. Next he turned to the Peripatetics, only to discover that they charged for sharing their "wisdom," which, in Justin's mind, discredited them completely. His third stop was with the Pythagoreans, who demanded a thorough knowledge of music, astronomy, and geometry since, according to them, it was only by pursuing those "otherworldly" disciplines that the soul could be prepared for contemplation. Justin abandoned them in despair, turning finally to the Platonists, who were much more satisfactory. As he explained:

> I spent as much of my time as possible with [a Platonist] who had lately settled in our city. . . . and I progressed, and made the greatest improvements daily. And the perception of immaterial things quite overpowered me, and the contemplation of ideas furnished my mind with wings, so that in a little while I supposed that I had become wise; and such was my

---

4. Tatian is best known for his *Diatessaron*, an attempt to harmonize the four gospels into one. He was a proponent of extreme asceticism, which most other Christians rejected.

5. Justin Martyr, *Dialogue with Trypho*, 2.

stupidity, I expected immediately to look upon God, for this is the end of Plato's philosophy.[6]

As Justin discovered, not all the philosophical schools were of equal worth, but the Platonists were closest to what he desired—and to what he eventually found in Christianity. Justin became a Christian after a chance encounter with an old man who persuaded him that the Hebrew prophets were better guides to the truth than any philosopher. It was from that perspective that he would later view the classical Greek tradition.[7] It was therefore important for him to argue that of all the pagans, Plato was nearest to the truth, even though he had not attained it.[8]

Justin lived fairly happily in Rome under Antoninus Pius (138–161), but under his successor, Marcus Aurelius (161–180), Justin was arrested, put on trial, and executed. The date of his martyrdom is not certain, but it was probably between 164 and 167. He has left us three significant works, two *Apologies* and a *Dialogue* with the Jewish rabbi, Trypho.[9] According to Justin, Trypho had based himself at Corinth after the Jewish revolt in Palestine, but the *Dialogue* is set some years before in Ephesus, shortly after Justin's conversion to Christianity. It is Justin's longest work by far, about four times the length of the *First Apology*.

APOLOGETIC WORKS

The dates and order of Justin's works are uncertain, but most people assume that the *First Apology* is the oldest of them and that it was written sometime around 145–155. It may have been followed a few years later by the *Second Apology* and then by the *Dialogue*, which would then be an account of an incident that had occurred twenty to thirty years earlier. The *Second Apology*, which is the shortest of Justin's works, is usually presented as an appendix to the *First*, but as it is considerably more specific in intention and less sophisticated in content, this appended location seems doubtful. In addition to scope and style as problematic reasons for thinking the *Second Apology* was originally a portion of the first, this second work contains virtually no references to the Bible, and its description of the fall owes nothing to the Genesis account.[10] There is also no

---

6. Ibid.

7. Ibid., 3.

8. In his *Second Apology*, 13, Justin wrote, "I confess that I both boast and with all my strength strive to be found a Christian; not because the teachings of Plato are different from those of Christ, but because they are not in all respects similar. . . . Whatever things were rightly said among all men, are the property of us Christians."

9. Trypho has been identified by some as Tarphon, supposedly one of the leading rabbis of his time; but most modern Jewish scholars believe Justin invented him.

10. Martyr, *Second Apology*, 5. Justin writes that the angels "were captivated by love of women, and begot children who are those called demons . . . afterward [they] subdued the human race to themselves, partly by

serious engagement with Greek philosophy, though the Cynics and the Stoics are mentioned briefly, as is Plato.[11] Perhaps it was an early attempt by Justin at writing an apology, or even the work of someone else who was less learned, but we have no way of knowing that for sure.

Justin was not the first Christian to write an apology defending the Christian faith, and the genre itself was of pagan origin, but he made it a standard form of Christian literature and is now generally regarded as the father of the Christian apologetic tradition.[12] Some of the speeches of the apostle Paul recorded in Acts are very similar in style and intention, and so Justin had an apostolic precedent for his approach. The *Dialogue with Trypho* is not an apology in the literary sense, but it fulfills a similar function and is a defense of Christianity against Judaism. It is of interest not only because it is one of the relatively few examples of a Christian attempt to persuade Jews to accept their Messiah in the postapostolic period but also because it comes from a time when Marcion and his followers were trying to distance Christianity from Judaism as much as possible. By second-century gentile Christian standards, Justin was unusually close to the Jewish world and appreciated its strengths more than most. That is not to say his understanding of Judaism was very accurate or profound, but the space he devoted to refuting it shows that he took it more seriously than most of his Christian contemporaries did.

APOLOGETIC RESPONSE AND METHODOLOGY

Justin's apologetic writings are of interest to us because of their two-edged approach, which reflects Justin's proximity to the church situation in New Testament times. From his perspective, the Jews had the truth but were blind to it, whereas the gentiles, who did not have God's revelation, were often willing to accept it when it was proclaimed to them. He is the only ancient writer who addressed both the Jewish and the gentile worlds on more or less equal terms, so his work lends itself to a comparison of the methods and arguments used in each case. With Jews, "dialogue" could only mean discussion about the right interpretation of Scripture, which both sides believed was the written Word of God. With gentiles, a different approach was required because they lacked the same familiarity with the biblical text and did not automatically accept its spiritual

---

magical writings, and partly by fears and the punishments they occasioned." It is hard to believe the mature Justin would have written something as obviously nonbiblical as this.

11. Ibid., 3, 8, 12.

12. For earlier Christian apologists such as Quadratus, Aristides of Athens, and Aristo of Pella, see the brief notices in Johannes Quasten, *Patrology: The Beginnings of Patristic Literature* (Leiden: Brill, 1950), 190–96.

authority. Somewhat ironically, Justin's approach was to persuade gentiles of the validity of Judaism before he would talk to them about Christianity, an important observation and one that contradicts the facile assumption that the church quickly embraced a Hellenic view of the world and distanced itself from its Jewish roots.

Justin gave pride of place to Greek philosophy in his apologetic for Christianity, perhaps because it was the route he himself followed into the faith. In pursuing this philosophical line of argument in his *Dialogue with Trypho*, Justin adopted the position of a Platonist who finds himself in conversation with an old man who appears out of nowhere. The old man discerns that Justin is a philosopher seeking to discover the truth and proceeds to interrogate him. Justin assures him that philosophy is the way to happiness because it is the knowledge of what really exists, combined with a clear perception of the truth, and happiness is the reward that comes from such knowledge and wisdom.[13] God, Justin goes on to explain, is a being who is eternally the same and who is the cause of everything else that exists. He can be known by human beings, but not in the way that other things are known. In other branches of learning, sight and experiment play a key role in determining what we believe, but this is not how we come to know God, who can be discerned by the mind alone.

The old man is skeptical of this and asks Justin whether a human mind can see God without the aid of the Holy Spirit. In this way, the old man slips a Christian concept into the discussion, but Justin does not immediately take him up on it. Instead, he cites Plato's doctrine of the rational soul as the basis for saying that man can attain knowledge of God. Animals are beings with a soul, but they cannot see God because they do not have a mind in the way humans do. But not all human beings see God, because that is a privilege reserved for those few who "live justly, purified by righteousness, and by every other virtue."[14] It thus transpires that the knowledge of God is not purely intellectual but demands moral rectitude. That can be attained to some degree in this life, but only when the soul is set free from the body is real progress possible.

The old man presents the argument that souls cannot be immortal because they are begotten. They partake of created nature, so they are not naturally linked to the divine. All souls are mortal, but that does not mean they necessarily die. As the old man puts it, the souls that have lived a life worthy of God do not perish, because that would be a victory for the power of evil. On the other hand, the souls that have not lived a life pleasing to God will also be kept in existence but punished

13. Martyr, *Dialogue with Trypho*, 3.
14. Ibid., 4.

for their wrongdoing. They are mortal according by nature but preserved in being because it is right for them to suffer for the evil they have committed.

At this point, Justin refers to what Plato said in the *Timaeus*, a treatise which Christians would later regard as the pagan writing that comes closest to the teaching of the Bible.[15] According to Plato, the world is subject to decay because it has been created, but the will of God will keep it in being, despite its inherent mortality. The soul belongs to this world of decay and death because if it were immortal, it would be like God, unable to sin or to fall away from him. Yet clearly there are many souls that know nothing of God and do not share his immortality. If the soul has life, it is because it partakes in a life that is not its own. Plato did not appreciate this moral dimension to the life of the soul, and his claim that it does not die cannot be sustained. Platonism, in other words, has some helpful insights into the nature of the soul, but the truth-seeker must go further than Plato did.[16]

It is at this point, when Justin realizes the inadequacy of even the best philosophy, that the old man steps in with another suggestion. The one who would find the truth must look elsewhere, to those whom he refers to as "prophets." The prophets are superior to the philosophers because they are more ancient in origin, because they are righteous in the sight of God, because they spoke by the power of God's Spirit, and because they foretold the future in a way that we are now seeing unfold before our eyes. What Justin needs, says the old man, is a revelation that can be given to him only by God. He concludes the conversation with the advice that the "real" Justin wants his readers to absorb: "Pray that, above all things, the gates of light may be opened to you; for these things cannot be perceived or understood by all, but only by the man to whom God and his Christ have imparted wisdom."[17]

It was by discovering the messages of the prophets that Justin found the peace of mind and soul that he had been looking for and became the philosopher that he had always wanted to be. For him, the wisdom imparted by prophetic revelation was the true philosophy, the one system of thought that makes sense of the universe and that combines both the intellectual and the moral in a harmonious synthesis.[18] Those who receive it are not merely enlightened by

---

15. It was the only Platonic dialogue available in Latin during the Middle Ages, and as such, it exerted considerable influence on a number of medieval theologians and philosophers, who interpreted it in a Christian sense. Especially notable in this respect were Thierry of Chartres and William of Conches, who were both active in the twelfth century.

16. In his *Second Apology*, 12, Justin describes his own journey out of Platonism as partly due to the fearlessness of Christians in the face of death. In his words: "When I was delighting in the doctrines of Plato, and heard the Christians slandered, and saw them fearless of death . . . [I] perceived that it was impossible that they could be living in wickedness and pleasure.

17. Martyr, *Dialogue with Trypho*, 7.

18. See Oskar Skarsaune, *The Proof from Prophecy: A Study in Justin Martyr's Proof-Text Tradition* (Leiden: Brill, 1987).

the truth but are also saved from their sins. As Justin puts it: "The words of the Savior . . . are sufficient to inspire those who turn aside from the path of rectitude with awe, while the sweetest rest is afforded those who make a diligent practice of them. If, then, you have any concern for yourself, and if you are eagerly looking for salvation, and if you believe in God, you may—since you are not indifferent to the matter—become acquainted with the Christ of God, and, after being initiated, live a happy life."[19]

With this, Justin concludes his exposition. To sum up what he says, an honest person such as Justin will naturally look to philosophy for an answer in a quest for the truth. After sampling the many different kinds on offer, they will eventually settle for Platonism because it is the highest and purest form of philosophical thought. But logical examination of Plato's teaching will reveal its inherent weaknesses and its inability to deliver on its promise of leading the enquiring soul into the presence of God. For that, it is necessary to look to the prophets God inspired and whose words reveal him to us. The person who turns to them will be led to Jesus Christ, whose coming the prophets foretold. The teaching of Christ is the truth, and those who receive it are the authentic philosophers, having reached the goal toward which the ancient Greeks had striven but which they had not attained.

Justin developed this argument in his *Dialogue with Trypho*, which is an odd place for it since Trypho presumably agreed with him about the inadequacy of the philosophical approaches with which he starts. But like many Hellenized Jews of that time, Trypho believed that Platonism was the best a gentile could hope for and that it was better to stick with that than to follow the teaching of a false Messiah, which is what they thought Jesus was. Justin had to point out to his fellow gentiles that Platonism was not enough even to give them the degree of wisdom the Jews possessed. Trypho possessed the truth but could not see it, whereas the gentiles did not possess it, even if they could receive it if it was proclaimed to them. That, of course, was the task to which the Christian church was dedicated, and Justin's *Apologies* must be understood and evaluated in that light.

THE APOLOGETIC FROM CHRISTIAN VIRTUES AND CHRISTIAN HOPE

Justin was fortunate to live in the time of the "five good emperors" who reigned from AD 96 to 180 and gave the Roman Empire a peace and stability that it had not known before and was not to experience again.[20] Marcus Aurelius,

---

19. Martyr, *Dialogue with Trypho*, 8.
20. The emperors were Nerva (96–98), Trajan (98–117), Hadrian (117–138), Antoninus Pius (138–161), and Marcus Aurelius (161–180). Justin lived under the last four of them.

the last of them, is the one best known today because of his reputation as a philosopher.[21] But his predecessors also claimed to govern on enlightened principles, and they were more tolerant of Christianity than Marcus Aurelius was. We do not know whether Justin's *Apologies*, addressed to Antoninus Pius and to the Roman senate, reached their destination or were read by those for whom they were theoretically intended, but the atmosphere of the time was such that writing to them in this way was not a waste of time. Justin's approach to the emperor was an appeal both to his office as head of state and to his conscience as a man of philosophical principles. He even addressed the emperor's two adopted sons as philosophers, adding that the younger one was "a lover of learning."[22] This form of address was clearly intended as an appeal to them to act in a way that would be consonant with their reputation and gave Justin the excuse he needed to base his case on principles that he assumed would be congenial to all concerned.

Justin claimed to be arguing on behalf of "those of all nations who are unjustly hated and wantonly abused," of whom he was one. Before elaborating on this, he made it clear that "reason directs those who are truly pious and philosophical to honor and love only what is true" and that such a person would rather die than fail to do the right thing. The use of the words *pious* and *philosophical* is particularly pointed, and Justin was subtly hinting that nobody to whom such epithets belonged would ever persecute Christians.[23]

The problem was that Christians were condemned merely for calling themselves Christians. That went back to the great fire of Rome in AD 64, which Nero, seeking a scapegoat, blamed on them. Somehow his proscription remained on the statute book, though nobody knew why. In AD 111 Pliny the Younger, who was governor of Bithynia, wrote to Emperor Trajan about how to handle accusations made against Christians, and his letter is interesting reading. Pliny did not know why they were illegal, and his investigations into their practices uncovered nothing criminal. He did not know what to do with them, but the emperor's reply was not much help. Trajan merely said that anonymous accusations against them must not be accepted, but he did nothing to challenge the law.[24]

The Christians were understandably unhappy with this imperial judgment. As Justin pointed out, a name by itself is neither good or bad. He did not ask that Christians should be acquitted simply because they were Christians, but he did

---

21. His *Meditations*, a work of Stoic philosophy written in Greek, still survives.
22. Martyr, *First Apology*, 1. The salutation is confusing. The second son, Lucius, is certainly Lucius Verus, himself a scion of the imperial family and adopted by Antoninus. The other is named simply as "Verissimus" ("most true") and is Marcus Aurelius, also adopted by Antoninus.
23. Ibid., 2.
24. Pliny the Younger, *Letters*, 10.96–97.

expect the authorities to try to convict them on the basis of some crime they had committed. If they were guilty, then they should be punished as evildoers, but if they had done nothing wrong, they ought not to be punished—a conclusion that one might expect any reasonable person to agree with.[25]

In reality, Christians suffered persecution because demonic forces seduced those in authority and blinded them to the truth. Justin brings this out clearly in his *Second Apology*, composed after Urbicus, the prefect of Rome, instigated a particularly outrageous attack on believers.[26] In Justin's words: "The evil demons, who hate us, and who keep such men as these subject to themselves, and serving them in the capacity of judges, incite them, as rulers actuated by evil spirits, to out us to death."[27]

The only thing Christians were guilty of was "atheism," but that was not a straightforward accusation. Justin argued that the gods worshipped by the Greeks and Romans were demons that had appeared to their ancestors and terrified them into acclaiming them as gods and worshipping them. Christians were by no means the first people to reject this kind of religion. As Justin pointed out, that had been done long before by Socrates (469–399 BC). But: "When Socrates endeavored, by true reason and examination, to bring these things to light, and deliver men from the demons, then the demons themselves, by means of men who rejoiced in iniquity, compassed his death, as an atheist and a profane person, on the charge that 'he was introducing new divinities', and in our case they display a similar activity."[28]

Socrates had been Plato's mentor and hero, and long before Justin's time, he had become a byword for a man who had been unjustly persecuted by ignorant bigots. Justin even claimed him as a kind of Christian before the coming of Christ because he had borne witness in his own way to the Word of Truth.[29] Yet despite his virtue, nobody had ever worshipped Socrates or tried to follow him. With Christ things were very different. Not only had educated people believed in him, but so had those of little or no learning, and in Justin's mind that proved his superiority in comparison to even the greatest of the philosophers: "No one trusted in Socrates so as to die for this doctrine, but in Christ, who was partially known even by Socrates (for he was and is the Word who is in every man, and who foretold the things that were to come to pass both through the prophets and in his own person when he was made of like passions, and taught

25. Martyr, *First Apology*, 4, 7.
26. He served in that office from 146 to 160.
27. Martyr, *Second Apology*, 1.
28. Martyr, *First Apology*, 5.
29. Ibid., 46: "Those who lived reasonably are Christians, even though they have been thought atheists, as among the Greeks, Socrates and Heraclitus, and men like them."

these things), not only philosophers and scholars believed, but also artisans and people entirely uneducated.[30]

Furthermore, many philosophers were skeptical of pagan religion and might well be called "atheists," but no harm ever came to them. Christians, on the other hand, were ardent worshippers of "the most true God, the Father of righteousness and temperance and the other virtues, who is free from all impurity."[31] They worshipped God as Father, Son, and prophetic Spirit, "knowing them in reason and truth, and declaring without grudging to everyone who wishes to learn, as we have been taught."[32]

Christian worship was very different from its pagan counterpart because it was grounded in reason. God does not want or need the sacrifices and libations that formed the substance of so much pagan worship because, as the maker of the universe, he already owns everything in it. Christians saw themselves as citizens of a heavenly kingdom, whose coming in glory they eagerly awaited, but they were not on that account subversives or rebels against the state. If they were, they would be engaged in clandestine activities and keep themselves well concealed, but they had nothing to hide. In fact, Justin pointed out, for a Christian to try to obtain earthly power would be to deny Christ, whose kingdom is not of this world.[33]

The truth about Christians was easy to discover, but the Roman authorities did not bother to check the facts. Had they done so, they would soon have realized that the high moral standards that Christians required of one another were important benefits to the state.[34] The bad reputation of the Christians was not due to anything they did but to the influence of demons who had deceived the public into thinking the opposite of the truth.[35] Christian teachings and practices were not secret rituals but were written down in books that anyone could read.

At this point, Justin expounded the basics of Christian moral teaching by quoting extensively from the Synoptic Gospels, and from Matthew in particular. This shows that he knew the Synoptic tradition and regarded it as authoritative. There is no indication that he had read the fourth gospel, and he did not make use of the rest of the New Testament, though it is impossible to say why, other than that he preferred to quote the precise words of Jesus and went no further than that. Probably he wanted to impress the Master's teaching on his readers,

30. Martyr, *Second Apology*, 10.
31. Martyr, *First Apology*, 6.
32. Ibid.
33. Ibid., 11.
34. Ibid., 12.
35. Ibid., 14.

none of whom would have been familiar with Christian Scripture. What we see here is Justin's judicious use of source material that he selected to support his argument. The words of Jesus mattered because his direct teaching was meant to impress pagans with his authority.[36]

The Christian virtues that Justin stressed are apparent from the *First Apology*. The first thing he mentioned was chastity, perhaps because this was a highly prized virtue among many philosophers but almost nonexistent in pagan religion, which was often little more than a fertility cult. After that came patience, unadorned truthfulness, and civil obedience.[37] Justin could have mentioned many other things, but it is clear that his desire to impress his audience informed his choices. The virtues he lauds in his coreligionists were those of the philosophers, a fact that should have evoked their sympathy and made them realize how irrational their anti-Christian prejudices were.

Justin went on from everyday ethics to the more difficult question of death and resurrection. Many pagans refused to believe a dead person could come back to life, but Justin refuted them in two ways. First, he appealed to pagan practices such as necromancy and their widespread belief that the souls of the dead could influence the behavior of the living. If that is true, argued Justin, what is to prevent such souls from coming back to life in the body, as Christians believe they will?[38] The second argument he took from human life. If a drop of human sperm can mutate into a grown human being, what is to stop a corpse from coming back to life if God so chooses? Both things are miracles because we can produce neither of them ourselves, but as we see babies being born every day, why should we doubt the possibility of a resurrection from the dead? This argument was not particularly strong, and Justin did not dwell on it, but he was not afraid to appeal to a commonly recognized mystery of human life in order to justify one that was rare and so far confined to Jesus Christ.

THE APOLOGETIC BASED ON THE UNIQUENESS OF CHRISTIANITY

Justin did not hesitate to compare pagan religious practices with Christian ones, sometimes to show that there were similarities between them and sometimes to show the exact opposite. The similarities of course were meant to prove that pagans were not totally wrong about everything—some elements of the truth were still present in their minds, and they occasionally surfaced, especially in the teachings of the great philosophers. As Justin put it: "On some points we

36. See Arthur J. Bellinzoni, *The Sayings of Jesus in the Writings of Justin Martyr* (Leiden: Brill, 1967).
37. Martyr, *First Apology*, 15–17.
38. Ibid., 18.

teach the same things as the poets and philosophers. . . . and on other points [we] are fuller and more divine in our teaching."[39] He showed this with reference to the life of Jesus, pointing out that pagan myths tell stories of virgin births and ascensions into heaven, to go no further. Modern critics might be tempted to say that the Christians borrowed these ideas from pagan sources and applied them to Christ, but Justin had a ready answer for them. He believed that evil spirits who corrupted the minds of pagans by taking elements of the truth and distorting them caused similarities of this kind. As he said, although there were many "sons of Zeus/Jupiter" who did extraordinary things, there is no suggestion that any of them were ever crucified—the central event in the life of Christ is entirely absent from pagan mythology.[40]

On the other hand, Justin also believed that Plato had gotten his basic ideas from Moses and that in the *Timaeus* he had even predicted the crucifixion of Christ when he wrote: "He [God the Father] placed him [Christ] crosswise in the universe."[41] Modern readers find that a bit of a stretch, to put it mildly, but it shows how Justin was determined to link Platonism to the biblical revelation. Justin was also aware that there were similarities between Christianity and some of the mystery cults that were popular in his time, but once again, he attributed this not to Christian borrowing from paganism but to the activities of evil spirits who were corrupting the truth. His discussion of the Christian eucharist, for example, describes it as a rite: ". . . which the wicked devils have imitated in the mysteries of Mithras, commanding the same thing to be done. For . . . bread and a cup of water are placed with certain incantations in the mystic rites of one who is being initiated."[42]

Observations of this kind do not prove that Christians borrowed anything from their pagan surroundings, and although sensationalist writers today sometimes cite such "evidence" to that effect, serious scholars generally dismiss it. But Justin's remarks show that some of his contemporaries were accusing Christians of such borrowing, and he knew that he had to refute them, even if the argument he chose for doing so is not one that we would use today.

One of the big differences between pagan myths and the gospels was that the former were disjointed and unhistorical, whereas the latter were systematically organized around a single individual, and eyewitnesses had verified their accounts in relatively recent times. Jesus Christ was a real person in a way that the main characters of Greek mythology were not, and both his teaching

39. Ibid., 20.
40. Ibid., 55.
41. Ibid., 60.
42. Ibid., 66.

and his behavior were far more moral than anything to be found among the Olympian gods, who had no teaching to speak of and whose misdeeds were often atrocious.[43]

As for the notion that Jesus was a kind of magician, the truth was that that designation belonged more readily to men who had risen up in opposition to him. There were quite a few of those, and one of them, Simon Magus, had even gone to Rome and been deified there after his death. True Christians rejected all such people and regarded them as demon-possessed.[44] Justin did not hesitate to claim that the same evil spirits who had corrupted the truth about God by producing pagan myths were doing exactly the same thing by raising up magicians such as Simon.[45]

THE APOLOGETIC BASED ON JEWISH/ CHRISTIAN PROPHECY

The main plank in Justin's apologetic platform was his reliance on the claim that Old Testament prophecy was fulfilled in Christ. It is at this point that his defense of Christianity against the pagans meets his defense of Christianity against the Jews. The prophecies had been translated from Hebrew into Greek long before the coming of Christ and had been readily available for anyone who cared to read them.[46] It was therefore possible to show that they had not been made up after the events they described. They were credible in a way that pagan myths were not, and it was possible to link what they said to things that had happened in the life, death, and resurrection of Jesus. It was on those ties that Justin's apologetic arguments ultimately rested.

One of the proofs on which Justin relied was the extreme antiquity of prophecy. According to him, it went back as much as five thousand years and had been revived at periodic intervals in Israel's history. It was not a one-off phenomenon from the distant past but a living tradition that had begun in the mists of time and continued until only a few centuries before it was fulfilled in Christ. Here, of course, Justin was exaggerating. Even on the most generous reckoning, the prophetic tradition did not go back more than about two thousand years (to Abraham), and Justin himself did not claim even that much. For example, he quoted Moses, whom he described as the first of the prophets, as saying, "The sceptre shall not depart from Judah, nor a lawgiver from between his feet,

---

43. Ibid., 23–25.
44. Ibid., 26. Interestingly, Justin claimed to have had a list of all these "heresies," which he would produce on request! If that was true, his cataloging activity preceded that of Irenaeus by a generation.
45. Ibid., 56.
46. Ibid., 31.

until he come for whom it is reserved; and he shall be the desire of the nations, binding his foal to the vine, washing his robe in the blood of the grape."[47]

As far as Justin was concerned, this prophecy (and others like it) foretold the coming of Christ, the supreme lawgiver of Israel, and undoubtedly it was intended to be a prophecy of some kind. What is surprising is that he attributed it to Moses, when in fact he was quoting the words of Jacob. Since that would have added more than four hundred years to the prophecy's antiquity, why did he not mention that? The reason must be that Justin was concentrating on the *written* character of the prophecy, which was very important to him. Jacob may have spoken the words, but it was Moses who recorded them, thereby putting them in the public domain. For Justin, who knew that the ancient Greek and Roman "prophecies" and oracles were cryptic and communicated orally, making their meaning uncertain, this was a key difference between paganism and Judeo-Christian religion. Biblical prophecies were history even before they occurred, which to Justin's mind greatly increased their authority.

As we would expect, much of Justin's evidence comes from the gospels, and especially from Matthew, which specializes in the theme of fulfilled prophecy, but he went beyond the verses quoted as such in the New Testament. He was especially partial to Isaiah and the Psalms, which he regarded as largely prophetic books. Occasionally he could be quite creative, as when he quoted Psalm 96:10 as "The Lord has reigned from the tree," meaning "from the cross," even though neither the original Hebrew nor the Greek translation contains the last three words. Where Justin got them from is a mystery. His reading may reflect a variant that was circulating in his lifetime, though there is no evidence for it.[48] What is certain is that Justin knew that most versions of the text did not have these extra words, which he claimed was because of censorship exercised by "the rulers of the people."[49]

Arguments about the true interpretation of Hebrew prophecy were obviously going to play a more central role in Justin's "dialogue" with Jews than in his arguments against pagans, if only because here Jews and Christians were on common ground. Occasionally, as in the example just given, they were reading different texts, and when that happened, Justin's approach was to claim that the Jewish version was inaccurate because it had been "doctored" by Jews.[50] But most of the time he allegorized the Old Testament to make it speak of Christ, even when it does not.[51] Modern readers are understandably embarrassed by such claims

47. Ibid., 32. The quotation is from Genesis 49:10.
48. Ibid., 41.
49. *Dialogue with Trypho*, 73.
50. Ibid., 70, 72–73.
51. Ibid., 40–43.

since they are almost always demonstrably false, but in fairness to Justin, he also realized that such "proofs" were unconvincing and was determined to show that Christ fulfilled the ancient prophecies in their literal and historical sense.[52]

The main point of difference between Justin and Trypho concerns the nature of the "literal" fulfillment of prophecy. Trypho, presumably echoing the general Jewish opinion of his time, claimed that the words of David (in the Psalms) and Isaiah referred to current events and not to some distant future. They may have "predicted" something about Solomon or Hezekiah but not about a Messiah whose coming would be delayed by hundreds of years. Justin's response was to show that Trypho's interpretation was wrong because what the prophets said went far beyond anything that Solomon or Hezekiah could have "fulfilled."[53] He also dismissed Trypho's claim that pagan myths had influenced Christians, using the same arguments that appear in his *First Apology*.[54]

From a modern point of view, Justin was on stronger ground when he argued against Trypho that it is not necessary to keep the Mosaic law, even though it was a divine revelation, because its purpose has been fulfilled in Christ.[55] His extensive treatment of this subject can be read as similar to what Paul said in Romans, though Justin never indicated that he knew the apostle's writings.[56] He was also aware that Jesus Christ did not completely fulfill all the prophecies, a point that Trypho made to discredit the Christian claims. In answer to that, Justin said Christ would come again, and then the fullness of the prophetic message would be accomplished.[57]

Most important, Justin focused on the cross, which to his mind was the ultimate proof that Jesus was the promised Messiah.[58] Closely tied to that were the prophecies of Christ's subsequent resurrection from the dead, which Justin also mentioned.[59] Interwoven with his explanations of these key events are lengthy arguments to show that the Old Testament foreshadows the revelation of the Trinity in God, though Justin never used that word. But he did distinguish the God who revealed himself to Moses from the Father of Jesus Christ (who remains eternally transcendent and reveals himself to no one directly) and claimed that references to the Word of God in the Old Testament are also

---

52. Ibid., 55.

53. Ibid., 33–34, 83–84.

54. Ibid., 67, 69–71.

55. Ibid., 10–30.

56. This does not mean he was ignorant of them but that he did not use them in his dialogue with Trypho, who would not have accepted them as evidence of divine revelation. Justin was adapting his approach to the beliefs and prejudices of his addressee, a typical apologetic maneuver.

57. Martyr, *Dialogue with Trypho*, 31–32, 110–11.

58. Ibid., 86, 89–91, 94–99, 104–05.

59. Ibid., 106–07.

christological.[60] Justin's aim was to show that the prophecies revealed in the Old Testament were fulfilled in Christ and that the church is the true inheritor of the promises that God made to Abraham. Judaism is true as far as it goes, but it does not go far enough and was never intended to be definitive. From the beginning, it was a stopgap that was meant to prepare the way for the coming of the Messiah. Christians believe that Jesus was that Messiah. Jews do not accept that, and this has been the occasion of bitterness and ill-feeling between us and them.[61] In modern times, dominant Christian powers have discriminated against Jews, but in the early days of the church, the will to persecute was very much on the other foot.

Justin did not approve of Christians who anathematized Jewish converts if they continued to observe their traditional Jewish ways. Trypho questioned him about that, and while he had to admit that there were some Christians who were intolerant in that way, he was not one of them. As far as he was concerned, keeping the Jewish law was a matter of indifference as long as nobody tried to force it on Christians as necessary for their salvation. That, of course, was the attitude of the apostle Paul, but in the second-century it was a sign of open-mindedness on Justin's part that would become rare as time went on. Justin's attitude toward Jews was to try to persuade them to see how their Scriptures ought to be interpreted and to pray for them, despite their hardness of heart.[62] It is an approach from which we have much to learn, and in this respect at least, Justin is our contemporary just as much as he was Trypho's.

CONTRIBUTIONS TO THE FIELD OF APOLOGETICS

We must ask ourselves what Christians can learn, today, from Justin Martyr's apologetic. His world was very different from ours, and in many ways his approach seems irrelevant and inapplicable now. But if we look more deeply, we shall see that there are lessons we can learn from him if we distinguish between his principles and their application in the circumstances of his time. There is much we can affirm and embrace in his thought, even as we must discard a good deal of his biblical interpretation.

For a start, Justin made a serious effort to understand those whom he was addressing. He did not presume that his readers understood Christianity already or approach them in a way that would have made no sense to an unbeliever. In dealing with those trained in Greek philosophy, he extolled the virtues of the

---

60. Ibid., 56–63.
61. Ibid., 39, 108, 115.
62. Ibid., 133.

philosophers and pointed out that Christians often agreed with them, especially on moral issues. He appealed to rationality as the basis of truth because that was a principle that was theoretically common to both. Christians, he argued, were the philosophers' best allies; in fact, they were the *true* philosophers, so educated Greeks ought to make common cause with them and refrain from persecuting people who shared so many of their own ideals.

Having made that point, Justin then reminded them that for all their virtues, the philosophers were unable to agree among themselves, even though they all recognized that there is only one truth. Christianity, he claimed, had a system that could embrace the fullness of truth, which was found in Christ, in whose teaching intellectual integrity and moral probity come together. As the Creator God, Christ is the source of all knowledge, and as the Redeemer who suffered and died on the cross, he overcame and defeated the power of sin that prevents us from realizing our potential as God's creatures. Christ not only preached the way of truth, he walked it all the way to the cross, and by doing so he brought real change and renewal to those who believe in him.

In dealing with Jews, Justin recognized the common basis of Scriptural revelation that unites Christians to them and argued that it made sense only in the person and work of Christ. Many of his examples strike us as far-fetched, but the basic principle is fundamental to Christianity. We cannot move away from the Old Testament, which forms the framework for our faith, but neither can we be tied to it in a way that excludes the revelation God has given us in Christ. Interpreting the Hebrew Bible christologically is not optional for us—it is essential. Whether we are in dialogue with Jews, who share our interest in the true meaning of the text as God's Word, or whether we are dealing with Christians who have no particular love for Israel or understanding of its abiding importance in the plan of God for our salvation, interpreting the Old Testament in the light of Christ remains foundational for our faith and for our apologetic too.

Finally, Justin's aim was to defend the Christian faith, not to impose it on people who were not persuaded by it. The pagans to whom he wrote did not accept what he said, and Trypho went away unconvinced. This does not mean that Justin's apologetic was a failure, but it is a reminder that conversion is a work of the Holy Spirit, not the result of clever or convincing argument. As Paul said when he wrote to the Corinthians: "I planted the seed, Apollos watered it, but God has been making it grow" (1 Cor 3:6). Justin saw himself as walking in the footsteps of Paul and/or Apollos, and he knew that his efforts would bear fruit only if and when God blessed them with the power of his Holy Spirit. So it was then, and so it is now, and in this way Justin remains a model for us of how we should bear witness to the faith that is in us.

BIBLIOGRAPHY
Texts and Translations
Falls, T. B. *Justin Martyr: Dialogue with Trypho*. Washington, DC: Catholic University of America Press, 2003 (translation only).

Goodspeed, E. J., ed., *Die ältesten Apologeten*. Göttingen: Vandenhoeck und Ruprecht, 1914 (critical text only).

Minns, D. and P. Parvis, eds., *Justin, Philosopher and Martyr: Apologies*. Oxford: Oxford University Press, 2009 (critical edition with translation).

Roberts, A., and J. Donaldson, ed., *Ante-Nicene Fathers*, I, 159–270. Edinburgh: T&T Clark, 1867 (translation only).

Studies
Allert, C. D. *Revelation, Truth, Canon and Interpretation: Studies in Justin Martyr's Dialogue with Trypho*. Leiden: Brill, 2002.

Barnard, L. W. *Justin Martyr: His Life and Thought*. Cambridge: Cambridge University Press, 1967.

Bellinzoni, A. J. *The Sayings of Jesus in the Writings of Justin Martyr*. Leiden: Brill, 1967.

Parvis, S., and P. Foster, *Justin Martyr and his Worlds*. Minneapolis: Fortress, 2007.

Quasten, J. *Patrology*. Vol 1 of *The Beginnings of Patristic Literature*. Utrecht: Spectrum, 1950.

Shotwell, W. A. *The Biblical Exegesis of Justin Martyr*. London: SPCK, 1965.

Skarsaune, O. *The Proof from Prophecy: A Study in Justin Martyr's Proof-Text Tradition*. Leiden: Brill, 1987.

IRENAEUS OF LYONS

Anti-Gnostic Polemicist

STEPHEN O. PRESLEY

During the second century, the church faced the formidable challenge of various Gnostic figures working to undermine the teaching of the apostles. Irenaeus (ca. 130–200) focused his apologetic efforts on the careful analysis and critique of these Gnostic thinkers. He composed a theological method aimed at countering the basic assumptions of the Gnostic myth, and his applied apologetic arguments relied heavily on rhetorical strategies that exposed the contradictions and inconsistencies in their views. Through his work, Irenaeus helped navigate the threat of Gnosticism in the second century and helped preserve the faith of the church.

HISTORICAL BACKGROUND

Irenaeus was born in Smyrna ca. AD 130 and at a young age became a disciple of Polycarp before he migrated west to Gaul and settled in Lyons.[1] In AD 177 the churches near Lyons and Vienne experienced violent persecutions, and Pothinus, the leader of the church in Lyons, was martyred.[2] A letter describing these brutal acts of persecution was drafted and sent with Irenaeus to Bishop Eleutherus in Rome to report the church's faithfulness in the midst of suffering and to encourage the Christian community there. When he returned to Lyons after the events subsided, Irenaeus assumed pastoral care of the church. During his ministry, he tried to heal church divisions and maintain unity, especially amid the Montanist

---

1. Eusebius, *Hist. eccl.* 4.14. Citations of Eusebius are from: Eusebius, *Ecclesiastical History*, trans. C. F. Crusé (Peabody, MA: Hendrickson, 2000). See also Irenaeus, *Haer.* 3.3.4. For more background on Irenaeus's life, see: Hubertus R. Drobner, *The Fathers of the Church: A Comprehensive Introduction* (Grand Rapids: Baker Academic, 2007), 117–22. Much of what we know of his life comes down to us from Eusebius, see Eusebius, *Hist. eccl.* 5.4–25.
2. Eusebius, *Hist. eccl.* 5.1.29.

Image: Statue of Irenaeus of Lyons, Frederick's Church, Copenhagen

and Quartodeciman controversies. But there were some Gnostics who were active among his congregation, and there were others who rejected the teaching of the apostles and the basic convictions of the church's faith. Unlike the earlier Christian apologists of the second century who wrote petitions to civic leaders or public intellectuals, Irenaeus is remembered for his apologetic efforts against this growing tide of Gnostic thinkers who threatened the early Christian communities.[3]

While Irenaeus's pen was rather active, only two of his works survive: a five-volume refutation of Gnosticism entitled *The Refutation and Overthrow of Knowledge Falsely So-Called* (or its shorter title, *Against Heresies*) and a small catechetical manual entitled the *Demonstration of the Apostolic Preaching*.[4] Eusebius reports that Irenaeus wrote a number of other works, including a work titled *Concerning Knowledge*, written against the Hellenes; a book on the Wisdom of Solomon and Hebrews; some letters written to Florinus entitled *On the Sole Sovereignty*, or *That God Is Not the Author of Evil*, and *On the Ogdoad*; and a letter written to Blastus called *On Schism*.[5] The topics and themes in these titles, along with the two extant works mentioned above, capture Irenaeus's apologetic, ecclesiastical, and theological concerns. These works bear out the reality that Irenaeus was, above all, a pastor with a local congregation and deeply concerned about the heretical teachings infiltrating the rank and file Christians in Lyons and beyond.

Tracing Irenaeus's apologetic contribution must begin by situating him within the theological milieu of the second century and the basic contours of Gnostic thought. This helps explain the historical and theological contexts that frame his arguments and his own theological method. Irenaeus spends a good bit of time carefully detailing the interconnected streams of Gnosticism flowing from various teachers. In his defense of the faith, Irenaeus is not afraid to draw on his secular education and use some basic philosophical arguments, though he relies much more on classical Greco-Roman rhetorical strategies.[6] For his

3. Robert M. Grant, *Greek Apologists of the Second Century* (Philadelphia: Westminster, 1988), 186.
4. English translations of *Against Heresies* 1–3 are from: Dominic J. Unger and John J. Dillon, *St. Irenaeus of Lyons: Against the Heresies (Book 1)*, ACW 55 (New York: Newman, 1992); Dominic J. Unger, John J. Dillon, and Michael Slusser, *St. Irenaeus of Lyons: Against the Heresies (Book 2)*, ACW 65 (New York: Newman, 2012); Dominic J. Unger, John J. Dillon, and Matthew Steenberg, *St. Irenaeus of Lyons: Against the Heresies (Book 3)*, ACW 64 (New York: Newman, 2012). English translations of *Against Heresies* 4–5 are from: A. Roberts and J. Donaldson, *Ante-Nicene Fathers. Vol. 1* (Peabody, MA: Hendrickson, 1994).
5. Eusebius, *Hist. eccl.* 5.20.1.4–8; *Hist. eccl.* 5.24.11–17; *Hist. eccl.* 5.26.
6. Robert M. Grant, "Irenaeus and Hellenistic Culture," *Harvard Theological Review* 42 (1949): 41–51; William R. Schoedel, "Philosophy and Rhetoric in the Adversus Haereses of Irenaeus," *Vigiliae Christianae* 13 (1959): 22–32; Pheme Perkins, "Irenaeus and the Gnostics: Rhetoric and Composition in Adversus Haereses Book One," *Vigiliae Christianae* 30 (1976): 193–200; Anthony Briggman, "Literary and Rhetorical Theory in Irenaeus, Part 1," *Vigiliae Christianae* 69 (2015): 500–27; Anthony Briggman, "Literary and Rhetorical Theory in Irenaeus, Part 2," *Vigiliae Christianae* 70 (2016): 31–50.

apologetic efforts, Irenaeus remains one of the most important theologians of the second century and a key representative of the way the early church fathers defended the faith.

THEOLOGICAL CONTEXT

The primary focus of Irenaeus's apologetic defense is a loosely connected set of religious teachers and communities called "Gnostics." These Gnostics drew on a complex mixture of pagan philosophy, Hellenistic Judaism, and Christian thought, with every teacher or community concocting their own blended worldview. While there is evidence of concerns for incipient Gnostic thought in the New Testament, the major schools of Gnosticism flourished in the second century. The opening lines of *Against Heresies* contain an allusion to 1 Timothy 1:3–4 that describes his opponents as "discarding the Truth and introducing deceitful myths and endless genealogies." This envisions his Gnostic opponents as a manifestation of Paul's warning.[7] Irenaeus tells us that he was well-acquainted with Gnostics; he had read some of their works and had personal conversations with them.[8] He was motivated to respond when he found them trying to persuade Christians, including those in his congregation, to abandon the church and the teaching of the apostles.[9]

In contemporary scholarship, the label "Gnostic," or "Gnosticism," has become highly controversial, with several works arguing that we should reject the term because no coherent definition can circumscribe the diversity of so-called Gnostic views.[10] To a certain degree, this is correct. The teachings of the various Gnostic writings are so varied that corralling them into a coherent definition is challenging.[11] Even Irenaeus complains that new Gnostic texts and teachers are always springing up like mushrooms.[12] But despite this challenge, there is a discernible set of assumptions and a basic dualistic worldview that pervades most of the Gnostic texts. In his introduction to Gnosticism, Christoph Markschies drafted a simple

---

7. Irenaeus, *Haer.* 1.pf.1. The title of his principle work, *The Refutation and Overthrow of Knowledge Falsely So-Called*, also alludes to 1 Timothy 6:20.

8. Irenaeus, *Haer.* 1.pf.2.

9. Ibid.

10. Karen King, *What is Gnosticism?* (Cambridge: Harvard University Press, 2003); Michael A. Williams, *Rethinking "Gnosticism": An Argument for Dismantling a Dubious Category* (Princeton: Princeton University Press, 1996).

11. The situation has become more complex since the discovery of a collection of ancient Gnostic texts in 1945 called the Nag Hammadi Library. The number and diversity of these texts makes any strict definition more difficult. For introduction and translation of the Nag Hammadi Library, see: Marvin Meyer, ed., *The Nag Hammadi Scriptures: The Revised and Updated Translation of the Sacred Gnostic Texts* (New York: HarperCollins, 2008).

12. Irenaeus, *Haer.* 1.29.1.

typological definition that lists a "particular set of ideas or motives" found in the various Gnostic works. These basic Gnostic assumptions include:

> 1) The experience of a completely other-worldly, distant, supreme God; 2) the introduction, which among other things is conditioned by this, of further divine figures, or the splitting up of existing figures into figures that are closer to humans than the remote supreme God; 3) the estimation that the world and matter as evil creation and an experience, conditioned by this, of the alienation of the gnostic in the world; 4) the introduction of a distant creator God or assistant: within the Platonic tradition he is called 'craftsman'—Greek *demiurgos*—and is sometimes described as merely ignorant, but sometimes also as evil; 5) the explanation of this state of affairs by a mythological drama in which a divine element falls from its sphere into an evil world slumbers in human beings of one class as a divine spark and can be freed from this; 6) knowledge ('gnosis') about this state, which, however, can be gained only through a redeemer figure from the other world who descends from a higher sphere and ascends to it again; 7) the redemption of human beings though the knowledge of 'that God (or the spark) in them' . . . and finally; a tendency toward dualism in different types which can express itself in the concept of God, in the opposition of spirit and manner, and in anthropology.[13]

Weaving these points together are a set of dualisms that flow from these Gnostic assumptions, including a *metaphysical* dualism that separates the spiritual world above from the material world below; a *theological* dualism that separates the Supreme God from the creator, or demiurge, and the division of the aeons in the Pleromic system; a *christological* dualism that distinguishes the figures of Christ and Jesus and the Logos and Savior; an *anthropological* dualism that distinguishes between spiritual ones who have knowledge of the divine spark and those who do not; a *canonical* dualism that separates the unity of Scripture, especially the Old and New Testaments; and a *soteriological* dualism that celebrates the salvation of the spiritual element and rejects the bodily resurrection.[14] This set of Gnostic motives and assumptions, along with the dualisms that emanate from them, compete with the basic contours of the Christian worldview grounded in Scripture. Furthermore, even though the Gnostics rejected the authority of the Old and

---

13. Christoph Markschies, *Gnosis: An Introduction* (New York: T&T Clark, 2003), 16–17.
14. Gérard Vallée, "Theological and Non-Theological Motives in Irenaeus's Refutation of the Gnostics," in E. P. Sanders, *Jewish and Christian Self-definition, 1: The Shaping of Christianity in the Second and Third Centuries* (Philadelphia: Fortress, 1980), 179–80.

New Testaments, they often integrated them into their writings as they explained and defended the views mentioned above. So, for example, in many Gnostic accounts, the Creator in Genesis is often viewed as a wicked deity who created the material world and who foolishly assumed he was the only God (Isa 45:5).[15] They also appeal to other texts, such as 1 Corinthians 15:50: "Flesh and blood cannot inherit the kingdom of God," as a defense against a bodily resurrection.[16]

In his principle work, Irenaeus wastes little time before beginning his summary and critique of Gnosticism in the first two books of *Against Heresies*. Beginning in *Against Heresies* 1, he systematically walks through each of the major schools of Gnosticism, including the Valentinians (*Haer.* 1.1–8), Marcus and the Marcosians (*Haer.* 1.13–20), Simon Magus and Menander (*Haer.* 1.23), Saturninus and Basilides (*Haer.* 1.24), Carpocrates, Cerinthus, and the Ebionites (*Haer.* 1.25), Nicolaitans (*Haer.* 1.26), Cerdo and Marcion (*Haer.* 1.27), Encratites and Tatian (*Haer.* 1.28), the Barbeliotes (*Haer.* 1.29), Ophites (*Haer.* 1.30), and the Cainites (*Haer.* 1.31).[17] Modern scholars debate Irenaeus's summary of Gnostics and question the accuracy of his descriptions, but studies continue to show that Irenaeus's presentation is fair.[18] In each case, he describes the origins and beliefs of each group with intermittent critiques layered with rhetorical flourish. In a few instances in *Against Heresies* 1–2, he discusses the church's faith and interjects his own theological perspective (cf. *Haer.* 1.8–10, *Haer.* 1.22), but he reserves a developed treatment of his own thought for *Against Heresies* 3–5. Of all these Gnostic thinkers, Valentinus, an eloquent and persuasive teacher, was the primary focus of Irenaeus's polemic, and the description of the Valentinian system spans eight chapters.[19]

APOLOGETIC METHODOLOGY AND RESPONSE

Irenaeus's response to Gnosticism stands in the line of several other Greek apologists of the second century. His contribution is the earliest response to the Gnostic systems that we now have. At the same time, his response to Gnosis is not merely

---

15. Stephen O. Presley, *The Intertextual Reception of Genesis 1–3 in Irenaeus of Lyons* (Leiden: Brill, 2015), 49–50.

16. Ibid., 191.

17. For an introductory reader with selections of Christian responses to Gnosticism and other early Christian heresies, see: Arland J. Hultgren and Steven A. Haggmark, eds., *The Earliest Christian Heretics: Readings from Their Opponents* (Minneapolis: Fortress, 1996).

18. Matthew C. Steenberg, *Irenaeus on Creation: The Cosmic Christ and the Saga of Redemption* (Leiden: Brill, 2008), 11–12.

19. Valentinus came to Rome in the mid-second century and actively sought to become bishop of the church, but after he was rejected, he left the church and started his own communities. He may be the author of *Gospel of Truth*, discovered among the texts of the Nag Hammadi library, though many other writings in the same collection resemble his thought.

polemical but also constructive; he outlines the orthodox faith of the church that was handed down from the apostles and argues that this faith precedes any heretical deviation. This is why an appreciation for Irenaeus's apologetic efforts must begin with a broader understanding of his general theological method that situates his polemic within an epistemological humility and grounds his theology in a doctrine of Scripture. Under the direction of this theological method, Irenaeus's applied apologetic arguments are often dependent on Greco-Roman rhetoric drawn from his education. He utilized a number of different rethorical terms and other apologetic strategies to refute his Gnostic interlocutors.

APOLOGETIC AND THEOLOGICAL METHOD

Turning first to Irenaeus's theological method, after cataloging all the various Gnostic groups in *Against Heresies* 1, in *Against Heresies* 2 he cycles back for a more focused response to some of the principal beliefs of Gnosticism. Within this refutation of Gnosis, specifically *Against Heresies* 2.25–28, Irenaeus offers something that William Schoedel has famously called an Irenaean "tractate on theological method."[20] The first point of his theological method is an appeal to epistemological humility, because God's creatures must come to appreciate the limits of empirical knowledge and recognize what God has revealed that is within the grasp of human cognition, or, in Irenaeus's words, what is placed "under our eyes."[21] The Gnostics do not begin with this assumption and instead present themselves as learned and intellectually skilled, rejecting the warning of Paul that "knowledge puffs up while love builds up" (1 Cor 8:1).[22] Certainly Irenaeus recognizes that not every theological and philosophical question is answerable with the revelation given (in nature or Scripture), and furthermore, not all revelation is equally clear and comprehensible. So he writes, the "sound and safe and religious and truth-loving mind" will apply itself to sensible and perceptible revelation through a proper "method of investigation."[23]

Second, this "method of investigation" recognizes that God reveals knowledge of himself in two forms: creation and Scripture. Irenaeus believes there are things in creation that are evident, such as the fact that creation exists or the sinfulness of God's creatures, but not all is made known.[24] For example, no Scripture passage or empirical observation of the natural order reveals what God was doing before he created the world or how God produced matter and from what

---

20. William Schoedel, "Theological Method in Irenaeus ("Adversus Haereses" 2.25–28)," *The Journal of Theological Studies*, vol 35.1 (1984): 31–49.
21. Irenaeus, *Haer.* 2.27.1.
22. Irenaeus, *Haer.* 2.26.1.
23. Irenaeus, *Haer.* 2.27.1–2.
24. Irenaeus, *Haer.* 2.28.7.

source.[25] The Gnostics, on the other hand, choose to seek after another god to explain these mysteries and presume to know what is beyond the available revelation.[26] According to Irenaeus, the only revelation that is definitive is "expressed in the Scared Scriptures clearly and unambiguously by the words themselves."[27] This is why he believes special revelation ought to take preference over the attention to general revelation, and Scripture itself says, "We know in part and we prophesy in part" (1 Cor 13:9). The safest and surest revelation is that which is given in Scripture, and this revelation should be the basis for any theological reflection or apologetic response.

But when Irenaeus writes that the knowledge of God is expressed "clearly and unambiguously in the words of Scripture," he does not mean that all Scripture is equally clear. There are parables and enigmatic sayings, especially in the Old Testament and the gospels, that require special attention. A Scripture interpreter should never adapt "ambiguous" matters, such as the Gnostic myth, to the enigmatic sayings in Scripture because that will only distort the totality of Scripture and render both the enigmatic and the clear, unclear.[28] The only option is to read the unclear with the clear, the obscure with the evident, and the perplexing with the simple. So Irenaeus writes:

> And so the parables may not be adapted to ambiguous matters. That way both he who interprets them will interpret them safely, and the parables will be explained by all in a similar manner. Thus, the body of Truth will continue entire, harmonious in its members and unshaken. But to combine things that are not expressed openly or placed under our eyes with the explanations of the parables, explanations that anyone excogitates at will, is unreasonable. It would result in no one's having a Rule of the Truth. On the contrary, as many interpreters of the parables as there would be, just so many truths would be seen at war with each other and setting up contradictory opinions, as is the case with the questions of the pagan philosophers.[29]

Here Irenaeus casts the unity of the "body of truth" in contrast to the disunity, disharmony, and multiplicity of the Gnostic interpretations. When unclear

---

25. Irenaeus, *Haer.* 2.27.3, *Haer.* 2.28.3, 7. As Schoedel notes, Irenaeus is not a thoroughgoing empiricist because his vision of the world is forged with an eschatological expectation, which shapes his Scripture reading as well. See Schoedel, "Theological Method," 36.

26. Irenaeus, *Haer.* 2.28.6.

27. Irenaeus, *Haer.* 2.27.1.

28. Ibid.

29. Ibid.

texts or parables are read in continuity with other unclear propositions, particularly those outside Scripture and found in the pagan philosophers, the result is an unending multiplicity of readings that lack any unity or coherence. It creates a cacophony of hermeneutical voices in conflict and discord, not only distorting the parables in Scripture but also contradicting what is taught in the clear passages. Instead, if the Christian reads Scripture with the "rule of truth," the Scriptures will be found "harmonious" and "unshaken," organized through the clear illuminating the unclear. Though there are a diversity of Scripture passages, "through the many voices of the passages there will be heard among us one harmonious melody that hymns praises to God who made all things."[30] For Irenaeus, the Gnostics err by rejecting this basic method by which one can know anything about God. They are prideful in their understanding of creation and philosophical reasoning, and they privilege the wrong kind of revelation. They distort the clear teaching of the Christian Scriptures and deconstruct the Scriptures by conforming them to their system.

A RHETORICAL APOLOGETIC

While some patristic writers drew on philosophical arguments, Irenaeus is more interested in utilizing rhetorical strategies. This does not mean he avoids using philosophical arguments; older studies suggest his limited use of philosophy indicates he had only a superficial knowledge derived from doxographical sources, or introductory works on philosophical topics. Recent treatments paint a more balanced picture of Irenaeus "as aware of general philosophical positions, as trained in rhetorical arts, and able to well utilize certain philosophical methods in his argumentation."[31] On balance, Irenaeus is clearly more interested in rhetoric than philosophy.[32] From the opening pages of *Against Heresies*, he shows his dependence on classical rhetorical modes of argument when he insists that he is *not* skilled in rhetoric, saying, "From us who live among the Celts and are accustomed to transact practically everything in a barbarous tongue, you cannot expect rhetorical art, which we have never learned, or the craft of writing, in which we have not had practice, or elegant style and persuasiveness, with which

---

30. Irenaeus, *Haer.* 2.28.3.

31. Anthony Briggman, "Revisiting Irenaeus' Philosophical Acumen," *Vigiliae Christianae* 65 (2011): 115–24. On occasion, Irenaeus will charge the Gnostics with plagiarizing the philosophers, and in one instance he suggests that Plato's thought is superior to Marcion. See *Haer.* 2.14.2–6 and *Haer.* 3.25.5. For criticisms of philosophy, see: Irenaeus, *Haer.* 2.14.2 and *Haer.* 2.33.2–4. There is little doubt that Irenaeus's relationship to philosophy would be clearer if some of his other works were discovered, such as his work on the problem of evil mentioned by Eusebius. Christopher Stead, *Philosophy in Christian Antiquity* (Cambridge: Cambridge University Press, 1994), 90.

32. Robert M. Grant, "Irenaeus and Hellenistic Culture," in *After the New Testament* (Philadelphia: Fortress, 1967), 164.

we are not familiar."[33] Irenaeus's use of rhetoric is complex and varied, witnessed in a variety of terms, illustrations, and concepts that put forth contradictions, objections, and insults against his opponents.[34] In the hands of Irenaeus, rhetoric is a tool to serve his theology, and three key rhetorical terms stand out—though several happen to be scriptural terms as well—including hypothesis (*hypothesis*), economy or dispensation (*oikonomia*), and recapitulation (*anakephalaiôsis*).[35]

Hypothesis: The Presentation of a Plot

The first rhetorical term is *hypothesis*, which is "the presentation (sometimes in a summary) of a plot or structure intended by an author such as Homer."[36] In the ancient context, Sextus Empiricus uses the term to describe the "argument" or "plot" of a drama.[37] In Irenaeus's thinking this term describes the argument of Scripture as a whole, which he implies when he criticizes the interpretive methods of the Valentinian Gnostics through the illustration of the hypothesis of a Homeric cento. A cento was a pedagogical tool in Greco-Roman education where a student selected isolated phrases or words from a famous poem or writing, such as Homer, Hesiod, Virgil, or Ovid, and pieced them together, in any arrangement of the student's choosing, to communicate their own poem or narrative.[38] Irenaeus cites a cento, with lines of unconnected sayings from Homer's works, and then compares the cento to the tendency for Gnostics to compose their own hypothesis from unconnected lines of Scripture, saying:

> After having entirely fabricated their own system, they gather together sayings and names from scattered places and transfer them, as we have already said, from their natural meaning to an unnatural one. They act like those who would propose themes [*hypothesis*] which they chance upon and then try to put them to verse from Homeric poems, so that the inexperienced think that Homer composed the poems with that theme, which in reality are a recent composition. . . . What simple minded person would not be misled by these verses and believe that Homer composed them in that manner for that very theme? One who is well-versed in Homeric themes will recognize the verses, but he will not recognize the theme, since he

---

33. Irenaeus, *Haer.* 1.pf.3. Schoedel, "Philosophy and Rhetoric," 27. Schoedel suggests that the structure of *Adversus haereses* in Books 1–5 follows roughly the models of Hellenistic rhetoric, including: *exordium, narratio, divisio, confirmatio, confutatio,* and *peroratio.* Schoedel, "Philosophy and Rhetoric," 27–28.

34. Perkins, "Irenaeus and the Gnostics," 195.

35. Grant, *Irenaeus of Lyons,* 46–53.

36. Ibid., 47.

37. Ibid., 48. Briggman, "Literary and Rhetorical Theory in Irenaeus, Part 1," 502–03.

38. Robert L. Wilken, "The Homeric Cento in Irenaeus, 'Adversus Haereses' 1.8.4," *Vigiliae Christianae* 21 (1967): 25–33.

knows that some of them were spoken of Ulysses, others of Hercules himself, others still of Priam, others of Menelaus and Agamemnon. However,
if he takes them and puts each one back into its own [theme], he will make
their fabricated theme disappear. In the same way, anyone who keeps
unchangeable in himself the Rule of Truth received through baptism will
recognize the names and sayings and parables from the Scriptures, but this
blasphemous theme of theirs he will not recognize.[39]

In Irenaeus's thinking, the Gnostics string together a set of unconnected
phrases from Scripture, as someone composing a Homeric cento, and compose
an altogether different hypothesis. They draw isolated words, verses, or expressions from Scripture and arrange them into a new plot, in continuity with their
own myth described above, and ultimately communicate a completely new
story, a story that is distinctive from the true hypothesis of Scripture.[40] Anyone
aquainted with Homer's writings (or Scripture and the rule of faith), Irenaeus
contends, would immediately recognize that the verses are taken out of the
context of their Homeric plot and then remove them and place them back into
their appropriate place in their original narratives. In the same way, the Christian, who has Scripture and the true hypothesis, or "rule of truth," will not be
deceived by the way the Gnostics use Scripture to prop up their system.[41]

Irenaeus's appeal to the hypothesis, or rule of faith, has long been a focus of
studies of his thought.[42] Immediately after his discussion of the Homeric cento,
Irenaeus recounts the key points of this rule of faith (that are themselves derived
from Scripture), which are oriented around the three heads of Father, Son, and
Spirit and detail the plotline of the economic activities of each, saying:

The Church, indeed, though disseminated throughout the world, even
to the ends of the earth, received from the apostles and their disciples the
faith in one God the Father Almighty, the Creator of heaven and earth and
the seas and all things that are in them; and in the one Jesus Christ, the
Son of God, who was enfleshed for our salvation; and in the Holy Spirit,
who through the prophets preached the Economies, the coming, the birth

39. Irenaeus, *Haer.* 1.9.4.
40. This dissection of Scripture also points to Irenaeus's concern with the way Gnostics allegorize the
text, especially their use of numerology or gematria. They gave special attention to the symbolic meaning of
numbers in Scripture and conformed those numbers to their system. See: Irenaeus, *Haer.* 1.1.3; *Haer.* 1.18–19;
Haer. 2.20–25; and *Haer.* 5.35.1–4. D. Bruno Reynders, "La polémique de saint Irénée: Méthode et principes,"
Recherches de théologie ancienne et médiévale 7 (1935): 5–27.
41. Grant, *Irenaeus of Lyons*, 49.
42. Philip Hefner, "Theological Methodology and St. Irenaeus," *Journal of Religion* 44.4 (1964): 294–309.

from a Virgin, the passion, the resurrection from the dead, and the bodily ascension into heaven of the beloved Son, Christ Jesus our Lord, and His coming from heaven in the glory of the Father to recapitulate all things, and to raise up all flesh of the whole human race, in order that to Christ Jesus, our Lord and God, Savior and King, according to the invisible Father's good pleasure, *Every knee should bow* [of those] *in heaven and on earth and under the earth, and every tongue confes*s Him, and that He would exercise just judgement toward all; and that, on the other hand, He would send into eternal fire the spiritual forces of wickedness, and the angels who transgressed and become rebels, and the godless, wicked, lawless, and blasphemous people; but, on the other hand, by bestowing life on the righteous and holy and those who kept His commandments and who have preserved in His love—both those who did so from the beginning and those who did so after repentance—He would bestow on them as a grace the gift of incorruption and clothe them with everlasting glory.[43]

Irenaeus does not believe his church alone confesses this faith but every church, regardless of geographical location. It is not the Gnostics who confess this faith but "the Church, as we have said before, though disseminated throughout the whole world, carefully guards this preaching and this faith which she has received, as if she dwelt in one house. She likewise believes these things as if she has but one soul and one and the same heart; she preaches, teaches, and hands them down harmoniously, as if she possessed but one mouth."[44] Just as the sun shines over all the earth, Irenaeus continues, so the preaching of this faith shines on everyone in the church, and no Christian teacher, however gifted, will teach differently from this faith.[45] This appeal to a unified confession forms the orienting purpose of Irenaeus's apologetic; the church, in whatever age or location, is called to receive, defend, and pass on this faith.

Economy: The Arrangement of the Plot

The second term, *economy*, depicts the "'arrangement of a poem or the purpose and direction of the plot."[46] This implies that episodes of the story can be arranged (or rearranged) in coordination with the hypothesis of the narrative. The rhetorician Quintilian cites Homer's practices of beginning a story in the

---

43. Irenaeus, *Haer.* 1.10.1. For other descriptions of the rule of faith in Irenaeus, see: Irenaeus, *Haer.* 1.22.1, *Haer.* 3.11.1, and Irenaeus, *Epid.* 6.
44. Irenaeus, *Haer.* 1.10.2.
45. Ibid.
46. Grant, *Irenaeus of Lyons*, 49.

middle or the end based on the necessity of the storyline.[47] In this sense, *hypothesis* and *economy* are closely connected in rhetorical works, since "the intention of a whole literary or rhetorical work resides in its hypothesis, then an economic arrangement presupposes the hypothesis—it takes the hypothesis as its starting-place."[48] The notion of economy becomes the "logical basis for Irenaeus' polemic against Gnostic interpretation of Scripture" so that the hypothesis of Scripture articulated in the rule of faith above frames the economic activity of God oriented toward the telos of beholding the glory of God.[49]

The problem with the Gnostics, Irenaeus suggests, is that they blend and adapt the plot of Scripture to conform to their own peculiar hypothesis. The Valentinians "gather their views from other sources than the Scriptures" and weave together Scripture with these sources, which ignores "the order and the connection of the Scriptures" and destroys the truth.[50] The language of economy is not explicit but implied in this context as the underlying plot that fashions the order and connection of the Scriptures and characterizes the unity of God's activity within creation. The problem with the Gnostics is that they transfer passages and rearrange them, adapting and accommodating them to conform to a different hypothesis and thus creating an entirely different economic arrangement.

Irenaeus confirms this a few chapters later when he describes the way the divine economy, including the nature and activities of Father, Son, and Spirit, are oriented toward the fulfillment of human salvation. Scripture ought not be distorted and conformed to a different conception of God and God's activity but instead ought to explain "God's dealings and Economy, which He made for the sake of the human race."[51] Contrary to the Gnostic who thinks up another god besides the Creator of all things, Irenaeus argues that the meaning of Scripture is rooted in the ordered connections between the economy, comprised of God's dealings, and the hypothesis, or rule of truth. The various episodes of the divine economy unite to support the hypothesis, which details the salvific events of Scripture that culminate in the person and work of Christ.

Recapitulation: The Concluding Summary

The third term is *recapitulation*, which was often used in rhetorical contexts to refer to a "concluding summary" of an act, speech, or literary work.[52] In Irenaeus's theology, the term points to the summary of the work of Christ that

---

47. Briggman, "Literary and Rhetorical Theory in Irenaeus, Part 1," 517.
48. Ibid., 518.
49. Ibid., 523.
50. Irenaeus, *Haer.* 1.10.3.
51. Ibid.
52. Grant, *Irenaeus of Lyons*, 50. This is an important Pauline term found in Ephesians 1:10.

knits together the narrative and explains Christ's work of salvation within Scripture's hypothesis. He writes that it was necessary that "the Lord, when coming to the lost sheep and making recapitulation of so great an economy, and seeking out His handiwork, should save the very man who was made according to His image and likeness."[53] *Recapitulation*, therefore, is a summary term for Irenaeus's Christology that unites the divine economy (the argument of the plot) into one person and one work of salvation. It draws a unity between Adam and Christ, as well as between the deity and humanity of Christ that refutes the various Gnostic dualisms mentioned above.

OTHER APOLOGETIC STRATEGIES

Finally, a series of other apologetic strategies shape Irenaeus's defense and show how the Gnostic views are inconsistent, improbable, and even absurd.[54] These methods include: a basic pattern for analyzing heretical perspectives, using questions and dilemma, parody, critiquing their sources, and critiquing their immorality. These strategies are some of the variety of ways Irenaeus uses the tools at his disposal to defend the church's faith and expose the fallacies of the Gnostic system.

First, in many cases Irenaeus's description of Gnosticism and critique of specific Gnostic sects follows a discernable pattern. For example, in *Against Heresies* 1.23–28, his analysis of each Gnostic heresy follows the same basic outline, including: (1) rejection of the God of the Old Testament, (2) supposition that evil angels or an inferior power created the world, (3) false teaching about Jesus—especially docetic Christology, (4) the magical practices of its adherents, (5) the idolatry and other forms of immoral practices by its adherents, (6) the claim made by its adherents that they have been liberated from obedience to the evil angels and/or the creator.[55] Irenaeus not only catalogs these heresies but also follows the apologetic strategy of *paradosis* that creates a historical genealogy of the heretics and traces their roots to the teaching of Simon Magus (*Haer.* 23, see Acts 8:9–24).[56] Above all, his critique of Gnosticism is a model of careful analysis of Christian heresies and sets the context for his applied apologetic methods throughout the rest of his work.

Second, one of Irenaeus's main apologetic strategies is the use of dilemma and question, though he also has instances of parody when rational arguments

53. Irenaeus, *Haer.* 3.23.1. See also: Irenaeus, *Haer.* 3.21.10–22.2, Irenaeus, *Epid.* 6, and *Epid.* 30.
54. Perkins, "Irenaeus and the Gnostics," 195.
55. Perkins, "Irenaeus and the Gnostics," 198. Perkins created this list using the common arguments in each chapter.
56. Ibid.

are exhausted and he resorts to discussing the absurdity of the Gnostic myth.[57] Throughout his refutation, Irenaeus never really makes use of syllogisms but instead consistently poses competing propositions, or intellectual dilemmas, for his opponents. Nearly every chapter of *Against Heresies* 2 contains instances of question and dilemma.[58] For example, in *Against Heresies* 2.1.1–5, Irenaeus begins comparing the nature of the one true God with the variety of Gnostic gods emanating from the highest God in the pleroma, saying:

> For it is necessary either that there be one who contains all others and who made within his own realm each creature that was made, just as he willed; or that there be in turn many and interminable Makers and Gods, beginning with each other and ending in each other on every side; and that all others that are outside be contained by some other who is greater. And it would be necessary to acknowledge that each one of them be, as it were, enclosed and remaining in his own realm. However, none of all these would be God, for each one of them would be deficient since that one possesses only a very small portion in relation to all the rest. And so the name Omnipotent would be destroyed, and such an opinion would of necessity fall into impiety.[59]

The intellectual dilemma raises the problem of the highest Gnostic deity containing all other spiritual realities, because either the divine emanations must extend *ad infinitum*, or there must be a God who is greater. For the Christian, there is only one God who formed and made all things by his Son and Spirit. This is the one God who is above all and has created all things.

Irenaeus also combines this strategy of dilemma with a constant barrage of questions that interrogate his opponents' views and raise more intellectual problems. For example, in *Against Heresies* 2.15.2, he questions the number and division of the thirty aeons in the Valentinian pleroma that are divided into groups of eight, ten, and twelve, called an Ogdoad, a Decad, and a Duodecad.[60] Irenaeus asks, "Why indeed is it divided into three parts, namely the Ogdoad, a Decad, and a Duodecad and not some other number different from these? And the division itself, why are there just three, and not four, or five, or six, or into some other number?" Cycles of questions likes this appear again and again

---

57. Reynders, "La polémique de saint Irénée," 8–9.
58. Ibid., 9. For example, see: Irenaeus, *Haer.* 2.1.1–5, *Haer.* 2.3.1, *Haer.* 2.4.1, and *Haer.* 2.5.1–3.
59. Irenaeus, *Haer.* 2.1.5.
60. See also Irenaeus, *Haer.* 2.11.2.

throughout his arguments as he raises questions of inconsistencies and contradictions in their myth.

There are still other times within his use of question and dilemma when Irenaeus finds the Gnostic myth so absurd that he resorts to parody or irony.[61] In these instances, he often suggests new erroneous explanations of their views or ridicules the inanity of their beliefs. For example, when Valentinians suggest that the world was created from the product of the rebellion of an aeon named Achamoth, whose tears created water, he asks how this deity created both salt water and fresh water from tears, when tears are only salty. Irenaeus makes the sarcastic proposal that perhaps Achamoth's tears produced salt water and that his perspiration produced the fresh water.[62] In another instance, he ridicules the Valentinian system by suggesting new names and titles because the name for their deities are created without meaning and connection to their system. He suggests, for example, calling the highest God in their system the Gourd, and the second power he names Utter-Emptiness, who together produce a new deity he calls "Cucumber" and "Pumpkin." Together "these powers—Gourd, Utter-Emptiness, Cucumber, and Pumpkin—begot the rest of the multitude of delirious Pumpkins of Valentinus."[63]

Third, Irenaeus poses several arguments for the source of their errors, including both pagan philosophers and demons. Contrary to other Christian theologians before him, Irenaeus is not enamored of pagan philosophy and generally assumes that the Gnostics have erroneously based their views on it rather than on a right reading of Scripture.[64] The Gnostics' ideas are not original but were said before them "by those who are ignorant of God and who are called philosophers."[65] In *Against Heresies* 2.14.2–7 Ireneus cites, among others, Anaxagoras, Democritus, Epicurus, Empedocles, Pythagoreans, Cynics, Plato, and Aristotle and mentions in passing how each of these philosophers influenced elements of the Gnostic system. In doing so, they present doctrines that have been sewn together with ancient philosophy as "a kind of cento out of many and worst rags, and so, by a subtle style, they prepare for themselves a fictitious cloak."[66] And Irenaeus does not stop there. In certain instances, he suggests that spiritual warfare may also explain the origins of the Gnostic system. The Gnostics are "altogether full of deceit of every kind, apostate inspiration, demoniacal working, and the

---

61. Reynders, "La polémique de saint Irénée," 25–6.
62. Irenaeus, *Haer.* 1.4.4; *Haer.* 2.10.3.
63. Irenaeus, *Haer.* 1.11.4.
64. Irenaeus, *Haer.* 1.25.6; *Haer.* 2.14.2–7; *Haer.* 2.27.1; *Haer.* 2.32.2.
65. Irenaeus, *Haer.* 2.14.2.
66. Ibid.

phantasms of idolatry."[67] They are, in Irenaeus's view, endowed with a "spirit of wickedness" that endeavors to lead those of the church astray.[68]

Fourth, Irenaeus attacks their morality and stresses their depraved, libertine behavior, which also invokes classical *ad hominem* arguments.[69] The Valentinians believe they are saved by nature, and therefore, nothing they perform in the material body can corrupt them. Even the "perfect among them shamelessly do all the forbidden things, about which the Scriptures give guarantee that 'they who do such things shall not inherit the kingdom of God'"[70] (Gal 5:21).They have no problems eating food sacrificed to idols, are the first to gather at every pagan religious festival or gladiatorial game, and participate in all kinds of sexual immorality.[71] Irenaeus reports that they even have some firsthand accounts from those who participated in this immoral behavior and later converted to the church.[72] Like the Valentinians, Carpocratians also boast of "practicing every kind of impious and godless deed" because their souls must depart from this world satisfied that they have experienced every kind of freedom.[73] Irenaeus remarks that the things they practice are so immoral that those in the church would not dare speak or even think of such behaviors.[74]

CONTRIBUTIONS TO THE FIELD OF APOLOGETICS

There is no doubt that in the waning years of the second century, Irenaeus's impact on apologetics in the early church was immense. John Behr writes, "By the time of his death, Irenaeus had done more than anyone else to expose those who had departed from the Church for what they were and to refute their teachings."[75] Throughout Irenaeus's apologetic response, he stressed the importance of the faith handed down from the apostles and the preservation of its unity and purity. Irenaeus's detailed analysis of the streams of Gnostic thought modeled the kind of careful theological reflection that a Christian apologist ought to practice. This response to Gnosticism framed his theological method, which argued

---

67. Irenaeus, *Haer.* 2.31.3.
68. Ibid.
69. Reynders, "La polémique de saint Irénée," 9–10. Perkins, "Irenaeus and the Gnostics," 195. George W. Macrae, "Why the Church Rejected Gnosticism," in *Jewish and Christian Self-definition, 1: The Shaping of Christianity in the Second and Third Centuries*, ed. E. P. Sanders (Philadelphia: Fortress, 1980), 128–30.
70. Irenaeus, *Haer.* 1.6.3.
71. Ibid.
72. Ibid.
73. Irenaeus, *Haer.* 1.25.3.
74. Irenaeus, *Haer.* 1.25.4. *Haer.* 1.25.5.
75. John Behr, *Irenaeus of Lyons: Identifying Christianity* (Oxford: Oxford University Press, 2013), 70.

that amid all revealed knowledge, the revelation of Scripture is the only clear and certain revelation. In order to defend the faith and explain the faith revealed in Scripture, Irenaeus was not afraid to employ rhetorical strategies derived from his secular education.[76] Above all, Irenaeus's apologetic arguments helped the church navigate the threat of Gnosticism in the second century and helped preserve the faith of the church.

BIBLIOGRAPHY

Primary Sources

Eusebius. *Ecclesiastical History*. Trans. by C. F. Crusé. Peabody, MA: Hendrickson, 2000.

Roberts, A., and J. Donaldson. *Ante-Nicene Fathers*. Vol. 1. Peabody, MA: Hendrickson, 1994.

Unger, Dominic J., and John J. Dillon. *St. Irenaeus of Lyons: Against the Heresies (Book 1)*. Ancient Christian Writers 55 New York: Newman, 1992.

Unger, Dominic J., John J. Dillon, and Michael Slusser. *St. Irenaeus of Lyons: Against the Heresies (Book 2)*. Ancient Christian Writers 65 New York: Newman, 2012.

Unger, Dominic J., John J. Dillon, and Matthew Steenberg. *St. Irenaeus of Lyons: Against the Heresies (Book 3)*. Ancient Christian Writers 64 New York: Newman, 2012.

Secondary Sources

Behr, John. *Irenaeus of Lyons*. Oxford: Oxford University Press, 2013.

Briggman, Anthony, "Literary and Rhetorical Theory in Irenaeus, Part 1." *Vigiliae Christianae* 69 (2015): 500–27.

———. "Literary and Rhetorical Theory in Irenaeus, Part 2." *Vigiliae Christianae* 70 (2016): 31–50.

———. "Revisiting Irenaeus's Philosophical Acumen." *Vigiliae Christianae* 65 (2011): 115–24.

Drobner, Hubertus R. *The Fathers of the Church: A Comprehensive Introduction*. Grand Rapids: Baker Academic, 2007.

Grant, Robert M. *Greek Apologists of the Second Century*. Philadelphia: Westminster, 1988.

———. *Irenaeus of Lyons*. New York: Routledge, 1997.

———. "Irenaeus and Hellenistic Culture." *Harvard Theological Review* 42 (1949): 41–51.

Hefner, Philip. "Theological Methodology and St. Irenaeus." *Journal of Religion* 44.4 (1964): 294–309.

Hultgren, Arland J., and Steven A. Haggmark, eds. *The Earliest Christian Heretics: Readings From Their Opponents*. Minneapolis, MN: Fortress, 1996.

King, Karen. *What is Gnosticism?* Cambridge, MA: Harvard University Press, 2003.

Markschies, Christoph. *Gnosis: An Introduction*. New York: T&T Clark, 2003.

Meyer, Marvin, ed. *The Nag Hammadi Scriptures: The Revised and Updated Translation of the Sacred Gnostic Texts*. New York: HarperCollins, 2008.

Perkins, Pheme. "Irenaeus and the Gnostics: Rhetoric and Composition in Adversus Haereses Book One." *Vigiliae Christianae* 30 (1976): 193–200.

Presley, Stephen O. *The Intertextual Reception of Genesis 1–3 in Irenaeus of Lyons*. Leiden: Brill, 2015.

Reynders, D. Bruno. "La polémique de saint Irénée: Méthode et principes." *Recherches de théologie ancienne et médiévale* 7 (1935): 5–27.

Schoedel, William R. "Philosophy and Rhetoric in the Adversus Haereses of Irenaeus." *Vigiliae Christianae* 13 (1959): 22–32.

———. "Theological Method in Irenaeus ('Adversus Haereses' 2.25–28)." *The Journal of Theological Studies* 35.1 (1984): 31–49.

Stead, Christopher. *Philosophy in Christian Antiquity*. Cambridge: Cambridge University Press, 1994.

Steenberg, Matthew C. *Irenaeus on Creation*. Leiden: Brill, 2008.

---

76. Grant, "Irenaeus and Hellenistic Culture"; William R. Schoedel, "Philosophy and Rhetoric"; Perkins, "Irenaeus and the Gnostics"; Briggman, "Literary and Rhetorical Theory in Irenaeus, Part 1"; Briggman, "Literary and Rhetorical Theory in Irenaeus, Part 2."

Vallée, Gérard. "Theological and Non-Theological Motives in Irenaeus's Refutation of the Gnostics." Pages 174–84 in *Jewish and Christian Self-definition, 1: The Shaping of Christianity in the Second and Third Centuries.* Ed. by E. P. Sanders. Philadelphia: Fortress, 1980.

Wilken, Robert L. "The Homeric Cento in Irenaeus, 'Adversus Haereses' 1.8.4." *Vigiliae Christianae* 21 (1967): 25–33.

Williams, Michael A., *Rethinking 'Gnosticism': An Argument for Dismantling a Dubious Category.* Princeton, NJ: Princeton University Press, 1996.

Young, Frances. "Greek Apologists of the Second Century." Pages 81–104 in *Apologetics in the Roman Empire: Pagans, Jews, and Christians.* Ed. by Mark Edwards, Martin Goodman, and Simon Price. New York: Oxford University Press, 1999.

ATHENAGORAS OF ATHENS

Greek Philosophy as Arbiter of Christian Beliefs

W. BRIAN SHELTON

Second-century Roman society held misperceptions that Christians practiced cannibalism, incest, and atheism. These growing popular attitudes put believers in social jeopardy and at court tribunals for their faith, sometimes resulting in their death. In two works addressed to the highest authority of the Roman Empire, Athenagoras (ca. 133–190) marshalled popular philosophy and literature, conventional techniques of argumentation, and a reasonable petition to establish a case for Christianity. He posits that the ethics practiced by Christians were equal to or superior to other Roman citizens, while doctrines like the resurrection had logical and scientific validation for belief.

HISTORICAL BACKGROUND

The second century was the inaugural era of formal Christian apologetics. Among the principal articulators in defense of the faith was the erudite Hellenistic philosopher Athenagoras. When pagan philosophers mocked the new faith and the populous promoted misinformed opinions about Christian religious practices, this church father took an approach to a ministry of apologetics based on contemporary intellectual standards and logical deduction in defense of the faith. Historically, little is known of the personal background of Athenagoras. He was likely born about AD 133 in the city of Athens and was of Greek origin. The city was held in high regard as both the birthplace of Greek philosophy and the symbolic center of its legacy. His obscure career likely ended there about AD 190. Only two of his apologetic writings survive, one in defense

Image: 1682 Oxford edition of the works of Athenagoras

of Christianity against the accusations of contemporary critics and another in defense of the resurrection.

The primary manuscript for these two works contains the appellation "Athenagoras of Athens, a Christian philosopher" and was written "concerning Christians." The successive appearance of two works in the codex suggests that both works were attributed to Athenagoras from antiquity. They are addressed to "Emperors Marcus Aurelius Antoninus and Lucius Aurelius Commodus, Armenian and Sarmatian Victors, and, what is more, philosophers," and this places their writing some time during the imperial father and son regency of AD 176–180.[1] Barnard suggests that Athenagoras may have presented the general apologetical work to the emperors in person on his imperial eastern tour, and the resurrection work seems to "be based on public lectures given to a regular audience."[2]

But what we know about this philosopher of Athens is limited. Clement of Alexandria, Tertullian, Eusebius, Jerome, and Suidas do not mention him, although this era does not commonly see Christian writers referencing their contemporaries.[3] Methodius of Olympus quotes Athenagoras one hundred years later, and even later Epiphanius and Photius repeat the fragment and explicitly name him. Philip of Side, a deacon under Chrysostom, provides a rare and exceptional biography:

> Athenagoras was the first director of the School at Alexandria; his *floruit* [flourishing] was about the time of Hadrian and Antoninus, to whom he dedicated his *Embassy* on behalf of the Christians. He was a man who professed Christianity while still wearing the philosopher's garb and was the leading man in the Academy. Before Celsus did so he had planned to write against the Christians, but, reading the Holy Scriptures to make his attack more telling, he was so won over by the Holy Spirit as to become, like the great Paul, a teacher and not a persecutor of the faith he was attacking. Philip says that Clement, author of the *Stromateis*, was his disciple and Pantaenus Clement's. Pantaenus too was an Athenian, and being a Pythagorean in his philosophy.[4]

While Clement and Pantaenus are well known for their headship of the Alexandrian catechetical school, Philip's claim that this philosopher was its

---

1. Leslie W. Barnard, *Athenagoras: A Study in Second Century Christian Apologetic* (Beauchesne: Paris, 1972), 19–20.
2. Ibid., 17–18.
3. Ibid., 16.
4. David Rankin, *Athenagoras: Philosopher and Theologian* (New York: Routledge, 2016), 5–6.

inaugural head does not find clear substantiation.[5] Particularly valuable in this short biography is the account of the conversion of Athenagoras, who Philip compares to the apostle Paul. It appears that this philosopher read Christian writings to contest the Christian faith before realizing the worth of its teachings. Perhaps his philosophical approach to evaluating Christianity required meritorious calculation of the Christian view of culture, logic, and writing that was only just emerging during this time. Somehow, the merit of Christianity took hold of Athenagoras, redirecting his efforts against the religion, and instead he supported it. Philip expresses the reason for his intellectual conversion: "He was won over by the Holy Spirit."[6]

Whatever the case, a possible sojourn in Alexandria would have provided more sympathy for his philosophical approach to Christianity than the culture of Athens. Christianity soon found a foothold in this cosmopolitan city, and evidence of the influence of Philo can be seen in Athenagoras's writings.[7] A range of ancient Greek philosophical appeals is evident in his thinking and demonstrates principles foundational to Pythagoreanism, Stoicism, Epicureanism, and Middle Platonism.[8] These philosophies were part of the intellectual milieu of the age, and Athenagoras was both aware of and comfortable in their employment. This is important, knowing the philosophical predilection of the imperial leadership, which was the intended audience for these treatises.

THEOLOGICAL CONTEXT

Both extant works of Athenagoras reflect a milieu of hostility toward the Christian faith, and his response in this context places him squarely among the greatest of the early apologists. This antagonism comes from two audiences: philosophers, who employed logic and rhetoric against the new religion, and common folk, who employed more unfounded and base allegations against it. This is the

---

5. Since Eusebius suggests that Pantaenus had two periods of oversight at the catechetical school (Eusebius, *Hist. eccl.* 6.14), perhaps knowledge of the role of Athenagoras there is simply lost. Furthermore, Barnard is correct in recognizing that while the succession of rule at the school is questionable and Philip's reference to Antoninus is a likely confusion with Marcus Aurelius Antoninus, other historical details deserve recognition (Barnard, *Athenagoras*, 14–15). While early fifth-century Socrates profiles Philip as excessively detailed, he does not suggest he is inaccurate (Socrates, *Hist. eccl.* 27; NPNF2 2:168). Pouderon concludes: "It is thus not a negligible testimony, merely an unsafe source, which must be used with infinite precaution." (Bernard Pouderon, "Les écoles chrétiennes de Rome, Athènes, Alexandrie et Antioche à l'époque des Antonins: Remarques sur la circulation des maîtres et de leurs disciples," *Bulletin de Littérature Ecclésiastique* 113 [2012]: 387. Translation by chapter author.)

6. Rankin, *Athenagoras*, 5–6.

7. Rankin, *Athenagoras*, 9–10. He concludes that no "substantial Alexandrian connection whatsoever" can be made, including the philosopher's presence in Alexandria, p. 9.

8. David Rankin, "Athenagoras, Philosopher and First Principles," *Studia Patristica* 45 (2010): 420–23.

period in which we find critics such as Celsus, whose *On True Doctrine,* or *The True Word,* criticized Christianity through a range of topics, from an absurd biography of Jesus to a mockery of his followers. Along philosophical lines, Celsus remarks: "There is nothing new or impressive about their ethical teaching; indeed, when one compares it to other philosophies, their simplemindedness becomes apparent."[9] Likewise, "In truth there is nothing at all unusual about what the Christians believe, except that they believe it to the exclusion of more comprehensive truths about god."[10] In *ad hominem* fashion, he also criticizes the believers of the faith: "It is clear to me that the writings of the Christians are a lie, and that your fables are not well-enough constructed to conceal this monstrous fiction: I have heard that some of your interpreters . . . are on to the inconsistencies and, pen in hand, alter the originals writings, three, four and several more times over in order to be able to deny the contradictions in the face of criticism."[11]

Origen attributes to Celsus an accusation of blind, even stupid, faith among Christians: "He asserts that certain persons who do not wish either to give or receive a reason for their belief, keep repeating, 'Do not examine, but believe!' and, 'Your faith will save you!'"[12] While the thoughts of Aristotle and Plato do find evidence in the writings of Athenagoras, we do not find any direct engagement with Celsus. Still, this critic's attitude likely mirrors the outlook of many pagan philosophers of the age and could be one of the reasons that led to Athenagoras's own writings in response.

There were other critics at this time who also shaped public opinion about Christians. Two such critics were Lucian, a satirist and rhetorician in Samosata of Roman Armenia, and Galen, a physician and philosopher in Pergamon. Lucian describes Christians' beliefs: "They are all brothers of one another after they have transgressed once for all by denying the Greek gods and by worshipping that crucified sophist himself and living under his laws . . . receiving such doctrines traditionally without any definite evidence."[13] Galen criticizes Christians' lack of erudition: "Most people are unable to follow any demonstrative argument consecutively; hence they need parables . . . just as now we see the people called Christians drawing their faith from parables."[14]

Among the accusations against Christianity at this time were several

9. Celsus, *On the True Doctrine*, 2.
10. Ibid., 121.
11. Ibid., 37.
12. Origen, *Cels.* 1:9.
13. Lucian, *Peregr.*, cited in W. H. C. Frend, *Martyrdom and Persecution in the Early Church: A Study of a Conflict from the Maccabees to Donatus* (New York: New York University Press, 1967), 202.
14. Frend, *Martyrdom and Persecution*, 238.

beliefs and practices viewed as odd by society. From Athenagoras we learn that fellow citizens accused Christians of immorality based on a misunderstanding of their faith. Society charged them with atheism for their lack of belief in the Greco-Roman gods commonly accepted at the time. Others charged them with engaging in incest because of the practice of a commemorative agape feast where Christian believers called each other brothers and sisters in Christ. Some charged them with cannibalism because they ate Christ's metaphorical body and blood.[15] Eusebius seems to validate these latter two claims of accusation when he cites how the church in Gaul was "charged with the feasts of Thyestes, and the incests of Oedipus."[16]

Along with this philosophical and cultural antagonism against Christianity, a mid-second century resident would likely be familiar with various social and imperial persecutions. Eusebius describes how the reign of Marcus Aurelius hosted "the greatest persecutions excited in Asia,"[17] which Frend describes as "having the full weight of public opinion behind them."[18] The emperor's reputation as a Stoic philosopher amplified popular traditions of Greco-Roman thought. Christians of this time underwent the martyrdoms of Justin in Rome, Polycarp in Smyrna, Sagaris in Laodicea, Papylas and Carpus in Pergamum, the citizens of Lyons and Vienne, and Apollonius in Rome. Emperor Marcus Aurelius is noted for his promotion of cultic state religion in conjunction with high ideals of philosophy for the sake of the empire.[19] Athenagoras addresses his apology to Marcus and Commodus, emperors during these persecutions.

Yet we should note that the *sitz im leben* was not merely one of Christian trials and persecution but also of Christian theological engagement. Logic and rhetoric were emerging alongside the deaths of martyrs in defense of the faith and directly engaged the arguments made by religious and social philosophers. Athenagoras is among these writers, making his contribution to the first age of apologists. The difference between the approach of the martyrs and the apologists has been seen as a variance between dissociative and integrative approaches to culture.[20] Martyrdom, monastic, and apocalyptic responses dissociated from

---

15. Athenagoras, *Embassy*, 3.
16. Eusebius, *Hist. eccl.* 5.1.14. Both allusions would be familiar to the ancients. In Greek mythology, King Atreus of Mycenae saw his kingdom and the affections of his wife go to his brother, Thyestes. In an act of revenge, Atreus killed his brother's sons and served them to him at a feast, which Thyestes unwittingly ate. Likewise, the Sophoclean tragedy of Oedipus sees the main character solve the riddle of the sphinx to win the throne of Thebes, innocently marrying the widowed queen, his mother.
17. Eusebius, *Hist. eccl.* 4.15.1.
18. Frend, *Martyrdom and Persecution*, 197.
19. Frank McLynn, *Marcus Aurelius: A Life* (Boston: Da Capo, 2010), 227–28.
20. W. Brian Shelton, "Learning from Patristic Responses to Culture," *The Contemporary Church and the Early Church: Case Studies in Resourcement*, ed. Paul Hartog (Eugene, OR: Wipf & Stock, 2010), 104–28.

culture, while legal rejoinders and philosophical syntheses integrated culture to offer testimony for the faith. For Athenagoras, his apologetic response was of the latter type, and it attempted to employ the ideals of Greek philosophy both in argumentation and in expression and to appeal to the minds of the philosophical elite of his era.

APOLOGETICAL RESPONSE AND METHODOLOGY

Athenagoras's two extant works refute the prevailing cultural views about Christianity and vindicate the meaning of misunderstood Christian practices. While both works represent a defense of the faith against contemporary critics, the *Embassy* is an exoneration of Christianity using conventional pagan and Jewish sources, while the *Resurrection* is an exposition on a central Christian doctrine.

Vindication of Christianity

The first treatise by Athenagoras is an apologetic for Christianity against the Roman cultural and legal persecution of the church and her beliefs. Commonly referred to as the *Embassy*, the work has also been named *A Plea for the Christians*. Historically, the term "embassy" or *presbeía* is a commission sent between rulers of states through ambassadors. The spirit of the work is an ambassadorial appeal to leading Romans whose perspective about Christianity is ill-informed. In particular, Athenagoras's intent is to refute the common charge of atheism that had been levied against Christians who would not join in the worship of the emperor or the Roman pantheon of gods. In addition to this general defense, the work also addresses the evidence of higher moral living among Christians and defends against the charges of cannibalism and incest. The logic and reason for particular Christian behaviors is explained, while the illogical and unreasonable treatment of Christians is questioned as incongruent with the prevailing values of the culture and the emperors themselves. His explanation seeks to vindicate the church to the ruling pagan philosopher of the state through logic, reason, Greek standards, and Greek literature.

The strategy used by Athenagoras has several elements to engage and refute the charges that had been made against Christianity. First, the work is addressed to "Emperors Marcus Aurelius Antoninus and Lucius Aurelius Commodus, Armenian and Sarmatian Victors, and, what is more, philosophers."[21] By writing to the emperor himself, Athenagoras hopes that the rulers of the day would

---

21. Barnard, *Athenagoras*, 19–20.

eventually extend leniency to Christians through their legislation, writings, and influence. The recognition of the accomplishments of the emperors is equally strategic, appealing both to their achievements as sovereigns and their wisdom as philosophers. They are addressed as philosophers, honoring their erudition that was a source of pride while setting up Athenagoras's own method for appeal as a colaborer in wisdom. They are called the "greatest of kings" with "gentle and mild natures,"[22] acclaimed as "illustrious and benevolent and most learned sovereigns"[23] and attributed to "excel all men in intelligence."[24] They are recipients of the hope that "the succession of your reign may grow and increase as all men become subject to you."[25] Such attributed honors are typical for the regal ethos that ambassadors would provide.

Secondly, Athenagoras strategically and artfully acknowledges that Christians are obligated by the same civic order that the pagan emperors seek from their citizens. Social policies are repeatedly recognized from one who implies that he is an obedient citizen. Christians pray for the emperor, government, and imperial succession, even if they are provided "in the interests of Christians themselves."[26] Christianity offers peace and order to the state by conforming to the will of God, which is congruent with conforming to the will of state. This congruence is stated explicitly: "This is also to our advantage that we may lead a quiet and peaceful life and at the same time may willingly do all that is commanded."[27] Barnard reflects on this approach as an appeal "to a common ground shared with his readers and propounds a *modus vivendi*," or mode of living, which characterizes the ideal Roman citizen.[28]

This ideal is honored by Christian citizens who respect moral religious teachings that also respect the state. Christians love their enemies rather than return vengeance when done wrong against them, reducing conflict, violence, and litigations. They strive to live a life of purity to honor God, calling each other "brother and sister" and sharing a kiss of salutation while remaining sexually uncorrupted. They prioritize fidelity in marriage, while some remain virgins to honor God. They object to gladiatorial games as murder, proving for

---

22. Athenagoras, *Embassy* 1.1, 1.2; *Leg.* and *Res.*, ed. and trans. William R. Schoedel (New York: Oxford University Press, 1972), 3.

23. Athenagoras, *Embassy* 2.1 (ANF 2:130). While these editors entitle the work *A Plea for the Christians*, the title *Embassy* will be retained throughout for consistency.

24. Athenagoras, *Embassy* 6.2, 31.3 (ANF 2:131, 145).

25. Athenagoras, *Embassy* 37.2; *Leg.* 87.

26. Claudio Moreschini and Enrico Norelli, *Early Christian Greek and Latin Literature* (Peabody, MA: Hendrickson, 2005), 1:207. Athenagoras, *Embassy* 37.2; *Leg.* 87.

27. Athenagoras, *Embassy* 37.3; *Leg.* 87.

28. Leslie W. Barnard, "The Father of Christian Anthropology," *Zeitschrift für die neutestamentliche Wissenschaft und die Kunde der älteren Kirche* 63 (1974): 257.

Athenagoras that the charge of cannibalism cannot stand.[29] Without citing the gospel writings, the philosopher echoes the words of Jesus that Christians will be known by their attribute of love (John 13:35). While Athenagoras appeals through philosophical means, he admits that some Christians "are unable in words to prove the benefit of our doctrine, yet by their deeds exhibit the benefits arising from their persuasion of its truth" when they love their neighbors as themselves. He unashamedly admits that they are not academically oriented, naming "uneducated persons, and artisans, and old women" as model citizens who live their faith in compatibility with the desirable ethics of society.[30]

Athenagoras is so confident in this claim that he invites imperial punishment to any who deserve it, logically thus permitting and even protecting Christians if they are correspondingly undeserving of punishment. For example, concerning the charges of cannibalism and incest, he remarks: "If these charges are true, spare no class: proceed at once against our crimes; destroy us root and branch, with our wives and children, if any Christian is found to live like the brutes." Likewise, on the other hand: "If these things are only idle tales and empty slanders, originating in the fact that virtue is opposed by its very nature to vice . . . it remains for you to make inquiry concerning our life, our opinions, our loyalty and obedience to you and your house and government, and thus at length to grant to us the same rights (we ask nothing more) as those who persecute us."[31]

Thirdly, Athenagoras connects theological similarities between the Greek philosophers and various Christian writers. Euripides, Plato, Aristotle, Stoics, Socrates, and the Pythagoreans all find reference by name as evidencing monotheism, and thus potentially the Christian God.[32] Quotations of recognizable works function to support the church in its worship of the one true, living God. Here he represents Pythagoras when he insists "God is one and 'above matter.'"[33] He profiles the Stoics when he depicts God as partless or simple.[34] He employs the notion of God as first principle when he names Epicurus in articulation of "ultimate indivisibles," which Athenagoras attributes to God alone.[35] While there is evidence that Athenagoras was a Platonist before his conversion, Rankin finds Platonic compatibility, but with clear variations that augment Christian thinking. He describes how, for Athenagoras, God and his Word is a first principle, while matter is not. "In this Athenagoras would claim (though somewhat

---

29. Positive ethics of Christians are laid out in Athenagoras, *Embassy* 11, 31–35.
30. Athenagoras, *Embassy* 11.4 (ANF 2:134).
31. Athenagoras, *Embassy* 3.2 (ANF 2:130).
32. Athenagoras, *Embassy* 5–8.
33. Rankin, "Athenagoras, Philosopher and First Principles," 421. Athenagoras, *Embassy* 6.1.
34. Ibid., 421.
35. Ibid.

dubiously) the witness and support of Plato."[36] Yet through this process, his argument affirms certain philosophical and theological tenets that would be recognizable and appreciated by his educated Greco-Roman audience.

He then synthesizes this testimony with the Hebrew prophets, namely Moses, Isaiah, and Jeremiah, who uttered their oracles "by the impulses of the Divine Spirit."[37] The "prophetic Spirit" testifies even to the reign of the two emperors as resting in the hand of God.[38] Bingham has remarked how Athenagoras locates the prophets and divine inspiration as "rational, doctrinal Christian authorities above the poets, philosophers, and human opinions."[39] Athenagoras's rhetoric is biblical when he marshals the Greek philosophers, and his rhetoric is philosophical when he marshals the biblical prophets.

FURTHER ASSIMILATION WITH GREEK PHILOSOPHY

This marshalling of philosophers leads Athenagoras to insist that Christians are not atheists but that they worship only one God, who is in fact Creator of all things and Judge of all people.[40] The Platonic thought that is often attributed to Athenagoras finds justification here, as Christians neither offer sacrifices, worship the universe, nor construct idols, because they distinguish God from matter: "We do not hold the pottery of more worth than him who made it, nor the vessels of glass and gold than him who wrought it; but if there is anything about them elegant in art we praise the artificer, and it is he who reaps the glory of the vessels: even so with matter and God—the glory and honor of the orderly arrangement of the world belongs of right not to matter, but to God, the Framer of matter."[41]

In this fashion, he can disprove the charge of atheism while not accepting a system of polytheism, instead landing in the middle with a belief of monotheism.

The influence of Justin Martyr on Athenagoras and his apologetic strategy is evident. Justin was a teacher in Rome before his martyrdom (about AD 165), and he was also noted for crafting works defending Christianity. Both his patristic apologies are addressed to the Roman emperor, both defend Christianity as misunderstood, and both object to its persecution merely for being called Christian. They similarly declare that the pious pursuit of truth will likely come at the price of their lives. Defense speeches are fundamental to their method.

---

36. Ibid., 424.
37. Athenagoras, *Embassy* 9.1 (ANF 2:134).
38. Athenagoras, *Embassy* 10.4, 18.2. *Leg.* 3, 37.
39. D. Jeffrey Bingham, "'We Have the Prophets': Inspiration and the Prophets in Athenagoras of Athens," *Zeitschrift für antikes Christentum* 20 (2016): 211.
40. Athenagoras, *Embassy* 3–4, 12.
41. Athenagoras, *Embassy* 15.3 (ANF 2:135).

Their works integrate popular philosophical and civic thinking into their appeals, and their writings are both characterized by stylistic excellence. They provide excellent examples of oratory targeting a synthesis of past traditions and centered on monotheistic belief.

In counterpoint fashion, Athenagoras also presents the inconsistent reasoning within the Greco-Roman pantheon in order to demote the logic of pagan persecution against Christianity. Various nations under Roman rule have various deities that contradict other systems.[42] People who make idols are either inventing a god who is unworthy of deity, or else they are like Christians when they reach for something beyond matter, yet they often find demons.[43] Much of the *Embassy* is dedicated to marshalling the teachings of philosophers and poets who share compatibility with Christian teaching while rejecting as absurd the inconsistencies and irrational beliefs of other religious philosophers. The Stoic Emperor Marcus Aurelius would surely have found a dual affirmation of both the best and the worse of Greco-Roman tradition. In synthetic fashion, Athenagoras even boldly compares the rule of Aurelius and Commodus to divine rule of the Father and Son: "So to the one God and the Logos preceding from Him, the Son, apprehended by us as inseparable from Him, all things are in like manner subjected."[44]

For Athenagoras, the most important principle in the use of philosophy is that skills of rhetoric, persuasion, and logic are not theologically contrary to the design and will of the Christian God. As one trained and experienced in philosophy as an art, Athenagoras likely viewed philosophical skills as divinely provided, far more than evangelistic techniques to protect the faith or convert others. Rankin remarks, "Athenagoras never employs the term 'philosophy' in a pejorative sense . . . because this is the game in which he is engaged. Philosophy is theology is philosophy; it all has to do with the love of truth and of certain, attainable knowledge."[45]

RATIONALIZING THE RESURRECTION

The second work of Athenagoras is *On the Resurrection*, sometimes called *The Treatise of Athenagoras*. The centrality of the doctrine of the resurrection was well established in Christian thought by the second century, anchored squarely in Jesus's resurrection as a prototype and hope for all believers. The apostle Paul had both articulated its centrality in 1 Corinthians 15:42–57 and encountered

42. Athenagoras, *Embassy* 1, 14.
43. Ibid., 15–27.
44. Athenagoras, *Embassy* 18.2 (ANF 2:137).
45. Rankin, *Athenagoras*, 70.

in skepticism among Athenian Greek philosophers in Acts 17:15–31. Athenagoras seems to echo the confrontation by Paul with this same audience in Athens, defending the resurrection as part of the overall economy of God in his creation. He employs logical precision, appealing to principles of philosophy, including burden of proof, the cause of common sense, and the underpinning of cause and end, all valued by the two emperors. Barnard has suggested that Marcus Aurelius's preoccupation with death in his *Meditations* lends itself to the receipt of a work describing the hope of the Christian resurrection.[46] The authorial comment in the *Embassy* reading "But let us defer the discourse concerning the resurrection"[47] helps justify the authorial connection with the *Resurrection* treatise on the manuscript.

Creation is a frequent topic of argumentation for Athenagoras, as he posits that the one who created matter from nothing "can reunite what is dissolved, and raise up what is prostrate, and restore the dead to life again, and put the corruptible into a state of incorruption."[48] The constitutional nature of humankind finds support of a resurrection, as the soul cannot be dissolved.[49] Likewise, judgment becomes a complementary argument for Athenagoras, who posits that the one who commands order and fairness must also judge to accomplish it, especially as the source and steward of human creation. The cause of human existence means that an "argument from rectitude, which represents God as judging men according as they have lived well or ill, derives its force from the end of their existence."[50] This fairness sees young children not at judgment but still resurrected. For Athenagoras, judgment functions to promote justice, but the condition of these young ones is seen as neither evil nor good behavior.[51] For all humanity eligible for virtue, "the examination relates to individuals, and the reward or punishment of lives ill or well spent is proportioned to the merit of each."[52] Both the beginning and end of the human body buttress the defense of the resurrection from the dead, since logic warrants that the being and behavior of humankind "must by all means be accompanied by an end in accordance with nature." The virtue of humanity must be regulated by a final cause.[53] Athenagoras's method again deserves recognition, as the classical Stoic curriculum was

---

46. Leslie W. Barnard, "Athenagoras, Galen, Marcus Aurelius, and Celsus," *The Church Quarterly Review* 168 (1967): 174.

47. Athenagoras, *Embassy* 36.3 (ANF 2:148).

48. Athenagoras, *Res.* 3.2 (ANF 2:150); cf. *Res.* 12–13.

49. Athenagoras, *Res.* 20; cf. *Res.* 15, 18, 21–23, 25.

50. Athenagoras, *Res.* 18.1 (ANF 2:158).

51. Athenagoras, *Res.* 14.

52. Athenagoras, *Res.* 25.5 (ANF 2:162).

53. Athenagoras, *Res.* 24.4 (ANF 2:162).

to start with logic and ethics and to end with physics.[54] Athenagoras employs all three of these qualities in his treatise on the resurrection to the Stoic philosopher Marcus.

Christianity finds validation through the writings of Athenagoras as he negotiates with intellectual dignity to plead for deserving mercy. He adopts the posture and rhetoric of an ambassador, conversing with the imperial court while representing citizens under duress. He is a religious advocate, explaining how Christian practices are harmonious with the Roman ideals of citizenship rather than as barbaric or loathsome. He is a philosopher, reasoning to recognize matter as a creation by the biblical God. When the prevailing Platonic dualism of the day precluded a material resurrection, Athenagoras maintains this basic worldview, then marshals virtuous logic to necessitate resurrected bodies at the final judgment. His apologetic response displays a deep conviction that this suspicious religion is valuable, meritorious, and justified while remaining respectful and self-effacing to the society that persecutes it.

CONTRIBUTIONS TO THE FIELD OF APOLOGETICS

Athenagoras shaped the thinking of the early church through his recognition of the compatibility between Christianity and the contemporary Roman value system. Like other associative theologians of his time who believed that pagan religion and philosophy could evidence a genuine search for truth that reaches for Christianity, Athenagoras did not disparage the pagan sources and methodologies but rather acknowledged and employed them. In modern church history, thinkers would label this phenomenon "common grace," in which "God's gracious work causes even nonbelievers to act mercifully, create systems of justice, and contribute to the general welfare of society."[55] When pagans act or think with goodness, they evidence the goodness of God. Their reach in this direction not only evidences a longing for truth, it also proves and defends the legitimacy of Christianity.

This methodology also allows for a strategic audience connection rather than the disconnect that sometimes characterizes Christian apologetics. In the spirit of Paul, Athenagoras became all things to all people (1 Cor 9:22), primarily to defend the faith, but not withstanding the winning of some to faith as well. Analysis of Athenagoras's contributions should also include his use of

---

54. Robert M. Grant, *Greek Apologists of the Second Century* (Philadelphia: Westminster, 1988), 51.
55. W. Brian Shelton, *Prevenient Grace: God's Provision for Fallen Humanity* (Wilmore, KY: Asbury, 2014), 158.

Scripture in his context and his accepted anthropology as instructional for the faith. Four methodological appeals emerge from his two extant works.

APPEAL TO CULTURAL CONVENTION

Athenagoras acknowledges the ideals of Roman social structure and civic obedience before he posits that Christianity finds congruence with these ideals. Like an ambassador, the apologist is respectful and conventional in his recognition of the audience he hopes to persuade. Athenagoras shows cultural acumen when he wisely employs the accepted social techniques for his context. These techniques create a case for Christianity, simply making the appeal using conventional standards. He writes directly to the emperor, employing political acumen to battle for his cause. He employs appropriate ambassadorial accolades that are culturally appropriate to an austere audience and more effectively persuasive. Young describes how prayer for the emperor was also a rhetorical technique of the time, calling Athenagoras's patriotic approach, "loyalist statements."[56]

Like an exemplary citizen, this advocator of Christianity presents believers as model inhabitants who obey the laws of the land. His defense of Christians as Roman citizens involves demonstrating the compatibility of their faith with the mandates of the empire in which they dwell. They offer peace when they conform to the will of God and the will of the state simultaneously. The religious morals of Christianity, like morals of other accepted religions under Roman rule, show respect for the state. Christianity goes even further to offer more consistent and even counter-culture, pro-state values, such as not returning evil for evil. But for Athenagoras, these appeals to show conformity and compatibility do not compromise the dissimilarity or holiness of Christianity nor its inherent superior system of truth and love. Philosophically speaking, other religions can be inherently inconsistent, and he reasonably does not affirm their systems fully. This ongoing tension between affirmation and refutation of other religions is maintained as he makes his case for the Christian faith. In this, Athenagoras is instructional to contemporary Christians who may be prone to cultural separatism. Rather than promoting distinction from culture for the sake of holiness, Athenagoras highlights cultural similarities and even an idealization of contemporary culture among Christians. Yet his efforts at synthesis have limits, such as in the case of Christian rejection of the bloodthirsty gladiatorial games. Biblical values always reject ungodly cultural activities while wedding themselves to the support of other cultural activities.

---

56. Frances Young, "Greek Apologists of the Second Century," *Apologetics in the Roman Empire: Pagans, Jews, and Christians*, eds. Mark Edwards, Martin Goodman, and Simon Price (New York: Oxford, 1999), 87.

APPEAL TO PHILOSOPHICAL CONVENTION

Athenagoras strategically employs Greek philosophy to match the interest of his intellectual audience. This helps him to find favor with the pagan reader prior to persuading them of the case for Christianity. The tenets of reason, logic, and good judgment that underpin social philosophical thinking all find a place as he makes the case for the faith, yet in using these techniques, Athenagoras remains fully Trinitarian. He articulates God's activities in this Greek milieu.[57]

Athenagoras utilizes a consistent methodology, employing literary and philosophical authorities through direct references as well as broader, ideological principles. All of this is at work in the two treatises. He establishes an obligation for the emperors' attention and sympathy by appealing to reason, the ideal tool for the philosophical foundation of culture, empire, and the pride of the emperors themselves. His use of the Greco-Roman heroes of thought displays a wide familiarity and generous affirmation of reason in support of political latitude and religious sympathy for Christianity. Young remarks of Athenagoras's sources, "These works seem to have a variety of different literary antecedents."[58] The antecedent to the teachings of Jesus or Paul are not employed as directly as a contemporary apologist might, but his restraint in this regard seems to be a strategic attempt to avoid arguing for Christianity from itself, preferring to argue for the merits of the faith on the basis of the emperors' own values. This concept of epistemology is explained below in more detail.

Once again we find that Athenagoras's efforts are not intellectually compromising; despite his effort at synthesis, Athenagoras is not concessional. Concerning his persecutors, he declares: "For we shall then conquer them, unhesitatingly surrendering, as we now do, our very lives for truth's sake."[59] Moreschini and Norelli describe how he recognizes primary and secondary differences, makes cultural accommodation, and makes concession for persuasion: "He professes a devotion to their rule, although without yielding on the matter of their divinity."[60]

APPEAL TO COMPATIBLE EPISTEMOLOGY

Athenagoras's use of Scripture also informs our understanding of the application of the Bible in the theater of apologetics. Scholars have debated the precise knowledge Athenagoras had of the New Testament and his view of inspiration

---

57. Pui Him Ip, "Re-Imagining Divine Simplicity in Trinitarian Theology," *International Journal of Systematic Theology* 18 (2016): 278–79.

58. Young, "Greek Apologists," 87.

59. Athenagoras, *Embassy* 3.2 (ANF 2:130).

60. Moreschini and Norelli, *Early Christian Greek and Latin Literature*, 1:207.

when he alludes to Jesus's sayings without citing or quoting them and his lack of reference to Jesus by name.[61] One explanation for this usage may be his understanding of the Jewish Scriptures.

Athenagoras used the Old Testament in his two apologetic works, varying between approval and separation from Judaism. He agues that the law and prophets anticipate Christian teaching and are foundational to Jesus's teaching. The Greco-Roman value that a religion requires roots in some ancient tradition is sustained by demonstrating that Christianity finds its origins in the Old Testament law and prophets. But Bingham has shown that polemical reasons may have restrained Athenagoras from excessive or direct citations from Jesus's teaching.[62] This approach avoids the problem of merely appealing to a Christian's own Scriptures as authoritative while still using the Scriptures in the acknowledged form of philosophical reasoning. His employed epistemology, or source of knowledge, is one that is acceptable to his audience without alienating his audience. The Jewish law becomes the moral standard for Christians, with veiled references to Jesus's teaching, which clearly draw from the law. The Greek term *Logos* refers to both Old and New Testament teaching, given by the God who created and who expects good living. Bingham explains: "The teachings of Jesus are presented as continuous with those of the prophets. The connection is seamless. The words of the prophets are those of Jesus, the divine Spirit produces them both."[63]

Athenagoras's strategy seems to show some restraint from direct application of too much Jewish heritage or Christian teaching, a balanced rhetoric and wise employment of language, and a consistent awareness of the audience's need for connection to ancient tradition. Rankin insists: "The [*sic*] Athenagoras' use of non-Christian sources in the *De Resurrectione* is not significant and occurs primarily in the area of language rather than concept."[64] Athenagoras employs biblical values insofar as they would be received by two Greco-Roman imperial thinkers, without being too Jewish or Christian. He avoids being unbiblical while arguing with accepted philosophical techniques.

APPEAL TO ANTHROPOLOGY

Barnard suggests that Athenagoras deserves the title of the first Christian anthropologist for his articulation of humanity in its relationship to its Creator:

---

61. Bingham, "We Have the Prophets," 211–42; Rankin, *Athenagoras*, 11–12.
62. D. Jeffrey Bingham, "Scripture as Apology in Athenagoras of Athens," *Studia Patristica* 45 (2010): 430.
63. Ibid., 431.
64. Rankin, *Athenagoras*, 12.

the ethic to live in purity and righteousness in light of our relationship to the Judge, our purpose to live an intelligent life, and our composition in relationship to the image of God. Athenagoras argues from creation and the human composition to secure intellectual support for a resurrection.

For example, the first part of *On the Resurrection* defends against the claim that God is unable to resurrect because it is unworthy of him.[65] Against the argument that some humans have become digested food for animals, Athenagoras argues that nonnatural foods such as human bones are eliminated and do not become part of animal composition. Besides, the omnipotence of God is capable of overcoming such obstacles as these in the resurrection. The second part of *On the Resurrection* argues that the event logically fits the creation purposes of humans.[66] In creation, the human composition includes body and soul, not just soul. In judgment, the justice of God ensures that the whole person should find rewards or punishments. While the origin of the soul does not find explicit pronunciation, the *Embassy* and *On the Resurrection* petition the Platonic view of matter and the Stoic view of physics. Ethics follows from the physical creation in both schools of thought.

Science is employed as part of the overall argument for Christian beliefs. The ancients speculated about human nature more than they studied it empirically, but science was still a component of thought. In a lesson for contemporary apologists, Athenagoras viewed positively the substance and nature of this world, which was never separated from the attributes of God and which was destined for redemption. For his contribution, Barnard places Athenagoras on the same level as the medical pioneer Galen: "Athenagoras is the earliest Christian thinker to attempt to harmonize theology with the medical science of his day."[67]

CONCLUSION

The work of Athenagoras perfectly represents the era of second-century apologists, matching the style and method of the better-known apologist Justin Martyr. This was a time of pagan misunderstanding and accusations against Christianity, and this compelled educated Christians such as Athenagoras to engage the culture using the same intellectual standards of logic and reason in defense of the faith. Skilled in Hellenistic thought, this Athenian apologist answered the worst of religious accusations with the best of religious engagement.

---

65. Athenagoras, *Res.* 1–10.
66. Ibid., 11–25.
67. Barnard, "Athenagoras, Galen, Marcus Aurelius, and Celsus," 172.

Athenagoras marshaled philosophical figures, references, and tenets to battle the enemies of Christianity, even as they marshaled those same instruments against the faith. He kept his arguments sound and rational and pleaded to the sovereign of the empire, who saw himself as a champion of these same tenets. Athenagoras boasted how Christians were model citizens, promoting the finest values of the society that the emperor administrated. And while the charges against Christianity are occasionally confronted directly, the majority of his two essays seeks to logically refute the alleged discontinuity between this new religion and other accepted religions. Greek philosophy becomes an arbiter for Christian beliefs.

By employing a strategic restraint from using Scriptures or the teachings of Jesus or the apostles, Athenagoras was able to remain on the same terms as his audience. Christianity can stand when probed from within or without. Anthropology finds a role for further compatibility between Christianity and ancient tradition, while reason is the means to demonstrate arguments for the resurrection central to this misunderstood religion. Athenagoras is certain that goodness, wisdom, and beauty find their origin in the Christian God, so appealing to them is a means of supporting the truth of Christianity. Sadly, the wonderful work of Athenagoras was soon forgotten by many in the patristic era, leading Barnard to declare, "In anthropology, as in other matters, Athenagoras was a pioneer—and it is the fate of pioneers to be forgotten."[68]

Whether or not Athenagoras was ever a headmaster, he teaches the student of contemporary apologetics important tenets for engagement. An understanding of culture is necessary as a foundation for dialog in defense of the faith. An erudite employment of those values begins by seeking compatibility with Christianity while noting the exceptional incompatibility with Christianity as well. Athenagoras models a "common grace" approach to the divine provision of truth and goodness, suggesting that finding these among the pagans is not a threat but a reinforcement of the Christian claims about creation. If these rules are honored, Athenagoras believed Christianity could find a legitimate space, even within a society that actively persecuted the church. In all this, Barnard notes that his "object was apologetic, not dogmatic."[69] His context forced him to realize that truth carries its own merit and employs its own power of persuasion rather than the doctrinaire attitude of rectitude.

---

68. Barnard, "Father of Christian Anthropology," 279.
69. Ibid., 269.

BIBLIOGRAPHY

Primary Sources

Athenagorae. *De Resurrectione Mortuorum*. In vol. 53 of Supplements to *Vigilae Christianae*. Ed. by Miroslav Marcovich. Boston: Brill, 2000.

Athenagorus. *A Plea for the Christians*. In vol. 2 of *The Ante-Nicene Fathers*. Ed. by Alexander Roberts and James Donaldson. Repr. Edinburgh: T&T Clark; Grand Rapids: Eerdmans, 2001.

———. *Legatio* and *De Resurrectione*. Ed. and trans. by William R. Schoedel. New York: Oxford University Press, 1972.

———. *The Resurrection of the Dead*. In vol. 2 of *The Ante-Nicene Fathers*. Ed. by Alexander Roberts and James Donaldson. Repr. Edinburgh: T&T Clark; Grand Rapids, Eerdmans, 2001.

Celsus. *On True Doctrine*. Trans. by R. Joseph Hoffman. Oxford: Oxford University Press, 1987.

Eusebius. *Ecclesiastical History*. Trans. by C. F. Crusé. Peabody, MA: Hendrickson, 2000.

Origen. *Contra Celsus*. In vol. 4 of *The Ante-Nicene Fathers*. Ed. by Alexander Roberts and James Donaldson. Grand Rapids: Eerdmans, 1994.

Socrates. *Ecclesiastical History*. In vol. 2 of *The Nicene and Post-Nicene Fathers*, Series 2. Trans. by Philip Schaff and Henry Wace. Edinburgh: T&T Clark; Grand Rapids: Eerdmans, 1997.

Secondary Sources

Barnard, Leslie W. *Athenagoras: A Study in Second Century Christian Apologetic*. Beauchesne: Paris, 1972.

———. "Athenagoras, Galen, Marcus Aurelius, and Celsus." *The Church Quarterly Review* 168 (1967): 168–81.

———. "The Father of Christian Anthropology." *Zeitschrift für die neutestamentliche Wissenschaft und die Kunde der älteren Kirche* 63 (1974): 254–70.

Bingham, D. Jeffrey. "Scripture as Apology in Athenagoras of Athens." *Studia Patristica* 45 (2010): 425–31.

———. "'We Have the Prophets': Inspiration and the Prophets in Athenagoras of Athens." *Zeitschrift für antikes Christentum* 20 (2016): 211–42.

Frend, W. H. C. *Martyrdom and Persecution in the Early Church: A Study of a Conflict from the Maccabees to Donatus*. New York: New York University Press, 1967.

Grant, Robert M. *Greek Apologists of the Second Century*. Philadelphia: Westminster, 1988.

Ip, Pui Him. "Re-Imagining Divine Simplicity in Trinitarian Theology." *International Journal of Systematic Theology* 18 (2016): 274–89.

Marcovich, Miroslav. *Introduction to De Resurrectione Mortuorum, by Athenagorae*. In vol. 53 of *Supplements to Vigiliae Christianae*. Ed. by Miroslav Marcovich. Boston: Brill, 2000.

McLynn, Frank. *Marcus Aurelius: A Life*. Boston: Da Capo, 2010.

Moreschini, Claudio, and Enrico Norelli. *Early Christian Greek and Latin Literature*. 2 vols. Peabody, MA: Hendrickson, 2005.

Pouderon, Bernard. "Les écoles chrétiennes de Rome, Athènes, Alexandrie et Antioche à l'époque des Antonins: Remarques sur la circulation des maîtres et de leurs disciples." Part 1 of *Bulletin de Littérature Ecclésiastique* 113 (2012): 385–400.

Rankin, David. "Athenagoras, Philosopher and First Principles." *Studia Patristica* 45 (2010): 419–24.

———. *Athenagoras: Philosopher and Theologian*. New York: Routledge, 2016.

Schoedel, William R. *Introduction to Legatio and De Resurrectione, by Athenagoras*. New York: Oxford University Press, 1972.

Shelton, W. Brian. "Learning from Patristic Responses to Culture." Pages 100–30 in *The Contemporary Church and the Early Church: Case Studies in Ressourcement*. Ed. by Paul Hartog. Eugene, OR: Wipf & Stock, 2010.

———. *Prevenient Grace: God's Provision for Fallen Humanity*. Wilmore, KY: Francis Asbury, 2014.

Young, Frances. "Greek Apologists of the Second Century." Pages 81–104 in *Apologetics in the Roman Empire: Pagans, Jews, and Christians*. Ed. by Mark Edwards, Martin Goodman, and Simon Price. New York: Oxford University Press, 1999.

TERTULLIAN OF CARTHAGE

African Apologetics Enters the Fray

BRYAN M. LITFIN

By the time Tertullian (ca. 160–ca. 220) was actively writing, the Christian faith had become well known but was not well liked. Anti-Christian writers such as Galen, Lucian, Fronto, and Celsus had begun to criticize Christianity for its beliefs and practices. To many pagans the new-fangled faith that celebrated a crucified criminal seemed alien and suspect. At times, the widespread public dislike of Christianity could break into outright persecution. Yet the followers of traditional Greco-Roman religion were not the only opponents of the ancient church. Apologists such as Tertullian also faced challenges from pseudo-Christian sects, such as the Gnostics, or from Jews who contested the meaning of the Old Testament. The turn of the third century was a dangerous moment for the Christians. Such precarious times called for a bold and fearless defender of the faith such as Tertullian.

HISTORICAL BACKGROUND

Tertullian was opinionated. Because of this, we know a lot more about his thoughts than about the man himself. He is mentioned only rarely by other church fathers. One later writer, Bishop Cyprian of Carthage (d. AD 258), certainly revered him. It is said that the bishop would never go a day without reading Tertullian. In fact, he would send his secretary to fetch the books with the request, "Give me the master."[1]

But other than some questionable references in a few Christian writers, the little we can know about Tertullian's life must be constructed from his own writings. Fortunately, we have a lot of them. They paint a picture of a man whose fiery personality entertains us and repulses us at the same time. Tertullian's intellect

---

1. Jerome, *Vir. ill.* 53.

was brilliant, and his wit was sharp. He demands admiration for his sheer audacity. At the same time, he could be narrow-minded and cold-hearted, especially toward the end of his writing career. Tertullian is an enigma—a hero of ancient Christianity whose works were deemed worthy of preserving, yet also one of the few church fathers never to be granted the title of "saint."[2]

Tertullian was an African, and he stands at the beginning of a long line of eminent African theologians. The region we are talking about here is North Africa, which is modern day Morocco, Algeria, Tunisia, and Libya.[3] Later African figures such as Minucius Felix,[4] Cyprian, Lactantius, and Augustine all drew from the theological legacy of Tertullian. So too the great martyrs of the African church, such as the illustrious Perpetua, owe an intellectual debt to Tertullian's obstinate resistance to any form of capitulation to Greco-Roman religion.

Except for a brief account of some martyrs penned by an anonymous writer,[5] Tertullian is the first Christian author whose works survive in the original Latin. From the time prior to him, only Greek Christian writings are extant today. As the fountainhead of an illustrious tradition of ecclesiastical Latin, Tertullian bequeathed to the later church some important terminology, including the word *trinitas* to describe the triune God as well as the term *novum testamentum*, or New Testament.

The city of Carthage appears to have been Tertullian's lifelong home and the only place in which he lived and worked. It was a large, thriving metropolis, the capital of the province of Africa Proconsularis. Though once an ancient foe of the Roman Republic, Carthage was eventually captured and destroyed by the Romans in 146 BC. Yet it was rebuilt in the age of the emperors as a new Roman outpost in North Africa. By the turn of the third century, it was a populous and prosperous capital with a busy harbor and a vibrant Christian church.

Scholars debate exactly how Christianity first arrived in Carthage, whether from Rome or Alexandria, Jewish converts or gentile, or from Latin-speaking

---

2. Toward the end of his life, Tertullian left the catholic church for the sect now known as "Montanism" (it was called the New Prophecy in his day). Because of this identification with a group perceived as heterodox and schismatic, Tertullian was never considered for canonization within the Roman Catholic Church. In this way he is like Origen, who likewise deserves highest esteem as a thinker and apologist yet whose life did not demonstrate the full orthodoxy and fidelity to the institutional church necessary for sainthood.

3. Egypt is also in the continent of Africa, of course, but the Nile had a unique civilization that was a blend of multiple cultures, so it was somewhat distinct from ancient North Africa.

4. Minucius Felix is probably, though not certainly, from Africa. He lived and wrote at Rome. His only surviving book, the *Octavius*, was written around the time Tertullian was active, and it may have drawn from Tertullian's works—or it may have influenced Tertullian in a reverse relationship. Modern scholars debate the question of literary dependence between the two authors.

5. The deaths of twelve martyrs from the African town of Scilli in AD 180 is recorded in a text called the *Acts of the Scillitan Martyrs.* I offer a translation of this work in chapter 7 of Bryan Litfin, *Early Christian Martyr Stories* (Grand Rapids: Baker Academic, 2014). Although this sparse narrative is the first surviving example of a Christian text in Latin, it was Tertullian who would most shape the future of Latin theological discourse.

missionaries or Greek. In such a large and diverse port city with far-flung international trade, any singular hypothesis of Christian origins probably needs to give way to a more complex theory in which different types of missionaries planted a Jesus-based faith in Roman North Africa. In any case, by Tertullian's day, around AD 200, the proto-orthodox church was a well-known cultural force; yet elements from Gnostic, Jewish, and ecstatic-prophetic belief systems also influenced the Carthaginian church.

Older biographical treatments of Tertullian claim he was a centurion's son who grew up to become a famous jurist and a priest, but those theories have been debunked, and scholars now make no firm claims about such matters.[6] One of the more certain facts about Tertullian is that he received an excellent education. He knew both Greek and Latin, and he shows himself in his thirty-one surviving writings to be well acquainted with the cultural myths and religious and philosophical literature of his day. Tertullian's skill in language is both an innate talent and the product of an elite education. Many scholars also think he had some kind of legal training because he shows expertise in Roman law and familiarity with a lawyer's method of argumentation.[7] In light of this background, perhaps it was inevitable that Tertullian would engage in high-level apologetics, but what were the apologetic challenges he faced?

THEOLOGICAL CONTEXT

Tertullian is often called a *controversialist*. This term means more than that he never shrank from arguments and disputes. It is probably safe to say that out of Tertullian's thirty-one extant writings, all of them are written against a specific opponent or a false set of ideas. He has left us no warm, tender-hearted essays to uplift his flock. We find in his corpus no pastoral exegesis of Scripture for the simple task of encouragement. Tertullian wrote only controversial treatises that state a definitive case. Even his letter to Christian martyrs awaiting death in prison challenges them to stand strong and remain firm—as if what they really needed in jail was a robust admonition to keep them on track! Tertullian was quite fond of telling people what they ought to believe.

The corpus of Tertullian can be divided into three main categories: (1) apologetic works, (2) controversial treatises, and (3) disciplinary, moral, and ascetic

---

6. For the rebuttal of the traditional account that has become the modern scholarly consensus, see Timothy D. Barnes, *Tertullian: A Historical and Literary Study*, 2nd ed. (Oxford: Clarendon, 1984), 3–59.

7. See David J. Rankin, "Was Tertullian a Jurist?" *Studia Patristica* 31 (Louvain: Peeters, 1997), 335–42. Rankin argues that Tertullian may have been trained as an "advocate" who pleaded cases in court and knew the techniques of rhetoric.

works.[8] This threefold division makes it seem that apologetics was just one-third of what Tertullian wrote about. But the reality is that all of Tertullian's writings made an *apologia*, a defense of an idea against those who might disagree. In essence, he had four main opponents: Greco-Roman pagans, Gnostic or heretical Christians, Jews, and Christians within his own church who held—whether through simple ignorance (more forgivable) or obstinate error (more blameworthy)—false notions that required rebuttal. This fourth category, since it is directed internally toward fellow Christians needing correction, would not be considered "apologetics" in the traditional sense of defending the faith to outsiders. That leaves pagans, heretics, and Jews as Tertullian's primary apologetic adversaries. Each of these and their thought-world will be considered below.

THE PAGANS

The term *pagan* originally meant a village-dweller, and by implication, a rustic hillbilly or a country hick. The use of this word to describe the followers of traditional Greco-Roman religion reflects that Christianity was primarily an urban phenomenon in its early centuries. The new faith spread from city to city until it eventually became the official religion of the Roman Empire in the late fourth century. But while Christianity was adopted as the ostensible faith of the urban elites, most of the countryside retained its adherence to the old religion of the gods, so the word *pagan* came to describe these people. But in Tertullian's day, those whom we now call pagans were not social outcasts. They adhered to the prestigious and dominant religion of the day, an expansive system that covered everything from mighty Jupiter with a thunderbolt in his hand down to the tiniest spirits of everyday life. Roman civil religion was a cultural means of appeasing one's patron gods more than a pious attitude of the heart. Emperor worship also functioned to keep the citizenry loyal to the state. Paganism was so intertwined with Roman government, culture, education, and monumental architecture that we must picture Tertullian's faith as a minority group: a marginal religious cult that few people understood and many people despised.[9]

---

8. See the Table of Contents in Johannes Quasten, *Patrology*, vol. 2 (Westminster, MD: Newman, 1950; repr. Allen, TX: Christian Classics), x.

9. A modern parallel to this scenario would not be the USSR in the heyday of Communist atheism, when a nonreligious empire persecuted small, secretive sects of religious people. Instead, North Korea would be a better example, where the cult of the leader's personality is strictly enforced and any Christian opposition to the state's totalitarianism is met with violent suppression. Another modern example might be a Middle Eastern country where intense devotion to Islam makes life hard, indeed dangerous, for the vulnerable Christian minority. When Tertullian took on Greco-Roman paganism, he was confronting no superficial enemy but a fearsome religious system that was entrenched in the power structures of his society from top to bottom.

THE HERETICS

Tertullian's second group of apologetic opponents were heretics such as the Gnostics.[10] *Gnosticism* is a catchall term for the various thinkers and sects in ancient times whose version of Christianity did not center on the life, death, and resurrection of the incarnate Son of God but focused instead on Jesus's role as a teacher of secret mysteries. The Gnostics considered themselves to be the elite believers, the truly spiritual Christians who understood what the simpletons of the church did not: that salvation came through *gnosis* (knowledge), not through the communal rituals and practices that celebrated the death and bodily resurrection of Jesus. In other words, Christianity was not about devoted adherence to the community Jesus founded but about inner awakening and mystical exploration of secret myths from the angelic world. Faith in Christ's atoning work on a Roman cross did not save; it was the esoteric wisdom that he passed secretly to the disciples (recorded in extra Gnostic "gospels") that brought salvation when humans interpreted these heavenly teachings correctly. Many people found great appeal in this elitist and seemingly intellectual approach to Christianity.

THE JEWS

Tertullian also argued against the Jews. Obviously, the rabbis of the ancient period did not accept Jesus as God's Messiah, so any Jewish scriptures that might be interpreted as speaking about him were instead given other interpretations. To rebut this position, the ancient apologists listed Old Testament "testimonies" that were claimed to have predicted Israel's true Savior in advance. Other Christian arguments tried to show that salvation could not be found through law-keeping or that the Jewish leaders were wrong to be complicit in sending Jesus to a Roman executioner's cross. Taken together, such treatises and arguments formed an early Christian genre that bears the name of one of Tertullian's works: *Adversus Judaeos* literature, which means "against the Jews." In addition to Tertullian, other apologists such as Justin Martyr and John Chrysostom also penned such works or delivered anti-Jewish critiques in sermons. It was common in this theological context for the early Christians to face off against the rabbis who still saw Christianity as heretical.

The *Adversus Judaeos* apologetic genre can be categorized in different ways—sometimes appropriate and sometimes not. We must recall that Scripture

---

10. Not all the heretics whom Tertullian confronted were Gnostics. One of his major opponents was Marcion, a false Christian who took a negative view toward earthly, material existence as the Gnostics did. Therefore, the Creator God of the Old Testament was said to be a tribal deity of the Jews, entirely different from the good and loving Father revealed by Jesus. Marcion believed Jesus came to tell us about a brand-new God who was much better than Yahweh of Israel. Tertullian rebutted Marcion in five huge books filled with biblical exegesis.

itself says reliance on Jewish practices for salvation is antithetical to the gospel of grace. "I, Paul, tell you that if you let yourself be circumcised, Christ will be of no value to you. . . . You who are trying to be justified by the law have been alienated from Christ; you have fallen away from grace" (Gal 5:2, 4). The Jewish leaders took the bloodguilt of Christ's death upon Israel (Matt 27:25), and now they wear a veil that blinds their minds to the Old Testament (2 Cor 3:14). Wrongly, they trust in Moses, for they cannot see that the Old Testament predicts Christ; yet as he himself said, "Moses wrote about me" (John 5:45–46; cf. Luke 24:27). Sometimes the early Christian *Adversus Judaeos* literature engaged positively with rabbinic thought and confronted Jewish readings of the Old Testament that made no room for prophetic prediction of Christ. In this way they called Israel to receive her true Messiah. But other times, it must be admitted, some church fathers delved into scurrilous attacks and anti-Jewish slurs that have no place in Christian discourse. The *Adversus Judaeos* literature had difficulty distinguishing the line between biblical refutation of works salvation and anti-Semitism that grieves the heart of God.

All of these currents of thought were circulating in Carthage when Tertullian was writing around AD 200. As a man blessed with a sharp intellect, a bold disposition, and the rhetorical training to make a sound argument, he took it upon himself to defend the Christian faith against all who might stand opposed. It is to his apologetical response that we now turn.

APOLOGETIC RESPONSE

APOLOGY: REFUTATION OF THE PAGANS

Historically speaking, the *Apology* is Tertullian's most widely respected work. It is well known as a rhetorical masterpiece, a fine example of the great Latin tradition of public debate and deliberative discourse.[11] Johannes Quasten, the eminent scholar of early Christianity, put it succinctly when he calls the *Apology* "the most important of all Tertullian's works."[12] Because of its importance, it appears in "by far the largest numbers of manuscripts."[13] It was even translated into Greek, a privilege accorded to few ancient Latin works. In other words, it is not only modern scholars but ancient readers and subsequent copyists who judged the *Apology* to be the best of what Tertullian had to offer.

The text is addressed to the governors of the Roman Empire in an attempt

---

11. For a comprehensive look at Tertullian's rhetorical skill, see Robert Dick Sider, *Ancient Rhetoric and the Art of Tertullian* (Oxford: Oxford University Press, 1971).

12. Quasten, *Patrology*, vol. 2, 256.

13. Ibid., 260.

to set the record straight about what Christianity really is—not a weird cult that deserves persecution but a useful and productive contributor to society and indeed the very truth of God. Yet Tertullian does not launch into theological argumentation at the outset. One of the most significant aspects of his apologetic approach is that he begins with *morality*. The governors of the empire, reflecting widespread public opinion, have an irrational hatred for Christianity because they think it is morally corrupt. Relying on rumor and misinformed opinion, they despise anyone who goes by the name of Christian, even if that person has committed no crime. Tertullian calls on his society to take a step back and find out what Christianity really is before judging it worthy of scorn. Reason and truth must prevail, not slanderous gossip and lurid innuendo.

When Christianity is truly understood, its morality will be recognized not only as good and right but even as superior to pagan practice. For example, the Lord's Supper—which the early church practiced in secret and offered only to baptized believers—was the object of much pagan suspicion. They assumed it was some kind of cannibalistic ritual that slaughtered babies for human consumption or feasted on the blood of helpless victims. Tertullian not only denies that such atrocities take place, he quits playing defense and goes on the offensive against the pagans. Pointing his finger at his society, he rails against its own murderous bloodlust: human sacrifice and other bloody rituals, the unfair torture and execution of Christians, and of course, the cruel gladiator games—including the strange practice of eating the animals of the arena as wild game meat, when those animals themselves had just eaten human beings! It is you pagans, Tertullian says, who hunger for human blood, while the feasts of the Christians are simple meals of fellowship and love.

This "offensive" approach to apologetics in which the worldview of the unbelievers is shown to be immoral continues as Tertullian ridicules the pagan gods and their silly stories. To believe in them is nothing but superstition, and the rituals of pagan worship are absurd. In contrast to this, Tertullian offers his own God as worthy of faith. "The object of our worship is the one God, who, out of nothing, simply for the glory of his majesty, fashioned this enormous universe."[14] Grounded in Judaism and therefore respectably ancient, Christianity testifies to a God whose holiness and worthiness outshines the crude pagan gods. Yet unlike Judaism, Christianity also teaches that this one God sent forth his Word to become incarnate as Jesus Christ. The so-called gods of the pagans are actually demons who stand opposed to—and will be judged by—the Lord Jesus.

---

14. Tertullian, *Apol.* 17.1 in Rudolph Arbesmann, Emily Joseph Daly, and Edwin A. Quain, *Tertullian: Apologetical Works and Minucius Felix: Octavius* (New York: Fathers of the Church, 1950), 52.

Tertullian finishes his essay by insisting at great length that Christians can respect the emperor's dignity and right to rule without participating in the imperial cult. Prayer for the emperor is far more helpful than sacrifices to him. Here Tertullian is back on defense again. He rebuts the charge that Christians are a political threat by showing their heartfelt appreciation for law and order. They do not need to worship the emperor to prove it. By worshiping the one true God and living moral lives, they are best equipped to aid the emperor through prayer. Even if they do not partake in certain public rituals or immoral businesses such as prostitution or fortune-telling, the Christians are good, law-abiding citizens who pay their taxes and live peaceably among the people. Though philosophers may mock them and the mob may clamor for their blood, Christianity produces good citizens who are moral, upstanding, obedient, and virtuous.

In a final appeal to the imperial governors, Tertullian dares them to try and stamp out Christianity. "But carry on, good officials; you will become much better in the eyes of the people if you sacrifice the Christians for them. Crucify us—torture us—condemn us—destroy us! Your iniquity is the proof of our innocence."[15] It is in this context that Tertullian utters one of his most famous slogans. Though often recorded as "The blood of the martyrs is the seed of the church," what Tertullian actually exclaimed was, "We become more numerous every time we are hewn down by you: the blood of Christians is seed."[16] In other words, though Christians ought not be condemned—Tertullian has spent his whole essay making this point—when they *are* mistreated or even martyred, they conduct themselves with such dignity that onlookers cannot help but admire the faith of the martyrs, even to the point of getting converted themselves. Whether by a moral life or a noble death, Christians present a truly winsome face to a watching world.

PRESCRIPTION AGAINST HERETICS: REFUTATION OF THE UNORTHODOX

The ancient pagans of Roman society were not the only opponents against which Tertullian directed his considerable rhetorical firepower. He also took on the heretics in many of his apologetic works. Unlike the pagans, the heretics claimed to represent a form of Christianity. But these troublemakers were unorthodox; they held doctrines not taught by the original apostles, nor found in the Holy Scriptures, nor in line with the creeds of the church, nor approved

---

15. Tertullian, *Apol.* 50 (Arbesmann et al., 125).
16. Ibid. The expression "The blood of the martyrs is the seed of the church" came into popular Christian parlance when it was incorporated into a worship song by Steve Green called *The Faithful* (1998).

by the respectable bishops. To exclude the false teachers from claiming true doctrine, Tertullian wrote *Prescription against Heretics*.

To understand this work, we must comprehend what is meant by the term *praescriptio*. It was a Roman legal term, derived specifically from the field of real estate law. The *praescriptio longi temporis* refers to ownership of property by right of longtime possession. When a plot of land has been held by a possessor for a substantial time, a newcomer cannot come along and litigate about the property. Even if he has a deed to show, he has never exercised his right of ownership, so he has lost his claim to the land. Another party has been there for too long, so the newcomer is prevented from disputing about it. He is barred from the court at the outset. The parcel of land belongs to another and has for many years. Case dismissed.

In a brilliant piece of argumentation, Tertullian applies this legal premise to the heretics. The "property" under dispute is the Bible; and Tertullian is saying with a wave of his hand, "Get off my land, you interlopers." He knows he could defeat the heretics in a head-to-head exegetical debate. Elsewhere he engages them in arguments about the Bible, not least in his massive five-volume work *Against Marcion*, which refutes that apostate teacher verse by verse. But here he is using the shortcut of the *praescriptio* to rule the heretics out of court before they can even start making arguments. Tertullian aims to show that only the true church traces back to the apostles, having held the biblical writings in its possession from the beginning. In other words, Tertullian is appealing to long-standing Christian tradition against newfangled heretical ideas that have cropped up more recently.

To prove that his church holds the apostolic faith, while heretics invent novelties and run after imaginative speculations, Tertullian appeals to what is known as the rule of faith. In the ancient church, the rule of faith was a brief summary of doctrine taught to candidates for baptism. Since most early Christians were illiterate, they were asked to memorize short creeds and recite them back to the bishop in the water. Prior to baptism, skilled teachers instructed the candidates about the meaning of these sacred words. Today's Apostles' Creed was not written by the apostles but comes from the early Middle Ages; yet it is a direct descendant of the second-century rule of faith that the ancient church fathers knew.

Tertullian used the baptismal rule as a convenient summary of the original apostolic faith, the faith he still held in good standing. In contrast, the heretics had clearly diverged from it. "We Christians are forbidden to introduce anything on our own authority or to choose what someone else introduces on his own authority," Tertullian writes. "Our authorities are the Lord's apostles. . . .

They faithfully passed on to the nations the teaching which they had received from Christ."[17] By continuous possession from the beginning, the true church owns the Bible and its unchanged message. The church only interprets the Bible according to the accepted ideas found in creedal summaries. This prevents heretics such as the Gnostics from barging in later with crazy myths that have nothing to do with the original teaching of Jesus and his disciples. The job of the Christian is to believe what has already been settled, not to invent new ideas that the church has never heard before.[18] "To know nothing against the Rule is to know everything."[19]

It is in the context of rejecting the philosophical speculations of heretics that Tertullian lets loose one of his most widely quoted quips: "What has Jerusalem to do with Athens, the Church with the Academy, the Christian with the heretic?"[20] This rhetorical outburst has often been taken to show that Tertullian rejected the use of philosophy in defense of Christianity—a mistaken idea that we will dismantle shortly. Yet the famous slogan does show that Tertullian had little patience for pseudointellectual musings from so-called Christians. If a doctrine is not found in the Bible as viewed through the lens of historic orthodoxy, the person advocating this false teaching must be branded a heretic. Theoretically, the principle of the *praescriptio* would exclude such interlopers from exegetical debate. Yet Tertullian certainly did engage the heretics on scriptural grounds, even if he should not have had to. He was a master of biblical interpretation against heterodox ideas. But as we now examine his apologetic handling of the Bible, let us look not at his refutation of heretics but at his engagement with his third major opponent: the Jews who disputed the meaning of the Old Testament.

AGAINST THE JEWS: REFUTATION OF THE RABBIS

As we have already seen, the genre of *Adversus Judaeos* literature was widespread in the ancient church.[21] At times it could swerve into anti-Semitism. But not every objection raised against Jewish interpretation can be taken as nefarious. The New Testament itself tells us that the "minds [of the followers of Moses] were made dull, for to this day the same veil remains when the old

---

17. Tertullian, *Praescr.* 6 in S. L. Greenslade, *Early Latin Theology* (Louisville: Westminster, 1956), 34.
18. This does not mean Tertullian rejected good theological debate among Christians. Nevertheless, orthodoxy provides the boundaries for Christian discussions. There are certain doctrinal essentials that cannot be disputed. He writes, "Provided the essence of the Rule is not disturbed, you may seek and discuss as much as you like" (Ibid., 14; Greenslade, 40).
19. Ibid.
20. Ibid., 7 (Greenslade, 36). Here, the "Academy" refers to the school of Plato.
21. For an overview of this literature, see A. Lukyn Williams, *Adversus Judaeos: A Bird's-Eye View of Christian Apologiae Until the Renaissance* (Cambridge: University Press, 1935).

covenant is read. It has not been removed, because only in Christ is it taken away. Even to this day when Moses is read, a veil covers their hearts. But whenever anyone turns to the Lord, the veil is taken away" (2 Cor 3:14–16). In Tertullian's apologetics toward the rabbis, he tried to remove this obscuring veil by clarifying the true christological meaning of the Jewish Scriptures.

Before turning to the sacred text itself, let us note that hermeneutics was the main issue here. The real question was, "What interpretive principles do you bring to the text?" and "What does it mean if your opponent does not interpret the Bible by those same principles?" Geoffrey Dunn, the foremost expert on Tertullian's *Adversus Judaeos*, writes, "At the heart of the early Christian understanding of the Hebrew Scriptures is this question of the relationship between Christianity and Judaism. Tertullian's *Against the Jews* is a *tour de force* in christological exegesis. It is one of the most scripturally based treatises he wrote and it should be important to us for this reason alone."[22] As we dig into the work, we will see that proper biblical interpretation was a major part of Tertullian's apologetics—but only when his opponent accepted the Scriptures as a source worth debating about. The Jews certainly did, so Tertullian met his rabbinic opponents head-on in the Old Testament.

A real-life event prompted the pamphlet *Against the Jews*. Historians know there was a large population of Jews in Carthage, so it would not have been unusual for Christians to encounter their Jewish brethren in daily life. A debate had taken place between a Christian and a gentile who had converted to Judaism. The debate dragged on throughout the day. Eventually the bystanders were interjecting their opinions and drowning one another out. Prompted by this cacophony, Tertullian decided to compose a treatise that would clearly lay out the Christian case against Judaism. His goal was not only to convert Jews to Christ (either by their own direct reading of his work or by giving Christians good ammunition for apologetics) but even to prevent the surprisingly common practice of Christians abandoning their faith for Judaism.[23]

In Tertullian's day, the heretic Marcion was trying to force a distinction between Israel's God and the God of the Christians. Tertullian abhorred this idea. His voluminous refutation of Marcion in five large books has the central purpose of tying Christianity inextricably to the God of the Jews. So when

---

22. Geoffrey D. Dunn, *Tertullian* (London: Routledge, 2004), 68.
23. Williams, *Adversus Judaeos*, 43. For a more detailed look at the text's rhetorical purpose and readership, see Geoffrey D. Dunn, *Tertullian's* Adversus Judaeos: *A Rhetorical Analysis* (Washington, DC: Catholic University of America Press, 2008), 26–27, 56–57, 175–76. On the real likelihood that ancient Christians might convert to Judaism, see Robert L. Wilken, *John Chrysostom and the Jews: Rhetoric and Reality in the Late 4th Century* (Berkeley: University of California Press, 1983).

Tertullian engages the Old Testament against the rabbis,[24] he does this not by rejecting the one Creator God but by claiming to be the true possessor of this God's promises through Jesus Christ. Therefore, it was essential to find prophecies of the coming Messiah in the pages of the Old Testament.

Many prior Christians had already recognized this point. To help with the task of easily accessing Messianic prophecies, it appears that books of "testimonies" circulated in the ancient church. These were excerpts of the Old Testament that were understood by the church fathers to predict Jesus and/or the rise of Christianity. Tertullian seems to have been using such a work when he composed his anti-Jewish treatise. Many of the standard messianic proof texts appear in the work:

> The dual sacrifices of Cain and Abel, only one of which is acceptable to God (Gen 4:3–16; cf. Mal 1:10–11)
> The divine curse on those "hanged on a tree" (Gal. 3:13; cf. Deut 21:22–23, ESV)
> The horrors of crucifixion (Ps 22)
> The prediction of the Virgin Birth (Isa 7:13–15)
> The Suffering Servant (Isa 53)
> The promise of a new covenant (Jer 31:31–32)
> The seventy "weeks" of Daniel before the arrival of the Messiah (Dan 9:21–27)

These are just representative examples. The list goes on and on as Tertullian works his way through the Old Testament to show its fundamental conjunction with the New.

Yet beyond mere proof texts, what we see on display here is Tertullian's christological reading of the biblical text. Although the present chapter is not the place to engage the immense subject of patristic hermeneutics, we can at least point out that he was reading the Bible in a very different way from the Jewish leaders.[25] Broadly speaking, rabbinic exegesis tended to be literal. It focused on the Hebrew letters themselves or on the text's practical significance for Jew-

---

24. Though Tertullian doesn't specifically mention the rabbis, we have to keep in mind that this sort of educated, literate debate about the meaning of texts could have been conducted only among a few intellectual leaders such as himself and the rabbis of the Carthaginian synagogues. For the majority of people in the ancient world, texts were "oral" entities that were encountered through the ear as they were read aloud. Only the elites could read and write at this high level.

25. For more on this, see Charles Kannengiesser, *Handbook of Patristic Exegesis: The Bible in Ancient Christianity* (Leiden: Brill, 2006).

ish life, such as matters of religious purity. In contrast, all forms of Christian exegesis—whether the more conservative approach of Antioch or the more allegorical school of Alexandria—allowed for spiritual meanings to be hidden beneath the biblical text. In this way, Jesus Christ could be found in the Old Testament, fulfilling his own words: "You study the Scriptures diligently because you think that in them you have eternal life. These are the very Scriptures that testify about me" (John 5:39).

APOLOGETIC METHODOLOGY

To understand Tertullian as an apologist, we must first break down a caricature that has been drawn of him too often. Many writers, unfamiliar with his entire thirty-one volume corpus, lend far too much weight to his famous quip, "What hath Athens to do with Jerusalem?" This lone statement—coming from an author in love with exaggerated rhetorical flourishes!—is viewed as programmatic for his entire apologetic approach. The claim is made that Tertullian utterly divorced philosophy from theology, and perhaps even rejected reason altogether.

For example, in the widely-used *Documents of the Christian Church* by Henry Bettenson and Chris Maunder, a section appears on "Christianity and Ancient Learning."[26] In it, Justin Martyr and Clement of Alexandria are put forward as "liberals" who are open to philosophy and integrative in spirit; but Tertullian's quip is cited as representing a "negative" view in which a stodgy fundamentalist rejects the wisdom of the world. Another popular textbook similarly concludes that Tertullian "places a deep chasm between the enterprise of philosophy and the Christian religion."[27] While there is truth in these characterizations, upon further examination, the issue becomes more complex. Tertullian was suspicious of philosophy for sure; yet he used it for Christian apologetic purposes more frequently than he sometimes let on.

Tertullian is also associated in surveys of apologetics with *fideism*. According to *The Stanford Encyclopedia of Philosophy*, this term "can be defined as an 'exclusive or basic reliance upon faith alone, accompanied by a consequent disparagement of reason and utilized especially in the pursuit of philosophical or religious truth.' . . . [A] fideist is someone who 'urges reliance on faith rather

---

26. Henry Bettenson and Chris Maunder, *Documents of the Christian Church*, 4th ed. (Oxford: Oxford University Press, 2011), 5–7.

27. William Edgar and K. Scott Oliphint, *Christian Apologetics Past & Present: A Primary Source Reader, Volume 1, to 1500* (Wheaton: Crossway, 2009), 117.

than reason, in matters philosophical and religious' and who 'may go on to disparage and denigrate reason.'"[28] In other words, a fideist puts all their emphasis on a leap of faith (*fides* means faith), even when the thing believed is irrational or absurd. To a fideist, the more absurd it is, the better, for this highlights the extremity of one's faith.

The reason Tertullian gets tagged with the unfavorable label of fideism is, once again, because of a pithy rhetorical quip. Somehow his supposed statement has morphed over the centuries into *credo quia absurdum*, "I believe [it] because it is absurd." What he actually said was, *certum est, quia impossibile*, "It is certain, because it is impossible." This makes it sound as though sheer absurdity leads to believability. But the context of this statement is important. The full statement appears in Tertullian's work *On the Flesh of Christ*: "The Son of God was crucified. There is no shame [in believing this], because it is indeed shameful. And the Son of God died. It is surely to be believed, because it is absurd. And having been buried, he rose again. It is certain, because it is impossible."[29] Here Tertullian is refuting a teaching of Marcion called Docetism: the belief that Christ did not actually suffer any human indignities—especially not death—because his ghostly body was unreal and only seemed to be human. Tertullian wants to prove that Jesus's true human body suffered on a cross, died, and was raised from the dead. But Tertullian is not staking his claim on an irrational leap of faith. Rather, he is quoting the apostle Paul's description of God's topsy-turvy way of doing things: "God chose the foolish things of the world to shame the wise; God chose the weak things of the world to shame the strong" (1 Cor 1:27). This statement does not express fideism but affirms only that God tends to work through things that humans find repulsive, foolish, or absurd. Paul was no fideist, and neither was Tertullian.

Interestingly, far from rejecting philosophy, Tertullian seems to have had a Greek philosopher in mind: Aristotle, who argues that when something is highly improbable, yet many people believe it anyway, that thing is likely to be true, for who would invent something so unbelievable?[30] While this is not a sound argument, we should still note that Tertullian was following good Aristotelian logic—precisely the opposite of what a fideist would do!

The fact of the matter is that Tertullian's apologetics—and indeed, his entire theological system, to the extent he had one—relied heavily on philosophical

---

28. Richard Amesbury, "Fideism," in *The Stanford Encyclopedia of Philosophy*, ed. Edward N. Zalta (Fall 2017 Edition). Retrieved online.

29. Tertullian, *Carn. Chr.* 5 (translation my own).

30. *Rhetorica* 2.23.21.

constructs. In particular, Tertullian had an affinity for Stoicism, especially its ethics. Stoicism believed that "right reason" governed the universe, so all things worked together for a higher purpose. Endurance was required in the face of hardship because the Stoic's mind perceived a divine rationale behind the suffering, enabling the body to persevere. For Tertullian, a philosophy built on such a premise fit nicely with Christian thought, especially in an age of persecution. Far from insisting on blind faith, Tertullian revered logic and reason, and he incorporated philosophy into his argumentation often.[31] At the same time, his spiritual temperament kept him from ever allowing human philosophical musings to trump the clear teachings of Scripture.

CONTRIBUTIONS TO THE FIELD OF APOLOGETICS

As we reflect on and summarize Tertullian's approach to apologetics, four applications of his method may be useful to modern Christians:

Be bold. Believe it or not, a "politically correct" mindset is no more prevalent today than it was in Tertullian's time. The demand for absolute submission to cultural norms was as vociferous in the third century as it is now. And ancient society widely scorned the Christian faith (at least in its more dogmatic forms), just as it does in the contemporary setting. Into this culture of hostility toward the gospel, Tertullian marched boldly with the truth of God. His apologetic method was to stake his claim on his possession of absolute, timeless truth that all humans must hear to achieve salvation. He did not dither; he did not waver; he did not dance around the issues. Tertullian defended his faith in the risen Christ with courageous honesty and firm conviction. So must we.

Emphasize morality. It is not enough in today's world to defend Christianity from intellectual attack, as if we hold to a set of abstract doctrines whose successful defense through logic will win converts. Misconceptions about

---

31. Eric Osborn in *Tertullian: First Theologian of the West* (Cambridge: Cambridge University Press, 1997) has investigated these matters in detail, and his conclusions are worth quoting at length. It is necessary, writes Osborn, "to show that Tertullian was not a fideist. Not only did he never say, 'credo quia absurdum', but he never meant anything like it and never abandoned the claims of Athens upon Jerusalem" (27–28). "Tertullian is the most improbable fideist; no one has [ever made arguments] so irrepressibly" as him (29). "Tertullian does not reject or accept philosophy as a whole. He knows his philosophers better than do most Greek [church] fathers. The points where philosophy has hit on the truth may be used to convince educated pagans that the gospel is true" (31). Tertullian's "concepts of being, soul, knowledge, God and goodness bear clear marks of Stoic influence. The same reason which is applied to natural questions must also be applied to the intelligent exploration of God. Because Tertullian sees the need for rational theological inquiry, he has been placed among the first philosophical Christians" (35). Clearly this was a man who, far from rejecting reason, proved his faith by rational support!

Christian morality abound in modern society. We are considered hateful people who are arrogant and hypocritical. While no one suspects us of orgies and cannibalism as in the ancient church, our morality is nonetheless called into question. Many Christians who hold to simple, time-honored values are painted with the brush of intolerance to look like spiteful bigots. It is time to stop being silent and accepting of this accusation. As Tertullian did, modern Christians should speak forthrightly about the true morals and ethics of our faith.

Use human reason as much as possible. Though morality is important, so too is a rational defense of the faith. Too often, Christians function with an unwarranted suspicion of secular science and/or philosophy. We tend to create our own distinct versions of each, in an attempt to purify them of worldly connections or implications. But as we have seen, Tertullian was no fideist who emphasized faith at the expense of reason. He was highly educated and knew his culture's scientific and philosophical presuppositions very well. While he never let pagan ideas contradict the clear teachings of Scripture, he was certainly willing to enter into reasoned discourse with his opponents about the great ideas of his day. By knowing non-Christian learning as well as his interlocutors did, Tertullian was able to use human reason in defense of the gospel. It was a wise and appropriate strategy.

Proclaim Christ in the Word. Biblical argumentation has its place, at least with those who claim to accept the Word of God as authoritative. But in the end, it is not about the minutiae of theology but about Christ. The task of searching the Scriptures is an important one. Theological discourse is a noble task, but when it comes to apologetics toward cults and sects that claim allegiance to the Bible, it is better not to get bogged down on extraneous matters. Tertullian understood that both Testaments present a single, coherent narrative about God and his work in the world. This work culminates with Jesus Christ. When digging into the Scriptures as part of an apologetic enterprise, do not let the heretics derail you into side questions. Instead, point the unbeliever to the Lord Jesus, letting his majesty shine forth from every page of Scripture. For as he himself said, "I, when I am lifted up from the earth, will draw all people to myself" (John 12:32).

BIBLIOGRAPHY

Texts and Translations

Arbesmann, Rudolph, Emily Joseph Daly, and Edwin A. Quain. *Tertullian: Apologetical Works and Minucius Felix: Octavius.* New York: Fathers of the Church, 1950.
Dunn, Geoffrey D. *Tertullian.* London: Routledge, 2004.
Greenslade, S. L. *Early Latin Theology.* Louisville: Westminster, 1956.

Studies

Barnes, Timothy D. *Tertullian: A Historical and Literary Study*. Oxford: Clarendon, 1971, 2nd ed. 1984.

Burrows, Mark S. "Christianity in the Roman Forum: Tertullian and the Apologetic Use of History." *Vigiliae Christianae* 42:3 (1988): 209–35.

Dunn, Geoffrey D. *Tertullian's* Adversus Judaeos*: A Rhetorical Analysis*. Washington, DC: Catholic University of America Press, 2008.

Edwards, Mark J., Martin Goodman, Simon Price, Chris Rowland, eds. *Apologetics in the Roman Empire: Pagans, Jews, and Christians*. Oxford: Clarendon, 1999.

Livermore, Paul. "Reasoning with Unbelievers and the Place of the Scriptures in Tertullian's *Apology*." *The Asbury Theological Journal* 56:1 (Spring 2001): 63–75.

Osborn, Eric. *Tertullian: First Theologian of the West*. Cambridge: Cambridge University Press, 1997.

Riggs, David L. "The Apologetics of Grace in Tertullian and Early African Martyr Acts." Pages 395–406 in *Studia Patristica, ed. Markus Vinzent, vol. 65*. Leuven: Peeters, 2013.

Sider, Robert Dick. *Ancient Rhetoric and the Art of Tertullian*. Oxford: Oxford University Press, 1971.

ORIGEN

An Innovator in Apologetic Sophistication

A. CHADWICK THORNHILL

Origen (ca. 185–254) was one of the most prolific authors of his day and the first to provide a large-scale philosophical defense of the Christian faith. His major apologetic work addressed the criticisms of paganism against Christianity as well as the criticism of Judaism, through the lens of an imagined interlocutor. His body of work also included numerous theological and exegetical writings. While Origen is often remembered for his allegorical exegesis and disputed eschatology, his apologetic legacy undoubtedly shaped future generations of apologists, and modern apologists still use some of his arguments and evidences.

HISTORICAL BACKGROUND

Origen is hailed as the originator of many scholarly accomplishments within Christian history. He is often recognized as the first systematic theologian, the first Christian philosopher, the founder of the first Christian university,[1] and one of the most prolific authors in all Christian history. Much of what is known of Origen's life comes from Eusebius's *Ecclesiastical History* (*Historia Ecclesiastica*). Origen was born in Alexandria, a city of intellectual fortitude in the ancient world. According to Eusebius, Origen's father, Leonides, himself a literary instructor,[2] was beheaded during the persecutions of Emperor Severus when Origen was seventeen.[3] This event led Origen to have a zeal for martyrdom, though his mother interceded to prevent him from seeking after it.[4]

By the ordering of his father, Origen was educated in the liberal arts as well

---

1. Of those listed, this is perhaps the least well known of Origen's many accomplishments. See John A. McGuckin, "Caesarea Maritima as Origen Knew It" in *Origeniana Quinta*, ed. Robert J. Daly (Leuven: Leuven University Press, 1992), 3–25.

2. John A. McGuckin, "The Life of Origen," in *The Westminster Handbook to Origen*, ed. John A. McGuckin (Louisville: Westminster John Knox, 2004), 3.

3. Eusebius, *Hist. eccl.* 6.1.1; 6.2.12.

4. Ibid., 6.2.1–6.

as in the Scriptures, "busying himself with deeper speculations"[5] concerning their truths. He was a student of Ammonius Saccas, who was the father of Neoplatonism and teacher of Plotinus.[6] Eusebius writes that even as a young man Origen despised heretical teachings and held firmly to the rule of the church.[7] Origen lectured at the catechetical school in Alexandria, which he would eventually oversee, and his reputation grew as one informed in philosophical matters but also full of "kindness and goodwill," particularly to those facing martyrdom.[8] Eusebius records that Origen lived a disciplined life, eschewing the accumulation of material possessions, frequently fasting, and refusing the comfort of a bed.[9] Perhaps the most famous example of his zeal and discipline is his reported, though historically uncertain, self-castration so as to remove any opportunity for temptation or scandal.[10]

Eusebius reports that all of Origen's time, in leisure and occupation, was spent in teaching and studying the Scriptures,[11] so much so that he learned Hebrew and investigated other translations of the sacred texts.[12] He famously, and no doubt painstakingly, compiled the Hexapla, which critically compared the Hebrew text with several Greek translations.

Origen was instrumental in Ambrose of Alexandria's acceptance of the orthodox doctrines of the church and, according to Eusebius, was a much sought-after instructor by heretics, philosophers, and Christians alike.[13] He was respected among the philosophers for his comprehension and proficiency in Greek literature and Greek philosophical systems.[14] His fame was so vast, according to Eusebius, even the mother of Emperor Alexander Severus, Julia Mamaea, reportedly called on him to teach in Antioch.[15]

Ambrose of Alexandria eventually became Origen's sponsor and provided Origen with amanuenses, copyists, and the financial means to produce his extensive writings, including his commentaries on Scripture.[16] Because of his sponsor, Origen produced a vast collection of writings. As a result, both the primary and secondary literature surrounding Origen's life and theological

---

5. Ibid., 6.2.9.
6. Avery Dulles, *A History of Apologetics* (San Francisco: Ignatius, 2005), 42.
7. Eusebius, *Hist. eccl.*, 6.2.14. But Eusebius is often criticized for his apparent exaggerations.
8. Ibid., 6.3.3.
9. Ibid., 6.3.9–13.
10. Ibid., 6.8.1. Though Eusebius reports that this was because of his interpretation of Matthew 19:12, Origen's own commentary on Matthew mocks such an interpretation of that text (*Comm. Matt.* 15.1–5). Whether Origen actually arranged his castration or not is debated (e.g., McGuckin, "The Life of Origen," 7).
11. Ibid., 6.8.5–6.
12. Ibid., 6.16.1–4.
13. Ibid., 6.18.1–2.
14. Ibid., 6.19.1–8.
15. Ibid., 6.21.3.
16. Ibid., 6.23.1–4.

articulations is vast. Around the age of forty-five, and likely due to ever-growing tensions with the local bishop, Demetrios,[17] likely over Origen's growing influence in the church and some of his theological positions,[18] Origen traveled to Caesarea and was ordained as presbyter. There he instructed Theodorus (also known as Gregory Thaumaturgus) and his brother Athenodorus, among many others.[19] He continued his production of commentaries there[20] and worked to found a school and grow the ecclesial library.[21] At the age of sixty, he produced his response to Celsus's *The True Discourse* in his major apologetic work, *Against Celsus*. According to Eusebius, Origen was imprisoned and tortured extensively near the end of his life but did not renounce his faith.[22] He was released prior to martyrdom because of the emperor's death and died at the age of sixty-nine.[23]

Origen is credited with producing the first "systematic theology" in his *On the Principles* (*De Principiis*), which explained the major tenets of the Christian faith. Among his other many literary achievements (which according to Epiphanius number six thousand books and according to Jerome number two thousand)[24] were the production of commentaries on Song of Songs, Ezekiel, the Gospels of Matthew and John, Romans, and largely lost commentaries on Genesis, Kings, Psalms, Isaiah, Lamentations, Ezekiel, a portion of the minor prophets, Luke, Acts, Galatians, Ephesians, Philippians, Colossians, Thessalonians, Hebrews, Titus, and Philemon. Other major works include his *Hexapla, Dialogue with Heracleides, On Prayer, Exhortation to Martyrdom*, and a lost *Treatise on the Resurrection*. A large number of Origen's letters and homilies survive as well. Origen's theological influence left an imprint on many of the most influential church fathers, including Basil of Caesarea, Gregory of Nazianzus, Ambrose of Milan, and Jerome. Origen's later denunciation by the church for allegedly holding to a form of universalism and to the eternality of the soul resulted in many of his works being lost to history.

THEOLOGICAL CONTEXT

Because of his philosophical, philological, and literary capabilities, Origen was certainly an apologetic force to be reckoned with. He received exceptional

---

17. McGuckin, "The Life of Origen," 9–13.

18. Henry Chadwick, *Early Christian Thought and the Classical Tradition* (Oxford: Oxford University Press, 1966), 99–100.

19. Eusebius, *Hist. eccl.*, 6.23.4; 6.26.1.; 6.30.1.

20. Ibid., 6.32.1–3.

21. McGuckin, "The Life of Origen," 16.

22. Eusebius, *Hist. eccl.*, 6.39.5.

23. Ibid. 7.1.1.

24. John A. McGuckin, "The Scholarly Works of Origen," in *The Westminster Handbook to Origen*, 26.

training in both philosophy and literature, and his reputation for discipline no doubt contributed both to his intellectual rigor as well as to his vast literary productions. As is the case with many of the fathers of the church, Origen's context was complicated both by external factors (paganism, Hellenistic philosophy, Roman persecution, and Christian heresies) as well as by his own personal history (his father's martyrdom, his philosophical training in Platonism, and his willingness to explore ideas with some fairness). For these reasons, framing his own thought is no easy task. As Crouzel and Prinzivalli observe, commenting on Origen's *De Principiis*, "Origen often examines several interpretive options and does not always indicate which he favors."[25]

The danger with reading Origen, as with many other great and prolific theologians, is that in his often-focused writing, he often does not counterbalance a statement. Thus, certain ideas, when read in isolation and without consideration of the whole of his work, have led to some interpreting his work with heretical force.[26] Origen is also quite famous for his allegorical method of interpretation, which, though may seem strange and fanciful to the modern reader, is rooted in his firm belief that the Scriptures are spiritual texts and thus must be interpreted as such. For Origen, Scripture has a plain or corporeal sense, a "psychical" or moral sense, and an allegorical or spiritual sense (*De Principiis* 4.11–12). But these meanings are less exegetical layers that exist in every text than significant in their ability to impart spiritual edification, for that is the meaning Origen wishes the Spirit to impart. Part of his hermeneutical restraint was recognizing that the whole of Scripture, or perhaps more narrowly the rule of faith, must constrain what could be said of a given passage.

While not strictly apologetic in nature, his *De Principiis* certainly has, as part of its aim, an explanation and defense of the rule of faith against the Marcionites, Gnostics, Docetists, and Arians of his day. He upholds the value of the Old Testament; the continuity of the God found in both Testaments; the authentic, full humanity of Jesus; the eternal generation of the Son; and the unity of God; and the triunity of the three divine persons.[27] Though lacking some of the formalized language, which would come through later councils, Origen is thoroughly orthodox in his expression of the nature of God and the nature of Christ.

Perhaps most prominent in his context was the influence of Middle Platonism and Stoicism, as a part of his philosophical training, on his theological

---

25. Henri Crouzel and Emanuela Prinzivalli, "Origen," in *Encyclopedia of Ancient Christianity*, Vol. 2, ed. Angelo Di Berardino (Downers Grove, IL: IVP Academic, 2014), 979.

26. Ibid.

27. Ibid., 981.

framework. The question of the relationship between philosophy and theology is not simply a modern one but one that created tensions even in Origen's day and was likely at least part of the conflict between Origen and Demetrios.[28] The question may be boiled down to whether Platonic thought had a clarifying or corrupting influence on Christianity (e.g., Harnack), and the question comes to the forefront with Origen. Though Origen was less overtly enthusiastic about Plato than Clement of Alexandria,[29] according to Henry Chadwick, Origen accomplished an "even profounder synthesis between Christianity and Platonism" than did Clement.[30] For Origen, philosophy was a part of the process of enlightening the mind toward knowledge of Christ.[31] He can thus appeal to the opinions of the philosophers at times and at other times critically evaluate them without seeing the need to use them as a means of verifying or reinterpreting the rule of faith.[32] Thus, Origen by his account does not seem entirely beholden to a Platonic system, though he clearly benefitted from many of its beliefs and perhaps underestimated how much they influenced his theological work.[33]

APOLOGETIC RESPONSE

Origen's primary apologetic writing is *Against Celsus* (*Contra Celsum*), in which Origen dialogues with the pagan philosopher Celsus, who had written an extensive assault against Christianity in his work *The True Discourse*. Celsus's work is mostly lost to history, so what survives is primarily found within Origen's response, meaning Origen's correct representation of Celsus's arguments would provide the primary means for accessing Celsus's work. Though Celsus wrote before Origen was even born (AD 178), his work provided fuel for the polemical fires of those opposed to Christianity. At the urging of Ambrose, Origen set out to rebut Celsus's arguments point by point and thereby stifled the objections Celsus raised. Origen wrote *Against Celsus* near the end of his life.

Celsus's arguments against Christianity are offered in two forms—first from a Jewish perspective, which Celsus adopts as a means of argument, not as

---

28. See McGuckin, "The Life of Origen," 7–10.
29. Salvatore Lilla, "Platonism and the Fathers," in *Encyclopedia of Ancient Christianity*, Vol. 2, 212.
30. Chadwick, *Early Christian Thought and the Classical Tradition*, 102.
31. As Chadwick quotes, "Discover the image of God within your own soul by introspection and withdrawing the mind from the distractions of sense" (Origen, *Hom. Gen.* 13.4, quoted in Chadwick, *Early Christian Thought and the Classical Tradition*, 105).
32. See Chadwick, *Early Christian Thought and the Classical Tradition*, 105.
33. For a compact yet detailed comparison of Middle and Neoplatonic overlap with Origen's theology, see Lilla, "Platonism and the Fathers," 213–15.

his own system of belief, and second from the perspective of a pagan philosopher, which Celsus undoubtedly was. Frede suggests that Celsus was likely the first pagan philosopher to compose an entire treatise against Christianity.[34] Celsus clearly did his homework in compiling his polemic, drawing on common objections and arguments against Christianity while also likely adding to and refining them.[35] It is difficult to determine the extent to which Celsus's work influenced either pagans or Christians, but the fact that his work was still circulated several decades after it was written and was bothersome enough to Ambrose that he implored Origen to author a response suggests it had maintained some cultural influence.

Origen describes his work as an "apology" numerous times in *Against Celsus*, which evokes a legal image and no doubt is connected to Celsus's assertion that Christians have a legal case to answer in that Christianity was not a recognized religion (i.e., was illegal).[36] The objections that Celsus raised against Christians, which were no doubt common ones, concerned "their morality, their education, and their rationality—in short, their civic respectability—objections which might well be endorsed by Roman magistrates or even the emperor."[37] Much of Origen's response addresses not legitimate objections to Christianity (though those are present as well) but misrepresentations of what Christians actually believe.[38] Though Celsus declares himself an expert on Christian belief and writings, his articulations often seem based on popular opinions about Christians rather than widely-held Christian beliefs.[39] Origen ultimately operates not in the legal realm, making an appeal to the authorities to reconsider the illegality of Christianity, but rather in the personal realm, appealing to the reader to decide whether the case for the truth of Christianity has been adequately made.[40] Eusebius thought so highly of Origen's argumentation in *Against Celsus* that he asserted that it answered all objections to Christianity, including those that would come in the future.[41]

Origen's lengthy response to Celsus integrates much from the Platonic and Stoic traditions in answering the objections raised. While biblical and theological

---

34. Michael Frede, "Origen's Treatise *Against Celsus*," in *Apologetics in the Roman Empire: Pagans, Jews, and Christians*, ed. Mark J. Edwards, Martin Goodman, Simon Price, and Chris Rowland (New York: Oxford University Press, 1999), 133.

35. Ibid.

36. Ibid., 136.

37. Ibid., 137.

38. E.g., Origen, *Cels*. 1.6, 9, 13, 26.

39. Ibid., 1.12–13.

40. Ibid., 138.

41. Eusebius, *Hier*. 1.

considerations certainly factored into Origen's argumentation, his response is thoroughly indebted to Greek philosophical thought, perhaps more than even he realized.[42] Origen is also a somewhat reluctant apologist, responding because of the urgings of Ambrose rather than from his own conviction that such a response was necessary or beneficial. In fact, in the preface, he seems opposed to the idea that such an effort is necessary. He explains his apologetic apprehension, saying, "I have no sympathy with anyone who had faith in Christ such that it could be shaken by Celsus . . . or by any plausibility of argument," and "I do not know in what category I ought to reckon one who needs written arguments in books to restore and confirm him in his faith."[43] In spite of this, he does see the potential value that his work holds for those reluctant about Christianity or for young Christians unsure about some of the doctrines of the faith.[44] At the conclusion of his response, Origen leaves it to the reader to decide whether his responses or Celsus's articulations are better representations of the truth and better exhortations to a virtuous life.[45]

Perhaps contrary to many modern inclinations, for Celsus, the novelty and recentness of Christian beliefs about Jesus count against its veracity. If it is new, it must certainly be wrong. A religion that lacks tradition or corrupts the traditions of others is an abomination. Not only have the Christians misunderstood and corrupted Jewish beliefs and practices, Celsus charges, but they have likewise done so with pagan beliefs. As Chadwick documents, Celsus challenges Christian beliefs about judgment, ethics, virtue, the kingdom of God, heaven, Satan, Jesus's identity as the "Son of God," nonresistance, objections to images and idols, and God's existence as spirit. To Celsus, these Christian beliefs bastardize pagan, Platonic, and Stoic beliefs about the same matters.[46] Thus, leaving Christianity unchecked would be disastrous to the empire and would unsettle the religious and civic foundations of Rome.

One of Origen's first defenses of the legitimacy of Christian belief about Jesus is the transformed lives of his followers. Origen considers both the astounding rate at which Christianity has grown and the piety and commitment of its

---

42. Henry Chadwick, *Origen: Contra Celsum* (Cambridge: Cambridge University Press, 1953), xii-xiii. As an example, Origen adapted the Neoplatonic conception of *hypostases* to his expression of the Trinity to distinguish the Father, Son, and Spirit as three *hypostases*. Though Origen's subordinationist tendencies have been debated and disputed, his conceptual integration formed the foundation by which the Cappadocian Fathers would explicate the doctrine of the Trinity. Their articulation of the doctrine would dominate the Christian tradition from then onward (Origen, *Comm. Jo.* 2.10.75).

43. Origen, *Cels.* Pref. 4.

44. Ibid., Pref. 4–6.

45. Ibid., 8.76.

46. Chadwick, *Origen: Contra Celsum*, xx-xxi.

adherents as a proof for Christian claims about Jesus.[47] Jesus's own life, miracles, and success in the face of major political opposition despite his ignoble personal circumstances further validate Christian belief.[48]

A major part of Origen's response to Celsus's Jewish objections involves his case for the prophetic foresight of the Old Testament as it relates to Jesus, his mission, and his death and resurrection. Origen sees Isaiah 35:5–6 as validating Jesus's performing of miracles.[49] Likewise, he sees the predictions of the prophets concerning the virgin conception of Jesus and the place of Jesus's birth as verifying the truthfulness of his identity.[50] Origen discounts Celsus's treatment of Jesus's miracles as works of sorcery and, in responding to the Jewish interlocutor Celsus portrays, notes that the same types of miracles Jesus performed were performed in the Old Testament and were predicted of the Messiah and therefore cannot be dismissed as works of sorcery.[51] Indeed, Origen charges that the same objections of sorcery could be laid at Moses's feet.[52]

Celsus also lays this charge of incredulity against claims of Jesus's resurrection, suggesting that the account merely replicates the myths about other figures who came back from the dead or was conceived from the grief, delusion, or hysteria of Jesus's followers.[53] Origen answers these charges by noting that Jesus's public death cannot be likened to the myths and is thus verifiable, as were his public appearances.[54] Furthermore, the suffering and martyrdom, which many of Jesus's disciples endured for proclaiming the actuality of his resurrection is unthinkable if they knew it to be only a myth or charade.[55]

Celsus viewed the incarnation as an affront to the conception of God, given that in becoming human, God would change "from good to evil, from virtue to vice, from happiness to misery, and from best to worst."[56] Origen responds that, in taking a human body and soul, God did not undergo change as it relates to the divine essence.[57] In defending the nature of the incarnation, Origen points to Paul's description in Philippians 2:5–9 and asserts that the incarnation was necessary to bring healing to the sick and diseased souls of humanity.[58]

---

47. Origen, *Cels.* 1.26.
48. Ibid., 1.28–31.
49. Ibid., 2.48.
50. Ibid., 3.2.
51. Ibid., 2.52.
52. Ibid., 2.53.
53. Ibid., 2.55.
54. Ibid., 2.56.
55. Ibid., 2.56.
56. Ibid., 4.14.
57. Ibid., 4.18.
58. Ibid., 4.19.

Also worth mentioning is that, though not written specifically as an apologetic exercise, Origen's concluding section of *On the Principles* offers a defense and articulation of the Trinity that would become influential, if not controversial, in the later definition of orthodox belief. Origen expresses within this section concepts that would find similar expression in later creedal formulations, such as the eternal generation of the Son, the oneness of the Son and Father in essence, the simplicity of the divine essence, the reality of the incarnation without any loss of divine properties, the sinlessness of the incarnate Christ, and the unity of the Father, Son, and Spirit. Influential as it was, Origen's articulations of the Trinity were used on both sides of the debate in later doctrinal controversies. Some of Origen's articulations tended toward a subordinationist view of Christ (though they were qualified), and he also rejected the use of *homoousios* to describe the relation of the Father and the Son, making his writings forceful fuel for the Arians. Origen, however, denied that there were two gods or two natures, or that the Son was not eternally one with the Father, and he also denied that there was any internal subordination to the Trinity, though there existed a hierarchy of actions between them.[59] Thus, though the terminology changed, Markschies notes: "The development of Trinitarian theology in all parts of the church over the two centuries following him did little other than develop the schema he himself had first sketched out, by clarifying the loose ends of his concept."[60]

APOLOGETIC METHODOLOGY

There is much more we could say regarding Origen's voluminous responses to Celsus's many objections. But due to the point-for-point nature of Origen's reply, perhaps more beneficial for the present-day apologist is to step back to see the forest of *Against Celsus* for the trees of Origen's responses. There is much in Origen's work, both in content and method, that can shape the efforts of apologists in the present.

Origen is perhaps most remembered as a Christian theologian for his allegorical method of interpretation, which to modern interpreters often seems fanciful, strange, and quite frankly, misguided. But often Origen does not appeal to a deeper or spiritual sense of the text when offering a defense of Christian beliefs. This seems particularly true when arguing for the validity of Christian beliefs about Jesus based on Old Testament prophecy. In many cases, Origen's interpretation roughly aligns with more conservative, present-day Christian

---

59. See Christoph Markschies, "Trinitarianism," in *The Westminster Handbook to Origen*, 207–09.
60. Ibid., 209.

interpretations. As Martens has cataloged, one of Origen's virtues for interpretation was being careful with the text, and considering all the broad nuances of a text during the interpretive process, this is certainly a value worth emulating.[61]

As Chadwick notes, Origen, following the lead of some of his Christian apologetic predecessors, also inherited from Jewish apologists a line of thinking that argued that Moses and the prophets contained the same expressions of truth that the Greek philosophers and poets articulated, and thus Moses and the prophets were a more reliable source of truth since they predated those later thinkers.[62] Origen was not afraid to recognize overlaps in his worldview and Celsus's worldview while also not giving into Celsus's objections on matters central to Christian belief. Indeed, Origen seems to prove himself a fairer interpreter of Greek philosophical beliefs as represented by Celsus than Celsus proves himself an interpreter of Christian doctrines.

Origen is also a thoroughgoing integrationist in regard to his apologetic method. Widely read and well-educated, Origen felt equipped to deal with matters of theology, philosophy, ethics, history, philology, and science in his apologetic responses. His integration was not born out of an ignorant willingness to enter any debate regardless of his preparation but was based on years of reading, study, and preparation. Origen, for example, does not shy away from using negative apologetics against Greek myths in response to charges of similarities or deficiencies of Jesus in comparison or negative apologetics against Stoic or Platonic beliefs. As Dulles describes, Origen is "the first apologist who seems prepared to take on any objection that can be urged against the Christian faith, whether from the standpoint of history, or philosophy, or of the natural sciences."[63] He is able to reference and analyze the Greek poets, philosophers, and historians perhaps as well as any of his contemporaries could. And he did not shy away from knowledge of these "secular" fields of inquiry despite his first and foremost concern and passion being for the interpretation and application of the Christian Scriptures. In spite of this, and though his integration of Neo-Platonic and Stoic ideas into Christian theology is well established, he does not describe Greek philosophy with great enthusiasm, viewing Scripture as the primary and greatest source of truth, though perhaps he underestimated how influential Greek thought was on his systemization of Christian doctrine.[64] Indeed, though

---

61. Peter W. Martens, *Origen and Scripture: The Contours of the Exegetical Life* (Oxford: Oxford University Press, 2012), 168–78. According to Martens, Origen also valued faithfulness, humility, inquisitiveness, fairness and open-mindedness, exertion, and focused effort.

62. Chadwick, *Origen: Contra Celsum*, ix–x.

63. Dulles, *A History of Apologetics*, 46.

64. David T. Runia, "Philosophy," in *The Westminster Handbook to Origen*, 172.

Origen no doubt knew the benefits of philosophical inquiry, he does not view them as a necessity for Christian faith.[65]

Origen also recognizes the limitations of certain fields of inquiry, thus exhibiting epistemic humility. For example, concerning the account of the Spirit descending at Jesus's baptism, Origen notes of historical inquiry: "Before we begin the defense, we must say that an attempt to substantiate almost any story as historical fact, even if it is true, and to produce complete certainty about it, is one of the most difficult tasks and in some cases is impossible. . . . [And thus] readers need an open mind and considerable study, and, if I may say so, need to enter into the mind of the writers to find out with what spiritual meaning each event was recorded."[66]

Rather than overstating his case, or denying such limitation, Origen humbly accepts the limitations of this field of inquiry. Origen certainly could have asserted the surety of Christian beliefs about the historicity of the Old and New Testaments but is aware both of the difficulties within the texts themselves and the limitations that historical inquiry contains in general, for both pagan and Christian writings. By analogy, Origen asks how one might respond in being asked to prove beyond doubt that the Trojan War occurred. The best the reader can do is to attend carefully to the texts and try to make reasonable judgments about their claims.

What may be most surprising for modern readers is that for Origen, the success of the apologetic endeavor is measured not only in the demonstration of philosophical truth but also the spurring on toward the virtuous life.[67] Origen did not pursue his scholarship, as abundant as it was, for accolades or intellectual accomplishment. Origen's scholarship, be it philosophical or exegetical, was always in service of spiritual growth. As Crouzel and Prinzivalli observe, Origen used his training in philosophy, philology, and history to illuminate the Scriptures and provide spiritual nourishment for himself and his learners.[68] This also provides for Origen a litmus test for truth. Origen does not undertake the apologetic enterprise for a cold, logical, empirical examination of truth, but rather sees the measure of truth in what it is able to produce. Origen would no doubt have objected to a worldview that was rationally defensible but spiritually deficient. The livability and virtuousness produced by one's beliefs are a necessary measure of whether they are true.

---

65. Ibid.
66. Origen, *Cels.* 1.42.
67. Ibid., 8.76.
68. Crouzel and Prinzivalli, "Origen," 979.

CONTRIBUTIONS TO THE FIELD
OF APOLOGETICS

In moving from the third century to the present, we should ask what a present-day apologist might learn from Origen. As we compare contexts, there is certainly much that emerges as unfamiliar between our postmodern, post-truth, secular age and Origen's Greek-Roman philosophical landscape. The tools of Neoplatonism and allegorical exegesis do not seem to make for likely instruments for the modern apologist to convince their skeptical neighbors. But there is much of the spirit, and even content, of Origen's apologetic that shows itself valuable for our context today.

First, and perhaps foremost, Origen evidences an epistemic humility that was perhaps not common enough among his apologetic contemporaries. Origen knew, for example, that argumentation, evidences, and reason could only get him so far. Rather than overstating his case, or denying such limitation, Origen humbly accepted the limitations of the fields of inquiry in which he worked, particularly noting that history does not offer irrefutable proofs of the events of the past but rather incomplete sets of data, which only present themselves as probable. There is no "foolproof" argument to validate that the Trojan War happened or that Jesus rose from the dead. This is perhaps a lesson too often lost on many modern-day apologists who may too quickly assert the "undeniable" or "beyond doubt" nature of their verdicts. Indeed, for Origen, some matters are more surely grounded in faith than in argument, as the cumulative case for Christianity, including one's personal experience and life change, need not depend on logic or argumentation alone.

Origen seemed to take the time to represent his interlocutor fairly, even perhaps when Celsus himself did not represent Christian beliefs with fairness. We cannot be too sure of this, since all we know of Celsus's words are what Origen presents of them, but Origen frequently quotes his dialogue partner at length before interacting with the arguments presented. And while Celsus often resorts to ad hominem attacks against the Christians, Origen does not return the same vigor of slander against his pagan conversation partner.

Origen was honest about the challenges facing Christianity, recognizing and interacting with the differences between the gospels, the differences between Genesis 1 and 2, the issue of continuity/discontinuity between the two Testaments of the Christian Bible, text critical problems, etc.[69] While his allegorical

---

69. John Anthony McGuckin, *The Westminster Handbook to Patristic Theology* (Louisville: Westminster John Knox, 2004), 136.

method of exegesis, grounded in his belief that believers possessed an enlight-ened mind that they received through the Holy Spirit in their rebirth, was often employed in resolving these issues, Origen was not dismissive of the challenges nor naive that simple solutions were always readily available.

Origen also lived a life of thoughtful, modest, and fervent devotion to God. While Origen is known for his philosophical and interpretive traits, his ascet-icism provided a foundation for the later monastic movements in the ancient church.[70] Though Origen certainly did not shy away from intellectual work and rigor in analyzing, describing, and defending Christian beliefs, he thought the life of the Christian to be an equally, if not more so, forceful confirmation of the truthfulness of Christianity. Eusebius once quipped of Origen that "they say that his manner of life was as his doctrine, and his doctrine as his life."[71] The virtues of the Christian life were for Origen a powerful confirmation of the validity of its beliefs, and he considered it unthinkable for a Christian to lack a commitment to a virtuous life. In his preface to *Against Celsus*, Origen holds Jesus as a model of answering objections in that, when faced with his accusers, he deemed his life to be a stronger refutation of their accusations than any speech of validation he might give. So too for the Christian, an argument could weaken one's case rather than strengthen it when a more powerful testimony could be rendered from their virtuous life. If nothing else, Origen's analogy offers the Christian a warning against entering too lightly or self-assuredly into the apolo-getic enterprise.

Finally, Origen was perhaps the most thorough early Christian integration-ist. While he may not have said it in the same words, Origen likely would be content with the common expression that "all truth is God's truth." For Origen, supreme truth could be found only in the Scriptures, which are the clearest and most definitive revelation of God to humanity. Despite this, Origen was also content to find truth wherever it could be found. Trained as he was in Greek phi-losophy, philology, natural science, and reading the Scriptures, Origen was able to draw effectively on multiple fields of inquiry as he developed his theological and apologetic positions. After hearing Origen lecture, Gregory Thaumaturgus praised Origen for his command not only of philosophy and the Scriptures but also of the natural sciences, mathematics, geometry, ethics, and astronomy.[72] Further, as Chadwick observes, Origen was content to allow Celsus's claim that

---

70. David Turner, OSB, "Christianity," in *Encyclopedia of Monasticism*, ed. William M. Johnston (New York: Routledge, 2015), 287.

71. Eusebius, *Hist. eccl.* 6.3.7.

72. Stewart Dingwall Fordyce Salmond, *Gregory Thaumaturgus: Oration and Panegyric Addressed to Origen*, 6–8.

Christian ethical teachings are not entirely unique from that of the philosophers, responding only that this confirms moral intuitions and that Christianity thus corresponds to what is ethically true.[73] In his writings, Origen willingly appropriated from the Neoplatonists, Stoics, and Gnostics when helpful but was not beholden to their systems. Heine, for example, comments on Origen's knowledge of Stoicism: "Origen has employed some of the most sophisticated tools of his day for the analysis of thought. The unobtrusive way in which he uses it shows that he has internalized the subject so thoroughly that it shapes the way he thinks about texts and about the way others have interpreted those texts."[74]

But Origen was not uncritical in these adaptations. He advocated caution in interacting with philosophy and reliance on divine grace in building knowledge of God in a secular context.[75] He thus expressed a charitable orthodoxy, finding common ground and even learning from unorthodox systems while not denying the rule of faith or the clear teachings of Scripture.

Origen likewise understood this integration not merely to be accessible to Christian elites, but rather as central to the mission of the church to be a cultural influencer in the world. He saw a larger cultural mission as integral to the identity of the church. For Origen, enlightening the mind was essential to Christian life and to Christian growth and to engagement with outsiders. McGuckin eloquently describes this aspect of Origen's career as "the first exemplar of how the church ought to be vested as a major center of learning, as part of its essential mission to the world."[76] Origen famously developed libraries in the churches where he worked, first at Alexandria and then at Caesarea, both to sharpen his own study and to help tutor those being brought up in the faith. McGuckin further asserts: "The principle had been established throughout Byzantine Christianity—that the church leadership ought to base its cultural mission around a nexus of higher education services. It is largely to Origen that Christianity owes this insight and its practice for centuries following."[77]

As Rankin notes, speaking broadly of the fathers, though certainly applicable to Origen as well, the fathers were able to adopt, adapt, and criticize the thought structures and frameworks of their contemporaries. There is a degree to which they, like we, were influenced by their culture and communicated in ways

---

73. Chadwick, *Early Christian Thought and the Classical Tradition*, 105.
74. Ronald E. Heine, "Stoic Logic as Handmaid to Exegesis and Theology in Origen's Commentary on the Gospel of John," *Journal of Theological Studies* 44.1 (April 1993): 117.
75. David Ivan Rankin, *From Clement to Origen: The Social and Historical Context of the Church Fathers* (New York: Routledge, 2016), 138. Rankin, among others, notes it is unclear if Origen was aware of just how much Stoic and Neoplatonic thought influenced his approach to the task of theology.
76. McGuckin, "The Life of Origen," 16.
77. Ibid., 16.

that made sense to their world. They could appreciate the good that their culture offered, such as the benefits of the empire—education, commerce, or societal organization. They could also recognize and reject the aspects of those cultural artifacts that were contrary to their Christian beliefs, such as immorality, materialism, paganism, certain culturally accepted activities, the imperial cult, etc.[78]

The extent to which Origen allowed the influence of Neoplatonic and Stoic doctrines to dominate his approach to Christian thought has and will be debated. That Origen shows awareness of the tension is certainly to his credit. Indeed, the life of the Christian is one lived in the tension of progressing in the knowledge of God as revealed in the Scriptures and practicing introspection to determine how one might best live in their cultural moment. This is as true for the apologist today as it was for Origen. The virtues often ascribed to Origen of discipline, piety, peace, and wisdom are surely virtues that must aid the apologist of our cultural moment. As we peruse the life and work of Origen, we find a model of commitment to knowing the thought forms of one's secular contemporaries in order to leverage those thought forms for the clarifying effect they can have on the Scriptures as well as to critique them from the stand point of Christian doctrine. It is this tension in which the Christian must constantly operate, and the more aware they are of its existence, the better equipped they are to truly seek the things above and not the things on earth. And for Origen, that may be the best apologetic the church has to offer to the world around it.

BIBLIOGRAPHY

Texts and Translations

Chadwick, Henry. *Origen: Contra Celsum*. Cambridge: Cambridge University Press, 1953.
McGiffert, Arthur Cushman. "Eusebius: Church History." In *Nicene and Post-Nicene Fathers*, Second Series, Vol. 1. Ed. by Philip Schaff and Henry Wace. Buffalo, NY: Christian Literature Publishing Co., 1890. Revised and edited for New Advent by Kevin Knight. http://www.newadvent.org/fathers/2501.htm.
Salmond, Stewart Dingwall Fordyce. "Gregory Thaumaturgus: Oration and Panegyric Addressed to Origen." In *Ante-Nicene Fathers*, Vol. 6. Ed. by Alexander Roberts, James Donaldson, and A. Cleveland Coxe. Buffalo, NY: Christian Literature Publishing Co., 1886. Revised and edited for New Advent by Kevin Knight. http://www.newadvent.org/fathers/0604.htm.

Studies

Chadwick, Henry. *Early Christian Thought and the Classical Tradition*. Oxford: Oxford University Press, 1966.
Crouzel, Henri, and Emanuela Prinzivalli. "Origen." Page 979 in *Encyclopedia of Ancient Christianity*, Vol. 2. Ed. by Angelo Di Berardino. Downers Grove, IL: IVP Academic, 2014.
Dulles, Avery. *A History of Apologetics*. San Francisco: Ignatius, 2005.
Frede, Michael. "Origen's Treatise *Against Celsus*." Pages 131–56 in *Apologetics in the Roman Empire:*

---

78. Rankin, *From Clement to Origen*, 145.

Pagans, Jews, and Christians. Ed. by Mark J. Edwards, Martin Goodman, Simon Price, and Chris Rowland. Oxford University Press, 1999.

Heine, Ronald E. "Stoic Logic as Handmaid to Exegesis and Theology in Origen's Commentary on the Gospel of John." *Journal of Theological Studies* 44.1 (April 1993): 90–117.

Lilla, Salvatore. "Platonism and the Fathers." Pages 589–98 in *Encyclopedia of Ancient Christianity*, Vol. 2. Ed. by Angelo Di Berardino. Downers Grove, IL: IVP Academic, 2014.

Markschies, Christoph. "Trinitarianism." Pages 207–8 in *The Westminster Handbook to Origen*. Ed. by John Anthony McGuckin. Louisville: Westminster John Knox, 2004.

Martens, Peter W. *Origen and Scripture: The Contours of the Exegetical Life*. Oxford: Oxford University Press, 2012.

McGuckin, John A. "Caesarea Maritima as Origen Knew It." Pages 3–25 in *Origeniana Quinta*. Ed. by Robert J. Daly. Leuven: Leuven University Press, 1992.

———. "The Life of Origen." Pages 1–23 in *The Westminster Handbook to Origen*. Ed. by John A. McGuckin. Louisville: Westminster, 2004.

———. "The Scholarly Works of Origen." Pages 25–44 in *The Westminster Handbook to Origen*. Ed. by John A. McGuckin. Louisville: Westminster John Knox, 2004.

———. *The Westminster Handbook to Patristic Theology*. Louisville: Westminster John Knox Press, 2004.

Rankin, David Ivan. *From Clement to Origen: The Social and Historical Context of the Church Fathers*. New York: Routledge, 2016.

Runia, David T. "Philosophy." Pages 171–5 in *The Westminster Handbook to Origen*. Ed. by John Anthony McGuckin. Louisville: Westminster John Knox Press, 2004.

Turner, David, OSB. "Christianity." Pages 286–90 in *Encyclopedia of Monasticism*. Ed. by William M. Johnston. New York: Routledge, 2015.

ATHANASIUS OF ALEXANDRIA

The Logos as Reason to Believe

JONATHAN MORGAN

If the fourth century was the most pivotal era for the development of early Christian theology, Athanasius of Alexandria (ca. 295–373) was its leading figure. As bishop, he presided over one of the most important sees in the empire during a tumultuous period that was rife with doctrinal tensions over the nature of the Trinity, the deity of Christ, and the identity of the Holy Spirit. Though two ecumenical councils bookended the century, with Nicaea confessing the Son as *homoousious* with the Father and Constantinople affirming the full personhood and deity of the Holy Spirit, the position that would be declared "orthodox" came about through a dizzying series of advancements and setbacks, often owing to whoever happened to be wielding imperial control. In spite of the oscillations of power among various theological and political camps, Athanasius never wavered from his firm doctrinal convictions affirmed in the Nicene tradition. The slogan "Athanasius contra mundum" is indicative of his unshakable commitment to what he believed was the truth of the gospel, regardless of who stood with or against him.

HISTORICAL BACKGROUND

Athanasius came into the world at a time of momentous change, not only for the church but also for the Roman Empire. He was only a child, but he was old enough to remember the Diocletian persecution at the beginning of the fourth century. This occasion rattled Athanasius's Christian community and likely impacted his psyche, though, as Gwynn observes, there is no evidence that the violence personally affected him.[1] In the span of a decade, the church's fortunes

---

1. David Gywnn, *Athanasius of Alexandria: Bishop, Theologian, Ascetic, Father* (Oxford: Oxford University Press, 2012), 2.

Image: Icon of Athanasius, Hosios Loukas Monestary, Boeotia, Greece

shifted dramatically when Emperor Constantine converted to Christianity. The authenticity of Constantine's conversion and personal piety has been long debated.[2] But regardless of his motives for associating himself with the new religion, his passage of an edict of toleration in 313 and personal beneficence toward the church changed the church's trajectory toward social and economic prosperity and ensured advantageous ties with the state going forward.[3] Almost overnight the Christian community found itself in the mainstream, no longer a marginalized, misunderstood minority religion.

Even with the putative assurance of peace, Athanasius's long episcopate was anything but peaceful. As Athanasius's era was marked by turbulence, so was his life.[4] After serving as a trusted deacon to Alexander, bishop of Alexandria, and despite being chosen by Alexander as his successor, Athanasius endured a contested election to the office of bishop on account of his age. Upon becoming a prominent bishop of firm theological convictions and dogged determinism, he made formidable enemies, ranging from other bishops to, on certain occasions, the emperor. Some accused him of bribery, and once he was charged with murder, though he was later acquitted when he produced in-person the man he was suspected of killing. Five times Athanasius was exiled from his see in Alexandria, for a total of seventeen years out of his forty-five-year episcopacy. In his later years he found common ground and reconciliation with some of his former opponents.[5] After returning to his see from his fifth and final exile, Athanasius lived the last seven years of his life in peace, having secured his place in the church as a standard-bearer of orthodoxy.[6]

---

2. On Constantine's life and legacy, particularly in relation to the church, see Timothy Barnes, *Constantine and Eusebius* (Cambridge: Harvard University Press, 1981) and *Constantine: Dynasty, Religion, and Power in the Later Roman Empire* (Malden, MA: Wiley-Blackwell, 2011). For a more sympathetic treatment see Peter Leithart, *Defending Constantine* (Downers Grove: IVP Academic, 2010).

3. Though the church enjoyed favored status in the empire throughout the fourth century, beginning with Constantine, the one exception was emperor Julian "the apostate," who, for a very brief time, made life difficult for the Christian community.

4. No comprehensive biography of Athanasius exists. But much has been written on his life, the political and theological challenges he faced, his exiles, and victories, and I do not attempt to repeat them here. For recent studies that provide biographical information, see the pertinent sections in Timothy Barnes, *Athanasius and Constantius: Theology and Politics in the Constantinian Empire* (Cambridge: Harvard University Press, 1993); Khaled Anatolios, *Athanasius: The Early Church Fathers* (London: Routlege, 2004); Thomas Weinandy, *Athanasius: A Theological Introduction* (Burlington, VT: Ashgate, 2007); David Gwynn, *Athanasius of Alexandria: Bishop, Theologian, Ascetic, Father, op.cit.*; Thomas Weinandy and Daniel Keating, *Athanasius and His Legacy: Trinitarian-Incarnational Soteriology and its Reception* (Minneapolis: Fortress, 2017).

5. John Behr notes that with Athanasius "there is no indication of vindictiveness, but rather a desire to make peace, so that by the time of his death he had become reconciled with most of his earlier enemies." See John Behr, *Formation of Christian Theology*. Vol. 2, *The Nicene Faith* (Crestwood, NY: St. Vladimir's Seminary Press, 2004), 21.

6. Behr, *Formation of Christian Theology*, 167, asserts that "Nicene Christianity exists by virtue of his [Athanasius's] constancy and vision." For a similar sentiment among Athanasius's contemporaries, see Gregory of Nazianzus, *Or. Bas.* 21.26 who named Athanasius "the pillar of the church." See J. P. Migne, *Patrologia Graeca*, Vol. 35 (Paris: E. Typographeo Reipublicae, 1857), 1112 (hereafter, *PG*).

THEOLOGICAL CONTEXT

For all the twists and turns in Athanasius's life, he is best known for his defense of the full divinity of the Son of God in opposition to what came to be known as Arianism.[7] The heresy was named after Arius, a presbyter in Alexandria, who emphasized the singularity and transcendence of God, teaching that the Son, while divine, was not *as* divine as the Father. The "begotten" Son was best understood as a creature whom God the Father made. Thus, there was a time when the Son did not exist. This made the Son temporal and therefore unequal with God.[8] The bishops at the Council of Nicaea condemned Arius and his view of the Son, confessing that the Son is coeternal with the Father ("begotten, not made") and "of the same substance (*homoousious*)" with the Father.[9] The majority of Athanasius's literary corpus, including his voluminous *Against the Arians*, is dedicated to defending the full divinity of the Son.[10] Though he became a chief adversary of Arianism in the decades after Nicaea, Athanasius's actual role in the proceedings of the Council is unclear. Gregory's tribute given seven years after Athanasius's death paints a portrait of the young deacon holding high rank at the Council on account of his virtue rather than office. He said Athanasius "stopped the disease (τὴν νόσον ἔστησεν)" of the Arian heresy almost single-handedly.[11] But there is little doubt that Gregory is speaking in hyperbole. While Athanasius likely "had the ear" of his bishop and may have influenced whatever contributions Alexander made in the debates, it is unlikely that he, as a young deacon in his twenties, would have had meaningful opportunities to engage in the polemical dialogues with such an assembly of episcopal dignitaries.[12] He may have had no formal role in the

---

7. Athanasius levels the name "Ariomaniacs" against his opponents, who, from his perspective, reduce the deity of the Son, whether or not they self-identify with Arius.

8. A wealth of scholarship exists on Arius and Arianism. See especially Robert Gregg and Dennis Groh, *Early Arianism: A View of Salvation* (Augsburg: Fortress, 1981); Robert Gregg, ed. *Arianism: Historical and Theological Reassessments* (Philadelphia: The Philadelphia Patristic, 1985); Charles Kannengiesser, *Arius and Athanasius: Two Alexandrian Theologians* (London: Variorum, 1991); Michel Barnes and Daniel Williams, eds. *Arianism after Arius: Essays on the Development of the Fourth Century Trinitarian Conflicts* (Bloomsbury: T&T Clark, 1994); Rowan William, *Arius: Heresy and Tradition* (Grand Rapids: Eerdmans, 2002).

9. Studies abound on the Council of Nicaea, its history, and the theological and political implications that followed. Three standard studies include R. P. C. Hanson, *The Search for the Christian Doctrine of God: The Arian Controversy, 318–381* (Edinburgh: T&T Clark 1988); Lewis Ayres, *Nicaea and its Legacy: An Approach to Fourth-Century Trinitarian Theology* (Oxford: University Press, 2004); Frances Young, *From Nicaea to Chalcedon: A Guide to the Literature and its Background*, 2nd ed. (Grand Rapids: Baker Academic, 2010).

10. In addition to *Against the Arians*, later dogmatic works in which Athanasius draws on similar themes include *On the Councils of Ariminium and Seleucia*, *On the Defense of the Nicene Definitions*, and *Letter to the Bishops of Egypt and Libya*. See C. Moreschini and Enrico Norelli, *Early Christian Greek and Latin Literature: A Literary History*, vol. 2 (Peabody, MA: Hendrickson, 2005), 33–34.

11. *Or.* 21.14 (PG 35, 1096).

12. Young, *From Nicaea to Chalcedon*, 49. See also Gwynn, *Athanasius of Alexandria*, 5, who notes that Athanasius makes no claim in his writings to have participated in the debates.

proceedings, but Athanasius clearly understood the theological significance of the Council and defended its theological content throughout his lifetime.

APOLOGETIC RESPONSE

Though Athanasius has secured his place in church history as a polemicist and dogmatic theologian, less attention has been given to his work as a pastor and apologist.[13] The dichotomies between the academy and the church, theologian and practitioner, doctrine and practice that are so prevalent in the modern era were unknown in the ancient world. The doctrinal matters taken up by bishops and intellectuals such as Athanasius were never intended as exercises in ivory-tower speculation but had immediate bearing on the lives of everyday Christians. Athanasius's doctrinal disputations were always intended for the good of the church. For him, right doctrine mattered because the gospel was at stake. As a bishop and a pastor, he was concerned that those under his care understood truth and why it mattered for their faith. Gwynn's observation is apt: "It is perhaps the greatest strength of Athanasius as a theologian that he could express concepts of such importance in language that everyone could understand and never lost sight of why the questions mattered for the wider Christian world."[14]

The best example of Athanasius's doctrinal clarity, pastoral sensibility, and apologetic aptitude is his double treatise, *Contra Gentes-De Incarnatione* (*Against the Heathen-On the Incarnation*).[15] It is ironic that Athanasius is best known for his defense of the Nicene faith against Arianism, yet *CG-DI*, what is perhaps his most celebrated work, is silent about the controversy. The absence of any mention of Arius or Arianism has led some scholars to believe Athanasius wrote it before the outbreak of the controversy and thus before Nicaea,[16] though that opinion is no longer the consensus. While no precise date is possible to attach to the double treatise, Anatolios makes a strong case that it was written between 328 and 335.[17]

---

13. On Athanasius's role as pastor, see Gwynn, *Athanasius of Alexandria*, 131–58, as well as Nathan Ng, *The Spirituality of Athanasius: A Key for Proper Understanding of this Important Church Father* (Bern: Peter Lang, 2001) and G. Demacopoulos, *Five Models of Spiritual Direction in the Early Church* (Notre Dame: University of Notre Dame Press, 2007), 21–49.

14. Gwynn, *Athanasius of Alexandria*, 56.

15. Throughout this essay I will refer to the double-treatise according to its traditional Latin title in abbreviated form, thus *CG-DI*.

16. Cf. Bernard de Montfaucon, *Athanasii achiepiscopi Alexandrini opera Omnia quae extant*, J. P. Migne, *PG*, 1 and E. P. Meijering, *Athanasius: Contra Gentes: Introduction, Translation and Commentary* (Leiden: Brill, 1984), 1–4.

17. Khaled Anatolios, *Athanasius: The Coherence of his Thought* (London: Routledge, 2005), 26–29. The dating of *CG-DI* has been a matter of scholarly debate for over a century. For several important studies, see Charles Kannengiesser, "La date de l'Apologie d'Athanase *Contre les Païens* et *Sur l'Incarnation du Verbe*," in *Recherches de Science Religieuse* 58 (1970): 383–428; J. C. M. Van Winden, "On the Date of Athanasius's Apologetical Treatises," in *Vigiliae Christianae* 29 (1975): 291–295; Alvyn Pettersen, "A Reconsideration of the Date of the *Contra Gentes-De Incarnatione* of Athanasius of Alexandria," in *Studia Patristica* 18 (1982): 1035–36.

Given this date range, Athanasius would have been a young man in his thirties as the newly elected bishop of Alexandria at the time of composition.

For the remainder of this essay I will focus on *CG-DI* for two reasons. First, as the earliest of Athanasius's major works, it is the foundational text for all his later writings. Frances Young observes that although one can trace minor developments in Athanasius's corpus in terms of details and ways of expressing ideas, "the central core of his position was never touched. His earliest writings are in fact the key to his life and his dogmatic argumentation."[18] Second, the twofold treatise is the only one in Athanasius's literary corpus that properly fits the designation "apologia," or defense of the faith.[19] Weinandy asserts that *CG-DI* serves, in part, as an "evangelistic apologetic" that "confirms the faith of the believer and so equips such a believer for adequately engaging in the defence and proclamation of the Gospel."[20] While there is a good deal of catechesis for Christians in *CG-DI*, Athanasius desired to engage a non-Christian audience as well, particularly pagan and Jewish critics. He thus anticipated a mixed audience.[21]

The aim and purpose of *Contra Gentes-De Incarnatione* is important to explore. Writing such a treatise as the newly minted successor to Alexander would have gone a long way to prove Athanasius's theological and ecclesial mettle, especially to those suspicious of the young bishop.[22] But this is ancillary to his main concern. Athanasius states with clarity the purpose for writing this double *apologia*; namely, to show that faith in Christ is not irrational.[23] Barnes conjectures that Porphyry's *Against the Christians*, which portrays Christianity as a religion for the benighted, may have provoked Athanasius to take up his pen in response.[24]

---

18. Young, *From Nicaea to Chalcedon*, 52. Gwynn, *Athanasius of Alexandria*, 6, concurs, noting, "*Contra Gentes—De Incarnatione* represents the initial staging point for all analysis of Athanasius's theology. His later doctrinal works remained grounded in the principles he expressed in that first treatise."

19. Apologetic writings were less common in Athanasius's day than in previous centuries. In the Constantinian era, the church had less need to defend itself against a critical government and hostile populace and more need for clear, insightful works on dogma. Moreschini and Norelli observe that Athanasius's *Contra Gentes* in particular is "a late example of a literary genre that had almost disappeared." See Moreschini and Norelli, *Early Christian Greek and Latin Literature*, 35.

20. Weinandy, *Athanasius: A Theological Introduction*, 12. Cf. Meijering, *Athanasius: Contra Gentes*, 5.

21. See Athanasius's introductory remarks in *DI* 25. Cf. Robert Thomson's introduction in *Athanasius: Contra Gentes and* De Incarnatione (Oxford: Clarendon, 1971), xxii. All citations in this essay from *CG* and *DI* are taken from Thomson's critical edition.

22. Gwynn, *Athanasius of Alexandria*, 65–66.

23. *CG* 1, 1. See also *DI* 1, 134, where Athanasius acknowledges those who mock Christianity as "impossible," "unsuitable," and merely "human." He sets out to show that, on account of Christ, the opposite is true. Cf. Anatolios, *Athanasius: The Coherence*, 28.

24. Barnes, *Constantine and Eusebius*, 206. Barnes's suggestion is even more likely if, as some scholars argue, paganism was on the rise in Athanasius's day. A pagan resurgence emboldened by works such as Porphyry may have incited Athanasius to respond in kind. Anatolios, *Athanasius: The Coherence*, 28, cites J. Roldanus and P. Camelot as representing this line of thought.

Whether or not this is the case,[25] Athanasius sets out to prove that the incarnation of the Logos has revealed the God that Christianity affirms. Those who believe in Christ know the truth, but that those who reject the Logos do not follow the truth and are thus irrational (ἄλογον).

"Exhibit A" in Athanasius's arsenal of evidence supporting Christianity is history. It is worth repeating that Athanasius lived in a pivotal time, a time that witnessed the inclusion of Christianity into the mainstream of Roman society and its ascendancy to the highest positions of sociopolitical power and influence, coinciding with the demise of paganism. For Athanasius, these two historical trajectories—the rise of Christianity and the decline of paganism—did not occur by happenstance. Rather, they are proof that Jesus Christ is alive, is reigning now, and is bringing about his purposes in the world. For Athanasius, these purposes include doing away with the idolatry of paganism and bringing about redemption in the world.[26] Athanasius thus provides a christological interpretation of history that makes sense of the profound societal developments of his day by underscoring the veracity of what the Son of God revealed and accomplished in the flesh; namely, salvation. What follows is a more detailed treatment of Athanasius's argument that Christianity is true and thus superior to paganism.

The entirety of *Contra Gentes-De Incarnatione* has a basic twofold structure. In the first three-quarters of the work (all of *CG* and roughly half of *DI*), Athanasius makes his case that Christianity offers a far more compelling view of reality than does paganism. The main thrust of his argument is that Christianity is reasonable, while paganism is not. In the final quarter of the double treatise (the last half of *DI*), Athanasius offers a rebuttal to Christianity's critics, both Jewish and pagan. Following Paul's observation that the crucified Christ is a scandal to the Jews and foolishness to the gentiles (1 Cor 1:23), Athanasius takes both sets of challenges in turn, demonstrating that the incarnation is both biblical and suitable to the character of God.

THE SUPERIORITY OF CHRISTIANITY OVER PAGANISM

In setting out to prove his case that Christianity is true and worthy of acceptance, one of Athanasius's strategies is to highlight important pagan beliefs and compare them with Christian doctrines. His aim in doing so is to use paganism as a foil, depicting it as illogical, inconsistent, and void of meaning compared

---

25. It is noteworthy that Athanasius indicates throughout *CG-DI* that paganism was on the decline and limping along because of Christ. Conversely, paganism thrived before Christ's advent. This lies at the heart of Athanasius's entire argument. See the brief but helpful discussion in Anatolios, *Athanasius: The Coherence*, 28.

26. Cf. Discussions in Gwynn, *Athanasius of Alexandria*, 66; Anatolios, *Athanasius: The Coherence*, 28–29; Weinandy, *Athanasius: A Theological Introduction*, 11–13.

with the beauty and rationality of Christianity. When all sides are considered, Athanasius assumes, there will be a clear winner.

Christianity as Superior in Explaining Creation

In the opening sections of *DI*, Athanasius considers creation. One's beliefs about the origin and nature of the cosmos are inseparable from one's assumptions about God's character and whether creation is ordered or has a *telos*. He notes that views of creation are diverse and idiosyncratic. First, he singles out the Epicureans, who believe all things came about by chance. He moves next to followers of Plato, who insist that God formed and fashioned the universe out of preexisting matter, though that substance had no distinct form. Finally, Athanasius takes aim at certain Gnostic sects that assert another creator apart from the Father of Jesus Christ.[27]

After a brief description of the three views, he judges each as "idle talk."[28] The Epicurean view is faulty on account of denying providence. How, Athanasius asks, could something as fundamental as differentiation exist without a God who holds everything together? The universe is filled with a variety of things that maintain their proper order. This would not be possible without providence.[29] Likewise, Platonism depicts a God who is weak. Human beings create out of material that already exists, such as a carpenter who makes tables out of wood. But, Athanasius insists, if God is truly the Maker and Creator of *all* things, it means he created the very matter from which everything is made. If God could create only out of primordial raw materials, he would be a mere craftsman, not the Creator.[30] Finally, the Gnostics, who propose the existence of a demiurge besides God the Father, are simply blind. Scripture nowhere supports their view but teaches that all things were made through Christ.[31]

By contrast, the biblical account of creation describes a God who created the universe out of nothing, on his own accord. The Christian doctrine of creation begins not with a "what" but a "who." The focus is not the universe nor the process by which it came about but on the benevolent God who created because he wanted to. Athanasius observes, "God is good—or rather the source of goodness—and the good has no envy [φθόνος] for anything. Thus, because he envies nothing its existence, he made everything from nothing [ἐξ οὐκ ὄντων]

---

27. *DI* 2, 136–138.
28. *DI* 3, 138.
29. *DI* 2, 136.
30. *DI* 2, 138.
31. *DI* 2, 138. Cf. John 1:3.

through his own Word, our Lord Jesus Christ."[32] God, who truly *is*, gave existence to that which *was not*, on account of his goodness and power.

Christianity as Superior in Answering the Problem of Evil

In addition to the universe, Athanasius discusses another observable phenomenon within the universe; namely, evil. He appeals to shared assumptions that recognize the difference between virtue and vice. People in Athanasius's day knew that humans are capable of good but also of great evil. The question is why. Athanasius takes on the origin and nature of evil in the early chapters of *Contra Gentes*. From the start, he is adamant that evil is not eternal and has no being of its own. It is best conceived as a lack or privation of being. Evil is the antithesis of God, who is truly real. Far from being a product of creation, evil came about through humans, who, having fallen from God,[33] imagined it themselves.[34] Athanasius is clear:

> Now, reality is the good, unreality what is evil. I call reality what is good because it has its exemplar in God who is real [ἐκ τοῦ ὄντος]; and I call unreality what is evil because what has no real existence has been invented by the conceits of men. For although the body has eyes in order to view creation and through its harmonious order to recognize the Creator, although it also possesses hearing in order to listen to the divine saying and the laws of God, and has hands too, in order to do necessary actions and to stretch them out to God in prayer, yet the soul abandoned the contemplation of the good and virtuous activity, and was from then on deceived and moved in the opposite direction.[35]

Evil has no purpose except to turn humans away from pursuing good. Athanasius notes that "men in their effrontery paid regard not to what was expedient

---

32. *DI* 3, 141. Cf. Alvyn Pettersen, "A Good Being Would Envy None Life: Athanasius on the Goodness of God," in *Theology Today* 55 (1998): 59–68.

33. When Athanasius discusses the Fall in *CG* he describes the soul's turn away from God and on to itself, thus forgetting God and clinging to sensible (physical) things. In *DI* he rehearses the biblical account of the fall of Adam and Eve, who disobeyed God's command in the Garden of Eden. It is likely for apologetic reasons that Athanasius offers varying accounts. The account of the soul's failure to maintain its contemplative posture before God in *CG* would certainly have appealed to those of his readers with Platonic sensibilities. See Jonathan Morgan, "The Soul's Forgetfulness of God in Athanasius's Doctrine of the Fall," in *St. Vladimir's Theological Quarterly* 60, 4 (2016): 473–88.

34. *CG* 2, 4–6. Cf. *CG* 7, 19, where Athanasius insists that "evil neither came from God nor was in God, nor did it exist in the beginning, nor has it any independent reality. But men, rejecting the notion of the good, began to think up for themselves and invent objects which to not exist as the fancy struck them."

35. *CG* 4, 11–13. Cf. *DI* 4, 145, where Athanasius affirms that "what does not exist is evil, but what does exist is good since it has been created by the existent God" to explain why humans, having turned from God, were deprived of immortality.

and proper, but to what was within their grasp, and began to do everything in reverse (τὰ ἐναντία)."[36] After providing examples of deeds done "in reverse," such as murder, adultery, disobedience, and gluttony, he observes, "All these things are evil and sins of the soul, but they have no other cause save the turning away from better things."[37] Thus, Athanasius maintains that evil has no prior existence to creation or true existence since it did not come from God. It came about through the twisted machinations of human beings, who turned from God and set their wills on themselves. As a result, humans do terrible things to satisfy their godless desires. In this way, Athanasius provides an explanation for the existence of evil in the world apart from God, who did not create it and has no affiliation with it.

In contrast to the Christian view, Athanasius attacks "some Greeks" for their belief that evil is an entity. But this idea creates a catch-22 for its adherents. If evil exists on its own, these Greeks would either have to admit that (1) the demiurge (creator) did not create everything and is not the lord of all things, or (2) the creator is the author of evil and is not good.[38] Athanasius next turns to Marcionites, who posit the existence of two gods, with the demiurge creating the world and being responsible for the existence of evil. Athanasius claims these "heretics" are easy to refute from Scripture, which clearly teaches one God, who is the creator of heaven and earth.[39] He also poses challenging questions to this view: How can a good god and an evil god exist simultaneously? If they are equal in power, do they not cancel out one another since they both exist against the will of the other and suffer events that are contrary to their intentions? Further, Athanasius observes that if the visible world is the work of the evil god, the good god has nothing to show for himself. Since the creator is known by his works, how would we know that the good god exists if there are no works by which he can be understood?[40] Through such criticism, Athanasius shows the irrationality of those whose concept of evil takes no account of what Christ revealed.

Christianity as Superior to Idolatry

Out of all the pagan beliefs that Athanasius considers foolish, none is more absurd than idolatry. His basic assumption is that the worship of idols and the rationale behind using them is *mythology* (inventing mythic tales and legends) rather than *theology*.[41] Two examples of his many critiques are in order. First, Athanasius points to the behavior of the gods whom the idols represent. Far from

---

36. *CG* 5, 13.
37. Ibid. See also *CG* 47, 131–33.
38. *CG* 6, 14.
39. Athanasius quotes Deut 6:4 and Matt 11:25.
40. *CG* 6–7, 14–16.
41. *CG* 19, 54. See the entry for μῦθολογὲω in *Liddell & Scott*.

being impassible and constant in holiness and virtue, the gods are irascible and violent, unpredictable and weak. They can violate natural law and basic decency, carrying out vile behavior that would make most humans blush.[42] Further, belief in such gods leads to wicked and chaotic societies rather than peaceful ones. For example, some gods desire human sacrifices in worship. People who imagine that their gods delight in the killing of humans, Athanasius maintains, are led to imitate what the gods desire. So they commit "murder, infanticide, and all kinds of licentiousness," filling their cities with wickedness that the laws condemn.[43] Fundamentally, the gods represent the irrationality and unreasonable passions that plague sinful human minds and are thus unworthy of worship.[44]

A second critique Athanasius offers is his observation that once humans turned from God, they gradually descended into lower forms of idolatry, first paying honor to celestial bodies, then the ether, then the elements, then men (both dead and living), then stone, wood, reptiles, and finally to the wild, irrational animals.[45] The further they wandered from God, the more they degraded themselves by what they worshipped. Athanasius also charges them with committing sacrilege because they ascribe the honor due God to the images themselves. He underscores the unrighteousness of exalting signs over what are signified.[46] But even more, he can't help but point out the folly of it all:

> Furthermore, they do not see in worshipping stones and wood that they are calling gods pieces of things similar to what they walk on and burn. That which a short time previously they put to use, they foolishly carve and venerate, not seeing or understanding at all that they are worshipping not gods but the skill of the sculptor. As long as the stone remains unpolished and the matter unworked they tread on them and put them to their own uses, often even the most ordinary ones. But when the artist has imposed the measure of his skill on them and formed the matter into the shape of a man or woman, expressing their gratitude to the artist, from then on they worship the statues as gods, after buying them from the sculptor for a fee. And often the sculptor himself, as if he had forgotten what he himself had made, prays to his own works; and what a short time previously he had polished and sculpted, after expending this art he calls gods.[47]

---

42. *CG* 11–12, 32–36.
43. *CG* 25, 68.
44. *CG* 19, 53.
45. *CG* 9, 22–24.
46. *CG* 21, 56–58. See also Gwynn, *Athanasius of Alexandria*, 67: "Athanasius' attack on idolatry in the *Contra Gentes* represents paganism as a product of that turn towards evil."
47. *CG* 13, 37. One is reminded here of Ps 115:4–8.

With these withering criticisms in hand, Athanasius intends for his readers to conclude that pagan gods are not real. If the gods act in despicable ways, if the poets created the myths of the gods, and if the images depicting the gods are made of common material merely sculpted by humans, then on what basis does one believe in them? Why pretend the gods are real? In fact, Athanasius chides, the pagans are the true "atheists" because they worship what has no existence at all instead of the true God.[48]

Comparing and contrasting pagan and Christian beliefs is an important part of Athanasius's strategy to show that Christianity is superior to paganism. But this is only one wave of his attack. The second wave amounts to rehearsing the biblical narrative of the creation, the fall, and humanity's redemption through the incarnation of the Son of God. Athanasius believes that this narrative makes perfect sense and best accounts for (1) the reality of death and wickedness in the world and (2) the historical trajectory of the predominance of Christianity coinciding with the decrease and demise of paganism throughout the world. Athanasius is not content to share mere propositions about God. Rather, he tells the story of God's creating and re-creating activity in a compelling way. For Athanasius, the biblical narrative, compounded with the historical realities of the fourth century, depicts the truth, goodness, power, and love of God.

The Superiority of God's Saving Activity

In *DI* 4–5 Athanasius explains the creation of humanity as a springboard to discuss the incarnation of the Son of God. As he created everything else, God created human beings out of nothing (ἐξ οὐκ ὄντων) but granted them the special gift of divine life through the grace of the Logos.[49] Since humans were created from nothing, they were naturally unstable and corruptible. Left to themselves, they would return to nonexistence. But as long as the Word indwelt them, they remain incorruptible and immortal, just as God had willed.[50] But humankind fell from fellowship with God by disregarding his commandments and stopped comprehending him. They turned their minds toward themselves and sought temporal pleasures rather than union with God.[51] Their senses became disordered when their contemplative vision shifted from God to themselves. In this

---

48. *CG* 14, 41. "How then could those who are condemned by the Divine Scripture of impiety not be judged by all to be atheists (ἄθεοι)? Or how could they not be demon-possessed who are so clearly refuted as worshipping lifeless things instead of the truth? And what hope or pardon could they have who trust in irrational and immovable objects, which they venerate instead of the true God?"

49. *DI* 5, 144.

50. *DI* 4, 142.

51. *CG* 3, 8; *DI* 4, 142–44.

sense, their own bodies became idols.[52] They forgot their Creator[53] and invented evil deeds to satiate their twisted desires. As a result, they died, and corruption took hold of them.[54] Then, having been given over to death, they continued inventing more ways to sin, becoming "insatiable in sinning."[55] Athanasius sums up the tragic situation of humanity's fall: "For these reasons death held greater sway and corruption stood firm against men; the race of men was being destroyed, and man who was rational and who had been made in the image was being obliterated; and the work created by God was perishing."[56]

In light of the pressing situation, Athanasius asks, "What was God to do?"[57] Some scholars describe this as the "divine dilemma."[58] God, of course, never faces an actual predicament. But Athanasius observes two problems confronting the Creator. On the one hand, since God cannot lie or falsify himself, he could not simply wave off death as if the fall had never occurred. He warned Adam and Eve that if they disregarded his commandment in the garden that death would be the penalty. Death must, therefore, run its course in devouring the human race. "For God would not have been truthful, if after he had said we would die, man had not died."[59] On the other hand, God is good. It would be unfitting that what he made should be brought to nothing, especially humans whom he made rational and in his own image through his Word. A beneficent God could not remain idle and allow human beings to remain in death and corruption on their slide back to nonexistence.[60] Thus, again, Athanasius's question: "What was God to do?"

The solution to the dilemma is the incarnation of the Word. For Athanasius, the "incarnation" is not simply the moment of the Son's assumption of human nature, but the *totus Christus*—the entire life and work of Christ from his conception to his ascension.[61] The Son of God assumed a physical, passible body, suffered death, and rose to new life to banish death and restore humanity to new life and incorruptibility. The incarnation was the only way for God to uphold

---

52. Behr, *Formation of Christian Theology*, 177. "With their souls directed toward the body, in, by, and for itself, the body is now the very point of human separation from God, not because of its materiality but because it has become an idol."

53. *CG* 3, 8.

54. *DI*, 5, 144.

55. *DI* 5, 147. Cf. *CG* 3, 10.

56. *DI* 6, 147.

57. Athanasius poses this question in *DI* 6, 148 and *DI* 13, 164.

58. Despite the ubiquity of this phrase, Athanasius never actually uses it. The phrase was inserted into the text as a subtitle in *On the Incarnation* translated by a religious of CSMV in the 1953 edition published by A. R. Mowbray. It has since enjoyed common usage in secondary studies on *CG-DI*.

59. *DI* 6, 149.

60. *DI* 6, 149.

61. See Weinandy, *Athanasius: A Theological Introduction*, 28–36.

his word, maintain his honor, and bestow his goodness and mercy, because it both satisfies death and frees humanity from death.[62] The incarnate Son of God took a body like ours and, free from all blemish by virtue of his deity, offered to death his own body and thereby destroyed death for all. When death tried to swallow the Son of God, it took in more than it could handle! What was owed to death was paid. In the death of Christ, death finally ran its course, and through the resurrection, Christ restored humanity to incorruption.[63] Repentance alone would not have sufficed, Athanasius claims. It may have absolved people of sinful deeds, but it would not root out the *natural consequences* of sin; namely, corruption and death.[64] Only the saving work of the incarnation could free humans from both the existential *and* ontological consequences of sin. The consequences of sin on humanity are profound, but God's solution in the incarnation is more than enough to reverse those consequences and restore us to incorruption and life. Near the end of *DI*, Athanasius sums up the purpose of the incarnation: "He became man that we might become divine; and he revealed himself through a body that we might receive an idea of the invisible Father; and he endured insults from men that we might inherit incorruption."[65] The incarnation re-creates us according to the divine image, renews in us knowledge of God, and restores to us the incorruptibility we had before the fall. In demonstrating God's truth and goodness, the incarnation is rational and fitting with God's character.

The Superiority of the Cross of Christ

While Athanasius acknowledges the saving work of Christ prior to Calvary,[66] he insists that the death of Christ is "the chief point" (κεφάλαιον) of the Christian faith.[67] At the beginning of both *CG* and *DI*, Athanasius upholds the cross—the very thing the pagans mock and decry as irrational—as the symbol of Christ's victory, the power of which has "filled the universe."[68] Again, Athanasius's main argument is that through the cross, Christ destroyed death and corruption on our behalf. He insists that "the death of all was fulfilled in the

---

62. *DI* 10, 154–156. Cf. Anatolios, *Athanasius: The Coherence*, 39, who maintains that "Athanasius wants to show that the face of the incarnation is consistent with who God is, and with God's general way of relating to creation from the beginning."

63. *DI* 9, 154. Cf. *DI* 20, 182.

64. *DI* 7, 150.

65. *DI* 54, 269.

66. For example, see *DI* 14, 168. In the incarnation the Son of God becomes sensible—that is, tangible and physical—to reveal the Father. Athanasius notes that the "eyes" of humans, having fallen from God, are no longer directed upward toward God but cast downward. In other words, humans chase after tangible, physical things. Thus, in the incarnation the Son came "down" where humans were looking and, becoming physical, entered our field of vision to get our attention and redirect our gaze upward.

67. *DI* 19, 180.

68. *CG* 1, 2.

Lord's body, and also death and corruption were destroyed because of the Word who was in it."[69] At the same time, Athanasius is keenly aware of his audience. He sets out to explain why the cross was the only fitting way for Christ to die. To non-Christian readers who may ask why Jesus did not select a more noble way to die, Athanasius retorts that crucifixion at the hands of Christ's enemies showed his superiority over human weakness. Because he was the Word and Life itself, he could not die on his own from natural causes. Further, it would be inappropriate, Athanasius claims, for Christ to have died of bodily disease or sickness, because he healed diseases and strengthened those who were weak. Therefore, because of his divine power, he could not die without giving himself to his executioners to fulfill the reason for which he came to earth.[70] Athanasius observes that the Son "accepted the death imposed by men in order to destroy it completely when it came to his own body."[71] Further, crucifixion was the most fitting way for Christ to die because it was public. Had Christ died alone or in private, then risen from the dead and appeared to everyone, recounting that he had indeed died and resurrected as the victorious Lord, no one would have believed him. But the fact that people witnessed Christ's death gave credence to his resurrection.[72]

To believers who have honest questions about the manner in which Christ died, Athanasius maintains that Christ had to die on the cross to bear our curse according to Deuteronomy 21:23. No other method of death would fulfill this passage. Second, insofar as Christ's death reconciles all people, both Jews and gentiles (Eph 2:14), to himself, the cross was the most suitable way for Christ to die since on it his hands were stretched out. Symbolically, one arm summons the gentiles while the other welcomes the Jews, both peoples uniting in Christ. Third, on the cross Christ was hoisted up into the air. This implies his victory over the devil, who, according to Paul, is the "ruler of the kingdom of the air" (Eph 2:2). Christ was uplifted from the earth that he might "purify the air" and put the devil to flight. Finally, Athanasius observes that the cross reopens the way to heaven, creating a kind of pathway whereby we might have access to God's very dwelling.[73] In all these ways, Athanasius claims, Christ's death on the cross was "suitable and fitting, and its cause appeared to be eminently reasonable [λογισμούς]."[74]

---

69. *DI* 20, 185.
70. *DI* 21, 186–88.
71. *DI* 22, 189.
72. *DI* 23, 190.
73. *DI* 25, 194–96.
74. *DI* 26, 197.

The Superiority of Christ's Resurrection

If Christ's death on the cross is the chief point of the Christian faith, Athanasius treats the resurrection as the culmination. The resurrection alone accounts for the fearlessness with which Christians face death and explains why Christianity had become dominant within an empire once hostile to it. If Christ were still dead, Athanasius reasons, the world would not be changing and taking on a more Christian ethos, sinners would not be transformed, and those who follow Christ wouldn't be intrepid in the face of death. A dead Jesus could not act or affect anything. But Athanasius points out the obvious—the socio-political landscape was changing hands from paganism to Christianity, evildoers of various stripes (murderers, adulterers, sorcerers, drunkards) were leaving behind their sinful ways and embracing Christ, and Christians, particularly the martyrs, had already proved the power of the resurrection by facing death without fear.[75] Though it is natural for humans to fear death, it is not so for Christians.[76] Even women and children who belong to Christ run toward death because they know that death is powerless, and they look forward to the life they will inherit on account of the resurrection.[77]

REFUTATIONS AGAINST THE JEWS AND THE GREEKS

In finalizing his case for the reasonableness of Christianity, Athanasius ends his double treatise by rebutting specific criticisms levied against Christians by Jews and Greeks (pagans). Specifically, he takes the Jews to task because of their unbelief and the Greeks because of their mockery. Objections from both camps that the incarnation was unbecoming (ἀπρεπὲς) of God were still formidable points of debate that Christians had to answer. But Athanasius is confident, claiming that Christians have "distinct proofs" against their theological opponents.[78]

To engage his Jewish critics, Athanasius employs the Hebrew Bible because both Jews and Christians affirm its divine authority. His strategy is to show that the "inspired books" describe Jesus and what he accomplished. This includes his virgin birth (Isa 7:14), incarnation (Num 24:5–7, 17; Isa 8:4), journey out of Egypt (Isa 19:1; Hos 11:1; Matt 2:13–15), substitutionary death (Isa 53:3–8), superiority over nature (Isa 53:8–10), the cross as the means of his death (Deut 28:66; Ps 22:17–18; Jer 11:19), and that he has been made known to the nations

---

75. *DI* 30–31, 208–10.
76. *DI* 27, 198–200.
77. *DI* 29, 204.
78. *DI* 33, 214. The refutations against the Jews in *DI* take up sections 33–40; those against the Greeks include sections 41–55.

(Isa 11:10). Jesus alone fits these prophetic descriptions.[79] In this way, Athanasius shows that "all of Scripture is filled with refutations of the unbelief of the Jews."[80] His main argument is that Christ is the reality to which the Old Testament symbols point.[81] Since Christ has come, there are no more prophecies, no more temple, no more Israelite kings, and no more holy city as the central place of God's activity. Now gentiles are coming to know the God of Abraham through Christ, not the old Jewish institutions. This, Athanasius pleads, should convince even the most obstinate that Christ the Messiah has come.[82]

Athanasius then turns his attention to the Greeks, who advance different challenges. To those who question why the Logos would appear in such a humble way, Athanasius counters that the Son of God did not come to dazzle and impress but "to heal and to teach those who were suffering."[83] Further, only humans are fallen. Everything else in creation has maintained its proper order. Thus, the Word had to become human because it was humans that needed saving.[84] To others who wonder why God could not have simply willed salvation with a "nod" if he was so powerful, Athanasius answers that the Word had to enter what already existed in order to heal it. A "nod" was fitting when nothing existed, but once things were given existence, the Word had to come and interweave life back into what was made; namely, humans. A command might keep death away but would not change humankind from being mortal and corruptible by nature. So the Word became corporeal to free humans from corruption. Through the incarnation, humans are "joined to life" and given immortality.[85]

The most important proof of the incarnation that Athanasius brings against the pagans is that pagan worship and idolatry were crumbling while, at the same time, more and more people were turning to Christ.[86] Athanasius provides a "before and after" digest comparing the former ways that deceived humanity with the incarnation that has revealed the truth and changed everything. Formerly, the "wisdom of the Greek" drove people to idolatry; now, on account of Christ, people are abandoning the old superstitions and worshipping God. Formerly, oracles deluded nations everywhere; now, on account of Christ, the madness has ceased. Formerly, the demons deceived men with illusions;

---

79. *DI* 33–35, 214–20.
80. *DI* 35, 220.
81. *DI* 40, 232–33. Athanasius asks, "For when he who was announced was come, what need is there of those who announce; when the truth is at hand, what need is there of the shadow?"
82. *DI* 40, 234.
83. *DI* 43, 240.
84. *DI* 43, 242.
85. *DI* 44, 244–46.
86. *DI* 46, 250. "When did men begin to abandon the worship of idols except since the true Word of God came to men?"

now their lies have ceased as believers make the sign of the cross to drive them away. Formerly, magic was admired among many as powerful; now, since Christ has been revealed, magic has lost its potency and influence.[87] Athanasius then sums up his findings: "So if the Savior is not a mere man, nor a magician nor a demon, but by his divinity has destroyed and eclipsed the suppositions of the poets and the illusions of the demons and the wisdom of the Greeks, it should be clear and will be admitted by all that he is truly the Son of God, being the Word and Wisdom and Power of the Father."[88]

APOLOGETIC METHODOLOGY

Athanasius's attempts to prove the rationality and superiority of Christianity in his response to the theological challenges of his day reveal a number of significant features of his apologetic methodology. First, it is noteworthy that Athanasius takes the cross as his starting point. He does not begin with natural law or other commonly shared assumptions and from there argue for specific Christian doctrines. Athanasius asserts that through the cross of Christ, God has revealed himself and his purposes for the world. The entire account of CG-DI is given from this perspective.[89] Because the cross is the foundation for his entire apologetic, Athanasius's method is to draw from the inspired Scriptures because, he believes, they are "sufficient for the exposition of the truth."[90] He is confident that if his critics read the Scriptures, they will come to believe what Athanasius is trying to persuade them to believe.[91]

While the Scriptures, not metaphysical speculation, form Athanasius's epistemological basis, he is not unaware of the intellectual currents of his day.[92] As the bishop of Alexandria, he lived in a well-educated metropolis and knew how to engage his learned interlocutors. As Hart notes, Athanasius drew on his culture's "plausibility structures" (that is, what a society considers credible given its assumptions and beliefs) but never subordinated Christian doctrine to those structures. Instead, he filled the vocabulary common with the reigning

---

87. DI 46–47, 250–54.

88. DI 48, 257. Cf. DI 55, 272.

89. CG 1, 2–4. See also Behr, Formation of Christian Theology, 23.

90. CG 1, 3.

91. CG 45, 124.

92. Thomson, introduction in Athanasius: Contra Gentes and De Incarnatione, xix. Anatolios, Athanasius: The Coherence, 30–31, observes that Athanasius was driven by the Scriptural narrative of the incarnation for the renewal of humanity but also had recourse to the concepts and vocabulary of Middle-Platonic ontology in his articulation of the Christian faith. On this point, see especially E. P. Meijering, Orthodoxy and Platonism in Athanasius: Synthesis or Antithesis? (Leiden: Brill, 1968). Meijering analyzes the extent to which Athanasius was familiar with and used the Platonic tradition in CG-DI.

plausibility structures with new meaning. That is, he used terminology familiar to people of his time but redefined it in order to advance Christian teaching.[93] For instance, parts 35–39 of *CG* are heavily indebted to Stoic influences. As Anatolios observes, they were helpful to Athanasius "insofar as they provided a vocabulary and certain conceptual tools for articulating notions of the divine providence, omnipresence, and intimate involvement in the world—in a word, immanence."[94]

Athanasius points to the relationship between difference and harmonious order in the natural world. The universe is composed of parts, bodies, and forces, each in harmony with the others. As a musician combines the sounds of each string into a harmony, so God beautifully orchestrates and orders all things, resulting in a well-functioning, well-ordered universe. From this it is evident that there is only one God. Many gods would mean either chaos in the world (in the way many captains steering a ship would lead to disarray) or the existence of multiple worlds. These options are absurd for Athanasius. Creation is a single entity, and its order is one, thus one may deduce that it has one Lord and Creator.[95] That the one universe was created with "reason, wisdom, and understanding and has been arranged with complete order" is evidence that its order belongs to the Logos of God.[96]

Finally, Athanasius includes testimonies of believers, followed by an invitation to his hearers to embrace faith in Christ. While he has strong words for his critics, Athanasius's genuine concern is for them to come to know the true God through the Word made flesh. In *DI* 28 Athanasius points to the lives of those who had put on Christ and no longer fear death. He then holds out an invitation to skeptics to accept the truth of Christ: "He who does not believe in the victory over death let him accept the faith of Christ and come over to his teaching, and he will see the weakness of death and the victory won over it. For many at first disbelieved and mocked, but later believing, so despised death that they even became Christian martyrs."[97] With such language, Athanasius bolsters the faith of believers while extending an invitation to those outside the faith. His aim was for his opponents to undergo a paradigm shift by recognizing the truth of Christianity and embracing Christ.[98]

---

93. See Trevor Hart, "The Two Soteriological Traditions of Alexandria," in *Evangelical Quarterly* 61:3 (1989), 239–259.
94. Anatolios, *Athanasius: The Coherence*, 49.
95. *CG* 38–39, 104–08.
96. *CG* 40, 110.
97. *DI* 28, 203. Cf. *DI* 41, 236.
98. Hart, "The Two Soteriological Traditions," 246.

CONTRIBUTIONS TO THE FIELD
OF APOLOGETICS

As an apologist for the Christian faith, Athanasius was concerned with equipping the faithful and engaging the faithless. His aim in *CG-DI*, his only apologetic treatise, was to show that faith in Jesus Christ is reasonable and true, while other ways of believing are not. He provided a careful analysis of fundamental beliefs held by pagans and compares these beliefs with Christian doctrines. In every case, Christianity is clearly superior, while paganism is found wanting. Athanasius knew how to connect with his audience because he recognized what they valued and was familiar with their conceptual framework. Thus, he engaged the Jews with the Old Testament and the Greeks with recourse to Stoic and Platonic sources. He also knew that pointing to contemporary events in history that everyone could observe carried persuasive power. All could see that Christianity was growing while paganism was in decline, and Athanasius stressed that the two historical phenomena were inseparable. But above all, Athanasius rested his argument on the persuasive power of the narrative of the incarnate Word, who restored humanity through his own death and resurrection. Overall, Athanasius never watered down the truth of salvation. He began his *apologia* with the scandal of the cross and argued uncompromisingly from that position. Hart observes, "What we must never forget is that it is precisely insofar as the gospel is a scandal to human wisdom that it confronts men and women in all its relevance. To the extent that we seek to lessen that scandal, therefore, we hinder rather than aid its cause."[99] Athanasius began and ended with the crucified Christ and thereby furthered the cause of the gospel.

BIBLIOGRAPHY
Primary Source
Athanasius: Contra Gentes and *De Incarnatione*. Ed. by Robert W. Thomson. Oxford: Clarendon, 1971.

Secondary Sources
Anatolios, Khaled. *Athanasius: The Coherence of his Thought*. London: Routledge, 2005.
———. *Athanasius: The Early Church Fathers*. London: Routledge, 2004.
Barnes, Timothy. *Constantine and Eusebius*. Cambridge: Harvard University Press, 1981.
Behr, John. *Formation of Christian Theology*. Vol. 2 of *The Nicene Faith*. Crestwood, NY: St. Vladimir's Seminary Press, 2004.
Gwynn, David. *Athanasius of Alexandria: Bishop, Theologian, Ascetic, Father*. Oxford: Oxford University Press, 2012.
Hart, Trevor. "The Two Soteriological Traditions of Alexandria." *Evangelical Quarterly* 61:3 (1989): 239–59.
Meijering, E. P. *Athanasius: Contra Gentes: Introduction, Translation and Commentary*. Leiden: Brill, 1984.
Weinandy, Thomas. *Athanasius: A Theological Introduction*. Burlington, VT: Ashgate, 2007.
Young, Frances. *From Nicaea to Chalcedon: A Guide to the Literature and its Background*. 2nd ed. Grand Rapids: Baker Academic, 2010.

---

99. Ibid., 258–59.

AUGUSTINE OF HIPPO

Apologist of Faith and Reason Seeking Understanding

CHAD MEISTER

Aurelius Augustine, or Saint Augustine of Hippo (354–430) as he is commonly known today, is widely recognized as the most influential Christian thinker, outside the biblical writers, in world history.[1] His genius and vast literary corpus have made him one of the most important western thinkers of all time, as well as one of the most significant defenders of the Christian faith. His famous reflection, "our heart is restless until it rests in you"[2] is followed by eighty thousand carefully crafted Latin words that are still widely read and studied today. And they reflect a deeply pious and thoughtful individual, a man who seems to have believed what he taught and lived what he believed. His writings, especially the *Confessions* (ca. 400) and *The City of God* (ca. 413–426), have inspired countless millions of readers throughout the centuries. Through them we are introduced to a masterpiece in western literature, to an articulate and comprehensive Christian worldview, and to some of the most creative and imaginative prose and arguments in world history.[3]

---

1. While this is undoubtedly true of his influence on Western Christianity, Augustine's influence on Eastern Orthodox Christianity was much less significant. One reason for this is that his writings were not translated from Latin into Greek until the fourteenth century. But Augustine is understood to be a saint by the Orthodox. For more on this, see Fr. Seraphim Rose, *The Place of Blessed Augustine in the Orthodox Church*, 3rd ed. (Platina, CA: St. Herman, 2007).

2. Augustine, *Conf.*, 1.1.1. The Latin text comes from James O'Donnell and can be found at this site: http://faculty.georgetown.edu/jod/latinconf/1.html. The English translation is from the translation by Henry Chadwick, *Saint Augustine—Confessions* (Oxford: Oxford University Press, 1998).

3. While Augustine was a brilliant metaphysician who provides many tightly argued altercations in his writings, Augustine scholar Robert O'Connell maintains that "Augustine constructed more through a play of his teeming imagination than by the highly abstract processes of strict metaphysical thinking." Robert O'Connell, *Imagination and Metaphysics in St. Augustine* (Milwaukee: Marquette University Press, 1986), 3.

Image: *Saint Augustine Disputing with the Heretics*, circa 1470–86, Museu Nacional d'Art de Catalunya, Barcelona

HISTORICAL BACKGROUND

Augustine was born on November 13, AD 354, in a modest town in Roman North Africa called Tagaste (modern Souk Ahras, Algeria), about forty miles from the Mediterranean coast. His father, Patricius, was a Roman pagan, and his mother, Monica, a baptized Christian. Monica was especially influential in Augustine's life. In fact, Augustine attributes his own interest in intellectual matters and the quest for truth to his praying mother.[4] As Augustine describes her, Monica prayed incessantly for him—that he would come to faith in Christ and that he would be a powerful orator for the defense of Christianity. Her requests were eventually satisfied, but there was an intellectual journey that Augustine would undergo before his restless heart would find the satisfaction for which it so longed.

Augustine's parents were middle class. They were not wealthy by the standards of imperial Rome, but neither were they poor. They were able, for example, to provide for Augustine a first-rate education (albeit with connections and the assistance of a wealthy benefactor). While Augustine had at least one brother and one sister, his parents apparently sent only him to be educated, perhaps recognizing how precocious he was, even as an infant. He first studied in Tagaste, then in Madauros, and finally in Carthage, a leading city of Roman Africa. Augustine became highly trained as a rhetorician, but his subjects of study also included Greek, Latin, philosophy, and literature, among others. In his philosophical studies he would have encountered many different schools of thought, including Platonism, Manichaeism, and skepticism. When his education was complete, he taught for a short time in Tagaste before returning to Carthage to teach rhetoric.

While pursuing his education in Carthage, at the age of nineteen, Augustine encountered the works of the Roman thinker Cicero. It was Cicero's work *Hortensius* that especially inspired Augustine to love wisdom—that is, to be a philosopher: "The book changed my feelings. It altered my prayers, Lord, to be toward you yourself. It gave me different values and priorities. Suddenly every vain hope became empty to me, and I longed for the immortality of wisdom with incredible ardour in my heart I began to rise up to return to you."[5]

Hortensius, which is sadly lost to posterity, set Augustine on the path of true wisdom. In reading this work, he concluded that he would follow Cicero's advice "not to study one particular sect but to love and seek and pursue and hold fast

---

4. See Augustine, *Ord.* 2.10.52. *St. Augustine: On Order (De Ordine)*. Trans. by Silvano Borruso (South Bend, IN: St. Augustine's Press, 2007). This work is, in a sense, Augustine's introduction to philosophy.

5. Augustine, *Conf.* 3.4.7.

and strongly embrace wisdom itself, wherever found."[6] But this path of wisdom seemed to be a circuitous route until Augustine discovered the cross.

AUGUSTINE THE MANICHAEAN

Shortly after reading *Hortensius*, Augustine encountered the teachings of the Manichaeans. The founder of Manichaeism was the Persian prophet Mani (AD 216–277), who was known as the "Apostle of Light" by his followers. Mani saw himself as the final successor in a line of prophets that began with Adam and included the Buddha, Zoroaster, and Jesus. Earlier religious beliefs and teachings were limited, Mani believed, and he was the prophet to transmit the true, universal religion that would replace all others.

Manichaeism was one of the Gnostic religions that flourished in imperial Rome at this time. The Gnostic religions (from the Greek term *gnosis*, which means "knowledge") offered adherents a secret knowledge, hidden from non-adherents, that provided the path of salvation. As with all forms of Gnosticism, Manichaeism taught that life in this world is full of pain and evil. An inner illumination (*gnosis*) reveals to the true seeker of wisdom that the soul (the immaterial aspect of the person), which shares in the divine nature, has fallen into the nefarious world of matter. This mingling of spirit and matter in a human being clouds one's knowledge of the true nature of oneself. Attaining the secret knowledge that one is truly united with the divine provides the path of salvation. The salvific knowledge of God, human beings, and human destiny in Manichaeism is expressed in a mythology of a fall from the heavenly realm, an entanglement of spirit/light and matter/darkness, and the freeing of the self from matter/darkness for those who seek and follow truth, and the transmigration of the self for those who do not seek truth but dwell in fleshly desires.

The Manichaean community was divided into two groups: the elect, who followed a rigorous ascetic rule, and the hearers, who provided financial and other support for the elect. Augustine was himself a Manichaean hearer for almost a decade, and in his *Confessions* he refers to Manichaean practices and beliefs on a number of occasions. But his adherence to this belief system would not last. He had too many philosophical and theological questions that Manichaeism could not answer.

AUGUSTINE THE SKEPTIC AND NEOPLATONIST

In 384 Augustine left Africa at roughly thirty years of age to take up a career in teaching in Rome. He was there as a teacher for only a short time

---

6. Augustine, *Conf.* 3.4.8.

before landing the prestigious post of professor of rhetoric in the imperial court of Milan. At that time Milan was, for all intents and purposes, the capital of the Western Roman Empire. It was the place to be if one desired a prominent, powerful, and lucrative career. And Augustine had such aspirations, as did his parents for him. It was during this time in Rome that Augustine became sympathetic to the academic skepticism of Cicero (notably his *De Natura Deorum* and *Academica*), Carneades, and others. Academic skepticism was so named because of its origin among scholars working in Plato's Academy. These skeptics would argue for both sides of an issue in an attempt to undermine the dogmatic confidence of their interlocutors. In doing so, they maintained that certitude in any arena is unattainable. Their reasoning persuaded Augustine, for a period.[7]

It was also during his time in Milan that Augustine came across the bishop of the city, Ambrose. Ambrose was in his mid-forties at the time, and Augustine was thirty. Ambrose was well schooled in philosophy, especially Neoplatonism. A member of the Roman aristocracy, he had at this point been bishop of Milan for ten years. He also had a peace about him and a confidence in his Christian faith that Augustine desired. Ambrose was a part of a community whose members consisted of Platonist Christians, and Ambrose himself was a Platonist of sorts. Ambrose and his cohorts held that Platonism was consistent with, and in some ways an anticipation of, Christianity. His sermons were deeply reflective, beautiful in oratory, and accessible to the common folk. They were unlike anything Augustine had heard before, and they impressed him, both in content and style of speech.

Inspired by the creative wit and interpretive skills of Ambrose, Augustine read various Neoplatonic works (most likely those of Plotinus and Porphyry). This, along with his discussions with Ambrose and other Neoplatonist Christians, convinced Augustine that Neoplatonism was vastly superior to Manichaeism in its philosophical insights and spirituality and that many Christian beliefs were not inconsistent with it.

Neoplatonism, as the term implies, has roots in the works of Plato (ca. 428– ca. 347 BC). A central aspect of Platonism is the assertion that reality is divided into two domains: the visible and the intelligible. The visible realm contains the particular, sensible things (things seen with the physical eyes but not "intellected"—grasped by the mind's eye). The intelligible realm contains the Forms/Ideas (things that are "intellected" but not seen with the physical eyes). Forms/Ideas are universal, objective, stable, absolute, and real. The visible world

---

7. As John Rist points out, Augustine was one of the few thinkers of late antiquity who took this radical skepticism seriously. See John Rist, *Augustine: Ancient Thought Baptized* (Cambridge: Cambridge University Press, 1994), 42–43.

consists of particulars, which are individual, dependent, fleeting, and less real. A brown dog, for example, is a particular, whereas brownness is a universal Form. For Plato, the transitory world that human beings inhabit is an imperfect manifestation of a perfect and unchanging reality that the senses cannot perceive; only the mind or intellect can grasp this more real aspect of what is.

Through the work of later Platonist philosophers, such as Plotinus (ca. AD 205–270), a new form of Platonism emerged. Utilizing the ideas found in the writings of Plato, Plotinus developed a spiritual cosmology referred to as Neoplatonism that is founded on three fundamental principles: the One (or "God" or "the Good"), the Intellect (or "Mind" or "Logos"), and the World-Soul. From these three fundamental principles, all existence emanates. Augustine was taken by Neoplatonism. It provided answers to profound questions that Manichaeism could not, such as the problem of evil. Augustine found Neoplatonism to contain many significant ideas and teachings that were consistent with Christianity, with the crucial exception that it did not acknowledge Christ as Messiah. Given these new Neoplatonic convictions, Augustine's skepticism began to dissipate. Neoplatonism thus brought about a kind of intellectual conversion for Augustine—a shift in his thinking that allowed him to consider the claims of Christianity as plausible possibilities. Yet what was still missing was a conversion of his will.

AUGUSTINE THE CHRISTIAN

This conversion of will occurred in a famous scene, which Augustine describes in detail in the *Confessions* (VII, 12). Leading up to his conversion was a reflection on his lascivious past. He had been a lustful young man, as he describes himself, and he laments one of his prayers during that youthful period: "But I was an unhappy young man, wretched as at the beginning of my adolescence when I prayed you for chastity and said, 'Grant me chastity and continence, but not yet.' I was afraid you might hear my prayer quickly, and that you might too rapidly heal me of the disease of lust which I preferred to satisfy rather than suppress."[8]

Overwhelmed by shame from a long hesitancy to give up his passion and illicit sexual practices for a prestigious career and to become a servant of the Lord, in August 386, in a garden—a real garden, he insists, not a mere metaphoric reference to the Garden of Eden—he rushed in and threw himself down beneath a fig tree. He then heard these words, which sounded like the voices of children: "*Tolle lege*," Latin words that can be translated "Take up and read."

---

8. Augustine, *Conf.* 8.7.17.

Augustine picked up his Bible and opened its pages. His eyes fell on these words: "Let us conduct ourselves becomingly as in the day, not in reveling and drunkenness, not in debauchery and licentiousness, not in quarreling and jealousy. But put on the Lord Jesus Christ, and make no provision for the flesh, to gratify its desires" (Rom 13:13–14 RSV).

These words spoke directly to him, as if God himself were speaking. Augustine's reply was this: "I had no wish to read further and no need. For in that instant, with the very ending of the sentence, it was as though a light of utter confidence shone in all my heart."[9] Augustine, at the age of thirty-one, was now fully committed to the Christian faith. Ambrose baptized Augustine and his son Adeodatus—a son born to him and his concubine (wife by common-law marriage)[10]—at the next Easter Vigil.

Augustine's mother died shortly after this event. Tragically, his son Adeodatus died shortly afterward as well. It was perhaps because of these events that Augustine gave up on his plans of married life, gave away his wealth to the poor, and converted his house into a monastic community for himself and a group of fellow believers. From the ashes of these tragedies, a new way of seeing the world was born for Augustine. A life devoted to God and family was changed into a life devoted to celibate ministry.

Ordained a priest in 391, Augustine founded a new community in Hippo (modern Annaba, Algeria). Five years later he became bishop there, and for the next thirty-five years, he was an influential writer and preacher, teaching about the Christian faith and life and often speaking against his former religion of Manichaeism. Augustine lived in Hippo from his late thirties until his death in 430, almost forty years later. During these years he engaged in a host of pastoral tasks and wrote theological and philosophical works. In the spring of 430, the Vandals—a "barbaric" Germanic people who would later sack Rome—invaded Roman Africa. On August 28, 430, while the city of Hippo was under siege, Augustine fell ill and died. The Vandals burned much of Hippo, though fortunately Augustine's library survived.

Augustine's life occurred during a period of history in the Mediterranean world called Late Antiquity, a transition period from Classical Antiquity to the

---

9. Augustine, *Conf.* 8.12.30.

10. When Augustine was nineteen, he began a long-term relationship with a woman. We do not know her name because Augustine never mentions it. She was from a lower social class, and Augustine never officially married her, perhaps because of her station in life. But she did provide Augustine a son, Adeodatus, which means "gift of God." Augustine's mother eventually persuaded him to give up his relationship (common-law marriage) with this woman to marry a young woman from the same social class as Augustine. While he initially agreed, he was in turmoil in severing ties with his former lover. He eventually ended his marriage plans and became a celibate priest.

Middle Ages. In fact, Augustine himself was one of the founders of the medieval world. Immensely influential in the development of Christian thought, he was canonized in 1298 by Pope Boniface VIII.[11]

APOLOGETIC RESPONSE AND METHOD

FAITH AND REASON

After his conversion, Augustine wrote about philosophical and theological issues having to do with ideas he previously held or with which he struggled.[12] One early writing was entitled *Against the Academicians*, in which he defended the possibility of knowledge against those successors of Plato who affirmed a form of skepticism.[13] For Augustine, obtaining certain, eternal truths was a central philosophical goal. But according to these academic skeptics, nothing can be known, so we should not offer our assent to any truth claims whatever.[14] Indeed, for some of them, it was the *pursuit* of knowledge, rather than knowledge itself, that led to wisdom and the good life. Augustine disagreed. For him, to be wise and happy, one must have knowledge, certain knowledge.

A basic strategy of the skeptics with whom Augustine disagreed was to first get their opponent to agree that knowledge of a truth claim is possible only if it could not be mistaken. Consider the appearance of some object. Suppose, for example, that the internal mental image of a particular palace includes the image of a large pillar next to it. If it is *possible* that a dream or hallucination caused the image of the pillar, argue the skeptics, then one cannot *know* that the pillar is next to the palace, even if the pillar is in fact next to the palace. With such austere causal demands for knowledge, the skeptics maintained that nothing at all can be known, for we cannot be certain that what we claim to know is not information obtained in a dream.

Augustine argued that there are propositions about which there cannot be any doubt, and since there is such certain knowledge, the skeptics were mistaken. In making his argument, Augustine focused on several questions in physics that

---

11. Giovanni Catapano provides an excellent and concise overview of Augustine's thought in his "Augustine," in Lloyd P. Gerson, *The Cambridge History of Philosophy in Late Antiquity* (Cambridge: Cambridge University Press, 2010), 552–81. Avery Dulles offers a helpful though quite brief overview of Augustine's role in the history of apologetics in his *A History of Apologetics* (Eugene, OR: Wipf & Stock, 1999), 59–70. For a more extended work on Augustine's thought and influence, see the classic work by Peter Brown, *Augustine of Hippo*, new ed. (Los Angeles: University of California Press, 2000).

12. What follows is a sketch of his influence as a Christian apologist, though the scope of his work in these areas spans beyond apologetics. He wrote voluminously, and it would be an impossible task to include here everything that Augustine wrote that is relevant to Christian apologetics. Judiciousness demands that only a select group of topics be included.

13. Augustine referred to this group of skeptics as the "New Academy."

14. Augustine, *Acad.* 3.10.22.

had divided philosophers for centuries. One of these questions is this: Is there only one world, or is there not only one world? Augustine recognized the difficulty in answering this question with any sort of certainty, yet he maintained that there is still something we can know about the matter: "Although I am still a long way from being wise, I know something in physics. I am certain that the world is either one or not. And if it is not one, then there is either a finite number of worlds or an infinite number of worlds."[15]

So even if we are unable to provide a direct answer to the question that is certain, we know there are two matters related to it about which we can have certain knowledge in physics: (a) either there is only one world or there is more than one world, and (b) if there is more than one world, then there is either a finite or an infinite number of them. So we *can* have certain knowledge about physics in this case and in others as well, in particular in cases of exhaustive disjunction. Since we can have such certain knowledge in the realm of physics, the skeptics are refuted.

The skeptic may respond with an external world skepticism in which knowledge of external reality itself is questioned. In other words, while the disjunctions Augustine provided may well provide a plausible response to the skeptic if there is an external world, perhaps there is no such world. Or perhaps the disjunctions do not match the external world. The disjunctive claims cannot be known to be true if it cannot be known that there is an external world, or if they match the external world. Augustine's argument against skepticism would thus seem to fail.

Augustine's response to this counterargument was that one has "seemings" of the external world that reflect and constitute the world. For example, I seem to see clouds in the sky today. The skeptic will grant that (1) I could be mistaken about what I see (this possibility of error is a central reason for skeptical doubt) and that (2) skepticism itself requires that there are such events. In fact, seemings are *required* for there to be error (I am either mistaken about the clouds being there, or I am not). Augustine offered a helpful example of this "subjective knowledge," saying, "When a man tastes something, he can swear in good faith that he knows that this is sweet to his palate. . . . and no Greek sophism can deprive him of that knowledge."[16] So one can have *certain* knowledge about such subjective experiences; if something seems to taste sweet, it does taste sweet to me, and we can know that it does. So once again, we can have certain knowledge in at least some areas, contrary to what the skeptics beleive, and this opens up the possibility for further metaphysical and other truths.

---

15. Augustine, *Acad.* 3.10.23. Trans. by Peter King (Indianapolis: Hackett, 1995).

16. Augustine, *Acad.* 3.11.26. Trans. by Peter King (Indianapolis: Hackett, 1995). This point was noted in John Rist, "Faith and Reason," in Eleonore Stump and Norman Kretzmann, eds., *The Cambridge Companion to Augustine* (Cambridge: Cambridge University Press, 2001), 28.

Augustine dealt with epistemological issues in other works beyond *Against the Academics*. For example, consider these proto-Cartesian words from *The City of God*:

> I am certain that I am, that I know that I am, and that I live to be and to know. . . . In the face of these truths, the quibbles of the skeptics lose their force. If they say, "What if you are mistaken?"—well, if I am mistaken, I am. For, if one does not exist, he can by no means be mistaken. Therefore, I am, if I am mistaken. . . . I am most certainly not mistaken in knowing that I am. Nor, as a consequence, am I mistaken in knowing that I know. For, just as I know that I am, I also know that I know.[17]

As with Descartes, who appears much later in the history of western thought, for Augustine, knowledge begins with the self. And with the certainty that arises with this internal kind of knowing, one can come to know that skepticism is wrong. There is certain knowledge, and knowing this, one can plausibly begin the search for additional truths in other areas.

In his more developed epistemology, Augustine used his theory of divine illumination to establish certain knowledge, like the Forms of Plato, in which the ideas of God provide the foundation of human certitude. Augustine used the Platonic analogy between physical perception and mental vision in which the divine light is to the mind of human beings as the sun is to the eyes of human beings.[18] This is how the mind can know eternal and necessary truths.[19] For example, while the physical eyes could never "see" every case of the principle of noncontradiction, or every case of two things being added to three things, which makes five things, it can know necessarily that something can't both be and not be, and that $2 + 3 = 5$. How so? The mind is capable of seeing eternal objects, such as laws of logic and mathematical truths, provided that they are bathed in divine light.[20] What Augustine seems to be saying is that one must first look inward and examine the interior depths of the mind to get an impression of necessary and eternal truths. But in going inward one must then glance upward, looking to the God of lights, who is shining above the self, to receive the illumination of these truths that is requisite for understanding them and attaining

---

17. Augustine, *City of God*, trans. Gerald G. Walsh and Grace Monahan (Washington, DC: Catholic University Press of America, 1952), 11.26, 228–29. See also his *On the Trinity*, ed. Marcus Dodds, trans. Arthur West Haddan (Edinburgh: T&T Clark, 1873), 10.10.14, 256.

18. Augustine, *Solil.* 1.6.12; 8.15.

19. Augustine, *Trin.* 14.15.21.

20. Augustine, Aurelius. *The Trinity*. Trans. by Stephen McKenna in *The Fathers of the Church: A New Translation*, vol. 45. (Washington, DC: The Catholic University of America Press, 1963), 12.15.24.

certitude—first inward, then upward. That is an epistemic move that Augustine gleaned from the Neoplatonists, though he did so from within a Christian purview, one in which the God of the Bible is the ultimate revealer of all truth.[21]

Another significant difference between the Neoplatonists' approach and Augustine's approach to knowledge is that, for Augustine, reason requires faith to function properly. Reason is incomplete without faith. The mind is not a dispassionate, morally indifferent data-processing device. The way our hearts and our desires are orientated affects our minds, and whether we have faith or not makes a difference to our understanding. As he puts it, "Faith seeks, understanding finds; whence the prophet says: 'Unless ye believe, ye shall not understand.'"[22]

In reading Augustine, one is struck by his profound appreciation for divine grace for all good things, including one's own faith.[23] Accordingly, if faith is a gift of God, it may seem that reason plays no role in coming to believe that God exists or in coming to faith in Christ. Augustine does say, after all, "I believe in order that I may understand." And he adds, "For if we wanted to know first, and then believe, we should not be able either to know or to believe."[24] Yet for Augustine, matters are more complicated than they might first appear.

In examining the role of faith and reason in Augustine, two important points are worth reflecting on. First, he generally discussed the relationship between reason and authority rather than reason and faith.[25] Faith depends on authority, for Augustine, and this authority primarily comes through Scripture and the church. But second, reason is required to determine whether this authority is genuine. As noted earlier, reason must be used to respond to the skeptical challenges to knowledge. But the heart must be right before God before reason can appropriately be used in the quest for truth, especially regarding truth about God, the human condition, and salvation. Augustine emphasized the role of reason in believing: "For who cannot see that thinking is prior to believing? For no one believes anything unless he has first thought that it is to be believed?"[26] And further: "For however, rapidly, some thoughts fly before the

---

21. For a careful analysis of Augustine's notion of inwardness, see Phillip Cary, *Inner Grace: Augustine in the Traditions of Plato and Paul* (New York: Oxford University Press, 2008). See also Ronald Nash, *The Light of the Mind: St. Augustine's Theory of Knowledge* (Lexington: University Press of Kentucky, 1969), and Peter King, "Augustine on Knowledge," in David Vincent Meconi and Eleonore Stump, *The Cambridge Companion to Augustine*, 2nd ed. (Cambridge: Cambridge University Press, 2014), 142–65.

22. Augustine, *On the Trinity*, trans. Arthur Hadden and William Shedd, vol. 8 of *A Select Library of Nicene and Post-Nicene Fathers of the Christian Church*, ed. Philip Schaff (Grand Rapids: Eerdmans, 1956), 15.2.2.

23. Augustine, *Enchir.* 31. Philip Schaff, ed., Nicene and Post-Nicene Fathers, Vol. 3 (Peabody, MA: Hendrickson, 1994), 247.

24. Augustine, *Tract. Ev. Jo.* 27.9. New Advent: http://www.newadvent.org/fathers/1701027.htm.

25. See Rist, "Faith and Reason," 26–28.

26. Augustine, *Praed.* 1.5. New Advent. http://www.newadvent.org/fathers/15121.htm.

will to believe . . . it is yet necessary that everything which is believed should be believed after thought has led the way; although belief itself is nothing other than to think with assent. . . . Everyone who believes, thinks—both thinks in believing, and believes in thinking."[27]

So reason is involved in both thinking and believing; one cannot know anything without believing something, and believing is central for the right kind of thinking. Faith is thus necessary in everyone's life, religious believer or unbeliever, as is reason.

Augustine maintained that reason can go far without proper faith. The Neoplatonists, for example, were excellent philosophers because they focused not only on epistemology and the general causes of things but also on the cause of the universe as such. This philosophical approach led them to the belief that God exists, and Augustine himself developed an argument for the existence of God using logical principles gleaned from the Greek thinkers. So non-Christian ideas can be used in acquiring knowledge, even knowledge of God. Nevertheless, one cannot get a clear understanding of God without faith and love of God; indeed, one cannot get a clear understanding of many central truths without the right kind of faith.[28]

THE EXISTENCE AND NATURE OF GOD

For Augustine, while faith is a prerequisite for knowledge of God (for faith illumines all theological and philosophical matters), there are also evidences in both the natural world and in reflection on the nature of the eternal truths of reason for the existence of God. He notes, for example, that the structure and beauty of the created order speaks to the existence of the Creator:

> But why did God choose then to create the heavens and earth which up to that time he had not made? If they who put this question wish to make out that the world is eternal and without beginning, and that consequently it has not been made by God, they are strangely deceived, and rave in the incurable madness of impiety. For, though the voices of the prophets were silent, the world itself, by its well-ordered changes and movements, and by the fair appearance of all visible things, bears a testimony of its own, both that it has been created, and also that it could not have been created save by God, whose greatness and beauty are unutterable and invisible.[29]

---

27. Ibid.
28. For more on Augustine's view of faith and reason, see Nash, *The Light of the Mind*, chapter 3.
29. Augustine, *Civ.* 11.4. Schaff, ed., Nicene and Post-Nicene Fathers, 207.

This paragraph is basically the extent to which we find Augustine offering an argument from the natural world to the existence of God. It is not a proof so much as it is a reflection on evidence from the natural world that points toward the creator of the world. It is similar to what is found in Psalm 19, where the psalmist notes that the heavens declare the glory of God (v. 1).

Augustine's proof for the existence of God was more Platonic in nature, one that relied not on the senses to give us true and certain knowledge but in which the eye of the mind could see the eternal truths of reason, such as those that can be found in mathematics. It is in his great work on theodicy and free will that Augustine developed what he took to be this proof for God's existence. His argument can be delineated in three steps:[30]

1. There are timeless and immutable truths.
    a. Absolute doubt is impossible (we know we are doubting).
    b. We know that we exist, that we think, and that $7 + 3 = 10$.
2. Immutable truth cannot be caused:
    a. by sensible things (for the unchanging and independent cannot be caused by the changing and dependent).
    b. by finite minds (for it is independent of our minds, and our minds are ruled by it).
3. Therefore, there must be a timeless and immutable Mind causing these immutable truths.

While this argument was never widely accepted in Christian apologetics as a serious contender for a persuasive philosophical argument for the existence of God, the general approach he formulated, using timeless and immutable truths, has been used in various forms throughout Christian history. And the very notion of a rational argument for the existence of God has been part and parcel of Christian apologetics ever since.[31]

While Augustine did try to show the existence of God through evidence, he spent much more time articulating and defending the nature of the Christian God than he did trying to prove that God exists. He used his training in rhetoric

---

30. Augustine, *Lib.* 2.1–15. *Augustine: On the Free Choice of the Will, On Grace and Free Choice, and Other Writings*, ed. and trans. by Peter King (Cambridge: Cambridge University Press, 2010). This three-step delineation is offered in Norman Geisler and Winfried Corduan, *Philosophy of Religion*, 2nd ed. (Grand Rapids: Baker, 1988), 154.

31. Philosophical historian Frederick Copleston provides a concise overview of Augustine's attempts to demonstrate the existence of God in his *A History of Philosophy*, vol. 2 (New York: Doubleday, 1985), 69–73. For a history of apologetics arguments, see William Edgar and K. Scott Oliphint, eds., *Christian Apologetics: Past and Present*, vols. 1 and 2 (Wheaton, IL: Crossway, 2009).

and logic to articulate and defend the Christian doctrine of God—a God who is not only transcendent in certain respects but is also knowable, describable, and involved in the world and in the life of the Christian. One particularly significant aspect of the doctrine of God on which Augustine spent much time is that of the Trinity. He spent almost thirty years crafting the multivolume book on the subject, entitled *On the Trinity*.[32] In this important theological work, he affirms the Nicene trinitarianism of his forefathers, but he builds on it to produce a distinctively western version of the doctrine.[33]

Augustine did his writing on the Trinity after the church had already officially established the Trinitarian doctrine, though there were continued challenges to it, notably from two camps: those who were arguing that it was a form of tritheism and those who denied the deity of Jesus Christ. The latter, those who affirmed Arianism, argued that since the Son was begotten (most everyone agreed with this claim), he was made; in other words, the Son was created. There was a time, Arius claimed, that he (the Son) was not. Since there was a time when he was not, he could not be the eternal Creator God. Augustine tried to dispel these false, heretical positions of Arius and others about the Trinity and to show that, while each member of the Trinity has the same divine nature, there is only one God.

From his writings we can glean a clear set of statements on the Trinity:[34]

The Father is God.
The Son is God.
The Holy Spirit is God.
The Father is not the Son.
The Son is not the Holy Spirit.
The Holy Spirit is not the Father.
There is only one God.

---

32. Augustine scholars widely believed that he began working on this book in the year 400 and continued refining it up until 428.

33. Nicene trinitarianism was produced at the Council of Nicea, the first of seven ecumenical councils that represented an attempt by church leaders from across the Roman Empire from the fourth to the eighth centuries to reach a consensus on core Christian beliefs about God, Christ, and other matters and to develop a unified Christendom throughout the empire. The seven ecumenical councils are: Nicaea (325), Constantinople (381), Ephesus (431), Chalcedon (451), Constantinople II (553), Constantinople III (680), and Nicaea II (787). Augustine was a young man during the Council of Constantinople and died the year before the Council of Ephesus. He was specially invited by the emperor to the latter, though he died before it officially began. Nevertheless, his work did influence the conclusions of the Council, as Pelagianism, which Augustine had long fought against, was officially condemned.

34. Philip Cary extracts these seven statements from Augustine's writings in his "The Logic of Trinitarian Doctrine," http://templetonhonorscollege.com/publications/logic-trinitarian-doctrine. For Augustine's actual statements, see the following: *Doctr. chr.* 1:5. New Advent: http://www.newadvent.org/fathers/12021.htm and *Trin.*, Book 1:4.

The first three propositions specify God as revealed in Scripture; the next three demarcate the persons from each other; and the last proposition is a clear affirmation of monotheism.

A question that arose in the mind of many Christians at the time was this: If there are not three gods, then of what are there three?[35] Augustine's reply is that there are three *personae*, which is a Latin term meaning "individual rational being," (or, in Greek, three *hypostases*, which means "individual being").[36] What Augustine concluded is that what demarcates the Father, Son, and Holy Spirit is not a set of unique essences, for they have the same divine essence. They are not three different natures. Nor are they three different persons in the contemporary sense of "person," in which a person consists of a mind, a will, a consciousness, and so on, for the Father, Son, and Holy Spirit have the same will. Rather, what demarcates the Father, Son, and Holy Spirit is their relations to one another: the Father *begets* the Son, the Son is *begotten* by the Father, and the Holy Spirit *proceeds* from the Father and the Son. We can thus describe the central idea of the Trinity in the following sentence: within the nature of the one God are three eternal, distinct, and coequal persons (*personae*): Father, Son, and Holy Spirit.

Augustine was fully aware that it is difficult to conceive of this trinitarian doctrine and that the biblical theophanies are not much help in imagining such a conception. What Augustine proposed, and this was unique to him, is that the human soul provides insights into the trinitarian nature of God. Utilizing the notion of the *imago dei*, that human beings are made in the image of God, along with his Neoplatonic leanings, Augustine suggested once again that we turn inward and then upward. As we do so, we recognize that we have a tripartite soul. We remember, we understand, and we act as moral and spiritual agents. Furthermore, "Since, then, these three, memory, understanding, will, are not three lives, but one life; nor three minds, but one mind; it follows certainly that neither are they three substances, but one substance."[37] As human beings, we are three in one in a manner akin to the divine Trinity; yet we are a lower image of this divine image.[38]

---

35. Phillip Cary examines this question in his article, "Historical Perspectives on Trinitarian Doctrine," in Religion and Theological Studies Fellowship Bulletin, Nov./Dec. 1995. http://templetonhonorscollege.com/publications/historical-perspectives-trinitarian-doctrine.

36. It is important to note that the term *person* in English is not equivalent to the Greek term *hypostases* or to the Latin term *personae*. For more on this, see Chad Meister, "Rethinking the Trinity: On Being Orthodox and Au Courant," *Philosophia Christi* 18.2 (2016): 271–80.

37. Augustine, *Trin.* 10.11.18. Schaff, ed., *Nicene and Post-Nicene Fathers*, 142.

38. For more on Augustine's view of the Trinity, see Lewis Ayers, *Augustine and the Trinity* (Cambridge: Cambridge University Press, 2010).

THE CHRISTIAN LIFE

It is arguably the case that Augustine's most significant work as a Christian apologist, and as a Christian thinker in general, can be found in his two most influential books, *Confessions* and *The City of God*.[39] In his *Confessions*, though certainly a work of confession, or perhaps more aptly *profession*, Augustine tries to persuade readers of the beauty of God, of the goodness of following God and the Christian path, and of the madness of following someone or something else. Not only was the *Confessions* widely read when Augustine was alive, but it was read widely and even imitated throughout the Middle Ages, Renaissance, and Reformation eras. It influenced such luminaries as Anselm, Aquinas, Dante, Martin Luther, and John Calvin.

Though autobiographical in nature, the *Confessions* is so much more than a story about Augustine's life. In it he covers such themes as sin, friendship, faith and reason, Neoplatonism, the nature of truth, the nature of time and eternity, memory, biblical hermeneutics, the role of pagan learning in the Christian life, and much more. The book speaks to the human condition not only in Augustine's day but in any day. It is the story of a youthful soul who turns away from God and truth, but it reflects all souls who turn away. And it points to the soul's journey home to God and eternal happiness, not only Augustine's soul but all souls who can follow this journey. Reading about his conversion inspires one to be converted. It is evangelistic, and it is apologetic.

In *The City of God*, we have, as with the *Confessions*, one of the most significant books ever written in Western civilization. For in this work Augustine responds to major objections to the Christian faith, but he also offers a new and unique vision of history and the responsibilities of human beings living in this world of which God is Creator and King.[40] The book is a response to Roman pagan charges that the sack of Rome and the degeneration of the Roman Empire were due to the Christians. Augustine argues at length why this is not true, and he pushes forward to explain how Christians should understand what life should be like in this world. In doing so he expounds on the nature of a human society that has fallen into sin and ruins (the "Earthly City") and one that has been restored to its proper place before God (the "City of God"). He makes the further case that the role of the church is to be God's instrument on earth for the

---

39. It was wise of William Edgar and K. Scott Oliphint to include portions of the *Confessions* and *The City of God* in their book, *Christian Apologetics: Past and Present*, Vol. 1, ch. 10.

40. For an excellent presentation and exposition of *The City of God*, see Charles Mathewes, *Books that Matter: The City of God*, Teaching Company Course (Chantilly, VA: The Great Courses, 2016). Mathewes's book *The Republic of Grace: Augustinian Thoughts for Dark Times* (Grand Rapids: Eerdmans, 2010) is also worth reading, as it takes core virtues of Augustinian thought and shows their relevance, and significance, for today.

propagation of the good, the true, and the beautiful and that it has indeed been such a force. In this book Augustine shows Christian truths and practice not only through the arguments he offers but also through the pedagogical style of his approach.

Beyond these two classic writings, Augustine authored many other books that have been major works of apologetics about Christian life, teaching, and practice. Included in them are writings against what he took to be false religious systems, such as Manichaeism, and on heretical systems, such as Donatism and Pelagianism.[41] He was thus an apologist in articulating what should be believed about the faith and life of a Christian and also in responding to those false teachings that were masquerading as truth claims about God and salvation.

THE PROBLEM OF EVIL

Another significant and lasting effort of Augustine is his work on the problem of evil. The problem as generally discussed in the contemporary literature on the subject can be captured in the following question: How can one make sense of the claim that God, if God exists, is all-powerful, all-knowing, and omnibenevolent, while evil, pain, and all manner of suffering exist in a world that such a God allegedly created? This question is often crafted into an argument against the existence of God. But this was not precisely the problem that Augustine had in mind.[42] For Augustine, the word for "evil" he used is the Latin term *malum*, which means both "bad" and "evil." This includes anything defective, ill-formed, or flawed in any way or anything that becomes defective or flawed. Augustine's term for something becoming defective or bad is "corruption" (*corruptio* in Latin). Consider a rotten pear or a rusted vehicle or a wicked soul. In each of these cases, something good (pear, vehicle, soul) became corrupted, and each became so in a manner unique to its nature.

For Augustine, God created everything in the universe, and he created everything good. So the problem of evil for Augustine is primarily this: How can anything in the universe become bad (evil, corrupted) if everything was created good? This was a vexing matter for Augustine. Early on as a Manichaean, he believed the problem of how both good and evil could coexist in the world was solved through Manichaean theology: the existence of both good and evil are

41. His writings against the Manicheans and the Donatists can be found at http://www.documentacatholicaomnia.eu/03d/1819–1893,_Schaff._Philip,_2_Vol_04_The_Anti-Manichaean_And_Anti-Donatist_Writings,_EN.pdf. His anti-Pelagian writings can be accessed here: https://www.ccel.org/ccel/schaff/npnf105.html

42. For more on Augustine and evil with regard to this point, see Phillip Cary, "A Classic View," in Chad Meister and James K. Dew Jr., *God and the Problem of Evil: Five Views* (Downers Grove, IL: InterVarsity Press, 2017), 13–36.

understood to be fundamental and eternal aspects of reality. But this "solution" was ultimately not satisfying for Augustine, for it seemed to elevate evil to the level and power of the divine. Augustine came to see evil in a much different light. His insights about the reality of evil are derived from the Neoplatonic tradition (Plotinus in particular), though he rejected the Neoplatonic view that material reality is evil.[43] On his view, God created the material world, and it was created good. So what is evil, according to him, and how can it be explained?

In order to understand Augustine's answers to these questions, we need to know something of his ontology. On his view of what is, which he discusses for example in book seven of the *Confessions*, while God created everything good, he also created everything corruptible. To be corruptible is not to be corrupted. Something that is corrupted is bad; but to be corruptible is to be *potentially* bad. So God created everything good, though potentially bad. Why did God do so? Because that is what a created thing is by nature. God, unlike created things, is unchangeable. Nothing other than God is unchangeable. To be changeable is to be corruptible, Augustine thought, for if something can change, it can change for the worse. And to be able to change for the worse is to be able to be corrupted. So all created things are changeable (mutable, as he puts it), and all changeable things are corruptible.

So God, being perfectly good, created the world, and it consisted of all good things. "Whatever things exist are good," he says.[44] But being corruptible by nature, all things eventually became corrupted. What brought about this corruption, this evil, in the world? Augustine, who continued to use aspects of Platonic and Neoplatonic philosophical principles even as an elderly Christian bishop, maintained that evil (corruption) is not a *thing* at all; it is not a substance in and of itself. Evil is not a form of being but a lack of being what a thing should be. Consider a very rusted vehicle again. The vehicle is not what it should be; there are holes where there should be metal. The vehicle itself is a good thing, but the lack of metal where it should be is bad. The evil itself, then, is not a thing or substance, but rather it is a lack of a thing or substance. Evil, to use medieval terminology, is a privation. It is what occurs when some good thing is privated of (deprived of) some good quality that it ought to have but does not. Evil, then, is not some*thing* that God has created, but it is still *real*; it is a real lack. A hole in a sock has no being, but it is still a real hole. But the question still remains: What brought about evil?

---

43. For more on this, see Erik M. Hanson, "Augustine," in Andrew Pinsent, ed., Chad Meister and Charles Taliaferro, series eds., *The History of Evil in the Medieval Age*, vol. 2 (London: Routledge, 2018), 10–22.

44. Augustine, *Conf.* 7.12.18. Trans. Chadwick, *Saint Augustine—Confessions*, 124–25.

The origin of evil, for Augustine, turns out to be will. As one of the great thinkers of free will in late antiquity, Augustine spent much time pondering and writing on the nature of the will. He maintained that human will, as a created thing, is itself corruptible. And through its own power, it became corrupted. God gave human beings the power to choose the good, and this ability to choose is what is responsible for ushering evil into the world. Augustine also held that angels were given free will, and some of them used it to turn against God and the good.

Augustine used this notion of the will to develop a full-orbed theodicy—an explanation for how evil could exist in a good world that God created. This free will theodicy can be concisely delineated in the following six statements:

1. God created the universe, and everything in it was good.
2. While God is in control of the universe, and nothing happens in it outside his permitting will, some of God's creation—namely *people*—were given the good gift of freedom of the will (having freedom of the will in the universe is better than not having it, since a moral universe requires it, and a moral universe is better than a nonmoral or amoral universe).
3. Some of these created persons—first angels, and then human beings—freely chose to turn from God's goodness; that is, they "sinned" and fell from their state of perfection (i.e., the "fall" of humanity).
4. This turning of the will, or sinning, brought evil (corruption) into the universe.
5. Evil, though brought about by created persons, is not a thing or entity; it is a metaphysical deprivation, or corruption, or lack, or privation, of the good (a *privatio boni*—"privation of good," to use a medieval Latin term).
6. God will finally rectify evil when he judges the world, ushering into his eternal kingdom those persons who have been saved through Christ and sending to eternal hell those persons who are wicked and disobedient.

There is yet another way of understanding the presence of evil, for Augustine; namely, that what we often consider evil is actually an instrumental way of accomplishing the good. Consider the example of going to the dentist and having a cavity removed. This can be a painful and anxiety-producing event. Yet the result is something good: a healthy tooth. In a similar manner, Augustine maintained that the adversities we face can cause us to reflect on what is truly significant and also to think about the afterlife, which can produce a healthy soul.[45]

---

45. See *Civ.* 1.8, 22.22.

There is much in Augustine's work on evil that remains relevant today beyond mere interest in historical philosophy and theology. And many contemporary Christian thinkers continue to use aspects of Augustine's thinking and theodicy in their responses to the problem of evil.[46]

CONTRIBUTIONS TO THE FIELD OF APOLOGETICS

Augustine marks the transition between the ancient world and the medieval one. His incorporation of classical thought into Christian ideas created a powerful philosophical-theological system of lasting influence, an influence that spans the three great streams of Christianity: as "Saint" in the Eastern Orthodox Church; as both "Saint" and "Doctor of the Church" in Roman Catholicism; and as one "most revered" by the great Protestant Reformers and influencers, such as Martin Luther, John Calvin, and John Wesley. The impact of Augustine on Western thought cannot be overstated, and his defense of Christian ideas and doctrines has been paramount.

His engagement with doubt, faith, and reason provided a philosophical and biblical basis for refuting skepticism and offering certain knowledge. In doing so, it gave faith pride of place, yet it also allowed reason a role in acquiring, developing, and confirming that faith. In other words, it provided a grounding for warranted belief.

His arguments for the existence of God, in particular his proof from the eternal truths of reason, showed a rational approach to the topic that many apologists have since emulated. And his work on the doctrine of God, especially his work on the Trinity, has been used throughout the centuries to articulate and defend the orthodox view of the Godhead.

Augustine's works on the Christian life and faith, especially his two most celebrated books, *Confessions* and *The City of God*, provide both persuasive arguments and a persuasive writing style that have stood as exemplars of Christian thought and writing. In them he contrasts the Christian life with the non-Christian and beautifully expresses the goodness and profundity of the former. And his vast corpus of works against heretics and false religious systems would prove to be an effective inoculation against such ideas throughout church history.

Finally, his work on the problem of evil is still studied widely, and Christian philosophers, theologians, and apologists today still use core elements of his

---

46. See, for example, Phillip Cary, "The Classical View," and John Hick, *Evil and the God of Love* (Basingstoke, England: Palgrave Macmillan, 2010).

points and arguments, such as the free will theodicy, evil as privation, and the role of evil in soul-making.

There is much more that could be included here regarding Augustine's influential, apologetical work. For example, his insights on the self and personal identity, soul-body dualism, miracles, biblical hermeneutics, original sin and the human condition, and just war theory, to name a few, are significant topics about which Augustine had something exceedingly important to add that have had lasting influence on Western thought and culture in the articulation and defense of the Christian faith. Faith and reason, God, the Christian life, and the problem of evil are four of the most significant apologetics issues, both historically and today, and Augustine's work on them continues to inspire.

Fifteen hundred years ago Augustine was a force to be reckoned with. Through his many well-crafted arguments, his beautiful Latin prose, and his poetic imagery, Augustine formed and reformed much of Christian thought and culture. Today his works and his ideas stand as models of Christian thought and cultural engagement, and they continue to influence yet another generation of readers and thinkers. His legacy as a Christian thinker and apologist is one that very few philosophers or theologians have achieved in world history; he is in a league of one. He was indeed a philosopher, a theologian, and a Christian apologist in the best senses of those terms.

BIBLIOGRAPHY

Sources for Augustine's Works

Against the Academicians: *Augustine: Against the Academicians / The Teacher*. Trans. by Peter King. Indianapolis/Cambridge: Hackett, 1995.

City of God. Vol. 2 of *Nicene and Post-Nicene Fathers*. Trans. by Gerald G. Walsh and Grace Monahan. Washington, DC: Catholic University Press of America, 1952.

Confessions. Trans. by Henry Chadwick. Oxford: Oxford University Press, 1998.

Enchiridion. Vol. 3 of *Nicene and Post-Nicene Fathers*. Ed. by Philip Schaff. Peabody, MA: Hendrickson, 1994.

On Christian Doctrine: New Advent: http://www.newadvent.org/fathers/12021.htm; Philip Schaff, ed., Nicene and Post-Nicene Fathers, Vol. 2. Peabody, MA: Hendrickson, 1994.

On Order: *St. Augustine: On Order (De Ordine)*. Trans. by Silvano Borruso. South Bend, IN: St. Augustine's Press, 2007.

On the Free Choice of the Will: *Augustine: On the Free Choice of the Will, On Grace and Free Choice, and Other Writings*. Ed. and trans. by Peter King. Cambridge: Cambridge University Press, 2010.

On the Gospel of John: New Advent: http://www.newadvent.org/fathers/1701027.htm.

On the Predestination of the Saints: New Advent: http://www.newadvent.org/fathers/15121.htm.

On the Trinity: Marcus Dodds, ed., *On the Trinity*. Trans. by Arthur West Haddan. Edinburgh: T&T Clark, 1873; *On the Trinity*. Trans. by Arthur West Hadden and William Shedd. Vol. 8 of *A Select Library of Nicene and Post-Nicene Fathers of the Christian Church*. Ed. by Philip Schaff. Grand Rapids: Eerdmans, 1956.

Soliloquies: Any translation.

Many of Augustine's works can be found online in English at the Christian Classics Ethereal Library, located at: https://www.ccel.org/node/70 and at New Advent: http://www.newadvent.org/cathen/02089a.htm.

Secondary Sources

Dutton, Blake D. *Augustine and Academic Skepticism: A Philosophical Study.* Ithaca, NY: Cornell University Press, 2016.

Edgar, William, and K. Scott Oliphint, eds., *Christian Apologetics: Past and Present*, Vol. 1. Wheaton, IL: Crossway, 2009.

Geisler, Norman, and Winfried Corduan, *Philosophy of Religion*, 2nd edition. Grand Rapids: Baker, 1988.

Hanson, Erik M. "Augustine." Pages 10–22 in *The History of Evil in the Medieval Age*, Vol. 2. Ed. by Andrew Pinsent, Chad Meister, and Charles Taliaferro. London: Routledge, 2018.

Hick, John. *Evil and the God of Love.* Basingstoke: Palgrave Macmillan, 2010.

King, Peter. "Augustine on Knowledge." Pages 142–65 in *The Cambridge Companion to Augustine.* 2nd ed. Ed. by David Vincent Meconi and Eleonore Stump. Cambridge: Cambridge University Press, 2014.

Lawhead, William. *The Voyage of Discovery: A History of Western Philosophy.* New York: Wadsworth, 1996.

Mathewes, Charles. *The Republic of Grace: Augustinian Thoughts for Dark Times.* Grand Rapids: Eerdmans, 2010.

Meconi, David Vincent, and Eleonore Stump, eds. *The Cambridge Companion to Augustine.* 2nd ed. Cambridge: Cambridge University Press, 2014.

Meister, Chad. "Rethinking the Trinity: On Being Orthodox and Au Courant." *Philosophia Christi* Vol. 18.2 (2016): 271–80.

Montgomery, John Warwick. "A Short History of Apologetics." Pages 21–28 in *Christian Apologetics: An Anthology of Primary Sources.* Ed. by Khaldoun Sweis and Chad V. Meister. Grand Rapids: Zondervan, 2012.

Nash, Ronald. *The Light of the Mind: St. Augustine's Theory of Knowledge.* Lexington: University Press of Kentucky, 1969.

O'Connell, Robert. *Imagination and Metaphysics in St. Augustine.* Milwaukee: Marquette University Press, 1986.

Plantinga, Alvin. "Reason and Belief in God," Pages 16–93 in *Faith and Rationality: Reason and Belief in God.* Ed. by Alvin Plantinga and Nicholas Wolterstorff. Notre Dame: University of Notre Dame Press, 1983.

Rist, John. *Augustine: Ancient Thought Baptized.* Cambridge: Cambridge University Press, 1994.

———. "Faith and Reason." Pages 26–39 in *The Cambridge Companion to Augustine.* Ed. by Eleonore Stump and Norman Kretzmann. Cambridge: Cambridge University Press, 2001.

Rose, Seraphim. *The Place of Blessed Augustine in the Orthodox Church.* 3rd ed. Platina, CA: St. Herman Press, 2007.

Sweis, Khaldoun, and Chad V. Meister, eds. *Christian Apologetics: An Anthology of Primary Sources.* Grand Rapids: Zondervan, 2012.

Part Two

MEDIEVAL APOLOGISTS

The collapse of the Roman Empire in the western Mediterranean led to significant changes in the situation of western Christianity, which could no longer rely on the protection of the Roman state. In the eastern Mediterranean, however, the situation was significantly different. Constantine had established the city of Constantinople as the capital of the eastern empire, which remained intact and viable after the collapse of the empire in the west and would survive for nearly a thousand more years. During this period Christian theology in Greece and Asia Minor (modern-day Turkey) developed its own distinct agenda, often known as "Byzantine" theology. Perhaps the most important apologist of this age was **Gregory Palamas**, whose arguments for the direct perception of God—rather than an undue reliance on rational argument—continue to be important in some schools of apologetics and spirituality.

The fall of the Roman Empire in the west was followed by the rise of Islam in the Arabian Peninsula. During the period following the death of Mohammad, Islam expanded rapidly by military conquest. By 640, the Caliphate had extended to Mesopotamia, Syria, and Palestine; by 642, to Egypt; and by 643, to the Persian Empire. Many of these regions were former strongholds of Christianity—such as the cities of Damascus, Alexandria, and Antioch. Islamic expansion continued until the city of Constantinople was conquered in 1453.

Christian apologists now found themselves confronted with a new intellectual and cultural rival. The Islamic emphasis on the absolute "oneness" (Arabic: *tawhid*) of God led to Islamic apologists calling into question both the Christian doctrine of the Trinity and the divinity of Christ. **John of Damascus** was the first significant Christian theologian to try to build intellectual bridges to Islam and demonstrate the rational credibility of the gospel. As a high-ranking civil servant in the court of the caliph of Damascus during the eighth century, John was able to ensure he represented Islam fairly while at the same time offering significant defenses of the divinity of Christ that would carry weight with an Islamic audience. Around the same time, **Timothy of Baghdad** produced his *Apology*—a defense of Christianity in response to questions raised by Mahdi, the caliph of Baghdad at the time. This document came to serve as a training manual for the ninth-century church on how to respond to Islamic concerns about the gospel.

By the ninth century, Arabic was firmly established as the public language of many parts of the Islamic world, including Syria. Christian apologists realized the need for apologetic works in Arabic that could engage Islamic writers in constructive dialogue and demonstrate the rationality of the Christian faith. The most successful of these writings were by northern Syrian bishop **Theodore Abu Qurrah**. In his writings, Theodore offered significant defenses of Christian beliefs, particularly the incarnation, an idea that Islam condemns as blasphemous. Theodore stated that it was necessary for God to assume a human existence and experience suffering in order to free human beings from their sins.

Christianity in western Europe had survived the collapse of the western Roman Empire and played a major role in reestablishing centers of learning during the Carolingian period. By the eleventh century, some degree of political stability had been restored to western Europe, leading to the formation of universities and an increasingly sophisticated urban culture. Monasteries played an important role in meeting the intellectual needs of the church. The Benedictine monastery of Bec in Normandy was particularly significant in this respect. **Anselm of Canterbury**—an eleventh-century archbishop of Canterbury who was originally a monk at Bec—championed an intellectual renewal of Christian theology, showing how core beliefs, such as the incarnation and atonement, could be affirmed and defended rationally. For Anselm, the inherently rational character of Christian doctrines meant that they were capable of public defense.

The University of Paris emerged as one of the most significant centers of learning in western Europe, attracting large numbers of Christian, Jewish, and Islamic scholars. **Thomas Aquinas**, one of the most important thirteenth-century theologians, was a major presence at Paris and recognized the importance of offering a rational defense of Christianity to Jewish and Islamic readers. Like Anselm before him, Aquinas held that Christian beliefs were fundamentally rational, even if they transcended the limits of reason, and were thus able to form a coherent and rationally defensible system. His *Summa Contra Gentiles* is clearly apologetic in both its general tone and approach. Whereas Aquinas's best-known work, the *Summa Theologiae*, is a detailed compendium of Christian theology, clearly written with the needs and concerns of believers in mind, the *Summa Contra Gentiles* anticipates questions that might be raised by Jewish, Islamic, or secular readers. It remains an important resource for modern apologists, not least on account of its thoughtful defense and articulation of core beliefs.

Neither Anselm nor Aquinas, however, appear to have had significant cultural and intellectual encounters with representatives of alternative religious traditions, such as Judaism or Islam. Like many medieval writers, their knowledge of such rival religious beliefs was generally indirect. Fourteenth-century writer **Ramon Lull** is of particular importance in that he had direct personal contact with such alternative religious outlooks, particularly Islam. This is reflected in his apologetic writings such as *The Book of the Gentile and the Three Wise Men*, which adopts a general rational defense of Christianity while being attentive toward the beliefs of specific audiences—such as Muslims.

Although the rise of "Christendom" as a settled Christian region in Europe diminished the role of apologetics, it is clear that some significant writers of the medieval period recognized the need for the effective and persuasive presentation of Christian ideas across religious and cultural boundaries—a task that remains important to this day.

JOHN OF DAMASCUS

Preparing Christians for the Coming Age of Islam

DANIEL J. JANOSIK

John of Damascus (675–749) played a significant role in apologetics to the Muslims because of his unique position as a Christian in the court of the caliph, Abd al-Malik. His testimony as an involved observer not only gives an insider's view of the development of Islamic theology but also provides insight into the Christian-Muslim debates that took place in the first one hundred years of Islam.[1] Reflections from his life and his writings show the perspectives of early Christians toward Muhammad, the Qur'an, and Islam. As one of the first major theologians to confront the "heresy of the Ishmaelites," John believed it was his duty to protect believers from what he viewed as false beliefs.[2] His apologetic approach, as an extension of his theology, was first to instruct Christians in orthodox beliefs and second to provide a model for defending their beliefs and refuting the false doctrine of others.

HISTORICAL BACKGROUND

The year of John's birth is significant because it is tied to whom he may have known and what he might have witnessed. Most scholars place his year of birth in either 674 or 675,[3] and the traditional date of his death is December 4, 749.[4]

---

1. See Daniel J. Janosik, *John of Damascus: First Apologist to the Muslims, The Trinity and Christian Apologetics in the Early Islamic Period* (Eugene, OR: Pickwick, 2016), 201–02.

2. Andrew Louth, *St. John Damascene: Tradition and Originality in Byzantine Theology* (Oxford: Oxford University Press, 2002), 77. Sidney Griffith points out that Anastasios in the 690s, as did John at a later time, also considered Islam as a kind of Christian heresy: Sidney Griffith, *The Church in the Shadow of the Mosque* (Princeton: Princeton University Press, 2008), 31–32.

3. Daniel Sahas, "John of Damascus on Islam. Revisited." *Abr-Nahvain* 23 (1984): 106. Robert Hoyland, *Seeing Islam as Others Saw It: A Survey and Evaluation of Christian, Jewish, and Zoroastrian Writings on Early Islam* (Princeton, NJ: Darwin, 1997), 482.

4. Frederic Chase, *St. John of Damascus: Writings*, The Fathers of the Church: Vol. 37 (Washington, DC: The Catholic University of America Press, 1958), xvii, n. 32. See also, Ernest Simmons, *The Fathers and Doctors of the Church* (Milwaukee: Bruce, 1959), 96.

Thus, John's life would have spanned a seventy-five year period that included the following Umayyad caliphs: Mu'awiyah I (661–680), Yazid I (680–683), Mu'awiyah II (683), Marwan I (684), 'Abd al-Malik (685–705), al-Walid I (705–715), and possibly up through Sulayman ibn Abd al-Malik (715–717) and Umar II (717–720).[5]

John of Damascus's grandfather, Mansur ibn Sarjun, was the financial governor of Damascus when the Arabs besieged the city in 635.[6] After six months, he apparently capitulated to the Arab leader, Khalid b. al-Walid, yielding the city after receiving favorable terms of surrender.[7] Since all Syrian financial transactions were under the Greek Byzantine system, John's grandfather not only retained his position as *"logothetes,"*[8] a position that implied the collection of land taxes, but was also able to pass the position on to John's father, Sargun b. Mansur (or Sergius). It then was handed on to John during the caliphate of 'Abd al-Malik (685–705),[9] who apparently was a good friend of John's father.[10]

John's family was probably Semitic, and "Mansur" most likely means "victorious,"[11] though other renderings are "ransomed"[12] or "saved."[13] John was known to the Arabs as Mansur ibn Sarjun, though in his later life, he was also known as Yuhanna b. Mansur b. Sarjun.[14] To the Christians, John was known by his Christian name and place of origin: John of Damascus or John Damascene.[15] Theophanes (758–817), a Byzantine chronicler, referred to John of Damascus as the one "who has well been called 'Chrysorrhoas' because of the golden grace of the Spirit that is reflected in his speech."[16] John's facility with Greek verse

    5. Ibn Warraq, *The Quest for the Historical Muhammad* (New York: Prometheus, 2000), 550.
    6. Hoyland, *Seeing Islam as Others Saw It*, 480.
    7. Daniel Sahas, *John of Damascus on Islam* (Leiden: Brill, 1972), 17–19.
    8. "Originally, logothetes were accountants. As Byzantine bureaucracy evolved and many Late-Roman offices disappeared during the crises of the seventh and eighth centuries, logothetes began to fill their functions, and the title came to mean 'minister.'" Harry Turtledove, trans., *The Chronicle of Theophanes* (Philadelphia: University of Pennsylvania Press, 1982), translator's note, 212.
    9. Sahas, *John of Damascus on Islam*, 26–29.
    10. Theophanes attests to this (Annus Mundi 6183 (Sept 1, 691—Aug 31, 692): "Abd al-Malik also sent orders to rebuild the temple at Mecca. He wanted to take way pillars from holy Gethsemane, but Sergios the son of Mansur (a Christian who was public finance minister and was very friendly with Abd al-Malik) and his co-leader of the Palestinian Christians, Patricius (surnamed Klausus), asked him not to do this, but to persuade Justinian through their request to send other columns in place of these. This was done." Turtledove, trans., *The Chronicle of Theophanes*, 64.
    11. Chase, *St. John of Damascus: Writings*, ix.
    12. Phillip Schaff, *History of the Christian Church*, vol. 4 (Grand Rapids: Eerdmans, 1910), 627.
    13. Sahas, *John of Damascus on Islam*, 5.
    14. Ibid., 8.
    15. Sahas, "John of Damascus on Islam. Revisited," 105.
    16. Minge, PG 94 (Paris 1860), 108.841A. Frederic Chase adds that the term *Chrysorrhoas* can be translated "golden-flowing" and probably refers to the name of the river that ran through Damascus (Chase, *St. John of Damascus: Writings*, xiv–xv). Louth gives a slightly different rendition of Theophanes's words, relating that Theophanes called him "John Chrysorrhoas ('flowing with gold'), 'because of the golden gleam of spiritual grace that bloomed both in his discourse and in his life'" (Louth, *St. John Damascene*, 6).

and prose shows that he had some type of classical education, and this clearly provided the foundation not only for his work as a "presbyter and monk"[17] but even more as one of the greatest writers of theology, poetry, and hymns in the Eastern Orthodox Church.[18] Frederic Chase, who translated John's *Fount of Knowledge*, says that John's understanding of classical Greek philosophy and science is amply demonstrated in his first portion of the *Fount of Knowledge*, a section known as the *Dialectica*, for it not only provides the "first example of a manual of philosophy especially composed as an aid to the study of theology" but "has remained to the present day indispensable for a proper understanding of Greek theology."[19] Chase also concludes that John's writings are "sufficient to show that his traditional reputation as an eloquent, learned, and devout preacher is fully justified."[20]

John grew up in the city of Damascus, which the Arabs conquered in AD 635.[21] Many Christians thought this invasion by the Arabs was punishment from the Lord for their unfaithfulness.[22] Some minority Christian sects, such as the Nestorians and the Monophysites, at first welcomed the change of leadership since it brought lower taxes and less persecution than they had experienced at the hands of their former Byzantine rulers. The Orthodox Melkite sect, to which John belonged, lost a great deal of influence but still retained some prominence because Byzantine Christians were needed to oversee economic policies and tax collection, which were still conducted in Greek. In AD 661 Damascus became the center of the Umayyad Empire, and it was there that John served as the *logothetes*, or chief tax collector.

As an administrative officer, theologian, and eyewitness observer, John was uniquely placed. J. W. Sweetman refers to this unique placement when he states that "perhaps no individual Christian thinker is so important in a comparative study of Islamic and Christian theology as John of Damascus."[23] Of John's influence on both the Christian and Islamic communities of his time, Daniel Sahas writes, "John of Damascus's short writings on Islam have had indeed a very long history, as well as a profound influence upon other Christian writers who dealt with or wrote about Islam. His exposition of Islam made Islam known to the

---

17. Turtledove, trans., *The Chronicle of Theophanes*, 100.
18. Louth, *St. John Damascene*, 13.
19. Chase, *St. John of Damascus: Writings*, xxviii.
20. Ibid., xv.
21. Fred Donner, *Early Islamic Conquests* (Princeton: Princeton University Press, 1981), 130–32.
22. Walter Emil Kaegi, "Initial Byzantine Reactions to the Arab Conquest," *Church History* 38, 2 (June 1969): 139–49.
23. J. W. Sweetman, *Islam and Christian Theology: A Study of the Interpretation of Theological Ideas in the Two Religions*, Part I: Vol. 1 (London: Origins Lutterworth Press, 1945), 63.

Christian community and, therefore made interfaith 'dialogue' part of the history and the development of Islam as well as of Christianity."[24]

John of Damascus, then, was a Christian theologian in dialogue with Islam, and through his writings, modern readers of his works may gain greater insight into the beginnings of Islam. In addition, careful students of John's work will gain a greater understanding of the role of apologetics in regard to theological preparation, the defense of the faith, and the refutation of what is considered to be in error.

THEOLOGICAL CONTEXT

John was of the Melkite tradition and was a supporter of the orthodoxy of the Byzantine king (which in Syriac is *malka*).[25] John is probably best known for his writings, which fall into three categories: theological exposition and defense of the Orthodox faith, sermons and homilies, and liturgical poetry and hymnody.[26] His work in theology, *De Fide Orthodoxa*, for example, was considered a type of *Summa Theologica*.[27] Over time, it became one of the standard theological texts for the Eastern Orthodox Church. John was also one of the "greatest liturgical poets" of the Church. Some of his hymns are still used today, and his poetry still graces the pages of Orthodox liturgy.[28] The works for which he was best known in his own lifetime were the three treatises against the iconoclastic Emperor Leo III (written between 726 and 730). The clear logic and force of John's arguments became widely known throughout the eastern world, and even today they are considered "such a complete defense of the veneration of sacred images based upon Scripture, tradition, and reason" that it would be hard to add anything to it.[29]

In defending the orthodox position, John apparently felt the need to summarize the doctrine of the Christian church up through the eighth century and then to develop an appropriate apologetic approach that would defend as well as refute. John's work in recontextualizing the doctrine of the Trinity in his defense of Christianity against Islam was significant in his own time, but it also

---

24. Sahas, "John of Damascus on Islam. Revisited," 114.

25. Louth, *St. John Damascene*, 12

26. Ibid., 9.

27. Sahas, *John of Damascus on Islam*, 53, Note 1. The purpose of John's theological compilation may have been to provide a summary of Christian theology from the previous seven centuries to provide Christians under the rule of Islam with a basis for their beliefs as well as an understanding of doctrines in contra-distinction to Islamic theology so that Christians would stand firm and not convert to Islam. See also Schaff, *History of the Christian Church*, vol. 4, 588, 635.

28. Ibid., 13.

29. Chase, *St. John of Damascus: Writings*, xiii.

had far-reaching effects on his successors. He systematically summarized Christian doctrine based on prior work done by theologians who were also apologists. In addition, he was the first major theologian to engage in a written apologetic against Islam. This resulted in two works specifically crafted to defend Christianity against what he referred to as the "heresy of the Ishmaelites."[30]

John Tolan, a historian of medieval religious and cultural relations, in his chapter on *Early Eastern Christian Reactions to Islam*, notes that the extant body of John's writings is over 1,500 pages. Surprisingly, only about twelve of those pages deal directly with Islam.[31] However, because of John's situation, it is possible that he wrote most of his works with Islam in mind.[32] Moreover, Tolan underscores the importance of this material when he proposes that these "dozen pages on Islam provide a key glimpse at the formation of an apologetic Christian response to Islam, and they were to be read and reread by scores of later Christian writers as they attempted to come to terms with Islam."[33] The text that contains this material on Islam is part of John's *Fount of Knowledge*, which he probably wrote in AD 743.[34] It is divided into three major sections: *The Philosophical Chapters*, *On Heresies*, and *Orthodox Faith*.[35] The *Philosophical Chapters*, also known as the *Dialectica*, consist of sixty-eight chapters and provide the philosophical and rational basis for John's theological work. These chapters systematically summarize the orthodox conclusions of the key theologians who lived before John, most notably the three Cappadocian Fathers: Gregory of Nazianzus, Gregory of Nyssa, and Basil the Great. His main concern in this section is that he would "destroy deceit and put falsehood to flight."[36] The falsehood that John refers to is found in the middle part, called *On Heresies* (*De Haeresibus*), and it is made up of one hundred chapters. Most of these short chapters on heresies are probably summaries of an earlier work that can be traced back to Epiphanius (fourth century), but the last three are probably written by John.[37] Of these three, the particular heresy that focuses on Islam is titled *Heresy*

---

30. Louth, *St. John Damascene*, 77. See also Andrew Saperstein, "Encounters with Islam," *Christian History & Biography* 94, (2007): https://christianhistoryinstitute.org/magazine/article/encounters-with-islam (accessed November 3, 2019). (Referring to John's works: *The Heresy of the Ishmaelites* and the *Disputation between a Christian and a Saracen*).

31. John Tolan, *Saracens: Islam in the Medieval European Imagination* (New York: Columbia University Press, 2002), 51.

32. Daniel J. Janosik, *John of Damascus: First Apologist to the Muslims*, 168–69.

33. Tolan, *Saracens*, 51.

34. Chase, *St. John of Damascus: Writings*, 3. The book was dedicated to Cosmas upon his installation as a bishop of Maiuma in AD 743. But Andrew Louth disputes this date and concludes that with the scant information we have, we will have to hold the date as questionable. (Cf., Louth, *St. John Damascene*, 33.)

35. The *Dialectica, de Haeresibus* and *De Fide Orthodoxa*.

36. Chase, *St. John of Damascus: Writings*, 6.

37. Ibid., xxxi. Chase refers to the chapters on the *Ishmaelites, the Iconoclasts and the Aposchistae*, a "sect which rejected the sacraments and the priesthood."

of the Ishmaelites, one of the primary names given to the Arabs who would later be called "Muslims."

The third part of John's *Fount of Knowledge* is titled *Orthodox Faith*. It consists of one hundred chapters divided into four books that follow the order of the Nicene Creed.[38] The first book deals with God in unity and Trinity, the second book deals with God's creation, the third book focuses on Christology, and the fourth book discusses a number of theological issues such as faith, baptism, the Eucharist, and the resurrection. Regarding *Orthodox Faith*, Chase writes that "the whole is a surprisingly successful synthesis of traditional Catholic teaching as handed down by the Greek Fathers and the ecumenical councils."[39]

While the book basically follows the order of the Nicene Creed, most of these core doctrines were the ones that the early Muslims challenged. Together with the way that John constructed the philosophical arguments in the *Dialectica* and the section on heretical views, it is very possible that he was consciously collecting the best of the philosophical, theological, and apologetic material to secure a foundation for the Christian church as it faced the new challenges of Islam.

This intentional focus may be seen in the way that John explored the doctrine of the Trinity. He not only brought together the best arguments from the previous eight centuries, but he also shaped his defense of the Triune God in such a way that his arguments could be fleshed out in his more popular-level apologetic works to counter the heretical views coming from Muslims. This focus also permeated some of his apologetic works against other non-Christian groups, such as the Manicheans, and may have served as proxy arguments against the heretical views of the Muslims. In this way, it may be said that much, if not all, of John's writings were a response to the growth of Islamic theology and hegemony. This was especially the case in some of his popular-level works.[40]

In his main treatise against Islam, *Heresy of the Ishmaelites*, John addressed the Saracens' denial of the divinity of Christ and their absolute rejection of the triune nature of God, which they considered the greatest of blasphemies. In his treatise the *Disputation between a Christian and a Saracen*, John used the Qur'an's acceptance of Jesus being the Word and Spirit of God to show a fatal flaw in Islamic theology. If Jesus was indeed the Word and Spirit of God, then he must also be eternal, since God would be incomplete without his Word and his Spirit. Therefore, Jesus must be as eternal as God, and since Saracens recognized only one God, Jesus must also be that one God. This argument was a favorite for Christian apologists for centuries, but the premises of this argument were

38. Chase, *St. John of Damascus: Writings*, xxxii.
39. Ibid., xxxiii.
40. Janosik, *John of Damascus*, 189.

based on John's foundational theological work formulated first in his book the *Orthodox Faith*. In fact, it is reasonable to conclude that the primary motivation for John to write his great theological works was because he realized that the new heresy of the Ishmaelites was a serious challenge to Christianity. Christians needed to have a firm theological foundation for defending their beliefs as well as refuting the errors presented to them by Islam. His apologetic treatises, then, were based on his theological works and written as practical ways to help Christians understand the specific threats of the new religion and provide arguments for the defense of the core doctrines of Christianity that were under attack.[41]

APOLOGETIC RESPONSE

John's main work regarding Islam was the *Heresy of the Ishmaelites*, written around AD 740.[42] It was the last entry in his section of one hundred heresies in the *Fount of Knowledge*. When John wrote his main work regarding Islam, the *Heresy of the Ishmaelites* (740), the Arab conquerors were not referred to as Muslims but rather Saracens, Hagarenes, or Ishmaelites.[43] John considered the religion of the Ishmaelites to be contrary to the Bible and a distortion of its truth. He also referred to it as "a strange admixture of twisted, erroneous beliefs coming from both Judaism and Christianity—in other words, a heresy."[44] This treatise indicates that John was familiar with some stories about Muhammad, whom he called a "false prophet," as well as some parts of the Qur'an (Surahs 2, 3, 4, and 5), though he never referred to the "writings" of Muhammad as the "Qur'an." Throughout the six pages or so of his treatise, John raised relevant questions and tried to give convincing theological answers. However, his main concern seems to have been a desire to equip his fellow Christians with an understanding of the erroneous Muslim beliefs so they could prepare a ready defense of the Christian faith.

DISPUTATION BETWEEN A CHRISTIAN AND A SARACEN

The *Disputation between a Christian and a Saracen* was probably intended as a training manual for Christian apologetics and was primarily written to help Christians answer the theological questions that the Saracens were raising.[45] As a

---

41. Ibid., 191.
42. Ibid., 92, 251.
43. Ibid., 98.
44. Ibid., 99. See also Sahas, "John of Damascus on Islam. Revisited," 112–14.
45. Cf. Douglas Pratt, *The Challenge of Islam: Encounters in Interfaith Dialogue* (Burlington, VT: Ashgate, 2005), 103–04. This also shows that if the author is indeed John, then he was familiar with the issues that were currently being debated in the middle of the eighth century.

high-ranking civil servant in the court of the caliph, John was aware that the Muslims were already applying considerable political and economic pressure on Christians to accept the new religio-political policies. Thus, this dialogue may have been written to Christians so that they would not succumb to the religious demands of the new Arab regime. Daniel Sahas confirms that "the *Disputatio* is a kind of manual for a dialectic confrontation of a Christian with a Muslim."[46] He goes on to say, "This short treatise is a valuable source of information about the earliest stage of Muslim-Christian dialogue, of the development of Muslim theology and the theological inquiries and divisions inside the Muslim community."[47] The dialogues reveal that the author had insight into the development of the new religion, an awareness of the theological challenges, and a concern for Christians' preparedness in defending their beliefs against these insurgent religious ideas.

APOLOGETIC APPROACH TO ISLAM

John's two works on Islam, the *Heresy of the Ishmaelites* and the *Disputation between a Christian and a Saracen*, highlighted the dangers of Islam's teachings, showed the rational basis of Christianity, and provided a model for refuting Islam's theological challenges.

John's grandfather, Mansur ibn Sarjun, ruled over the city of Damascus when it was a leading center of the Byzantine Christian empire. However, John grew up knowing only the ever-increasing domination of Islam and the diminishing influence of Christianity. No doubt he would have heard many stories from his father and grandfather concerning the "good old days," as well as the lament from other Christians who viewed the Muslim conquests as a punishment for their sins and their lack of following Christ.[48] As the Arabs first took control of Palestine and Syria, the Jews, as well as the Nestorians and Jacobites, seemed to fare better under Saracen rule than under Byzantine rule, which favored the Orthodox Melkites. However, after a time, they realized that the new regime was becoming increasingly hostile to any form of belief system other than its own.[49] As the pressure and persecution grew, more Christians succumbed to the call of Islam and followed the path of the new religion. As the number of conversions increased, John recognized the need to stem this flow of Christians converting

---

46. Sahas, *John of Damascus on Islam*, 121.
47. Ibid., 121.
48. Kaegi, "Initial Byzantine Reactions to the Arab Conquest," 139–49. See also Abdul-Massih Saadi, "Nascent Islam in the Seventh Century Syriac Sources," chap. in *The Qur'ān in Its Historical Context*, Gabriel Reynolds, ed., Routledge Studies in the Qur'ān (London: Routledge, 2008), 219.
49. John Lamoreaux, "Early Eastern Christian Responses to Islam," chap. in John Tolan, *Medieval Christian Perceptions of Islam: A Book of Essays* (New York: Garland, 1996), 3–31.

to Islam. If this assessment is accurate, then he would have written his dialogues to highlight the dangers of Islam's teachings and show how Christians could give reasonable responses to the theological issues the Saracens raised.

One of the concerns in developing an adequate apologetic approach with Islam is that amid a number of common elements, there are also many differences between the two belief systems. Norman Daniel wrote, in regard to Christianity and Islam, "There are irreducible differences between non-negotiable doctrines. . . . The Christian creeds and the Qur'ān are simply incompatible and there is no possibility of reconciling the content of the two faiths, each of which is exclusive, as long as they retain their identities."[50]

John understood these irreconcilable differences. Therefore, to provide Christians with a rational basis of their own beliefs, as well as a way to contrast what he considered the heresy of the Saracen beliefs, it is reasonable to assume that he developed his extensive work on Christian doctrine in his theological book, the *Fount of Knowledge*, to provide a foundation for his apologetics. The Christians could then use this knowledge to make a reasonable defense of their faith when they were tempted to convert to Islam or were confronted with Islamic doctrine.

Second, in his two treatises on Islam, John developed a model for refuting Islam's theological challenges which provided Christians with an understanding of Islamic beliefs so that they would recognize the false teaching, reject the heresy, and regain their hope and trust in the God of the Bible. With this background in mind, John's apologetic approach can be categorized under the three terms: understand, defend, and refute. First, John states what the Ishmaelites believe and compares this with Christianity. He then defends the Christian beliefs with Scripture and doctrine, as well as a defense guided by reason. Finally, he refutes the Muslim beliefs and even argues that they are inferior and irrational in comparison to Christian doctrine. John's audience is mostly Christian, so his goal in this approach is to promote orthodox Christian belief in his Christian readers rather than offering detailed arguments against the new "heresy," though he is interested in countering what he considers to be a false belief system.

APOLOGETIC METHODOLOGY

FIRST STEP: UNDERSTAND

John's position as a respected civil servant in the Umayyad Caliphate would have given him privileged access to the leaders in the government as well

---

50. Norman Daniel, *Islam and the West* (Oxford: Oneworld, 1993), 335–36.

as opportunities to engage the theologians in dialogue. In this regard, Robert Hoyland affirmed that John was "well informed" about the "Islam" of his day, and noted that John's arguments in *Heresy of the Ishmaelites* dealt knowledgably with subjects such as "Christology, Muhammad's prophethood and scripture, worship of the cross, . . . Muslim licentiousness, . . . and the description of paradise."[51] This firsthand knowledge fit in well with the first step in his apologetic approach, which was to gather and learn as much as possible about the beliefs and traditions of the group that he was assessing and then pass this on to his Christian readers.

In the *Heresy of the Ishmaelites*, we see some traditions of the developing religion that came to be known as Islam. These are the practices and disputes that John would want to share with fellow Christians so that they would better understand Muslim beliefs. First, John explained that the Ishmaelites worshiped one God and claimed to be within the tradition of religions that looked back to Abraham as their spiritual father. They believed that Muhammad was a prophet in this same tradition and that he was chosen to reveal the final revelation from God. John is aware of at least parts of this revelation in written form since he refers to the "writings" that came down to Muhammad. However, he references only a few of the verses that come mostly from the later Medinan Sūrahs, which tend to deal with administrative, theological, and legal matters (Sūrahs 2–5, and perhaps Sūrahs 112 and 19). John was familiar with some narrative information about Mary, the mother of Jesus, as well as about Jesus. He understood that the Ishmaelites believed that Christ was created in the womb by God and born to a virgin, but he also recognized that they believed Jesus to be only a created being, a servant of God and not divine. In addition, he was aware of the verse that states that Jesus was not crucified, but rather he was taken by God to heaven, where he denied that he was the "Son of God and God" (Q. 5:116–117).

In response to verses such as this, John's strongest critique focused on the passage of Islamic writing that deals with Jesus Christ as God's Word and Spirit (Q. 4:169, 171). The Ishmaelites were adamant that Jesus could not be God. The presence of this particular dialogue with the Saracens may reflect the years of John's witness to his Saracen employers and their rejection of his beliefs. Andrew Louth acknowledges that these comments may represent actual conversations that John may have had and states, "Given that these are issues that engaged his Muslim contemporaries, and the fact that John at one point seeks to respond to problems raised by the Christian doctrine of the Trinity, one might conjecture that this dialogue was indeed a rhetorical exercise, composed when John was in

---

51. Hoyland, *Seeing Islam as Others Saw It*, 488.

contact with Muslims, with his ears full of their debates and their taunts against Christianity."[52]

There are a number of other important aspects of Islam that John would want Christians to understand. At one point, John mentions that Muhammad "composed many absurd stories and gave a title to each one."[53] John mentions four of these titles, the book on *The Woman*, the book of *The Table*, the book of *The Heifer*, and one that is not in the Qur'an, the book of *The Camel of God*. The fact that these were specified as separate books may indicate that the Qur'an had not yet been compiled in book form at this time. At the least, this verifies that John was aware of scriptures of some sort and that they were in a written form. From the book on *The Woman*, John recounts that there is legal provision for a man to take up to four wives and up to a thousand concubines. He is also aware of some of the relatively simple divorce and marriage procedures that contrast greatly with the intent of Christian marital practices.

John concludes with a list of practices that Muhammad apparently ordered Muslims to follow: circumcision for men and women, regulations on what to eat or not to eat, refraining from keeping the Sabbath and from being baptized, and forbidding the drinking of wine.[54] These things were written to inform Christians of the practices of the Ishmaelites—especially to show how inferior the practices were in comparison to Christianity.

In his dialogues, John reveals that quite a bit was known about this new heresy. Through his theological works, such as *Orthodox Faith*, John informed Christians of the foundational doctrines of Christianity. Together, these two pathways of understanding provided knowledge of the differences between the two religions so that Christians would be able to make informed choices and to also stand firm in their own faith. Thus, understanding both sides provided the foundation so that a better defense could be made of the gospel.

SECOND STEP: DEFEND

The second step in John's apologetic approach was designed to help Christians defend their beliefs by providing answers to objections that were commonly raised, as well as giving a defense of the reasonableness of Christianity in contrast to Islam. This is where the dialogue format offered a superior way for Christians to defend their beliefs within a framework of logic and sound theology.

52. Louth, *St. John Damascene*, 71.
53. Janosik, *John of Damascus*, HER, 95–96 (author's translation of John of Damascus, *Heresy of the Ishmaelites*, lines 95–96), 260–68, translated from the Greek text from the critical edition compiled by Bonifatius Kotter, *Die Schriften Des Johannes Von Damaskos*, IV (New York: De Gruyter, 1981).
54. HER, 153–156.

The dialogues also offered a way that John could control the content and raise the issues that would provide answers to the questions that Saracens were asking Christians. These questions dealt with core issues of Christian doctrine, such as the Trinity, the deity of Christ, the crucifixion, the trustworthiness of the New Testament, and a number of other important beliefs. Through these dialogues, John was able to model not only ways that Christians could answer questions in defense of their faith but also ways to ask questions that would reveal the illogical and heretical beliefs of the Saracens. For example, in the *Heresy of the Ishmaelites*, John first deals with the origin of the "heresy" and states that it is a forerunner of the Antichrist, developed by a false prophet named "Mamed," who misunderstood the truth of the Old and New Testaments and instead led his people astray with "heretical pronouncements . . . worthy of laughter."[55]

His reference to biblical themes such as the "Antichrist" and "false prophets" allowed John to highlight the errors of Islam in key theological areas. He was then able to defend Christianity and raise the status of the Bible by contrasting it with the writings of the Ishmaelites to reveal the deficiencies of what he called a "heresy." In addition, the reference to the Antichrist may have alerted the Christians of his time to the dangers of these new beliefs, since there seemed to be a heightened interest in the end times, and apocalyptic teaching was widespread.[56] In this context, John could then condemn Muhammad as one of the false prophets that Jesus said would appear and deceive the people during the last days (Matt 24:11). John builds on history and on the authority of the Bible to refute the prophethood of Muhammad. He shows that God publicly validated the prophethood of Moses, and just as all the rest of the biblical prophets did, he "foretold the coming of Christ."[57] However, Muhammad and the Saracens denied the incarnation, the deity of Christ, and the crucifixion as well. Therefore, these were areas that Christians needed to defend. Thus, in the dialogue, when John related that Muhammad had claimed that God had "neither been begotten nor has begotten,"[58] John asked the Saracen how his prophet could be from God if his message contradicted the earlier prophecy. The Saracen, not having an answer, can offer only that "God does as he pleases."[59] John then points out to his readers that the Qur'an not only denies the deity of Jesus but also seems to deny that Jesus was crucified by the Jews, or the Romans, at all,

---

55. HER, 10–16.
56. Jonathan P. Berkey, *The Formation of Islam: Religion and Society in the Near East, 600–1800* (Cambridge: Cambridge University Press, 2003), 98.
57. HER, 38–41.
58. HER, 17–18.
59. HER, 46.

and even suggests that God instead raised Jesus into heaven without his ever having experienced death (Q. 4:157).[60] However, without the crucifixion of Jesus and his subsequent resurrection, hope in eternal life would be futile for a Christian.

Throughout the dialogue, John made the Christian position seem much stronger than the Saracen one, but judging by how subsequent apologists used them, they were also effective for giving the Christian reader courage to engage in similar dialogues and even to ask some of the same questions. For example, one of John's strongest arguments against the Saracens, which later apologists often used, involved the nature of Jesus Christ. Christians were called "associators" by the Saracens because Christians were said to associate Christ with God, which was an abomination for the Saracens. John addresses these objections by developing a logical argument used by Christian apologists for centuries afterward. John asked, If the Saracens call Christ the "Word" and "Spirit" of God (Q. 4:171), then why do they accuse the Christians of being associators? The Word of God and the Spirit of God are inseparable from God, John maintains, and therefore the "Word of God is in God" and must be God. If the Word and the Spirit were outside of God, then "God is without Word and Spirit," and this would be impossible.[61] Consequently, John continues, the Saracens have mutilated God by tearing out his Word and Spirit, and John calls them "mutilators of God."[62] John concludes his argument by saying that "it would be far better for you to say that He had a partner, rather than mutilate Him."[63]

Arguments such as these were mostly developed for building up the faith of Christian believers and not necessarily for the conversion of Muslims. The pattern of presenting the Muslim claim and then having the Christian respond in defense of the truth of Christian doctrine represents one of the main purposes of apologetics, which is to educate Christians so that they not only understand the beliefs of other religions but also have a much better understanding of their own beliefs. This certainly seems to be one of the main goals expressed in John's writings and his apologetic approach.

THIRD STEP: REFUTE

In the third step of John's apologetic approach, he refutes the accusations of the Saracens to show that the beliefs of Christians are more logical. He also

---

60. HER, 22–25.
61. HER, 71–73.
62. HER, 77.
63. HER, 74–75.

uses ridicule to show how the Saracen beliefs are not even worthy of being followed. To set up this part of the dialogue, John has the Saracen ask questions that challenge Christian beliefs or accuse Christians of error. He then portrays Christians as skilled apologists who demand evidence and eyewitness accounts, rely on the OT prophecies and argue from the prophets, and know enough about Saracen writings to point out heretical statements. This technique was helpful because it allowed the Christian to refute the Saracen through logic, common sense, and even Scripture. For example, when the Saracen accused the Christian of polytheism for believing in three gods, John used logic and Scripture to develop the argument previously explained regarding "associators" and "mutilators" in regard to the Word of God and the Spirit of God. Since he was able to thereby show that even the book supposedly revealed to Muhammad could not match the established word of God found in the Old and New Testaments, he was able to argue persuasively for the superiority of Christianity. If his goal had been to create an aversion to the Saracen beliefs among his Christian readers through logical arguments as well as ridicule, then it seems that he accomplished that purpose as well. However, if John's desire was also to inform his Christian audience of the main teachings of the Saracen beliefs to prevent Christians from converting, then these aspirations too were achieved. Ultimately, John provided his readers with crucial information on the beliefs and practices of his opponents so that Christians would be able to refute error and defend their faith.

CONTRIBUTIONS TO THE FIELD OF APOLOGETICS

John lived through the coming of age of Islam. During his time in the court of the caliph, John witnessed the control of Damascus passing from Christian hands into the grip of the Saracens (Muslims). He saw veneration of Muhammad replacing faith in Jesus Christ, and he experienced the passing of religious authority from the Bible to the Qur'an. He also bore witness to the martyrdom of those who refused to submit to the new regime.

Given John's position during such a theological maelstrom, it is conceivable that these experiences impelled him to prepare fellow Christians to stand firmly against the growth of Islamic theology and hegemony. To build up Christians' knowledge of their own faith, John compiled a summary of the major doctrines of the church from the first century up to his own. This early *Summa Theologica* provided the foundation for a solid understanding of the intricacies and the depth of the doctrines of the church.

In addition, to help Christians understand the beliefs of the Saracens, John constructed a series of dialogues, in which the main beliefs and practices of the Saracens were introduced and critiqued. This provided Christians with an understanding of what John called "the heresy of the Ishmaelites." It was important for Christians to have an understanding so that they would not be drawn over to Islam or weakened in their own beliefs.

John taught the Christians of his time to first understand their own faith so that they could better understand the beliefs of their opponents. He then trained them to point out the weaknesses of the other side and promote the strengths of their own arguments. Even today, through his writings, this unpretentious priest and monk reaches across time with his three-corded approach to help Christians understand, defend, and refute.

BIBLIOGRAPHY

Primary Texts and Translations

Chase, Frederic H., trans. *St. John of Damascus: Writings*. Vol. 37 of *The Fathers of the Church*. Washington, DC: The Catholic University of America Press, 1958.

Janosik, Daniel. *John of Damascus, First Apologist to the Muslims, The Trinity and Christian Apologetics in the Early Islamic Period*. Eugene, OR: Pickwick, 2016. Trans. of *The Heresy of the Ishmaelites* (Appendix C, 260–68), and the *Disputation between a Christian and a Saracen* (Appendix D, 269–76).

John of Damascus. *Disputation between a Christian and a Saracen*. Found in Bonifatius Kotter, *Die Schriften Des Johannes Von Damaskos*, IV. New York: De Gruyter, 1981.

———. *Heresy of the Ishmaelites*. Found in Bonifatius Kotter, *Die Schriften Des Johannes Von Damaskos*, IV. New York: Walter De Gruyter, 1981.

Secondary Sources

Armour, Rollin. *Islam, Christianity, and the West: A Troubled History*. New York: Orbis, 2002.

Berkey, Jonathan P. *The Formation of Islam: Religion and Society in the Near East, 600–1800*. Cambridge: Cambridge University Press, 2003.

Daniel, Norman. *Islam and the West*. Oxford: OneWorld, 1993.

Donner, Fred. *Early Islamic Conquests*. Princeton: Princeton University Press, 1981.

Griffith, Sidney. *The Church in the Shadow of the Mosque*. Princeton: Princeton University Press, 2008.

Hoyland, Robert. *Seeing Islam As Others Saw It: A Survey and Evaluation of Christian, Jewish, and Zoroastrian Writings on Early Islam*. Princeton: Darwin, 1997.

Janosik, Daniel. *John of Damascus, First Apologist to the Muslims, The Trinity and Christian Apologetics in the Early Islamic Period*. Eugene, OR: Pickwick, 2016.

Kaegi, Walter Emil. "Initial Byzantine Reactions to the Arab Conquest." *Church History* (American Society of Church History) 38, 2 (June 1969): 139–49.

Kotter, Bonifatius. *Die Schriften Des Johannes Von Damaskos*. II. New York: De Gruyter, 1973.

———. *Die Schriften Des Johannes Von Damaskos*. IV. New York: De Gruyter, 1981.

Lamoreaux, John. "Early Eastern Christian Responses to Islam." Pages 3–31 in *Medieval Christian Perceptions of Islam: A Book of Essays*. Ed. by John Tolan. New York: Garland, 1996.

Le Coz, Raymond. *Jean Damascene: Ecrits Sur L'Islam*. No. 383. Sources Chretiennes. Paris: Les Editions du Cerf, 1992.

Louth, Andrew. *St. John Damascene: Tradition and Originality in Byzantine Theology*. Oxford: Oxford University Press, 2002.

Pratt, Douglas. *The Challenge of Islam: Encounters in Interfaith Dialogue*. Burlington, VT: Ashgate, 2005.

Sahas, Daniel. *John of Damascus on Islam*. Leiden: Brill, 1972.

―――. "John of Damascus on Islam. Revisited." *Abr-Nahrain* 23 (1984): 104–18.

Saperstein, Andrew. "Encounters with Islam." *Christian History & Biography*, Issue 94 (2007), https://chris tianhistoryinstitute.org/magazine/article/encounters-with-islam.

Schaff, Philip. *History of the Christian Church*, Vol. 4. Grand Rapids: Eerdmans, 1910.

Sweetman, J. W. *Islam and Christian Theology: A Study of the Interpretation of Theological Ideas in the Two Religions.* Part I: Vol. I. London: Lutterworth, 1955.

Tolan, John. *Saracens: Islam in the Medieval European Imagination.* New York: Columbia University Press, 2002.

Turtledove, Harry, trans. *The Chronicle of Theophanes.* Philadelphia: University of Pennsylvania Press, 1982.

Warraq, Ibn. *The Quest for the Historical Muhammad.* New York: Prometheus, 2000.

THEODORE ABU QURRAH

Defending Christian Doctrines during the Rise of Islam

BYARD BENNETT

Theodore Abu Qurrah (ca. 750–ca. 820) was one of the earliest Christian theologians to write in the Arabic language. His works offered a thoughtful and nuanced response to Muslim criticisms of the Christian faith and helped shape the later trajectory of Christian-Muslim dialogue. Responding to Muslim objections to the Trinity, the incarnation, and Christ's atoning work on the cross, Theodore defended the divinity of the Son and showed that it was necessary for the Son to become incarnate if human beings were to be freed from their sins.

HISTORICAL BACKGROUND

Theodore seems to have been born in Edessa in northern Syria in the second half of the eighth century AD.[1] Theodore served as the Melkite (Chalcedonian) bishop of Harran and was active in the second decade of the ninth century AD. The city of Harran was located about thirty miles southeast of Edessa and had a religiously diverse population that included pagans, Jews, Muslims, and various Christian communities.[2] In the ninth century, members of these religiously

---

1. For a discussion of what little is known about Theodore's life, see John C. Lamoreaux, *Theodore Abū Qurrah* (Provo, UT: Brigham Young University Press, 2005), xiii-xviii. For detailed bibliographies relating to Theodore's life and works, see Samir Khalil Samir, *Abū Qurrah. Vida, bibliografía y obras*, trans. Juan Pedro Monferrer Sala (Córdoba: Universidad de Córdoba, 2005); David Thomas and Barbara Roggema, eds. *Christian-Muslim Relations: A Bibliographical History. Volume 1 (600–900)* (Leiden: Brill, 2009), 439–91.

2. On the religious situation in Harran, see Tamara M. Green, *The City of the Moon God: Religious Traditions of Harran* (Leiden: Brill, 1992); Jürgen Tubach, *Im Schatten des Sonnengottes: der Sonnenkult in*

Image: Arabic page from Theodore Abu Qurrah

diverse communities began to shift toward using Arabic as a common language to express and communicate theological and philosophical ideas.

CULTURAL AND THEOLOGICAL CONTEXT

Syria had been a part of the Byzantine Empire prior to the Islamic conquest in AD 634–638. After the conquest, the Muslim rulers of the Umayyad Caliphate (AD 661–750) were primarily interested in conducting further military expeditions to expand the territory they controlled. The administrative system inherited from the Byzantine Empire remained in place, and Christians continued to hold government positions. During this period, Muslim rulers seem to have had a limited understanding of the religion of their Christian subjects. Although the Umayyad rulers imposed certain restrictions on non-Muslims, Christians were often allowed to retain possession of their churches, provided that they paid the tax (*jizya*) levied on non-Muslims.[3]

The rise of the 'Abbasid Caliphate (AD 750–1258) changed the conditions under which Christians lived in the Middle East. Between the second half of the eighth century and the tenth century, Arabic increasingly became the language of public discourse; members of non-Arab groups began to speak Arabic so that they could engage in commercial transactions, interact with the changing administrative structures of the civil government, and participate in broader intellectual discussions. The rapid development of Islamic theology in the ninth century was accompanied by the production of polemical treatises in which Muslim theologians attacked Christian beliefs as being irrational and contrary to the true faith.[4] By the middle of the ninth century, Christians also became subject to increasing restrictions under the caliph al-Mutawakkil (847–861). As a result of Arabization and the changing political situation, urban public spaces and intellectual discourse were increasingly defined by Islamic culture, with a corresponding gradual conversion of formerly Christian peoples to Islam.[5]

Edessa, Ḥarrān und Ḥaṭrā am Vorabend der christlichen Mission (Wiesbaden: Harrassowitz, 1986); Jan Hjärpe, *Analyse critique des traditions arabes sur les sabéens ḥarraniens* (Uppsala: Skriv Service AB, 1972).

3. The Qur'an (*Al-Tawbah*, 9:29) commended the payment of *jizya* by non-Muslims living under Muslim domination.

4. See Ali Bouamama, *La littérature polémique musulmane contre le christianisme depuis ses origines jusqu'au XIIIe siècle* (Algiers: Entreprise Nationale du Livre, 1988); David Thomas, *Anti-Christian Polemic in Early Islam: Abū 'Isā al-Warrāq's "Against the Trinity"* (Cambridge: Cambridge University Press, 1992); David Thomas, *Early Muslim Polemic Against Christianity: Abū 'Isā al-Warrāq's "Against the Incarnation"* (Cambridge: Cambridge University Press, 2002).

5. Conversions from Islam to Christianity also occurred throughout this period, though in much smaller numbers due to severe sanctions against apostasy from Islam; see Christian C. Sahner, "Swimming against the Current: Muslim Conversion to Christianity in the Early Islamic Period," *Journal of the American Oriental Society* 136 (2016): 265–84.

Christians living under Islamic rule struggled to adapt to these changes. First it became necessary to find ways to express Christian concepts in Arabic and then to translate a vast number of texts (the Bible, liturgical texts, homilies, theological treatises, and documents relating to church councils) from Greek and Syriac into Arabic.[6] Since Islamic religious culture increasingly shaped public discourse, Christians writing for a broader audience had to take account of Qur'anic phraseology and Islamic patterns of thought while avoiding language that would be perceived as antagonistic by Muslims.[7]

Christians' ability to adapt to these changed conditions was hindered by their division into three separate confessional groups— Melkite (Chalcedonian), West Syrian (Monophysite), and East Syrian ("Nestorian"/Church of the East).[8] After the Muslim conquest, no one Christian group could claim an official endorsement by the state; the division of Christians into separate, competing groups in fact facilitated Muslim rule over their disunited subjects. The division among Christians also made it difficult for them to maintain a united front in responding to increasingly aggressive Muslim criticisms of Christianity.[9]

These criticisms tended to center on two fundamental issues. First, the Qur'an affirmed that God must be distinguished from everything else and that he had no partner, nor could anything be associated with him.[10] To attribute offspring to God would associate God with human practices of begetting and would raise up another lord alongside him, which was incompatible with the Islamic understanding of monotheism.[11] Muslims therefore did not accept the Son as a second principle within the divine life and rejected the incarnation (i.e., that God had entered into Jesus in a unique way and fully and permanently indwells

6. See Sidney H. Griffith, *The Bible in Arabic: The Scriptures of the "People of the Book" in the Language of Islam* (Princeton: Princeton University Press, 2013); Kate Leeming, "The Adoption of Arabic as a Liturgical Language by the Palestinian Melkites," *ARAM Periodical* 15 (2003): 239–46; Alexander Treiger, "The Fathers in Arabic," in *The Wiley Blackwell Companion to Patristics*, ed. Ken Parry (Chichester, West Sussex: John Wiley & Sons, 2015), 442–55; Najib George Awad, *Orthodoxy in Arabic Terms: A Study of Theodore Abu Qurrah's Theology in Its Islamic Context* (Berlin: De Gruyter, 2016).

7. See Mark N. Swanson, "Apologetics, Catechesis, and the Question of Audience in 'On the Triune Nature of God' (Sinai Arabic 154) and Three Treatises of Theodore Abū Qurrah," in *Christians and Muslims in Dialogue in the Islamic Orient of the Middle Ages*, ed. Martin Tamcke (Beirut: Orient-Institut Beirut, 2007), 113–34. In his Arabic works, Theodore is normally careful not to directly identify his opponents. When he does identify his opponents, he often claims to be responding to Jewish criticisms of Christianity, though the context suggests that he also has Muslim opponents in view.

8. These three confessional groups emerged as a result of Christological controversies in the fifth century; by the sixth century, these groups had become separate institutional churches.

9. See Karl Piggéra, "Konfessionelle Rivalitäten in der Auseinandersetzung mit dem Islam. Beispiele aus der ostsyrischen Literatur," *Der Islam* 88 (2012): 51–72.

10. *Al-Nisā'* 4:48; *Al-Tawbah* 9:31.

11. *Al-Isrā'* 17:111; *Al-Furqan* 25:2; *Al-Nisā'* 4:171. See Mark Beaumont, *Christology in Dialogue with Muslims: A Critical Analysis of Christian Presentations of Christ for Muslims from the Ninth and Twentieth Centuries* (Carlisle: Paternoster, 2005), 8; Mark Beaumont, "Speaking of the Triune God: Christian Defence of the Trinity in the Early Islamic Period," *Transformation* 29 (2012): 111–12.

Jesus's humanity).[12] Second, Muslim polemicists argued that an incarnation was not necessary, for salvation was not accomplished by one human being for another.[13] Only the person who repented, believed in Allah and his messenger, and performed righteous deeds might hope to find mercy with God.[14] If Christians do not accept this view and offer a different account, Muslims argued, it is because the Christians have corrupted their Scriptures and do not understand their meaning.[15]

APOLOGETIC WORKS

Before discussing Theodore's arguments in defense of the faith, it will be helpful to briefly identify the major works in which Theodore sought to respond to Muslim criticism of Christian beliefs.[16] Constantin Bacha's 1904 edition of ten short Arabic treatises by Theodore stimulated scholarly interest in Theodore's Arabic writings.[17] Georg Graf published a German translation of these ten treatises in 1910.[18]

Even before Bacha's edition appeared, Johannes Arendzen had prepared an edition of an Arabic treatise by Theodore concerning the veneration of icons and published this with a Latin translation.[19] Arendzen's edition of the text was also

---

12. Cf. Qur'an, *Al-Mā'idah* 5:72.

13. See Steven J. McMichael, "The Death, Resurrection, and Ascension of Jesus in Medieval Christian Anti-Muslim Religious Polemics," *Islam and Christian-Muslim Relations* 21 (2010): 160.

14. Cf. Qur'an, *Al-Qaṣaṣ* 28:67.

15. On early Islamic discussions of the corruption of Scripture, see Ryan Schaffner, "The Bible Through a Qur'ānic Filter: Scripture Falsification (*Taḥrīf*) in 8th-and 9th-Century Muslim Disputational Literature" (PhD diss., Ohio State University, 2016); Mark Beaumont, "'Ammār al-Basrī on the Alleged Corruption of the Gospels", in *The Bible in Arab Christianity*, ed. David Thomas (Leiden: Brill, 2007), 241–55.

16. Some of Theodore's writings still remain unedited; for a description of the extant but unpublished works, see Georg Graf, *Geschichte der christlichen arabischen Literatur*, vol. 2 (Vatican City: Biblioteca Apostolica Vaticana, 1947), 15–16; Joseph Nasrallah, "Dialogue islamo-chrétien à propos de publications récentes," *Revue des études islamiques* 46 (1978): 129–32; Joseph Nasrallah, *Histoire du mouvement littéraire dans l'église melchite du Ve au XXe siècle: Contribution à l'étude de la littérature arabe chrétienne. Vol. II, Tome 2: 750-Xe S.* (Louvain: Peeters, 1988), 122–24; Samir Khalil Samir, "Al-jadīd fī sīrat Thāwudūrus Abī Qurra wa-āthārihi," *Al-Mashriq* 73 (1999): 417–49.

17. Constantin Bacha, *Les oeuvres arabes de Théodore Aboucara, évêque d'Haran=Mayāmir Thāwudūrus Abī Qurra usquf Ḥarrān* (Beirut: Maṭba'at al-fawā'id, 1904). In the following year, Bacha republished one of these treatises (*The Treatise on the Authority of the Law of Moses and of the Gospel*) with a French translation; see Bacha, *Un traité des oeuvres arabes de Théodore Abou-kurra, évêque d'Haran* (Tripoli: L'évêché grec-catholique, 1905).

18. Georg Graf, *Die arabischen Schriften des Theodor Abû Qurra, Bischofs von Ḥarrān (ca. 740–820)* (Paderborn: Ferdinand Schöningh, 1910), 88–277. Bacha and Graf used different schemes for numbering the treatises; for the relationship between the two numbering schemes, see Adel-Théodore Khoury, *Les théologiens byzantins et l'Islam. Textes et auteurs (VIIIe-XIIIe S.)* (Louvain: Nauwelaerts, 1969), 85 n. 10. When one of these ten treatises is cited below, after the title *Maymar* (Arabic for "treatise") the number in Bacha's edition will be given in Arabic numerals; the number in Graf's translation will then be given in Roman numerals. Theodore is particularly concerned to address Muslim objections in treatises 1 (IX), 2 (III), 7 (VII), and 10 (VI).

19. Johannes Arendzen, *Theodori Abū Ḳurrah De cultu imaginum libellus a codice Arabico nunc primum editus Latine versus illustratus* (Bonn: Drobnig, 1897).

translated into German by Graf.[20] After the publication of a new critical edition of the Arabic text by Ignace Dick in 1986, translations into Italian, English, Finnish, Romanian, and Spanish have also appeared.[21]

In 1912 Louis Cheikho produced an edition of the Arabic text of Theodore's longest and most systematic work, *The Treatise on the Existence of the Creator and the True Religion*.[22] Graf published a German translation of this work the following year.[23] Ignace Dick later produced a new edition of the Arabic text and a French translation.[24] In the last sixty years, Dick and other scholars have published editions of several minor works of Theodore.[25] John Lamoreaux has also recently published an English translation of selections from Theodore's writings.[26]

Theodore's works covered a wide variety of topics. These included not only a defense of Christian doctrines in response to Muslim criticism but also debates with non-Chalcedonian Christian theologians and a discussion of certain questions about free will that were of interest to contemporary Christian and Islamic philosophical writers.[27] Theodore may also have composed works in languages other than Arabic, since he refers to a treatise (now lost) that he produced in

20. Graf, *Die arabischen Schriften*, 278–333 (=*Maymar* XI).

21. Ignace Dick, *Théodore Abu Qurra: Traité du culte des icônes-Introduction et texte critique*, Patrimoine Arabe Chrétien 10 (Jounieh: Librairie Saint-Paul, 1986); Paola Pizzo, *Teodoro Abū Qurrah: La difesa delle icone. Trattato sulla venerazione delle immagini* (Milan: Jaca, 1995); Sidney H. Griffith, *Theodore Abū Qurrah: A Treatise on the Veneration of the Holy Icons* (Louvain: Peeters, 1997); Serafim Seppälä. *Theodoros Abu Qurra: Ikonien Kunnioittamisesta* (Helsinki: Maahenki, 2008); Lidia Rus, *Abu Qurra: Despre cinstirea Sfintelor Icoane* (Bucharest: Editura Univers Enciclopedic, 2012); Rocio Daga-Portillo, *Teodoro Abū Qurra: Tratado sobre la veneración de los iconos* (Granada: Nuevo Inicio, 2017).

22. For a brief description of this work and a detailed bibliography, see Thomas and Roggema, *Christian-Muslim Relations*, 448–50. For Louis Cheikho's edition of the Arabic text, see "Maymar li-Tādurus Abī Qurrah fi wujūd al-khāliq wa l-dīn al-qawīm," *Al-Mashriq* 15 (1912): 757–74, 825–42.

23. Georg Graf, *Des Theodor Abū Ḳurra Traktat über den Schöpfer und die wahre Religion* (Münster: Aschendorff, 1913).

24. Ignace Dick, "Théodore Abuqurra, évêque melkite de Harran (750?-825?); introduction générale, texte et analyse du *Traité de l'existence du Créateur et de la vraie religion*" (PhD diss., Université Catholique de Louvain, 1960). Dick's revised edition of the Arabic text was later published in *Théodore Abu Qurra: Traité de l'existence du Créateur et de la vraie religion-Introduction et texte critique*, Patrimoine Arabe Chrétien 3 (Jounieh: Librairie Saint-Paul, 1982). An unpublished English translation is given in George Hanna Khoury, "Theodore Abu Qurrah (c. 750–820): Translation and Critical Analysis of His 'Treatise on the Existence of the Creator and on the True Religion'" (PhD diss., Graduate Theological Union, 1990).

25. Ignace Dick, "Deux écrits inédits de Théodore Abuqurra," *Le Muséon* 72 (1959): 53–67; Sidney H. Griffith, "Some Unpublished Arabic Sayings Attributed to Theodore Abū Qurrah," *Le Muséon* 92 (1979): 29–35; John C. Lamoreaux, "An Unedited Tract Against the Armenians by Theodore Abū Qurrah," *Le Muséon* 105 (1992): 327–41; Alexander Treiger, "New Works by Theodore Abū Qurra Preserved under the Name of Thaddeus of Edessa," *Journal of Eastern Christian Studies* 68 (2016): 1–51.

26. Lamoreaux, *Theodore*.

27. On the christological debates with non-Chalcedonian theologians, see Sidney H. Griffith, "'Melkites', 'Jacobites' and the Christological Controversies in Arabic in Third/Ninth-Century Syria," in *Syrian Christians Under Islam. The First Thousand Years*, ed. David Thomas (Leiden: Brill, 2001), 32–53. For Theodore's discussion of free will, see Paola Pizzo and Samir Khalil Samir, *Teodoro Abū Qurra. Trattato sulla libertà* (Turin: Zamorani, 2001); Thomas and Roggema, *Christian-Muslim Relations*, 451–52.

Syriac.[28] A number of short works attributed to Theodore exist in Greek;[29] many of these works also appear in a Georgian translation.[30]

APOLOGETIC RESPONSE

Throughout his writings, Theodore argued that the differences between competing religions could be rationally adjudicated. By the careful use of reason, one may overcome doubt and arrive at certainty about what is right and just, discerning the religion by which God wishes to be worshiped.[31] Theodore begins his

---

28. See *Maymar* 3 (Bacha, 60,20) = VIII.21 (Graf, 212), where Theodore speaks of having composed thirty *mayāmir* "in Syriac, in praise of the position of [Chalcedonian] orthodoxy and the words [*Tome*] of the holy St. Leo, the bishop of Rome" (ET Lamoreaux, *Theodore*, 119). Lamoreaux follows Samir Khalil Samir ("Le traité sur les icônes d'Abū Qurrah mentionné par Eutychius," *Orientalia Christiana Periodica* 58 (1992): 469–72) in understanding the thirty *mayāmir* to be the thirty chapters within a single theological treatise, perhaps a doctrinal florilegium.

29. In 1606 the Jesuit theologian Jakob Gretser published an edition of forty-two Greek works attributed to Theodore; see Jakob Gretser, *Anastasii Sinaitae Patriarchae Antiocheni . . . Dux viae* (Ingolstadt: Adam Sartorius, 1606), 376–547. Gretser's edition included Latin translations previously made by scholars working from different Greek manuscripts; Gretser then supplied a corresponding Greek text for all but one of these works from a single sixteenth-century Greek manuscript that was available to him (Munich, Bayerische Staatsbibliothek, *gr.* 66). Migne (PG 97, 1461–1602) reproduced the forty-two works in Gretser's edition. Migne also added a further Greek treatise *De unione et incarnatione* (PG 97, 1601–10), which had previously been published with a Latin translation in Andreas Arnold, *S. Athanasii . . . Syntagma doctrinae* (Paris: Martin & Boudot, 1685), 56–81 and reproduced in Andreas Gallandi, *Bibliotheca veterum patrum*, vol. 13 (Venice: G.B. Albrizzi, 1779), 286–89. Graf (*Die arabischen Schriften*, 67–77) questioned the authenticity of many of the works that had been included in Gretser's edition and reproduced by Migne. A new edition of the Greek works attributed to Theodore and a German translation appeared in Reinhold Glei and Adel Theodor Khoury, *Johannes Damaskenos und Theodor Abū Qurra. Schriften zum Islam* (Würzburg: Echter Verlag, 1995), 86–165; from this new edition, a Dutch translation of Theodore's Greek works was prepared by Michiel Op de Coul and Marcel Poorthuis, *Johannes Damascenus & Theodorus Abū Qurra. De eerste christelijke polemiek met de Islam* (Zoetermeer: Meinema, 2011), 84–169. On the origin and transmission of the Greek works attributed to Theodore, see John C. Lamoreaux, "Theodore Abū Qurrah and John the Deacon," *Greek, Roman, and Byzantine Studies* 42 (2001): 361–86; Lamoreaux, *Theodore*, xxviii-xxx; Ina Süß, *Christus im Diskurs mit Muhammad. Das Ringen um religiöse Identität: Die Auseinandersetzung der syrischen Christen mit dem Islam anhand ausgewählter Texte des Johannes Damaskenos und des Theodor Abū Qurra* (Chemnitz: Universitätsverlag Chemnitz, 2015), 118–56.

30. On the translation of Theodore's works into Georgian, see Marie-Felicité Brosset, "Histoire et littérature de la Géorgie," *Recueil des Actes de la séance publique de l'Académie Impériale des Sciences de Saint-Pétersbourg* (St. Petersburg: n.p., 1838), 135–36; Gregor Peradze, "Die altchristliche Literatur in der georgischen Überlieferung," *Oriens Christianus* 30 (1933): 192–94; Graf, *Geschichte*, 20–21; Dick, *Traité*, 89–92; Ivane Lolašvili, *Arsen Iq'altoeli* (Tbilisi: Metsniereba, 1978), 112–13; Roussoudane Gvaramia, "Bibliographie du dialogue islamo–chrétien (auteurs chrétiens de langue géorgienne, VIIe–XIVe siècles)" *Islamochristiana* 6 (1980): 290–91; Michael Tarchnišvili, *Geschichte der kirchlichen georgischen Literatur* (Vatican City: Biblioteca Apostolica Vaticana, 1955), 129, 206, 208–9, 366, 370–71, 375, 380, 385. The works of Theodore that were translated from Greek into Georgian by Arsen Iq'altoeli († c. 1127) have been published by Leila Datiašvili, *Teodore Abuk'ura. T'rakt'at'ebi da dialogebi targmnili berdznulidan Arsen Iq'altoelis mier* (Tbilisi: Metsniereba, 1980), 24–115. It has been debated whether some of the Greek works ascribed to Theodore originated as translations from Georgian into Greek; see Graf, *Geschichte*, 21; Bernadette Martin-Hisard, "La *Vie de Jean et Euthyme* et le statut du monastère des Ibères sur l'Athos," *Revue des études byzantines* 49 (1991): 86; Annie Mahé and Jean-Pierre Mahé, *La sagesse de Balahvar. Une vie christianisée du Bouddha* (Paris: Éditions Gallimard, 1993), 26; Elguja Khintibidze, *Georgian Literature in European Scholarship* (Amsterdam: Adolf M. Hakkert and W. Kos, 2000), 17–18.

31. Cf. *Maymar* 2 (III) (ET Lamoreaux, *Theodore*, 192).

defense of the Christian faith by discussing the nature of reason and the criteria that should be used in discerning the true religion. Theodore then shows that it was both reasonable and necessary that God the Father should give life to the Son and share with him all things (every power and perfection, even his very being). Theodore next examines the reasons people may have for choosing a religion and notes that some of these reasons are unworthy and self-serving and lead one into error. Christianity, however, does not appeal to unworthy, self-serving motives. Instead, it presents a new way of life that is unfamiliar and requires self-denial; indeed, no one would embrace such a way of life unless they had seen the miracles done by Jesus's power, which compelled them to believe and to surrender themselves to God. Theodore concludes by showing that it was necessary for the Son of God to enter into a human life to bring about our salvation and that only by this means could God's love and justice both be preserved.

DISCERNING THE TRUE RELIGION

Given the fact of religious diversity, how was one to identify the true religion? Theodore explores this question in the second section of his *Treatise on the Existence of the Creator and the True Religion*.[32] Theodore invites the reader to join him in a thought experiment. He begins by imagining that he had grown up on a mountain where he knew no other people. When he descends to seek the company of others, he finds them to be divided into competing religions. Each group claims to have a prophet who spoke the truth about divine matters. Each group also warns Theodore not to pay attention to the claims made by any other religion, since other religions do not possess the truth.

The claims made by each religious group are similar in form, Theodore notes. Each group points to the action of God toward them, describing how God (or the gods) intervened for their people or performed miracles in their midst. Each group also refers to the benefits that will be received by those who follow the practices prescribed by their particular religion and the punishment that will be suffered by those who do not act in the required way.

Theodore compares this situation to that of a sick man who receives conflicting advice from others about what is healing and what is harmful. When confronted with a diversity of opinions, the mind must find criteria for deciding between competing accounts. Since human beings are created in the likeness of God, the mind must reason from what is highest and best in human nature to understand the character of God, who is the source of our life and

---

32. Dick, *Traité de l'existence*, 199–258. For an English translation of this section of the work, see Lamoreaux, *Theodore*, 1–25. A French translation and commentary are given in Guy Monnot, "Abū Qurra et la pluralité des religions," *Revue de l'histoire des religions* 208 (1991): 49–71.

our reason.[33] As the mind contemplates all that is virtuous in human life and finds the source of these virtues in different aspects of God's own goodness (God's attributes), one also gains a sense of what is truly good (and ought to be done) or evil (and ought to be avoided).

The greatest virtue, Theodore argues, is to give the best things one has to another so that the other can share in them and enjoy them.[34] The most important thing one can give to another is life itself, since, without life, virtuous activity is not possible; the virtues can be realized only in one who is living, not in one who is dead. Furthermore, it is better to give life to another who is the same type of being as oneself and is therefore able to be virtuous in the same way and to the same degree as oneself. This is precisely what we see in the order of nature: a man begets a son who is like him and shares in his nature and has the capacity for the same virtues.[35]

Since we are created in the likeness of God, our minds are capable of recognizing what is truly good; in the same way, we also have an instinctive sense of what is wrong and ought not to be done. When someone deceives us or harms us, we dislike this and regard it as evil. Since we have an instinctive sense of the harm done by evil, we should not treat another in a way that we ourselves would not wish to be treated. We should instead treat another person in the same way that we wished the other person to treat us.

Above all, Theodore argues, we wish to be treated with love, and we therefore ought to treat others in the same way. Love involves preferring another person to oneself and being willing to set aside one's own interests to help the other person. The highest form of love is that which extends itself to all people and wishes the best for them, regardless of their current moral condition. Rather than retaliating against those who treat us wrongly, we should instead treat them with kindness and wish for them to be changed for the better and to be

---

33. Cf. *Maymar* 5 (IV) (ET Lamoreaux, *Theodore*, 159–61). There is, of course, a difference between the way good things exist in God and the way good things exist in created beings. Good things exist in God in the best possible way, without any limit or qualification and without any possibility of corruption or loss. In created beings, however, good powers and virtuous qualities are present only in a limited and qualified way and can be corrupted and lost. For Theodore, the fact that goods exist only in a qualified, imperfect way in the created world shows that the source of these goods lies beyond this world, i.e., in a perfect being in whom every good exists in its original (i.e., fullest and purest) form.

34. This argument was later further developed by the Monophysite Christian theologian Yaḥyā ibn 'Adī († AD 974); see Samir Khalil Samir, "Christian Arabic Literature in the 'Abbasid Period," in *Religion, Learning and Science in the 'Abbasid Period*, eds. M. J. L. Young, J. D. Latham and R. B. Serjeant (Cambridge: Cambridge University Press, 1990), 454.

35. Theodore's arguments for the necessity and propriety of begetting within the divine life were criticized by the tenth-century Muslim theologian 'Abd al-Jabbār; the latter may have been drawing on an earlier work (now lost) by Abū Mūsā 'Īsā b. Ṣabīḥ al-Murdār († AD 841) entitled "Against Abū Qurrah the Christian." See Christian Boudignon, "Logique aristotélicienne et *kalām 'alā-l-naṣārā*: la réponse à Abū Qurra dans le *Mugnī* de 'Abd al-Ğabbār," *Arabica* 58 (2011): 519–44.

well. Rather than despising or hating another person, we should desire that they receive from God every good thing that a creature can have.

Theodore contends that when one examines the various religions, one can see that only Christianity offers guidance that conforms to the principles stated above. Christians believe that God, because he is supremely good, wished to give the best things he had to another. God did this by giving life to another who was like himself in every way, having the same nature and possessing every virtue and excellence that is proper to God. If God had not given life to one who was like himself but had only given life to lesser beings, God would be missing something that is good. Since even human fathers can give life to one who is like themselves and capable of sharing in the same virtues, God would be lacking a good that human fathers have, and thus God would be inferior to human fathers in this respect. Since, however, God lacks nothing that is good, he was pleased to give life to his Son and to share with him every good thing that he himself possesses.

When one compares the way of life that Christ commanded with the guidance given by other religions, one can see that Christ's teaching alone matches the rational principles discussed above. It was noted earlier that love is the greatest good and the best kind of love is one that extends to all people and seeks their good despite their past and present evils. Christ's teaching alone conforms to this principle, since he commanded his followers to love everyone, even their enemies, and to do them good (Luke 6:35). By acting in this way, Christ's followers showed that they were children of God, who makes his sun rise on both the evil and the good and sends his rain down on both the just and the unjust (Matt 5:45).

By contrast, Theodore observes, other religions teach that retaliation against others is justified. The desire for retaliation arises from a resentment one feels when one is deprived of certain pleasures. The force of this resentment leads one to respond in ways that are excessive and lack measure or restraint, rejecting the claims of both love and justice. To respond in this way is contrary to our nature and corrupts our nature. God, however, does not desire our nature's corruption but rather its goodness; God would never command things that degrade us and lead to condemnation.

That retaliation is an evil also becomes clear when the principle of discernment is considered: one should act in the way one wishes to be treated by others. No one would wish to have others retaliate against them. Why then, Theodore asks, should anyone think that it is good to retaliate against others? The final judgment, in any case, belongs not to human beings but to God, and what God requires is this: that one should believe in the Son and keep his commandments. This includes the commandment to love even one's enemies. In conclusion, then, the true religion is that which is characterized by the greatest other-regarding love, a love so universal that it extends to all people regardless of their current moral state, and it is God's self-revelation in Jesus Christ that best fulfills this requirement.

How People Choose Religions

If it is indeed possible for one to discern the true religion, why do so many other religions continue to exist? Theodore argues that people may choose a religion for a variety of reasons, not all of which are of equal value or in conformity with the truth.[36] For example, one might choose a religion because it is permissive in character and allows one to pursue things that one finds pleasing, such as ease, wealth, or sensual pleasures. One might also choose a religion because it allows one to gain power over others and fulfill one's ambitions. Other people might choose a religion based on tribal zeal, since the one promoting the religion is a member of their group, and they stand to gain power or status through their association with him. Still other people might adopt a religion because of compulsion, fearing that those in power would harm them if they did not change their religion. In each of these cases, a religion can also seem more plausible if it offers simple ideas that are familiar from earlier religions or are unreflectively accepted in that society.

Theodore points out that the Christian religion could offer none of these benefits as incentives for conversion. Instead of being permissive, it commanded a life of self-restraint and warned that anyone who followed Jesus would have to endure hardship and even suffer death for his sake.[37] Furthermore, Jesus and his followers had no wealth or worldly power that they could offer to others. Neither could tribal zeal have been an incentive for conversion, for the apostles were Jews and left their families to preach the gospel to gentiles in many nations. The apostles had no power or rule over others, so they could not have compelled others to adopt their religion.[38] The religion Jesus and his followers proclaimed

---

36. Theodore develops the following argument concerning unworthy reasons for adopting a religion in the third section of his *Treatise on the Existence of the Creator and the True Religion* (Dick, *Traité de l'existence*, 259–70; ET Lamoreaux, *Theodore*, 41–47) and in *Maymar* 4 (II) (Bacha, *Les oeuvres arabes*, 71–75; ET Lamoreaux, *Theodore*, 49–53). See Sidney H. Griffith, "Comparative Religion in the Apologetics of the First Christian Arabic Theologians," *Proceedings of the PMR Conference* 4 (1979): 63–87; Sidney H. Griffith, "Faith and Reason in Christian Kalām: Theodore Abū Qurrah on Discerning the True Religion," in *Christian Arabic Apologetics During the Abbasid Period (750–1258)*, eds. Samir Khalil Samir and Jørgen S. Nielsen (Leiden: Brill, 1994), 1–43; Mark N. Swanson, "Apology or Its Evasion?: Some Ninth-Century Arabic Christian Texts on Discerning the True Religion," *Currents in Theology and Mission* 37 (2010): 389–99.

37. Lamoreaux ("Theodore," 379–380) discusses the role played by this argument in Theodore's Arabic works and in a Greek treatise (*op.* 21; Glei and Khoury, 106.92–93,105–110) that is clearly dependent on these Arabic sources.

38. For the development of this theme in other ninth-century Arab Christian writers, see Samir Khalil Samir, "Liberté religieuse et propagation de la foi chez les théologiens arabes chrétiens du IXe siècle et en Islam," in *Witness of Faith in Life and Worship. Tantur Yearbook 1980–1981* (Jerusalem: Ecumenical Institute for Theological Research, 1981), 93–164.

also contained many things that were not found in previous religions and were contrary to what was unreflectively accepted in contemporary society (for example, Jesus's prohibition of retaliation and his command to love one's enemies).[39] It is clear, then, that the Christian religion spread not by appealing to worldly incentives but because its unique claims were supported by demonstrations of divine power.

SIGNS OF DIVINE POWER ATTEST TO THE TRUTH OF THE CHRISTIAN RELIGION

Theodore noted that in the Gospels, Jesus taught and commanded many things that were surprising or shocking to those who heard him. His hearers nonetheless received his teaching when they saw him do things that could not be done without God's help, including raising the dead to life.[40] Furthermore, Jesus did these things on his own authority; he had no need to wait until God suggested something to him, nor did he have to pray and wait for God's permission.[41] The same was true of Christ's disciples; they did not have to first seek permission from God, but rather they acted immediately to heal by the power of Jesus's name. These manifestations of divine power gave credence to Jesus's claims to be the Son of God and caused the people to believe that he bore the cross and every other suffering for the sake of God and our salvation.

THE NECESSITY OF THE INCARNATION

But why did the Son need to take on a human existence and endure these sufferings? Theodore offers two arguments to explain why this was necessary.[42] Theodore first argues that because God is immaterial, invisible, and not confined to any place, he needed to assume a created form to communicate effectively with

---

39. For a similar argument in another early ninth-century Arabic Christian apologetic work, *The Disputation of the Monk Abraham of Tiberias*, see Karl Vollers, "Das Religionsgespräch von Jerusalem (um 800 D)," *Zeitschrift für Kirchengeschichte* 29 (1908): 63; Giacinto Būlus Marcuzzo, *Le dialogue d'Abraham de Tibériade avec 'Abd al-Raḥman al-Hāšimī à Jérusalem vers 820* (Rome: Pontificia Universitas Lateranensis, 1986), 399–401.

40. Theodore develops this argument in *Maymar* 4 (II) (ET Lamoreaux, *Theodore*, 51–53), the first section of *Maymar* 9 (I) (ET Lamoreaux, *Theodore*, 27–36), and the third section of the *Treatise on the Existence of the Creator and the True Religion* (ET Lamoreaux, *Theodore*, 46–47).

41. *Maymar* 9 (I) (ET Lamoreaux, *Theodore*, 29). Theodore is responding to the claim made in the Qur'an (*Āl-'Imran* 3:49; *Al-Mā'ida* 5:110) that Jesus performed miracles only by God's permission. An argument similar to Theodore's is found in an anonymous Arabic Christian apologetic text of the ninth or tenth century; see Sidney H. Griffith, "*Answers for the Shaykh*: A 'Melkite' Arabic Text from Sinai and the Doctrines of the Trinity and the Incarnation in 'Arab Orthodox' Apologetics," in *The Encounter of Eastern Christianity with Islam*, eds. Emmanouela Grypeou, Mark N. Swanson, and David Thomas (Leiden: Brill, 2006), 293, 297.

42. Theodore develops this argument in *Maymar* 6 (V) (Bacha, *Les oeuvres arabes*, 83–91; ET Lamoreaux, *Theodore*, 129–35); see Jean Rivière, "Un précurseur de Saint Anselme: La théologie rédemptrice de Théodore Abû Qurra," *Bulletin de littérature ecclésiastique* 6 (1914): 337–60.

created beings. God, Theodore explains, wished for his creatures to focus their attention on him. The minds of created beings, however, are limited and have difficulty concentrating on things that have no limit or place. For this reason, when God revealed himself as present, he often used something created to direct and retain the attention of his hearers. When God revealed himself to Moses, he used a burning bush as something on which Moses could fix his attention and to which Moses could direct his words. Later God revealed himself to Israel in the form of a ruler sitting on a throne. He did this not because he needed a throne but because it gave created minds a place to direct their worship.[43] In the same way, God made the body of Jesus the place of his dwelling, allowing the people to focus their attention on the place in which God was revealing himself.[44]

Theodore then argues that it was necessary for God to assume a human existence and endure sufferings if he was to free human beings from their sins while also upholding the justice of the law. The law, he observes, demands absolute and unqualified devotion to God; no action falls outside of this and can be considered merely discretionary. As a result, when human beings fail to do as they ought, there is no way that they can make restitution by offering in compensation something that was not required. By taking on a human existence, Jesus was able, as a human being, to offer the total devotion that other human beings had not offered. As the Son of God, he was also able to act in a way that made restitution for what others had not done and paid the debt that others were unable to pay.

Theodore developed this argument as follows: the law of God commanded human beings to love God with all their hearts, with all their might, with all their souls, and with all their wills. What then can be done when one falls short of offering to God all that one has? There is no way to make up for what was

---

43. Cf. *Maymar* 10 (VI) (ET Lamoreaux, *Theodore*, 136). Theodore is aware that the Qur'an, while emphasizing God's transcendence of spatial limitations, also repeatedly speaks of God as sitting on a throne (see, e.g., *Yūnus*, 10:3) and that the proper interpretation of these passages was a matter of controversy in the early Islamic period. Theodore uses the Qur'anic image of God sitting on a throne to show that it was both reasonable and necessary for God to take on a created form in the incarnation. Theodore develops this argument as follows: in his mercy, God wished to become visible to his creatures and this required him to take on a created form that exists in a place. God did this by accepting certain freely chosen limits yet without reducing his divinity and his divine power in any way. Thus, although no creature can directly perceive the being of God, created beings can know the character of God when he assumes a created form and likeness, and this occurred most completely and perfectly when God assumed human form in the incarnation. For a discussion of this argument, see Seppo Rissanen, *Theological Encounter of Oriental Christians with Islam during Early Abbasid Rule* (Åbo: Åbo Akademi University Press, 1993), 122–24; Beaumont, *Christology*, 33–36; Vasile-Octavian Mihoc, *Christliche Bilderverehrung im Kontext islamischer Bilderlosigkeit: Der Traktat über die Bilderverehrung von Theodor Abū Qurrah (ca. 755 bis ca. 830)* (Wiesbaden: Harrassowitz, 2017), 158–63.

44. Theodore makes a similar argument in his *Treatise on the Veneration of the Holy Icons* 11 (ET Griffith, *Treatise*, 58–59): Even though God is not limited or confined by any place, it is still appropriate to direct honor toward the place from which God becomes known to people.

not done by doing something else that was not required. All our devotion was required, but not all was given. There is thus a debt that remains unpaid, and there is nothing further one can offer that would clear that debt.

In this situation, Theodore argues, there are two ways God might respond. First, he might, without condition, simply forgive the sins and set aside the penalty appropriate to sin. This would require God to disregard the law he had instituted and to regard sins as if they were not an evil, which would be contrary to God's justice.[45] It is clear, then, that the law must be upheld, and if sins are to be forgiven, there must be a just cause for doing so.

Second, God himself might supply a way for human beings to be forgiven. Justice requires that the evil of sin should be punished with an appropriate penalty, and a penalty involves suffering. God's nature does not admit of suffering, for his power is infinite, and he cannot be oppressed or injured by any other. Only a created being, whose power and nature are limited, could suffer. God therefore sent his Son to take upon himself a human nature, a nature that was capable of suffering.[46]

> He went forth into the world and allowed himself to experience the punishment that each of us merited because of our sins, namely being beaten, being humiliated, being crucified, and experiencing death. If he had not become incarnate, there would have been no way for him to experience such pains, for in his divine essence he is neither seen nor touched, nor is he affected by suffering, pain, or harm. By becoming incarnate, however, he made it possible for himself to experience such suffering by exposing his body to it. His back he allowed to be beaten with whips, his head to be struck, his face to be spat upon, his hands and his feet to be nailed, his side to be pierced by a lance. He truly underwent these sufferings in his body. . . . It is thus that he accomplished our salvation.[47]

By assuming a human nature, the Son was able to fulfill all that the law commanded of human beings and was also able to suffer the punishment that human beings deserved under the law on account of their sins.

---

45. *Maymar* 6 (V) (ET Lamoreaux, *Theodore*, 130).
46. Cf. *Treatise on the Veneration of the Holy Icons* 5, 12 (ET Griffith, *Treatise*, 39, 63): "[W]e accord God the purest attributes, but we also recognize his descent, in his mercy, into something other than what is in harmony with the transcendence of his being—wherein is our salvation for which we thank him . . . [Depictions of Christ are therefore appropriate because they remind Christians] to express gratitude to the Messiah for having become incarnate for the sake of their salvation."
47. *Maymar* 6 (V) (ET Lamoreaux, *Theodore*, 131).

Let those who are listening hear and understand that when the Father saw that Adam and his children had fallen into sin and were being jostled about in it as if by waves and that through it destruction had overwhelmed them, he said to his Son, "I see that Adam, who is in our image and likeness, as well as his offspring, have come under sin's dominion. The just claim of sin that stands against them has excluded them from the state of blessedness for which they were created. The law cannot be made void, however; it must receive its claims in full, from every single human being. Come, take a body. Through it, manifest yourself in the world and expose yourself to the punishments that human beings merit because of their sins. Let those punishments befall you, for when this happens there will be forgiveness of sins for those who, for their sins, offer to me your pains. For them there will be an escape from every punishment they merit because of my law. In this way, you will have nullified the just claims of sin and the devil its sponsor and fulfilled the claims of my law without its becoming null and void. At that same time, you will have opened the door for all of Adam's offspring who wish deliverance for themselves, preparing for them a forgiveness that they will be able to obtain without trouble, by faith in you and by the offering of your pains."[48]

Thus far Theodore has shown that the savior needed to take on a human life if he was to act on behalf of humanity through his suffering. At the same time, Theodore argues, the savior also needed to be more than human if what he achieved was to be made available to all people. If an individual human being were able to fulfill the law, what was achieved would be limited, pertaining only to that individual and not to anyone else. What the Son was and what he was able to offer were far greater than what anyone who was only human could be or offer. The one who suffered for sinners was in fact the blameless Son of God, the Father's equal and his beloved. For such a person to offer himself for sinners was an act so remarkable that nothing could be of greater value. The act of one person who was only human could achieve a limited good and receive a proportional benefit, a benefit which affected only one person. What the Son of God achieved was an unlimited good and a proportionally greater benefit, one so great that it could affect innumerable lives.

You, my pure Son, are my equal and share my essence. Not even the whole of humanity could be your equal or could be compared to you in any way

---

48. *Maymar* 6 (V) (ET Lamoreaux, *Theodore*, 132–33).

because of the incomparable glory of your divinity. Thus, when you have suffered for their sakes just once the punishment merited by them an innumerable number of times, you will have caused the law to receive in full its claims on them and infinitely more as well . . . In that the Son is incomparably better than the whole world . . . it was he who was sacrificed for the whole world. He was sufficient to give the law its claims in full; indeed, he was immeasurably more than sufficient.[49]

CONTRIBUTIONS TO THE FIELD OF APOLOGETICS

Theodore Abu Qurrah made a significant contribution to Christian apologetics by responding to contemporary Muslim criticisms of the Christian faith. Theodore took seriously the plurality of religions existing within Middle Eastern society and developed a reasoned account of how one could evaluate the claims made by competing religions. He was also keenly aware of the changing linguistic and social context, using his works to show how the Christian faith could be expressed in the Arabic language and in a manner that took account of Islamic thought and culture. While agreeing with Muslim theologians that God transcends the created world, Theodore showed that it was also necessary for God to enter into creation and assume our humanity. Only in this way, he argued, could the sins of humanity be forgiven in a way appropriate to God's perfect justice and all-surpassing love.

Theodore's apologetic works helped strengthen and encourage generations of Arabic-speaking Christians who lived under the dominance of Islam, and his writings are still read with appreciation today in the Middle East. In the last century, his works have also become better known in Europe and North America and offer Christians living in the West resources for explaining their faith to Muslims and engaging in constructive dialogue.[50]

BIBLIOGRAPHY

Arendzen, Johannes. *Theodori Abū Ḳurrah De cultu imaginum libellus a codice Arabico nunc primum editus Latine versus illustratus.* Bonn: Drobnig, 1897.
Arnold, Andreas. *S. Athanasii . . . Syntagma doctrinae.* Paris: Martin & Boudot, 1685.
Awad, Najib George. *Orthodoxy in Arabic Terms: A Study of Theodore Abu Qurrah's Theology in Its Islamic Context.* Berlin: De Gruyter, 2016.

---

49. *Maymar* 6 (V) (ET Lamoreaux, *Theodore*, 133).
50. For the use of Theodore's works as a resource in contemporary Christian dialogue with Muslims, see Beaumont, *Christology*, 200–12; Mark N. Swanson, "The Trinity in Christian-Muslim Conversation," *Dialog: A Journal of Theology* 44 (2005): 256–63.

Bacha, Constantin. *Les oeuvres arabes de Théodore Aboucara, évêque d'Haran=Mayāmir Thāwudūrus Abī Qurra usquf Ḥarrān.* Beirut: Maṭbaʿat al-fawāʾid, 1904.

———. *Un traité des oeuvres arabes de Théodore Abou-kurra, évêque d'Haran.* Tripoli: L'évêché grec-catholique, 1905.

Beaumont, Mark. *Christology in Dialogue with Muslims: A Critical Analysis of Christian Presentations of Christ for Muslims from the Ninth and Twentieth Centuries.* Carlisle: Paternoster, 2005.

———. "'Ammār al-Basrī on the Alleged Corruption of the Gospels." Pages 241–55 in *The Bible in Arab Christianity.* Ed. by David Thomas. Leiden: Brill, 2007.

———. "Speaking of the Triune God: Christian Defence of the Trinity in the Early Islamic Period." *Transformation* 29 (2012): 111–27.

Bouamama, Ali. *La littérature polémique musulmane contre le christianisme depuis ses origines jusqu'au XIIIe siècle.* Algiers: Entreprise Nationale du Livre, 1988.

Boudignon, Christian. "Logique aristotélicienne et *kalām ʿalā-l-naṣārā*: la réponse à Abū Qurra dans le *Mugnī* de ʿAbd al-Ǧabbār." *Arabica* 58 (2011): 519–44.

Brosset, Marie-Felicité. "Histoire et littérature de la Géorgie." Pages 119–78 in *Recueil des Actes de la séance publique de l'Académie Impériale des Sciences de Saint-Pétersbourg* (St. Petersburg: n.p., 1838).

Cheikho, Louis. "Maymar li-Tādurus Abī Qurrah fī wujūd al-khāliq wa l-dīn al-qawīm." *Al-Mashriq* 15 (1912): 757–74, 825–42.

Daga-Portillo, Rocio. *Teodoro Abu Qurra: Tratado sobre la veneración de los iconos.* Granada: Nuevo Inicio, 2017.

Datiašvili, Leila. *Teodore Abuk'ura: T'rakt'at'ebi da dialogebi targmnili berdznulidan Arsen Iq'altoelis mier.* Tbilisi: Metsniereba, 1980.

Dick, Ignace. "Deux écrits inédits de Théodore Abuqurra." *Le Muséon* 72 (1959): 53–67.

———. "Théodore Abuqurra, évêque melkite de Harran (750?–825?); introduction générale, texte et analyse du *Traité de l'existence du Créateur et de la vraie religion.*" PhD diss., Université Catholique de Louvain, 1960.

———. *Théodore Abu Qurra: Traité de l'existence du Créateur et de la vraie religion-Introduction et texte critique.* Patrimoine Arabe Chrétien 3. Jounieh: Librairie Saint-Paul, 1982.

———. *Théodore Abu Qurra: Traité du culte des icônes-Introduction et texte critique.* Patrimoine Arabe Chrétien 10. Jounieh: Librairie Saint-Paul, 1986.

Gallandi, Andreas. *Bibliotheca veterum patrum.* Vol. 13. Venice: G. B. Albrizzi, 1779.

Glei, Reinhold, and Adel Theodor Khoury. *Johannes Damaskenos und Theodor Abū Qurra. Schriften zum Islam.* Würzburg: Echter Verlag, 1995.

Graf, Georg. *Die arabischen Schriften des Theodor Abû Qurra, Bischofs von Ḥarrān (ca. 740–820).* Paderborn: Ferdinand Schöningh, 1910.

———. *Des Theodor Abû Ḳurra Traktat über den Schöpfer und die wahre Religion.* Münster: Aschendorff, 1913.

———. *Geschichte der christlichen arabischen Literatur.* Vol. 2. Vatican City: Biblioteca Apostolica Vaticana, 1947.

Green, Tamara M. *The City of the Moon God: Religious Traditions of Harran.* Leiden: Brill, 1992.

Gretser, Jakob. *Anastasii Sinaitae Patriarchae Antiocheni . . . Dux viae.* Ingolstadt: Adam Sartorius, 1606.

Griffith, Sidney H. "Some Unpublished Arabic Sayings Attributed to Theodore Abū Qurrah." *Le Muséon* 92 (1979): 29–35.

———. "Comparative Religion in the Apologetics of the First Christian Arabic Theologians." *Proceedings of the PMR Conference* 4 (1979): 63–87.

———. "Faith and Reason in Christian Kalām: Theodore Abū Qurrah on Discerning the True Religion." Pages 1–43 in *Christian Arabic Apologetics During the Abbasid Period (750–1258).* Ed. by Samir Khalil Samir and Jørgen S. Nielsen. Leiden: Brill, 1994.

———. *Theodore Abū Qurrah. A Treatise on the Veneration of the Holy Icons.* Louvain: Peeters, 1997.

———. "'Melkites', 'Jacobites' and the Christological Controversies in Arabic in Third/Ninth-Century Syria." Pages 9–55 in *Syrian Christians Under Islam. The First Thousand Years.* Ed. by David Thomas. Leiden: Brill, 2001.

———. "*Answers for the Shaykh*: A 'Melkite' Arabic Text from Sinai and the Doctrines of the Trinity and the Incarnation in 'Arab Orthodox' Apologetics." Pages 277–309 in *The Encounter of Eastern Christianity with Islam.* Ed. by Emmanouela Grypeou, Mark N. Swanson, and David Thomas. Leiden: Brill, 2006.

———. *The Bible in Arabic: The Scriptures of the "People of the Book" in the Language of Islam.* Princeton: Princeton University Press, 2013.

Gvaramia, Roussoudane. "Bibliographie du dialogue islamo–chrétien (auteurs chrétiens de langue géorgienne, VIIe–XIVe siècles)." *Islamochristiana* 6 (1980): 287–95.

Hjärpe, Jan. *Analyse critique des traditions arabes sur les sabéens ḥarraniens.* Uppsala: Skriv Service AB, 1972.

Khintibidze, Elguja. *Georgian Literature in European Scholarship.* Amsterdam: Adolf M. Hakkert and W. Kos, 2000.

Khoury, Adel-Théodore. *Les théologiens byzantins et l'Islam. Textes et auteurs (VIIIe-XIIIe S.).* Louvain: Nauwelaerts, 1969.

Khoury, George Hanna. "Theodore Abu Qurrah (c. 750–820): Translation and Critical Analysis of His 'Treatise on the Existence of the Creator and on the True Religion.'" PhD diss., Graduate Theological Union, 1990.

Lamoreaux, John C. "An Unedited Tract Against the Armenians by Theodore Abū Qurrah." *Le Muséon* 105 (1992): 327–41.

———. "Theodore Abū Qurrah and John the Deacon." *Greek, Roman, and Byzantine Studies* 42 (2001): 361–86.

———. *Theodore Abū Qurrah.* Provo, UT: Brigham Young University Press, 2005.

Leeming, Kate. "The Adoption of Arabic as a Liturgical Language by the Palestinian Melkites," *ARAM Periodical* 15 (2003): 239–46.

Lolašvili, Ivane. *Arsen Iq'altoeli.* Tbilisi: Metsniereba, 1978.

Mahé, Annie, and Jean-Pierre Mahé. *La sagesse de Balahvar: Une vie christianisée du Bouddha.* Paris: Éditions Gallimard, 1993.

Marcuzzo, Giacinto Būlus. *Le dialogue d'Abraham de Tibériade avec 'Abd al-Raḥman al-Hāšimī à Jérusalem vers 820.* Rome: Pontificia Universitas Lateranensis, 1986.

Martin-Hisard, Bernadette. "La *Vie de Jean et Euthyme* et le statut du monastère des Ibères sur l'Athos." *Revue des études byzantines* 49 (1991): 67–142.

McMichael, Steven J. "The Death, Resurrection, and Ascension of Jesus in Medieval Christian Anti-Muslim Religious Polemics." *Islam and Christian-Muslim Relations* 21 (2010): 157–73.

Mihoc, Vasile-Octavian. *Christliche Bilderverehrung im Kontext islamischer Bilderlosigkeit: Der Traktat über die Bilderverehrung von Theodor Abū Qurrah (ca. 755 bis ca. 830).* Wiesbaden: Harrassowitz, 2017.

Monnot, Guy. "Abū Qurra et la pluralité des religions." *Revue de l'histoire des religions* 208 (1991): 49–71.

Nasrallah, Joseph. "Dialogue islamo-chrétien à propos de publications récentes." *Revue des études islamiques* 46 (1978): 121–51.

———. *Histoire du mouvement littéraire dans l'église melchite du Ve au XXe siècle: Contribution à l'étude de la littérature arabe chrétienne. Vol. II, Tome 2: 750-Xe S.* Louvain: Peeters, 1988.

Op de Coul, Michiel, and Marcel Poorthuis. *Johannes Damascenus & Theodorus Abū Qurra. De eerste christelijke polemiek met de Islam.* Zoetermeer: Meinema, 2011.

Peradze, Gregor. "Die altchristliche Literatur in der georgischen Überlieferung." *Oriens Christianus* 30 (1933): 180–98.

Pinggéra, Karl. "Konfessionelle Rivalitäten in der Auseinandersetzung mit dem Islam. Beispiele aus der ost-syrischen Literatur." *Der Islam* 88 (2012): 51–72.

Pizzo, Paola. *Teodoro Abū Qurrah. La difesa delle icone. Trattato sulla venerazione delle immagini.* Milan: Jaca, 1995.

Pizzo, Paola, and Samir Khalil Samir, *Teodoro Abū Qurrah. Trattato sulla libertà.* Turin: Zamorani, 2001.

Rissanen, Seppo. *Theological Encounter of Oriental Christians with Islam during Early Abbasid Rule.* Åbo: Åbo Akademi University Press, 1993.

Rivière, Jean. "Un précurseur de Saint Anselme: La théologie rédemptrice de Théodore Abû Qurra." *Bulletin de littérature ecclésiastique* 6 (1914): 337–60.

Rus, Lidia. *Abu Qurra: Despre cinstirea Sfintelor Icoane.* Bucharest: Editura Univers Enciclopedic, 2012.

Sahner, Christian C. "Swimming against the Current: Muslim Conversion to Christianity in the Early Islamic Period." *Journal of the American Oriental Society* 136 (2016): 265–84.

Samir, Samir Khalil. "Liberté religieuse et propagation de la foi chez les théologiens arabes chrétiens du IXe siècle et en Islam." Pages 93–164 in *Witness of Faith in Life and Worship. Tantur Yearbook 1980–1981.* Jerusalem: Ecumenical Institute for Theological Research, 1981.

———. "Christian Arabic Literature in the 'Abbasid Period." Pages 446–60 in *Religion, Learning and Science in the 'Abbasid Period.* Ed. by M. J. L. Young, J. D. Latham, and R. B. Serjeant. Cambridge: Cambridge University Press, 1990.

———. "Le traité sur les icônes d'Abū Qurrah mentionné par Eutychius." *Orientalia Christiana Periodica* 58 (1992): 461–74.

———. "Al-jadīd fī sīrat Thāwudūrus Abī Qurra wa-āthārihi." *Al-Mashriq* 73 (1999): 417–49.

———. *Abū Qurrah. Vida, bibliografía y obras.* Trans. by Juan Pedro Monferrer Sala. Córdoba: Universidad de Córdoba, 2005.

Schaffner, Ryan. "The Bible Through a Qur'ānic Filter: Scripture Falsification (*Taḥrīf*) in 8th-and 9th-Century Muslim Disputational Literature." PhD diss., Ohio State University, 2016.

Seppälä, Serafim. *Theodoros Abu Qurra: Ikonien Kunnioittamisesta*. Helsinki: Maahenki, 2008.

Süß, Ina. *Christus im Diskurs mit Muhammad. Das Ringen um religiöse Identität: Die Auseinandersetzung der syrischen Christen mit dem Islam anhand ausgewählter Texte des Johannes Damaskenos und des Theodor Abū Qurra*. Chemnitz: Universitätsverlag Chemnitz, 2015.

Swanson, Mark N. "The Trinity in Christian-Muslim Conversation." *Dialog: A Journal of Theology* 44 (2005): 256–63.

———. "Apologetics, Catechesis, and the Question of Audience in 'On the Triune Nature of God' (Sinai Arabic 154) and Three Treatises of Theodore Abū Qurrah." Pages 113–34 in *Christians and Muslims in Dialogue in the Islamic Orient of the Middle Ages*. Ed. by Martin Tamcke. Beirut: Orient-Institut Beirut, 2007.

———. "Apology or Its Evasion?: Some Ninth-Century Arabic Christian Texts on Discerning the True Religion." *Currents in Theology and Mission* 37 (2010): 389–99.

Tarchnišvili, Michael. *Geschichte der kirchlichen georgischen Literatur*. Vatican City: Biblioteca Apostolica Vaticana, 1955.

Thomas, David. *Anti-Christian Polemic in Early Islam: Abū 'Īsā al-Warrāq's "Against the Trinity."* Cambridge: Cambridge University Press, 1992.

———. *Early Muslim Polemic Against Christianity: Abū 'Īsā al-Warrāq's "Against the Incarnation."* Cambridge: Cambridge University Press, 2002.

Thomas, David, and Barbara Roggema, eds. *Christian-Muslim Relations: A Bibliographical History. Vol. 1 (600–900)*. Leiden: Brill, 2009.

Treiger, Alexander. "The Fathers in Arabic." Pages 442–55 in *The Wiley Blackwell Companion to Patristics*. Ed. by Ken Parry. Chichester, West Sussex: John Wiley and Sons, 2015.

———. "New Works by Theodore Abū Qurra Preserved under the Name of Thaddeus of Edessa." *Journal of Eastern Christian Studies* 68 (2016): 1–51.

Tubach, Jürgen. *Im Schatten des Sonnengottes: der Sonnenkult in Edessa, Ḥarrān und Ḥaṭrā am Vorabend der christlichen Mission*. Wiesbaden: Harrassowitz, 1986.

Vollers, Karl. "Das Religionsgespräch von Jerusalem (um 800 D)." *Zeitschrift für Kirchengeschichte* 29 (1908): 29–71, 197–221.

TIMOTHY I OF BAGHDAD

A Model for Peaceful Dialogue

EDWARD L. SMITHER
TREVOR CASTOR

Timothy of Baghdad (727–823) was an early apologist answering questions relevant to Christian-Muslim dialogue necessary for cultural engagement today. The questions, Do Christians worship three gods? How can God have a son? and Did Jesus die on the cross? continue to pose problems for Muslims when they hear the Christian message. Through his discussions with the Muslim Caliph Mahdi (ca. 744–785), Timothy, who served as the Church of the East bishop in Baghdad, answered many Muslim concerns about the gospel. He shows that it is possible to engage in peaceful dialogue with Muslims without compromising the essentials of the Christian faith.

HISTORICAL BACKGROUND

Timothy was born into a wealthy family, and his uncle served as a bishop. Following the holistic Church of the East study program, Timothy prepared for the ministry by completing studies in hermeneutics, theology, philosophy, and medicine. He studied theology in both Syriac (his mother tongue) and Greek and became well-versed in the writings of Theodore of Mopsuestia (350–428), Diodore (d. 390), Origen (185–254), the Cappadocians (fourth century), and Gregory the Great (d. 604). He also developed proficiency in Persian. His studies in Greek philosophy, particularly Aristotle, gave him a framework with which to dialogue with Muslim thinkers in Baghdad.

In addition to his skills in theology, Timothy proved to be a capable leader and reformer within the Church of the East. His first place of service was in Bet

---

Image: Painted figure of an Eastern Patriarch at Jausaq, Samarra, Iraq

197

Bägash (southeastern Turkey), a church that his uncle previously led. After eight years, Timothy put his name forward to lead the church at Baghdad. Because simony (purchasing bishoprics) was common in the eastern church, Timothy arrived in Baghdad with sacks (presumably filled with gold) for the bishops overseeing the election. Once he was appointed, he revealed that the sacks were filled with stones. This action symbolized his ability to navigate church politics and also to put new reforms in place.

Though the Church of the East faced allegations of being theologically Nestorian, Timothy regarded his community as faithful guardians of orthodoxy. Well-read in the Syriac, Greek, and Latin church fathers, Timothy hosted church councils in 790 and 804 in which the faith of Nicaea was affirmed.[1]

Timothy began leading the church in Baghdad in 762, a little over a decade after the Abbasid Dynasty established its caliphate in the city. The Church of the East was eager to establish a presence in the city to keep an eye on what the Muslim leaders were doing. Many Christians served in various roles within the court of the caliph. Ironically, Church of the East Christians enjoyed more freedom under Muslim rule than they had under the recently defeated Byzantine Empire. As a result, Timothy secured permission from the caliph to send missionaries to the formerly Christian lands in Central and East Asia. Timothy used the Church of the East monasteries in Persia as training centers, where monks studied theology, philosophy, medicine, and linguistics to preach, care for physical needs, and translate Scripture. Timothy also set apart bishops for new churches in Central Asia, Tibet, and China.[2]

THEOLOGICAL CONTEXT

CHURCH OF THE EAST

Because of a supposed connection to the fifth-century bishop Nestorius of Constantinople (ca. 386–451), who was condemned for his christological views, the Church of the East has often been incorrectly referred to as the Nestorian Church. Lieu and Parry argue that this title is a misnomer: "So-called Nestorianism is an erroneous Byzantine construct resulting from the christological debates and ecclesiastical politics centered on Constantinople in the fifth century. It has

1. See Samuel H. Moffett, *A History of Christianity in Asia, Volume I: Beginnings to 1500* (Maryknoll, NY: Orbis, 1998), 352.

2. See Frederick W. Norris, "Timothy I of Baghdad, Catholicos of the East Syrian Church, 780–823: Still a Valuable Model." *International Bulletin of Missionary Research* 30:3 (2006): 133–135; also Edward L. Smither, *Missionary Monks: An Introduction to the History and Theology of Missionary Monasticism* (Eugene, OR: Cascade, 2016), 143–145; and Dale T. Irvin and Scott W. Sunquist, *History of the World Christian Movement Volume 1: Earliest Christianity to 1453* (Maryknoll, NY: Orbis, 2001), 285.

little bearing on the Christian communities in Central Asia, China, and India."[3] For our purposes, the Church of the East refers to Syrian and Persian Christians who originally lived between Edessa and Nisibis in the border region between the Roman and Persian Empires and who submitted to the leadership of the Patriarch of Seleucia-Ctesiphon.[4]

The Church of the East emerged as the gospel spread eastward from Antioch to Edessa—a city on the Old Silk Road connecting traveling merchants between Rome, Persia, Armenia, and Arabia. In the late second century, the Scriptures were translated into Syriac by the eastern church father Tatian of Mesopotamia (d. ca. 185). In the early third century, a bishop was set apart for the church at Edessa.[5] Because of Edessa's position on the Silk Road, the gospel quickly moved east toward the Persian regions, largely through the witness of business people.[6] Between the third and sixth century, displaced and deported Christians were also entering Persia from Antioch, Syria, Cilicia, and Cappadocia.[7]

After the rise of the Sassanid Empire in Persia in 225, the Church of the East developed more of a Persian identity. The church was based at the Persian capital of Seleucia-Ctesiphon, and its theological school was located at Nisibis. This did not mean that Christianity gained official acceptance in Persia. Despite a brief period of toleration in the early fifth century, the Zoroastrian-dominated government discriminated against and at times persecuted the church from the fourth to sixth century. Persian Christians were often associated with the Romans, who had tolerated and embraced Christianity as an imperial religion in the fourth century. In response to a letter from Emperor Constantine (d. 337) in 315 requesting that Persian Christians be protected, Shah Shapur II (309–379) launched a brutal persecution against the Persian church. Over time such discrimination and pressure led many Persian believers to leave their homeland and to immigrate to places such as Arabia.[8]

In addition to producing one of the earliest translations of Scripture, the

---

3. Samuel N. C. Lieu and Ken Parry, "Deep into Asia," in *Early Christianity in Contexts: An Exploration across Cultures and Continents*, ed. William Tabbernee (Grand Rapids: Baker Academic, 2014), 147; also Moffett, *A History of Christianity in Asia*, xiv; Aziz S. Atiya, *History of Eastern Christianity* (Piscataway, NJ: Gorgias, 2010), 241–242; and Wilhelm Baum and Dietmar W. Winkler, *The Church of the East: A Concise History* (London: Routledge, 2000), 3–5.

4. See Irvin and Sunquist, *History of the World Christian Movement*, 197; also Baum and Winkler, *Church of the East*, 7–9.

5. See Moffett, *History of Christianity in Asia*, 46, 72–77.

6. John Stewart, *Nestorian Missionary Enterprise: The Story of a Church on Fire* (Edinburgh: T&T Clark, 1928), 9.

7. See Baum and Winkler, *Church of the East*, 9–12.

8. See Moffett, *History of Christianity in Asia*, 92, 112, 117, 137–45, 157–61; also Irvin and Sunquist, *History of the World Christian Movement*, 199–203; and Stewart, *Nestorian Missionary Enterprise*, 16–35, 50–51.

Church of the East developed its own rich theological tradition. With theological schools at Edessa and Nisibis, the church was known for thinkers such as Ephraem of Syria (306–373), who articulated theology in the form of hymns and poetry. Though the Church of the East began to be more identified with Nestorian theology in the fifth century, they never affirmed Nestorius's christological ideas. Instead, they were guilty by association because they followed the theological tradition of Antioch and its greatest thinker, Theodore of Mopsuestia. The Church of the East rejected the Formula of Chalcedon of 451, which articulated the hypostatic union of Christ. They opposed this not out of allegiance to Nestorius but in opposition to the Greek manner that it was articulated, which seemed to alienate the Semitic-minded Syrians. The Church of the East did separate from the other Syrian churches, but this was more due to political division than theological differences.[9]

Following the rise and expansion of Islam in the sixth and seventh centuries, the Church of the East was one of the few Christian communities to flourish in the Middle East and Central Asia. By Timothy's day, there were as many as ten million believers in the Church of the East scattered across Asia.[10]

Muslim Context

Timothy led the Christian community in Baghdad, where the Abbasid Caliphate—the global ruling center for Islam—was located. After the death of the Muslim prophet Muhammad (570–632), caliphs (spiritual, political, military, economic leaders) based in Medina led the Muslim community. From 661 to 750, the Umayyad Dynasty governed the Muslim world from Damascus. In 750 Caliph Mansur (714–775) built the city of Baghdad on the Tigris River and established the Abbasid Caliphate there. The Abbasids ruled from Baghdad for five hundred years.

While Arab culture dominated the Umayyad Caliphate, the Muslim community became more diverse and global during the Abbasid period. Through the work of traders and merchants, Islam spread to new parts of Africa, including Sudan (East Africa) and Gambia and Senegal (West Africa). Muslim missionaries from India spread the faith to Indonesia. Spanning from Spain to Indonesia, the Abbasid Caliphate grew in wealth and power during this period.[11]

The Muslim world also enjoyed a golden age of learning under the Abbasids.

9. See Irvin and Sunquist, *History of the World Christian Movement*, 197–201; also Moffett, *History of Christianity in Asia*, 154, 169–80, 200–205; Baum and Winkler, *Church of the East*, 7, 11, 19–32; and Lieu and Parry, "Deep into Asia," 148.
10. See Norris, "Timothy I of Baghdad," 133.
11. See Moffett, *History of Christianity in Asia*, 348–349.

Building on the work of the Greeks and Persians, Muslim thinkers made advancements in philosophy, medicine, astronomy, math, and science. They translated and assimilated Aristotle's works in medieval Islamic philosophy, and the mathematician Muhammad ibn Musa al-Khwarizmi (d. 850) pioneered the study of Algebra and the use of algorithms.

APOLOGETIC RESPONSE

According to Michael Penn, Church of the East Christians had a history of engaging in dialogue with Muslims through the form of disputation letters. Muslim leaders initiated the correspondence with brief questions. Their Christian counterparts then responded with extended answers. The most common questions raised concerned the nature of God (particularly the Trinity), the life and death of Christ, Christian views of Muhammad and the Qur'an, and other Christian beliefs and practices.[12] Timothy's two-day dialogue with Caliph Mahdi in 781 followed the pattern of these letters and dealt with many of the same questions.

Sometime after the encounter, at the request of a Christian colleague, Timothy recorded *The Apology of Timothy the Patriarch before the Caliph Mahdi*.[13] While the document contains Timothy's perspective and bias on the discussion, it also serves as a training manual for the eighth-century church on responding to Muslim concerns about the gospel.

A guest in the court of the caliph and a leader of the minority faith community in Baghdad, Timothy treats his host with honor, referring to Caliph Mahdi as a "God loving king."[14] While Timothy confesses that there is only one God and one Lord Jesus Christ (1 Cor 8:6), his starting point with the caliph is the common belief held by Muslims and Christians of God's eternal nature. From there, he addresses a number of questions, four of which we will focus on in this chapter: Is Jesus the Son of God? What is the Trinity? Did Christ die? Is Muhammad mentioned in the Bible?

IS JESUS THE SON OF GOD?

The caliph responds to Timothy's opening proclamation about the eternal nature of God with a question: "O Catholicos [patriarch or bishop], a man like

---

12. See Michael Phillip Penn, *When Christians First Met Muslims: A Sourcebook on the Earliest Syriac Writings on Islam* (Berkeley: University of California Press, 2015), 15.

13. See Alphonse Mingana, *The Apology of Timothy the Patriarch before the Caliph Mahdi* (Cambridge: Woodbrooke Studies Vol. 2, 1927–1934), 11.

14. Mingana, *Apology of Timothy*, 18 (note: all English translations of the *Apology of Timothy* are from Mingana).

you who possesses all this knowledge and utters such sublime words concerning God, is not justified in saying about God that He married a woman from whom He begat a son."[15] This common objection from Muslims comes straight from the Qur'an: "The Creator of the heavens and earth! How could He have children when He has no spouse, when He created all things, and has full knowledge of all things?" (Surah 6:101).[16]

Much to the caliph's surprise, Timothy agrees that it is impossible for God to have a literal child. He explains that whoever suggests that Christ is the offspring of a sexual union between God and Mary speaks blasphemy. Orthodox Christian teaching has never made such a claim. The Qur'an (Surah 5:116) also denies this possibility.

The caliph has no problem with Christ being born of a virgin or with the angel Gabriel's announcement of Christ's birth, since the Qur'an affirms both (Surah 3:42–49; 19:16–26). But Mahdi's concern is with Christ (and also the Holy Spirit) being divine. The Muslim leader is unwilling to accept that the Son and Spirit have eternal natures, insisting that they are created beings. He further denies the possibility that an eternal God can be born into space and time.

Timothy explains that Mary did not give birth to the divine Jesus. Interestingly, during the fifth century, the church wrestled with a similar question: Was Mary the God-bearer (*theotokos*) or the Christ-bearer (*Christotokos*)? Did Mary give birth to divinity? Timothy tries to clarify Christ's identity by saying, "Christ is the Word-God, who appeared in the flesh for the salvation of the world."[17] Timothy may have chosen these titles (Christ and Word) because they are both used in the Qur'an to describe Jesus (Surah 3:45). Also, in the Church of the East, these were common ways to distinguish between Christ's divine nature (Word, or *logos*) and his human nature (flesh). Using this framework, Timothy explains the unity of these natures in one person, saying, "He is one with His humanity, while preserving the distinction between His invisibility and His visibility, and between His Divinity and His humanity. Christ is one in His sonship, and two in the attributes of His natures."[18] In short, the Word is eternally begotten of the Father in his divine nature, while Christ is begotten from Mary in space-time in his human nature.

When the caliph pressed further and asked whether Timothy called Jesus the Son of God, Timothy responded, "O King, Christ is the Son of God, and I confess Him and worship Him as such. This I learned from Christ Himself in

---

15. Ibid., 17.
16. All English references to the Qur'an are taken from M.A.S Abdel Haleem (2008).
17. Mingana, *Apology of Timothy*, 17.
18. Ibid., 20.

the Gospel and from the Books of the Torah and of the Prophets, which know Him and call Him by the name of 'Son of God' but not a son in the flesh as children are born in the carnal way, but an admirable and wonderful Son."[19]

Rooting his argument in the Christian Scriptures, Timothy asserts that the entire testimony of Scripture affirms Christ as the Son of God. His reference to Isaiah 9:6 is important because it dispels the Muslim misconception that the Son of God is a New Testament idea that Christ's disciples propagated.

Bewildered by Timothy's attempt to explain the hypostatic union (Christ was fully God and fully man), Caliph Mahdi asks the bishop to further clarify. Timothy responds by explaining the nature of Christ through a series of metaphors and similes, including the image of the sun. Before offering these, Timothy gives the important caveat: "O our King, that He is a Son and one that is born, we learn it and believe in it, but we dare not investigate how He was born before the times, and we are not able to understand the fact at all, as God is incomprehensible and inexplicable in all things."[20] Confessing that Jesus is the Son of God and resting in the witness of Scripture, Timothy is content to relate to the caliph that this is ultimately a mystery that only God understands.

WHAT IS THE TRINITY?

The caliph asks Timothy if he believes in the Father, Son, and Holy Spirit. Timothy replies, "I worship them and believe in them."[21] Unable to accept this confession, Mahdi accuses Timothy of tritheism.

Timothy appeals to analogies to explain the eternal relationship within the Trinity. His preferred analogy is to liken the Father, Son, and Holy Spirit to the sun. He argues: "As light and heat are not separable from the sun, so also (the Word) and the Spirit of God are not separable from Him. If one separates from the sun its light and its heat, it will immediately become neither light-giver nor heat-producer, and consequently it will cease to be sun."[22]

Following the Greek and Eastern church tradition, Timothy emphasizes the relational nature of the godhead instead of its shared essence, which the Western church stressed. While the Father begets the Son and the Holy Spirit proceeds from the Father, the godhead is understood through the relationships of the three persons of the Trinity.

Timothy's relational godhead argument prompted the caliph to ask the bishop for support from the Christian Scriptures about the eternal relationship

19. Ibid., 17.
20. Ibid.
21. Ibid., 22.
22. Ibid., 23.

among the Father, Son, and Holy Spirit. Timothy responded with a litany of texts (with my emphasis added) to support his claim. From the Psalms he cited:

> By the *word* of the LORD the heavens were made,
>   their starry host by the breath of his mouth. (Ps 33:6)

> Forever, O LORD, your *word*
>   is firmly fixed in the heavens. (Ps 119:89 ESV)

> When you send forth your *Spirit*, they are created,
>   and you renew the face of the ground. (Ps 104:30 ESV)

From the prophet Isaiah, he referenced:

> The grass withers, the flower fades,
>   but the *word* of our God will stand forever. (Isa 40:8 ESV)

From the New Testament, he cited the prologue of John's gospel: "In the beginning was the *Word*, and the *Word* was with God, and the *Word* was God. He was in the beginning with God. All things were made through him, and without him was not any thing made that was made" (John 1:1–4 ESV). Finally, he cites Jesus's commissioning words in Matthew: "Go therefore and make disciples of all nations, baptizing them in the name of the Father and of the Son and of the Holy Spirit" (Matt 28:19 ESV).[23] Timothy argues that the Psalmist, prophets, Christ, and the gospel writers agree that God the Father, the Word, and the Spirit are all eternally united in relationship.

Continuing to struggle with the Son's divinity within the godhead, the caliph retorted: "By the fact that you say that He [Christ] worshipped and prayed, you deny His divinity, because if He worshipped and prayed He is not God; if He was God, he would not have worshipped and prayed."[24] The Qur'an objects to Christ's divinity by highlighting his human limitations, such as the need to eat (Surah 5:75). Timothy responds by reminding the caliph of their common conviction that God created the heavens and the earth by his Word (Surah 2:17; 3:59). He also mentions the shared Muslim-Christian belief that Christ is a Word from God (Surah 3:45; 4:171). Timothy argues that since everything was created by the Word of God, Christ is Lord of everything and needs nothing.

---

23. Timothy also cited Ps 56:10 and John 17:5.
24. Mingana, *Apology of Timothy*, 30.

Finally, Timothy appeals to the common Muslim-Christian idea that Jesus lived a sinless life. Though Jesus did not need baptism, prayer, or worship, Timothy asserts that the Lord did these things to model how to live the Christian life.

DID CHRIST DIE?

When Timothy mentions the death of Christ, the caliph appeals to the Qur'an and argues that Christ did not die on the cross. It only appeared as though he died (Surah 4:157). Timothy responds by citing two other Qur'anic passages that mention Christ's death (Surah 19:33; 3:55); but Mahdi counters that these passages refer to Christ's eventual death when he returns for the day of judgment.

Timothy continues the dialogue by appealing to Old Testament prophecies about the Messiah dying by crucifixion (Ps 22; Zech 13:7; Isa 53:5; Dan 9:26). The caliph reasons that the prophets must have also seen an illusion of the crucifixion. Timothy then asks Mahdi, Who would be responsible for this illusion? Did God deceive the prophets? Did he deceive the disciples to believe that Christ died and was raised from the dead? Will God hold them accountable for what they believed through deception? For Timothy, God could not deceive the prophets or disciples with such an illusion because that would be contrary to his nature.

The caliph suggests that Christ's suffering on the cross was against God's nature. God would not allow his servant to be delivered to the Jews for crucifixion (Surah 3:55). Timothy responds that according to the Qur'an (Surah 2:87; 3:21; 3:112; 5:70), the Jews had killed other prophets before Christ. Timothy adds that the Jews did not take Christ's life. Instead, he laid it down on his own accord (John 10:18). If the one who caused the earth to shake, the sun to darken, and the dead to rise through his crucifixion had wanted to stop it, then he could have (Matt 27:51–54; Mark 15:33). Christ died and he did so willingly.[25]

IS MUHAMMAD MENTIONED IN THE BIBLE?

Following Timothy's extensive use of Scripture to show the eternal relationship of the persons of the Trinity, the caliph asks why biblical passages that mention Muhammad are ignored: "How is it that you accept Christ and the Gospel from the testimony of the Torah and of the prophets, and you do not accept Muhammad from the testimony of Christ and the Gospel?"[26] Caliph Mahdi's claim that Muhammad is mentioned in both the Old and New Testaments originates from the Qur'an (Surah 7:156).

---

25. Cf. Ibid., 41–43.
26. Ibid., 32.

Timothy responds by appealing to Scripture again. He focuses on Old Testament prophecies concerning the virgin birth (Isa 7:14), messianic titles (Isa 9:6), miracles (Isa 35:5), suffering and death (Isa 53:5), Christ's resurrection (Ps 16:10), his ascension (Ps 47:5), and his future return (Dan 7:13–14). More than an obscure reference to Christ, these Old Testament prophecies affirm the identity, person, and work of Christ. Timothy continues: "These and scores of other passages of the prophets show us Jesus Christ in a clear mirror and point to Him. So far as Muhammad is concerned I have not received a single testimony either from Jesus Christ or from the Gospel which would refer to his name or to his works."[27]

The caliph continues by asserting that the New Testament refers to Muhammad as the Paraclete (helper, comforter, counselor). Timothy argues that the Paraclete shares God's nature, allowing him to search, know, and reveal the depths of God. The Paraclete is spirit and not bound by space or time (Luke 24:39). He also participated in the work of creation (Ps 33:6). Finally, the Paraclete's primary work is to remind Christ's disciples of his teachings and to empower them for ministry (John 14:26). Since Muhammad possessed only a human nature, was bound by space and time, denied the Trinity, and did not perform miracles, he cannot be identified as the Paraclete from Scripture.

The caliph appeals to the Torah and argues that the prophet mentioned in Deuteronomy 18:15 (a prophet like Moses that would be sent by God) must have referred to Muhammad. Mahdi supports this claim by stating that the Ishmaelites, or Arabs, are the Israelites' brethren, and that, as Moses did, Muhammad also brought a law. Timothy responds, explaining that the prophet mentioned in the Torah would come from the tribes of Israel and would go to them as a prophet. Muhammad did not originate from Israel, and he did not go to Israel—he went only to the Arabs. Unlike Moses, Muhammad did not perform miracles. Timothy concludes that if Muhammad were mentioned in the Old Testament, he would have been highlighted as clearly as Christ had been through the many noted prophecies. Finally, Timothy confesses that if Scripture had spoken about Muhammad in such a clear way, then Timothy would have left Christianity and embraced Islam.[28]

Though Timothy concludes that Muhammad is not mentioned in the Scriptures, he still speaks highly of the Muslim prophet: "Muhammad is worthy of all praise by all reasonable people, O my sovereign. . . . Muhammad taught about God, His Word and His Spirit, and since all the prophets had prophesied

27. Ibid., 33.
28. Cf. Ibid., 51.

about God, His Word and His Spirit, Muhammad walked, therefore, in the path of all the prophets."[29]

Timothy praises Muhammad's teaching on the unity of God. He also compares Muhammad's use of the sword against the Meccan idolaters to Moses's instructions to kill the Israelites who worshiped the golden calf (Exod 32:27).

APOLOGETIC METHODOLOGY

Despite being the leader of the minority Christian community in Baghdad, Timothy was given a voice and invited to dialogue with the ruling Muslim caliph, Mahdi. We could argue that the caliph was offering the bishop an early form of academic freedom. Passionate about sending missionaries to the rest of Asia, Timothy did not shy away from proclaiming the gospel and defending historic Christian teaching in his own community. We now summarize his apologetic principles that will also prove helpful for contemporary Christians as they converse with Muslims.

A Cultural Insider. Timothy was not a foreigner spreading a foreign faith. Baghdad was his home. In addition to his native language of Syriac, he spoke Arabic and probably some Persian. He looked at the world from an Asian and Semitic perspective, which allowed him to craft metaphors and analogies that enabled him to connect with his Muslim neighbors. His training in philosophy also helped him grasp the intellectual world of Muslim intellectuals and to adequately respond to the questions of Caliph Mahdi.

He Understood the Qur'an. As his dialogue with Caliph Mahdi shows, Timothy grasped very well the Muslim holy book. He was able to appeal to it when needed and also to answer the caliph's arguments that were based on verses from the Qur'an.

He Appealed to Scripture. Timothy succeeds in offering clarity on the question of the Son of God, the Trinity, the death of Christ, and the Christian understanding of Muhammad. While he knew the Qur'an and could appeal to it when needed, he knew his Bible even more. Time and time again, Timothy based his answers in the historic teaching of Scripture and even invited his conversation partner, the caliph, to gain a deeper understanding of Scripture.

The differences between Timothy and Caliph Mahdi came down to what they accepted as divine revelation. When the caliph asks Timothy if he believed the Qur'an was inspired by God, the bishop responded with his conviction about the Christian Scriptures: "It is not my business to decide whether it is from God

---

29. Ibid., 61.

or not. But I will say something of which your Majesty is well aware, and that is all the words of God found in the Torah and in the Prophets, and those of them found in the Gospel and in the writings of the Apostles, have been confirmed by signs and miracles; as to the words of your Book they have not been corroborated by a single sign or miracle."[30]

He Built Bridges. While standing firmly on historic Christian teaching from Scripture, Timothy emphasized common beliefs between Christians and Muslims. His dialogue was founded on the shared belief in God's eternal nature. He could also speak positively about Islam, including his praise for Muhammad. Upon hearing Timothy's thoughts about Muhammad, Caliph Mahdi invited the bishop to recite the *shahada* (declaration to become a Muslim), especially the first part, which states that "God is one and there is no other beside Him." Though not converting to Islam, Timothy replied that he already believed these words: "This belief in one God, O my Sovereign, I have learned from the Torah, from the Prophets and from the Gospel. I stand by it and shall die in it."[31]

Timothy recognized the stark differences between Islam and Christianity; yet he postured himself as a fellow seeker of truth. Timothy likened spiritual truth to a pearl that had fallen on the ground in a dark house. Muslims and Christians alike are seeking that truth and trusting that when light enters the house, they will possess it.

CONTRIBUTIONS TO THE FIELD OF APOLOGETICS

The four apologetic principles Timothy used are quite relevant to Christians today in their engagement with Muslims. Although many Christians may not have the cultural insider status that Timothy enjoyed, they would be wise to learn and even master the language, culture, and worldview of their Muslim friends. Christians should also develop a grasp of the Qur'an, Hadiths, and other Islamic literature so they can have meaningful conversations. More than that, Timothy's model teaches Christians to know their own Scriptures to defend against false teaching and also to clarify the person of Christ, the godhead, and the essence of the gospel. Finally, while Timothy presented a bold witness, he did not communicate from a position of power. He was the leader of the minority faith community who built bridges of understanding toward Muslims while presenting himself as a fellow seeker of truth.

---

30. Ibid., 36.
31. Ibid., 62.

BIBLIOGRAPHY

Abdel Haleem, M. A. S., trans. *The Qur'an*. Oxford World Classics. Oxford: Oxford University Press, 2008.

Atiya, Aziz S. *History of Eastern Christianity*. Piscataway, NJ: Gorgias, 2010.

Baum, Wilhelm, and Dietmar W. Winkler. *The Church of the East: A Concise History*. London: Routledge, 2000.

Irvin, Dale T., and Scott W. Sunquist. *History of the World Christian Movement Volume 1: Earliest Christianity to 1453*. Maryknoll, NY: Orbis, 2001.

Lieu, Samuel N. C., and Ken Parry. "Deep into Asia." Pages 143–180 in *Early Christianity in Contexts: An Exploration across Cultures and Continents*. Ed. by William Tabbernee. Grand Rapids: Baker Academic, 2014.

Mingana, Alphonse. *The Apology of Timothy the Patriarch before the Caliph Mahdi*. Cambridge: Woodbrooke Studies Vol. 2, 1928.

Moffett, Samuel H. *A History of Christianity in Asia, Volume I: Beginnings to 1500*. Maryknoll, NY: Orbis, 1998.

Norris, Frederick W. "Timothy I of Baghdad, Catholicos of the East Syrian Church, 780–823: Still a Valuable Model." *International Bulletin of Missionary Research* 30:3 (2006): 133–36.

Penn, Michael Phillip. *When Christians First Met Muslims: A Sourcebook on the Earliest Syriac Writings on Islam*. Berkeley: University of California Press, 2015.

Smither, Edward L. *Missionary Monks: An Introduction to the History and Theology of Missionary Monasticism*. Eugene: Cascade, 2016.

Stewart, John. *Nestorian Missionary Enterprise: The Story of a Church on Fire*. Edinburgh: T&T Clark, 1928.

ANSELM OF CANTERBURY

Apologetics and the
Ratio Fidei

EDWARD N. MARTIN
STEVEN B. COWAN

Public Domain

In the eleventh century, there were not yet "universities," there was no rebirth of Aristotle's texts, and the Norman Conquest prominently took place in England, making for significant changes in Europe after 1066. The sites of great learning in Europe were in the monasteries, and Anselm (1033–1109) would find his home in the monasteries of France and England for nearly his entire career. Sometimes called "The Second Augustine," Anselm sought to defend the faith "entrusted to God's holy people" (Jude 3) through a careful use of logic or "dialectic." Through his particular Scripture-affirming rationalistic apologetic method, which he developed over his career of writing and teaching, Anselm surmounted such subjects as faith and reason, God's existence, the philosophical theology of the incarnation and the Trinity, foreknowledge and free will, truth, the logical use of language and communication, and allied topics.

HISTORICAL BACKGROUND

Anselm was born in Aosta, in northwestern Italy in 1033. According to Martin Rule, Anselm was likely related to the marquis of Susa, Manfred the First. Manfred was an uncle on his mother's side to Arduin, the marquis of Ivrea, who served as king of Italy for thirteen years. Thus, there is a connection from Anselm to the family line of Boniface, marquis of Tuscany, who was the father of perhaps the most powerful woman in medieval times, Matilda.[1] It was at Matilda's Canossa Castle where the famous standoff between the Holy Roman Emperor Henry IV of Germany and Pope Gregory VII took place in 1077—part of the Investiture Controversy that would later visit Anselm when he served

---

1. Martin Rule, *The Life and Times of St. Anselm: Archbishop of Canterbury and Primate of the Britains*, 2 vols. (London: Paul, Trench, and Company, 1883), vol. 1, 1.

in Canterbury. The excommunicated king, barefoot and penitent, stood in the snow during a three-day snowstorm, seeking entry to Matilda's castle grounds where Gregory was staying. At last Henry was admitted entry, begged forgiveness of Pope Gregory, was granted absolution of said excommunication, and the three of them partook of communion together that evening in Matilda's castle.[2]

Anselm moved about as a wandering scholar in his early twenties and finally settled and was accepted as a novitiate at the Benedictine monastery at Bec in Northern France. When he arrived in 1059, at the age of twenty-six, his primary attraction to the monastery at Bec was the scholarly prior Lanfranc, who headed one of the most important centers of learning in Europe at that time—a time before universities. Monasteries were very important as places of learning, not only for active teachers in theology and the liberal arts but also for their libraries and for the copyists who made and distributed copies of important texts of Scripture, learning, and history.

Anselm, known for his acute mind and religious devotion, quickly advanced at Bec. When Lanfranc left for Caen in 1063 (later to become archbishop of Canterbury before Anselm), Anselm was elected as his replacement as prior. Though the post brought administrative headaches from time to time, Anselm enjoyed much stability there ranging over his thirty-year stay. In 1089, having served for nineteen years as archbishop, Lanfranc died, and the archbishopric remained open for some four years, as the English kings after William the Conquerer (William Rufus, etc.) plundered the monetary assets of the church more easily without an archbishop around. Anselm did not invite a promotion; indeed, he was loath to travel to England at all for fear that he might be seen as a candidate for the promotion to take over Lanfranc's position once again. But travel he did, regretfully, at the invitation of various individuals, making it clear that he did not want the office and its administrative tasks. Anselm was well regarded at Canterbury by the religious and secular community. William Rufus seemed satisfied to let the office lay open until he fell terribly ill in 1092, and fearing that this was a divine punishment for how he had plundered the funds of the church in recent years, he called for the one man those in command recommended to him most as the obvious successor to Lanfranc—Anselm. Thus, despite his attempts to avoid it, Anselm was eventually enthroned as the thirty-sixth archbishop of Canterbury in 1093 and served until his death on April 21, 1109.

---

2. For more on the controversy, see *The Correspondence of Pope Gregory VII: Selected Letters from the Registrum*, trans. Ephraim Emerton (New York: Columbia University Press, 1932); *The Papal Reform of the Eleventh Century: Lives of Pope Leo IX and Pope Gregory VII*, trans. I. S. Robinson (Manchester: Manchester University Press, 2004); and I. S. Robinson, *Henry IV of Germany 1056–1106* (Cambridge: Cambridge University Press, 2000).

THEOLOGICAL CONTEXT

During Anselm's time at Canterbury, he authored two apologetic works of note. The first was written in reply to a heretic named Roscelin of Compiegne. Roscelin had held that if the Christ was incarnate, and the doctrine of the Trinity was correct, then surely the Father and the Holy Spirit also were incarnated. This episode led to Roscelin's eventual recantation and then the recantation of that recantation. Anselm's apologetic response was an extended letter named *On the Incarnation of the Word*, written to Pope Urban II.[3] The second work he authored is his famous *Cur Deus Homo*, a dialogue between teacher (Anselm) and student (Boso) on why it was necessary for God to become a human being to save humankind. Could God not have simply forgiven us just with his say-so? No, said Anselm. In order to satisfy divine justice, humans must make recompense; but only God has what it takes to bear the sins. So, Anselm argues, it must be a God-man who provides this atonement.[4] Notice that though there are two uses of the word *must* in these descriptions, this act of salvation is ultimately the free exercise of divine grace. *If* God chooses to save some of us, that is by divine prerogative. But *if* we are to be saved, *then* this incarnation, Anselm reckons, is what *must* take place. These terms signal a creative interplay of the "must" that logic leads one to and the "free will" with which God exercises his grace or mercy. Here Anselm also presents his notion of satisfaction or "substitutionary atonement," a significant advancement on that doctrine.

During this time, Anselm went into exile twice. The first was from 1097 to 1100, until King William Rufus died; the second from 1103 to 1106, after which a bargain was worked out with the new king, Henry I. This second exile was due to the ongoing controversy, mentioned above, known as the "Investiture Controversy." Once returned from his second exile, Anselm wrote his last work, *De Concordia*, on the compatibility of human freedom with divine foreknowledge, God's grace, and God's predestination.

APOLOGETIC METHODOLOGY

For those interested in apologetics, the question of how faith and reason ought to relate to each another in the life of the believer is a perennial topic for discussion and debate. It was no different in Anselm's day.[5] There were warring

---

3. Sandra Visser and Thomas Williams, *Great Medieval Thinkers: Anselm* (Oxford: Oxford University Press, 2009), 8.
4. See *Cur Deus Homo*, bk. 2, ch. 6.
5. See this debate played out well in the medieval monastery setting in Umberto Eco, *The Name of the Rose* (New York: Mariner, 1980).

factions: those who repudiated the use of philosophy in matters theological and those who tended to accept it positively to varying degrees. Anselm very much accepted the use of logic to explicate the propositions of theology, and he did so because he found that a faith that sought further illumination was one best guided by a rational and logical method of inquiry.

The essential features of dialectic that Anselm brought to bear as a tool for the explication of theological content were the laws of logic and the search for middle terms in syllogisms.

Laws of Logic

The most basic law, or principle, of logic is *the law of noncontradiction.* Applied to things, it states: *a thing cannot both be and not be at the same time and in the same sense.* Applied to propositions, it states: *a proposition* (a statement that can be true or false) *cannot both be true and not true at the same time and in the same sense.* Thus, if a single statement both affirms some truth T and denies T at the same time and in the same sense, that statement is a contradiction. When two or more propositions are taken together and compared, if accepting them all as true leads to a violation of the law of noncontradiction (LNC) (e.g., if one statement says, "John owns this car" and another says "it's not the case that John owns this car"), we say that these statements are *logically inconsistent.* That is, there is no possible world in which both propositions are true. Christianity, as a theological position, affirms many propositions (e.g., it affirms that God created the world *ex nihilo*; that God was in Christ, reconciling the world to himself; that the holy Scriptures are inspired by God's Holy Spirit; and that human beings are made in the image of God). So in this way, surely our Christian faith must be logically consistent; our believing all that our faith affirms cannot violate the LNC.

The Search for the "Middle Term"

Aristotle, the "father of logic," had categorized the wide array of arguments or *syllogisms* in the formal logic that he knew. In a syllogism, the major premise is given first, then the minor premise, followed by the conclusion. There was a major term (predicate of the conclusion) and a minor term (subject of the conclusion). There was also a middle term, which in the premises showed up twice but disappeared from the conclusion. By Boethius's time, the focus in logic, especially as applied to theology, was in finding the middle term in arguments. Ian Logan writes: "The purpose of [Aristotle's work *Topics*] is to provide an exhaustive framework for the discovery of arguments. According to Boethius, 'every argument is expressed by a syllogism or an enthymeme.' An 'argument is nothing other than the discovery of an intermediate [term], for an intermediate will be able to conjoin the extreme, if an affirmation is being maintained, or to disjoin them, if a negation is being asserted.'"[6]

What Logan is reporting means that in a syllogism there are three terms, A, B, and C, and one premise asserts "A is __ to B," another that "B is __ to C," and the conclusion is drawn, "so A is __ to C," where "__" indicates usually some term indicating a relation. The glue that binds terms A and C together in a syllogism is B, the middle term. This middle term is, for Boethius, the intermediate. A familiar example might be useful:

1. All humans are mortal.
2. Socrates is a human.
3. So Socrates is mortal.

Here, the middle term is *humans*; it is what binds "mortal" (the major term) and "Socrates" (the minor term) together, as seen in the conclusion. Also, we say that this argument is *valid*, that is, it is an argument whose form is such that it is *impossible* for all the premises (here 1–2) to be *true* and yet for the conclusion to be *false*. This argument's validity, then, means that the truth of premises 1–2 entails the truth of the conclusion. Notice the strength of the wording here: if the premises are true, it is *impossible* for the conclusion to be false. This is the strongest form of necessity that is available in the human language—logical necessity.

It is to be noted that logical relations are the sorts of relations that are necessary and *a priori*. Thus, when Anselm speaks of the "necessary reasons" during the elucidation of the Christian faith by logical, rational analysis, it is the logical necessity that binds the major, minor, and middle terms together.

An example of the above "search for the middle term" might reasonably be seen to be employed by Anselm in his *Cur Deus Homo,* "Why God Had to Become a Man," mentioned above. Consider how the search for the "middle term" of the argument pervades the heart of the gospel and incarnation. First, humankind was created in relationship to God, but humans sinned against God, incurring a debt they could not pay. Any power of penance or righteousness they might muster could only be to pay *what they normally owe* God out of allegiance to him. Second, God demanded payment for the sin. Recompense must be made. And yet God wants humans (and created humans with the purpose) to be happy—to find their fulfillment in him. But third, what is the *binding agent*

---

6. Eleonore Stump, *Boethius's In Ciceronis Topica* (Ithaca: Cornell University Press, 1988), 31–32. Cited in Ian Logan, *Reading Anselm's Proslogion: The History of Anselm's Argument and its Significance Today* (London: Routledge, 2016), 14–15.

(middle term) that connects an affronted yet reconciling God to a sinful humanity who cannot be reconciled to God through their own power? The *middle
term* sought for is, Anselm tells us, *the God who becomes a human being.* If one
has a gulf of debt between God and humans, the link (a sort of *middle term*)
between the two is a God-human, the God-Man, Christ Jesus. Anselm used logic
to express these necessary relations within the Godhead and in God's relations
to his fallen creation.

Methodologically, we see how Anselm relied on the power of reason for his
Christian apologetics. Anselm held that good, hard thinking could show one the
"necessary reasons" for our faith, and for the essentials of our Christian belief.
He held this position, with some very good reasons (but perhaps not indefeasible
reasons). To prepare for Anselm's *ratio fidei,* let us return briefly to the issue of
the autonomy of logic over theology. The main issue here is this: What is the
temporal, logical, ontological, moral, and hierarchical relationship of the eternal God to an eternal logical law like that of the law of noncontradiction? That
is, which came first, the Deity or the law? Is God *above* the law of logic? If so,
could God have established different laws? Is the LNC just random or arbitrary,
then—merely the result of the whim of the ultimate sovereign, God? Or is God
below the law of logic? If so, does that not imply that God is lacking in power
and authority? Perhaps (more reasonably, it seems), God is on the same level as
the law of logic. This model could be worked out in a variety of ways.[7] Of course,
laws of logic are propositions, and if Augustine's argument from truth is on the
right track,[8] then propositions, in modern language, are dependent beings, for
they depend on a mind to be thought. Augustine's insight is that if propositions
are eternal, immutable, stable, intentional and yet *mind-dependent,* then the
mind that "thinks" them must be eternal, immutable, stable, intentional (i.e.,
something people have: thoughts that are consciously *about* something else),
and mental in nature. But most everyone admits that propositions exist; so there
must exist such a mind to explain, undergird, and make possible the existence
of such entities. Augustine's argument is strong. For if one denies the existence
of propositions, one appears to be expressing the proposition that there are no
propositions. This means that one affirms the existence of propositions in the
very act of denying the existence of propositions—which means that they definitely exist. This "proof" of the existence of propositions is similar to that of the

---

7. See the recent book where up to six possible models are set out, mostly by Christian philosophers.
See Paul M. Gould, ed., *Beyond the Control of God?: Six Views on the Problem of God and Abstract Objects*
(New York: Bloomsbury, 2014).

8. See Saint Augustine, *On Free Choice of the Will*, ed. Thomas Williams (Indianapolis: Hackett,
1993), ch. 2.

reality of truth. Suppose one denies that truth exists. In that denial, one is saying that it is true that there is no truth—which is not a very promising avenue.

So since there exist propositions, Augustine reasons, there must exist an eternal, personal, immutable, stable, intentional mind, which everyone understands to be God. What this means is that laws of logic such as the LNC form an eternal logical law that would exist in any way the world would have gone, that is, at "every possible world." Thus, laws of logic are *necessarily true*. But as logic tells us, each necessary truth is logically *independent* of any other necessary truth. Thus, it is logically independent of God, who is a necessarily existent being. But the laws of logic depend on an eternal mind—God's mind—for their existence, for being thought. So these laws are eternal yet dependent, which seems altogether coherent. If an eternal being thought a thought eternally, the thought would exist eternally, and thus "necessarily," but would be dependent on that mind (and not the other way around) for its existence. God would thus be, arguably, sovereign over the laws of logic since there would be an asymmetric dependence relation of the laws (including the LNC) on God. Yet because the laws reflect the eternal, immutable thoughts of God, the laws *could not be different from the way they are*. Another way of thinking of this relation would be that God has maximal power, maximal wisdom, and maximally perfect cognitive proper function. God would thus self-legislate the laws of logic (if that is the best model to adopt here), or at least God would just think as a maximally perfectly properly functioning cognizer would think, and thus the laws would be a by-product of that thought, reflective of God's eternal cognitive thinking. Just as God is good in both a descriptive and prescriptive way (good is the way God is, and thus being that way is the way good things *ought to* be), so also the laws of logic are reflective of (i.e., descriptive of) God's natural thinking, which itself is prescriptive in nature, setting the pace for how all rational people *ought* to think and the strictures within which rational, consistent dialogue can take place.

APOLOGETIC RESPONSE

RATIONAL FAITH SEEKING UNDERSTANDING

Anselm is often called "The Second Augustine." Anselm, both literally and figuratively, speaks the language of Augustine—Latin—and in many ways that of Plato, and the moral and metaphysical realism that comes with Augustine's Christian Platonism. Anselm, as an extension of Augustine's Christian Platonism, models great respect for the Holy Scriptures. In the preface to the *Monologion,* his first book, written at Bec in 1076–1077, he says, "In the course of frequent rereadings of this treatise I have been unable to find anything which is inconsistent with the writings of the Catholic Fathers, and in particular with those of the Blessed Augustine."[9]

Like Augustine, Anselm had a very high regard for human reason. Every theologian before him—and every theologian since him—had expressly stated that *rationality* was the chief, or one of the chief, attributes of humankind as made in the *imago Dei*. We "image" God; God is perfectly rational; so other things being equal, we are made with the capacities and states of being rational beings. So though sin may have marred that image and marred the functioning of our rationality, still there was a hope and trust that through reason we could see what was presented to us, we could "picture" mentally the "Forms" of things within us—the Forms themselves being like divine thoughts or exemplars that God had given to us to understand—and thus arrive at a sort of godlike state of understanding, other things being equal.[10] As Sandra Visser and Thomas Williams point out, this viewpoint Anselm called the "reason of faith," or *ratio fidei*.[11] Our understanding of Anselm's meaning to "the reason of faith" is impacted by how we interpret the degree to which Anselm gave a due, or undue, autonomy or hegemony to *ratio* over *fides*. If Anselm means something like *logic* by his use of *ratio*, then the *logic of faith* sounds like something internal to the believer: our faith is coherent and doesn't violate the LNC. If we interpret *ratio* as the "rational evidences or foundation of *fides*," then that sounds like something external: the grounds for our faith that come from observation and reflection on those data. Visser and Williams recommend not an *either/or*, but a *both/and*. "Anselm's *ratio fidei* means both of these things at once; it refers to the intrinsically rational character of Christian doctrines in virtue of which they form a coherent and rationally defensible system."[12] The vital thing to see here is the reason why Anselm had such faith in reason, as it were: it is because of God, not because of us or our operation on or use of *ratio*. God is everywhere rational; God is everywhere in operation. This universe he made is a rational universe; it is orderly and exhibits laws: moral laws reflecting his nature (Rom 2:14–15), scientific laws reflecting his order, logical laws reflecting the proper function of his own perfect cognition. God made us in his image, and so he (or at least his work, design, purposes) is at work in us. Thus, we can discover and use reason to investigate things pertaining to belief, faith, and the divine nature. These reflections

---

9. Anselm, *Monologion,* in *Anselm of Canterbury: The Major Works,* edited with an introduction by Brian Davies and G. R. Evans (Oxford: Oxford University Press, 1998; reissue edition, 2008), 6.

10. Obviously there is the issue of Eph 4:18, our "darkened" understanding, but Anselm seems to think that God's illumination of the mind would or could overcome any setbacks that the sinful nature had brought to our epistemic condition. See also Col 3:10 in this context.

11. Sandra Visser and Thomas Williams, *Great Medieval Thinkers: Anselm,* 13–14.

12. Ibid., 14.

gave Anselm encouragement, and we might say emboldenment, for the "reason of faith."[13] One should not miss, as well, the notion of "order" and "orderliness" of one's meditations that come about within the setting of the monastery, where Anselm would constantly have been engaged in the *lectio divina*, teaching, learning, writing, memorization, recitation, and cross-checking, whose purposes were, in many ways, to "hide the word in one's heart" and to erase any error and mishap in the process of transmission.

Anselm famously saw himself as defending the view *faith seeking understanding* (*fides quaerens intellectum*), a phrase he got from Augustine and is cited in *Proslogion* (ch. 1): "For I believe this also, that 'unless I believe, I shall not understand.' [Isa. 7:9]"[14] He adds in the preface that an earlier title he had thought to give the work, *Proslogion*, was "*Faith in the Quest of Understanding.*"[15] And yet, with these statements, though it might seem that the context is that *Proslogion* is a Christian apologetic work that is designed to take the already faithful person on to "understanding," this phrase seems to mollify the more potent "reason of faith" approach to apologetics, seen above, that we see Anselm offering in his first work, *Monologion*, just one year before *Proslogion*. The setting for the works is important, and Anselm's prefaces to his works tell us a lot about the context for writing, possible names of treatises, his intention for writing, and the like. In *Monologion*, Anselm relates that some of the brothers specifically asked him for a treatise, reflecting the teaching he had already been doing among them "on the subject of meditating upon the essence of the divine." These brothers requested that "nothing whatsoever to be argued on the basis of the authority of Scripture, but the constraints of reason concisely to prove, and the clarity of truth clearly to show, in the plain style, with everyday arguments, and down-to-earth dialectic, the conclusions of distinct investigations."[16]

It should be noted here that Anselm is not saying that once one gets to understanding, one will be able or permitted to set aside one's faith. No, it remains true, for Anselm, as the New Testament teaches, that "without faith it is impossible to please God" (Heb 11:6). Anselm agreed wholeheartedly with Augustine's notion of "the ladder of faith," a ladder which, unlike Wittgenstein's, does not get pitched away once one escapes from the hole. Rather, the ladder is always guiding and leading. Augustine wrote, "The hidden things and secrets of the Kingdom of God first seek out believing men, that they may make them understand. For faith is understanding's ladder, and understanding is

13. Visser and Williams, *Great Medieval Thinkers*, 14.
14. Anselm, *Proslogion,* in *Anselm of Canterbury: The Major Works*, 87.
15. Ibid., 83.
16. Anselm, *Monologion,* in *Anselm of Canterbury: The Major Works*, 5.

faith's reward."[17] This being said, Anselm was no sloth when it came to seeking understanding of his faith. In the commendation of his *Cur Deus Homo* to Pope Urban II, Anselm depicts his goals:

> Many of our holy Fathers and teachers, following the Apostles, speak frequently and on a grand scale about the logical principles [*rationes*] of our faith. Their aim in doing so is to confute unwisdom, to shatter the rigid resistance of unbelievers and to nourish those who, with cleansed hearts, already take delight in this same logic of the faith, for which, once we have reached certitude about it, we ought to hunger. Given the greatness and frequency of their utterances on this subject, neither in our times nor in times to come can we hope for anyone who will be their equal in the contemplation of the truth. All this I grant. *Nevertheless, I do not think that anyone deserves to be rebuked, if, after becoming well-grounded in the faith, he has conceived a desire to exercise himself in the investigation of its logic.*[18] [emphasis added]

One detects Anselm's apologetic emphasis, "to shatter the rigid resistance of unbelievers." But our study and evidences are also to "nourish those ... hearts [who] take delight in this same logic of the faith." Anselm says that one should be "well-grounded in the faith" properly to do the sort of logical analysis of Christian faith that he undertakes in his works.

ARGUMENTS FOR GOD'S EXISTENCE

Arguments for God's existence come in two varieties: *a priori* and *a posteriori* arguments. *A priori* arguments have no premises that require one to consult sense experience to justify those premises. In *a posteriori* arguments, at least one of the premises requires some sort of experience to verify. In *Monologion*, Anselm offers cosmological-type arguments for God's existence, while his famous ontological argument is found in *Proslogion*. The order Anselm wrote these books is important and noteworthy.

Cosmological Arguments in Monologion

Anselm's various arguments here can be called cosmological arguments because of their appeal to certain causal structures or effects that lead one back

---

17. Augustine, Sermon CXXVI.1.1. Cited in Kretzmann, "Faith Seeks," 12.
18. Anselm, from the Commendation of *Cur Deus Homo* to Pope Urban II by Anselm, in *Anselm of Canterbury: The Major Works*, 260.

to the single cause of those effects—God. In the ancient world, the master of causality was Aristotle and his doctrine of the four causes.

If we ask what was the cause of X, Aristotle was the first to break down that question and say that we really could mean one of four things: *the material cause* (out of what matter or substance is it?); *the formal cause* (what is the formal or intellectual cause, planning, intentions, etc. that go into that thing coming about?); *the efficient cause* (what we mostly mean by "cause"—the actual oomph that brings something about, moving parts about, etc.); and *the final cause* (the answer to the reason *why did this thing come about?*).[19]

One of the cosmological arguments for God's existence that Anselm gives in *Monologion* is based on gradations. This argument at the beginning of the book bears interesting resemblances to Thomas Aquinas's Fourth Way. Anselm seemed in this argument to have derived some straightforward inspiration from Boethius's *Topics*. Eleonore Stump comments that Boethius maintained that "'Where there is something greater and lesser, there must also be something greatest or maximal', drawing the inference that there exist maximal propositions, which are the topics (i.e., the *loci*, the places) where the other propositions are located, in the same way as bodies are located in physical places. These maximal propositions are the 'universal and most known propositions from which the conclusion of syllogisms is derived.'"[20]

Compare Anselm's argument in *Monologion*:

> Of all things that exist, there is one nature that is supreme. It alone is self-sufficient in its eternal happiness, yet through its all-powerful goodness it creates and gives to all other things their existence and their goodness. . . . Quite certain, indeed, and clear to all who are willing to see, is the following: take some things that are said to be (say) X, and relative to each other are said to be less, more, and equally X. It is through this X that they are said to be so, and this X is understood as the very same thing in the various cases and not something different in each case (whether X is considered to be in them equally or not equally). Take, for example, some things that are said . . . to be, either equally, or more, or less just. They cannot be understood

---

19. Cf. Suppose one of us were to buy a new mailbox kit at the local hardware store, hoping to replace our current failing unattractive and rickety mailbox. I find an opening in my schedule, read the directions, construct and install the new box, and am impressed at how much nicer it looks. The material cause is the actual metal and plastic that make up the box and post. The formal cause is the intention I have, the planning and purchasing just the right sized box for the job. The efficient cause is the actual mechanical movement and muscle work I use to shape and install the new box; and finally, the final cause, the reason that drives me to replace the old one (the old one is falling apart and having a good mailbox is essential to receive and protect important documents, etc.).

20. Stump, *Boethius's In Ciceronis Topica*, 31. Cited in Logan, *Reading Anselm's Proslogion*, 15.

to be just except through justice, and justice is not something different in each of the various cases. Therefore, since it is certain that all good things when compared with each other are either equally or not equally good, necessarily all good things are good through something, and this something is understood to be the same thing in each of various good things.

Different good things may none the less appear to be called good through different things. [21]

Anselm now explains that ultimately, if a thing is good, it must be made good by the good—a unitary source. But what is it that unifies all the Platonic perfect forms into one source? It will be a substance whose justice is its goodness, whose power and truth are its justice and being, etc. There is a particular causal independence that will signal this one's presence and reality: it will be self-existent, not caused by another. Anselm here takes Aristotle's four causes, and asks about two of them, the material cause and the efficient cause: is the material cause of this most excellent of substances, the greatest, the best, the most just *out of itself, out of nothing, or out of some other thing?* As for efficient cause: is the thing *through (the agency of) itself, through nothing, or through (the agency of) some other thing?* He concludes that the greatest substance, the best and most excellent being exists *per se* (through itself) and *ex se* (out of itself).

Necessarily, therefore, everything beneficial or excellent is, if it is truly good, good through the same one thing through which all good things necessarily are good, whatever that thing may be. And who would doubt that that through which all things are good is a great good? Because, then, it is that through which every good thing is good, it is good through itself. It therefore follows that all the other good things are good through something other than what they themselves are, while this thing alone is good through itself. But nothing that is good through something other than itself is equal to or greater than that good which is good through itself. The one thing, therefore, that is good through itself is the one thing that is supremely good. For the supreme is that which so overtops the others that it has no equal and no superior. But what is supremely good is also supremely great. There is therefore one thing that is supremely good and supremely great, and this is of all the things that exist, the supreme. [22]

---

21. Anselm, *Monologion,* in *Anselm of Canterbury: The Major Works,* 11–12.
22. Anselm, *Monologion* in *Anselm of Canterbury: The Major Works,* 12. Noted that 175 or so years later, when Aquinas writes his Five Ways (five arguments for God's existence) in the *Summa Theologica,* as well as in *Summa Contra Gentiles,* Aquinas uses this sort of "causal elimination" type of argumentation, which finds direct development here in Anselm.

Whatever we make of Anselm's argument, we should note its Platonic Form-based argumentation. Since there is only one ultimate *Form* of "the Good," all good things must be made good by imitating or participating in that Form. When translated to Christian theism, there must be one source of Good that makes all things good. Anselm believes logical inference leads to this conclusion, and it is reasonable to conclude something like that. For we acknowledge that God is good and "every good and perfect gift is from above, coming down from the Father of the heavenly lights, who does not change like shifting shadows" (Jas 1:17). We should note that in this causal argument in *Monologion,* the being Anselm proves is the greatest *actual* being, but in his next publication, *Proslogion,* he hits on the idea that God is not only the best actual being—he is in fact the best or greatest *possible* being.

Ontological Arguments in Proslogion *and* Reply

The cosmological argument above was an *a posteriori* argument. There, Anselm said that there are some things that we see to be, that are said to be, just (say). Some are more just; some less. By contrast, the "one single argument" Anselm presents in *Proslogion* (ch. 2) is an *a priori* argument. By *a priori* it is meant that none of the premises require any experience to evaluate their truth claim; rather, one relies on conceptual analysis and one's inner intuitions alone to judge the argument. Anselm's great insight of the single argument in *Proslogion* 2, that later Kant would call *the ontological argument* (from Greek *ontos*, "being"), was similar to an insight in modern modal logic that says that the best way to tell what is possible *is by what is actual.* Anselm's related insight is this: if X is a necessary being, then X must be an *actual* being. Usually logic tells what is possible, contingent, impossible, and necessary—not what is *actual.* His insight is that the term *necessary,* when used in the phrase "necessary being," entails real existential truths, namely that those necessary beings exist in this actual possible world. What this means is that it is possible to have, as Stephen Davis calls it, an *a priori* existential argument: an argument whose conclusion is that there actually exists a particular being but none of whose premises demand any sort of *a posteriori* appeal to experience.[23]

Anselm houses this argument within the framework of a prayer. Having written the much longer *Monologion,* Anselm says he was thinking it would be convenient if he could provide "one single argument" [*unum argumentum*] that "for its proof required no other save itself, and that by itself would suffice to prove that God really exists, that He is the supreme good needing no other and

---

23. Stephen Davis, *God, Reason, & Theistic Proofs* (Grand Rapids: Eerdmans, 1997), 21.

is He whom all things have need of for their being and well-being, and also to prove whatever we believe about the Divine Being."[24]

That is a tall order. There are four criteria here. First, the argument would be sole and solitary, standing on its own. There would be no need for a chain of arguments; it would be self-sufficient. Since Anselm thought that God is through himself and out of himself, i.e., God is *a se*, he has aseity, and he is ontologically independent and self-existent, perhaps this inspired Anselm to think there just might be a proof itself (not self-existent, perhaps, but at least self-standing or self-sufficient). It is interesting that in Scripture, while we are invited to name our children and to name the animals, *we do not name God—God must name himself.* Why? For the name reveals the essence of something, and only God knows his own essence and nature well enough to capture that essence in his name. When Moses asks in Exodus 3 who he should say has sent him, God tells Moses to say, "*I AM* has sent me to you" (v. 14). God reveals his covenantal name, as God says that he is the being whose essence is *to be.* The name of God is, in some sense, the insight that Anselm had: God *is.* Thus, if you define him logically as one who is and in fact must be, since it is his *nature* to exist, this means God cannot not be. When we grasp God's covenantal name given in Exodus 3:14, it seems that we are 90 percent there when it comes to Anselm's wonderfully brilliant ontological argument. Second, the argument would indeed show that God exists, so long as we thought that God is the being "than which nothing greater can be conceived." And indeed we do: for this phrase can be taken to mean also that God is the *perfect* being, since there can only be one, unique, best, perfect being. Such a being is one that would be worthy of worship, and one to whom we could pray as the sole sovereign. These are properties that Anselm felt he had proved of God in the *Monologion*.[25] Third, the "supreme good . . . and well-being" criterion here seems to be inspired by the *Monologion* argument we referred to above. In light of what Anselm says in his preface to *Proslogion*, perhaps the brothers were complaining that their apologetic was too top-heavy and had too many premises. Finally, fourth, the argument was also to prove whatever we think and believe about the divine being.

Again, Anselm thought modally and Platonically, and according to David Beck, he thought like a Stoic too. Beck claims that it is likely from the Stoic Seneca that Anselm got his famous formula for God's nature, Anselm's definition of God, that God is "*qua nihil maius cogitari potest*": that which nothing greater can be thought.[26] Anselm's argument, in the form of a prayer of "faith seeking

---

24. Anselm, *Proslogion,* in *Anselm of Canterbury: The Major Works*, 82.
25. Anselm, *Monologion,* in *Anselm of Canterbury: The Major Works*, last section (sec. 80).
26. In Seneca, *On Providence*, 1, 13. From W. David Beck, *The Reality of God: A Narrated History of the Case* (Downers Grove, IL: InterVarsity Press, 2020), 233 (MS draft copy).

understanding," introduces God, then, as that than which nothing greater can be thought. Anselm assumes one can form a concept of something in one's mind, and when one goes through this process, there is a sense in which the concept certainly "exists" in the mind—which Anselm calls "existing in the understanding."[27] In Platonic epistemology, there are Forms that do, and Forms that do not, have a corresponding reality. For example, consider Thomas and Gena Jones's fourth daughter. If the Jones only have three children, then this concept does not have a corresponding reality. *Ceteris paribus*, it is a good thing for a person to exist, being an image bearer of God. If a person only exists in thought and not in reality, there is a state that would be better; namely, if the person existed both as a concept/idea *and* in reality. Anselm here is using a *Greatness Principle* (GP). Anselm thinks we make this sort of judgment all the time and that our intuitions alone tell us that, in effect, existence in reality is a "great-making property," a property better to have than to lack. Let's now consider his argument.

> And so, Lord, do thou, who dost give understanding to faith, give me, so far as thou knowest it to be profitable, to understand that thou art as we believe; and that thou art that which we believe. And, indeed, we believe that thou art a being than which nothing greater can be conceived. [Anselm's definition for God is given here.] Or is there no such nature, since the fool hath said in his heart, there is no God? (Ps. 14:1) But, at any rate, this very fool, when he hears of this being of which I speak—a being than which nothing greater can be conceived—understands what he hears, and what he understands is in his understanding; although he does not understand it to exist.
>
> For, it is one thing for an object to be in the understanding, and another to understand that the object exists. When a painter first conceives of what he will afterwards perform, he has it in his understanding, but he does not yet understand it to be, because he has not yet performed it. But after he has made the painting, he both has it in his understanding, and he understands that it exists, because he has made it.
>
> Hence, even the fool is convinced that something exists in the understanding [namely, the concept of God as the being than which none greater can be conceived or thought]. For, when he [the fool] hears of this, he understands it. And whatever is understood, exists in the understanding. And assuredly that, than which nothing greater can be conceived, cannot

---

27. As we will see below, this concept plays a central role in Anselm's presentation of his ontological argument in *Proslogion*, chapter 2.

exist in the understanding alone. For, suppose it exists in the understanding alone; then it can be conceived to exist in reality, which is greater.

Therefore, if that, than which nothing greater can be conceived, exists in the understanding alone, the very being, than which nothing greater can be conceived, is one, than which a greater can be conceived. But obviously this is impossible. [Notice the strong modal term, invoking a *reductio ad absurdum* argument: when one assumes God exists in the mind alone but not in reality, it leads to a violation of the LNC; thus, one's assumption is false and the negation of one's assumption is proved true.] Hence, there is no doubt that there exists a being, than which nothing greater can be conceived, and it exists both in the understanding and in reality.[28]

The argument we can draw from *Proslogion* 2 is as follows: (1) God is a conceivable being, i.e., a possible being (assumption); (2) there are three types of possible beings: possible beings that exist that might not exist, possible beings that do not exist, possible beings that *must* exist, i.e., necessary beings (definitions); (3) GP (Anselm's *A priori* "Greatness" Principle): If X is a possible being that could have existed in reality but does not, then X would have been a greater being had it existed (key intuitive principle Anselm uses); (4) God is a possible being, a greater than which is not possible (definition of GCB). (5) Suppose God existed only conceptually in the understanding (supposition of a *reductio ad absurdum* argument). (6) If God existed only conceptually in the understanding and not in reality, then God would have been a greater being than he is (GP). (7) As a result, a possible being, a greater than which is not possible, would be a being greater than which *is* possible (definition of "God" and Application of GP). (8) But this is a contradiction (violation of LNC), showing our initial *reductio* assumption false; (9) thus, it's not the case that God exists only conceptually in the understanding, i.e., God exists both conceptually in the understanding and in reality.

One can sense that Anselm's argument, if successful, will meet the four criteria outlined above. The argument would be self-sufficient; would show that God really existed; would show that we need God (which would follow because we need good that must come from outside us, and God is found to be the unified source of all that is good—if God were not, I could conceive of a greater being who is the unified source of all good); and would show the other omni-properties of God too. This follows because the Anselmian method, based on the definition of God, is like a sieve: it helps to determine and crank out, as it

28. Anselm, *St. Anselm: Basic Writings*, trans. by S. N. Deane, 2nd ed. (La Salle, IL: Open Court, 1962), 53–4.

were, just what sorts of properties would, and what would not, be present in the greatest conceivable being.

Whether or not the argument is successful pivots on the extent to which we can accept both Anselm's Greatness Principle (GP) and premise 1, that God is a possible being. These are questions that are part of the long and complex history of this argument. A testimony to the greatness of Anselm's argument is that every generation of thinkers since the eleventh century has continued to create new types and versions of ontological arguments. Anselm sought to defend the God he believed in and thought that once one gets a hold of, "understands," the being that God is (cf. his name, *I am*), one will see that God necessarily exists come what may (even if there were no physical universe, no causal activity in any sense in the entire world of contingent beings—there being no contingent beings at all would not change the true reality that God *is*). Of course, *our coming to know that fact*, our being properly situated epistemically with respect to the proposition, "God exists," is different from the metaphysical reality that *God is the great "I am."* In the case of God's name, God had to reveal the name to us; our rationality couldn't have predicted or come to have known that fact or that name.

ANSELM'S CRITICS AND THE LEGACY OF HIS ONTOLOGICAL APOLOGETIC

In Anselm's time, after the publication of *Proslogion*, a monk named Gaunilo of Marmoutiers issued a reply to Anselm's argument, *Pro Insipiente*, "On Behalf of the Fool." Gaunilo tried to show Anselm's argument to be ineffective by arguing that one can apply Anselm's thinking to prove all sorts of things *we know do not exist* must exist. If this were the case, this would successfully show that Anselm's argument misses the mark. For example, Gaunilo asks us to suppose the idea of a greatest conceivable island. Suppose we had an idea of this most excellent of islands. Gaunilo proceeds: "You can no longer doubt that this island which is more excellent than all lands exists somewhere, since you have no doubt that it is in your understanding. And since it is more excellent not to be in the understanding alone, but to exist both in the understanding and in reality, for this reason it must exist. For if it did not exist, any land which really exists will be more excellent than it; and so the island already understood by you to be more excellent will not be more excellent."[29]

The problem with this argument is that the greatest conceivable island cannot possibly pass as an instance of the greatest conceivable *being*, because

---

29. Gaunilo, "On Behalf of the Fool," in *St. Anselm: Basic Writings*, 309.

(1) islands don't admit of intrinsic maximal states of excellence, for one can always add more value to a finite spread-out island, e.g., add another Jack Nicholas-designed golf course, another aquarium, another soccer stadium, another Van Gogh art gallery, etc. and (2) things that don't admit of intrinsic maximal states of excellence cannot possibly be the *greatest conceivable being*. Reflection shows only *persons* could possibly be greatest, because only persons can possess all (or the greatest co-possible set of) the *great-making properties* all at once. A "great-making property" (GMP) is a property that, *ceteris paribus*, is better to have than to lack. Having wisdom is a GMP. Having knowledge of Chicago Cubs baseball history, while sometimes handy and endlessly fascinating, is not a GMP. Having power is a GMP; then, having maximal power is a GMP. But so is having consciousness, being a person, thus—and so greatest conceivable islands cannot possibly be greatest conceivable beings, simply because islands don't have the right natures: its nature does not have essential properties allowing it to have maximal goodness, maximal power, maximal knowledge, omnipresence, etc.

Kant's famous objection in 1781 was that existence is not a predicate, so it cannot be a great-making property. Kant, in effect, is attacking Anselm's GP. Existence is different from that, Kant says. The thought is that first one must have an existing being, *then* we can talk about the properties of such a being. "Being is obviously not a real predicate, that is, it is not a concept of something which could be added to the concept of a thing. It is merely the positing of a thing, or of certain determinations, as existing in themselves."[30] Philosophers of religion Michael Peterson, William Hasker, et. al, challenge this Kantian objection: "Unfortunately, Kant's understanding of a real predicate actually undercuts his own argument that existence is not a real predicate. For Kant synthetic propositions contain real predicates. Since 'A greatest possible being exists' is a synthetic proposition, 'exist' would be a real predicate."[31]

Others have developed *modal ontological arguments*, finding inspiration for a second ontological argument in *Proslogion* 3, in which God is said to be a being whose "nonexistence" is not possible. Here it is not existence that is the GMP but rather *necessary existence*. Alvin Plantinga famously posited that the following is possible: that there be a being with maximal greatness (one who necessarily is omniscient, omnipotent, and omnibenevolent, for starters) in every possible world.[32] In many ways, the current argument has come down to a point

30. Immanuel Kant, *Critique of Pure Reason*, trans. Norman Kemp Smith (New York: St. Martin's, 1965), 504; A 598/B 626.

31. Michael Peterson et. al., *Reason & Religious Belief: An Introduction to the Philosophy of Religion,* 5th ed. (New York: Oxford University Press, 2013), 83.

32. See Alvin Plantinga, *God, Freedom and Evil* (Grand Rapids: Eerdmans, 1989), 108, proposition 25.

that G. W. Leibniz made in the eighteenth century: if God is a possible being, then God is a necessary being. So naturally the discussion has often come back to whether or not the concept of God, or of a greatest conceivable being, is in fact a logically coherent concept. If it is, then God is a possible being and the argument will go through. It all depends on that concept: is it possible for God to have all the great-making properties in maximal fashion, all at once? Or at least, is there a greatest conceivable being (is that a coherent notion) that exhibits necessarily the greatest instantiation of co-possible GMPs? Theists tend to say yes and that God is that being.

There are many good discussions of Anselm's argument and the modal ontological argument today. The authors Stephen Davis, William Rowe, Alvin Plantinga, Graham Oppy, Michael Tooley, and Keith Yandell are a few of the reliable names for future research.

CONTRIBUTIONS TO THE FIELD OF APOLOGETICS

Eadmer, Anselm's biographer, wrote of his "hero" that he, "being continually given up to God and to spiritual exercises . . . attained such a height of divine speculation that he was able by God's help to see into and unravel many most obscure and previously insoluble questions."[33] Two contributions are worth noting here.

The ontological argument if successful plays a very important role in our thinking about Christian theism. This is because while the other arguments for God's existence establish only some of the putative properties of the divine being, the ontological produces an entire set of properties. For example, if we infer that "God is a designer" from the design argument, we still don't know for sure what the moral standing of the designer is. Is the designer morally indifferent to us? Or is this being all good, or something else? The point is that the ontological argument fills in every good-making property in the divine being, because *each* of those properties is co-constitutive of the greatest conceivable being. In this way, the ontological argument gives us that God is good, the creator, sovereign, wise, powerful, a person, an agent, and so forth. But even more, it tells us that God is wise to the superlative degree, that he is all-wise, all-knowing, and all-good. These are very important results that the ontological argument brings to the philosophical theologian, even perhaps if there is no valid and sound

---

33. Eadmer, *Vita Sancti Anselmi*, trans. R. W. Southern as *The Life of St. Anselm: Archbishop of Canterbury* (Nashville: Nelson, 1962), 12.

ontological argument, simply based on the insight that God is a being whose essence is to exist, as his covenantal name reveals.

Another of Anselm's undeniable contributions to the field of apologetics and philosophical theology is the method of "perfect being theology." Augustine and Boethius before Anselm, to be sure, had a concept of a perfect being; even Plato's definition for why God would be immutable is based on the idea of a perfect being type of theology, in some sense. But Anselm's method, stemming from Anselm's definition of God as "the being than which none greater can be thought" continues to bear much fruit. The method can be shown by an example. Suppose we wonder about God's relationship to *time*, i.e., whether God is atemporal, as Anselm, Augustine, Boethius, and Aquinas thought, or whether God is *everlasting*, i.e., whether God exists *at all times and through all time*. Is it fitting for Christian apologists to defend that God is temporal? Or are Anselm and Augustine correct to think that part of the majesty of God, being a perfect being, is that one is not caught up in the "tooth" of time. Boethius's definition of eternity looms large here: "*Aeternitas igitur est interminabilis vitae tota simul et perfecta possessio.*"[34] ("Eternity, therefore, is the perfect possession of unbounded life all at once.") If one is in time, *it makes one less of a being than one could be*, the thought goes, since one's life yesterday is "gone" and is no longer accessible and present-able to one *now*. The method of perfect being theology might say the following. Perhaps the Scriptures *underdetermine* the exact relationship that God has to time; we just have not been told enough. *But given God is perfect, we can rest assured:* whatever relationship is the optimal relationship for the greatest conceivable being to have toward time, *that is the one* God has.[35] It might seem a bit underwhelming to come to this conclusion, but in light of "seeing through a glass darkly," the Anselmian answer may be one that fits best with our own psychological health and well-being as apologists and theologians. And certainly this result, even apart from the insights the method yields elsewhere, signals some positive reasons in favor of our adopting its methodology.

BIBLIOGRAPHY

Adams, Robert. "The Logical Structure of Anselm's Arguments." Pages 221–42 in *The Virtue of Faith and other Essays in Philosophical Theology*. New York: Oxford University Press, 1987.

Anselm of Canterbury. *Monologion*. Pages 5–81 In *Anselm of Canterbury: The Major Works*. Ed. by and with an introduction by Brian Davies and G. R. Evans. Reissue ed. Oxford: Oxford University Press, 2008.

---

34. Boethius, *The Consolation of Philosophy* (Middlesex, England: Penguin, 1969), book V.6. Translation by the author.

35. See Thomas V. Morris, *Our Idea of God* (Downers Grove, IL: InterVarsity, 1991), 138.

————. *Proslogion*. Pages 82–104 in *Anselm of Canterbury: The Major Works*. Ed. by and with an introduction by Brian Davies and G. R. Evans. Reissue ed. Oxford: Oxford University Press, 2008.

Boethius. *The Consolation of Philosophy*. Middlesex, England: Penguin, 1969.

Davis, Stephen. *God, Reason, & Theistic Proofs*. Grand Rapids: Eerdmans, 1997.

Eadmer. *Vita Sancti Anselmi*. Trans. by R. W. Southern as *The Life of St. Anselm: Archbishop of Canterbury*. London: Nelson, 1962.

Gould, Paul M., ed. *Beyond the Control of God?: Six Views on the Problem of God and Abstract Objects*. New York: Bloomsbury, 2014.

Kant, Immanuel. *Critique of Pure Reason*. Trans. by Norman Kemp Smith. New York: St. Martin's, 1965.

Lewis, C. S. *The Problem of Pain*. New York: Macmillan, 1960.

Logan, Ian. *Reading Anselm's Proslogion: The History of Anselm's Argument and its Significance Today*. London: Routledge, 2016.

Morris, Thomas V. *Our Idea of God*. Downers Grove, IL: InterVarsity, 1991.

Peterson, Michael, William Hasker, Bruce Reichenbach, and David Basinger, *Reason & Religious Belief: An Introduction to the Philosophy of Religion*. 5th ed. New York: Oxford University Press, 2013.

Plantinga, Alvin. *God, Freedom, and Evil*. Grand Rapids: Eerdmans, 1989.

Robinson, I. S. *Henry IV of Germany 1056–1106*. Cambridge: Cambridge University Press, 2000.

Rowe, William. *Philosophy of Religion: An Introduction*. 4th ed. Belmont, CA: Wadsworth/Thomson Learning, 2007.

Rule, Martin. *The Life and Times of St. Anselm: Archbishop of Canterbury and Primate of the Britains*. 2 vols. London: Kegan Paul, Trench, and Company, 1883.

Saint Augustine. *On Free Choice of the Will*. Ed. by Thomas Williams. Indianapolis: Hackett, 1993.

————. Letter CXX, 1, 3. Cited in Normal Kretzmann, "Faith Seeks, Understanding Finds: Augustine's Charter for Christian Philosophy." Pages 1–36 in Thomas Flint, ed. *Christian Philosophy*. Notre Dame: Notre Dame University Press, 1990.

Stump, Eleonore. *Boethius's In Ciceronis Topica*. Ithaca: Cornell University Press, 1988.

Tooley, Michael. "Plantinga's Defense of the Ontological Argument." *Mind* 90 (1981): 422–27.

The Correspondence of Pope Gregory VII: Selected Letters from the Registrum. Trans. by Ephraim Emerton. New York: Columbia University Press, 1932.

The Papal Reform of the Eleventh Century: Lives of Pope Leo IX and Pope Gregory VII. Trans. by I. S. Robinson. Manchester: Manchester University Press, 2004.

Visser, Sandra, and Thomas Williams. *Great Medieval Thinkers: Anselm*. Oxford: Oxford University Press, 2009.

Williams, Thomas. "Saint Anselm." *The Stanford Encyclopedia of Philosophy*. Spring 2016 edition. Edward N. Zalta, ed. https://plato.stanford.edu/entries/anselm/.

Yandell, Keith. *Philosophy of Religion: A Contemporary Introduction*. 2nd ed. New York: Routledge, 2016.

SAINT THOMAS AQUINAS

Defending Reason and *Faith*

FRANCIS J. BECKWITH

SHAWN FLOYD

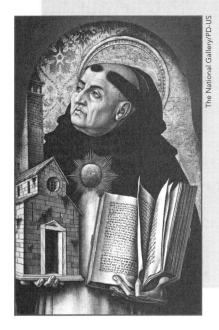

By the thirteenth century, Christianity had permeated every aspect of life in the Western world. This era also marked the ascendancy of the great universities of Europe, the rediscovery of the works of Aristotle, and the founding of the great mendicant religious orders—the Franciscans and the Dominicans. Amid all this emerged Thomas Aquinas (1225–1274), the most important Christian thinker of the second millennium. Seeking to appropriate the best of Aristotle into the rich theological inheritance from the Church's first millennium, Aquinas, a Dominican priest, explored in his works virtually every question on which Christian thought could provide insight, including the relationships between faith and reason, nature and grace, virtue and holiness, law and morality, body and soul, and God and creation.

HISTORICAL BACKGROUND

Roccasecca is a small municipality or *commune* in the Italian province of Frosinone. Just beyond its perimeter are ruins of a tenth-century castle whose initial purpose was to help protect the Abbey of Montecassino, a Benedictine monastery some sixteen miles southeast of Roccasecca. The complete history of the castle's occupancy is unclear, but from 1100 onward, it was the residence of various branches of the d'Aquino family. In 1220, the castle was home to Landulf d'Aquino, a knight who governed land claimed by the king of Sicily, Frederick II. Historians indicate that Landulf was not without means or political connections. He was, however, of lower nobility even though his roots extended back to more elevated peerage.[1]

---

1. James Weisheipl, OP. *Friar Thomas D'Aquino: His Life, Thought, and Works* (Washington, DC: Catholic University Press, 1983), 6.

Of Landulf's many children (we're told he had eight or nine), it was his youngest, Thomas (b. 1225), whose towering intellect and piety would make him perhaps the most influential theologian in the Western world. Between 1230 and 1231, the young Aquinas entered the Abbey at Montecassino as an oblate, and there he received an education in reading, writing, and basic monastic life.[2] This practice will no doubt seem foreign to readers, but as Jean-Pierre Torrell explains, it was not uncommon for noble families to prepare their youngest son for a vocation within the church.[3]

The proximity of the Abbey made it a natural place for Aquinas's schooling. It was also one of the most premiere centers of education in Europe. Yet the Abbey was situated in a region of perpetual conflict between King Frederick II and the Papal States. By 1239 those conflicts had intensified, and Aquinas's parents sent him to continue his studies at a new *studium* in Naples.[4] There, his studies most likely consisted of the seven liberal arts: the *trivium* (grammar, rhetoric, and logic) and the *quadrivium* (arithmetic, geometry, music, and astronomy). It is also likely that he became familiar with the writings of Aristotle (384–322 BC).[5] Apart from Aristotle's *Categories*, which had been available for centuries, many of his works had been translated into Latin during the mid-twelfth century. By the time Aquinas had arrived in Naples, those works were read widely and had spawned a heightened interest in science, medicine, and Arabic astronomy throughout southern Italy.[6]

While in Naples, Aquinas grew in his appreciation for the Dominican order and eventually joined. His family did not receive the decision well, as they intended for him to join the order of Saint Benedict and perhaps, according to Torrell, become abbot of Montecassino.[7] There were politically delicate issues at work here too. The d'Aquino family was allied with Frederick II, who by now was excommunicated and had previously expelled some of the abbey's monks.[8] The Dominicans in Naples were intent on shielding Aquinas from his family's attempts to interfere. They relocated him first to Rome, then Bologna. Despite their efforts to keep him hidden, a small regiment of soldiers (led by his own brother) eventually apprehended Aquinas and confined him to the grounds of the family castle. For the better part of a year, they implored him to renounce

---

2. Jean-Pierre Torrell, OP. *Saint Thomas Aquinas: The Person and His Work, Volume 1*, trans. Robert Royal (Washington, DC: Catholic University Press, 1996), 5.

3. Ibid., 4.

4. Ibid., 5.

5. Weisheipl, *Friar Thomas D'Aquino*, 16.

6. Torrell, *Saint Thomas Aquinas*, 6.

7. Ibid., 9.

8. Weisheipl, *Friar Thomas D'Aquino*, 12.

his vocation with the Dominicans. He showed no resentment or ill will toward his family; he instead is reported to have been serene and in constant prayer. Eventually, his family relented and released him to the Dominican priory in Naples.[9]

For reasons that are not completely clear, Aquinas would not remain in Naples for long. Perhaps the existing political conflicts made him vulnerable to further trouble.[10] He was again relocated and resumed his studies at the University of Paris in 1245. Some speculate that he completed his studies and attained a master of arts (a prerequisite for advanced studies in law, medicine, or theology). Yet some dispute this possibility because, as a Dominican, he could not have been enrolled at a secular institution such as the University of Paris. As Weisheipl explains, monastic law prohibited the religious from studying classical texts under the direction of arts faculty without permission.[11] How Aquinas managed to complete the required MA need not concern us here. What we do know is that it was in Paris where Aquinas commenced a demanding journey toward becoming a *magister in sacra pagina*—master of the sacred page.

Becoming a master in theology required the completion of various tasks under the supervision of an established theological master. These included teaching and writing commentaries on sacred Scripture as well as on Peter Lombard's four-volume compendium of Christian doctrine, the *Sentences* (ca. 1252–1257). Students would also participate in formal debates or "disputations" on perennial questions in theology. Once these requirements were met, the student would prepare and present his inaugural lecture.[12] Aquinas's inaugural lecture took place in 1256.

A brief remark about Aquinas's body of work is in order. Most of his writings emerged in the context of his teaching.[13] These include biblical commentaries, commentaries on Aristotle and Neoplatonic writings, collected disputations, polemical writings, and theological syntheses. The latter category includes his commentary on the *Sentences*, the eight-hundred-page *Summa Contra Gentiles* (1259–1265), and the three-thousand-page *Summa Theologiae* (1265–1274, though never completed). The two *Summas* are particularly important for us as they provide Aquinas's definitive account of theology and philosophy's respective domains and connection.

---

9. Ibid., 11. The drama of this episode is described more thoroughly by Weisheipl and Torrell. Our brief account follows their narrative.

10. Ibid., 18.

11. Weisheipl, *Friar Thomas D'Aquino*, 38.

12. These tasks are described with varying degrees of detail by Torrell, Weisheipl, and Ralph McInerny and John O'Callaghan, "Saint Thomas Aquinas," in *The Stanford Encyclopedia of Philosophy* (Summer 2018 Edition), ed. Edward N. Zalta, https://plato.stanford.edu/archives/sum2018/entries/aquinas/.

13. McInerny and O'Callaghan, "Saint Thomas Aquinas."

THEOLOGICAL CONTEXT

While most of Aquinas's theological education occurred in Paris, it will be helpful to note a formative stint spent at the University of Cologne (1248–1252).
There the Dominican order had established a *studium generale*, and Aquinas
was to accompany a theological master sent to preside over it.[14] The master was
Albertus Magnus ("Albert the Great") (1200–1280), a German Dominican
bishop who also taught at the University of Paris. As a mentor, there was none
better for Aquinas. Copleston describes him as "a man of open mind" with
"wide intellectual interests and sympathies."[15] Weisheipl claims that in terms of
Albert's "breadth of scholarship . . . and thoroughness," he exceeded Aquinas.[16]
And much of Aquinas's understanding of and appreciation for Aristotle is no
doubt due to Albert's influence. While Aquinas would have already been familiar with Aristotle prior to Paris and Cologne, it was Albert who "augmented
Thomas's knowledge [of Aristotle] and encouraged its growth."[17]

In both the universities and the church-sponsored *studium*, the study of
Aristotle did not occur without controversy. A brief discussion of these controversies can shed some light on Aquinas's theological milieu and help clarify
ongoing disputes over theology's relationship to philosophy. For Albert, there
was no conflict between philosophy and theology. He saw them as independent
yet compatible sciences distinguished by different investigative methods. While
he thought philosophical reason was not the theologian's point of investigative departure, he nevertheless believed it "can be of real utility in a secondary
capacity when dealing with objections brought by" those hostile to Christian
teaching.[18] In this way, philosophy remains an independent science whose contributions to theology are salutary.

Not everyone shared Albert's understanding of philosophy's value. Some
argued that philosophy could not achieve its investigative ends without the assistance of theology. Bonaventure (1221–1274), a Franciscan and contemporary
of Aquinas, offered a view along these lines. While he agreed that philosophy
and theology involved different investigative methods, he also thought the most
mature philosophical system would be woefully incomplete and even erroneous
without the light of faith.[19] Other theologians were even more incredulous of

---

14. Weisheipl, *Friar Thomas D'Aquino*, 38.
15. Frederick Copleston, SJ, *A History of Philosophy, Vol. 2: Medieval Philosophy* (Garden City, NJ:
Image Books, 1962), 293.
16. Weisheipl, *Friar Thomas D'Aquino*, 39.
17. Ibid.
18. Copleston, *A History of Philosophy*, 296.
19. Ibid., 245–6.

philosophy's value. Of course, opposition to philosophy was nothing new among Christian thinkers. As far back as the patristic era, one can find those who thought philosophy's pagan origins were a sufficient reason for eschewing its lessons. As Tertullian (ca. 160–ca. 220) rhetorically asked, "What indeed has Athens to do with Jerusalem? What concord is there between the Academy and the Church?"[20] While the thirteenth-century church rejected such a severe view, concerns about heresy occasionally led to censuring particular philosophical theses or even whole texts. Even then, proscriptions on teaching censured texts usually applied in certain universities where they were rarely enforced, at least during Aquinas's time.[21]

While others viewed Aristotle's philosophy with varying degrees of skepticism, there were thinkers who had an exceedingly high regard for it. These were the "Latin Averroists," a term ascribed to university faculty who lauded Aristotle as interpreted by the Islamic philosopher Averroes (1126–1198). On their view, Aristotle's thought represented the pinnacle of human knowledge even though his views included theses clearly antithetical to Christian doctrine (two of which being the eternity of the world and the denial of the human soul's subsistence). Unlike Albert, whose endorsement of Aristotle was highly qualified,[22] the Averroists construed Aristotle's teaching "as being identical with the whole truth attainable by human reason."[23]

The aforementioned disputes were in full swing during Aquinas's time in Paris and Cologne. His own efforts to resolve them transcended particular disputes over Aristotle. For Aquinas, broader questions were in play. How should we assess what natural human reason tells us about God, humanity, and the purpose for which humanity exists? Are the deliverances of human reason commensurate with revealed truth? If so, what does theology disclose that reason cannot discover? The apologetic tasks Aquinas undertook would often be within the context of these questions. His treatment of them would effectively transform how the church demarcated theology and philosophy.

APOLOGETIC RESPONSE

Aquinas's treatment of the aforementioned questions is expressive not only of his profound sensitivities as a theologian but as a remarkable thinker capable of

20. Tertullian, *The Prescription Against the Heretics (De praescriptione haereticorum)* (c. 200), trans. Peter Holmes, chapter 7, from *Ante-Nicene Fathers*, vol. 3, eds. Alexander Roberts, James Donaldson, and A. Cleveland Coxe (Buffalo, NY: Christian Literature, 1885), http://www.newadvent.org/fathers/0311.htm (revised and edited for New Advent by Kevin Knight).
21. Torrell, *Saint Thomas Aquinas*, 7.
22. Weisheipl, *Friar Thomas D'Aquino*, 42.
23. Ibid., 272.

systematizing broad strands of thought into an elegant worldview. As Copleston notes, Aquinas, "with his genius for systematization, saw clearly the use that could be made of the principles of Aristotle in achieving a systematic theological and philosophical synthesis."[24] Of course, Aquinas's appropriation of Aristotle's thought was (unlike the Latin Averroists) qualified by his Christian commitments. Even where Aquinas departed from Aristotle, he remained convinced that natural human reason was fully compatible with sacred teaching and useful in rendering its particular elements coherent. Similarly, Aquinas was convinced that Christian faith could provide a richer understanding of what one can know apart from what God reveals about himself.

In short, both reason and faith—the "instruments" employed by philosophy and theology, respectively—are reliable sources of divine truth. As Aquinas notes, "Some truths about God exceed all the ability of the human reason. Such is the truth that God is triune. But there are some truths which the natural reason also is able to reach. Such are that God exists, that He is one, and the like. In fact, such truths about God have been proved demonstratively by the philosophers, guided by the light of the natural reason."[25]

The linkage between "truths known by means of reason" and "demonstratively proven truths" is important here. The truths at which the philosopher aims are those resulting from scientific demonstration (*scientia*). In scholastic thought, a demonstration is a kind of reasoning that yields conclusions that are necessary and certain. According to Aquinas, reason can demonstrate not only that God exists but that God—the first Being—exists in a peculiar way in comparison to all other beings. God is not simply the greatest possible being, but the source of all contingent being, including the categories by which we understand and conceptualize the created order. For this reason, Aquinas believes that God cannot be fully captured by these categories. Any description we may have of God (whether by way of our natural reason or imparted to us by revelation), though taking the form of a subject/predicate statement (e.g., "God is omnipotent, wise, and so forth"), does not tell us what God is in his essence: "Although by the revelation of grace in this life we cannot know of God 'what He is,' and thus are united to Him as to one unknown; still we know Him more fully according as many and more excellent of His effects are demonstrated to us, and according as we attribute to Him some things known by divine revelation, to which natural reason cannot reach, as, for instance, that God is Three and One."[26]

---

24. Copleston, *A History of Philosophy*, 423.

25. *Summa Contra Gentiles (SCG), Book One: God, trans. Anton C. Pegis (Notre Dame: University of Notre Dame Press, 1975)*, I.3.2.

26. St. Thomas Aquinas, *Summa Theologiae (ST)* I, Q12, a13, a1, 2nd and rev., literally translated by Fathers of the English Dominican Province (1920), online edition, http://www.newadvent.org/summa/ *(ST)*.

We might sum up Aquinas's view by employing the oft-cited phrase "reason can tell us *that* God is, not *what* he is." This description, while apt, may suggest that the purview of faith concerns only what lies beyond the parameters of human reason. For Aquinas, however, the matter is more interesting. To see why, consider the ambiguity of the term *reason*. Our discussion thus far has concerned only *demonstrative* reason. In instances of demonstrative reason, a person who understands and believes the premises of a demonstration cannot fail to assent to its conclusion. To use a simple illustration: if I understand that (1) all marsupials are suckled in a natural pouch and (2) an opossum is a marsupial, then I cannot help but conclude that an opossum is suckled in a natural pouch. Similarly, demonstrations for God's existence produce conclusions that are necessary and certain for those who understand and believe the demonstrations' premises. The apparent necessity of the conclusion *induces* our assent.

This point partially explains why our assent to the conclusion of a theistic demonstration is not a matter of faith (although it may be for those who don't know or understand demonstrations). The assent of faith is voluntary; it involves a willingness to believe what God has revealed to us about himself. Yet for those who know God's existence by means of demonstration, their assent will not be voluntary but compelled by the obviousness of what reason concludes.

Apart from establishing the demonstrable fact of God's existence, is reason able to contribute anything else to our understanding of God or Christian teaching? Answering this question requires us to take note of the distinction between reason's *demonstrative* and *persuasive* functions.[27] While reason cannot demonstrate that, for example, God is triune, it can make use of analogies and arguments in an effort to show that what Christianity teaches about God isn't contrary to reason. In other words, persuasive reason can function apologetically by combatting error and defending the coherence of Christian doctrine.[28] Moreover, persuasive reason cannot compel our assent, but it can give us good reasons for assenting. On this point, John Jenkins notes that "persuasive reasoning" consists of "credibility arguments" that corroborate the truth of sacred teaching but are unable "to move one to assent to the articles of faith."[29] In other words, persuasive reason does not destroy the merit of faith by rendering faith unnecessary; rather, it is a salutary means of promoting, encouraging, and defending faith to those who may not be convinced of the veracity of Christian teaching.

27. St. Thomas Aquinas, "Commentary of Boethius's *De Trinitate*," in *Aquinas On Faith and Reason*, ed. Stephen Brown (Indianapolis: Hackett, 1993), QII.art.1 *ad* 5. Shawn Floyd also discusses this distinction and its implications for theological knowledge in his article "Achieving a Science of Sacred Doctrine," *The Heythrop Journal* 40, vol. 2 (2006): 1–15.

28. *De Trinitate* QII.art.1 *sed contra* 1–4.

29. John Jenkins, *Knowledge and Faith in Thomas Aquinas* (Cambridge: Cambridge University Press, 1998), 185–86.

APOLOGETIC METHODOLOGY

To God, from What Is "Better Known to Us"

How does Aquinas use demonstrative reason to prove God's existence? The approach Aquinas uses to prove God's existence through demonstrative reason is entirely sensible. As in any search for explanations, we begin with facts about the world that are most accessible to us and attempt to demonstrate the cause on which they depend. To illustrate, imagine trying to enter your home through the front door. The key seems to work, but when you try to push the door open, it just won't budge. You surmise that there is something interfering with the door's mechanism. It could be that the hinges are broken, that there is a heavy object on the other side of the door, or that someone put a substance (like industrial-strength superglue) between the frame and the door strong enough to prevent the door from opening. You then inspect around the door and eliminate the broken hinges and superglue theories. You conclude that there is a heavy object on the other side of the door. For all you know, it could be an anvil, a pile of bricks, or the offensive line of the Dallas Cowboys. You don't know precisely *what* is hindering your entrance, but you do know that there is *something* there and that it has enough mass to prevent you from opening your front door.

Demonstrating God's existence is not unlike determining that there is an obstruction behind the door. We begin with the "effects" or observable realities within our experience and then proceed to establish their cause. As Aquinas writes, "When an effect is better known to us than its cause, from the effect we proceed to the knowledge of the cause. And from every effect the existence of its proper cause can be demonstrated, so long as its effects are better known to us; because since every effect depends upon its cause, if the effect exists, the cause must pre-exist. Hence the existence of God, in so far as it is not self-evident to us, can be demonstrated from those of His effects which are known to us."[30]

This sort of reasoning, argues Aquinas, has approval in Scripture: "The Apostle says: 'The invisible things of Him are clearly seen, being understood by the things that are made' (Rom 1:20)."[31] In other words, we can know God's existence by first identifying some uncontroversial aspect of our experience, such as motion (or change), efficient causality, possibility and necessity, gradation of being, or the end-directed nature of the universe. These are the "effects" (or "the things that are made"). From there we can conclude that there is a cause of those effects ("the invisible things of Him"[32])—an ultimate explanation that

---

30. *ST*, I Q2.art2, *respondeo.*
31. *ST*, I Q2.art2, *sed contra.*
32. Aquinas also believes that even though most people do not reason to God (as a philosopher might),

Aquinas describes (very generally) as a first cause or mover (or, as he puts it, what "everyone understands to be God"[33]).

DEMONSTRATING GOD'S EXISTENCE[34]

The previous subsection provides a general overview of Aquinas's method of demonstrating God's existence. As for the demonstrations themselves, there are five summarized in the *Summa Theologiae* (often called "the five ways").[35] These are intended to be (as it were) "CliffsNotes" versions of more developed arguments that one can find in *Summa Contra Gentiles* and *On Being and Essence*.[36]

Let's consider the second of Aquinas's five ways—the argument from the order of efficient causes. He first points out that a thing cannot be the efficient cause of itself. You currently exist because other things have brought you into and sustain your existence, e.g., your parents, the environment, oxygen, available sustenance, etc. If those things did not exist, you would not exist. Yet each of *those* things cannot be the efficient cause of their own existence any more than you can be the cause of your existence. They too require an efficient cause (or causes) to bring them into and sustain their existence.

What we have here, then, is an *order* of efficient causes, each of which is causally dependent on something prior to itself. To be clear, the order of causes Aquinas has in mind is not a *temporally* ordered series of causes. That is, they are not events whose occurrence come about by virtue of some other event preceding them in time. Rather, the series consists of causes that exist simultaneously in an order of causal subordination. As Copleston explains, "When Aquinas talks about an 'order' of efficient causes he is not talking of a series stretching back into the past, but of a hierarchy of causes, in which a subordinate member is here and now dependent on the causal activity of a higher member."[37]

To illustrate this point, consider a lamp sitting on one's desk. Assuming it is like most lamps, its ability to provide light is powered by electricity, which

---

they still have a general sense of God's existence and attributes through "the things that are made." Writes Aquinas: "To know that God exists in a general and confused way is implanted in us by nature, inasmuch as God is man's beatitude. For man naturally desires happiness, and what is naturally desired by man must be naturally known to him. This, however, is not to know absolutely that God exists; just as to know that someone is approaching is not the same as to know that Peter is approaching, even though it is Peter who is approaching..." (*ST*, I Q2.art1.ad1).

33. *ST*, I Q2.art3, *respondeo*.

34. Shawn Floyd offers a more detailed account of the ideas in this and the following subsection in his article "Aquinas's Philosophical Theology" *The Internet Encyclopedia of Philosophy*, Jim Fieser and Bradley Dowden eds., hosted by the University of Tennessee at Martin. https://www.iep.utm.edu/aq-ph-th/.

35. *ST*, I Q2.art3.

36. *SCG*, 1.13; St. Thomas Aquinas, *De Ente et Essentia* (*On Being and Essence*) (*De ente*), 88–98, adapted and edited by Joseph Kenny, OP, http://dhspriory.org/thomas/DeEnte&Essentia.htm.

37. Frederick Copleston SJ, *Thomas Aquinas* (Baltimore: Penguin, 1955), 122.

in turn is supplied by functioning wires, cables, and pylons. The pylons supply electricity distributed from transformers, and the transformers depend for *their* operation on the electricity the power plant supplies. The power plant—whose own operations involve simultaneously running furnaces, boilers, and turbines—converts natural resources into electrical energy. Of course, we could trace the causal history of those natural resources too, but perhaps the point is clear enough. One's working lamp is part of a causal order of dependency, and the causes within that order—from the functioning lamp to the initial conversion of natural resources into electrical energy—exist simultaneously to produce the observable effect (emitting light).

This way of describing a causal order helps us see why its component causes are of an intermediate and instrumental nature. That is, they depend for their existence on some prior cause while also enabling succeeding causes to exist. Edward Feser calls causal orders of this sort "essentially ordered causal series" because each cause within the series depends necessarily for its existence on an antecedently sustaining cause.[38] Moreover, this account helps explain why causal series of this sort cannot be infinite (that is, essential ordered causal series cannot be series for which there is no "first"). For without a first efficient cause, there would be no subsequent instrumental causes and thus no causal order for us to observe.

The key idea here is that the power of intermediate causes is entirely derivative. They exist only by virtue of a principle cause of which they are an instrument, and this is why their power "must ultimately be traced to the simultaneous activity of a first mover."[39] As Aquinas argues, in the absence of a first mover or cause, there can be no ultimate effect "nor any intermediate efficient causes; all of which is plainly false. Therefore it is necessary to admit a first efficient cause, to which everyone gives the name of God."[40]

Here is an important observation about this argument many people miss. Just as this argument does not concern a series of temporally ordered causes, neither does it require that the universe have a temporal beginning (as one finds in the Kalām cosmological argument).[41] That argument's second premise—"The universe began to exist"[42]—depends on establishing philosophically (or scientifically) that the universe had a *temporal* beginning. For Aquinas, however, one cannot know that the universe began to exist through philosophy or science since neither can provide a demonstrable argument for such a claim.

---

38. Edward Feser, *Aquinas: A Beginner's Guide* (London: Oneworld, 2009), 78.
39. Ibid.
40. *ST*, I Q2.art3, *respondeo*.
41. William Lane Craig, *The Kalām Cosmological Argument* (London: Macmillan, 1979).
42. Ibid., 63.

One believes it, argues Aquinas, solely on the authority of Scripture.[43] So even if the universe had always existed or was of an infinite duration, it would still need a First Cause in the sense of needing a principle or ultimate source of causal power to keep it going.[44]

TALKING ABOUT GOD

Although we can demonstrate the existence of God (understood in terms of a first cause), there is much about God that our demonstrative efforts cannot prove. For Christians especially, the most important truths about God are matters of faith communicated to us through sacred Scripture. Even so, the demonstrations of God's existence yield conclusions from which additional truths can be inferred. In both the *Summa Contra Gentiles* and the *Summa Theologiae*, Aquinas argues that being First in the order of causality requires that God also be simple, good, one, infinite, eternal, perfect, immutable, and omnipresent.[45]

In order to see why, consider whether God might be a material substance. If God were material, then he would be subject to being moved or acted on by things other than himself. In other words, he would not be "first" in the order of causality. Moreover, material substances are composite entities that invariably depend on something else for their existence. If God was a composite of this sort, there would have to be something causally prior to himself capable of sustaining his existence. In fact, Aquinas insists that God is not even a composite of properties or attributes. God's being must be simple and undivided.

By describing God as simple, Aquinas means that the characteristics we often attribute to God are not something *in addition to* the divine life. To make this point a bit clearer, consider the attributes of "goodness" and "existence." For creatures like us, goodness is not an all or nothing affair. We have it to some degree; and we also lose or gain goodness depending on how we deliberate and act over time. For God, however, "goodness" is not a property that God *has* or possesses in addition to who he is. Rather, he is his *own* goodness.[46] We can make a similar point about God's existence. As a first cause, God's existence is not derived from or dependent on some antecedent cause. God is his *own* existence.[47]

---

43. *ST,* I Q46.art2, *respondeo.*
44. "To understand this we must consider that the efficient cause, which acts by motion, of necessity precedes its effect in time; because the effect is only in the end of the action, and every agent must be the principle of action. But if the action is instantaneous and not successive, it is not necessary for the maker to be prior to the thing made in duration as appears in the case of illumination. Hence they say that it does not follow necessarily if God is the active cause of the world, that He should be prior to the world in duration; because creation, by which He produced the world, is not a successive change . . ." (*ST,* I.Q46.art2, a1).
45. *SCG,* 1.14–44; *ST,* I Q3–13.
46. *SCG* I.3.8.
47. *ST* I 3.4.

Aquinas engages in a similar analysis to arrive at the other attributes; that is, he shows that if God is indeed the *first* cause, he must not only be immaterial but must lack nothing, depend on nothing, and be the source of all contingent existence. If this account of being first and uncaused is correct, then God must be good, one, infinite, eternal, perfect, immutable, and omnipresent. Yet we must keep in mind here that these descriptors (e.g., being good, powerful, eternal, and so forth) cannot refer to God in the way they sometimes refer to us. Human language is a complicated mechanism we use to describe or refer to finite physical creatures existing in time. When using those terms to describe God, then, we must understand them not univocally but analogically.

The idea of analogy is complicated, and many medieval thinkers did not always understand analogical language in the same way.[48] But the general idea here is that while the *terms* we use to describe both God and creatures may be the same, they nevertheless have varied but related meanings. For example, if we say God is "intelligent" or has the characteristic of a "mind," we cannot assume that God is (like other intelligent creatures) a rational agent who possesses a body or who deliberates about what goodness or wisdom requires. This characterization would require that God exist in time, be limited, acquire knowledge he currently doesn't have, and undergo change—all of which is inconsistent with the divine nature. We thus attribute "intelligence" to God knowing that it cannot be the same *kind* of intelligence we attribute to creatures. God's mode of being far surpasses that which we experience in this temporal world; we cannot know God in his essence this side of eternity.[49] When we ascribe intelligence to God, then, we mean that God's intelligence is *like* human intelligence (that is, it is analogous).

The Preambles of Faith and the Articles of Faith

Having addressed what demonstrative reason permits us to say about God, we can now speak more clearly about how reason is related to the faith-related claims we affirm about God. According to Aquinas, the truths of God that we can know by reason are called *the preambles of faith*. We call them "preambles" not because one must first know them by reason to have faith but because they are beliefs—though demonstrable by reason—that the believer must presuppose when assenting to the *articles of faith*—the specific teachings about God as revealed to us through sacred Scripture. In other words, demonstrable truths about God are assumed to be true when assenting to teachings that are more explicitly theological.

---

48. E. Jennifer Ashworth, "Medieval Theories of Analogy," in *The Stanford Encyclopedia of Philosophy* (Fall 2017), Edward N. Zalta, ed., https://plato.stanford.edu/archives/fall2017/entries/analogy-medieval/.

49. Aquinas does hold that the blessed will see God in his essence in heaven. See *ST*, Suppl., Q92.

In some instances, a demonstrable truth will be a matter of faith, particularly for those who are unfamiliar with or incapable of thinking through demonstrative arguments. Yet even in these cases, God's existence is presumed true when assenting to sacred teaching. As Aquinas writes: "Things which can be proved by demonstration are reckoned among the articles of faith, not because they are believed simply by all, but because they are a necessary presupposition to matters of faith, so that those who do not know them by demonstration must know them first of all by faith."[50]

By way of illustration, consider the cases of Mr. Reason and Mr. Pious. Mr. Reason, who first comes to know God's existence by rational argument, is moved by the grace of God to assent to the articles of faith (which must include the existence of God, since one must assent to the doctrine that Jesus is God's Son), and then seeks reception into the Church by means of Baptism. On the other hand, Mr. Pious always believed there is a God (but not because of a rational demonstration). He attended church with his family, prayed occasionally, and so forth. He never questioned God's existence and never sought to demonstrate it either. Yet like Mr. Reason, Mr. Pious is eventually moved by God's grace to assent to the articles of faith (which must include the existence of God, since one must assent to the doctrine that Jesus is God's Son), and then seeks reception into the Church by means of Baptism.

Contrary to what some critics claim,[51] Aquinas does not believe that the preambles of faith must be held as *demonstratively* true or as a kind of first or foundational step for one to have authentic faith. As he notes: "The existence of God and other like truths about God, which can be known by natural reason, are not articles of faith, but are preambles to the articles; for faith presupposes natural knowledge, even as grace presupposes nature, and perfection supposes something that can be perfected. *Nevertheless, there is nothing to prevent a man, who cannot grasp a proof, accepting, as a matter of faith, something which in itself is capable of being scientifically known and demonstrated*" (emphasis added).[52]

Aquinas's distinction between the preambles and the articles of faith follows from his view that philosophy and theology are distinct yet complementary realms of inquiry. They are complementary insofar as they reinforce and illuminate each other. The preambles of faith, though knowable by reason, may be believed without rational demonstration. The articles of faith, though not

50. *ST*, II-II.Q1, art. 5, ad. 3
51. For example, the evangelical theologian Carl F. H. Henry writes, "In developing the empirical case for theism, Aquinas's larger aim was to prepare the natural man, once convinced of God's existence by his own reason and apart from divine revelation, to accept supernaturally revealed truth" (Carl F. H. Henry, *God, Revelation and Authority*, 6 vols. [Wheaton, IL: Crossway, 1999; originally published in 1976], II: 105).
52. *ST*, I.Q2, art. 2, ad. 2, (emphasis added).

knowable by rational demonstration, may be better understood by reason insofar as reason assists the theologian in the task of answering the heretics' misunderstandings as well as the difficulties raised by those who reject the faith outright.

In this regard, the *Summa Contra Gentiles* is Aquinas's crowning achievement. Unlike that of the *Summa Theologiae*,[53] its primary purpose is (according to many commentators) apologetic: "I have set myself the task of making known, as far as my limited powers will allow, the truth that the Catholic faith professes, and of setting aside the errors that are opposed to it."[54]

There are three different categories of non-Christians to which Aquinas is responding, each requiring a different approach. In replying to heretics, he can appeal to the New Testament. In answering Jews, he has the authority of the Old Testament. In speaking with pagans and Muslims (or what he calls "Mohammedans"), neither of which accepts the Hebrew-Christian Scriptures, he has "recourse to the natural reason, to which all men are forced to give their assent," though he admits that "in divine matters the natural reason has its failings."[55] And yet as Aquinas points out, "to proceed against individual errors, however, is a difficult business."[56] For this reason, the four books of the *Summa Contra Gentiles* address four general theological categories—God, creation, providence, and salvation—rather than each individual group of non-Christians. Under each category, Aquinas responds to various challenges posed by each group, requiring him to weave a tapestry of arguments that appeal to both Scripture and natural reason.

Consider, for example, Aquinas's discussion of the Christian God. He first conscripts natural reason to show that the existence of the one true God is rationally demonstrable.[57] But in his extended examination of what has been specially revealed about God—that God is a triunity of three divine persons—he generously cites and carefully exegetes Scripture while also employing natural reason in making subtle philosophical distinctions to show that the idea that three divine persons are one God is not conceptually incoherent.[58]

---

53. This is not to say *ST* is not an apologetic work, for it most certainly is. But that is not its primary purpose. It was written for beginning theology students, as Aquinas notes in the prologue to *ST*: "Because the doctor of catholic truth ought not only to teach the proficient, but also to instruct beginners (according to the Apostle: *As unto little ones in Christ, I gave you milk to drink, not meat*—1 Cor 3:1–2), we purpose in this book to treat of whatever belongs to the Christian religion, in such a way as may tend to the instruction of beginners." (*ST*, prologue).

54. *SCG*, 1.2.2.

55. Ibid.

56. Ibid.

57. *SCG*, 1.13.

58. Thomas Aquinas, *Summa Contra Gentiles* (*SCG*), *Book Four: Salvation*, trans. Charles J. O'Neil (Notre Dame: University of Notre Dame Press, 1975), 4.1–55.

The Articles of Faith and Historical Apologetics

According to Aquinas there are fourteen articles of faith,[59] seven of which refer to the Godhead and seven of which refer to Christ's human nature: (1) God is one, (2) God is Father, (3) God is Son, (4) God is Holy Spirit, (5) God is Creator, (6) God is the source of grace for our redemption, (7) God will raise us to everlasting life, (8) Christ was conceived by the Holy Spirit, (9) Christ was born of the Virgin Mary, (10) Christ suffered, died, and was buried, (11) Christ descended into hell, (12) Christ was raised from the dead, (13) Christ ascended into heaven, and (14) Christ will judge the living and the dead.

As we have already noted, Aquinas maintains that we come to believe the articles of faith (by the authority of God via special revelation) in a way different from how we come to know the preambles of faith (by rational demonstration) even though some of what we assent to by faith may also be known by reason. Yet in the era of modern apologetics, many Christian thinkers have offered a variety of arguments that try to show that some, if not all, of the other articles of faith may be rationally defended as well. For example, one finds arguments based on historical and literary evidence for everything from Christ's resurrection to the trustworthiness of Scripture. The point of these arguments is to make the case that if historical and literary evidence can show that it is reasonable to believe that Christ rose from the dead and that we can trust Scripture, then some, if not all, of the articles of faith—which all ultimately come from Christ and Scripture—are supported by reason as well.[60]

It is clear that Aquinas would not in principle object to the use of such evidence by Christians, since in several places he does in fact appeal to certain occurrences as showing divine action in history.[61] However, he would likely issue several clarifications. First, he would not classify arguments of this sort as demonstrative proofs. Appeals to historical evidence or putative miracles are by their nature probabilistic and (using Aquinas's term) *persuasive* in nature since evidentiary appeals of this sort cannot compel the mind's assent.[62] After all,

59. *ST*, II-II.Q1, art. 8, *respondeo*.
60. See, e.g., William Lane Craig, *Reasonable Faith: Christian Truth and Apologetics*, 3rd ed. (Wheaton, IL: Crossway, 2008), chapters 5–8; R. Douglas Geivett and Gary R. Habermas, eds., *In Defense of Miracles: A Comprehensive Case for God's Action in History* (Downers Grove, IL: InterVarsity Press, 1992); John Warwick Montgomery, "The Theologian's Craft: A Discussion of Theory Formation and Theory Testing in Theology," *Concordia Theological Monthly* 37.2 (1966): 67–98; J. P. Moreland, *Scaling the Secular City: A Defense of Christianity* (Grand Rapids: Baker, 1987), chapters 5 and 6; and N. T. Wright, *The Resurrection of the Son of God* (Minneapolis: Fortress, 2003).
61. See, e.g., *ST*, III.Q43.art4; *SCG*, 1.6.1–4.
62. Aquinas writes:
The word "proof" is susceptible of a twofold meaning: sometimes it is employed to designate any sort "of reason in confirmation of what is a matter of doubt" [Tully, Topic. ii]: and sometimes it means a sensible sign employed to manifest the truth; thus also Aristotle occasionally uses the

even the miraculous works Christ performed to substantiate his divinity were not sufficient to induce faith in those who witnessed them.[63] Plenty of witnesses dismissed the evidence or provided alternative explanations for what they saw (e.g., "He is demon-possessed and raving mad" [John 10:20 NRSV]).

Second, one does not need historical evidence for the sort of faith necessary for salvation. In other words, the evidence that persuasive reason (e.g., evidence for Christ's bodily resurrection) provides is no more necessary for faith than being able to demonstrate God's existence is for believing sacred teaching. Such evidence may provide an occasion for God's grace to move one's will, but it is the Holy Spirit and not the intellectual acceptance of evidence that moves the pilgrim to assent to the articles of faith.[64]

Third, while Aquinas is clear that reason and argument are often necessary to instruct the faithful, combat error, and defend Christian teaching, their most important role is to facilitate union with God; namely, by providing us with the means necessary to contemplate and take delight in divine things.[65] Similarly, reasoning of this sort can console and encourage believers when they experience doubt or have difficultly addressing the objections of nonbelievers. In short,

term in his works [Cf. Prior. Anal. ii; Rhetor. i]. Taking "proof" in the first sense, Christ did not demonstrate His Resurrection to the disciples by proofs, because such argumentative proof would have to be grounded on some principles: and if these were not known to the disciples, nothing would thereby be demonstrated to them, because nothing can be known from the unknown. And if such principles were known to them, they would not go beyond human reason, and consequently would not be efficacious for establishing faith in the Resurrection, which is beyond human reason, since principles must be assumed which are of the same order, according to 1 Poster. But it was from the authority of the Sacred Scriptures that He proved to them the truth of His Resurrection, which authority is the basis of faith, when He said: "All things must needs be fulfilled which are written in the Law, and in the prophets, and in the Psalms, concerning Me": as is set forth Luke 24:44.

But if the term "proof" be taken in the second sense, then Christ is said to have demonstrated His Resurrection by proofs, inasmuch as by most evident signs He showed that He was truly risen. Hence where our version has "by many proofs," the Greek text, instead of proof has *tekmerion*, i.e. "an evident sign affording positive proof" [Cf. Prior. Anal. ii]. (*ST*, III.Q55.art5, *respondeo*).

63. *ST*, II-II.Q.6.1. As Brian Davies notes about Aquinas's discussion of miracles in *ST*, III.Q43.art3, "[Aquinas] does not speak of demonstration at all in [III.Q43.art4]. He does not even employ the verb *probare* ('to prove'). Instead he relies on the verb *ostendere* (to show) and other Latin words with a similar significance, speaking of Christ's miracles 'showing forth' or 'manifesting' his divinity or as being an 'argument' for it. He does not speak of Christ's miracles as furnishing us with a scientific proof that Christ is necessarily God." (Brian Davies, *Thomas Aquinas's* Summa Theologiae: *A Guide and Commentary* [New York: Oxford University Press, 2014], 318.)

64. Aquinas says as much when he writes:

God enables man to work miracles for two reasons. First and principally, in confirmation of the doctrine that a man teaches. For since those things which are of faith surpass human reason, they cannot be proved by human arguments, but need to be proved by the argument of Divine power: so that when a man does works that God alone can do, we may believe that what he says is from God: just as when a man is the bearer of letters sealed with the king's ring, it is to be believed that what they contain expresses the king's will.

Secondly, in order to make known God's presence in a man by the grace of the Holy Ghost: so that when a man does the works of God we may believe that God dwells in him by His grace. Wherefore it is written (Galatians 3:5): "He who giveth to you the Spirit, and worketh miracles among you." (*ST*, III.Q43.art1, *respondeo*).

65. *De Trinitate* I.2.

reason and inquiry are often for the sake of the *believer's* edification and not the refutation of the unbeliever's arguments.[66] With these considerations in mind, it seems fair to say that although Aquinas would welcome today's emphasis on historical apologetics, he would categorize this project as a probabilistic enterprise—that is, a venture in persuasive rather than demonstrative reason.

CONTRIBUTIONS TO THE FIELD OF APOLOGETICS

The influence of Aquinas—or at least Thomistic approaches—in twentieth- and twenty-first-century Christian apologetics can be seen in a variety of areas and among a diversity of thinkers in both Protestant and Catholic circles. Probably the most important Christian apologist of the twentieth century, the Anglican C. S. Lewis (1898–1963), who did not think of himself as a Thomist, was nevertheless inspired by Aquinas's view of natural law, as any close reading of *The Abolition of Man* would reveal.[67] Lewis was a great lover of not only Dante's *The Divine Comedy* but the Christian medieval worldview that gave it its depth and breadth. There is little doubt that through Dante—whose work is deeply Thomistic—Lewis indirectly appropriated Aquinas's sensibilities more than he realized.[68]

One of the great interpreters of Lewis, the philosopher Peter Kreeft, a former Protestant turned Catholic, has been the most prodigious exponent of Aquinas's work for apologetic purposes.[69] His *Handbook of Christian Apologetics* (coauthored with R. K. Tacelli, SJ) and his abridged version of the *Summa Theologiae, Summa of the Summa,* are widely used texts among both evangelicals and Catholics.[70] Philosopher Edward Feser is another Catholic writer who has been in the forefront of employing Aquinas's apologetics to both popular and professional audiences.[71] If one is looking for a recent and substantive introduction to Aquinas, Feser's work is an excellent place to start.

---

66. Aquinas also worries that arguments intended to teach and encourage believers might be construed by theological adversaries as demonstrative proofs, and poor ones besides. "[T]here are certain likely arguments that should be brought forth in order to make divine truth known. This should be done for the training and consolation of the faithful, and not with any idea of refuting those who are adversaries. For the very inadequacy of the arguments would rather strengthen them in their error, since they would imagine that our acceptance of the truth of faith was based on such weak arguments." (*SCG*, 1.9.2).

67. C. S. Lewis, *The Abolition of Man* (New York: Harper One, 1947).

68. Dudley Howe Miles, "Dante and Aquinas," *The Romanic Review* 2 (1911): 85–89.

69. Peter Kreeft, *C. S. Lewis: A Critical Essay,* 3rd ed. (Front Royal, VA: Christendom Press, 2011).

70. Peter Kreeft and R. K. Tacelli, S. J., *A Handbook of Christian Apologetics* (Downers Grove, IL: InterVarsity Press, 1994); St. Thomas Aquinas, *Summa of the Summa: The Essential Philosophical Passages of St. Thomas Aquinas' Summa Theologica Edited and Explained for Beginners,* ed. and annotated by Peter Kreeft (San Francisco: Ignatius, 2004).

71. Edward Feser, *Five Proofs of the Existence of God* (San Francisco: Ignatius, 2017); Edward Feser, "The New Atheists and the Cosmological Argument," *Midwest Studies in Philosophy* 37 (2013).

In recent years, several evangelical thinkers have identified themselves as Thomists in differing degrees. J. P. Moreland defends what he calls a Thomistic view of the soul in response to the challenges of materialist views of the mind,[72] while R. C. Sproul and Norman L. Geisler borrow generously from Aquinas's natural theology and wider metaphysical views as part of their defenses of Christian theism.[73] Even some who do not identify as Thomists, such as Stuart Hackett and William Lane Craig,[74] have been instrumental in introducing robust defenses of natural theology into evangelical apologetics, a project that Doug Erlandson, a Reformed thinker, has argued is Thomistic in spirit.[75]

Analytic Thomism is a burgeoning school of thought in contemporary philosophy. It has its roots in the work of British philosophers Elizabeth Anscombe and Peter Geach. Some of its leading figures include Eleonore Stump, John Haldane, Brian Leftow, and Alexander Pruss. Although they would likely not describe their work in terms of apologetics, their use of the tools of analytic philosophy to defend traditional Christian doctrines (or traditional philosophical views that inform those doctrines) from a Thomistic perspective certainly contributes to supporting the rationality of Christian belief.[76] Even Alvin Plantinga, a Reformed analytic philosopher who at one time was critical of Thomism and natural theology,[77] looks to Aquinas in his effort to defend the Christian faith in his monumental work *Warranted Christian Belief.*[78] Plantinga attributes this change of mind to his professional interaction with several Thomist philosophers.[79]

---

72. J. P. Moreland and Scott B. Rae, *Body & Soul: Human Nature & the Crisis in Ethics* (Downers Grove, IL: InterVarsity Press, 2000). See also J. P. Moreland, *The Recalcitrant* Imago Dei: *Human Persons and the Failure of Naturalism* (London: SCM, 2009). It should be noted that Moreland does not consider himself a Thomist on other matters, such as the nature of God.

73. R. C. Sproul, John Gerstner, and Arthur Lindsley, *Classical Apologetics: A Rational Defense of the Christian Faith and a Critique of Presuppositional Apologetics* (Grand Rapids: Zondervan—Academie, 1984); Norman L. Geisler, *Christian Apologetics* (Grand Rapids: Baker, 1976); Norman L. Geisler, *Thomas Aquinas: An Evangelical Appraisal* (Grand Rapids: Baker, 1991). For an analysis of how Sproul, Gerstner, and Geisler misread Aquinas on the doctrine of justification, see Francis J. Beckwith, "Doting Thomists: Evangelicals, Thomas Aquinas, and Justification." *Evangelical Quarterly* 85.3 (July 2013): 211–27.

74. Stuart Hackett, *The Resurrection of Theism: Prolegomena to Christian Apology* (Grand Rapids: Baker, 1957); and Craig, *Reasonable Faith*, chapters 3 and 4.

75. Doug Erlandson, "The Resurrection of Thomism," *Antithesis* 2, 3 (May/June 1991).

76. See, e.g., Eleonore Stump, *Atonement* (New York: Oxford University Press, 2018); John Haldane, *Reasonable Faith* (New York: Routledge, 2010); Brian Davies, *Thomas Aquinas on God and Evil* (New York: Oxford University Press, 2011); Alexander R. Pruss and Joshua L. Rasmussen, *Necessary Existence* (New York: Oxford University Press, 2018); Brian Leftow, *God and Necessity* (New York: Oxford University Press, 2015).

77. See Alvin Plantinga, "Is Belief in God Properly Basic?" *Noûs* 15.1 (March 1981): 41–51; Alvin Plantinga, "Reason and Belief in God," in *Faith and Rationality*, eds. Alvin Plantinga and Nicholas Wolterstorff (Notre Dame: University of Notre Dame Press, 1983), 16–93.

78. Alvin Plantinga, *Warranted Christian Belief* (New York: Oxford University Press, 2000), 167. Although he calls the Christianity he is defending the Aquinas/Calvin (A/C) model, Plantinga is far from being a Thomist, most especially because he rejects Aquinas's classical theism. See Plantinga, *Warranted Christian Belief*, 319–23; and Alvin Plantinga, *Does God Have a Nature?* (Milwaukee, WI: Marquette University Press, 1980).

79. Plantinga writes: "In 'Reason and Belief in God,' I suggested that Aquinas was also an evidentialist in this sense; various people (Alfred Freddoso, Norman Kretzmann, Eleonore Stump, Linda Zagzebski, and

There is much more we could add here. The secondary literature on Aquinas is voluminous. Our selective review of recent Aquinas-influenced apologists woefully underrepresents many of the important works both scholars and curious readers have been reading for many years. Frederick Copleston, W. Norris Clarke, Josef Pieper, Ralph McInerny, Vernon Bourke, Anton Pegis, Jacques Maritain, Étienne Gilson, Norman Kretzmann, Herbert McCabe, Marie-Dominique Chenu, Reginald Garrigou-Lagrange, Benedict M. Ashley, Alfred Freddoso, and others all deserve mention here.[80] Yet given the apologetic focus of this chapter, we've decided to offer a more selective summary of material. Of course, if one wishes to understand more of what Aquinas has to say about the matters addressed in this chapter, one could do no better than to read the work of the *magister in sacra pagina* yourself.

SELECTED BIBLIOGRAPHY[81]

This bibliography is not a complete record of all the works and sources that have been consulted.

Aquinas, Thomas. *De Ente et Essentia (On Being and Essence)*. Adapted and edited by Joseph Kenny, OP. http://dhspriory.org/thomas/DeEnte&Essentia.htm.

———. *Summa Contra Gentiles, Book One: God*. Trans. by Anton C. Pegis. Notre Dame: University of Notre Dame Press, 1975.

———. *Summa Contra Gentiles, Book Two: Creation*. Trans. by James F. Anderson. Notre Dame: University of Notre Dame Press, 1975.

———. *Summa Contra Gentiles, Book Three: Providence*. Trans. by Vernon J. Bourke. Notre Dame: University of Notre Dame Press, 1975.

———. *Summa Contra Gentiles, Book Four: Salvation*. Trans. by Charles J. O'Neil. Notre Dame: University of Notre Dame Press, 1975.

———. *Summa of the Summa: The Essential Philosophical Passages of St. Thomas Aquinas' Summa Theologica Edited and Explained for Beginners*. Edited and annotated by Peter Kreeft. San Francisco: Ignatius, 2004.

———. *Summa Theologiae*. 2nd and revised ed. Trans. by Fathers of the English Dominican Province. 1920. http://www.newadvent.org/summa/.

Beckwith, Francis J. *Never Doubt Thomas: The Catholic Aquinas as Evangelical and Protestant*. Waco, TX: Baylor University Press, 2019.

Copleston, Frederick, SJ. *A History of Philosophy, Vol. 2: Medieval Philosophy*. Garden City, NY: Image, 1962.

John Zeis in "Natural Theology: Reformed?" in *Rational Faith: Catholic Responses to Reformed Epistemology*, ed. Linda Zagzebski [Notre Dame: University of Notre Dame Press, 1993], 72) remonstrated with me, pointing out that things were much more complicated than I thought. The fact is that Aquinas is an evidentialist with respect to *scientia*, scientific knowledge. But it doesn't follow that he thought a person could properly accept belief in God, say, only if he had (or there are) good theistic arguments. On the contrary, Aquinas thought it perfectly sensible and reasonable to accept this belief on faith" (Plantinga, *Warranted Christian Belief*, 82 n. 17).

80. There are, of course, important and influential Aquinas scholars who do not explicitly identify as either Catholic or Christian, e.g. Robert Pasnau and Anthony Kenny.

81. A special thank you to Benjamin Rusch (PhD student, Baylor University) for his assistance in compiling this bibliography and verifying references. Thanks also to Richard Eva (Phd student, Baylor University) for his help in proofing this chapter.

Floyd, Shawn. "Aquinas's Philosophical Theology." *The Internet Encyclopedia of Philosophy*. Ed. by Jim Fieser and Bradley Dowden. Hosted by the University of Tennessee at Martin. https://www.iep.utm .edu/aq-ph-th.

McInerny, Ralph, and John O'Callaghan. "Saint Thomas Aquinas." *The Stanford Encyclopedia of Philosophy*. Ed. by Edward N. Zalta. Summer 2018 Edition. https://plato.stanford.edu/archives/sum2018 /entries/aquinas/.

Torrell, Jean-Pierre, OP. *Saint Thomas Aquinas: The Person and His Work, Volume 1*. Trans. by Robert Royal. Washington, DC: Catholic University Press, 1996.

Weisheipl, James, OP. *Friar Thomas D'Aquino: His Life, Thought, and Works*. Washington, DC: Catholic University Press, 1983.

RAMON LULL

Apologetics as the Art of Arts

GREG PETERS

By the later thirteenth century, the Muslim dominance in Visigoth Spain came to an end, creating an opportunity for Christian apologists to evangelize their Muslim neighbors. At the same time, the new universities of Paris and Bologna, for example, were training philosophers and theologians in the art of scholasticism, making use of the recently rediscovered works of Aristotle. As if this were not enough, there was also, in the early thirteenth century, the creation of the mendicant orders, men whose apostolate was the active life, to travel throughout Europe preaching and teaching the Christian faith. These friars also made ideal missionaries to the Jews and Muslims of Europe, North Africa, and the Middle East. It was in this rich intellectual and missional environment that Ramon Lull (1232/1233–1316) ministered.

HISTORICAL BACKGROUND

Most medieval philosophers and theologians did not write autobiographies. In fact, many of them are known primarily through hagiographical texts that often do not withstand close historical scrutiny. That is *not* the case with Ramon Lull, who wrote his *Vita coaetanea* ("Contemporary Life") five years before his death in 1316.[1] Though it is from his own hand, there are three historical gaps in the text: that of nine years (1265–1274), eleven years (1276–1287), and the final five years of his life (that is, from the time he finished the *Vita* to his death). And the five years from 1302 to 1307 are dealt with only superficially.

Lull was born in 1232 or early 1233 in Palma, Majorca, which is the capital city of the main island of the Balearic Islands, due east of Valencia, Spain. From the eighth to the early thirteenth century, this area of the world belonged to various Muslim empires. But from 1226 to 1248, the Muslim territories in the

---

1. An English translation of the Life is available in Anthony Bonner, ed. and trans., *Doctor Illuminatus: A Ramon Lull Reader* (Princeton: Princeton University Press, 1985), 11–40.

Iberian Peninsula were reduced to the small kingdom of Granada. Thus, Lull was raised on Christian land in the kingdom of Majorca, with Catalan as his first language. Likely of noble origin, Lull received an education appropriate for his class. He spent his early days writing troubadour poetry, in service to the king, and, he says, living a decadent life. He was married before September 1257, a union that resulted in two children. Around this same time he entered the service of James II of Majorca, the future king, serving as the administrative head of the royal household. Lull begins his *Vita* around this same time.

In short, Lull's long life, which lasted into his eighties, can mostly be boiled down to three main activities: writing, traveling, and preaching/teaching, all in an attempt to convert Muslims and Jews to the Christian faith. Around the age of thirty (in 1263), Lull had a series of visions of Jesus Christ on the cross, eventually understanding "with certainty that God wanted him . . . to leave the world and dedicate himself totally to the service of Christ."[2] In time Lull further concluded that he "would have to write a book, the best in the world, against the errors of unbelievers."[3] To accomplish this goal, he adopted "three intentions": (1) a willingness to die for the sake of converting others to Christ, (2) to write the above-mentioned book, and (3) to admonish the church and Christian kings to establish monasteries for the training of Christian missionaries to the Muslims and Jews. After setting his affairs in order, Lull left his wife and children permanently and spent nine years (1265–1274) studying philosophy, theology, the Bible, the Qur'an, and the Arabic language. Then, in 1274, while in retreat at the Cistercian monastery of La Real near Palma, the "Lord suddenly illuminated [Lull's] mind, giving him the form and method for writing the aforementioned book against the errors of the unbelievers."[4] It was in 1287 that he visited the Papal Court for the first time. About five years later, in Genoa, while en route to North Africa, he had a deep psychological crisis, fearing that the Muslims would kill him. But he overcame these fears and continued in his travels to Tunis. He was expelled from the country a year after his arrival. Lull became a wide traveler through Europe and the Mediterranean world, perhaps even making it to Jerusalem in 1302. He regularly met with ecclesiastical and governmental officials, arguing for the creation of schools and monasteries to train missionaries to the Muslims and Jews. During this time he would teach his Art (see below) in various universities and monasteries, but most of his time was spent writing.[5]

---

2. *Vita coaetanea* 4; Bonner, ed. and trans., *Doctor Illuminatus*, 12.
3. *Vita coaetanea* 6; Bonner, ed. and trans., *Doctor Illuminatus*, 13.
4. *Vita coaetanea* 14; Bonner, ed. and trans., *Doctor Illuminatus*, 18.
5. Lull's *Art* will be discussed below in greater detail, but Josep Rubio describes it as "a single omnivalent method of generating a theoretically endless number of meaningful propositions . . . although the Art may be itself reduced to a single text in Llull's [*sic*] corpus, it nonetheless represents a single method, since it is always

In 1307, at the age of about seventy-five, Lull traveled to Bougie in North Africa, where he was imprisoned for six months and then expelled, suffering shipwreck off Pisa on his way back to Europe. He returned to Tunis in his early eighties. By the time of his death, he had written no less than 265 works, 237 of which are extant. These works vary in genre, from philosophy to natural science to medicine to apologetics for the Crusades, but nearly each one of them presupposes a knowledge of Lull's *Art*, and all of them, in some way, were meant as tools for evangelizing the Muslims and Jews.

THEOLOGICAL AND CULTURAL CONTEXT

There were two main influences in the life and ministry of Lull that must be understood before considering his thought and apologetic philosophy and strategy: (1) the geographical context of his life and ministry, and (2) the religious culture of this geographical context. Rarely does one think of Majorca as a major player in medieval history; yet, according to Anthony Bonner, "the small island of Majorca was strategically placed at the center of the commercial wheel of the western Mediterranean, and probably only a handful of thirteenth-century European cities were more cosmopolitan."[6] Once the Muslim influence over Majorca faded in the thirteenth century, the island came under the control of the Aragonese monarchy, though the island itself was part of the kingdom of Majorca that included Roussillon (a passable portion of the eastern Pyrenees mountains on the border of Spain and France), Montpellier in southern France, and the Balearic Islands. Because Catalan was the main language, Lull lived under the cultural influence of the southern French troubadour movement that used Provençal, which is similar to Catalan. By 1300 Catalan was a common language throughout much of the Mediterranean.

Majorca itself was quite international, having been settled by people from Catalonia, Aragon, Montpellier, Marseille, Genoa, and Pisa. Upward of a third of the population on the island were Muslim slaves, and the smaller community of Jews were heavily involved in banking and in the gold trade. Majorca's port was an ideal stopping place for ships traversing throughout the western Mediterranean, and around the turn of the fourteenth century, Majorcans began to travel to England using the Strait of Gibraltar. Thus, Lull grew up not on an isolated island with a narrow local perspective but on a truly international island

present either explicitly or implicitly in the whole length and breadth of Llull's extant *oeuvre*" (Josep E. Rubio, "Llull's 'Great Universal Art'" in Amy M. Austin and Mark D. Johnston, eds., *A Companion to Ramon Lull and Lullism* [Leiden: Brill, 2018], 81).

6. Bonner, ed. and trans., *Doctor Illuminatus*, 2.

that exposed him to the life and thought of Muslims and Jews and also to the intellectual life of continental Europe by way of Majorca's connections to southern France and Italy.

As has been stated, Lull was in near constant contact with Muslims and Jews, those whom he later hoped to convert to the Christian faith. By the time of Muhammad's death in 632, Muslims controlled more than half of Arabia (the area east of the Red Sea and south of the Persian Gulf). The Islamic conquests of the mid-seventh century, including the conquest of Jerusalem in 637 greatly enlarged the Muslim world (e.g., the rest of the Arabian peninsula, Syria, and Egypt). The next wave of conquest led the Muslims through the Straits of Gibraltar, and by 711 they had conquered most of Visigoth Spain. During their conquest of Egypt, the Muslims "encountered and absorbed the legacy of western classical culture" through the books that came into their possession.[7] For example, Alexandria was home to one of the greatest libraries in the world, at one time containing works of the Greek literary, philosophical, and scientific traditions. Though these works were no longer housed in the Alexandrine library and were scattered across the newly conquered Muslim kingdom, this availability of western learning caused the Muslims to not only look to the east (e.g., Persia and India) for intellectual enrichment but also to the west. Their "discovery of the western intellectual and cultural tradition meant that the Muslim world shifted much of its orientation" so that "for several centuries the Muslim world was in fact the chief preserver and continuator of the classical tradition."[8]

It was into this fertile intellectual tradition, which had only grown richer in the five centuries since the Muslims arrived in Spain, that Lull was born and raised. But according to Lull, "while still a young man and seneschal to the king of Majorca, [I] was very given to composing worthless songs and poems and to doing other licentious things."[9] In other words, Lull was more interested in the troubadour tradition of southern France than he was the intellectual tradition of Spain. Of course, Lull is likely exaggerating his licentiousness for dramatic (or hagiographic) effect. But he does record that once he was converted to the idea of evangelizing Muslims and Jews, he needed to devote nine years to studying philosophy, theology, the Bible, and Arabic. In other words, despite the intellectual wealth of newly re-Christianized Spain, Lull took little advantage of it until his conversion at age thirty.

---

7. Clifford R. Backman, *The Worlds of Medieval Europe, Second Edition* (New York: Oxford University Press, 2009), 127.

8. Ibid.

9. *Vita coaetanea* 2; Bonner, ed. and trans., *Doctor Illuminatus*, 11.

Though the Muslims on Majorca during Lull's lifetime were mostly slaves, he still understood that Islamic culture was one of great intellectual depth and that the way to the Muslims was through rational apologetic argument. But this was not the view of all medieval Muslim evangelists, causing tension between Lull and, for example, the Dominican Order.[10] Ramon Martí was a Dominican friar born around 1215 who had studied philosophy and theology in Paris (possibly under Albert the Great and as a student alongside Thomas Aquinas) and Arabic in Tunis for the purpose of evangelizing the king of Tunis. On five separate occasions, in five different works spanning nearly thirty years, Lull makes a point of saying that Martí's mission to the king was a failure.[11] As the story goes, "Martí went to Tunis and logically proved to the king that the religion of Muhammad was false, so that he was ready to abandon it. The friar [Martí] responded that 'the faith of the Christians is so transcendent that it cannot be proved by necessary reasons; it is only to be believed, nothing else.'"[12] This did not sit well with the king, who grew angry with Martí for convincing him of the falsity of Islam without proving the veracity of Christianity. Martí was banished from the kingdom. Lull, unlike Martí and his Dominican confreres, thought Christian truth could be proved through "necessary reasons."[13] In other words, Lull thought that "the superiority of Christianity to Islam can be demonstrated rationally."[14] It was this conviction that led to Lull's *Art*.

APOLOGETIC METHODOLOGY AND RESPONSE

LULL'S ART OF ARTS

Lull believed that Muslims and Jews would come to Christian faith through positive argument; that is, he would start with what they already believed rather than attacking their beliefs. To do this, Lull needed to show that "all truths concord and that no knowledge contradicts the ultimate truth."[15] The way to do this, records Lull, came to him directly from God, who "illuminated his

---

10. On the Dominicans in general see Benedict M. Ashley, *The Dominicans* (Collegeville, MN: Liturgical, 1990).

11. Joachim Ch. Lavajo, "The Apologetical Method of Ramon Marti, according to the Problematic of Raymond Lull," *Islamochristiana* 11 (1985): 158.

12. John V. Tolan, *Saracens: Islam in the Medieval European Imagination* (New York: Columbia University Press, 2002), 256.

13. Gilles Emery, "The Doctrine of the Trinity in St Thomas Aquinas," in Thomas G. Weinandy, Daniel A. Keating, and John P. Yocum, eds., *Aquinas on Doctrine: A Critical Introduction* (London: T&T Clark, 2004), 47: The Dominican "Thomas Aquinas rejects in equal measure the apologetic project linked to 'necessary reasons' by which certain theologians have tried to show the necessity of the Trinity for the reasoning believer."

14. Tolan, *Saracens*, 256.

15. Ibid., 267.

mind, giving him the form and method" of his Art.[16] Initially, Lull referred to his method as the *Ars major* (the Great Art) but later used the generic name *Ars generalis* (the General Art). In time, as evidenced in his *Vita coaetanea*, he simply referred to it as "the Art."[17] In summary, Lull's Art "synthesizes a vast range of techniques for private meditation, scriptural exegesis, and apologetic argument into a single system for 'discovering' how all knowledge and being reveals divine truth."[18] In essence, Lull likens all knowledge to the Word of God. He does this by establishing "nine Divine Dignities or attributes, which are the Absolute Principles of all being and knowledge. Nine additional Relative Principles explain the operation of the Absolute Principles at nine levels of existence called Subjects. In addition, nine heuristic questions called Rules help guide inquiry regarding the Principles and Subjects."[19] On this foundation, the "Great Art generates knowledge by combining groups of these letters in circular or tabular diagrams . . . and then explicating the meaning of those combinations."[20]

At its core, Frances Yates concluded, the Art "is a kind of logic," though Lull claimed it was more than that since it could show truth in all areas of human inquiry, including law, medicine, theology, and the sciences.[21] At the same time, this way of finding truth "depends heavily, if not completely, on correct understanding of the terms" involving "careful interpretive work, guided by unswerving fidelity to the fundamental tenets of Catholic dogma."[22] The Art did not rely on the citation of authorities, common in Scholastic philosophy and theology, to support the arguments, which Lull thought was a good thing since Muslims, Jews, and Christians would not all recognize the same authorities. This gave Lull's Art a kind of universal grounding and universal applicability. Nonetheless, Lull believed "all knowledge exists for the sake of theology," whereas "philosophy prepares the explanation of theology." In this sense, as was so common in the Middle Ages, philosophy was the handmaiden of theology.[23]

Though Lull spawned a school of thought known as Lullism, his whole system soon fell out of favor, though whether it had ever been in favor is questionable.[24] To the modern reader, Lull's system comes across as convoluted and nearly

---

16. *Vita coaetanea* 14; Bonner, ed. and trans., *Doctor Illuminatus*, 18.

17. For example, see *Vita coaetanea* 14.

18. Mark D. Johnson, *The Evangelical Rhetoric of Ramon Lull* (New York: Oxford University Press, 1996), 12.

19. Ibid.

20. Ibid., 13.

21. Frances A. Yates, "The Art of Ramon Lull: An Approach to it through Lull's Theory of the Elements," *Journal of the Warburg ad Courtauld Institutes* 17 (1954): 117.

22. Johnson, *The Evangelical Rhetoric of Ramon Lull*, 13.

23. See Malcolm de Mowbray, "Philosophy as Handmaid of Theology: Biblical Exegesis in the Service of Scholarship," *Traditio* 59 (2004): 1–37.

24. See Austin and Johnston, eds., *A Companion to Ramon Lull and Lullism*.

impenetrable.[25] Whereas Thomas Aquinas's theology became, by the twentieth century, *the* theology of the Roman Catholic Church, Lull's philosophy and theology largely remained at the edges, and his "rediscovery" is much more recent.[26] Yet despite its abstruse nature, Lull's thought was sometimes "packaged" in ways that were more accessible to his reader. For example, *The Book of the Gentile and the Three Wise Men* is not only Lull's most important apologetic work, but he explicitly states elsewhere that it is also "based on the methodology of the Art."[27] According to Bonner, "The *Book of the Gentile*, however, is not a work *of* the Art, but rather a popular presentation of Lull's apologetic arguments in accordance with the method and structure of the Art."[28] Thus, an examination of *The Book of the Gentile* will illuminate Lull's apologetic method.

THE BOOK OF THE GENTILE AND THE THREE WISE MEN

The Book of the Gentile was originally written between 1274 and 1276 in Catalan and deals with the three major religions in the west at the time: Christianity, Judaism, and Islam. But it was translated during Lull's lifetime into French and Latin and in 1378 into Spanish. Its importance in the history of Christian-Muslim discourse is evident, helping explain its popularity and the rich manuscript tradition. The text begins, as do many of Lull's treatises, with images, in this case five trees: (1) a tree of the twenty-one divine virtues, (2) a tree of the created and uncreated virtues, (3) a tree of divine virtues and the seven mortal sins, (4) a tree of virtues, and (5) a tree of the virtues and vices. These illustrations are for the purpose of showing how the Divine Dignities and Relative Principles relate to one another. The premise of the book is that an unhappy gentile (i.e., someone who has no religion and no knowledge of God) is roaming around, lacking direction in his life. He happens upon three wise men: a Jew, a Christian, and a Muslim. Looking for contentment, he enters a discussion with them and agrees that after listening to each of them he will, in the end, choose one of their faiths and find happiness. Each one takes their turn explaining their religion, and then, at the end, they eagerly anticipate his decision. But instead of

25. Tolan, *Saracens*, 262: "The *Art*, an arcane matrix of interwoven concepts, presented in a complex system of geometrical figures and tree diagrams, has daunted and discouraged many of Lull's readers from the thirteenth century to the present."

26. See, for example, J. N. Hillgarth, *Ramon Lull and Lullism in Fourteenth-Century France* (Oxford: Clarendon, 1971), 135: "Interest in many of Lull's works, particularly in his more strictly philosophical, as opposed to his 'literary' writings, is relatively recent. The nineteenth-century revival of interest in Scholasticism did not lead ultimately to an objective revaluation of the Art of Lull." On Lullism in general, see Anthony Bonner, ed. and trans., *Selected Works of Ramon Lull (1232–1316), Volume I* (Princeton: Princeton University Press, 1985), 71–89.

27. Bonner, ed. and trans., *Selected Works of Ramon Lull*, 97. See Lull's *De fine*, lines 1214–1217 in Aloisius Madre, ed., *Raimundi Lull Opera Latina 120–122* (Turnholt: Brepols, 1981), 287.

28. Ibid.

adopting any of the religions, the gentile says he has experienced an outpouring of faith and understands the way that will lead him to God. The gentile fascinates the three interlocutors so much that they agree to continue talking with one another until they come to one truth and unite under one single faith.

From the start, Lull says that his goal is to find "a new method and new reasons" (i.e., the Art and "necessary reasons") so that those who are in error may be corrected and brought to eternal life. He knows that "every science requires words by which it can best be presented, and this demonstrative science needs obscure words unfamiliar to laymen; but since we are writing this book for laymen, we will here discuss this science briefly and in plain words" (Prol.; 110).[29] The work is divided into four books: book 1 proves the existence of God, in book 2 the Jew tries to prove the truthfulness of his belief, followed in book 3 by the Christian, and then the Muslim in book 4. Lull's project then comes into focus: (1) *The Book of the Gentile* is meant for laypeople as (2) a practical exercise in applying the Art for the purpose of (3) converting non-Christians to the truth of the Christian faith.

Immediately after meeting the gentile in the text, the reader expresses great sympathy for his condition, detailed so well by Lull:

> By divine dispensation it came to pass that in a certain land there lived
> a gentile very learned in philosophy, who began to worry about old age,
> death, and the joys of this world. This gentile had no knowledge of God,
> nor did he believe in the Resurrection, nor did he think anything existed
> after death. Whenever the gentile thought about these things, his eyes
> filled with tears and weeping, and his heart with sighs and sadness and
> pain, for he was so fond of this worldly life, and he found so terrible the
> thought of death and the notion that after death he would be nothing, that
> he was unable to console himself or stop crying, nor could he drive the sad-
> ness from his heart. (Prol.; 111)

In an attempt to alleviate his suffering, the gentile decides to go into another land, seeking a remedy for his sadness. Upon arriving, he follows a path that leads him into a verdant forest "full of springs and lovely fruit-bearing trees by which the life of the body could be sustained" (Prol.; 111). Sitting among the trees, springs, and wild animals, the gentile hopes that the smells and the beauty around him will provide a cure, but they do not: "When the Gentile tried to

---

29. Parenthetical references throughout refer to the book and chapter (or Prologue) of *The Book of the Gentile*, followed by its page number in Bonner, ed. and trans., *Selected Works of Ramon Lull*. By "laymen," Lull is simply referring to one who has not been schooled in academic philosophy and theology.

console and cheer himself with what he saw, heard, and smelled, there came to him the thought of death and of the annihilation of his being, and then pain and sadness increased in his heart. . . . The farther he went and the more beautiful the places he found, the stronger the thought of death weighed down on him" (Prol.; 112).[30]

Fortunately for the gentile, while he agonizes in the forest, three wise men leave the city and meet up with one another on the road. They befriend one another, hoping to refresh themselves after long seasons of study. As they walk, they talk "about their respective beliefs and about the things they taught their students," eventually coming into "a lovely meadow with a lovely spring watering five trees," which were depicted at the beginning of the book (Prol.; 113). Also in the meadow, next to the spring, is a nobly-dressed lady sitting on a palfrey that drinks from the stream. When asked her name, she replies that she is Intelligence, so they ask her to explain the meaning of the writing on each of the flowers of the five trees. This provides Lull the opportunity to lay the groundwork for his Art.

Lull spends three paragraphs describing what Lady Intelligence says about the trees, and this is at the core of his overall project. This forms the interpretive grid of the Art, for Lull almost always uses a chart or graph, that readers might visualize his method. In this case, five trees are described with leaves that end up depicting what, in other texts, are graphs and grids of letters.[31] In *The Book of the Gentile*, the trees contain the following:

Tree 1 has (a) twenty-one flowers that represent God and his "essential, uncreated virtues." (b) There are two conditions to this tree: "One is that one must always attribute to and recognize in God the greatest nobility in essence, in virtues, and in action; the other condition is that the flowers not be contrary to one another, nor one be less than another."[32]

Tree 2 has (a) forty-nine flowers that have written on them the "seven virtues of the first tree and the seven created virtues, by means of which the blessed achieve eternal blessedness."[33] (b) There are also two conditions to

30. It is possible that Lull is presenting a kind of inverse Garden of Eden in this depiction of the gentile's torment in such strikingly beautiful nature. Though it was in a garden in which humankind first sinned, the Scriptures and subsequent Christian tradition taught that nature had the ability to teach someone about the existence of God and even about his attributes and salvific nature. See Rom 1:19–20 and, for example, Basil of Caesarea's sermons *On the Hexaemeron*.

31. For example, see Yates, "The Art of Ramon Lull," 8 and the Plates XII-XIV in Bonner, ed. and trans., *Selected Works of Ramon Lull*.

32. Bonner, ed. and trans., *Selected Works of Ramon Lull*, 114.

33. The seven "created virtues" are the three theological virtues (faith, hope, and love) and the four

this tree: "The first is that the created virtues be greater and nobler where they most strongly symbolize and demonstrate the uncreated virtues; the second condition is that the uncreated and created virtues not be contrary to one another."[34]

Tree 3 also has (a) forty-nine flowers, though they are now a combination of the seven virtues from Tree 1 along with the seven deadly vices "by which the damned go to eternal fires." (b) Two more conditions prevail: "The first is that the virtues of God not be concordant with the vices; the second is that everything which causes the virtues of God to be better represented to the human understanding by means of the vices should be affirmed."[35]

Tree 4 has (a) twenty-one flowers inscribed with the seven created virtues and (b) the following two conditions: "The first is that none of the these virtues be contrary to another; the second is that whatever enhances them or, by their agency, causes man to have greater merit, must be true, and the contrary must be false."[36]

Tree 5 has (a) another forty-nine flowers "on which are written the seven principal created virtues and the seven deadly sins." (b) Again, there are two conditions: "The first is that the virtues and vices not be concordant with one another; the second is that the virtues most contrary to the vices be most lovable, and the vices most contrary to the virtues be most detestable."[37]

Lull concludes this section by stating that the "above-mentioned ten conditions are themselves governed by two other conditions or principles. One is that all these conditions be directed toward a single goal; the other is that they not be contrary to this goal. And this goal is to love, know, fear, and serve God."[38] At their most basic, then, these trees establish the ground rules by which the gentile and the three wise men will be governed during their conversation. Anything

---

cardinal virtues (prudence, justice, temperance, and courage). Combining these seven with the seven "uncreated virtues" of Tree 1 yields 49 ($7^2 = 49$) possible combinations (i.e., Lull's "forty-nine flowers").

34. Bonner, ed. and trans., *Selected Works of Ramon Lull*, 114.

35. Ibid., 115.

36. Ibid.

37. Ibid.

38. Ibid. As Bonner rightfully notes, these ten conditions attached to the five trees are, in essence, the Art itself: "Tell me, fool: in what way can you know that the Catholic faith is true and that the faith of Jews and Saracens is false and wrong?—He replied: In the ten conditions of the *Book of the Gentile and the Three Wise Men*" (from Lull's *Book of the Lover and the Beloved*; cited in Bonner, ed. and trans., *Selected Works of Ramon Lull*, 115, n. 17).

that is said that contradicts one of these conditions will be judged to be false. The three wise men realize that because they do not share a pool of common authorities, they will have to appeal to these shared first principles, or, again, in Lull's language, "necessary reasons."

Once he establishes these ground rules in the prologue, Lull moves on to the first book, whose purpose is to prove the existence of God. This is an important and necessary step, though one that would be uncontroversial to the three wise men who each come from a monotheistic religion. Nonetheless, it shows that Lull's Art is dependent on there being a god; that is, it is a theistic system of demonstration. Without the existence of a god, there would be no way to complete the Art, and it would fail as a system. At the same time, this is a typical medieval apologetic in the sense that Thomas Aquinas's *Summa Contra Gentiles*, which also has an evangelistic purpose, begins with demonstrations of God's existence that are heavily dependent on Aristotle.[39]

In book 3, the Christian is given the opportunity to speak. He speaks second because Christianity is younger than Judaism but older than Islam. Before speaking, he makes the sign of the cross, paying "homage to the divine Unity and Trinity." He then states that he will put forward fourteen articles of religion.[40] In article 1, he says that God is one, simple, and perfect and defers back to the Jew's proof for God's existence. He then moves to articles 2 through 4, concerning the Trinity and the incarnation of the Son of God. These are the two sticking points, thinks Lull, for Christian belief and the two areas in which the above-mentioned Dominican missionaries, for example, failed to prove them and instead insisted on faith. As stated above, Lull rejected this typically Dominican form of evangelism, convinced that his Art could demonstrate the Trinity and the truth of the incarnation. Simply put, picking the flower of "goodness, greatness" from tree 1, the Christian interlocutor will "prove, according to the conditions of the five trees, that God must necessarily exist in trinity."[41] And by proving the Trinity, the Christian will also prove the persons of the Father, Son and Holy Spirit. Notice that this demonstration works only *if* one accepts the ten aforementioned conditions of the trees. If one accepts those conditions, then one can come to understand that the true (i.e., Christian) God is one and three. The Christian wise man (and, thereby, Lull) lays out the argument for the Trinity as follows:

---

39. See Anton C. Pegis, trans., *Saint Thomas Aquinas: Summa Contra Gentiles, Book One: God* (Notre Dame: University of Notre Dame Press, 1975).

40. Compared with the Jew's eight and the Muslim's twelve.

41. Bonner, ed. and trans., *Selected Works of Ramon Lull*, 193.

a) God's goodness, greatness is either finite or infinite eternity, power, wisdom, love.
b) If finite, it is contrary to perfection; if infinite, it accords with perfection.
c) According to the condition of the trees, God's goodness, greatness cannot be contrary to perfection.
d) Thus, God's goodness, greatness is infinite eternity, power, wisdom, love, perfection.

a) The greater the good, the more strongly it accords with eternity, power, wisdom, love.
b) The lesser the good, the closer to imperfection, which is contrary to perfection.
c) Thus, if there exists in God one "begetting good," which is infinite goodness, greatness, etc., then it must too be God since things that exist "in God" are greater than things that do not exist in God.

a) This begetting good exists in God and is infinite goodness, greatness, etc.
b) If this begetting good "issues forth" another good infinite in goodness, greatness, etc.,
c) Then this issued-forth good must also exist in God and be God.

Therefore, Lull concludes, "The above-mentioned things [are] as good or as great by all the flowers of the tree as would be God's unity without the existence in it of trinity. And since, according to the conditions of the tree, one should grant God the greatest good, therefore the Trinity, by what we have said above, is demonstrable."[42] For the educated reader, it is clear that Lull is making an argument for the Trinity along the lines of the Nicene-Constantinopolitan Creed, wherein the Son is "eternally begotten" of the Father and the Holy Spirit "proceeds" from the Father (and perhaps also the Son). Though it is debatable whether Lull is successful here, the point is to show how he puts his Art into action. In the end perhaps the most telling aspect of his methodology is in the phrase "according to the conditions of the tree" (used twice here). If one rejects the trees, then Lull's argument fails. In this way, Lull's Art was all-encompassing, a powerful tool "against the errors of the unbelievers."[43]

---

42. Ibid., 194.
43. *Vita coaetanea* 14; Bonner, ed. and trans., *Doctor Illuminatus*, 18.

LULL'S OTHER MISSIOLOGICAL STRATEGIES

Though Lull's main apologetical approach to converting Jews and Muslims was his Art, this was not his only approach to the evangelization of unbelievers. Two other strategies deserve discussion: (1) the construction of monasteries as houses of study to prepare others for the evangelization of Jews and Muslims and (2) crusading.

Already, in his *Vita coaetanea*, Lull had written about founding houses to train future missionaries:

It then occurred to him that he should go to the pope, to kings, and to Christian princes to incite them and get them to institute, in whatever kingdoms and provinces might be appropriate, monasteries (*monasteria*) in which selected monks (*personae religiosae*) and others fit for the task would be brought together to learn the languages of the Saracens and other unbelievers, so that, from among those properly instructed in such a place, one could always find the right people to be sent out to preach and demonstrate to the Saracens and other unbelievers the holy truth of the Catholic faith, which is that of Christ.[44]

Though Lull's suggestion was not wholly novel, it was a plan that he returned to again and again throughout his life.[45] Around 1275 Lull "obtained an agreement from the . . . king of Majorca that a monastery be built in his kingdom, that it be endowed with sufficient property, and that thirteen Franciscan friars be sent there to learn Arabic for the purpose of converting unbelievers."[46] About 1288, in his book *Felix, or the Book of Wonders*, Lull imagines a conversation between a "noble prelate" and a minstrel, in which the prelate asks the minstrel how he can honor faith. The minstrel replies "saying that he should build a monastery where monks could learn Arabic and then go off to honor the faith in the Holy Land overseas."[47] In 1294 Lull petitioned the newly elected Pope Celestine V to take seriously the conversion of unbelievers and to do the following to reach the lost: (1) set aside 10 percent of the church's wealth for crusades and missionary work until the Holy Land was recovered, (2) appoint a cardinal of the church

---

44. *Vita coaetanea* 7; Bonner, ed. and trans., *Doctor Illuminatus*, 13.
45. The Franciscan Roger Bacon (d. 1292), for example, also advocated for the teaching of languages to reach non-Christians: "Many infidels would be converted if missionaries were trained according to Bacon's proposals. Study of languages would provide them with the necessary skills to acquire knowledge and to communicate with non-Christians" (E. Randolph Daniel, *The Franciscan Concept of Mission in the High Middle Ages* [Lexington, KY: University Press of Kentucky, 1975], 61).
46. *Vita coaetanea* 17; Bonner, ed. and trans., *Doctor Illuminatus*, 19.
47. Bonner, ed. and trans., *Selected Works of Ramon Lull, Volume II*, 885–86.

to travel the world looking for the best Christian preachers, "holy men, religious and secular alike, who to honor our Lord would fain suffer death,"[48] (3) teach these preachers the languages spoken in the world so that they can reason with all unbelievers, (4) reconcile with Eastern Christian schismatics (*Schismaticos*— probably the Nestorians, for example), who are well-placed to convert Muslims, (5) write letters to all Muslim rulers to send some of their learned scholars to be instructed in true Christian belief (particularly the Trinity and the incarnation, with the assumption, it seems, that they would, in turn, be converted themselves, especially through the Art), and (6) found colleges to teach foreign languages.[49]

For Lull, these monasteries would not be places of contemplative vocation but would be active, as the Franciscans' were. Men would come to learn philosophy and theology, but most importantly they would study the requisite languages for doing effective evangelization. In many ways, Lull was ahead of his time in stressing the need for missionaries to be conversant in the language of the people group to which they are sent. Concerning Muslims, Lull was persuaded that they could be convinced of the truthfulness of Christianity *if* they could be persuaded using the Art, but that persuasion needed to be in their own language.

Though it is difficult in the twenty-first century to think of crusading as anything other than a militarily motivated activity, in the High Middle Ages it was thought of in missiological terms as well. Recovery of the Holy Land was not only a military objective but was thought of evangelistically as a means of converting Muslims and Jews. Early in his career Lull seemed uninterested in the question of the crusades, much less an advocate of them, though this changed throughout his career.[50] By the time of his death, he was much more open to entertaining the apologetic value of the Crusades. In his early work *Book on the Contemplation of God*, written in Catalan, Lull says that the Holy Land should be retaken "by love and prayers and the shedding of tears and blood." This was the manner, wrote Lull, "in which You [God] and Your apostles have conquered it."[51] In 1291, with the fall of Acre in May of that year, Lull was in Rome, where he wrote his first work in support of the Crusade—the *Libre de passatge*, which contained the *Petition to Nicholas IV* and the *Treatise on the Mode of Converting Infidels*. In the *Treatise*, Lull argues for both intellectual conversion and the use of force, suggesting that the military orders (such as the Knights Templar, Hospitallers, and the Teutonic Knights) should amalgamate to present a more united

---

48. Slightly adapted from E. Allison Peers, *Ramon Lull: A Biography* (London: Society for Promoting Christian Knowledge, 1929), 253.

49. Peers, *Ramon Lull*, 253.

50. On Lull's crusading ideology in general, see José Goñi Gaztambide, *Historia de la bula de la cruzada en España* (Vitoria: Editorial del Seminario, 1958), 234–62.

51. Cited in Tolan, *Saracens*, 261.

front for the holding of the Holy Land and for the conversion of the Muslims. In 1305, in his *Liber de fine*, Lull lays out his most detailed crusading plans. Here too he continues to advocate for the intellectual conversion of Muslims and Jews but also lays out plans for the unification of the crusading military orders and the forced retaking of Christian lands. Without a doubt, Lull advocated for the Crusades but, interestingly, was not a strong advocate for forced conversions through compulsory evangelization.[52] Until his death, Lull preferred to see unbelievers come to faith through their own intellectual conversion, even if those unbelievers had been conquered through the Crusades. And until his death, Lull believed in the apologetic persuasion of his Art.

BIBLIOGRAPHY
Ashley, Benedict M. *The Dominicans*. Collegeville, MN: Liturgical, 1990.
Backman, Clifford R. *The Worlds of Medieval Europe, Second Edition*. New York: Oxford University Press, 2009.
Bonner, Anthony, ed. and trans. *Doctor Illuminatus: A Ramon Lull Reader*. Princeton: Princeton University Press, 1985.
———. *Selected Works of Ramon Lull (1232–1216), Volumes I–II*. Princeton: Princeton University Press, 1985.
Daniel, E. Randolph. *The Franciscan Concept of Mission in the High Middle Ages*. Lexington, KY: University Press of Kentucky, 1975.
De Mowbray, Malcolm. "Philosophy as Handmaid of Theology: Biblical Exegesis in the Service of Scholarship." *Traditio* 59 (2004): 1–37.
Emery, Gilles. "The Doctrine of the Trinity in St Thomas Aquinas." Pages 45–65 in *Aquinas on Doctrine: A Critical Introduction*. Ed. by Thomas G. Weinandy, Daniel A. Keating, and John P. Yocum. London: T&T Clark, 2004.
Gaztambide, José Goñi. *Historia de la bula de la cruzada en España*. Vitoria: Editorial del Seminario, 1958.
Hillgarth, J. N. *Ramon Lull and Lullism in Fourteenth-Century France*. Oxford: Clarendon, 1971.
Johnson, Mark D. *The Evangelical Rhetoric of Ramon Lull*. New York: Oxford University Press, 1996.
———. "Ramon Llull and the Compulsory Evangelization of Jews and Muslims." Pages 3–37 in *Iberia and the Mediterranean World of the Middle Ages: Studies in Honor of Robert I. Burns S.J., Volume 1—Proceedings from Kalamazoo*. Ed. by Larry J. Simon. Leiden: Brill, 1995.
Lavajo, Joachim Ch. "The Apologetical Method of Ramon Marti, according to the Problematic of Raymond Lull." *Islamochristiana* 11 (1985): 155–76.
Madre, Aloisius, ed. *Raimundi Lull Opera Latina 120–122*. Turnholt: Brepols, 1981.
Peers, E. Allison. *Ramon Lull: A Biography*. London: Society for Promoting Christian Knowledge, 1929.
Pegis, Anton C., trans. *Saint Thomas Aquinas: Summa Contra Gentiles, Book One: God*. Notre Dame: University of Notre Dame Press, 1975.
Tolan, John V. *Saracens: Islam in the Medieval European Imagination*. New York: Columbia University Press, 2002.
Yates, Frances A. "The Art of Ramon Lull: An Approach to it through Lull's Theory of the Elements." *Journal of the Warburg ad Courtauld Institutes* 17 (1954): 115–73.

52. Mark D. Johnston, "Ramon Llull and the Compulsory Evangelization of Jews and Muslims" in Larry J. Simon, ed., *Iberia and the Mediterranean World of the Middle Ages: Studies in Honor of Robert I. Burns S.J., Volume 1—Proceedings from Kalamazoo* (Leiden: Brill, 1995), 3–37.

GREGORY PALAMAS

Defending the Authority and Evidential Value of Religious Experience in Eastern Orthodoxy

BYARD BENNETT

Gregory Palamas (ca. 1296–1357) was one of the most important theologians of the Byzantine period, and his theological proposals have helped shape Eastern Orthodox theology in the modern period. Some of Gregory's most influential apologetic works were written during an extended debate with a contemporary philosopher, Barlaam of Seminara. The debate began with a discussion of how faith and reason were related and, more specifically, whether logical arguments could establish with certainty what God is like and how he exists. Barlaam believed that created beings could have a true but limited knowledge of God, but he denied that logical demonstration could be used to prove that certain things were necessarily true of God. Gregory believed that the biblical understanding of faith required a far more robust sense of certainty than Barlaam's account allowed. One could arrive at this kind of certainty, Gregory argued, only by seeing God act and being affected by God's action; certainty thus depends on a personal experience of God. The debate between Gregory and Barlaam therefore shifted its focus; the central issue then became the authority and evidential value of religious experience. Gregory's defense of the authority and significance of religious experience helped shape the character of later Byzantine and Eastern Orthodox theology.

HISTORICAL BACKGROUND

Gregory was born in Constantinople, probably in 1296.[1] His father was a member of the court of Emperor Andronicus II Palaeologus (r. 1282–1328) and also

---

1. For a discussion of Gregory's life and works and an extensive bibliography, see Robert E. Sinkewicz, "Gregory Palamas," in *La théologie byzantine et sa tradition II (XIIIe-XIXe s.)*, eds. Carmelo Giuseppe Conticello

Image: Byzantine fresco of Gregory Palamas, Monastery of Vatopedi, 1371

266

served as tutor for the emperor's grandson, the future Andronicus III Palaeologus (r. 1328–1341). Although Gregory's father died before Gregory turned seven, Gregory's family continued to enjoy the favor of the emperor, and Gregory was able to secure a first-rate education from the renowned scholar Theodore Metochites (1270–1332).[2]

Around 1316 Gregory left the court and became a monk on Mount Athos in northeastern Greece. As the fourteenth century progressed, Mount Athos experienced an increasing number of raids by Turkish pirates, causing many monks to leave the area; this led to a decline in the quality of monastic life. In about 1326 Gregory himself left Mount Athos with eleven other monks and settled in Thessaloniki. He was later ordained to the priesthood and became the leader of a monastic community in Veria, about forty miles west of Thessaloniki.

Due to repeated raids by "Illyrians" (i.e., the Albanian nomads of Thessaly), monastic life in Veria eventually became untenable, and by 1331 Gregory had returned to Mount Athos.[3] There he began to compose works that promoted the ideals of the monastic life as it was observed on Mount Athos, emphasizing the need for unceasing prayer as a means to union with God.[4]

THEOLOGICAL CONTEXT

Even though Gregory had withdrawn to a secluded place to pursue the monastic life, he was eventually drawn into a conflict that was taking place at the imperial court. This conflict was political in origin but had important religious implications. After

and Vassa Conticello (Turnhout: Brepols, 2002), 131–88. Critical editions of Gregory's works can be found in Γρηγορίου τοῦ Παλαμᾶ Συγγράμματα, 5 vols., ed. Panagiotes K. Chrestou (Thessaloniki: Kyromanos, 1962–1992). In this chapter, I will focus the discussion primarily on Gregory's *Triads* and his *One Hundred and Fifty Chapters*. For the *Triads*, I have used the critical edition and French translation of Jean Meyendorff, *Grégoire Palamas: Défense des saints hésychastes*, 2 vols., 2 ed. (Leuven: Spicilegium Sacrum Lovaniense, 1973). For the *One Hundred and Fifty Chapters*, I have used the critical edition and English translation of Robert E. Sinkewicz, *The One Hundred and Fifty Chapters* (Toronto: Pontifical Institute of Mediaeval Studies, 1988).

2. On Theodore Metochites's contributions to the study of astronomy and Aristotelian philosophy, see Karin Hult, *Theodore Metochites on Ancient Authors and Philosophy: Semeioseis gnomikai 1–26 & 71* (Göteborg: Acta Universitatis Gothoburgensis, 2002); Börje Bydén, *Theodore Metochites' Stoicheiosis astronomike and the Study of Natural Philosophy and Mathematics in Early Palaiologan Byzantium*, 2 rev. ed. (Göteborg: Acta Universitatis Gothoburgensis, 2003); Marina Bazzani, "Theodore Metochites, a Byzantine Humanist," *Byzantion* 76 (2006): 32–52; Emmanuel Paschos and Christos Simelidis, *Introduction to Astronomy by Theodore Metochites (Stoicheiosis astronomike 1.5–30)* (Singapore: World Scientific, 2017).

3. Antonio Rigo, "La Vita di Pietro l'Athonita (*BHG* 1506) scritta da Gregorio Palama," *Rivista di studi bizantini e neoellenici* 32 (1995): 181 n. 19.

4. See Rigo, "Vita," 177–90; Ioannis Polemis, "Neoplatonic and Hesychastic Elements in the Early Teaching of Gregorios Palamas on the Union of Man with God: The *Life of St. Peter the Athonite*," in *Pour une poétique de Byzance. Hommage à Vassilis Katsaros*, eds. Stephanos Efthymiadis, Charis Messis, Paolo Odorico, and Ioannis Polemis (Paris: Éditions De Boccard, 2015), 205–21; Mihail Mitrea, "'Old Wine in New Bottles'?: Gregory Palamas' *Logos* on Saint Peter of Athos (*BHG* 1506)," *Byzantine and Modern Greek Studies* 40 (2016): 243–63.

losing several major battles with the Turks, Emperor Andronicus III had appealed to Pope Benedict XII for military assistance. The negotiations included discussions regarding the reunification of the Eastern (Greek Orthodox) and Western (Roman Catholic) churches. The proposal to reunite the churches was very unpopular in the Greek East. The need to secure military assistance was nonetheless so pressing that the emperor could not simply dismiss or ignore the discussions concerning the reunion of the churches that the pope demanded. A number of learned men connected with the imperial court protested vigorously against these discussions and composed works that opposed church reunion. Their works, however, showed that they did not all share the same assumptions, hindering the creation of a common front against the proposed reunification of the churches.

BARLAAM OF SEMINARA:
CAN ONE PROVE TRUTHS ABOUT GOD?

One of the principal contributors to the discussion of church reunion was Barlaam of Seminara (c. 1290–1348). Barlaam was born in southern Italy, where for centuries there had been a large Greek presence. After being ordained to the Orthodox priesthood, he traveled east to Constantinople, where he pursued philosophical studies before becoming a monk. Having gained favor at the imperial court, he was appointed to a position of monastic leadership and also held a post teaching philosophy to advanced students.

In 1334 Barlaam began to devote much of his time to the question of church reunion, meeting with the envoys sent by Pope John XXII and later writing a series of treatises opposing the reunion of the churches.[5] Barlaam's opinion carried significant influence, not only because he was a learned man and favored by the court but also because he understood the Latin language and had some knowledge of the theology of the Western church.

Gregory also opposed the reunification of the churches but had reservations about the arguments Barlaam was advancing to support this position. Gregory was particularly concerned about Barlaam's view of reason and Barlaam's criticism of the use of rational proofs in theology.

Before examining why Gregory had reservations about Barlaam's views, it will be helpful first to understand the original context of Barlaam's arguments.[6]

---

5. A critical edition and Italian translation of Barlaam's treatises *Against the Latins* are given in Antonis Fyrigos, *Barlaam Calabro. Opere contro i Latini*, 2 vols. (Vatican City: Biblioteca Apostolica Vaticana, 1998). See also John A. Demetracopoulos, "Further Evidence on the Ancient, Patristic, and Byzantine Sources of Barlaam the Calabrian's *Contra Latinos*. À propos de A. Fyrigos, ed., *Barlaam Calabro, Opere contro i Latini*," *Byzantinische Zeitschrift* 96 (2003): 83–122.

6. For a more detailed discussion, see Robert E. Sinkewicz, "The Doctrine of the Knowledge of God in the Early Writings of Barlaam the Calabrian," *Mediaeval Studies* 44 (1982): 181–242.

The envoys sent by the pope had criticized the way the Greek church understood the procession of the Holy Spirit. In making these criticisms, the papal envoys had advanced a number of syllogistic arguments drawn from the works of the scholastic theologian Thomas Aquinas.[7] Aquinas had understood theology to be a demonstrative science, and the arguments cited by the papal envoys thus depended on a certain understanding of how one could reason deductively about the nature of God. Rather than refute each of the arguments the envoys had advanced, Barlaam felt that it would be easier to refute the assumptions on which his opponents' arguments rested. Once these assumptions were seen to be false, any arguments based on these assumptions would be seen to fail as well.

Barlaam and the papal envoys agreed on the formal requirements for demonstrating the truth of a proposition but differed on whether truths about God could be demonstrated in this same manner. In Aristotelian logic, the conclusion of a syllogistic argument has been demonstrated (i.e., shown to be necessarily true) when the following conditions are met:

(1) The premises of the argument, which affirm or deny something (a predicate) of something else (a subject), must be true and primary.[8]
(2) A premise is primary when
   (a) it is previously known as a fact and is indemonstrable,[9] and
   (b) it precedes and causes the conclusion that follows from it, so that the latter is necessarily the case.[10]

As an example of a premise that is true and primary, Aristotle offered a universal geometrical truth: "The diagonal of a square is commensurable with the sides."[11] In other words, for any square, the length of the diagonal of the square will be the length of the side of the square multiplied by the square root of two. If a geometrical figure is a square, then it follows necessarily that the diagonal of the square will be of just such a length.[12]

In Aristotle's account, the capacity to prove that something is necessarily

7. See Robert E. Sinkewicz, "The *Solutions* Addressed to George Lapithes by Barlaam the Calabrian and Their Philosophical Context," *Mediaeval Studies* 43 (1981): 165 with n. 74.

8. Aristotle, *An. pr.* 1.1, 24a16–17; 24b17–18; *Top.* 1.1, 100a27–28.

9. For Aristotle, a proposition about X is considered "indemonstrable" if it is known immediately, being true by definition in every instance of X, and is essential to understanding what X is. Aristotle cited mathematical definitions and geometrical axioms as examples of indemonstrable propositions. Propositions of this type do not need demonstration but are epistemically basic and serve as the foundational principles from which new knowledge can be produced by means of deduction; see Aristotle, *An. post.* 1.2, 71b17–23.

10. Aristotle, *An. post.* 1.2, 71b20–35; 1.3, 72b19–25; cf. *An. pr.* 1.1, 24b18–22.

11. Aristotle, *An. post.* 1.2, 71b26–27.

12. Cf. Aristotle, *An. post.* 1.2, 71b9–12; 1.30, 87b22–25.

so depends on first grasping what is universal and previously known (i.e., not discovered by demonstration). But how does one grasp what is universal? Aristotle argued that while sight can look only at particular things, the mind can look beyond the particular thing to grasp the universal, i.e., that X is the case in all instances of Y, where Y are things that are of the same kind and have the same essence.[13] Universals therefore exist as concepts or principles in the mind, indicating what things are and how they come into being; as concepts, universals do not have an existence apart from the particular individual things which they define and explain.

Barlaam accepted that Aristotelian logic could help human beings gain a systematic understanding of how the created world was structured. He doubted, however, that it could help one understand the nature of the uncreated God or arrive at certainty about divine matters. Aristotelian logic was concerned to examine created things and grasp the axioms and ratios that define and bring about things of a certain kind. God, however, is superior to all created things. What God is, Barlaam argued, exceeds the limits of our senses and can never be fully comprehended by created minds. Aristotle's account of grasping the universal by abstraction from sensible objects cannot help one understand a God who is unseen and immaterial and exceeds all the limited conceptions we might try to apply to him.

Furthermore, Barlaam noted, Aristotle's account of universals aimed to identify the features that characterize members of a class. God, however, is not one member of a broader class of beings that can be called "God." There is only one particular individual who is God, and the attributes of God belong to him alone. Aristotle had accepted that a definition could be given that fit all the members of a class (e.g., one could give a definition of what a human being is, specifying the characteristics that every human being will necessarily possess). Aristotle nonetheless held that one could not give a definition of a particular individual man, e.g., Socrates; the attributes that make Socrates an individual are idiosyncratic and subject to no general rule.[14] Now if there is no definition for an individual (showing what must necessarily be the case in all instances), neither can there be any demonstration in the case of individuals (showing what necessarily follows and must always be the case). Thus, Barlaam argued, Aquinas and the Latin envoys were mistaken in thinking one could use demonstrative syllogisms to prove anything regarding the nature of God; just as their method was flawed, so too were the conclusions they drew from this.

13. See the texts and discussion in Richard Sorabji, *The Philosophy of the Commentators 200–600 AD: A Sourcebook. Volume 3: Logic & Metaphysics* (London: Duckworth, 2004), 264–65.
14. See Aristotle, *Metaph.* 7.10, 1036a2–6; 11.2, 1059b26; *De an.* 2.5, 417b22–23.

APOLOGETIC RESPONSE AND METHODOLOGY

GREGORY PALAMAS: ONE CAN PROVE TRUTHS ABOUT GOD, BUT THESE PROOFS PRESUPPOSE EXPERIENTIAL KNOWLEDGE OF GOD

Barlaam's argument was carefully reasoned and initially appeared to offer an effective criticism of the papal envoys' assumptions and method of argumentation. Like Barlaam, Gregory believed that the logic applicable to created realities had limited value in establishing what the uncreated God is like. Still, the direction taken in Barlaam's argument and the consequences this might have for certainty in matters of faith troubled Gregory. If one could show that a proposition was necessarily true, then one could know with certainty that what the proposition asserts will always be true. But if, as Barlaam affirmed, one cannot show that statements about God are necessarily true, does this mean that one can no longer know with certainty what God is like? And if one cannot know with certainty what God is like, would it still be possible to have a true and lasting faith? Perhaps Barlaam's argument was so conditioned by Aristotelian thought that Barlaam risked giving up things that were important to the Christian faith. If faith is indeed "confidence in what we hope for and assurance about what we do not see" (Heb 11:1), then surely one must be able to have certainty regarding what has been taught concerning God (cf. Luke 1:4).

At the time of the conflict between Gregory and Barlaam, some philosophers at the imperial court were discussing the limitations of what could be known by sense-perception and whether one could affirm with certainty the truth or falsity of statements about the objects of sense-perception.[15] Gregory may have understood Barlaam's discussion of the limits of what can be demonstrated to be a sign of a broader skeptical stance, i.e., as casting doubt on what could be known about God or even what could be known at all.[16]

---

15. On the defense of skepticism in Theodore Metochites's *Semeioseis gnomikai* (c. 1326), see Börje Bydén, "'To Every Argument There Is a Counter-Argument': Theodore Metochites' Defence of Scepticism (*Semeiosis* 61)," in *Byzantine Philosophy and Its Ancient Sources*, ed. Katerina Ierodiakonou (Oxford: Clarendon, 2002), 183–217. On the use of skeptical arguments by Nicephorus Gregoras (1293/94–1360/61) and the response by Nicholas Cabasilas Chamaetos (1322/3–1392), see John A. Demetracopoulos, Νικολάου Καβάσιλα Κατὰ Πύρρωνος. Πλατωνικός φιλοσκεπτικισμός καὶ ἀριστοτελικὸς ἀντισκεπτικισμὸς στὴ βυζαντινὴ διανόηση τοῦ 14ου αἰώνα (Athens: Parousia, 1999), 311–17. Like Barlaam, Theodore Metochites and Nicephorus Gregoras also believed that Aristotelian logic and demonstrative syllogisms could not be used to gain certain knowledge of God's nature and attributes; see Robert E. Sinkewicz, "A New Interpretation for the First Episode in the Controversy between Barlaam the Calabrian and Gregory Palamas," *Journal of Theological Studies* 31 (1980): 493–95; Bydén, "To Every Argument," 185, 189 n. 20, 190; Katerina Ierodiakonou, "The Anti-Logical Movement in the Fourteenth Century," in *Byzantine Philosophy and Its Ancient Sources*, ed. Katerina Ierodiakonou (Oxford: Clarendon, 2002), 222–23.

16. In reality Barlaam seems to have avoided skepticism regarding the objects of sense-perception. Barlaam held, with the Neoplatonic tradition, that universal concepts were present in the mind prior to sense-perception. The human mind, Barlaam argued, had received these universal concepts from the previously-existing divine

As a monk and an advocate for spiritual renewal, Gregory believed that it was important to affirm that one could know God and arrive at certain knowledge of God.[17] If one sought a knowledge of God that was true and primary (i.e., knowable before and apart from demonstration) and could lead to certainty, this could come only from personal experience of seeing God act.[18] By directly perceiving God's action, one could move beyond the shifting and conflicting reasonings advanced by supposedly enlightened philosophers.[19] One should therefore accept as primary and certain the testimonies of those who have been inspired by God (the authors of Scripture) and the teachings of those whose minds were enlightened by God and moved by the Holy Spirit (the Holy Fathers).[20] Furthermore, through self-denial and prayer, one should seek to gain a similar personal, experiential knowledge of God, for only a mind enlightened by God can understand what the Scriptures and the Holy Fathers have taught.

HESYCHASM AND GREGORY'S ARGUMENT FOR THE AUTHORITY OF RELIGIOUS EXPERIENCE

Gregory's arguments for the authority of religious experience presupposed a specific model of prayer that was gaining increasing influence in monastic circles during the thirteenth and fourteenth centuries. This model of prayer, called "hesychasm," was particularly influential on Mount Athos, the monastic center that had played an important role in Gregory's own spiritual formation.[21]

Hesychasm represented a development of certain teachings on prayer and religious experience that had been advanced by Evagrius of Pontus, one of the Desert Fathers who had lived in Egypt at the end of the fourth century AD. Evagrius had divided the spiritual training of monks into two stages. In the initial stage, one became aware of the evil reasonings and disordered desires that led one to sin, and began to fight against these. Later, through vigilance and discipline, one was able to rise above the distractions created by mental pictures of things

mind (δημιουργικὸς νοῦς) that created and ordered all things. A universal concept, already present within the mind, is aroused and awakened when the individual sees an object that falls under that universal concept. Thus, for example, seeing a square will arouse within the mind a preexisting concept of what a square is; this preexisting concept exists within the mind immaterially and can be remembered or forgotten but not lost. For a reconstruction of Barlaam's position, see Sinkewicz, "Barlaam's *Solutions,*" 167–71. On this foundation, Barlaam could also offer a way of showing how the human mind could arrive at a secure knowledge of divine matters: Because the human mind (i.e., individual intellect) is an image of the mind of the Creator and is informed and illuminated by the latter, it is possible for created beings to have true but limited knowledge of God and to assent to this knowledge.

17. See Gregory Palamas, *Ep. 1 to Akindynos* 8,13; *One Hundred and Fifty Chapters* 141.
18. Gregory Palamas, *Triads* 3.1.32.
19. Gregory Palamas, *Ep. 2 to Akindynos* 5; *Ep. 1 to Barlaam* 22,34–36,41.
20. Gregory Palamas, *Ep. 1 to Akindynos* 8–9; *Ep. 1 to Barlaam* 31; *One Hundred and Fifty Chapters* 2.
21. For a comprehensive bibliography of publications relating to hesychasm, see Sergey S. Horujy, ed. *Hesychasm: An Annotated Bibliography* (Moscow: Institute of Human Studies of the Russian Academy of Sciences, 2004).

one craves or fears and sinful reasonings about how one ought impulsively to respond. Evagrius taught that in this later stage, one became able to pray without ceasing (1 Thess 5:17), focusing one's undivided attention on God without being diverted by distractions. As one continued in unceasing prayer, one's mind could begin to perceive God's gracious action toward the world in a way that was analogous (but superior) to sense-perception.[22] Evagrius held that in this state, God's gracious action could be perceived as light, for Scripture testifies that God is light (1 John 1:5) and that he dwells in unapproachable light (1 Tim 6:16).[23] Only when one's mind was illuminated by God could one begin to know God, Evagrius argued, for it is written, "In your light we see light" (Ps 36:9) and "For God, who said, 'Let light shine out of darkness,' made his light shine in our hearts to give us the light of the knowledge of God's glory" (2 Cor 4:6).

Evagrius's teaching remained popular among the hesychast monks of the Byzantine period.[24] To help focus the mind and maintain uninterrupted prayer, hesychast monks also made use of certain practical helps. First, a short phrase, based on Scripture and appealing for the help of Christ, was continually repeated throughout the day (e.g., "Lord Jesus Christ, have mercy on me"). This practice of "monologistic prayer" (prayer using the repetition of a single phrase) had already been recommended by Evagrius and other Desert Fathers of the late fourth and early fifth centuries. In the thirteenth and fourteenth centuries, certain visualization and breathing exercises were added.[25] In these exercises, the person praying was to see the mind descending to the heart and resting there. This descent signified the mind's concentration of its attention on God and the stilling of all the functions of the mind by which mental pictures, concepts, and discursive reasonings had formerly been produced.[26]

---

22. Cf. Gregory Palamas, *Triads* 1.3.21; 2.3.36–37; 3.1.22,35–36.

23. For a discussion of Evagrius's teaching and its influence on later monastic writers, see Hans-Veit Beyer, "Die Lichtlehre der Mönche des vierzehnten und des vierten Jahrhunderts," *Jahrbuch der Österreichischen Byzantinistik* 31 (1981): 473–512; Columba Stewart, *Cassian the Monk* (Oxford: Oxford University Press, 1999), 97, 197 n. 91; Augustine Casiday, *Reconstructing the Theology of Evagrius Ponticus: Beyond Heresy* (Cambridge: Cambridge University Press, 2013), 180–85. On the use of citations from Evagrius in the debate between Gregory Palamas and his opponents, see Antonio Rigo, "De l'apologie à l'évocation de l'expérience mystique. Évagre le Pontique, Isaac le Syrien et Diadoque de Photicé dans les oeuvres de Grégoire Palamas (et dans la controverse palamite)," in *Knotenpunkt Byzanz: Wissenformen und kulturelle Wechselbeziehungen*, eds. Andreas Speer and Philipp Steinkrüger (Berlin: De Gruyter, 2012), 85–108.

24. On the development of hesychastic teaching in the late Byzantine period, see Dirk Krausmüller, "The Rise of Hesychasm," in *The Cambridge History of Christianity. 5: Eastern Christianity*, ed. Michael Angold (Cambridge: Cambridge University Press, 2006), 101–26. Antonio Rigo has provided Italian translations of some of the most important late Byzantine works on hesychastic prayer; see his *I padri esicasti. L'amore della quiete (ho tes hesychias eros). L'esicasmo bizantino tra il XIII e il XV secolo* (Magnano: Qiqajon, 1993). Gregory's relation to these earlier hesychastic writers is discussed by Luca Bianchi, *Monasteri icona del mondo celeste. La teologia spirituale di Gregorio Palamas* (Bologna: EDB, 2010).

25. Antonio Rigo, "Le tecniche d'orazione esicastica e le potenze dell'anima in alcuni testi ascetici bizantini," *Rivista di studi bizantini e slavi* 4 (1984): 75–115.

26. See Theoleptus of Philadelphia, *Discourse* 1.16 and Gregory Palamas, *Triads* 1.3.17–18, which draws

The hesychast monks believed that purification from sinful reasonings and illumination by God were part of a process by which God renewed sinful human beings and made them partakers of the divine nature (2 Pet 1:4).[27] When the mind was illuminated by God's grace, it was filled with divine light and remained attached to the good, in spite of outward hardships and temptations.[28] In the same way that two people are united in marriage, the uncreated divine light fused itself with the soul and, by dwelling in the soul, caused the soul to participate in its divine qualities.[29] Because of the soul's union with the body, the body itself was also illuminated and transformed by God's grace.[30] This divine illumination and transformation of the soul and body was shown to the apostles when Christ was transfigured (Matt 17:2; Mark 9:2); in the Transfiguration, the divinity of Christ was seen as an uncreated light that glorified the body conjoined with it.[31]

BARLAAM'S CRITICISM OF ARGUMENTS BASED ON RELIGIOUS EXPERIENCE

Barlaam was skeptical of the hesychast monks' claim that they had gained an experiential knowledge of God, a claim that Gregory had endorsed. The hesychast monks, Barlaam argued, say they have seen a divine light and sensed a warmth or certain movements within their bodies.[32] God, however, does not

on ps.-Dionysius, *On the Divine Names* 1.5 (PG 3, 595B) to argue that the cessation of intellectual activity is a precondition for the spiritual perception of God's activities. In *Triads* 2.2.8–9, Gregory draws on ps.-Dionysius, *Mystical Theology* 1.3 (PG 3, 1000C) to develop a similar argument; see also Gregory's briefer discussion in *Triads* 2.3.36 and *Ep. 1 to Barlaam* 42.

27. On the concept of *theosis* (deification) in patristic and Byzantine spirituality, see Norman Russell, *The Doctrine of Deification in the Greek Patristic Tradition* (Oxford: Oxford University Press, 2004) and the essays collected in *Partakers of the Divine Nature: The History and Development of Deification in the Christian Traditions*, eds., Michael J. Christensen and Jeffery A. Wittung (Grand Rapids: Baker Academic, 2007), 95–174; *Visions of God and Ideas on Deification in Patristic Thought*, eds. Mark Edwards and Elena Ene D-Vasilescu (London: Routledge, 2017), 53–170; *Mystical Doctrines of Deification: Case Studies in the Christian Tradition*, eds. John Arblaster and Rob Faesen (London: Routledge, 2018). Gregory's understanding of *theosis* is discussed in M.-J. Monsaingeon and J. Paramelle, *Saint Grégoire Palamas, De la déification de l'être humain, suivi de Georges I. Mantzaridis, La doctrine de Saint Grégoire Palamas sur la déification de l'être humain* (Lausanne: L'Âge d'Homme, 1990); Yannis Spiteris, *Palamas: la grazia e l'esperienza. Gregorio Palamas nella discussione teologica* (Rome: Lipa, 1996), 71–123; Reinhard Flogaus, *Theosis bei Palamas und Luther: Ein Beitrag zum ökumenischen Gespräch* (Göttingen: Vandenhoeck & Ruprecht, 1997); A. N. Williams, *The Ground of Union: Deification in Aquinas and Palamas* (Oxford: Oxford University Press, 1999).

28. Cf. Theoleptus of Philadelphia, *Ep.* 3: "Just as sparks burst out when steel is struck by iron, in the same way when a God-loving soul is attacked by temptations from the outside, it glows with the [lights] emanating from the divine illuminations and becomes all light and can illuminate those who approach it as they see the lights flashing from the endurance for the love of God and from the gentleness and kindness towards all" (ET Angela C. Hero, *The Life and Letters of Theoleptos of Philadelphia* [Brookline, MA: Hellenic College Press, 1994], 75).

29. Gregory Palamas, *Ep. 1 to Barlaam* 43–44; cf. *Triads* 1.3.20; 2.3.36,68; *One Hundred and Fifty Chapters* 92.

30. Gregory Palamas, *Ep. 1 to Barlaam* 44; *Triads* 2.2.12; 2.3.9; *One Hundred and Fifty Chapters* 146.

31. Gregory Palamas, *Triads* 1.3.5; 2.3.20; 3.1.15,19,33. Compare *One Hundred and Fifty Chapters* 83, where Gregory concludes that the activity "of God manifest from created things is uncreated" (ET Sinkewicz, *One Hundred*, 181).

32. For a description of the claims made by the hesychast monks, see Antonio Rigo, "*L'Epistola a Menas*

have a bodily existence, so he cannot be perceived with the senses in the way that the monks claim. It is clear then, Barlaam argued, that what the monks saw was not God himself but merely a created light that their senses were adapted to perceive.[33] In the same way, any warmth or movements that the monks felt within their bodies did not represent unmediated contact with God. If not a result of purely natural causes, such sensations were only created effects that occurred when God acted indirectly on the physical world through the mediation of the angels.[34] In conclusion, Barlaam argued, no one should claim to have seen God with bodily eyes, for such a teaching is contrary to reason and accepted only by heretical movements whose beliefs the church has condemned.[35] In 1337 Barlaam publicly denounced hesychastic teaching as unorthodox and appealed to the Standing Synod in Constantinople to condemn it, but the Synod declined to act.

Although Barlaam's criticisms were not directed at Gregory, they did raise doubts about whether personal religious experience could be treated as authoritative and whether it could lead to certain knowledge of God, as Gregory had claimed. Gregory later came to Thessaloniki and in 1338 to 1340 wrote a series of treatises (the *Triads*) defending the hesychast monks against Barlaam's criticisms.[36]

GREGORY'S DEFENSE OF THE AUTHORITY AND SIGNIFICANCE OF RELIGIOUS EXPERIENCE

In the *Triads*, Gregory argued that the monks' claims to have seen and directly experienced God were true; experiences of this type provided knowledge of God that was certain and did not need to be justified by any independent

di Gregorio Palamas e gli effeti dell'orazione," *Cristianesimo nella storia* 9 (1988): 57–80; Rigo, *L'amore*, 19–20; Barlaam, *Ep. 5 to Ignatius the Hesychast* 16 (Antonis Fyrigos, *Dalla controversia palamitica alla polemica esicastica* [Rome: Antonianum, 2005], 386–89); Gregory Palamas, *Triads* 1.3.22; 2.3.35; 3.1.33.

33. See Gregory Palamas, *Triads* 1.3; 2.3.12,20; 3.1.11. Barlaam made a strong distinction between God and everything other than God; see Gregory Palamas *Triads* 3.1.24. Palamas understood Barlaam to be arguing that (a) God was identical with his essence, and (b) all that was not God was a product or effect brought about by God in the created realm. Barlaam's actual position may have been more nuanced. It is also possible that Barlaam was influenced by the Neoplatonic philosopher Proclus's view that all forms of light were corporeal, in which case even the most transcendent forms of light could not be identified with God, who is incorporeal. On Proclus's account of light, see Richard Sorabji, *The Philosophy of the Commentators 200–600 AD: A Sourcebook. Volume 2: Physics* (London: Duckworth, 2004), 275–84; Byard Bennett, "The Physics of Light, Darkness, and Matter in John the Grammarian's *First Homily Against the Manichaeans*: Early Byzantine Anti-Manichaean Literature as a Window on Controversies in Later Neoplatonism," in *Mani in Dublin: Selected Papers from the Seventh International Conference of the International Association of Manichaean Studies in the Chester Beatty Library, Dublin 8–12 September 2009*, eds. Siegfried G. Richter, Charles Horton, and Klaus Ohlhafer (Leiden: Brill, 2015), 19–33.

34. Cf. Gregory Palamas, *Triads* 3.3.5; compare 2.2.9.

35. See Antonio Rigo, *Monaci esicasti e monaci bogomili. Le accuse di messalianismo e bogomilismo rivolte agli esicasti ed il problema dei rapporti tra esicasmo e bogomilismo* (Florence: Olschki, 1989); Rigo, "Messalianismo = Bogomilismo. Un'equazione dell'eresiologia medievale bizantina," *Orientalia Christiana Periodica* 56 (1990): 53–82.

36. An English translation of selections from the *Triads* has been produced by Nicholas Gendle, *Gregory Palamas. The Triads* (New York: Paulist, 1983).

process of rational demonstration. Barlaam's criticisms were unjustified. Barlaam had posited a sharp distinction between God and created things but had given an inadequate account of how God mediated his grace to the created world.

In biblical literature, God is described as being surrounded by glory (Ezek 1:27–28) and sending forth light (Ps 43:3); this glory and light belong to God and reveal his presence and character (Deut 5:24; 2 Chron 5:14; Ezek 8:4; 10:19; 11:22; 28:22; 43:2; 1 Tim 6:16; 2 Pet 1:17; Rev 15:8; 21:11, 23).[37] Even though God is by nature invisible (Col 1:15; 1 Tim 1:17; 6:16), he makes it possible for us to see his glory (Ezek 8:4; Acts 7:55), which we perceive as light (Ps 36:9; Acts 22:11). Since this light belongs to God and reveals his presence and power, this light is truly divine and uncreated.[38]

Rather than focusing on the distinction between what God is (God's essence) and what created things are, as Barlaam did, one should instead make a distinction between God's essence (i.e., the properties that make him God and that no other beings can possess) and God's activities (those aspects of God's life and power by which God creates, preserves, rules over, and transforms all other beings).[39]

It is true, Gregory admitted, that created minds can never fully comprehend God's essence; i.e., all the peculiar properties that make God who God is.[40] For example, how could a created mind know what it meant for God to be infinite or immaterial? Words such as *infinite* and *immaterial* tell one only *that* God is free from limits but not *how* God exists in his freedom from limits. God exists in a way that transcends every conception we might form of God, and we cannot share in these unique features of God's existence.

In spite of our limitations as created beings, God nonetheless wishes to show us something of his nature by the way he acts. These activities are not separate from God but are expressions of God's life and represent his power to bring things

---

37. Gregory's use and interpretation of these biblical themes is discussed by Fadi A. Georgi, "The Vision of God as a Foretaste of Eternal Life," in *Gotteserlebnis und Gotteslehre: Christliche und islamische Mystik im Orient*, ed. Martin Tamcke (Wiesbaden: Harrassowitz, 2010), 147–56.

38. Gregory held that the divine light belonged to all three persons of the Trinity (*Triads* 3.1.12) but was principally an activity of the Spirit, by which the Spirit gives life to created beings and sanctifies them (*Triads* 3.1.9, 33). For a discussion of the relation between Gregory's pneumatology and his distinction between essence and activity, see Jacques Lison, *L'Esprit répandu: la pneumatologie de Grégoire Palamas* (Paris: Cerf, 1994).

39. Gregory Palamas, *Triads* 3.1.29, 34; 3.2.14; *One Hundred and Fifty Chapters* 75, 78, 84, 87, 91, 105, 107, 125, 144. The historical background of the essence-activity distinction is discussed in Alexis Torrance, "Precedents for Palamas' Essence-Energies Theology in the Cappadocian Fathers," *Vigiliae Christianae* 63 (2009): 47–70; Torstein Theodor Tollefsen, *Activity and Participation in Late Antique and Early Christian Thought* (Oxford: Oxford University Press, 2012); Susanne Hausammann, *Das lebenschaffende Licht der unauflösbaren Dunkelheit. Eine Studie zum Verständnis von Wesen und Energien des Heiligen Geistes und der Schau des göttlichen Lichtes bei den Vätern der Orthodoxen Kirche von Origenes bis Gregor Palamas* (Neukirchen-Vluyn: Neukirchener Verlagsgesellschaft, 2011).

40. Gregory Palamas, *Triads* 2.3.8–9, 33, 66; *One Hundred and Fifty Chapters* 81–82.

into existence and give them life.[41] Since the power to bring things into existence and give them life belongs to God alone, God's activities must be regarded as fully divine and not, as Barlaam thought, merely effects brought about in the created realm.[42] Furthermore, these activities are an eternal and inalienable part of God's existence, for no essence is without its activity;[43] God could no more be without his activity than one could be a human being without being alive.

Gregory argued that God's gracious action toward us gives us life and draws us into communion with him so that we are able to know and share in his goodness, wisdom, and holiness. Although we cannot share in those things that make God uniquely who he is (his essence), God's activities make it possible for us to share in every good quality God possesses that is not unique to his own individual existence.[44] The hesychast monks' claim that they had directly perceived God was true, Gregory argued; unmediated contact with God not only provides certain knowledge of God but also allows human beings to participate in God's goodness and to be transformed into God's likeness.

THE AFTERMATH OF THE CONTROVERSY BETWEEN GREGORY AND BARLAAM

Gregory was able to gain support for his position from the monks of Mount Athos, and this led to Barlaam being condemned by the Patriarchal Synod in 1341.[45] Between 1341 and 1347, Gregory nevertheless had to defend himself against other opponents who felt that the language Gregory had used to distinguish between God's essence and activity was incautious.[46] By distinguishing between incommunicable properties peculiar to God and activities by which God shared his communicable properties with other beings, Gregory seemed to be teaching that there was a fundamental division in God between a superior

---

41. Gregory Palamas, *One Hundred and Fifty Chapters* 87, 133.

42. Gregory Palamas *Triads* 1.3.23, which draws on ps.-Dionysius *On the Divine Names* 11.6 (PG 3, 956A).

43. Gregory Palamas, *Triads* 3.1.24; *One Hundred and Fifty Chapters* 88, 136–137, 139, 143.

44. Cf. Gregory Palamas, *Triads* 2.3.15: "Thus to our human nature He has given the glory of the Godhead, but not the divine nature; for the nature of God is one thing, His glory another, even though they be inseparable one from another. However, even though this glory is different from the divine nature . . . it belongs to the divine nature in an ineffable manner" (ET Gendle, *Gregory Palamas*, 60).

45. For an English translation of the *Tomos of the Holy Mountain*, indicating the Athonite monks' support for Gregory's position, see Sinkewicz, "Gregory Palamas," 183–88.

46. For the criticisms made of Gregory's position, see Angela Constantinides Hero, *Letters of Gregory Akindynos* (Washington, DC: Dumbarton Oaks, 1983); Juan Nadal Cañellas, *Gregorii Acindyni refutationes duae operis Gregorii Palamae cui titulus Dialogus inter Orthodoxum et Barlaamitam*, CCSG 31 (Turnhout: Brepols, 1995); Cañellas, "Gregorio Akíndinos," in *La théologie byzantine et sa tradition II (XIIIe–XIXe s.)*, eds. Carmelo Giuseppe Conticello and Vassa Conticello (Turnhout: Brepols, 2002), 189–314; Cañellas, *La résistance d'Akindynos à Grégoire Palamas. Enquête historique, avec traduction et commentaire de quatre traités édités récemment*, 2 vols. (Leuven: Peeters, 2006).

form of divinity (God's transcendent essence) and an inferior form of divinity (God's self-communication to lesser beings through his activities).[47] Gregory's opponents argued that, in making these distinctions, Gregory had failed to adequately affirm the oneness of God.[48] During these years, which coincided with a major political conflict and a civil war within the Byzantine Empire, Gregory fell from political favor and was imprisoned.

At the conclusion of the civil war, Gregory was exonerated and appointed to a senior ecclesiastical position, becoming metropolitan of Thessaloniki. Gregory then produced a detailed defense of the distinction he had made between God's essence and activity (the *One Hundred and Fifty Chapters*).[49] Although the philosopher Nicephorus Gregoras and a number of bishops continued to oppose Gregory's teaching, a synod convened in 1351 endorsed the principal features of Gregory's position.[50]

As the polemics against his theology subsided, Gregory was able to devote most of his time to preaching and pastoral work. After being briefly imprisoned by the Turks in 1354–1355, Gregory died in 1357 and was proclaimed a saint of the Greek church in 1368.[51]

CONTRIBUTIONS TO THE FIELD OF APOLOGETICS

Gregory's apologetic works had a significant influence on later Byzantine and Eastern Orthodox theology. As the Byzantine Empire drew to a close, Gregory's defense of hesychasm and his distinction between God's essence and activities helped Orthodox Christians define their identity and respond to the alternative

---

47. See Gregory Palamas, *Ep. 3 to Akindynos* (in Hero, *Letters*, xv–xvi n. 44); Sinkewicz, "Gregory Palamas," 134.

48. For Akindynos's charge of ditheism, see Gregory Palamas, *One Hundred and Fifty Chapters* 147.

49. On this work, see Robert E. Sinkewicz, "Christian Theology and the Renewal of Philosophical and Scientific Studies in the Early Fourteenth Century: The *Capita 150* of Gregory Palamas," *Mediaeval Studies* 48 (1986): 334–51.

50. See Aristeides Papadakis, "Gregory Palamas at the Council of Blachernae, 1351," *Greek, Roman and Byzantine Studies* 10 (1969): 333–42. On Nicephorus Gregoras's opposition to Gregory and the hesychast monks, see Demetrios N. Moschos, Πλατωνισμός ἢ Χριστιανισμός; Οἱ φιλοσοφικές προϋποθέσεις τοῦ Ἀντιησυχασμοῦ τοῦ Νικηφόρου Γρηγορᾶ (1293–1361) (Athens: Parousia, 1998).

51. An account of the miracles Gregory performed during his pastoral work at Thessaloniki was composed by Philotheos Kokkinos in the 1360s, apparently in support of the canonization process. An English translation is given in Alice-Mary Talbot and Scott Fitzgerald Johnson, *Miracle Tales from Byzantium* (Cambridge: Harvard University Press, 2012), 301–405. On Gregory's captivity and his debates with Muslims at the court of the Turkish sultan, see G. Georgiades Arnakis, "Gregory Palamas among the Turks and Documents of His Activity as Historical Sources," *Speculum* 26 (1951): 104–18; Anna Philippidis-Braat, "La captivité de Palamas chez les Turcs: dossier et commentaire," *Travaux et mémoires* 7 (1979): 109–222; Daniel J. Sahas, "Captivity and Dialogue: Gregory Palamas (1296–1360) and the Muslims," *Greek Orthodox Theological Review* 25 (1980): 409–36.

approaches taken by Catholicism and Protestantism.[52] Although Gregory's influence waned during the post-Byzantine period, there was a revival of interest in his works in the first half of the twentieth century.[53]

Gregory's work has been appreciated by contemporary Orthodox theologians because Gregory did not make Christian theology narrowly dependent on some preconceived account, drawn from non-Christian sources, of what is reasonable or logical. In rejecting Aristotelian philosophy and scholastic theology, which was concerned to show the harmony of faith and reason, Gregory wished to make faith the sole basis for knowing anything of God's nature. Faith, Gregory argued, is necessary if one is to know God, and there can be no real knowledge of God apart from religious commitment.[54]

For Gregory, what confirms and validates faith is a certain kind of religious experience that involves perceiving and being affected by God's action.[55] Gregory described this spiritual perception of God's action as being analogous in some respects to sense-perception, but superior to the latter. Gregory noted that a logical demonstration is not required to establish that objects of sense-perception exist and have certain qualities. The same, he argued, is true in the case of spiritual perception; logical demonstration is not needed to establish that the objects of spiritual perception exist and have certain properties. Furthermore, since logical demonstration need not precede religious experience, the study of logic should not be regarded as essential to the life of faith.[56] Neither, he argued, was it

---

52. For the use and interpretation of Gregory's essence-activity distinction in later Byzantine writers, see John A. Demetracopoulos, "Palamas Transformed. Palamite Interpretations of the Distinction between God's 'Essence' and 'Energies' in Late Byzantium," in *Greeks, Latins and Intellectual History 1204–1500*, eds. Martin Hinterberger and Chris Schabel (Leuven: Peeters, 2011), 263–372.

53. On Palamas's decreased influence in post-Byzantine literature, see Marcus Plested, "Gregory Palamas," in *The Wiley Blackwell Companion to Patristics*, ed. Ken Parry (Chichester, West Sussex: John Wiley & Sons, 2015), 297–99. For the reappropriation of Gregory's theology as a basis for Orthodox theology in the modern period, see Aidan Nichols, *Light from the East: Authors and Themes in Orthodox Theology* (London: Sheed & Ward, 1995), 41–56 ("John Meyendorff and Neo-Palamism"); Norman Russell, *Gregory Palamas and the Making of Palamism in the Modern Age* (Oxford: Oxford University Press, 2019). Among the contemporary Orthodox theologians who have carefully studied Gregory's conceptions of knowledge and theological method and have made these a point of departure for their own theological proposals, one might note especially Bishop Atanasije Jevtić and Father Nikolaos (Nicholas) Loudovikos. See Athanase Jevtitch, *Études hésychastes*, trans. Jean-Louis Palierne (Lausanne: L'Âge d'Homme, 1995), 7–72 ("Prolégomènes à une gnoséologie hésychaste: L'amour, fondement de la connaissance"); Nikolaos Loudovikos, Ὁ μόχθος τῆς μετοχῆς. Εἶναι καὶ μέθεξη στὸν Γρηγόριο Παλαμᾶ καὶ τὸν Θωμᾶ Ἀκινάτη (Athens: Armos, 2010); Loudovikos, "Initiating the Discussion—'For the Fall and Rising of Many': St. Gregory Palamas at the Crossroads of Interpretation," *Analogia* 3:2 (2017): 3–7.

54. Cf. *Triads* 3.1.32, where Gregory affirms that the only one who knows the activities of the Spirit is he "who has learnt of them through *experience*. As for the man who seeks knowledge before works, if he trusts in those who have had the experience, he obtains a certain image of the truth. But if he tries to conceive of it by himself, he finds himself deprived even of the image of truth" (ET Gendle, *Gregory Palamas*, 87; emphasis his).

55. For further discussion, see Britta Müller-Schauenburg, *Religiöse Erfahrung, Spiritualität und theologische Argumentation: Gotteslehre und Gottebenbildlichkeit bei Gregorios Palamas* (Stuttgart: Kohlhammer, 2011).

56. Barlaam had argued that the study of logic and natural science was useful in training the mind and freeing it from ignorance and false opinions, thus helping prepare the mind to ascend toward God. Gregory

necessary to validate religious experience by reference to some prior conceptions imposed by human reason.

Authentic experience of God, Gregory contended, can nonetheless be seen to have certain characteristic features. First, since it is written that the pure in heart will see God (Matt 5:8), the person claiming to have this experience must have worked to combat sinful thoughts, root out vices, acquire the virtues, and engage in unceasing prayer.[57] Second, the person must have previously stilled the functions of the mind by which mental pictures, concepts, and discursive reasonings were produced. Otherwise, any perceptions could reasonably be assumed to arise from the recipient's own mind and not from God's action.[58] Third, the experience of God must be so qualitatively different from sense-perception and intellectual perception that it could only be explained by God's supernatural action.[59] The hesychast monks had often held that perceiving God's uncreated light might be accompanied or followed by miraculous phenomena such as foreknowledge of future events and the gift of healing.[60] Gregory accepted this but placed greater emphasis on the qualitative and quantitative differences discernable in the objects of spiritual perception themselves (e.g., the light that is seen is limitless, infinite in extension, and able to comprehend all things while itself transcending comprehension by the mind and the senses).[61]

In conclusion, the extended debate with Barlaam led Gregory to develop a systematic account of the Christian life that emphasized the authority and evidential value of religious experience.[62] This model regarded faith and religious

rejected the idea that such intellectual training could facilitate union with God. Gregory argued that since God is uncreated, he wholly transcends both the mind and the physical senses of created beings; spiritual perception is thus brought about by God's action alone and not by any powers that belong by nature to the mind and the senses. Cf. *Triads* 3.1.36, where Gregory argues that "you should hold that intellectual activities are entirely bypassed by the light of union and by the action of this light" (ET Gendle, *Gregory Palamas*, 91). For a further discussion of the views of Barlaam and Gregory on this subject, see Dirk Krausmüller, "Do We Need to Be Stupid in Order to Be Saved? Barlaam of Calabria and Gregory Palamas on Knowledge and Ignorance," in *Salvation According to the Fathers of the Church: The Proceedings of the Sixth International Patristic Conference, Maynooth/Belfast, 2005*, eds. D. Vincent Twomey and Dirk Krausmüller (Dublin: Four Courts, 2010), 143–52; Michele Trizio, "'Una è la verità che pervade ogni cosa.' La sapienza profana nelle opere perdute di Barlaam Calabro," in *Byzantine Theology and Its Philosophical Background*, ed. Antonio Rigo (Turnhout: Brepols, 2011), 108–40.

57. Cf. *Triads* 1.3.22: "The vision is granted him in proportion to his practice of what is pleasing to God, his avoidance of all that is not, his assiduity in prayer, and the longing of his entire soul for God" (ET Gendle, *Gregory Palamas*, 39).

58. *Triads* 1.2.3–4. In *Triads* 1.3.22 and 3.1.36, Gregory again links stillness of mind with the presence of God, when he says that any true vision of the uncreated light will not be accompanied by agitation or disturbance in the soul but rather by peace, rest, joy, and humility.

59. *Triads* 3.1.36.

60. *Triads* 3.1.33. Compare *Triads* 3.1.35: "Do you not see that they will acquire the same energy as the Sun of Righteousness? This is why various divine signs and the communication of the Holy Spirit are effected through them" (ET Gendle, *Gregory Palamas*, 89).

61. *Triads* 3.1.33.

62. Cf. A. M. Allchin, "The Appeal to Experience in the *Triads* of St. Gregory Palamas," in *Studia Patristica Vol. VIII*, ed. F. L. Cross (Berlin: Akademie-Verlag, 1966), 323–28.

commitment (expressed through spiritual struggle and unceasing prayer) as the only way to attain certain knowledge of God's nature. This knowledge arose from contact and union with God and was produced by God's unmediated action, transcending the natural human faculties of sensation and reason. Gregory's account of mystical union and the immediate and certain knowledge of God that transcends reason has sometimes been compared to Western medieval traditions of contemplative prayer.[63]

Gregory's account thus differed in important ways from the Western medieval tradition of scholastic theology, which aimed to be a demonstrative science that showed the harmony of faith and reason. In Gregory's view, it is not necessary to validate Christian teaching by reference to human reason since true knowledge of God transcends the limits of sense-perception, concepts, and discursive reasoning. Although one might be able to demonstrate the coherence of Christian doctrines to the unconverted, such a demonstration would not be sufficient to bring about the mind's conversion and return to God. Conversion and transformation occur only when God graciously acts supernaturally on a person, creating incontrovertible certainty and producing a holy life. In the end, this holy life is the best apologetic for the truth of the faith.[64]

BIBLIOGRAPHY

Allchin, A. M. "The Appeal to Experience in the *Triads* of St. Gregory Palamas." Pages 323–28 in *Studia Patristica Vol. VIII*. Ed. by F. L. Cross. Berlin: Akademie-Verlag, 1966.

Arblaster, John, and Rob Faesen, eds. *Mystical Doctrines of Deification: Case Studies in the Christian Tradition*. London: Routledge, 2018.

Arnakis, G. Georgiades. "Gregory Palamas among the Turks and Documents of His Activity as Historical Sources." *Speculum* 26 (1951): 104–18.

Bazzani, Marina. "Theodore Metochites, a Byzantine Humanist." *Byzantion* 76 (2006): 32–52.

Bennett, Byard. "The Physics of Light, Darkness, and Matter in John the Grammarian's *First Homily Against the Manichaeans*: Early Byzantine Anti-Manichaean Literature as a Window on Controversies in Later Neoplatonism." Pages 19–33 in *Mani in Dublin: Selected Papers from the Seventh International Conference of the International Association of Manichaean Studies in the Chester Beatty Library, Dublin 8–12 September 2009*. Ed. by Siegfried G. Richter, Charles Horton, and Klaus Ohlhafer. Leiden: Brill, 2015.

Beyer, Hans-Veit. "Die Lichtlehre der Mönche des vierzehnten und des vierten Jahrhunderts." *Jahrbuch der Österreichischen Byzantinistik* 31 (1981): 473–512.

Bianchi, Luca. *Monasteri icona del mondo celeste. La teologia spirituale di Gregorio Palamas*. Bologna: EDB, 2010.

---

63. See, e.g., Kallistos Ware, "The Nearness Yet Otherness of the Eternal in Meister Eckhart and St. Gregory Palamas," *Eckhart Review* 9 (2000): 41–53; Emmanuel Cazabonne, "Gregory Palamas (1296–1359): Monk, Theologian, and Pastor," *Cistercian Studies Quarterly* 37 (2002): 303–33; Russel Murray, "Mirror of Experience: Palamas and Bonaventure on the Experience of God—A Contribution to Orthodox-Roman Catholic Dialogue," *Journal of Ecumenical Studies* 44 (2009): 432–60.

64. Cf. *Triads* 1.3.13: "But we hold that the true opinion is not the knowledge found through words and syllogisms, but that which is demonstrated through deeds and [one's] life and it alone is not only true, but also certain and secure. For it is said, 'Every word contends with a word,' but what contends with a life?"

Bydén, Börje. "'To Every Argument There Is a Counter-Argument': Theodore Metochites' Defence of Scepticism (*Semeiosis* 61)." Pages 183–217 in *Byzantine Philosophy and Its Ancient Sources*. Ed. by Katerina Ierodiakonou. Oxford: Clarendon, 2002.

———. *Theodore Metochites' Stoicheiosis astronomike and the Study of Natural Philosophy and Mathematics in Early Palaiologan Byzantium*, 2 rev. ed. Göteborg: Acta Universitatis Gothoburgensis, 2003.

Casiday, Augustine. *Reconstructing the Theology of Evagrius Ponticus: Beyond Heresy*. Cambridge: Cambridge University Press, 2013.

Cazabonne, Emmanuel. "Gregory Palamas (1296–1359): Monk, Theologian, and Pastor." *Cistercian Studies Quarterly* 37 (2002): 303–33.

Chrestou, Panagiotes K., ed. Γρηγορίου τοῦ Παλαμᾶ Συγγράμματα. 5 vols. Thessaloniki: Kyromanos, 1962–1992.

Christensen, Michael J., and Jeffery A. Wittung, eds. *Partakers of the Divine Nature: The History and Development of Deification in the Christian Traditions*. Grand Rapids: Baker, 2007.

Demetracopoulos, John A. Νικολάου Καβάσιλα Κατὰ Πύρρωνος. Πλατωνικός φιλοσκεπτικισμός καί ἀριστοτελικός ἀντισκεπτικισμός στὴ βυζαντινή διανόηση τοῦ 14ου αἰῶνα. Athens: Parousia, 1999.

———. "Further Evidence on the Ancient, Patristic, and Byzantine Sources of Barlaam the Calabrian's *Contra Latinos*. À propos de A. Fyrigos, ed., *Barlaam Calabro, Opere contro i Latini*," *Byzantinische Zeitschrift* 96 (2003): 83–122.

———. "Palamas Transformed. Palamite Interpretations of the Distinction between God's 'Essence' and 'Energies' in Late Byzantium." Pages 263–372 in *Greeks, Latins and Intellectual History 1204–1500*. Ed. by Martin Hinterberger and Chris Schabel. Leuven: Peeters, 2011.

Edwards, Mark, and Elena Ene D-Vasilescu, eds. *Visions of God and Ideas on Deification in Patristic Thought*. London: Routledge, 2017.

Flogaus, Reinhard. *Theosis bei Palamas und Luther: Ein Beitrag zum ökumenischen Gespräch*. Göttingen: Vandenhoeck & Ruprecht, 1997.

Fyrigos, Antonis. *Barlaam Calabro. Opere contro i Latini*. 2 vols. Vatican City: Biblioteca Apostolica Vaticana, 1998.

———. *Dalla controversia palamitica alla polemica esicastica*. Rome: Antonianum, 2005.

Gendle, Nicholas. *Gregory Palamas. The Triads*. New York: Paulist, 1983.

Georgi, Fadi A. "The Vision of God as a Foretaste of Eternal Life." Pages 147–56 in *Gotteserlebnis und Gotteslehre: Christliche und islamische Mystik im Orient*. Ed. by Martin Tamcke. Wiesbaden: Harrassowitz, 2010.

Hausammann, Susanne. *Das lebenschaffende Licht der unauflösbaren Dunkelheit. Eine Studie zum Verständnis von Wesen und Energien des Heiligen Geistes und der Schau des göttlichen Lichtes bei den Vätern der Orthodoxen Kirche von Origenes bis Gregor Palamas*. Neukirchen-Vluyn: Neukirchener Verlagsgesellschaft, 2011.

Hero, Angela C. *Letters of Gregory Akindynos*. Washington, D.C.: Dumbarton Oaks, 1983.

———. *The Life and Letters of Theoleptos of Philadelphia*. Brookline, MA: Hellenic College Press, 1994.

Horujy, Sergey S., ed. *Hesychasm: An Annotated Bibliography*. Moscow: Institute of Human Studies of the Russian Academy of Sciences, 2004.

Hult, Karin. *Theodore Metochites on Ancient Authors and Philosophy: Semeioseis gnomikai 1–26 & 71*. Göteborg: Acta Universitatis Gothoburgensis, 2002.

Ierodiakonou, Katerina. "The Anti-Logical Movement in the Fourteenth Century." Pages 219–36 in *Byzantine Philosophy and Its Ancient Sources*. Edited by Katerina Ierodiakonou. Oxford: Clarendon Press, 2002.

Jevtitch, Athanase. *Études hésychastes*. Translated by Jean-Louis Palierne. Lausanne: L'Âge d'Homme, 1995.

Krausmüller, Dirk. "Do We Need to Be Stupid in Order to Be Saved? Barlaam of Calabria and Gregory Palamas on Knowledge and Ignorance." Pages 143–52 in *Salvation According to the Fathers of the Church: The Proceedings of the Sixth International Patristic Conference, Maynooth/Belfast, 2005*. Ed. by D. Vincent Twomey and Dirk Krausmüller. Dublin: Four Courts, 2010.

———. "The Rise of Hesychasm." Pages 101–26 in *The Cambridge History of Christianity. 5: Eastern Christianity*. Edited by Michael Angold. Cambridge: Cambridge University Press, 2006.

Lison, Jacques. *L'Esprit répandu: la pneumatologie de Grégoire Palamas*. Paris: Cerf, 1994.

Loudovikos, Nikolaos. Ὁ μόχθος τῆς μετοχῆς. Εἶναι καὶ μέθεξη στὸν Γρηγόριο Παλαμᾶ καὶ τὸν Θωμᾶ Ἀκινάτη. Athens: Armos, 2010.

———. "Initiating the Discussion—'For the Fall and Rising of Many': St. Gregory Palamas at the Crossroads of Interpretation." *Analogia* 3:2 (2017): 3–7.

Meyendorff, Jean. *Grégoire Palamas. Défense des saints hésychastes*. 2 vols. 2 ed. Leuven: Spicilegium Sacrum Lovaniense, 1973.

Mitrea, Mihail. "'Old Wine in New Bottles'?: Gregory Palamas' *Logos* on Saint Peter of Athos (*BHG* 1506)." *Byzantine and Modern Greek Studies* 40 (2016): 243–63.

Monsaingeon, M.-J. and J. Paramelle, *Saint Grégoire Palamas, De la déification de l'être humain, suivi de Georges I. Mantzaridis, La doctrine de Saint Grégoire Palamas sur la déification de l'être humain*. Lausanne: L'Âge d'Homme, 1990.

Moschos, Demetrios N. Πλατωνισμός ἤ Χριστιανισμός; Οἱ φιλοσοφικές προϋποθέσεις τοῦ Ἀντιησυχασμοῦ τοῦ Νικηφόρου Γρηγορᾶ (1293–1361). Athens: Parousia, 1998.

Müller-Schauenburg, Britta. *Religiöse Erfahrung, Spiritualität und theologische Argumentation: Gotteslehre und Gottebenbildlichkeit bei Gregorios Palamas*. Stuttgart: Kohlhammer, 2011.

Murray, Russel. "Mirror of Experience: Palamas and Bonaventure on the Experience of God—A Contribution to Orthodox-Roman Catholic Dialogue." *Journal of Ecumenical Studies* 44 (2009): 432–60.

Nadal Cañellas, Juan. *Gregorii Acindyni refutationes duae operis Gregorii Palamae cui titulus Dialogus inter Orthodoxum et Barlaamitam*. CCSG 31. Turnhout: Brepols, 1995.

———. "Gregorio Akíndinos." Pages 189–314 in *La théologie byzantine et sa tradition II (XIIIe-XIXe s.)*. Edited by Carmelo Giuseppe Conticello and Vassa Conticello. Turnhout: Brepols, 2002.

———. *La résistance d'Akindynos à Grégoire Palamas. Enquête historique, avec traduction et commentaire de quatre traités édités récemment*. 2 vols. Leuven: Peeters, 2006.

Nichols, Aidan. *Light from the East: Authors and Themes in Orthodox Theology*. London: Sheed and Ward, 1995.

Papadakis, Aristeides. "Gregory Palamas at the Council of Blachernae, 1351." *Greek, Roman and Byzantine Studies* 10 (1969): 333–42.

Paschos, Emmanuel, and Christos Simelidis, *Introduction to Astronomy by Theodore Metochites (Stoicheiosis astronomike 1.5–30)*. Singapore: World Scientific, 2017.

Philippidis-Braat, Anna. "La captivité de Palamas chez les Turcs: dossier et commentaire." *Travaux et mémoires* 7 (1979): 109–222.

Plested, Marcus. "Gregory Palamas." Pages 293–305 in *The Wiley Blackwell Companion to Patristics*, ed. Ken Parry (Chichester, West Sussex: John Wiley and Sons, 2015).

Polemis, Ioannis. "Neoplatonic and Hesychastic Elements in the Early Teaching of Gregorios Palamas on the Union of Man with God: The *Life of St. Peter the Athonite*." Pages 205–21 in *Pour une poétique de Byzance. Hommage à Vassilis Katsaros*. Edited by Stephanos Efthymiadis, Charis Messis, Paolo Odorico, and Ioannis D. Polemis. Paris: Éditions De Boccard, 2015.

Rigo, Antonio. "Le tecniche d'orazione esicastica e le potenze dell'anima in alcuni testi ascetici bizantini." *Rivista di studi bizantini e slavi* 4 (1984): 75–115.

———. "L'*Epistola a Menas* di Gregorio Palamas e gli effeti dell'orazione." *Cristianesimo nella storia* 9 (1988): 57–80.

———. *Monaci esicasti e monaci bogomili. Le accuse di messalianismo e bogomilismo rivolte agli esicasti ed il problema dei rapporti tra esicasmo e bogomilismo*. Florence: Olschki, 1989.

———. "Messalianismo = Bogomilismo. Un'equazione dell'eresiologia medievale bizantina." *Orientalia Christiana Periodica* 56 (1990): 53–82.

———. *I padri esicasti. L'amore della quiete (ho tes hesychias eros). L'esicasmo bizantino tra il XIII e il XV secolo*. Magnano: Qiqajon, 1993.

———. "La Vita di Pietro l'Athonita (*BHG* 1506) scritta da Gregorio Palama." *Rivista di studi bizantini e neoellenici* 32 (1995): 177–90.

———. "De l'apologie à l'évocation de l'expérience mystique. Évagre le Pontique, Isaac le Syrien et Diadoque de Photicé dans les oeuvres de Grégoire Palamas (et dans la controverse palamite)." Pages 85–108 in *Knotenpunkt Byzanz: Wissenformen und kulturelle Wechselbeziehungen*. Ed. by Andreas Speer and Philipp Steinkrüger. Berlin: De Gruyter, 2012.

Russell, Norman. *The Doctrine of Deification in the Greek Patristic Tradition*. Oxford: Oxford University Press, 2004.

———. *Gregory Palamas and the Making of Palamism in the Modern Age*. Oxford: Oxford University Press, 2019.

Sahas, Daniel J. "Captivity and Dialogue: Gregory Palamas (1296–1360) and the Muslims." *Greek Orthodox Theological Review* 25 (1980): 409–36.

Sinkewicz, Robert E. "Christian Theology and the Renewal of Philosophical and Scientific Studies in the Early Fourteenth Century: The *Capita 150* of Gregory Palamas." *Mediaeval Studies* 48 (1986): 334–51.

———. "The Doctrine of the Knowledge of God in the Early Writings of Barlaam the Calabrian." *Mediaeval Studies* 44 (1982): 181–242.

———. "Gregory Palamas." Pages 131–88 in *La théologie byzantine et sa tradition II (XIIIe-XIXe s.)*. Ed. by Carmelo Giuseppe Conticello and Vassa Conticello. Turnhout: Brepols, 2002.

————. "A New Interpretation for the First Episode in the Controversy between Barlaam the Calabrian and Gregory Palamas." *Journal of Theological Studies* 31 (1980): 489–500.

————. *The One Hundred and Fifty Chapters.* Toronto: Pontifical Institute of Mediaeval Studies, 1988.

————. "The *Solutions* Addressed to George Lapithes by Barlaam the Calabrian and Their Philosophical Context." *Mediaeval Studies* 43 (1981): 151–217.

Sorabji, Richard. *The Philosophy of the Commentators 200–600 AD: A Sourcebook. Volume 2: Physics.* London: Duckworth, 2004.

————. *The Philosophy of the Commentators 200–600 AD: A Sourcebook. Volume 3: Logic & Metaphysics.* London: Duckworth, 2004.

Spiteris, Yannis. *Palamas: la grazia e l'esperienza. Gregorio Palamas nella discussione teologica.* Rome: Lipa, 1996.

Stewart, Columba. *Cassian the Monk.* Oxford: Oxford University Press, 1999.

Talbot, Alice-Mary, and Scott Fitzgerald Johnson, *Miracle Tales from Byzantium.* Cambridge: Harvard University Press, 2012.

Tollefsen, Torstein Theodor. *Activity and Participation in Late Antique and Early Christian Thought.* Oxford: Oxford University Press, 2012.

Torrance, Alexis. "Precedents for Palamas' Essence-Energies Theology in the Cappadocian Fathers." *Vigiliae Christianae* 63 (2009): 47–70.

Trizio, Michele. "'Una è la verità che pervade ogni cosa.' La sapienza profana nelle opere perdute di Barlaam Calabro." Pages 108–40 in *Byzantine Theology and Its Philosophical Background.* Ed. by Antonio Rigo. Turnhout: Brepols, 2011.

Ware, Kallistos. "The Nearness Yet Otherness of the Eternal in Meister Eckhart and St. Gregory Palamas." *Eckhart Review* 9 (2000): 41–53.

Williams, A. N. *The Ground of Union: Deification in Aquinas and Palamas.* Oxford: Oxford University Press, 1999.

Part Three

EARLY MODERN
APOLOGISTS

The early modern period designated an important era in Christian apologetics in which reason was increasingly seen as a criterion of acceptability. The Enlightenment is a complex movement, probably best seen as a family of movements that believed the European wars of religion were an indicator of the need to find a more reliable basis for communal reasoning and decision-making than that traditionally found in religion. The Enlightenment took quite different forms in England, France, Germany, and the Low Countries, leading apologists to temper their approaches to these local variations.

Although the Enlightenment was often presented in the past as an anti-religious movement, recent scholarship has reversed this trend, pointing out the close connection between the movement and religion. Nevertheless, the new emphasis on reason as the most reliable public authority of judgment made it inevitable that religious apologists now tended to find rational common ground with their audiences. A rational framework for faith having been established, the fine theological and spiritual detail could be added later.

In England, Christian apologetics faced two particularly significant challenges in the eighteenth century. The rise of the movement known as "deism" led to growing interest in minimally counterintuitive forms of religion. Deism, by limiting God's role to the act of creation of the universe and the provision of human moral guidance, seemed to offer educated English society a form of religion that avoided what were seen as the rational difficulties of traditional Christian ideas such as the doctrine of the Trinity or the divinity of Christ.

This perception was given added force through the growing impact of the scientific revolution, which seemed to point to a God who was known through the regularities of the world rather than through the specific history of Jesus Christ. The perceived threat of atheism arising from the natural sciences was countered in several ways, including the famous Boyle Lectures of the early eighteenth century. These apologetic sermons stressed the harmony of the Christian faith and the new scientific discoveries of Newton and his successors.

Joseph Butler—often known simply as Bishop Butler—was one of the most influential apologists of the early eighteenth century. Aware of the growing demand for evidence or "proof" of religious beliefs, Butler argued that probability was a more reliable guide to truth in such matters than rational demonstration. While apologetic arguments can never hope to secure certainty of conviction, they are nonetheless probable.

Butler's approach involved working with the deists' argument that the justification of Christian belief must rest on ordinary methods of reasoning that would be used in everyday life. Butler argued that using such forms of argument or standards of evidence takes us much further than is generally realized, in that they are able to establish the probability of some core Christian beliefs.

William Paley took this position further in his influential work *Natural Theology*, arguing that these ordinary methods of reasoning could be used to consider the origins and implications of biological complexity in the natural world. Paley pointed to the complexity of such biological structures as the human eye and argued that it was in many respects analogous to watches, telescopes, and the machines constructed during the British Industrial Revolution. The eye shows evidence of having been designed and constructed for a specific purpose. The most probable explanation of biological complexity was divine creation. Paley's argument, given imaginative appeal through the controlling analogy of a watch, was highly effective and had a significant impact in the first half of the nineteenth century.

Elsewhere, apologetic approaches were devised to cope with the increasingly rationalist cultural mood in most parts of western Europe. In his *De veritate*, Dutch jurist and apologist **Hugo Grotius** set out to demonstrate the superiority of Christianity over rival religions, specifically paganism, Judaism, and Islam. In doing so, he set out reasons for his assertion that he believed met the criteria now expected for rational acceptance of a specific religious tradition. The use of such rational criteria was not, of course, without risks. One concern that critics of the approach noted was that it risked reducing Christianity to a rational philosophy and failed to respect its spiritual and affective aspects.

This concern was addressed with particular force in France by **Blaise Pascal**, a prominent Jansenist theologian and mathematician. As the result of a spiritual experience during the night of November 23, 1654, Pascal spoke of his faith in "God of Abraham, God of Isaac, God of Jacob—not of the philosophers and scholars." Pascal's apologetics are eminently reasonable but emphasize the limited capacity of reason to grasp reality and the importance of the human heart in discovering religious faith. "The heart has its reasons of which reason knows nothing. It is the heart which perceives God and not the reason." Pascal does not endorse irrationalism here, but rather highlights the role of the emotions and intuitions in the direct perception of God. Many recent apologists have found Pascal's approach helpful, and he remains one of the most influential contributors to the development of apologetics.

This period also witnessed the emergence of a distinctively American approach to apologetics, especially in the writings of **Jonathan Edwards**. Although Edwards was remarkably well informed about trends in European philosophy, his apologetic approach was clearly grounded in the cultural realities of the American colonies. Edwards developed several apologetic approaches, mingling rational and affective approaches. He argued that the signs of beauty, design, and unity in the world were an indication of divine design, yet he also emphasized the importance of engaging "religious affections" rather than merely offering "external arguments" for faith.

The early modern period saw apologetics become increasingly important. Although external challenges—such as other religions—remained an important motivation for apologetics, these were supplemented by growing skepticism about certain core themes of Christianity within Western culture. This trend continued in the nineteenth century, resulting in increased attention to apologetic issues in most major Christian denominations, both in western Europe and North America.

HUGO GROTIUS

Reason, Evidence, and Unity as the Means of Apologetics

BRYAN BAISE

While Hugo Grotius (1583–1645) is undoubtedly known for his writings on international law and rights, he was also a deeply committed Christian. His apologetic, *De Veritate*, sought to demonstrate the superiority of Christianity when compared with her rivals. Grotius's interesting contribution is shown through a constant irenic apologetic. While the circumstances that formed his apologetic are unique, the spirit embodied in his apologetic is both a product of his era and one that we should laud. The question that arises from *De Veritate* is how much of an irenic spirit would stifle a clear Christian apologetic message? Grotius assuredly meant to demonstrate that Christianity speaks a better word, but it is unclear as to how much of that better word is unveiled. Grotius's contributions point us toward a spirit of charity and unity with fellow believers and a strategy of comparing rival worldviews while considering the limitations of a bare-bones apologetic strategy disentangled from an apologetic grounded first in revelation.

HISTORICAL BACKGROUND

Hugo Grotius may not immediately come to mind when one thinks of a Christian apologist. He was considered the "father of international law," and his writings on the nature of law, rights, and justice are well known, yet Grotius was also a deeply committed Christian living in a contested era. Born in 1583 to a wealthy family in Delft, Holland, the young Grotius demonstrated remarkable intellectual abilities at a very young age, writing Latin by the age of eight. He entered Leiden University at eleven,[1] and by the time he was fifteen, Grotius traveled to

---

1. Henk J. M. Nellen, ed., *Hugo Grotius: A Lifelong Struggle for Peace in Church and State, 1583–1645* (Leiden: Brill, 2007), 33–34.

Image: *Hugo de Groot, Hugo Grotius,* by Michiel van Mierevelt, 1631, Prinsenhof, Delft, Netherlands

France, where King Henry IV labeled him "the miracle of Holland."[2] He became the Latin historiographer of the United Provinces by the time he was eighteen.[3] While in France he earned a doctor of laws degree from the University of Orleans and returned after graduation to Holland to practice law. The young man showed remarkable promise, excelling at everything he attempted.

Grotius began practicing law at the Hague and, as with his previous endeavors, was wildly successful. He represented several distinguished individuals and companies, one of which was Prince Maurice of Nassau. Grotius excelled in his representation, and when the position of attorney general became available in 1607, the prince tabbed Grotius for the role.[4] A year later, in 1608, he married Maria van Reigersberch.[5] Grotius served as attorney general with distinction until 1613, when he was appointed pensionary of Rotterdam.[6] Yet not all of Grotius's life was full of success. After his promotion to Rotterdam, he was embroiled in legal and theological controversies that eventually led to his imprisonment.[7] After three years in jail, he escaped to France in a book chest sent by his wife and lived the rest of his life in exile until his death in 1645.

Grotius lived through a significant shift in history in which long-held theological assumptions were being uprooted and challenged by new ideas. A central commitment of Grotius, reflected in his apologetic writings, was an irenic spirit that desired unity among the faithful rather than further theological backbiting and quarreling.

THEOLOGICAL CONTEXT

Living at the dawn of the post-Reformation era meant there were numerous opportunities for theological scuffles and arguments. Grotius originally wrote his defense of the Christian faith in a 1620 poem while he was serving as a prisoner in a castle at Loevestein. The Latin edition, *De Veritate Religionis Christianae* ("*De Veritate*"[8] heretofore), was published in 1640. Theological controversies were pulsating throughout Europe. In the Netherlands alone, Dutch Protestantism was aflame with heated debates between Calvinists and Arminians. The latter, gaining their name from University of Leiden professor Jacobus

2. René Jeffrey, *Hugo Grotius In International Thought* (New York: Palgrave Macmillan, 2006), 4.
3. Jeffrey, *Hugo Grotius*, 92.
4. Charles S. Edwards, *Hugo Grotius, The Miracle of Holland: A Study in Political and Legal Thought* (Chicago: Hall, 1981), 1–2.
5. See Nellen, *Hugo Grotius*, 99–100.
6. At the time of Grotius's appointment, a pensionary was one of the highest offices in the land, somewhat equivalent to prime minister.
7. The controversies will be spelled out in detail in the next section.
8. Translation: "On Truth"

Arminius, stressed the necessity of the freedom of the will, albeit in a chastened sense. Indeed, Arminius did not imagine the will as playing a *primary* role in salvation. Instead, he taught that the will contributed nothing toward one's salvation "without the liberating grace of God, which precedes and permeates the decision."[9] And yet, according to Arminius, humans can reject, resist, and spurn the grace of God.[10] Arminius still believed that God chose whom he would save before the foundations of the world, but he maintained that such a truth does not discount a person's free will.[11]

By constructing his theological account in this way, Arminius contested the contemporary emphasis on the irresistible nature of grace, and this view led to political troubles. The Netherlands was solidly Reformed and Protestant, and during this era of history, the relationship between church and state was more symbiotic than in our contemporary liberal societies.[12] Engaging in a battle with the church put oneself in contest with the state, to some extent.

In 1607 various conferences were held in Holland to discuss Arminius's views, and Arminius defended himself. In 1609 another conference was held with no resolution, and later that year, Arminius died. One of the central questions at hand was whether those holding to this theological commitment should be allowed to teach within established churches.[13] Holland contained a large contingency of "Remonstrants" (those sympathetic to Arminius's teaching), while the rest of the Netherlands were opposed to his teachings (Counter-Remonstrant). Here is where Grotius and his writings became known. Grotius wrote a pamphlet entitled *Ordinum Pietas* in 1614, and in this first publication, he sought to defend Holland and the Remonstrants from the charge of heresy, suggesting that the church should not indiscriminately take sides on this matter but should tolerate a variety of views. Grotius tried to show that "the state of Holland had the competence to decide upon theological disputes legitimately."[14] This was a defense of the existing religious policy in Holland and the willingness of the

---

9. Kevin D. Stanglin and Thomas H. McCall, ed., *Jacob Arminius: Theologian of Grace,* (London: Oxford University Press, 2012), 158.

10. Stanglin and McCall, *Jacob Arminius,* 156–57; 169–70.

11. David McCollough, "His great act of rebellion was to move from these very guarded statements (about man's accountability before God with respect to salvation) to dent the irresistibility of God's grace; in other words, to say that alongside those whom God has eternally decreed to be elect to salvation there are those who choose to reject the offer of God's grace, and fall away into damnation." David McCullough, *The Reformation* (London: Viking, 2003), 365.

12. Though we should say they were not synonymous. There are key distinctions made in the Reformed churches at the time that would distinguish church from state. See Karel Blei, *The Netherlands Reformed Church, 1571–2005* (Grand Rapids: Eerdmans, 2006), 25–36.

13. Again, Blei is instructive here. See Ibid., 24–25.

14. Christopher A. Stumpf, "The Christian Society and Its Government," in *Church as Politeia: The Political Self-Understanding of Christianity,* eds. Christopher A. Stumpf and Holger Zaborowski (New York: De Gruyter, 2000), 158.

state to tolerate charity with theological dogmas to obtain peace in the church.[15] The desire for peace and order is a key element to understanding Grotius and his apologetic strategy. Throughout his public life, Grotius was driven by the hope of peace within the church whenever he debated political and theological matters. Like many of his fellow public servants, he wanted to ensure that resolution to the conflict was beneficial for all and did not adversely affect the common good of the city. This disposition was part of Grotius's overall apologetic method, for he was deeply concerned about the unity of the faith in Holland.[16]

Just a few years later, in 1619, the Synod of Dort took up the Arminian controversy again and eventually outlawed Arminianism in the churches. Remonstrant sympathizers were arrested, and Grotius found himself imprisoned at the castle in Lovestein. Here he began work on what he was most widely known for in his lifetime, his apologetic work *De Veritate*. Published in 1640, the book was an apologetic on two fronts: internal (within the Protestant church) and external (with other religions). The former was where Grotius's irenic temperament was fully displayed. Grotius wanted to bring peace and orderly discussion to the church's various theological disputes, and he promoted and defended doctrines that could be assented to from a variety of theological camps. While his intentions were good, his execution was less well-received.

In addition to this internal apologetic, Grotius also wanted to demonstrate the superiority of Christianity among rival religions, specifically paganism, Judaism, and Islam. In his discussion of paganism, Grotius had in mind a kind of polytheism. In the opening of section 2 of his refutation against paganism, he writes: "And first, against the heathens we say,—If they suppose many gods, eternal and equal, this is sufficiently confuted in the first book."[17] Each of the major non-Christian religions has their own section devoted to what Grotius saw as the essential arguments for defeating that worldview. Grotius's writings show his interest in defending the Christian faith internally and externally, both *in* the house of faith and *against* the house of faith.

APOLOGETIC RESPONSE

Grotius's primary intention in *De Veritate* was to demonstrate that the Christian faith is true and that it should be preferred to other religions, such as

---

15. See Hugh Dunthorne, "History, Theology and Tolerance: Grotius and his English Contemporaries," *Grotiana* 34 (2003): 107–19.

16. For more information related to this, see J. P. Heering, *Hugo Grotius as Apologist* (London: Brill, 2004), 65–66.

17. Citations for *De Veritate* are from Hugo Grotius, *The Truth of the Christian Religion*, trans. John Clarke, ed. Maria Rosa Antognazza (Indianapolis: Liberty Fund, 2012). See Section II.

Judaism and Islam.[18] In the seventeenth-century this might seem like a foregone conclusion, yet Grotius's humanist roots led him to view "closed-circuit tests" based solely on revelation as insufficient proof.[19] It was the dawn of the Enlightenment, and in the midst of a scientific revolution, European society was beginning to require all claims, including religious ones, to be scrutinized under the light of reason and science.

In *De Veritate*, Grotius defends the Christian faith with each work dealing with a separate topic and audience, including: Christianity and the authority of the Bible, testimony and the witness of the Bible, Paganism, Judaism, and "Mohametism" (Islam). Each book utilizes the same methodology: an appeal to unity combined with a search for historical evidences that demonstrate truths of the Christian faith. In his writing, Grotius suggests the Christian faith is superior to its rivals and seeks to serve Christians who may have found themselves in the crosshairs of contending faiths. He sought to be helpful to his fellow citizens, and this is evident throughout *De Veritate*. Throughout the work, Grotius consistently displays his humanist roots and a measure of theological irenicism.[20] As Heering notes:

Book One of *De Veritate* develops with the existence of God, the eternal nature of souls, and man's need to seek true religion. Grotius developed his argument in two stages. The first suggests an argument from causality. Grotius believed reason dictated the conclusion that there are a series of causes and consequences, and thus one must conclude that there was a first cause. This principle cause must be itself uncaused and one ascribes a name to this kind of "uncaused cause": God.[21] As one will see moving forward, each book of *De Veritate* was dependent upon previous arguments developed from earlier philosophers and theologians.[22] Indeed, one can find this kind of causality formulation all the way back to Aristotle and Thomas Aquinas.[23] No doubt this kind of argument was a commonly held conviction at the time and Grotius' employment of it suggests not only his awareness, but belief in its effectiveness.[24]

---

18. Gunther Lottes, "The Transformation of Apologetic Literature in the Early Enlightenment: The Case for Grotius's *De Vertitate.*" *Grotiana* 35 (2014): 70.

19. Ibid., 80.

20. The "irenic ideal" related to Grotius's apologetic is well documented. See Henk Nellen, "Minimal Faith and Irenic Ideals in Seventeenth-Century Scholarly Circles: Hugo Grotius as a Guardian of Isaac Casaubon's Legacy," *Church History and Religious Culture* 94:4 (2014): 444–78.

21. *De Veritate*, I.II

22. This is not intended as a *judgment* but rather an observation of Grotius's deeply embedded humanism where he retrieves classical sourcing to solidify his argumentation.

23. See *Summa Contra Gentiles*, I.IX for Aquinas's formulation.

24. See Heering, *Hugo Grotius as Apologist*, 94.

The second stage of his argument assumed a universal agreement that God exists. Grotius believed that regardless of one's culture or place, all humanity has some understanding of God's existence and that all people shape their lives around this conviction. Those who deny this are refusing to accept the clear conclusion of reason out of their vanity or pride.[25]

In *Book I* Grotius draws several conclusions about God's unity. God's being the first cause of all things has implications for his nature, his perfections, and the structure of the cosmos—including those that dwell within it.[26] For Grotius, the providential ordering of the universe does not merely suggest an intelligent designer but also points to God's guidance of nations, political events, and is most fully evidenced through miracles and the fulfillment of prophecy.[27] He points to miraculous events, which confirmed the strength of the Jewish faith within "the books of Moses" (the Pentateuch), and argues that these events serve as a strong indicator of God's providential ordering. Even the Greeks, Grotius imagines, drew their laws from the Jewish faith.[28] Furthermore, Grotius did not believe the existence of evil disproved the providence of God. Instead, he argued that evil's existence merely proves that God is at work in the midst of evil. God's providential ordering and keeping of the cosmos would necessarily include his making right the wrongs of evil. This should lead us to conclude that the one who governs the cosmos is worthy of people's praise and is the fruit of all genuine search for true religion and salvation. Human reason can provide only rough estimations of the redemption provided through revelation.

In *Book II* Grotius demonstrates that Christianity is the true religion that most fully comports with human reason. He begins his argument on historical grounds by suggesting that Christianity can be demonstrated through the historical documentation of Jesus's life and ministry. Various claims beyond the Bible reveal the veracity of the historical Christ.[29] Jesus suffered an "ignominious death,"[30] and those who followed him—including the early church—were people of great wisdom and intelligence. That such people followed Jesus, Grotius imagines, provides strong evidence that Jesus performed the miraculous, which "cannot be ascribed to any natural or diabolical power, but must be from God."[31] The resurrection is the greatest miracle Christ performed and the ground of Christian faith. If Christ's followers were indeed wise people (as is evident),

25. Ibid., 49.
26. *De Veritate*, I.III-VII.
27. Ibid., I.X-XII.
28. Ibid., I.XIV-XVI.
29. *De Veritate*, Book II.I-II.
30. Ibid., I.II.
31. Book II.V. Here again we see the humanist Grotius, a lover of letters and wisdom.

they would not have believed something false or something that could have been falsified. Thus, Grotius concludes that the historical reports from these reliable witnesses are trustworthy and their accounts of the life, death, and resurrection of Jesus can be trusted.[32]

Grotius offers the perfection of Jesus as an additional piece of evidence. He compares both Muhammad and Moses to Jesus, arguing that since both men were not free from sin nor its consequences, the perfection of Jesus is an exemplar of his uniqueness. Furthermore, the rightness of Christianity is also evidenced in the widespread growth of the religion against her rivals.[33] "It was agreeable," writes Grotius, "to Divine Providence to cause that to spread the furthest, which is in itself best."[34] Grotius ends with an appeal to those who may not be satisfied with what he has offered as argumentation to this point in his work. He suggests that different kinds of objections and arguments require different proofs, imploring the reader not to commit a category error in rejecting all arguments because some are not convincing. Grotius wants readers to see that there are different criterion that are contingent on the different questions being asked. Mathematics, for example, sets different kinds of questions than what he calls "matters of fact."[35] Grotius wants the skeptic to realize that the questions explored in Christianity establish sufficient evidence to convince people of the truth of the faith, but this evidence cannot make them believe it. Evidence can persuade, but it cannot secure faith. It is a "touchstone, to try men's honest dispositions by."[36] One must follow the evidence with obedience in faith.

Book III argues for the credibility of the Bible. Grotius consideres four primary themes: authenticity, reliability, confirmation, and the truth and purity of the text. He suggests that we can trust the authors of each biblical text because their writings are confirmed by external witnesses (Jewish and pagan both) as well as the early Christians. The authors knew what they were writing and were knowledgeable about the events surrounding their accounts.[37] They would not say something false, because this would not be consistent with God's providence over his revelation. Grotius writes, "If it be granted that God takes care of human affairs, and especially those that concern his own honor and worship, it is

---

32. Ibid., II.VI.
33. Ibid., II.IX.
34. This is a dangerous argument, but Grotius does present this as a strong indicator of Christianity's truth. Ibid., II.XVIII.
35. *De Veritate,* Book II.XIX.
36. Ibid., II.XIX , 136.
37. Book III.V.

impossible he should suffer a multitude of men, who had no other design than to worship him with sincerity, to be deceived by false books."[38]

Even though errors might be found in translation of these inspired books, such errors do not lead to significant doctrinal deviations.[39] For Grotius, this yet again reveals God's providence over his revelation. Yet "as soon as any of the apostles, or apostolic men, published anything, doubtless the Christians took great care to have many copies of it."[40] Grotius closes book three with an apologetic for the Old Testament. These "records of the Jewish religion"[41] provide tremendous testimony to the Christian faith. One can trust that the names attached to their respective books are those who wrote them. The New Testament writers were no strangers to these texts, as they cited them extensively in their own writings.

A treatise against paganism is the central theme of *Book IV*. Here Grotius appeals to the unity of God, the unworthiness of evil spirits and those who worship the dead, as well as abstractions and unintelligent animals. The principal aim for a Christian after reading this section of his work is to "assist others, who wander in various crooked paths of error, and to make them partakers of the same happiness."[42] After this encouragement, Grotius first considers paganism, writing that since there is one God, created beings are not to be worshipped. If indeed there are multiple gods, they must be created beings, and one must discern whether they are good or evil. The spirits to whom the pagans give their worship are clearly evil because they do not direct their worship to the Supreme God. Thus, worshipping these false gods, and even more so, the worship of the dead, is wrong and unnecessary, as neither has demonstrated any power to bring petitions to fruition. "What is worst of all is," writes Grotius, "that those men who are thus bad in honour, are found to have been remarkable for very great vices."[43]

The worship of gods and spirits extends to the heavens as well, but this falls short, for they have no capacity to actualize anything from one's worship of them; they are "only signs to judge of beings by."[44] Similarly, stars were designed for people's use, not for their worship. They have no real existence as what Grotius calls "abstractions"—concepts like fear, anger, hope, health, and good fortune. Because they do not exist, they have no claim on us; they have no knowledge of our prayers, and thus it would be "disagreeable to right reason to worship them

---

38. Book III.IX.
39. For his discussion about the nature of these "errors," see Book III.XV.
40. Ibid., III.IX, 157.
41. Book III.XVI.
42. Book IV.I, 169.
43. *De Veritate,* Book IV.IV.
44. Ibid., IV.V.

as God."[45] One of Grotius's more interesting arguments in this book is his belief that pagan philosophers have little reason to stand against Christianity because their best truths are also found in Christianity: "There is less reason for the heathens to oppose the Christian religion," wrote Grotius "because all parts of it are so agreeable to the rules of virtue, that, by their own light, they do in a manner convince the mind." [46] Grotius believed that the universal agreement of pagan philosophy with Christianity demonstrated the veracity of the Christian faith.

Grotius's focus shifts to Judaism in *Book V*. Here he addresses the miracles of Jesus, how Jesus used Mosaic Law in his teaching, and Jesus's identity as the promised Messiah. Grotius believes Jews should recognize the historicity of the miracles in the New Testament because the it contains so many of the truths of the Old Testament. The same God at work in the Old is also at work in the New. The locale of these miracles may have been different, but the one performing them, God, is the same. That they would recognize miracles in the Old Testament but not in the New led Grotius to believe that the Jews are blinded by sin.[47] He wrote that "God cannot more effectually recommend the authority of any doctrine delivered by man, than by working miracles."[48] For Grotius, the same God who providentially ordered the cosmos is the same one who performed miracles, and Jesus is a continuation of God's work in this world. Rather than seeing these miracles as performed through the help of devils, Grotius implores his Jewish interlocutors to see Jesus's miracles as having their sources in *their* divine law. He writes, "For God has said in the 18th chapter of Deuteronomy, that he would raise up other prophets besides Moses, which the people were to hearken to; and threatens heavy punishment if they did not."[49]

Grotius addresses two primary charges Judaism makes against Christianity, concluding that the first—Christians worship more than one God—is based on wrong interpretation. Grotius wonders why this same charge is not brought against Philo, a Jew, who said there are three "things" in God?[50] He also points out that Christians are not worshipping human nature. Instead, Christians are honoring their Messiah, and that does not "tend to the lessening of God the Father."[51]

In his final book, Grotius engages with Islam, focusing on its origins and comparing Christian doctrines with those of Islam. After Constantine embraced

---

45. Ibid., IV.VII.
46. Ibid., IV.XII.
47. Ibid., V.VI–VII.
48. Ibid., V.II.
49. Ibid., V.V.
50. Ibid., V.XXI.
51. Ibid., V. XXII.

Christianity, the world entered the church in greater numbers, and this mass movement produced several quarrels and "religion was made an [*sic*] Art."[52] Because of their division and strife, God saw fit to judge his people by allowing Muhammad to start a new religion, and this new religion moved beyond the borders of Arabia into the rest of the world. In his description of Islam's origins, Grotius's irenic spirit emerges yet again. He traces Islam's beginning to the quarrelsomeness of Christians—their focus on dogmatic concerns without a corresponding love for unity.

Grotius then implores the reader to compare the life of Muhammad with the life of Jesus to see that Jesus's life was far superior. Such considerations should focus not just on the life of the leaders but also on their followers and methods. Jesus's disciples "patiently endured [*sic*] Hardships and Torments,"[53] while Muhammad's followers neither worked miracles nor endured grievous troubles or severe deaths. Instead, Grotius points out that Islam spread by conquest. Similarly, when the ethical demands of the two religions are compared, Grotius believes Christianity's ethic of patience and kindness toward another subverts Islam's appeal to revenge.

Grotius ends his apologetic work by defending Christianity's description of Jesus as the Son of God, writing that the word *Son* has an understanding that goes beyond the biological. In the final section, Grotius appeals to fellow Christians, admonishing them to lift their hearts to God, who made all things. God cares for his creation and guides it with his providence, so he can be trusted to be the God revealed to us in the Bible. Grotius encourages the reader to read the Scriptures, to keep their teachings, and to come to mutual agreement so there "be no [*sic*] Sects or Divisions amongst them."[54] Grotius's organization of *De Vertitate* suggests that his approach to defending the faith advocates the right use of reason and historical evidence to appeal for Christian unity, rather than dividing over theological minutiae.

APOLOGETIC METHODOLOGY

RIGHT REASON AND HISTORICAL EVIDENCE

Throughout *De Veritate* Grotius suggests that what is false is that which goes against "right reason," or what contradicts that which is plainly known. Grotius had been steeped in Christian humanism, and he felt the defense of the Christian faith required this. But unlike some of his reformational counterparts,

---

52. Ibid., VI.I.
53. Ibid., VI.VII.
54. *De Veritate*, VI.XI.

Grotius went beyond the theological differences Christianity has with rival religions. Multiple sections of *De Veritate* suggest that Grotius's deep concern went beyond people believing in Christianity to having their beliefs affixed with *reasonable trust* in the veracity of the Bible's account of humanity, sin, and Jesus Christ. He defends the historicity of the Old and New Testaments, Jesus's existence, and miracles, and even takes significant steps to defend the *names* on the books of the Bible. Grotius takes pains to ensure that the reader feels the Christian faith is grounded in evidential veracity, demonstrating his desire and need to ensure that Christian commitments are *rational*. A defense of the names of the books of the Bible, for Grotius, stems from an underlying belief that faithful testimony and witness are pillars necessary to solidify the claims of the Christian faith. In emphasizing these external testimonials and the veracity of the New Testament documents as the substance of his apologetic strategy, he implies that what is preventing non-Christians from repentance and faith is a *lack of evidence*. As Sarah Mortimer writes, "[U]nderpinning *De Veritate* is the assumption that human beings are in a position to make choices about their faith and matters of salvation. Grotius did not start with men created by God and now failed and corrupted, as theologians assumed they were, but with human beings able to make choices, who are free and '*sui iuris*' [of one's own right]."[55]

For Grotius, free will was essential to what it means to be human. The execution of right reason is not irrevocably tempered by the fall of humanity, rather "God made man a free agent, and at liberty to do well or ill."[56] The use of right reason allows those investigating the claims of Christianity to see evidentiary support in a clear light and then to decide if they are compelling. The New Testament claims are based on the apostle's testimony, so Grotius spent significant space demonstrating that we can trust the Old and New Testament documents. If the documents can be trusted, then the accounts can be trusted, and these accounts contain the truths of Christianity. Notice the emphasis is not on supernatural wonders described in the New Testament. Rather, Grotius emphasizes that what is contained within the New Testament accounts is trustworthy. He wants the reader to believe what is written within the Scriptures, but he begins with an appeal to historicity and testimony and reliability. Again, Mortimer is instructive, "For Grotius, human beings are able to evaluate the various ethical and theological claims they encounter, be it Christian, Jewish, Muslim or pagan, and they can accept or refuse such claims as they see fit. Christianity, for Grotius, fulfills and surpasses the moral and ethical values which we have as humans,

55. Sarah Mortimer, "De Veritate: Christianity and Human Nature," *Grotiana* 35 (2014): 88.
56. *De Veritate,* Book I, Section XIX, 86.

but he insists that it remains external to them. This religion is beyond nature, but it is our free will, and not grace, that enables us to reach it."[57]

The post-Reformation era led to several significant theological skirmishes, and the debate over the nature of grace and free will was central among them. Even today an emphasis on the need to read, apprehend, and discover the truths of Christianity for oneself divides Protestant theologies and draws several clear separations between Catholic and Protestant thought. Though space does not permit us to fully articulate the debate in this chapter, this sets the broader context for Grotius's emphasis on will and right reason. Grotius believed it was a free will, guided by the exercise of right reason, that would lead the reader to pursue unity among brothers and sisters in the faith.

APPEAL TO CHRISTIAN UNITY

In the preface to *De Veritate,* Grotius states one of the goals of his apologetic: to demonstrate the superiority of Christianity over the rival worldviews of the time—the "pagan," the deists, the Jews, and the Muslims. At the same time, he also made it clear that he was not going to enter into questions about disputes "which Christians have among themselves, but confines wholly to the other."[58] If an unbeliever found themselves convinced of Christianity, Grotius felt they would be "exceedingly at a [*sic*] Loss to know what Society of Christians to join himself with; so miserably divided are they amongst themselves . . . [t]his is a very great scandal to the Christian Religion."[59] The divisions that exist in Christianity are largely shaped around doctrinal controversies, and as such, the battle lines, Grotius believed, were drawn around theological minutiae. Grotius's distaste for these debates is due not to thinking that the debates and disagreements aren't real but in his overriding concern that presenting a unity of the faith to the world is the best means of displaying Christian truth.

This desire for unity is especially striking when we consider that Grotius wrote *De Veritate* while a prisoner in castle Lovestein. Grotius had been charged with "disturbing the religious peace," and this event seems to have shaped the contours of his writings.[60] There is a conciliatory tone in *De Veritatae* that is inseparable from its context, as Grotius focused on demonstrating what separated Christianity from rival religions. In dealing extensively with Judaism and Islam, Grotious desired to show them wanting so that the superiority of Christianity would be clearly seen. We should also notice how Grotius's appeal to Chris-

---

57. Mortimer, "De Veritate: Christianity and Human Nature," 88.
58. *De Veritate,* Preface, 14.
59. Ibid., 14.
60. Frun, *Verhorren,* "Memorie," 72, cited in Heering, *Grotius as Apologist,* 64.

tianity is grounded in doctrines agreed on by the majority of Christians rather than novel or narrow doctrinal views. This displays an irenic, unifying spirit that seeks to appeal to a true faith, unified beyond myopic theological and dogmatic disputes. Grotius wished for the union of brothers and sisters in Christ, and any form of Christianity that did not evidence such love, he believed, was misguided. Grotius acutely sensed that the theological controversies that had placed him in prison were the fruits of Christendom gone bad. As a Dutch humanist with an eye toward unity, "the most important part of religion consists of ethics, to which doctrine must be subordinated,"[61] and Grotius clearly wanted peace and order to mark the Christian faith. "Truth," he writes, "was indissolubly linked with peace: where there was no peace there could be no truth."[62]

Grotius's goal in writing *De Veritate* was to invite Christians to demonstrate the essential truths of their faith in such a manner that a nonbeliever will see the truths of faith brought forth in unity. Where this is lacking, it simply means Christianity has more work to do toward this end, not that Christianity has failed. By distinguishing Christianity from her rivals and appealing to unity among the faithful, Grotius embodied the spirit of the Christian humanist: the pursuit of peace and order before division by doctrine.

CONTRIBUTIONS TO THE FIELD OF APOLOGETICS

Grotius lived in a time in which the claims of Christianity were increasingly subject to rational investigation. As we have seen, both the format and structure of *De Veritate* reveals that Grotius wanted readers of his apologetic to see how rival worldviews fell flat so that the superiority of Christianity would shine forth all the brighter. Yet it is worth asking when reading *De Veritate* precisely what kind of Christianity emerges from this attempt. The constant emphasis throughout the work on the need for peace and order may frustrate some readers. It may even stifle discussion about doctrines critical to the Christian faith. Take, for example, the notable absence of any trinitarian discussion within *De Veritate*. There is no description, explanation, or defense of this critical and essential doctrine of the faith. Grotius shaped his apologetic work by pursuing only the most *basic* tenets of Christian faith, truths that can be apphrended by reason, and then *comparing* those tenets with rival beliefs. *Book I* of *De Veritate* is a summation of major doctrines that might be common to all religions, yet the absence of

---

61. Heering, *Grotius as Apologist*, 69.
62. Ibid., 72.

trinitarianism here does not mean Grotius believes the Trinity is nonessential. Rather, it suggests a belief that right reason alone cannot adjudicate its truth. In other words, it's better to compare apples-to-apples (common features) than apples-to-oranges (clearly distinct features).

De Veritate embodies a familiar apologetic format. Grotius's focus is less on providing sufficient answers to questions of the scientific revolution—given that this was still in the early stages—but on the questions Christians would encounter when interacting with people of other religious views. As the limits on traveling across the globe were beginnning to shrink, encounters with new people and new beliefs were increasing, and it is likely Grotius had this in mind. To those who travel by sea and encounter various perspectives he "envisages a competition of world religions among which the Christian merits in his view to be preferred to all others."[63]

Consistent with the expectations of his time, Grotius attempted to show how Christianity was historical, veridical, and internally consistent.[64] For example, when considering the resurrection, Grotius appealed only to what he described as "credible evidence."[65] Though the resurrection cannot be *historically* verified, the historicity of the event has been used by Christians throughout history as a ground for their faith, and the only way this is possible is if those who experienced the truth passed these events on to others. No one in their right mind, Grotius imagined, would promulgate such ideas unless they were true, and no one would believe it unless it were true. For Grotius, the truth of the resurrection is adduced from the idea that the resurrection had to occur because no one would have believed it otherwise. Furthermore, those advancing the doctrine of Christ's resurrection had nothing to gain from propagating a falsity. Grotius was convinced that this established internal consistency and historicity, and it serves as an early example of an attempt to explain the arguments for the resurrection through a historical process.[66]

These appeals to historical processes go beyond his work in *De Veritate*. In a previous work in 1625 entitled *On The Law of War and Peace (De jure belli ac pacis)*, Grotius writes that "the truth of the Christian religion, in so far as it makes a considerable addition to natural and primitive religion, cannot be proven by purely natural arguments, but rests upon the history of both the resurrection of Christ and of the miracles performed by Him and His apostles. This is

---

63. Lottes, "The Transformation of Apologetic Literature," 66–74, 67.
64. Ibid., 70.
65. *De Veritate*, II.VI.
66. Lottes, "The Transformation of Apologetic Literature," 72.

a question of fact, proven long ago by irrefutable testimonies, and of fact already very ancient."[67]

For Grotius, arguments from history and testimony provided solid ground for rational arguments and could lend apologetic strength to one's existing faith. Yet his constant appeals to the historicity of resurrection and miracles seem hollow as *substantive* grounds of the faith. As one writer has suggested, nonbelievers who might read Grotius's tract in hopes of being converted would not find much to convert to![68] Certainly we should commend Grotius for his efforts, but one can argue that Grotius's context influenced his apologetic in a way that proved detrimental to his overall project of Christian unity. To be sure, his historical context is not the only or even primary reason Grortius diminishes the essential Christian doctrines in pursuit of unity.[69] And yet if his goal was to place the *sine qua non* of Christianity into the hands of sailors and common people to help them defend the faith, it would have been helpful to have included several more central, key doctrines of Christianity in *De Veritate*. But he does not. Instead, he focuses on the reasonableness of the faith and hopes that such congenial yet rational appeals will win over skeptics and provide Christians with enough to be an effective apologist. It's not clear that he succeeded in this. Indeed, Grotius himself was charged with holding unorthodox views, not because he advocated for them but because he did not believe it was necessary to clarify what he considered "theological minutiae."[70]

One lesson we can learn from Grotius is that to defend the faith, the *faith* must be present both in action and in specific doctrine. While neither the former nor the latter can encapsulate the totality of the Christian faith, an emphasis on action (ethics) at the expense of key doctrinal matters all but guarantees that the faith we are attempting to deliver will be stamped with a return to sender. This is a sobering reminder to pursue faithfulness rather than the latest controversies and to place our confident hope in the work of the Holy Spirit. As the guarantor of his Word, the Spirit promises it will not return void.

Grotius was a remarkable man, a devoted Christian, and rightfully concerned about Christian unity and its witness to a watching world. Yet this latter

---

67. Stephen C. Neff, *Hugo Grotius On the Law of War and Peace: Student Edition* (London: Cambridge University Press, 2012), 290.

68. Fiammetta Palladini, "The Image of Christ in Grotius's *De Veritate Relgionis Christianae*: Some Thoughts on Grotius's Socinianism," *Grotiana* 33 (2002): 58–69.

69. For more, see Bas De Gaay Fortman, "Between Principles and Practice: Grotius' Commitment to *Religious Peace* in a Contemporary Context," *Grotiana* 34 (2013): 25–40.

70. On this, see Henk Nellen, "Minimal Religion, Deism and Socinianism: On Grotius's Motives for Writing *De Veritate*." *Grotiana* 33 (2002): 25–27. Cf. "Grotius and Socinianism" in *Socinianism and Armenianism: Antitrinitarians, Calvinists, and Cultural Exchange in Seventeenth-Century Europe*, eds. Marla Muslow and Jan Rohls (London: Brill, 2005), 121–47.

concern seems to have led him to delimit several doctrinal essentials. And such desires—without a clear and distinct Christian theological framework to support them—may sadly end up divorcing demonstrations of the rationality of Christian doctrine from the distinct ways we are called to live out our faith. We need an approach that roots Christian ethical response in Christian doctrinal belief. A watching world needs a clear Christian message. *De Veritate,* laudable as it may have been at the time, missed this very crucial mark.

BIBLIOGRAPHY

Blei, Karel. *The Netherlands Reformed Church, 1571–2005.* Grand Rapids: Eerdmans, 2006.

Dunthorne, Hugh. "History, Theology and Tolerance: Grotius and his English Contemporaries." *Grotiana* 34 (2003): 107–19.

Edwards, Charles S. *Hugo Grotius, The Miracle of Holland: A Study in Political and Legal Thought.* Chicago: Nelson Hall, 1981.

Fortman, Bas De Gaay. "Between Principles and Practice: Grotius' Commitment to *Religious Peace* in a Contemporary Context." *Grotiana* 34 (2013): 25–40.

Grotius, Hugo. *The Truth of the Christian Religion.* Trans. by John Clarke. Ed. by Maria Rosa Antognazza. Indianapolis: Liberty Fund, 2012.

Heering, J. P. *Hugo Grotius as Apologist.* London: Brill, 2004.

Jeffrey, René. *Hugo Grotius in International Thought.* New York: Palgrave Macmillan, 2006.

Lottes, Gunther. "The Transformation of Apologetic Literature in the Early Enlightenment: The Case for Grotius's *De Vertitate.*" *Grotiana* 35 (2014): 66–74.

McCullough, David. *The Reformation.* London: Viking, 2003.

Mortimer, Sarah. "De Veritate: Christianity and Human Nature." *Grotiana* 35.1 (2014): 75–94.

Muslow, Marla, and Jan Rohls, eds. *Socinianism and Arminianism: Antitrinitarians, Calvinists, and Cultural Exchange in Seventeenth-Century Europe.* London: Brill, 2005.

Neff, Stephen C. *Hugo Grotius On the Law of War and Peace: Student Edition.* London: Cambridge University Press, 2012.

Nellen, Henk J. M. ed., *Hugo Grotius: A Lifelong Struggle for Peace in Church and State, 1583–1645.* Leiden: Brill, 2007.

———. "Minimal Faith and Irenic Ideals in Seventeenth-Century Scholarly Circles: Hugo Grotius as a Guardian of Isaac Casaubon's Legacy." *Church History and Religious Culture* 94:4 (2014): 444–78.

———. "Minimal Religion, Deism and Socinianism: On Grotius's Motives for Writing *De Veritate.*" *Grotiana* 33 (2002): 25–27.

Palladini, Fiammetta. "The Image of Christ in Grotius's *De Veritate Relgionis Christianae*: Some Thoughts on Grotius's Socinianism." *Grotiana* 33 (2002): 58–69.

Stanglin, Kevin D., and Thomas H. McCall, ed., *Jacob Arminius: Theologian of Grace.* London: Oxford University Press, 2012.

Stumpf, Christopher A. "The Christian Society and Its Government." Pages 151–176 in *Church as Politea: The Political Self-Understanding of Christianity.* New York: De Gruyter, 2000.

BLAISE PASCAL

Wagering the Truthfulness of Christianity

TYLER DALTON MCNABB
MICHAEL R. DEVITO

One of the most interesting, and often neglected, figures within the history of apologetics is the French polymath Blaise Pascal (1623–1662). The combination of a father's influence and a life filled with bodily infirmities resulted in one of the most brilliant minds our world has ever seen. Within his short thirty-nine years of life, Pascal is noted for inventing the first calculator, Europe's first transportation system, and discovering the existence of an empty vacuum. After a powerful religious experience at age thirty-one, Pascal left behind academia, refocusing his genius on to matters of theology and apologetics. As one would expect, Pascal had the same impact in these domains as he did in the world of academics. Most famous of Pascal's contributions to apologetics is what is known as "Pascal's Wager." Pascal uses decision theory to argue that if a subject S wants to avoid the risk of eternal hell and put herself in the best position to achieve eternal reward, S should put herself in a position to where she is likely to commit herself to the proposition that theism is true.

HISTORICAL BACKGROUND

Born in Clermont, France, on June 19, 1623, Blaise Pascal was son to Etienne, a brilliant man who was a lawyer by vocation but who was also "proficient in Latin and Greek, a dabbler in natural philosophy, and an expert mathematician."[1] Pascal's mother, Antoinette Begon, passed away when he was three years old, causing Etienne to abandon his high status career to better care for Blaise and his two sisters (Gilberte and Jacqueline). Etienne was deliberate and intentional with his children's education, and one of his first acts as sole caretaker of his household

---

1. David Simpson, "Blaise Pascal (1623–1662)," *Internet Encyclopedia of Philosophy*, https://www.iep.utm.edu/pascal-b/#SH8b.

was to up and move his family to Paris to provide them an environment that "offered greater intellectual and cultural stimulation."[2]

Blaise received his education primarily from his father, whose educational approach was both unique and impactful. Instead of textbooks and lectures, Etienne took a "problem-oriented approach to teaching,"[3] challenging Blaise to hands-on problem-solving, which used his creativity and intuition. It is noted in Gilberte's writings that Etienne "would always keep his lessons at a level just above the level of the work his students were capable of."[4] As Thomas Morris points out, "It was no accident that such a background produced an experimental scientist of the first rank."[5] It wasn't exclusively Etienne's pedagogical approach that transformed Blaise into a genius. Gilberte also tells of a young Blaise "who asked questions far beyond his years and held conversations that would seem appropriate to an adult."[6]

Also distinctive of Etienne's educational approach was his attitude toward mathematics, which he believed to be too provocative and stimulating for young Blaise to venture into until he was more mature. Etienne first wanted Blaise to get a good grasp on the arts, humanities, and the classics. He did not want mathematics to distract him from these other studies. Morris writes, "Etienne was afraid that once he got a peek at [mathematics], Blaise would become so entranced that he would neglect everything else."[7] Legend has it that despite his father's efforts, young Blaise had become so captivated and entranced with mathematics that at twelve years old he discovered much of Euclid's geometry (the first thirty-two propositions) on his own. It was at this point that Etienne realized that Blaise was much more than just a smart child—he was a genius. A mathematician and friend of Etienne's, Jacques Le Pailleur, after seeing Blaise's mathematical work, advised Etienne to "abandon his course of study and to introduce the boy to mathematics at once."[8]

Another key aspect of Pascal's education that worked in conjunction with his homeschooling was his father's inclusion of him in weekly discussion groups that functioned as a kind of Socratic discourse.[9] These meetings included prominent intellectuals from a variety of fields, including Rene Descartes and Pierre

2. Thomas V. Morris, *Making Sense of It All: Pascal and the Meaning of Life* (Grand Rapids: Eerdmans, 1992), 3.
3. Ibid., 4.
4. James A. Connor, *Pascal's Wager: The Man Who Played Dice with God* (New York: HarperCollins, 2006), 20.
5. Morris, *Making Sense of It All*, 4.
6. Connor, *Pascal's Wager*, 20.
7. Morris, *Making Sense of It All*, 4.
8. Connor, *Pascal's Wager*, 24.
9. Ibid.

de Fermat, Blaise's future collaborator in discovering probability theory.[10] The discussions were held at scientist Pere Mersenne's residence and would eventually evolve into the Academy of Paris.[11] At each meeting a different individual would present a cutting-edge thesis from their area of expertise and then defend it from the criticism and critiques of the rest of the group. It was at age sixteen that Pascal first presented his own thesis, an essay on conic sections, and he received "a great deal of admiration on the part of the older, established members of the group, and his talents soon became legendary."[12]

In addition to his unorthodox educational upbringing, another defining characteristic of Blaise's life was his extremely poor health. In his childhood he "often seemed on the verge of death,"[13] and throughout the vast majority of his brief time on earth, Blaise wrestled with constant bodily ailment. As Gilberte noted, "after his 18th birthday Pascal never lived a day of his life free from pain or from some sort of illness or medical affliction."[14] It is unclear as to exactly what the root cause (or causes) of Pascal's medical conditions were, with David Simpson stating: "The most common medical opinion is that he contracted gastrointestinal tuberculosis in early childhood and that manifestations of the disease, along with signs of possible concurrent nephritis or rheumatoid arthritis, recurred periodically throughout his lifetime. The accounts of his pathology are also consistent with migraine, irritable bowel syndrome, and fibromyalgia—a complex of illnesses often found together and which also frequently occur in combination with symptoms of anxiety, depression, and emotional distress."[15]

Interestingly, Simpson points out that one of the reasons for the interest in Pascal's medical history is the correlation between disability or disease with "added motive or accelerator for high-level creative achievement,"[16] citing Stephen Hawking and Isaac Newton (among many others) as examples. Connor seems to provide some support for this thesis, noting that Pascal's "life alternated between rounds of intense scientific investigation and months of languishing in his bed from one of his many illnesses."[17]

Financial troubles hit the Pascal family hard when the French government, under the rule of Cardinal Richelieu, decided to fund the war declared on the Holy Roman Empire[18] and in turn neglected to make payments on the

10. Ibid., 25.
11. Ibid.
12. Morris, *Making Sense of It All*, 5.
13. Simpson, "Blaise Pascal."
14. Ibid.
15. Ibid.
16. Ibid.
17. Connor, *Pascal's Wager*, 68.
18. Ibid., 42. Etienne's wealth decreased from 65,665 livres to less than 7,296.

government bonds that French citizens, including Etienne, had invested in. When Etienne and other investors protested this move, Richelieu responded by imprisoning those who opposed him.[19] This forced Etienne to flee Paris, leaving his family behind. It was Etienne's daughter Jacqueline who came to the rescue. Jacqueline, being a talented poet, captivated Richelieu with some of her poems "that had been written in praise of him and his administration"[20] and then pleaded with him to help their family by having mercy on Etienne. The cardinal was more than favorable toward the daughter, giving Etienne the position of tax collector, with military protection, in Upper Normandy. Not to be outdone by his sister, Blaise, to help his father be more efficient calculating taxes (an extremely time-consuming endeavor at this point in history) invented the first calculator, which "has been recognized as a precursor of modern computers."[21] It is evident that Etienne's investment in his children's education provided him an exponential return.

THEOLOGICAL CONTEXT

The seventeenth century was a truly unique time in academia. Starting with the scientific discoveries of Copernicus and Galileo, followed by the work of Rene Descartes, the sparks that would eventually ignite the fires of the Enlightenment began to flicker. Connor describes the intellectual climate of the times, stating, "The medieval universe was fading away, and the old divine certainties were losing ground. The scientists and philosophers of France were busy casting about for something new to bet their souls on, a new ground of order, a new way to make the universe spin properly, and for most of them, that something was mathematics."[22]

This was the backdrop of Pascal's intellectual life, and its effects can be seen in his own work. Pascal argued vehemently against the old Aristotelian thought that had been status quo for centuries. Thus, many of the scientific discoveries made by Pascal laid the foundations for empirical science as we know it today. In addition to his monumental discovery of the calculator, which would have been enough to solidify his legacy as a genius, Blaise also devised scientific experiments to show that (contrary to the recent philosophical arguments put forth by Descartes) the existence of a vacuum in nature was possible; he invented modern decision theory (a topic that will be addressed in more detail below);

---

19. Ibid.
20. Ibid., 44.
21. Morris, *Making Sense of It All*, 7.
22. Connor, *Pascal's Wager*, 24.

and he designed Europe's first public transportation system. As James Conner writes, "You cannot walk ten feet in the twenty-first century without running into something that Pascal's thirty-nine years of the seventeenth century did not affect in one way or another."[23]

Pascal's religious upbringing was one of traditional Catholicism that took somewhat of a dramatic pivot in his early twenties as the result of his father needing to see a pair of doctors because of slipping on ice and breaking his hip.[24] The two surgeons happened to be followers of Cornelius Jansen, a Dutch Catholic bishop "who had written a big book on Saint Augustine in which he stressed the importance of the grace of God in the economy of salvation and the necessity for living out one's faith on a daily basis."[25] The duo of bonesetters connected Etienne with a neighboring priest and vicar of Rouville named M. Guillebert, who persuaded Etieene, and in turn Blaise and the rest of the Pascal family, in the truth of the Jansenist sect of Catholicism.

Jansenist thought arose out of a strict reading of Augustine's work (as opposed to much of the Catholic doctrine of the time, which followed the more Aristotelian thought of Thomas Aquinas).[26] This more Calvinist flavor of Catholic theology appealed to those "who seek to find God outside of human experiences, who distrust reason, [and] who think that the world is a shipwreck and that people are no damn good."[27] These theological doctrines permeate the majority of Pascal's writings, highlighting the profound effect Jansenism had over his outlook on the world. The deep impact of the Jansenist doctrine on the Pascal family can also be seen in its effects on Blaise's sister Jacqueline, who was a sister in the Jansenist order and a major influence throughout the course of Blaise's life.[28]

Preceding his father's death, Pascal went through what historians have called a "worldly period" at the age of twenty-nine.[29] This was probably because of being separated from both his father and his sisters "and thrown for the first time on his own resources."[30] During this time, which lasted about two years, Pascal gave in to his concupiscence, enjoying many of the social pleasures of life that would have been prohibited under the Catholic ethic of the time. Yet as Connor points out, the term *worldly* is relative, and what would have been

23. Ibid., 2.
24. Ibid., 70.
25. Morris, *Making Sense of It All*, 8.
26. Connor, *Pascal's Wager*, 73.
27. Ibid.
28. Ibid., 122.
29. Ibid., 131–36.
30. *Pensees*, xiii.

considered sinful living "in and around Port-Royal would seem the height of religious austerity to most modern Americans."[31] Nevertheless, this period in Pascal's life was uncharacteristic of the devout religious lifestyle to which he had adhered in the past.

While Pascal might have been able to abandon some of his piety, there was no escaping his genius. The insights Pascal gained from this worldly period not only "played an important role in his diagnosis of the human condition that figures so powerfully in the *Pensees*"[32] but also led to his discovery of probability theory and decision theory. During this time Pascal became friends with the duc de Roannez, who in turn introduced him to the chevalier de Mere, Antoine Gombaud, and Damien Mitton, both of whom were quasi-Catholic companions of the duke that cared a great deal more about gambling than theology or academics.[33] Their love of gambling, coupled with their recent losing streak, motivated de Mere to ask Pascal, "the 'mere' mathematician,"[34] a series of questions regarding not only what his odds were of winning a given throw of the dice but also how two men who are forced to stop in the middle of a dice game should divide the money. Connor remarks that Pascal's answer and his future correspondence with Pierre Fermat on these questions birthed the science of both probability theory and decision theory. "From that day on," Connor explains, "the world would no longer turn to the oracles to cast a dim light on the future, for the gods had been replaced by mathematics, and risk was no longer something people suffered, but something they managed."[35]

Pascal's worldly indulgences came to an abrupt end on the night of November 23, 1654, when he had a profound religious experience, one powerful enough to reignite his passion for Christ and the Catholic church.[36] Biographers have termed this experience the "Night of Fire," because of the opening line of Pascal's record of the event. The details of what exactly triggered this religious experience are speculative, probably because, as the majority of historians believe, Pascal didn't share this experience with anyone during the course of his lifetime, with the only reference of the event being found sewn inside his coat after he died.

It is important to note that the changes that occurred in Pascal's life as a result of the "Night of Fire" were not changes in his external behavior (for, as Gilberte noted, Pascal still accompanied his gambling friends and kept servants

---

31. Connor, *Pascal's Wager*, 133.
32. Morris, *Making Sense of It All*, 9.
33. Connor, *Pascal's Wager*, 134–35.
34. Ibid., 136.
35. Ibid.
36. Ibid., 143–48.

for work around his home)[37] but more methodological. Connor explains: "In a world where doubt had become intellectually fashionable, where theological ideas once bolstered by cosmology had been overturned, Blaise had learned that one could become certain of God's existence and of God's nature by direct encounter, bypassing reason altogether. . . . Piety was no longer an empty practice, and reason was no longer a royal road to truth."[38]

As a result of the demotion of the status of reason, Pascal abandoned the majority of his intellectual endeavors and shifted his focus toward theology and apologetics.

APOLOGETIC CONTEXT

Pascal's renewed religious passion combined with his previous theological outlook led him to write one of his most popular works, the *Provincial Letters*, which was a polemic aimed at a rival of the Jansenists, the Jesuits. Originally written under the pseudonym Louis de Montalte,[39] these letters were carefully and eloquently constructed so that "readers with no special knowledge or qualifications in theology or casuistry could have such matters explained to them in such a way that they felt competent to pass judgment on the practices and abuses attributed to the Jesuits."[40] Pascal's literary weapon of choice in attacking the Jesuits was mockery, focusing specifically on the laxity of the Jesuit teaching. Pascal "created the myth of the clever Jesuit and associated all casuistry with a cynical practice of making excuses for sinners."[41] The success of Pascal's letters eventually led to him being declared a heretic and the letters being put on the forbidden books list by Louis XIV and ordered to be burned.[42]

Another result of this mystical experience and Pascal's subsequent repentance back to Christianity was his writing of the *Pensées* (or "Thoughts"), which was a Christian apologetic trying to persuade his nonbelieving interlocutors into the truth of the Christian faith. Pascal began taking notes and organizing them by topic. Unfortunately, he died before he was able to finish the project, succumbing to the sicknesses that had plagued him his entire life.[43] His notes were further organized after his death and published two years later.

---

37. Ibid., 151.
38. Ibid., 152.
39. Ibid., 171.
40. A. J. Krailsheimer, "Introduction," Blaise Pascal, *Pensées*, trans. A. J. Krailsheimer (New York: Penguin, 1995), ix.
41. Connor, *Pascal's Wager*, 173.
42. Ibid.
43. Krailsheimer, "Introduction," xvii.

In the *Pensées*, Pascal writes of the wretchedness of the human condition, the limits of reason, the vital role of the heart, and the need for God (and specifically Jansenist theology) to transcend reason. Contrary to the arguments for God seen in the likes of Aristotle, Aquinas, and Anselm, Pascal, while not completely dismissing the usefulness of these arguments, set out to "create an apology not of the mind but of the heart."[44] For Pascal, it is through the heart that we know the truth of "first principles . . . like space, time, motion, number. . . . And it is on such knowledge . . . that reason has to depend and base all its arguments."[45] In addition to providing the foundations of reason, the heart also provides the only mechanism through which one can assent to knowledge of God. Pascal writes of this interplay between reasoning and the heart as it relates to his apologetic methodology, stating, "That is why those to whom God has given religious faith by moving their hearts are very fortunate, and feel quite legitimately convinced, but to those who do not have it we can only give such faith through reasoning, until God gives it by moving their heart, without which faith is only human and useless for salvation."[46]

This understanding of reasoning and the central role of the heart within Pascal's writing can be traced back to the work of Saint Augustine, who had a major influence on Pascal's thought.[47]

A product of Pascal's apologetic methodology, the *Pensées* contain Pascal's most popular argument—The Wager: a pragmatic argument based on decision theory that states that one is rationally compelled to believe in God apart from evidence because one has an infinite utility to gain and only a finite utility to lose by doing so. Pascal gained the insights for this argument from his time spent around gambling—specifically, the idea that "if [people] could risk their wealth, their honor, and their reputations as part of the game, a mere sport, would they

---

44. Connor, *Pascal's Wager*, 181.

45. Blaise Pascal, *Pensees*. Trans. A. J. Krilsheimer (London: Penguin, 1995), (110), 28.

46. Ibid. (282), 29.

47. Outside of the *Pensées*, Pascal's essay *The Art of Persuasion* provides an interesting look at the interplay between the heart and mind as it relates to his apologetic. As mentioned in the *Pensées*, Pascal recognizes that when it comes to truly persuading one on the knowledge of divine truths, "God alone can place them in the soul" (3). That said, Pascal then lays out a rhetorical methodology that focuses on persuading both one's heart and one's mind, which, according to Pascal, "are as doors by which [truths] are received into the soul" (5). When it comes to persuading the heart, Pascal argues that pleasing one's interlocutor is just as important as providing convincing proofs because, according to Pascal, "so much more are men governed by caprice than by reason" (18). When it comes to convincing one's mind, Pascal's art of persuading "is simply the process of perfect methodical proofs, consist[ing] of three essential parts: of defining the terms of which we should avail ourselves by clear definition; of proposing principles or evident axioms to prove the thing in question; and always mentally substituting in the demonstrations of the definition in the place of the thing defined" (25). Pascal argues that if one follows these rules of definitions, axioms, and demonstrations, one's argument can never "be subject to the slightest doubt" (27).

not also be willing to risk the same on the possibility of eternal life?"[48] This argument was aimed at "the rational doubter"[49] to show not only that Christians are rationally justified in their belief that God exists but also that the skeptic is not justified in disbelieving in God because of the stakes. What Pascal was after was what philosophers call a means-end rationality.[50] A belief is considered rational insofar as it enables a subject to achieve their goal.

After laying out the Wager, Pascal then puts forth his Christian apologetic, arguing that Christianity is the best religion to wager on. Jeff Jordan explains: "It is likely that Pascal had in mind a two-step apologetic strategy. The first step consisted primarily of the Wager employed as an ecumenical argument in support of theism generally, with the second step being arguments for Christianity in particular."[51] This is not to say Pascal thought one could just believe that the Christian God exists. For Pascal, the primary aim of the *Pensées* was trying to convince his audience to live out the "apparently meaningless practices"[52] of the Catholic Church in hopes that they would in turn "over come the passions, especially pride, which have been [their] greatest obstacle to belief."[53] Ultimately, Pascal's hope was not only that the nonbeliever would come to believe in God "but in so doing to become a full member of the Catholic church,"[54] apart from which he believed there was no salvation.

The beginning of the 1660s marked a rapid diminishing of Pascal's health, probably as the result of a number of external factors.[55] First, King Louis XIV and Pope Alexander VII ordered the official condemnation of Jansenist theology in 1661. The emotional impact of this proclamation not only had a profoundly negative effect on Pascal, it also took a massive toll on his sister Jacqueline Pascal, who died on October 4, 1661, from what Pascal believed to be "a broken heart."[56] The combination of the loss of his sister with the loss of the status of his beloved Jansenist theology was inevitably too much for Pascal's already fragile constitution to handle. After uttering his final words, "May God never abandon me!" Pascal "fell into a coma, and at one o'clock in the morning on Saturday, August 19, 1662, he died in his bed."[57]

---

48. Connor, *Pascal's Wager*, 182.
49. Ibid.
50. Alvin Plantinga, *Warranted Christian Belief* (New York: Oxford University Press, 2000), 115–16.
51. Jeff Jordan, *Pascal's Wager: Pragmatic Arguments and Belief in God* (New York: Oxford University Press, 2006), 9.
52. A. J. Krailsheimer, "Introduction," xxvi.
53. Ibid.
54. Ibid.
55. Connor, *Pascal's Wager*, 188–95.
56. Ibid., 192.
57. Ibid., 202–03.

APOLOGETIC METHODOLOGY

Pascal's contributions to the advancement of science and mathematics are numerous, and it is up for debate as to which of his discoveries was most impressive. While Pascal did address a wide variety of issues in apologetics, such as the problem of divine hiddenness, the problem of evil, and the relationship between faith and reason, it is Pascal's Wager that stands alone as his most forceful argument for belief in God. In contrast to theoretical arguments for the existence of God, which generally conclude with the premise "Therefore, God exists," Pascal's Wager is a pragmatic argument that works independently of whether God exists or not. Pascal argued that one is rationally compelled to believe that God exists (specifically Christianity) regardless of the evidence because one has an infinite amount to gain and only a finite amount to lose by doing so. In this section we first provide a quick overview of decision theory because of its direct application to the Wager. Next, we lay out a basic version of the Wager in detail, discussing many of its key components. Lastly, we look at two popular objections to the Wager and provide counter arguments to each objection.

DECISION THEORY

Central to understanding the force behind Pascal's Wager is to first understand the logic on which the argument is built—namely, decision theory. Decision theory is the process that a rational agent undergoes when trying to decide among competing possible actions under conditions of uncertainty or risk. Unlike cases of objective probability, where empirical frequencies are known (for example, flipping a coin one hundred times will generally lead to an outcome of the coin landing on heads half the time and tails half the time), many times an agent's knowledge is limited to the likelihood of a possible outcome and must assign possible probabilities to competing states of affairs (known as subjective probabilities).[58] To choose the best course of action, an agent must also assign a value (or utility) to each possible outcome, with higher utilities for more desirable outcomes and lower (or negative) utilities for less desirable outcomes. To better illustrate this idea, Jeff Jordan uses the following decision matrix:[59]

---

58. To clarify, by subjective probability, we don't mean a subject's unconstrained subjective probability, which is merely based on the credence that the agent has for her belief.
59. Jordan, *Pascal's Wager*, 11–12.

	State 1	State 2
Act 1	F1	F2
Act 2	F3	F4

In this example, "Act" represents a possible action an agent can take, "State" represents possible states of affairs (ways the world might be), and "F[number]" represents the utility based on the choice of a certain act in a certain state of affairs (outcome). To further illustrate this point, Jordan provides an example of a decision under risk where an agent is deciding whether she should carry an umbrella. There is a 50 percent chance it will rain, and the agent assigns a utility of 10 to carrying an umbrella and it raining, a utility of 2 to carrying and it not raining, a utility of 1 to not carrying and it raining, and a utility of 5 to not carrying and it not raining. The decision matrix is labeled as follows:[60]

	Rain	No rain
Carry	10	2
Do not carry	1	5

In order to determine the expected utility of each act, one must multiply the utility of each outcome with the probability of each state of affairs and sum the totals. The underlying principle motivating the agents decision is what Jordan calls the Expectation rule, which states, "For any person S, and any number of alternative actions, α and β, available to S, if α has a greater expected utility than does β, S should chose α."[61] So the expected utility of carrying the umbrella is $1/2(10) + 1/2(2) = 6$. The expected utility of not carrying the umbrella is $1/2(1) + 1/2(5) = 3$. Because there is a higher expected utility to carry than not to carry, the agent should chose to carry the umbrella.

In conjunction with decision under risk, there are also occasions when an agent must make a decision in which knowledge of the probabilities of outcomes is unknown. This is known as decision under uncertainty. Rota gives an example of an agent trying to decide whether he should lock up his friend's borrowed bicycle while he goes into a store. The agent is in a good part of town where crime rarely happens, and he will be able to see the bike from the storefront. Rota asks,

---

60. Ibid., 12.
61. Ibid., 11.

"So, should you lock the bike up? You don't have any precise knowledge about the probability of theft in the circumstances, and while you could estimate the value of the bike, there is no obvious way to calculate the disvalue your friend would experience if your negligence got his bike stolen."[62] Rota details this scenario in the following decision matrix:[63]

	A thief will happen by	A thief won't happen by
Lock	Nothing bad happens	Nothing bad happens
Don't Lock	Bike stolen (probably)	Nothing bad happens

To determine whether the agent should lock the bicycle, decision theorists try to determine which action dominates. An action *weakly dominates* the other if: "for any person S, if one of the actions, α, available to S has an outcome better than the outcomes of the other available actions, and never an outcome worse than the others, S should choose α."[64] An action *strongly dominates* the other if: "for any person S, and action α, if in each state α has a better outcome than the alternatives in that state, S should choose α."[65] In the case of locking the bike, the action to lock the bike weakly dominates the action not to lock the bike because nothing bad happens in either state of affairs, making the act of locking the bike better if a thief happens by than not locking the bike, and equal if a thief doesn't happen by. With these basics of decision theory laid out, we can now properly analyze Pascal's Wager.

PASCAL'S WAGER

Most philosophers agree that within the *Pensées*, Pascal lays out three versions of the Wager,[66] but the central thesis of his argument proceeds as follows: "Let us weigh up the gain and the loss involved in calling heads that God exists. Let us assess the two cases: if you win you win everything, if you lose you lose nothing. Do not hesitate then; wager that he does exist."[67]

---

62. Michael Rota, *Taking Pascal's Wager: Faith, Evidence, and the Abundant Life* (Downers Grove, IL: InterVarsity Press, 2016), 28.

63. Ibid.

64. Jordan, *Pascal's Wager*, 13.

65. Ibid.

66. See Jordan, *Pascal's Wager*, 7–36. Jordan believes a fourth version can also be found in the *Pensees*, which he calls the Jamesian Wager. Jordan argues that this version is both valid and defensible against numerous objections commonly put forth against the Wager.

67. Pascal, *Pensees*, 123.

In other words, as Rota concisely states, "It is rational to seek a relationship with God and live a deeply Christian life, because there is very much to gain and relatively little to lose."[68] As mentioned above, Pascal's argument, unlike common theoretical arguments for God's existence, is a pragmatic argument that doesn't depend on propositional evidence. Rather, the Wager is designed to show that one is rationally compelled to believe in God and that unbelief is "rationally impermissible."[69] Motivating Pascal's apologetic was the belief that, unlike his contemporary, Descartes, you couldn't reason to belief in God. Pascal writes, "'Either God is or he is not.' But to which view shall we be inclined? Reason cannot decide this question. . . . Reason cannot make you chose either, reason cannot prove either wrong."[70] For Pascal, it wasn't about the evidences one would have for believing that God did or did not exist. Rather, it was about "having reason to induce the belief in [the] proposition" that God exists because "forming the belief in the proposition may be the rational thing, all things considered, to do."[71] Let's look at two brief caveats to the Wager and then turn to the relationship between the Wager and decision theory to draw out this point.

Following the thought of William Rowe, Jordan argues that Pascal's apologetic approach likely consisted as first an argument for expanded theism, which is "the view that [God] exists, conjoined with other significant religious claims, claims about sin, redemption, a future life, a last judgment, and the like," proceeded by an argument for "full-blown Christian belief" supported by "miracle reports and satisfied prophesies."[72] Thus the Wager, according to Jordan, is a wager between expanded theism and naturalism.[73]

It is also important to note that the Wager is forced, meaning "wagering about the existence of God is unavoidable: 'you have to wage.' Wagering is forced, since refusing to wager is tantamount to wagering against."[74] Everyone who has ever existed, whether they have realized it or not, has wagered on the existence of God.

With these two points in mind, we can now set up a decision matrix to better illustrate how the Wager works.[75]

68. Rota, *Taking Pascal's Wager*, 12.
69. Jordan, *Pascal's Wager*, 7.
70. Pascal, *Pensees*, 122.
71. Jordan, *Pascal's Wager*, 7.
72. Ibid., 10.
73. Ibid.
74. Ibid., 17.
75. This matrix is a modified version of the one found in Rota, *Taking Pascal's Wager*, 32.

	God exists	God doesn't exist
Wager God exists	WG (Wager and God exists)	W(~G) (Wager and God doesn't exist)
Wager God doesn't exist	~W(G) (Wager against and God exists)	~W(~G) (Wager against and God doesn't exist)

In the case of outcome WG, if God exists and one commits to believing in God, they are much more likely to spend eternity with God, as well as receiving benefits on this side of eternity, such as answered prayer, and therefore Pascal assigns it an infinite utility. At first glance, outcome W(~G) is normally thought to have a negative utility. If one commits to God and God does not exist, then one wasted time going to church, praying, tithing, etc. But as Rota explains in detail, modern psychological and sociological studies have shown that the benefits of believing in God are far superior when compared with not believing.[76] For example, those who believe in God generally tend to live longer,[77] contribute more to charity,[78] and experience an overall greater satisfaction with life[79] when compared with their atheist counterparts. It would seem then, looking at recent data, that W(~G) should still be assigned some positive finite utility. The naturalist could (and most likely will) object to this conclusion and possibly cite studies that show the opposite is true, so the value assigned to W(~G) is up for debate.

When it comes to wagering that God doesn't exist, ~W(G) results in the opposite outcome of WG. One would be minimizing their flourishing while alive and, more importantly, minimizing their chances at eternal life. Pascal mentions nothing of hell or of an infinite disutility in the *Pensées*, but it is clear that ~W(G) should be assigned a significant disutility. Considering the studies mentioned above, it would seem that one would also experience a disutility on ~W(~G), although obviously significantly less than ~W(G), because of all the potential social and psychological benefits that come with belief in God.

Depending on what one assigns W(~G), the Wager (as stated above) shows that wagering for God either weakly dominates (if W(~G) is assigned a

---

76. See Rota, *Taking Pascal's Wager*, 35–42.

77. See M. E. McCullough et al., "Religious Involvement and Mortality: A Meta-Analytic Review," *Health Psychology* 19.3 (2000): 211–22. Quoted in Rota, *Taking Pascal's Wager*, 41.

78. See Robert D. Putnam and David E. Campbell, *American Grace: How Religion Divides and Unites Us* (New York: Simon & Schuster, 2010), 446. Quoted in Rota, *Taking Pascal's Wager*, 41.

79. See Harold Koenig, Dana King, and Verna B. Carson, *Handbook of Religion and Health*, 2nd ed. (Oxford: Oxford University Press, 2012), 131. Quoted in Rota, *Taking Pascal's Wager*, 37.

disutility) or strongly dominates (if W(~G) is assigned a positive utility) wagering against God. This conclusion, which is a decision under uncertainty, is also true for any probability assigned to the possible existence of God (or a decision under risk) as long as the probability assigned to God's existence is greater than zero. This can be seen in the following matrix, where p is some positive probability:[80]

	God exists	God doesn't exist
Wager God exists	p, ∞	1—p, (finite utility or disutility)
Wager God doesn't exist	p, (infinite disutility)	1—p, (finite utility or disutility)

Because W(G) has an infinite utility, no matter what the probability assigned to God's existence is, the expected value of wagering for God's existence will be infinite as opposed to wagering against God, which will compute to some finite expected value. Therefore, as Jordan puts it, "As long as the existence of God is judged to be greater than zero, believing will always carry an expected utility greater than that carried by nonbelief."[81] In other words, as long as the probability is greater than 0, it will always be more rational to wager in favor of God's existence. But note there are those who defend the Wager by way of arguing that the probability needs to be at least around .5.[82] Doing this might make defending the Wager less complicated, but of course, this creates a bigger burden for the advocate of the Wager. It's easier to show that the probability of God's existence is not 0 than to show that it is at least near the .5 mark.

As previously stated, there are at least three versions of the Wager in the *Pensées*, and many different versions, along with various counterarguments, have been proposed throughout the course of the past four hundred years. The version laid out above provides many of the elements present in the family of Wager arguments, but it should not be considered exhaustive. Nevertheless, it is clear that, at least at first glance, the Wager is a powerful argument for belief in the existence of God. Let us now analyze two common objections to the Wager and show how, ultimately, they fall short.

---

80. This is a modified version of the matrix found in Jordan, *Pascal's Wager*, 23.
81. Ibid., 22.
82. For example, see Rota, *Taking Pascal's Wager*.

OBJECTIONS
Many Gods Objection

The most common objection to the Wager is known as the "many gods" objection, which argues that because of the diversity of religious belief, it is wrong to assume that the belief being wagered on is either Christianity or naturalism. What about Islam, Judaism, or Hinduism? If any one of these belief systems (or one of the various other world religions) were correct, then belief in the Christian God would result in the same outcome (in most cases)[83] as belief in naturalism—a significant disutility. Thus, the 2 x 2 decision matrix does not accurately represent the landscape of the person wagering. It must include each world religion that adheres to some version of the doctrine of the afterlife.

Initially, this objection seems to present a serious problem for Pascal's Wager. Yet upon further reflection, this is not the case. Rota correctly points out that "nothing in the objection . . . challenges the conclusion that it is better to commit to God in a Christian way than not be religious at all."[84] All this objection has shown, according to Rota, is that the Wager presented above gives us no way to choose between Christianity and other world religions. "That's true enough," Rota continues, "but it hardly follows that there is no way to choose between [other religions] and Christianity. The way is clear: practice the religion that seems to you, on careful examination and reflection, to be most likely to be true."[85] The initial force behind the Wager is to show that, despite the evidence for or against, it is more prudent to believe in God than not to believe. Yet one should consult the available evidence when it comes to determining which religion seems most likely to be true. This is where, for the Christian, the argument for the resurrection, the historical reliability of the gospels, and other apologetic resources can tip the scales for Christianity in a significant way. Nevertheless, all the "many gods" objection has shown is that more work needs to be done once the conclusion of the Wager is reached, not that the diversity of the world's religions undermine the Wager in any way.

Doxastic Volunteerism

A second common objection to the Wager comes by way of doxastic volunteerism, the epistemological thesis that an agent has direct control over their beliefs, or in other words, "that one can believe at will."[86] This philosophical doctrine seems highly unlikely. Can one force themselves to believe in God any more

83. This would exclude religions that do not have a doctrine of the afterlife (i.e., heaven and hell).
84. Rota, *Taking Pascal's Wager*, 67.
85. Ibid.
86. Jordan, *Pascal's Wager*, 18.

than one can force themselves to believe in Santa Claus in hopes of increasing their chances of getting presents at Christmas? Jordan highlights James 2 to draw this point out further, saying, "The devils believe that God exists and they shudder . . . but presumably, even though they believe and shudder, the devils do not reform, they do not act appropriately."[87] If this is the case, and doxastic volunteerism is incorrect, is not the Wager seriously undermined because the people wagering cannot force themselves to believe in God?

This objection is based on a faulty understanding of Pascal's aim for the Wager. Pascal was not a doxastic voluntarist. Remember, Pascal held to a Jansenist theology that emphasized humanity's wretchedness and inability to choose God. Knowing that this objection would inevitably have been raised to the Wager, Pascal writes: "'Yes, but my hands are tied and my lips are sealed; I am being forced to wager and I am not free; I am being held fast and I am so made that I cannot believe. What do you want me to do then?' . . . You want to find faith and do not know the road. You want to be cured of unbelief and you ask for the remedy: learn from those who were once bound like you and who now wager all they have . . . follow the way by which they began. They behaved just as if they did believe, taking the holy water, having masses said, and so on."[88]

In short, Pascal acknowledges that one cannot force themselves to believe, yet because one is rationally compelled to believe by the Wager, one should "fake it till you make it." Pascal advised his interlocutor to go to church, pray, and to follow the lead of other Christians, no matter how meaningless these activities seem, because by doing these things, one increases their chances of coming to a genuine belief in God. Therefore, "no Pascalian need be . . . a doxastic voluntarist. A Pascalian Wager neither entails nor assumes that belief is under our direct control."[89] Rather, Pascal argued that the compelling force of the Wager should motivate one to live for God despite their beliefs, in hopes that eventually they would truly believe.

CONTRIBUTIONS TO THE FIELD OF APOLOGETICS

As referenced above, there have been new defenses to Pascal's Wager. Pascal's argument is still taken seriously among contemporary philosophers of religion. What has changed recently are some innovative applications that philosophers

87. Ibid.
88. Pascal, *Pensees*, 124–25.
89. Jordan, *Pascal's Wager*, 19.

Blaise Pascal's famous *Pensées* (*Thoughts*), we have today only the rough notes for Edwards's apologetic system but not the finished writing that he had intended. The difference is that Edwards's notebooks are perhaps ten or twelve times as long as Pascal's *Pensées*. They are a veritable goldmine of apologetic insights, and the essay that follows is only a brief overview of some of Edwards's varied contributions to Christian apologetic argumentation.

THEOLOGICAL CONTEXT

The eighteenth century was an era of apologetics. For the first time since late antiquity, leading Western thinkers no longer took the basic truthfulness of the Christian religion for granted. Instead Christianity was now something to be defended. Beginning in the 1690s, the English deists cast doubt on many basic Christian beliefs, including Jesus's divinity, the Trinity, the historical accuracy of the Bible, the possibility of miracles, Jesus's fulfillment of Old Testament prophecies, Jesus's atoning death, Jesus's bodily resurrection, Jesus's second coming, and the providential origins of the Christian church. In response to a relatively small number of deistic books, orthodox authors published hundreds of treatises in response, arguing that the Christian faith was more "reasonable" than its deistic alternative. A nineteenth-century commentator noted that "the title of Locke's treatise, *The Reasonableness of Christianity* [1695], may be said to have been the solitary thesis of Christian theology in England for the great part of a century."[3] Though small in numbers, the opponents of orthodoxy largely succeeded in determining the agenda for eighteenth-century theologians.

Like many of his theological contemporaries, Jonathan Edwards argued against deism and for the credibility of the Christian faith. Yet this aspect of Edwards's authorship is not well known, except among scholarly specialists. Edwards is more widely recognized as a defender of particular—especially Calvinistic—doctrines in works such as *Freedom of the Will* and *Original Sin* than as a defender of Christianity in general. In part this is because (as noted above) Edwards did not live to write the comprehensive theological work that he intended, which was to merge dogmatic theology with apologetic argumentation into a kind of *dogmatics-as-apologetics*. This unique approach to defending the Christian faith is another reason for the relative lack of attention given to Edwards as an apologist. While Edwards's writings contain many of the more familiar and traditional arguments for God's existence, he often sought to show

---

3. Mark Pattison, "Tendencies of Religious Thought in England, 1688–1750," in *Essays and Reviews*, 8th ed. (London: Longman, Green, 1861), 258.

the validity of Christian beliefs by demonstrating their necessary interconnection with other accepted truths or their entailment with one another. This "implicit apology" for the faith involved a rethinking of academic disciplines to show their hidden reliance on and connection with Christian truths. In this way Edwards sought not only to uphold Christian theological claims, but—in an even more ambitious fashion—to set biblical truth at the center of an entire panoply of human arts and sciences. Not since the Middle Ages, perhaps, had any Christian thinker so boldly tried to situate theology at the center of all human knowing and intellectual inquiry.[4]

The remainder of this chapter will begin with a treatment of the modern intellectual context to Edwards's theological and apologetic writings, followed by an analysis of his apologetic response and methodology. This includes an examination of the external apologetic argument, based on both rational and evidential reasoning; the internal argument, based on the nature of religious experience; and finally, the implicit argument, based on a rethinking of academic disciplines. While his contributions to the field of apologetics were cut short by his early death, we still can see the broad outlines of Edwards's position vis-à-vis the dominant, early-modern traditions of Christian apologetics and his incomplete effort at construing the narrative of God's redemptive work in history as a form of apologetics.

THE INTELLECTUAL CONTEXT OF EARLY MODERNITY

Since Christian apologetics is, in its very nature, a response to certain arguments or objections to the Christian faith, it may be helpful to consider Edwards's intellectual context.[5] Brian A. Gerrish described the early modern period as "the retreat of God." By small degrees, God gradually receded from the thinking of European intellectuals and ended up as an unnecessary hypothesis. It would be "not so very far from the truth," wrote Gerrish, "if we said that the story begins with a God who does everything, moves on to a God who acts occasionally, and ends with a superannuated God who need not exist at all."[6] Many of the locations or functions assigned to God were no longer tenable by the 1700s. The idea of "innate ideas," implanted into human minds by the Creator, was less credible

4. On Edwards's apologetics generally, see the works listed in the bibliography at the end and the concise but penetrating comments in Ava Chamberlain, "Editor's Introduction," in WJE 18:24–34; Amy Plantinga Pauw, "Editor's Introduction," in WJE 20:11–17; and Douglas A. Sweeney, WJE 23:10–29.

5. Paul Tillich wrote of systematic theology as "answering theology," so that "apologetics . . . is an omnipresent element and not a special section of systematic theology" (*Systematic Theology*, 3 vols [Chicago: University of Chicago Press, 1951–63], 1:31). Such a comment fits Edwards, in that his entire exposition of Christian doctrine was shaped by the desire to respond to deistic objections to orthodoxy.

6. B. A. Gerrish, *A Prince of the Church: Schleiermacher and the Beginnings of Modern Theology* (Philadelphia: Fortress, 1984), 54–55.

in light of John Locke's *Essay Concerning Human Understanding* (1690). Locke's empirical philosophy affirmed that the human mind is stocked with ideas through sense experience. Yet the idea of God, for Locke, was neither innate nor derived directly from sense experience. The claim that human beings can possess a valid idea of God became problematic. Moreover, in the physical universe no less than the mental, God's status came into question. When Isaac Newton developed his celebrated laws of motion, he showed that the planets and other astronomical bodies could continue in motion without being acted on from without. No longer was there any need for an Aristotelian "first mover." At one swoop, God's role in astronomy was forever altered.

If one could not find God through ordinary cognition or through the functioning of the physical universe, one might seek a route through direct religious experience or mysticism. Yet by 1700, reliance on religious experience had become unacceptable to mainstream intellectuals. Bloody religious conflicts, waged in the name of rival creeds, rent the heart of European civilization from the mid-1500s until the mid-1600s. These wars of religion undermined confidence in the competing orthodoxies of Catholicism and Protestantism and, with them, belief in the claims of divine revelation that underlay them. Great Britain underwent social upheaval and dislocation in the mid-1600s because of religious rivalries. Consequently, there were few notions in the early eighteenth century more unpopular than the idea that God communicates truths to a select few. Locke's critique of "enthusiasm"—the eighteenth-century term for this idea— was one of the most influential chapters of his *Essay*. The words of the Anglican bishop Joseph Butler to John Wesley are emblematic of the era: "Sir, the pretending to extraordinary revelations and gifts of the Holy Ghost is a horrid thing, a very horrid thing."[7]

Compounding the problem yet further was the rise of the English deists, who had an "extraordinary effect . . . on the whole intellectual life of the eighteenth century." Professing their "honest desire for truth" and "moral seriousness," the deists set about to thoroughly reexamine and criticize all existing beliefs and practices in the name of "reason."[8] Whatever did not stand the test of "reason" as they understood it was to be revised or rejected. Yet "gradually becoming more conscious of their divergence from historic Christianity, they transformed themselves into the champions of natural, as opposed to revealed,

---

7. Joseph Butler, as quoted in J. M. Cohen and M. J. Cohen, eds., *The Penguin Dictionary of Quotations* (Harmondsworth, UK: Penguin, 1960), 85.

8. Ernst Cassirer, *The Philosophy of the Enlightenment*, trans. Fritz C. A. Koelln and James P. Pettegrove (Boston, MA: Beacon, 1955), 174.

religion."[9] The deists were thus insiders who became outsiders. As deism developed, there was a sharpening opposition between natural religion and revealed religion. The more radical deists came to see Christian doctrines as unnecessary and the Bible as an inferior, limited expression of truths available to all persons through the light of natural reason. Because deists shared with orthodox thinkers many of the same presuppositions and a common intellectual culture, it was often difficult for the orthodox to argue against and to differentiate themselves from these opponents. The deists claimed that God is beyond the world, having created it and established its natural laws but now no longer involved in its day-to-day functioning. The Trinity, the incarnation, the atonement, miracles—these were nonessential or perhaps even harmful beliefs. The Bible is valuable primarily or exclusively because of its ethical teaching, since God is a moral being who rewards the virtuous. Such, in brief, was the deist challenge.

Edwards opposed deism with every particle of his being. Indeed, it would be hard to imagine a Christian view more antithetical to deism than his theology. While they sought to distance God from the world, he upheld a perspective that was *radically God-centered.* Consequently, Edwards led a frontal assault on the deists' concept of reason, notion of reason's sufficiency, argument against the Bible's authority, and denial of the miraculous. Edwards attributed the deists' influence to the spiritual declension of his time, an era "distinguished from all other ages of the Christian church for deadness in the practice of religion and for practical licentiousness and so of the absence of the Spirit of God."[10] The corrupt Zeitgeist had distorted the church's thinking. Because Edwards affirmed that sound theology would always be associated with genuine virtue, the moral decay of the early 1700s was to him a convincing argument against the latest theological trends.

APOLOGETIC RESPONSE AND METHODOLOGY

EDWARDS'S APOLOGY, I—THE EXTERNAL ARGUMENT

Edwards's most sweeping argument against deism was his assertion of the insufficiency of natural reason and the consequent necessity of revelation.

---

9. G. C. Joyce, quoted in J. K. S. Reid, *Christian Apologetics* (Grand Rapids: Eerdmans, 1969), 147. On the debates concerning deism, see Avery Dulles, *A History of Apologetics* (New York: Corpus, 1971) and Alan Richardson, *Christian Apologetics* (London: SCM, 1947). The paragraph above on deism is, of course, a vast simplification, and Paul Hazard notes: "There was not one deism, but several, all different, all mutually opposed, and even at daggers drawn with one another. Pope's deism is not Voltaire's, and Voltaire's was worlds away from Lessing's" (*European Thought in the Eighteenth Century: From Montesquieu to Lessing* [New Haven, CT: Yale University Press, 1954], 393).

10. Edwards, WJE 18:546.

"Were it not for divine revelation," writes Edwards, "I am persuaded that there is no one doctrine of that which we call natural religion [but] would, notwithstanding all philosophy and learning, forever be involved in darkness, doubts, endless disputes and dreadful confusion." If there had been no revelation, then "the world would be full of disputes about the very being of God." No one would know if there were one God or many and whether God's nature was personal or impersonal. "Ten thousand schemes there would be about it."[11] The philosophers of ancient Greece and Rome, for all their brilliance, never came to any consensus about the gods. Instead, the "infinite contradictions and uncertainties among the ancient philosophers" led to skepticism.[12] Not even the "ingenious Chinese"—whom Edwards regarded highly—came to any settled knowledge of God through natural reason alone.[13] Furthermore, it was not the mere existence of God but God's will for human life that people needed to learn. This is where deism was an abysmal failure. What kind or worship does God seek? Why do human beings sin against God? How can sin be compensated for? Is there such a thing as forgiveness? If so, how is forgiveness obtained? What is the nature of life after death? To such queries the deists had no reply. The deists themselves formed no church for "public worship," and this was another indication of the insufficiency of deism as a foundation for religious practice.[14]

A key reason for the deists' errors regarding reason is that they failed to distinguish between *a priori* deduction of religious truths and *a posteriori* vindication. "It is one thing to see that a truth is exceeding agreeable to reason, after we have been told it and have had it explained to us," writes Edwards, "and another to find it out and prove it of ourselves."[15] In religious matters no less than secular, familiarity breeds contempt: "We are ready to despise that which we are so used to . . . as the children of Israel despised manna."[16] All that was true and valuable in deism was borrowed—or rather stolen—from Christianity. The same was true of Islam, according to Edwards. This religion contained many truths adopted from the Bible, and yet Muhammad inconsistently rejected the biblical testimony to Jesus's divinity—just as the deists did.[17]

A confusion may arise for the reader because Edwards speaks stridently

---

11. WJE 13:421–3.
12. WJE 23:448.
13. WJE 23:439.
14. WJE 13:291.
15. WJE 13:421.
16. WJE 18:140.
17. Edwards described Islam as a "great kingdom of mighty power and vast extent that Satan set up against the kingdom of Christ" (WJE 9:415). While many of Edwards's contemporaries shared his view of Islam, McDermott judges that Edwards was "unusually vitriolic" against Islam because "the deists . . . were using Islam as a stick to shake at their orthodox opponents" (McDermott, "The Deist Connection," 39, 43).

against the deists' reliance on reason and yet often relies on rational argument to support his own points. As John Gerstner noted, "He tended to explain rationally what most other Reformed theologians were inclined to leave in 'mystery.'"[18] Not once did he display the fear or distrust of philosophy that sometimes crops up in the writings of Martin Luther, Søren Kierkegaard, and Karl Barth. The answer to this puzzle lies in Edwards's *sharp distinction between regenerate and unregenerate reason*. There was indeed a sizeable scope for the exercise of human reason in the sphere of theology, but this was to happen only after reason had embraced the truths of Christian revelation by faith. Edwards concurred with Anselm's principle of "faith seeking understanding" (*fides quaerens intellectum*). Faith, far from constraining reason, freed it to explore the boundless mysteries of God and God's revelation. Edwards could thus assert both the insufficiency of natural reason and the indispensability of regenerate reason in theological reflection.[19]

The classical arguments for God's existence—ontological, cosmological, teleological—all appear within Edwards's *Miscellanies*. The essay "Of Being" presents a kind of ontological argument. The inconceivability or nonexistence of nothingness shows the existence of a necessary being or God. "God is a necessary being, because it's a contradiction to suppose him not to be. No being is a necessary being but he whose nonentity is a contradiction. We have shown that absolute nothing is the essence of all contradictions."[20] A related argument, connected with Edwards's idealism, was that God, or "Being in general," must not only exist but be conscious, "for how doth one's mind refuse to believe, that there should be being from all eternity without its being conscious to itself that it was."[21] Edwards's cosmological argument for God derives from his strict notion of universal cause-and-effect relationships, as presupposed in *Freedom of the Will*: "'Tis acknowledged to be self-evident, that nothing can begin to be without a cause."[22] Both the world's existence and its particular mode of existence demand some sort of cause.

The presence of design and unity in the world is also a demonstration of God's existence. "The world is evidently so created and governed as to answer

---

18. John Gerstner, "An Outline of the Apologetics of Jonathan Edwards," *Bibliotheca Sacra* 133 (1976): 4. Gerstner himself highlights Edwards's theological rationality in *The Rational Biblical Theology of Jonathan Edwards*, 3 vols. (Powhatan, VA: Berea / Orlando, FL: Ligonier Ministries, 1991), esp. 1:94–139. McClymond criticizes Gerstner for failing to situate and interpret Edwards's apologetics in its historical, eighteenth-century context (McClymond, *Encounters*, 154, n. 70).

19. Philosopher William Wainwright observed the "apparent ambiguity" in Edwards's remarks on reason but noted that "grace is needed to reason properly" (Wainwright, *Reason and the Heart: A Prolegomenon to a Critique of Passional Reason* [Ithaca, NY: Cornell University Press, 1995], 7–54, citing 7, 11).

20. WJE 13:213. See also WJE 6:202–7, 350–2; 13:256, 436; 18:122; 18:190–1.

21. WJE 13:188.

22. WJE 13:254–5. Compare with WJE 1:180–5. Elsewhere Edwards notes that our imperfect ideas concerning God prevent us from understanding how God exists without being caused (WJE 18:190–91).

but one design in all the different parts of it, and in all ages."[23] What is more, it is not only the large-scale structure of the world that shows a divine design but also the intricate forms and functions of living creatures. He writes that "the contrivances of the organs of speech is peculiarly wonderful" and that human souls themselves are "pieces of workmanship" more elaborate than any man-made machines.[24]

One finds the general outline of a moral argument for God in Edwards's assertion of an "inward testimony ... of the being of God" implied in the awareness that "when we have done good or evil, we naturally expect from some superior being reward or punishment."[25] He even says that "the being of God may be argued from the desirableness and need of it," for the world can scarcely be so defective as to lack a universal governor to relieve the miseries and correct the injustices of human life.[26] In connection with his view of God as moral governor, Edwards sought to establish the credibility of life after death. Many notebook entries treat "immortality" or the "future state." Like most other eighteenth-century authors, Edwards held that a clear and definite expectation of future rewards and punishments was needed to keep people from becoming "negligent, dull and careless" about religion.[27] A life beyond the present was a necessity so that human beings could find fulfillment of their innate capacity for the enjoyment of God. In a manner reminiscent of Thomas Aquinas and C. S. Lewis, Edwards argued that "God provides some proper good for the satisfaction of the appetites and desires of every living thing" and that the same must apply to "the desires of virtue and love to God."[28] The present life presents many hindrances to the full enjoyment of God, and only in heaven will these encumbrances be removed. Heavenly love will know no limits of intensity or duration, and it is only reasonable to think God intends for such a state to exist.[29]

Like other Christian apologists, Edwards insisted on the divine inspiration and authority of the Bible. Edwards viewed the Bible, as did John Calvin, as self-authenticating, with words that strike the mind as God-given. Despite its lack of "rhetorical ornaments," the Bible "shines brighter with the amiable simplicity of truth."[30] The phraseology of the Bible is so expressive that human wisdom alone

---

23. WJE 18:191. See also WJE 18:392–8 and WJE 20:154–5, 280–6.
24. WJE 13:334, 337–8. See also WJE 13:373–4.
25. WJE 13:375.
26. WJE 13:375.
27. WJE 13:294.
28. WJE 23:126.
29. On the happiness of heaven, see WJE 13:275, 303, 329, 331, 336–7, 369–70; WJE 20:455–6; and the extended treatment in WJE 8:366–97.
30. WJE 13:202–3. Similarly John Calvin wrote that the Bible possesses an "uncultivated and almost rude simplicity," which nonetheless "inspires greater reverence for itself than any eloquence" (*Institutes of the*

could not have contrived it, as in the "strange system of visions" in the book of Revelation.[31] Edwards also appealed to external attestations of the Bible's veracity: "'Tis proof that Scripture [is true], that the geography is consistent."[32] A long notebook entry discusses the canon of the New Testament writings and the substantial agreement of early Christian writers as to which books were inspired.[33]

Like Paley, Edwards appealed to historical evidences to confirm the truth of Christianity. The Jews' monotheism and the forms of worship they used bear witness that they worshiped the true God and worshiped him truly.[34] While the gods of the ancient pagans have long since been abandoned, multitudes still acknowledge the God of Abraham. The survival of the Jewish people—despite the attempts to exterminate them and the cultural pressures that could have caused them to assimilate to the idolators around them—makes them a "standing evidence" for God.[35] Another line of argument is based on miracles. There is a strong presumption in favor of Jesus's miracles since he performed them publicly, and "if the matters of fact had been false, they would have been denied by Jesus's contemporaries."[36] Christ's miracles show that "the whole course of nature" was "subject to his command."[37] More than all other miracles, it was the resurrection that confirmed Jesus's teaching and his divinity.[38] One notebook entry argues that Jesus was truly dead after his crucifixion and had not passed into a deathlike "swoon."[39] The history of the apostles corroborates the truth of Christianity. The dramatic change in the attitude of the apostles—from fear and dismay to boldness and confidence—shows the truth of Jesus's resurrection and his continuing presence among them.[40] Moreover, the spread of Christianity in the Roman Empire without the aid of human power, wealth, or learning is itself a kind of miracle. Nothing as remarkable has happened before or since.[41]

Many of Edwards's later notebook entries dealt with "heathen traditions" that anticipated or paralleled the teachings of Christianity. These included extracts from various authors of Edwards's day on world religions. Taken together, these

Christian Religion, ed., John T. McNeill, trans., Ford Lewis Battles, 2 vols. [Philadelphia: Westminster, 1960], 1:82–3, 90–91 [Bk. 1, Ch. 8, Secs. 1–2].)

31. WJE 13:335–6. Compare with comments on the story of Joseph, WJE 13:339.
32. WJE 13:338. See also WJE 13:376.
33. WJE 20:396–427.
34. WJE 13:448.
35. WJE 23:334–40.
36. WJE 13:293.
37. WJE 13:352–3.
38. WJE 13:394–5.
39. WJE 13:302–3.
40. WJE 13:507.
41. WJE 13:293.

notebook entries run to hundreds of pages.[42] Gerald McDermott has shown that Edwards in the 1700s did more research in the as-yet-embryonic field of comparative religions than anyone else in colonial America. In these pages Edwards is more tolerant and open-minded toward non-Christian religions than one might have expected. Yet Edwards's attitude toward Islam was considerably more harsh than toward pre-Christian religions. He associated Islam with deism because he regarded both as post- and anti-Christian developments that originated from a willful rejection of biblical revelation concerning Christ.[43]

One of the more striking entries from Edwards discusses whether "heathen philosophers" did not have "some degree of inspiration of the Spirit of God." He goes on to say that "inspiration is not so high an honour and privilege as some are ready to think. It is no peculiar privilege of God's special favorites." In effect, Edwards implied that inspiration was not an all-or-nothing affair but appeared in history in varying degrees. Socrates and Plato, he suggested, may have had "some degree of inspiration as well as the wise men from the East who came to see Christ when an infant."[44] Edwards's thinking on non-Christian religions stood in a line of liberalizing Christian thought that stretched from Origen to Clement of Alexandria to Erasmus and Zwingli among the Reformers as well as many of the Renaissance humanists. He discussed the "heathen traditions" that paralleled Christian beliefs on the Messiah, evil spirits, the Trinity, the incarnation of deities in physical objects, original sin, infused grace, the Sabbath day, the immortality of the soul, the future judgment, the resurrection of the body, and the final conflagration. Divine revelation to the gentile nations occurred by means of ancestral traditions—an idea McDermott identifies with a technical term not used by Edwards, *prisca theologia* ("ancient theology"). What the heathen possessed, then, was not a natural theology but instead a revealed theology. Religious truths given by God among the ancients—perhaps at the time of Noah and his sons—became a part of the common lore of various nations. In this way Edwards was able to maintain his antideistic position that all true knowledge of God comes through revelation and yet also to explain the existence of true religious beliefs and traditions among the gentile nations that had no direct contact with the ancient Israelites or with early Christianity.

---

42. WJE 20:227–31, 239–54, 275–80, 287–96, 302–9, 321–3, 343–58, 365–6, 456–8; and WJE 23:95–104, 123, 171, 176–7, 190–4, 214–5, 432–81, 543–75, 640–713.

43. Gerald McDermott, "The Deist Connection: Jonathan Edwards and Islam," in Stephen J. Stein, ed., *Jonathan Edwards's Writings: Text, Context, Interpretation* (Bloomington, IN: Indiana University Press, 1996), 39–51.

44. WJE 23:84–5.

EDWARDS'S APOLOGY, II—THE INTERNAL ARGUMENT

We turn now to the internal argument. Edwards's teaching on *spiritual perception*—what he called the "new sense," or "the sense of heart"—supported his apology for the truth of Christianity. This is the aspect of Edwards most directly linked to such thinkers as Samuel Taylor Coleridge and Friedrich Schleiermacher. Edwards presented the spiritual sense of the saints as a kind of *evidence for God, immediately present to the mind and more certain and reliable than ordinary rational argumentation for God's existence.* Enlightenment thinkers generally emphasized direct experience of the world. Immanuel Kant defined *enlightenment* as "man's release from his self-incurred tutelage" and stressed that each individual must "dare to know."[45] Yet Edwards turned Enlightenment empiricism to the advantage of God. Faith, he held, was a form of seeing for oneself and not a secondhand belief or a reliance on another's authority. Those who saw God's "beauty" or "excellency" had as good a reason to be convinced of God's reality and beauty as any person had to be convinced of the reality of the physical objects around them.

The significance of Edwards's approach to spiritual perception becomes clearer if we view it against the backdrop of Locke's philosophy. Locke had denied the existence of innate ideas. He further insisted that all human ideas originated either through sensation or through the mind's reflection on ideas derived from sensation. The consequence, for Locke, was that no idea could ever be directly perceived as coming from God. Divine revelation could only reinforce ideas and principles already known through sense experience of the world. Locke's more radical disciples—i.e., the deists—immediately grasped the implications of their master's teaching, and they denied that there could be any distinctive religious experience reserved for saints alone. For his part, Locke allowed that there could be "inspiration" that brought "original revelation" to the mind of an inspired individual or prophet. Yet this sort of inspiration was only knowledge, in the true sense, within the mind of the person who first experienced it. For everyone else it was simply a tradition passed down. Locke wrote: "For whatsoever truth we come to the clear discovery of, from the knowledge and contemplation of our own ideas, will always be certainer to us than those which are conveyed to us by traditional revelation."[46] A religion, such as Christianity, claiming to be based on a revelation of God transmitted through historical records, such as the

---

45. Immanuel Kant, "What is Enlightenment?," quoted in James C. Livingston, *Modern Christian Thought: From the Enlightenment to Vatican II* (New York: Macmillan, 1971), 1.

46. John Locke, *An Essay Concerning Human Understanding*, 4.18.4. Locke's chapters "Faith and Reason" and "Enthusiasm" (*Essay* 4:18–19), were profoundly influential in the eighteenth century, and they are indispensable to understanding Edwards's intricately articulated position on spiritual perception.

Bible, was at a disadvantage in Locke's philosophy. The skeptic could argue that he would always be more certain of his *present* experiences than of any claims to *past* miracles, inspiration, or revelation.

In one of his earliest writings, Edwards argued that the perception of God in faith was itself a "testimony" to God's reality:

> There may undoubtedly be such a thing as is called the testimony of faith, and a sort of certainty of faith that is different from reason, that is, is different from discourse by a chain of arguments, a certainty that is given by the Holy Spirit; and yet such a belief may be altogether agreeable to reason, agreeable to the exactest rules of philosophy. . . . He is certain that what he sees and feels, he sees and feels; and he knows that what he then sees and feels is the same thing he used to call God. . . . Now no man can deny but that such an idea of religion may possibly be wrought by the Holy Spirit. 'Tis not unphilosophical to think so.[47]

Spiritual perception carries immediate certainty because it is a firsthand experience. As the truism goes, seeing is believing: "When a person sees a thing with their own eyes, it gives them the greatest certainty they can have of it, greater than they can have by any information of others."[48] In *Religious Affections* Edwards wrote: "The gospel of the blessed God don't go abroad a begging for its evidence, so much as some think; it has its highest and most proper evidence in itself."[49]

Edwards, in his sermon *Divine Light*, describes the illumination of the mind as both a scriptural and a rational teaching: "The evidence that is this way obtained, is vastly better and more satisfying than all that can be obtained by the arguings of those that are most learned."[50] Here Edwards stands Locke on his head, for he uses Locke's empiricist principle—that everyone must see with their own eyes—to establish that *the intellectual certitude of the believer's spiritual perception is greater than the certitude gained by ordinary human reasoning about God.* For Edwards, the soul in conversion comes into immediate contact with God and gains a new knowledge that it could never previously have attained. The Bible describes conversion as the opening of the eyes of the blind, the unstopping of the ears of the deaf, and even the raising of the dead back to

---

47. WJE 13:177–8.
48. WJE 17:65. Compare WJE 2:305–7, where Edwards discusses Christians as "witnesses" to God.
49. WJE 2:307.
50. WJE 17:423.

life.[51] God "illumines" the mind of the saint, "infuses" his grace, and "indwells" the body of the believer through the Holy Spirit.[52] Revelation does not merely "enlarge" natural reason—as Locke had claimed—but transcends it, conferring that which the human mind could not attain by its own resources. Nonetheless, the illumination of the believer's mind and heart was not an instance of "inspiration" or "enthusiasm"—as Locke's logic seemed to suggest. Edwards thus sought to vindicate a genuine religious knowledge based on a direct encounter with God that was not "enthusiastic." His idea of spiritual perception was a response to the Enlightenment's challenge to provide rational justification for belief in God.

EDWARDS'S APOLOGY, III—THE IMPLICIT ARGUMENT

In speaking of an implicit argument, we refer to Edwards's strategy to appropriate and reinterpret various academic disciplines or genres of thought to bring them back into relationship with God and with theological truth. Norman Fiering commented that "his purpose, contrary to that of the *philosophe*, was to turn the best thought of his day to the advantage of God."[53] Thus, Edwards sought to turn the tables on the Enlightenment by absorbing the best ideas of skeptical thinkers and adapting them for Christian use.

One expression of Edwards's implicit apology appears within a short paper entitled *A Rational Account of the Main Doctrines of the Christian Religion Attempted*. The jottings here were recorded over some stretch of time, perhaps as long as fifteen years.[54] Edwards states that the preface to the *Rational Account* was "to shew how all arts and sciences, the more they are perfected, the more they issue in divinity, and coincide with it, and appear to be as parts of it."[55] What he envisaged was nothing less than a comprehensive system of the sciences, with theology as the capstone of them all. No modern-period major thinker— with the possible exception of G. W. F. Hegel—ever tried such a thing. One is tempted to think of the *Rational Account* as "medieval" in the way it relates all human sciences to theology, as in Bonaventura's thirteenth-century treatise on *The Reduction of the Arts to Theology*.[56] Yet Edwards's system would assuredly

---

51. WJE 21:159–64.

52. WJE 2:206.

53. Norman Fiering, *Jonathan Edwards's Moral Thought and Its British Context* (Chapel Hill: University of North Carolina Press, 1981), 60–1.

54. WJE 6:396–7, with Anderson's comments at WJE 6:394.

55. WJE 6:36.

56. "Since every science," wrote Bonaventure, "and particularly [though not only] the science contained in the Holy Scriptures, is concerned with the Trinity before all else, every science must necessarily present some trace of this same Trinity" (quoted in Jaroslav Pelikan, *The Christian Tradition: A History of the Development of Doctrine; Volume 3: The Growth of Medieval Theology [600–1300]* [Chicago: University of Chicago Press, 1978], 282, cf. 305–7).

have been a post-Lockean, post-Enlightenment effort at unifying the human sciences around theology and yet based on empirical principles.

Edwards's reflections on metaphysics are an implicit argument for God. The dominating question in *The Mind*, as Wilson Kimnach states, was the following: "How could one convince the most sophisticated audience that he had identified a functioning spiritual system as surely as Newton had identified the true physical system?"[57] In effect, Edwards used metaphysics as an instrument to establish the supremacy of God and the spiritual as compared with material realities, thus reversing the commonly accepted notions of the philosophers that matter was real, while spirit was tenuous and ethereal. In Edwards's bold reinterpretation, matter was the mere shadow of spiritual reality. Moreover, God is ultimate reality, "the prime and original being, the first and the last, and the pattern of all."[58] Edwards's metaphysics showed a strong unifying tendency since every entity in the universe stood in a direct and constant relationship with God.

Another intellectual discipline Edwards sought to appropriate and reinterpret for theological purposes was British moral philosophy—a field of study fast departing from its theological underpinnings during the 1700s. Lord Shaftesbury and Francis Hutcheson separated moral reflection from any essential linkage to God or theological notions. Their "moral sense" theories grounded ethics in human nature, not God's nature. Yet Edwards sought to arrest and reverse this process. The project of Edwards's *End of Creation* was the ethicizing of the divine, while that of Edwards's *True Virtue* was the divinizing of ethics. Both treatises presumed that God was the proper and true aim of all right actions. The argument of these two writings was a slap in the face for Enlightenment humanists, who held that human beings should seek their own happiness and that God's great aim was simply to promote creatures' well-being. Where Enlightenment thinkers sought to reduce religion to morality, Edwards's *True Virtue* turned the tables. Not only was religion *not reducible* to morality or virtue, argued Edwards, but virtue could not even exist in the proper sense apart from love to God. Edwards's reinterpretation of eighteenth-century moral philosophy thus reestablished the theological underpinning for ethics.

Yet another discipline that fell within Edwards's implicit argument was history. The general thesis of the *History of Redemption* was the unity of history.[59] Edwards compared God's providence to "a large and long river, having innumerable branches beginning in different regions . . . at length discharging themselves at one mouth into the same ocean." Yet our limited, human perspective makes

---

57. Wilson Kimnach, "Editor's Introduction," in WJE 10:189.
58. WJE 6:363.
59. Perry Miller, *Jonathan Edwards* (New York: Sloane, 1949), 313.

it difficult for us to perceive the unity of the whole: "The different streams of this river are ready to look like mere jumble and confusion to us because of the limitedness of our sight." Edwards affirms that in the end "not one of all the streams fail of coming hither at last."[60] Essentially, *History of Redemption* is a book about intiellectual and spiritual discernment and is not a mere compilation of facts.[61] The work was organized so that the reader could trace the stepwise progress of God's redemptive plan. Edwards conceived history eschatologically; that is, backward from the end, not forward from the beginning. History was like a novel in which the final chapter explained all that preceded. Properly interpreted, then, the course of world affairs would become a means of "seeing" God and an implicit apology for the reality and activity of God.

CONTRIBUTIONS TO THE FIELD OF APOLOGETICS

As noted already, the "New Divinity" authors in the generation succeeding Edwards, who were self-consciously indebted to Edwards (e.g., Samuel Hopkins, Joseph Bellamy, Jonathan Edwards Jr., Nathaniel Emmons) were largely unaware of the vast extent of the apologetic argumentation that was contained in the private notebooks or *Miscellanies*. The so-called "New England Theology" of the nineteenth century had ever-looser links to Edwards's ideas, ran its course in the nineteenth century, and eventually converged with liberalizing theological influences emanating from Germany.[62] For this reason, an Edwards-inspired or Edwards-influenced version of Christian apologetics remains to some extent a matter of conjecture and what one might call "a road untraveled" rather than something that can readily be documented from the writings of the last two and a half centuries.

Apologetic responses to the deist challenge from the early 1700s to the early 1800s might be divided into two categories that could be termed *evidentialist* and *experientialist*. The *evidentialists*, epitomized by William Paley's *A View of the Evidences of Christianity* (1794), made their case for Christianity by appealing to the historical evidences of fulfilled prophecy in Christ's coming, the Bible's historical accuracy, and the positive moral and cultural impact of Christianity in western history. Paley's discussion of "antecedent probability" rebutted David

---

60. WJE 9:520.
61. John F. Wilson, "Editor's Introduction," in WJE 9:72–4.
62. Oliver Crisp and Douglas A. Sweeney, eds., *After Edwards: The Courses of the New England Theology* (New York: Oxford University Press, 2012); and Douglas Sweeney and Allen C. Guelzo, eds., *The New England Theology: From Jonathan Edwards to Edwards Amasa Park* (Eugene, OR: Wipf & Stock, 2015).

Hume's renowned argument against miracles, his treatment of "direct historical evidence" defended the credibility of the Bible, and his approach to "auxiliary evidences" expounded the morality of the gospel message, the uniqueness of Christ's character, and the remarkable spread of Christianity despite the many obstacles it encountered during its formative period.[63]

In distinction from the evidentialists, the *experientialists* are epitomized by Friedrich Schleiermacher's *On Religion* (1799) and—better known among English-speakers—Samuel Taylor Coleridge's *Aids to Reflection* (1825). Coleridge declared that "the mode of defending Christianity adopted by . . . Dr. Paley" had only increased the level of unbelief. This was because both the skeptics and Paley himself encouraged people to be "always looking out"—i.e., seeking to find God in the external world. What they discovered was a "lifeless Machine whirled about by the dust of its own Grinding." Far better, said Coleridge, was for everyone to "look into their own souls."[64] Schleiermacher had argued similarly in his *Speeches*. In fact, Schleiermacher went much further than Coleridge did in claiming that a "miracle" was not a special event but a special way of looking at everything. All mundane events were "miracles"—for those who had eyes to see. Religion did not consist in a form of intellectual *knowing* (as the evidentialists imagined) nor in virtuous *doing* (as moralists and deists proposed) but rather in devout *feeling*, that is, a "contemplation of . . . all finite things, in and through the Infinite."[65] This "sense," or "taste," for the infinite was the essence of all true religion and, for Schleiermacher, an intrinsic element of the human consciousness and experience of the world. No evidence could disprove it. No logical argument could overturn it. Religion itself was thus invulnerable to any sort of intellectual assault.[66]

Against this historical backdrop, Edwards's apology for Christianity is remarkable in integrating different argumentative strategies. Edwards avoided

---

63. Paley's Evidences is included as volume 2 in William Paley, *The Works of William Paley*, 5 vols. (Boston, MA: Belcher, 1810). For further exposition, see D. L. LeMahieu, *The Mind of William Paley: A Philosopher and His Age* (Lincoln, NE: University of Nebraska Press, 1976).

64. Samuel Taylor Coleridge, *The Collected Writings of Samuel Taylor Coleridge, Volume 9: "Aids to Reflection,"* ed. John Beer (Princeton: Princeton University Press, 1993), xliv, lxxxviii, 405–8. Coleridge stated that he did not "deny" miracles or regard them as "useless," though he sought to "build the miracle on the faith, and not the faith on the miracle" (xliv).

65. Friedrich Schleiermacher, *On Religion: Speeches to Its Cultured Despisers*, trans. John Oman (New York: Harper & Row, 1958 [1893]), 36. For background, see Richard E. Crouter's "Introduction" to his new translation *On Religion* (Cambridge: Cambridge University Press, 1988), 1–73.

66. Schleiermacher's apologetics has been criticized for making belief in God invulnerable to intellectual assault and yet at too high a price—i.e., by denying the cognitive status of theological assertions. See Wayne Proudfoot, *Religious Experience* (Berkeley: University of California, 1985). Edwards, in contrast, affirmed that theological assertions *have cognitive content and make objective truth claims*. Intellectual content blended with affective experience in Edwards's teaching on the "sense of the heart": "The heart cannot be set upon an object of which there is no idea in the understanding" (WJE 22:88).

the cut-and-dried objectivism of Paley's evidentialism as well as Schleiermacher's problematic subjectivism. Tucked away in the *Miscellanies* one finds extensive presentations of Christian evidences, discussions regarding the possibility of miracles, treatments of biblical history, and reconstruals of the rational arguments for God's existence (e.g., ontological, cosmological, teleological). Yet decades before Schleiermacher or Coleridge, Edwards anticipated Coleridge's call for people to "look into their own souls." Many aspects of the Romantics' internal argument for Christianity found a place in Edwards, appealing as he did to an inner sensibility that established the credibility of Christian belief. While Edwards displayed some crucial differences from Schleiermacher, there were affinities as well.[67] This may be one reason for Edwards's surprising appeal among Schleiermacher's twentieth-century progeny—viz., the self-consciously liberal or modernist theologians. (Jonathan Edwards's books are assigned reading at Harvard Divinity School as well as Dallas Theological Seminary. How many other modern theologians are read at both seminaries?) Edwards's in-depth analysis of religious experience—not to mention his affirmation of its evidential and apologetic value—has made him an appealing figure for theological revisionists who otherwise have little interest in his doctrinal Calvinism or his defenses of traditional doctrines.[68]

In his later years Edwards seems to have arrived at the view that the best apologetics is a good dogmatics and that dogmatics ought to take the form of narrative or history. During the 1730s Edwards developed, in the words of Ava Chamberlain, a "growing conviction that salvation history—grounded in the fulfillment of both prophetic and apocalyptic projections of the future of the church—represented Christianity's best line of defense against the deists."[69] It was not that he gave up the rational defense of the Christian faith, but he sought to show faith's rationality by an appeal to historical rather than solely logical or philosophical arguments. At the time that Edwards wrote to the college trustees in New Jersey (for what was later to be called Princeton University), Edwards's early project for the *Rational Account* had been superseded by his plans for the *History of the Work of Redemption*—like the previously planned work—was to defend the faith and "to confute deist claims."[70] In Edwards's unwritten *History of the Work of Redemption*, the timeless truths of the dogmaticians were some-

---

67. One crucial difference is that Edwards proposed that the "sense of the heart" or "spiritual sense" was possible only among the regenerate, who had received God's special grace, while Schleiermacher's *Gefühl* ("feeling"), or "sense and taste for the infinite," was possible for all human beings, without exception.

68. Richard R. Niebuhr has sought to link Edwards with Schleiermacher in *Streams of Grace: Studies of Jonathan Edwards, Samuel Taylor Coleridge, and William James* (Eugene, OR: Wipf & Stock, 2011).

69. Ava Chamberlain, "Editor's Introduction," in WJE 18:34.

70. Ava Chamberlain, "Editor's Introduction," in WJE 18:24–34, citing 30.

how to be translated into the form of narrative. Stephen Clark writes: "Edwards's insight is that Christian doctrine is not given whole, but emerges, revealing an organic nature as the history of redemption unfolds, and as the biblical revelation develops."[71]

Had Edwards not died when he did (from a badly administered smallpox inoculation), it is possible that his "great work" on the *History of Redemption* would have provided his intellectual heirs with a model of apologetic engagement that differed from any other they had encountered. Edwards was strictly orthodox in his commitment to a Calvinist conception of human sin and divine grace, together with the fundamental doctrines concerning God and Christ that were formulated in the early church era. Yet the tendency of the later notebooks was toward an appreciation of God's presence and activity in non-Christian contexts. Edwards's twentieth-century follower H. Richard Niebuhr called for nothing less than a universal history of God's redeeming work: "The Christian community must turn . . . from the revelation of the universal God in a limited history to the recognition of his rule and providence in all events of all times and communities."[72] Niebuhr's *The Meaning of Revelation* (1941), with its stress on theology as narrative, influenced faculty at Yale Divinity School during the 1980s and 1990s, including Hans Frei, George Lindbeck, David Kelsey, and others. The "narrative theology" that then took hold at Yale forged an inseparable union between theological reasoning and narrative form. While Karl Barth contributed much to this trend, it was Niebuhr's interpretation of Edwards that served as a key point of departure for the so-called "new Yale School," with its focus on "narrative theology."[73]

When one considers Edwards's well-planned but never-completed *History of the Work of Redemption* among the major trends in modern Christian theology and apologetics—Paley's evidentialism, Schleiermacher's experientialism, Hegel's reconstrual of the arts and sciences, and the narrative theologies of Karl Barth and the "new Yale school"—the overall effect is striking. The Harvard University historian Perry Miller may well have been correct in insisting that Edwards anticipated a number of crucial theological and philosophical developments long before they arrived.

---

71. Stephen M. Clark, "Jonathan Edwards: The History of Redemption" (PhD diss., Drew University, 1986), 406.

72. H. Richard Niebuhr, *The Meaning of Revelation* (New York: Macmillan, 1941), 87.

73. Continuing Niebuhr's and hence Edwards's legacies was Hans Frei's *The Eclipse of Biblical Narrative: A Study in Eighteenth and Nineteenth Century Hermeneutics* (New Haven: Yale University Press, 1974). On "narrative theology" at Yale see Mark I. Wallace, *The Second Naivete: Barth, Ricoeur, and the New Yale Theology*, 2nd ed. (Macon, GA: Mercer University Press, 1995).

BIBLIOGRAPHY

Cassirer, Ernst. *The Philosophy of the Enlightenment*. Translated by Fritz C. A. Koelln and James P. Pettegrove. Boston, MA: Beacon, 1955.

Coleridge, Samuel Taylor. *The Collected Writings of Samuel Taylor Coleridge, Volume 9: "Aids to Reflection."* Edited by John Beer. Princeton: Princeton University Press, 1993.

Crisp, Oliver, and Douglas A. Sweeney, eds. *After Edwards: The Courses of the New England Theology*. New York: Oxford University Press, 2012.

Crouter, Richard E. "Introduction" to translation *On Religion*. Cambridge: Cambridge University Press, 1988.

Dulles, Avery. *A History of Apologetics*. New York: Corpus, 1971.

Fiering, Norman. *Jonathan Edwards's Moral Thought and Its British Context*. Chapel Hill: University of North Carolina Press, 1981.

Frei, Hans. *The Eclipse of Biblical Narrative: A Study in Eighteenth and Nineteenth Century Hermeneutics*. New Haven: Yale University Press, 1974.

Gerrish, B. A. *A Prince of the Church: Schleiermacher and the Beginnings of Modern Theology*. Philadelphia: Fortress, 1984.

Gerstner, John. "An Outline of the Apologetics of Jonathan Edwards." *Bibliotheca Sacra* 133 (1976): 3–10, 99–107, 195–201, and 291–98.

———. *The Rational Biblical Theology of Jonathan Edwards*, 3 vols. Powhatan, VA: Berea Publications/ Orlando, FL: Ligonier Ministries, 1991. See especially, 1:94–139.

Hazard, Paul. *European Thought in the Eighteenth Century: From Montesquieu to Lessing*. New Haven: Yale University Press, 1954.

Heimert, Alan. *Religion and the American Mind, from the Great Awakening to the Revolution*. Cambridge: Harvard University Press, 1966.

LeMahieu, D. L. *The Mind of William Paley: A Philosopher and His Age*. Lincoln, NE: University of Nebraska Press, 1976.

Livingston, James C. *Modern Christian Thought: From the Enlightenment to Vatican II*. New York: Macmillan, 1971

McClymond, Michael J. *Encounters with God: An Approach to the Theology of Jonathan Edwards*. New York: Oxford University Press, 1998.

McDermott, Gerald. "The Deist Connection: Jonathan Edwards and Islam." Pages 39–51 in *Jonathan Edwards's Writings: Text, Context, Interpretation*. Ed. by Stephen J. Stein. Bloomington, IN: Indiana University Press, 1996.

Miller, Perry. *Jonathan Edwards*. New York: Sloane, 1949.

Niebuhr, Richard R. *Streams of Grace: Studies of Jonathan Edwards, Samuel Taylor Coleridge, and William James*. Eugene, OR: Wipf & Stock, 2011.

Paley, William. *The Works of William Paley*. 5 vols. Boston, MA: Belcher, 1810.

Pattison, Mark. "Tendencies of Religious Thought in England, 1688–1750." *Essays and Reviews*. 8th ed. London: Longman, Green, 1861.

Pelikan, Jaroslav. *The Christian Tradition: A History of the Development of Doctrine; Volume 3: The Growth of Medieval Theology [600–1300]*. Chicago: University of Chicago Press, 1978.

Proudfoot, Wayne. *Religious Experience*. Berkeley: Univerisity of California, 1985.

Reid, J. K. S. *Christian Apologetics*. Grand Rapids: Eerdmans 1969.

Richardson, Alan. *Christian Apologetics*. London: SCM, 1947.

Schleiermacher, Friedrich. *On Religion: Speeches to Its Cultured Despisers*. Trans. by John Oman. New York: Harper & Row, 1958 [1893].

Sweeney, Douglas, and Allen C. Guelzo, eds. *The New England Theology: From Jonathan Edwards to Edwards Amasa Park*. Eugene, OR: Wipf & Stock, 2015.

Wainwright, William. *Reason and the Heart: A Prolegomenon to a Critique of Passional Reason*. Ithaca, NY: Cornell University Press, 1995. See pp. 7–54.

Wallace, Mark I. *The Second Naivete: Barth, Ricoeur, and the New Yale Theology*. 2nd ed. Macon, GA: Mercer University Press, 1995.

WILLIAM PALEY

Apologetics of Design and for Culture

CHARLES TALIAFERRO

William Paley (1743–1805) was a Christian apologist, a philosopher, an essayist, and an Anglican priest. While highly educated and active as a young scholar in university life, he chose to do his research and writing from an early point in his career outside the university, earning a living for himself and his family through public speaking, his publications, and his income as a priest. Contemporaries praised him for taking philosophy outside the academy and into common life. He was an apologist who was oriented to addressing not just the highly educated but a wide audience receptive to the God of Christianity and for whom Paley desired what he saw as God's calling to enhance the happiness of all people. He put a premium on rational deliberation in his case for theism (as a general worldview) and in his case for Christian revelation in particular. On this point, Paley was different from apologists who appeal to passion and paradox and who shun the appeal of impartially acquired evidence. Paley believed that the reality of God is evident to an impartial, inquiring mind. In terms of good and evil, Paley thought that God intends for sentient creatures to be happy. He also thought Christians should not simply seek the salvation of others but should be highly committed to confronting social injustice. His spirituality involved a dual commitment to the well-being of soul and body for individuals and society as a whole. For Paley, evangelism that does not include striving for justice, especially for the vulnerable, is spurious, or at least deeply tarnished.

HISTORICAL BACKGROUND

William Paley was born in Peterborough, England, the eldest son of William and Elizabeth Paley. Contemporaries describe his mother as having a strong, active intellect.[1] His father was a canon at Peterborough and headmaster of

---

1. The complete works of William Paley, as well as a life of Paley, is available online. See: http://onlinebooks.library.upenn.edu. All references to Paley are from this site.

Giggleswick School. After graduating from Giggleswick, the younger Paley was educated at Cambridge University, graduating from Christ's College in 1763. In 1766 Paley was appointed a fellow of Christ's College and then appointed as one of the college's tutors in 1768. He was ordained a priest in the Anglican Communion in 1767. Paley continued as an academic at Christ's College until 1774, when he then left university life, continuing his studies and writing as an active pastor-priest. In 1792 he turned down the offer to become the master of Jesus College, Cambridge, thereby committing his ministerial and apologetic services to those outside the academy.

While at Cambridge University, Paley lectured on early modern philosophers such as Joseph Butler, John Locke, and Samuel Clarke and on the New Testament and moral theory. His lectures on morality led to the publication of his book *The Principles of Moral and Political Philosophy* in 1785. In it, Paley defended a version of theistic utilitarianism, according to which God has created and sustained people for the sake of everlasting happiness. This work was immensely popular, released in fifteen editions during Paley's lifetime.

Paley held a series of increasingly prominent positions in the Church of England, culminating in his becoming the archdeacon of Carlisle, a canon of Saint Paul's, subdeacon of Lincoln, and then rector of Bishopwarmouth. Paley married twice, first to Jane Hewitt, with whom he had eight children. She died in 1791. Paley then was married to Miss Dobinson in 1795. Paley died in Lincoln late in the day, May 25, 1805, in tranquility, surrounded by family.

Contemporaries largely described Paley as cheerful, pleasant, and outgoing. As a student, he displayed an inquiring mind, raising vexing questions (such as the question of whether capital punishment is justified) and having a penchant for debate. He was very much in demand as a lecturer or public speaker until an illness in 1800 forced him to give it up. His lectures and sermons have been described as not strong on grace but strong on content, amiable, and focused on his audience, without condescension. He was aware that when people engage in reasoning, it is important to have genuine openness to the reasons offered, for he once observed: "Who can refute a sneer?" Apparently, he was known for not putting a priority on being smartly dressed. He was somewhat eccentric in his mannerisms. Throughout his life, he was not interested in sports (he was described as not a very good horse rider), unlike many of his peers. While there is strong evidence of his integrity and discipline as a Christian (he placed a premium on clergy's setting an example of virtue), he was not above amusements such as card playing. Paley urged Christians to recognize and tolerate other Christians. In his lifetime, only Anglicans were permitted to attend Cambridge and Oxford Universities. Paley argued that this was too restrictive. He seems to have favored what C. S. Lewis would later describe as "mere Christianity," a position that affirmed Christian teaching without arguing that any one denomination or communion should be favored over others. On this last point, he urged the full acceptance (or toleration) of Roman Catholics and of the acceptance of nonconformists into Oxford.

THEOLOGICAL CONTEXT

William Paley stands in a long tradition of Christian philosophers who argued that the belief that there is a God is evident to honest, impartial inquirers, without requiring appeal to special revelation. On this front, Paley continued a tradition that was established by a group of philosophers and theologians who flourished at Cambridge University in the seventeenth century known as the Cambridge Platonists. These included Benjamin Whichcote, Henry More, Ralph Cudworth, Nathaniel Culverwell, John Smith, Peter Sterry, and Anne Conway.[2] These were the first people to publish extensive philosophical work in English. Earlier work in Britain was published in Latin and Greek. They advanced a range of arguments to the effect that there are features of our cosmos—its contingency (the fact that the cosmos does not exist necessarily), its stable laws of nature, the emergence of life, and especially the emergence of conscious life and objective values—that are more reasonable to expect given theism rather than nontheistic (or atheistic) naturalism. That is, they believed that theism offers an account of the existence and continuation of the cosmos that alternative, atheistic accounts leave unexplained. The Cambridge Platonists then (as Paley would afterward) used the general evidential case for theism to bolster the case for special revelation. After all, if impartial inquiry had led us to conclude it is unreasonable to believe in God, this would undermine the claims that there is a God revealed in human history. Conversely, a positive case for the reality of God should incline us to be open to the probability of there being a divine revelation. The contemporary Christian philosopher Richard Swinburne uses an analogy with astrophysics: if you have a well-grounded theory according to which stars do not explode, one would need very good evidence that some debris in space came from an exploding star, but on the other hand, if you have good grounds to believe that sometimes stars do explode, one would need less stringent evidence that some debris observed in space came from an exploding

---

2. For more on these Christian Platonists of Cambridge, see my works, *Cambridge Platonist Spirituality* (Paulist Press, 2004); *Evidence and Faith: Philosophy and Religion since the Seventeenth Century* (Cambridge University Press, 2005); and *The Golden Cord: A Short Book on the Secular and Sacred* (University of Notre Dame Press, 2012).

star. From Paley's perspective, because we have good grounds for thinking there is a God, this should open us up to considering the evidence that God is revealed in human history. This was a stance shared by John Locke (whom Paley lectured on), who, after laying down a case for theism, authored *The Reasonableness of Christianity*.

APOLOGETIC RESPONSE

Paley's first book of apologetics, *Horae Paulinae, or the Truth of the Scripture History of St. Paul*, was published in 1790 and was a largely exegetical work, defending the coherence and plausibility of the New Testament. His most famous work of apologetics are *View of the Evidences of Christianity* and *Natural Theology; or, Evidence of the Existence and Attributes of God*. In addition to these, Paley's work on natural theology was highly influential in promoting the interaction among the sciences and philosophy and theology. But Paley is unique among those in the history of apologetics, for he was concerned not only with philosophical and theological argument but also with social apologetics and cultural engagement. What follows is a summation of both, his contributions to apologetics from reflections on design and his holistic approach to apologetics, which includes his strenuous opposition to slavery, his opposition to the vast inequalities of wealth in his day, and his view that the true value and end of life is happiness.

Arguments from Design

Paley's most memorable contribution to the history of ideas is his argument from design. The first few pages of his book *Natural Theology* summarize his approach famously well.

> In crossing a heath, suppose I pitched my foot against a stone and were asked how the stone came to be there, I might possibly answer that for anything I knew to the contrary it had lain there forever; nor would it, perhaps, be very easy to show the absurdity of this answer. But suppose I found a *watch* upon the ground, and it should be inquired how the watch happened to be in that place, I should hardly think of the answer which I had given, that for anything I knew the watch might have always been there. Yet why should not this answer serve for the watch as well as for the stone; why is it not admissible in that second case as in the first? For this reason, and for no other, namely, that when we come to inspect the watch, we perceive—what we could not discover in the stone—that its several parts are framed and put together for a purpose, e.g., that they are so formed and adjusted as to

produce motion, and that motion so regulated as to point out the hour of the day; that if the different parts had been differently shaped from what they are, or placed in any other manner or in any other order than that in which they are placed, either no motion at all would have carried on in the machine, or none which would have answered the use that is now served by it.

This mechanism being observed . . . the inference we think is inevitable, that the watch must have had a maker—that there must have existed, at some time and at some place or other, an artificer or artificers who formed it for the purpose which we find it actually to answer, who comprehended its construction and designed its use.

Nor would it, I apprehend, weaken the conclusion, that we had never seen a watch made; that we had never known an artist capable of making one; that we were altogether incapable of executing such a piece of workmanship ourselves, or of understanding in what manner it was performed; all this being no more than what is true of some exquisite remains of ancient art, of some lost arts, and, to the generality of mankind, of the more curious productions of modern manufacture.[3]

The popularity of Paley's work was immense. Paley's work was widely read at Cambridge University for almost one hundred years. Its many admirers included Charles Darwin:

In order to pass the B.A. examination, it was, also, necessary to get up Paley's *Evidences of Christianity*, and his *Moral Philosophy*. . . . The logic of this book and as I may add of his *Natural Theology* gave me as much delight as did Euclid. The careful study of these works, without attempting to learn any part by rote, was the only part of the Academical Course which, as I then felt and as I still believe, was of the least use to me in the education of my mind. I did not at that time trouble myself about Paley's premises; and taking these on trust I was charmed and convinced of the long line of argumentation.[4]

Paley's argument from design, developed extensively throughout his *Natural Theology*, highlights the functional nature of particular organs, such as the eye of a human or nonhuman animal, which he contends (rightly) have functions in

---

3. William Paley, *Natural Theology* (Indianapolis: Bobbs-Merrill, 1802/1963), ch. 1.
4. Charles Darwin, *Autobiography* (New York: Collier, 1961), 34–35.

living things. They constitute nonmoral virtues or powers making up the health of beings. They are virtues or good powers, though not, narrowly speaking, moral virtues such as courage.

The argument from design that Paley developed is an argument from analogy. The cosmos resembles things we have reason to believe are designed by mindful causes. Therefore, we have reason to believe that the cosmos was designed by mindful causes (albeit such a cause would be immensely more powerful and knowledgeable than mere human watchmakers!). The argument from design was popular in his day among Christian theists and deists alike. According to deism, there is a Creator-God, but God has not revealed himself in human history. Many deists denied the reality of miracles, but many of them (including the harsh critic of Christianity, Thomas Paine) believed in an afterlife.

The argument from design received serious criticism from David Hume in his *Dialogues Concerning Natural Religion*. Through one of the characters in the dialogue, the argument from design is developed with the analogy that the cosmos resembles not a clock but a house. Objections include the proposal that if the cosmos is like a house and houses have lots of builders, perhaps we should conclude that there are many designers or gods, not only the God of Christianity. Also, isn't the cosmos more like an animal or plant rather than a house [or watch]? And what are we to make of the evil we observe? If there is a designer, do we have reason to believe that the designer is good? There are other objections as well. But perhaps the most important objection to note here comes from Charles Darwin's theory of evolution and subsequent Darwinian biologists such as Richard Dawkins. From a Darwinian point of view, all of what we take to be the teleological (purposive) nature of the world is the result of mindless, purposeless forces. Dawkins's case against the argument from design is observed in the title of his 1986 book, *The Blind Watchmaker*. Therein, he argues that the cosmos does resemble something like a watch, but such a cosmos came about through "blind"—that is, mindless, nonpurposive—causes.

Paley was aware of Hume's critique of the argument from design but found it wanting. He thought the goodness of the cosmos called for an explanation in terms of forces that had some prevision (purpose) of what it was bringing about.

> It is a happy world after all. The air, the earth, the water teem with delighted existence. In a spring noon, or a summer evening, on whichever side I turn my eyes, myriads of happy beings crowd upon my view. "The insect youth are on the wing." Swarms of new-born flies are trying their pinions in the air. Their sportive motions, their wanton mazes, their gratuitous activity,

testify their joy and the exultation which they feel in their lately discovered faculties.... The whole winged insect tribe, it is probable, are equally intent upon their proper employments, and under every variety of constitution, gratified, and perhaps equally gratified, by the offices which the author of their nature has assigned to them.[5]

This was a far more cheerful estimation of the goodness of the cosmos than was shared by Hume and, later, Darwin and Dawkins.[6]

Three points highlight the value of Paley's work in teleological argumentation. First, the line of Paley's reasoning is most plausible when one focuses on the existence of the cosmos as a whole, with stable laws of nature that enable life, including conscious life in beings with ethical and moral values. Rather than attend to single objects, such as eyes, one needs to appreciate the abundant laws and elements that make any life (including sighted animals with thoughts, intentions, sentience, and so on) possible. This broader teleological argument has been advanced today as the "fine-tuning" argument. Our cosmos appears to be so "finely tuned" that if some of the constants were even slightly different, there would be no stars and planets, let alone sites where life could emerge. Given theism, we would have an account of why there is such a cosmos rather than not, whereas secular naturalism seems straddled with the view that the extraordinary, life-supporting cosmos "just is," without an account.[7]

Second, teleological arguments, whether in the tradition of Paley or in the context of more broad teleological arguments, are strengthened when combined with other theistic arguments, such as the cosmological argument. In the text cited at the outset of this section, Paley seemed content with recognizing the existence and continuation in existence of a stone as requiring no explanation. In most forms of the cosmological argument, it is proposed that a full explanation of contingently existing beings must rest in a necessary being. God, as a necessarily

5. Paley, *Natural Theology*, 236.

6. I have replied to Hume, Darwin, and Dawkins elsewhere. See especially chapter 4 in *Evidence and Faith: Philosophy and Religion from the Seventeenth Century* (Cambridge: Cambridge University Press, 2005).

7. See Robin Collins, "Evidence for Fine-Tuning" in *God and Design: The Teleological Argument and Modern Science*, ed. Neil A. Manson (New York: Routledge, 2003), 178–99; "The Teleological Argument: An Exploration of the Fine-Tuning of the Universe," in *The Blackwell Companion to Natural Theology*, eds. William Lane Craig and J. P. Moreland (Chichester: Wiley-Blackwell, 2009), 202–81; and "Modern Cosmology and Anthropic Fine-Tuning: Three Approaches," in *Georges Lemaître: Life, Science and Legacy*, eds. Rodney D. Holder and Simon Mitton (Berlin: Springer, 2012), 173–91. For an argument from the other side, see Thomas Nagel, an atheist, expressing his deep satisfaction with naturalism in accounting for the cosmos, especially the emergence of consciousness, in *Mind and Cosmos*. While I defend a broad teleological theistic argument, some philosophers today (often under the title Intelligent Design) defend a design argument that focuses on the emergence of organisms very much in the tradition of Paley, such as Michael Behe, *Darwin's Black Box* (New York: Free Press, 1996).

existing being, can offer an account of the contingent that is not available in secular naturalism.[8]

A third point engages the worries expressed by Hume, Darwin, and Dawkins about the problem of evil. Each of these thinkers embraced a worldview in which the horrors of this life are natural elements in our world. Unhappiness, murder, rape, and so on, are not violations of the intention and will of a holy God. In *The Descent of Man*, Darwin even described what he predicted would be the extermination of weaker races by stronger races as natural, a position that later Nazi biologists welcomed.[9] Paley's theism bolsters instead the view that extermination campaigns, injustice, and so on are elements that are in violation of the purpose of the created order, which is for us to care for one another, seeking justice. A fuller treatment of the problem of evil will have to take place elsewhere but has been dealt with by philosophers and apologists from Augstine to Plantinga and will continue to be addressed by the next generation of apologists.[10] Paley was himself a strong defender of the idea that people have free will and are morally responsible for their kind as well as cruel acts.[11]

SOCIAL APOLOGETICS AND CULTURAL ENGAGEMENT

Paley was not just an apologist to save souls but someone deeply committed to rectifying the injustices of his day. Paley was an abolitionist; he was passionately committed to the belief that enslaving fellow human beings was a sin. He supported the American Revolution, in part, because he believed the revolution would lead to the freeing of slaves in North America. By contrast, David Hume (in a way, Paley's nemesis in terms of the history of the argument from design) was a white supremacist, and his work was cited by defenders of the African slave trade.

Paley did not argue for the radical redistribution of all property during his day. But he did contend that the wealthy have Christian obligations to give generously to assist the destitute. He held that God created us for happiness—happiness that is not just temporary but that is everlasting, beginning in this life and extending to the next. When we deprive others (including depriving nonhuman animals) of happiness, we are acting against the will of God. The property

---

8. For an excellent defense of this position, see Alexander Pruss and Joshua Rasmussen, *Necessary Existence* (Oxford: Oxford University Press, 2018).

9. See "Eugenics" by K. Ludmerrer in *Encyclopedia of Bioethics*, ed. Mark Lappe (New York: Free Press, 1978), 457.

10. For a good introduction to various views on this topic, see Chad Meister and James K. Dew Jr., eds., *God and the Problem of Evil: Five Views* (Downers Grove, IL: InterVarsity Press, 2017).

11. For more on a free will defense, see Alvin Plantinga, *God, Freedom, and Evil* (Grand Rapids: Eerdmans, 1989).

owners who have abundance have obligations of charity to ensure the happiness of others.

Paley's stress on the importance of happiness is interesting from the standpoint of apologetics. In Paley's view, a Christian apologist should not be interested primarily in converting people to have "the right beliefs about God" but in the happiness of all people, Christian and non-Christians alike, which is very similar to C. S. Lewis's own approach.

In the history of ethics in modern European thought, the ethical theory of utilitarianism, which supposes that ethics should be situated around bringing about the greatest happiness for the greatest number of people, is associated with secular philosophers such as Jeremy Bentham (an atheist) and John Stuart Mill (who thought there might be a God). What is less well known is that quite independent of Bentham (and predating Bentham's published work), Anglican clergy, including William Paley, advocated a vigorous form of utilitarianism that put God and happiness at the core. Because of their Christian theism, these utilitarians grounded their understanding of God-directed happiness in the framework of divine covenants and divine commands, such as the duty to love one's neighbor as oneself. They thereby bypassed some of the challenges facing their secular utilitarians, who worried about whether it would be morally right to cause great misery to the vulnerable if that made the majority of people overwhelmingly happy.[12]

APOLOGETIC METHODOLOGY AND CONTRIBUTIONS TO THE FIELD OF APOLOGETICS

Paley was an apologist who valued impartial reason. Paley had a major impact in drawing together science and theology. His major contribution to apologetics was his publication *Natural Theology*, which is credited for inspiring ten volumes of Bridgewater treatises in the 1830s, with contributors including William Whewell (who came up with the term *scientist*).[13] Paley's output became the educational foundation of the apologists who followed him and spurred the building of defenses for Christian theism, natural theology, and God's goodness.

Some Christian philosophers in the modern era have criticized Paley's

---

12. See Graham Cole, "Theological Utilitarianism and the Eclipse of the Theological Sanction" *Tyndale Bulletin* 42, no 2. (Nov 1991): 226–44.

13. See Charles Babbage, *Ninth Bridgewater Treatise: A Fragment* (London: Murray, 1838); and William Whewell, *Astronomy and General Physics Considered with Reference to Natural Theology* (London: Pickering, 1834).

methodology of first striving to make the case for theism prior to assessing revelational claims (upheld by the Cambridge Platonists, John Locke, William Paley, and Richard Swinburne, among many others).[14] The most ardent critic today is Paul Moser. According to Moser, to appeal to the evidential case for theism involves what he calls "spectator evidence."[15] It is evidence that is cut off from the challenge of being confronted by the radical call of God to renounce our self-interest and commit ourselves passionately to the lordship of Jesus Christ. Moser argues that a morally perfect God would desire that people come to know God through a process of moral and personal transformation. In the course of committing ourselves to Jesus of Nazareth as revealed in the New Testament, our lives will be transformed, and in a sense, our changed, love-centered lives will become evidence of the truth of Christian revelation. Moser sees himself developing a theology of evidence inspired by the apostle Paul, Søren Kierkegaard, and Reinhold Niebuhr. He laments that natural theology can contribute to vanity and haughtiness rather than spur us on to seek out sites in which God has been manifested in human history.

Four brief rebuttals are valuable here to show why Paley's project is a worthy one. First, in reply to Moser, it needs to be acknowledged almost *anything* (including natural theology) can be a source of human vanity and haughtiness. Paul Moser is an exemplary person with evident virtues (a humble, nonegotistical friend), but it is *conceivable* that his massive record of publishing (advancing his case for humility and a Christ-centered life, especially stressing Christ crucified) by highly prestigious presses (such as Cambridge University Press) could be a source of vanity and haughtiness. Speaking personally (and not making this point about Moser), if I had such an awesome record of Cambridge University Press publications, I would be tempted to let an inordinate number of people know about my books. So I propose that the danger that natural theology might lead to vices is a danger in almost any worthwhile endeavor.[16] Second, I suggest that natural theology would give people independent reasons to explore Moser's challenge rather than seeking to give one's life over to other sources, such as following the Buddha or seeking to live in harmony with the Dao or following

14. For a good critical overview of Paley and his detractors, see Alister E. McGrath, *Darwinism and the Divine: Evolutionary Thought and Natural Theology* (Oxford: Whiley-Blackwell, 2011).

15. Paul Moser, "Christian Philosophy and Christ Crucified: Fragmentary Theory in Scandalous Power" in *Christian Philosophy: Conceptions, Continuations, and Challenges*, ed. Aaron Simmons (Oxford: Oxford University Press, 2019), 209–28.

16. It might be countered that there is a different kind of arrogance or vanity involved in, say, one's professional accomplishments and in claiming that the belief in God is backed up by the evidence of natural theology, but I suggest they can be of the same kind or species; both can be objects of an inordinate desire for praise or prestige. And, other things being equal, I suggest that Moser's defense of his positions and Paley's of his can equally reflect epistemic humility.

the teachings of Spinoza. Third, if Paley is right, one has good reason to reject secular naturalism, which is probably the closest philosophical alternative to Christian theism today. Lastly, it is not clear that the apostle Paul would disdain natural theology. Probably the most widely cited Scripture that has been used to invite the quest of natural theology is Paul's letter to the Romans (1:20): "Since the creation of the world, God's invisible qualities—his eternal power and divine nature—have been clearly seen, being understood from what has been made, so that people [those who deny God] are without excuse."

What Paley requested of his readers (or listeners) is to be open to his reasoning, for, he believed, that once one combines natural and revealed theology, we are on the true path to happiness: "the doing of good to mankind, in obedience to the will of God, and for the sake of everlasting happiness."[17]

BIBLIOGRAPHY

Babbage, Charles. *Ninth Bridgewater Treatise: A Fragment*. London: Murray, 1838.
Behe, Michael. *Darwin's Black Box*. New York: Free Press, 1996.
Cole, Graham. "Theological Utilitarianism and the Eclipse of the Theological Sanction." *Tyndale Bulletin* 42.2 (November 1991): 226–44.
Collins, Robin. "Evidence for Fine-Tuning." Pages 178–99 in *God and Design: The Teleological Argument and Modern Science*. Ed. by Neil A. Manson. New York: Routledge, 2003.
———. "Modern Cosmology and Anthropic Fine-Tuning: Three Approaches." Pages 173–191 in *Georges Lemaître: Life, Science and Legacy*. Ed. by Rodney D. Holder and Simon Mitton. Berlin: Springer, 2012.
———. "The Teleological Argument: An Exploration of the Fine-Tuning of the Universe." Pages 202–81 in *The Blackwell Companion to Natural Theology*. Ed. by William Lane Craig and J. P. Moreland. Chichester: Wiley-Blackwell, 2009.
Dawkins, Richard. *The Blind Watchmaker*. New York: Norton, 1987.
Ludmerer, K. "Eugenics." Page 457 in *Encyclopedia of Bioethics*. Ed. by Mark Lappe. New York: Free Press, 1978.
McGrath, Alister E. *Darwinism and the Divine: Evolutionary Thought and Natural Theology*. Oxford: Wiley-Blackwell, 2011.
Meister, Chad, and James K. Dew Jr., eds. *God and the Problem of Evil: Five Views*. Downers Grove, IL: InterVarsity Press, 2017.
Moser, Paul. "Christian Philosophy and Christ Crucified: Fragmentary Theory in Scandalous Power." Pages 209–28 in *Christian Philosophy*. Ed. by J. Aaron Simmons. Oxford: Oxford University Press, 2019.
Paley, William. *Natural Theology*. Indianapolis: Bobbs-Merrill, 1802/1963.
———. *The Principles of Moral and Political Philosophy*. Indianapolis: Library Fund, 1785/2002.
———. *A View of the Evidence of Christianity*. Annotations by R. Whatley. New York: Miller, 1794/1860.
Plantinga, Alvin. *God, Freedom, and Evil*. Grand Rapids: Eerdmans, 1989.
Pruss, Alexander, and Joshua Rasmussen. *Necessary Existence*. Oxford: Oxford University Press, 2018.
Taliaferro, Charles. *Cambridge Platonist Spirituality*. New York: Paulist, 2004.
———. *Evidence and Faith: Philosophy and Religion since the Seventeenth Century*. New York: Cambridge University Press, 2005.
———. *The Golden Cord*. Notre Dame: University of Notre Dame Press, 2013.
Whewell, William. *Astronomy and General Physics Considered with Reference to Natural Theology*. London: Pickering, 1834.

---

17. Paley, *The Principles of Moral and Political Philosophy*, 25.

JOSEPH BUTLER

Defending the Probability of Christianity against Deism

DAVID MCNAUGHTON

Joseph Butler (1692–1752) had as his principal target in his *Analogy of Religion* the deists, who accepted that the world must have an intelligent creator and designer but typically denied the specific doctrines of Christianity, such as miracles, the incarnation, and a final judgment. They argued that no credence should be attached to the biblical narrative, which should be rejected both on historical grounds and on grounds of good taste. The God of the Bible is not the God shown to us in the regular operations of nature. Butler's response is threefold. First, by study of the world around us, we can glean much more about God's nature; viz., that he is a righteous judge who will ultimately treat each of us according to our deserts. Second, that there is nothing in revelation that is inconsistent with what we find in nature. Third, while the conclusions of natural theology are never certain, they are probable. In practical matters it is reasonable, when our futures are at risk, to act even on very low probabilities. Anyone who accepts that there is some likelihood that a righteous God exists should amend their life accordingly.

HISTORICAL BACKGROUND

The main public events in Butler's fairly uneventful life can be quickly delineated. Of his private life or opinions, we know little, since he ordered all his papers to be burned upon his death. Born on May 18, 1692, into a Presbyterian family dwelling in Wantage, Berkshire, he was educated first at the local grammar school and later at the Dissenting Academy in Gloucester, probably with the intention of entering the Presbyterian ministry. The curriculum included Greek and Latin, logic, mathematics, geography, and biblical studies. It was here that Butler met Thomas Secker, later to become archbishop of Canterbury, and began his correspondence with Samuel Clarke.

By 1714 Butler had decided to conform to the Established Church of England and was thus eligible to enter the ancient universities, which were then closed to nonconformists. In 1715 he entered Oriel College, Oxford, where, as was not uncommon in the eighteenth century, he found the education he received deficient. He was ordained to the priesthood in 1718. The following year he was appointed preacher at the Rolls Chapel, by Sir Joseph Jekyll, master of the Rolls. The chapel, in Chancery Lane, London, served both as a repository for legal records (preserved on rolls of parchment—hence the name) and as a place of worship for the lawyers and clerks who worked in the Court of Chancery, which dealt with matters of equity rather than with common law. The *Fifteen Sermons*, first published in 1726, were originally preached to this especially well-educated audience. A second edition followed in 1729, containing a long preface intended to summarize, explain, and amplify Butler's argument.

In 1721 Butler obtained his bachelor of common law degree from Oxford and was soon given one of the richest benefices in the country—Stanhope in County Durham. His income now allowed him to resign the Rolls preachership, and he resided entirely at Stanhope until 1733, working on the *Analogy of Religion*. Secker, fearing that Butler was becoming too isolated in Stanhope, recommended him to Queen Caroline. She expressed some surprise, having supposed him dead. The archbishop of York is reputed to have quipped: "No, Madam; but he is buried."[1] In 1736 *The Analogy* was published, and the queen duly appointed Butler as her clerk of the Closet. His duties included attendance on the Queen for two hours each evening for theological discussion. After Queen Caroline's death, Butler was elevated to the see of Bristol in 1738 and appointed to the bench of bishops in the Lords. In 1746 Butler was appointed clerk of the Closet to the king, and in 1750 he was elevated to the see of Durham, a position he did not long occupy, dying in 1752.

Butler was a scrupulous and conscientious clergyman, somewhat prone to melancholy. He was well known for his charitable giving: it is reported that he found it difficult to resist giving alms to anyone who begged. He spent the majority of his income on refurbishing ecclesiastical buildings, buying land for a church for the working poor, and aiding the development of infirmaries at Bristol and Newcastle upon Tyne. As far as we know, he was a thoroughly orthodox member of the Church of England, though one who thought the outward forms of religion important in imparting and supporting faith.[2]

---

1. Thomas Bartlett, *Memoirs of the Life, Character and Writings of Joseph Butler* (London: Parker, 1839), 38.
2. For fuller biographical details, see Christopher Cunliffe "Butler, Joseph (1692–1752)," in *Oxford Dictionary of National Biography* (Oxford: Oxford University Press, 2008).

THEOLOGICAL CONTEXT

The Church of England in the eighteenth century is often thought of as not only worldly and complacent but also theologically unexciting. After the great upheavals of the seventeenth century, it rested secure, supported by an established Protestant monarchy. This picture is misleading in many ways.[3] The established church was challenged on the one flank by Methodism and the dissenting churches and on the other by the issue of Nonjuring High Churchmen (who felt they could not, in good conscience, break their oath of allegiance to James II by swearing a new one to William III and his successors) and the threat of the reinstatement of the Jacobite dynasty by armed rebellion. Theological and doctrinal disputes abounded, especially about the exact nature of the real presence of Christ in the Eucharist. On these matters Butler's views are unknown. The other great challenge it faced was the rise of deism, and it is this issue that Butler's *Analogy of Religion* addresses.

DEISM, THEISM, AND CHRISTIANITY

Deists and many orthodox theists held certain beliefs in common. Both believed there is an intelligent First Cause of the universe, whom we may call God. As a rational being, God designed the universe to be orderly and to work according to intelligible principles. These laws of nature are found to govern the behavior of everything there is, from the smallest atom to the movements of stars and planets. Since a rational being prefers beauty to ugliness, and harmony to disharmony, he will create a universe that displays these qualities. Nature is not a chance collocation of atoms but an intelligible and organized whole. Natural theology helps us understand God's nature, both when we consider nature in its external aspect, as organized cosmos, and when we look at human nature. For we are made in God's image, especially in respect of the inner light of reason that has been given to each human.

Deists characteristically rejected a number of claims that are distinctive of the great monotheistic religions: Judaism, Christianity, and Islam. They denied that God directly intervenes in human history, either by performing miracles, inspiring prophets, or by revealing truths about himself that could not be known merely from the examination of his creation. They rejected the specifically Christian doctrines of the incarnation, the Trinity, and the atonement. The God of the deists is not someone with whom each of us can have a personal

3. B. W. Young, "Theology in the Church of England" in *The Oxford History of Anglicanism, Vol. II*, ed. Jeremy Gregory (Oxford: Oxford University Press, 2017), 392–428.

relationship. Theirs is not a God to whom we can pray for guidance or help. We might summarize the distinction by saying that deists accept a general but not a particular providence. That is, for the deist, God administers the world wisely by general laws but does not provide guidance or succor to each individual.

Deism had its roots in the strong rationalism of the early Enlightenment and the rise of modern science. Thus, for example, countenancing miracles would conflict with the belief that God works through the regularities of nature. The need for a perfect being to give an occasional "tweak" to the orderly progress of nature would detract from the perfection of his handiwork. Deists aimed to strip away the accretions of mystery, superstition, and "priest craft" with which, in a more barbarous age, Christianity had become encrusted in order to reveal the pure underlying religion of reason. Only when thus cleansed would Christianity be a view that reasonable people could accept. The deists also had moral objections to the idea of revelation. It was *unfair* that important truths—truths necessary for salvation—should be vouchsafed to some but not to others. Nor is it morally acceptable to suppose that God might have favorites, such as the children of Israel. Surely, a wise and loving God would be, as it were, an equal opportunity revealer of truth.

Many influential deists were professing Christians, although some were not. They saw themselves as reforming, rather than as denying, Christianity. Naturally, they differed somewhat as to precisely which elements of traditional Christianity they rejected. Someone who accepted only the claims listed in the first paragraph of this section would be subscribing to a very austere version of deism. Some who bore the label were more accommodating to elements of theism than others. Samuel Clarke, in his *Discourse Concerning the Unchangeable Obligations of Natural Religion*, listed four types of deists.[4]

The first, and most austere, restricted themselves to the belief that God is an eternal, infinite, independent, and intelligent being who created the world. The second allowed that God exercises a continuing providential government over the world, but this government is not a *moral* one. The third group accepted that God is a moral governor but denied immortality. The fourth accepted that there is a future life and judgment in which virtue is rewarded and vice punished. All denied that we need revelation to discover the truth of any of these claims.[5]

Thus, Lord Herbert of Cherbury, an early deist, offered five essential marks of natural, or uncorrupted, religion. Sometimes known as the Five Articles of Deism, these are: (1) A belief in the existence of the deity, (2) The obligation to

---

4. I take this from Terence Penelhum, *Butler* (London: Routledge & Kegan Paul, 1985), 100.
5. Ibid.

reverence such a power, (3) The identification of worship with practical morality, (4) The obligation to repent of sin and to abandon it, and (5) Divine recompense in this world and the next.[6] The fifth mark, of course, implies belief in an afterlife, which, as we have seen, is not shared by all deists.

A key figure in the development of deism was John Locke. Though not himself a deist, his tests for a credible revelation tended to lead in the direction of deism. What is revealed must come from a tradition that is fully accredited by internal and external evidence, and crucially, any revelation must be capable of *post hoc* justification. That is, such mysteries as it purports to reveal must, once revealed, be accepted only if they are reasonable.

Later deists built on this foundation. John Toland, in his *Christianity Not Mysterious*, maintained that the content of revelation must neither contradict nor transcend the dictates of reason. Revelation does not impart truths that could not otherwise be ascertained. Where it is reliable, it is simply a convenient source of knowledge that could be acquired by other, perhaps more laborious, routes. Anthony Collins, in his *Discourse of Freethinking*, held that practical morality is independent of dogma, which has brought about much evil. He went so far as to claim that Christ and the apostles never appealed to supernatural authority but offered clear and simple instructions about how to live. Finally, Matthew Tindal, in *Christianity as Old as the Creation, or the Gospel a Republication of the Religion of Nature*, argued that though Judaism and Christianity contain genuine revelations, what is revealed is something everyone can accept: the law of nature, which consists in the practice of morality in obedience to the will of God.[7]

APOLOGETIC METHODOLOGY

Butler offers an *internal* response to deism. That is, he accepts the deists' premises and their claim that we must justify Christian belief using ordinary methods of reasoning that we would employ in everyday life. He argues that those methods will take us much further than deists supposed: they can be used to show that many of the fundamental claims of theism can be thus established and that traditional Christian orthodoxy, as revealed in Scripture, is in line with what

---

6. I am indebted in this section to the anonymous "deism" entry in the *Internet Encyclopedia of Philosophy* https://www.iep.utm.edu/deismeng/. Useful discussions of deism in the context of Butler's apologetic can be found in the following: David Brown, "Butler and Deism" in Christopher Cunliffe, ed., *Joseph Butler's Moral and Religious Thought* (Oxford: Oxford University Press, 1992), 7–28, and Albino Babolin, "*Deus Absconditas*: Some Notes on the Bearing of the Hiddenness of God upon Butler's and Pascal's Criticism of Deism", 29–36, in the same volume. See also the chapter by Michael McClymond in this volume for a helpful outline of deism.

7. Ibid.

we know of the world. Internal critiques of a view are, of course, very powerful. External critiques of a view can be rejected because they adopt a flawed methodology that proponents of that view do not accept. But if Butler can show that, on the deists' own assumptions, they should accept doctrines that they reject, then their whole project is undermined.[8]

Butler's response relies on two claims about how we reason. The first is that, at best, nearly all the conclusions we reach are merely probable. Certainty is not to be had. The second is that ordinary reasoning is frequently analogical: we learn something in one context and then apply those conclusions in a similar, but somewhat different, context, making allowances for any dissimilarities. These two points are related. As Butler says, "That which chiefly constitutes probability is expressed in the word *likely*, *i.e.* like some truth, or true event; like it, in itself, in its evidence, in some more or fewer of its circumstances. For when we determine a thing to be probably true, suppose that an event has or will come to pass, it is from the mind's remarking in it a likeness to some other event, which we have observed has come to pass."[9]

That is, what is *likely* to happen is something that is *like* what we have observed before.

The full title of Butler's book is *The Analogy of Religion, Natural and Revealed, to the Constitution and Course of Nature*. The first part expounds what we can glean from our knowledge of ourselves and the world about the nature of our Creator. The second part argues, using the same methodology, that there is nothing surprising, unfair, or unreasonable in the idea of a *special* revelation—that is, one given to some rather than to others—and that the Christian revelation is itself eminently reasonable and plausible. The first part is positive and constructive—showing what natural religion gives us grounds to believe. The second part is defensive—showing that there are no good grounds to reject the Christian revelation.

Taking as his starting point the most austere deist position—that the universe has an intelligent designer—Butler successively argues that we have good reason to believe that:

- There is an afterlife in which people will be punished or rewarded depending on whether they have lived virtuous or vicious lives.

---

8. There are no editions of Butler's *Analogy* currently in print. The standard edition (now very rare) is edited by J. H. Bernard, who helpfully numbers Butler's paragraphs. There are various online copies available, none of which are entirely satisfactory. My own edition (with Oxford University Press) should be appearing in 2020.

9. All references to Butler's *Analogy* are by part, chapter number, and paragraph, except in the case of the introduction, where only a paragraph number is given. Introduction, 2.

- This life is a probation or trial through which we must pass to attain virtue and fit ourselves for the kingdom of heaven.
- These conclusions are unaffected by whether we accept free will or think that everything comes about by necessity.
- We inevitably understand only a small part of God's purposes. We know enough to know what God expects of us, but many parts of his plan will seem puzzling.
- The question of whether Christianity is true is of enormous practical importance.
- A revelation, by its nature, is miraculous and is likely to be accompanied by confirming miracles. But there is nothing in what we know of the world that justifies skepticism about the miraculous.
- It is understandable, given the current human condition, that only a mediator and advocate could save us.
- The objections against a special revelation are unsound. Given our ignorance, it is understandable that we are required to do certain things to be saved without our fully comprehending why God has chosen these means to salvation.

PROBABILITY

In this life there are virtually no certainties. At best, we may have good grounds for thinking that some particular event is very likely to happen; at worst, we may know only that there is a range of probable outcomes, with no clear guidance as to which is the most likely. By contrast, God knows with certainty. "Probable evidence, in its very nature, affords but an imperfect kind of information; and is to be considered as relative only to beings of limited capacities. For nothing which is the possible object of knowledge, whether past, present, or future, can be probable to an infinite Intelligence; since it cannot but be discerned absolutely as it is in itself, certainly true, or certainly false. But to us, probability is the very guide of life."[10]

We might suppose that we should take action only when we have a better than even chance of securing the outcome we desire. But that, Butler argues, would be a mistake. How we should act is determined by *two* things: the likelihood of the desired outcome *and* the value of that outcome. If we want a very great good, or if we seek to avoid a catastrophe, we would be warranted in acting even though the probability of the good, or of the bad, outcome was very low. Thus, we insure our houses against fire, even though the likelihood

---

10. *Analogy* (Introduction), 3.

of that happening is very low, because if our home burned down, the loss would be extremely damaging. Similarly, it would be crazy not to apply for a job you wanted simply because your chances were slim. "For numberless instances might be mentioned respecting the common pursuits of life, where a man would be thought, in a literal sense, distracted, who would not act, and with great application too, not only upon an even chance, but upon much less, and where the probability or chance was greatly against his succeeding."[11]

This point will turn out to be crucial when Butler considers what we might call practical religion: How should we shape our religious practices in the face of some uncertainty as to whether there is a God and, if so, what his purposes may be?

Analogical Reasoning

Arguments by analogy start from a known pattern of events and argue that in a similar but not identical situation, we will find a similar pattern. Butler's main arguments start with our earthly life and move to life after death. In this life we find that, for example, folly and vice are often punished and virtue rewarded. Given the assumption Butler shares with the deist—that this is God's world—we would expect a similar pattern in the life to come.

APOLOGETIC RESPONSE

Life after Death

It is crucial for the remainder of Butler's argument that he persuade the deist that we have good reason to believe we shall survive death. For, after all, if we do not survive, questions about how God will treat us in a future existence are empty. He begins by invoking a general principle that is based on experience; namely, that we have good reason from experience to expect a thing to go on existing unless there is some cause that puts a stop to it. If we can show that there is no reason to think that bodily death will bring about the dissolution of the mind, then we have good reason to suppose that the mind will naturally continue after death. He then argues that diminution of our body, or our bodily powers, does not affect the mind. So there is no reason to suppose that the dissolution of the body will affect the mind. The matter that constitutes our bodies is constantly changing, but this does not affect our minds, nor does the loss of a limb or an eye affect the mind. Our body and sense organs are mere instruments by which the mind relates to the world and could be replaced by artificial legs,

---

11. Ibid.

arms, eyes, etc. Impending death may rob us of various bodily functions, but dying people can retain mental clarity until the end. We have good, but of course not conclusive, reason to suppose that our minds are simple and nonspatial and therefore likely to survive the death of the material body.

This argument is open to serious objections. What Butler has shown is that many parts of our body can be lost without damage to our mental powers. But from this, one cannot infer that *all* parts of our body might be destroyed without mental damage or destruction, for two reasons. First, it is generally unsound to argue that because something could continue existing without any one particular kind of part, it could continue existing without *any* parts of that kind. Because I can skip any particular meal without detriment does not mean I can skip all meals without dying. Second, there does seem to be one part of the body, namely the brain, that when damaged does affect mental functioning. If my visual cortex is destroyed, then I cannot see, even if my eye is functioning properly. And similarly for other parts of the brain. So this particular organ does not seem to be a mere instrument for the use of the mind but something whose proper functioning is integral to mental functioning. In that case, it seems likely that death of the brain and death of consciousness go hand in hand. Of course, this does not prove that we could not survive death, but it does undermine Butler's argument that study of the relation between mind and body suggests that life after death is natural and probable.

MORAL GOVERNMENT OF GOD

Leaving these problems aside for a while, let's turn to the heart of Butler's analogical argument. In this life we have considerable, though not total, control over how our lives turn out. We can certainly ruin ourselves by folly and vice, and we are more likely to flourish if we live prudently and virtuously. Deists and Christians agree that this is God's world, so we can assume that the principles on which it runs come from God. How we behave in earlier stages of our lives deeply affects what happens to us as we grow older. Even if the natural consequences of our actions are long postponed, they often catch up with us later on. By analogy, in a future life, we would expect the same, or at least similar, principles to apply. So we can infer that vice will be punished and virtue rewarded in the life to come. Where someone has failed to pay the penalty for their sins in this life, we may anticipate, with reasonable confidence, that they will get their due in the next. Similarly, the virtuous who are unrewarded here may expect reward later.

Butler admits that *in this life* the correspondence between sin and punishment on the one hand, and virtue and reward on the other, is less than perfect. So why should we expect the next life to be more just than the current one?

364   EARLY MODERN APOLOGISTS

Butler's reply is that we must not forget that we are part of nature, and we are moral beings, knowing the difference between good and evil. This gives us a unique insight into the mind and purposes of the Creator. That we care about justice is grounds for thinking that he who created us does also.

Butler adds that the *natural* tendency of virtue is to make our own lives, and those of others, happier, and the natural tendency of vice is the opposite. The same can be said of other processes in nature: water naturally flows downhill; the immune system naturally fights invading organisms. But accidental circumstances can frustrate these natural tendencies. Humans may dam rivers or pump water up hills. In autoimmune diseases the body's defenses attack its own cells. If we are to understand the principles on which the world runs, we should look at the natural tendency of things rather than the accidental exceptions. Similarly, the natural tendency of exercise and a good diet is to promote a healthy, long life. The enthusiastic jogger may be run over by a bus, while the flabby couch potato is saved from heart disease by a triple bypass, but such exceptions do not undermine the claim that the natural tendency of exercise is to make you healthier, happier, and therefore live longer. Equally, a society of the virtuous will tend to be happier and more successful than a society of villains, even if the villains occasionally win. Moreover, vice is parasitic on virtue; it can only succeed where most are trusting, generous, etc. A confederacy of people without a shred of decency or trustworthiness will inevitably fail. If virtue prevails slowly and with difficulty against obstacles in this life, we may assume that in the much longer term of a future life, it will ultimately triumph.

TRIAL AND TRIBULATION

Looking at this world, with its many horrors, we might think God is neither benevolent nor just. Disease, famine, and flood destroy the righteous and the wicked alike. Sometimes the innocent suffer, and, on occasion, the wicked flourish like the green bay tree. This is the infamous problem of evil: if God is good, whence all this suffering and injustice? Butler's reply is that the existence of suffering is implied in the notion of moral government. In a world where nothing and no one went wrong, there would be no need for *government* of any kind. This life, he contends, should be seen as a testing ground in which we are given the opportunity to develop as virtuous, fulfilled human beings or to sink into sloth and sin. It is thus, as Butler puts it, a state of probation: our conduct will determine whether we are rewarded or punished at the end of our probationary period. If this life is to be a genuine test of character, there must be temptations and obstacles to overcome. No merit attaches to doing right when there is nothing attractive about going wrong. We can display patience and fortitude only when trouble comes. We are imperfect beings who come into the world with few abilities. To acquire what are now called "life skills," we must face challenges. Where there is no possibility of failure, there cannot be success.

What Butler offers here is a theodicy—an account of the divine purpose that seeks to justify the ways of God to humanity. He admits that it is only a partial theodicy: there are evils it does not explain. Many fall by the wayside, sometimes through no fault of their own, and this waste of life is distressing, though no more surprising than the failure of many seeds to germinate or the high mortality rate among young animals. Since this is God's world and, so Butler has argued, under God's moral governance, such facts must be consistent with God's goodness, though we cannot see how. Our ignorance in these matters is no evidence against God's existence. It would be absurd to suppose that we, with our limited knowledge, could understand the reason for everything. It would be folly to suppose that we know better than God how things should be run. It is sufficient that we can understand the general outline of God's plan for us.

Suppose that we are not entirely convinced of God's moral government. Suppose, indeed, that we think it rather unlikely that prudence and virtue will bring reward, not only imperfectly in this life but also perfectly in the next. Nevertheless, from the point of view of practice, we might have as good a reason to follow God's ordinances as we would if we were fully convinced. For, as Butler points out at the beginning of his work, what it is sensible to do depends not only on the probability of a hoped-for outcome but on its value compared with the probability and value of the alternatives. Though it is unlikely that my house will burn down, it would be a disaster if it did, and the premiums are not inordinately burdensome. Similarly, even if one is not fully persuaded by Butler's case for a future life or for God's moral government, it would be the merest folly to risk one's possible future life, and perhaps incur God's wrath, unless what was required of you was too demanding. But the demands, though perhaps difficult to live up to, are reasonable. First, you need to repent of folly and wrongdoing and live a sober, virtuous, and godly life. Second, since the natural consequence of sin is punishment, you need to accept the gracious mercy made available to you through Christ's mediation and sacrifice. This is Butler's version of Pascal's Wager: in deciding how to live, consider both the odds and what is at stake either way.

That concludes Butler's positive account of natural religion. But before turning to his discussion of revelation, we should briefly examine an important defensive move of his. Suppose, as some contend, that everything that happens does so necessarily. There is no chance and no free choice. Would this invalidate Butler's conclusions? It would certainly not undermine arguments that might be offered for God's existence. If a watch shows evidence of intelligent design, the inference to a (human) designer is not undermined just because the designer had no choice. Similarly for the design of the universe.

Is the view that excludes chance and choice inconsistent with God's rewarding and punishing in the next world? No, because we see that he punishes folly and vice and rewards prudence and morality in *this* world. On the supposition that everything that happens in our world is determined, we can infer, therefore, that his approval or condemnation of our actions does not depend on our choices being free. But if he is not inhibited, by our lack of freedom, from punishing and rewarding in this life, then we have no reason to suppose he will be prevented from doing so in the next.

The final worry Butler addresses is this: even if we have reason to believe God will reward and punish in a future life, would it be just or benevolent for him to do so? If we are fully convinced that someone could not help but violate the law, we are inclined to exonerate him from blame. Should not a just and merciful God do the same? Butler's response is that what is sauce for the goose is sauce for the gander. If *everything* happens by necessity, then so do God's actions, as well as ours. If the offender necessarily offends, then God necessarily punishes. If the necessity of all actions exonerates the offender from blame, then the necessity of God acting in accordance with his nature exonerates him from blame. If, conversely, the necessity of our actions does not exonerate from blame, then the offender is to blame, and God is not to blame for punishing.

Ingenious though this defense is, Butler has overlooked one possibility: maybe *our* actions are necessitated, but God's are not. In that case, it may strike some that it would be unjust for God to punish us, given that we could not help ourselves.

REVELATION

The truths we can work out by reflecting on the world God has created may also be communicated to us directly by God, either by physical manifestations, such as the tablets of the Law, or by inspired prophecy. That the world is under the moral government of God and that we shall be judged in a future life are indeed claims that are revealed in Scripture, as well as by natural reason. But the Bible purports also to reveal much that could not otherwise be known, including especially the role of Christ in our salvation. It is with these claims that the second half of the *Analogy* is concerned. The strategy of this part of the work is necessarily more defensive than the first. Whereas in the first part Butler contends that what is revealed to us about God's moral purpose is also independently *supported* by what we observe of the way the world is run, in the second part he seeks to show only that what is revealed about the method of our salvation is *compatible* with what we know about the workings of this world. That distinction is built into the enterprise. For what can be known only by revelation cannot be independently supported by natural religion.

To deists and other people of the Enlightenment, the Bible, on which the specific doctrines of Christianity were based, seemed an implausible mishmash of myth, miracle, and divine mediation produced in a barbarous and superstitious age. In the second part of the *Analogy*, Butler addresses a number of these criticisms.

1. Revelation is superfluous.
2. No rational person could, or should, believe in miracles.
3. The role of Christ as Redeemer is both incomprehensible and unnecessary.
4. Revelation should be universal; if not, it is discriminatory and morally objectionable.
5. Appeals to mystery and to our ignorance are a shallow subterfuge to conceal how ridiculous are some aspects of the Bible in general, and of Christianity in particular.

Butler's strategy in responding to each of these objections is the same. We are necessarily ignorant of a great part of God's scheme in creation. So we must not assume that he will order things in the manner that seems sensible to us, with our limited and partial understanding. We may not always understand *why* God has done things this way rather than that. But we can see that God governs *this* world by the very principles to which objection is made when it comes to revelation. Since deists accept that this world manifests signs of God's intelligent and righteous governance, they cannot consistently reject a revelation that operates along similar lines.

First, to suppose that we stand in no need of revelation is to suppose that we need nothing more than to follow the precepts of natural religion to stand in a right relation to God. But it is clear that we cannot work out our own salvation and need "supernatural instruction and assistance."[12] In addition, revelation reinforces the evidence for natural religion and supplies answers to worrying questions that natural reason cannot answer.

Second, the performance of miracles by the founder of Christianity and his followers is crucial to establishing the authority of revelation. Without miracles, we would have no reason to accept their message rather than any other. But, the objection runs, to be credible, don't reports of miracles require *much more*

---

12. *Analogy*, II, i, 2.

evidence in their favor than testimony to everyday occurrences, not least because they violate the laws of nature? Butler responds with two main arguments. First, miracles are not unusual in being unlikely. There is an equally strong presumption against many ordinary nonmiraculous events. But we do not require much by way of evidence to believe them. It is very unlikely that any particular person should win a national lottery. Yet we happily, and rightly, accept reports of who the winner is this week, without demanding extraordinary proof. Second, the special or peculiar events that accompany and attest to a revelation need not be thought of as *violations of the laws of nature*. We cannot be sure whether the course of nature has always been the same; nor can we be sure what it now is. Many phenomena once thought to be physically impossible have later been discovered to be not only possible but actual.[13] What is significant about the miracles of our Savior and the apostles is that they exhibit a power not given to ordinary people; a power that we may assume, from the context, to be of divine origin.

Third, there is no presumption, from the analogy of nature, against the idea that God would reconcile himself to the world through a mediator. For the human animal, as with every other animal, comes into existence and is preserved by the mediation of parents and others. So there is no reason to suppose that the same does not apply to our spiritual existence.

But why, it might be asked, is mediation required? Surely God could simply forgive the repentant. Butler's answer is that no doubt he *could*, but the analogy of nature suggests that he *may not*, for reasons we cannot now comprehend. We see that misfortune and disaster often, but not inevitably, follows from deeds of folly or vice. Sometimes, indeed, there are remedies, ways to prevent the bad consequences of our actions. But not always. Repentance and sorrow may be of no avail, and one foolish act in our youth may cause ruin to ourselves and others, however much we later regret it. If this is how things pan out in this world, why suppose it will be different in the next? We might suppose that according to the general laws of divine government, sinners will be punished, however repentant they may be, *unless someone interposes and mediates between us and God*. Nothing in the analogy of nature renders this unlikely.

Fourth, why was revelation made to some but not to others and at a particular point in history? Surely such favoritism is unworthy of God. Butler's response is, as always, to appeal to the analogy of nature. We do not find in this world, which is under the moral government of God, that all are treated equally and that no favors are bestowed. So why should we suppose that revelation would be distributed on different principles?

---

13. Butler cites electricity and magnetism as examples.

Finally, Butler raises the following objection: it is, surely, a feeble defense to try "to solve difficulties in revelation, by saying, that there are the same in natural religion; when what is wanting is to clear both of them, of these their common, as well as other their respective, difficulties."[14] He replies as follows:

1. "It would be absurd to give up reasoning in areas where certainty is unavailable, and difficulties remain. Is it not a poor thing, for a physician to have so little knowledge in the cure of diseases, as even the most eminent have? To act upon conjecture and guess, where the life of man is concerned? Undoubtedly it is: but not in comparison of having no skill at all in that useful art, and being obliged to act wholly in the dark."[15]
2. It is disingenuous for people to say they only have objections to revealed, but not to natural, religion. For in truth their objections are objections to both.
3. If we have good reason to be prudent in respect of our temporal affairs, even though there is much we do not know about how things will turn out, there is equally good reason to take care of our spiritual welfare, despite our considerable ignorance.
4. People object that if Christianity were true, the evidence would not be so doubtful. To Butler, this is another example of our supposing that God *must* act in a certain way because *we* think he should. But the uncertainty under which we have to make decisions in this life shows that this is not how God organizes things.
5. The purpose of the *Analogy* is "not to vindicate the character of God, but to shew the obligations of men."[16]
6. Butler's defensive apologetic has employed only the principles conceded by the deists. There are other things that he firmly believes that would strengthen the case for Christianity, but those fall outside the scope of this work.

CONTRIBUTIONS TO THE FIELD OF APOLOGETICS

Almost all commentators on the *Analogy* begin by conceding that Butler's argument might be thought to have only historical significance since deism died out in the mid-eighteenth century. But they go on (mostly) to say that, despite this, parts of it can still be "rescued."[17] This concession is historically misleading. It is

---

14. *Analogy*, II. viii. 2.
15. *Analogy*, II. viii. 4.
16. *Analogy*, II. viii. 8.
17. See, for example, in addition to the articles in *Moral and Religious Thought* already cited, C. D.

true that *deism*, as a serious theological movement, no longer exists, but that does not mean the ideas behind it are dead. Far from it. Surveys suggest that there are a very large number of ordinary people who are "spiritual but not religious." They believe in some transcendent creative power that is also, perhaps, immanent in the world, and they seek communion with that power by a variety of spiritual practices. But to seek is not necessarily to know where to look, still less to find. And Butler's sober arguments, if sound, should be a crucial guide for such seekers. In particular, he puts forward three central claims that, though perhaps unpopular, should be taken seriously. First is his claim that this power is a *moral* being who rewards and punishes according to merit. The idea of God as righteous judge is not much in evidence among the "spiritual but not religious," who tend to like their spirituality warm and fuzzy, but that is all the more reason for considering it. Second, the claims of Christianity are not as fanciful, or as ill-supported by the evidence, as many modern people believe. Third, and perhaps most importantly, we need to respond to Butler's version of Pascal's Wager. In practical matters, it is folly to wait for all the evidence to be in before making a decision or a commitment. Our own well-being, and that of others, requires us to make the best bet, even when the chances of winning are low. In Butler's view, it would be a brave person who bet against there being a righteous judge. If there is such a judge, we should live virtuously—but that is something we have good reason to do anyway. Equally, it is only sensible to examine the claims of Christianity very seriously and to consider whether we can hope to be reconciled to a righteous Governor solely by our own efforts or whether we need divine aid.

But how strong are Butler's arguments? If there is no life after death, then the rest of his case becomes of merely academic interest. Without a postmortem existence, there can be no final judgment. Unfortunately, as we have seen, this part of Butler's case is by far the weakest. Even a superficial knowledge of the brain suggests that it is the seat of consciousness and that as it is damaged or decayed, so rational thought and awareness are impaired. We can reasonably infer, on the basis of these observations, that once the brain is dead, the person is also. Survival after death is not the *natural* next stage of our lives.

Can a different case be made for Butler's conclusion? Everyday biological observation will not, as Butler supposed, support the claim that we survive death. But such survival is not, of course, impossible. God may miraculously raise us from the dead, as Scripture claims. Thus, Butler may simply have miscategorized the proper source of a confidence in life after death. It should be seen

---

Broad, "Bishop Butler as Theologian" in C. D. Broad, *Religion, Philosophy and Psychical Research* (London: Routledge & Kegan Paul, 1953), 202–19; E. C. Mossner, *Bishop Butler and the Age of Reason* (New York: Macmillan, 1936), 231.

not as a conclusion of natural theology but rather as a part of revealed religion, to be assessed along with the other parts of the Christian revelation. Or we could appeal to observational evidence for surviving death, but of a different kind from the sort that Butler offers.

If we accept that there is a real possibility, albeit fairly small, of survival after death, then the rest of Butler's case is pretty strong. If we want to know more about the creative power behind the universe, where else can we look but at the world, including—centrally for Butler—our own consciousness and conscience? The existence of conscience, especially, is a strong reason for believing that we are the product of a Being who cares about justice, honesty, and benevolence.

Butler's most important legacy, in my opinion, is his discussion of the influence that probable reasoning should have on practice. Employing these insights, he builds a powerful case for what we might term Butler's Wager. Given the gravity of what is at stake, the evidence from natural religion, and the testimonial support for the Christian revelation, it would be a brave person who dismissed those claims without careful thought.[18]

BIBLIOGRAPHY

Anon. "Deism." In the *Internet Encyclopedia of Philosophy*. https://www.iep.utm.edu/deismeng/. See also the chapter by Michael McClymond in this volume for a helpful outline of deism.

Babolin, Albino. *"Deus Absconditas*: Some Notes on the Bearing of the Hiddenness of God upon Butler's and Pascal's Criticism of Deism". Pages 29–36 in *Joseph Butler's Moral and Religious Thought*. Ed. by C. Cunliffe. Oxford: Oxford University Press, 1992.

Bartlett, Thomas. *Memoirs of the Life, Character and Writings of Joseph Butler*. London: Parker, 1839.

Bernard, J. H. *The Works of Bishop Butler vol. 2*. London: Macmillan, 1900.

Broad, C. D. "Bishop Butler as Theologian." Pages 202–19 in *Religion, Philosophy and Psychical Research*. Ed. by C. D. Broad. London: Routledge & Kegan Paul, 1953.

Brown, David. "Butler and Deism." Pages 7–28 in *Joseph Butler's Moral and Religious Thought*. Ed. by C. Cunliffe. Oxford: Oxford University Press, 1992.

Butler, Joseph. *The Analogy of Religion, Natural and Revealed, to the Constitution and Course of Nature. To which are added, Two Brief Dissertations: I. Of personal identity. II. Of the nature of virtue*. Second edition: (corrected): London: John & Paul Knapton, 1736.

Collins, Anthony. *Discourse of Freethinking. London*, 1713.

Cunliffe, Christopher., ed. *Joseph Butler's Moral and Religious Thought*. Oxford: Oxford University Press, 1992.

———. "Butler, Joseph (1692–1752)." *Oxford Dictionary of National Biography*. Oxford: Oxford University Press, 2008, https://www-oxforddnb-com.proxy.lib.fsu.edu/view/10.1093/ref:odnb/9780198614128 .001.0001/odnb-9780198614128-e-4198.

McClymond, Michael J. "Jonathan Edwards: Dogmatics as Apologetics" Pages 324–343 in *The History of Apologetics*. Grand Rapids: Zondervan, 2020.

Mossner, E. C. *Bishop Butler and the Age of Reason*. New York: Macmillan, 1936.

Penelhum, Terence. *Butler*. London: Routledge & Kegan Paul, 1985.

Tindal, Matthew. *Christianity as Old as the Creation, or the Gospel a Republication of the Religion of Nature*. London, 1730.

Toland, John. *Christianity Not Mysterious*. London, 1696.

Young, B. W. "Theology in the Church of England." Pages 392–428 in *The Oxford History of Anglicanism, Vol. II*. Ed. by Jeremy Gregory. Oxford: Oxford University Press, 2017.

---

18. I am grateful to Ben Forrest, Eve Garrard, and David White for comments on earlier drafts.

Part Four

NINETEENTH-CENTURY APOLOGISTS

The nineteenth century was marked by turbulence across much of western Europe. The legacy of the French Revolution of 1789 was political instability and intellectual uncertainty across much of Europe as French revolutionary armies aimed to extend their revolution to Germany and Italy. The Napoleonic Wars created further instability, leading to political revolt in parts of Germany, inspiring writers such as Karl Marx to develop radical political philosophies. Both the French Revolutionaries and Marx saw religion as a baleful and unnecessary legacy of the past, which perpetuated the interests and concerns of the ruling elites. Christianity was faced with a series of new intellectual challenges, which demanded apologetic responses.

John Henry Newman illustrates this new importance of apologetics in Great Britain. Newman served as vicar of the University Church of St. Mary, Oxford, and was highly regarded as a preacher. Newman was alarmed by what he saw as a dangerous drift toward political and theological liberalism in England during the 1830s and used his university pulpit to reassert the rationality and moral coherence of the Christian faith. The eight volumes of Newman's "Parochial and Plain Sermons" delivered in the University Church in Oxford from 1835 to 1841 are packed with apologetic insights. As an apologist, Newman was aware of the importance of establishing a distinctively Christian academic institution that was capable of connecting Christianity with its teaching and research across disciplines. Newman's *Idea of a University* remains a landmark in the recognition of the place of educational institutions in apologetics.

Others, alarmed at the political drift of this period and concerned that Christianity had become preoccupied with institutional concerns, set out to reconnect the Christian faith with the subjective lives of individuals. Such strategies had already been developed in the late seventeenth and early eighteenth century, when pietism secured a significant influence over evangelical Christians in England, Germany, and America. Pietism appealed to the "logic of the heart" and opened up new forms of apologetics based on the transformation of the individual—a demonstration, in effect, that Christianity was *real* and not simply *true*.

One of the most important developments of this approach is found in Danish writer **Søren Kierkegaard**, now widely seen as a forerunner of existentialism. Kierkegaard was skeptical about the apologists of his day who tried to demonstrate that the truths of Christianity were rationally acceptable. For Kierkegaard, Christianity was about more than mere intellectual assent; it was about the transformation of the experiential world of the believer. There was, in his view, a serious risk of impoverishing Christianity by reducing it to rational principles and failing to appreciate its relational and transformational aspects. A purely objective or historical apologetic approach cannot do justice to the central themes of Christianity.

Kierkegaard's critique of reason has led some to suppose he was irrational; a more reliable assessment is that, like Pascal before him, he demonstrated the limitations of certain forms of rationalist apologetics. In emphasizing the subjectivity of truth, Kierkegaard was not lapsing into some form of relativism but pointing to the need for an individual to be inwardly transformed by the truth of the gospel, not simply persuaded of its correctness. Kierkegaard's impact on apologetics did not become significant until after World War I, when his works began to be translated into English and German. Writers such as Emil Brunner realized how Kierkegaard opened the way to relational and existential approaches to apologetics, allowing them to map central biblical themes to his existential framework.

Yet others felt it was important for Christians to engage the specific challenges raised by biblical criticism and evolutionary theory during the nineteenth century. Scottish theologian **James Orr** is one of the most important British examples of this approach to apologetics. Although Orr offered significant defenses of traditional approaches to the Christian understanding of the nature of God or the authority of Scripture in light of modern challenges, his apologetic significance lies more in his appeal to Christianity as a worldview capable of accommodating the many aspects of our experience of the world. In his classic work *The Christian View of God*, Orr highlighted the importance of concentrating on the "exposition and vindication of the Christian view of things as a whole" rather than treating Christianity as a collection of unrelated beliefs.

The American Revolution, unlike its French counterpart, did not have an explicitly antireligious agenda. A number of issues lay behind this revolution, including the burdens of taxation, the lack of due representation, and the desire for freedom from the British Crown. Yet while much criticism was directed against the Church of England as the colonial religious establishment, there was no hostility toward Christianity as such. Indeed, in important ways, the Great Awakening had deepened the hold of faith on the American colonies and may have helped create a strong sense of values that were hostile to British Crown rule, such as a growing sense that all people were created equal by God.

American apologists thus engaged questions that were quite distinct from those of their European counterparts during the nineteenth century. The growing public consensus on the importance of law in public life was reflected in the emergence of schools of apologetics, which focused on evidential apologetics. This is particularly well represented in **Simon Greenleaf**, who applied the criteria of legal evidence to the gospel writers and concluded that the case for the truth of Christianity could be proven beyond a reasonable doubt. Greenleaf's innovative approach in applying legal criteria and strategies in apologetics has had a particular resonance within North America and has been widely applied by his successors.

A theme of many Protestant apologists of the nineteenth century is the need to avoid doctrinal innovation and to affirm and demonstrate the historical reliability and spiritual authenticity of traditional formulations of faith. This strategy is perhaps best seen in the Old Princeton School through the writings of **B. B. Warfield**. For Warfield, apologetics serves as a prolegomenon to systematic theology. This close interconnection of apologetics and theology is one of the most distinctive themes of Warfield's approach. Yet for many, the most important aspect of Warfield's apologetics lies in his recognition that the trustworthiness of Christianity rests on the trustworthiness of its foundational documents, so that the defense of the historical and theological reliability of Scripture is to be seen as being of critical theological importance. This insight remained important for many American Protestant apologists in the early twentieth century, to be considered in the next part of this work.

SIMON GREENLEAF

A Defense That Never Rested

CRAIG A. PARTON

Simon Greenleaf (1783–1853), the greatest living authority of his day on the common law rules of evidence and one of the foundational faculty members of Harvard Law School, is the father of what has come to be known today as the school of "juridical," or "legal," apologetics. Applying the laws of legal evidence to the gospel writers, Greenleaf concluded that their testimony would stand up in any common law trial court and that the case for the truth of Christianity could be proven to a legal certainty. Greenleaf's innovative methodology and application of legal techniques in the defense of Christian truth claims has given birth to a vibrant effort on the part of the legally-trained to establish the truth of Christianity "beyond a reasonable doubt." Greenleaf is a particularly superb example of a Christian who saw the insights of his vocation as the opportunity to defend "many convincing proofs" (Acts 1:3) that God was "reconciling the world to himself in Christ" (2 Cor 5:19).

HISTORICAL BACKGROUND

Simon Greenleaf was born in Newburyport, Massachusetts, in 1783. Shortly thereafter his parents moved to Maine. Greenleaf stayed in Massachusetts, where he was raised by his grandfather. He attended Latin school and became proficient in the Greek and Roman classics, which he read in the original languages. He also analyzed an attack on Christianity done in French by a physician. That attack focused on the trial of Christ and its supposed incongruity with first-century Jewish legal procedure.[1]

At the age of sixteen, Greenleaf rejoined his parents in Maine, and two years later, in 1801, he joined the law office of Ezekiel Whitman. It was under Whitman

---

1. Joseph Salvador, *Historie des Institutions de Moise et due Peuple Hebreu*, 4 vols. (1828–1830). This work as it relates to the trial of Christ is commented on by Greenleaf in chapter 4 of Greenleaf's classic apologetical work, *The Testimony of the Evangelists.*

that Greenleaf received his tutelage since formal education in law was essentially unavailable. Only the College of William & Mary had a functioning law school at the time. It was not until 1817 that Harvard Law School was founded.

Whitman would later be elected to Congress and then became the chief justice of the Maine Supreme Court. Greenleaf followed Whitman to the Maine Supreme Court, where Greenleaf became its reporter, or clerk. He compiled the key cases of the Maine Supreme Court from 1820 to 1832. Greenleaf also served in the first Maine legislature to which he was elected in 1820. His career then took a fortuitous turn when the fledgling Harvard Law School approached him about a professorship in law.

Harvard Law School (HLS) had first opened its doors in 1817 pursuant to a grant from Isaac Royall Jr.[2] The school struggled initially and had only six students enrolled in 1829. The famed United States Supreme Court Justice Joseph Story changed the trajectory of HLS when he joined the faculty in 1829 as Dane Professor of Law, a chair that Greenleaf himself occupied beginning in 1846 and shortly after Story's death in 1845.

Greenleaf came to HLS in 1833, assuming the chair of Royall professor of law, named for the founder of the school. Greenleaf would eventually become internationally recognized as the greatest authority on common law evidence in the English-speaking world.[3] Writers and professors in the field today still reference his *Treatise on the Laws of Evidence*, which consisted of three volumes and was published between 1842 and 1853. Greenleaf was recognized for his scholarship by receiving an honorary doctorate from Harvard in 1834, one from the University of Massachusetts-Amherst in 1845, and then a third from the University of Alabama in 1852. In recognition of Greenleaf's influence in the area of the integration of law and theology, the Simon Greenleaf School of Law was founded in 1980 and was later assumed by Trinity International University. It focuses on training students in the areas of law, theology, human rights, and apologetics.[4]

While at Harvard, and because of his interest in foreign missions, Greenleaf spent time assisting with the writing of the Constitution for the new nation of Liberia

---

2. The Royall Professorship in Law at Harvard is the oldest continuously endowed chair of law in the country.

3. Ross Clifford, *Leading Lawyers Case for the Resurrection* (Edmonton, Canada: Canadian Institute for Law, Theology and Public Policy, 1996).

4. The Simon Greenleaf School of Law was founded in 1980 with fifteen initial faculty members focusing, as noted, on the areas of law, theology, apologetics, and human rights. The inaugural edition of the *Simon Greenleaf Law Review* reprinted Boston University Law School Dean Edmund Bennett's careful work examining alleged errors and contradictions in the gospels, along with a critique of Thomas Paine's *The Age of Reason*. The first dean of the Simon Greenleaf School of Law was the renowned and controversial legal scholar John Warwick Montgomery, holder of eleven earned degrees in history, law, theology, and philosophy and a legal apologist who has dedicated his professional life to the integration of law, theology, and human rights.

in 1846–47. Greenleaf's broadly orthodox Christian theology is evident in this Constitution, which at one point recognizes "with devout gratitude, the goodness of God, in granting to us the blessings of the Christian religion, and political, religious and civil liberty." It speaks of all people having the right to worship God "according to their conscience" and makes explicit that there would be no religious test for holding political office.[5] Greenleaf also wrote into that Constitution an explicit prohibition against slavery and affirmed the right of women to own property. He served for many years while at Harvard as president of the Massachusetts Bible Society. In addition, and while at Harvard, he successfully argued the United States Supreme Court case of *Charles River Bridge v. Warren Bridge* 36 U.S. (11 Pet.) 420 (1837), which dealt with the construction and interpretation of public contracts.[6]

THEOLOGICAL CONTEXT

Greenleaf's integration of his legal training with the defense of the gospel stems directly from an orthodox theology of vocation—seeing Christ as center and circumference of all of life and seeing the points of integration between one's vocation and one's calling as a Christian believer in a secular society. From his earliest years in law, Greenleaf displayed an interest in integrating legal reasoning into a defense of the Christian faith. Beginning in 1817 he delivered a series of lectures on the popular subject of Freemasonry and whether it was consistent with biblical revelation.[7] After an exhaustive analysis of the historical origins of Masonry found in Greek, Latin, and Egyptian sources, Greenleaf concludes that a true Mason must become a Christian to properly understand the teachings of Masonry: "To this comprehensive view of Masonry, we should add, that . . . the character of a mason is never complete till he becomes also a Christian."[8]

Professor Greenleaf also worked with a set of volumes originally published in Paris by Joseph Salvador (*Histoire des Institutions de Moise et due Peuple Hébreu*) and in particular a section of that work entitled "The Jewish Account of the Trial of Jesus." Greenleaf critiqued Salvador's work and concluded that the trial of Jesus was indeed "judicial murder" and was in violation of the applicable criminal procedural rules developed in the Old Testament as, at least in theory, held to by the religious authorities of the time.

---

5. See Art. I, sections 2 and 3 of the Declaration of Rights in the Constitution of Liberia.

6. Interestingly, opposing Greenleaf in that case was none other than Daniel Webster.

7. Simon Greenleaf, *A Brief Inquiry into the Origins and Principles of Free Masonry* (Portland: Shirley, 1820). The volume has been reprinted by Facsimile Publishers of New Delhi, India, 2016. We note later Greenleaf's familiarity with some of the solid apologetical works of his time as is reflected in his annotations at the conclusion of *Testimony of the Evangelists*. See *infra*, at ft. 44.

8. Greenleaf, *A Brief Inquiry*, 72.

APOLOGETIC RESPONSE AND METHODOLOGY

Greenleaf begins *The Testimony of the Evangelists* (written in 1846) by first noting that of all vocations, the legal profession is uniquely committed to the concept of "evidence."[9] Lawyers deal with all classes of people, from cradle to grave, and they should be expected to give special and close attention to the evidences produced in favor of Christianity. From the start, Greenleaf, as C. S. Lewis after him, allows no "moral teacher" label for Jesus if he is found *not* to have risen from the dead. Jesus, if not God, is an imposter and enslaver of people and an enemy of human liberty throughout the world. But if Jesus is who he claims to be, there are enormous consequences in this life and the next.[10]

Greenleaf next discusses the nature of the factual case for Christianity. Christianity professes only to convince the candid and serious inquirer and does not present a deductive case rising to the level of 100 percent, or absolute, certainty.[11] This is a critical apologetical point: *Christianity is based on verifiable facts, and those facts are contained in the eyewitness accounts.* The case for Christianity must be built on a factual foundation and not on presuppositions that require the nonbeliever to assume material facts as true. The case for Christianity is built from the bottom up, not from the top down.

Importantly, Greenleaf grounds his discussion of the reliability of the testimony on the critical accuracy of the text that contains that testimony. If the documents in which this testimony resides are corrupted, or "plastic,"[12] there can be no confidence in what that record contains. The documents either have come down to us in a reliable manner, or the defense of Christianity is totally futile: "That the text of the Four Evangelists has been handed down to us in the state in which it was originally written, that is, without having been materially corrupted or falsified, either by heretics or Christians; are facts which we are entitled to assume as true, until the contrary is shown. The genuineness of these writings really admits of as little doubt, and is susceptible of as ready proof, as that of any ancient writings whatever."[13]

Thus, as a first principle one must know if the document containing the testimony of the witnesses is genuine—that is, has come down to us in the form

---

9. Simon Greenleaf, *The Testimony of the Evangelists: Examined by the Rules of Evidence Administered in Courts of Justice* (Grand Rapids: Kregel, 1995), 9–10 (hereafter referred to as "*Testimony*").

10. Greenleaf, *Testimony*, 10.

11. Greenleaf points out that "proof of matters of fact rests upon moral evidence alone," and not upon evidence excluding the possibility of error such as mathematical formulas. Greenleaf, *Testimony*, 28.

12. A term unfortunately used recently by theologian Jeffrey Kloha to describe the biblical text. Kloha would end up leaving his theological faculty appointment at Concordia Seminary St. Louis after his position was thoroughly exposed and devastated in a public debate with lawyer John Warwick Montgomery.

13. Greenleaf, *Testimony*, 16.

in which it was originally written or has instead suffered material corruption. Greenleaf calls this his "first rule" and contends it applies "with equal force to all ancient writings."[14] Thus, the biblical writers are subject to the exact same treatment as Tacitus, Suetonius, and Plato. The law requires that any document whose admissibility is sought must be genuine or "authentic" (that is, what it purports to be). Fail to prove the genuineness or authenticity of a document, and it will not be admissible to prove the truth of its contents. In support, Greenleaf cites to the "ancient document rule" as formulated in the law of evidence: "Every document, apparently ancient, coming from the proper repository or custody, and bearing on its face no evident marks of forgery, the law presumes to be genuine, and devolves on the opposing party the burden of proving it to be otherwise."[15]

A document is said to come from the proper repository when "it is found in the place where, and under the care of persons with whom, such writings might naturally and reasonably be expected to be found."[16] If the document is found in that proper place and in that proper custody and shows no evidence of forgery, "the law presumes they are genuine, and they are permitted to be read in evidence, unless the opposing party is able successfully to impeach them. . . . The presumption of law is the judgment of charity."[17]

As for Scripture in general and the gospels in particular, the pertinent manuscripts have been used in the church from "time immemorial" and thus are found where they would be expected to be found (as opposed to being found, for example, in a hunting lodge in Moose, Wyoming). Greenleaf cannot help himself at this point, jabbing at Mormon revelation by saying that the biblical claim is not that the Scripture was written on golden plates and transported directly down to earth and back to heaven by angels.[18] The fact that we do not have originals of the gospels is not a problem because there is a rich manuscript lineage and a Christian community that had an interest in accurate copies being made from which the original could be faithfully reconstructed. Stamping *QED* to the argument,[19] Greenleaf reminds the reader that the sixth-century Roman civil law code for all of Europe (*Corpus Juris Civilis*) is received as authentic and genuine on far less manuscript evidence than that of the gospels.[20]

---

14. Greenleaf, *Testimony*, 16–17.
15. Greenleaf, *Testimony*, 16.
16. Ibid.
17. Ibid.
18. Greenleaf, *Testimony*, 17. He later characterizes Mormonism as in the highly dubious class of "pretender revelation." *Testimony*, 48–49, at note 8.
19. *Quad Erat Demonstrandum*, "that which has been demonstrated."
20. Greenleaf, *Testimony*, 17–18.

Only after arguing that the gospels are authentic and genuine does Greenleaf move to his classic five-part test to analyze the writers' veracity, since establishing a document as genuine and authentic does not mean its content are true.[21]

Testimony of the Evangelists: Examined by the Rules of Evidence Administered in Courts of Justice is now widely known as a seminal text in legal apologetics. It is important to first note the focus of Greenleaf's inquiry in this work—or more specifically what his focus is *not*. Greenleaf's approach does not focus on the so-called traditional arguments for the existence of God. Creation is not the focus and neither are end-time events. Nor is the focus on the Pauline Epistles, the general epistles, or the Old Testament. Instead, his focus is on the words of Matthew, Mark, Luke, and John and, in particular, the facts relating to the life, death, and resurrection of Jesus Christ. Greenleaf makes clear that this thoroughly christocentric apologetic is also fully fact-infused: "The foundation of our religion is a basis of fact—the fact of the birth, ministry, miracles, death, resurrection, and ascension of Jesus Christ."[22]

In this magnum opus, Greenleaf proceeds to set forth a five-part test to determine the accuracy of the testimony of these four witnesses: (1) are the witnesses *honest*?; (2) do the witnesses have the *ability* to accurately record the facts they recite?; (3) are there a sufficient *number* of witnesses, and are they *consistent* in what they record?; (4) does the testimony *conform* with our experience?; and (5) does the testimony *conform with other facts* known about that period of history?

APOLOGETIC TEST 1: ADMISSIONS AGAINST INTEREST

The *first test* to apply is "to the witnesses themselves, to see who and what manner of men they were."[23] In other words, is their character trustworthy, and are they honest about themselves and others? Here Greenleaf focuses in on the natural human proclivity to shade the truth when talking about one's own conduct or the conduct of close associates or to always see one's own actions in the most favorable light. The law talks about "admissions *against* interest"[24] as one of the strongest signs that a witness is telling the truth.

The gospel writers made such admissions against interest repeatedly and dramatically and otherwise gave indicia of their credibility. For example, Mark, who is generally thought to have had direct contact with Peter, wrote of Peter's

---

21. The Qur'an, for example, may be authentic and genuine (that is, we may have what was originally recorded and the document comes without significant time lag), but that hardly requires that we concede that its *contents* are true.

22. Greenleaf, *Testimony*, 12.

23. Greenleaf, *Testimony*, 13.

24. See, for example, California Evidence Code section 1220. Admissions against interest are not barred by the rule against the admissibility of hearsay testimony.

cowardice before a little girl and Peter's betrayal shortly after claiming a kind of hyperloyalty to Jesus. In addition, Mark mentioned Jesus's prophesy that Peter would deny him, as well as recounted Jesus's direct and less than complimentary statement that Satan was directly using Peter. As an example of the kind of detail and credibility we would expect from truthful witnesses, Greenleaf notes that Luke was a physician (Col 4:14), and it is in his gospel that medical details are abundant. Luke indeed supplied the kind of detail one would expect from a doctor,[25] especially details about the crucifixion that establish Jesus's death on the cross. In addition, the gospel writers did not shy away from recording the harsh words of Jesus. Such examples are throughout the gospels and include that he is the only way to the Father (John 14:6), that some were to give away all their possessions in order to follow him (Matt 19:21), that some would die violent deaths (John 21:18–19) that some would be forced to forsake mother and father (Matt 19:29), and that the whole world would hate them for following him (John 15:18–25).

Greenleaf's conclusion was that the gospel writers were honest and "hide nothing"—if they were trying to gloss over their sins and weaknesses, they failed miserably. Their staggering and repeated "admissions against interest" are indicia of their reliability.

APOLOGETIC TEST 2: ABILITY FOR HONEST REPORTING

Second in Greenleaf's analysis of the testimony of the evangelists is whether the gospel writers had the ability to get the story straight. The ability of these writers to record the truth is directly dependent on their opportunity to either observe the facts directly or interview those who did and check out their testimony for themselves.

In this regard, Matthew, John, and Peter (via Mark) as disciples had repeated opportunities to personally observe the events they recorded. For example, John carefully recorded the execution of Jesus and noted his own presence at the foot of the cross (John 19:16–37). The record is also clear that Peter was present at Jesus's trial and crucifixion (Matt 26:56–75; Luke 23:49). John and Peter went to the empty tomb (John 20), and Matthew, John, and Peter all saw the resurrected Christ (Matt 28:16-17; John 20:25; 2 Pet 1:16). In addition, Greenleaf notes that Matthew and Luke were in professions in which attention to detail

---

25. Greenleaf notes that in Luke we get the detail expected of a trained physician. Thus, Luke does not just say the hand of a man was shriveled but that his "*right* hand was shriveled" (Luke 6:6) and not just that a person had leprosy but that he was "covered with leprosy" (Luke 5:12). In addition, Luke records the "woman with a hemorrhage," Jesus and his sweating of blood in the garden, and a follower cutting off the ear of the servant of the high priest and Jesus's healing of that ear on the spot (Luke 22:44–51). Greenleaf, *Testimony*, 24–25.

was built into their practices. Matthew was a tax collector and well-versed in the world of fraud and deception—not one likely to have a big-fish story pulled off on him. Luke, as a physician, was professionally trained in careful analysis in order to prescribe remedies and, again, was not likely to be superficial or naive about the observable world.[26] Trial lawyer Walter Chandler summarizes it nicely when he says that "the writings themselves indicate extraordinary mental vigor, as well as cultivated intelligence" and that Luke and John have "the invariable characteristics of intellectual depth and culture. The 'ignorant fishermen' idea is certainly not applicable to the Gospel writers."[27]

APOLOGETIC TEST 3: SUFFICIENCY AND CONSISTENCY OF THE WITNESSES

Greenleaf's third test to apply to the evangelists is whether there are sufficient witnesses and whether those witnesses are consistent or are colluding. This test is concerned with whether there are enough differences in the gospel accounts to rule out collusion and yet enough commonality to conclude that the gospels can be harmonized to present the life of Christ in polyphonic harmony.

Lawyers have carefully studied the art of detecting when a witness is lying or colluding with other witnesses and how to expose this type of collusion at trial. First, Greenleaf notes that testimony is generally presumed to be truthful unless impeached or otherwise successfully attacked on cross-examination. This is consistent with the way we assume people are telling the truth and not perjuring themselves unless the evidence indicates otherwise. As just one example of work on witness perjury in the legal context, we note the fourfold construct by McCloskey and Schoenberg that has been called "the finest work on that subject."[28] That construct involves the following factors: "*internal* and *external* defects in the *witness himself* on the one hand and in the *testimony itself* on the other."[29] This construct is already found in Greenleaf's five-part test for determining the credibility of a witness.

Second, do the witnesses give sufficient detail to allow cross-examination? Lying or untruthful witnesses usually testify in little detail or at least reserve detailed testimony for that part of their examination that is not central to their perjury. In the case of the gospel writers, the four accounts are rich in overlying

---

26. Greenleaf, *Testimony*, 19–25.

27. Walter M. Chandler, *The Trial of Jesus from a Lawyer's Standpoint* (New York: Empire, 1908), 19.

28. Alan Saltzman, "Criminal Law: How to Expose Perjury through Cross-Examination," *Los Angeles Daily Journal*, 4 November 1982.

29. Patrick L. McCloskey and Ronald L. Schoenberg, *Criminal Law Advocacy*, vol. 5 (New York: Bender 1984), para. 12.01[b]. This construct is applied to the New Testament writers to vindicate their integrity by John Warwick Montgomery in *Human Rights and Human Dignity* (Grand Rapids: Zondervan, 1986), 140ff.

detail that can be readily cross-examined. For example, Luke could easily have avoided all attempts at future verification of his accuracy and said *"once upon a time* the word of God came to John the Baptist." Rather, he put it this way: "In the fifteenth year of the reign of Tiberius Caesar—when Pontius Pilate was governor of Judea, Herod being tetrarch of Galilee, his brother Phillip tetrarch of Ituraea and Trachonitis, and Lysanias tetrarch of Abilene—during the high-priesthood of Annas and Caiaphas, the word of God came to John son of Zechariah in the wilderness" (Luke 3:1–2).

No single gospel author claimed to give a definitive account of the life of Jesus, and John explicitly disavowed claims to exhaustive records of the life and ministry of Christ (c.f., John 20:30–31; 21:25). In fact, lawyers such as Greenleaf have noted that the presence of four different but not inconsistent versions of events is one of the strongest evidences of the integrity and general reliability of the gospel writers.

There is a widely held perception among nonlawyers that lying is fairly easy to pull off in a court of law. Nothing is further from the truth, and the Gospel writers, if trying to collude and conjure up a fraud, set their own death traps by giving abundant detail capable of verification or falsification. Legal scholars after Greenleaf have described in great detail the tortuous labyrinth that a deceptive witness must navigate to escape the clutches of skillful cross-examination.[30] And as for the argument that the gospel writers were not formally cross-examined in a court of law, Greenleaf notes that the Romans and religious leaders of the time had the "means, motive and opportunity" to decimate the apostolic witnesses if indeed they could.[31]

APOLOGETIC TEST 4: CONFORMITY TO EXPERIENCE

Greenleaf's fourth test centers on whether the testimony conforms with experience. Do the writers record events and human behavior in a plausible manner? The gospel writers presented the events and human reactions to those events in a relentlessly believable manner. Take the resurrection, for example. The apostles are hardly presented in a flattering light. Some have already gone back to fishing, others are scared to death of the religious authorities, and none of them believe the first witnesses' testimony, presumably at least in part because it is evidence presented by women. The apostles needed a tactile experience with Jesus Christ to conquer their unbelief (John 20).

Thus, when the gospel writers come in contact with, for example, miraculous healings by Jesus, Greenleaf notes as follows:

---

30. Richard A. Givens, *Advocacy* (New York: McGraw-Hill, 1980), 12.
31. Greenleaf, *Testimony*, 31 *et seq*. We note also that California Evidence Code sections 412 and 413 reflect that failure to explain or deny unfavorable evidence may suggest that the evidence is true.

In every case of healing, the previous condition of the sufferer was known to all; all saw his instantaneous restoration; and all witnessed the act of Jesus in touching him, and heard his words. All these, separately considered, were facts, plain and simple in their nature, easily seen and fully comprehended by persons of common capacity and observation. If they were separately testified to, by different witnesses of ordinary intelligence and integrity, in any court of justice the jury would be bound to believe them; and a verdict, rendered contrary to the uncontradicted testimony of credible witnesses to any of these plain facts, separately taken, would be liable to be set aside, as a verdict against evidence.[32]

APOLOGETIC TEST 5: CONFORMITY TO HISTORY

Greenleaf's fifth test is summarized by the question: does the testimony coincide with contemporaneous facts and circumstances? In short, do Matthew, Mark, Luke, and John speak accurately about the historical, legal, sociological, and geographical facts of their day? The answer, says Greenleaf, is a resounding yes.

Much study has been done about the structure of the legal system in first-century Palestine under Roman rule. Greenleaf himself wrote extensively on the subject and concluded that the gospel accounts of the trial of Jesus are consistent with what we know of Roman judicial procedure and consistent with how the Jewish religious leaders of the day ignored Jewish procedural law to secure the execution of Jesus.[33] Greenleaf even took on a contemporary of his day who had tried to establish the unreliability of the gospels because they recite actions by the Sanhedrin that seemed contrary to established Jewish law of that day (e.g., trials at night, condemnation on the sole basis of a forced confession elicited after physically abusing the accused, striking the accused in open court, holding a trial on a feast day, and sentencing the accused on the same day as the conviction).[34] Greenleaf methodically analyzes each objection and finds them unsupportable—the religious leaders of that day in general wanted Jesus eliminated, and only the secular authority could administer the death penalty.[35] We note three brief and more recent examples of external verification of the accuracy of the gospel writers:

---

32. Greenleaf, *Testimony*, 41–42.
33. Greenleaf, "An Account of the Trial of Jesus," found in *Testimony*, chapter 3.
34. Joseph Salvador, *The Jewish Account of the Trial of Jesus*, critiqued by Greenleaf in *Testimony*, chapter 4.
35. For a lawyer's analysis of the efforts of other lawyers such as Nicodemus, Joseph of Arimathea, and Gamaliel to try to intervene on Jesus's behalf, see John J. Bombaro, Adam S. Francisco, eds. *The Resurrection Fact: Responding to Modern Critics* (Irvine, CA: New Reformation, 2016), 88–116.

The Pavement: John records that the Roman trial of Jesus by Pilate took place in a location by the name of The Pavement.[36] If such a place never existed, it would cast some doubt on the accuracy of John's account of the various trials of Jesus. For centuries there was no archaeological verification of this site. The location has been only relatively recently unearthed and definitively shown to be the courtyard where Pilate tried Jesus.[37]

The Pool at Bethesda: Mentioned by John, this pool is not referenced in any other historical accounts. Again, this architectural feature was only relatively recently discovered.[38]

Pontius Pilate: Though mentioned in the gospels and part of the ecumenical creeds of Christendom, no historical reference was ever found to Pontius Pilate. That ended in 1961 with the discovery of the so-called Pilate Inscription at Caesarea Maritima, now housed at the Israel Museum in Jerusalem.

Finally, it is fascinating to see that lawyers have scrutinized Greenleaf's approach to determine its consistency with current federal rules of procedure and have found it to be fully consistent with contemporary federal civil procedure. Greenleaf's five-part test results in a fully vindicated eyewitness testimony to the life, death, and resurrection of Jesus Christ as recorded by the gospel writers.[39] In short, the basic evidentiary principles that Greenleaf outlined over a century ago continue to be utterly valid today.

CONTRIBUTIONS TO THE FIELD OF APOLOGETICS

Greenleaf stands in a long line of lawyer-apologists, but he is also the linchpin to an entire apologetics school. His unique contribution in applying the laws of legal evidence to the gospel writers initiated what has come to be known as "juridical," or "legal," apologetics. This discipline traces its origins to the New Testament itself, where we find lawyers involved in many of the central issues

36. John 19:13.
37. See William F. Albright, *The Archaeology of Palestine*, rev. ed. (London: Pelican, 1960), 41. Albright establishes that this was the courtyard of the Roman military headquarters in Jerusalem, was destroyed in the siege of Jerusalem in AD 66–70, and only recently discovered in 1961.
38. F. F. Bruce, "Archaeological Confirmation of the New Testament." *Revelation and the Bible*, ed. C. Henry (Grand Rapids: Baker, 1969), 329.
39. See appendix B to Montgomery's *Law Above the Law* (Irvine, CA: New Reformation, 2015). It contains a fascinating article entitled "Seeking Truth on the Other Side of the Wall: Greenleaf's Evangelists Meet the Federal Rules, Naturalism and Judas," by Nancy J. Kippenhan.

of the life and ministry of Jesus Christ. Indeed, the Old Testament encourages the development of legal structures to handle disputes as a means of controlling human depravity. From the *theological* use of the law to show humanity's need for redemption to the centrality of contracts and criminal procedure and the orderly transfer and preservation of real and personal property (the so-called *civil* use of the law), the Bible has law and legal procedure embedded in it from stem to stern. The Old Testament introduces Moses as the first law-giver and highlights the activities of military judges such as Deborah and Ezra, along with lawyer-like counselors such as Daniel and Jonathan, who served as trusted advisors to their clients.[40]

In the New Testament, and particularly in its focus on the last week of the life of Jesus Christ, lawyers play a noteworthy role—from the apostle Paul and his legal training as a trial lawyer and prosecutor under the renowned law professor Gamaliel (chief justice of the Jerusalem Supreme Court, known as the Sanhedrin) to fellow Jerusalem Supreme Court member Joseph of Arimathea to Nicodemus, another member of the Supreme Court and "Israel's teacher" (John 3:10; Acts 22:3). In terms of substantive and procedural legal process, legal argumentation and the legal profession are prominently featured in the New Testament.[41]

Of particular interest to lawyers has been Christianity's direct challenge that to refute the resurrection of Christ is to destroy and discredit the religion *in its entirety* (1 Cor 15:12–19). Many have taken up this challenge and have become Christians while trying to refute the evidence for the resurrection.[42]

There are now books by well over one hundred lawyers on the truth of the Christian faith as vindicated by the rules of evidence.[43] In fact, the first textbook on apologetics was done in the sixteenth century by Hugo Grotius, the so-called Father of International Law.[44] Grotius applied the laws of legal

---

40. Ethelbert Callahan, *The Lawyers of the Bible* (Indianapolis: Hollenbeck, 1912), 28ff.

41. This is all explained in detail in Bombaro and Francisco, *The Resurrection Fact*, 88–116 and the article therein entitled "The Case Against *The Case Against Christianity:* When Jerusalem Came to Athens" by Parton.

42. For a work by a skeptic who examined the evidence for the resurrection with the intent of destroying Christianity and in the process became a Christian, see Frank Morison, *Who Moved the Stone: The Evidence for the Resurrection* (New York: Barnes & Noble, 1963). The first chapter is appropriately titled "The Book that Refused to be Written."

43. See Philip Johnson, "Juridical Apologetics 1600–2000 A.D.: A Bio-Biographical Essay," *Global Journal of Classical Theology* 3 (March 2002): 1–25; see also Ross Clifford, *John Warwick Montgomery's Legal Apologetic: An Apologetic for All Seasons* (Bonn: Culture & Science, 2004), "Appendix I: Table of Lawyers' Apologetical Writings," which lists over thirty-five trial lawyers who have analyzed the various truth claims of Christianity. Clifford's *Leading Lawyers' Case for the Resurrection* has a chapter devoted to Greenleaf.

44. Hugo Grotius, *De Veritate Religionis Christianae*—"On the Truth of the Christian Religion," trans. John Clarke (London: Baynes, 1825), see esp. bk. 2, sec. 6 ("The resurrection of Christ proved from credible testimony"), 85–88.

evidence to the claims of Christianity and found that the case was established "beyond a reasonable doubt." Sir Matthew Hale, Lord High Chancellor under King Charles II in the seventeenth century, was a committed Christian who wrote on the truth of Christianity. The great systematizer of the English common law, William Blackstone, was a believing Christian who wrote that every lawyer should begin his study of the law with a study of God's Word because that Word is revelatory and thus transcendent, and no human law should ever contradict it.[45]

In more contemporary times, Lord Hailsham, former Lord High Chancellor of England, wrote on the defense of the Christian faith,[46] and Sir Norman Anderson, an English barrister in the twentieth century was one of the great authorities on world religions in general and on Islam in particular.[47] This partial list would not be complete without mentioning John Warwick Montgomery— English barrister, American attorney, author of over sixty books in six languages on the evidence for the Christian faith, and a trial lawyer handling some of the most important religious liberty cases before the International Court of Human Rights sitting in Strasbourg, France.

It is not mere coincidence that lawyers and legally trained professionals are attracted to Christian truth claims. Instead, it is the facticity of those religious truth claims and their openness to being checked out and refuted that has led so many lawyers to examine the central claims of Christianity.

CLOSING ARGUMENTS

Greenleaf concludes that it would be "incredible that bad men should invent falsehoods to promote the religion of the God of truth. The supposition is suicidal. If they did believe in a future state of retribution, a heaven and a hell hereafter, they took the most certain course, if false witnesses, to secure the latter for their portion."[48] We have seen that Greenleaf's legal apologetic is Christocentric as it ultimately builds from the reliability of the gospel accounts to the overwhelming strength of the factual claim of the resurrection and that none of this "was done in a corner" (Acts 26:26). Greenleaf notes that the factual evidence never rises to 100 percent certainty but, if fairly sifted, leads the skeptic to

---

45. William Blackstone, *Commentaries on the Laws of England*, vol. 1 (London: University of Chicago Press, 1979), 41. Blackstone's comments in this regard are part of his discussion of the "Rights of Persons," which became Volume 1 of his commentaries and was originally published in 1765.

46. See especially Lord Hailsham, *The Door Wherein I Went* (London: Collins, 1975).

47. See Norman Anderson's *A Lawyer among the Theologians*; *The Evidence for the Resurrection*; *Jesus Christ: The Witness of History*; and *Christianity and World Religions*.

48. Greenleaf, *Testimony*, 33.

the inevitable conclusion that at the cross God indeed was reconciling the world unto himself.

Greenleaf sums the case up this way:

> All that Christianity asks of men on this subject is that they would be consistent with themselves; that they would treat its evidences as they treat the evidence of other things; and that they would try and judge its actors and witnesses, as they deal with their fellow men, when testifying to human affairs, in human tribunals. Let the witnesses be compared with themselves, with each other, and with surrounding facts and circumstances; and let their testimony be sifted, as it were given in a court of justice, on the side of the adverse party, the witness being subjected to rigorous cross-examination. The result, it is confidently believed, will be an undoubting conviction of their integrity, ability and truth. In the course of such an examination, the undesigned coincidences will multiply upon us at every step in our progress; the probability of the veracity of the witnesses and of the reality of the occurrences which they related will increase, until it acquires, for all practical purposes, the value and force of demonstration.[49]

Simon Greenleaf never rested in establishing the case for Christianity and Christ crucified "beyond a reasonable doubt." That he reached that conclusion as the greatest living authority of his time on common law evidence should give pause to even the most extreme of skeptics.

BIBLIOGRAPHY

Blackstone, William. *Commentaries on the Laws of England*. Vol. 1. London: University of Chicago Press, 1979.

Bombaro, John J., and Adam S. Francisco, eds. *The Resurrection Fact: Responding to Modern Critics*. Irvine, CA: New Reformation, 2016.

Bruce, F. F. "Archaeological Confirmation of the New Testament." Pages 319–31 in *Revelation and the Bible*. Edited by C. Henry. Grand Rapids: Baker, 1969.

Callahan, Ethelbert. *The Lawyers of the Bible*. Indianapolis: Hollenbeck, 1912.

Chandler, Walter M. *The Trial of Jesus from a Lawyer's Standpoint*. New York: The Empire, 1908.

Clifford, Ross. *John Warwick Montgomery's Legal Apologetic: An Apologetic for All Seasons*. Bonn, Germany: Culture and Science, 2004.

———. *Leading Lawyers' Case for the Resurrection*. Edmonton, Canada: Canadian Institute for Law, Theology and Public Policy, 1996.

Givens, Richard A. *Advocacy*. New York: McGraw-Hill, 1980.

---

49. Greenleaf, *Testimony*, 41–42. Greenleaf's notes at the end of *Testimony* reflect his familiarity with the best apologetical texts of his time (references abound to William Paley, Richard Whately, Bishop Daniel Wilson, and Dr. Thomas Chalmers and to the latest works refuting the "deductivistic" and wholly circular argument against miracles circulating from the pen of David Hume).

Greenleaf, Simon. *The Testimony of the Evangelists: Examined by the Rules of Evidence Administered in Courts of Justice*. Grand Rapids: Kregel, 1995.

Grotius, Hugo. *De Veritate Religionis Christianae—"On the Truth of the Christian Religion."* Trans. by John Clarke. London: Baynes, 1825.

Hailsham, Lord (Quentin McGarel Hogg). *The Door Wherein I Went*. London: Collins, 1975.

Johnson, Philip. "Juridical Apologetics 1600–2000 A.D.: A Bio-Biographical Essay." *Global Journal of Classical Theology* 3 (March 2002): 1–25.

McCloskey, Patrick L., and Ronald L. Schoenberg. *Criminal Law Advocacy*. Vol. 5. New York: Bender, 1984.

Montgomery, John Warwick. *Human Rights and Human Dignity*. Grand Rapids: Zondervan, 1986.

Morison, Frank. *Who Moved the Stone? The Evidence for the Resurrection*. New York: Barnes & Noble, 1963.

Parton, Craig A. "The Case Against *The Case Against Christianity:* When Jerusalem Came to Athens." Pages 89–116 in *The Resurrection Fact: Responding to Modern Critics*. Ed. by Bombaro and Francisco. Irvine, CA: New Reformation, 2016.

Saltzman, Alan. "Criminal Law: How to Expose Perjury through Cross-Examination." *Los Angeles Daily Journal*. (November 4, 1982): 4.

Salvador, Joseph. *Historie des Institutions de Moise et due Peuple Hebreu*, 4 vols. Paris: Michel Levy, 1862.

Additional Recommended Reading

(All works are by judges or lawyers.)

Casteel, Herbert. *Beyond a Reasonable Doubt: A Judge's Verdict on the Case for Christian Faith*. Joplin, MI: College Press Publishing, 1992.

Ewan, Pamela B. *Faith on Trial: Analysis of the Evidence for the Death and Resurrection of Jesus*. Nashville: Broadman & Holman, 2013.

Lamb, Francis. *Bible Miracles Examined by the Methods, Rules and Tests of the Science of Jurisprudence as Administered Today in Courts of Justice*. Oberlin, OH: Bibliotheca Sacra, 1909.

Linton, Irwin H. *The Sanhedrin Verdict*. New York: Loizeaux Brothers, 1943.

Moen, John T. "A Lawyer's Logical and Syllogistic Look at the Facts of the Resurrection." *Simon Greenleaf Law Review* 8 (1987–88): 81–110.

Montgomery, John Warwick. *Christ Our Advocate: Studies in Polemical Theology, Jurisprudence and Canon Law*. Bonn, Germany: Culture and Science, 2002.

———. *Defending the Gospel in Legal Style: Essays on Legal Apologetics and the Justification of Classical Christian Faith*. Bonn, Germany: Culture and Science, 2017. See also Montgomery's *Law Above the Law* (Irvine, CA: New Reformation, 2015), which includes *Testimony of the Evangelists* as an appendix along with a contemporary analysis of Greenleaf's method and its utter consistency with modern-day federal civil procedure.

Morison, Charles Robert. *The Proofs of Christ's Resurrection: From a Lawyer's Standpoint*. Andover, MA: Draper, 1882.

Parton, Craig A. *The Defense Never Rests*. 2nd ed. St. Louis: Concordia, 2015.

———. *Religion on Trial: Cross-Examining Religious Truth Claims*. St. Louis: Concordia, 2018.

Sherlock, Thomas. *The Tryal of the Witnesses of the Resurrection of Jesus*. London: Roberts, 1729. Reproduced in John Warwick Montgomery's *Jurisprudence: A Book of Readings*. Strasbourg: International Scholarly, 1980.

Smith, Graeme. *Was the Tomb Empty? A Lawyer Weighs the Evidence for the Resurrection*. Grand Rapids: Monarch, 2014.

JOHN HENRY NEWMAN

Apologetics for the Clear-Headed and Holy-Hearted

CORNELIU C. SIMUŢ

John Henry Newman (1801–1890) is known for his contribution to the Oxford movement and then, more famously, for his conversion to Catholicism. Newman was both an extremely complex personality and an assiduous defender of traditional Christianity against the rising tide of theological liberalism. An ardent apologist, he fought theological liberalism and sought to preserve the foundations of Christianity within their original metaphysical boundaries. Newman dedicated his entire life not only to safeguard Christianity's most precious tenets, including the resurrection of the dead and eternal life, but also to raise awareness of the devastating consequences of accepting theological liberalism. He opposed the demotion of doctrine from an essential truth to an individual view, which—to quote Richard Harding—"was seriously endangering the future existence of Christianity."[1] Newman was keenly aware of this threat and acted to oppose it through various writings against the secularizing tendencies of Christian theology. In so doing he embarked on an academic, ecclesiastical, and pastoral journey that lasted almost six decades. He was canonized as a saint in the Roman Catholic Church in October 2019.

HISTORICAL BACKGROUND

John Henry Newman was born in 1801, and his life spans a significant, and turbulent period in the history of Christian theology, a fact that cannot be overstated in examining his life. The rise of theological liberalism shaped his entire career. In Newman's formative years (until 1832, when he completed *The Arians*

---

1. Richard J. Harding, *John Henry Newman: The Resolution of a Dilemma* (Lincoln, NE: iUniverse, 2000), 70.

of the Fourth Century), Hegel was developing his religious philosophy, turning Christianity into just another mere religion among several others.[2] In Newman's more mature years (until 1864, when he published *Apologia pro vita sua*), Ferdinand Christian Baur used Hegel's religious philosophy to create further dissonance within Christian circles by positing the existence of Jewish and gentile factions within the Christian religion, factors which promoted supernatural as well as natural perspectives on doctrine.[3] In Newman's final years (until his cardinalate in 1879 and his death in 1890), Adolf von Harnack emerged as one of the informal leaders of theological liberalism, cementing the spread of antisupernatural understandings of Christian dogmas throughout the academy and the broader Christian church.[4]

Newman's apologetic and theological activity developed and matured in the context of the unrest created by theological liberalism, and this reality also shaped his personal life. Jay Newman has argued—although apparently with some bias against Newman's understanding of theological liberalism—that Newman's preoccupation with defending the Christian religion took place later in his life when "he became more bitter and frustrated" and viewed "as liberals all progressive Christians whose interpretation of Scripture and attitude toward the church differed even slightly from his own."[5] Certainly there is not much to be found in his twenties to foreshadowe his apologetic career. We know that he was fully immersed in the life of the church and the academy. As Ian Ker summarizes, Newman was ordained a deacon in the Church of England and then appointed curate at Saint Clement's Church in Oxford in 1824. In 1825, he was appointed vice-principal of Alban Hall and ordained a priest. A year later, in 1826, he was appointed tutor of Oriel College, followed in 1828 by his decision to assume vicarage of Saint Mary's, the official church of the University of Oxford.[6]

Newman's apologetic concerns regarding theological liberalism may have been first triggered by a political shift that occurred in 1830 when the

---

2. Stephen Thomas provides an exceptional comparison between Newman's idea of revelation, which "remains unchanged," and Hegel's perspective on "subject and object, *Geist* and world," which "mutually modify—or participate in—one another as the very process of coming-to-be." For details, see Stephen Thomas, *Newman and Heresy: The Anglican Years* (Cambridge: Cambridge University Press, 1991 [2002]), 242.

3. Ben F. Meyer places Newman and Baur in the same cultural milieu. See Meyer, *Critical Realism and the New Testament* (Eugene, OR: Wipf & Stock, 1989), 99–100.

4. Trevor Hart shows that for Harnack, Newman's approach was "much too influenced by prior dogmatic commitment," but disagreements with one another's approaches must have been shared mutually. See Trevor Hart, "Creeds, Councils, and Doctrinal Development," in *The Early Christian World*, vol. 1, ed. Philip F. Esler (London: Routledge, 2000), 656.

5. Jay Newman, *The Mental Philosophy of John Henry Newman* (Waterloo, ON: Wilfried Laurier University Press, 1986), 30.

6. Ian Ker, ed., *The Genius of John Henry Newman. Selections from His Writings* (Oxford: Oxford University Press, 1989), xvii-xviii.

conservative Tories lost power in British politics. Their power was assumed by the more liberal Whigs, who were extremely eager to reform British society (even in religious matters) and decisively convinced that their best chance to achieve their policy objectives lay in combining religious liberalism and utilitarian Benthamism.[7] Both of these philosophies staunchly rejected supernaturalism and actively promoted naturalistic views of life, and they were critical of anything with a hint of divine origin, especially natural law and natural rights. Such liberal convictions within the new governing party led to fears of new social reforms that could potentially sweep across the Commonwealth, affecting the entire spectrum of political, educational, and religious institutions. The church at this moment was caught between a rock and a hard place. The bishops of the Church of England were warned "to set their house in order and prepare to meet the coming storm" by the prime minister himself—Charles Grey, the Second Earl Grey. Unfortunately, Lord Grey's words were taken out of their original context, which included not only courteous assurances of his sincere attachment "to the maintenance of all the rights and privileges of the church" but also equally firm promises to uphold "the purity of her doctrines and soundness of her discipline." Still, the spread of this quote within the church leadership caused horror and discouragement throughout the church, especially among those like Newman, who worked for the church and felt trapped by a series of political decisions apparently aimed at destroying the institution he loved and served.[8]

The new government's Reform Bill was fiercely debated, and a large majority of bishops voted against it in 1831. Two years later, in 1833, the social reform that the Whigs initiated progressed through the suppression of ten Irish sees and several bishoprics of the established church, the reorganization of ecclesiastical revenues, and the placement of church finances under the authority of the Ecclesiastical Commissioners.[9] Countless fears and unsubstantiated rumors about the government's intentions to seize church property and possibly cancel the church's endowments circulated all over Britain. It seemed only normal for the clergy—Newman included—to take immediate action, not only to preserve the institution of the church from the interference of the state but also to defend the church's traditional doctrines against such liberal policies.[10]

---

7. Vincent F. Blehl, SJ, ed., *The Essential Newman: The Central Writings of the Master of English Prose Who Infused New Vigor into the Nineteenth-Century Catholic Church* (New York: Mentor-Omega, 1963), 12.

8. George M. Trevelyan, *Lord Grey of the Reform Bill, Being the Life of the Charles, Second Earl of Grey* (New York: Longman's, Green & Co., 1920), 307–08.

9. "Speech of the Right Reverend Henry, Lord Bishop of Exeter in the House of Lords (on Thursday, July 18, 1833) on Second Reading of the Church Temporalities (Ireland) Bill", in *Mirror of Parliament*, Part CCXXXVI (London: Proprietors of "The Mirror of Parliament", 1833), 24.

10. Brian Martin, *John Henry Newman: His Life and Work* (London: Continuum, 1982 [2000]), 51.

THEOLOGICAL CONTEXT

The liberal policies of the British government were not fully implemented across the Commonwealth, at least not to the degree that the clergy of the established church had feared. As church leaders turned to focus on religious issues rather than political concerns, Newman soon realized that there was just as much at stake in the field of Christian theology, as modern philosophies—such as Hegel's idealism—were intersecting with long-held Christian doctrines and infiltrating the hearts and minds of clergymen and laypeople alike. By the early 1830s, Newman had been a Christian believer for about fifteen years. Gerard Magill writes that he had converted to evangelical Christianity in 1816 under the influence of Reverend Walter Mayers[11] but was now feeling drawn toward High Church dogmatics after he met with people such as Hurrell Froude and John Keble, who became leading figures of the Oxford movement. Remaining in the evangelical camp, Newman was also affected by the theology of John Wesley and George Whitefield, whose thinking led to the emergence of the evangelical party within the Church of England. The core theological teachings that occupied Newman, shaping his thinking as an evangelical, were the sinfulness of humanity,[12] the necessity of genuine conversion,[13] and the reality of Christ's atonement.[14] As Newman's theological reflection matured, he came to realize that the awakening of a person's feelings were an essential goal of sermons, exhortations, and conversion. All of this was in line with the Wesleyan tradition.[15]

Newman later studied theology more formally—first between 1817 (when he entered Trinity College, Oxford) and 1820 (when he obtained his bachelor's degree), and then again between his graduation in theology and 1822, when he was elected fellow of Oriel College, Oxford. Newman began to realize that there was more to the study of theology than what he had known from his early evangelical upbringing, largely dominated by Calvinist and Puritan convictions such as predestination to damnation and justification associated with certainty of salvation. While he could never stomach the former, he embraced the latter doctrine throughout his life and this frequently prompted him to react against theological liberalism when it appeared in the Church of England and in the Roman

---

11. Gerard Magill, *Religious Morality in John Henry Newman: Hermeneutics of Imagination* (Dordrecht: Springer, 2015), 14–15.

12. Sinfulness is present even in man's "just causes." Newman, *Apologia pro vita sua* (New York: Appleton, 1865), 77.

13. Newman, *Apologia pro vita sua*, 386.

14. Christ's atonement is mentioned by Newman among the main doctrines of Protestantism and Catholicism. See Newman, *Apologia pro vita sua*, 147.

15. Timothy F. Sedgwick, *The Christian Moral Life: Practices and Piety* (New York: Seabury, 1999 [2008]), 47.

Catholic Church. But he reacted more with the mind than with the heart. Avery Dulles goes as far as to claim: "At no point in his career did he undergo anything resembling the sudden conversion of the heart to which the followers of Wesley customarily appealed."[16]

For Newman, theological liberalism was incompatible with the Christian faith because it sought to show that "there is no positive truth in religion, but that one creed is as good as another."[17] It was also problematic in implying that all theological views should be accepted as mere opinions or individual convictions that, although essentially important for certain people, were not meant to be mandatory for everybody. Such an understanding of Christian doctrine and practice was considered acceptable at Oriel College in the late 1820s. Even if ideas like this were promoted by High Church clergymen in good standing within the Anglican community and with no leanings toward theological liberalism, Newman was convinced their approval of these ideas would only spell trouble. Following a serious illness in 1827 and the death of his sister Mary in 1828, Newman consistently rejected anything with a leaning toward theological liberalism. According to John Connolly: "At this point in his life, Newman turned away from liberalism for good and aligned himself with the High Church Anglican party."[18]

Theological liberalism, already a serious concern in the late 1820s, was soon followed by the political liberalism promoted by the Whig government in the early 1830s. Although it proved to be less damaging than originally feared, the emergence of liberal political ideas was enough to prompt Keble to deliver his famous sermon on "National Apostasy," which John Griffin calls "perhaps the most famous sermon in the history of English ecclesiastical writing."[19] The preaching of this sermon marked the beginning of the Oxford Movement in July 1833. As political fears faded away (when the Whig party decided not to implement its entire program of liberal political reform) the Oxford Movement—which started with Newman, Froude, and Keble—shifted its focus to preventing the expansion of theological liberalism within the Church of England. In September 1833 Newman began writing the *Tracts for the Times*,[20] a series of theological essays that came to define the Oxford movement. After publication, its members were called Tractarians. This publication provided them with an ear-

---

16. Avery Dulles, *John Henry Newman* (London: Continuum, 2009), 28.

17. John Henry Newman, "Biglietto Speech," in W. P. Neville, *Addresses to Cardinal Newman and His Replies* (London: Longmans, 1905), 64.

18. John R. Connolly, *John Henry Newman. A View of Catholic Faith for the New Millenium* (Lanham, MD: Sheed & Ward / Rowman & Littlefield, 2005), 3.

19. John R. Griffin, *John Keble, Saint of Anglicanism* (Macon, GA: Mercer University Press, 1987), 82.

20. John Henry Newman, et al., *Tracts for the Times* (London: Rivington, 1833, etc.).

nest impetus to fight for the traditional and supernatural doctrines of the church against the pernicious consequences of theological liberalism.[21] Craig Townsend writes that the *Tracts* called for "the renewal" of the church "by restoring the importance of dogmatic tradition and placing a greater emphasis on piety."[22] Newman and the Tractarians turned to the church's past and attempted to reclaim several sixteenth- and seventeenth-century divines—most notably Richard Hooker (1554–1600). But they also reached further back in history, drawing from patristic theology and highlighting figures from the first centuries of the church. Newman was not a novice in this field of study, having already published his first book, *The Arians of the Fourth Century*, in 1832 with the intention of igniting religious devotion in the Church of England according to the model that the early church provided.[23] According to Benjamin King, Newman's book made "doctrinal history available in the present not as antiquarian scholarship but as living wisdom."[24]

As Newman delved deeper—both dogmatically and historically—into the patristic period, he shifted away from the Protestantism of the high church movement toward Catholicism. The shift was not at all sudden, gradually occuring over the course of a decade. Yet eventually, Newman left Protestantism and embraced Catholicism. The first signs of his shift appeared publically in 1841 with the publication of *Tract 90*,[25] which in broad terms affirmed that the Protestant *Thirty-Nine Articles* of the Church of England were intended to criticize only *popular belief* about Catholic doctrine,[26] not Catholic doctrine per se, including—as shown by Emmeline Garnett—the doctrines of purgatory and transubstantiation.[27] Newman's promotion of this idea created havoc within the University of Oxford and throughout the Church of England, but his motive was sincere. Newman sought to root the church in its traditional history and doctrines as they had developed across centuries of faithful witness for Christ and his salvation. It would be yet another four years before Newman eventually left the Church of England in 1845 and was formally received into the Roman

---

21. According to Newman, God bestows upon the church "outward supernatural aid." See Newman, *Tracts for the Times*, vol. 1 for 1833–1834 (London: Rivington, 1840), 9.

22. Craig D. Townsend, *Faith in Their Own Color: Black Episcopalians in Antebellum New York City* (New York: Columbia University Press, 2005), 111.

23. In Newman, devotion is compulsory in the service of God. See Newman, *The Arians of the Fourth Century* (Leominster: Gracewing, 2001 [1833]), 148.

24. Benjamin J. King, *Newman and the Alexandrian Fathers: Shaping Doctrinei in the Nineteenth-Century England* (Oxford: Oxford University Press, 2009), 251.

25. John Henry Newman, *Tract 90* (Oxford: Baxter, 1841).

26. For Newman, this is "Romish" doctrine. See Newman, *Tract XC on Certain Passages in the XXXIX Articles* (Oxford: Rivington, 1865 [1841]), 25.

27. Emmeline Garnett, *Tormented Angel: A Life of John Henry Newman* (New York: Ariel / Ferrar, Straus, & Giroux, 1966), 84–85.

Catholic Church, where he served for the rest of his life as priest (from 1847), rector of the Catholic University of Ireland (1851–1858), and cardinal (after 1879). In his ongoing fight against theological liberalism, Newman always defended the apostolicity and the catholicity of the Christian communion, first as a member of the Church of England and then of the Roman Catholic Church. To quote Vincent Blehl, his utmost intention was to instill a "deep and genuine spiritual life"[28] across British society by works that addressed not only the institution of the church (*An Essay on the Development of Christian Doctrine*, *Apologia pro vita sua*, and *Via Media*) but also institutions of higher education (*Discourses on the Scope and Nature of University Education* and *The Idea of a University*).[29]

APOLOGETIC RESPONSE

As we have tried to show in this brief summary, Newman's times were complex and difficult, leading to shifts in Christian theology as church leaders sought to confront modernistic approaches to philosophy and religion aimed at dismantling the supernatural elements of traditional Christianity in favor of more naturalistic approaches based exclusively on rational investigation. These developments were wrapped up in the theological liberalism, which Newman felt compelled to oppose throughout his life, and he led this charge by trying to explain and clarify the connection between faith (the main preoccupation of traditional theology) and reason (the key focus of theological liberalism). Gerald Bednar believes that Newman approached this relationship "in more personal terms,"[30] which he hoped would allow for a more facile reception of his ideas.

Since Newman's initial evangelical convictions, influenced by the Wesleyan tradition, were rooted in feelings of the heart and less on theological authority, Newman looked back in church history to find additional support for his attempts to counter theological liberalism. He found the support he was looking for in the writings of the church fathers and the early church tradition. This discovery convinced him that the subjective reality of the conversion of the heart must be supplemented by the more objective reality of apostolic succession, which, as Ian Ker reveals, he believed to have been "clearly taught in Scripture."[31] To put it simply: a Christian cannot be saved only because they feel the Lord's presence in their heart; they must also stand within the church's tradition along-

---

28. Blehl, *The Essential Newman*, 14.
29. For details, see Edward Short, *Newman and His Family* (London: Bloomsbury, 2013), xvii-xviii.
30. Gerald J. Bednar, *Faith as Imagination: The Contribution of William F. Lynch, S. J.* (Kansas City, MO: Sheed & Ward, 1996), 16.
31. Ian Ker, *John Henry Newman: A Biography* (Oxford: Oxford University Press, 2010 [1988, 2009]), 160.

side all those who were saved before them. Newman addressed these concerns early in his career, especially in his early work *The Arians of the Fourth Century*, where his intention was to anchor the church in what William Sachs calls "the authority of ancient creeds and liturgies,"[32] an authority which in turn is rooted in the authority of the Bible and the authority of God himself.[33]

Second, having established the need for the church to anchor its doctrine and practice in the history and teachings of the early church, Newman's fight against theological liberalism centered on what the church must now do today. In the early 1830s, Newman felt a clear call to action was needed. In the new liberal politics of the Whig party, which had garnered support from religious liberals, and the rise of Bentham's utilitarian philosophy, which denied the divine character of natural law and natural rights, Newman and his colleagues strongly insisted that the church should be left alone to walk on its own path— without political or social reformation by the British government. They argued that Christianity is a religion with its own history and future, and it is based on divine revelation, human reason, and a high degree of mystery, which cannot be investigated by human methodologies. The Christian character of Christianity's adherents is something that the state cannot regulate. Newman explored many of these issues in *Tracts for the Times*, hoping to incite a response within the church.[34] While Joyce Sugg thinks some of the titles were rather "gloomy but stirring," his essays "Repent while Yet There is Time" or "Sinner, Hearken to the Voice of the Lord" were titled in this manner to drive home the need for immediate action. Newman felt this was necessary if the church was to survive its clash with "the tide" of theological liberalism.[35]

After leaving the Anglican Communion and joining the Catholic Church, Newman realized that just as his own religious understandings had changed, so too had the church's doctrines changed and shifted throughout history. He reasoned that the doctrines of the church change over time because the church is faced with new challenges as history unfolds toward its end. Newman believed Christianity was the universal religion with the capacity to accommodate itself to any historical period and any location in the world. But for the church to adapt to various times and places, doctrines would need to develop, if not in content, then at least in the way they were presented to the world. For these doctrines to develop in an orderly fashion and according to the proper pattern (one that is in line with

---

32. William L. Sachs, *The Transformation of Anglicanism: From State Church to Global Communion* (Cambridge: Cambridge University Press, 2002 [1993]), 162.

33. Newman, *The Arians of the Fourth Century*, 79–80.

34. Newman, *Tracts for the Times*, vol. 1, 48.

35. Joyce Sugg, *John Henry Newman: Snapdragon in the Wall* (Leominster: Gracewing, 2001 [1965]), 60, 143.

apostolic teaching), the church must have an infallible authority that checks and regulates the development of doctrine. Newman focused on how this works in *An Essay on the Development of Christian Doctrine*, which James Earnest and Gerard Tracey say presents a theory of "doctrinal development" focused on "assigning responsibility for development" to "the whole church" as collective consciousness,[36] a rather exceptional way to convey the idea of infallible authority.[37]

Newman also believed that yet another way to combat theological liberalism was through education, and in particular, university education. In *Discourses on the Scope and Nature of University Education* and then in *The Idea of a University*, Newman investigated the idea of truth as the object of any kind of knowledge. Since Christianity upholds the final Truth, knowledge is compulsory for one's effort to fully understand the doctrinal and practical realities of the Christian religion, even if the knowledge of truth presupposes a wide range of collateral investigations.[38] As highlighted by Colin Barr, Newman believed the church needs universities *and* universities need the church.[39] Human beings need to exercise their minds to know the truth, and it is through the effort to acquire knowledge that both truth and *the* Truth are investigated, appropriated, and then disseminated to others. This can be done through the church, of course, but also through the university, whose chief preoccupation should be, in Newman's own words, "the education of the intellect."[40] While Newman believed knowledge was not the same as Christian virtue, he also appreciated that knowledge could assist human beings in growing in Christian virtue, understanding doctrine, and practicing their faith in a better and more fulfilling way. Thus, while Newman resented theological liberalism, he actively promoted liberal education, which, in the words of Hu Xianzhang and Cao Li, "centered on classical liberal arts education, rational thinking, and self-education" and could assist the individual in discerning the complex ways of the modern world.[41]

Newman focused his writing quite extensively on the relationship between the church and the modern world, and he investigated the connections among

36. James D. Earnest and Gerard Tracey, "Editors' Introduction," in *John Henry Newman: Fifteen Sermons Preached before the University of Oxford between A. D. 1826 and 1843*, eds. James D. Earnest and Gerard Tracey (Oxford: Oxford University Press, 2006), cvii.

37. John Henry Newman, *An Essay on the Development of Christian Doctrine* (London: Toovey, 1846 [1845]), 171.

38. Newman, *The Idea of a University*, 176.

39. Colin Barr, *Paul Cullin, John Henry Newman, and the Catholic University of Ireland, 1845–1865* (Leominster: Gracewing, 2003), 84.

40. Newman, *The Scope and Nature of University Education*, 175.

41. Hu Xianzhang and Cao Li, "Meaning and Methods: Some Thoughts on the Role of General Education and Curriculum Design," in *General Education and the Development of Global Citizenship in Hong Kong, Taiwan, and Mainland China: Not Merely Icing on the Cake*, eds. Xing Jun, Ng Pak-Sheung, and Cheng Chunyan (London: Routledge, 2013), 62.

faith, reason, and philosophy. Later in life he wrote *Via Media*, in which he discusses the task of the church in the modern world as an effort to harmonize the church's official doctrines with its practical devotion and its involvement in world politics by promoting the foundational idea of revelation.[42] The church does this work through individual Christians who exercise their freedom of conscience in such a way that they hear God's voice and see his eternal law, not through a false sense of freedom in which they express their own personal opinions. Reinhard Hütter has noted that, in Newman, freedom of conscience means that one should never go against one's conscience by ignoring the transcendent and personal God. Newman warned that freedom of conscience—or just human freedom for that matter—should never lose "its clear imprint."[43] In his *An Essay in Aid of a Grammar of Assent*, which he wrote rather late in life, Newman investigated how the church could involve itself in the modern world by countering the crisis of belief brought on by theological liberalism, which focused exclusively on humans' reason in order to believe only in truths verified by reason and accepted in certainty.[44] He began researching what Peter Wilcox believes to have been "a variety of inadequate solutions to the problem of faith and reason under the general term of 'liberalism.'"[45] Newman wrestled with the connection between faith and reason, humans' capacity to understand and believe mysteries that cannot be fully explained rationally, and humans' need for certainty as they believe the unbelievable by means of formal and informal reasoning. All of these are interconnected with human conscience, which Robert Spitzer believes to have "a personal-dialogical character"[46] in Newman, who promoted a vivid interaction among mind, heart, and conscience. The mind, Newman argued, works with the conscience, which is capable of aligning feelings with reason so that the reality of God is comprehended and accepted by the human being as both transcendent and personal, and not exclusively as a rational idea promoted by theological liberalism.

APOLOGETIC METHODOLOGY

In defending the traditionalism of the church, especially the supernatural character of Christianity in doctrine and practice, Newman adopted four distinct

---

42. John Henry Newman, *The Via Media of the Anglican Church*. London: Pickering, 1877, 56.
43. Reinhard Hütter, *Bound to Be Free: Evangelical Catholic Engagements in Ecclesiology, Ethics, and Ecumenism* (Grand Rapids: Eerdmans, 2004), 111.
44. John Henrey Newman, *An Essay in Aid of a Grammar of Assent* (New York: The Catholic Publication Society, 1870), 331–32.
45. Peter C. Wilcox, STD, *John Henry Newman, Spiritual Director, 1845–1890* (Eugene, OR: Pickwick, 2013), 140.
46. Robert Spitzer, SJ, *Finding True Happiness. Satisfying Our Restless Hearts* (San Francisco: Ignatius, 2015), 122.

methodologies: theological, homiletical, philosophical, and educational. In the words of Anthony Kenny, Newman wanted "to prove to the world that not just belief in God, but the acceptance of a specific religious creed was a completely rational activity."[47] These four areas are not only fields of inquiry or domains of research but rather ways to counter the pervasive influence of theological liberalism, which—given its anthropological preoccupations for the rationality of the human being as detached from divinity and the supernatural realm of God— was more likely to reach the whole of society more quickly and with greater ease than the traditionalism of the Christian religion. This is why Newman thought it was best if he could address as many problematic issues as they presented themselves to him, and he sought to engage society through the channels that allowed him to reach as many people as possible, namely through theology, preaching, philosophy, and education.[48]

In using theology to oppose theological liberalism, Newman—as an Anglican—focused on doctrine and the need for the church to pay attention to its doctrinal formulas. These are more than just a cluster of dry sentences; they are affirmations of the reality of human salvation, not only within the church but also beyond it. They are based on God's revelation in all the world's religions, not only in Christianity, an idea already present in his work *The Arians of the Fourth Century*. This conviction allowed Newman to defend Christianity and its teachings not only as an apologist but also as an active and genuine promotor of Christian values more broadly in his interactions with other religions. As Terrence Merrigan notes, the *whole* range of soteriological economies is rooted in the life and work of Christ.[49] At the same time, this theological methodology, which focused on arguments and rational approaches to doctrine and practice, prompted Newman to move away from mere emotions and speculation to concentrate on the rational validity of doctrine that would unite people rather than divide them.[50] This is why his *Lectures on the Doctrine of Justification* sought to present what Chris Castaldo has dubbed "the proper trajectory of Anglicanism"[51] as a *via media* between Catholicism and Protestantism by appealing to the necessity that Christians should go back to Scripture and the church fathers

47. Anthony Kenny, *Philosophy in the Modern World*, vol. 4 (Oxford: Oxford University Press, 2007), 29.

48. James Olney, *Metaphors of Self: The Meaning of Autobiography* (Princeton: Princeton University Press, 1973), 203.

49. Terrence Merrigan, "Revelation," in *The Cambridge Companion to John Henry Newman,* eds. Ian Ker and Terrence Merrigan (Cambridge: Cambridge University Press, 2009), 56.

50. In Newman, doctrine appears to be a mature intellectual effort; to be believed, doctrines need to be "exact and fully developed." See Newman, *The Arians of the Fourth Century*, 46.

51. Chris Castaldo, *Justified in Christ. The Doctrine of Peter Martyr Vermigli and John Henry Newman and Their Ecumenical Implications* (Eugene, OR: Pickwick, 2017), 92.

because the latter were "expositors" of the former.[52] As a Catholic, Newman wrote about the responsibility of the church to address the problems of society, irrespective of whether they deal with science or other matters. Thus, in *Via Media*, Newman insisted that all offices of the church—prophetical, regal, and sacerdotal—must work together in harmony for the sake of the laity who must never be left without proper ecclesiastical and scholarly education in the face of theological liberalism.[53]

Second, in his promotion of homiletics as a means of countering theological liberalism, Newman insisted over and over again on the indwelling of the Holy Spirit. This is evident in his work *Parochial and Plain Sermons*. As an Anglican, Newman insisted that the Spirit does not work only through faith but also through obedience, and every Christian must be aware of these pneumatological channels because the indwelling of the Spirit is an objective reality that helps human beings move beyond what Ian Ker considers to be "ordinary moral respectability."[54] For Newman, sermons were real occasions to caution people and tell them exactly what to do, that they should seek holiness through practicing humility and living daily life with a genuine sense of zeal, an aspect John Crosby has noted.[55] A true Christian must be consistent, not pretentious, because doing one's duty every day is the essence of true religion. All Christians must be zealous for the gospel.[56] Moreover, consistency in daily life provides people not only with a proper sense of religiosity but with an acute sense of vigilance. This vigilance helps them identify false manifestations of religion, such as theological liberalism.

As a Catholic, Newman continued to be interested in promoting spirituality by addressing special occasions (such as feasts, funerals, or important holidays), which were common ways to speak to people in Catholicism. These special occasions were opportunities to engage with some of the most pressing matters of the day, especially the need to live out the great truths of Christianity in an age of reason dominated by theological liberalism.

Third, by utilizing philosophy to engage theological liberalism, Newman sought to explain the relationship between faith and reason. In his Anglican years, he insisted that faith is not opposed to reason because faith is a *form* of reason. Faith is not different from any other manifestation of intellectual

52. Newman, *Lectures on the Doctrine of Justification*, 134.
53. See, for instance, how Newman presents the church as "witness of Heaven." Details in Newman, *Via Media*, lxxx.
54. Ian Ker, *The Achievement of John Henry Newman* (London: Collins, 1991), 91.
55. John F. Crosby, *The Personalism of John Henry Newman* (Washington, DC: The Catholic University of America Press, 2014), 10.
56. Newman, *Parochial and Plain Sermons*, vol. 1, 60–61.

404 NINETEENTH-CENTURY APOLOGISTS

engagement except that, in its capacity as a form of intellectual activity, faith is dependent on morality. This idea was present in *Sermons, Chiefly on the Theory of Religious Belief, Preached before the University of Oxford*,[57] which also defined a complex notion of faith that includes both explicit and implicit aspects. Newman did not use the concept of faith to oppose the notion of reason promoted by theological liberalism;[58] on the contrary, he sought to present faith as a broader perspective on reason. In the words of Martin Moleski, Newman saw "reason as waiting to be placed in the service of something beyond itself."[59] As a Catholic, his use of philosophy focused on the notion of certainty, further described in *An Essay in Aid of a Grammar of Assent*.[60] In this work, Newman investigates the state of the human mind as it seeks to reach certainty beyond logic and reason while also, as Vincent Blehl has explained, working with logic and reason.[61] This is why Newman's philosophical methodology is an enterprise in religious philosophy. He finds ways to justify religious belief as a matter of personal conviction based on proofs that are not confirmed by the scientific reason of theological liberalism but by the right judgment of Christian belief.

Fourth, Newman utilized educational work in the fight against theological liberalism, though his experiences in this regard were more substantial as a Catholic than an Anglican. But this is secondary to the notion that core to the role of education is the unquestionable value of knowledge, which, according to Juan Vélez, has the capacity to unite reason and faith in dialogue and harmony.[62] Knowledge seeks to discover the truth, so education and religion must always go hand in hand. This is so not only because they both inform ethics but because they can transform society for the better. As Terrence Merrigan has shown, this combination of the intellectual and the ethical leads to accountability before God.[63] In a society dominated by theological liberalism, with its focus on reason and scientific proof—especially that God does not exist—Newman's *The Idea of a University* insisted that through proper education human beings can acquire knowledge and encounter God as Creator. This is possible because all forms of knowledge are part of the same unique universe God has created.[64]

---

57. John Henry Newman, *Sermons, Chiefly on the Theory of Religious Belief, Preached before the University of Oxford* (London: Rivington, 1844 [1843]).

58. Newman, *Sermons, Chiefly on the Theory of Religious Belief*, 20–21.

59. Martin X. Moleski, SJ, *Personal Catholicism: The Theological Epistemologies of John Henry Newman and Michael Polanyi* (Washington, DC: The Catholic University of America Press, 2000), 179.

60. Newman, *An Essay in Aid of a Grammar of Assent*, 189.

61. Vincent F. Blehl, *Pilgrim Journey: John Henry Newman, 1801–1845* (London: Burns & Oates, 2001), 326.

62. Juan R. Vélez, *Holiness in a Secular Age: The Witness of Cardinal Newman* (New York: Scepter, 2017), chapter 11, ebook.

63. Terrence Merrigan, *Clear Heads and Holy Hearts: The Religious and Theological Ideal of John Henry Newman* (Louvain: Peeters, 1991), 4.

64. Newman, *The Idea of a University*, 99.

CONTRIBUTIONS TO THE FIELD OF APOLOGETICS

The four methodologies outlined in the previous section give us a starting point for assessing how Newman built his apologetic arguments in favor of Christian traditionalism. United by his consistent opposition to theological liberalism, his primary contributions to apologetics are summarized in these four areas: theological, homiletical, philosophical, and educational. Newman defended the supernaturalism of traditional Christian doctrine against the anthropologization that theological liberalism promoted. He did so by revealing the importance of ecclesiastical tradition (especially the early church), the responsibility of the church to engage in society, and the necessity of the Holy Spirit's presence in the life of the Christian. Newman also underlined the key role of a personal spirituality marked by faith, obedience, zeal, and consistency, the significance of the relationship between faith and reason, and the meaningfulness of human efforts to go beyond logic and reason. And he spent a lifetime promoting the paramount value of knowledge and education, as well as the compulsory nature of Christian ethics as a means to transform society and the world.

Newman's contributions to theology, homiletics, philosophy, and education are likely far too complex for the average person who has little interest in academic theology, and it is very likely his theological, homiletical, philosophical, and educational writings will remain beyond the grasp of ordinary people. John T. Ford notes that "ordinary people must trust in order to live their everyday lives," which means that "it is reasonable to assume that they must be guided by faith in religious matters,"[65] just as they would in any matter of daily life. In light of this, it seems fair to say that Newman's greatest contribution to the field of apologetics may be his effort to make his apologetic endeavors available to common people through his belletristic literature. In his capacity as a writer, which surfaced in his Catholic period after 1845, Newman wrote a novel and a poem that presented the Christian religion in all its complexity, beauty, and hope. These works were written, in Gertrude Himmelfarb's words, "in a common language and reflecting common values."[66] In his novel *Callista*,[67] Newman emphasizes the attraction Christianity exerts on the pagan mind, the necessity of conversion from paganism to Christianity, and the possibility of personal

---

65. John T. Ford, "Biography: John Henry Newman (1801–1890)," in *John Henry Newman. Spiritual Writings,* ed. John T. Ford, CSC (Maryknoll, NY: Orbis, 2012), 24.

66. Gertrude Himmelfarb, "The Essay as Genre," in *The Spirit of the Age Victorian Essays,* ed. Gertrude Himmelfarb (New Haven, CT: Yale University Press, 2007), 24.

67. John Henry Newman, *Callista: A Sketch of the Third Century* (London: Burns, Oates, & Co., 1869 [1855]).

martyrdom[68] for the cause of Christ, which became a reality so often throughout the history of the church. Amy K. Hirschfeld is of the opinion that, for Newman, "the sufferings of the martyrs were emblematic of the trials that all Christians must undergo to gain salvation,"[69] hence his preoccupation to explain what Christianity entails in as simple terms as possible. In his poem *The Dream of Gerontius*,[70] Newman insists on the reality of death, on how human beings often face it, and on what happens just before and after the event of death.[71] In this work, Newman's apologetic is profoundly eschatological as he expounds the reality of angels, demons, and the existence of the soul beyond the natural world and physical death, as well as the impending character of God's judgment, the beatific vision of Christ crucified, the role of purgatory as preparation for heaven, and the eager anticipation of God's actual presence. What Newman sought to achieve in these works was to teach ordinary people about "the image of the area beyond the door of death" and to give him useful instructions about how to place "himself into God's hands" as he embarked on his "heavenward pilgrimage."[72]

These themes were presented in a way that makes them accessible to common people. They also made him into one of the nineteenth century's most effective apologists in defending the supernatural dimension of Christian doctrine and practice. Newman sought to provide his readers with hope to combat against the secularizing forces of theological liberalism.

CONCLUSION

Newman's entire apologetic activity was masterfully summarized by Owen Chadwick, who once wrote that Newman "was the first theorist of the Christian doctrine to face the challenge of modern historical enquiry."[73] Regardless of whether Newman was, in fact, the first to have done so is neither important nor useful, but this phrase points to his lifelong dedication in opposing theological liberalism, the fruit of modern historical criticism. Although he may have done this "despite himself," as Chadwick notes, Newman was determined and consistent throughout his entire career, both as Anglican and as Catholic, in seizing opportunities to vigorously criticize theological liberalism. Whenever he did so,

---

68. Ibid., 331.
69. Amy K. Hirschfeld, "An Overview of the Intellectual History of Catacomb Archaeology," in *Commemorating the Dead: Texts and Artifacts in Context. Studies of Roman, Jewish, and Christian Burials*, eds. Laurie Brink, OP, and Deborah Green (Berlin: de Gruyter, 2008), 24.
70. John Henry Newman, *The Dream of Gerontius* (Oxford: Oxford University Press, 1903 [1865]).
71. Ibid., 25.
72. Julien Chilcott-Monk, *John Henry Newman and the Path to Sainthood* (Norwich: Canterbury, 2010), 9.
73. Owen Chadwick, *Newman* (Oxford: Oxford University Press, 1989 [1983]), 1.

Newman encouraged ordinary people to contemplate the beauty and hope of Christianity "in a world which looked to be about to reject religion as behind the times."[74] Though he may at times have been viewed as a theologian, preacher, philosopher, and educator, Newman's apologetic efforts cannot be limited to any of these fields alone. It is better to see Newman, in Ian Ker's words, as a "supremely imaginative writer"[75] who never made a real distinction among his efforts in theology, preaching, philosophy, and education but employed them all to defend the traditional supernaturalism of Christian teaching and practice against the secularizing tendencies of theological liberalism. In doing so, he provided Christianity with a unified apologetic effort, bringing together academic theology, homiletics, philosophy, and education. He also reached ordinary people and their mundane concerns through his novel and poetry. Newman's apologetics is, perhaps, best described in his own words. He sought to defend Christianity against theological liberalism by inspiring people to pursue truth, hope, and holiness with "clear heads and holy hearts."[76]

SELECTED BIBLIOGRAPHY

Listed here are only the writings that have been cited multiple times within the chapter. This bibliography is not a complete record of all the works and sources that have been consulted.

Primary Sources

Newman, John Henry. *An Essay in Aid of a Grammar of Assent*. New York: The Catholic Publication Society, 1870.

———. *An Essay on the Development of Christian Doctrine*. London: Toovey, 1846 [1845].

———. *Apologia pro vita sua*. New York: Appleton, 1865.

———. *Callista: A Sketch of the Third Century*. London: Burns, Oates, & Co., 1869 [1855].

———. *Lectures on the Doctrine of Justification*. London: Rivington, 1874 [1838].

———. *Parochial and Plain Sermons*. London: Rivington, 1875 [1834–1843].

———. *Sermons, Chiefly on the Theory of Religious Belief, Preached before the University of Oxford*. London: Rivington, 1844 [1843].

———. *The Arians of the Fourth Century*, with an Introduction and Editor's Notes by Rowan Williams. Leominster: Gracewing, 2001 [1833].

———. *The Dream of Gerontius*. Oxford: Oxford University Press, 1903 [1865].

———. *The Idea of a University*. London: Longmans, Green, & Co., 1919 [1873].

———. *The Scope and Nature of University Education*. London: Longmans, 1859 [1852].

———. *The Tracts of All Times*. London: Rivington, 1833, etc.

———. *The Via Media of the Anglican Church*. London: Pickering, 1877.

———. *Tract XC on Certain Passages in the XXXIX Articles*. Oxford: Rivington, 1865 [1841].

———. "Biglietto Speech". In W. P. Neville, *Addresses to Cardinal Newman and His Replies*. London: Longmans, 1905. Pages 61-70.

74. Chadwick, *Newman*, 4.
75. Ker, *The Genius of John Henry Newman*, xii.
76. Newman, *Via Media*, lxxv.

Secondary Sources

Barr, Colin. *Paul Cullin, John Henry Newman, and the Catholic University of Ireland, 1845-1865*. Leominster: Gracewing, 2003.

Bednar, Gerald J. *Faith as Imagination: The Contribution of William F. Lynch, S. J.* Kansas City, MO: Sheed and Ward, 1996.

Blehl, Vincent F., ed. *The Essential Newman: The Central Writings of the Master of English Prose Who Infused New Vigor into the Nineteenth-Century Catholic Church*. New York: Mentor-Omega, 1963.

Blehl, Vincent F. *Pilgrim Journey: John Henry Newman, 1801–1845*. London: Burns & Oates, 2001.

Castaldo, Chris. *Justified in Christ: The Doctrine of Peter Martyr Vermigli and John Henry Newman and Their Ecumenical Implications*. Eugene, OR: Pickwick Publications, 2017.

Chadwick, Owen. *Newman*. Oxford: Oxford University Press, 1989 [1983].

Chilcott-Monk, Julien. *John Henry Newman and the Path to Sainthood*. Norwich: Canterbury Press, 2010.

Connolly, John R. *John Henry Newman: A View of Catholic Faith for the New Millenium*. Lanham, MD: Sheed & Ward / Rowman & Littlefield, 2005.

Crosby, John F. *The Personalism of John Henry Newman*. Washington, DC: The Catholic University of America Press, 2014.

Dulles, Avery. *John Henry Newman*. London: Continuum, 2009.

Earnest, James D., and Gerard Tracey. "Editors' Introduction." Pages xiii-cvix in James D. Earnest and Gerard Tracey, eds. *John Henry Newman: Fifteen Sermons Preached before the University of Oxford between A. D. 1826 and 1843*. Oxford: Oxford University Press, 2006.

Ford, John T. "Biography: John Henry Newman (1801-1890)". Pages 1-31 in John T. Ford, C. S. C., ed. *John Henry Newman: Spiritual Writings*. Maryknoll, NY: Orbis, 2012.

Garnett, Emmeline. *Tormented Angel: A Life of John Henry Newman*. New York, NY: Ariel / Ferrar, Straus, & Giroux, 1966.

Griffin, John R. *John Keble: Saint of Anglicanism*. Macon, GA: Mercer University Press, 1987, 82.

Harding, Richard J. *John Henry Newman: The Resolution of a Dilemma*. Lincoln, NE: iUniverse, 2000.

Hart, Trevor. "Creeds, Councils, and Doctrinal Development." Pages 636–659 in Philip F. Esler, ed. *The Early Christian World*. Vol. 1. London: Routledge, 2000.

Himmelfarb, Gertrude. "The Essay as Genre." Pages 17–30 in Gertrude Himmelfarb, ed. *The Spirit of the Age: Victorian Essays*. New Haven, CT: Yale University Press, 2007.

Hirschfeld, Amy K. "An Overview of the Intellectual History of Catacomb Archaeology." Pages 11–38 in Laurie Brink, O. P., and Deborah Green, eds. *Commemorating the Dead: Texts and Artifacts in Context. Studies of Roman, Jewish, and Christian Burials*. Berlin: Walter de Gruyter, 2008.

Hütter, Reinhard. *Bound to Be Free: Evangelical Catholic Engagements in Ecclesiology, Ethics, and Ecumenism*. Grand Rapids: Eerdmans, 2004.

Kenny, Anthony. *Philosophy in the Modern World*. Vol. 4. Oxford: Oxford University Press, 2007.

Ker, Ian, ed. *The Genius of John Henry Newman: Selections from His Writings*. Oxford: Oxford University Press, 1989.

Ker, Ian. *The Achievement of John Henry Newman*. London: Collins, 1991.

Ker, Ian. *John Henry Newman: A Biography*. Oxford: Oxford University Press, 2010 [1988, 2009].

King, Benjamin J. *Newman and the Alexandrian Fathers: Shaping Doctrinei in the Nineteenth-Century England*. Oxford: Oxford University Press, 2009.

Magill, Gerard. *Religious Morality in John Henry Newman: Hermeneutics of Imagination*. Dordrecht: Springer, 2015.

Martin, Brian. *John Henry Newman: His Life and Work*. London: Continuum, 1982 [2000]), 51.

Merrigan, Terrence. "Revelation." Pages 47–72 in Ian Ker and Terrence Merrigan, eds. *The Cambridge Companion to John Henry Newman*. Cambridge: Cambridge University Press, 2009.

Merrigan, Terrence. *Clear Heads and Holy Hearts: The Religious and Theological Ideal of John Henry Newman*. Louvain: Peeters, 1991.

Meyer, Ben F. *Critical Realism and the New Testament*. Eugene, OR: Wipf & Stock, 1989.

Moleski, S. J., Martin X. *Personal Catholicism: The Theological Epistemologies of John Henry Newman and Michael Polanyi*. Washington, DC: The Catholic University of America Press, 2000.

Newman, Jay. *The Mental Philosophy of John Henry Newman*. Waterloo, ON: Wilfried Laurier University Press, 1986.

Olney, James. *Metaphors of Self: The Meaning of Autobiography*. Princeton, NJ: Princeton University Press, 1973.

Sachs, William L. *The Transformation of Anglicanism: From State Church to Global Communion*. Cambridge: Cambridge University Press, 2002 (1993), 162.

Sedgwick, Timothy F. *The Christian Moral Life: Practices and Piety.* New York: Seabury, 1999 (2008).

Short, Edward. *Newman and His Family.* London: Bloomsbury, 2013.

Spitzer, S. J., Robert. *Finding True Happiness: Satisfying Our Restless Hearts.* San Francisco, CA: Ignatius, 2015.

Sugg, Joyce. *John Henry Newman: Snapdragon in the Wall.* Leominster: Gracewing, 2001 (1965).

Thomas, Stephen. *Newman and Heresy: The Anglican Years.* Cambridge: Cambridge University Press, 1991 (2002).

Townsend, Craig D. *Faith in Their Own Color: Black Episcopalians in Antebellum New York City.* New York: Columbia University Press, 2005.

Trevelyan, George M. *Lord Grey of the Reform Bill, Being the Life of the Charles, Second Earl of Grey.* New York: Longman's, Green, & Co., 1920.

Vélez, Juan R. *Holiness in a Secular Age: The Witness of Cardinal Newman.* New York: Scepter, 2017.

Wilcox, S. T. D., Peter C. *John Henry Newman, Spiritual Director, 1845–1890.* Eugene, OR: Pickwick, 2013.

Xianzhang, Hu, and Cao Li, "Meaning and Methods: Some Thoughts on the Role of General Education and Curriculum Design". Pages 61–80 in Xing Jun, Ng Pak-Sheung, and Cheng Chunyan, eds. *General Education and the Development of Global Citizenship in Hong Kong, Taiwan, and Mainland China: Not Merely Icing on the Cake.* London: Routledge, 2013.

SØREN KIERKEGAARD

Apologetic of Christianity for Christendom

SEAN A. TURCHIN
CHRISTIAN KETTERING

Søren Kierkegaard (1813–1855) has often been presented as the existentialist, irrationalist philosopher of "leap of faith" fame who did great damage to the true intellectual appeal of Christianity. Interestingly, this is also the same Søren Kierkegaard known to be a Christian philosopher who serves as a prime example as to why Christians have little use for philosophy. These two caricatures of Kierkegaard represent how two segments of the Christian community are critical of certain dispositions found in other Christians. The former caricature is linked to the academics, who are generally disturbed by the severe deficiency in the common Christian to provide a reasonable explanation for their belief in Christ. The latter caricature represents a disposition of Christians who are professionals in nonacademic fields and are often skeptical of academic thought. For them, Kierkegaard's "leap of faith" demonstrates that Christian philosophical endeavors are a waste of time. Francis Schaeffer would serve as a prominent example of someone who understood Kierkegaard in light of both caricatures.

In this chapter, a distinct view of Kierkegaard will be presented. Søren Kierkegaard is an example of a person who dedicated his entire existence—intellectual, emotional, and social—to presenting and upholding the life-changing truth found in faith in Christ. Indeed, if an apologist is one who dedicates one's life to protecting, preserving, and witnessing to the core elements of Christian theology, then one might dare call Kierkegaard an apologist. If in this way Kierkegaard can be considered an apologist, surely he is also the apologist's apologist. For if the apologist ever loses their own way in emphasizing logical, evidential equations in defense of Christianity, the dialectical thought of Kierkegaard will be there to prick their life back to the life-changing, existence-altering offer of Christ.

HISTORICAL BACKGROUND

Born May 5, 1813, in Copenhagen, Denmark, the "melancholy Dane," Søren Kierkegaard, lived a life ridden with personal guilt, depression, and tragedy. Throughout his youth he searched to find his own place in the world, searched to what task he would employ his literary, philosophical, and theological genius. It was the question as to his purpose in life that later birthed a prolific authorship of literary and theological-philosophical works. And although his work covers a number of topics, from that of existence to that of various social critiques of his day, the enduring theme throughout his authorship was that of Christianity, namely, what it means to be a Christian.

This task proved so central that, coupled with his melancholy, in 1841 he broke off his engagement to his beloved Regine Olsen. Kierkegaard did this out of fear that she would not be able to bear the weight of his task or his depression. After a short life, Kierkegaard died, largely unsuccessful in his reform, at the age of forty-two on November 11, 1855. In this relatively short span of time, Kierkegaard is estimated to have written over thirty works as well as thousands of pages of journal entries. Additionally, most of these works offer consistent yet multilayered messages interacting with and challenging some of the most influential philosophical minds in history.

THEOLOGICAL CONTEXT

Leading theologians of Kierkegaard's Denmark, such as Hans Lassen Martensen, found alliance with influential philosophical systems of the time. A former student at the Univeristy of Copenhagen and Kierkegaard's tutor for a time, Martensen was influential in introducing Hegel's philosophy to Denmark, specifically the use of Georg Wilhelm Friedrich Hegel's philosophy in making sense of theological problems. Martensen's position was that modern Christianity need no longer operate as the "older supernaturalism," whereby supernaturalism and rationalism stood in stark contrast to each other.[1] Martensen's position implies that although theology had at one time maintained a separation between knowledge and faith, rationalism and supernaturalism, reason and revelation, this opposition is no longer necessary for Christian thought (in light of Hegel's philosophy), since the incarnation is seen as providing a supreme model of mediation.[2]

---

1. Jakob Peter Mynster, "Rationalism, Supernaturalism" in *Mynster's 'Rationalism, Supernaturalism' and the Debate about Mediation*, ed. and trans. Jon Stewart, Texts from *Golden Age Denmark*, Vol. 5 (Soren Kierkegaard Research Centre, University of Copenhagen: Museum Tusculanum Press, 2009), 95. Quote also in Bornemann's review, 61.

2. Hans Lassen Martensen, "Rationalism, Supernaturalism and the *principium exclusi medii*" in *Mynster's 'Rationalism, Supernaturalism' and the Debate about Mediation*, 130, 133. Preceding this quotation, Martensen argues that the law of excluded middle, "cannot be a final court of appeals for theology . . . when we see how Christianity continually sublates it."

Martensen found the thought of Hegel useful particularly in mediating the logical law of excluded middle and therefore the supposed problem of Christ as God and man.[3] Kierkegaard was skeptical of such mediation or overcoming of logical barriers. For Kierkegaard, such mediation is shown to be epistemologically unsound in actual existence, regardless of what thinkers can achieve on paper. In other words, an abstract ideation of the assurance of the possibility of God as man does not translate into existence. For example, it did not translate into existence for the disciples, who saw Jesus walk on water and yet was rejected by his own religious leaders. Nor does such "rational" exuberance assist those who live after Christ. Kierkegaard also sees this overreaching exaltation of human reason as an afront to God's own purposeful revelation, which makes room for faith, a passionate movement of one's whole being, rather than mere propositional acknowledgment.

Kierkegaard saw this move by Martensen as an epistemologically suspect elevation of reason, leading to a perversion of theology as well as a conflation of what Kierkeggard considered the polite secular ethical life of universal values with the Christian life and its claim of a direct relationship with God.

Kantian and Fichtean ethical viewpoints were also assimilated into the Christian viewpoint of Kierkegaard's day. Kierkegaard saw this noncritical acceptance of secular philosophy as something of a trojan horse that would leave Christianity as a shallow shell without the life-changing message of Christ. Kierkegaard measured Hegel's unbounded unfolding of reason as flawed and, even worse, damaging to the core of Christianity. For Kierkegaard, the ethics and faith of revelation through Abraham to Christ are quite distinct from Kant and Fichte's faith in human reason and their conflation of the ethical and the divine.[4] Kierkegaard argued that the church leaders of his Denmark were trading the treasure of Christ for the follies of human reason and, what is more, in the name of furthering Christianity.

APOLOGETIC CONTEXT

For those familiar with the works of Kierkegaard, it is well known that he had a disdain for Christian apologetics, namely, any attempt to make the truths of Christianity rationally acceptable whereby such truths demand nothing more from the individual than mere intellectual assent. Accordingly, to make

---

3. Sean A. Turchin, "Introducing Christianity into Christendom: Investigating the Affinity between Søren Kierkegaard and the Early Thought of Karl Barth," (PhD diss., University of Edinburgh, 2011), 31.

4. Christian Kettering, "Abraham as Existential Archetype in Kierkegaard's *Fear and Trembling*" (PhD diss. to be presented, North-West University), 207.

Christianity a truth equal to that of a mathematical proposition would be to rob Christianity of its very essence, namely, the demand for the individual to accept the paradoxical truth claims of Christianity against the absurdity of its claims and the offense to reason that follows, thus making way for faith. For Kierkegaard, only faith is able to come to terms with the paradoxical nature of Christianity, specifically the "absolute paradox"—that in the person of Jesus Christ, God became man.[5]

As we shall see, a human's ability to make "rational" sense of the incarnation comes to a halt when faced with the absolute paradox. Reason is faced with what only appears as an absurdity—"that the eternal truth has come into existence in time, that God has come into existence, has been born, has grown up, etc., has come into existence exactly as an individual human being, indistinguishable from any other human being."[6]

But Kierkegaard's estimation of the powers of human reason in relation to the tenets of Christianity does not mean Kierkegaard thought Christianity offers no rational basis for its beliefs.[7] Furthermore, Kierkegaard's dislike for apologetics does not necessarily conclude that he offered no apologetical defense for his own understanding of Christianity. Just because Kierkegaard painstakingly argued for the limits of human rationality and historical investigation in relation to "knowing" the truth claims of Christianity does not mean he believed Christianity was without historical basis and that its truths were indefensible. As Myron Penner argues in his work *The End of Apologetics*, "Kierkegaard's rejection of apologetics (and its use of reason) is to be seen as part and parcel of his rejection of the modern conception of reason—not of reason altogether."[8] The key to Penner's observation is the "modern conception" of reason, not what reason essentially is or offers. This is to say Kierkegaard's epistemological viewpoint of humility does not apply only to Christianity but to all endeavors. For Kierkegaard, uncritical celebration of human reason *en masse* was a recipe for

---

5. Kierkegaard, *Practice in Christianity* (hereafter *PC*), ed. and trans. Howard V. Hong and Edna H. Hong (Princeton: Princeton University Press, 1991), 125; Søren Kierkegaard, *Journals and Papers* (hereafter *JP*), vol. 4, ed. and trans. Howard V. Hong and Edna H. Hong (Bloomington, IN: Indiana University Press, 1970, 401.

6. Søren Kierkegaard, *Concluding Unscientific Postscript to Philosophical Fragments* (hereafter *CUP*), ed. and trans. by Howard V. Hong and Edna H. Hong (Princeton: Princeton University Press, 1992), 210.

7. Against those who view Kierkegaard as endorsing some form of irrationalism, George Pattison, in his work, *The Philosophy of Kierkegaard* (Durham, UK: Acumen, 2005), holds that "If we read Kierkegaard as a whole he does in fact create a context in which the Christian claims are meaningful, if not reasonable." He adds, "It is merely intellectual laziness to declare that Kierkegaard is a fideistic irrationalist;" see pp. 134, 165. Furthermore, most debates concerning Kierkegaard's understanding of the rationality of Christianity inevitably revolve around his presentation of Christian tenets as being paradoxical. In this light many understand Kierkegaard as an irrationalist.

8. Myron Penner, *The End of Apologetics: Christian Witness in a Postmodern Context* (Grand Rapids: Baker Academic, 2013), 11.

one to miss the eternal significance of one's own life as well as lead to the broader degradation of society. Johannes Climacus explains, "Lo, we have become so objective that even the wife of a civil servant argues from the whole, from the state, from the idea of society, from geographic scientificity to the single individual. It follows so automatically that the single individual is Christian, has faith etc. that it is flippant to make so much ado about it, or certainly capricious."[9]

HISTORICAL VS. PROPOSITIONAL APOLOGETICS

Concerning historical truth, even that of the history of Christianity, Kierkegaard argued that such truth is established by historical evidences or reports, whereas philosophical truth is established in relation to the "eternal truth."[10] The question, for Kierkegaard, is in what sense are such notions of truth related to Christianity? It is not that he believed Christianity existed without objective or historical truth as if it were a mere belief divorced from reality. Concerning the historicity of Christianity, Kierkegaard says, "Objectively viewed Christianity is a given fact,"[11] meaning, "Christianity is a historical truth; it appears at a certain time and certain place and consequently it is relevant to a certain time and place."[12] Nevertheless, his concern is with the inevitable consequences from which the "inquiring, speculating, knowing subject accordingly asks about the truth but not about the subjective truth, the truth of appropriation"[13] and to what extent, if any, historical investigation and rationalism inhibit or promote appropriation. Thus, for Kierkegaard, "The objective issue, then, would be about the truth of Christianity. The subjective issue is about the individual's relation to Christianity."[14] All things considered, if the discipline of apologetics is to offer a defense of Christianity, then one can easily see Kierkegaard's writings as offering such a defense; he tries to explicate what Christianity is and what it means to be a Christian against what he sees as the "counterfeit" Christianity of his day. What Kierkegaard does not seek to do, indeed what he does not think it is possible to do, is to improve or make more appealing all that is encompassed in God's self-revealing in Christ.

---

9. Kierkegaard, *CUP*, 51.
10. Ibid., 21.
11. Ibid.
12. Kierkegaard, *JP*, vol. 2, 232.
13. Kierkegaard, *CUP*, 21.
14. Ibid., 17. For Kierkegaard, if Christianity is not about objective adherence but rather about subjective appropriation, true Christian living, then the obsessive efforts of theological scholarship and historicism fail to even understand the history of Christianity regarding its infiltrating the world. He asks, "Or was it perhaps objective doctrine, the objective, which triumphantly penetrated the whole world? What infinite nonsense! No, the objective has nothing to do with such things; it never moves from the spot. No, it was not doctrine, it was not the objective which conquered the world, but it was the blood of the martyrs and the sacrifices of the faithful—in short, it was the subjectivities who triumphantly fought the doctrine through" (357). See Kierkegaard's *JP*, vol. 4.

CONTEXTUAL APOLOGETICS

Apologists from Justin Martyr's day to the modern day respond to the pressing questions of their time. So also is the case with Kierkegaard. In the context of his time, perhaps somewhat equal to ours, Kierkegaard believed that the application of Hegelian logic to the Christian tenets of faith was contra to the very essence of Christianity. Thus, Kierkegaard stood against the efforts of Danish Hegelians such as Hans Lassen Martensen and Johan Ludvig Heiberg,[15] whose efforts sought to rid Christianity of its contradictions to make doctrine palatable to reason.

Kierkegaard argued that faith, and not a mere intellectual assent to the message of Christianity, was essential since reason cannot mediate the truths found through faith. Martensen explained his Hegelian approach to theology, stating, "In theology both rationalism and supernaturalism are antiquated standpoints which belong to an age which has disappeared."[16] Martensen's position implies that although theology had at one time maintained a separation between knowledge and faith, rationalism and supernaturalism, reason and revelation, this opposition is no longer necessary for Christian thought (in light of Hegel's philosophy), since the incarnation is seen as providing a supreme model of mediation.[17] But Christianity demands the adherence to Christ's nature as being both human and divine. But this adherence does not entail a logical explanation as to the rationality of this union in Christ. To this end, it was against the attempts of the Hegelians to explain away Christian mystery and paradox that Kierkegaard employed concepts that insist on the limitation of human reason. These concepts are designed to show that in relation to the central tenets of Christianity, reason comes to a halt.[18] To his own "apologetic" efforts, Kierkegaard employed pseudonyms to address the threat that speculative philosophy posed to Christianity. As Jon Stewart states, "Here Climacus argues against Heiberg's (and Martensen's) claim that mediation is the principle of Christianity, and that dogmas such as the Incarnation and the Trinity cannot be made sense of without it. Climacus' central plea is to avoid confusing

15. For a full account of Kierkegaard's thought in relation to his contemporaries and the issues that consumed the day, see Jon Stewart, *Kierkegaard's Relations to Hegel Reconsidered* (Cambridge: Cambridge University Press, 2003).

16. Jakob Peter Mynster, "Rationalism, Supernaturalism," in *Mynster's 'Rationalism, Supernaturalism' and the Debate about Mediation*, 95. Quote also in Bornemann's review, 61.

17. Hans Lassen Martensen, "Rationalism, Supernaturalism and the *principium exclusi medii*" in *Mynster's 'Rationalism, Supernaturalism' and the Debate about Mediation*, 130, 133. Preceding this quotation, Martensen argues that the law of excluded middle "cannot be a final court of appeals for theology ... when we see how Christianity continually sublates it."

18. George Pattison, *The Philosophy of Kierkegaard* (Durham, UK: Acumen, 2005), 134.

the two spheres and attempting to apply the principle of mediation to the sphere of actuality or Christian faith."[19]

So, Kierkegaard as an apologist? Again, in countering the defense (apologetics) of Christianity at the hands of the speculative rationalism of his day by means of his own dialectical methodology, then, yes, Kierkegaard can be seen as an apologist, one who aimed at a defense of true Christianity. Indeed, if his defense is to be equated with a modern conception of apologetics, whereby, perhaps, one seeks to "prove" the rational superiority of Christianity, Kierkegaard would have a problem with such a defense. Highlighting Kierkegaard's problem with an abuse of Christian apologetics, Penner states, "Kierkegaard is not against apologetics because he is a fideist who thinks Christian belief negates human reason, or that faith is opposed to any critical reflection on beliefs whatsoever. He objects to the entire modern epistemological paradigm that produces modern apologetics, because it attempts to ground faith in genius or secular reason."[20]

Kierkegaard is convinced that there is something much better as the ground of Christian truth and revelation than this genius or secular reason.

APOLOGETIC RESPONSE

Kierkegaard offered several considerations as to why rational and historical investigations into the truths of Christianity ultimately find themselves at a loss for providing us certainty or rational ease. Here, Kierkegaard's critique may seek to remind us of our inevitable epistemological limitations and thus offer a humble approach to modern apologetical endeavors.

In Kierkegaard's defense of the truth of Christianity, he employed several themes or concepts for consideration: the limitations of human reason due to the effect of sin, the knowledge of history as an approximation, and the paradoxical nature of the incarnation as one that offends human reason. All such themes aim to place speculative rationalism and historicism of Christianity beyond a human's own powers to make known what only God can fully know. We shall explore these themes below in relation to Kierkegaard's attack on the

---

19. Jon Stewart, "Johan Ludvig Heiberg: Kierkegaard's Criticism of Hegel's Danish Apologist" in *Kierkegaard and His Danish Contemporaries, Tome I, Philosophy, Politics and Social Theory Vol. 7*, ed. Jon Stewart (Farnham, Surrey, England:Ashgate, 2009), 63.

20. Penner, *The End of Apologetics*, 58. Although I argue in my PhD dissertation against a fideist reading of Kierkegaard, I take Penner's point to be that though Kierkegaard was himself engaged with rational reflection and reasoning of Christianity, these cannot provide epistemological security for those who are deliberating on whether Christianity is true. Indeed, I believe, perhaps shifting slightly away from Penner's critique, that modern apologetics can be useful in its rational and historical investigations, but such investigations must understand their inevitable limitations—limitations that the ancient texts of Scripture openly proclaimed and therefore, even in the face of the miraculous, nonetheless called for faith.

exaggerated use of rationalism and historicism in seeking to grasp the truths of the Christian faith.

REASON AND CHRISTIANITY

Indispensable to understanding Kierkegaard's conception of the limitations of human reason, and thus all its methods of employment to rationally justify Christianity, is the Christian concept of *sin* and its effect on our relationship to the truth. Not only are humans and God infinitely qualitatively different (hereafter IQD), but because of sin they remained relationally separated.[21] Consequently, the IQD serves Kierkegaard in reminding humanity of both its ontological difference from God as well as its relational separation from God, but this is not its only purpose. With this knowledge, the self thus despairs over this abyss separating oneself and God. The self thus despairs insofar as this separation serves in revealing to oneself that it is not a true self, for a true self is one that exists in relation to God. Or as Kierkegaard maintains, one can truly come to know oneself only before "the mirror of the Word. . . . To stand before the mirror means to stand before God."[22]

So, against the Socratic definition of "sin is ignorance,"[23] Kierkegaard states, "Christianity begins in another way: man has to learn what sin is by revelation from God; sin is not a matter of a person's not having understood what is right but of his being unwilling to understand it, of his not willing what is right."[24] Our willing and knowing need to be confronted with the truth since no such truth is attainable by our own rational and volitional powers.

Left to its own powers, the self exists both without God and true selfhood, thus consumed in the despair brought on by the IQD. But amid this discussion of the sheer negativity of the self, divorced from selfhood and God, grace has been present. In his insisting that revelation is needed to overcome the IQD's effects—that the self needs the "Savior" to both receive the condition for the truth and the truth itself—Kierkegaard does not leave the self to its own ruin in the abyss.

---

21. Søren Kierkegaard, *The Sickness unto Death* (hereafter *SUD*), ed. and trans. Howard V. Hong and Edna H. Hong (Princeton: Princeton University Press, 1983), 126. Kierkegaard repeatedly expresses the *IQD* in his *Eighteen Upbuilding Discourses*, with the phrase, "You are on earth and God is in heaven." Note that it is not merely in his pseudonymous literature that Kierkegaard concerns himself with the God-relation but also in his signed Discourses. See "To Need God is a Human Being's Highest Perfection" and "To Gain One's Soul in Patience" in Søren Kierkegaard, *Eighteen Upbuilding Discourses*, ed. and trans. Howard V. Hong and Edna H. Hong (Princeton: Princeton University Press, 1990), 307.

22. Kierkegaard, *JP*, vol. 4, 287.

23. Kierkegaard, *Philosophical Fragments* (hereafter *PF*), ed. and trans. Howard V. Hong and Edna H. Hong (Princeton: Princeton University Press, 1985), 87.

24. Kierkegaard, *SUD*, 95.

With the impossibility of the offence maintained by the IQD being breached on this side of eternity, humanity is "reminded that God has accomplished 'the impossible;' a gift which requires the consent, not of human comprehension, but the consent of the free will to a forgiveness which is revealed by God."[25] Kierkegaard heeds us to take comfort in the divine possibility, whereby, as he states, "The self is healthy and free from despair . . . when, precisely by having despaired, it rests transparently in God.[26] Kierkegaard was concerned with the possibility that his intentions with the self would be misunderstood. He states, "This self is no longer the merely human self but is what I, hoping not to be misinterpreted, would call the theological self, the self directly before God. And what infinite reality the self gains by being conscious of existing before God, by becoming a human self whose criterion is God!"[27]

In sum, the theological implications of Kierkegaard's presentation should be quite clear. Humanity is born into sin and thus is without hope by means of its own efforts. They are without hope because they lack not only the truth but also the condition to receive it. Thus, for Kierkegaard, Christ is both the teacher and Savior, who saves humanity from its condition. By virtue of the Savior's initiation, the individual can now come to Christ and follow him in truth. In this light, the "teacher is the way, the truth, and the life."[28] This to say that through the paradoxical revelation of God as man, Jesus of Nazareth, one is confronted with one's own sin and limitation. In philosophical terms, sin enhances the IQD both ethically and epistemologically, and yet in Jesus of Nazareth, one is called to faith in the absolute infinite being who can break into one's finite subjectivity

---

25. Ibid., 128.
26. Ibid., 30.
27. Ibid., 79.
28. T. H. Croscall, *Kierkegaard Studies* (London: Lutterworth, 1948), 141. At the conclusion of this section, it is important to note that much of the interpretation of Kierkegaardian subjectivity, in the relative or fideist sense, is derived from the infamous passage found in a journal entry dated 1835, in which Kierkegaard says, "The thing is to find a truth which is true for me, to find the idea for which I can live and die. What would be the use of discovering so-called objective truth, of working through all the systems of philosophy and [being able] to review them all and show up the inconsistencies within each system? What good would it do me to be able to develop a theory of the state and combine all the details into a single whole, and so construct a world in which I did not live? What good would it do me to explain the meaning of Christianity if it had no deeper significance for me and for my life? What good would it do me if truth stood before me, cold and naked, not caring whether I recognized her or not, and producing in me a shudder of fear rather than a trusting devotion? I certainly do not deny . . . an imperative of understanding and that through it one can work upon men, but it must be taken up into my life." The fact that this entry was recorded in 1835 and *PF* was not written until 1844 could lead some to conclude a form of relativism in the strict subjective sense of Kierkegaard's early thought. But even if one is to adopt this view, it is clear that Kierkegaard refutes this particular philosophy derived from the statement that "the thing is to find a truth which is true for me" in *PF*. This form of truth, as we shall see later is the Socratic Truth. Truth, as seen in *PF*, does not lie in the subject, as Socrates taught, but is foreign to the subject and hence must be brought to the subject. The subject is confronted with the object of belief and therefore appropriates the objective in the act of belief, being the act of subjectivity. Therefore, the idea of Kierkegaard endorsing subjectivism as a form of relativism from this entry is clearly incorrect.

and restore one's designed self in relation to a transcendent and wholly other God. Christ is indeed the bridge across the IQD, though in the revelation of Christ, God has chosen to require faith.

Given Kierkegaard's position of the inefficiency of human reason in obtaining knowledge of our condition and thus the remedy of that condition, it is no surprise that he extends this inefficiency to our mere rational attempts of knowledge of God in general. We are unable to transcend from what is known to that which is unknown. Yet human understanding continually desires to transcend its own innate epistemological barriers. In fact, in the name of human reason, the possibility of revelation from God has been denigrated or outright dismissed. Kierkegaard's dialectical IQD also suggests that human reason has no grounds for such a claim against the possibility of God and his revelation.[29] Kierkegaard spends significant ink outlining human reason's push toward that which is infinite and absolute, as ethically-minded people sense hints of this within themselves. Kierkegaard's verdict is bleak: human reason never gets beyond its own subjectivity, trapped in finitude and limitation, and sadly it is comfortable and happy to be so.[30]

The unknown exists, as Kierkegaard says, as "the frontier that is continually arrived at."[31] It is the frontier of the "absolutely different." But this distinction of that which is absolutely different is not a distinction arrived at outside the understanding itself. Rather, it is the understanding that "consequently thinks the difference in itself, which it thinks by itself. It cannot absolutely transcend itself and therefore thinks as above itself only the sublimity that it thinks by itself."[32]

In the end, human reason affords us nothing about our knowledge of God. Given what has been stated above, it is no wonder that Kierkegaard thinks apologetical arguments for proving God's existence are useless; again, this is not saying he would have a problem, per se, with proofs, understood in the rightful context of rational considerations. But it is not merely the inadequacy of human reason and its sinful condition that make such arguments or proofs ultimately unprofitable. Kierkegaard believed that demonstrations for God's existence betray a contradiction in the desire to demonstrate God to begin with. He writes, "If, namely, the god [Guden] does not exist, then of course it is impossible

29. Kettering, "Abraham as Existential," 149.

30. Søren Kierkegaard, *Fear and Trembling: Repetition*, ed. and trans. Howard V. Hong and Edna H. Hong (Princeton: Princeton University Press, 1983), 60. Kierkegaard's pseudonym *Johannes de Silentio* states, "The person who denies himself and sacrifices himself because of duty gives up the finite in order to grasp the infinite and is adequately assured; the tragic hero gives up the certain for the even more certain, and the observer's eye views him with confidence. But the person who gives up the universal in order to grasp something even higher that is not the universal, what does he do?"

31. Kierkegaard, *SUD*, 44.

32. Kierkegaard, *SUD*, 45. See Kierkegaard, *SUD*, 99, 117, 126, 127.

to demonstrate it. But if he does exist, then it is foolishness to want to demonstrate it, since I, in the very moment the demonstration commences, would presuppose it not as doubtful—which a presupposition cannot be, inasmuch as it is a presupposition—but as decided, because otherwise I would not begin easily perceiving that the whole thing would be impossible if he did not exist."[33]

What Kierkegaard finds amusing is that in seeking to prove God's existence, one must possess the presupposition that God first exists, otherwise the desire to demonstrate it would have never been initiated. In short, "the whole process of demonstrating continually becomes . . . an expanded concluding development of what I conclude from having presupposed that the object of investigation exists."[34] Kierkegaard's criticisms of the proofs for God's existence stand under some of his harsher criticisms of apologetics. This is not to say that theism is paradoxical or even against reason. Rather, for Kierkegaard, if one's emphasis is on a supposedly reasonable formula to affirm God's existence, one is not heeding the revelation of the Christian viewpoint in the right way. Kierkegaard says, "The fool says in his heart there is no God, but he who says in heart or to others: Just wait a little and I will prove it to you—ah, what a rare wise man he is!"[35] Kierkegaard is a philosopher of the gospel: he sees, succinctly sizes up complex philosophers, pokes holes in their argument, and then presents the gospel—stylized with authentic philosophical clothes—as a better solution. If Kierkegaard could prove Jesus was God, he would not do it, for faith is what is called for. Faith is not a consolation of last resort for Kierkegaard. On this point he mocks the church leaders of his day. In the least, faith is by design.[36]

If one were to create a "Kierkegaardian" apologetic, it would be rooted in revelation and the teleological and logical nature of continual calls for faith, even in light of the miraculous, when discussing an infinite God and finite humanity. This insight can be found in a close study of Kierkegaard. Even so, Kierkegaard, who is aware of every detail and inuendo of his own authorship, does not make this point. Rather, and not unlike the modern Billy Graham, Kierkegaard is quite anxious about getting to witnessing to his faith that the eternal God has come to us in time, made us aware of our sin, and offered salvation from it through faith in Christ.[37] In this message, Kierkegaard finds the life-altering truth for one's existence.

---

33. Ibid., 40.

34. Ibid.

35. Søren Kierkegaard and Charles E. Moore, *Provocations: Spiritual Writings* (Plough Publishing House, 2014), 75.

36. Kettering, "Abraham as Existential," 195.

37. Bent Rohde, *Kierkegaard's Journals and Notebooks, Volume 7* (Princeton: Princeton University Press, 2014), 290. Kierkegaard writes, "Ah, if only we could remain clear about what Christianity is! That it is not a

HISTORICAL EVIDENCE AND "OBJECTIVE TRUTH"

According to Kierkegaard, when it comes to "truths" of history or "truths" of the past, the best we can enjoy, in terms of what we can know, is an approximation. But where one's eternal fate is concerned, an approximation is not good enough. Hence, those who seek to be fully assured of the truth of Christianity by means of historical evidence will be greatly disappointed. Arguing against a mere historical/objective approach to Christianity, Kierkegaard states:

> The objective view . . . continues from generation to generation precisely because the individuals (the observers) become more and more objective, less and less infinitely passionately interested. On the assumption that one would in this way continue to demonstrate and seek a demonstration of the truth of Christianity, something remarkable would finally emerge, that just as one was finished with the demonstration of its truth, it would cease to exist as something present: it would have become something historical to such a degree that it would be something past, whose truth, that is, whose historical truth, had now been brought to the point of reliability.[38]

It cannot be otherwise, for history has to do with the past. Those who live in the present can never know for sure the actual events of the past, and this applies to Julius Caesar with equal vigor as Christ. Add to this Christianity's claim that the eternal came into existence at a past moment in time, and the situation becomes utterly untenable.

If Christian truths exist in a way that parallel empirical truths, then Kierkegaard believed the outcome would consist of a position of constant deliberation, whereby one would continually seek to ascertain more knowledge about the credibility of the object. Thus, the result would be a dispassionate and blasé relation to Christianity. Since Christianity makes claims that could never be historically or conceptually verified, Kierkegaard believed that the objective position was not only untenable but that it also stood in stark opposition to what was central for the Christian faith, subjectivity (i.e., active Christian living).

---

doctrine, but an existence; that what is needed is not professors, but witnesses—then we would be free of all this self-important scholarliness, these fine men who are scholars—whom Christianity now needs. No, Christ did not need scholars, but could be satisfied with fishermen, so what is really needed now is many more fishermen. For, precisely because Christ was present, the danger would not have been so great if Christianity had fallen into the hands of students. The error is not the studying; rather, the error is that the emphasis continually falls on the wrong thing: on fathoming and presenting—so that it becomes ridiculous, a triviality, to do any of it. On the other hand, a simple man has no distractions. In this case one immediately focuses on his life: if he is without significance in this respect, he is without any significance whatever. But this simplification is extremely important with respect to drawing up the account."

38. Kierkegaard, *SUD*, 32.

The significance of this objective/subjective distinction originated from Kierkegaard's central concern presented in the work preceding *Concluding Unscientific Postscript (CUP)*, namely, *Fragments*. There Kierkegaard is concerned with the relation of historical evidences and scholarship to Christianity. At the beginning of *Fragments*, he asks, "Can a historical point of departure be given for an eternal consciousness; how can such a point of departure be of more than historical interest; can an eternal happiness be built on historical knowledge?"[39] Kierkegaard answers the question in the affirmative in both *Fragments* and *CUP*. The Christian's eternal happiness is built on the historical, and this is the absurd.[40] In *CUP* Kierkegaard explains, "The individual's eternal happiness is decided in time through a relation to something historical that furthermore is historical in such a way that its composition included that which according to its nature cannot become historical and consequently must become that by virtue of the absurd."[41]

In *CUP*, with succinct clarity, Kierkegaard addresses the issues he had posed earlier in *Fragments*. In sum, Kierkegaard considered *objectivity*, which represents impersonal, uninterested acceptance, the antithesis of true Christian faith. Faith had become a hybrid of an acceptance of historical facts and continual speculation, which sought to ascertain the historical truth more secularly, by way of evidence and demonstration. In sum, he says historical evidence and rationalism cannot provide any objective certainty about Christianity. If it did, it would deem faith superfluous. Kierkegaard sums up the whole problem of objective adherence to Christianity, stating, "The entire confusion and tragedy of the modern age can be expressed in one sentence: it has taken Christianity in vain."[42] Kierkegaard's criticism is twofold, in the first place Christianity is not historically certain, nor is anything else. History can always be fabricated with additions and subtractions. Additionally, even if Christianity has one of the surest historical foundations, which Kierkegaard does not deny, that the eternal infinite God became man in time is itself a paradox.

So it is that Kierkegaard sees his contemporaries as duped into an intellectual assent of Christian truth that does not lend itself to mere assent, for faith is required. Kierkegaard is quite clear that intellectual acknowledgement of

---

39. Kierkegaard, *PF*, 3.

40. Ibid.,109. In *PF* Kierkegaard's Climacus explains, "As is well known, Christianity is the only historical phenomenon that despite the historical indeed, precisely by means of the historical has wanted to be the single individual's point of departure for his eternal consciousness, has wanted to base his happiness on his relation to something historical" (Kierkegaard, *PF*, 109).

41. Kierkegaard, *CUP*, 385.

42. Søren Kierkegaard, *JP*, vol. 1, A–E, ed. and trans. Howard V. Hong and Edna H. Hong (Bloomington: Indiana University Press, 1967), 187.

supposed facts is not a characteristic of the life-altering passionate faith of Abraham and Christ. The witness and testimony of the church and Scripture serve as a historical basis. But this historical basis brings Kierkegaard's contemporaries no further than the people in the first century who saw a man, Jesus of Nazareth, do the miraculous.[43] The witness of Christians is held in the highest esteem by Kierkegaard, but this witness and the historical basis of it brings the listener to the paradox, to their own moment before God with the opportunity for faith.

KNOWLEDGE OF GOD IN CHRIST

For Kierkegaard, "God cannot be an object for man, since God is subject."[44] Therefore, the *Deus revelatus* is also the *Deus absconditus*, the hidden and the revealed God.[45] Since "God is pure Subjectivity,"[46] the absolute, the unconditioned, it seems he must make himself known in a way that also guards his divine subjectivity. God's veiling and unveiling of himself is achieved in his taking on of human flesh to be an object for human knowing, all the while remaining hidden in human flesh. It is the taking on of human flesh whereby God remains "incognito" within time. Kierkegaard writes, "He is God but chooses to become this individual human being. This . . . is the most profound incognito or the most impenetrable unrecognizability that is possible, because the contradiction between being God and being an individual human being is the greatest possible, the infinitely qualitative contradiction."[47] That God becomes man moves beyond the sheer paradoxes of the Christian faith to take its place as the "absolute" paradox. We must wonder what Kierkegaard means by stating that the truths of Christianity are paradoxical. For clarification, he looks to Gottfried Wilhelm Leibniz.

Leibniz makes a distinction between that which is above reason and that which is against reason.[48] This distinction relegates faith to that which is above reason. Furthermore, for Leibniz, there is a causal chain linking a cause to its effect. But, and this is where Kierkegaard thinks the problem exists for a demonstration of Christianity, the truths of the Christian faith possess no

---

43. Kierkegaard, *Practice in Christianity*, 41. Anti-Climacus in *Practice in Christianity* writes, "Yet he, the miracle worker, is still the lowly man who literally does not have a place to lay his head."

44. Kierkegaard, *JP*, vol. 2, F-K, 99.

45. For an in-depth study of Kierkegaard's use of the "veiling and unveiling" God, and its relation to Luther's thought, see Craig Hinkson's "Luther and Kierkegaard: Theologians of the Cross," *International Journal of Systematic Theology* 3.1 (2001): 25–45, and "Kierkegaard's Theology: Cross and Grace: The Lutheran and Idealist Traditions in His Thought" (PhD diss., University of Chicago, 1993), chaps. 1–3.

46. Kierkegaard, *JP*, vol. 3, L–R, 121. See also, pp. 121, 122, 265, 275, 284, 345, 270, 370, 404, 412–413, 420, 421.

47. Kierkegaard, *PC*, 131.

48. *SKS* 19, 390 / *Pap*. IV C 29 / *JP* 3, 3073.

such chain. Its truths exist beyond what reason is able to examine. Therefore, for Kierkegaard, these truths can be expressed only as a paradox.[49] But the lack of causality between a Christian truth and its cause does not qualify it as irrational, only above the rational. Kierkegaard believes that from the perspective of eternity, these paradoxes do not exist.[50]

According to Kierkegaard, the absurd, or paradox, denotes a concept that human reason gives to something it cannot dissolve. In short, "reason has no power at all to dissolve it in nonsense and prove that it is nonsense."[51] On the other side of the dialectic, reason cannot just simply dissolve it until it makes sense. Therefore, for Kierkegaard, the paradox, the absurd, "is a symbol, a riddle, a compounded riddle about which reason must say: I cannot solve it, it cannot be understood, but it does not follow thereby that it is nonsense."[52] Since reason can neither make sense or nonsense of the riddle, Kierkegaard thinks the inevitable result is reason's despair. Thus, "the absurd is the expression of despair: that humanly it is not possible."[53]

In the most empirical and rational sense, the notion "that an individual human being is God, that is, claims to be God, is indeed the offence [in an eminent sense],"[54] because, as Kierkegaard states, it "conflicts with all (human) reason."[55] For Kierkegaard, the conflict emerges "by placing the eternal, essential truth together with existing."[56] Therefore, in light of the IQD between God and a human being, reason has nothing at its disposal to logically unite these two opposing concepts. In neglecting the difference between God and humanity, speculative philosophy incorrectly perceived the incarnation as an object, or idea, open to scrutiny.

Kierkegaard writes, "If God and man resemble each other to that degree, if they are to that degree kindred, consequently essentially within the same quality, then the conclusion 'ergo it was God' is humbug; for if to be God is nothing else than that, then God does not exist at all."[57] He states further, "He [Jesus Christ] could say it [that he is God] to someone present, because someone present, by seeing the speaker, this individual human being, through this contradiction would nevertheless not receive a direct communication, since the contradiction

49. Ibid.
50. *SKS* 7, 196–7 / *CUP1*, 214.
51. Kierkegaard, *JP*, vol. 1, A–E, 5.
52. Ibid., 5.
53. Ibid., 6.
54. Kierkegaard, *PC*, 26.
55. Ibid., 26.
56. Kierkegaard, *CUP*, 209.
57. Kierkegaard, *PC*, 28.

is between what is said and what is seen, that is, who the speaker is according to appearances."[58]

If reason has no categories at its disposal to overcome the logical contradictions emerging from uniting the terms *God* and *man*, historical investigation appears futile in making it sensible.[59] That God had entered history in Christ "conflicts with all (human) reason."[60] Therefore, Kierkegaard asks, "Can it be demonstrated from history that Christ was God?"[61] Insofar as historical knowledge can only provide an approximation, to those who would seek to prove the logic of the incarnation by historical means, the best history can offer is that Christ "was a great man, perhaps the greatest of all."[62] And yet Kierkegaard is appalled that "history is the very thing that people have wanted to use to demonstrate that Christ was God."[63] "If the paradox [Christ] is explained objectively by speculative philosophy, then it ceases to be an object of faith and becomes the object of scientific knowledge."[64] Thus, faith believes against the understanding. Instead of trying to explain and render "probable" the paradox, faith exists in tension with reason and is therefore subject to spiritual trial. It believes that which is absurd, the God-man, and ventures to follow him. Since historical knowledge is at best an approximation, and evidence is unable to "prove" the deity of Jesus, deliberation must be brought to an end, and a leap of faith must take place.[65] In the explanatory work *CUP*, Kierkegaard describes faith as "the objective uncertainty with the repulsion of the absurd, held fast in the passion or inwardness which is the relation of inwardness intensified to its highest. This formula fits only the one who has faith, no one else, not even a lover, or an enthusiast, or a thinker, but solely and only the one who has faith, who relates himself to the absolute paradox."[66] Kierkegaard is keen to distinguish faith from *vapeurs* (vagaries, hysterical feelings, or fantasies). Rather it is a movement of one's whole being, and in this, rationality's role, though at times antagonistic, is not excluded.

---

58. Ibid., 94.
59. Kirmmse notes, "Reason can come to the understanding that all these attempts to understand the key to divinity as being lodged in history, etc. are unreasonable and wrong, while faith, on the other hand, can see that these efforts to limit God's absolute transcendence by assimilating him to human categories of understanding are mockery of God, blasphemy." See Bruce H. Kirmmse, *Kierkegaard in Golden Age Denmark* (Bloomington and Indianapolis: Indiana University Press, 1990), 384–389 for further discussion.
60. Kierkegaard, *PC*, 26.
61. Ibid.
62. Ibid., 27.
63. Ibid., 31.
64. Stewart, *Kierkegaard's Relations to Hegel Reconsidered*, 471.
65. Kierkegaard, *CUP*, 262. Kierkegaard's Johannes Climacus in unpacking the concept of faith found within *Fear and Trembling* explains, "The ethical is the temptation; the relationship with God has come into existence; the immanence of the ethical despair has been broken; the leap has been posited, the absurd is the notification."
66. Kierkegaard, *CUP*, 611.

CONTRIBUTIONS TO THE FIELD
OF APOLOGETICS

In light of the problems that Danish Hegelianism presented, Kierkegaard's task can be described as offering a rational defense of the limits of Christian knowledge. Just as Luther had demurred the reduction of Christian life to nothing more than habitual practices divorced from true spiritual significance, so Kierkegaard believed that the philosophy of Hegel, at the hands of his followers, had damaged the Christianity of the early nineteenth century. Drawing on Luther's context as an analogy for the problems facing Danish Christianity, Kierkegaard's pseudonym, Johannes Climacus, describes pre-Reformation Catholicism as one characterized by a surfeit of objectivity: "Did not the papacy have objectivity and objective definitions and the objective, more of the objective, the objective in superabundance? What did it lack? Appropriation, inwardness."[67] This latter quote gets to the heart of Kierkegaard's mission, which is that the life-changing power of the revelation of Christ would not be erased from the church. The individual subject must alone before God take on or appropriate in faith the revelation of Christ. The revelation of Christ is that one in sin is in total and complete reliance on God for all aspects of one's existence.

But why should Kierkegaard find objective Christianity so appalling? It would seem that adherence to a faith without objectivity would be more appalling in that such a faith would be rationally unwarranted. All things considered, Kierkegaard's own dislike for the apologetics of his day spurred him on to offer his own defense of what Christianity is and, more importantly, what it is to be a Christian. For Kierkegaard, a witness to faith in Christ is the highest of existences. While many might marvel that Billy Graham could walk into a stadium and simply preach the gospel of Christ, resulting in the subsequent tears of thousands, Søren Kierkegaard would be utterly pleased.

At the beginning it was suggested that Kierkegaard is the apologist's apologist. Kierkegaard is more than willing to point out the logical inconsistencies and errors in both secular and Christian thinkers' works. In some of his pseudonymous works, he even seems to take on the position of a neutralist to combat his opponents at their strongest. Remember that, for Kierkegaard, Christianity is unique in its historical foundation for an eternal happiness. Even so, Kierkegaard argues that rational endeavors, or what might be called evidentialism, whether secular or Christian, will never get beyond faith and may result in a flabby, ever-manipulated faith. Objects of knowledge may be added or removed,

---

67. Ibid., 366.

but the revelation of God entering time in Christ will alter one's existence in time and for all eternity.

Kierkegaard's purpose in engaging in debate is to safeguard the faith called for by the God of Abraham, the faith of Christ. One has heard of church leaders who were at one time utterly resolved in their belief in Christianity, only to be crushed into utter doubt and despair by the daily erosion of the weight of life. This is where Kierkegaard begins, with doubt and despair, with the revealing and often incomprehensible God of Abraham offering a relationship if one can trust walking on seventy thousand fathoms of water with Christ. Many, it would seem, begin with this faith and their utter lostness before God. But if one begins in a context immersed in the utter reasonableness of Christianity only to come into a tailspin of doubt, or if along life's journey one is left cold in the calculation of the truth of Christianity, Kierkegaard, the apologist's apologist, is there to remind one that the God of Abraham, Christ, has called for faith in him from the outset! Kierkegaard seeks to remind the church that faith is not a consolation; faith is a prize.

BIBLIOGRAPHY

Croscall, T. H. *Kierkegaard Studies*. London: Lutterworth, 1948.

Hinkson, Craig. "Kierkegaard's Theology: Cross and Grace. The Lutheran and Idealist Traditions in His Thought." PhD diss., University of Chicago, 1993.

———. "Luther and Kierkegaard: Theologians of the Cross." *International Journal of Systematic Theology* 3.1 (2001): 25–45.

Kettering, Christian. *Abraham as Existential Archetype in Kierkegaard's Fear and Trembling*. South Africa: North-West University, dissertation to be presented.

Kierkegaard, Søren, and Charles E. Moore. *Provocations: Spiritual Writings*. Walden, NY: Plough, 2014.

Kierkegaard, Søren. *Concluding Unscientific Postscript to Philosophical Fragments*. Ed. and trans. by Howard V. Hong and Edna H. Hong. Princeton: Princeton University Press, 1992.

———. *Eighteen Upbuilding Discourses*. Ed. and trans. by Howard V. Hong and Edna H. Hong. Princeton: Princeton University Press, 1990.

———. *Fear and Trembling: Repetition*. Ed. and trans. by Howard V. Hong and Edna H. Hong. Princeton: Princeton University Press, 1983.

———. *Journals and Papers*. Vol. 1, A–E. Ed. and trans. by Howard V. Hong and Edna H. Hong. Bloomington: Indiana University Press, 1967.

———. *Journals and Papers*. Vol. 2, F–K. Ed. and trans. by Howard V. Hong and Edna H. Hong. Bloomington: Indiana University Press, 1970.

———. *Journals and Papers*. Vol. 4, S–Z. Ed. and trans. by Howard V. Hong and Edna H. Hong. Bloomington: Indiana University Press, 1975.

———. *Philosophical Fragments*. Ed. and trans. by Howard V. Hong and Edna H. Hong. Princeton: Princeton University Press, 1985.

———. *Practice in Christianity*. Ed. and trans. by Howard V. Hong and Edna H. Hong Princeton: Princeton University Press, 1991.

———. *The Sickness unto Death*. Ed. and trans. by Howard V. Hong and Edna H. Hong Princeton: Princeton University Press, 1983.

Martensen, Hans Lassen. "Rationalism, Supernaturalism and the *principium exclusi medii*." Pages 127–44 in *Mynster's 'Rationalism, Supernaturalism' and the Debate about Mediation*. Ed. and trans. by Jon Stewart. Texts from *Golden Age Denmark*, Vol. 5. Søren Kierkegaard Research Centre, University of Copenhagen: Museum Tusculanum Press, 2009.

Mynster, Jakob Peter. "Rationalism, Supernaturalism." Pages 93–110 in *Mynster's 'Rationalism, Supernaturalism' and the Debate about Mediation*. Ed. and trans. by Jon Stewart, Texts from *Golden Age Denmark*, Vol. 5. Søren Kierkegaard Research Centre, University of Copenhagen: Museum Tusculanum Press, 2009.

Pattison, George. *The Philosophy of Kierkegaard*. Durham, UK: Acumen, 2005.

Penner, Myron. *The End of Apologetics: Christian Witness in a Postmodern Context*. Grand Rapids: Baker Academic, 2013.

Rohde, Bent. *Kierkegaard's Journals and Notebooks*. Vol. 7. Princeton: Princeton University Press, 2014.

Stewart, Jon. "Johan Ludvig Heiberg: Kierkegaard's Criticism of Hegel's Danish Apologist." Pages 35–71 in *Kierkegaard and His Danish Contemporaries, Tome I, Philosophy, Politics and Social Theory Vol. 7*. Ed. by Jon Stewart. Farnham, Surrey, England: Ashgate, 2009.

———. *Kierkegaard's Relations to Hegel Reconsidered*. Cambridge: Cambridge University Press, 2003.

Turchin, Sean A. "Introducing Christianity into Christendom: Investigating the Affinity between Søren Kierkegaard and the Early Thought of Karl Barth." PhD Diss., University of Edinburgh, 2011.

JAMES ORR

Defender of the Christian Worldview

RONNIE P. CAMPBELL JR.

Perhaps no British theologian during the late nineteenth and early twentieth centuries did more in promoting the need for a comprehensive and coherent Christian world- and life-view than the Scotsman James Orr (1844–1913). The turn of the nineteenth century was plagued with various currents of thought that stood in opposition to Christianity. German liberal theology, textual criticism, Hume's attack on miracles, and Darwinian evolution all confronted Christian orthodox teaching. Throughout his apologetic career, Orr sought to defend the Christian faith against such attacks by focusing on a defense of the whole of the Christian worldview. All the while, Orr never lost focus of the need for ministering to the wider Christian public in his defense of the Christian faith.

HISTORICAL BACKGROUND

Born in Glasgow on April 11, 1844, James Orr was the son of an engineer, which placed him in the Scottish lower-middle class. But tragedy befell him, and young James found himself orphaned at a young age and was primarily raised by his relatives. Because of his circumstances, Orr became an apprentice to a bookbinder, which delayed his entrance into university. Not until the age of twenty-one did Orr enroll in the University of Glasgow, with intentions of going into Christian ministry.

In 1870 Orr graduated with first-class honors with a master of arts in mental philosophy. He had also won the coveted Ferguson Scholarship, which allowed for winners to study abroad. Rather than going to Oxford or Cambridge, as many Ferguson scholars often did, Orr chose to remain at the University of Glasgow, where he opted to study divinity from 1870 to 1872. After graduating with a bachelor of divinity, Orr accepted a call in 1873 with the East Bank United Presbyterian Church, where he served in ministry for seventeen years.

Along the way, Orr learned German and later earned the doctor of divinity degree from Glasgow, which he defended by oral examination. In 1891 Orr gave the Kerr Lectures at the United Presbyterian Theological College. It took Orr three years to prepare for the lectureship. Orr's Kerr lectures were later published into what would become his most famous work, *The Christian View of God and the World, as Centering in the Incarnation*. In the same year as his Kerr lectures, he was appointed to professor of church history at the United Presbyterian Divinity Hall. To round out his academic career, in 1900 Orr became professor of apologetics and dogmatics at the newly founded Trinity College of Glasgow, where he remained until his death.[1]

Orr's church background was evangelical and reformed. It was through the local YMCA and Sydney Place Church that Orr received his evangelical heritage. The YMCA not only provided an atmosphere for learning but was also involved in evangelistic outreach. Sydney Place Church, pastored by John Kerr, was denominationally United Presbyterian (UP), and though reformed, it held its Calvinism somewhat loosely.[2] The UP denomination was more democratic in nature and focused heavily on training pastors and ministers for "pioneer, colonial, and missionary work."[3] It was within this tradition that Orr made his home. Before going to university, Orr also served at the Glasgow City Mission, ministering to the local poor. The mission was evangelical and interdenominational, as was the YMCA.[4]

While at the University of Glasgow, Orr studied under John Veitch, a defender of commonsense realism, and Edward Caird, a Hegelian idealist. While most of Orr's classmates gravitated toward Caird, Orr aligned himself more closely with Veitch's commonsense assumptions. Despite this, Orr's epistemological position was mediating enough that Caird publicly commended one of Orr's essays on David Hume, which later won a university prize and eventually became his 1903 book, entitled *David Hume and His Influence on Philosophy and Theology*. While working on his bachelor of divinity, Orr studied under other such reputable professors as Duncan Weir, professor of Oriental languages, John Caird, older brother to Edward Caird and professor of divinity, and John

1. Glenn G. Scorgie, "James Orr," in *Handbook of Evangelical Theologians*, ed. Walter A. Elwell (Grand Rapids: Baker, 1993), 12–13; Scorgie, *A Call for Continuity: The Theological Contribution of James Orr* (Macon, GA: Mercer University Press, 1988), 19–54; Gary J. Dorrien, *The Remaking of Evangelical Theology* (Louisville: Westminster John Knox, 1998), 43; William Edgar and K. Scott Oliphint, *Christian Apologetics Past and Present (Volume 2, From 1500): A Primary Source Reader* (Wheaton, IL: Crossway, 2011), 361; D. F. Kelly, "Orr, James," in *Evangelical Dictionary of Theology*, 2nd ed., ed. Walter A. Elwell (Grand Rapids: Baker Academic, 2007), 871–72.

2. Scrogie, *A Call for Continuity*, 20–21.

3. Ibid., 24.

4. Ibid., 21.

Cairns, who taught theology. It was John Caird who would introduce Orr to the works of German theologian Isaak August Dorner, who is quoted extensively in Orr's work *The Christian View of God*. Dorner emphasized the need to make Christology the central integrating feature of one's theological system, and this was what Orr aimed to do, especially as he sought to defend Christian orthodoxy in *The Christian View of God*.[5]

THEOLOGICAL CONTEXT

Orr was well aware of his environment. The popularity of deism grew in England throughout the seventeenth and eighteenth centuries, eventually collapsing into what is now known as classical Protestant liberalism, which prevailed up until World War I. Because of the efforts of deists and, especially, the philosophical works of Immanuel Kant and David Hume, miracles and the supernatural were now seen as an impossibility. Moreover, "Life of Jesus" studies boomed and dominated the second half of the nineteenth century. Early on, many of the so-called "Life of Jesus" works were rationalistic in nature, eschewing Christian dogma and supernatural elements in the gospels, while maintaining a positive view of the moral life and example of Jesus. In 1835 that all changed when the German critical scholar David Friedrich Strauss published *The Life of Jesus Critically Examined*. The focus shifted from rationalistic attempts that still recognized the gospels—apart from the supernatural and dogmatic elements—as overall historically accurate to seeing the gospels as primarily mythological.[6] In Orr's own day, the orthodox teaching on the Chalcedonian understanding of the God-man faced opposition from such New Testament critics as Kirsopp Lake, Hermann Gunkel, and T. K. Cheyne.[7]

At the end of the 1800s and into the turn of the early twentieth century, the theological world was inundated by numerous currents of thought that, in many ways, stood antithetical to Christian orthodoxy. German liberal theology, textual criticism, Hume's case against miracles, and Darwinian evolution all provided avenues of attack against Christian supernaturalism. As we'll see below, in one way or another, Orr had a hand in responding to each of these throughout his academic career, especially as he sought to defend orthodox Christianity and the fundamentals of the Christian faith, indeed, as he saw it,

---

5. Ibid., 25–28, 48–51; Scrogie, "James Orr," 12.
6. R. Douglas Geivett and Gary R. Habermas, *In Defense of Miracles* (Downers Grove, IL: InterVarsity Press, 1997), 11–12; Scorgie, *A Call for Continuity*, 133.
7. James Orr, *The Resurrection of Jesus* (1908; repr., Joplin, MO: College Press, 1973), 9–30.

the Christian worldview.[8] What ultimately motivated Orr to respond apologetically to such challenges to the Christian faith was his deep sense of responsibility to the Christian public, which was somewhat characteristic and fostered among Scottish theologians in Orr's day.[9] As Glen Scorgie put it, there was an expectation that "theologians should be servants of the Church."[10]

APOLOGETIC METHODOLOGY AND RESPONSE

When it comes to apologetic method, some have labeled Orr as an evidentialist. As an apologist trying to defend Christianity, Orr certainly was concerned with appealing to the facts and evidence,[11] but not to brute facts alone.[12] Orr saw Christianity as a comprehensive system that best explains all aspects of our world, and it is this system as a whole that needs defending.

DEFENSE OF THE CHRISTIAN WORLDVIEW

In the introductory chapter to *The Christian View of God*, which some consider to be his magnum opus, Orr recognized two ways of defending Christian truth. On the one hand, the apologist may appeal to the particulars of Christian doctrine. While commendable, given the "signs of the time," Orr saw it more beneficial to approach the task in a second way—defending the entirety of the Christian system.[13] He explains,

> The opposition which Christianity has to encounter is no longer confined to special doctrines or to points of supposed conflict with the natural sciences,—for example, the relations of Genesis and geology,—but extends to the whole manner of conceiving of the world, and of man's place in it, the manner of conceiving of the entire system of things, natural and moral, of which we form a part. It is no longer an opposition of

---

8. See James Orr, *Ritschlianism: Expostory and Critical Essays* (London: Hodder & Stoughton, 1903); Orr, *The Problem of The Old Testament: Considered with Reference to Recent Criticism* (James Nisbet & Co. Limited, 1908); Orr, *The Bible Under Trial: In View of Present-Day Assaults on Holy Scripture* (New York: A. C. Armstrong & Son, 1907); Orr, *Revelation and Inspiration* (New York: Scribner's Sons, 1910); Orr, *David Hume and His Influence on Philosophy and Theology* (Edinburgh: T&T Clark, 1903); Orr, *Sin as a Problem of Today* (London: Hodder & Stoughton, 1910).

9. Scorgie, *A Call for Continuity*, 127.

10. Ibid.

11. Take for example Orr's work in *The Resurrection of Jesus*.

12. Kenneth D. Boa and Robert M. Bowman Jr, *Faith Has Its Reasons: An Integrative Approach to Defending Christianity*, 2nd ed. (Waynesboro, GA: Paternoster, 2005), 145.

13. Though, Orr certainly was not opposed to the defense of particular doctrines of the Christian faith. Two particular doctrines often defended in Orr's works include the doctrine of humanity and the doctrine of sin. See *Sin as a Problem of Today* and *God's Image in Man, and Its Defacement in the Light of Modern Denials* (London: Hodder & Stoughton, 1905. Repr., Bibliolife, nd).

detail, but of principle. This circumstance necessitates an equal extension of the line of the defence. It is the Christian view of things in general which is attacked, and it is by an exposition and vindication of the
Christian view of things as a whole that the attack can most successfully
be met.[14]

An avid reader of German theology, Orr noticed the continual recur-
rence of the word *Weltanschauung*, which, at times in the literature, was used
interchangeably with another compound word, *Weltansicht*. Both words carry
the English equivalent of "view of the world." Whereas the English is often
understood in more physical terms, the German has the "force of a technical
term, denoting the widest view which the mind can take of things in the effort
to grasp them together as a whole from the standpoint of some particular philosophy or theology."[15] Orr's purpose, then, in *The Christian View of God* was to
make a case for Christianity as providing the "highest point of view," especially
in comparison with other philosophical and theological systems.

Orr recognized that in postulating Christianity as a worldview, it is neither
a scientific system nor a philosophy in its own right, though as a worldview, it
certainly must reconcile with the "established results of science" and must "be
in harmony with" the conclusions of "sound reason."[16] In summarizing Orr's
work in *The Christian View of God and the Word*, Scorgie put it this way: "It is
the coherency of the Christian worldview, its harmony with reason and moral
experience that makes it compelling."[17] He continues:

> Thus the systematic presentation of evangelical doctrine (which is nothing
> other than the setting forth of this worldview) is in fact the most compre-
> hensive apologetic for the Christian faith. Accordingly, *The Christian View*
> does not begin with an apology for Scripture and then proceed to confident
> deduction therefrom. To the contrary, Scripture is not treated at all. The
> Christian system of belief is commended on the basis of its own intrinsic
> merits and the correspondence assumed to exist between its claims and
> humanity's capacity to recognize truth intuitively and rationally. In this
> sense, then, the Christian faith is self-authenticating.[18]

---

14. James Orr, *The Christian View of God and the World* (1893; repr., Middletown, DE: CreateSpace,
2017), 4.
15. Ibid.
16. Ibid., 7.
17. Scorgie, "James Orr," 14.
18. Ibid.

In an appendix to his first lecture in *The Christian View of God*, Orr outlines the following as the central tenets of the Christian worldview:

- God is personal, ethical, and self-revealing.
- God created the world, is both immanent and transcendent, and governs the world toward moral ends.
- Human beings, as divine image bearers, are spiritual in nature, have dignity and worth, and are destined to be in a "perfected relation of sonship."
- The fall of humanity introduced sin and disorder to the world, which was not part of God's original design for the world, and thus, the fall did not occur by necessity. Yet against the modern understanding, the doctrine of the fall stands as the presupposition to the Christian doctrine of redemption, as understood from Scripture.
- God has revealed himself and his plan for salvation historically through the patriarchs and Israel and most fully in the person and work of his Son, Jesus Christ.
- Jesus was not merely a man but the eternal Son of God, who took on our humanity and in whom the fullness of the godhead dwelled in bodily form.
- Redemption of the world comes through the act of atonement, is appropriated by faith, and is available to all who do not willfully reject God's act of grace.
- The work and aim of Christ's work was for the founding of God's kingdom on earth, which includes both spiritual salvation for individuals and a new order for society.
- History has a goal, and the present order of things as we know it will cease—the Son of Man will judge the world, the dead will be raised, the righteous and wicked will be separated, and we will enter the eternal ages.[19]

The above summary sets the stage for the case Orr makes throughout *The Christian View*. He saw each of the above postulates as needing defending, and that is what he set out to do.

Orr is not opposed to the use of natural theology in his defense of the Christian worldview. He employs the use of the cosmological, teleological, and moral arguments in building a case for the supernatural ordering of the universe. Yet Orr recognized that theism can only remain a "bare" theism for so long. Part of the ethos of the world at that time demanded a serious reflection on a God who manifests himself in the world in both word and deed, hence the need for

---

19. The above are a summary of Orr's distinguishing points in *The Christian View*, 23–24.

revelation. Orr believed that one of the great strengths of the Christian view of God is the close connection it has with divine revelation. On this, Orr writes:

> Here, accordingly, it is the Christian view of God has ifs [*sic*] strength against any conception of God based on mere grounds of natural theology. It hinds together, in the closest reciprocal relations, the two ideas of God and Revelation. The Christian doctrine, while including all theif [*sic*] the word Theism ordinarily covers, is much more than a doctrine of simple Theism. God, in the Christian view, is a Being who enters into the history of the world in the most hiving way. He is not only actively present in the material universe,—ordering, guiding, controlling it.—but He enters also in the most direct way into the course of human history, working in it in His general and special providence, and by gradual and progressive Revelation, which is, at flue same time, practical discipline and education, giving to man that knowledge of Himself by which he is enabled to attain the highest ends of his own existence, and to co-operate freely in the carrying out of Divine ends; above all, discovering Himself as the God of Redemption, who, full of long suffering and mercy, executes in loving deeds, and at infinite sacrifice, His gracious purpose for salvation of mankind.[20]

The theism Orr defends is not one dissociated from divine revelation; rather, it is one that is completed in the fullness of the Christian worldview.[21] At the center of the worldview is the divine revelation that comes through the nature, person, and work of the incarnate Son of God.

Though Orr does not begin *The Christian View* with Christology, for him, following Dorner,[22] the incarnation—especially as represented by historical orthodox Christianity—plays a significant role in setting the Christian faith apart from other philosophical and religious systems and is central to the internal logic of the Christian worldview.[23] Orr maintained that the doctrine of the incarnation sheds new light on the following areas of Christian doctrine: (1) the Trinity, (2) creation, (3) human nature, (4) the purpose of God in creation and redemption of humanity, and (5) divine mercy in relation to redemption.[24] Given Orr's stance on natural theology and the tight connection in Christianity

---

20. Ibid., 57.
21. Ibid.
22. "A Christian system which is unable to make Christology an integral part of itself, has pronounced its own judgment; it has really given up the claim to the title of Christian." I. A. Dorner, *History and Development of the Doctrine of the Person of Christ*, 49, as quoted in Orr, *The Christian View*, 31.
23. Orr, *The Christian View*, 30.
24. Ibid., 23.

between God and revelation, one cannot merely defend theism against its alternatives, but rather, one must consider "a divine Christ" and the alternatives. The Christ of Scripture stands against various philosophies, including those of humanitarianism, agnosticism, pantheism, and skepticism.[25]

Throughout the remainder of *The Christian View*, Orr tackles a variety of other issues related to the Christian worldview but specifically the doctrines of humanity and sin. Orr believed one's views on God and humanity "stand or fall together."[26] The doctrine of humanity is closely associated with the doctrine of creation, which also must be defended. For Orr, the doctrine of creation—the belief that all things are ultimately derived from and originate through God as the source of its being—is not only fundamental to the teaching of Scripture but is immensely practical. It opposes all forms of dualism, views that stress logical derivation of the cosmos from God (e.g., as in Spinoza and Hegel), and atheist assumptions on the self-subsistence and eternality of the universe.

In working out the Christian view on creation, humanity, and sin, Orr was concerned with humanity's place in creation, especially in light of the challenges raised by Darwinian evolution. Any theologian worth their weight in salt would have been aware of the challenges Darwinism brought against Christianity, and for many, such challenges called into question the accuracy of the Genesis account. While Orr did not find it necessary to defend a literal interpretation of the first chapter of Genesis,[27] he nevertheless affirmed that the narrative of Genesis—from creation to the flood—was not myth and that it should be understood as containing "knowledge of memory of real transactions."[28] Moreover, he saw no major disagreement between Scripture and science, for, "in the original picture in Genesis we have, as in nature, a gradually ascending series of creations. We have man at the top of the scale; man as the latest being of all, and distinguished from all by the fact that he alone bears his Creator's image;

---

25. Ibid., 30–50.

26. Ibid., 88.

27. Scorgie, *A Call to Continuity*, 109.

28. "It is clear that the narratives of Creation, the Fall, the Flood, are not myths, but narratives enshrining the knowledge of memory of real transactions. The creation of the world was certainly not a myth, but a fact, and the representation of the stages of creation dealt likewise with facts. The language used was not that of modern science, but, under divine guidance, the sacred writer gives a broad, general picture which conveys a true idea of the order of the divine working in creation. Man's fall was likewise a tremendous fact, with universal consequences in sin and death to the race. Man's origin can only be explained through an exercise of direct creative activity, whatever subordinate factors evolution may have contributed. The flood was an historical fact, and the perseveration of Noah and his family is one of the best and most widely attested of human traditions. In these narratives in Genesis and the facts which they embody are really laid the foundation of all else in the Bible. The unity of revelation binds them up with the Christian Gospel." James Orr, "The Early Narratives of Genesis," in *The Fundamentals*, vol. 1, eds. R. A. Torrey and A. C. Dixon (1909; repr., Grand Rapids: Baker, 1973), 240.

man set at the head of the lower orders of creatures, as God's rational vicegerent and representative. Science corroborates all this."[29]

Orr was not opposed to evolution and, upon observing the scientific literature, believed some kind of organic evolution was likely.[30] His views on creation centered more on the dependency of all things on God and less on the process of how God brought it all about. But Orr did see the need to make certain modifications to the Darwinian understanding of evolution, rejecting any view incompatible with the traditional understanding of the *imago Dei* and the endowment of those faculties setting human beings apart from other creatures. Orr also believed Darwinism could never explain human moral history.[31] As Scorgie explains, "Theories of moral evolution made sin a natural necessity, not a fault for which humanity was entirely and personally responsible."[32] Orr spent a good portion of his apologetic energy in *The Christian View*—and elsewhere— making sense of the dialogue between faith and science while also seeking to maintain a proper unity between the truths gained through both general and special revelation.

Though Orr's apologetic method in *The Christian View* primarily focused on a defense of the entirety of the Christian worldview, he certainly was not opposed to defending the particulars of the Christian faith. He, along with other committed, orthodox scholars, such as B. F. Westcott,[33] J. Sparrow Simpson,[34] R. A. Torrey,[35] and William Milligan,[36] took up the challenge of responding to critical objections to the orthodox teaching on Jesus's resurrection from the dead. His evidentialist methodology is most clearly seen in his work *The Resurrection of Jesus*, to which we now turn.

DEFENSE OF THE RESURRECTION

Orr spent quite a bit of his apologetic focus on defending the Scriptures and answering objections raised through higher textual criticism. This was especially true with the resurrection of Jesus. But Orr was not an inerrantist, and at times he chided his fellow Christians for putting too much stock in such an

---

29. Orr, *The Christian View*, 97. See also Orr, "Science and Christian Faith" in *The Fundamentals*, vol. 1, 334–47, and Orr, *Revelation and Inspiration*, 168.

30. Scorgie, *A Call to Continuity*, 108.

31. Orr, *The Christian View*, 71. Scorgie, *A Call to Continuity*, 108–111.

32. Scorgie, *A Call to Continuity*, 111.

33. Brooke Foss Westcott, *The Revelation of the Risen Lord*, 3rd ed. (London: Macmillan, 1884); Westcott, *The Gospel of the Resurrection: Thoughts On Its Relation to Reason and History*, 6th ed. (London: Macmillan, 1888).

34. W. J. Sparrow Simpson, *Our Lord's Resurrection*, 2nd ed. (London: Longmans, Green, & Co., 1909).

35. R. A. Torrey, *Evidence for the Resurrection* (London: Revell, 1904).

36. William Milligan, *The Resurrection of Our Lord*, repr. (New York: Macmillan, 1927).

438 NINETEENTH-CENTURY APOLOGISTS

"overstrained theory."[37] Consider his words in *Revelation and Inspiration*, "One may plead, indeed, for 'a supernatural providential guidance' which has for its aim to exclude all, even the least, error or discrepancy in statement, even such as may inhere in the sources from which the information is obtained, or may arise from corruption of anterior documents. But this is a violent assumption which there is nothing in the Bible really to support. It is perilous, therefore, to seek to pin down faith to it as a matter of vital moment."[38]

In such a line of argumentation, some see Orr as conceding too much to higher criticism. But as Scorgie points out, Orr's denial of inerrancy was more of a tactical move than a substantive one. Scorgie says,

> He did not wish to be trapped in an awkward corner, but he was really unwilling to concede very much at all. He held that even the assurance of Scripture's profitability in Second Timothy 3:16 presumed a very high degree of historical and factual accuracy. He held, in fact, that the Bible manifested such a high degree of accuracy that the phenomenon was itself an argument for the supernatural origin of Scripture. Moreover, he sympathized with the general direction of the inerrantists' regard for Scripture and believed that it was in line with apostolic conviction and historic Christianity.[39]

Though Orr denied the doctrine of inerrancy, he maintained deep commitment to Orthodox Christian teaching, especially Chalcedonian Christology, and held to a high view of the Scriptures. He even contributed to the famed *Fundamentals*, a four-volume set first published in 1909 and edited by A. C. Dixon and R. A. Torrey that included a number of scholarly articles authored by respectable evangelical academics such as B. B. Warfield, G. Campbell Morgan, and H. C. G. Moule.[40]

Orr recognized that historical criticism was not all wrong, and he commended recent efforts in retrieving the humanity of Christ, over against those theories that were more "docetic" in nature. But rather than beginning with the Trinity, a top-down approach, he believed it better to begin with the historical data, building a case from the bottom up, or as he put it, from the "solid ground."[41] He conceded to the critics that certain "details in the Resurrection narratives themselves might be, probably were, inaccurate;" yet he maintained

---

37. Orr, *Revelation and Inspiration*, 73.
38. Ibid., 213–14.
39. Scorgie, *A Call for Continuity*, 99.
40. See James Orr, "The Holy Scriptures and Modern Negations," "The Early Narratives of Genesis," and "Science and Christian Faith" in *The Fundamentals*, vol. 1.
41. Scorgie, *A Call for Continuity*, 123–25.

that "the central facts—the empty grave, the message to the women, the appearances to the disciples, sustained as these were by the independent witness of Paul in I Corinthians xv. 7, the belief of the whole Apostolic church—stood secure."[42]

Orr began *The Resurrection of Jesus* by surveying the modern landscape of the Life of Jesus studies. The times had changed, and what Christian apologists were up against was quite different from previous generations. The apologetic literature was familiar with a variety of naturalistic theories—"theories of imposture, of swoon, of subjective hallucination or visions, of objective but *spiritual* manifestations"[43]—all of which, he believed, had been defeated, leaving room for only one remaining hypothesis: that Jesus raised from the dead. But with the rise of new critical methods, especially with greater emphasis on the study of the "religious history of mankind," "comparative study," and "growth of religious myth," Orr believed the older ways of defending the faith were "obsolete."[44] This modern mindset was no longer open to entertaining the possibility that Jesus raised from the grave bodily. This new school of thought, often called the "Pan-Babylonian" movement, was spearheaded by such a work as J. G. Frazer's *Golden Bough* and developed by other British and German critical scholars, such as H. Winckler, A. Jeremias, H. Gunkel, P. Jensen, and T. K. Cheyne. It taught that certain concepts that developed in Babylon had spread throughout the East and eventually influenced first Judaism and later Christianity. But the Pan-Babylonian movement was not the only school of thought Orr was up against. Some critics, such as Kirsopp Lake and Theodor Keim, recognized that the appearance claims of 1 Corinthians 15:4–8 were highly attested and sought to explain the resurrection in spiritual terms. Though Christ's body lay in the ground, the disciples received visions of Jesus from life beyond the grave. These were not hallucinations, as Strauss thought, but objective visions of Christ, who Lake and Keim believed was raised spiritually.[45]

Having considered the modern theological setting, Orr then defended the nature of the resurrection as miraculous and bodily. Critics were virtually unanimous in Orr's day that the resurrection stood as the central teaching of the early church. But the problem was twofold: (1) what, then, was the nature of the resurrection? and (2) to what extent are miracles possible? In response to the first question, Orr argued that the resurrection was not a change from bodily existence to a "spiritual, incorruptible, and immortal"[46] existence, as Lake believed;

42. Orr, *The Resurrection of Jesus*, 11–12.
43. Ibid., 12.
44. Ibid., 13.
45. Ibid., 13–27.
46. Ibid., 40.

rather, based on Paul's testimony in 1 Corinthians 15, along with such passages as Romans 8:11, 23; Ephesians 1:19–20; and Philippians 3:10–11, 21, the evidence points to a bodily resurrection. Orr writes, "On a fair view of the evidence, therefore, it seems plain that the belief of the Apostolic Church was belief in true bodily Resurrection of Jesus Christ, and it is as little open to doubt that, if such an event took place, it was a *miracle*, i.e., a true supernatural intervention of God, in the strictest sense of the word."[47]

But why should we even think miracles are possible? On this, Orr recognized the central difficulty was a worldview problem. Any worldview (e.g., atheism, Spinozism, materialism, monism, etc.) that dismisses "a Living Personal God as the Author and Upholder of the world"[48] cannot but conclude that miracles are impossible. The question, then, is not whether miracles are possible given atheism, pantheism, or any other system, but whether miracles are possible given a theistic view of the world.

Throughout the remainder of *The Resurrection of Jesus*, Orr set out to accomplish several other tasks. He built a case for the general reliability of the facts surrounding the gospel message. Even if one were to admit the alleged discrepancies found in the gospel narrative, such discrepancies would "hardly touch the *main* facts of the combined witness."[49] Orr then set his sights on defending the credibility of the burial of Jesus, the Easter message, and the postresurrection appearances. Finally, having established the case for the historical facts, Orr considered two naturalistic theories that tried to explain the data—visional-apparitional theories and Neo-Babylonian theories.

For any objection to the resurrection, two key pieces of evidence must be explained—the empty tomb and the appearances. Orr believed the visional-apparitional theories to be inadequate at explaining either of the two pieces of evidence. Regarding the empty tomb, there is a fact that the critics cannot explain; namely, that within weeks from the crucifixion, the disciples changed from a state of despair to a joyful, confident message. And they proclaimed in the streets of Jerusalem, where Jesus had been crucified, that he had raised from the dead, even in the face of persecution. At any time, the rulers could have produced the body, as Orr explains:

> Yet not the least attempt was made, either by the rulers, or by anyone else interested, to stay the movement, and silence the preachers, as might easily have been done, had their testimony been false, by pointing to where the

47. Ibid., 42.
48. Ibid., 48.
49. Ibid., 59.

body of Jesus still lay, or by showing how it had come to be removed from the tomb in which it had, after the Crucifixion, to the knowledge of all, been deposited. *Did not* in this case spells *could not*, and the empty tomb remains an unimpeachable witness to the truth of the message that the Lord had risen.[50]

As for the appearances, subjective hallucination or objective-apparitional vision theories had several difficulties in explaining the data. To make their theory work, vision theorists often broke with tradition and suggested that the visions must have taken place in Galilee instead of Jerusalem. The obvious advantage of changing the locale is that such a move on the part of the critic is to separate the visions from the events of Easter morning, allowing more time for the development and spread of the visions. But Orr believed such a view stands against "nine-tenths" of tradition and has no real basis in the facts alleged to support the view. After all, neither Matthew, Mark, or John give any indication that the disciples fled to Galilee from Jerusalem, and even Luke records one of the appearances in Jerusalem. Moreover, such theories have difficulty explaining the nature, timing, and various accounts of the appearances. And not all critics took the appearances to be subjective. Keim argued that the visions were objective in nature, "telegrams from heaven," sent from beyond the grave, assuring the disciples that Jesus was still alive. This theory relied heavily on the evidence from the Society for Psychical Research on apparitions of the dead.[51] Keim believed that taking the appearances to be apparitions or objective visions saved the resurrection while also accommodating much of the evidence from tradition, even if the resurrection was not bodily.[52] But such a view, Orr believed, rested too much on "*data* so elusive, precarious, and . . . misleading."[53] Furthermore, the apparitional view of the resurrection, taken by Keim, Lake, and others, stood in contrast to the "proper Scriptural idea of the Resurrection," mistaking survival of the soul with the resurrection.[54] Finally, Keim's telegraph view, Orr argued, does not explain the empty tomb, nor does it ultimately escape supernaturalism.[55]

But what of the Neo-Babylonian theories? Supporters of those theories, such as Gunkel, Cheyne, A. Jeremias, and Jensen, believed that the mythologies of the

---

50. Ibid., 213–14.
51. The Society for Psychical Research (SPR) was established in 1882 with the purpose of scientific investigation into psychical and spiritualist phenomena. Henry Sidgwick served as the first president of SPR, and various other key British thinkers were involved in the society, such as Edmund Gurney and Frederic Myers. For more information on SPR, see www.spr.ac.uk/about/our-history.
52. Orr, *The Resurrection of Jesus*, 217–27.
53. Ibid., 228.
54. Ibid., 228–29.
55. Ibid., 229–30.

ancient religions were the keys to unlocking the understanding of the Old and New Testaments. Orr argued that such attempts at comparing the various myths to the Old and New Testaments, and especially the resurrection, were thin and weak, and they were often grounded more in assumption than in facts and evidence. Furthermore, the methods for arriving at such conclusions were often arbitrary.[56]

CONTRIBUTIONS TO THE FIELD OF APOLOGETICS

While some have taken Orr's overall contribution to theology to be minimal, one can hardly examine his scholarly works and doubt his apologetic impact.[57] As an apologist, Orr was aware of the various currents of thought, and his chief concern was to engage Christianity's critics to defend orthodox Christian theology. There is much we can learn from Orr's work as an apologist.

One significant area of contribution was Orr's use of worldview in defending the Christian faith. Orr was one of the first English-speaking theologians to relate the notion of a *Weltanschauung* to Christianity.[58] As William Edgar and Scott Oliphint put it, "While it might be difficult to see how radical this was, it should be remembered that hardly anyone was thinking in these terms during this time, especially in the area of apologetics and theology.[59] Today most apologists engaging with their critics think in terms of the concept of worldview. Orr paved the way for others, such as Edward J. Carnell and Carl F. H. Henry, in thinking of Christianity not only as a system that needs defending but also as a system that best explains the whole of reality.[60]

Another area of contribution, linked closely to Orr's emphasis of worldview, was the importance of seeing truth as unitive. Though Christianity is not a philosophical or scientific system, it should, nevertheless, cohere with those truths gleaned from science and reason. Orr was willing to accept those areas of science that were most probable and appropriately aligned with the Christian worldview; yet he was unwilling to budge on theories that stood contradictory to orthodox Christian teaching. We see this most readily in his willingness to accept certain aspects of evolutionary theory while rejecting other strands that were contrary to the Christian faith, specifically when related to the orthodox teaching on the *imago Dei*, the origin of sin, and human moral history.

---

56. Ibid., 247.
57. David K. Naugle, *Worldview: The History of a Concept* (Grand Rapids: Eerdmans, 2002), 13.
58. Ibid.
59. Edgar and Oliphint, *Christian Apologetics*, 362.
60. Dorrien, *The Remaking of Evangelical Theology*, 44.

In defending the resurrection, Orr's emphasis on a ground-up approach can still be seen among evidentialist apologists today, especially in the works of Gary Habermas, Michael Licona, and William Lane Craig. Though Orr was not the first apologist to defend the resurrection in this manner, he certainly saw the need to begin with the facts surrounding the resurrection and then to show why naturalistic theories fail at explaining the evidence.

Finally, though Orr spent the early part of his career giving lectures and producing academic works, he devoted much of his latter career educating the broader public. Orr believed that theology and the defense of Christianity was not something only for the elite or for those in academia but for all Christians. He never lost sight of the importance of reaching the broader Christian public. Orr, along with the other faculty at the United Free Church College in Glasgow, usually spent their Sundays speaking at local churches. Furthermore, Orr, along with James Denney, edited *The United Free Church Magazine* to provide an avenue for reaching church folk within their homes. From 1906 on, Orr dedicated much of his efforts to popular works.[61]

Throughout his academic and ministerial career, Orr remained true to his evangelical heritage. He never lost sight of his calling, devoting his life to the defense of orthodox Christian teaching. Orr's overall contribution to apologetics and theology was not found in his brilliance or originality but in his tenacity for defending the Christian worldview.[62]

BIBLIOGRAPHY

Boa, Kenneth D., and Robert M. Bowman Jr. *Faith Has Its Reasons: An Integrative Approach to Defending Christianity*. 2nd ed. Waynesboro, GA: Paternoster, 2005.

Dorrien, Gary J. *The Remaking of Evangelical Theology*. Louisville: Westminster John Knox, 1998.

Edgar, William, and K. Scott Oliphint. *Christian Apologetics Past and Present (Volume 2, From 1500): A Primary Source Reader*. Wheaton, IL: Crossway, 2011.

Geivett, R. Douglas. *In Defense of Miracles: A Comprehensive Case for God's Action in History*. Downers Grove, IL: InterVarsity Press, 1999.

Kelly, D. F. "Orr, James." Pages 871–72 in *Evangelical Dictionary of Theology*. 2nd ed. Ed. by Walter A. Elwell. Grand Rapids: Baker, 2007.

Milligan, William. *The Resurrection of Our Lord*, repr. New York: Macmillan, 1927.

Naugle, David K. *Worldview: The History of a Concept*. Grand Rapids, MI: William B. Eerdmans Publishing Co., 2002.

Orr, James. *David Hume and His Influence on Philosophy and Theology*. Edinburgh: T&T Clark, 1903.

———. *God's Image in Man, and Its Defacement in the Light of Modern Denials*. London: Hodder & Stoughton, 1905. Repr., Bibliolife, nd.

———. *Revelation and Inspiration*. New York: Scribner, 1910.

———. *Ritschlianism: Expository and Critical Essays*. London: Hodder & Stoughton, 1903.

———. "Science and Christian Faith." Pages 334–47 in *The Fundamentals*. Vol. 1. Ed. by R. A. Torrey and A. C. Dixon. 1909. Repr. Grand Rapids: Baker, 1973.

---

61. Scorgie, *A Call for Continuity*, 137–39.
62. Ibid., 155.

———. *Sin as a Problem of Today*. London: Hodder & Stoughton, 1910.

———. *The Bible under Trial: In View of Present-Day Assaults on Holy Scripture*. New York: Armstrong, 1907.

———. *The Christian View of God and the World*. 1893. Repr. Middleton, DE: CreateSpace, 2017.

———. "The Early Narratives of Genesis." Pages 228–40 in *The Fundamentals*. Vol. 1. Ed. by R. A. Torrey and A. C. Dixon. 1909. Repr. Grand Rapids: Baker, 1973.

———. "The Holy Scriptures and Modern Negations." Pages 94–110 in *The Fundamentals*. Vol. 1. Ed. by R. A. Torrey and A. C. Dixon. 1909. Repr. Grand Rapids: Baker, 1973.

———. *The Problem of the Old Testament: Considered with Reference to Recent Criticism*. London: James Nisbet & Co. Limited, 1908.

———. *The Progress of Dogma*. Repr. Vancouver, BC: Regent College Publishing, 2000.

———. *The Resurrection of Jesus*. 1908. Repr. Joplin, MO: College Press, 1973.

Scorgie, Glen G. *A Call for Continuity: The Theological Contribution of James Orr*. Macon, GA: Mercer University Press, 1988.

———. "James Orr." Pages 12–25 in *Handbook of Evangelical Theologians*. Ed. by Walter A. Elwell. Grand Rapids: Baker, 1993.

Simpson, W. J. Sparrow. *Our Lord's Resurrection*. 2nd ed. London: Longmans, Green, and Co., 1909.

Torrey, R. A. *Evidence for the Resurrection*. London: Revell, 1904.

Westcott, Brooke Foss. *The Revelation of the Risen Lord*. 3rd ed. London: Macmillan, 1884.

———. *The Gospel of the Resurrection: Thoughts on Its Relation to Reason and History*. 6th ed. London: Macmillan, 1888.

B. B. WARFIELD

The Lion of Princeton

KIM RIDDLEBARGER

circa 1920, Special Collections, Princeton Theological Seminary

Benjamin Breckinridge Warfield (1851–1921) was an American Presbyterian theologian who for many years taught at Princeton Theological Seminary (1887–1921). Known for his scholarly and erudite defense of an inerrant Bible, the historical Jesus, and Jesus's bodily resurrection, Warfield sought to ground the truth of Christianity in the person and work of Jesus Christ as revealed in the pages of the New Testament.

HISTORICAL BACKGROUND

Benjamin Breckinridge Warfield was born near Lexington, Kentucky, on November 5, 1851.[1] His paternal line is often characterized as "good Puritan stock," while his mother, Mary Cabell Breckinridge, was the daughter of a capable old school Presbyterian theologian, Robert J. Breckinridge, who served as professor at Danville Theological Seminary. Warfield's maternal uncle, John Cabell Breckinridge, was a two-term congressman and later vice president of the United States during the Buchanan administration. John C. Breckinridge would later serve as a general and cabinet member of the Confederate States of America. Although Kentuckians, the Warfield family maintained their Whig sympathies and allegiance to the Union.

Warfield's upbringing was impressive if typical of the well-connected families of the day. He was educated by the best instructors available and, along with his siblings, memorized both the Westminster Larger and Shorter Catechisms by age six, followed by memorization of the Scripture proofs. At age sixteen, Benjamin made his profession of faith in the Second Presbyterian Church of Lexington, Kentucky. He entered the College of New Jersey (Princeton) in 1868, excelling at mathematics and physics, making near-perfect

---

1. Additional biographical details for Benjamin Warfield can be found in Hugh Thomson Kerr, "Warfield: The Person behind the Theology," Annie Kinkead Warfield Lecture for 1982, ed. William O. Harris (1995).

marks before graduating in 1871. Rather than take an experimental fellowship to hone his budding scientific interests, Warfield heeded his father's advice and, in February 1872, studied abroad at the universities of Edinburgh and Heidelberg.

His mother, who hoped at least one of her sons would enter the ministry, found her prayers answered when Benjamin, then twenty-one, wrote home from Heidelberg that summer announcing his desire to enter the ministry. The news surprised his family and friends, especially when Warfield confirmed his intention by enrolling at Princeton Theological Seminary in 1873. Just as his father William Warfield had been, the younger Warfield was reticent to speak about personal spiritual matters. While in Heidelberg, Warfield "realized the paramount claims of God and religion upon him"[2] and soon found himself in the Princeton Seminary classroom of famed Presbyterian theologians Charles Hodge and his son, Caspar Wistar Hodge.

After completing his course work at Princeton Theological Seminary, Warfield declined a call to pastoral ministry in Dayton, Ohio, and returned to Europe to pursue additional theological education. Upon advice from C. W. Hodge, and with the endorsement of noted church historian Philip Schaff, Warfield enrolled in the University of Leipzig for a year of study (1876–1877).[3] Warfield's intended mentor, Heinrich Merkel, died shortly before Warfield's arrival. Apparently unfazed, Warfield undertook a course of study with Erlangen School Old Testament scholar Franz Delitzsch and confessional Lutheran Christoph Ernst Luthardt, who devoted much energy to refuting the critical scholarship of David Strauss and Ernest Renan. Both Delitzsch and Luthardt had written substantial apologetics works in response to the sustained attacks on the authority and historical accuracy of the Bible then sweeping across Europe. This course of study, no doubt, prepared Warfield for his future endeavors in the fields of New Testament and polemical theology.[4]

Before leaving for Leipzig, Warfield married Annie Pearce Kinkead, the daughter of a prominent Lexington attorney. While walking in the Harz Mountains, the newlyweds were caught in a violent thunderstorm. Annie Warfield was nearly struck by lightning and sustained a severe shock to her nervous system, leaving her traumatized and in declining health over the course of her life. Mrs. Warfield bore no children. Her husband provided her with constant and

---

2. W. J. Grier, "Benjamin Breckinridge Warfield," *Banner of Truth* 89 (Fall 1971): 4.
3. Letter from C. W. Hodge to B. B. Warfield, June 6, 1876, papers of B. B. Warfield, Speer Library, Princeton Seminary.
4. James Samuel McClanahan, "Benjamin B. Warfield: Historian of Doctrine in Defense of Orthodoxy, 1881–1921" (PhD dissertation, Union Theological Seminary in Virginia, 1988), 19.

tender care—something Warfield's eulogizers recall fondly. Given his wife's frail condition, Warfield rarely left home for more than two hours at a time until her death in 1915, leaving little opportunity for speaking engagements, pulpit supply, or church committee work.

While at Leipzig, Warfield was offered his first professorship—professor of Old Testament at Western Theological Seminary in Allegheny, Pennsylvania, which he declined. He was also offered a pastoral call as assistant at the First Presbyterian Church in Baltimore, which he accepted. After serving that congregation for one year, Western Theological Seminary called again, this time asking Warfield to assume duties as professor of New Testament exegesis and literature. In September 1880, Warfield was ordained to the Presbyterian ministry and installed as professor. Within two years, the College of New Jersey awarded Warfield the doctor of divinity degree on the strength of the young professor's first wave of publications, completed after beginning his tenure at Western (1880–1886).

As Warfield rose to prominence in Presbyterian circles, A. A. Hodge, a close friend of Warfield's who had succeeded his father Charles as professor of systematic theology at Princeton, died unexpectedly in November 1886. Although Warfield was a New Testament professor and had not labored in the field of systematic theology, he was extended a call to fill A. A. Hodge's chair. Warfield enthusiastically accepted, in effect extending the life of what has come to be known as the "Old Princeton Theology" for another thirty-three years—until Warfield's death from an apparent heart attack on the evening of February 16, 1921.

Confined to Princeton because he had to take care of his wife, Warfield took up the life of a busy professor. The massive amount of material Warfield published is nothing short of astonishing. The list includes ten published volumes of collected essays, numerous articles and book reviews, plus two additional volumes of essays, two handwritten scrapbooks, and fifteen volumes of collected *opuscula*. One of his most important works, *An Introduction to the Textual Criticism of the New Testament* (1886), was reprinted nine times. There are three volumes of sermons, several small commentaries, an important investigation of popular religious movements, *Counterfeit Miracles*, as well a book on the deity of Jesus, *The Lord of Glory* (1907). Warfield also completed several hundred essays and book reviews (many quite substantial), some for publication in encyclopedias, journals, and in the three Princeton theological quarterlies over which he exercised editorial control until shortly before his death. Add to this many thousands of letters and pieces of personal correspondence. As Hugh Kerr observed, Warfield's body of published work equals that of Augustine, Aquinas, Luther,

Calvin, and Barth.[5] J. Gresham Machen once opined—correctly perhaps—that Warfield did the work of ten men.[6]

THEOLOGICAL CONTEXT

B. B. Warfield is not primarily considered to be an apologist per se, although much of his career as professor of polemical and didactic theology at Princeton (1887–1921) was spent defending the faith, specifically the facticity and historicity of Christianity. The Lion of Princeton's task was to pounce on any deviation from Reformed orthodoxy that came to his attention—a task for which he was well suited. Warfield wrote occasionally (topically), so there are no systematic or complete texts from which to glean his apologetic method. There is no "early" Warfield, nor are there any signs that Warfield's views about apologetics changed significantly over the course of his career. In 1908 Warfield produced a substantial article on "apologetics" for the *New Schaff-Herzog Encyclopedia of Religious Knowledge*, laying out in systematic form many of his widely scattered convictions. We can also trace four distinct phases in Warfield's career and the issues he addressed, which serve as a useful guide to consider the context in which Warfield worked, as well as his many and varied contributions to the defense of the faith.[7]

Although often overlooked by his interpreters, Warfield began his lengthy career as a professor of New Testament at Western Theological Seminary. In the first decade of his career (1880–1890, including his time at Western and then his early years at Princeton), Warfield focused on the text and canon of the New Testament, publishing more than sixty articles, essays, and reviews dealing with developments in text criticism, New Testament background, canonicity, word studies, exegetical issues, and studies in patristics.[8] Warfield was primarily concerned with issues of the reliability of the manuscript tradition underlying the New Testament text, as well as questions regarding the inspiration and authority of Scripture.[9] In 1881 Warfield coauthored *Inspiration* with A. A. Hodge, defending the inspiration and authority of the Bible. Several years later Warfield

5. Kerr, "Warfield: The Person behind the Theology," 12–13.

6. Ned B. Stonehouse, *J. Gresham Machen: A Biographical Memoir* (Philadelphia: Westminster Theological Seminary, 1977), 220.

7. Wilber B. Wallis, "Benjamin B. Warfield: Didactic and Polemical Theologian," *The Presbyterion: Covenant Seminary Review*, Part I (Spring 1977): 14.

8. John E. Meeter and Roger Nicole, *A Bibliography of Benjamin Breckinridge Warfield, 1851–1921* (Phillipsburg, NJ: P&R, 1974).

9. See his joint essay with A. A. Hodge: A. A. Hodge and B. B. Warfield, "Inspiration," *The Presbyterian Review* (April 1881): 225–60; repr. in A. A. Hodge and B. B. Warfield, *Inspiration*, ed. Roger Nicole (Grand Rapids: Baker, 1979), 5–71.

published an essay in historical apologetics, "The Resurrection of Christ: A Historical Fact" (1884).

His second decade of labor (1890–1900) saw Warfield direct his attention to controversies then arising within the Presbyterian church over the inspiration and authority of the Bible as well as matters of biblical and historical apologetics. Warfield was a key figure in the famous "Briggs controversy." C. A. Briggs, a professor at Union Theological Seminary in New York, challenged the orthodoxy of the Princeton theology and denied the full authority and inerrancy of the Bible, leading to his eventual suspension from the Presbyterian ministry. During this phase Warfield was compelled to rebut the influential church historian A. C. McGiffert, whose views on "primitive Christianity" echoed German liberal Albrecht Ritschl's. McGiffert contended that "primitive Christianity" mutated into "catholic Christianity" during the latter part of the second century, a development that McGiffert felt distorted the purity of the ethical teachings of Jesus. Warfield accused McGiffert of "a speculative reconstruction of the primitive church [to] set aside the authority of the New Testament altogether, and enthrone in its place the supreme authority of an 'inner light.' This is excellent Quaker teaching, but it is a direct assault upon the very basis of Reformed, and indeed, of the whole of Protestant theology."[10]

During the third phase in Warfield's career (1900–1915), Warfield addressed christological controversies, especially in response to higher-critical reconstructions of the life of Jesus and his person and work. In those essays now collected in *Christology and Criticism*, Warfield took direct aim at those efforts that tried to ground the Christian faith in human reason apart from divine revelation (rationalism) or in religious experience (mysticism). He was not impressed with those utilizing various higher-critical tools to chip away at the historicity and authority of Scripture. Warfield once quipped about such critics, "The difference between them is very much a matter of temperament, or perhaps we may even say of temperature. The Mystic blows hot, the Rationalist cold. Warm up a Rationalist and you inevitably get a Mystic; chill down a Mystic and you find yourselves with a Rationalist on your hands."[11] But the issue was a serious one. He explained, "A Christianity to which Christ is indifferent is, as a mere matter of fact, no Christianity at all. For Christianity, in the core of the matter, consists in just, 'Jesus Christ and Him as crucified.'"[12] American churches and seminaries

---

10. B. B. Warfield, "The Latest Phase of Historical Rationalism," *The Presbyterian Quarterly* 9 (1895): 36–67, repr. in B. B. Warfield, *Christology and Criticism* (Grand Rapids: Baker, 1981), 589–90.

11. Reprinted in B. B. Warfield, *Critical Reviews* (Grand Rapids: Baker, 1981), 366–67.

12. Compare with the idea of "lives of Jesus" evaluated in Warfield's essay "Christless Christianity" from *The Harvard Review* 5 (October 1912): 423–473, repr. in B. B. Warfield, *Christology and Criticism* (Grand Rapids: Baker, 1981), 367.

were beginning to embrace higher-critical methods and antisupernatural presuppositions of German theologians and biblical scholars, and Warfield would spend much of his formidable intellectual capital confronting this rising tide.

The fourth phase in Warfield's career (1915–1921) is in many ways the most important aspect of his ongoing legacy within American Reformed and Presbyterian circles. Warfield was now focused on the application of redemption and the Christian life—issues with great impact on church life, doctrine, and preaching of the church. It was during this latter phase of his career that Warfield took aim at the famed Second Great Awakener Charles Finney, completing his two volumes dealing with perfectionism (1919–1921) and offering his stinging review of Dallas Theological Seminary founder L. S. Chafer's book *He That Is Spiritual* (1918). Warfield also published his popular book comparing theological systems, *The Plan of Salvation* (1915), and composed his response to early Pentecostal manifestations, *Counterfeit Miracles* (1918). Warfield's final years were marked by a decline in apologetic writings in favor of polemical responses to non-Reformed doctrine making inroads into Reformed and Presbyterian churches.

APOLOGETIC RESPONSE

Perhaps a reflection of his postmillennial optimism, Warfield understood apologetics not merely as a "defensive" science reflected in the various "apologies" offered in response to objections raised by non-Christians but also as an offensive science that has as its aim the "Christianizing of the world."[13] Warfield defines Christian theology as the "science of God," concluding that Christianity cannot be grounded in the subjective experiences of individuals or in rationalistic systems conjured forth by human reason. It is instead grounded in that which Warfield identifies as an "objective body of facts"—the revelation given by God in historical events, which culminates in the person and work of Jesus Christ. If the knowledge of God is the object of theology, then the theological system must be built on the foundation of the objective facts that God revealed in redemptive history and in the explanatory word (Scripture). Establishing the truth of this revelation falls to the science of apologetics.[14]

According to Warfield, apologetics has three distinct branches: "Philosophical, Psychological, and Historical, [which] presents God, Religion, Christianity,

---

13. B. B. Warfield, "Review of Herman Bavinck's *De Zekerheid des Geloofs*," *Princeton Theological Review* 1 (Jan 1903): 120.
14. B. B. Warfield, "Apologetics," *New Schaff-Herzog Encyclopedia of Religious Knowledge*, ed. S. M. Jackson (New York: Funk & Wagnalls, 1908), I, 236.

and the Bible" to the theologian, who, in turn, does the work of exegesis, biblical and systematic theology. In this sense, apologetics serves as prolegomena to the theological system.[15] Warfield took issue with his noted Dutch Reformed colleagues, Abraham Kuyper and Herman Bavinck. Warfield lamented that Kuyper made "too little of apologetics" by burying apologetics as a subset of a subset deep within the theological disciplines, allowing Christianity to remain "the great assumption."[16] Warfield was also critical of Bavinck, who, in Warfield's estimation, followed Kuyper in treating apologetics as a truncated discipline buried within the theological encyclopedia. Warfield acknowledged the fallacy of assuming that "Apologetics will of itself make a man a Christian" but nevertheless chides Bavinck that apologetics has a role in the triumph over unbelief, not as a defensive last resort—"to protect an isolated body of Christians from annoyance from the great surrounding world"—but as an offensive weapon with "tremendous fertility in attack and defense."[17]

Warfield's early career was marked by efforts to establish the autographic text of the New Testament as trustworthy and therefore a suitable foundation for claims to biblical authority. Warfield's inaugural address at Western Theological Seminary set the tone for much of his subsequent career. Identifying the question he would answer in the body of his address, Warfield asked, "Is the church doctrine of the plenary inspiration of the New Testament endangered by the assured results of modern biblical criticism?"[18] Answering his own question, Warfield stated, "Modern biblical criticism has not disproved the authenticity of a single book of our New Testament." In what would become a hallmark of Warfield's defense of the inspiration and authority of the Bible, Warfield used the same higher-critical methods used to attack the reliability of the Bible against its critics, concluding, "It is a most assured result of biblical criticism that every one of the twenty seven books which now constitute our New Testament is assured genuine and authentic."[19]

That critical tools of biblical scholarship when used without antisupernatural biases could be a boon to defending the faith was evident in Warfield's 1886 review of B. F. Westcott and F. J. A. Hort's groundbreaking book *The New Testament in the Original Greek*. As Westcott and Hort showed, Warfield

15. B. B. Warfield, "The Idea of Systematic Theology," *The Presbyterian and Reformed Review* 7 (April 1896): 243–71, repr. in *Studies in Theology* (Grand Rapids: Baker, 1981), 74.

16. B. B. Warfield, "Introductory Note," to Francis Beattie's *Apologetics*, vol. 1 (Richmond: Presbyterian Committee on Publications, 1903), 19–32, repr. in *Selected Shorter Writings*, vol. 2, 95–96.

17. Warfield, "Review of Herman Bavinck's *De Zekerheid des Geloofs*," 120.

18. B. B. Warfield, "Inspiration and Criticism," repr. in *Revelation and Inspiration* (Grand Rapids: Baker, 1981), 396.

19. Warfield, "Inspiration and Criticism," 408.

notes, "The authors furnish us for the first time with a really scientific method" of reconstructing the original autographic text of the New Testament. "They reduce guesswork . . . and substitute for it a sound inductive procedure."[20] It was now apparent that "if we compare the present state of the New Testament text with that of any other ancient writing, we must render . . . and declare it to be marvelously correct."[21]

This is an important consideration in Warfield's use of historical apologetics because Christians should not begin the apologetic task by naively assuming the inspiration and authority of Scripture when this is the very point of contention with non-Christians, who reject all such claims. Warfield contends that "we cannot raise the question where God has given us an absolutely trustworthy record of the supernatural facts and teaching of Christianity, before we are assured that there are supernatural facts and teaching to be recorded. The fact that Christianity is a supernatural religion and the nature of Christianity as a supernatural religion, are matters of history; and are independent of every theory of inspiration."[22]

Since the autographic text of the New Testament has been substantially recovered using the tools of lower (textual) criticism, the best place to defend the faith is the biblical testimony within those documents to the bodily resurrection of Jesus Christ. If Jesus rose from the dead, then the supernatural claims of the Christian faith are sufficiently established. Warfield asserts, "The empty grave is alone enough to found all Christianity upon."[23] Understanding the relationship between the fact of the resurrection and Christian doctrine is vital. "It is somewhat difficult to distinguish between doctrines and facts. The doctrines of Christianity are doctrines only because they are facts." The relationship between the two is such that "the facts of Christianity become its most indispensable doctrines."[24] For Warfield, the resurrection is "the cardinal doctrine of our system: on it all other doctrines hang."[25] If Jesus rose bodily from the dead, then he is God in human flesh, and the foundation for Christianity as a revealed and supernatural religion is established. If Jesus did not rise, Christianity's truth claim collapses. In light of this, Warfield identified the chief enemy of Christi-

20. B. B. Warfield, "The Greek Testament of Westcott and Hort," *The Presbyterian Review* 3 (April 1882): 355.

21. B. B. Warfield, *An Introduction to the Textual Criticism of the New Testament* (New York: Whittaker, 1887), 12.

22. B. B. Warfield, "The Church Doctrine of Inspiration," repr. in *The Inspiration and Authority of the Bible* (Phillipsburg, NJ: P&R, 1948), 121.

23. B. B. Warfield, "The Resurrection of Christ a Historical Fact," in *Selected Shorter Writings of Benjamin B. Warfield*, vol. 1, ed. John E. Meeter (Phillipsburg, NJ: P&R, 1980), 190.

24. Warfield, "The Resurrection of Christ a Historical Fact," 178.

25. Ibid.

anity as the skepticism created by the twin foes rationalism and mysticism, since both approaches "must be rid of the resurrection of Christ. It has recognized the necessity and has bent all its energies to the endeavor."[26] The resurrection of Jesus, then, is Christianity's chief and most fundamental fact.

Warfield understood that non-Christian presuppositions often led to assuming and then asserting that miracles such as the resurrection of Jesus are impossible. He raises the critical question that someone holding antisupernatural presuppositions must reckon. "The real dilemma, then, is clearly between the world-view we have formed for ourselves and the facts that come to us, accredited by testimony sufficient in itself to prove their reality—apart that is, from the presumption cherished against them in our minds on the credit of our worldview." Warfield presses the point further. "Are the facts that are permitted to occur in the universe to be determined by our precedently conceived world-view? Or is our world-view to be determined by a due consideration of all the facts that occur in the universe? And it is just clearly the dilemma between an *a priori* determination of facts or an *a posteriori* determination of theory.[27] For Warfield, the best way to overcome the intellectual standoff between what one assumes *can* occur and what *did* occur is to challenge a priori determinations with facts to the contrary.

Warfield sought to expose a priori antisupernaturalism by using the critical methods against those who champion them when attacking the veracity of the New Testament. One approach Warfield used in dealing with skepticism about the historical character of the New Testament was to begin by acknowledging from the beginning those writings that critics universally accept. Warfield notes that "the most extreme schools of scepticism admit that the Book of Revelation is by St. John; and that Romans, 1 and 2 Corinthians, and Galatians are genuine letters of St. Paul." Although "most leaders of anti-Christian thought admit other epistles also . . . we wish to confine ourselves to the narrowest ground." Even when taking the narrowest of ground, the apologist is able "to show that the testimony of these confessedly genuine writings of the apostles is enough to establish the fact of the resurrection."[28] The Pauline Epistles, which are accepted by most as genuine, "have a great deal to say about the resurrection."[29] The resurrection of Jesus was "universally believed in the Christian Church," as the original followers of Christ, including his apostles, claimed to be "eye-witnesses of

---

26. Ibid.
27. B. B. Warfield, "The Question of Miracles," in *The Bible Student*, 7 (March, April, May, June 1903): 121–26, 193–97, 243–50, 314–20, repr. in *Selected Shorter Writings*, vol. 2, 181.
28. Warfield, "The Resurrection of Christ a Historical Fact," 181.
29. Ibid.

the fact of his resurrection." Furthermore, "over two hundred and fifty of these eye-witnesses were living when Paul wrote," and the early church clearly "owed its life, as it certainly owed its continued existence and growth, to its firm belief in this dogma."[30]

The resurrection of Jesus Christ is sufficient to establish Christianity as a supernatural religion. Warfield presses home the point that such a risen Savior also establishes the authority of the Bible. "We believe this doctrine of the plenary inspiration of Scriptures primarily it is the doctrine which Christ and the apostles believed, and which they have taught us. It may seem difficult to take our stand frankly by the side of Christ and his apostles. It will always be found safe."[31] Since the one raised from the dead confirms Scripture's absolute authority, Christians have a potent means of arguing for the inspiration and authority of the Bible without assuming it.

Warfield's historical apologetic and the case for the resurrection of Jesus Christ is further developed in his discussion of faith and its relationship to the work of the Holy Spirit. Warfield distinguishes between the objective truth of Christianity apart from faith—which the fallen children of Adam sinfully suppressed—and the subjective capacity to believe what one knows to be true but sinfully rejects. Defining faith as an absolute reliance on Jesus Christ for salvation, Warfield notes that "it is from its object"—the person and work of Jesus Christ—"that faith derives its value. . . . The saving power of faith resides not in itself but in the almighty Savior on whom it rests."[32]

Since the object of saving faith is Jesus Christ, and since sin has hardened the human heart, non-Christians may refuse to believe what the facts tell them. This in no way weakens the case for Christianity but requires us to understand "no man . . . was ever reasoned into the kingdom of heaven. It is the Holy Spirit alone who can translate us into the kingdom of God's dear Son."[33] Yet we ought not neglect the case for the truth of biblical revelation, because "there are excellent reasons why every man should enter the kingdom of heaven; and these reasons are valid in the form of every rational mind, and their validity can and should be made manifest to all."[34] Unbelief is the irrational and sinful attempt to suppress what is factually true—i.e., the Christian truth claim.

Faith in Christ, then, is not an irrational act. "Though faith is the gift of

30. Ibid., 187.
31. Warfield, "The Church Doctrine of Inspiration," 128.
32. B. B. Warfield, "The Biblical Doctrine of Faith," repr. in *Biblical Doctrines* (Grand Rapids: Baker, 1981), 502.
33. B. B. Warfield, "Calvin's Doctrine of the Knowledge of God," in *The Princeton Theological Review* 7 (April 1909): 219–325; repr. in B. B. Warfield, *Calvin and Augustine* (Philadelphia: P&R, 1956), 124, n. 99.
34. Ibid.

God, it does not in the least follow that the faith which God gives is an irrational faith, that is, a faith without cognizable ground in right reason. We believe because it is rational to believe in Him, not even though it be irrational." As a Calvinist who takes seriously the noetic effects of sin, Warfield qualifies his previous comment. "Of course mere reasoning cannot make a Christian; but that is not because faith is not the result of evidence, but because a dead soul cannot respond to evidence. The action of the Holy Spirit in giving faith is not apart from the evidence, but along with the evidence; and in the first stage consists in preparing the soul for the reception of the evidence."[35]

While necessary to establish the ground for faith, the inability of right reason to exercise saving faith apart from the work of the Holy Spirit does not depreciate the role or importance of apologetics. On the one hand, Warfield asserts that "it is easy, of course, to say that a Christian man must take his standpoint not above the Scriptures, but in the Scriptures. He very certainly must." The Scriptures come to us with divine authority, not an appeal to human rationality. Yet, says Warfield, every believer "must first have the Scriptures, authenticated to him as such, before he can take his standpoint in them. It is equally easy to say that Christianity is attained, not by demonstrations, but by a new birth. Nothing could be more true."[36]

On the other hand, Warfield adds, "But neither could anything be more unjustified than the inferences that are drawn from this truth for the discrediting of apologetics." The objective truth of the Christian faith provides a necessary but not a sufficient condition for saving faith. There must be a supernaturally supplied subjective capacity to believe the sufficient conditions (regeneration). "It is beyond all question only the prepared heart can fitly respond to the 'reasons'; but how can even the prepared heart respond when there are no 'reasons' to draw out its action?" Warfield concludes, "The Holy Spirit does not work a blind, an ungrounded faith in the heart. What is supplied by his creative energy in working faith is not a ready-made faith, rooted in nothing and clinging without reason to its object; nor yet new grounds of belief in the object presented; but just a new ability of the heart to respond to the grounds of faith, sufficient in themselves, already present to the understanding."[37] Christian evidences establish objective and factual grounds for faith, while the Holy Spirit enables those dead in sin to believe what they know to be true (saving faith) yet apart from the Spirit's work would otherwise refuse to believe.

---

35. Warfield, "Apologetics," 15.
36. Warfield, "Introductory Note," to Beattie's *Apologetics*, 98–99; this same statement appears almost word-for-word in Warfield's "Review of Herman Bavinck's *De Zekerheid des Geloofs*," 115).
37. Warfield, "Introductory Note," to Francis Beattie's *Apologetics*, 98–99.

APOLOGETIC METHODOLOGY

Although often associated with so-called "classical apologetics," Warfield never used any of the classical proofs for God's existence in his own apologetic writings. But Warfield did endorse the classical arguments when others used them.[38] In an encyclopedia entry, "God," written for the *Davis Dictionary of the Bible* (1898)—the one place in his writings in which he addressed the subject of "proofs" for God's existence—Warfield explains the complementary relationship between natural and special revelation in which God reveals himself in the natural order but primarily in Scripture. In nature, God's existence is revealed to all humanity—his invisible power and divine perfections (cf. Rom 1). God's supreme revelation is in redemptive history, beginning with the events recorded in the Old Testament, which culminate in the incarnation of Jesus, until finally, in the completed revelation of God (the biblical canon), the triune God fully reveals himself.

The classical proofs, says Warfield, are "derived from the necessity we are under of believing in the real existence of the infinitely perfect Being, of a sufficient cause for the contingent universe, of an intelligent author of order, and of a lawgiver and judge for dependent moral beings."[39] Although Warfield praised the efforts of those who engage in what he identifies as "philosophical apologetics," as noted, Warfield's own interests and energies were devoted to historical and biblical apologetics in defense of special revelation, not the so-called "classical proofs" for the existence of God. Warfield made clear his preference for historical apologetics in a sermon entitled "The Risen Christ" when he flatly declared, "The resurrection of Christ is the fundamental fact of Christianity."[40]

One source of controversy among Warfield's interpreters has to do with the influence of Thomas Reid (1710–1796) and Scottish common sense realism (SCSR) on Old Princeton in general and Warfield in particular. Those who find SCSR problematic criticize Old Princeton's philosophical foundation as a departure from Calvin's biblicism.[41] Others seek to distance Warfield and the Old Princetonians from what they consider SCSR's rationalistic tendencies (Paul Helseth and Fred Zaspel) stressing that SCSR's influence on the Princeton theologians is overstated, as evident in Warfield's stress on supernatural conversion

---

38. Ibid.

39. B. B. Warfield, "God," in John Davis, ed., *Bible Dictionary* (Philadelphia: Westminster, 1898), 110–11.

40. B. B. Warfield, "The Risen Christ," in *Saviour of the World* (New York: Hodder & Stoughton, 1914), 191–213, repr. in *The Person and Work of Christ* (Philadelphia: P&R, 1950), 543.

41. This would include Jack Rogers, Donald McKim, John VanderStelt, and Cornelius Van Til and to a lesser degree, American church historians George Marsden and Mark Noll.

and the illumination of the Holy Spirit. The principle architects of "Reformed epistemology," Alvin Plantinga and Nicholas Wolterstorff, find much of value in Thomas Reid's epistemology and SCSR when developing their thesis that "belief in God as properly basic" and that the Christian truth claim is "warranted belief."

Paul Helm observes that there is nothing in the basic epistemological tenets of SCSR that argue either for or against Reformed orthodoxy.[42] Whatever one concludes about SCSR and its influence on Old Princeton and Warfield (good, ill, or nil), Warfield's apologetic arguments used basic SCSR tests for truth—internal coherence and eternal correspondence to facts. Warfield's well-developed doctrine of the "witness of the Holy Spirit" allowed him to argue on the one hand that Christianity is factually true and therefore capable of "reasoning" its way to dominion (because it is objectively true). On the other hand, he could argue that unless and until the Holy Spirit enables someone to embrace these facts not just intellectually (assent) but as a matter of trust, there can be no saving faith, i.e., trust in Jesus Christ's person and work as the sole object of such faith. The objective truth of Christianity, which can be established by apologetic arguments, cannot issue in faith unless the Holy Spirit grants the subjective capacity to believe (regeneration).

In distinguishing the complementary roles of general revelation and special revelation, Warfield, seeing the former as an important element of theological prolegomena, tacitly endorsed the arrangement found among the Reformed scholastics (i.e., Francis Turretin) and in a number of dogmatics texts from the Scottish theologians John Dick, Thomas Chalmers, and William Cunningham, as well as his Princeton mentors, Charles and A. A. Hodge, all of whom contend that natural revelation was indeed sufficient to provide the human race with a general and universal knowledge of God. Yet sinfully and inevitably suppressed by our fallen race *post lapsis*, such natural revelation serves the divine purpose of rendering all people under God's just condemnation, leaving them without excuse. Special revelation (Scripture) provides the fallen human race with "the entire body of saving truth," was revealed first to the patriarchs, then to Israel, then to the entire human race, and has for its design "to save man." Such revelation is made "through the instrumentality of deeds," God also providing the "explanatory" word to such deeds, making special revelation "itself a redemptive act."[43]

---

42. Paul Helm, "Thomas Reid, Calvinsim, and Common Sense," in Hendrik Hart, Johan Van Der Hoeven, and Nicholas Wolterstorff, eds. *Rationality in the Calvinian Tradition* (Lanham: University Press in America, 1983), 71–89.

43. B. B. Warfield, "The Biblical Idea of Revelation," in *Inspiration and Authority of the Bible* (Phillipsburg, NJ: P&R, 1948), 78–81.

Warfield's stress on the function of apologetics to establish the truth of biblical revelation is still debated within the Reformed tradition between so-called "evidentialists" and "presuppositionalists"—the latter held forth as the consistent "Reformed" view by Cornelius Van Til (1895–1987) of Westminster Theological Seminary and his followers. Presuppositionalists consider Warfield's use of historical apologetics as compromising the defense of faith by allowing "right reason" to stand in judgment over divine revelation. Nevertheless, Warfield's understanding of the relationship between reason and faith, along with his insistence on necessity of regeneration prior to the exercise of faith, clearly places him well within the Augustinian/Reformed tradition.

CONTRIBUTIONS TO THE FIELD OF APOLOGETICS

B. B. Warfield was a polemicist whose job was to respond to any deviations from Reformed orthodoxy, but that should not disqualify him from consideration as a well-known defender of the faith. Warfield's many and varied contributions to the discipline of apologetics came at a time when the church found itself under constant assault from new critical methodologies—many reflecting the antisupernatural theological liberalism of German universities. Warfield felt that those critical methods not intrinsically anti-Christian could be aimed at the critics themselves to establish the Christian claim to possess a supernatural revelation in the twenty-seven books of the New Testament with a fully reconstructed autographic text underlying them. Warfield's work in textual criticism opened the door to the use of lower criticism to establish the reliability of the New Testament text—an apologetic task that continues to the present.

Believing apologetics to be an offensive science, and not merely a defensive one, Warfield contended that apologetics occupies an important role in theological prolegomena. It was the apologist's task to pass on to the biblical and systematic theologian the knowledge of God, the religious nature and need of humanity, the supernatural nature of Christianity, as well as a factually grounded revelation of God in the Bible. This could best be done, Warfield argued, by establishing that Jesus rose bodily from the dead. Jesus Christ's self-attestation regarding his person and work and his endorsement of the Old Testament and the soon to be written New Testament as the Word of God and in its own right a redemptive act would ensure that theologians could begin their work presupposing that the material for doing biblical and systematic theology (Scripture) was not something merely asserted to be divine revelation but shown to be so by none other than God incarnate.

Perhaps Warfield's most significant contribution was his development of the doctrine of the witness of the Holy Spirit. According to Warfield, Christianity is founded on historical events and is therefore objectively true. But the effects of Adam's fall render all people darkened in their understanding and thoroughly and sinfully predisposed to reject Christian truth claims. It is the work of the Holy Spirit to create the subjective capacity to believe the evidences for the truth of Christianity given by God (not humanly devised) already present in the mind. The Holy Spirit does not supply additional reasons to believe but does supply the subjective capacity to believe those evidences already divinely given. The Spirit illumines the mind, softens the heart, and "quickens" the will through regeneration.[44] This provides those in Augustinian and Reformed traditions with a suitable way to relate faith and reason without exalting reason above revelation, as well as provides a means of returning Christian evidences to the apologetic arsenal of Reformed Christians, without unwittingly compromising the faith they seek to defend.

BIBLIOGRAPHY

Grier, W. J. "Benjamin Breckinridge Warfield." *Banner of Truth* 89 (Fall 1971): 3–9.

Hodge, A. A., and B. B. Warfield. "Inspiration." Pages 225–60 in *The Presbyterian Review* (April 1881); reprinted in A. A. Hodge and B. B. Warfield, *Inspiration*. Ed. by Roger Nicole. Grand Rapids: Baker, 1979, 5–71.

Kerr, Hugh Thomson. "Warfield: The Person Behind the Theology." Annie Kinkead Warfield Lecture for 1982. Ed. by William O. Harris (1995).

McClanahan, James Samuel. "Benjamin B. Warfield: Historian of Doctrine in Defense of Orthodoxy, 1881–1921." PhD dissertation, Union Theological Seminary in Virginia, 1988.

Meeter John E., and Roger Nicole. *A Bibliography of Benjamin Breckinridge Warfield, 1851–1921*. Phillipsburg, NJ: P&R, 1974.

Stonehouse, Ned B. *J. Gresham Machen: A Biographical Memoir*. Philadelphia: Westminster Theological Seminary, 1977.

Wallis, Wilber B. "Benjamin B. Warfield: Didactic and Polemical Theologian." Pages 3–19 in *The Presbyterion: Covenant Seminary Review*. Part I (Spring 1977).

Warfield, B. B. "Apologetics." Pages 3–21 in *New Schaff-Herzog Encyclopedia of Religious Knowledge*. Ed. by S. M. Jackson. New York: Funk & Wagnalls, 1908.

———. "The Biblical Doctrine of Faith." Pages 467–508 in *Biblical Doctrines*. Grand Rapids: Baker, 1981.

———. "The Biblical Idea of Revelation." Pages 71–102 in *Inspiration and Authority of the Bible* (Phillipsburg, NJ: P&R, 1948).

———. "Calvin's Doctrine of the Knowledge of God." Pages 219–325 in *The Princeton Theological Review* 7 (April 1909); repr. in B. B. Warfield, *Calvin and Augustine*. Philadelphia: P&R, 1956).

———. "Christless Christianity." *The Harvard Review* Vol. 5 (October 1912); reprinted in B. B. Warfield, *Christology and Criticism*. Grand Rapids: Baker, 1981, 423–473.

———. "The Church Doctrine of Inspiration." Reprinted in *The Inspiration and Authority of the Bible*. Phillipsburg, NJ: P&R, 1948.

———. *Critical Reviews*. Grand Rapids: Baker, 1981.

———. "God." Pages 251–53 in *Bible Dictionary*. Ed. by John Davis. Philadelphia: Westminster, 1898.

———. "The Greek Testament of Westcott and Hort." *The Presbyterian Review* 3 (April 1882): 325–46.

---

44. Warfield, "Introduction to Francis Beattie's *Apologetics*," 100–101.

————. "The Idea of Systematic Theology." *The Presbyterian and Reformed Review* 7 (April 1896): 243–71; reprinted in *Studies in Theology*. Grand Rapids: Baker, 1981.

————. "Inspiration and Criticism." Pages 395–425 in *Revelation and Inspiration*. Grand Rapids: Baker, 1981.

————. *An Introduction to the Textual Criticism of the New Testament*. New York: Whittaker, 1887.

————. Introductory Note to *Apologetics*, Vol. 1, by Francis Beattie. Richmond: Presbyterian Committee on Publications, 1903.

————. "The Latest Phase of Historical Rationalism."Pages 36–67, 185–210 in *The Presbyterian Quarterly* 9 (1895); reprinted in B. B. Warfield, *Studies in Theology*. Grand Rapids: Baker, 1981.

————. "The Question of Miracles." *The Bible Student* 7 (March, April, May, June 1903): 121–26, 193–97, 243–50, 314–20.

————. "The Resurrection of Christ a Historical Fact." Pages 178–192 in *Selected Shorter Writings of Benjamin B. Warfield*. Vol. 1. Ed. by John E. Meeter. Phillipsburg, NJ: P&R, 1980.

————. "Review of Herman Bavinck's *De Zekerheid des Geloofs*." *Princeton Theological Review* 1 (Jan 1903): 138–48.

————. "The Risen Christ." Pages 191–213 in *Saviour of the World*. New York: Hodder & Stoughton, 1914; repr. in pages 535–46 in *The Person and Work of Christ*. Philadelphia: P&R, 1950.

Part Five

TWENTIETH-CENTURY AMERICAN APOLOGISTS

In the twentieth century, apologetics increasingly became characteristic of English-speaking Christianity, with American voices shaping a conversation that had hitherto been dominated by European writers. This is to be seen as the natural outcome of the large number of seminaries and Christian colleges that emerged in the United States and as a concern for Christian higher education that is particularly—though not uniquely—characteristic of American Protestantism. It may also be linked with the phenomenon of "culture wars" in the United States (which has no direct equivalent in Europe or Australasia), in which an increasingly aggressive secular culture pursues an agenda that demands an apologetic response from Christian pastors and academics. The five apologists included in the fifth part of this work reflect these factors. Most reflect a Reformed perspective on apologetics that has popularly come to be known as "presuppositionalism" but is better described using other terms.

One important approach to apologetics built on the approach developed by B. B. Warfield and is particularly associated with **J. Gresham Machen**. Like Warfield, Machen saw the critique of theological liberalism as integral to the apologetic task, which at times he saw as equivalent to the defense of theological orthodoxy. Machen was appointed to a chair of apologetics and ethics at

Princeton Seminary in 1926, although his most important work as an apologist followed his departure from Princeton as a result of the emerging "fundamentalist" controversy, leading to the establishment of Westminster Theological Seminary. Although Machen emphasized the biblical foundations of orthodox Christianity, his main apologetic strategy in his best-known work, *Christianity & Liberalism*, was to show that historic Christianity and liberalism taught vastly different doctrines and were thus to be considered distinct religions.

Cornelius Van Til began to teach apologetics at Westminster Theological Seminary in the summer of 1930, just one year after the founding of the new seminary. His approach is widely designated as "presuppositionalist," although this description is not particularly helpful. Van Til himself saw his approach as focusing primarily on the Bible as the ultimate criterion for truth, thus distinguishing between those (such as Joseph Butler) who believe there is a neutral basis or shared ground between the Christian and non-Christian that can serve as the basis for apologetics and those who do not. True knowledge of God is impossible outside the Bible, so the apologist is obliged to presuppose the truth of Christianity from the outset.

This point was contentious and caused a significant rift between Van Til and **Gordon Haddon Clark**, who had taught Christian philosophy at Wheaton College before becoming ordained in the Orthodox Christian Church. This controversy began in 1944 and appears to have focused on the question of whether there was any correlation between human and divine modes of reasoning. Van Til denied any such possibility, whereas Clark argued that it was both possible and necessary. Clark was clear that if there was no fundamental identity between human and divine thought, it was impossible to have access to truth.

An unbeliever can grasp truth through reason. Clark, therefore, emphasized the importance of logical consistency as a criterion to judge worldviews, arguing that non-Christian worldviews could be defeated by exposing their incoherence or logical inconsistency. A Christian worldview could be partly validated by demonstrating its consistency. To his critics, this suggested that Clark was making the concept of coherence a neutral or common principle, shared by both Christians and non-Christians.

Clark's approach is partly reflected in the writings of perhaps the most significant popular American apologist of the 1960s and 1970s, **Francis A. Schaeffer**. For Schaeffer, there are two central elements to apologetics: "The first is defense. The second is to communicate Christianity in a way that any given generation can understand." Schaefer fine-tuned both his knowledge of Western culture and his apologetic method during his time at l'Abri in Switzerland. The apologist had to help nonbelievers find the point of tension or internal contradiction in their own way of thinking and then discover how Christianity offered a more coherent way of thinking. Schaeffer's influence on evangelicalism has been considerable, particularly in developing a better understanding of culture as a precondition for effective apologetic engagement.

The apologetic method of **Edward John Carnell** can be seen, at least in some respects, as a reversion to the classic apologetic strategies of the past—aiming to find common ground with audiences beyond the Christian community. Carnell is widely seen as a representative of the form of neoevangelicalism that emerged in the postwar period. He was inspired by writers such as Billy Graham and Carl F. H. Henry and was linked with institutions such as Fuller Theological Seminary. Setting to one side the fundamentalist refusal to engage with wider culture because of the danger of intellectual or spiritual contamination, Carnell set out to champion a "classical orthodoxy" (rather than the "cultic orthodoxy" more characteristic of fundamentalism) and developed an apologetic approach that emphasized the rationality of faith and the need to engage wider culture with the basic themes of the gospel. Carnell's first apologetic treatise, *An Introduction to Christian Apologetics*, is a landmark in contemporary American evangelical apologetics, paralleling Henry's *Uneasy Conscience of Modern Fundamentalism*, both in terms of what it chose to leave behind and what it chose to affirm.

Carnell served as president of Fuller Theological Seminary between 1954 and 1959, stamping his views on cultural engagement on the fledgling institution. The importance of this point is too easily overlooked in that most of the distinctively American approaches to apologetics to emerge in this period were linked with Westminster Theological Seminary and were shaped to varying extents by the framework developed by Cornelius Van Til. The emergence of a distinct and more culturally engaged form of apologetics at Fuller Seminary offered American evangelicalism an alternative approach to apologetics and catalyzed the emergence of a wider range of apologetic strategies in the following decades.

J. GRESHAM MACHEN

Saving Christianity from Christians

D. G. HART

By the spring of 1926, J. Gresham Machen (1881–1937) had taught at Princeton Seminary for two decades. He began in 1906 as a lecturer in New Testament Greek after receiving an education at Johns Hopkins University in classical Greek, at Princeton Seminary in the standard curriculum for ministerial preparation with some upper level seminars in New Testament, and then a year of independent study in Germany at Marburg and Goettingen Universities, where he listened to lectures in theology and the Bible. He went on to teach at Princeton Seminary until the liberalism of the Presbyterian Church (USA) led him to start a new seminary and then a new denomination of Presbyterianism, the Orthodox Presbyterian Church.

HISTORICAL BACKGROUND

Machen was the son of a highly regarded Baltimore attorney. He was born in 1881 and grew up in wealthy and influential circles. The Machen family entertained Woodrow Wilson when he was a student in Baltimore and vacationed in Maine with the Rockefellers. Machen's social location may explain in part his reluctance to return to Princeton after his studies in Germany. He experienced further ambivalence about the ministry before resolving doubts by 1914, when he pursued ordination in the Presbyterian Church (USA), a step necessary for appointment as assistant professor of New Testament at Princeton. He liked to travel to big cities and visit theaters, bookstores, and concert halls. To be a minister and a seminary professor implied a life of constraint, one that conformed to a congregation's expectations for godly living (and avoiding worldliness).

Over time, Machen made his peace with teaching at Princeton, preaching in local churches, and even beginning to make his voice heard in church politics. His most popular and controversial book, *Christianity and Liberalism*, was published in 1923 when the modernist-fundamentalist controversy was gaining coverage in the newspapers and occupied the time of church committees. Machen's argument in that book, one of the best summaries of the issues involved according to some observers, was that Christianity and liberal Protestantism were two religions, with distinct understandings of God, human sin, salvation, the Bible, and the church. As provocative as the argument was, it was an attempt to present the issues as fairly as possible.

Machen's popularity and intellectual gifts were responsible for the board of directors' decision at Princeton Seminary in the spring of 1926 to promote Machen to the chair of apologetics and ethics. The determination seemed to be a welcome way to fill a gap and make use of Machen's well-recognized gifts. But when the recommendation went to the General Assembly of the Presbyterian Church (the highest body in Presbyterianism's system of oversight and courts), the committee responsible for theological education opted to postpone the promotion. The reason had in part to do with opposition from liberal church officials who did not want to see Machen's conservatism rewarded. It also stemmed from moderate evangelicals who looked down on polemics and disagreement as indications of substandard piety.

Another factor was Machen's vote at a spring meeting of his presbytery (the regional body to oversee church life) in New Jersey on a motion to support the federal government's policy of Prohibition. Although he recognized that drunkenness was a sin, Machen also believed the Bible had little to say about the specific policies and laws that regulated the sale and distribution of alcohol in a specific country such as the United States. As sensible as his outlook may have been, it ran contrary to the dominant position in the Presbyterian Church and cost Machen his promotion and appointment as apologist. After all, as some Presbyterians reasoned, how could a man with such dubious politics be entrusted to teach ethics (part of the job description at Princeton for teaching apologetics) to young people aspiring to the ministry?

Even if Machen never taught apologetics in the classroom, his entire career as a seminary professor and churchman involved the defense of Christianity. He began by defending the truthfulness of the New Testament teachings about Christ. He later defended Christian doctrine over against efforts by liberals to harmonize Christianity with modern thought. And even later he advanced the cause of Presbyterian rights to challenge church decisions that went against the teaching of Scripture and rules of church government. In fact, for the decade after his failure to be promoted as professor of apologetics, Machen spearheaded efforts to maintain and preserve the theological and educational traditions of Princeton Seminary, first in 1929 by founding Westminster Seminary, then in

1933 by leading the formation of the Independent Board for Presbyterian Foreign Missions, and then in 1936 by starting a new Presbyterian communion, the Orthodox Presbyterian Church. Thanks to those endeavors, Machen remains one of the foremost spokesmen for historic Christianity in the United States during the first half of the twentieth century.

THEOLOGICAL CONTEXT

Although he reluctantly came to the vocation of teaching at Princeton, Machen became one of the last proponents of the so-called Princeton Theology. Founded in 1812 as the first Presbyterian seminary, Princeton emerged through the likes of Archibald Alexander, Samuel Miller, and Charles Hodge, the school's first three faculty, and later carried on by professors such as A. A. Hodge and B. B. Warfield as the bastion of Reformed orthodoxy in the United States. Other schools such as Andover Seminary, Yale Divinity School, or Union Theological Seminary in New York City may have begun with commitments to defend and preserve the main features of Calvinism. But Princeton did so for the better part of 125 years because of its adherence to the Presbyterian church's confessional standards—the Westminster Confession and Catechisms—its commitment to Scripture as God's infallible Word and the final arbiter of religious truth, its awareness of Protestant history in relation to earlier church developments, and its mission to train pastors. Through its theological journal (which had several names), the *Princeton Theological Journal*, its faculty and writers of similar outlook commented on major trends in church life, theological and biblical studies, literature, and society. Through it all, Princeton's faculty gained a reputation for defending Calvinist orthodoxy against all explicit and implicit threats.

In the specific area of apologetics, Princeton tried to harmonize the belief that faith begins with the work of the Holy Spirit and a commitment to reasoned arguments on behalf of Scripture's truthfulness and Christianity's plausibility. Later on, with the rise of presuppositional apologetics in Dutch Calvinism (most evident in the works of Cornelius Van Til), Princeton's reliance on reason came in for criticism. Defending Christian truth by rational argument seemed to contradict the more basic point of human sinfulness and the impossibility of persuading unregenerate people of the Bible's teaching apart from a prior work of God. The debate over methods that developed during the middle decades of the twentieth century between evidentialism (e.g., R. C. Sproul and John Gerstner) and presuppositionalism (Van Til) was an outworking of the different ways in which Old Princeton and Abraham Kuyper's institutions in the Netherlands reacted to and appropriated the Enlightenment. Machen himself followed the

Old Princeton tradition but was not doctrinaire. In 1932, during a series of lectures on apologetics that he gave in London (more below), Machen explained his approach to the defense of Christianity. After giving a talk on the truth of the resurrection or the deity of Christ, Machen said, he commonly received comments from Christians who appreciated his argument but admitted that they already believed the Bible and so did not need to be convinced. Machen's response in these settings was to agree that he would prefer to make presentations to "as many skeptics as possible." Even if such people were not present, his arguments were not in vain. His purpose in apologetics was not to convince skeptics or people opposed to the faith but "to give Christian people"—parents, Sunday school teachers—"materials that they can use . . . in dealing with their own children or with pupils in their classes, who . . . are troubled by the hostile voices on every side."[1]

APOLOGETIC RESPONSE

Machen's emergence as a popular speaker who defended the basic truths of Christianity took a while. His first venture into the world of apologetics was a circuitous one. After serving as a YMCA secretary in France during World War I, in which he satisfied a desire to be useful in the great conflict that disrupted Europe, Machen returned to the United States to prepare a series of lectures on the apostle Paul to be given at Union Presbyterian Seminary in Richmond, Virginia. Eventually published as *The Origin of Paul's Religion*, Machen's aim was to enter the debates in New Testament studies about Pauline theology and whether it represented a departure from the simpler teachings of Jesus (or whether Paul was the founder of a new form of Christianity). The book was filled with references to the most relevant and recent scholarly literature on the subject. Reviewers of the book recognized Machen's scholarly accomplishment and praised him for interacting with all the relevant sources and schools of interpretation.

At the same time, reviewers also understood the thrust of Machen's book, which was to take Paul at his word, not as a religious genius who used Jesus to develop a new series of reflections about God and salvation but as a follower of Christ who tried to explain the significance of Jesus's death, resurrection, and ascension in relation to Old Testament Judaism. Machen was well aware that biblical studies had long since rejected supernaturalism, which left scholars trying to explain miracles, divine revelation, and beliefs about Christ's deity as

---

1. Machen, "Christian Scholarship and the Defense of the Faith," in D. G. Hart, ed., *J. Gresham Machen: Selected Shorter Writings* (hereafter *Selected Shorter Writings*) (Phillipsburg, NJ: P&R, 2004), 145.

products of a primitive, prescientific culture. In contrast, Machen was determined to take Paul at face value and so to try to explain the apostle's teaching about Jesus as a divine being whose death and resurrection brought salvation to sinners. In other words, instead of trying to explain away the aspects of Paul's epistles that were incompatible with the modern mind, Machen argued that the church's historic interpretation of the New Testament was plausible. An important reason was that modern scholars had yet to arrive at a theory that adequately explained Paul's outlook by tracing it to first-century developments in history, comparative religion, or philosophy. Paul's teaching was uniquely the product of divine revelation and the historical truth of Christ's life, death, and resurrection.

The Origin of Paul's Religion may have been a form of apologetics in the realm of New Testament studies, but its audience was largely confined to scholars and pastors. Machen's foray into writing for a popular audience came with two important books from the 1920s, published at the peak of the fundamentalist controversy: *Christianity & Liberalism* and *What Is Faith?* The former drew the most attention and remains a book that many believers continue to read. Together, though, Machen used both books to defend historic Christianity over against its modern and liberal competitor. Simply put, he argued in *Christianity & Liberalism* that Protestantism was not Christian but an entirely different religion. In *What Is Faith?*, Machen portrayed liberalism as inherently anti-intellectual by reducing faith to feelings or experience and denying its intellectual (and doctrinal) aspects.

As simplistic as the assertion that Christianity and liberalism are two distinct religions might have appeared—and it was especially provocative during the 1920s—Machen's contention tried to avoid animus or psychological manipulation. *Christianity & Liberalism* simply (even as Machen conceded his conservative beliefs) laid out the major points of Christian doctrine—God, human nature, sin, Scripture, salvation, and the church—and showed that historic Christianity and liberalism taught vastly different doctrines. For instance, while Christians had historically professed that the Bible was the Word of God, liberalism reduced the Bible to human imaginings and aspirations about spiritual matters. And while the church had always taught that Jesus was God and man, one person with two distinct natures, liberals reduced Christ's divinity to the ways his followers tried to take an ordinary though remarkable teacher and turn him into the founder of a new religion. On salvation, Machen saw the strongest divergence of ideas. While for conservatives (and the Bible) Christianity offered a way of salvation based on the gracious work of Christ, for liberals redemption relied on human efforts, following Jesus's teaching, to live a good life. Machen wrote for Christian and secular readers and admitted that his nonreligious audience might sympathize more with liberalism than Christianity. But either way, he hoped to show that what liberalism amounted to was not any religion recognizable as Christian. It was a program for a virtuous life with vague associations to a spiritual (but not supernaturalistic) realm.

What Is Faith? built on *Christianity & Liberalism* by starting with the position Machen had laid out in the first book, namely, that doctrine was essential to understanding Christianity and its differences from other religions. Because doctrine was so basic to Christianity, faith, the way by which a person came to trust in Christ, was bound up with intellect or understanding, the way by which someone became convinced of truths about Christ. For instance, Machen defended the position of making the terms for church membership harder than they were. Someone might claim to have accepted Christ as her personal savior and yet have no adequate understanding of what words such as *Christ* and *savior* mean. This point prompted Machen to defend the practice of catechetical instruction as well, especially as practiced by Lutheran communions in the United States. By teaching the Protestant churches' catechisms to believers seeking church membership, ministers (as well as parents) would make up for the doctrinal illiteracy that afflicted both evangelical and liberal Protestants. Such doctrinal awareness, of course, did not ensure genuine faith, but it did address the all-too-common assumption that faith and knowledge were distinct aspects of Christian experience. True faith depended on correct knowledge of those truths to which Christians entrusted their eternal destiny. As such, faith could never be blind. The genuine article always involved basic knowledge about God, sin, Christ, and salvation.

The arguments Machen made on behalf of the Bible and basic Christian teaching placed him clearly on the fundamentalist side of the modernist-fundamentalist controversy. That identification became even more apparent with his last scholarly book, *The Virgin Birth of Christ* (1930), a product of almost twenty-five years of investigation. In 1925 the doctrine of the virgin birth had almost split Machen's denomination, the Presbyterian Church U.S.A. (northern). At previous general assemblies, the church had affirmed the virgin birth as an essential and necessary article of faith in response to the rise of biblical criticism and liberal theology. But the Presbytery of New York, the center of modernist theology among Presbyterians and Baptists, had ordained two pastors who had refused to affirm the doctrine. In response to that controversy, the 1925 general assembly considered a motion to declare the virgin birth once again to be a fundamental article of Christianity. When commissioners from New York threatened to leave the denomination, the moderator, Charles Erdman, a colleague of Machen's at Princeton Theological Seminary who taught practical theology, called for a committee to study the causes behind theological controversies among Presbyterians. That committee eventually resulted in changes at Princeton Seminary that forced Machen to leave and in 1929 to found a new institution, Westminster Theological Seminary in Philadelphia.

The coincidence of Machen's book with these developments may have led some readers to think he was writing in response to the Presbyterian controversy. But Machen had written about the New Testament accounts of Jesus's birth while a seminarian, and it was a topic he continued to monitor in his classroom and research responsibilities. He considered *The Virgin Birth of Christ* his "magnum opus," his most significant achievement as a biblical scholar. Like *The Origin of Paul's Religion*, it was a defense of the truthfulness of the New Testament narratives. To try to explain away the supernatural elements of the virgin birth did not make sense of either the earliest manuscripts of the gospels, the original teachings of the apostles, or the prominence of Christ's birth account in the first Christian creeds. Machen conceded that belief in the virgin birth ultimately depended on faith and the work of the Spirit. At the same time, his book offered reasons for taking the Bible and its doctrine seriously, not as the spiritual longings of prescientific people but as serious assertions about the nature of salvation according to the Christian religion.

Although Machen's writings throughout the 1920s identified him as a fundamentalist—and he became one of the main spokesmen for conservative Protestantism when editors or journalists needed a quote or an essay—the Princeton professor was uncomfortable with the term and what it represented. William Jennings Bryan asked Machen to testify at the Scopes Trial, but Machen declined, partly because he did not believe he qualified as an expert on the Genesis creation accounts and partly because he sensed the courtroom proceedings could devolve into a circus atmosphere. Machen remarked that he considered himself not a fundamentalist but a Calvinist, that is, an adherent of Reformed Protestantism. If forced to choose simply between modernist and fundamentalist, then he had no hesitation in siding with the latter camp. Even so, what he tried to do in defending Christianity was more than simply covering the basics of the faith. Machen also wanted Christians to know the Bible and doctrine in greater detail than fundamentalism's brief statements of faith allowed. As he explained at the opening of Westminster Theological Seminary in 1929, "We rejoice in the approximations to that body of truth which other systems of theology contain; we rejoice in our Christian fellowship with other evangelical churches." But, he explained, this sort of theological consensus would not deter the new seminary from teaching Reformed theology. "We cannot consent to impoverish our message by setting forth less than what we find the Scriptures to contain." Machen even believed that his best service to other Protestants was not to teach and defend "some vague greatest common measure among various creeds, but that great historic faith that has come through Augustine and Calvin to our own Presbyterian church."[2]

So instead of using the credibility and reputation he had built during the 1920s as a defender of the New Testament and historic Christian doctrine, Machen spent the remainder of his relatively short life (he died at the age of fifty-six) trying to preserve the witness of the Presbyterian Church (U.S.A.). The first leg of this journey came in 1929 with the formation of Westminster Theological Seminary. Machen was convinced, along with donors and trustees, that the controversy at Princeton and the administrative changes to restore peace in the faculty had compromised the ability of faculty there to hold church officials accountable to the communion's doctrinal standards. He also believed that Princeton was no longer a place to train the kind of pastors the times required. Westminster, then, became in Machen's mind the successor to Princeton's tradition of scholarly theological rigor. Next came the formation of the Independent Board for Presbyterian Foreign Missions in 1933, which was Machen and fellow conservatives' response to a report on US Protestant foreign missions that whitewashed the presence of liberalism on the mission field and even proposed a rationale for missions based on humanitarianism and cooperation with non-Christian religions. Once again, Machen brought his arguments on behalf of historic Christianity to bear on the concrete task of starting an agency to support and send out reliable missionaries. Executives in the Presbyterian Church regarded this initiative as a rebuke to the denomination's integrity and orchestrated measures to bring Machen (along with other members of the Independent Board) to trial for ecclesiastical insubordination. Once found guilty by the Presbytery of New Brunswick, a verdict upheld by the 1936 general assembly, Machen led a small group of conservatives to form the Orthodox Presbyterian Church, a communion that claimed to be the spiritual successor to the Presbyterian Church (U.S.A.).

APOLOGETIC METHODOLOGY

Throughout these church conflicts, Machen's abilities as a defender of the faith were still evident. Not only did he continue to argue for the infallibility and authority of Scripture or the truthfulness of the church's witness in its creeds and catechisms about God, human sinfulness, and salvation through Christ alone,

---

2. Machen, "Westminster Theological Seminary: Its Purpose and Plan," in *Selected Shorter Writings*, 191.

Machen also defended the basic convictions of Protestantism about church government and need to be vigilant in keeping pastors, elders, and denominational officials true to the vows they had taken to uphold the church's doctrinal standards. His argument on behalf of Protestantism was arguably best summarized in testimony he gave during his trial when he explained why he could not be simply loyal to the agencies of the Presbyterian Church:

> I could not promise to support even the very best and soundest of human agencies as a condition of my being ordained. It is at the very heart and core of my ordination pledge, in accordance with the law of the Presbyterian church, that I should repeatedly examine any agency that appeals to me for support in light of the Word of God, and support it only if it is in accord with that blessed Word.[3]

Machen added that his conscience, not the "pronouncements of any human councils or courts," guided him to take this position, which was, of course, akin to the logic that Protestants used in the sixteenth century against submitting to the papacy and Roman Catholic bishops.

Even as he spearheaded new Presbyterian institutions and tried to defend his actions within the Presbyterian Church, in 1932 Machen gave a series of lectures in London that supplied the theory behind his years of applied apologetics. In the first of those talks, "Christian Scholarship and Evangelism," Machen observed how views of education and knowledge had seeped into Christian circles only to erode doctrinal literacy and study of the Bible. As a critic of modern theories of education, such as those associated with John Dewey, who stressed the importance of helping students figure out how to think rather than imparting definite knowledge about a subject, Machen let his audience know what he thought of this "child-centered notion of education." It had resulted in the oxymoronic notion that "it is possible to think with a completely empty mind."[4] This wrongheaded theory of education was responsible for the decline of American public education, Machen argued, but it was also infecting the church through the implementation of "religious education." The premise for this method of teaching in the church was that the teacher "is not to impart knowledge of a fixed body of truth which God has revealed, but to train the religious faculty of the child."[5] The means by which teachers developed a child's religious faculty could include any number of doctrinal or spiritual aids. The danger, for Machen, was that such

3. Machen, "Statement to the Presbytery of New Brunswick," in *Selected Shorter Writings*, 349.
4. Machen, "Christian Scholarship and Evangelism," in *Selected Shorter Writings*, 136.
5. Ibid., 137.

an approach gave up "the search for objective and permanent truth" about God and salvation. Such a view of education was also at odds with the Bible since it "presents a body of truth which God has revealed," and a pastor or teacher's duty was, then, to pass on and explain those truths.[6]

From these comments on education and knowledge in the church and schools, Machen proceeded to make his case for the importance of scholarship to evangelism. The faith that a pastor or evangelist determined to cultivate in a new believer depended on knowledge, objective truth. No matter how much devout Christians might promote a "simple faith," genuine belief was never isolated from knowledge about Christ. Why else would someone put their trust in a person who might turn out to be, because of insufficient knowledge, untrustworthy. In fact, to have faith in Christ required knowing precisely that he was the son of God whose death on the cross and resurrection could pay the penalty for sin (and remedy the predicament of humankind going all the way back to the fall). Simple faith required a fair amount of knowledge, Machen argued, and the New Testament itself gives many examples. Paul and Silas spoke "the word of the Lord" (Acts 16:32) to the jailer in Philippi, after telling him to believe in Christ. So too, Christ's example with the Samaritan woman in John 4 indicates that instruction about God, worship, and salvation was basic to evangelizing the lost. Machen also pointed to the example of Paul in Thessalonica, in which Machen explained the preaching Paul used to evangelize unbelievers: "Ye turned to God from idols"—there is theology proper. "And to wait for His Son from heaven"—there is Christology. "Whom He raised from the dead"—there is the supernatural act of God in history. "Even Jesus"—there is the humanity of our Lord. "Which delivereth us from the wrath to come"—there is the Christian doctrine of sin and the Christian doctrine of the cross of Christ.[7]

Over and over in the New Testament came the direct tie between faith and knowledge. The lesson was that "out of a great underlying fund of Christian learning . . . true evangelism springs."[8]

If Machen's first lecture reinforced his argument in *What Is Faith?*, his second, "Christian Scholarship and the Defense of the Faith," echoed his point in *Christianity and Liberalism*. He was particularly concerned to undermine the idea that the Bible, as God's Word, needed no defense or that Christianity, as wonderful as it was, could simply win people by virtue of its grandeur. Machen believed that such naive notions were symptomatic of "an anti-intellectualistic, nondoctrinal Modernism." The reason such religion needed no defense was

---

6. Ibid., 137.
7. Ibid., 140.
8. Ibid., 141.

because it was thoroughly in tune with the spirit of the age.[9] Machen knew and conceded that argument "alone" was insufficient "to make a man a Christian." The best arguments in the world were all in vain "unless there is one other thing: the mysterious, creative power of the Holy Spirit in the new birth."[10] But insufficiency did not mean unnecessary. Sometimes God used apologetics directly and sometimes indirectly to generate saving faith. Either way, apologetics was a means to a right understanding of the Christian religion, which, of course, was crucial to the knowledge on which faith depended.

Such arguments for the truth of Christianity, Machen explained, invariably produced controversy and polemics. A defense of the gospel would inevitably lead to combat against false views of salvation or timid presentations of Christianity. During the fundamentalist controversy Machen had heard plenty of laments about fighting in the church and the optimistic notion that what would remedy the church's weakness was not contention with error but revival. Here Machen shot back that any presentation of the gospel involved contending for the correct view of salvation. Again, knowledge was necessary for faith. He added that the entire history of the church in the New Testament was filled with controversy thanks to the apostles' efforts to oppose defective or erroneous understandings of the gospel. Even Paul's hymn of love in 1 Corinthians 13, Machen observed, comes in a polemical passage in one of the most confrontational books in the Bible. He concluded by pleading for prayer that God would raise up defenders of the faith who knew and were sufficiently courageous to confront the "mighty conflict against the Christian religion" that dominated modern society.[11]

In his final lecture in London, "Christian Scholarship and the Building Up of the Church," Machen continued his defense of the faith along doctrinal and intellectual lines. He addressed particularly the importance of philosophy, which had traditionally been an important aid to theologians in their endeavors to systematize biblical teaching and to arrive at orthodox notions about God and his ways. In other words, the Bible did not necessarily teach philosophy, but its revelation did involve truths about the sorts of subjects that philosophers studied. It was common for liberal and fudamentalists in Machen's day to take the view that metaphysics were of little concern to a Christian because religion was a different order of human existence than philosophy. Machen countered this and defended the importance of philosophy as an aid to apologetics, first, by insisting that the doctrine of creation implied an understanding of reality bound up with the most important philosophical questions. Everything in the Bible, Machen argued,

9. Machen, "Christian Scholarship and the Defense of the Faith," in *Selected Shorter Writings*, 144.
10. Ibid., 144–45.
11. Ibid., 152.

"is based upon the stupendous metaphysic" of Genesis 1:1—namely, that "God is the maker and Ruler of the world" and that this God is personal.[12] The same sort of reflections went into the "second great mystery" of the Bible—"The mystery of man."[13] The creation accounts in Genesis distinguish humans from the rest of creation in an elevated status as image-bearers of God, and those documents also reveal the fall and the toll that sin took on human nature. The character of human nature, another aspect of philosophical inquiry, was another subject that philosophers and theologians shared. Machen's conclusion was that such considerations were so important to understanding the gospel and to defending Christianity from false ideas about God and human nature that believers were foolish to emphasize a simple, experiential faith. Christianity was indeed accessible to the simplest of people. But the Bible's teachings were also so profound that Christians had incredible resources for addressing the questions that vexed the greatest minds.

CONTRIBUTIONS TO THE FIELD OF APOLOGETICS

To conclude that Machen was one of the early twentieth century's most formidable Protestant apologists would be to overestimate only one aspect of his career and writing. Machen was a New Testament scholar, churchman, seminary administrator, and an apologist. At the same time, a pattern emerges throughout his career as a New Testament scholar, seminary professor, and writer; namely, that Machen throughout his professional life tried to make historic Christianity intelligible to those Americans (and some Europeans) who believed modern times made religion (at least in its older forms) obsolete. In the introduction to his book *Christianity and Liberalism*, Machen admitted that some readers would fling the book aside because they had already made up their minds that Christianity was false and its defense was a "hopelessly" lost cause.[14] But even these skeptics and agnostics, Machen believed, should consider that older truths about humanity and social relations were not so readily dismissed. Science may have yielded many improvements in human existence—even as it challenged truths revealed in Scripture, but a mechanistic and materialistic world had also resulted in an "unprecedented decline in literature and art."[15] The predominance of science had also changed politics such that socialism minimized commitments

---

12. Machen, "Christian Scholarship and the Building Up of the Church," in *Selected Shorter Writings*, 156.
13. Ibid., 157.
14. J. Gresham Machen, *Christianity and Liberalism* (New York: Macmillan, 1923), 9.
15. Ibid., 15.

to individual freedom in order to improve the collection of citizens and even humanity itself. Even in education, pedagogical theories were prevailing that denied the uniqueness and peculiarities of individual students only to provide a curriculum that bred conformity and social stability. Machen tried to convince hostile readers to give his arguments attention if only to recognize that Christianity was opposed to "the materialistic paternalism of the present day" and so worthy of more consideration than some might assume. A defense of Christianity, he argued, might "restore mankind to something of the glories of the past."[16]

Another audience Machen had in view were those who believed the church had become too deeply invested in Progressive politics. The era in which he worked was one in which politicians in both major parties implemented reforms in the federal government to regulate big business, as well as other sectors of American life. In most cases, the politics of Progressivism was bound up with the social gospel of the mainline churches. As a states' rights Democrat and civil libertarian, Machen opposed these political measures in a variety of settings— letters to editors, testimony before legislators, membership in political organizations. His understanding of the spirituality of the church was another ingredient in his political outlook. Machen held that the church was a spiritual institution with spiritual means (word and sacrament) for spiritual ends (salvation). As such, he declared, "You cannot expect from a true Christian church any official pronouncements upon the political or social questions of the day, and you cannot expect cooperation with the state in anything involving the use of force." Individual Christians, of course, could serve as police or politicians. But the church's weapons against evil were spiritual, "not carnal." Consequently, if the church became a political lobby "through the advocacy of political measures whether good or bad," the church would be guilty of "turning aside from its proper mission, which is to bring to bear upon human hearts the solemn and imperious, yet also sweet and gracious, appeal of the gospel of Christ."[17]

Such a defense of the church's calling—with its explicit rejection of politics and social activism for the church as an institution—was not a popular position either with fundamentalists or modernists. In fact, it was largely responsible for the Presbyterian Church's failure to promote Machen to the chair of apologetics at Princeton Seminary in 1926. He believed the church should not take sides in policy, legislation, or political campaigns—unless Christians had a clear biblical warrant. Machen voted against the church's support for Prohibition, not because he favored alcohol or drunkenness but because the Bible said nothing about

16. Ibid.
17. Machen, "The Responsibility of the Church in the New Age," in *Selected Shorter Writings*, 375.

how to legislate (whether at the national or state level) the sale and distribution of alcohol.

That vote was largely responsible for opposition to Machen's academic promotion, which in turn meant that he was never technically an apologist. At the same time, his defense of the church's task—as one that was spiritual, not political—was of a piece with the rest of his career and work. Machen may not have written about schools of apologetics or argued for one school of philosophy over another as the best way to defend Christian truth. But from his biblical scholarship and popular books to his lectures and even his understanding of church-state relations, Machen was usually engaged in arguments to defend the Bible, doctrine, and the church against misunderstanding and error.

BIBLIOGRAPHY

Hart, D. G. *Defending the Faith: J. Gresham Machen and the Crisis of Conservative Protestantism in Modern America*. Baltimore: Johns Hopkins University Press, 1994.

Hart, D. G., and John R. Muether. *Seeking a Better Country: 300 Years of American Presbyterianism*. Phillipsburg, NJ: P&R Publishing, 2007.

Helseth, Paul Kjoss. *"Right Reason" and the Princeton Mind: An Unorthodox Proposal*. Phillipsburg, NJ: P&R Publishing, 2010.

Hutchison, William R. *The Modernist Impulse in American Protestantism*. Cambridge: Harvard University Press, 1976.

Loetscher, Lefferts A. *The Broadening Church: A Study of Theological Issues in the Presbyterian Church since 1869*. Philadelphia: University of Pennsylvania Press, 1954.

Longfield, Bradley J. *The Presbyterian Controversy: Fundamentalists, Modernists, and Moderates*. New York: Oxford University Press, 1991.

Machen, J. Gresham. *The Christian Faith in the Modern World*. New York: Macmillan, 1937.

———. *The Christian View of Man*. New York: Macmillan, 1936.

———. *Christianity and Liberalism*. New York: Macmillan, 1923.

———. *The Origins of Paul's Religion*. New York: Macmillan, 1921.

———. *Virgin Birth of Christ*. New York: Harper & Brothers, 1930.

———. *What is Faith?* New York: Macmillan, 1925.

Marsden, George M. "The Collapse of American Evangelical Academia." Pages 219–64 in Alvin Pantinga and Nicholas Wolterstorff, eds. *Faith and Rationality: Reason and Belief in God*. Notre Dame: University of Notre Dame Press, 1983

———. *Fundamentalism and American Culture: The Shaping of Twentieth-Century Evangelicalism*. New York: Oxford University Press, 1980.

Noll, Mark A. *Between Faith and Criticism: Evangelicals, Scholarship, and the Bible in America*. San Francisco: Harper & Row, 1986.

———. *Princeton and the Republic, 1768–1822: The Search for A Christian Enlightenment in the Era of Samuel Stanhope Smith*. Princeton: Princeton University Press, 1989.

———, ed. *The Princeton Theology, 1812–1921: Scripture, Science, and Theological Method from Archibald Alexander to Benjamin Warfield*. 1983; Repr.; Grand Rapids: Baker, 2001.

Vander Stelt, John C. *Philosophy and Scripture: A Study in Old Princeton and Westminster Theology*. Marlton, NJ: Mack, 1978.

CORNELIUS VAN TIL

Presuppositional Apologist

K. SCOTT OLIPHINT

Throughout the course of his four decades of teaching pastors, Cornelius Van Til (1895–1987) focused his apologetic method on the reality that no one is autonomous and that all of us suffer from the same spiritual disease. Since sin has radically affected every aspect of our human character, nothing short of regeneration—bringing the spiritually dead to life—is necessary. The task of Christian apologetics (as well as of evangelism), according to Van Til, is to incorporate the power of God, in his Word, as we seek to persuade those who are outside of Christ. Van Til reminded us that apologetics begins with the reality that all people are responsible to submit to the God who is known by all (Rom 1:18–20) and that this submission will happen only when the truth of God's Word is applied by his Spirit to human hearts.

HISTORICAL BACKGROUND

Cornelius Van Til was born in 1895, the sixth of eight boys, in Grootegast, Netherlands. Reared in the Dutch Calvinist tradition, he was regularly and routinely exposed to the Scriptures, in both family and corporate worship. His father was a farmer and eventually followed his two eldest sons to the United States, when Cornelius was ten, to begin farming in Indiana. Cornelius was, by all accounts, a skilled farmer himself, and it was assumed that he would continue the family tradition.

Eventually it became clear that Cornelius was adept at academics. He graduated from Calvin College in 1922, from Princeton Theological Seminary in 1925, and from Princeton University with his PhD in 1927. He served as the pastor of the Christian Reformed Church in Spring Lake, Michigan, from 1927 to 1928 and was instructor of apologetics at Princeton Theological Seminary from 1928 to 1929. After one year, Princeton offered him a full appointment. Van Til inquired of J. Gresham Machen as to what he should do, and Machen informed him that the seminary was now lost. So Van Til did not accept the appointment. Instead, Van Til returned to his former pulpit in Spring Lake, Michigan,

479

which was still vacant, in June 1929. After returning to pulpit ministry, Machen sent an initial telegram to Van Til asking him to join him in the newly founded Westminster Theological Seminary in Philadelphia. Initially, O. T. Allis was sent to Michigan to persuade Van Til to come to Philadelphia. Van Til first declined the offer, stating that his decision was "irrevocable." So at the urging of the new New Testament professor of Westminster, Ned Stonehouse, Machen himself went out to Michigan and convinced Van Til to come, assuring him that the appointment could be temporary. Van Til left Michigan, again, in September 1929 and became the professor of apologetics at Westminster Theological Seminary in Philadelphia. He remained there for the rest of his life, retiring from full-time teaching in 1972. Van Til was the last of the founding faculty of Westminster Seminary.[1]

Most influential in Van Til's theological upbringing were the Dutch theologians Abraham Kuyper and Herman Bavinck. He devoured their works before moving to Princeton to study. At Princeton, he was influenced heavily by Geerhardus Vos, Caspar W. Hodge, and J. Gresham Machen. Because of Van Til's Princeton studies, he had great admiration for the work of B. B. Warfield. In his doctoral work, Van Til studied under the idealist philosopher A. A. Bowman. Van Til's dissertation, *God and the Absolute*, showed the bankruptcy of absolute idealism, as well as pragmatism. Along with the theological giants who molded Van Til's thought, his extensive knowledge of idealism would shape his writing and his approach to apologetics and theology for the rest of his life.

Van Til's writings are extensive; many were written syllabuses that were published virtually unedited. With minor exceptions, the bulk of Van Til's academic career can be summed up under two interrelated headings: apologetics and Barthianism. In apologetics, Van Til was a bloodhound, uniquely capable of sniffing out unbelief no matter where it purported to hide. In Barthianism, Van Til was a bulldog, tenaciously exposing the "neo" of Barth's neoorthodox theology, showing its utter antithesis from biblical orthodoxy. In both cases, Van Til's passion was for the purity of the gospel, especially in its academic contexts. He recognized, in a way that few have, how easy it is for those who love the life of the mind to go astray, even if inadvertently, and he was continually calling his readers back to the "self-attesting Christ of Scripture."

At the end of his career, Van Til reflected on his academic contributions. He asked himself whether he had been consistent with his own desires. He began this way:

---

1. Some of this material is taken from John R. Muether, *Cornelius Van Til: Reformed Apologist and Churchman* (Phillipsburg, NJ: P&R, 2008). This book should be the first consulted for a helpful overview of Van Til's life and career.

When I ask myself such questions as these I think that as far as the manner of presentation is concerned, I have often not lived up to my own motto on this point of *suaviter in modo* [mild in manner]. I beg forgiveness of those whom I have hurt because of this sin of mine. Then, so far as content is concerned, I have often not lived up to my own motto on this point either. I have not always made perfectly clear that in presenting Christ to lost men, we must present Him for what He is. He has told us what He is in the Scriptures. Apparently I have given occasion for people to think that I am speculative or philosophical first and biblical afterward.[2]

THEOLOGICAL CONTEXT

It was Cornelius Van Til's unrelenting and rock-solid commitment to a robust Reformed theology that drove everything he did and everything he was. When Van Til first began to prepare to teach his Evidences course in the summer of 1930, just one year after the founding of Westminster Theological Seminary, he was tendentious and uneasy about it. His discomfort stemmed from his desire to please his mentor, the founder of Westminster, J. Gresham Machen. Specifically, Van Til was aware that his Evidences course would need to distance itself from the teaching that Van Til had received as a student in his apologetics instruction at Princeton Theological Seminary.[3] He was concerned that Machen would not approve of Van Til's disagreement with the content of those courses, given that Westminster was founded to be the continuation of Old Princeton, not its nemesis. So Van Til wrote to Machen that summer to ensure that he would prepare and teach the course in a way that Machen could approve.

The response from Machen to Van Til was most encouraging. Machen began the letter "by relating that he held but the 'vaguest kind' of thoughts on the matter . . . of evidences." He then assured Van Til, "Your choice of topics is sure to be better than mine ever would be," to which Machen added this encouragement: "I wish I could take your course in Evidences. I need it, and I am sure it is greatly to the benefit of the Seminary that you are offering it."[4] In this encouragement, Van Til was confident that he could try, in this syllabus, to critique the method of apologetics that he had learned as a student at Princeton Seminary.

---

2. Cornelius Van Til, *Toward a Reformed Apologetics* (n.p., 1972), 1.
3. It is important to remember that Van Til's critique of Princeton Seminary's theology and apologetic approach was not a product simply of his reading. His initial discomfort came when he sat, as a student, in classes at Princeton, in which were taught methods and ideas foreign to the Reformed theology that Van Til had learned and affirmed. His critique, then, is not first of all that of a scholar of Old Princeton, but of a student. It came out of his own experiences at Princeton.
4. Muether, *Cornelius Van Til*, 70f.

It is crucial to remember that there was a conscious and determined effort by Machen, as he began Westminster Seminary, that there would be significant and substantial theological continuity between Old Princeton and the new Westminster. Westminster was founded to continue the Reformed theological tradition that Princeton had squandered. In the area of apologetics, Van Til was convinced that there had to be significant *discontinuity* between the two institutions. With Machen's encouragement, Van Til set out to offer what would be a new, and more radically consistent, theological approach to the topic of "evidences" in apologetics.

It was clear to Van Til as he prepared for the second of two required apologetics courses in the curriculum at Westminster that (1) a course on evidences was crucial and central to the training of people for pastoral ministry and that (2) he would need to reorient the topic to make it more consistent with the Reformed theology that was the trademark of Old Princeton and the new Westminster.

The apologetics training Van Til had received at Princeton, from William Brenton Greene Jr., was not compatible with the theology that Van Til had imbibed at Calvin and then at Princeton Seminary. Taking his cue from Warfield and others, the apologetic approach taught by Greene at Princeton in the second decade of the twentieth century had borrowed too heavily from an approach that was, at its root, less than Reformed in its theological foundation. Van Til knew that his task as a new professor of this new seminary was to change that apologetic "glitch" in Princeton's approach. It was this first syllabus on "Evidences" that began, in earnest, Van Til's Reformed reorientation and reformation of Christian apologetics. Though the syllabus was revised over several decades of teaching, the substance of it remained fundamentally unchanged, as Van Til set the topic of evidences within the context of the empiricism of David Hume and especially the evidential apologetic of Bishop Joseph Butler.[5]

Even with Van Til's deep appreciation for his time at Princeton Seminary, and for the men who influenced him there, he also recognized, especially because of his upbringing and his training at Calvin College, that there were elements of Princeton's theology, and its apologetic, that were not consistent with everything he had read and learned previously. Specifically, Princeton was not duly aware or appreciative, in its apologetic approach, of how radical the Reformation was in its theological depth. Through Kuyper and Bavinck, and especially through John Calvin, Van Til recognized the all-encompassing and universal implications of Paul's teaching that every person, by virtue of being created in the image

---

5. Thus far, the material in this section has been used with permission from my "Preface" to Cornelius Van Til, K. Scott Oliphint, ed. *Christian-Theistic Evidences*, In Defense of the Faith VI (Phillipsburg, NJ: P&R, 2016).

of God, was a person who possessed, and suppressed (apart from Christ), the true knowledge of the true God. It was this possession-suppression dynamic in all people that focused Van Til's assessment of his Princeton mentors and their influence on him.

Van Til's "revered teacher" at Princeton, whom Van Til referred to as "the sainted William Brenton Greene, Jr.,"[6] had taught Van Til an apologetic method that was inconsistent with the Reformed theology that flowed through every inch of his theological veins. As Van Til reflected on his own development of a Reformed apologetic approach, he said at one point, "Deciding, therefore, to follow the Reformers in theology, it was natural that I attempt also to do so in apologetics. I turned to such Reformed apologists as Warfield, Greene, and others. What did I find? I found the theologians of the "self-attesting Christ," defending their faith *with a method which denied precisely that point!*"[7]

It was this inconsistency that motivated Van Til's lifelong career of seeking to bring the discipline of apologetics more directly in line with the Reformed theology that should inform it. As Van Til prepared for his course on the place and influence of "evidences" in apologetics, he recognized that "Greene follows the traditional method of apologetics as worked out by Bishop Butler and others."[8] The "traditional method" had underneath it a theology that was less than Reformed. Its view of sin and depravity was weak, and that meant its view of human abilities and strengths was greatly exaggerated. Bishop Butler's *Analogy of Religion*, for example, argued that anyone, regenerate or unregenerate, could adequately grasp the principles offered. Anders Jeffner has suggested that one of the key and most self-destructive features in Butler's argument is the "aspiration to a reasonable theology." This aspiration emerges in Butler in two ways. The first is an endeavor to accept a religious doctrine, revealed or not, only if it is based on arguments that people can test *regardless of their religious status*. The second is an attempt to use only such scientific results as are achieved without any theological or metaphysical premises. So, says Jeffner, "If Hume's arguments against Butler are valid, he has demonstrated in an important field that the aspiration to a reasonable theology leads to the dissolution of theology."[9] In other words, once it is thought that a person's mind is virtually intact, even after the fall, then the

---

6. Cornelius Van Til, *Defense of the Faith* ed. K. Scott Oliphint (Phillipsburg, NJ: P&R, 2008), 368.

7. Cornelius Van Til, *The Reformed Pastor and the Defense of Christianity and My Credo* (Phillipsburg, NJ: P&R, 1980), 82, my emphasis.

8. Van Til, *Defense of the Faith*, 353. Van Til notes that Greene recommends an apologetic approach set out in George P. Fisher's *The Grounds of Theistic and Christian Belief*, which itself did not offer a Reformed apologetic.

9. Anders Jeffner, *Butler and Hume on Religion: A Comparative Analysis* (Diakonistyrelsens bokforlag, 1966), 20.

extent of sin, of darkness, of foolishness (cf. Rom 1:21f.) is inevitably subdued or denied.

It was into this theological context—a context for which Van Til was most appreciative, even as he was bound to be critical—that Van Til's thought began to develop. He was a young professor beginning his career in a new seminary. That seminary was to be the continuation of Old Princeton, since the new Princeton was infected with liberalism. But there was one significant area in which Old Princeton itself had to be reformed. That area had escaped the attention of Princeton's finest and ablest theologians. It became the lifelong focus of Van Til's thought. In that way, Van Til pioneered a merger of Reformed theology with apologetics that had been, by and large, only inchoate and undeveloped since the time of the Reformation.

APOLOGETIC RESPONSE

Van Til's opposition to his Princeton mentors, due to his unwavering commitment to Reformed theology, began in earnest in his "Evidences" syllabus and continued unabated throughout his career.[10] Perhaps the best way to frame Van Til's approach is by noting his relationship to two of his theological heroes, Abraham Kuyper and B. B. Warfield.

There are many reasons for singling out these two men. They were, by any standard, true giants in their respective endeavors, they were contemporaries, and they both had significant influence on those who were the founders of Westminster Seminary, especially on Van Til and the apologetic tradition of Westminster. Most importantly, for our purposes, an understanding of the differences in these two men will help us understand just what it was that Van Til was doing in apologetics.

The point of dispute between Kuyper and Warfield, and which Van Til sought to reconcile in his own approach, can be focused on the nature of the theological antithesis that obtains between believer and unbeliever. We can begin with Kuyper's view of that antithesis: "If this fact of 'being begotten anew,' coming in from without, establishes a radical change *in the being of man*, be it only potentially, and if this change exercises at the same time an influence upon his *consciousness*, then as far as it has or has not undergone this transformation, there is an abyss in the universal human consciousness across which no bridge can be laid."[11]

---

10. For an analysis of Van Til's commitment, see K. Scott Oliphint, "The Consistency of Van Til's Methodology," *Westminster Theological Journal* 52/1 (1990): 27–49.

11. Abraham Kuyper, *Encyclopedia of Sacred Theology: Its Principles* (New York: Scribner's Sons, 1898), 152.

Kuyper lays emphasis here on one of his primary points of argumentation, that is, that the situation as it now obtains, since the fall into sin, is not normal but abnormal. Whatever else we want to affirm about the antithesis, we must recognize that it has come about because of a cosmic rift in what was originally a unified cosmic, including human, condition. Our condition was universal, first in Adam as our covenant representative, and then later, through Adam, in the universal effect of the fall. And it is regeneration that mitigates this universality and that creates an "unbridgeable chasm." Kuyper then goes on to illustrate his meaning:

> It is like this with a group of wild fruit trees, some of which you graft, and the others you do not. From the moment of that grafting, if successful and the wild trees are properly pruned, the growth of the two kinds of trees is completely different, and this difference is not merely relative and a matter of degree, but *specific*. It is not a better and tenderer growth in one tree producing a richer fruit, while the other tree thrives less prosperously, and consequently bears poorer fruit, but it is a difference *in kind*. However luxuriantly and abundantly the non-grafted tree may leaf and blossom, it will *never* bear the fruit which grows on the grafted tree. But however backward the grafted tree may be at first in its growth, the blossom which unfolds on its branches is *fruit blossom*. No tree grafts itself. The wild tree cannot change from its own kind into the kind of the grafted tree, unless a power which resides outside of the sphere of botany enters in and effects the renewal of the wild tree. This is no relative transition. A tree is not one-tenth cultivated and nine-tenths wild, so that by degrees it may become entirely cultivated; it is simply grafted or not grafted, and the entire result of its future growth depends on this fundamental difference.[12]

Additionally, Kuyper acknowledges the weakness of every metaphor, but then makes the application for us: "If in the orchard of humanity a similar operation or grafting takes place, by which the character of the life-process of our human nature is potentially changed, a differentiation between man and man takes place which divides us *into two kinds*."[13]

Perhaps it will help to translate the problem a bit further. Kuyper's point is that the antithesis between believer and unbeliever is so radical, due to the deep effects of regeneration, that an abyss is established between the two "across which

---

12. Ibid., 152–53.
13. Ibid., 153.

no bridge can be laid."[14] In other words, when Kuyper emphasizes the differences *in kind* between the two groups, those differences are so deep as to be virtually unbridgeable. This has significant import for the discipline of apologetics.

As Kuyper argues for the place of apologetics, he can see its use only in the context of the false claims of philosophy. Just as there is an antithesis between *two kinds* of science, there remains an unbridgeable gap between believer and unbeliever in every intellectual engagement. Apologetics, therefore, is relatively useless; it is near the bottom of theological disciplines. The absolute character of the antithesis demands as much, according to Kuyper.

It was this notion of antithesis about which Warfield had serious concerns. He was afraid an emphasis on the antithesis as an antithesis of *kind* would effectively destroy communication between the two parties. Not only so, but how could there be cooperation in science, for example, if there is an unbridgeable chasm between the two? Warfield, in responding to Kuyper, said it this way:

> There certainly do exist these "two kinds of men" in the world—men under the unbroken sway of sin, and men who have been brought under the power of the palingenesis. And the product of the intellection of these "two kinds of men" will certainly give us "two kinds of science." But the difference between the two is, after all, not accurately described as a difference in kind—*gradus non mutant speciem* [change in degrees does not change a thing's nature]. Sin has not destroyed or altered in its essential nature any one of man's faculties, although-since it corrupts *homo totus*—it has affected the operation of them all. The depraved man neither thinks, nor feels, nor wills as he ought; and the products of his action as a scientific thinker cannot possibly escape the influence of this everywhere operative destructive power. . . . Nevertheless, there is question here of perfection of performance, rather than of kind. It is "science" that is produced by the subject held under sin, even though imperfect science—falling away from the ideal here, there and elsewhere, on account of all sorts of deflecting influences entering in at all points of the process. . . . The science of palingenesis is only a part of the science of sinful humanity.[15]

In other words, for Warfield, if we begin with the discipline of science and move from there to those who engage in it, we ought to recognize that both believer and unbeliever are doing *science*. Just because one may do it less

---

14. Kuyper, *Encyclopedia of Sacred Theology*, 152.
15. B. B. Warfield, *Selected Shorter Writings of B B Warfield*, 2 (Phillipsburg, NJ: P&R, 1976), 100.

perfectly than another does not change the nature of science itself (i.e., *gradus non mutant*). Warfield's concern, then, is that Kuyper's view of the antithesis as *absolute* with respect to the *disciplines* in which one is engaged has led him to the conclusion that it is useless and futile to try to bring those disciplines together. They exist in an unbridgeable gap.

Not only so, but with respect to apologetics, if the antithesis is absolute in the sense that Warfield takes it to be in Kuyper, then it is futile to engage the intellectual battle with unbelief. Warfield's concern is that, for Kuyper, there is such a great chasm fixed between unregenerate and regenerate people that there is no avenue, no bridge, by which one might engage unbelief. If sin affects the whole person, how can we possibly expect to travel, as it were, over to the side of unbelief and engage in argument?

Warfield had good reason to be nervous about Kuyper's view of the antithesis and its relationship to apologetics. In Kuyper's massive, three-volume *Encycloaedie Der Heilige Godgeleerdheid* (*Encyclopedia of Sacred Theology*), in which he discusses and delineates the proper order of theological disciplines, Kuyper leaves the discipline of apologetics to the third volume, and then discusses it only in terms of that which can address "pseudo-philosophy." Kuyper explains it this way: "That which [apologetics] must defend is Dogma, either in its specific details, or in the grounds wherein the Dogma rests, or in the conclusions (*gevolgtrekkingen*), which follow from the Dogma. It is not diathetical, since it does not describe Dogma, it is not thetical, since it does not postulate Dogma, nor prove it, but it is antithetical, since it directs its plea in behalf of Dogma over against that which pseudo-philosophy raises against Dogma, its grounds or effects. Its place is thus not before but after Dogmatics and Ethics."

Then, a bit later, Kuyper says, "From this it follows that Apologetics is confined to two tasks. In the first place to disqualify pseudo-theology from its *vitium originis*, which men come to adopt from the side of philosophy,: and in the second place to maintain the principles which are inseparable from Dogma, as actually the only trustworthy ones to maintain, over against false principles of wayward Philosophy."[16]

For Warfield, this relegates the discipline of apologetics to a "subdivision of a subdivision"[17] in the theological curriculum. That is to say, if Kuyper's classification

---

16. Abraham Kuyper, *Encyclopædie Der Heilige Godgeleerdheid* (Amsterdam: Wormser, 1894), 3:459, 461.

17. Warfield's discussion of Kuyper can be found in "Introduction to Francis R. Beattie's Apologetics," in *Selected Shorter Writings of Benjamin B. Warfield*, ed. John Meeter (Phillibsburg, NJ: P&R, 1970-1973). We will be using William Edgar and K. Scott Oliphint, eds., *Christian Apologetics Past and Present: A Primary Source Reader, From 1500*, vol. 2 (Wheaton, IL: Crossway, 2011): 391–403, which contains Warfield's essay. See Edgar and Oliphint, *Christian Apologetics Past and Present*, 396. See also Cornelius Van Til, *A Christian Theory of Knowledge* (Phillipsburg, NJ: P&R, 1969).

and delineation of the task of apologetics is correct, then Christianity remains, according to Warfield, "the great assumption."[18] By this Warfield means to say that if one holds to Kuyper's theological taxonomy, many crucial tasks are initiated first—tasks such as exegesis, church history, and systematic theology—without ever dealing with the truthfulness of Christianity itself. By placing apologetics so far down on the list of theological disciplines, all these crucial areas in Christian theology can, and according to Kuyper should, be carried out while, at the same time, there has yet to be a defense of the truth of Christianity at all.

Thus, for Kuyper, according to Warfield, the work that is entailed in all these prior theological disciplines "has all hung, so to speak, in the air."[19] Warfield means by this that because apologetics is so far down on the encyclopedic list, the status of truth and of the faith on which exegesis, church history, and systematic theology all rest has yet to be fleshed out. While work has been done, for example, in biblical exegesis, the question of whether Christianity is true or whether it is simply a vain hope has not been, and according to Kuyper should not be, broached. That question, Warfield is protesting against Kuyper, cannot even enter the discussion until other disciplines have spoken: "Not until all their labor is accomplished do they pause to wipe their streaming brows and ask whether they have been dealing with realities, or perchance with fancies only."[20] This view, says Warfield, (together with the Ritschlianism prevalent in his day) accounts for the "widespread misprision of apologetics."[21]

Once we recognize these two positions and take into account these two giants of Reformed thinking, we can begin to see, in part, what motivates Van Til in his reformation of Reformed apologetics. In navigating this debate among his two mentors, Van Til states, "Hence Warfield was quite right in maintaining that Christianity is objectively defensible. And the natural man has the ability to understand intellectually, though not spiritually, the challenge presented to him. And no challenge is presented to him unless it is shown him that on his principle he would destroy all truth and meaning. Then, if the Holy Spirit enlightens him spiritually, he will be born again 'unto knowledge' and adopt with love the principle he was previously anxious to destroy."[22]

Van Til seeks to resolve at least a part of this disagreement on the antithesis and its application to apologetics by agreeing on two aspects of its essential nature. He then went on to qualify the antithesis with one crucial qualification.

---

18. Edgar and Oliphint, *Christian Apologetics Past and Present*, 397.
19. Ibid.
20. Ibid.
21. Ibid., 395.
22. Van Til, *Defense of the Faith*, 352.

First, Van Til agrees with Kuyper that the antithesis is absolute. The word *absolute* can cause problems because it might mean that it is unqualified. But in this context it means it is not a relative affirmation; it is not the case that sin is more or less present in people. Or, to put it another way, it is not that people can be partly Christian and partly non-Christian. That is, the antithesis is not a relative matter, somehow depending on circumstances or contexts. One is either Christian or non-Christian.

Secondly, Van Til agrees that this absolute antithesis is true *in principle*. That is, it is the *principle* of the antithesis, regardless of the consequent applications, that is being discussed here. Just *how* that principle is applied is another, worthy, discussion. But *that* there is a "chasm" between believer and unbeliever, with respect to their *basic foundation* (i.e, principle or *principium*), must be affirmed. The antithesis, in its basic *principle*, is absolute.

But there is one key addition that must be remembered and that always, whether spoken or not, goes hand in hand with this notion of an absolute antithesis. Van Til qualifies and clarifies Kuyper's language by insisting that the antithesis is *ethical*.[23] By this, Van Til means to distinguish it from any kind of metaphysical notion of the antithesis. An absolute *ethical* antithesis is one in which there are not two worlds but two kinds of people in one world; two activities—*in principle*—that are associated with these people. To use the language of Reformed theology, there is a *covenantal* antithesis between believer and unbeliever. All people are either *in Adam* or *in Christ*. These are the two, and *only* two, covenantal representatives whom God has appointed. Our basic identity is in one of the two, for now and into eternity.

It is understandable that Warfield took Kuyper's view the way that he did. Kuyper's relegation of apologetics to a "subdivision of a subdivision" was surely an application of his view of the antithesis. But in fairness to Kuyper, his illustration (above) of the two kinds of trees—grafted and ungrafted—surely shows that he was not thinking *metaphysically*. The two kinds of trees were, after all, still *trees*, even as some were influenced from without while others were not. In both aspects—Kuyper's assigned place of apologetics and his fruit tree illustration—Kuyper was not as clear as he needed to be.

Van Til takes what he sees as the best of Kuyper and of Warfield in his own development of a consistently Reformed apologetics. Christianity is, indeed, defensible, and should be defended and commended; its place should be front and center, not a subdivision of a subdivision, in the theological curriculum.

---

23. I prefer the term *covenantal* rather than *ethical*. For reasons why, see K. Scott Oliphint, *Covenantal Apologetics: Principles and Practice in Defense of Our Faith* (Wheaton, IL: Crossway, 2013).

Its defense should not be relegated to a miniscule task at the bottom of a theological encyclopedia. So, says Van Til, "I am unable to follow [Kuyper] when from the fact of the mutually destructive character of the two principles he concludes to the uselessness of reasoning with the natural man."[24] Again, his comments on this topic illuminate how he understood the potential of apologetics:

> When he [the unregenerate man] studies nature, a man must not read his Bible. But if he wants to study nature fruitfully and intelligently, he must not harbor a philosophy of being and knowledge that does not enable him to distinguish one fact from another and that cannot account for the relevance of hypothesis to fact.
>
> Again, the claim is not that the believer by being a believer is transformed 'into an expert botanist or physicist.' To become an expert botanist or physicist one must study botany or physics. Once more, the question is not, whether the non-believer knows botany, physics or any other science. The question is that of the two principles, the Christian and the non-Christian, which are opposed to one another. *As far as an ultimate point of view is concerned*, the sinner has been mistaken in his interpretation of the physical universe no less than in his interpretation of God (emphasis added).[25]

APOLOGETIC METHOD

From this discussion on the antithesis, we can highlight the salient points of Van Til's apologetic method. Given that there remains an absolute, ethical (or covenantal) antithesis between believer and unbeliever, there remains an ethical (or covenantal) gap between the two. Not only so, but the noetic effects of sin are such that, apart from Christ, we are dead in our trespasses and sins (Eph 2:1); our minds are hostile toward God and not able to submit to him (Rom 8:7); and apart from the Holy Spirit, we are not able to understand the gospel (1 Cor 2:13–14). If apologetics is going to be done, that gap must somehow be bridged. How might we bridge the gap between believer and unbeliever?

At this point, Van Til takes his cue primarily from Calvin (following Paul), whose emphasis on the *sensus divinitatis* was reformational in its application and scope. Because people are made in the image of God, they always and everywhere, inevitably, dynamically, and immediately *know* the true God truly

---

24. Van Til, *Defense of the Faith*, 351.
25. Ibid., 280.

(c.f., Rom 1:20).[26] The gap between believer and unbeliever is bridged by God, who is constantly revealing himself to all people through everything he has made.

Given that all people everywhere know God, any appeal that the apologist makes to the true God will resonate with them because the God of whom we speak, and whose existence we defend, is already known at the outset.

There is, of course, a deep and pervasive problem inherent in this knowledge that God gives to all people. Again, following Calvin (who follows Paul), Van Til recognized that all who refuse to follow God will suppress this true knowledge of him. That suppression, says Paul, is the reason for the revelation of God's wrath (Rom 1:18), and will be the foundation of our inexcuseability on the day of judgement (Rom 1:20).

So the situation looks like this. There *is* a bridge that crosses the chasm of belief and unbelief. God built and sustained that bridge. The problem is that those who reject God refuse to recognize the reality of what the world is like, who they are, why they reject him, what they should be doing, etc. The suppression of the truth causes them to create an illusion, a false world, even as they use and borrow from those good gifts that God has given to all people. To put it succinctly, they reject God but presume on his goodness in giving them life and breath and all things (Acts 17:25).

How, then, does one defend the Christian faith in such circumstances? To what does the apologist appeal when the covenantal chasm is so deep and entrenched? One appeals to the knowledge of God, the *sensus divinitatis*, that all people have (because God *gives* it to all people). That knowledge of God is displayed in two general ways. First, it is displayed when people "borrow" from Christianity to make sense of, or try to interpret, their own experience, their own lives, or their own understanding of the world. When Paul told the Athenians that "in him we live and move and have our being" (Acts 17:28), he was using a poetic phrase from one of their own poets. That phrase was utterly false in that context because "in him" meant "in Zeus." But the entire reason that such a phrase was put forth was because there was a true knowledge of God, but that knowledge was suppressed. The suppression led to idolatry, but that idolatry itself presupposed true knowledge of God. So Paul's appeal to their poetry recognized that they had "borrowed" from Christian truth to build a false religion. Second, whenever aspects of Christian truth are "borrowed" from unbelievers, those aspects can never be consistent, or at home with, the principles or foundations on which unbelief rests. Someone who claims, for example, that stealing

26. For an exegetical analysis of the *sensus divinitatis*, see K. Scott Oliphint, "The Irrationality of Unbelief," in *Revelation and Reason: New Essays in Reformed Apologetics*, eds. K. Scott Oliphint and Lane G. Tipton (Phillipsburg, NJ: P&R, 2007), 59–73.

is wrong cannot, outside Christianity, find a solid foundation for such a claim. Apart from God's revelation, it is an arbitrary law. And any arbitrary law can just as arbitrarily be changed or broken. Therefore, there is no foundation available to anyone outside of Christ; apart from Christ, all is relative. And despite protestations to the contrary, no one can or does live as if all things are relative. A red traffic light cannot mean that some must stop and others may go.[27]

All of this is to say that when the apologist comes to challenge those who reject Christ, it must be done on the basis (1) of God's universal revelation, which itself produces a universal knowledge of God and (2) the fact that everyone suppresses such knowledge, apart from the regenerating work of the Holy Spirit. When we engage in apologetics, we must recognize, and never oppose, the following:

1. The triune God is the foundation of all that exists. Apart from him, there would be nothing—no people, no language, no world, etc.
2. God's revelation, both natural and special, is self-attesting—this truth allows us to recognize that all people know God through the things he has made (natural) and that his spoken Word, in Scripture, carries with it the authority of God himself. No other authority can claim such a thing.
3. The problem of sin is spiritual death. The only way the spiritually dead can rise is through the life-giving power of the truth of Scripture. The goal of apologetics is to communicate that truth so that people might come to Christ.

CONTRIBUTIONS TO THE FIELD OF APOLOGETICS

Some readers might recognize that I have studiously avoided the term *presuppositionalism* in my discussion thus far. That is for good reason. The term has become so muddy, so misunderstood, so maligned that its usefulness has ceased as a description of a Reformed apologetic approach. Instead, we might label the approach as "covenantal."[28] The focus of that term should turn us toward the depth and richness of a robust Reformed theology, which itself provides the foundation for any approach to apologetics that seeks to be Reformed. This has at least two implications.

27. In *Covenantal Apologetics*, I construct a number of possible dialogues, including one using a version of the cosmological argument, to show how one might engage unbelief in the context of this methodology.
28. See K. Scott Oliphint, *Covenantal Apologetics: Principles and Practice in Defense of Our Faith* (Wheaton, IL: Crossway, 2013)s

First, it should help us recognize that this approach aligns with a robustly Reformed theology. Apologetics should be, in the first place, a *theological* discipline, and so should be dependent on one's theology for its methodology.

Second, those who love and embrace Reformed theology would be best served by analyzing and applying Van Til's apologetic method in light of that theology. In this method the Reformed doctrine of God and doctrine of Scripture are applied. In this method there is meant to be a seamless connection between a strong defense of Christianity and the truth of the gospel as it is found in Christ. There is no "bare theism" attached to this method. What is defended is a full-orbed *Christian* theism. Apart from such a defense, the gospel simply comes in as a supplement, a kind of "concluding unscientific postscript." Such a conclusion, in the end, compromises the glories of the gospel, even as it is satisfied with a generic god.

B. B. Warfield once noted that Calvinism is "Christianity come to its own."[29] Similarly, Reformed apologetics is apologetics come to its own.[30] It challenges the root cause of sin's rebellion, and it offers to people the one and only hope of Jesus Christ crucified, raised, ascended and now reigning, until all his enemies are made a footstool for his feet.

BIBLIOGRAPHY

Kuyper, Abraham. *Encyclopedia of Sacred Theology: Its Principles*. New York: Scribner's Sons, 1898.
Muether, John R. *Cornelius Van Til: Reformed Apologist and Churchman*. Phillipsburg, NJ: P&R, 2008.
Oliphint, K. Scott. "The Consistency of Van Til's Methodology." *Westminster Theological* Journal 52/1 (1990): 27–49.
———. *Covenantal Apologetics: Principles and Practice in Defense of Our Faith*. Wheaton, IL: Crossway, 2013.
———. "The Irrationality of Unbelief." Pages 59–73 in *Revelation and Reason: New Essays in Reformed Apologetics*. Ed. by K. Scott Oliphint and Lane G. Tipton. Phillipsburg, NJ: P&R, 2007.
———. *Thomas Aquinas (Great Thinkers)*. Phillipsburg, NJ: P&R, 2017.
Van Til, Cornelius. *Toward a Reformed Apologetics*. n.p., 1972.
———. *Why I Believe in God*. Philadelphia: Committee on Christian Education of the Orthodox Presbyterian Church, 1948.
———. K. Scott Oliphint, ed. "Christian-Theistic Evidences." Phillipsburg, NJ: P&R, 2016.
———. K. Scott Oliphint, ed. *Defense of the Faith*. Phillipsburg, NJ: P&R, 2008.
Warfield, B. B. *Selected Shorter Writings of B B Warfield*. Vol. 2. Phillipsburg, NJ: P&R, 1976.

---

29. Van Til, *Defense of the Faith*, 94–95.
30. Ibid., 306.

GORDON HADDON CLARK

Logic and Scripture in a Presuppositional Apologetic

ROBERT A. WEATHERS

Among Christian philosophers of the twentieth century, few were more influential than Gordon Haddon Clark (1902–1985). A prolific writer and popular professor, Clark addressed theological liberalism by advocating a rigorous use of logic in Christian philosophy and apologetics. He was an ardent Calvinist, a committed Presbyterian, and an influential figure in the rise of neoevangelicalism in the mid-twentieth century. His place in history is anchored by his work to promote biblical inerrancy, controversies that either included him or were centered on his work, and his advocacy of the Westminster Confession of Faith among Presbyterians, to name just a few. And as a Christian apologist, his influence is still felt through his many students, including Carl F. H. Henry and Billy Graham.

HISTORICAL BACKGROUND

Gordon Haddon Clark's life and work were woven into the rich heritage of Presbyterianism in America. Clark was born in 1902 into the second generation of Clarks who had immigrated from Scotland and brought their Presbyterian faith with them. His grandfather, James, was a product of the Disruption of 1843, a church controversy that split the established Church of Scotland and created the Free Church of Scotland, whose ministers were grounded in a deep Calvinist Presbyterianism. James and his wife, Margaret, sailed for the US and in 1859 had a son, David, who proved to be even more erudite in his studies and passionate for ministry than his father. In his first pastorate David met Elizabeth Yates Haddon, and the two were married in 1895. Gordon, an only child, was born in 1902. In the environment of his father's pastoral ministry, Gordon grew, studied, and thrived.

David passed along to his son a love for Christ, a passion for ministry, a commitment to the ideals of Presbyterian Calvinism, and a hunger for learning.

494

"David equipped his son with a set of competencies that other young students would not learn until seminary," biographer Douglas Douma writes, "including knowledge of Presbyterian history, church doctrine, and the nature of recent events in the church."[1] On top of that, Gordon gleaned insights into Princeton theology and theological education based on his father's firsthand experience. But most of all, David showed his son that academics and ministry should be wedded in the life of the pastor and teacher, and he showed Gordon how to live a life that exemplified his faith. As Douma emphasizes, the inspiration that Gordon gleaned from his father as a role model "cannot be overestimated."[2]

EDUCATION, MARRIAGE, AND MINISTRY

Gordon Clark first professed Christ as his Savior at a Billy Sunday crusade in Philadelphia in 1915.[3] He grew in his faith as he flourished in his education, learning the classics in the local public school and then leaving to attend the University of Pennsylvania. By that time "he had a strong Christian faith, was well read, and conscious of his Presbyterian identity."[4]

In 1924, Clark segued into the graduate school at the University of Pennsylvania to study philosophy. He would have preferred Princeton Theological Seminary, but the influence of modernism on the seminary faculty discouraged him. This decision provides an early glimpse of the conflicts with modernism that would shape Clark's teaching and writing ministry.

The philosophy faculty at Pennsylvania was impressive, and Clark prospered in that environment. In 1924, as a graduate student, Clark's teaching ministry was launched when he was invited to teach undergraduate courses at Penn. His fondness for logic took root and blossomed, and he wrote his dissertation on Aristotle's *De Anima*, which he would complete in 1929. While at the university, he met and married Ruth Schmidt, a fellow student. They had two daughters and were married for forty-eight years.[5]

Clark joined the philosophy faculty at Pennsylvania and remained there until 1936, when the new president of Wheaton College, J. Oliver Buswell,

---

1. Douglas J. Douma, *The Presbyterian Philosopher: The Authorized Biography of Gordon H. Clark* (Oregon: Wipf & Stock, 2016), 4.
2. Douma, *Presbyterian Philosopher*, 7. Cf. Carl F. H. Henry, "A Wide and Deep Swath," in *Clark and His Critics: The Works of Gordon Haddon Clark, Vol. 7* (Unicoi: The Trinity Foundation, 2009), 19.
3. Billy Sunday was a former professional baseball player turned evangelist. Douma notes the interesting irony of Clark's salvation experience in this environment, as Clark would later diverge from emotional appeals like Sunday's in favor of intellectual appeals and apologetics, which would one day lead to a disagreement in class with a young student named Billy Graham. Douma, *Presbyterian Philosopher*, 9, 44.
4. Ibid., 9.
5. Douma, *Presbyterian Philosopher*, 12. Interestingly, Clark's father baptized Ruth in 1907. Ruth's family was Methodist, so it is unclear why she was baptized by a Presbyterian pastor.

invited Clark to join their philosophy faculty. Even so, Buswell, along with some faculty, had some reservations. In particular, they questioned whether his strict Calvinism would be a problem for those who preferred to stress one's personal responsibility before God. But they determined a one-year trial was in order. The year went well, and in 1937 Clark was appointed associate professor of philosophy.[6]

Clark's tenure at Wheaton College lasted a relatively short seven years, but these seven years were arguably the most significant for measuring his influence as a Christian philosopher and apologist. Douma quips that a list of Clark's Wheaton students "reads like an honor roll of twentieth-century Christian intellectuals."[7] At a pivotal time in American Christian history, rising stars such as Billy Graham, Carl F. H. Henry, E. J. Carnell, and Harold Lindsell sat in Clark's classes. Clark's rigorous Christian philosophy stretched them, and together they shaped the future of evangelicalism, shepherding the rise of the neoevangelical movement in America. Some, such as Henry, even remained lifelong friends and colleagues with Clark. On the other hand, Clark's years at Wheaton were also the genesis of some of the most heated debates in the history of the Orthodox Presbyterian Church.

BUTLER AND BEYOND

In 1943 Clark resigned from Wheaton College, after which he was ordained as a minister in the Orthodox Presbyterian Church, and soon began teaching at Butler University in Indiana in what, he thought, would be a short-term commitment to fill a void in the faculty. Instead, he stayed at Butler for twenty-eight years, until 1973. In his time at Butler, Clark wrote prolifically and sharpened his skills in apologetics. In 1952 he published *A Christian View of Men and Things*, regarded by most scholars as Clark's most definitive example of his apologetic method.[8]

Clark formally retired from Butler at the end of the 1972–73 academic year, but he was in high demand as a teacher, and his retirement was short-lived. He eventually accepted a post at Covenant College in Georgia, where he began duties in the fall of 1974. His beloved wife, Ruth, died in 1977. Clark remained at Covenant until 1983, retired again and then, at the request of his son-in-law, Dwight Zeller, moved to Colorado to teach at Sangre de Cristo Seminary as "scholar in residence."

It was at Sangre de Cristo, in the fall of 1984, that Gordon Clark taught his

6. Ibid., 13, 38–41.
7. Ibid., 43.
8. Ibid., 167.

final course. He was hospitalized with stomach pain and then returned home knowing that his diagnosis was terminal. On the morning of April 9, 1985, Gordon Clark passed away from cirrhosis of the liver, not from alcohol—for he never drank—but from the effects of medication he had taken for forty years for his arthritis. He was eighty-two years old.[9]

THEOLOGICAL CONTEXT

In the twentieth century, a movement ignited among evangelicals to rebut the rising tide of theological modernism in America. Gordon Clark held a unique role in this critical period, due to his intentional influence and to the unintentional effects of his teaching and writing, as well as the residual effects surrounding his theology and apologetics.

Clark and his theology were central to three controversies, one while at Wheaton and two afterward. In turn, these would shape his place in history and the influence of his apologetics.

CALVINISM AND ESCHATOLOGY

Though a popular teacher, Clark made some of his colleagues at Wheaton uncomfortable with his rigorous Calvinism and his strict use of logic in philosophy. Then in 1940 Clark's shield against the flames of controversy vanished when Buswell, Clark's primary supporter, was dismissed as president. The new president, V. Raymond Edman, sided with those on the faculty and in the larger evangelical community who felt that Clark's Calvinism did not mesh with the evangelistic fervor that Wheaton wanted to foster among its faculty and students.[10]

In addition, Clark openly challenged the popular dispensational millennialism largely favored at Wheaton, and he advocated for Westminster Theological Seminary rather than the newly formed Faith Theological Seminary, which rankled many within the conservative Presbyterian movement, including popular personalities such as Francis Schaeffer. Furthermore, Clark actively promoted Reformed theology on campus.[11] In 1942 Henry C. Thiessen filed an official complaint against Clark with Wheaton's Board of Trustees. Seeing the tide turn against him, by 1942 Clark was already seeking other employment, and in February 1943 Clark resigned his position at Wheaton College.[12]

---

9. Ibid., 224–44.
10. Ibid., 47.
11. Ibid., 48.
12. Ibid., 52–55.

THE ORDINATION CONTROVERSY

In 1943, now unemployed, Clark considered that it served as an opportunity to nurture one of his young loves, pastoral ministry. His father had consistently shown that Christian theology should be wedded to practical ministry, and Clark had never lost sight of that. He had always been actively and lovingly involved in the local church. And now pastoral ministry offered an attractive opportunity for income while he was unemployed. So in 1942, at the age of forty, prior to his resignation at Wheaton, Clark started the application process for ordination in the Orthodox Presbyterian Church (OPC).[13] But Clark's application for ordination landed in the midst of a rising wave of debate over what many in the denomination perceived as the undue influence of Westminster Theological Seminary over OPC churches. Further, the controversy at Wheaton had illuminated Clark's theological views, generated bubbling discussion across the evangelical landscape, and had made Clark both a popular and a polarizing individual within the denomination.

As a result, the road to ordination for Gordon Clark was a long and winding ordeal that finally ended in Philadelphia two years after his original application. Clark was ordained in 1944 at a special session of the OPC, which, records show, was "the best-attended session in the history of the Philadelphia Presbytery."[14] Like his father and his grandfather before him, Gordon Clark was now an ordained pastor.

"THE COMPLAINT" AND THE VAN TIL CONTROVERSY

Despite his desire to move forward, Clark remained in the bullseye of a growing controversy in the OPC. Only three months after his ordination, twelve elders in the OPC and five Westminster faculty members lodged a complaint against Clark's ordination. This document was formally called *The Complaint*, and it targeted the ordination process itself, claiming that Clark was ordained at an illegal meeting and so the ordination should be nullified. But more significantly, *The Complaint* took issue with four of Clark's theological positions: the incomprehensibility of God, the relationship of the faculties of the soul, divine sovereignty and human responsibility, and the free offer of the gospel.[15]

Central to all four of these complaints was Clark's epistemology. Whereas other Calvinist theologians and apologists denied any efficacy in human reason, Clark believed that the Christian apologist could still appeal to human reason.

---

13. Ibid., 76–77. That is, rather than the Reformed Episcopal Church, which would have been another option for ordination in keeping with Clark's theological views.

14. Douma, *Presbyterian Philosopher*, 92.

15. Ibid., 110–27.

Clark's primary rival in this debate was Cornelius Van Til, professor of apologetics at Westminster Theological Seminary. The controversy began in 1944 and shadowed both men for the remainder of their careers. Whereas the controversy is often framed as focusing on the incomprehensibility of God, "the real issue was whether any human thought could be identical to any divine thought." [16] Van Til denied such identity was possible between humanity and God, while Clark argued that it was not only possible but also necessary. For Clark, "If there is no such identity, we have no access to truth."[17] This third controversy has become not only the best-known controversy in the biography of Gordon Clark but also the most influential for Christian apologetics.[18]

APOLOGETIC AND THEOLOGICAL RESPONSES

In most ways, Clark and Van Til agreed—theologically. They both upheld the inerrancy of Scripture, and they both sought to rally evangelicals against the growing tide of modernism and liberalism. But they disagreed on the starting point for Christian apologetics, a critical matter for epistemology. The question was: "On what foundation could a Christian apologist connect, if at all, with an unbeliever?" The two scholars locked horns on this prickly dilemma of common ground between a believer and an unbeliever. Van Til denied any such common ground, arguing that the fallen mind was unable to grasp truth. Clark, on the other hand, granted human logic the power to forge such common ground. This, he taught, was possible because of the fundamental fact that all people are created in God's image and that logic itself is necessary to live.

According to Clark, Van Til asserted that "there is a qualitative difference between the contents of the knowledge of God and the content of the knowledge possible to man." That is to say, Clark explained, Van Til believed that human knowledge and divine knowledge do not "coincide at any single point." Therefore, a proposition would not have the same meaning for God as it would for a person.[19] Clark disagreed with Van Til at this point and cautioned that the result of such reasoning was that a human being could have absolutely no truth at all. Clark asserted that Calvinism did not deny human reason. In fact, Clark instructed that Calvin himself affirmed that even fallen, sinful human beings

---

16. John M. Frame, "Cornelius Van Til," in *A History of Western Philosophy and Theology*, 1st ed. (Phillipsburg, NJ: P&R, 2015), 530.

17. Ibid.

18. Ibid., 35. Douma states, "Perhaps second only to the books he wrote, it is Clark's theological and philosophical stance maintained in [this] controversy for which he is best known today."

19. Gordon H. Clark, "Apologetics," in *Contemporary Evangelical Thought*, ed. Carl F. H. Henry (New York: Channel, 1957), 159.

retained the ability to reason.[20] Clark's presuppositional apologetic method developed from this significant distinction.

APOLOGETIC CONTEXT

Clark's approach to apologetics is best considered within the wider context of apologetics. Christian apologetics has typically fallen into two broad categories: classical apologetics and evidential apologetics. These methods assume common ground between the believer and the unbeliever and affirm the unbeliever's ability to reason effectively toward biblical truth, using logic and reason to move the unbeliever toward faith. In addition, these approaches generally hold a conviction that evidence should undergird any proposition.[21] Reasons justify faith, and the unbeliever can be led to faith through the effective use of apologetics, even apart from the Bible—if necessary. The primary role of apologetics, therefore, is preevangelism.[22]

Presuppositionalism

But for other apologists, especially those whose apologetic methods are informed by Calvinism and Reformed theology, the effort to convince the unsaved mind of the viability of the Christian faith is futile. Because the human mind is sinful and fallen, and ascents to false presuppositions, any epistemology that depends on human reasoning to reach the conclusion of God's existence is flawed at its core. Therefore, presuppositionalism, as it has come to be known,[23] advances that any true knowledge of God is impossible outside the Bible. Knowledge of God can be acquired only by his special revelation. Therefore, the presuppositionalist *presupposes* the truth of Christianity as a starting point.[24]

20. Ibid.

21. An excellent summary of these approaches can be found in Steven B. Cowan, ed., *Five Views on Apologetics*, Counterpoints Series, ed. Stanley N. Gundry (Grand Rapids: Zondervan, 2000), 7–20. Examples of approaches that affirm evidence as undergirding propositional claims include Lew Weider and Ben Gutierrez, *Consider* (Bel Air, MD: Academix Publishing Services, Inc., 2010), 33–34; Ronald H. Nash, *Faith and Reason: Searching for a Rational Faith* (Grand Rapids: Zondervan, 1988), 78. William Lane Craig writes, "Although we know our faith to be true primarily through the witness of the Spirit, we must show our faith to be true through rational argument and evidence." And he continues, "We shall be engaged not only in refuting objections that our view is incoherent or implausible in light of certain facts (defensive apologetics), but also in providing arguments and evidence that show that our view best explains the data (offensive apologetics)." William Lane Craig, "Classical Apologetics," in Cowan, *Five Views on Apologetics*, 43, 45.

22. Most classical and evidential apologists are careful to distinguish between apologetics and evangelism. For instance, while clarifying that apologetics is not "evangelism," Christian apologists agree that "it is a vital part of pre-evangelism," preparing the unbeliever to grasp and ascent to the claims of Christ. See R. C. Sproul, John Gerstner, and Arthur Lindsley, *Classical Apologetics: A Rational Defense of the Christian Faith and a Critique of Presuppositional Apologetics* (Grand Rapids: Zondervan, 1984), 21.

23. The term was coined in 1948 by J. Oliver Buswell, in a review of a book by E. J. Carnell. Douma, *Presbyterian Philosopher*, 68.

24. Norman L. Geisler, "Presuppositional Apologetics," *Baker Encyclopedia of Christian Apologetics*, Baker Reference Library (Grand Rapids: Baker, 1999), 607.

Speaking for presuppositionalists, theologian John Frame explains that presuppositionalists consider the truth of the Bible to be "our most fundamental conviction, our most basic commitment. We may also describe that commitment as our most ultimate *presupposition*, for we bring that commitment into all our thought, seeking to bring all our ideas in conformity to it. That presupposition is therefore our ultimate criterion of truth. We measure and evaluate all other sources of knowledge by it. . . . To say this is to say that for Christians faith governs reasoning just as it governs all other human activities."[25]

Presuppositionalism is most often associated with Van Til.[26] Van Til largely rejected classical apologetics, which he called "traditional apologetics," for its reliance on the philosophy of Thomas Aquinas as a starting point, since Thomism had its foundations in Aristotle. Instead, he declared that the starting point for apologetics must be the self-revelation of God in Scripture. He argued that any form of rationalism in apologetics must be rejected and that Thomism reduced apologetics to rationalism to make it more acceptable to sinful humanity.[27]

Clark's Presuppositionalism

Along with Van Til, Gordon Clark is regarded as a pioneer of presuppositional apologetics. Even so, Clark diverged from Van Til at the critical point of the efficacy of human reason. Unlike Van Til, Clark believed that reason could serve as a starting point for apologetics. Truth exists, and human beings, with or without regenerate minds, can know propositional truth through reason. Clark argued that presuppositions were analogous to axioms in mathematics. These axioms, by their nature, "are never deduced from more original principles. They are always tested in another way." That is to say, the axiom is a presupposition, or a first principle.[28] And the ultimate presupposition in Christianity is the propositional truth of Scripture.

Unlike other belief systems, Christianity is one consistent set of propositional truths. "Undoubtedly," Clark affirmed, "I hold the truth is a consistent system of propositions."[29] This system is revealed in Scripture. This claim sets the foundation for Clark's "scripturalism," or his view that the revelation of Scripture provides the only true axiom for theological discussion.

25. John M. Frame, "Presuppositional Apologetics," in Cowan, *Five Views on Apologetics*, 209. Emphasis in original.

26. Sproul, Gerstner, Lindsley, *Classical Apologetics*, 183.

27. Norman L. Geisler, "Van Til, Cornelius," *Baker Encyclopedia of Christian Apologetics*, 752–53. For a more thorough treatment of Van Til's thought, see chapter 27 in the present volume.

28. Gordon H. Clark, *An Introduction to Christian Philosophy* in *Christian Philosophy: The Works of Gordon Haddon Clark*, vol. 4 (Unicoi: The Trinity Foundation, 2004), 299.

29. Gordon H. Clark, "Reply to Gilbert Weaver," in *Clark and His Critics: The Works of Gordon Haddon Clark, Vol. 7*, 290. Cf. Clark, "Apologetics," 159.

"Revelation should be accepted as our axiom, seeing that other presuppositions have failed."[30]

Clark argued that knowledge requires certainty, which cannot be derived
from sense experience because of the inherent uncertainties of experience.
Experience, then, cannot be called "knowledge." Only knowledge derived from
Scripture can be called true knowledge. Clark argued that evidentialism and
classical apologetics, as well as any hybrids, cousins, or offspring, were based
on non-Christian philosophies and therefore were fundamentally flawed and
could not provide necessary axioms. Empirical arguments for God's existence
assumed the validity of sense perception, and whether in science or any other
discipline, including religion, this approach was defective for the simple reason
that it ignored the inability of humanity to gain knowledge of God apart from
God's revelation.[31]

For example, in the context of critiquing Kierkegaard's approach to historical
truth, Clark advanced that it was impossible to conclude the veracity of Christian truth by studying history. "History," he explained, "is an empirical study and
Empiricism makes knowledge impossible. . . . Suppose historical research proved
the Bible true. Would this help anyone who did not have faith? No, for faith is not
the result of scholarly inquiry. It does not bring a person one step closer to faith."[32]

Clark's point was that "no construction in philosophy is possible without
some sort of presupposition or *a priori* equipment." Empiricism fails to provide
this necessary presupposition because "Empiricism requires all universal judgements to be conclusions drawn from experience. But experience cannot give
universal judgements." That is to say, experience does not provide axioms or
presuppositions.[33]

But that does not mean evidentialism has no value. For Clark, evidentialism
has its place. "In this field," he conceded, "a great deal has been accomplished."
But he criticized evidentialists for being too loose in their definition and, hence,
their application of apologetics. The main flaw of evidentialism, he argued, was a
failure to distinguish its purpose from apologetics, or, that is, reasoning with the
unregenerate mind.[34] In addition, Clark complained that the reliance of apologetics on evidentialism often resulted in the assumption that apologetics and evi-

30. Clark, *An Introduction to Christian Philosophy*, 298; Gordon H. Clark, "The Axiom of Revelation:
Wheaton Lecture II," in *Clark and His Critics: The Works of Gordon Haddon Clark, Vol. 7*, 52.

31. Gordon H. Clark, "Secular Philosophy: The Wheaton Lecture I," in *Clark and His Critics: The
Works of Gordon Haddon Clark, Vol. 7*, 48.

32. Gordon H. Clark, *Three Types of Religious Philosophy* in *Christian Philosophy: The Works of Gordon
Haddon Clark, Vol. 7* (Unicoi: The Trinity Foundation, 2004), 73–74.

33. Clark, *An Introduction to Christian Philosophy*, 297.

34. Clark, *An Introduction to Christian Philosophy*, 273; Clark, "Apologetics," 140.

dentialism were the same thing. Evidentialism, he explained, handles "subsidiary matters." But apologetics is "more philosophical. It discusses broad, fundamental principles."[35] Since the existence of God is distinct from the universe, discussing matters of the created order do not help identify God or prove his existence. Methods such as evidentialism, then, represent a "piecemeal approach" that yields answers but does not move a person toward faith and, worse, masks the main problem.[36] In place of an attempt to merely "aggregate unrelated assertions," the apologist needs to advocate for a comprehensive worldview by demonstrating the logical inconsistencies of non-Christian worldviews.[37]

For Clark, the purpose of apologetics was not to compile disconnected facts in hopes that the unbeliever would be convinced of the truth. Instead, the purpose of apologetics was to show that the facts made sense only in the context of a system of truth and that Christianity was the only system that made sense of the facts.

APOLOGETIC METHODOLOGY

Having established that the unbeliever can grasp truth through reason, Clark's apologetic method hinged on a universal principle of logic, that is, the Aristotelian law of contradiction. In this law, Clark found a starting point to converse with non-Christians. If the law of contradiction is abandoned, any conversation, with or without evidences, is irrelevant. He agreed with classical and evidential apologists that the goal of apologetics was evangelism, but he considered the law of contradiction to be the logical starting point.[38] The law of contradiction asserts that the system most logical and consistent is that which is true. As Clark explained, it "would be impossible to have two self-consistent, mutually contradictory philosophies."[39] That is, both could not be true. One would have to be false and the other true, for which the truth would be revealed in its coherence and consistency. "Disconnectedness is no virtue; logical inconsistencies cannot be defended," he clarified.[40] So "if this coherence theory of truth should be established, then we could rely with confidence on this application of the law of contradiction."[41] Without the law of contradiction, "conversation becomes meaningless."[42]

35. Clark, *An Introduction to Christian Philosophy*, 273; Clark, "Apologetics," 151.
36. Clark, *An Introduction to Christian Philosophy*, 273.
37. Clark, "Reply to Gilbert Weaver," 290.
38. Clark, "Apologetics," 152.
39. Gordon Clark, *A Christian View of Men and Things: An Introduction to Philosophy* in *The Works of Gordon Haddon Clark, Vol. I* (Unicoi: The Trinity Foundation, 2005), 27.
40. Clark, *An Introduction to Christian Philosophy*, 274.
41. Clark, *A Christian View of Men and Things*, 27; Clark, "Apologetics," 151.
42. Clark, "Apologetics," 151.

Now undergirded by the law of contradiction, Clark applied a method that could be described as "define or discard."[43] He regarded a proper apologetic method to be one that dismantled other forms of theism and competing worldviews and then showed the superiority of the Christian worldview and its comprehensive truth. "The best general procedure," he wrote, "for one who wishes to recommend Christian theism is to show that other forms of theism are inconsistent mixtures."[44] Clark's application of this method consisted of two steps.

The first step was negative: "to lay bare the contradictions and inconsistencies in all non-Christian positions through application of the law of contradiction."[45] To this end, Clark used a method of *reductio ad absurdum*, exposing the fallacies within a non-Christian system, which results in self-contradiction. His second step was to exhibit to the unbeliever the "internal consistency of the Christian system" and then to "urge the unbeliever to repudiate the axioms of secularism and accept God's revelation. That is, the unbeliever will be asked to change his mind completely, to repent."[46]

Clark's book *A Christian View of Men and Things* demonstrates this method, and he used it again in his chapter "Apologetics," which he contributed to Carl F. H. Henry's *Contemporary Evangelical Thought*. First, Clark established his method by explaining that "Christianity *is* a comprehensive view of things."[47] He explains that it is not enough to pick apart or support "areas of special interest." It is not the particulars that matter as much as the comprehensive worldview and how those particulars fit into a comprehensive worldview. "It takes the world, both material and spiritual, to be an ordered system. Consequently, if Christianity is to be defended against the objections of other philosophies, the only adequate method will be comprehensive." The apologist needs to present the whole picture. To compare theories, one must have a "comprehensive apologia."[48]

Having confirmed his position, Clark proceeded to review various worldviews that contrast with a biblical worldview. He considered philosophies of history, politics, ethics, science, religion, and especially knowledge. He interacted with great thinkers in all these fields and offered that each fails because of its internal inconsistencies but that Christianity provides the only comprehensive worldview to address each of these areas.

Once the logical consistency of the Christian worldview was demonstrated,

43. Douma, *Presbyterian Philosopher*, 216.
44. Clark, *A Christian View of Men and Things*, 165.
45. Quoted in Gilbert B. Weaver, "Gordon Clark: Christian Apologist," in *Clark and His Critics: The Works of Gordon Haddon Clark, Vol. 7*, 270–71; Also, Clark, *A Christian View of Men and Things*, 27.
46. Quoted in Weaver, "Gordon Clark," 270–71.
47. Clark, *A Christian View of Men and Things*, 23. Emphasis in original.
48. Clark, *A Christian View of Men and Things*, 23.

then the unbeliever could be led toward faith. Clark viewed Christian apologetics in the service of evangelism as analogous to mathematics in the service of engineering. "Evangelism [is] compared with practical engineering that must adapt itself to the local conditions; while apologetics is similar to the mathematical theory which engineering applies. Therefore, the starting point here discussed is not a temporal but the logical starting point. This is elementary" he argued.[49]

Apologetics, rightly implemented, is carefully distinguished from the use of evidences and from an evangelistic sermon. The apologist's job is to advocate the comprehensive logic of the biblical worldview. Even so, the apologist, the evidentialist, and the evangelist have the same goal in mind—to advocate for the Christian faith that the unsaved might believe.[50]

CONTRIBUTIONS TO THE FIELD OF APOLOGETICS

Clark's contributions to twentieth-century apologetics and theology can be seen in three areas. First, Clark advocated the inerrancy of the Bible against the growing push of liberalism and modernism in America. He saw the rise of neoorthodoxy as a dangerous temptation within evangelicalism. To Clark, Karl Barth personified neoorthodox theology in all its hazardous glory. With Barth in his crosshairs, Clark was awarded a grant in 1959 to write *Karl Barth's Theological Method*, which would refute Barth's theology.[51] As it turned out, Clark's work on Karl Barth coincided with Barth's 1962 visit to America. One of Clark's former students, E. J. Carnell, was invited to be one of six young theologians to participate in a dialogue with Barth at the University of Chicago. Clark attended to cover the event for *Christianity Today*, and Clark was mortified by what he perceived as Carnell's concessions in the area of biblical inerrancy in his exchange with Barth. Clark not only expressed his disappointment with Carnell in his piece for *Christianity Today* but confronted Carnell later and rebuked his young protégé for this and, as Clark saw it, other concessions to orthodoxy and inerrancy.[52]

Clark did not limit his stand for orthodoxy and inerrancy to reactions against liberalism. His work included positive and proactive steps to ensure that future generations of evangelicals held a solid line against modernism as well.

---

49. Clark, "Apologetics," 152.
50. Ibid., 140.
51. Published in 1963 as Gordon H. Clark, *Karl Barth's Theological Method* (Nutley: Presbyterian and Reformed, 1963). See also Clark, *Three Types of Religious Philosophy*, 80–82.
52. Rudolph Nelson, *The Making and Unmaking of an Evangelical Mind: The Case of Edward Carnell* (Cambridge: Cambridge University Press, 1987), 112; Douma, *Presbyterian Philosopher*, 180.

For example, Clark participated in the founding of the Evangelical Theological Society in 1949, serving on its first executive committee and helping draft its belief statement, which requires its members to affirm the inerrancy of Scripture. He later served as the organization's vice president in 1964 and its president in 1965.[53]

Second, against that backdrop, Clark's influence is still felt in his insistence that Christian apologetics should establish the comprehensive nature of a biblical worldview. He fortified the role of the Bible in Christian apologetics. In addition, firmly positioned in the community of presuppositional apologists, his rationalism served as a counterbalance against the presuppositionalism of Van Til, as Clark continually insisted that apologetics was linked to evangelism and served to tear down the hindrances keeping the unbelieving mind from faith. Thus, he sought to keep classical and evidential apologetics in perspective, which set Clark apart in the community of presuppositional apologists.

But not all critics agree that Clark distanced himself far enough from Van Til. Sproul, Gerstner, and Lindsley, in their 1984 defense of classical apologetics, commended Clark's apologetic as a needed rationalism within presuppositionalism, especially when compared with Van Til's apologetics. Even so, they accused Clark of being so adamantly opposed to evidentialism and classical apologetics that fideism eventually leaked into his method. In the end, they charged, Clark's approach represents "absolute fideism," and they described Clark as "the most thoroughgoing presuppositionalist of them all."[54]

While Clark should be commended for his focus on the intellectual viability of Christianity in the context of an age of growing skepticism and for his insistence on applying evidentialism and classical apologetics within the overall context of a biblical worldview, Clark's emphasis on logic demoted the emotions that often motivate people toward faith. In a biblical worldview, these emotions are acknowledged and interpreted, not ignored. Clark disdained what he regarded as an artificial distinction between "the head and the heart" when speaking of evangelism, but he also attributed far more intellectual muscle to people than is warranted, while neglecting the power of emotions to motivate people toward faith.[55]

In addition, Clark did not reconcile his focus on reason in apologetics, and his dislike of empiricism, with the plain truth that the objects of human knowledge are tied to empirical reality. How does humanity encounter God apart from the empirical world? And if experience cannot be called "knowledge," how does

53. Douma, *Presbyterian Philosopher*, 171.
54. Sproul, Gerstner, Lindsley, *Classical Apologetics*, 185, 265–75.
55. Clark, "The Axiom of Revelation," 73.

one explain the assumption in Scripture that the opposite is true (in John 20:27, for instance)? While this problem does not divest Clark's apologetics of its significance, it haunts it from the background.[56]

Third, and perhaps most of all, Clark's legacy endures through a generation of scholars and preachers for whom he was a mentor, teacher, friend, and sometimes, a critic in the effort to answer the threat of theological liberalism in the twentieth century. To impact the academic discipline of apologetics is one thing, but to shape the apologists, the philosophers, the theologians, and the evangelists who speak to the objections of culture every day is quite another. Students recall Clark's presence and influence with a mixture of fondness and unease but always with respect. E. J. Carnell, whose path would lead him to the presidency of Fuller Seminary, acknowledged an "incalculable indebtedness" to Clark. Billy Graham, who as a student once courageously confronted Clark in class over issues of evangelism, recalled being intimidated when Clark would come to hear him preach at a church near Wheaton's campus. And Erwin Lutzer, who studied with Clark in Indiana, reports that Clark ignited his mind to think clearly about philosophy, increased his understanding of Calvinism, and "solidified many doctrines" that he had already come to accept.[57] In addition to these, his influence on the young mind of Carl F. H. Henry resulted in a lifelong academic and personal relationship that continues to impact evangelical theology into the twenty-first century. In the preface to *God, Revelation, and Authority*, Henry writes, "To no contemporary do I owe a profounder debt, however, than to Gordon Clark. . . . Since the thirties when he taught me medieval and modern philosophy at Wheaton, I have considered him the peer of evangelical philosophers in identifying the logical inconsistencies that beset nonevangelical alternatives and in exhibiting the intellectual superiority of Christian theism."[58]

Gordon Clark's legacy endures in the precision of his scholarship and the controversies of his life, as well as the influence of his personality and depth of his teaching. In addition, Clark bequeathed to generations of Christians, apologists, theologians, and pastors the unnerving, but always necessary, reminders that God is sovereign, apologetics serves evangelism, people are inconsistent in their thinking, and that truth is found only and always in God's Word.

---

56. Ronald H. Nash, "Gordon Clark's Theory of Knowledge," in *Clark and His Critics: The Works of Gordon Haddon Clark, Vol. 7* (Unicoi: The Trinity Foundation, 2009), 134.

57. Nelson, *The Making and Unmaking of an Evangelical Mind*, 211; Billy Graham, *Just As I Am: The Autobiography of Billy Graham* (San Francisco: HarperCollins, 1997), 66; Douma, *Presbyterian Philosopher*, 44, 179, 199–214.

58. Carl F. H. Henry, *God, Revelation, and Authority*, Vol. I, *God Who Speaks and Shows: Preliminary Considerations* (Waco, TX: Word, 1976), 10.

BIBLIOGRAPHY

Clark, Gordon H. "Apologetics." Pages 137–61 in *Contemporary Evangelical Thought*. Ed. by Carl F. H. Henry. New York: Channel, 1957.

———. "The Axiom of Revelation: Wheaton Lecture II." Pages 51–77 in *Clark and His Critics: The Works of Gordon Haddon Clark*. Vol. 7. Unicoi, TN: The Trinity Foundation, 2009.

———. *A Christian View of Men and Things: An Introduction to Philosophy. Pages 11–227* in *The Works of Gordon Haddon Clark*. Vol. 1. Unicoi, TN: The Trinity Foundation, 2005.

———. *An Introduction to Philosophy*. Pages 273–346 in *The Works of Gordon Haddon Clark*. Vol. 4. Unicoi, TN: The Trinity Foundation, 2004.

———. *Karl Barth's Theological Method* (Nutley, NJ: P&R, 1963).

———. *Modern Philosophy*. Pages 13-369 in *The Works of Gordon Haddon Clark*. Vol. 5. Unicoi, TN: The Trinity Foundation, 2008.

———. "Reply to Gilbert Weaver." Pages 287–94 in *Clark and His Critics: The Works of Gordon Haddon Clark*. Vol. 7. Unicoi, TN: The Trinity Foundation, 2009.

———. "Secular Philosophy: The Wheaton Lecture I." Page 48 in *Clark and His Critics: The Works of Gordon Haddon Clark*. Vol. 7. Unicoi, TN: The Trinity Foundation, 2009.

———. "Three Types of Religious Philosophy." Pages 15–103 in *Christian Philosophy: The Works of Gordon Haddon Clark*. Vol. 7. Unicoi: The Trinity Foundation, 2004.

Cowan, Steven B., ed. *Five Views on Apologetics*. Counterpoints Series. Ed. by Stanley N. Gundry. Grand Rapids: Zondervan, 2000.

Douma, Douglas J. *The Presbyterian Philosopher: The Authorized Biography of Gordon H. Clark*. Eugene, OR: Wipf & Stock, 2016.

Frame, John M. "Cornelius Van Til." Pages 526–29 in *A History of Western Philosophy and Theology*. 1st ed. Phillipsburg, NJ: P&R, 2015.

Geisler, Norman L. "Van Til, Cornelius." Pages 751–758 in *Baker Encyclopedia of Christian Apologetics*. Baker Reference Library. Grand Rapids: Baker, 1999.

Graham, Billy. *Just As I Am: The Autobiography of Billy Graham*. San Francisco: HarperCollins, 1997.

Henry, Carl F. H. *God, Revelation, and Authority*, Vol. I, *God Who Speaks and Shows: Preliminary Considerations*. Waco, TX: Word, 1976.

———. "A Wide and Deep Swath." Pages 17–24 in *Clark and His Critics: The Works of Gordon Haddon Clark*. Vol. 7. Unicoi, TN: The Trinity Foundation, 2009.

Nash, Ronald H. "Gordon Clark's Theory of Knowledge." Pages 105–41 in *Clark and His Critics: The Works of Gordon Haddon Clark*. Vol. 7. Unicoi, TN: The Trinity Foundation, 2009.

Nelson, Rudolph. *The Making and Unmaking of an Evangelical Mind: The Case of Edward Carnell*. Cambridge: Cambridge University Press, 1987.

Sproul, R. C., John Gerstner, and Arthur Lindsley. *Classical Apologetics: A Rational Defense of the Christian Faith and a Critique of Presuppositional Apologetics*. Grand Rapids: Zondervan, 1984.

Weaver, Gilbert B. "Gordon Clark: Christian Apologist." Pages 287–94 in *Clark and His Critics: The Works of Gordon Haddon Clark*. Vol. 7. Unicoi, TN: The Trinity Foundation, 2009.

FRANCIS A. SCHAEFFER

Cultural Apologist

WILLIAM EDGAR

In an era shaken by two world wars, genocides, and cultural revolutions, certain theologians, such as Karl Barth, developed the view that apologetics was a misguided endeavor, which only served to dignify unbelief. Instead, Barth argued, the church needed a dialectical approach that proclaimed a wholly other God who became wholly revealed in Jesus Christ. The "Christ event" did not occur in verifiable history but in an existential encounter. In response, a unique kind of apologetics emerged that was evangelical and Reformed but also capable of persuasion. Francis Schaeffer (1912–1984) arose to convince a generation that the Christian faith was true and could be lived out in every area of life, with God's help.

HISTORICAL BACKGROUND

Francis A. Schaeffer was born on January 30, 1912, in Germantown, a part of Philadelphia, Pennsylvania.[1] On his mother Bessie's side, he had English ancestry. His grandfather "Franz" emigrated from Germany in 1869. Franz's only son, known as Frank, was Francis August Schaeffer III. Frank and Bessie's only child, Francis August Schaeffer IV, called Fran, grew up excelling in school despite fairly severe dyslexia. He was strong and athletic and a decent carpenter. Albeit from a working-class background, he was intellectually curious, which led him to read Greek philosophy and take an interest in art and music. He read the Bible out of intellectual honesty, thinking how he might discard it, but instead found

---

1. Several biographies of Schaeffer exist. Colin Duriez, *Francis Schaeffer: An Authentic Life* (Wheaton: Crossway, 2008) is the best. Barry Hankins, *Francis Schaeffer and the Shaping of Evangelical America* (Grand Rapids: Eerdmans, 2008) compares him with supporters and critics. A quite lengthy account of his life within the context of the community he founded is by Edith Schaeffer, *The Tapestry: The Life and Times of Francis and Edith Schaeffer* (Waco, TX: Word, 1981). A much shorter account, ending in the late 1960s, by Edith Schaeffer is *L'Abri* (Wheaton: Tyndale, 1969).

himself drawn to its answers. In 1930 he wandered into an evangelistic tent meeting and gave his life to Christ unconditionally.[2]

Schaeffer graduated magna cum laude from Hampden-Sydney College in 1935, the same year he married Edith Seville, daughter of missionaries to China. Edith worked with him in every aspect of his life and ministry for more than fifty years. Together they had four children. Schaeffer resolved to go into the ministry, somewhat to the chagrin of his parents. That same year he enrolled at Westminster Theological Seminary, Philadelphia.

At Westminster, Schaeffer came under the sway of Cornelius Van Til (1895–1987), arguably the most original apologist of the twentieth century. His approach would have a lasting impact on Schaeffer, though the two men came to differ over several aspects of apologetics. In 1937 a faction at the seminary, led by J. Oliver Buswell and the fiery young Carl McIntire, led a group into the formation of a new seminary, Faith Seminary, and a new denomination, the Bible Presbyterian Church. The Schaeffers had become critical of Westminster's perceived strictness on doctrines such as predestination and also on its perceived looseness on matters of Christian liberty, alcohol, dancing, gambling, smoking, and the theater. At the center of the new movement was a commitment to a premillenarian interpretation of the end times. The Schaeffers would later regret some of the coldness with which they had conducted themselves. Schaeffer became the first person ordained in the new Bible Presbyterian Church. His first call was to a church in Grove City in western Pennsylvania. Here, and in his two succeeding parishes, Schaeffer showed extraordinary concern for families, especially for children.

Schaeffer became involved in the ACCC (American Council of Christian Churches) and then the ICCC (International Council of Christian Churches), alternative movements to the more pluralistic national and international ones. They represented the separated churches and would play a role in the Schaeffers' eventual opportunity to move to Europe. As World War II raged, and perhaps because of his German background but also because of his biblically-based love for the Jewish people, Schaeffer was especially anxious about what was happening in Europe. Combined with the Schaeffers' concern for children, these preoccupations led them to explore ministry in Europe. The family spent three months living in Holland with the ICCC, a visit that would change their lives. In Amsterdam, they met Hans Rookmaaker, an art historian who had converted during his stint in a German prison camp. The friendship with Rookmaaker would enrich both men and would later define the international flavor of L'Abri

---

2. Told in Duriez, *Francis Schaeffer*, 23.

movement. The Schaeffers moved to La Rosiaz, near Lausanne. In 1950 they moved up the mountain to Champéry and continued their travels and ministries from there.

In the spring of 1951, Francis Schaeffer underwent a serious spiritual crisis. It had been provoked by a number of factors and culminated in his putting into question the Buswell-McIntyre movement's lack of love. Schaeffer remained concerned throughout his life with the purity of the visible church but felt that his colleagues lacked *reality*, one of his favorite concepts. He basically put everything into question but, after an intense period of self-examination, emerged with a new conviction that combined biblical orthodoxy with a moment-by-moment trust in Christ's finished work on the cross.[3]

In 1955, after several years of working with children and students, the Schaeffers received a letter from the Swiss government ordering them to leave the country. The reason given was their "religious influence." Although the official position of the state was religious freedom, feelings between Roman Catholics and Protestants were still strong. Champéry was in the Roman Catholic canton of Valais. The fine print did provide that if they relocated to a Protestant canton, they could stay in Switzerland.[4] After many ups and downs, they were able to purchase a chalet in the canton of Vaud. And there, in 1955, they broke with their mission and began *L'Abri* (the shelter). From these humble beginnings developed a ministry of welcome, prayer, worship, and especially, giving biblical answers for the myriad questions posed by hundreds, and then thousands, of guests. Eventually, other branches of L'Abri were founded.

At first Schaeffer's impact was limited to personal conversations and his lectures around Europe. He also conducted a Bible study in a Lausanne café, which was recorded and had considerable impact. But when his talks and discussions were systematically recorded and widely distributed, the renown of L'Abri spread around the world. Then came the books. From his seminal texts, *Escape from Reason* and *The God Who Is There*, followed by *Death in the City* and *He Is There and He Is Not Silent*, came numerous other publications, many of them through Inter-Varsity Press, edited by the devoted James Sire. Then came the films. Two of them, produced by Schaeffer's son, Franky Schaeffer V, became classics, at least within the evangelical world. *How Should We Then Live?* was a ten-episode analysis of the rise and decline of the West. *Whatever Happened to*

---

3. As he writes in the preface to *True Spirituality*, Schaeffer had begun to sense a "lack of reality" in his life. He became disillusioned with "the Movement" and its lack of love. He realized in all honesty that he needed to "rethink my whole position." After several agonizing months he concluded that he had made the right decision in becoming a Christian years before. We are not sure of all the processes that led him back to "reality," but the story is recounted in Schaeffer, *The Tapestry*, 315f.

4. The events are marvelously recounted in Schaeffer's *L'Abri*, as well as in Duriez's *Francis Schaeffer*.

the Human Race was cowritten with C. Everett Koop, the pediatric surgeon who became the thirteenth surgeon general of the United States.[5]

In his final years, Francis Schaeffer continued his major emphases, but he also was courted by America's Christian right. Whereas Shaeffer had always held conservative political views, advocates of the so-called evangelical right, such as Cal Thomas, Jerry Falwell, D. James Kennedy, and Charles Colson, saw in him an intellectual defender of their positions. Each appropriated different parts of his output for their support. In 1981 Schaeffer wrote his book *A Christian Manifesto*, which was an explosive critique of tyranny, with suggestions on how to resist. It certainly sounded as though it could come from right-wing conservatism. How much of this alliance was shared by Schaeffer himself is the subject of considerable discussion.[6]

Schaeffer battled lymph cancer for six years. He spent a good deal of time at the Mayo Clinic. His last book was *The Great Evangelical Disaster*. It was a plea for "loving confrontation" with the cultural enemies of the time. He died on May 15, 1984, in Rochester, Minnesota, with Edith by his side.

THEOLOGICAL CONTEXT

The twentieth century was both the bloodiest of all times and the most innovative. Between the World Wars, the Cold War, the Vietnam War, and other events, hundreds of millions of people died or were wounded. At the same time, there were some remarkable advances in technology, healthcare, human rights, and education.

These trends deeply affected philosophy both descriptively and prescriptively. Most prominent philosophers repudiated any idea of an absolute truth. In Great Britain and in the German world, analytical philosophy reigned. Members of the so-called Vienna Circle were committed to a form of empirical verification in limited areas. The group included Rudolph Carnap, whose *Logical Structure of the World* was enormously influential, and Ludwig Wittgenstein, whose *Tractatus* changed much of the discussion about language. Francis Schaeffer was more interested in continental philosophy than analytical philosophy. He regularly cites in his works the existentialists, Albert Camus and Jean-Paul Sartre, as well as Marxists such as Herbert Marcuse.

---

5. While these films did not have the polish of great filmography, they were unique in that nothing of the kind existed.

6. Schaeffer even warned his audience to be wary of all humanism, whether it be from conservatives or liberals. He also cautioned not to wrap the American flag around the faith. At the same time it is clear that he had a part in shaping the views of the American right. Francis A. Schaeffer, *A Christian Manifesto* (Wheaton, IL: Crossway, 1981), 121.

The arts underwent radical upheavals in the twentieth century. Famously, the year 1913 saw the production of Igor Stravinsky's *The Rite of Spring*, whose subtitle is "Pictures of Pagan Russia in Two Parts." In the program, a young girl is selected for a sacrifice but dances herself to death instead. The undulating rhythms and strange orchestrations caused a small riot in the Champs-Élysées Theater upon its premiere. That same year the New York Armory Show featured Marcel Duchamps's *Nude Descending the Staircase*, a mechanical-looking abstract suggesting gradual motion. That year also saw Kazimir Malevich's *Bureau and Room* and Pablo Picasso's *Guitar*, both cubist works in which the subject is barely perceptible among the lines and colors. The twentieth century also brought out the works of Piet Mondrian, Jackson Pollock, the surrealists, and the abstract expressionists. Schaeffer was thoroughly conversant with these paintings and used them to illustrate his views on Western culture.

The developments in theology somewhat paralleled these expressions. Liberal theology, sometimes known as modernism, continued to grow and develop from its nineteenth-century roots. Based on critical approaches to the Bible, liberalism was wary of doctrine or church discipline. It stressed the more humanitarian teachings of Jesus and downplayed miracles. Paul Tillich, the "neo-liberal," considered the Christian faith in terms of existentialist philosophy and renamed God the "ground of being." He thought the horrors of the twentieth century required the "shaking of the foundations."[7] John A. T. Robinson (1919–1983), the Anglican bishop of Woolwich, began as a liberal theologian. In his *Honest to God*, he put all traditional doctrines into question, including ethics, proposing a "new morality" based on love, not rules (he later modified his view about the Bible and defended the authenticity of John's gospel).

Apparently contrasting liberalism, neoorthodoxy emerged early in the century as a corrective to an overly-human focus in theology. Karl Barth (1886–1968) published his commentary on the book of Romans in 1919 and frequently republished it. In it he argued that God could not be wedded to human cultures or accomplishments. Barth was a prolific writer, including his fourteen-volume *Church Dogmatics* in which he set forth most of the major Christian doctrines, but always from the perspective of dialectical theology, arguing that the "wholly other" God could be "wholly revealed" only in Jesus Christ. Barth sharply rejected apologetics, precluded any view that Scripture was inerrant, and was effectively a universalist. Thus, he was generally not well received by evangelicals, including Francis Schaeffer. A number of adherents belonged to the neo-orthodox school, also known as the "theology of crisis," or sometimes just "dialectical theology,"

---

7. Paul Tillich, *The Shaking of the Foundations* (New York: Charles Scribner's Sons, 1955).

including Emil Brunner, who was more open to natural revelation than Barth, and Reinhold Niebuhr, the American political realist.

APOLOGETIC RESPONSE

Schaeffer defined apologetics as having a twofold purpose: "The first is defense. The second is to communicate Christianity in a way that any given generation can understand."[8] What is striking about this definition is its concern both to answer the challenges to the Christian faith and also to commend it to a particular generation. Even the word *defense*, for him, was not meant primarily to sound combative.

To understand Schaeffer's response to the conflicts of his time, a word needs to be said about his diagnosis of the era. Although he spoke less deliberately about the theological underpinnings for apologetics, he did believe that God, the triune God revealed in Scripture, was the ultimate reality, or what he called the "final screen." God was rational and had made human beings after his image, and thus with rationality. This being so, the world after the fall into sin had rebelled against God, opting instead for an irrational universe. In several of his lectures and writings, he describes the history of thought and culture in the West as veering toward a "line of despair" before which most thinkers accepted absolutes and after which they abandoned the hope of having any absolutes, or of reconciling meaning and reason. He locates this line in the nineteenth century, focusing particularly on the philosophy of G. W. F. Hegel (1770–1831). Picking up on the popular view that Hegel's interpretation of history was the march from thesis to antithesis to synthesis, Schaeffer believed this was opening the door to relativism.[9] This analysis has been subject to question, particularly since Hegel thought of himself as a complete rationalist. Nevertheless, his critique of Hegel is not out of line with the conservative German rejections of his pantheism.[10]

Schaeffer places Søren Kierkegaard (1813–1855) next in the line, calling him the "father of all modern thinking." The reason is that when facing a difficult commandment from God, Kierkegaard advocated an irrational "leap in the dark."[11] This summary of Kierkegaard has also been disputed. No doubt in reaction to his critics, Schaeffer expanded his approach to Kierkegaard in the second edition of *The God Who Is There*, showing a nuanced view of his

---

8. Francis Schaeffer, *The God Who Is There* (Downers Grove, IL: InterVarsity Press, 1968), 139.
9. Schaeffer, *The God Who Is There*, 20–21.
10. See the interesting partial defense of Schaeffer by Andrew Hartman, "Plotting Hegel on Francis Schaeffer's 'Line of Despair'," https://s-usih.org/2014/11/plotting-hegel-on-francis-schaeffers-line-of-despair.
11. Schaeffer, *The God Who Is There*, 21–22.

understanding of faith, making him much more of an evangelical Christian who would not have been happy with the way later generations used him.[12] From there, Schaeffer goes on to show how the arts followed suit, using illustrations from Mondrian, Duchamp, Happenings, modern music, and the literature of Henry Miller and others.

And then theology comes in for a thrashing. Schaeffer believed that theology was a kind of caboose to the rest of these trends. He comments on the "older liberalism," which rejected miracles based on a naturalistic view of science. And he critiques neoorthodoxy for saying nothing particularly new but yet sounding more biblical. Throughout, he insists that in both liberalism and neoorthodoxy, it is not so much quibbles about biblical inerrancy that are at stake but the underlying methodology, which he calls "existentialist," because it accepts mysticism over against a reasonable view of the world. True to his big-picture view, he states, "If our American theologians had understood the Armory Show of 1913 in New York, when modern art was first shown in the United States, perhaps the big denominations in America would not have been captured by the liberals in the thirties." And he goes on to chide conservative theologians for being "far too provincial, isolated from general cultural thinking."[13]

In addition to his broad critique of modern culture and modern theology, Schaeffer also exhibited special interests in such issues as pollution. He wrote a prescient book, *Pollution and the Death of Man* (1970), in which he took aim at those who thought technology could save us and those who wanted, romantically, to live without it. He chided Christians for their blatant neglect of beauty in their surroundings. He also struck up a friendship with Léopold Senghor, the poet, cultural critic, and Senegal's first president. Senghor was a leader in the Négritude movement, a response to racism in various colonial countries. Senghor, Schaeffer affirms, is lucid about the "methodology" shared on both sides of the Iron Curtain and rejects the dialectical approach both in Marxism and in much of Western theology.[14]

APOLOGETIC METHODOLOGY

Two things may be said at the outset. First, Francis Schaeffer always maintained that his views on the Christian life were foundational to the entire enterprise of

12. Francis Schaeffer, *The God Who Is There*, 2nd ed. (Downers Grove, IL: InterVarsity Press, 1998), 35–36.

13. Schaeffer, *The God Who Is There*, 2nd ed., 74.

14. Schaeffer, *The God Who Is There*, 2nd ed., 64–65. See also Francis A. Schaeffer, *The God Who Is There*, in *The Francis Schaeffer Trilogy: Three Essential Books in One Volume* (Wheaton: Crossway, 1990) 41.

L'Abri. In an interview with Colin Duriez, Schaeffer affirmed that without all the struggles that led to *True Spirituality*, L'Abri would not have been born.[15] Thus, his apologetic method would not stand without his understanding of sanctification. Related to that, he strongly emphasized the role of the Holy Spirit and of prayer in doing apologetics.[16] Second, while certain themes can be teased out of his discourse, there does not seem to be a grand scheme nor one apologetic approach that is valid for every circumstance.[17] It's not that his method was eclectic, drawing from every source. Rather, so much of his approach was based on personal conversations, museum visits, and lectures in numerous universities; one cannot easily label what he was doing. He said it this way: "I'm only interested in an apologetic that leads in two directions, and the one is to lead people to Christ, as Savior, and the other is that after they are Christians, for them to realize the lordship of Christ in the whole of life. I don't believe there is any one apologetic that meets all the needs."[18]

Several recurrent themes do emerge from Schaeffer's work. (1) A strong commitment to *truth*. He believed the current age had largely surrendered any notion of truth and substituted it for what he called "an upper story" mysticism. Taking a cue from the enlightenment philosopher Immanuel Kant, who divided knowledge into a lower story (the *phenomenal*) of verifiable facts and an upper story (the *noumenal*) of unverifiable mystery, Schaeffer argued that much of modern thought was an escape from reason. He boldly stated that pleading for truth often had to come before appeals to conversion, since without a framework, such appeals could simply confirm people in their irrationalism. Truth, for Schaeffer, was not an abstraction. God was personal. Indeed, Schaeffer called the universe personal. One of the keys to God's being able to communicate with us is our shared personal qualities.[19]

(2) Schaeffer belonged, loosely, to the school of *presuppositionalism* as taught by Cornelius Van Til. This meant people did not simply confront raw data but that they were precommitted to a worldview within which such data could be interpreted. To give an example of how this view works in a conversation, he was often able to push, gently but firmly, unbelievers to become more rationally consistent with their presuppositions and thus farther from the real world.

15. Francis Schaeffer, *True Spirituality* (Wheaton: Tyndale, 1971). See Duriez, *Francis Schaeffer*, 221. See also William Edgar, *Francis Schaeffer on the Christian Life: A Countercultural Spirituality* (Wheaton: Crossway, 2012).

16. Schaeffer, *The God Who Is There*, 2nd ed., 173.

17. Bryan A. Follis, *Truth with Love: The Apologetics of Francis Schaeffer* (Wheaton: Crossway, 2006), 46.

18. Interview quoted in Duriez, *Francis Schaeffer*, 177.

19. When criticized for appearing to bring God down to the human level, he argued that God's personality was on a "high order" whereas ours belonged to the creature.

He was a committed realist. He called this procedure "taking the roof off" a person's house. (Van Til called it "ripping off the iron mask.") Schaeffer's plea for consistency was a part of his commitment to rationality. Yet he never asserted *rationalism*, or the deification of reason. When this tension is felt keenly, there is an opportunity to plead for another set of presuppositions, from God's world, leading to the gospel. Schaeffer warned that exposing people to such vulnerability was risky and if not handled well could lead to suicide. This tactic is at the heart of what Schaeffer did best.

(3) And while it may appear contradictory to presuppositionalism, though it really is not, Schaeffer had a strong commitment to evidences and verification. One of his most piercing critiques of modern theology was its willingness to part company with reliable proofs. For example, he loved to quote J. S. Bezzant, a liberal theologian who was nevertheless critical of neoorthodoxy. Against the claim that the truth of the gospel is free from the requirements of verification, he averred, "When I am told that it is precisely its immunity from proof which secures the Christian position from the charge of being mythological, I reply that immunity from proof can 'secure' nothing whatever except immunity from proof and call nonsense by its name."[20] Schaeffer strongly believed the events in the Bible were historical. He once remarked, with considerable excitement, that the Lord spoke to Paul on the Damascus road "in the Hebrew language," subject to grammars and lexicons, a language that could be understood.[21]

(4) Riffing on this last point, Schaeffer felt strongly that the language of evangelism should be understandable to the present generation. He labored to find ways to communicate to a culture that had given up on truth. Colorfully, he coined terms that were meant to get through. He referred to "the manishness of man" to emphasize what is unique about God's image-bearers. He talked about "moral motions" to stress the moral consciousness of human beings. Even identifying the deity as "the God who is there" helps reinforce the realism of his view that God exists. Some of his illustrations were poignant as well. He had a talk on "The Universe and Two Chairs."[22] It was meant to show how a Christian could live either in the "chair of unfaith" or the "chair of faith." The former is a believer who yet does not fully accept the reality of a supernatural universe, whereas the latter does. The difference is crucial, not for salvation but for the practice of the Christian life, which is led by the Holy Spirit and the reality of prayer.

(5) Finally, apologetics is useless if not driven by love—the love of God,

---

20. Schaeffer, *The God Who Is There*, 2nd ed., 120.
21. This is a Protestant affirmation. Ibid., 123.
22. The illustration can be found, among other places, in his *Death in the City* (Downers Grove, IL: InterVarsity Press, 1969), chapter 9.

of course, but particularly the love of each interlocutor. Many people came up to L'Abri intent on testing the patience of its leaders. As someone who benefitted from their longsuffering, I can attest that love was in the air, even through some very difficult trials. Schaeffer reflected a great deal on the church and its life. While L'Abri was not the church, he did try to shape a community that closely resembled the church. At its center was the grace extended to everyone there. It was not a formless grace, but one structured by the intellectual and biblical teaching that pervaded. Some of Schaeffer's critics have missed this element, which is yet a nonnegotiable of his apologetics.

CONTRIBUTIONS TO THE FIELD OF APOLOGETICS

One could speak of direct and indirect contributions to apologetics and the church by Francis Schaeffer. Directly, he effected a strong influence on a generation that interacted with him. This includes people and institutions. When one thinks of the people, many names come to the fore. Charles Colson, the former Watergate conspirator turned Christian prison reformer, considered Schaeffer to have been one of the two or three most significant influences on his thought. Particularly drawn to Schaeffer's worldview approach, Colson even titled one of his own books *How Now Shall We Live?* Perhaps the most fertile of Schaeffer's heirs is British scholar and social critic Os Guinness. Guinness worked with the Schaeffers for a number of years and then earned his DPhil from Oxford in the sociology of knowledge. He is the author of scores of books, including *The Last Christian on Earth* and *The Call*. One of Schaeffer's unsung spiritual children is Dick Keyes, until recently director of L'Abri in Southborough, Massachusetts. Among the most creative thinkers of our day, he has written on identity, heroism, cynicism, and has delivered hundreds of powerful lectures on the bearing of the Christian faith on our condition.[23] Nancy Pearcey should be counted as one of the most important apologists of our time. She is the author of several books, including *Total Truth* and the fascinating *Saving Leonardo*. The list goes on.

As for institutions, there are ten residential L'Abri communities and several nonresidential ones around the world today.[24] Each one has a specific character, though they are bound together and governed by the members. L'Abri in Rochester, Minnesota, sponsors a major conference every year in February. In addition,

---

23. Dick Keyes, *Beyond Identity* (Eugene, OR: Wipf & Stock, 2003); *True Heroism in a Wolrd of Celebrity Counterfeits* (Nashville: NavPress, 1995); *Seeing Through Cynicism* (Downers Grove, IL: InterVarsity Press, 2006);

24. See http://labri.org/.

Covenant Theological Seminary houses the Francis Schaeffer Institute, directed by Mark Ryan. There is also a Francis Schaeffer Foundation, based in Gryon, Switzerland. The Schaeffer archives are held at Southeastern Baptist Theological Seminary in Wake Forrest, North Carolina. The collection is enormous.[25]

Indirectly, though it is not possible to be certain, we can say a few things. Many people had their lives changed at L'Abri. Many who never visited L'Abri testify to the way their thinking was changed forever when they realized, by reading Schaeffer or listening to recordings, that Christians could think and engage the surrounding culture. He is still quoted in sermons, lectures, and different writings. Shortly after Schaeffer died, tributes came in abundantly from many people and many sources, including President Reagan and *Time* magazine.

Schaeffer has his critics. Certain scholars take issue with some of his judgments. George Marsden and Mark Noll, premier historians, have questioned his views of the founding of the American Republic.[26] Various evangelical scholars have disagreed with his views on philosophy, on history, and on the arts.[27] That his views have come under scrutiny is a testimony to the importance of the man and his voice.

Though Schaeffer was in his prime in the 1960s and 1970s, students today may still greatly benefit from his legacy. Some of the quotes and references may be dated, but the ideas, and especially the thrust of his work, remain vital.

BIBLIOGRAPHY

Duriez, Colin. *Francis Schaeffer: An Authentic Life*. Wheaton: Crossway, 2008.
Hankins, Barry. *Francis Schaeffer and the Shaping of Evangelical America*. Grand Rapids: Eerdmans, 2008.
Schaeffer, Edith. *The Tapestry: The Life and Times of Francis and Edith Schaeffer*. Waco, TX: Word, 1981.
———. *L'Abri*. Carole Stream, IL: Tyndale, 1969.
Schaeffer, Francis A. *A Christian Manifesto*. Wheaton: Crossway, 1981.
———. *Death in the City*. Downers Grove, IL: Inter-Varsity Press, 1969.
———. *Escape from Reason*. Downers Grove, IL: Inter-Varsity Press, 1968.
———. *The God Who Is There*. Downers Grove, IL: Inter-Varsity Press, 1968.
———. *The Great Evangelical Disaster*. Wheaton: Crossway, 1984.
———. *He Is There and He Is Not Silent*. Downers Grove, IL: Inter-Varsity Press, 1973.
———. *How Should We Then Live?* Old Tappan, NJ: Fleming Revel, 1976.
———. *Pollution and the Death of Man*. Carole Stream, IL: Tyndale, 1970.
———. *True Spirituality*. Carole Stream, IL: Tyndale, 1971.
Schaeffer, Francis A., and C. Everett Koop. *Whatever Happened to the Human Race?* Revised. Wheaton: Crossway, 1983.

---

25. See https://www.youtube.com/watch?v=TONMvOA5QMU.
26. See Barry Hankins, *Francis Schaeffer and the Shaping of Evangelical America* (Grand Rapids: Eerdmans, 2008), 208–27.
27. See *Reflections on Francis Schaeffer*, ed. Ronald Ruegsegger (Grand Rapids: Zondervan, 1986).

EDWARD JOHN CARNELL

Finding Common Ground for Apologetics

STEVEN A. HEIN

One of the most talented and influential pioneers in the neoevangelical movement in the middle of the twentieth century was the Baptist scholar of Fuller Theological Seminary, Edward John Carnell (1919–1967). His abiding desire was to show the intellectual vitality and attractiveness of orthodox Protestant Christianity. Central to Carnell's apologetic mission was affirming and exploring universal contact points, or "common ground," between the world of unbelief and the Christian faith. Human nature and experience involve a functioning "rational self" that seeks a unified universe, a "volitional self," or "free self," that seeks personal happiness, a "moral self" that is fulfilled in the attainment of personal rectitude, and a "vital self" that finds true peace and security in a mutual love relationship with God. With these as contact points within the sinful human condition, Carnell sought to defend the Christian faith by demonstrating that it alone fulfills the ultimate concerns of human existence.

HISTORICAL BACKGROUND

Edward Carnell was born in Antigo, Wisconsin, in 1919 as the son of a fundamentalist Baptist preacher. After a rather mediocre high school scholastic performance, manifesting ambivalence for scholarly interests, Carnell made a last-minute decision during the summer of 1937 to attend Wheaton College. Within fundamentalist circles Wheaton enjoyed the reputation of offering the finest in Christian higher education. But Carnell seemed more motivated by the partial tuition scholarship for which he was eligible, being the son of a Baptist minister.

At Wheaton, Carnell found himself intellectually. The greatest force behind Carnell's beginnings toward intellectual maturity was philosophy professor Gordon Hadden Clark. Clark came to Wheaton as a guest professor in 1936 from the University of Pennsylvania, joining the permanent faculty in 1937. His rigor and high standards of scholarly excellence had a profound effect on Carnell, helping to instill in him a love of things philosophical. They also developed a drive in the young Carnell for an intellectual preparedness and thoroughness that would settle for nothing but the best. Clark also nurtured in Carnell a keen interest in epistemological considerations and the necessity of defending the Christian theistic position through a rigorous application of the canons of logic. Carnell became an enthusiastic student, not of the older common sense realism but rather of Clark's presuppositional variety of Christian rationalism.[1]

After Wheaton, Carnell attended Westminster Theological Seminary, stating on his application that he believed Westminster "offered the most scholarly defense of the Gospel."[2] Nevertheless, after three years under the tutelage of Cornelius Van Til, Carnell broke with his seminary mentor because of his refusal to acknowledge any epistemological common ground between the believer and the unbeliever from which the Christian faith could be defended.[3] Graduating from Westminster, Carnell completed two doctoral programs—one at Harvard and a second at Boston University under the personalist philosopher E. S. Brightman. Brightman played a major role in molding Carnell's conviction that inconsistency is only sufficient to identify error but insufficient in its own right to verify what is true. Needed also is a "systematic coherence," a consistent picture of the totality of human experience. By experience, Carnell meant that which "embraces the entire rational, volitional, and emotional life of man, both within and without."[4] He called this test for truth "systematic consistency," a horizontal logical consistency and a vertical "fitting" of the facts of experience.[5] John Sims rightly observed that Carnell's test for truth was a combination of Clark's test of logical consistency and Brightman's requirement of empirical coherence.[6]

---

1. In Clark's system of thought, the axiom of the God who reveals himself in scriptural revelation is a worldview hypothesis that validates itself by a demonstration of inner consistency according to the canons of logic. All "facts" of experience gain their meaning and coherence from presupposed understandings on the metaphysical level. If you begin with the Christian position, maintained Clark, you can see that the theistic-biblical revelation hypothesis, as a system of thought, is more consistent and makes better coherence out of the facts of experience than any other worldview thought system. Thus, the faith has been defended. See Gordon H. Clark, *A Christian View of Man and Things* (Grand Rapids: Eerdmans, 1952); and Ronald Nash, *The New Evangelicalism* (Grand Rapids: Zondervan, 1963), 111–43.

2. As quoted in Rudolph L. Nelson, "Fundamentalism at Harvard: The Case of Edward John Carnell," *Quarterly Review* (summer 1982): 87.

3. In 1971, four years after Carnell's death, Van Til said: "Everything he wrote in his first book on apologetics and in those to follow he wrote with full consciousness of the differences which arose between us during his days at Boston." E. R. Geehan, ed., *Jerusalem and Athens: Critical Discussions on the Theology and Apologetics of Cornelius Van Til* (Grand Rapids: Baker, 1971), 368.

4. Edward John Carnell, *An Introduction to Christian Apologetics* (Grand Rapids: Eerdmans, 1948), 56.

5. Ibid., 106ff.

6. John A. Sims, *Edward John Carnell: Defender of the Faith* (Washington, DC: University Press of America, 1979) 57.

While still doing his study under Brightman, Carnell worked on his first apologetic treatise, *An Introduction to Christian Apologetics*, which was published in 1948. Relative to that year and the state of scholarly affairs in Protestant orthodox circles, the work was a magnificent piece of apologetic discourse. It showed a keen awareness of current philosophical and theological problems addressed by the more liberal spectrum of the marketplace of ideas. It also brought the option of orthodox Protestantism into the discussion with a noted degree of comprehensiveness and force. This was something that fundamentalism had been incapable of doing since the days of Warfield and Machen, and it was just what the infant neoevangelical movement needed.

When Carnell began teaching at Fuller Theological Seminary in Pasadena, he enthusiastically joined the effort to build and nourish an "evangelical Cal Tech" for the cause of a cleansed Protestant orthodoxy. He served at Fuller until his death in 1967, including the presidency between 1955 and 1959. Carnell was an admired and popular professor with the students at Fuller. He became an articulate spokesman for the seminary and for neoevangelicalism. During the first four years of his tenure, he was a prolific writer, authoring four major books and over a dozen scholarly articles. Over the course of his teaching and literary career, he would author nine books, six chapters in books, twenty-eight articles, and countless book reviews. His most abiding concern was Christian apologetics: commending and defending an orthodox Protestant understanding of the Christian faith.

THEOLOGICAL CONTEXT

After World War II, a number of second-generation fundamentalists sought to distance themselves from the anti-intellectual stereotype of the fundamentalist camp by producing literature that was scholarly, apologetic, and interactive with the general theological and philosophical currents of the day. Evangelicalism, or neoevangelicalism, was the label they preferred to identify their theological and ecclesiastical program. Perhaps the first published effort of these young second-generation conservatives to air publicly their dissatisfaction within fundamentalism and introduce a platform for renewal and change was Carl F. H. Henry's bombshell *The Uneasy Conscience of Modern Fundamentalism* in 1947. Henry detailed how his uneasy conscience was not directed toward the great biblical verities but rather "the frequent failure to apply them effectively to the crucial problems confronting the modern mind."[7] Needed was the development of com-

---

7. Carl. F. H. Henry, *The Uneasy Conscience of Modern Fundamentalism* (Grand Rapids: Eerdmans, 1947), Introduction.

petent literature in every field of study that would integrate and apply a biblically-based Christian worldview to the issues, problems, and societal applications relevant to each discipline. Moreover, Henry advocated that such scholarship be used in every segment and level of the church's educational ministry.

Harold Ockenga credited himself with first associating the term *neoevangelicalism* to this reform movement in connection with a convocation speech he made in Pasadena in 1948. While affirming its theological stance, he repudiated fundamentalism's separatist ecclesiology and called for "a new emphasis upon the application of the Gospel to the sociological, political, and economic areas of life."[8] Reflecting on the prolific publications of young scholars in the movement over the next decade, Union Seminary's Arnold Hearn reported that a "fundamentalist renascence" was taking place. These men were demonstrating "a capacity to make their case in terms more sensitive to the integrity of the modern mind."[9] Scholars who identified with the movement were a diverse group, with varied denominational backgrounds and diversity in theological interests and emphases. Perhaps Edward John Carnell's description of the movement as championing a "classical orthodoxy" instead of a "cultic orthodoxy" would be an accurate description of how these men saw their own theological commitments.[10] Agreeing with Carnell's description, Donald Bloesch added neoevangelicalism's stress on the defense and rationality of faith.[11] Perhaps no one in the neoevangelical camp did more to advance this dimension of the movement than Edward John Carnell. While a rational defense of the faith was utmost in Carnell's early apologetic interest, his later works sought to connect theological currents of his day that lay outside his conservative Protestant orthodox camp. His doctoral work in the thought of Reinhold Niebuhr and Søren Kierkegaard led to explorations of common ground and commendations of the Christian faith from more subjective aspects of the human condition. His treatment of the ethical dimensions of human existence drew heavily on Kierkegaard's emphasis of truth as inward moral decision. His exploration of the love of God for ultimate well-being and happiness reflected the positive influence of Niebuhr's *Nature and Destiny of Man.* If neoevangelicalism sought greater interaction with

---

8. Harold J. Ockenga's Foreword in Harold Lindsell's *Battle for the Bible* (Grand Rapids: Zondervan, 1976).

9. Arnold W. Hearn, "Fundamentalist Renascence," *The Christian Century* (April 31, 1958): 528–29.

10. Carnell charged that Fundamentalism (cultic orthodoxy) had erred; (1) by reverting to the Roman Catholic doctrine that faith is "reason with assent," (2) by believing that all issues concerning biblical inspiration and authority were neatly settled by orthodoxy during the fundamentalist/modernist controversy, (3) by practicing a separatist view of the Church, (4) by ignoring the social responsibilities in the Christian ethic, and (5) by failing to exhibit the love and humility of Christ with those who disagree. Edward John Carnell's chapter in Harold Fey's *How My Mind Has Changed* (New York: Meridian, 1960), 92–101.

11. Donald Bloesch, *The Evangelical Renaissance* (Grand Rapids: Eerdmans, 1973), 34–35.

the more liberal spectrum of contemporary religious thought, no greater positive example could be noted than the writings of Edward John Carnell.[12]

APOLOGETIC RESPONSE

Carnell's approach to commend and defend the Christian faith evolved over his literary career. What unified it was his belief that an adequate defense of the faith must explore significant contact points, or "common ground," between the world of unbelief and the verities of the faith. An effective apologetic must "make answer" to the questions and criticisms from the world of unbelief. For the answers to be adequate and meaningful, they must flow from elements of common ground between the questioner and the one who answers. Carnell tried to make contact between biblical revelation and truth that the unbeliever has discovered within their own culture. Much of the common ground he used revolved around two questions that were of abiding interest to him: (1) How can we *know* (in the critical sense of the term)? and (2) how can our lives be happy and fulfilled? The former question tapped Carnell's interest in epistemology; the latter, his natural interest in his own sense of well-being.

Carnell's method was to correlate the gospel with *a priori* categories of human thought, exploring questions and concerns he believed were important to human nature and existence. His ever-developing focus on the human condition reflected a creative synthesis of emphases drawn from such diverse thinkers as Kierkegaard, Reinhold Niebuhr, Gordon Clark, and Saint Augustine. Aspects of human nature provided the contact points by which he sought to defend the Christian faith. Unifying all his works were explorations of the effects of evil on the human condition and then how the God of the Christian faith overcomes them and provides lasting personal well-being.

The mature Carnell understood human nature and existence to participate in a fourfold environment: rational, aesthetic, moral, and spiritual. These provide univocal contact points between God and humanity.[13] Carnell's strategy was first to highlight significant human concerns that arise from these environ-

---

12. A more detailed exploration of Carnell's use of theological accents in Kierkegaard and Niebuhr will follow in our discussions of Carnell's use of the "third method" of knowing and his exploration of the law of love as the ultimate fulfillment of human existence.

13. For Carnell, these environments are grounded in the mind of God and reflect Augustine's threefold understanding of same as the *true*, the *good*, and the *beautiful*. The moral environment simultaneously puts one in contact with God, the ultimate Good. Carnell's apologetic projects explored the rational, moral, and spiritual contact points but largely avoided aesthetics in his defense of the faith. But he did believe that beauty is a God-endowed concept grounded in eternal standards resident in the mind of God. "God is beauty, for He is perfect harmony and symmetry." Beauty is "perceived in the intelligible soul" as lighted by the eternal Logos of God. Carnell, *Christian Apologetics*, 153, 168.

ments. Then he would connect them with our ideals and aspirations with arguments of how they are fulfilled only in the God of Scripture. His understanding of what constituted the most significant concerns and vitalities in the human self evolved throughout his career. His earliest apologetic mission reflected a strong desire to rethink the intellectual and rational foundations of orthodox Protestantism and make them intellectually viable in his contemporary world of unbelief. His approach defended the hypothesis that the God of Scripture is the one who "gives being and meaning to the many of the space-time universe." He is the supreme ontological truth.[14] "Through his power the world is explained; and through his justice the moral ought is explained; and through his mercy reconciliation is explained."[15]

Christian Apologetics reflected his initial conviction that the "real self" is the rational self. We are most satisfied and fulfilled in our existence when we can discover and hold a worldview that is internally consistent and best fits the world of human experience. He charged that our practical and theoretical predicaments "can only be solved by successfully combining the ideal and the empirical worlds in such a way that one can find hope for immortality, a rational view of the universe, and a proper knowledge of the truth."[16] The God of Scripture gives being and meaning to the time-space universe and constitutes the highest good.

Carnell moved away from the preeminence of the rational self in his second work, *A Philosophy of the Christian Religion*.[17] Here he declared that the vital self is the "free self" who chooses values for personal happiness. "Solving the dilemma of sin and guilt is far more important than resolving the origin and nature of the space-time universe." And he declared, "If God is able to satisfy the *heart, a fortiori* he can satisfy the mind."[18] *A Philosophy* surveyed human values and defended the conclusion that human existence is fulfilled only by living with moral uprightness in a loving fellowship with God. His analysis of the free self reflected Reinhold Niebuhr's dialectic that while the Law of Love defines righteousness as the ultimate value for self-fulfillment, sin has rendered us incapable of meeting its terms. Only the righteousness of Christ (and his perfect love) resolves the tension and fulfills our desire for an ultimate and lasting happiness. All commitments to lesser pleasures fail to provide happiness that is permanent and will not disappoint. The love of Christ mediates ultimate happiness and satisfaction for time and eternity. To know God or any person in a significant way

---

14. Carnell, *Christian Apologetics*, 124.
15. Ibid., 274.
16. Ibid., 45.
17. Edward John Carnell, *A Philosophy of the Christian Religion* (Grand Rapids: Eerdmans, 1952).
18. Ibid., 274.

is to know them in loving fellowship. Only such a knowing and fellowship with God can bring a fulfilling and lasting happiness.

Carnell entered his mature stage of thinking in his major work on ethics, *Christian Commitment: An Apologetic*.[19] Here he developed a "third method of knowing" as a point of contact with the moral and spiritual environment that can be explored without the need for rational confirmation. To understand the realities of the moral environment, each person must explore the realities to which the self is committed. In *Christian Commitment*, Carnell sought to establish a firm epistemological foundation for discerning the character of Kierkegaard's inward ethical truth. He later explained, "Since I have felt that the methodology of existentialism all too often has been left standing without a firm foundation beneath it, I have tried to develop an epistemology (theory of knowledge) to help provide such a foundation. This epistemology, which has much in common with the views of both Socrates and Kierkegaard, appeals to the realities which already hold a person by reason of existence itself."[20]

In addition to ontological and propositional truth, Carnell posited a third locus of truth: "the reflection of goodness and honesty in one's character."[21] He referred to this attribute as *rectitude* (moral uprightness), that which comes into existence only "when what one is coincides with what one ought to be . . . [when] essence and existence are united by right moral decision."[22] This subjective element in Carnell's understanding of truth drew heavily on the thinking of Kierkegaard for ethical and personal decision-making. Previously, his appeal was to *rationes aeternae* grounded in the image of God.[23] In *Christian Commitment*, his concern was not an intellectual understanding of moral concepts but the individual's subjective participation in the moral environment. Here our conduct often mirrors our understanding of what we believe is real. Judicially motivated judgements of others who wrong us are an indicator of the moral understandings to which we are committed.

Carnell used the illustration of a pear to describe how his epistemology broadened from his early rational emphasis. A pear may be known in three ways, each corresponding to an aspect of reality, and each providing an answer to important questions we may ask: (1) Is the pear actually a pear? (2) How does

---

19. Edward John Carnell, *Christian Commitment: An Apologetic* (New York: Macmillan, 1957).

20. Edward John Carnell, *The Burden of Søren Kierkegaard* (Grand Rapids: Eerdmans, 1956), 44n.

21. Carnell, *Philosophy*, 450.

22. Carnell, *Philosophy*, 451; Carnell, *Christian Commitment*, 16. While Carnell usually used the term *rectitude*, our discussion will use a more accessible term—*moral-uprightness*. By *rectitude*, Carnell meant the understanding and commitment of the sum of all human goodness of character.

23. Carnell borrowed *rationes aeternae* (eternal concepts) from Augustine's Neo-Platonist epistemology, in which the categories of human conceptional thought are grounded in the mind of God mediated by the eternal Logos. As God is truth, the *rationes aeternae* express absolute objective truth.

the pear taste? and (3) May I take the pear? Knowledge by inference answers to the mind and is necessary to establish the reality of the pear. Knowledge by acquaintance answers to our receptive faculties and is necessary to establish the taste of the pear. And knowledge by moral self-acceptance answers to our moral sense and is necessary to establish our ethical relation to the pear. Knowledge by rational reflection cannot know what the pear tastes like, and general experience of pears cannot tell us if it is all right to make off with the pear. Thus, a pear is known only by the whole self when all three ways of knowing are engaged.[24] These ways of knowing participate in a fourfold environment: rational, aesthetic, moral, and spiritual. They provide the univocal contact points between God and humans by which Carnell sought to commend and defend the Christian faith.

Unifying all his endeavors to defend the faith was the interest he presumed everyone has in their own personal well-being. At the end of his career, Carnell acknowledged that while some are troubled about rational objections to the faith, others are not. While identifying with the former, his later apologetic efforts were more concerned to connect with the interests and concerns of the average person on the street, regardless of interests in things theological. These efforts came to full fruition in his last major apologetic work, *The Kingdom of Love and the Pride of Life*. His desire was to make significant connection with the initially uninterested person who may well have a "who cares?" attitude about Christianity. Carnell's conviction was that the natural person will not listen to or heed the voice of the gospel until it interests them. And significant existential interest is tied to the discovery of profit for the self. Beginning with *A Philosophy*, Carnell wrestled with the question: What are humanity's greatest concerns in life, and how do they make contact with the truth of the gospel? His answer was that we all want happiness and a confident sense of well-being now and forever. This he understood as everyone's quest in life, and it shaped his entire apologetic career. He concluded his apologetic efforts defending the thesis that only living in a mutual loving relationship with the God of the Christian faith can provide ultimate well-being and a lasting happiness.[25]

APOLOGETIC METHODOLOGY

Carnell's apologetic methodology sought common ground with the scholar and the person on the street. His writings addressed those who did not acknowledge the truthfulness of Christianity and others who were just not interested.

---

24. Carnell, *Christian Commitment*, 125.
25. Ibid., 19.

He addressed some aspects of human nature to defend the veracity of the gospel and others to show its importance for lasting fulfillment of the human condition. He believed each person had a *rational self, free self, moral self,* and a *vital self.* Each of these domains of personhood became a common ground on which a bridge could be constructed to defend the rationality of the gospel and to demonstrate its lasting appeal.

THE RATIONAL SELF: A REFLECTION OF THE MIND OF GOD

Exploring common ground to defend the faith engaged Carnell's lasting interest in epistemology. How can we justify what should be believed and why should the unbeliever seriously consider the Christian faith? Carnell's first answer to this was that Christianity should be embraced because it presents a worldview that is demonstrably true. *An Introduction to Christian Apologetics* directed a defense of the faith to unbelievers as the only worldview that is internally consistent and coheres with universal human experience and the world. He called this dual starting point "systematic consistency." It involved a twofold test for truth that blended rational and empirical starting points. It was kind of a synthesis between Dutch Reformed presuppositional principles (Clark and Van Til) and the empirical foundations of the older common sense philosophy (Warfield and Machen). While he believed "Christianity can be accepted with the consent of all our faculties," the work presented an extended discussion of religious epistemology intended to justify biblical Protestant orthodoxy as offering the most systematically-consistent portrait of reality.[26] Equipped with divinely-endowed rationality and *rationes aeternae,* the reader can recognize that Christianity is the most rational worldview. "In this entire system of salvation," Carnell declared, "there is nothing impossible, immoral, absurd, nothing inconsistent with the corpus of well-attested truth."[27]

Moving away from the previous generation's commitment to the empirical starting point of Scottish common sense philosophy, Carnell's approach championed a "Christian rationalism" that grounded our conceptional and rational forms of thought in the mind of God.[28] Rationality forms the crucial univocal contact point between time and eternity as humans are rationally lighted by God through the mediating eternal Logos. Reason is intuitive in nature, innate and

---

26. Carnell, *Christian Apologetics,* 9.
27. Ibid., 179.
28. Carnell explained his term "Christian Rationalism" in an extended footnote to mean that some of our knowledge "can be learned by [logical] anticipation. Since every human being is born with *a priori* equipment as part of the image of God—an endowment which belongs to man qua man—our first acts of knowledge in nature are possible because we already know other truths prior to sense experience. . . . The image of God in man means at least that we are born with a clear knowledge both of God and his law. *Christian Apologetics,* 151.

grounded metaphysically in the mind of God. We can know God and receive rationally meaningful revelation as truth because God has endowed us with a mind enlightened by the Logos with *rationes aeternae* that enable us to think God's thoughts after him.[29]

> The rationality of God preserves our right to truth both in the validity of the *rationes* for tomorrow and to believe that the universe will continue regular and predictive. Creation cannot fail in the ends for which it was made, for the wealth of heaven and earth belongs to a rational God. Indeed, all men continue to act as if the minds of men and the universe about them will continue rational, but it is salutary to remind them that apart from the God Who has revealed Himself in Scripture, such optimism is rationally unfounded.[30]

The discrete facts of the material universe are related to each other by God's free purpose, not by some demonstrable necessity nor by mere sensory observation.[31] God, not logic "is the ultimate reason for things," for the mind of God "unifies the particulars in the space-time universe according to theology."[32] Facts simply tell us what God chose to do. "When we have properly construed the meaning of facts, we have discovered the purposes of God.... We know we have God's mind on the subject to the extent that our thought about it is noncontradictory and fits all the relevant data of experience."[33]

The intelligibility of God and his revelation is made possible by the mediating Logos. As epistemological Logos, he is the author of all meaning and mediator of meaning and truth to humans through the light that comprises the rational image of God. As "cosmological Logos," he is the author of the many facts we experience internally and externally. As the "soteriological Logos," Christ is the answer to soul sorrow and the basis for salutary faith. Added to the fragmented knowledge that we already have about God (natural knowledge), the rational self can know the saving Logos who reveals the personal compassionate love of God, the forgiveness of sin, and the possibility of a personal encounter with God. Carnell best summarized his case for Christianity directed to the rational

---

29. This understanding by Carnell draws heavily on Augustine and his early mentor Gordon Clark. He set it forth as a counter to a strict empiricism and the Kantian notion of the exclusive constructive role of reason. See Carnell's discussion in *Christian Apologetics*, 182–83.

30. Ibid., 183.

31. The problem with empiricism, charged Carnell, is that if nothing is in the intellect which was not in the senses, nothing can be known or meaningfully asserted about spiritual realities. It cannot take from sensory experience what is not there. See Carnell's critique in *Christian Apologetics*, 147–50.

32. Ibid., 39.

33. Gordon Lewis, *Testing Christianity's Truth Claims* (Chicago: Moody, 1976), 185–86.

person in his concluding remarks to *Christian Apologetics*: "If man rejects the solution to the riddle of the universe that Christ offers, and if he cannot believe in a system of philosophy which at least professes to answer the question of the rationality of the universe, to solve the dilemma of truth, and to provide a basis for personal immortality, how shall he answer Peter's question, 'to whom shall we go?' (John 6:68)."[34]

THE FREE SELF: THE WISDOM OF CHRISTIANITY FOR ULTIMATE, LASTING HAPPINESS

In the early 1950s Carnell recognized that the chief problem of the sinful self is not a matter of ignorance or incorrect belief. Rather, we suffer from "a moral defect" in our wills and affections such that "all human motives are tinctured by self-interest and all institution are morally ambiguous."[35] The transition away from the preeminent positioning of the rational self to the conditions of the human heart was first reflected in Carnell's second major apologetic work, *A Philosophy of the Christian Religion*. Three key thoughts guided his new thinking. First, the *essence* of Christianity is not offered by providing the best explanation of a rational universe. At its core, it offers a mutual love relationship with our Creator. This rather simple recognition had a profound impact on Carnell's thinking. The dimension of the personal is more important than the rationally inferential in biblical Christianity. Secondly, two types of knowledge must be distinguished: knowledge by inference, which is rational, and knowledge by acquaintance, which is existential, personal, and relational. "Perfection of knowledge is reached not by perceiving rational connections, but by enjoying intimate, personal acquaintance." And thirdly, "philosophy has never been able to formulate an approach to God which appeals to the man on the street."[36] For the rest of his apologetic career, Carnell would defend the faith by an appeal to the whole self, especially in its volitional, moral, and existential conditions.

While maintaining epistemological differences with Kierkegaard, Carnell agreed with him that Christianity emphasizes a "third locus of truth," truth in the heart. "Just as there is no perfection of knowledge beyond acquaintance, so there is no perfection of truth beyond the truthfulness of a good heart."[37] The "free self" can experience lasting happiness and fellowship with God in the context of three *loci* of truth. "Truth as reality makes up the environment of fellowship; truth as propositional correspondence to reality defines the criteria

34. Carnell, *Christian Apologetics*, 356–57.
35. E. J. Carnell in Harold Fey's *How My Mind Has Changed*, 100.
36. Carnell, *Philosophy*, 183.
37. Ibid., 452.

of true fellowship; while truth as goodness of character is the fellowship itself."[38] While fellowship is the greater value to fulfill the whole person, Carnell at this stage continued to maintain that the rational self must remain the final arbiter of all truth, including inward truth of the heart. The heart possesses no criteria of verification not subject to systematically consistent rationality. The heart may first experience the true value of fellowship, but only the thinking mind may pass judgment about its truthfulness.

In *A Philosophy*, Carnell commended the wisdom of biblical Christianity as the supreme value commitment for permanent and fulfilling happiness. His argument drew on Reinhold Niebuhr's analysis of the human condition and the essence of Christian love.[39] He commended Christianity by advancing Niebuhr's central thought that love alone can satisfy the self-transcending limits of human nature and freedom. Carnell's method was first to explore the effect that various value commitments in his contemporary culture have on the human condition in pursuit of happiness and well-being. His goal was to show that they either were not ultimate or lasting, or both.

Only by living in the law of love as freedom's supreme value commitment can the inner cravings of the human heart be satisfied. All other value commitments, if made ultimate, end in unhappiness and regret. While lesser values can produce some happiness, none can produce a lasting happiness. Living in the law of love "lead to nothing else, being itself the perfect end."[40] While only God can meet our need ultimately with his unfailing love, we are driven away from him by our own sinfulness. To admit the primacy of the law of love is to admit our sinfulness and deserved condemnation. Denial of this condition outrages and frustrates the free self's quest for a well-being that satisfies the heart.[41] Carnell's strategy was to appeal to sinful humanity's heightened self-interest as a contact point to build an appetite for the value of fellowship with the God of the Christian faith. He resolved the existential tension between our need for divine love and our prideful self-love in a Niebuhrian fashion by an appeal to the saving work of Christ, who solves the problem of sin and alienation. Carnell did not

---

38. Ibid., 453.

39. Carnell's conservative doctrinal distinctives were hostile to Niebuhr's use of dialectic, but he appreciated Niebuhr's conception of the free self, his analysis of sin, and the moral norm of *agape* love in the latter's classic work, *The Nature and Destiny of Man*. All of these are pivotal ideas in *Philosophy*. Carnell wrote his dissertation at Harvard on Niebuhr ("The Concept of Dialectic in the Theology of Reinhold Niebuhr"), which became the foundation of his work, *The Theology of Reinhold Niebuhr* (Grand Rapids: Eerdmans, 1950).

40. Carnell, *Philosophy*, 338.

41. Carnell believed it is a psychological impossibility for people to prefer what they believe will diminish their own happiness. The will and the commitment to self-love are tied together in human nature. "In every action, we overtly or covertly pledge obedience to the canons of personal interest and preference." Carnell, *Philosophy*, 15.

repudiate rationally-correct thinking. Rather, he moved it to a subordinate helping role. Of crucial importance is the quest for happiness, not correct thinking.
Rational thought may point to the reality that "there is pudding" (the Christian
option), quipped Carnell, but only a strong appetite in the heart will induce one
to partake. Creating this appetite became his chief goal throughout the rest of
his apologetic enterprise.

THE MORAL SELF: THE QUEST FOR MORAL UPRIGHTNESS

Noted in *A Philosophy*, Carnell added a third type of truth. In addition to
ontological and propositional truth, truth is also "a reflection of goodness and
honesty in one's character." He labeled this character, *rectitude*, or moral uprightness.[42] This is the stuff of "imperative essence" that describes all that we *ought*
to be. It can be fully known only when duty appears in the heart with a sense
of personal obligation. Responding to Kant's *Moral Imperative*, he conceded
that "I shall not steal" may well be rationally consistent, but why should one be
rationally consistent? Carnell's point was that "since people are free to decide
whether or not they want to be rational, a formal statement of duty can confront
the heart with nothing but *claims* to duty."[43]

Carnell employed his third method of knowing to facilitate an existential
journey by the reader that would clarify his participation in the moral and spiritual environment and nurture the "spiritual mettle" to meet God. Influenced
by Socrates and Kierkegaard, Carnell engaged the reader as a questioner who
offered also their own inner moral reflection as a sounding board and stimulus
for the reader to do the same. His strategy was to bring about a personal awareness of the gap between what one senses one ought to possess (moral uprightness)
and what one in fact reflects (sinful pride and pretense).

In *A Philosophy*, Carnell simply informed the reader that love is the law of
life and then defended loving fellowship as the supreme value in life. Here he
tried Socratically to bring readers to the awareness that they already accept love
as the law of life. From that awareness, Carnell showed the tension between that
acceptance and the loveless manner of their own lives. The law of love is the standard by which we judge others when they violate our sense of dignity. Judicially
motivated action most reliably reflects how we participate in the imperative
environment and our understanding of the character of moral uprightness.

Throughout his career, Carnell believed that a major problem in ethics was

---

42. Carnell, *Philosophy*, 451
43. Carnell, *Christian Commitment*, 21. Carnell's understanding of truth as inwardness where the heart
is captivated and held by a sense of ethical duty reflected the positive influence of Kierkegaard in his mature
thought.

how to unite a sense of duty with personal desire. Self-love grounds our desire to protect our own dignity and the obligation of others to do the same.[44] Therefore, instead of surveying the conscience, Carnell sought to clarify the reader's moral commitments by surveying what is demanded of others to protect our sense of self-dignity when they enter our circle of nearness. Whenever others offend our dignity, we judge them guilty by what Carnell called *judicial sentiment*. Our judgments about the guilt of those who violate our dignity reflect our demand that it be respected by moral absolutes.[45] Existentially speaking, duty and desire are united by judicial sentiment, and both participate in the moral environment.

Using common everyday events for the person on the street, Carnell sought to clarify that there are three standards of duty that others must respect to protect our dignity. The first is the *Law of Justice*. Justice is the standard of obligations that others have when they enter our circle of nearness simply by the recognition that we are a human being.[46] Justice is expressed by universal human rights and the principle of fairness. It answers to aspects of dignity shared by all simply because they are human beings. Obligations entailed in the Law of Justice are absolute and universal. They are always in force and apply to everyone. Nevertheless, maintained Carnell, justice alone does not define the full conditions of personal uprightness nor the core of the moral and spiritual environment.

There are aspects of our personal dignity that are unique to each of us as individuals. When others enter the circle of nearness, they must not respect only our rights (held in common with the race) but also those aspects of self that we reveal about our uniqueness. When elements of our individual self are revealed to others, they are aspects of our personal dignity that also must be respected.[47] The *Law of Consideration* comes into play as a moral obligation when our individuality is revealed to others, as when we humbly ask a favor. Obligation and culpability are valid only when elements of our individuality first have been disclosed.[48] Carnell summarized the relationship between justice and consideration:

---

44. Ibid., 97. Carnell believed that ethicists often make one of two mistakes. "Either they deny man's concreated sense of dignity, and so end up with a formalistic ethic that outrages the heart, or they recognize the omnipresence of self-love, but fail to anchor it in a sense of duty." Carnell believed that Kantian ethics commits the former error, while the pragmatic ethic of William James is guilty of the latter.

45. Ibid., 91ff.

46. Ibid., 172ff. "We are entitled to such things as a just share of the highway, or sidewalk, the privilege of walking through the city park, and a fair slice of the benefits and securities of citizenship.... If we pay for goods, we demand a just return for our money, if we sign a contract, we expect to have its terms honored." 173.

47. Carnell explained that "when others enter the circle of nearness, they are obligated to accept all of us, particularities and mysteries included. The reason for this is obvious. We are the sum of such mysteries and particularities. Whoever offends them offends us." Ibid., 189.

48. There is no moral guilt for offering peanuts to one with a severe allergy or wine to an alcoholic until such personal conditions have been revealed. But then, the obligations of the Law of Consideration must be observed. See Carnell's discussion and similar everyday common examples. Ibid., 188–95.

"Although our life is never materially identical with the race, it is formally identical most of the time. And it is this formal identity which makes it meaningful to speak of our just rights in society. . . . In every situation where nothing but the formal side of our life is revealed, the moral sense is satisfied with justice. But when our difference from the race is revealed, the judicial sentiment is aroused if those who enter the circle of nearness fail to pass from justice to consideration."[49]

While Carnell believed that consideration was closer to the core of the moral and spiritual environment than justice, it falls short of a perfect moral response. To fully respect the dignity of our person, even individual elements not revealed must be respected. Agreeing with Niebuhr, Carnell maintained that only love embraces and accepts the whole self, revealed and hidden. One who loves fulfills the core of the law of life and moral uprightness. "The total effort of the third method of knowing has been directed to a clarification of this one truth." Justice and consideration are valid expressions of law, but without love they lack moral worth. "I simply say that nothing has moral value unless it is done out of love."[50]

> Since personal rectitude forms the stuff of the third species of truth, and since the third species of truth comes into existence the moment an individual closes the gap between what he is (the descriptive essence) and what he ought to be (the imperative essence), it follows that love comprises the imperative essence, the law of life, the moral and spiritual environment and the essence of God. Love is the univocal element which makes it possible to say, "God is good," and "an upright man is good," for good is but another name for love.[51]

THE SPIRITUAL SELF: GOD'S CREATURE MADE FOR LOVE

Recognition of the guilt of others by judicial sentiment when they violate the *Law of Love* presents for us a moral predicament. When we judge others, we make ourselves liable to the same judgment. If the law of love by which we judge others is valid, is it not also the valid standard by which others judge our behavior? Secondly, while we are custodians of the law, none of us has authority to adjudicate the offenders.[52] There must exist, in reality, an *administrator of justice*. To deny the existence of an administrator of justice is either to conclude (1) that true justice does not exist or (2) our judicial sentiment is merely

---

49. Ibid., 204.
50. Ibid., 211.
51. Ibid., 208.
52. "Although we are custodians of the law, we have no authority to enforce the law. . . . Those who injure us are guilty; but the cycle of guilt is incomplete unless they are morally answerable for their transgression. . . . therefore, we reveal our belief in the administrator of justice." Ibid., 102–03.

a reflection of our subjective emotions or personal taste. Therefore, Carnell concluded, "As God judges others through us, he judges us through others. While judicial sentiment and conscience are not the same, they are related. 'Judicial rebuke for our failure to honor love with love is as certainly the voice of God as God's judicial rebuke of those who outrage our dignity.'"[53]

Carnell carried out an extended discussion about how the law of love reveals the predicament of our sinful condition. The law demands love as our supreme duty, but a sense of that duty can never truly motivate us to love. I must love my wife: it is my duty. But the more I am committed to my duty, the further away I become from freely and joyfully loving her. Love is a free spontaneous expression, while duty binds. Love is other-centered, while commitments to duty are self-centered. Striving to love is the evidence that it is still lacking, while we surely corrupt ourselves if we do not try.[54]

In his mature thinking, Carnell believed that the real vital self is the moral or loving self. While love defines the essential core of our vitality and nature, pride rules our affections. This condition he equated with original sin and "total depravity." We can understand this depravity when we see clearly that while we are committed to love and the law of life, sinful pride rules our hearts. If Kant would say on the basis of rational thinking, "I ought, therefore I can," Carnell confessed in the face of the law of love, "I ought, therefore I cannot." But if "indirect fulfillment" is included in Kant's dictum, Carnell would concede it. "Judged from within moral self-acceptance, an individual can satisfy rectitude in two different ways; either by spontaneously doing what is right or by spontaneously expressing sorrow for having failed. The penitent life is indirect fulfillment. Both satisfy the claims of the moral and spiritual environment."[55]

Sincere apologies and spontaneous expressions of sorrow provide humility and indirectly meet the demand of love and preserve or restore fellowship. But with God, apologies are not enough. We apologize for the occasional loveless things we have done, but before God we must repent of the whole manner of the person we have been. The third method of knowing can inform us that humble repentance is a precondition to restoring a relationship with God, but only the gospel of Christ can finally rescue us from our moral predicament. His propitiation of the guilt of our sin has satisfied the legal requirements of the law of life. "Christ propitiated the judicial sentiment in God, thus making it possible for God to pardon those who deserve condemnation; but the cycle of pardon

---

53. Ibid., 234.
54. See Carnell's discussion about the tension between the motive of duty and the true character of love, and then his discussion about how striving to love shows a lack of love. Ibid., 160–62, 212–13.
55. Ibid., 158.

is not completed until sinners humble themselves and repent."[56] Christ is the fulfillment of the law of love.

Fellowship with God fulfills our desire for lasting happiness and well-being, and love exhausts our free potentialities. In *Christian Commitment*, Carnell sought to convince the reader by the "use" of the negative element of judicial sentiment that the law of love as the essence of moral duty. In *The Kingdom of Love and the Pride of Life*, he simply described a loving and virtuous person as one who is kind and truthful. Love unlocks creative possibilities in a person that are intimate and far more fulfilling than mere data abstracted from natural law. Heart knowledge about others and the realities of love are found only in fellowship.[57] Ultimately, the self is fulfilled in the security of a love relationship found only in the unconditional love of Christ in the gospel.

As Carnell concentrated his later writings on the character of fellowship for personal well-being, he abandoned the abstract level of intellectual debate that characterized his early writings. His appeal was for the reader to consider the common, rather mundane events of ordinary life. Through an examination of social relations and contexts familiar to the person on the street and the scholar, he sought to make manifest the vitalities of love and our implicit commitment to them for our own well-being. The question for Carnell was: What is the reader's greatest concern in life, and how does it make contact with the verities of the gospel? His answer was that we all want happiness and a confident sense of well-being now and forever. This, Carnell presented not as a quest in life for us but as a blessing to be bestowed on the humble and repentant by God. The essence of joy in any activity in life that we are interested in and find personally fulfilling is love. Ultimate fulfillment is found in the reciprocal love of mutual fellowship. Since we fail to meet the conditions of love perfectly, only God ultimately can fulfill human existence.

CONTRIBUTIONS TO THE FIELD OF APOLOGETICS

Carnell's apologetic interest in the vitalities of love must be viewed within the larger context of his personal and professional life. As he joined a small vanguard evangelical movement, he soon realized that he had joined in a struggle to promote a conservative Protestant orthodoxy freed from the negativism and separatist ethos of fundamentalism. His early years at Fuller Seminary convinced

---

56. Ibid., 254.
57. Carnell, *The Kingdom of Love* (Grand Rapids: Eerdmans, 1960), 48–49.

him that conservative Protestant orthodoxy needed moral enlightenment and reform. Carnell's apologetic career helped early evangelicalism see that its fundamentalist heritage greatly needed revision when measured by the relational implications of the gospel and the law of love. The radical demands of love require more than avoiding certain forms of sinful behavior and avoiding those who do not share such zeal. It requires a joyful, spontaneous concern for the dignity and welfare of others. It presses toward the goal of relationships accented by love, the ultimate of which is with God through the gospel.

Carnell's combinational tests for truth had a rather minimal effect on how most conservative Protestant apologists defended the faith during the latter decades of the twentieth century. His approach neither removed nor modified the epistemological starting points for doing Christian apologetics within well-established presuppositional, rational, and Christian evidence camps. Perhaps Carnell's greatest influence after his death was on distinguished Denver Seminary apologist Gordon R. Lewis. Throughout his career Lewis championed systematic consistency and devoted half his work *Testing Christianity's Truth Claims* to summarizing Carnell's use of rational, relational, and moral tests for truth.[58] Moreover, the mature Carnell's defense of the faith for the tender-minded utilizing inwardness and appeals to the heart have been encouraged as supplemental apologetic strategies by even some of the most strident apologists and defenders within the Christian evidence camp.[59]

The reviewers of his works were quick to recognize lapses in points of doctrine and inconsistencies in argumentation. Some thought his positions too liberal, and others were disappointed with his conservatism. Most all recognized a competent scholar who was not unwilling to listen to those who differed from his tradition and to learn from them. His careful scholarship, attention to epistemological issues, and his championing of love as the law of life were breezes of fresh air that contributed much to the revitalization of orthodox Protestantism out of the demise of the fundamentalist movement. His career could best be depicted by his own description of a virtuous philosopher: "A virtuous

58. See Gordon R. Lewis, *Testing Christianity's Truth Claims*, 176–295. According to his colleague and successor at the Denver Seminary, Lewis used the term *verificationism* as his label when advocating this combinational test for truth: logical consistency, support of the facts, and existentially compelling. See Douglas Groothuis's celebratory remembrance of Gordon R. Lewis, https://www.christianitytoday.com/ct/2016/june-web-only/gordon-lewis-irenic-apologist.html. The influence of these tests for truth by Carnell can be seen (through Lewis) also in Groothuis's own apologetic work. See Douglas Groothuis, *Christian Apologetics: A Comprehensive Case for biblical Faith* (Downers Grove, IL: InterVarsity Press, 2011).
59. Strong advocates of a Christian evidence apologetic, such as Dr. John Warwick Montgomery and Dr. Rod Rosenbladt, have advocated developing and using supplemental tender-minded apologetic approaches that appeal to longings and yearnings of the heart as exemplified by the fiction of C. S. Lewis. They have also commended the apologetic works of Edward John Carnell to their students.

philosopher may never be celebrated as an original philosopher. But he will be praised as a good man who inspires good students. Having reminded himself that intellectual detachment becomes perverse whenever it usurps the office of love, he will make it his duty to remind others, too. 'The fear of the Lord is the beginning of wisdom' (Psalm 111:10)."[60]

BIBLIOGRAPHY

Bloesch, Donald. *The Evangelical Renaissance*. Grand Rapids: Eerdmans, 1973.

Carnell, Edward John. *The Case for Orthodox Theology*. Philadelphia: Westminster, 1959.

———. *The Burden of Søren Kierkegaard*. Grand Rapids: Eerdmans, 1956.

———. *Christian Commitment: An Apologetic*. New York: Macmillan, 1957.

———. *An Introduction to Christian Apologetics*. Grand Rapids: Eerdmans, 1948.

———. *The Kingdom of Love and the Pride of Life*. Grand Rapids: Eerdmans, 1960.

———. *A Philosophy of the Christian Religion*. Grand Rapids: Eerdmans, 1952.

———. *The Theology of Reinhold Niebuhr*. Grand Rapids: Eerdmans, 1950.

———. A chapter in Harold E. Fey, ed. *How My Mind Has Changed*. New York: Holt, Reinhart & Winston, 1962.

———. "Post-Fundamental Faith." *The Christian Century* (August 26, 1959): 971.

Clark, Gordon H. *A Christian View of Man and Things*. Grand Rapids: Eerdmans, 1952.

Geehan, E. R., ed., *Jerusalem and Athens: Critical Discussions on the Theology and Apologetics of Cornelius Van Til*. Grand Rapids: Baker, 1971.

Hearn, Arnold W. "Fundamentalist Renascence." *The Christian Century* (April 31, 1958): 528.

Henry, Carl F. H. *The Uneasy Conscience of Modern Fundamentalism*. Grand Rapids: Eerdmans, 1947.

Lewis, Gordon. *Testing Christianity's Truth Claims*. Chicago: Moody, 1976.

Lindsell, Harold. *Battle for the Bible*. Grand Rapids: Zondervan, 1976.

Nash, Ronald. *The New Evangelicalism*. Grand Rapids: Zondervan, 1963.

Niebuhr, Reinhold. *The Nature and Destiny of Man*. New York: Scribner's Sons, 1948.

Richardson, Alan. *Christian Apologetics*. New York: Harper & Bros., 1957.

Sims, John A. *Edward John Carnell: Defender of the Faith*. Washington, DC: University Press of America, 1979.

---

60. Carnell, *The Kingdom of Love*, 50.

Part Six

TWENTIETH-CENTURY EUROPEAN APOLOGISTS

The development of European apologetics during the twentieth century took a path significantly different from that of its North American counterpart. Whereas American Protestant apologetics tended to crystallize in the form of certain schools or methods—such as "evidentialism" or "presuppositionalism"— European apologetics took a less structured and more fluid approach, partly reflecting the diverse backgrounds and approaches of the individual thinkers who achieved prominence during this period. Although some leading European apologists of this period were ordained (such as Dietrich Bonhoeffer), the most influential writers were lay Christians (such as G. K. Chesterton, C. S. Lewis, and Dorothy L. Sayers) with established careers as writers and who saw themselves as called to use their literary gifts to defend and commend their faith.

Some, such as **A. E. Taylor**, drew on the classical philosophical tradition in defending morality's dependence on religious faith. In his *Faith of a Moralist*, Taylor argued that the ultimate good of humanity is nonsecular and eternal. God is to be seen as the absolute and final embodiment of good, pointing to an eternal destiny for the moral person whose aim is to pursue and attain this good. Taylor was widely regarded as one of the greatest philosophers of his day, and his arguments for the dependence of morality on the transcendent reality of God was influential in the period before World War II.

Others, however, preferred to appeal to the imagination and intuition in reaffirming the appeal and truthfulness of the Christian faith. Journalist **G. K. Chesterton** is widely regarded as having initiated this trend in the first decades of the twentieth century, which was continued by writers such as J. R. R. Tolkien, C. S. Lewis, and Dorothy L. Sayers. Chesterton developed an approach to apologetics that appealed to the imagination, showing how the core themes of the Christian faith—such as the incarnation—resonated deeply with human intuitions. For Chesterton, however, the appeal of Christianity lay not so much in any of its individual ideas but in the overall greater picture of reality that resulted when these were woven together. As a journalist, Chesterton recognized the importance of good communicative skills, which were particularly well deployed in his Father Brown detective novels.

Although Tolkien himself was an important literary apologist, many would argue that his chief apologetic significance lies in helping his fellow Oxford academic **C. S. Lewis** to discover the narrative character of the Christian faith. After an extended period as an atheist, Lewis began to experience the imaginative appeal of Christianity in the late 1920s, leading to his "reconversion"—a process described in his autobiography, *Surprised by Joy*. Encouraged by Tolkien, Lewis began to use narratives—such as the Chronicles of Narnia—to allow his readers to grasp the deep imaginative appeal of the Christian faith, and hence to explore its core ideas in more detail.

Lewis's distinctive apologetics combines a demonstration of the rationality of Christianity with an appreciation of its capacity to capture the human imagination. Although there were points at which Lewis demonstrated a strongly rational approach to apologetics (such as sections of *Mere Christianity*), his more general approach was to hold together an appeal to the imagination, the use of stories to demonstrate how faith can change individual lives, and a reassurance that Christianity makes sense of what we observe in the world and experience within us.

A similar theme is found in the writings of novelist **Dorothy L. Sayers**, who held that Christianity was able to disclose and illuminate the deeper patterns of reality. Sayers authored some of the best-known detective novels of the late 1920s and early 1930s, seeing the theme of a detective discovering a pattern lying behind events as paralleling the tasks of Christian apologetics. Both try to reach behind outward appearances and discover the deeper patterns of truth behind them.

It is widely agreed that the most significant European Protestant theological voice of the twentieth century was Karl Barth, a Swiss writer whose legacy continues to be widely discussed and appropriated. Barth was strongly critical of apologetics, arguing that the best apologetic was a good systematic theology. This view was controversial in the 1930s. Emil Brunner, a member of the "dialectical theology" movement that gathered around Barth, believed that theology was called on to challenge the assumptions of secular society and to present a Christian alternative. But Barth's views came to be influential in European and American mainline Protestant seminaries in the 1960s and beyond. **Dietrich Bonhoeffer**, who was close to Barth during the German church struggle over Nazi influence, shared Barth's concerns about apologetics. For Bonhoeffer, the core concern was to help someone encounter Christ, and thus his apologetics focused on a relational, not a logical or rhetorical, issue. While Christians are called on to bear witness to their faith, this is incapable of being expressed in the categories traditionally associated with apologetics.

The rise of postmodernism raised new apologetic concerns. One of the most important European apologetic engagements with postmodernism was due to missionary bishop **Lesslie Newbigin**. On returning to Europe from a long period of serving in India, Newbigin was struck by the extent to which traditional cultural assumptions had been eroded and saw the need to develop an apologetic response to this changed situation. Newbigin's response was the Gospel as Public Truth project, launched in 1992. Newbigin did not see this primarily in terms of the public defense of the rationality of the Christian faith, but rather it highlighted the relational aspects of faith and the importance of using narratives to render the capacity of the gospel to transform human lives.

Yet Newbigin also appreciated the importance of countering various forms of relativism and pluralism, both of which had gained influence in the 1960s. For Newbigin, it was important to appreciate that while Western culture was tending toward pluralism, this did not legitimate a pluralist ideology. The church was called to proclaim its unique and distinct message within a pluralist context, not to endorse such pluralism. Newbigin's strategy thus combined sociological realism about the increasing influence of secularism and the erosion of the Enlightenment worldview with a theological confidence in the unique identity and relevance of Christianity.

A. E. TAYLOR

Defending the Relationship between Morality and Religion

MICHAEL O. OBANLA

DAVID BAGGETT

A. E. Taylor (1869–1945) was an Oxford-trained philosopher whose voluminous writings added much to the history of apologetics. His story reveals a man who found merely immanent goods inadequate to account for the richness of moral experience. Unwilling to allow a naturalistic perspective to function as the default position, he followed evidence wherever it led, providing a model of moral apologetics that would provide a foundation for future apologists. Taylor's insights are both relevant and prescient to the contemporary discussion of apologetics generally and moral apologetics particularly, as well as to their broader cultural context.

HISTORICAL BACKGROUND

Alfred Edward Taylor, the son of Wesleyan Methodist parents, was born in the town of Oundle, Northamptonshire, in England on December 22, 1869.[1] His father, Reverend Alfred Taylor, was a minister in the Wesleyan Methodist Church in Oundle when Taylor was born and later served as a missionary in Gold Coast, Australia. The impact of Taylor's Methodist background would be felt strongly in his works. The Methodists are particularly known to focus on the role faith plays in the formation of a Christian's character. They also believe in imparted righteousness, the possibility of perfection through God's love, and the supremacy and authority of Scripture. Taylor would later join the Scottish Episcopal Church, a member of the Anglican Communion, but his later theology, which focused on morality and faith, divine grace, perfection in love, and the authority of religion as a reflection of God's authority, deeply reflected his Methodist heritage.

---

1. Portions of this chapter are used and adapted with permission from David Baggett and Jerry L. Walls, *The Moral Argument: A History* (New York: Oxford University Press, 2019).

Taylor received his early education at the Kingswood School in Bath, the oldest Methodist school in the world, founded by John Wesley in 1748 to educate the sons of Methodist clergymen. As a child, Taylor was said to be a voracious reader and was in the habit of hiding under the bed with a book to avoid being sent outside by his parents to play. He was also a good storyteller and writer, making up long stories to tell his siblings. Taylor lost his mother while he was still young, after which his father alone raised him with his brother and sister.

Taylor was admitted to Oxford University's New College in 1887, where he read classics and obtained a First Class in Honor Moderation[2] in 1889 and in 1891 a First Class in *Literae Humaniores*, colloquially known as the "Greats," an honors course in classics (Latin and Greek), philosophy, and the ancient history of Rome and Greece.[3] He preached in Methodist churches while attending Oxford's New College but upon graduation became a member of the Scottish Episcopal Church. In 1900, at the age of thirty, Taylor married Lydia Justum Passmore, the second daughter of Edmund Passmore of Ruggs, Somerset. She was an author who would eventually publish two novels in 1914 and 1915. They had one son named Francis. Taylor and Lydia were obviously very much in love judging from his reaction after her death in 1938. Although he lived seven more years after her death, it was a life of loneliness, which he tried to ameliorate by fully submerging himself in writing: an endeavor he carried out even up to the last night of his life, when he was said to be preparing an English reader's companion to Plato's *Republic*.

Taylor's professional career, which began with his being elected to a fellowship at Merton College of Oxford University in 1891 at the age of twenty-one, took him to various teaching positions in England, Scotland, and Canada. He remained a fellow at Merton College for seven years, which provided him the opportunity to continue his classical and philosophical studies and enjoy a daily close interaction with F. H. Bradley, a British idealist philosopher who greatly influenced Taylor's scholarship and with whom Taylor had a warm and cordial relationship.[4] In 1896 Taylor was appointed a lecturer in Greek and philosophy at Owens College, Victoria University (now University of Manchester), Manchester, UK, while still maintaining his connection to Oxford University.

---

2. *Honor Moderation,* or *Mods,* is the name given to the first part of an undergraduate course commonly known as the Classics at Oxford University that focuses on the study of Latin, ancient Greek, the history of ancient Rome and Greece, and philosophy.

3. See A. J. D. Porteous, "A. E. Taylor (1869–1945)," *Mind* 55 218 (April 1946): 187–91.

4. British idealism was very popular and influential in the late nineteenth and early twentieth centuries, especially the Bradleyan view that greatly influenced Taylor's early philosophical view. Perhaps, to showcase his appreciation and warm regard for Bradley, Taylor dedicated his first book to Bradley. But by 1908 Taylor had gradually started moving away from the Bradleyan philosophical view.

At Oxford, in 1899, he was awarded the Green Moral Philosophy Prizeman for which he had submitted "The Problem of Conduct," an essay he later published in 1901. The same year this essay was published, he was reelected to a fellowship at Merton College, a position he had earlier relinquished in 1898. He resigned his appointment at Owens College in 1903 to become the Frothingham Professor of Logic and Metaphysics at McGill University, Montreal, Canada, a position he held for five years. In 1908 he returned to the University of St. Andrews in Scotland to assume the Moral Philosophy chair that Bernard Bosanquet had vacated. He held that position until 1924, when the University of Edinburgh invited him to assume the position of the chair of moral philosophy, succeeding James Seth in the process. He held that position until his retirement as professor emeritus in 1941 but continued to teach until 1944, when his successor was finally appointed.

By the time he passed away in his sleep on October 31, 1945, Taylor had become an acclaimed authority in classical philosophy and moral apologetics. Taylor's vast and merited reputation rests on roughly twenty books for which he is highly honored in the academic world. He wrote with literary grace and philosophical perspicacity and profundity. His writings were inventive in the reach and depth of his knowledge of the subject matter and his meticulous attention to detail. Taylor was a philosopher, theologian, and apologist for the Christian faith, and his fame extended beyond the Anglican communion, of which he was a devout member.

THEOLOGICAL CONTEXT

Taylor's writings showed a variety of philosophical interests, especially Greek philosophy, ethics, philosophy of religion, and metaphysics. He was, perhaps, the most notable British idealist philosopher and an authority on Plato, especially for his work *Plato: The Man and His Work*. He was also considered a leading authority in moral philosophy and philosophy of religion, especially with respect to his 1926–1928 Gifford Lectures and the resulting publication, *The Faith of a Moralist*, considered to be his most decisive work of moral apologetics. His last work, *Does God Exist?*, is also widely acclaimed in moral apologetics, unshackled from the constraints of the Gifford Lectures. In that book Taylor presented "an essay of acute, cogent reasoning"[5] on a topical subject that has agitated the minds of philosophers and theologians ever since. His purpose for writing the book was "not to demonstrate 'the being of God', but only to argue that some alleged and

---

5. John E. Kuizenga, "Does God Exist?" *Theology Today* 4.4 (January 1948): 557.

widely entertained 'scientific' objections to theistic belief are unsound, and that it is unbelief (not belief) which is the unreasonable attitude."[6]

Taylor's moral argument in *Does God Exist?* is structured very much after Hastings Rashdall's argument for objective moral values, explained in the second volume of his 1907 treatise on moral philosophy[7] and on the moral argument of William Ritchie Sorley, delivered as a series of Gifford lectures in 1914 and 1915.[8] The locus of Taylor's argument was on God's grounding of moral value. This book was his last significant writing and something of an addendum to *The Faith of a Moralist*, allowing him to speak more freely than he could within the restrictions of the Gifford Lectures. For space constraints, the present treatment of Taylor will mostly draw from his magnum opus, *The Faith of a Moralist*, a book of which H. P. Owen wrote deserves "to be placed among the classics of philosophy."[9]

Several philosophical strands of thought contributed to the particular ideological milieu in which Taylor operated. He was greatly steeped in the classics: Plato, Aquinas, Butler, Clark,[10] and others. He was also a member of the Victorian age, and as such he was well aware of prevailing trains of thought and the reigning plausibility structures of his day. He was acutely cognizant of imminent shifts and incipient trajectories of dominant thought patterns in his native England and elsewhere, so he recognized that strong challenges to a theistic picture of reality were emerging. Taylor embarked on his academic career in the late 1800s, a time that saw the publication of Friedrich Nietzsche's *Thus Spake Zarathrustra* and described by some as the real start of the age of skepticism.

Before explicit nihilistic atheism developed more momentum in the twentieth century, a partially overlapping worldview development came to the fore. It was not so much the idea that because God does not exist, neither does objective morality. Instead, it was the idea that even if God *does* exist, he is irrelevant to morality. Much of the import of the *Enlightenment project* was to make just such a case: that God is an extraneous hypothesis when it comes to morality. Even if natural theology retained some of its value, on this view, the most that could be inferred is the existence of an intelligent divine designer of some sort,

6. A. E. Taylor, *Does God Exist?* (New York: Macmillan, 1947), v.

7. See Hastings Rashdall, *The Theory of Good and Evil: A Treatise on Moral Philosophy*, Vol. 2 (Oxford: Clarendon, 1907).

8. See William Ritchie Sorley, *Moral Values and the Idea of God* (Cambridge: Cambridge University Press, 1918).

9. H. P. Owen, *The Moral Argument for Christian Theism* (London: George Allen & Unwin, 1965), 7.

10. See Thomas Aquinas, *The Summa contra Gentiles* (Aeterna, 2015), Joseph Butler, *Analogy of Religion*, ed. Joseph Cummings (New York: Cosimo, 2005), and Samuel Clarke, *A Discourse Concerning the Being and Attributes of God, the Obligations of Natural Religion, and the Truth and Certainty of the Christian Revelation* (London: Knapton, 1732).

nothing like a loving heavenly Father or beneficent Being. The legendary Victorian moral sensibilities were arguably, increasingly, unmoored from grounding religious convictions as time wore on. They were perceived by increasing numbers instead as able to stand on their own footing, apart from the robust metaphysical foundations of theism, or even of a Socratic doctrine of the good and the ought.

Taylor thought that among the most significant and disquieting of all the social changes of the Victorian age was the "combination of universal state-enforced primary education with the transference of the work of the teacher to the hands of laymen under no effective ecclesiastical or theological control."[11] Challenges to authority were part of the air the Victorians breathed. This secularization of morality inevitably raised the practical question of whether moral conduct does not form a self-contained domain and whether ethics is a "wholly autonomous science, neither requiring support or completion from religion, nor affording rational ground for religious convictions of any kind."[12]

Indeed, something even more momentous was at stake: the question of what the ideal of life is for the whole of humanity. In light of the significant claims of religion in answer to this question, Taylor wrote, "A wrong answer to the question about the relations of morality and religion, once generally accepted, is certain, sooner or later, to be made the foundation of an educational policy, and adoption of a radically vicious educational policy means shipwreck for the spiritual future of mankind."[13]

For such reasons, Taylor saw the vital need to discuss the relationship between morality and religion. Misunderstanding their vital connection, he was convinced, yields huge problems, most importantly a misconstrual of what it is that is good for humanity. We risk domesticating morality, robbing it of its revelatory power, underestimating its evidential significance, if we sever and unmoor it from God too hastily. We also run the serious risk, by too quickly dismissing God from the moral equation, of selling ourselves short as human beings, settling for paltry substitutes for what constitutes our ultimate good rather than the real thing. Eventually, we even risk losing morality itself, if by removing God as its ultimate source and authority we erode its foundations and rob it of its prescriptive power. For this reason, Taylor saw the moral life as "not just an outward expression of one's moral personality, but a response to God's grace," thereby tying together the moral life and the religious life, especially the Judeo-Christian

---

11. A. E. Taylor, *The Faith of a Moralist* (New York: Macmillan, 1930), i.12.
12. Ibid.
13. Ibid.

548   TWENTIETH-CENTURY EUROPEAN APOLOGISTS

traditions, in a way that illuminates the temporal while focusing on the eternal.[14] In this way, he characterized morality "as a movement toward an eternal good," which in a way suggests a "dualistic dance, so to say, between the Creator and the created" that is reflective of the dualistic nature of human beings in their existence as both material and spiritual or mutable and abiding beings.[15]

Taylor saw all these tendencies as already taking root and finding expression, relegating theology to the backseat in the process. Even if religious belief was retained, it was often seen as not particularly important or existentially central. Even Kant's famous variant of the "moral argument" in the *Second Critique* took too circuitous a path from morality to God.[16] At most it was an effort to address the *First Critique*'s denial of theoretical knowledge of God. Theoretical reasoning ran into its limitations where God is concerned, on Kant's earlier view; owing to our lack of empirical evidence, we cannot form theoretical knowledge about the contents of the noumenal realm, which includes God. Later Kant would use morality to argue that we can and should practically postulate the existence of God to make sense of aspects of our moral experience, but such an approach was too tepid and indirect for Taylor. He thought the moral evidence for God was stronger and more direct than that, even if it did not attain to the level of a logical demonstration.

It was to Kant that Taylor most attributed the severing of fact and value. Of course, Kant was a complicated figure whose ideas cannot be easily encapsulated, but there was at least a salient strain of Kantian thought, Taylor argued, that had the effect of tearing God and nature asunder, along with the Socratic doctrine of the Good from the Christian doctrine of God. Followed to its logical conclusions, this influence culminated in separating facts from values, making their conjunction seem at best accidental. Taylor regarded it as "the most important problem in the whole range of philosophy" to examine this alleged lack of connection between reality, actuality, existence, or being, on the one hand,

---

14. Michael Obanla, "A. E. Taylor's Moral Apologetics: An Axiological and Teleological Argument for Rational Belief in God" (PhD diss. Liberty University, 2018), 7.

15. Ibid.

16. In the *Second Critique*, also known as *The Critique of Practical Reason* (*The Critique of Pure Reasaon* is known as the *First Critique*, while *The Critique of Judgment* is Kant's *Third Critique*), Kant sees morality as the efficient cause of happiness and the highest good as a state in which everyone is happy as a result of being virtuous. But human beings in their personal and collective existences are incapable of ensuring that being moral or virtuous would necessarily lead to happiness. The law of nature is also incapable of doing so. For this reason, Kant concludes that it is impossible to attain to the highest good unless one presupposes "the existence of a cause of nature, distinct from nature, which contains the ground of this connection, namely the exact correspondence of happiness with morality." (Immanuel Kant, *The Critique of Practical Reason*, trans. Werner S. Pluhar [Lexington, KY: Feather Trail, 2009], 71.) Thus, it is morally imperative to presuppose the existence of a transcendental and Supreme Being named God. Taylor carries Kant's argument further by focusing on the personality and purpose of God as the cause of the hope of immortality and that not only the soul but the whole person would assume immortality in line with the view of Christianity.

and goodness or value, on the other.[17] It was his work in this area that led to his importance in the history of moral apologetics.

Salvaging an intimate connection between fact and value was a crucial agenda for Taylor for several reasons. What confronts us in life is neither facts without value nor values attached to no facts. The sufficient reason for a value-charged universe, he thought, must combine both goodness and being, which assumes an organic connection between fact and value. Existence and value are also related in what "ought to be." The moral ideal stands as the goal of human purpose as it is realized in time by people. For such reasons Taylor was intent to use moral values as a window of insight into reality.

APOLOGETIC RESPONSE

Recall again what Taylor was up against: increasing secularism and skepticism, relegation of theology to an inferior epistemic position, a mounting resistance to authority, a primacy on temporal goods, a diminishing role for natural theology, and a severing of fact and value.

In the context of this rich history, Taylor provided an important response and a clarion call to ground morality in something beyond the empirical world. His response, in *Faith of a Moralist* and elsewhere, is to encourage close, careful examination of the evidence that morality provides. To do it justice, though, requires careful attentiveness, a steadfast refusal to water down the salient features and facets of morality and moral experience, and a rigorous willingness to follow the evidence where it leads. All of this was by way of combatting what the separation of fact and value, and God and morality, was normalizing, eroding morality at its core as a result.

Huw Parri Owen's book *The Christian Knowledge of God* identifies four dominant forms of the moral argument for theism, the fourth of which Taylor represents: "This form of the argument is one to which A. E. Taylor gave classical expression in the first volume of his *The Faith of a Moralist*. It is based on the present discrepancy between value and fact, aspiration and achievement, potentiality and actualization."[18]

COHERENCE OF ACTUALITY AND VALUE

Several fundamental inquiries guided Taylor's study, but we will direct our attention just to the first, a question from Kant's *Second Critique* (and Plato's

---

17. Taylor, *The Faith of a Moralist*, i.36.
18. Huw Parri Owen, *The Christian Knowledge of God* (London: Athlone, 1969), 95.

Philebus): What is the true character of good for humanity? For example, is the good eternal? Spiritual? Outside the temporal order? In tackling this question, Taylor saw that if an absolute and rigid divorce between fact and value is maintained, morality would have nothing to say about eternal life conceived in the Christian sense nor about an aspiration for total moral transformation and liberation from mutability.

But Taylor challenged this trend, insisting that dynamic religious faith simply must contain a large moral component. Where there is nothing to adore, there is no religion; adoration requires more than a valueless fact or an ideal admitted to be a mere figment of the imagination. The possibility of genuine worship and religion is absolutely bound up with a final coincidence of existence and value in an object "at once the Alpha, the primary and absolute source of being, and the Omega, the ultimate goal of desire and endeavor. No other object can rightly make the demand for the last and utter surrender which is worship in the spirit."[19]

Bertrand Russell's essay about a free man's worship was predicated on divorcing worth and fact, which left Taylor cold.[20] Taylor would insist that Russell's dismissal of the evidential significance of morality was premature. Taylor chalked up such a tendency to Kant's *First Critique*, but even Kant harbored reservations about too strict a severance of fact and value; and Taylor wanted to argue that though we cannot move too quickly from actuality to goodness, a case can be made for a close connection between actuality and value, after all. The point is that "value can only exist *in rebus*, i.e. in actual things or matters and that any value judgment, whether in ethics or aesthetics, must by necessity reference a personal activity."[21]

Taylor thought those implicated in a radical separation of value from actuality are often victims of a fallacy of diction, a false abstraction due to convenient but ambiguous habits of speech. Echoing William Sorley on this score, Taylor pointed out that the real objects to which we are ascribing the possession of value are the people offering the candid utterances, the generous acts, the creation of beauty, and the like.[22] It is not the concept of health that has value but the functioning of existing organisms. This is one important connection between value and actuality.

Taylor further argued that the ideals of good that historically have moved

19. Taylor, *The Faith of a Moralist*, i.32.
20. See Bertrand Russell, "A Free Man's Worship," in *Mysticism and Logic* (London: George Allen & Unwin, 1917), 46–57.
21. Michael Obanla, "A. E. Taylor's Moral Apologetics," 50. Also see Immanuel Kant, *The Critique of Pure Reason* [*1st Critique*] Trans. by Marcus Weigelt, (New York: Penguin, 2007).
22. See William Ritchie Sorley, *Moral Values and the Idea of God*. Gifford Lectures Delivered in the University of Aberdeen in 1914 and 1915 (Cambridge: Cambridge University Press, 1918). In the Gifford Lectures, Sorley argues for coherence between reality and value, claiming, "ethical ideas [values] are facts of the personal consciousness, and they are realized through the will, and in the character of persons." (Ibid.,

people to great efforts moved so powerfully only because they were not taken to be an addition imposed on the facts of life but to be the bones and marrow of life itself. "Serious living is no more compatible with the belief that the universe is indifferent to morality than serious and arduous pursuit of truth with the belief that truth is a human convention or superstition."[23] To divorce facts and values is like trying to separate the sounds of a great symphony from its musical quality. If this is so, it is merely arbitrary to assume that while our physical structure and its history throw real light on ultimate reality, our moral, aesthetic, and religious being throws no light whatever on the nature of the real.[24] In fact, it may well be that it is just this knowledge that brings us most directly into contact with the heart of reality.[25]

TEMPORALITY AND ETERNITY: BEING AND BECOMING

After arguing for the evidential significance of moral experience, Taylor emphasized that what is more important than *what we do* is *who we are*. What kind of people ought we to be? In answering this question, Taylor considered a "tension between the temporal and eternal," a tension discoverable only for beings who are neither simply eternal nor simply temporal but both at once.[26] The moral transformation we need involves gradual deliverance from our initial condition of change and mutability with which we begin. This shifting of interest from temporal to nontemporal good gives the moral life its characteristic coloring of struggle and conflict never finally overcome in this life. The moral life, robustly construed, involves people striving toward something yet unreached but also something known only in a dim sort of way. Taylor thus thought that the form of the good unavoidably remains somewhat vague and inchoate, perhaps even ineffable, which made him averse to any reductionist analysis of the good that would domesticate it and make it something less than what it seems to be.

This is a juncture at which Taylor realized his inability to provide anything like a logical proof of such a reality, since he was appealing to an almost intuitive or experiential sense of a transcendent good. Still, he stood foursquare with Plato in taking such a sense as a veridical insight into the nature of reality. Because of such a rich conception of the good, Taylor saw what needs explanation here as a robust phenomenon adequately accounted for only by an equally rich explanation.

185.) It was this and similar assertions that Taylor developed further into his argument about value existing only *in rebus*, i.e., in actual existents or beings.

23. Taylor, *The Faith of a Moralist*, i. 60.
24. Ibid., i.65.
25. Ibid., i.66.
26. Ibid., i.69.

The Problem of Evil, Human
Sinfulness, and Personal Guilt

Taylor admitted that the biggest weakness of ethical treatises is inadequate treatment of the problem of evil. It is barely mentioned in Moore's *Principia Ethica*, for example.[27] Taylor thought only Kant and Plato showed a keen sense of human sinfulness.[28] The contrition that makes itself heard in the "penitential" Psalms seems almost unknown to philosophical ethics.[29]

It is incredible that evil should ever be chosen just because it is recognized for what it is.[30] The Platonic explanation that the choice of evil is due to ignorance or mistake throws the difficulty back only one stage. The real difficulty for the epistemologist is created, as Plato suggests in the *Theaetetus*[31] and Descartes indicates more plainly in his *Fourth Meditation*,[32] not by true judgment but by error. Why do we ever judge falsely about anything?[33]

Taylor protested the domestication of moral wrongdoing for its unsound moral psychology. Our human expression of wrongdoing and guilt is so singularly unlike anything we can detect in the prehuman world that we are bound to treat it as something strictly *sui generis* and *human*, not generically animal. Moral phenomenology when we do wrong makes us directly and intimately acquainted with moral guilt. Taylor specified five familiar characteristics that distinguish our human experience of guilt and wrongdoing from anything that is to be found in the infrahuman world. First, it is characteristic of the human sense of guilt that it always involves condemnation of our own selves and our own doings and is thus radically different from any discontent with our surroundings.

Second, nothing is more characteristic of the human sense of guilt than its *indelibility*, its power of asserting itself with unabated poignancy despite all lapse of time and all changes in the self and its environment.[34] Old misdoings can haunt and torment us all through life. Rejecting the depiction of guilt as merely morbid, Taylor took at least characteristic instances of guilt as veridical. What is psychologically dysfunctional and unhealthy is someone blithely unworried about moral guilt while worried about trivial social blunders, which is analogous to becoming enraptured by abysmally poor music.[35] Nor are ascriptions of guilt a

27. George Edward Moore, *Principia Ethica* (Cambridge: Cambridge University Press, 1922).

28. Taylor, *The Faith of a Moralist*, i.163.

29. Ibid., i.165.

30. Ibid., i.166.

31. Plato, *The Theaettetuso of Plato* (Cambridge: Cambridge University Press, 1881).

32. Rene Descartes, "Mediation IV: Of the Truth and the False" in *The Philosophical Works of Descartes*, vol. 1 (Cambridge, UK: Cambridge University Press, 1911), 171–179.

33. Taylor, *The Faith of a Moralist*, i.167.

34. Ibid., i.174.

35. Ibid., i.177.

theological newcomer on the scene; the "poetry of Homer reveals there are some kinds of conduct regarded specially unpardonable and certain to provoke the anger of the gods, the unseen guardians of the moral law."[36]

Third, recognition of our guilt is regularly attended by what we may call a *demand* for punishment. The retributive character of punishment is a doctrine indispensable to sound ethics, and it has nothing to do with revengeful passion. We recognize the justice of a social penalty decreed on us only when and if we have already sat in judgment on ourselves. When people say God "must" punish wrongdoing, they are giving expression to a *demand* for punishment that they find in their own hearts. The gravity of forgiveness attests to this.[37]

Fourth, there is a recognition of the peculiarly *polluting* quality of moral guilt. All languages use the same words for what offends the conscience, what is defiling and loathsome to sight, touch, or smell. Wrongdoing is intuitively cast as filthy, dirty, stinking; it is the same specific emotional reaction characteristic of humanity in all ages and all levels of civilization. An occupational hazard of contemporary ethicists is thinking of morality only as obligations and thinking too little about the association between "sin" and "uncleanness."[38] In the realm of senses, dirt is a vehicle for infection and danger.[39]

Fifth, what is going on when we feel guilty or our sense of honor wounded? The sense of both is itself a product of the moralizing process. Truly returning to nature would require giving up shame, honor, and chivalry.[40] What is amiss in all of us is not just what we have done but that the fountain of our moral personality is poisoned. We are fallen creatures, and we know it. Our moral task is no mere business of canalizing or embanking the course of a stream; it has to begin higher up with the purification of the bitter waters at their source. We have not just broken a rule but insulted or proved false to a person of supreme excellence who is entitled to whole-hearted devotion.[41]

If we are to think adequately of the shame of disloyalty to our best spiritual ideal, we have to learn to think of that ideal as already embodied in the living and personal God and of falsehood as personal disloyalty and ingratitude to God. Many of our modern philosophical moralists are afraid to make the idea of God central in their theories of conduct, so their treatment of guilt is inadequate to the actual moral experiences of people with any depth of character.[42] "Thus once

---

36. Ibid.
37. Ibid., i.187.
38. Ibid., i.192.
39. Ibid., i.193.
40. Ibid., i.205.
41. Ibid., i.207.
42. Ibid., i.208.

more I find myself forced back on the conclusion that, to be truly itself, the moral life must have as its last motive love to God, and so become transfigured into the life of religious faith and devotion."[43]

Belief in the absolute reality of God, and love for the God in whom we believe, is at the heart of living morally. The good of our fellow people is unworthily thought of when we do not conceive that good as a life of knowledge of God and transformation by the knowledge into the likeness of God. And the love that arises from our belief is the one motive adequate to secure the full and wholehearted discharge of the duties laid on us by our ideal. "If a man is seriously convinced that of all facts those of our own moral struggle are the most immediately sure and certain, that we have more intimate assurance of the reality of love and hate, virtue and vice, than of the reality of atoms or electrons, I do not believe he is in much danger of reducing Theism to the level of a metaphysical speculation or a 'permitted' hypothesis."[44]

APOLOGETIC METHODOLOGY

This sample of Taylor's response to his cultural and theological milieu highlights several important aspects of his apologetic methodology, two of which will be accentuated here. First, *he spent a great deal of time suggesting that a close examination of morality itself—moral goods that do not admit of deflationary analyses or merely temporal significance, binding moral obligations, genuine moral guilt for wrongdoing—is semiotic, pointing beyond itself to something more ultimate.* This is the underlying logic of moral arguments for God's existence (and the afterlife): morality is taken to be a veridical insight into the nature of reality.

What often happens instead—among, say, a certain stripe of atheists—is this: they become convinced that the natural world exhausts reality, and then, predicated on that assumption, they presume to construct their ethical theory within the constraints and strictures imposed by their materialist assumptions. If they are not adamant in affirming metaphysical naturalism, they are often at least committed to *methodological naturalism*, which (at least in the realm of science) means they choose not to consider supernatural or transcendent causes, even as a remote possibility.

The result is largely the same either way: regarding ethical theory, they gravitate toward an analysis of morality that is amenable to naturalistic explanation. To do this they often have to adopt a somewhat deflationary account of what

---

43. Ibid., i.209.
44. Ibid., i.210.

morality is. They opt for a minimal analysis of what constitutes the arena of ethics. Sam Harris is a paradigmatic contemporary example of this modus operandi. Morality, in his view, is largely about promoting social harmony, effecting preferred consequences, promoting happiness, and minimizing pain.[45] These are all, one might say, earthly or temporal goods, and there is something unassailable and, in today's "secular" context in which all of us are steeped, highly intuitive about affirming such goals. What else do we want? As long as morality gets reduced to rules for getting along and promoting a kind of overall utility, an exclusive consideration of temporal goods strikes many as fundamentally correct. The cultural momentum right now is on the side of the "immanentists," not the "transcendentalists." The latter get accused of exercises in obscurantism and ontological gluttony, but this is just where the force of *Faith of a Moralist* can be felt.

By rigorous examination of moral phenomenology, Taylor accentuated the ineradicable shortfall of secular goods, obtainable only under temporal conditions, inadequate to "evoke and sustain this aspiration which gives the moral life its specific character as moral." He asked bluntly, "Can a satisfactory morality be anything but what is sometimes called by way of disparagement an *other-worldly* morality?"[46] Taylor was convinced that all the greatest moralists have answered the same way. Secular goods are seasonal, come and go, and are always tinged with regret; the same can be said about the common, or social, good; whatever good civilization gains, a good is surrendered.

Second, *Taylor's epistemology was laudably expansive.* He knew that human beings were not merely logic choppers, which likely contributed to his draw to an argument that appeals to both the intellect and affective—the full range of our relational, aesthetic, and imaginative faculties. Like William Sorley, John Henry Newman, and Clement Webb, Taylor could see that the head and heart must come together, that philosophy and literature must converge, and that an inquiry into truth requires the full panoply of our resources.

Taylor's magnum opus is a two-volume work generously peppered not just with tremendous erudition, ample references to Greek, German, Latin, and French vocabulary, detailed knowledge of the history of philosophy, and deft philosophical analysis but also with ubiquitous and adroit literary references. What the questions under consideration most demand, he saw, is not information or even dialectical ingenuity, as much as openness to the "whole wide range of suggestion with which all our active experiences are pregnant, combined

---

45. See Sam Harris, *The Moral Landscape: How Science Can Determine Moral Values* (New York: Free Press, 2010).

46. Taylor, *The Faith of a Moralist*, i.94.

with the sound and balanced judgment we popularly call common sense."[47] It is the book of a well-read genius with an expansive religious epistemology who spent his whole adult life pursuing a life of the mind and living with the moral argument—not as an argumentative strategy but as a pulsating passion with which he wrestled and struggled.[48]

In pondering life's realities, Taylor perceived an acute advantage for poetry as a medium of expression over "technical philosophy" because poetry conveys so well the epistemic need for tentativeness as we "grope our way in the half-light which is, after all, our 'master light.'"[49] Taylor was convinced that the closer we get to this good, the more we find ourselves closer to home. Again, this is less a logical or scientific demonstration than an appeal to a shared moral phenomenology that provides an internal sort of evidence that such a good is real and our proper telos.

In such ways he modeled what an expansive epistemology looked like, a needed corrective in today's fetish for myopia. He wrote, "Plato was so much more than the author of a philosophical theory; he was one of the world's supreme dramatists, with the great dramatist's insight into a vast range of human character and experience, an insight only possible to a nature itself quickly and richly responsive to a world of suggestion which narrower natures of the specialist type miss."[50]

CONTRIBUTIONS TO THE FIELD OF APOLOGETICS

A. E. Taylor's contributions and relevance are extensive. Two salient examples will presently suffice. It bears emphasis that Taylor wasn't simply appealing to the prejudices of his audience or exploiting the cultural momentum of his day. He had already begun to sense serious resistance to a classical theistic understanding of the world and account of moral truth. He was not just proclaiming his worldview—the terms of the Gifford Lectures precluded it—but vociferously arguing for its plausibility by pointing, in this case, to the evidence that morality itself provides that there is more to reality than meets the eye. He was a bit averse to being labeled an "apologist" since he was first a philosopher, and he was less interested in winning an argument than in discovering the truth. He also did not claim to provide a "logical proof" of his position, but he still thought the evidential significance of morality, rightly and robustly construed, weighed decidedly in favor of theism.

---

47. Ibid., i.16
48. See Baggett and Walls, *The Moral Argument: A History.*
49. Taylor, *The Faith of a Moralist*, i.71.
50. Ibid., i.16.

CRITIQUING NATURALISM

The model Taylor provided in making his case in *Faith of a Moralist* is significant and one of the great takeaways from consideration of his contribution. His work helped reveal some of today's emaciated caricatures of morality and its reigning deflationary analyses woefully inadequate to do justice to distinctive features of morality that cry out for adequate explanation. He would concur with the sentiment that so long as he is content to assume the reality and authority of the moral consciousness, the moral philosopher can ignore metaphysics; but if the reality of morals or the validity of ethical truth is once brought into question, the attack can be met only by a thoroughgoing inquiry into the nature of knowledge and of reality.

What makes certain thin conceptions of morality inadequate is not their fashionableness or lack thereof but their failure to come to terms with the implications and richness of our moral experience. Rather than deciding our metaphysics first and looking into ethics only later, thinkers such as Taylor and Rashdall would suggest that a close study of ethical truth can yield insight into the nature of reality.

Yet another prominent luminary in the history of the moral argument, whose work on the argument came to the fore in Gifford Lectures, was William Sorley. As Rashdall before him and Taylor after him, Sorley quoted, with approval, Hermann Lotze: "'The true beginning of metaphysics lies in ethics.' 'I admit,' he [Lotze] goes on to say, 'that the expression is not exact; but I still feel certain of being on the right track, when I seek in that which *should be* the ground of that which *is*.'"[51] The moral argument is based on this powerful idea: a close examination of morality in its distinctive features, its robust construal that is true to our rich and thick moral experiences, functions semiotically to point to something more ultimate than itself, functions evidentially to provide reasons to think that the merely temporal and finite goods of this world are not the most important goods there are to secure. For this reason, Taylor spent a lot of time tearing down a false dichotomy between facts and values.

Two salient problems attach to reductionist analyses of morality such as that of Harris. First, his commitment to something such as methodological naturalism is not neutral. It is problematically circular. A simplistic account of morality reduced to its bare minimum is clearly more likely on atheism than it is on theism, but most theists are not remotely tempted to adopt such a view of ethics. Second, and relatedly, his is an account that leaves too much out. By forcing morality into the procrustean bed of his sparse ontology, he simply has to ignore some of its most powerful and distinctive features least amenable to his

---

51. William Sorley, *Moral Values and the Idea of God*, 3rd ed. (Cambridge: Cambridge University Press, 1935), 2.

reductionist analysis. Harris's normative account of morality, recall, is at least in the close vicinity of utilitarianism.

Taylor argued forcefully that value is the explanatory principle of experience and that what we discover in our moral experience is a hierarchy of patterns for which our natural experience can't provide an ultimate ground or *raison d'être*. Commenting on this concept, Charles Mason wrote, "This major contention [of Taylor's] . . . is that man is in actual dependence upon a host of ideals, norms, presuppositions, and these enter into the warp and woof of his thinking and his acting. They are the ultimate rationales without which neither logical values, aesthetic values, nor ethical values have the slightest coercive cogency. The meaning of the fact is always in the universal. . . and it is for this reason that 'all secular good' is declared defective."[52]

Taylor showed that the problem with privileging a thin metaphysics is that it precludes following where the evidence of morality may well lead. It is a circular, even if unwitting, example of domestication. Steven D. Smith writes that it may be that "we can do science well enough within the iron cage of secular discourse" but that such an approach does not work when we try to address normative matters; and morality is a paradigm of normativity.[53] In general, the closer we move to an effort to understand the human condition and ultimate reality, the more evidence a naturalistic set of assumptions tends to ignore.

Interestingly enough, Taylor recognized that this can even happen within science. Contrary to a popular view, science is not always free of evaluations. Whether indications of intelligent design, for example, are taken to provide evidence for a Creator invariably depends on whether one accepts such a conclusion as rational or not, and rationality itself is evaluative. In foreseeing such a problem, Taylor showed remarkable prescience.

MORAL TRANSFORMATION AND THE POWER OF THEISTIC EXPLANATION

Taylor not only modeled a substantive critique of naturalism, he also demonstrated the causal efficacy of theism generally, and even Christianity specifically, to which we can but gesture here. One of the most important deliverances of morality, beyond mere rules for behavior, is its insistence on moral maturation, growth, and transformation. This is one of the features of morality on which Taylor spilled quite a bit of ink. Recall that he did not think a deep understanding of

---

52. Charles W. Mason, *The Value-Philosophy of Alfred Edward Taylor: A Study in Theistic Implication* (Washington, DC: University Press of America, 1979), 33.

53. Steven D. Smith, *The Disenchantment of Secular Discourse* (Cambridge: Harvard University Press, 2010), 25.

morality could be exhausted by focusing merely on marginal moral improvement in this life, or even aspirations toward earthly utopias. Invariably such efforts remain thwarted and incomplete and, ultimately, temporary.

Secular goods are inadequate to undergird morality's call to perfection, and its resources inadequate to provide a hope for total moral transformation that is anything more than a Pollyannaish pipedream. The whole good can't be experienced at any one time, and we are left with disconnected experiences of a "good" that we know to be ultimately unified. Our experience of moral value implies an eternal and unified fulfillment—whole, simultaneous, and complete fruition of a life without bounds—which can be accomplished by God, who is the ground of both value and being.

BIBLIOGRAPHY

Aquinas, Thomas. *The Summa Contra Gentiles*. Aeterna, 2015.
Baggett, David, and Jerry L. Walls. *The Moral Argument: A History* (New York: Oxford University Press, 2019).
Butler, Joseph. *Analogy of Religion*. Ed. by Joseph Cummings. New York: Cosimo, 2005.
Clarke, Samuel. *A Discourse Concerning the Being and Attributes of God, the Obligations of Natural Religion, and the Truth and Certainty of the Christian Revelation*. London: J. & J. Knapton, 1732.
Descartes, Rene. *The Philosophical Works of Descartes*. Vol. 1. Trans. by Elizabeth S. Haldane and G. R. T. Ross. Cambridge: Cambridge University Press, 1911.
Evans, Stephen C. *Natural Signs and Knowledge of God: A New Look at Theistic Arguments*. Oxford: Oxford University Press, 2010.
Harris, Sam. *The Moral Landscape: How Science Can Determine Moral Values*. New York: Free Press, 2010.
Kant, Immanuel. *Critique of Practical Reason*. Trans. by Werner S. Pluhar. Lexington, KY: Feather Trail, 2009.
———. *Critique of Pure Reason*. Trans. by Marcus Weigelt. New York: Penguin, 2007.
Kuizenga, John E. "Does God Exist?" *Theology Today* 4.4 (January 1948): 557–61. ATLA Religion Database with ATLASerials EBSCO*host*.
Mason, Charles W. *The Value-Philosophy of Alfred Edward Taylor: A Study in Theistic Implication*. Washington, DC: University Press of America, 1979.
Obanla, Michael Olaseni "A. E. Taylor's Moral Apologetics: An Axiological and Teleological Argument for Rational Belief in God." PhD diss., Liberty University, 2018.
Owen, H. P. *The Christian Knowledge of God*. London: Athlone, 1969.
———. *The Moral Argument for Christian Theism*. London: Allen & Urwin, 1965.
Plantinga, Alvin. "Methodological Naturalism." *Philosophical Analysis: Origin & Design* 18.1 (1997). https://www.calvin.edu/academic/philosophy/virtual_library/articles/plantinga_alvin/methodological_naturalism_part_1.pdf.
Porteous, A. J. D. "A. E. Taylor (1869–1945)." *Mind* 55.218 (April 1946): 187–91. http://www.jstor.org/stable/2250551.
Rashdall, Hastings. *The Theory of Good and Evil: A Treatise on Moral Philosophy*. Vol. 2. Oxford: Clarendon, 1907.
Russell, Bertrand, "A Free Man's Worship." Pages 46–57 in *Mysticism and Logic and Other Essays*. London: George Allen & Unwin, 1917. Repr. CreateSpace, 2010.
Smith, Steven D. *The Disenchantment of Secular Discourse*. Cambridge: Harvard University Press, 2010.
Sorley, William Ritchie. *Moral Values and the Idea of God*. Gifford Lectures Delivered in the University of Aberdeen in 1914 and 1915. Cambridge: Cambridge University Press, 1918.
———. *Moral Values and the Idea of God*. 3rd ed. London: Cambridge University Press, 1935.
Taylor, A. E. *Does God Exist?* New York: Macmillan, 1947.
———. *The Faith of a Moralist*. Series 1. *The Theological Implication of Morality*. Gifford Lectures Delivered in the University of St. Andrews, 1926–1928. London: Macmillan, 1951.
———. *Socrates*. Boston: Beacon, 1951.

G. K. CHESTERTON

Apologist of the Literary Imagination

RALPH C. WOOD

G. K. Chesterton (1874–1936) remains a powerful Christian apologist because he was gifted with a remarkable literary imagination. After an early period of wrenching doubt, he gradually worked his way back to orthodox faith. Because he had faced the worst kinds of unbelief, his apologetic work has vigor and strength that conventional defenses often lack. And because his artistic mind provided keen poetic sounds and images of everything he thought and believed, he was able to create a revolutionary kind of apologetics. He does not begin with God's own self-identification in Israel, Christ, and the Church nor with the awful fact of original sin and human misery. He argues, instead, that we humans are the most abnormal of animals because we are poets in the literal sense of *poesis* (the Greek word for "making"). The subhuman animals make things, often beautiful things, yet strictly as functional means of survival. Only our species creates nonutilitarian things for the sake of their transcendent beauty—or, alas, their demonic ugliness. We create because we are free and unique creatures of the Creator. Thereby do we imaginatively participate in—or else destructively refuse—the Reality that is at once natural, human, and Divine.

HISTORICAL BACKGROUND

Gilbert Keith Chesterton was born in London in 1874 to middle-class Anglican parents who were functional Unitarians. They shared the common Victorian assumption that doctrinal and sacramental Christianity would gradually give way to an ethical humanism that most people of good will would embrace. Schooled at venerable St. Paul's (where John Milton had studied two centuries earlier), Chesterton showed few early signs of his later religious convictions. Instead, he honed his rapierlike mind in vigorous and solemn debates with school friends who shared his humanist outlook. They were all convinced that the French Revolution had been the great freeing event of the modern world.

560

At St. Paul's, they established a lively forum for ideas called the Junior Debating Club, and they published a journal called *The Debater*. Styling themselves as revolutionaries and iconoclasts, they wrote thoughtful essays on important writers and artists and political questions. The youthful Chesterton numbered Rousseau, Whitman, and Whistler among his heroes. "We love [those] who have done with the churches," he wrote with impudent bravado, "we worship [those] who may not believe."[1]

Unlike his school friends who went up to Oxford or Cambridge, Chesterton attended the Slade School of Art at University College, London. He had been drawing and sketching from a young age, and he seemed destined to make his living as an artist. At the Slade he encountered the impressionist art that was then in vogue, and it threw him into a personal crisis. It led him to fear that "reality" is nothing other than a series of constantly shifting colors, of endlessly dissolving impressions, of virtually shapeless forms. He felt that he had been cast into a bottomless well of subjectivity, as if the universe had no final floor, as if nothing existed outside his own mind. This was not a case of typical late-teenage angst. It was a wrenching mental and spiritual battle unto death. He had discovered that if nothing exists beyond himself, then he is also the author of evil no less than good. In the face of such solipsism, young Chesterton considered suicide.

Chesterton would later recount his ordeal in a story entitled "The Diabolist." There he reports his encounter with a figure who, having indulged in every imaginable vice, contemplates a final denial of all virtue by discovering "in evil a life of its own." "What you call evil I call good," the nameless diabolist confesses. Yet he also admits that, if so, his diabolism would itself become meaningless since "I shan't know the difference between right and wrong." How will he even know when he is being diabolic? The man disappears as Chesterton contemplates the flames of Guy Fawkes Day, wondering whether the diabolist's confession had revealed "hell or the furious love of God." If the man persists in denying the distinction between good and evil, he will end in hell. If, by contrast, he confesses the priority and finality of good over evil, he will have been snatched as a brand from the burning.[2]

Chesterton came to see that he had gotten things exactly backward. He had regarded the mind as the arbiter of all things while ignoring the most obvious of all things—the exterior world. He noted that children, like poets, give rapt attention to even the simplest and most trivial objects. The pure thinker, by contrast, tries to impose a system of thought on the world's "blooming, buzzing confusion"

---

1. Garry Wills, *Chesterton: Man and Mask* (New York: Sheed & Ward, 1961): 16.
2. G. K. Chesterton, "The Diabolist," in *Tremendous Trifles* (New York: Sheed & Ward, 1955; first published 1909): 104.

(as William James called it), or else he sinks (like Chesterton) into the void of solipsistic delusion. Not the inward but the outward world, he came to see, is truly inexhaustible. Reality lies in the external created order, not in the mind's abyssal vortex of thinking. Nothing can be reduced to its static and defining forms as they are perceived by the mind; all things—by their very existence—are overflowing with boundless significance. Just as God creates the cosmos *ex nihilo*, so does the poetic imagination discern how all things are emerging out of nothingness into endlessly abundant life. Some of these newborn things clash and conflict, alas, and some human creations are plainly malevolent—as in the case of cruelties both great and small, both planetary and personal. Yet when such poetic making is in accord with the grain of the universe, it has enormous redemptive power.

Now in only his mid-twenties, Chesterton began to pour forth a virtual deluge of essays and poems, dramas and novels, that took London by storm. Who was this brazen upstart, nearly everyone was asking, who was turning the world upside down? Even more remarkable was Chesterton's unabashed self-identification as a Christian. It became evident that neither the utilitarian Christianity of his parents nor the secularism of its cultured despisers could answer his pressing questions, much less cure the dire ills of the modern world. Largely by observing the devout Christian practice of Frances Blogg, a high-church Anglican who would eventually become his wife, Chesterton returned to the Church. By the turn of the twentieth century, he had begun to use the word *Catholic* as a virtual synonym for Christianity.

Partly in deference to Frances, Chesterton was not received into the Roman Catholic Church until 1922, when he was forty-eight. He would die fourteen years later at age sixty-two, in 1936. Chesterton rightly regarded his conversion as a progressive and not a reactionary decision. It was not a nostalgic, backward-gazing act, a desperate desire to restore the glories of the Christian past. Over and again he confessed that he believed the Gospel simply because it is true, not because it met his emotional needs. Nor was his faith an intellectual exercise of formally subscribing to a set of ideas. On the contrary, it was rooted and grounded in human existence as created and re-created by God. Twice, says Chesterton, the world has been shaken with revolutionary force, first in the making of human beings and then in the coming of the God-man: "Once Heaven came upon the earth with a power or seal called the image of God, whereby man took command of Nature; and once again (when in empire after empire men had been found wanting) Heaven came to save mankind in the awful shape of a man."[3]

---

3. G. K. Chesterton, *Orthodoxy* (San Francisco: Ignatius, 1995; first published 1908): 152. All further references to this work will be cited as O.

Though sometimes a crank and often a curmudgeon, Chesterton never turned in revulsion against the disorders of his age. He sought instead to redress them by means of a feisty and witty kind of journalism. This was his single avowed profession. He wrote for *le jour* in the conviction that the diurnal is intimately related to the eternal. The Incarnation is evidence that God participates in the whole of human and natural—indeed of cosmic—life. Chesterton unleashed a torrent of essays (some 1,400), novels, poems, and dramas—a final total of more than 100 books. His aphorisms made him the most oft-quoted writer since Shakespeare. He was convinced that many of the world's best things—the ordinary even more than the exceptional—were either neglected or scorned. Already in *The Defendant* (1901), for example, he was standing up for skeletons, China shepherdesses, ugly things, penny dreadfuls, slang, farce, even baby worship. He took up whatever subject happened to interest him, seeking to explore its surprises.

Chesterton also addressed the clamant concerns of his time—from economics to eugenics, from sexual ethics to theological dogmas, from the causes of war to the means of peace. He also thundered against the maladies that afflicted the poor: the wage slavery that wedded workers to their jobs, the prohibitionism that would rob the destitute of bibulous relief from their drudgery, the nanny state that sought to manage even the hygiene of the needy. Together with Hilaire Belloc and Vincent McNabb, Chesterton devised an alternative to both capitalism and socialism; they called it Distributism, a scheme for reallocating land and property rather than money. Thus was Chesterton no mere nay-saying contrarian. The arc of his oeuvre is definitely upward and affirmative. The gladness of his apologetics becomes especially evident in his overtly theological works: *Orthodoxy* and *Everlasting Man*, plus his essays in *Heretics* and *The Defendant*, as well as his biographies of Saint Francis of Assisi and Saint Thomas Aquinas. Chesterton also gives convincing imaginative life to his core convictions in two long poems—*Lepanto* and *The Ballad of the White Horse*—as well as his fiction, especially *The Ball and the Cross*, *The Napoleon of Notting Hill*, and *The Man Who Was Thursday*.

THEOLOGICAL CONTEXT

Chesterton worked in an age whose religious atmosphere was exceedingly bleak and thin. The chief English theologian of note was the gloomy Dean of St. Paul's, William Inge. He was a neo-Platonist advocate of individualist mysticism, a despiser of Roman Catholicism and democracy alike, a supporter of nudism, animal rights, and eugenics. A lesser figure was R. J. Campbell, a liberal and hugely popular Congregationalist who doubted the historicity of many biblical events, who was smitten with Indian gurus and theosophy, and who believed in his own eventual reincarnation—though he later returned to orthodox Anglicanism. There was little in the Christianity of Inge and Campbell that could draw Chesterton to it. Yet the atheists of the time—Herbert Spencer, Julian Huxley, Charles Bradlaugh—were hardly more challenging. Chesterton found them so unpersuasive that, as he ironically confessed, they sowed his "first wild doubts of doubt." He thus turned the cynical sneer of King Agrippa at the Apostle Paul (in Acts 26) into a comical affirmation of their flaccid godlessness: "Almost thou persuadest me to be a Christian" (O, 90).

When the best exponents of both belief and unbelief were so invertebrate, it is not surprising that the humanism of G. B. Shaw and H. G. Wells won the attention of cultured people who took ideas seriously. Shaw's plays (*Man and Superman*, for instance) gave brilliant comic and dramatic life to the Nietzschean and Bergsonian case for the "Life Force." Working through "creative evolution," this cosmic power would create, Shaw believed, a race of "supermen" who would quicken the human species with new rigor and vision. Wells was an omnimath whose scores of books span almost all the literary genres, his major work being utopian fantasy and science fiction. In his immensely popular *Outline of History*, Wells set forth his faith in a brave new world built on continual progress via the sciences when, at last, they would be untrammeled by religion and superstition. Already in this brief description of Shaw and Wells as among the best minds of his time, we find a clue to Chesterton's apologetics: he did not regard them as his enemies but his friends. To him, our much-vaunted freedom of thought is bootless unless it issues in vigorous intellectual dialogue and disputation among serious interlocutors. In their debates at large public forums, Chesterton treated Wells and Shaw with utmost charity and good humor. To the slender vegetarian Shaw, Chesterton said, "Looking at you, Shaw, one would think there is a famine in the land." Not to be outdone by the rotund and outsized Chesterton, Shaw replied, "Looking at you, one would think you caused it." "If I were as fat as you," Shaw is said to have added, "I would hang myself." Replied Chesterton: "And if I had it in mind to hang myself, I'd use you as the rope."[4]

Chesterton often gained the sympathy of his audiences by self-mockery. For instance, in a newspaper contest seeking to identify the major problem facing modern society, he is said to have answered with this terse reply: "Dear Sir: I am. Yours truly, G. K. Chesterton." Chesterton rarely wielded his Christianity as an

---

4. Mardy Grote, *Viva la Repartee: Clever Comebacks and Witty Retorts from History's Great Wits and Wordsmiths* (New York: HarperCollins e-books, 2009): 88.

ax but almost always as a rapier. He never claimed that Christians have always been in the right nor did he deny that Christians have committed atrocities, even if they were committed in violation rather than obedience to the gospel. In *The Ball and the Cross*—the short fantasy novel that sums up the whole of Chesterton's vision—he has his Christian protagonist, Evan McIan, confess not only his own sinful devices and desires but also the evils perpetrated in the name of Christ: "The Church in its earthly action has really touched morbid things— tortures and bleeding visions and blasts of extermination. The Church has had her madnesses, and I am one of them. I am the massacre of St. Bartholomew. I am the Inquisition of Spain."[5] Such apologies, in this more conventional sense, are not only acts of humility, they also exemplify the contrition that should be intrinsic to all apologetics conducted in the name of the self-identifying God who both commands and forgives.

APOLOGETIC METHOD

Chesterton is a notoriously unsystematic but almost always consistent thinker, especially when he treats serious matters in comical guise. He formulated no method for defending the Christian faith against both its cultured and ignorant detractors. Yet it can be safely said that he does not begin with divine revelation—so as to make all truth depend on a prior encounter with God's definitive self-disclosure in Israel and Christ, in Church and Scripture and tradition. Nor does he have recourse to a so-called "Christian worldview," as if the Faith "once for all entrusted to God's holy people" (Jude 3) could be neutrally discerned and then set alongside other such worldviews, so as to evaluate them allegedly without presuppositions.

On the contrary, he saw the world through the lenses of Christian faith. At first his Christianity was largely an inherited thing, a late-Victorian cultural legacy he had absorbed almost unconsciously. But later he embraced it, quite deliberately, as the defining reality of his life. Thus did he participate in human and natural things so as to discern divine things at work within them. The rough order implicit in his apologetics thus proceeds as follows: (1) from his claim that the ailment of our age is not godlessness but insanity; (2) to his attempt to establish the uniqueness of human beings in the gift of imaginative creation, whether in prehistoric cave drawings or immemorial fantasies and fairy tales; (3) then to his conviction that, just as human beings stick out like a spike

---

5. G. K. Chesterton, *The Ball and the Cross* (Mineola, NY: Dover, 1995; first published 1909): 157. Later McIan adds: "Torture should be violently stopped, though the Church is doing it" (167).

from the processes of nature, so are the Incarnation and the Church the ultimate divine irruptions into the processes of history.

APOLOGETIC RESPONSE

Our Present Insanity

Orthodoxy is Chesterton's most celebrated work. Graham Greene described it as "among the great books of the age."[6] Dorothy L. Sayers was inspired to reclaim her childhood Christianity mainly by reading *Orthodoxy*. Even H. L. Mencken—there could hardly have been a figure more antithetical to Chesterton—praised *Orthodoxy* as "indeed, the best argument for Christianity I have ever read—and I have gone through, I suppose, fully a hundred."[7] The reason is not far to find: Chesterton doesn't begin by denouncing human sinfulness and misery as containing an implicit cry for the God of grace and salvation. "It is plainly not now possible (with any hope of a universal appeal) to start, as our fathers did, with the fact of sin," he confesses. "This very fact which was to them (and is to me) as plain as a pikestaff, is the very fact that has been specially diluted or denied" (O, 19). For Chesterton, the conviction of sin depends on an assumed metaphysical order, a transcendent hierarchy of goods in relation to which we are meant to combat vices and promote virtues. The shattering of this Great Chain of Being, as it was once called, is precisely the condition and curse of our age.

What, for Chesterton, is the source of the destruction and sadness that vex much of modern life? It is important to note that he does not attribute the modern calamity to a fist-shaking denial of God. Such an accusation would be far too easy for Christians to rebut since much of modern atheism is set against a sort of grandfather "god" whom William Blake rightly called Old Nobodaddy, one whom thoughtful Christians have never credited in the first place. Instead, Chesterton takes a surprising tack, declaring that our age is not godless so much as it is *insane*—indeed, doubly insane.

The first form of our unrecognized insanity is found in the rationalism that has become increasingly regnant since the seventeenth century. Gradually the West lost its vision of nature as a virtually inexhaustible realm of analogies and metaphors for naming the presence and character of the incarnate God. With the overwhelming influence of René Descartes, we have undergone a tectonic shift called "the turn to the subject." This means—to put the matter far too simply— that the human subject, the increasingly autonomous self, need no longer look to

---

6. Graham Greene, *Collected Essays* (New York: Viking, 1969): 137.
7. Quoted in S. T. Joshi, *God's Defenders* (Amherst, NY: Prometheus, 2003), p. 86.

divine self-revelation or to divinely-ingrained nature to discern the proper ordering of human life. Descartes regarded the thinking self, the disembodied mind,
the *cogito*, as ultimately authoritative. Only what can be subjectively thought and
empirically experienced is real. Enlightenment rationalism led, ironically, to a
new fixation on inner experience. Chesterton is one of its fiercest and funniest
critics, describing inner light as the worst kind of lighting:

> That Jones shall worship the god within him turns out ultimately to mean
> that Jones shall worship Jones. Let Jones worship the sun or moon, any-
> thing rather than the Inner Light; let Jones worship cats or crocodiles, if
> he can find any in his street, but not the god within. Christianity came
> into the world firstly in order to assert with violence that a man [has] not
> only to look inwards, but to look outwards, to behold with astonishment
> and enthusiasm a divine company and a divine captain. The only fun of
> being a Christian [is] that a man [is] not left alone with the Inner Light,
> but definitely [recognizes] an outer light, fair as the sun, clear as the moon,
> terrible as an army with banners. (O, 81)

The ultimate rationalist triumph occurs when the mind reduces nature to
a mechanical system awaiting human mastery and manipulation. Reason then
becomes an affair of purely rational calculation. Reality consists of those things
that can be tested and measured, so as to be demonstrated either by experimental
science or mathematical logic.[8] Much of our ordinary lives can be understood
in this way, and it must not be contemned. The Christian distinction between
the Creator and the creation means, among other things, the earth cannot be
regarded as inherently but rather as derivatively sacred. We shall hear Chesterton
define the earth as our sister rather than our mother. This critical and enabling
distance from the material world has wrought a wondrous series of scientific revolutions since the seventeenth century. We are beneficiaries of much-welcomed
breakthroughs in combating hunger and poverty, in creating medical advances
and labor-saving devices. Chesterton never cast stones at them.

Yet if the universe consists of nothing but matter and energy—of physical
causes alone—then we of all people have no transcendent freedom or hope.
We become malleable creatures who can be hammered into shapes of our own

---

8. Chesterton's attack on hyper-rationalism is not an attack on reason. Quite to the contrary: "It is idle to
talk always of the alternative of faith and reason. Reason is itself a matter of faith," Chesterton observes. "It is
an act of faith to assert that our thoughts have any relation to reality at all" (O, 38). We assume the rationality
of the world as the fundamental postulate and axiom of our very existence. That the world is rational rather
than irrational is the basis of everyday life: we could not engage in the most elementary communications and
relations if our words and concepts—our reason—had no truthful relation to reality.

devising. We become convinced, for example, that societal ills can be cured by applying scientific methods to them—only to discover that such utopias turn into tyrannies, whether in holocausts and gulags or maniacal consumerism.[9] In either fashion, physicalism turns into madness. A maniac, Chesterton shrewdly observes, is not the person who has lost his mind. "The madman is the man who has lost everything except his reason. . . . He [dwells] in the clean and well-lit prison of one idea" (O, 27)—the monomaniacal idea of scientific rationalism.

A second and equally dread form of derangement lies in the polar opposite of mechanistic physicalism: it is what Alasdair MacIntyre calls *emotivism*, "the doctrine that all evaluative judgments and more specifically all moral judgments are *nothing but* expressions of preference, expressions of attitude or feeling, insofar as they are moral or evaluative in character."[10] Emotivists refuse to make moral arguments. For them, all choices are arbitrary choices made by the omnicompetent ego. With remarkable prescience, Chesterton foresees the triumph of emotivist will: "Will, they say, creates. The ultimate authority, they say, is in will, not reason. The supreme point is not *why* a man demands a thing, but the fact *that* he does demand it. . . . They say choice itself is the divine thing" (O, 43; emphases added). Whereas hyper-rationalists regard truth as whatever can be autonomously reasoned and scientifically established, emotivists reduce truth to subjective choices for one's own autonomous self-construction, ignoring the freeing power of limits.

> The worship of will is the negation of will. To admire mere choice is to refuse to choose. . . . Every act of will is an act of self-limitation. To desire action is to desire limitation. In that sense every act is an act of self-sacrifice. When you choose anything, you reject everything else. . . . Every act is an irrevocable selection and exclusion. Just as when you marry one woman you give up all others, so when you take one course of action you give up all the other courses . . . Art is limitation; the essence of every picture is the frame. . . . The moment you step into the world of facts, you step into a world of limits. You can free things from alien or accidental laws, but not from the laws of their own nature. You may, if you like, free a tiger from his bars;

---

9. Chesterton was virtually a lone voice crying in the wilderness of modern eugenics fashionably advocated by such figures as Winston Churchill and Oliver Wendell Holmes, Shaw and Wells and Virginia Woolf. One of the first acts of Hitler's new regime in 1933 was to promulgate a Eugenic Sterilization Law, ordering doctors to sterilize those who were allegedly afflicted with hereditary diseases. In 1934, only two years before his death, Chesterton thundered against such evils in "The Fallacy of Eugenics," in *Avowals and Denials* (London: Methuen, 1934).

10. Alasdair MacIntyre, *After Virtue*, 2nd ed. (Notre Dame: University of Notre Dame Press, 1984): 11–12, emphasis in original.

but do not free him from his stripes. Do not free a camel from the burden of his hump: you may be freeing him from being a camel. (O, 44–45)

Such dehumanizing emotivism, Chesterton warns, will produce a people too intellectually meek "even to claim their inheritance." They will become so suspicious of large truth-claims that they will be dubious about even the smallest. Their lunacy, Chesterton declares, may be defined "as using mental activity so as to reach mental helplessness." "We are on the road," he wittily and alarmingly concludes, "to producing a race of men too mentally modest to believe in the multiplication table." "Swords will be drawn," he prophesies, "to prove that leaves are green in summer."[11] If scientific physicalists are filled with a mad, overweening presumption that they can know and control everything, then lunatic emotivists are imbued with a pseudo-modesty that everything is so subjective and relativized that they can know nothing for certain.

Chesterton saw it all coming already with the publication of *Orthodoxy* in 1908. Scientific rationalism gone mad is an apt description of what eventually happened to the Enlightenment project, while a deranged emotivism, in its denial of objective truth and its exaltation of arbitrary will, is an apt description of our post-Enlightenment culture.

ART AS THE SIGNATURE OF MAN

Chesterton was among the first to decry the immoral uses to which Darwinism was being put. Survival-of-the-fittest capitalists favored the competitive strong over the unambitious weak, while eugenicizing socialists sought to improve the species by eliminating the mentally inferior. As a result, Chesterton came to be deeply suspicious of monocausal evolution as a sufficient explanation for the uniqueness of the human species. To embrace natural selection based solely on efficient causes alone, he came to believe, is to affirm that *homo sapiens* differ from anthropoids only in continuous degree, not in discontinuous kind. Though the emergence of a distinctively human species may be glacially gradual, this hardly denies its uniqueness: "Evolutionists cannot drive us, because of the nameless gradation in Nature, to deny the personality of God, for a personal God might as well work by gradations as in any other way; but they do drive themselves, through those gradations, to deny the existence of a personal Mr. Jones, because he is within the scope of evolution and his edges are rubbed away."[12]

"Man is the ape upside down," Chesterton trumpeted. As superprimates

11. G. K. Chesterton, *Heretics* (New York: Lane, 1905): 305.
12. G. K. Chesterton, *Lunacy and Letters*, ed. Dorothy Collins (New York: Sheed & Ward, 1958), 192.

who are also subangels, our human kind does not look down at the ground like the other beasts. We are *anthropoi*, the upward-looking creatures who seek transcendent beauty and truth and goodness. We live and move and have our being as the other animals do not—namely, as siblings of nature rather than her children:

> The essence of all pantheism, evolutionism and modern cosmic religion is really in this proposition: that Nature is our mother. Unfortunately, if you regard Nature as a mother, you discover that she is a stepmother. The main point of Christianity [is] this: that Nature is not our mother: Nature is our sister. We can be proud of her beauty, since we have the same father. . . . This gives to the typically Christian pleasure in this earth a strange touch of lightness that is almost frivolity. Nature was a solemn mother to worshippers of Isis and Cybele. Nature was a solemn mother to Wordsworth or to Emerson. But Nature is not solemn to St. Francis or George Herbert. To St. Francis, Nature is a sister, even a younger sister: a little, dancing sister, to be laughed at as well as loved. (O, 119)

Unless there is a fundamental distinction between our species and the other animals, we have little reason to regard humans as anything *other* than beasts with big brains, having no unique dignity and worth—indeed, having little reason even to treat beasts humanely. Hence Chesterton's embrace of a much more modest kind of evolution: "If evolution simply means that a positive thing called an ape turned very slowly into a positive thing called a man, then it is stingless for most orthodox [believers]; for a personal God might just as well do things slowly than quickly, especially if, like the Christian God, *he were outside time*" (O, 39–40, emphasis added). It follows that, for Chesterton, humans are best understood as a *revolution* rather than an *evolution*—creatures who do not fold smoothly into the world's fluid processes, but who protrude from the rest of creation as the queerest of all creatures, a monstrosity.

Chesterton defines the particular nature of human uniqueness in *The Everlasting Man*. It is his single most important work of apologetics. C. S. Lewis said the book "baptized" his intellect as the work of George MacDonald had baptized his imagination. In a 1950 letter to Sheldon Vanauken, Lewis called it "the best popular apologetic I know."[13] Whereas Chesterton wrote *Orthodoxy* to explain how he returned to the faith by overcoming the twin insanities of hyper-rationalism and hyper-subjectivism, he penned *The Everlasting Man*, at least in part, to rebut H. G. Wells's *Outline of History*. There Wells had portrayed

---

13. Sheldon Vanauken, *A Severe Mercy* (New York: Harper & Row, 1977): 90.

human existence as an unbroken chain of progress from primitive animal dependence to modern scientific autonomy. The seamless forward movement of history would soon slough off religious belief as a useless appendage, Wells predicted, thus proving humans to be entirely self-sufficient beings.

Working seventeen years after the publication of *Orthodoxy*, Chesterton in *The Everlasting Man* resorts less to fantastic paradoxes than to careful arguments about human uniqueness. He locates it in the Paleolithic cave paintings of southwestern France. While it was natural for primitive people to draw pictures of animals, Chesterton argues, it is impossible to conceive of even the most intelligent monkeys drawing pictures of people. Almost from the beginning, man exhibited the remarkable fact that "he [is] a creator as well as a creature.... [S]omehow or other a new thing had appeared in the cavernous night of nature, a mind that is like a mirror because it is truly a thing of reflection. It is like a mirror because in it alone all the other shapes can be seen like shining shadows in a vision. Above all, it is like a mirror because it is the only thing of its kind.... Man is the microcosm; man is the measure of all things; man is the image of God."[14]

The emergence of this creative creature is unaccountable in scientific or historical terms: "It was not and it was; we know not in what instant or in what infinity of years. Something happened, and it has all the appearance of being a transaction outside time."[15] Only in humanity is there to be found anything akin to reflexive self-consciousness, the ability to stand outside ourselves, to behold ourselves as in a looking-glass, and thus to depict the nonhuman world as having its own existence, as something else than ourselves, something radically other. "Man's encounter with himself is always reflected in his portrayal of something else."[16] Hence Chesterton's lapidary claim: "Art is the signature of man."[17] Our species is *homo poetica*—humans are artists, makers, fabricators of secondary things for the sake of their beauty rather than their utility alone. Termites build magnificent mounds of magnificent intricacy but, so far as we know, they do not look upon their creations so as to declare, "And it was very good." Nor do termites regret what they have made, so as to be grieved in their hearts. Their making is strictly functional (or else nonfunctional).

Human *poesis* is of an entirely different order. Aquinas (who learned it from the Peripatetics and Aristotle) taught Chesterton that, as with the other animals, truth is rooted in our sensate perception and discovery of what is.

14. G. K. Chesterton, *The Everlasting Man* (New York: Doubleday Image, 1955; originally published 1925), 36. All further references to this work will be indicated as *EM*.

15. Chesterton, *EM*, 39. "[A] transition had occurred to which bones and stones cannot in their nature bear witness; and man became a living soul" (EM, 53).

16. Wills, *Chesterton*, 190.

17. Chesterton, *EM*, 34.

Hence the ancient motto: "Nothing is in the intellect that was not first in the senses." Yet the imagination breaks down the sense impressions received from the natural realm and reshapes them into newly perceived unities that amount to new worlds of meaning and significance. Humans, as the imaginative poets of the world attest, spiritualize material things while also giving material images and sounds to spiritual things. Without embarrassment, therefore, Chesterton embraces the dialectical character of the mind-world, grace-nature relation. God is not a solo performer but a symphonic conductor. He creates and re-creates his cosmos *with the free involvement of his creatures*. And when the fallen mind becomes unresponsive to the sheer givenness of the creation, it becomes the poet's task to reenchant the world by making it strange, fantastic, grotesque. Chesterton's work is rife with staggering surprises, burlesque chases and escapes, but also with nightmarish visions of evil. Chesterton has repeated recourse to mime and farce, to things eccentric and out of kilter; not for him the strict balance and harmony and proportion of classical aesthetics. But never does he resort to the outré for its own sake, never gratuitously, but always for a larger and deeper vision. Alison Milbank cites both Thomas Aquinas and Dionysus the Pseudo-Areopagite to explain Chesterton's desire to show how everything is signaling wildly to indicate its divine origin and final destiny. They both argue "that it is more appropriate for God to be presented by metaphors of a lower and bodily order than higher ones, 'for what He is not is clearer to us than what He is', and so 'similitudes drawn from things farthest away from God form within us a truer estimate that God is above whatsoever we may say or think of Him.'"[18]

In this reshaping of the world as the senses register it, the imagination does not abandon objective reality. On the contrary, there is a huge difference between the objective *vision* that discerns the strange otherness of things as over against the subjective *dream* that displaces the inexhaustibly interesting world with its own feverish phantasms:

> That strangeness of things, which is the light in all poetry, and indeed in all art, is really connected with their otherness; or what is called their objectivity. What is subjective must be stale. . . . [T]he selfish artist . . . shrinks from the world and lives only in his own mind. According to St. Thomas, the mind acts freely of itself, but its freedom exactly consists in finding a way out to liberty and the light of day; to reality and the land of the living. In the subjectivist, the pressure of the world forces the imagination

---

18. Alison Milbank, *Chesterton and Tolkien as Theologians: The Fantasy of the Real* (London: T&T Clark, 2007): 67.

inward. According to St. Thomas, . . . the energy of the mind forces the imagination outwards, but because the images it seeks are real things. All their romance and glamour, so to speak, lies in the fact that they are real things; things not to be found by staring inwards at the mind. The flower is a vision because it is not only a vision. Or, if you will, it is a vision because it is not a dream. This is for the poet the strangeness of stones and trees and solid things; they are strange because they are solid. . . . According to Aquinas, the object becomes a part of the mind; nay, according to Aquinas, the mind actually becomes the object. But . . . it only becomes the object and does not create the object. In other words, the object is an object; it can and does exist outside the mind, or in the absence of the mind. And *therefore* it enlarges the mind of which it becomes a part.[19]

For Chesterton the imaginative apologist, the world is teeming with analogies and metaphors, with narratives and rhymes, with images and patterns by which we creatively identify and participate in reality. Humans stand at the apex of God's good creation because of the mind's poetic powers of making and unmaking. This means that everyone is a poet. We are all engaged in the creative fulfillment or frustration of our divine potential. Everyone is participating, well or ill, in the divine reality. By extension, so are nations and peoples and cultures all engaged in *poesis*, whether for the enrichment or impoverishment of the human condition. This was the breakthrough insight Chesterton had discerned already in 1908 with the publication of *Orthodoxy*: "This is not a world, but rather the materials for a world. God has given us not so much the colours of a picture as the colours of a palette. But He has also given us a subject, a model, a fixed vision. We must be clear about what we want to paint. This adds a further principle to our previous list of principles. We have said we must be fond of this world, even in order to change it. We now add that we must be fond of another world (real or imaginary) in order to have something to change it to."[20]

Lest one fear that this "fixed vision" requires nothing more than the discernment of timeless and placeless patterns or shapes—so as to squeeze the complex and contingent things of the world into them, Procrustean fashion—Chesterton makes exactly the opposite case. The universe is an overflowing cornucopia of the divine presence that pushes the blooming buzzing potential of everything outward toward its ultimate fulfillment beyond the walls of the world. There is

---

19. G. K. Chesterton, *Saint Thomas Aquinas: The Dumb Ox* (New York: Doubleday Image, 1956; first published 1933): 184. Emphasis in the original.
20. Chesterton, *Orthodoxy*, 112.

not a dearth but an excess of meaning that prompts imaginative activity wherein true life consists:

> The *deceitfulness* of things which has had so sad an effect on so many sages, has almost a contrary effect on this sage [St. Thomas]. If things deceive us, it is by being more real than they seem. As ends in themselves they always deceive us; but as things tending to a greater end, they are even more real than we think them. If they seem to have a relative unreality (so to speak) it is because they are potential and not actual; they are unfulfilled, like packets of seeds or boxes of fireworks. They have it in them to be more real than they are. And there is an upper world of what the Schoolman called Fruition, or Fulfillment, in which all this relative relativity becomes actuality; in which the trees burst into flower or the rockets into flame.[21]

For those who learn to view the world through the prism of the Christian imagination, the world constitutes a gigantic allegory revealing how the super- natural works with "unspeakable energy" in the natural, thereby inviting our own poetic naming and enjoyment of it:

> I am sitting under tall trees, with a great wind boiling like surf about the tops of them, so that their living load of leaves rocks and roars in something that is at once exultation and agony. I feel, in fact, as if I were actually sit- ting at the bottom of the sea among mere anchors and ropes, while over my head and over the green twilight of water sounded the everlasting rush of waves and the toil and crash and shipwreck of tremendous ships. The wind tugs at the trees as if it might pluck them root and all out of the earth like tufts of grass. Or, to try yet another desperate figure of speech for this unspeakable energy, the trees are straining and tearing and lashing as if they were a tribe of dragons each tied by the tail. . . .
>
> In [this] little apologue or parable . . . the trees stand for all visible things and the wind for the invisible. The wind is the spirit which bloweth where it listeth; the trees are the material things of the world which are blown where the spirit lists. The wind is philosophy, religion, revolution; the trees are cities and civilisations. We only know that there is a wind because the trees on some distant hill suddenly go mad. . . .
>
> The wind is up above the world before a twig on the tree has moved. So there must always be a battle in the sky before there is a battle on the

---

21. Ibid., 180–81. Emphasis in the original.

earth. Since it is lawful to pray for the coming of the kingdom, it is lawful also to pray for the coming of the revolution that shall restore the kingdom. It is lawful to hope to hear the wind of Heaven in the trees. It is lawful to pray "Thine anger come on earth as it is in Heaven."[22]

In this final claim, Chesterton reveals that he is not a vitalist or a naturalist wanting his readers to join G. B. Shaw in celebrating the transmoral power of the Life Force. On the contrary, he was driven to acknowledge, not an impersonal Unmoved Mover, but a personal Presence acting both within and beyond the universe. The very givenness of creation implies a Creator. That the world has meaning implies someone who "means" it. Hence Chesterton's astonished confession: "There was something personal in the world, as in a work of art; whatever it meant it meant violently."[23] Although this personal Presence bids humans to participate freely as coworkers in making things more real than they seem to be, we can also refuse such wondrous liberty. Such refusal is the source of evil— i.e., the making of things hideously ugly and massively destructive, whether at the personal or political level. We can, alas, unmake the world; we can unweave the rainbow, as Keats said. Though the gifts of life are graciously given, they can just as readily be taken away.

The anonymous authors of certain primordial myths and ancient folk stories grasped the moral character of the universe. They discerned that one can enjoy the unexampled gift of natural and human existence only by way of obedient gratitude. "In the fairytale an incomprehensible happiness rests upon an incomprehensible condition. A box is opened, and all evils fly out. A word is forgotten, and cities perish. A lamp is lit, and love flies away. A flower is plucked, and human lives are forfeited. An apple is eaten, and the hope of God is gone."[24] As in the story of paradisal Eden, all good and perfect gifts are radically contingent; they depend on a proper response. Chesterton calls it the "condition of joy."

To live with obedient wonder and grateful joy is the ultimate act of poetic freedom. It enables us to order our loves and to govern our desires so that our choices eventually become our habits—our convictions having chosen us rather than the other way around. The ultimately free decision, Chesterton, the master of paradox declares, is "the liberty to bind myself."[25] Discipline and fidelity, oaths and obligations, are means rather than obstacles to joy. The making and keeping of promises, especially in marriage, provide the key to happiness. "Love is

22. G. K. Chesterton, *Tremendous Trifles* (London: Methuen, 1909): 104.
23. Chesterton, *Orthodoxy*, 70.
24. Chesterton, *Orthodoxy*, 61.
25. Ibid., 130.

not blind," Chesterton alliteratively observes. "Love is bound; and the more it is bound the less it is blind."[26] Morality is like art, we have heard him saying: it consists in drawing a line. The frame is the most important part of a picture. In humbly embraced limits, not in braggart will-to-power, lies true liberty. To receive such beneficent gifts entails not blind obedience but the right kind of thoughtfulness. "I would maintain that thanks are the highest form of thought," Chesterton argues, "and that gratitude is happiness doubled by wonder."[27] Such gratefulness should be given not only for obvious goods but also for ordinary things that should not be taken for granted: "The test of all happiness is gratitude. . . . Children are grateful when Santa Claus puts in their stockings gifts of toys or sweets. Could I not be grateful to Santa Claus when he put in my stockings the gift of two miraculous legs? We thank people for birthday presents of cigars and slippers. Can I thank no one for the birthday present of birth?"[28]

Thus was Chesterton's poetic apologetics already fledged in his twenty-fifth year, 1901: "The function of the imagination is not to make strange things settled, so much as to make settled things strange; not so much to make wonders facts as to make facts wonders."[29]

THE DIVINE IRRUPTION INTO THE HUMAN SPHERE

Though Chesterton is wearing Christian lenses, he is working within what is usually called natural theology; i.e., evidence for God as it is discerned apart from divine self-disclosure in Israel and Christ and the Church. One need not be a Christian to embrace his argument that modernity is not godless so much as deranged and that true sanity is to be found in a radical sense of human distinctiveness exhibited in artistic and moral works of the imagination. "Pessimism does not consist in being tired of evil," Chesterton declares, "but in being tired of good. Despair does not lie in being weary of suffering, but in being weary of joy."[30] Yet what happens when people become jaded with joy, saddened by sanity? Such was the condition of late antiquity, Chesterton argues. Hence the second and most drastic feature of Chesterton's apologetics: his conviction that, just as the creature who bears the image of God disrupts the system of nature, so in a second and final act God disrupts the sheer successiveness of history—the repetitious rise and fall of nations and empires, even civilizations—by becoming the everlasting Man with an everlasting Body.

---

26. Ibid., 76.
27. G. K. Chesterton, *A Short History of England* (London: Chatto & Windus, 1930; first published 1917): 59.
28. Chesterton, *Orthodoxy*, 60.
29. G. K. Chesterton, *The Defendant* (London: Dent & Sons, 1940; first published 1901), 84.
30. Chesterton, *EM*, 158.

What had first been born in a Paleolithic cave—the truth that man is the uniquely imaginative being—is now reborn in an even more obscure cave, the cattle shelter outside the village of Bethlehem. There extremes meet and the whole universe is turned upside down:

> All the eyes of wonder and worship which had been turned outwards to the largest thing were now turned inward to the smallest. . . . God who had been only a circumference was seen as a centre; and a centre is infinitely small. It is true that the spiritual spiral henceforward works inwards instead of outwards, and in that sense is centripetal and not centrifugal. The faith becomes, in more ways than one, a religion of little things. . . .
>
> It is not only true that such a subterranean chamber was a hiding-place from enemies; and that the enemies were already scouring the stony plain that lay above it like a sky. It is not only that the very horse-hoofs of Herod might in that sense have passed like thunder over the sunken head of Christ. It is also that there is in that image a true idea of an outpost, of a piercing through the rock and an entrance into an enemy territory. There is in this buried divinity an idea of undermining the world; of shaking the towers and palaces from below; even as Herod the great king felt that earthquake under him and swayed with his swaying palace.[31]

Christ brings not only the peace of unity and concord but also the sword of division and strife. Christianity is a fighting faith, as Chesterton never wearied of iterating. "Before Abraham was, I am" is not the confession of a platitudinous ethical teacher; it is an offensive saying, a scandalous claim made by One who speaks with ultimate Authority. So are the moral demands of Jesus truly impossible of human fulfillment, except that his followers are summoned and enabled to exceed the limits of the merely human. Such scandalous claims and commands made the early church intolerable; "and in a sense it is true to say that it was intolerable because it was intolerant. It was resented, because, in its own still and almost secret way, it had declared war. It had risen out of the Ground to wreck the heaven and earth of heathenism. It did not try to destroy all that creation of gold and marble [found in ancient Rome]; but it contemplated a world without it."[32] Garry Wills capitulates the matter clearly: "Christ among men is a paradox more absolute than the first mystery of man among the brutes. . . . Christ stands at the crossroads of man's life. He creates the crossroads, for before

---

31. Ibid., 184.
32. Ibid., 184–85.

him the different strata could not even conflict. To the philosophers he is the Logos, to the shepherds he is the Shepherd, to the demons he is an exorcist, to the monotheists he is the one God, to the poets he is one of the Persons who must exist in the highest activity of Love: to all men an absolute answer or a living blasphemy."[33]

This means that Christians are not delivered from the circumambient darkness into a world of heavenly light; they are swept up into the continuing action of Christ's life as it is manifest in history through his unique People. Chesterton is no religious pluralist. He does not regard Christianity as one option among many. "The Church contains what the world does not contain. Life itself does not provide as [the Church] does for all sides of life."[34] Yet neither is Chesterton a Christian triumphalist wanting the Church to trample its opponents with cocksure answers to serious questions. He is careful, therefore, to distinguish between the *ecclesia militans* and the *ecclesia triumphans*. The struggling, fighting church will always be the sinful and failing church, one characterized by fits and starts, by devastating mistakes and defeats that are answered only by temporary corrections and victories, before its final triumph "beyond the walls of the world," as Tolkien said. Assured that the gates of hell shall not prevail against the coming of the kingdom, the church remains the one thing that will stand when all else falls. Thus does Evan McIan the Catholic confess this Fact to his atheist interlocutor James Turnbull in *The Ball and the Cross*:

> "The Church is not a thing like the Athenaeum Club," [MacIan] cried. "If the Atheaeum Club lost all its members, the Atheaeum Club would cease to exist. But when we belong to the Church we belong to something which is outside all of us; which is outside everything you [Turnbull] talk about, outside [even] the Cardinals and the Pope. They belong to it, but it does not belong to them. If we all fell dead suddenly, the Church would still somehow exist in God. Confound it all, don't you see that I am more sure of its existence than I am of my own existence?"[35]

McIan also confesses, in a stunning paradox, that the Cross is the only thing that can never be defeated. Why? Because it is defeat itself. As the Orthodox liturgy declares, "By death he has trampled down death." Christians win by losing—losing the right battles for the right reasons at the right times and by the right means—namely, by wielding the instrument of suffering-unto-death that

33. Wills, *Chesterton*, 196–7.
34. Chesterton, *EM*, 180.
35. G. K. Chesterton, *The Ball and the Cross* (Mineola, NY: Dover, 1995; first published 1909), 38.

transforms sinners into saints. Hence Chesterton's insistence that the church should be

> . . . defined as an enormous private detective, correcting that official detective—the State. . . . The Church did, in an evil hour, consent to imitate the commonwealth and employ cruelty. But if we open our eyes and take in the whole picture, if we look at the general shape and colour of the thing, the real difference between the Church and the State is huge and plain. The State, in all lands and ages, has created a machinery of punishment, more bloody and brutal in some places than others, but bloody and brutal everywhere. The Church is the only institution that ever attempted to create a machinery of pardon. The Church is the only thing that ever attempted by system to pursue and discover crimes, not in order to avenge, but in order to forgive them. The stake and rack were merely the weaknesses of the religion; its snobberies, its surrenders to the world. Its speciality—or, if you like, its oddity—[is] this merciless mercy; the unrelenting sleuthhound who seeks to save and not slay.[36]

From having been generically Christian at the first, Chesterton became ever more distinctively Roman Catholic as he grew older. This on-going conversion meant no narrowing of his vision. The wideness of Chesterton's apologetics becomes evident in one of his last books, *Christendom in Dublin*, a short account of his participation in the International Eucharistic Congress held in 1932. There he discovered that the Church is the one multilingual, multiethnic, multicultural institution. It transcends time while being grounded in history. In Dublin, Chesterton heard the awakening cry that shatters the brazen silence of a world tossing and thrashing amid its own nightmare—a world that would soon be convulsed by a new and worse war, a war that would be global in its scope as the Great War was not. Chesterton was astonished that partisan politics played no part in this international celebration. The pageantry contained no exaltation of one nation over others. The great displays of color and light were present in the city slums no less than the thoroughfares. "It was like that celestial topsy-turvydom in which the first shall be last. . . . In that strange town [of Dublin], the poorer were the streets, the richer were the decorations." There were barely literate inscriptions and crudely drawn pictures hailing Saint Patrick and praising Christ the King. Among all the flags from all the peoples and nations of the earth, one stood out above all others: the papal pennant.

---

36. G. K. Chesterton, "The Divine Detective," http://www.online-literature.com/chesterton/2603/.

I looked again at the great gold-and-silver banner and suddenly forgot all the nonsense about national and political conquest; and the idiocy that imagines the Pope as landing on our shores with a pistol in each hand. I knew there was another Empire that has never declined nor fallen; and there rolled through the heavens of pure thought the thunder of the great Encyclicals, and the mind of the new Europe in which the new nations find that the Faith can make them free. The great flag began to flap and crackle in the freshening evening wind; and those who had been toiling on the little farm, those whose fathers had been hunted like vermin, those whose religion should have been burnt out like witchcraft, came back slowly through the twilight; walking like lords on their own land. . . . Whatever St. Dominic may have said in the irritation of the moment, I am not so sure that St. Peter has lost the power to say, "Rise and walk."[37]

Such a confession shows that Chesterton does not turn the Church into an impossible ideal, a rarefied thing so pure that it becomes more myth than reality. He roots and grounds his apologetics in the one universal community that is meant not to poison people with pride but to heal them with humility. Because the Church militant will not become the Church triumphant until the end, true freedom always lies ahead. Chesterton said it well already in 1908: "The mass of men always look backwards; . . . the only corner where they in any sense look forwards is the little continent where Christ has His Church."[38] The community of Christ casts its eye on the future, not in eschatological expectation alone, but also in the conviction that the kingdom already dwells in our midst, however sinfully and partially, as the Body of Christ. It remains the world's true revolutionary force. It constantly pushes the world forward toward a radical reordering of all human desires—at once individual and communal, both cultural and political. It alone, Chesterton believed, has the power that is not weakness, the militancy that is not militarism, the awakening cry that is not a scream of desperation, the patriotism that gathers all people to their true *patria*.

CONTRIBUTIONS TO THE FIELD OF APOLOGETICS

How are we to evaluate Chesterton's apologetics? If he were making stand-alone arguments, spun like a fascinating web out of his own genius, then we would

---

37. G. K. Chesterton, *Christendom in Dublin*, in *Collected Works of G. K. Chesterton*, Vol. 20 (San Francisco: Ignatius, 1986): 44.
38. Chesterton, *Orthodoxy*, 152.

have to admit that they are the product of his own time and culture—even if he believed them to be eternally valid. They would have relevance largely for the early decades of the twentieth century. There is considerable truth in this claim. Christians of every age must create defenses of the Faith that remain stable, at least for a while, amid the sandy soil of time. The good news is that Chesterton's imaginative apologetics break the bonds of time. They are often outlandish because the Gospel itself is outlandish. It is not obvious and predictable News but the scandalously good tidings of great joy. It turns everything upside down, much as Chesterton defined the function of paradox as truth standing on its head and waving its legs to get our attention. Though Chesterton is an enormously witty writer, he is not a mere stuntman and punster. His vision is comic in Dante's precise sense. Unlike tragedy, whose wisdom centers on death and its (often noble) consequences, comedy opens out to new life, to second chances (indeed, to seventy times the seventh), to banquets and weddings, even to heavenly feasts.

Chesterton knew well that conversions rarely come through the mind alone, that few people are argued into the Faith, and thus that even the finest apologetics serve chiefly to clear obstacles from its path. Intellectual clarity about matters doctrinal and ethical are the indispensable bases for the Christian life, but they are not the main means of conversion. Like Chesterton, converts are meant to be incorporated as actors in the divine drama by their participation in the sacramental and prophetic life of the church. Thus, is it fitting, I believe, to sketch the nature of the Christian life as Chesterton envisions it, especially in his epic poem *The Ballad of the White Horse*.

In a miraculous apparition, the Mother of God speaks to King Alfred about the fearful struggle awaiting him as he seeks to drive the invading Vikings out of England.

> "The gates of heaven are lightly locked,
> We do not guard our gold,
> Men may uproot where worlds begin,
> Or read the name of the nameless sin;
> But if he fail or if he win
> To no good man is told."[39]

To know in advance the outcome of life's battles (whether personal or cultural) would induce either despair or presumption, severing the nerve of both

39. G. K. Chesterton, *The Ballad of the White Horse*, ed. Bernadette Sheridan, IHM (Detroit: Marygrove College Press, 1993; first published 1911), 1:225–30.

faith and courage. For the "Christless chivalry" of the pagan Danes, by contrast, defeat is worse than death. The Blessed Virgin declares, by contrast, that those marked by the incarnate God's own death have no cause to fear either their earthly end or the judgment that lies beyond it. Having been marked by the emblem of suffering, and having drunk from the cup of life, they are abashed only by their insufficient service to the Crucified:

> "But the men signed of the cross of Christ
> Go gaily in the dark . . . .
> "But the men that drink the blood of God
> Go singing to their shame."[40]

The poem's central paradox lies in the sorrowful joy that enables Christians not to despair when confronting the nightmare horrors of human existence. The ballad's *leit motiv* is found in the unblinkered wisdom of the poem's most famous lines. They are twice spoken by the Queen of Heaven to Alfred the Great, King of the Saxons:

> "I tell you naught for your comfort,
> Yea, naught for your desire,
> Save that the sky grows darker yet
> And the sea rises higher."

> "Night shall be thrice over you,
> And heaven an iron cope.
> Do you have joy without cause,
> Yea, faith without a hope?"[41]

True faith and joy are not based on the promise of earthly victory or even the prospect of eventual relief from suffering. They are found, instead, in Saint Paul's praise of Abraham as the founder of God's people—the patriarch who in hope believed "against all hope" (Rom 4:18). Such supernal hope begins where all human hope ends, enabling the faithful to fare forward joyfully, without a fretful and paralyzing regard for the outcome. To create an opening to such faith and joy is the ultimate aim of G. K. Chesterton's work as an apologist of the literary imagination.[42]

---

40. Ibid., 1:233–34, 237–38.
41. Ibid., 1:254–61.
42. Portions of this article are derived from Ralph C. Wood, *Chesterton: The Nightmare Goodness of God* (Waco, TX: Baylor University Press, 2011). Used with permission.

BIBLIOGRAPHY

Brabazon, James. *Dorothy Sayers: A Biography*. New York: Scribner's & Sons, 1981.

Chesterton, G. K. *The Ball and the Cross*. Mineola, NY: Dover, 1995; first published 1909.

———. *The Ballad of the White Horse*. Ed. by Bernadette Sheridan, IHM. Detroit: Marygrove College Press, 1993; first published 1911.

———. *Christendom in Dublin*. In *The Collected Works of G. K. Chesterton*, Vol. 20. San Francisco: Ignatius, 1986.

———. "The Diabolist." In *Tremendous Trifles*. New York: Sheed & Ward, 1955; first published 1909.

———. "The Divine Detective." http://www.online-literature.com/chesterton/2603/.

———. *Everlasting Man*. New York: Doubleday, 1955; originally published 1925.

———. "The Fallacy of Eugenics." In *Avowals and Denials*. London: Methuen, 1934.

———. *Heretics*. London: Bodley Head, 1960; first published 1905.

———. *Lunacy and Letters*. Ed. by Dorothy Collins. New York: Sheed & Ward, 1958.

———. *Orthodoxy*. San Francisco: Ignatius, 1995; first published 1908.

———. *Saint Thomas: The Dumb Ox*. New York: Doubleday, 1956; first published 1933.

———. *A Short History of England*. London: Chatto & Windus, 1930; first published 1917.

Greene, Graham. *Collected Essays*. New York: Viking, 1969.

Grote, Mardy, *Viva la Repartee: Clever Comebacks and Witty Retorts from History's Great Wits and Wordsmiths*. New York: HarperCollins, 2009.

Joshi, S. T. *God's Defenders*. Amherst, NY: Prometheus, 2003.

MacIntyre, Alasdair. *After Virtue*. 2nd ed. Notre Dame: University of Notre Dame Press, 1984.

Wills, Garry. *Chesterton: Man and Mask*. New York: Sheed & Ward, 1961.

Wood, Ralph C. *Chesterton: The Nightmare Goodness of God*. Waco, TX: Baylor University Press, 2011.

DOROTHY L. SAYERS

Pursuing Truth through Stories and Patterns

AMY ORR-EWING

Well-known as a British author of detective fiction and religious plays and as translator of Dante, Dorothy L. Sayers (1893–1957) was also an insightful lay theologian and Christian apologist. She was an eloquent religious voice in her generation, articulating the Christian faith in an accessible and persuasive way. Speaking of Dorothy L. Sayers and C. S. Lewis, Regius Professor of Divinity at the University of Oxford Canon Oliver Quick wrote to Archbishop William Temple in 1943 describing them as: "The two people who seem really able to put across to ordinary people a reasonably orthodox form of Christianity."[1] Karl Barth recommended Sayers to a student, calling her one of the most "outstanding British theologians"[2] whose books he had read to help him learn English. Barth went on to translate three of Sayers's theological essays into German.[3]

HISTORICAL BACKGROUND

Dorothy Leigh Sayers was born on June 13, 1893. She was the only child of Reverend Henry Sayers and Helen Mary, and she was baptized July 15 in Oxford, at Christ Church Cathedral. Her name Dorothy means "gift of God," and Leigh was her mother's maiden name. Her father came from a long line of Church of England clergy, and Dorothy was brought up as an Anglican surrounded by the rituals and duties of the church.

While living at home and taking lessons from a governess, Dorothy made points of application between what she was learning and the material world around her. In her loosely biographical, unfinished novel *Cat O' Mary*, she described one

---

1. Private letter from Oliver Quick to William Temple, 24 July 1943; Lambeth Palace Library, William Temple Papers, vol. 39, fol. 269.
2. Unpublished letter from Arnold Ehrhardt to Sayers, September 1945: Wade DLS Letters Folder 9/9–10. Marion E. Wade Center, Wheaton College, Wheaton, Illinois.
3. Karl Barth, *Das grösste Drama aller Zeiten aus dem Englischen übersetzt und mit einem Geleitwort* (Evangelischer Verlag: Zollikon, 1959).

such incident from her own childhood through her character Katherine's words. Sayers and her governess had been searching in the old vicarage garden for the tennis court, which was completely overgrown. Sayers was able to use the geometric principles she had learned in the schoolroom to locate the hidden tennis court in the unkempt garden. She reflected through her character Katherine: "If the court had not been precisely laid out in the first instance, she might have had more difficulty, but the corner being accurately placed, the laws of geometry held good. In her heart of hearts Katherine was awe-stricken. To see a prophecy made on paper fulfilled on the back lawn is a very enlarging experience."[4]

This was part of a philosophical awakening for Sayers as she recognized that a preexisting pattern was being revealed in the specifics of life. The mundane lines of a tennis court took on a symbolic importance since the experience of applying geometry to everyday life showed that there was an intrinsic coherence to reality. An observation of ultimate truth being revealed in the specifics of day-to-day life was, for Sayers, a religious experience, a glimpse of divine beauty in the overall pattern itself as well as in the particulars of the given instance: "She had been brought face to face with beauty. It had risen up before her again—the lovely, satisfying unity of things: the wedding of the thing learnt with the thing done: the great intellectual fulfillment . . . nothing would ever quite wipe out the memory of that magnificent moment when the intersecting circles marched out of the page of the Euclid book and met on the green grass in the sun-flecked shadow of the mulberry tree."[5]

Sayers was a deeply intellectual young person, and this interest in the pattern and coherence of reality was already emerging from the root of her adolescent Christian faith.

Sayers attended Godolphin School as a teenager and left willingly when a serious illness caused her to return home in December 1911. After a significant few months of recuperation, during which she pursued private study with a tutor, Sayers won the highly prized Gilchrist Scholarship and studied modern languages at Somerville College, Oxford, in October 1912. Sayers flourished both academically and socially at Oxford, earning a first class degree and interacting with friends of differing religious and philosophical viewpoints.

In June 1915 Sayers sat for her final examinations at Oxford in French honors, specializing in the medieval period, and was awarded the highest grade possible—a "first." At the time, women at Oxford were granted only a "title to

---

4. Dorothy L. Sayers, "Cat O' Mary" in Barbara Reynolds, ed., *Dorothy L. Sayers Child and Woman of Her Time Volume Five: A Supplement to the Letters of Dorothy L. Sayers* (Cambridge: The Dorothy L. Sayers Society: Carole Green Publishing, 2002), 67.

5. Ibid.

a degree" rather than the honor of the degree itself, but this detail was settled in 1920 when Dorothy L. Sayers was among the first group of women upon whom an Oxford degree was officially conferred.

In May 1922, having applied for various jobs, Sayers secured a full-time position at S. H. Benson's advertising agency as a copywriter. She was grateful for the steady work, and she worked at Benson's for the following nine years while continuing to write her detective novels. Sayers had a gift for communicating with the general public and coined such slogans as "My Goodness My Guinness!" and "It pays to advertise!" The experience of working in a professional advertising agency focused on communicating with the general public in a persuasive and memorable way laid foundations of skills and insights in Sayers that she would draw on in her later popular and Christian apologetic writing, which enjoyed mass appeal.

In 1923 her first detective novel, *Whose Body*, was finally published, with her second book, *Clouds of Witnesses*, ready and waiting in the pipeline. But despite her success, this era proved to be both personally and spiritually challenging for Sayers. Sayers fell in love with the Bloomsbury set writer John Cournos. He wanted to have a sexual relationship with her outside of marriage using contraception. Sayers hoped not only to marry the man she loved but also to bear his children, and as a committed Anglican, her conscience would not allow her to use contraception. Cournos was adamant that he would never marry or have any children, which eventually caused their separation.

Sayers began a short-lived relationship with a motorbike mechanic, and because she neither loved him nor had any desire to bear his children, in her despair she did consent to using contraception. But she became pregnant and had a son. Her misery was compounded upon discovering months later that Cournos had gone to America, gotten married, and now had a child with his new wife. Sayers continued to work at Benson's, hiding the pregnancy with loose clothing. She sought to protect her parents from any scandal or disappointment: "They know nothing about it at home, and they must know nothing. It would grieve them quite unnecessarily."[6] She wanted to shield her son as well: "Whoever suffers over this business I'm quite clear it mustn't be John Anthony."[7] On January 3, 1923, Sayers gave birth, in secrecy, to a son whom she named John Anthony. She had arranged for her cousin Ivy, a professional foster mother, to take the child in.

Sayers suffered a good deal, not only emotionally, because of the strain of secrecy, but also professionally, because of her fear of exposure. Her reputation as a theological thinker might well have risen considerably during the 1940s and 50s

---

6. Dorothy L. Sayers letter to Ivy Shrimpton, 6 February 1924, in Reynolds, *Letters Volume One*, 210.
7. Dorothy L. Sayers letter to Ivy Shrimpton, late February 1924, in Reynolds, *Letters Volume One*, 211.

had it not been for the residual problem of having to keep her son's existence secret. Indeed, in 1943, upon the success of her religious play, *The Man Born to be King*, Archbishop of Canterbury William Temple wrote to Sayers offering to confer upon her a Lambeth doctorate of divinity, given the religious impact of her work. When Sayers received the offer, she was reluctant to accept: "Your Grace, Thank you very much indeed for the great honour you do me. I find it very difficult to reply as I ought, because I am extremely conscious that I don't deserve it. . . . A degree in Divinity is not, I suppose, intended as a certificate of sanctity, exactly; but I should feel better about it if I were a more convincing kind of Christian. . . . I shouldn't like your first woman D. D. to create scandal, or give reviewers cause to blaspheme."[8]

Having asked for some time to think the matter over, Sayers decided not to accept the DD.

She believed that any perception that she held an ecclesiastical position could undermine her effectiveness as a popular Christian apologist since her identification as a public intellectual or as a writer predisposed the public to make no assumption about her religion, meaning that her opinion might hold more sway with them. In reality, it seems likely that the underlying reason for rejecting the honor was a fear of the scandal of her illegitimate son being made known and bringing the church and the archbishop into disrepute.

In the intervening years, Sayers completed twelve detective novels, through which she attained personal financial independence. In April 1926 she married a divorced journalist named Atherton Fleming, commonly referred to as "Mac." He was at first a congenial, supportive husband, but his physical and mental health gradually deteriorated to the point that living with him placed Sayers under enormous strain. But with the financial independence gained from her career as a bestselling novelist, Sayers focused her energies from the late 1930s to the 1950s on Christian theology and apologetics through writing and broadcasting. She wrote plays, essays, articles, theological books such as *The Mind of the Maker* and *Creed or Chaos*, and she translated Dante's work from Italian into English.

THEOLOGICAL CONTEXT AND APOLOGETICAL RESPONSE

REALITY OF TRUTH

Although truth was central to Sayers's thought, alongside the cultural and intellectual challenges facing Christianity in the mid-twentieth century, the word

---

8. Dorothy L. Sayers letter to the Archbishop of Canterbury, 7 September 1943, in Barbara Reynolds, ed., *The Letters of Dorothy L. Sayers Volume Two 1937–1943: From Novelist to Playwright* (Cambridge: The Dorothy L. Sayers Society: Carole Green Publishing, 1997), 429.

became multilayered in its meaning. In her work as a creative writer, Sayers envisaged truth as that which the artist imagines and communicates when producing work that explores the unity of apparently disparate concepts: "The associative values of words, which make them such bad tools for the scientist, make them the right tools for the poet, for they facilitate the establishment of similarities between many widely differing concepts, and so make easy the task of the creative imagination building up its poetic truths."[9]

According to Sayers, truth was that which all genuine artistic endeavors reached for and revealed: "When we read the poem, or see the play or picture or hear the music it is as though a light were turned on inside us. We say: 'ah! I recognise that! That is something which I obscurely felt to be going on in and about me, but I didn't know what it was and couldn't express it' . . . This recognition of the truth that we get in the artist's work comes to us as a revelation of a new truth."[10]

Sayers viewed truth as critically important in the life of the writer because it was a concept that encapsulated the goal of all artistic creation.[11]

But Sayers, the theological thinker, also realized that truth could mean something slightly different. Her ideas of truth were not merely literary and creative; she had a theologically informed set of ideas about God and Christ that undergirded her understanding of the nature of truth. Ideas about Christ as "the truth" were not a narrow observation in Sayers's work—she believed they had universal purchase: "If Christ is the eternal truth, His coming should fulfil, not merely the Jewish prophecies but all prophecies—all the religious intuitions of man."[12] But this did not mean she understood religious truth as being "plural." In fact, Sayers contended that the truth about Christ made contradictory religious beliefs "incompatible." She argued that Jesus Christ is completely in his own Person, "wholly and uniquely God." She believed this was fundamental to the Christian faith and wished to see a return from nominal moralism to Christ-centered creedal Christianity. And she argued that any religious system that was otherwise founded would be completely alien from Christianity and "incompatible with it."[13]

---

9. Dorothy L. Sayers letter to the Archbishop of Canterbury, 24 September 1943, in Reynolds, *Letters Volume Two*, 19.

10. Dorothy L. Sayers, "Toward a Christian Aesthetic," in V. A. Demant, ed., *Our Culture: Its Christian Roots and Present Crisis,* Edward Alleyn Lectures 1944 (London: SPCK, 1944), 60–61.

11. She wrote: "The only thing that matters about a writer is whether he is qualified to deal with the subject or not, and whether what he says is false or true" Dorothy L. Sayers, *Begin Here* (London: Gollancz, 1940), 117.

12. Dorothy L. Sayers, "Worship in the Anglican Church," a lecture to the North London Presbyterian Fellowship of Youth at Regent Square Church on January 10, 1942, in *SEVEN: An Anglo-American Literary Review* 12 (1995): 31–48.

13. Dorothy L. Sayers, "Problems of Religious Broadcasting," *BBC Quarterly* (1947): 29–31.

Truth, for Sayers, was ultimately grounded in the person of Christ and was not contingent on individuals or communities affirming it; rather, it stood regardless of who recognized it. Sayers believed that faith and "truth" sometimes ran counter to an individual's personal preferences: "Faith is not primarily 'a comfort,' but a truth about ourselves. What we believe is not necessarily the theory we most desire or admire. It is the thing which, consciously or unconsciously, we take for granted and act on."[14] Sayers's convictions about Christ were founded, in part, in her belief that truth has historical dimensions: "That our vague dreams of a God in human form, dying and resurrected are true too—the thing did happen—it has an actual date in history."[15]

In her essay "A Vote of Thanks to Cyrus," Sayers described her surprise at realizing as a child that there was a continuity between the religious sphere and history. She concluded that "history was all of a piece and the Bible was part of it."[16] It mattered to Sayers that Christ came at a particular point in history: "In most theologies, the god is supposed to have suffered and died in some remote and mythical period of pre-history. The Christian story, on the other hand, starts briskly in St Matthew's account with a place and a date."[17]

Sayer's belief was in stark contrast with the theological legacy of the historical-critical movement, which called into question the connection between the Jesus of history and the Christ of faith. The movement to demythologize the historical Jesus is exemplified in the writings of David Friedrich Strauss's *Life of Jesus Critically Examined* and Ernest Renan's *Vie de Jésus*.[18] N. T. Wright comments that such theology offered "the world the pale and timeless Galilean,"[19] which was precisely the portrait of Jesus in the popular imagination that Sayers rejected with her insistence on the coalescence of the New Testament and what she regarded as historical truth.

Yet Sayers also sought to ground her ideas of the "truth" more broadly by trying to interact with the world of science. She wrote, "To the Scientist . . . Reason is valid and your methods are valid so far as they go. God is Truth, and any truth is God's truth; there is nothing irrational about God. But you must not try to make scientific tools do something they aren't fitted to do. It won't tell you about origin or purpose."[20]

14. Dorothy L. Sayers, "What Do We Believe?" in *Unpopular Opinions* (London: Gollancz, 1946), 17–18.
15. Dorothy L. Sayers, "Viewpoints of Various Worldviews" (Date unknown) Wade Center, Illinois. MS-471, 4.
16. Ibid., 24.
17. Dorothy L. Sayers, "The Greatest Drama Ever Staged" in *Creed or Chaos?* (London: Methuen, 1947), 2.
18. David Friedrich Strauss, *Life of Jesus Critically Examined* (New York: Blanchard, 1860), Ernest Renan, *Vie de Jésus* (New York: Modern Library, 1927) originally published, 1863.
19. N. T. Wright, *Jesus and the Victory of God* (London: SPCK, 1996), 18.
20. Sayers, "Viewpoints of Various Worldviews" MS-471, 5.

Sayers saw no conflict between "God's truth" and science.[21] In fact, she saw scientific discovery as a part of the broad landscape of truth: "One must not try to bolster up theological truth by denying or falsifying scientific truth and conversely: one must not try to bolster up scientific truth by denying or falsifying theological truth. There is only one truth in which all truths are unified."[22] Sayers claimed that science could provide evidence for the truth of her own particular religious beliefs: "The truth of Christianity ought to be ascertainable, by scientific method, from the observation of the phenomena. So it ought—so indeed it must be, which is why argument about Christian evidence is possible."[23] She believed in objective truth and the possibility of human minds accessing such truth by means of reason and logic.

But from Sayers's point of view, communication of Christian truth with the wider general public was far more important than detailed theological debates pertaining to the precise modes of human apprehension of truth. In a letter to Reverend Dom Ralph Russell on October 28, 1941, Sayers spoke of her frustration with so-called experts in theology who were not able to communicate truth in any meaningful way to ordinary people: "They *will* treat God as an elderly invalid who might collapse from shock if suddenly intruded on by a common person. . . . One of the lay apologist's great difficulties is the difference between the technical and every-day meaning of the words in the theological vocabulary."[24]

She hoped to connect transcendental truth with the day-to-day experience of real people. When Sayers's work is examined, it becomes clear that she had a high view of the potential of human reason to lead humans to discover the truth about God. Sayers resonated more closely with Aquinas's understanding of Christian faith as fundamentally rational but not limited by or dependent on human reason.

PATTERNS IN TRUTH

Throughout her work Sayers explored the possibility of recognizing truth within overarching structures or "patterns."[25] Sayers saw the true story about

---

21. It is interesting to compare Sayers with Dooyeweerd here in his *Prologomena* in H. Dooyeweerd, *A New Critique of Theoretical Thought: The Necessary Presuppositions of Philosophy*, eds. William S. Young and David H. Freeman (Phillipsburg, NJ: P&R,1969). His grounding of the *archos* in history and communicated through revelation is unpacked in different "spheres" of knowledge, such as science. See H. Dooyeweerd, *A New Critique of Theoretical Thought: The General Theory of the Modal Spheres,* eds. H. de Jongste and David H. Freeman (Phillipsburg, NJ: P&R, 1969).

22. Dorothy L. Sayers notes for a letter in reply to Kathleen Nott's *The Emperor's Clothes*, Marion E. Wade Center, Illinois. 1954, MS-345, 8.

23. Ibid., MS-345, 9.

24. Dorothy L. Sayers unpublished letter to Rev. Dom Ralph Russell, 28 October 1941, Wade DLS Letters, 406/78, Marion E. Wade Center, Illinois.

25. Sayers, "Creative Mind," MS-50, 19.

Christ entering the world he created as the defining pattern for humanity. Sayers's desire to perceive the pattern and then to be shaped personally and creatively by it was a critical aspect of her religious outlook. Sayers asserted that a "religious person is a person who tries to shape his life in every aspect so as to fit with the purpose for which the world was made."[26]

In Sayers's mind, the individual pieces of a given question should fit together within a whole.[27] The evidence leads to a conclusion within a particular framework where apparently disparate aspects when "arranged" make sense: "Here metaphor and analogy are both appropriate and necessary—for both these processes involve the arranging of things according to some quality that the dissimilars have in common."[28] The particular framework for truth may well take the form of a story, but it could also be a dogma, creed, or picture. Pattern meant a synthesis of truth; from Sayers's perspective, it was intentional. This stemmed from her intuition that the Creator has designed things to conform to a pattern. Pattern is characterized as human creativity, and patterns reflect the divine reality: "The same pattern inheres in my work as in myself; and I also find that theologians attribute to God Himself precisely that pattern of being which I find in my work and in me."[29]

In her essay "Oedipus Simplex," Sayers explained how her concept of pattern provided an undergirding structure for creativity and meaning. The pattern was an iteration of an artist's vision and will, providing a frame of reference and coherence within which logical consequences would follow:

> We shall observe it in certain fixed points; these are the nodes of necessity, through which the lines *must* pass in order to make the pattern. The nodes are determined by the artist, but the lines are self-determined, and may take any direction they choose, subject to two limitations. . . . The will of the maker readily submits to all these modifications, since the necessity laid upon the lines to come to the nodes means that all the possible modifications can only in the end produce a conditioned necessity of their own—just as, in a game of croquet, the path of every ball, however wildly it

---

26. Sayers, "Nature of God," MS-143, 2.

27. In her detective novels, characters find themselves persuaded to believe in something as evidence is pieced together within a framework; the pattern emerges as the story unfolds. The reader of her detective fiction conversely experiences the frustration of piecemeal evidence leading us down blind alleys. In her lecture "Aristotle on Detective Fiction" delivered at Oxford, 5 March 1935, Sayers explores the detective fiction writer's need to deploy imposter narratives before the "truth" becomes clear at the denouement. Sayers appeals to Aristotelian *Paralogismos* as "the art of the false syllogism . . . The art of framing lies . . . in the right way." Sayers, *Unpopular Opinions*, 230–231.

28. Sayers, "Creative Mind," MS-50, 19.

29. Dorothy L. Sayers, "Problem Picture" in *Mind*, 172.

may diverge under the impact or a bad shot . . . is governed by the absolute external necessity imposed on both sides alike of going through the right hoops in the right order.[30]

Sayers was clear that her understanding of pattern and the ensuing coherence of reality did not necessarily imply a deterministic outlook. Even from the perspective of a human author creating works of art, Sayers assumed that logic required an author to work within the constraints of what was believable— reasonable potentialities of possibilities about the plot. She envisaged a wheel with a rim and various spokes representing the characters. As the story developed and the spokes converged on the hub, the realms of possibility for multitudinous outcomes narrowed. Nonetheless, the freedom of the author was ultimately unimpaired, the plot was not predetermined in any genuine sense. Pattern was not a straitjacket imposed on the arts. Rather, for Sayers, acknowledging pattern was to embrace intrinsic coherence while still allowing author and characters' choice. A good author would acknowledge pattern but refrain from constantly referring to it: "I would add that, in order to make a good story it is advisable to *keep* the lines veiled; otherwise one will not achieve the desired effect of inevitability combined with surprise."[31]

Pattern was an undergirding concept for Sayers, with implications reaching beyond the creative process of making art. Pattern had important theological meaning. In her article "The Triumph of Easter," Sayers introduced a section under the heading Working the Pattern Out in which she argued: "The Church asserts that there is a Mind which made the Universe, that he made it because he is the sort of Mind that takes pleasure in creation, and that if we want to know what the Mind of the Creator is, we must look at Christ." Having described what Christ is like, Sayers concluded the section with the comment, "That is the bold postulate that the Church asks us to accept, adding that if we do accept it . . . the answers to all our other problems will be found to make sense."[32] Sayers believed that accepting the Christian view of God the Creator and Christ the incarnate Son, as described in the creeds, gave one a framework, a pattern, that had exhaustive elucidatory power and thus tremendous apologetic appeal.

In her wartime talk, "The Religions Behind the Nation," broadcast to the nation by the BBC, Sayers explored this explanatory power in the context of the sociopolitical context of her era. Taking contemporary discussions of the state

---

30. Dorothy L. Sayers, *The Poetry of Search and The Poetry of Statement and other Posthumous Essays on Literature, Religion and Language* (London: Gollancz, 1963), 258.

31. Ibid., 259.

32. Dorothy L. Sayers, "The Triumph of Easter," *The Sunday Times* (April 17 1938): 10.

of the nation as her starting point, Sayers noted that it was commonly agreed in Britain that people wanted to defend "our culture," but she wanted to ask the question: "What *is* our culture?"[33] She argued that the critical point at stake in defining the culture of a nation was not the ideologies preached or the religious outlook but "the assumptions we hold in common about what is GOOD . . . the things we take so much for granted that we never argue about them at all."[34] This speech was written and broadcast in 1941 in the midst of World War II, and Sayers reflected on the things that British culture presupposed: "All men and all races possess certain rights in common, just because they are men. We take it for granted that such things as freedom, mercy, charity, truth, tolerance, justice, and peace are Good Things."[35] By contrast, Sayers pointed out that the Nazis deny such assumptions by claiming that there are "inferior races . . . and that war is more desirable than peace."[36] Although seemingly "sheer barbarism,"[37] the core of such a reaction lay two basic but widely held assumptions that "reason cannot prove and for which science can offer no evidence."[38] These assumptions were "that both our conception of the good and our human reason are really valid."[39] Sayers examined Roman, Greek, and Enlightenment thinking and concluded that "the enlightened human reason can establish almost anything except those two basic suppositions on which a human culture depends: it cannot *prove* that goodness is not an illusion, and it cannot *prove* that reason itself is not an illusion."[40] By contrast, Sayers believed that Christian dogma could provide a coherent foundation for goodness and reason.

> It [Christian dogma] asserted that the things which man had believed about right and reason from the beginning of time, were neither idle dreams nor wishful thinking, but actually and earthily true. . . . It claimed in fact . . . that man's persistent belief in goodness and reason were justified; that such was the nature of God and the true nature of man—and that Christ was there to prove it. . . . Christianity offered the actual physical fact of the Incarnation. . . . Christianity took theology out of the realm of myth and allegory, and pegged it firmly down to history. It picked up, so to speak, all the scattered ideas about God and man and the universe which

---

33. Dorothy L. Sayers, "The Religions Behind the Nation" in *The Church Looks Ahead: Broadcast Talks* (London: Faber & Faber, 1941), 67.
34. Ibid.
35. Ibid., 68.
36. Ibid., 69.
37. Ibid.
38. Ibid., 70.
39. Ibid.
40. Ibid., 72.

had been lying about like loose beads—beautiful but disconnected—and ran through them, like a string, the historical personality of the God who was made flesh.[41]

This necklace Sayers envisaged, with the string of the incarnate Christ in history pulling the beads into a coherent shape, was a pattern. The specificity of Christ in history enacted a pattern on which western civilization was built and was able to flourish. But intellectuals have sought to do away with Christ—the very string holding the beads together.

> It is the pattern of those beads on that string that is the pattern of our own civilisation and culture. We have grown accustomed to the look of it. We have spent nineteen and half centuries polishing the beads. And during that time, we have been tempted to feel that the only thing that spoils the look of them is the ugly string of Christian dogma running through them. For the last three centuries, we have been snipping the string away, strand by strand—forgetting that it was the string that made the pattern in the first place. Let us be quite clear about that. The assumptions we take for granted about right and reason, which seem to us self-evident, are not self-evident at all . . . but the evidence for them is the evidence for Christianity, and if we reject the one we automatically reject the other. What we have been trying to do for some time is to keep the Christian ethic without the connecting thread of the Christian theology—the beads without the string. We can of course, hope or imagine that the pattern will hold together of its own accord, but we have no rational warrant for supposing that it will; indeed, the witness of history contradicts that supposition.[42]

APOLOGETIC METHODOLOGY

Throughout Sayers's writing career and across different genres, Sayers's deployed methodology was to pursue truth as discovered and revealed through stories and pattern.

DETECTIVE FICTION

In Sayers's detective fiction, readers are drawn into a story and persuaded to discover the truth of a particular matter by means of evidence being pieced

---

41. Ibid., 74.
42. Ibid., 74–75.

together within an idiosyncratic pattern that makes sense, among competing explanations. Recognition of the pattern is the paradigm for discovering truth. The reader experiences the frustration of piecemeal evidence leading down blind alleys, imposter stories that do not fit the pattern and cannot lead to the truth. In Sayers's presentation of plot, evidence needed to be pieced together into a big picture. Things would not make sense outside the true story, but there was a singular pattern within which the pieces would fit and everything could be explained. This was foundational to Sayers's understanding of apologetics and the Christian story. Evidence will lead to the truth. There is a true pattern, which makes sense of the whole. When we discover this truth, all the pieces will fit together.

PLAYS

In her religious plays for stage and radio, Sayers's theological insights flowed from her observation that "the Christian faith is the most exciting drama that ever staggered the imagination of man—and the dogma is the drama."[43] Sayers saw that stories enfleshed on the stage, including the stories of the gospels, pointed to the profound truth of God's revelation of himself in history. The process of incarnating her ideas beyond words on a page through living, breathing actors underscored the deeper truth that God has made himself known in Christ's incarnation. From Sayers's perspective, as she embarked on creating works of drama as opposed to novels, there could be nothing more stimulating for a playwright, nor for that matter an audience, than Christian dogma. She concluded that the story of the incarnation was not only a matter of Christian theology but that it would be made for gripping drama on the stage. "If the Incarnation had never happened, it would have been necessary for some dramatist to invent it." She called the incarnation "the most dramatic thing . . . that ever entered into the mind of man,"[44] so it made sense to her to create works of drama exploring this most explosive of stories. Sayers's interest in presenting the Christian faith in dramatic form was related to her conviction that the story inherently encapsulated the truth. Sayers never developed a theoretical narrative theology but was first a creative writer, and as such her theology was encapsulated in the drama on the stage.[45] She held that her role as a writer, as opposed to that of a professional

---

43. Dorothy L. Sayers, "The Greatest Drama Ever Staged is the Official Creed of Christendom," *Sunday Times* (3 April 1938): 1. This was later published in *The Triumph of Easter* (London: Hodder & Stoughton, 1938).

44. Dorothy L. Sayers to Father Herbert Kelly, October 4, 1937, in *The Letters of Dorothy L. Sayers*, vol. 2, ed. Barbara Reynolds (Cambridge: Dorothy L. Sayers Society, 1997), 43.

45. Sayers's direct practical engagement with writing theology as drama and her lack of analysis of her own approach in relative terms has contributed to her work being largely ignored by narrative theologians. But

preacher or a priest, gave her an unprecedented opportunity to expose people to this story: "Since it is not the playwright's business to argue but to present, the only thing one can do is to put it on the stage . . . and let it speak for itself."[46] Sayers was ready to communicate Christian doctrine through story in the form of drama, first by writing text on a page and then by helping actors animate that script on the stage or the radio.

Broadcasting on the BBC took Sayers's works to a considerable audience and significantly increased her influence in Britain. Sayers's plays also provided the national broadcaster with an opportunity to communicate its own "Christian" founding principles amid the political turmoil of the early years of World War II.[47] A. N. Wilson comments: "Sayers' religious plays had an enormous impact on the radio audiences of wartime England." Radio was a relatively new medium of communication that Sayers adeptly co-opted for her uncompromising commitment to present Christian dogma as truth to as large an audience as possible. The apologetic impact of her work was largely because she made "plausible, in a modern sense such scenes as Jesus walking on water or reappearing from the grave after three days."[48]

The director of religious broadcasting at the BBC, Dr. J. W. Welch, wrote to Sayers in February 1940 inviting her to write a series of plays on the life of Christ for broadcast on Sundays in the children's hour. This resulted in *The Man Born to Be King*. The motive of Dr. Welch in broadcasting Sayers's play cycle was clear: "Now the task of the Church in any age is to reveal Christ. It cannot do more, and it should not attempt less. To reveal Christ and to persuade men and women to respond to that truth is the whole task of the Christian Church."[49] Sayers was selected for the task on the basis that she had great ability as a Christian apologist. Her plays were commissioned with the expectation that Christian truth might

---

her strengths as a creative writer enabled her to engage a wide audience with theology and make a significant contribution to Christian apologetics in her own era.

46. Dorothy L. Sayers letter to Father Herbert Kelly, 4 October 1937, in Reynolds, *Letters Volume Two*, 43.

47. "The BBC did not interpret its task as the provision of entertainment alone; to supply entertainment by itself was thought of as the betrayal of trust. 'Education' in the broadest sense was thought of as an equally important objective." Asa Briggs, *The History of Broadcasting in the United Kingdom Volume 1: The Birth of Broadcasting* (London: Oxford University Press, 1961), 8. Reith wrote in 1924: "I think it will be admitted by all, that to have exploited so great a scientific invention for the purpose and pursuit of entertainment alone would have been a prostitution of its powers and an insult to the character and intelligence of the people." J.C.W. Reith, *Broadcast Over Britain* (London: Hodder & Stoughton 1925), 17. The construction of Broadcasting House in 1932 and the inscription in the arch DEO OMNIPOTENTI "To God Almighty" underlined the fact that while entertainment and public service were both integral to the output of the BBC, religion was also a stalwart component under the influence of Director General Lord Reith. Stobart wrote a few months before the Corporation was founded: "We began by assuming that we are living in a Christian land and that services were to be Christian and Catholic in the broadest sense." Asa Briggs, *The History of Broadcasting in the United Kingdom Volume II: The Golden Age of Wireless* (London: Oxford University Press, 1965), 227.

48. A. N. Wilson, "Complete with Spats," *London Review of Books* 15.10 (27 May 1993): 4.

49. Ibid., 11.

be communicated to a vast array of people. The truth in this context was focused on Christ and the story of his life. Welch hoped that *The Man Born to be King* play cycle would "chisel away the unreality which, for the majority, surrounds his person, might hurt some of the minority; yet the task was to destroy only the unnecessary and false, and so to release the true. Could we, for man today, and in the language of today, make Christ and his story live again? The answer lies in the plays printed in this book."[50]

The result was that over two million people heard the plays. Sayers had reached a huge audience with her work, using story brought to life by drama. Welch commented that "Miss Sayers has put the Christian Church in this country in her debt by making Our Lord—in her fine phrase—'Really real' for so many of us."[51]

As a creative writer and literary critic, Sayers believed in the power and theological resonance of any story well told, but in her plays she tried to go a step further and retell the truest of true stories on the stage. Sayers realized that a story could make for an excellent exploration of Christian dogma since theological, cosmological, and ontological truths are necessarily borne out and revealed in contingent specificities. Sayers understood that this is the nature of Christian revelation. Furthermore, she perceived that while Christian theology is making universal and comprehensive truth claims about reality, people come to know and experience this truth within space, time, and history, in real life experiences—even in stories.[52] She intuited that drama might be an ideal means for the exploration of the outworking of such particularities.[53] In this way, Sayers was able to bring the arts and theology together. What is more, she was able to reflect at more than a theoretical level on theology and the arts because she was a practitioner of both.[54] Sayers's unique position in this regard lends her

50. Ibid., 12.

51. Ibid., 16.

52. Sayers reflected in her Good Friday letter to Wren-Lewis, March 1954, in Reynolds, *Letters Volume Four*, that it was through the power of the brilliant story-telling of G. K. Chesterton that she herself became awakened to the truth and this had inspired her to do the same. "All I did was to tell the story in words of one syllable and insist that it was an exciting story.... Chesterton performed a like office for me when I was a sullenly unreceptive adolescent." Sayers' friend the theologian E. L. Mascall comments in an article on Sayers that Chesterton's writings had a similar effect on them both: "It was the sheer excitement of the drama, combined with its amazing power of intellectual synthesis, that convinced me that if any religion was true it must be historic, traditional, orthodox Christianity." E. L. Mascall, "What Happened to Dorothy L. Sayers?" *SEVEN An Anglo-American Literary Review* 3 (1982): 15.

53. Reflecting on this from the point of view of literary technique Sayers contrasted writing the specific details of a play with those in a novel: "People can turn back and verify, whereas in a play, points must be made once and for all so as to stick in peoples' minds." Dorothy L. Sayers, "Stage and Story" unpublished notes. Marion E. Wade Center, Wheaton College, Wheaton, Illinois. MS-207, 3., 1.203don"Dorothy L. ff.oce Wells. Press, 1941), looking forward to handing it in September.n. I have been working on this alongsid

54. Clemson argues that "It is as a dramatist more thoroughly and creatively than as an essayist, that she is a theologian." Frances Clemson, *Sayers' Dramatic Works*, unpublished doctoral thesis, 307.

perspective the potential to contribute to this increasingly important field of study for the contemporary church.[55] As Jeremy Begbie comments, "The arts are able to do their own kind of work in their own kind of way, articulating depths of the Word of the gospel and our experience of it that are otherwise unheard or unfelt, while nonetheless being responsible and faithful to the normative texts of the faith. . . . A major research agenda opens up here, as well as a major practical challenge to all who care about the arts in the Church."[56]

THE MIND OF THE MAKER

Sayers's deeper theological inquiry into human creativity as an outworking of the divine Trinity, *The Mind of the Maker*, was published in 1941. It was intended to be part of a wider project called "Bridgeheads" that Sayers and some of her friends conceived.[57] The aim was to give a rational Christian perspective on the big issues facing the nation—political, social, and economic. The series never took off, but *The Mind of the Maker* was an immediate success and is still in print today. C. S. Lewis commented that "much of her most valuable thought about writing was embodied in *The Mind of the Maker*: a book which is still too little read."[58] Sayers wrote to J. H. Oldham in September 1939:

> I don't think it's going to be enough merely to keep the Christian flag flying; I fancy that now or never is the time to bring it out and carry it ostentatiously down the street. In a sense Christianity is in a good position—even if it is only that of being able to say "I told you so." Materialism is dead, and the people who have been busy for the last fifty years secularising

---

55. Whilst Catholic and Orthodox traditions have historically strongly supported the coalescence of theology and the arts, for a flavor of the burgeoning of scholarship pertaining to theology and the arts within the Protestant tradition see Trevor Hart, *Between the Image and the Word: Theological Engagements with Imagination, Language and Literature* (London: Routledge, 2016); Trevor A. Hart and Ivan Khovacs, eds., *Tree of Tales: Tolkien, Literature and Theology* (Waco, TX: Baylor University Press, 2007); Belden C. Lane, *Ravished by Beauty: The Surprising Legacy of Reformed Spirituality* (Oxford: Oxford University Press, 2011); and Jeremy Begbie, ed., *Sounding the Depths: Theology Through The Arts* (London: SCM, 2002).

56. Jeremy Begbie, "The Future of Theology amid the Arts: Some Reformed Reflections" in Roger Lundin (ed.), *Christ Across the Disciplines: Past, Present, Future* (Grand Rapids: Eerdmans, 2013), 173.

57. "Bridgeheads" was advertised as "a series of books" responding to the intellectual and spiritual consequences of the "increasingly specialised, analytical, and disintegrated" modern world. Dorothy L. Sayers, *Why Work?* (London: Methuen), 23. Sayers wrote to Dr. Oldham 2 October 1939, explaining: "We are trying to get together a little group of people who will write, lecture, etc., on anything that comes to hand . . . to set forth in the accompanying expression of our common aims and beliefs. . . . Our idea is that we should each and all get our stuff published as far as possible through our usual channels and not call ourselves anything in particular." The group was mixed: "Of the three of us who started in, one is R. C., the other C. of E. and the third rather inclined to be anti-organised-religion of any kind, so that we can scarcely be called sectarian." Reynolds, *Letters Volume Two*, 138.

58. C. S. Lewis, *On Stories and Other Essays on Literature* (London: Harcourt, 1982, first published 1966), 92.

everything are now thoroughly frightened of the results when they see the idea being carried to its full conclusion. Even the intellectuals, whom the Church was foolish enough to lose, seem to be wavering. . . . I do think it is necessary to bring the statement of Christian doctrine into some sort of relation with reality.[59]

The Mind of the Maker was a theological exploration of the apologetic appeal of her tripartite pattern of human creativity in demonstrating the veracity of Christian faith by asserting that human creativity was demonstrably a reflection of this ultimate divine pattern. Sayers explained that she was trying to simply provide a commentary to the creeds of the church. In her view, these creeds were not mere "speculation" about truth but were written with the purpose of "finding a formula to define experienced truth under pressure of misapprehension and criticism."[60] *The Mind of the Maker* is predicated on Sayers's conviction that the Christian doctrine of the Trinity provided a foundation for truth, reality, and human creativity. Furthermore, God in his Trinitarian being is recognizably real for human beings since his reality is reflected in the specifics of humanity's known experience and in particular in the sphere of creative art. Sayers argued that a perceptible trifold pattern, constituting a framework that makes sense of everything, underlies reality. In *The Mind of the Maker*, she set out to show how this pattern was peculiarly reflected in a tripart specific process that she personally knew well—the work of an author and of human creativity more generally. A work of Christian apologetics, *The Mind of the Maker* was an attempt to make a rational connection between human experience and the reality of the divine. Sayers's "commentary" might also be described as an apologetic interpretation of the evidence of human experience for a Creator.[61]

ESSAYS

Sayers's essays on work and women serve as examples of this prominent genre of her writing. Her essays are concise pieces of prose pursuing truth. Sayers wrote three essays about work: "Living to Work," "Why Work?," and "Vocation in Work" and two essays on the place of Women: "Are Women Human?" and "The Human-Not-Quite-Human." In these essays, Sayers wrote with lucidity about the divine pattern for human dignity in work as well as about gender, leaving her

---

59. Dorothy L. Sayers letter to Dr. J. H. Oldham, 10 September 1939, in Reynolds, *Letters Volume Two*, 133.

60. Dorothy L. Sayers, *The Mind of the Maker* (London: Continuum, 2005, first published London: Methuen, 1941), 3.

61. Although Sayers opens the preface with the words: "This book is not an apology for Christianity," Sayers, Preface to *Mind*, 1.

readers with a greater clarity as to how she understood the relationship between ultimate truth and human experience. The apologetic appeal of her essays lies in Sayers's efforts at pointing readers to a divine pattern that humanity longs to emulate. The falling short of human experience is a misapplication of pattern—things are not as they should or could be—but Sayers opined that even this dissonance could point humanity to the Christian revelation. In her writing about work, Sayers was trying to suggest that her own generation had an opportunity both within the church but also in society at large to rethink human vocation. Sayers perceived of all work as belonging primarily to the creative rather than an exclusively economic sphere and thus as having theological importance. Humanity created in the image of a creative God images forth God by working: "Work is the natural exercise and function of man—the creature who is made in the image of his Creator."[62] Sayers believed that this conceptual, theological starting point for thinking about work would dramatically impact a worker's attitude toward their work along with the value of the work that was produced. Sayers regarded the church's failure to grasp the reality that work falls within the remit of a divine pattern for human life and flourishing, as leading inevitably to the church's impotency in speaking out publicly for the good of society. Sayers argued: "I am persuaded that the reason why the Churches are in so much difficulty about giving a lead in the economic sphere is because they are trying to fit a Christian standard of economics to a wholly false and pagan understanding of work."[63] Rather than pointing to a divine pattern, the church was, in Sayers's view, colluding with a pagan pattern of economics that was doomed to fail since it was not "true" to the way things actually are.

In her essays on the humanity of women, Sayers wanted to challenge the church and its hierarchy to see that this was an area where Jesus Christ had modeled something entirely different. Christ had not reduced women to their biology or to a particular sociological sphere, and yet the church was failing to follow her Lord in this matter. This conviction that Jesus demonstrated how women should be regarded and treated led to the apologetic finale of her essay "The Human-Not-Quite-Human" and thus presented the church with a serious challenge to consider:

Perhaps it is no wonder that the women were first at the Cradle and last at the Cross. They had never known a man like this Man—there never has been such another. A prophet and teacher who never nagged at them,

---

62. Ibid., 11.
63. Sayers, *Why Work?*, 12.

never flattered or coaxed or patronized; who never made arch jokes about them, never treated them as "The women, God help us!" or "The ladies, God bless them!"; who rebuked without querulousness and praised without condescension; who took their questions and arguments seriously; who never mapped out their sphere for them, never urged them to be feminine or jeered them for being female.[64]

Clearly Sayers's portrait of Jesus to a skeptical world recalling how women appreciated his inherent affirmation of their humanity (women "were first at the Cradle and last at the cross"), resounded with theologically orthodox movements affirming female humanity within the church, as well as women outside the church. Intriguingly, in the 1940s and 50s, a leading voice in theology pertaining to Christianity and culture and the communication of the church's creed to the world was a woman's voice who argued that Jesus Christ had uniquely affirmed the voice of women. Sayers's voice was listened to whether by her broadcast messages on BBC radio, her plays on stage and radio, or her books, which sold in their thousands because she was regarded as a clear, sensible, and coherent thinker regardless of her gender. Her ideas and her confidence in Christian truth as exciting, relevant, and foundational for the health of any society continue to resonate today.

CONTRIBUTIONS TO THE FIELD OF APOLOGETICS

Dorothy L. Sayers operated as a successful author, dramatist, essayist, and literary translator. But it is her unique contribution to the Christian apologetic witness of the church that has been undervalued. As a professional woman in the 1930s to 50s, she marshalled the medium of her day—the radio, drawing on lessons learned in mass communication through the advertising industry and successfully capturing the imagination of the general public for Christian theology. Her grasp of the power and vibrancy of story and the intrinsic coherence of pattern lent Sayers an apologetic edge such that her works reached millions of people. Her focus on dogma and the creeds of the church as a simple but irreducible core of Christian truth that inexorably connected with the known world of historical, scientific, philosophical, political, and moral reality in an identifiable pattern held genuine apologetic appeal in her day. Dorothy L. Sayers was able to

---

64. Dorothy L. Sayers, "The Human Not Quite Human," in *Unpopular Opinions* (London: Gollancz, 1946), 122.

speak sensibly and relevantly about Christian dogma. She repeatedly expressed her lack of confidence in her capacity to speak of any emotional or personal experience of God, instead focusing on what she called "the passionate intellect."

Sayers came to God through her love of the intellectual pattern of Christian faith, the dogmatic and doctrinal pattern expressed in the story of Christ. It was this irresistible interplay of pattern and story that gave rise to her "passionate intellect," that passion for truth. Thus, motivated and equipped, she was able to speak cogently and persuasively about theology to the church. She retold the Christian story in creative ways on stage and radio, argued for the Christian doctrine of the Trinity as a coherent foundation for truth and reality evidenced in everyday human experience, wrote about questions that deeply concerned the wider public, such as work and gender, and so became the best known and most effective female Christian apologist of the English-speaking world in the twentieth century.

BIBLIOGRAPHY

Barth, Karl. *Das grösste Drama aller Zeiten aus dem Englischen übersetzt und mit einem Geleitwort*. Evangelischer Verlag: Zollikon, 1959.

Begbie, Jeremy. "The Future of Theology amid the Arts: Some Reformed Reflections." Pages 152–82 in *Christ Across the Disciplines: Past, Present, Future*. Ed. by Roger Lundin. Grand Rapids: Eerdmans, 2013.

———, ed. *Sounding the Depths: Theology through the Arts*. London: SCM, 2002.

Briggs, Asa. *The History of Broadcasting in the United Kingdom Volume I: The Birth of Broadcasting*. London: Oxford University Press, 1961.

———. *The History of Broadcasting in the United Kingdom Volume II: The Golden Age of Wireless*. London: Oxford University Press, 1965.

Clemson, Frances. *Sayers' Dramatic Works*. Unpublished doctoral thesis.

Dooyeweerd, Herman. *A New Critique of Theoretical Thought: The General Theory of the Modal Spheres*. Ed. by H. de Jongste and David H. Freeman. Phillipsburg, NJ: P&R, 1969.

———. *A New Critique of Theoretical Thought: The Necessary Presuppositions of Philosophy*. Ed. by William S. Young and David H. Freeman. Phillipsburg, NJ: P&R, 1969.

Hart, Trevor. *Between the Image and the Word: Theological Engagements with Imagination, Language and Literature*. London: Routledge, 2016.

Hart, Trevor A., and Ivan Khovacs, eds. *Tree of Tales: Tolkien, Literature and Theology*. Waco, TX: Baylor University Press, 2007.

Lane, Belden C. *Ravished by Beauty: The Surprising Legacy of Reformed Spirituality*. Oxford: Oxford University Press, 2011.

Lewis, C. S. *On Stories and Other Essays on Literature*. London: Harcourt, 1982; first published 1966.

Mascall, E. L. "What Happened to Dorothy L. Sayers?" *SEVEN An Anglo-American Literary Review* 3 (1982): 9–18.

Reith, J. C. W. *Broadcast Over Britain*. London: Hodder & Stoughton, 1925.

Renan, Ernest. *Vie de Jésus* New York: Modern Library, 1927; originally published, 1863.

Reynolds, Barbara, ed. *The Letters of Dorothy L. Sayers Volume Two 1937–1943: From Novelist to Playwright*. Cambridge: The Dorothy L. Sayers Society: Carole Green Publishing, 1997.

———, ed. *The Letters of Dorothy L. Sayers Volume Four 1951–1957: In the Midst of Life*. Cambridge: The Dorothy L. Sayers Society: Carole Green Publishing, 2000.

———, ed. *Dorothy L. Sayers Child and Woman of Her Time Volume Five: A Supplement to the Letters of Dorothy L. Sayers*. Cambridge: The Dorothy L. Sayers Society Carole Green Publishing, 2002.

Sayers, Dorothy L. *Begin Here*. London: Gollancz, 1940.

———. "The Greatest Drama Ever Staged." *The Sunday Times* (April 3, 1938), 1.

———. "The Greatest Drama Ever Staged is the Official Creed of Christendom." *The Sunday Times*, (April 3, 1938), 1.

———. *The Mind of the Maker.* London: Continuum, 2005; first published London: Methuen, 1941.

———. *The Poetry of Search and The Poetry of Statement and other Posthumous Essays on Literature, Religion and Language.* London: Gollancz, 1963.

———. "Problems of Religious Broadcasting" *BBC Quarterly* (1947): 29–31.

———. "The Religions Behind the Nation." Pages 43–48 in *The Church Looks Ahead: Broadcast Talks.* London: Faber & Faber, 1941.

———. "Toward a Christian Aesthetic." Pages 50–69 in *Our Culture: Its Christian Roots and Present Crisis.* Edward Alleyn Lectures 1944. Ed. by V. A. Demant. London: SPCK, 1944.

———. "The Triumph of Easter." *The Sunday Times* (April 17, 1938), 1.

———. "What Do We Believe?" *The Sunday Times* (September 10, 1939), 8.

———. *Why Work?* London: Methuen, 1942.

———. "Worship in the Anglican Church." *SEVEN: An Anglo-American Literary Review.* 12 (1995): 31–48.

Strauss, David Friedrich. *Life of Jesus Critically Examined.* New York: Blanchard, 1860.

Wilson, A. N. "Complete with Spats." *London Review of Books* 15.10 (27 May 1993): 4.

Wright, N. T. *Jesus and the Victory of God.* London: SPCK, 1996.

C. S. LEWIS

Imaginative Apologetics
of a Reluctant Convert

ALISTER E. MCGRATH

The Oxford apologist C. S. Lewis (1898–
1963) remains one of the most widely
read and influential Christian apologists
of all time. After his conversion to Chris-
tianity, Lewis was able to deploy his skills as a literary scholar to write standard
works of apologetics, as well as novels with a strong apologetic dimension. One
of the most characteristic features of Lewis's apologetics is his appeal to the
imagination, which is especially evident in his celebrated Chronicles of Narnia.

HISTORICAL BACKGROUND

Clive Staples Lewis—'Jack' to his friends—was born in the Irish city of Belfast
on November 29, 1898. His father was a lawyer whose successful career allowed
the family to move to a large house ("Little Lea") on the outskirts of Belfast in
1905. Several years later Lewis's mother died of cancer, leaving his father to
look after Lewis and his elder brother, Warren. The two brothers spent hours
alone in the vast attic of the old house, inhabiting imaginary worlds of their
own making.

If Lewis ever had any Christian faith to start with, he soon lost it. After a
period of wartime service in the British Army, Lewis went to Oxford University
in January 1919. Like many, he found that the trauma and destruction of World
War I called into question the existence of God. Atheism, it seemed, was the
only serious option for a thinking person. Lewis had hopes to be remembered as
a "war poet" but gradually realized that he lacked the talent and focused instead
on his academic studies. Lewis gained first class honors in Greats (classics and
philosophy) in 1922 and first class honors in English the following year. After
a difficult period during which his future seemed uncertain, he was elected a
fellow of Magdalen College in the spring of 1925. This secured his academic and
financial future, as well as widening his network of contacts to include members
of the faculty of English literature at Oxford. One of the most significant results

of this was that Lewis developed a close friendship with J. R. R. Tolkien during the late 1920s. This friendship continued until Lewis's death in 1963.

During the 1920s Lewis had time to reconsider his attitude to Christianity. In the early 1920s, he seems to have regarded atheism as rationally plausible yet imaginatively and emotionally inadequate. The story of his return to faith is described in detail in his autobiography, *Surprised by Joy*. After wrestling with the clues concerning God that he found in human reason and experience, he eventually decided that intellectual honesty compelled him to believe and trust in God. He did not want to; but he felt he had no choice—and so found himself becoming "the most dejected and reluctant convert in all England."[1] Lewis dates this life-changing transition to the summer of 1929, although it is possible it took place in June 1930. Yet this conversion was really to a form of theism rather than to Christianity itself. The final stage of Lewis's conversion seems to have taken place in late 1931. Lewis offers an allegorical account of his conversion in his first published book, *The Pilgrim's Regress*.

After his conversion to Christianity, Lewis established his reputation as a leading authority on medieval and Renaissance English literature. *The Allegory of Love* is still regarded as a masterpiece. Alongside his scholarly writings, Lewis wrote books of a very different nature. Aiming at clarity and conviction, Lewis produced a series of works aimed at communicating the reasonableness of Christianity to his own generation. Lewis realized that his own transition from atheism to Christianity equipped him to function as an apologist. His first apologetic work, *The Problem of Pain*, did not arise from his own initiative but from an invitation from a publisher who was impressed by Lewis's writing style and ability to connect with a wider audience.

The success of *The Problem of Pain* caused Lewis to write more in the same vein, developing his own distinct apologetic method while gaining recognition as a reputable and accessible Christian voice in the nation during World War II. This growing reputation was cemented by a series of radio talks Lewis was invited to give on the BBC during the summer of 1941, which gained Lewis a wide following. The success of this series led to invitations to give three further series of addresses along the same lines. Lewis later edited the four series of talks and published them as *Mere Christianity*.

Throughout the 1940s Lewis consolidated his growing reputation as a Christian apologist. In 1942 he published *The Screwtape Letters*, whose wit and insight firmly established him as a leading defender of the Christian faith and helped him emerge as a new and distinctive Christian voice in the United States.

---

1. C. S. Lewis, *Surprised by Joy* (New York: HarperCollins, 2002), 279.

It was not long before Lewis had gained an increasingly numerous and increasingly appreciative American readership. On September 8, 1947, he appeared on the front cover of *Time* magazine, which declared that this bestselling author was "one of the most influential spokesmen for Christianity in the English-speaking world."[2]

Lewis was outspokenly critical of "Christianity-and-water"[3] (as he dubbed liberal versions of Christianity) and seems to have struck a deep chord of sympathy with his readers. The British cultural elite were irritated at his success. The writer and broadcaster Alistair Cooke described him as a "very unremarkable minor prophet"[4] who would soon be forgotten once World War II had ended—a prediction in which Cooke showed himself to be a very unremarkable and incompetent minor prophet.

After his conversion, Lewis became a regular member of the congregation at Holy Trinity Church, Headington Quarry. Yet although he regarded himself as a layman of the Church of England, Lewis chose to write as a representative of a broad and generous consensual Christian orthodoxy, which he later dubbed "Mere Christianity." Lewis conspicuously avoided becoming embroiled in the ecclesiastical controversies of his day, seeing his responsibility as a Christian apologist taking precedence over any specific denominational concerns or commitments.

Although Lewis's popular works brought him popular acclaim throughout the 1940s, they seemed to some influential Oxford academics to destroy his scholarly reputation. In 1946 he was passed over for the Merton professorship of English literature at Oxford. The pattern was repeated with other senior academic positions in 1947 and 1948. Lewis's realization that he was being marginalized by sections of Oxford's academic community led him to undertake a massive research project, leading to what was probably his most important scholarly work—*English Literature in the Sixteenth Century, Excluding Drama*. Lewis was elected a Fellow of the British Academy in recognition of the merits of this stellar study and was invited to take up the newly created Chair of Medieval and Renaissance English at Cambridge that same year. He remained in this post until the spring of 1963, when his declining health prevented him from carrying out his teaching duties.

Lewis died of cancer at his Oxford home at 5:30 p.m. on November 22,

---

2. "Don v. Devil." *Time* 50.10 (September 8, 1947): 65–74.
3. C. S. Lewis, *Mere Christianity* (New York: HarperCollins, 2001), 40.
4. Alister McGrath, "C. S. Lewis, Defender of the Faith," in *C. S. Lewis and His Circle: Essays and Memoirs from the Oxford C. S. Lewis*, eds. Roger White, Judith Wolfe, and Brendan N. Wolfe (New York: Oxford University Press, 2015), 7.

1963, a few hours before the world was shocked by the news of the assassination of President John F. Kennedy. Lewis is buried in the churchyard of Holy Trinity Church, Headington Quarry, which he attended from 1930 until his death.

APOLOGETIC METHODOLOGY

Lewis explicitly referred to himself as an apologist, seeing this as the natural and proper outcome of his own religious history. Lewis was an atheist who had become a Christian—and knew why he had done so. Lewis's capacity to empathize with an atheist worldview helped him develop apologetic strategies capable of engaging and challenging Atheism's core assumptions. His capacity to write in elegant, accessible, and engaging English secured him a wide readership who came to trust him as a reliable and faithful defender of the Christian faith, rather than of any specific denominational form of that faith.

Lewis's first work of apologetics was *The Problem of Pain*. Taking a slightly cerebral and detached approach to this emotionally charged issue, Lewis argued that the Christian faith was both able to accommodate the existence of pain and suffering in the world while at the same time enabling it to be seen in a new way. Lewis was clear that the only purpose of the book was to "solve the intellectual problem raised by suffering."[5] The emotional aspects of suffering were simply passed over. The book's best-known sentence is not representative of its overall argument: "God whispers to us in our pleasures, speaks in our conscience, but shouts in our pains: it is His megaphone to rouse a deaf world."[6] Although this is a subsidiary point, it is often incorrectly presented as if it were the total sum of Lewis's approach. For Lewis, pain can bring home to us the frailty and transience of our existence and thus helps shatter the illusion that "all is well," allowing God to plant "the flag of truth within the fortress of a rebel soul."[7]

Lewis argues that the map of reality offered by the Christian faith corresponds well to what is observed and experienced. Books of this type—including *The Problem of Pain* and *Miracles*—make a fundamental appeal to human reason. Although Lewis was far too sophisticated a thinker to believe he could prove the existence of God or the truth of Christianity, he nevertheless held that the fundamental reasonableness of the Christian faith can be shown by argument and reflection. Lewis's apologetic approach at this stage thus emphasizes the intellectual capaciousness of the Christian view of reality and how it is able

---

5. C. S. Lewis, *The Problem of Pain* (New York: HarperCollins, 1996), xii.
6. Ibid., 91.
7. Ibid., 94.

to "fit in" our observations of the world around us and our experiences and longings within us.

The approach can be summed up from the concluding sentence of a lecture Lewis delivered to the Socratic Club in Oxford in 1944: "I believe in Christianity as I believe that the Sun has risen, not only because I see it, but because by it I see everything else." Although Lewis here affirms the rationality of faith, he does so using an image that appeals primarily to the imagination. One of the most distinctive features of Lewis's approach to apologetics is to affirm the importance of both the reason and imagination in commending and defending Christianity. They play different roles but serve the same purpose. "Reason is the natural organ of truth, imagination is the organ of meaning."[8]

Lewis's most significant work of apologetics is *Mere Christianity*, now widely regarded as one of the most important and influential works on Christianity to have been published in the twentieth century. Although the work affirms the fundamental rationality of the Christian faith, Lewis's approach appeals primarily to the shared experience of ordinary people—such as a sense of moral obligation or a feeling of longing for something that is deeply satisfying yet is not delivered in or through anything that is finite or created. There is, Lewis suggested, a deep and intense feeling of longing within human beings that no earthly object or experience can satisfy. Lewis refers to this experience as "joy," and argues that it points to God as its source and goal (hence the title of his autobiography). Pleasure, beauty, and personal relationships all seem to promise satisfaction and fulfillment—and yet when we grasp them, we find that what we were seeking was not in them but lies beyond them. There is a "divine dissatisfaction" within human experience that prompts us to ask whether there is anything that may satisfy the human quest to fulfill the desires of the human heart.

In *Mere Christianity* Lewis argues that this is indeed the case. Hunger, he suggests, is an excellent example of a human feeling that corresponds to a genuine physical need. This need points to the existence of food by which the need may be met. Thirst is a further example of a human longing pointing to a human need, which in turn points to its fulfillment in drinking. Any authentic human longing, Lewis argues, points to a genuine human need, which in turn points to a real object corresponding to that need. Lewis thus suggests that it is reasonable to argue that the deep human sense of infinite longing that cannot be satisfied by any physical or finite object or person must point to a real human need that has both its origin and its fulfillment in God. In this he echoes a great theme of

---

8. C. S. Lewis, "Bluspels and Flalansferes," in *Selected Literary Essays* (New York: Cambridge University Press, 1969), 265.

traditional Christian thinking about the origin and goal of human nature. "You have made us for yourself, O Lord, and our hearts are restless until they find their rest in you"[9] We are made by God, and we experience a deep sense of longing for him, which only he can satisfy. Although Lewis's reflections on the desire he calls "joy" clearly reflect his own personal experience, it is evident that he considers this sense of longing to be a widespread feature of human nature and experience. Lewis's wide reading of literature—especially poets such as George Herbert and Thomas Traherne—helped convince him of the importance of this sense of longing.

Yet alongside his emphasis on the rationality of the Christian faith, Lewis argued that apologetics had to come to terms with the need for theological translation—the ability to be able to translate the great themes of Christianity into a language that could be understood by those outside the church. Although Lewis highlighted the importance of this at several points, he gave it particular attention in a lecture on "Christian Apologetics," delivered at a conference of youth leaders and clergy in 1945. "Our business is to present that which is timeless," he declared, "in the particular language of our own day." This means we must "learn the language of our audience"—something that has to be done by experience.[10]

Lewis learned this lesson the hard way. Although he excelled as a lecturer at Oxford throughout the 1930s—his lectures were among the best attended in the University—Lewis had little experience of speaking to a wider audience until 1941. In that year, the Dean of St Paul's Cathedral, London, asked Lewis to speak to Royal Air Force personnel about Christianity. Lewis accepted the offer, realizing that it would force him to translate his ideas into "uneducated language."[11] Lewis's first speaking engagement was at a Royal Air Force training base for Bomber Command based near Oxford. It was highly successful, and he was asked for more. Gradually, Lewis learned how to adapt his style and vocabulary to meet the needs of an audience he had never encountered before. As he put it in his lecture of 1945, he learned to "translate every bit of [his] theology into the vernacular."[12]

Yet Lewis's approach to apologetics took a new turn in the early 1930s, when he realized the important role that an appeal to the human imagination through fiction could play in Christian apologetics. Lewis never saw this as displacing or

9. Augustine, *Conf.* I.I.
10. C. S. Lewis, "Christian Apologetics," in *God in the Dock* (Grand Rapids: Eerdmans, 1970), 96.
11. Alister McGrath, *C. S. Lewis—A Life: Eccentric Genius, Reluctant Prophet* (Carol Spring, IL: Tyndale, 2013), 207.
12. Ibid., 208.

subverting his more rational approaches to apologetics; rather, he saw them as complementing each other, and extending his range as an apologist.

THE TURN TO THE IMAGINATION: THE CHRONICLES OF NARNIA

We have already seen how Lewis invites us to see Christianity as offering us a standpoint from which we may see things as they actually are and grasp their intrinsic coherence and interconnectedness. Lewis consistently uses a remarkably wide range of visual metaphors—such as sun, light, blindness, and shadows—to help us understand the nature of a true understanding of things and the condition of humanity, which prevents us from fully grasping this without divine assistance. Where some argue that rationality concerns the ability of reason to give an account of things, Lewis frames this more in terms of our ability to see their proper relationships.

This has two important consequences. First, it means Lewis sees reason and imagination as existing in a collaborative, not competitive, relationship. Reason without imagination is potentially dull and limited; imagination without reason is potentially delusory and escapist. Lewis develops a notion of "imagined"—not imaginary—reality, which is capable of being grasped by reason and visualized by the imagination. For Lewis, human beings need to be able to visualize things, however inadequately, if they are to make sense of them or relate to them.

Secondly, it means Lewis makes extensive use of verbal illustrations or analogies to enable us to *see* things in a new way. His famous apologetic for the doctrine of the Trinity in *Mere Christianity* suggests that our difficulties arise primarily because we fail to see it properly. If we see it another way—as, for example, an inhabitant of a two-dimensional world might try to grasp and describe the structure of a three-dimensional reality—then we begin to grasp its intrinsic rationality. Lewis's apologetic often takes the form of a visual invitation: "Try seeing it this way!" The rationality of the Trinity needs to be shown, not proved—and it is shown by allowing us to see it in the right way.

A further example is his illustration of the incarnation using the analogy of a diver descending into a deep and dark lake to retrieve treasure. In the same way, God descends into our world to take hold of us, to restore us to fellowship with him, and to assure us of our place in heaven. It is a recognizable—and imaginatively effective—reworking of Athanasius of Alexander's famous maxim: "God became man so that man might become God."[13]

---

13. Athanasius, *On the Incarnation*, 54.3.

While the intellectual capaciousness of the Christian faith can be rationally analyzed, Lewis hints that it is best imaginatively communicated. For Lewis, there is always a sense of a "beyond," a "numinous"—something of enormous significance that lies beyond our reason, sometimes hinted at more by intuition than logic. This point had been made earlier by the apologist G. K. Chesterton (who Lewis greatly admired and whose influence can be seen at many points in Lewis's writings). "Every true artist," Chesterton argued, feels "that he is touching transcendental truths; that his images are shadows of things seen through the veil."[14] Lewis himself had wrestled with this question of the significance of his deepest intuitions as a young atheist, as a passage from *Surprised by Joy* makes clear: "On the one side a many-islanded sea of poetry and myth; on the other a glib and shallow rationalism. Nearly all that I loved I believed to be imaginary; nearly all I believed to be real I thought grim and meaningless."[15]

It was thus natural and reasonable for Lewis to turn to literature as a means of engaging the imagination and helping his readers grasp the deeper reality that lay beyond reason. The apologetic potential of literature was the subject of both discussion and disagreement between Lewis and Tolkien. Although the Chronicles of Narnia and The Lord of the Rings are both apologetic works, they take very different forms. Yet each developed their own distinct approach on the basis of the fundamental idea that Christianity provided a "true myth" and that the writing of narrative fiction could be justified on its basis.

But what sort of literature would be appropriate? As a young man, Lewis enjoyed reading science fiction. While he admired this literary genre, he disliked what he regarded as the naive evolutionary optimism that seemed to be shared by leading writers in the field, such as H. G. Wells. So could a literary genre that was being used to advocate various forms of atheism and materialism be used instead to *critique* these viewpoints and advocate a Christian alternative? Lewis thought the experiment to be worth trying and set to work on his "science fiction" trilogy: *Out of the Silent Planet, Perelandra*, and *That Hideous Strength*. In these works Lewis shows that stories can be told that subvert some established truths of the day and expose them as shadows and illusions.

Although some suggest that Lewis's shift to works of fiction was a result of his perception of his own deficiencies in rational argument—as in the famous encounter with the philosopher Elizabeth Anscombe in February 1948—this is not so. Lewis's interest in the apologetic potential of fiction was evident in 1939. By the time of his encounter with Anscombe, Lewis had written three works

---

14. G. K. Chesterton, *The Everlasting Man* (San Francisco: Ignatius, 1993), 105.
15. Lewis, *Surprised by Joy*, 197.

of fictional apologetics and had begun to craft some of the early sections of the Chronicles of Narnia. Lewis had long admired the imaginative approach to theology and apologetics that he found in the writings of the Victorian preacher and novelist George MacDonald, involving a direct appeal to the imagination, and believed he was able to develop his own distinctive version of this approach.

Lewis saw such imaginative approaches as *supplementing* their rational counterparts, operating at different levels, and potentially appealing to different audiences. For Lewis, the human imagination was the gateway to the soul, enabling the apologist to evade the "watchful dragons" of rationalism. The Chronicles of Narnia represent Lewis's mature and most successful work of literary apologetics. Though cast in the form of children's stories, these seven works aim to capture their readers' imaginations and generate a new receptivity toward core themes of the Christian story.

The Chronicles of Narnia can be seen as an exploration of what Lewis called a "supposal." What might Christ become like if there really were a world like Narnia and he chose to become incarnate, die, and rise again in *that* world in much the same way as he has done in ours? Let us *suppose* that there was a land like Narnia and that the Son of God, who became a human being in our world, instead became a Lion there—and then imagine what would happen. This literary device has obvious apologetic implications in that Lewis can be seen as inviting his readers to "suppose" that the Christian faith is true and reliable and then to imagine what it would be like to inhabit such a space. What would the world look like when seen from this standpoint? Might this way of seeing things make more sense than materialist or naturalist alternatives?

We see this approach at several points in Lewis's "argument from desire" in *Mere Christianity*, which culminates in the conclusion that "if I find in myself a desire which no experience in this world can satisfy, the most probable explanation is that I was made for another world."[16] Lewis's point is that this experience is quite puzzling and that it needs explanation. Now suppose that the Christian way of thinking is right; if this is so, we would expect some kind of experience like this. And this is an indication—though not a proof—that Christianity is true.

But is this transcendent object of desire real? Lewis suggests that the pursuit of the clues offered by human desire makes sense only if there is a fourth dimension to human existence, served by the human imagination. The "watchful dragon" of human reason is hesitant to allow us to speak of anything that goes beyond experience. In order to deal with this question, Lewis turns to Plato's

---

16. Lewis, *Mere Christianity*, 136–37.

famous analogy of the cave. As Plato uses the analogy in his dialogue *The Republic*, we are asked to think of a group of people who have been confined within a cave for their entire lives. A fire is burning, and they see shadows thrown on the wall of the cave. The cave is the only world they have ever experienced, and so they naturally assume it is the real world—the *only* world. The shadows they see are all that there is to reality. Yet what if there is another world that transcends the one they know from experience?

Lewis develops this analogy in *The Silver Chair*, one of the later volumes in the Chronicles of Narnia. He tells of how a witch confronts a Narnian in a dark underground kingdom. The witch tries to persuade him that her underground kingdom is the real world and that Narnia is a fiction of his imagination. Hearing the Narnian speak about the sun, the witch invites him to tell her more about it. There is no equivalent in the underworld to which she belongs. The prince replies by constructing an analogy based on what he sees in the underground world: the sun is like a lamp that lights up the world. The witch responds that the sun is simply an imagined and invented notion based on a real object—a lamp. Knowing that his readers are perfectly aware that the sun actually exists, Lewis is thus able to show, through an appeal to the imagination rather than reason, the superficial sophistication of the witch's argument. It may seem clever and persuasive but is seriously flawed.

Yet perhaps the most important theme developed throughout the Chronicles of Narnia is the role stories played in creating systems of meaning and value. Lewis discovered this point in a long evening conversation with J. R. R. Tolkien in September 1931, in which Tolkien explained that Christianity was a "myth" in his own technical sense of the term—a narrative that conveyed a worldview. Lewis realized that this made sense of many things that otherwise puzzled him, such as a capacity of pagan mythology to make some limited sense of the world. It was an important moment in triggering Lewis's transition from a generalized theism to an authentic Christianity.

Throughout the Chronicles of Narnia, Lewis aims to show that multiple stories are told about ourselves and our world and that we have to make a choice about which of these is the most reliable. This is perhaps seen at its most effective in *The Lion, the Witch, and the Wardrobe*, which raises the question of how characters and stories are to be tested. Who is to be trusted? Which story about Narnia is to be believed? To make the right judgements about what they should do, the children need to discover and trust the true master narrative of the origins of the mysterious world into which they have stumbled and within which they seem destined to play such a significant role. Lewis offers a way of understanding the nature of Christian faith as entering into a true story and becoming part of it.

Yet many would argue that the greatest apologetic achievement of the Chronicles of Narnia is Aslan, who Lewis develops as a Christ-figure and the heart's desire. Aslan evokes awe and wonder and lies beyond the power of anyone to tame or reduce to bland categories. Lewis's description of the impact of Aslan on the children in *The Lion, the Witch, and the Wardrobe* brings out the individuality of each relationship while highlighting Aslan's capacity to evoke wonder, awe, and an unutterable love. Aslan overwhelms the children's ability to understand him. They simply cannot take him in and are able to grasp only something of his nature and purposes. Yet they learn to respect and trust him, even though they know they do not fully understand him. Lewis captures, far better than many others, what it feels like to know and be known by Christ.

Lewis clearly saw his story of Aslan as a retelling of the core Christian story of incarnation, crucifixion, and resurrection. The reader is invited to reflect on this story and to draw conclusions about Aslan's true identity and significance. While some feel that Lewis's theology of atonement is a little deficient (the only person to benefit from Aslan's death is Edmund), Lewis provides a narrative framework for exploring a series of core Christian ideas—especially those of the atonement and the Christian hope. Contemporary apologists have widely used Lewis's description of the "New Narnia" in *The Last Battle*, especially to explore the idea of "going home" to be with God. Jewel the Unicorn's words are of particular importance: "I belong here. This is the land I have been looking for all my life, though I never knew it till now."[17]

APOLOGETICS IN LEWIS'S CAMBRIDGE PERIOD

Lewis's most influential works of apologetics were written during 1939–1954, while he was based in Oxford. They were catalyzed by many factors, including his interaction with students and especially his central role as host of "The Inklings," a loose group of academics who were interested in Christianity and literature, which at its height included J. R. R. Tolkien and Charles Williams. Although Lewis returned to his home in Oxford on weekends during his Cambridge period (1955–1963), it is clear that Lewis's move allowed him to rethink his role as an apologist.

Lewis's popular writings of this period—such as *Reflections on the Psalms* and *The Four Loves*—deal with the exploration of an *assumed* faith, not the defense of a *challenged* faith. This new approach is set out clearly in the opening pages of Lewis's *Reflections on the Psalms*: "This is not what is called an

---

17. C. S. Lewis, *The Last Battle* (New York: HarperCollins, 2002), 213.

'apologetic' work. I am nowhere trying to convince unbelievers that Christianity is true. I address those who already believe it, or those who are ready, while reading, to 'suspend their disbelief.' A man can't always be defending the truth; there must be a time to feed on it."[18]

This final sentence needs to be read in the light of Lewis's frequently repeated assertions that he found defending Christian ideas draining and exhausting. Lewis seems to be arguing that the time had come for him to *enjoy* Christian ideas, rather than be constantly forced into battle on their behalf.

Lewis's changed apologetic focus during his Cambridge period represents a change of emphasis within his overall approach. During the 1940s and early 1950s, Lewis developed works of rational apologetics, such as *Miracles* and *Mere Christianity*, that offered a rational defense of the Christian faith to unbelievers. During the later 1950s, Lewis tended to focus on works, such as *Surprised by Joy*, that explored the imaginative and relational dimensions of faith, with a presumed Christian audience in mind. The shift in envisaged readerships may reflect Lewis's changing perceptions of the needs of the moment; yet there is no loss of the comprehensive vision of the Christian faith that became so characteristic of Lewis.

There is one aspect of Lewis's apologetics that he came to regard as inadequate during his Cambridge period. *The Problem of Pain* tended to treat suffering as if it were a logical puzzle, an intellectual anomaly that required theoretical resolution. Lewis came to realize the severe inadequacy of such an approach, which failed to recognize the emotional trauma that so often accompanied experiences of suffering and death. The event that triggered this process of realization was the death, from cancer, of Lewis's wife, Joy Davidman, on July 13, 1960. Lewis wrote one of his most powerful books in response to this event. *A Grief Observed* is saturated with raw and unresolved emotion, offering one of the most vivid and compelling accounts of the grieving process while at the same time raising apologetic questions that Lewis realized his earlier writings had not adequately resolved.

Lewis's powerful, frank, and honest account of his own experience in *A Grief Observed* secured it a wide readership. The work was initially published under a pseudonym, so some of Lewis's friends, quite unaware of its true origins, recommended it to him as a helpful account of the process of grieving. Yet the work is significant at another level: in exposing the vulnerability and fragility of a purely rational faith. Lewis seems to have realized that his earlier approach engaged with the surface of human life, not its depths. "Where is God? . . . Go to

---

18. C. S. Lewis, *Reflections on the Psalms* (New York: HarperCollins, 2000), 7.

him when your need is desperate, when all other help is vain, and what do you find? A door slammed in your face, and a sound of bolting and double-bolting on the inside. After that, silence."[19]

Yet *A Grief Observed* is a powerful apologetic work in its own right. It is perhaps the only one of Lewis's books to address apologetic issues arising from the emotional process of grief. *A Grief Observed* describes what Lewis regards as a process of testing—not a testing *of God* but a testing *of Lewis*. "God has not been trying an experiment on my faith or love in order to find out their quality. He knew it already. It was I who didn't."[20] And although *A Grief Observed* takes a quite different approach from that of *The Problem of Pain*, both end up focusing on the doctrine of the incarnation in holding together the core insights that can allow people to live meaningfully with pain or suffering. *The Problem of Pain* helps us understand suffering; *A Grief Observed* helps us cope with it.

The incarnational turning point in *A Grief Observed* resulted from Lewis's desire to be able to suffer instead of—indeed, in the place of—his dying wife. "If only I could bear it, or the worst of it, of any of it, instead of her."[21] The mark of the true lover is a willingness to take on pain and suffering so that the beloved might be spared it. Lewis then saw, in a moment of insight, that this is what God did on the cross. God *could* bear the suffering of those he loved. And God *did* bear the suffering of those he loved. That, in turn, allows us to bear the ambiguity and risks of faith, knowing that its outcome is secured. *A Grief Observed* is a narrative of the testing and maturing of faith, not simply its recovery—and certainly not its loss.

CONTRIBUTIONS TO THE FIELD OF APOLOGETICS

Lewis's approach to apologetics defies easy classification. Those who assign him to some predetermined "school" of thought end up distorting his approach, which resists the conveniences of categorization. Lewis's complex and creative understanding of the interaction of reason and imagination has gained him a large following. As his Oxford colleague Austin Farrer once remarked, Lewis makes us think we are "listening to an argument," when in reality "we are presented with a vision, and it is the vision that carries conviction."[22] Both modern

---

19. C. S. Lewis, *A Grief Observed* (New York: HarperCollins, 1994), 5–6.
20. Ibid., 52.
21. Ibid., 44.
22. Austin Farrer, "The Christian Apologist," in *Light on C. S. Lewis*, ed. Jocelyn Gibb (London: Geoffrey Bles, 1965), 37.

and postmodern readers find in Lewis much that they can agree with and apologetic approaches that can be adapted and applied within those structures. Above all, Lewis has helped us rediscover the power of narrative apologetics, allowing us to retell the Christian story to new audiences. Even though he died more than fifty years ago, Lewis remains the most widely read Christian apologist. His approaches are all capable of development and extension, and it is likely that we will see further refinements of his methods in years to come.

BIBLIOGRAPHY

Carpenter, Humphrey. *The Inklings: C. S. Lewis, J. R. R. Tolkien, Charles Williams, and Their Friends.* Boston: Houghton Mifflin, 1979.

Downing, David C. *Into the Wardrobe: C. S. Lewis and the Narnia Chronicles.* San Francisco: Jossey-Bass, 2005.

Edwards, Bruce L. *C. S. Lewis: Life, Works and Legacy.* 4 vols. Westport, CT: Praeger, 2007.

Gibb, Jocelyn, ed. *Light on C. S. Lewis.* London: Bles, 1965.

Jacobs, Alan. *The Narnian: The Life and Imagination of C. S. Lewis.* New York: HarperCollins, 2005.

King, Don W. *C. S. Lewis, Poet: The Legacy of His Poetic Impulse.* Kent, OH: Kent State University Press, 2001.

Lewis, C. S. *God in the Dock.* Grand Rapids: Eerdmans, 1970.

———. *A Grief Observed.* New York: HarperCollins, 1994.

———. *The Last Battle.* New York: HarperCollins, 2002.

———. *Mere Christianity.* New York: HarperCollins, 2001.

———. *The Problem of Pain.* London: HarperCollins, 1996.

———. *Reflections on the Psalms.* London: HarperCollins, 2000.

———. *Selected Literary Essays.* New York: Cambridge University Press, 1969.

———. *Surprised by Joy.* London: HarperCollins, 2002.

Loades, Ann. "C. S. Lewis: Grief Observed, Rationality Abandoned, Faith Regained." *Literature and Theology* 3 (1989): 107–21.

MacSwain, Robert, and Michael Ward, eds. *The Cambridge Companion to C. S. Lewis.* Cambridge: Cambridge University Press, 2010.

Markos, Louis. *Restoring Beauty: The Good, the True, and the Beautiful in the Writings of C. S. Lewis.* Colorado Springs, CO: Biblica, 2010.

McGrath, Alister E. *C. S. Lewis—A Life: Eccentric Genius, Reluctant Prophet.* Carol Stream, IL: Tyndale, 2013.

———. *The Intellectual World of C. S. Lewis.* Oxford: Wiley-Blackwell, 2013.

Phillips, Justin. *C. S. Lewis at the BBC.* London: HarperCollins, 2003.

Sayer, George. *Jack: A Life of C. S. Lewis.* London: Hodder & Stoughton, 1997.

DIETRICH BONHOEFFER

In Defense of Christian Witness

MATTHEW D. KIRKPATRICK

Dietrich Bonhoeffer (1906–1945) is known as much for his life as for his thought. He was executed just a few weeks before the end of World War II for his involvement in the German resistance and its assassination attempts on Hitler's life. Bonhoeffer's statue joins the likes of Max Kolbe, Óscar Romero, and Martin Luther King Jr. in the gallery of twentieth-century martyrs adorning the Great West Door of Westminster Abbey in London. Born in Germany in 1906, Bonhoeffer had a life largely punctuated by warfare or the fragile peace that existed around it. In many respects, Bonhoeffer's theology should be understood and contextualized by his environment. This is not to relativize it as relevant only within such a specific historical setting. Even a cursory understanding of Bonhoeffer's lasting legacy reveals just how relevant his thought remains even now.[1] Rather, it is to recognize that all his work was written in response to the constantly changing environment in which he found himself and the never-ending battles he felt compelled to fight with the ideological and social injustice he witnessed.

HISTORICAL BACKGROUND

Bonhoeffer was born into a privileged, upper-middle-class family. However, quite apart from embracing the conservative status quo, he and his siblings were taught to think for themselves and to stand apart from the crowd. Where many within the nation were easily swept up in the fervor of both World War I and the rise of National Socialism, the Bonhoeffer household watched with a clear and critical eye. During the 1920s and 1930s, Germany felt aggrieved by the loss of World War I but also by their treatment at the Treaty of Versailles, where,

---

1. Cf. Matthew D. Kirkpatrick, ed., *Engaging Bonhoeffer: The Impact and Influence of Bonhoeffer's Life and Thought* (Minneapolis: Fortress, 2016).

among other things, they had been forced to take sole responsibility for the war. Many Germans continued to feel the impact of such unjust treatment and looked at their victorious neighbors with suspicion and resentment. Promoted on a platform of national renewal, vitality, and romantic hope, it is no surprise that Hitler's National Socialism would have been so appealing. Although Bonhoeffer was not immune to the injustices of Versailles or sympathy for his nation, such feelings of naive nationalism never swayed him. Throughout his life, Bonhoeffer traveled far and wide, exposing himself to all manner of cultural, political, socioeconomic, and religious communities. It was only two days after Hitler's inauguration as Reich Chancellor that Bonhoeffer delivered a radio address attacking the concept of the führer and its hold on the younger generation.[2] Even as early as 1932, a year before Hitler had gained power, Bonhoeffer had already predicted the possibility of further war on the horizon.[3]

As can be seen from his first doctoral dissertation, *Sanctorum Communio*, one of Bonhoeffer's central concerns was the church. In opposition to the spirit of the age that viewed it with suspicion or derision, Bonhoeffer developed a comprehensive ecclesiology that considered the church as central not only to the imparting of revelation but also to God's action within the world. Quite in contrast to German isolationism, Bonhoeffer believed the church to be universal and threw himself into ecumenical work, traveling all around Europe to attend the meetings of various groups and working as an international youth secretary.[4] Although Bonhoeffer affirmed the importance of local churches, he believed it was the one great ecumenical church that had world historical significance, and it was precisely this church that could challenge any secular power.[5]

Much of Bonhoeffer's energy in the 1930s was spent trying to bring the ecumenical movement to an understanding of itself as church and to a recognition of its task and responsibility. But Bonhoeffer was no less exhaustive back home. Something of his understanding of the situation can be seen in a sermon he preached at the Kaiser Wilhelm Memorial Church in Berlin on May 28, 1933.[6] Here Bonhoeffer argued for the presence of two churches: the church of Aaron

---

2. Dietrich Bonhoeffer, *Berlin: 1932–1933* (Minneapolis: Fortress, 2009), 268–82.

3. Dietrich Bonhoeffer, *Ecumenical, Academic, and Pastoral Work: 1931–1932* (Minneapolis: Fortress, 2012), 375–81.

4. In stark contrast, two of Germany's most influential Lutheran theologians, Paul Althaus and Immanuel Hirsch, published an article in the *Hamburger Nachrichten* condemning any involvement with the churches of victorious nations as fundamentally at odds with the truth.

5. Cf. Dietrich Bonhoeffer, *London: 1933–1935* (Minneapolis: Fortress, 2007), 309. Note Bonhoeffer's threefold statement of the responsibilities of the church toward the states, which includes as its third point the need to bring it to a grinding halt (Bonhoeffer, *Berlin*, 365). This is especially noticeable as Luther's theology, on which Bonhoeffer's statement is based, denies the possibility of rebellion against the state (cf. Martin Luther, "On Temporal Authority" and "Whether Soldiers, too, can be Saved").

6. Bonhoeffer, *Berlin*, 472–76.

and the church of Moses. The first dresses itself up in its full regalia to proclaim a message that the people want to hear and create the god that they want to worship. The latter is obedient to the Word of God and proclaims his truth no matter what the consequences. For Bonhoeffer, this profound distinction would become manifest in the Nazi-backed *Reichskirche* and the Confessing Church established to stand against it respectively. The first confused the realms of the church and the state and affirmed the hand of God on the Volk and its leaders in bringing about his judgment and redemption on the earth. The latter recognized the authority of the state (according to Romans 13) but also defended the distinct responsibility of the church in standing under the Word of God in unwavering allegiance and responsibility to God.[7] From 1935 Bonhoeffer would lead the illegal Confessing Church seminary first at Zingst and then at Finkenwalde. And it is from his time here that he wrote two of Christianity's great spiritual classics, *Life Together* and *Discipleship*.

Tragically, the Confessing Church never truly became the church of Moses. Despite Bonhoeffer's efforts to mobilize it against the Nazi regime, and to recognize the state's true identity through its treatment of the Jews, the Confessing Church remained trapped in political wranglings and theological debate and chained to an illegitimate nationalism that crippled its effectiveness. Although the reasons behind his decision are more complex, Bonhoeffer finally saw evidence of righteous action, not in the church but in the nonreligious German resistance. And it is to this that he finally gave his life.

THEOLOGICAL CONTEXT

The eighteenth and nineteenth centuries represent a period of significant upheaval, not just politically but also philosophically and theologically. Up until this point, Christianity had maintained its influence over the West, and the church had retained its authority. But during this time both elements were slowly undermined and gave way to a growing individualization and secularization. This development was in large part precipitated and promoted by the growth of Protestantism, which affirmed as one of its central doctrines a liberty of conscience.[8] Such a newfound freedom promoted a critical eye to the past and a deconstruction of its authoritarian structures. But such a methodology would

---

7. This position is most powerfully expressed in the Barmen Declaration, written in 1934. Although primarily drafted by Karl Barth, Bonhoeffer became one of its most vociferous advocates and came to consider it a standard of authentic faith.

8. Cf. Owen Chadwick, *The Secularisation of the European Mind in the 19th Century* (Cambridge: CUP, 1975).

not remain the sole possession of Luther and the Reformers but would ultimately lead to the subservience of Christianity to morality in Kant, the transcending of Christianity to speculative philosophy in Hegel, the relativizing of Christianity to other religious expressions in Schleiermacher, and finally the annihilation of Christianity to "true" human nobility in Nietzsche. Although these represent more radical interpretations, in the face of the Enlightenment and the scientific method, more traditional theology also underwent a radical deconstruction. Perhaps most striking is the promotion of the historical-critical method in biblical scholarship that sought to strip away what was perceived as the corrupting elements of the biblical narrative to uncover the true character of Christ.[9]

Bonhoeffer was clearly aware of these movements and engaged with many of their leading proponents. But he believed that, despite the diversity of their views, each of these groups made one simple mistake—they all sought to do theology from below, by perceiving, testing, and critiquing everything from the perspective of the human mind. Whether through reason, emotions, zeitgeist, or texts, "revelation" was something to be figured out rather than received. And it is this perspective that rested at the heart of the liberal theology that Bonhoeffer stood so firmly against.

Although Bonhoeffer considered this liberal methodology to be generally flawed, the historical context reveals why he considered it problematic. During the period after the upheavals of World War I and the Treaty of Versailles, Germany had experienced a romantic revival and a harking back to its perceived "true" heritage. The German *völkische* movement believed that Germany's woes were the fault of foreign pollution and that Germany needed to regain its position in world history by purifying itself from these influences.[10] Such national enthusiasm gelled perfectly with the foundations of liberal theology, which also sought to strip away a perceived corruption. Consequently, *völkisch* theology quickly gained influence throughout the nation. In particular, it manifested itself in the powerful German Christian movement that sought to redeem Christ from the corrupting influence of the Jewish Old Testament and the rabbi Paul and to present Jesus as a conquering Aryan Christ who affirmed Germany's true promise as the people of God.[11] For Bonhoeffer, a theology that so easily justified

---

9. Cf. David Friedrich Strauss's *Life of Jesus* (1835), William Wrede's *The Messianic Secret* (1901), and Albert Schweitzer's *The Quest for the Historical Jesus* (1906).

10. For helpful introductions to the *Volkische* movement, and its development into *Volkische Theologie*, see Peter Matheson, *The Third Reich and the Christian Churches* (Edinburgh: T&T Clark, 1981); John A. Moses, *The Reluctant Revolutionary: Dietrich Bonhoeffer's Collision with Prusso-German History* (New York; Oxford: Berghahn Books, 2009); and Klauss Scholder, *The Churches and the Third Reich* (London: SCM, 1987–8).

11. For a fascinating exposé of the pervasive and revolutionary effect of *völkische* theology on University life, see Susannah Heschel, "For 'Volk, Blood, and God': The Theological Faculty at the University of Jena

a Hegelian *Machtstaat*, a Nietzschean master-slave morality, and which manifested itself in overt antisemitism and sweeping prejudice was simply the extension of a liberal theology from below. But for Bonhoeffer, this was no abstract extension *ad absurdium* but a murderous reality he witnessed all around him.

Bonhoeffer was clearly concerned with these different theological and philosophical elements and how they sought to abolish or distort Christianity. But despite his involvement in such academic disputes, Bonhoeffer's focus was not in doing battle with philosophers and wayward theologians. These errors are not, for Bonhoeffer, the product of a particular intellectual zeitgeist but of the fallen human condition. Consequently, where errors may be obvious within nefarious *völkische* forms of thought, they are the exact same dangers that normal, well-meaning Christians fall into on a day-to-day basis. Although this chapter will consider some of his more academic involvement, Bonhoeffer was not primarily an apologist for Christianity against atheism or secularism but an apologist for Christianity against Christians. It was in these far more subtle distortions that Bonhoeffer perceived Christianity's real enemy.

APOLOGETIC RESPONSE

Bonhoeffer's formal relationship with apologetics is not uncomplicated. But three apologetical arguments can be discerned within Bonhoeffer's thought that encapsulate something of his theology and offer us penetrating insight into his engagement with his context.

APOLOGETICS FOR A CHRISTOLOGICAL COMMUNITY

Bonhoeffer's earlier more academic works[12] are usually given far less attention than such spiritual classics as *Discipleship*, *Life Together*, and his *Letters and Papers from Prison*. But they provide an essential foundation for understanding Bonhoeffer's thought more generally and offer important contributions in their own right. In particular, they provide crucial insight into Bonhoeffer's understanding of sin that rests at the heart of his theology.

For Bonhoeffer, humankind's fall has an essentially epistemological character.[13] Drawing firmly from Augustine, Bonhoeffer argues that before the fall, Adam and Eve received all their knowledge from God directly. Rather than

During the Third Reich," in Wolfgang Bialas and Alison Rabinbach, eds., *Nazi Germany and the Humanities* (Oxford: Oneworld, 2007), 365–98.

12. Such as his doctoral dissertations, *Sanctorum Communio* and *Act and Being*, and lecture series, *Creation and Fall*.

13. Bonhoeffer's understanding of the fall is most fully elaborated in *Creation and Fall*, as well as the essay, "God's Love and the Disintegration of the World" in his *Ethics*.

storing up information themselves, they gained knowledge of reality from God in each moment, and their understanding and actions were in total harmony with him. But at the heart of both the garden and the story lies the Tree of the Knowledge of Good and Evil, which represents the decision that lies permanently before humankind: a life that gains its knowledge directly from God or, by taking the fruit, one that seeks to gain it from elsewhere. In choosing to eat from this tree, humankind reveals its rejection of a reliance on God and, in its decision against God, a reliance on its own judgment and perception.

The consequence of the fall is that humankind gains its wish and receives all knowledge. But as the human mind is limited, and now sinful, it has no ability to retain or grasp this knowledge, which now comes crashing down around it. Humankind is cursed to rely on its own ability to piece the shards of reality back together and to live out of its own abilities rather than God's.

With this foundation, Bonhoeffer offers a stunning attack on all philosophy, which relies on this limited and sinful mind.[14] First, regarding the mind's limitation, Bonhoeffer argues that if we live within a system of existence, there is no way of knowing what that system is. Only someone who can look down on it, seeing its beginning and end, its creation and telos, can know what it is. No matter what patterns may be rationally perceived or facts empirically discerned, without the full story, their true nature can never be known. All the systems we create for ourselves—even such apparently infallible systems such as mathematics—are ultimately meaningless as they have no grounding and have been divorced from their true origin.[15] Secondly, the systems we create for ourselves are also sinful. Consequently, they are not just the best systems we can come up with under the circumstances. We also design them to appear objective and absolute to offer ourselves a sense of security to overcome the profound anxiety at the heart of an anchorless existence.

In this way, Bonhoeffer argues that two realities now exist—the Reality of God that manifests his glory and the projected "reality" of humankind that reveals the nature of its fallen mind. Bonhoeffer's position is summarized in an early lecture delivered at Union Theological Seminary in 1931, where he states:

> The ego stands in the centre of the world, which is created, ruled, overpowered by the ego. The identification of the ego with the ground of

---

14. This can be found particularly within both *Sanctorum Communio* and *Act and Being*, but also the lectures "The Theology of Crisis and Its Attitude toward Philosophy and Science" and "The Anthropological Question in Contemporary Philosophy and Theology" *Barcelona, Berlin, New York: 1928–1931* (Minneapolis: Fortress, 2008), 389–408, 462–76.

15. Dietrich Bonhoeffer, *Creation and Fall: A Theological Exposition of Genesis 1–3* (Minneapolis: Fortress, 1997), 53.

everything which has been called God is inevitable. There are no limits for the ego, its power and its claim is boundless, it is its own standard. Here all transcendence is pulled into the circle of the creative ego. . . . Man knows himself immediately by the act of the coming of the ego to itself and knows through himself essentially everything, even God. God is in man, God is man himself.[16]

The only way out of this circularity of thought is through something transcendent breaking in.[17] For something to be truly transcendent, it cannot simply be different to thought or come from outside of thought. Otherwise, it simply remains a new thing to be perceived and assimilated into thought. It must be opposed to our ways of thinking and resist becoming objectivized.

For Bonhoeffer, this transcendence is found only in Christ. Drawing heavily on Kierkegaard, Bonhoeffer argues that in both the incarnation and crucifixion, we find Christ as a paradox that defies our systematization and objectification. He is both "a stumbling block to Jews and foolishness to Gentiles" (1 Cor 1:23), precisely because there is no way of knowing this ignoble, suffering man as God, except through faith. But by becoming so offensive to human reason, such faith is created only by reason's submission and a return to knowing only from and through God rather than ourselves. As Bonhoeffer explains in a journal article from 1932,

The main difference between a so-called revelation in the sphere of idea and a revelation in "once-ness" is that man always will be able to learn a new idea and to fit it into his system of ideas; but a revelation in "once-ness" in a historical fact, in a historical personality, is always anew a challenge to man. He cannot overcome it by pulling it into the system which he already had before. This is the reason why God reveals himself in history: only so is the freedom of his personality guarded. The revelation in history means revelation in hiddenness; revelation in ideas (principles, values, etc.) means revelation in openness.[18]

In this first section, Bonhoeffer highlights how Christianity not only reveals the epistemological problem at the heart of philosophy but also how it

---

16. Bonhoeffer, *Barcelona, Berlin, New York*, 471. Bonhoeffer's lecture was designed to introduce his lecturers and fellow students to the theology of Karl Barth and its dialectical methodology that he believed to be largely absent from their studies. But these thoughts very much represent the direction of his own thought.

17. Cf. Dietrich Bonhoeffer, *Sanctorum Communio* (Minneapolis: Fortress, 1998), 44–55.

18. Dietrich Bonhoeffer, "Concerning the Christian Idea of God," *The Journal of Religion* 12:2 (Apr 1932): 181.

offers something of a solution—even if this is not something philosophers might accept. But so far Bonhoeffer has not departed radically from such thinkers as Augustine, Luther, Kierkegaard, and Barth, even if his description extends their ideas. Bonhoeffer does, however, make a unique move.

Like other theologians at the earlier part of the twentieth century, Bonhoeffer shows an appreciation for the I-Thou school of thought, especially through the work of Eberhard Grisebach, which argued that a person, an "I," comes into existence only through confrontation with another being, a "thou."[19] For Bonhoeffer, Grisebach had correctly perceived the epistemological problem but had argued that ethical encounter with the will of a human thou provided the transcendence to break through and create the I. For Bonhoeffer, a human thou can never become truly transcendent, as it can always be interpreted by the I and enfolded into its own "reality." It is only in the absolute submission of faith that God breaks in as the Divine Thou and draws us out from nothingness into true existence, establishing our I.[20]

The distinctive move Bonhoeffer makes is in the recognition that God does not come to us as a disembodied spirit or voice. He comes to us through other people. Consequently, other humans become thou to us through the Divine Thou. As Bonhoeffer explains in *Sanctorum Communio*:

> One human being cannot of its own accord make another into an I, an ethical person conscious of responsibility. *God or the Holy Spirit joins the concrete You; only through God's active working does the other become a You to me from whom my arises. In other words, every human You is an image of the divine You.* . . . This is not to say that it is a borrowed attribute of God, and not really a You. Rather, the divine You creates the human You. And since the human You is created and willed by God, it is a *real, absolute, and holy You*, like the divine You.[21]

Bonhoeffer's point is that if we say we have faith in God, we must also have faith in the one imparting God to us. And it is in this disposition of open submission to one another that not only is my I created but true community is established. For Bonhoeffer, all philosophical attempts to define the person fail by either annihilating any concept of community as simply functional for the individual or, more commonly, subordinating the individual to the universal.

---

19. Although these ideas were made more well-known through Martin Buber's seminal work, *I-Thou*, Bonhoeffer's own exposure came through Grisebach's *Die Grenzen des Erziehers und seine Verantwortung*.

20. Cf. *Barcelona, Berlin, New York*, 398–99, 472.

21. Bonhoeffer, *Sanctorum Communio*, 54–55, Bonhoeffer's emphasis.

Rather, it is only in the concept of faith in this transcendent, paradoxical Christ, and so also in one another, that adequate anthropological and sociological descriptions may be found.

APOLOGETICS FOR A CHRISTOLOGICAL FAITH

Where Bonhoeffer's early work defined the concept of community, the main bulk of his writing sought to engage with this community and the ways in which humankind's fallenness continued to impact its life and knowledge.

A few more details of the fall narrative are important to draw out. For Bonhoeffer, the nature of the serpent's conversation with Eve is key. First, the serpent does not try to get Eve to rebel *against* God but rather *toward* him. In Adam and Eve's desire to be *sicut deus*—like God—their desire was not to throw God out. After all, why would they want to? Rather, the serpent seduces them to try and be with God, but now on their own terms.

The serpent's conversation also reveals how this is achieved. By asking Eve, "Did God really say . . . ?" the serpent gets Eve to stand in judgment of God's word rather than simply receiving it. For Bonhoeffer, the associations with the liberal theological method are hardly subtle. As Bonhoeffer describes it, in this story we find the first "religious" or "pious" conversation, as here, for the first time, God is the one being discussed as the object of knowledge rather than its source.[22] But liberal theology is simply an obvious manifestation of a fallen desire that rests within everyone, no matter what their theological affiliation. For Bonhoeffer, the projections of the limited and sinful mind are not exclusive to the philosophical world but find their most dangerous manifestation within traditional Christianity when it is no longer received as *transcendent revelation* but is converted into *imminent religion.*

In trying to grasp hold of its knowledge of God, the limited mind systematizes it into the realm of ideas and makes it comprehensible to itself. Here the incarnation is converted into a doctrinal conundrum to be figured out and Christ a series of conceptual principles or ethical rules to be analyzed, verified, and acknowledged as true. But the mind's limitation is never without its sinfulness. For beyond simple necessity, by converting Christ into a verified system, he becomes worthy of our appreciation and allegiance but not of our discipleship. For Bonhoeffer, systems produce admirers rather than true followers or imitators because a system has authority only because we have judged it and authorized it.[23] Furthermore, Christ as a religious system becomes homogenous

---

22. Bonhoeffer, *Creation and Fall*, 103–10.
23. Note that *Nachfolge*, the title of Bonhoeffer's famous work, means "discipleship" or "imitation."

with other systems of thought that are likewise authorized. Consequently, the essential conflict of Christianity with the world is annihilated. In both these ways, Christianity becomes the perfect religion to quieten our existential anxiety and convince us that we are saved, without undermining the life we want to live.

One of the most famous ways in which Bonhoeffer describes this corruption is found at the beginning of *Discipleship* and his discussion of "cheap grace."[24] For Bonhoeffer, the church has allowed itself to look like the world by having converted grace into a principle that is simply received and demands nothing from us. In this way the church has distorted Luther's principle of *sola gracia* by promoting the idea that not only are extraordinary works not required of us but such works even display a lack of true faith. Cheap grace allows Christians to continue to live their lives without spiritual duress and for the church to retain its popularity by preaching peace and comfort. If we recall Bonhoeffer's sermon from 1933, cheap grace is the hallmark of the church of Aaron. In contrast, in the church of Moses, costly grace is freely given but demands our entire lives in imitation to its giver. As Bonhoeffer states in that most famous of phrases, "When Christ calls a man, he bids him come and die."[25]

This distortion of Christianity is not the complex product of Christian philosophers but a danger of ordinary providence. All it requires is for Christians no longer to go to God for revelation but instead to take hold of his revelation and make it the mundane object of our knowledge. Such cheapening distortion can be found in such figures as the visionary Christian leader who sculpts their ministry around a Christian concept but no longer goes to God to receive it,[26] the preacher whose passionate sermons tell the congregation more about their own thoughts than those of Christ,[27] the ethicist who prefers developing Christian rules or programs to listening to what God may say to him or her in each moment,[28] or the evangelist who seeks to achieve something in someone rather than discerning God's will for that individual.[29] Bonhoeffer's intention is not to make God's revelation entirely subjective or to undermine the givenness of this revelation within Scripture. It is rather to highlight the danger of when this revelation no longer needs God. Bonhoeffer summarizes this tendency in

24. Dietrich Bonhoeffer, *Discipleship* (Minneapolis: Fortress, 2001), 43–56.
25. This became famous through the earlier translation by Reginald Fuller (Dietrich Bonhoeffer, *The Cost of Discipleship* [London: SCM, 1959], 89). A more faithful rendition is, "Whenever Christ calls us, his call leads us to death" (Bonhoeffer, *Discipleship*, 87).
26. Dietrich Bonhoeffer, *Life Together/Prayerbook of the Bible* (Minneapolis: Fortress, 2005), 34–36, 39–44.
27. Bonhoeffer, *Discipleship*, 37–40.
28. Dietrich Bonhoeffer, *Ethics* (Minneapolis: Fortress, 2005), 47–57, 76–82.
29. Bonhoeffer, *Discipleship*, 172.

a powerful speech to the World Alliance and the Ecumenical Council youth conference in 1932, where he charges, "Has it not become terribly clear, again and again, in all that we have discussed here with one another that we are no longer obedient to the Bible? We prefer our own thoughts to those of the Bible. We no longer read the Bible seriously. We read it no longer against ourselves but only for ourselves."[30] Christianity under the control of our limited and sinful minds becomes a source of epistemological and existential comfort because it does what we want it to rather than becoming a source of transcendent revelation that breaks through our epistemological circle.

If the source of Christianity as a religion is the human mind, as the first of our arguments has made clear, the source of true Christianity is the transcendent, paradoxical Christ. By becoming human and suffering on the cross, God makes himself impenetrable to rational gaze. As Bonhoeffer notes, "God himself dies and reveals himself in the death of a man, who is condemned as a sinner. It is precisely this, which is the foolishness of the Christian idea of God, which has been witnessed to by all genuine Christian thinking from Paul, Augustine, Luther, and Kierkegaard and Barth."[31]

In doing so, two things are achieved. First, Christ can be known only through faith. In his "Lectures on Christology," Bonhoeffer argues that Christianity as a religion asks of Christ "What?" and "How?"[32] Such questions are designed to make sense of Christ and to figure him out.[33] In contrast, the only true question of Christology is "Who?"[34] Such a question is asked by someone who acknowledges that all their knowledge and abilities have come to an end before Christ and submits themselves to Christ for him to reveal himself. "Who?" is the question of faith. Secondly, as described above, it is only by coming as the paradox, rather than systematic idea or manifesto, that Christ commands our absolute submission and brings us back into discipleship and imitation. For Bonhoeffer, faith and imitation are one and the same.[35]

Against the Christianity of majority rule, Bonhoeffer articulates a Christianity that requires absolute submission and discipleship, whose gift is costly grace, and whose only action is faithful obedience to the Word of God.

---

30. Bonhoeffer, *Ecumenical, Academic, and Pastoral Work*, 377–78.
31. Ibid., 184.
32. Published in different editions as *Christology* (1966), or *Christ the Centre* (1978).
33. Bonhoeffer argues that the essential error of the christological heresies is simply in trying to make Christ rationally comprehensible with regards to how God might be born, die, or exist in two complete natures. The creeds, on the other hand, simply state the truth rather than try to rationally explain it.
34. Bonhoeffer, *Berlin*, 302f.
35. For Bonhoeffer's discussion of the symbiotic relationship of faith obedience, see *Discipleship*, 43–56.

APOLOGETICS FOR A CHRISTOLOGICAL HUMANITY

So far, the first two apological positions rest on similar foundations—the radical nature of sin and our absolute reliance on God, which are themes that run throughout the majority of Bonhoeffer's work. But when we turn to *Letters and Papers from Prison*, written after Bonhoeffer's involvement in the *Abwehr* resistance and his subsequent imprisonment, we find a shift in his theology. Scholars have debated whether his prison theology represents a difference of emphasis or substance. What is clear is that the apparent unworldliness of such works as *Discipleship* is tempered here by Bonhoeffer's reflections on family, friendship, and the blessings that God has given us. These thoughts are precipitated, undoubtedly, by Bonhoeffer's sense of isolation and the space—perhaps for the first time in his hectic life—to reflect on their true meaning. And so it is here, in the darkness of the prison cell, that Bonhoeffer considers the light that God has given us.

In *Letters and Papers from Prison*, Bonhoeffer offers one of his most forceful attacks on the church. Throughout his authorship, Bonhoeffer had been as critical of the church as he was in affirming it. Given what has already been discussed of his attack on religion, a call for a "religionless Christianity" should be unsurprising.[36] The difference we find here is that where Bonhoeffer had focused on the ways in which humankind had manipulated God in their conception of him, now the focus was on the way in which the church had used this conception to manipulate humankind.

In letters to his close friend and confidant Eberhard Bethge, Bonhoeffer suggests that the church has converted God into a *deus ex machina*, or a "working hypothesis," to convince people that the only way in which they will understand life is through the answers God awards.[37] The point for Bonhoeffer is not that God's self-revelation does not also bring enlightenment to life but that the church has used this conception of God as a way of ensuring its own power within society as the keepers of God's revelation. Founded on the assumption of a religious *a priori*—that all people, deep down, have a sense of God and need for him—everyone has been made subservient to the church, needing its guidance and oversight. One of the most important ways it has done this is convincing them of their absolute sinfulness and so the need for the church's absolution.

But Bonhoeffer raises a series of controversial questions: What if there is no such thing as a religious *a priori*? What if people no longer need the answers of the church because they can rightly figure them out for themselves? What if

---

36. Dietrich Bonhoeffer, *Letters and Papers from Prison* (Minneapolis: Fortress, 2009), 362–64, 372.
37. Cf. Bonhoeffer, *Letters and Papers*, 366, 425–27, 450, 479.

the world has "come of age"?[38] For Bonhoeffer, the world has fundamentally changed, and with the march of the Enlightenment and the sciences, people are able to understand the world in ways that were inconceivable even a few hundred years earlier. Consequently, the church has unwittingly succeeded in doing two key things. First, by converting God into a religious concept, the church has been able to enslave people for a time. But in this new age, the religious God is no longer relevant and has been pushed ever more firmly out of our existence.[39] The seeds of the church's domination have become the foundation for its downfall. Secondly, through its demand for power, the church has worked against humankind's development and so has not only lost its control but has created an environment of hostility toward God as an epistemological oppressor.[40]

With this foundation, Bonhoeffer makes his audacious apologetic claim: if God had been understood correctly, the world would have come of age sooner because in the true God, we find the essence of human fulfillment.[41] In opposition to a purely secular mentality, it is only in Christianity that we find a true humanism. Quite apart from *Letters and Papers from Prison* presenting a theology at odds with his previous thought, it is in this claim that we find his two previous thoughts combined.

First, if we recall Bonhoeffer's argument from the start of his authorship, it is only in Christianity that an authentic understanding of both person and community can be understood. At its foundation, there is no way a secular philosophy (or any other philosophy for that matter) could be humanistic, because there is no way for it to know what a human actually is. Any attempt to promote the "human" will simply be the projection of what we consider humanity to be and will end up as limited and sinful as the mind that is projecting it.

But this first argument does not do enough to ground Bonhoeffer's position as properly humanistic, as what God reveals through his breaking into our minds has not yet been adequately defined. It is here that we are brought to the second argument. For although the idea of Christ as paradox may appear to take us further away from our experience of concrete human life, for Bonhoeffer, we must take seriously the essential content of the incarnation. While the union of the divine and human makes Christ incognito, we still find in him the fullness

---

38. Ibid., 361–65.

39. Ibid., 426.

40. It is not surprising that Bonhoeffer had read all of Nietzsche's work by the time he had completed his first doctoral dissertation. For Bonhoeffer, Nietzsche had understood something essential in his attack on Christianity and its apparent affirmation of human weakness and ignorance rather than strength. Nietzsche's error was in failing to distinguish between Christendom and what true Christianity stands for (Cf. Peter Frick, *Bonhoeffer's Intellectual Formation: Theology and Philosophy in his Thought* [Eugene, OR: Wipf & Stock, 2008], 175–76).

41. Bonhoeffer, *Letters and Papers*, 431.

of humanity, and that in relation to the divine. For Bonhoeffer, Christ is true humanity. In Pilate's statement, *ecce homo*—"Behold the man"—we hear the essence of Christ's human nature.[42] If we want to know what a true human being looks like, we must look to Christ and his relationships to both God and his neighbor. In our fallen existence we remain pseudohumans.

For Bonhoeffer, despite the tension that runs throughout his authorship between sin and the redeemed life, he rejects a dualism that sees a tension between the church and the world. Rather, the church is the true world, and in its existence it calls the world back to its true identity.[43] In the same way, Christ's life calls us to our true existence as humans, and that in relation to ourselves, to God, and to others. But this is achieved only by the breaking in of God's self-revelation within our lives.

Where the church may have worked against humankind, crippling it so that it would not mature beyond the church's authority, so for Bonhoeffer the whole point of salvation history is not just to save us spiritually but also redeem us as humanity. Although Bonhoeffer never undermines the importance of sin, sanctification is a process toward regaining our true lives in all their spiritual, existential, and intellectual glory. But this can be achieved only through the revelation of that one true human.

APOLOGETIC METHODOLOGY

Thus far it should be clear that Bonhoeffer presents a variety of interrelated apologetical arguments. But there is also a problem that is precipitated by the question of methodology. Bonhoeffer himself did not like apologetics. Revealed in his reflections on the preaching he witnessed while in the United States, warnings expressed to his students at Finkenwalde, and the final condemnations in his prison theology, Bonhoeffer's view of apologetics is that it represents a consistently dangerous form of theological thought and expression. In order to understand his perspective, it is helpful to reflect on the characterization presented at the beginning of Avery Dulles's *A History of Apologetics*, where he states:

> In the minds of many Christians today the term "apologetics" carries unpleasant connotations. The apologist is regarded as an aggressive, opportunistic person who tries, by fair means or foul, to argue people into joining the Church. Numerous charges are laid at the door of apologetics:

---

42. Bonhoeffer, *Ethics*, 82–96.
43. Ibid., 66–68, 97–102.

its neglect of grace, of prayer, and of the life-giving power of the word of God; its tendency to oversimplify and syllogize the approach to faith; its dilution of the scandal of the Christian message; and its implied presupposition that God's word should be judged by the norm of fallible, not to say fallen, human reason.[44]

As this weighty tome makes clear, there are many forms of apologetics. And this chapter presents Bonhoeffer in an apologetical guise. But Dulles's characterization goes a long way to describe Bonhoeffer's own definition and evaluation. As Bonhoeffer makes clear in his lectures on homiletics at Finkenwalde, he believed that apologetics made use of "logical and aesthetic tricks, flowery speech, rhetorical attempts to persuade and convince" and in the end did more to "justify its own existence" than in truly presenting the gospel.[45] In his *Letters and Papers from Prison*, Bonhoeffer takes his critique further to single out apologetics as one of the means by which the church wars against the world's coming of age. As he describes, "In very different forms the Christian apologetic is now moving against this self-confidence. It is trying to persuade this world that has come of age that it cannot live without 'God' as its guardian . . . I consider the attack by Christian apologetics on the world's coming of age as, first of all, pointless, second ignoble, and, third, unchristian."[46]

For Bonhoeffer, a robust hamartiology and Christology make clear that faith is not achieved by convincing someone of an idea but rather of them encountering Christ. All the theologian or evangelist can do is to help the individual become able to utter the question "Who?" This cannot occur by articulating ever more powerful arguments about Christ's plausibility but by destroying all preconceived ideas such that true submission before this paradoxical being may be realized.[47] In Bonhoeffer's mind, if apologetics seeks to "persuade and convince" that Christianity is true, it does the opposite of what God has sought to achieve in the incarnation. For Bonhoeffer, apologetics fails not just in its presentation of the gospel but also in its understanding of the gospel.

This point is brought across powerfully in Bonhoeffer's perspective of the

---

44. Avery Cardinal Dulles, *A History of Apologetics* (San Francisco: Ignatius, 1999), xix.

45. Dietrich Bonhoeffer, *Theological Education at Finkenwalde: 1935–1937* (Minneapolis: Fortress, 2013), 504.

46. Bonhoeffer, *Letters and Papers*, 426–27.

47. Bonhoeffer spends very little time dealing with those who don't believe. And this was rarely his pastoral context. But in *Discipleship*, Bonhoeffer advises pastors not to debate with the parishioner who states that they have lost their faith nor to try and convince them that Christianity is true. Rather, they should simply ask them to be obedient, as through this disposition before God they manifest a form of submission by which God may reveal himself once more (Bonhoeffer, *Discipleship*, 67–69).

absurdity of thinking the gospel could be stronger and more convincing than its subject matter, Jesus Christ. As he notes in *Discipleship*:

> All our urging, running after people, proselytizing, every attempt to accomplish something in another person by our own power is in vain and dangerous. . . . The driving restlessness of the group of disciples, who do not want to accept any limitation on their effectiveness, and their zeal, which does not respect resistance, confuses the word of the gospel with a conquering idea. An idea requires fanatics, who neither know nor respect resistance. The idea is strong. But the Word of God is so weak that it suffers to be despised and rejected by people. . . . Disciples who would know nothing about this weakness of the Word would not have come to know the secret of God's lowliness. This weak Word, which suffers contradiction by sinners, is the only strong, merciful Word, that can make sinners repent from the bottom of their hearts. The Word's power is unveiled in weakness. If the Word came in full, unveiled power, that would be the final judgment day.[48]

For Bonhoeffer, Christ's paradoxical nature is not simply an indication of his absolute heterogeneity with the world but also of what is needed for humankind to be saved. It is only this truly transcendent being that can break through the circularity of our limited and sinful minds and bring us back into absolute reliance on the reality of God. Christ could not come as the conquering ruler who appears so deserving of our esteem. Rather, he comes in weakness, ignominy, and offence, and only in this way can he save us and draw us back into the relationship with God that the creation account reveals.[49]

This does not undermine the content of theology or the relative truth of gospel statements. Bonhoeffer spent much of his time developing and promoting creedal formulas.[50] It simply means that Christian doctrine is not the sum total of faith but the human formulation and expression of the faith that is created by encounter with Christ. Christ does not call us to agreement with a manifesto but submission to a person. Bonhoeffer's own apologetical arguments are not designed to convince anyone into relationship with God. Rather, they are forms of argument that God may use to convict believers (or potentially nonbelievers)

---

48. Bonhoeffer, *Discipleship*, 172–73.

49. As Bonhoeffer notes from prison, "God is weak and powerless in the world and in precisely this way, and only so, is at our side and helps us" (Bonhoeffer, *Letters and Papers*, 479).

50. In addition to his affirmation of the Barmen Declaration, Bonhoeffer helped pen the initial drafts of the Bethel Confession that likewise sought to counter the nationalistic faith of the German Christians.

of their need to continue to submit to God and, once submitted, to aid in understanding what God has achieved in his reality, not ours.

How then should we understand Bonhoeffer's methodology? In contrast to apologetics, Bonhoeffer offers us his concise answer: "Do not defend the word of God but rather witness it."[51] This position is affirmed at the end of his life, in a tantalizing outline for a future book, where he states, "The church's word gains weight and power not through concepts but by example."[52] For Bonhoeffer, such a position was necessary to confirm, given the church's obvious guilt and failure in this regard.[53] But, again, it was far more so given humankind's general fallen state. If we recall Bonhoeffer's first apologetical position, we become thou to each other not when we utter abstract words but when we truly manifest the Divine Thou and actually become Christ to one another.

CONTRIBUTIONS TO THE FIELD OF APOLOGETICS

Bonhoeffer's relationship with apologetics is complex and uneasy. The arguments presented here should not be understood as diminishing this tension, as Bonhoeffer would remain decidedly concerned about many forms of apologetics practiced today. But this perhaps makes Bonhoeffer's contribution to apologetics even more important.

Positively, Bonhoeffer's work draws us to consider the way in which the Christian gospel helps us see with greater clarity how our lives are impacted here and now in ways that no other worldview can. It calls us to consider a Christology beyond the moments of Christ's death and resurrection that tend to preoccupy our attention. Instead, it presents the way in which only this Christ might break through our sinfulness to bring us to faith and, further, to new life here and now.

Negatively, Bonhoeffer's work warns of the dangers at the heart of our research and ministry. For there is nothing more dangerous than converting someone to an idea. If humans in their sin are looking for a sense of belonging, distraction, or security in the face of their spiritual anxiety, there are many who want to sign up to Christianity as a social group, philosophical school, or spiritual exercise. But faith comes about only through an encounter with Christ, not with a preacher or apologist. Bonhoeffer calls us at every moment to question our motivations and our goals. Is someone convinced or converted because of

---

51. Bonhoeffer, *Theological Education at Finkenwalde*, 344; cf. 344 n. 22.
52. Bonhoeffer, *Letters and Papers*, 504.
53. Much of Bonhoeffer's *Ethics* and *Letters and Papers from Prison* concern the church's guilt. See especially the essay "Guilt, Justification, Renewal," in Bonhoeffer, *Ethics*, 134–45.

our physical presentation, the speed or fluency of our speech, or the following we appear to have? If so, are they meeting Christ, or signing up to something that is simply attractive? For Bonhoeffer, there is nothing stronger than the weakness of Christ. And all Christian ministry must strive with all its strength to become just as weak.

BIBLIOGRAPHY

Bonhoeffer, Dietrich. *Barcelona, Berlin, New York: 1928–1931*. Minneapolis: Fortress, 2008.

———. *Berlin: 1932–1933*. Minneapolis: Fortress, 2009.

———. "Concerning the Christian Idea of God." *The Journal of Religion* 12.2 (Apr. 1932): 177–85.

———. *The Cost of Discipleship*. London: SCM, 1959.

———. *Creation and Fall*. Minneapolis: 1997.

———. *Discipleship*. Minneapolis: Fortress, 2001.

———. *Ecumenical, Academic, and Pastoral Work: 1931–1932*. Minneapolis: Fortress, 2012.

———. *Ethics*. Minneapolis: Fortress, 2005.

———. *Letters and Papers from Prison*. Minneapolis: Fortress, 2009.

———. *Life Together/Prayerbook of the Bible*. Minneapolis: Fortress, 2005.

———. *London: 1933–1935*. Minneapolis: Fortress, 2007.

———. *Sanctorum Communio*. Minneapolis: Fortress, 1998.

———. *Theological Education at Finkenwalde: 1935–1937*. Minneapolis: Fortress, 2013.

Chadwick, Owen. *The Secularisation of the European Mind in the 19th Century*. Cambridge University Press, 1975.

Dulles, Avery Cardinal. *A History of Apologetics*. San Francisco: Ignatius, 1999.

Frick, Peter. *Bonhoeffer's Intellectual Formation: Theology and Philosophy in his Thought*. Eugene, OR: Wipf & Stock, 2008.

Heschel, Susannah. "For 'Volk, Blood, and God': The Theological Faculty at the University of Jena During the Third Reich." Pages 365–98 in *Nazi Germany and the Humanities* Ed. by Wolfgang Bialas and Alison Rabinbach. Oxford: Oneworld, 2007.

Matheson, Peter. *The Third Reich and the Christian Churches*. Edinburgh: T&T Clark, 1981.

Moses, John A. *The Reluctant Revolutionary: Dietrich Bonhoeffer's Collision with Prusso-German History*. New York: Berghahn, 2009.

Scholder, Klauss. *The Churches and the Third Reich*. London: SCM, 1987–8.

LESSLIE NEWBIGIN

Missionary Apologist

KRISH KANDIAH

James Edward Lesslie Newbigin (1909–1998) was arguably the greatest missionary theologian of his generation. His work as a cross-cultural missionary in India pioneered new models of ecclesial unity and cooperation, and his role as a global missionary statesman demonstrated innovative thinking in the integration of evangelism, mission, and apologetics. He was also a prolific author, writing on a huge range of cultural, apologetic, philosophical, and theological issues. Many would see Newbigin as the grandfather of the missional church movement; his thought leadership certainly provides rich resources and challenge for contemporary apologetics.

HISTORICAL BACKGROUND

Lesslie Newbigin was born in 1909 in Northumbria, England. The son of a Presbyterian businessman, he attended a Quaker boarding school and went on to study geography and economics at Cambridge University. Newbigin recounts that his conversion took place during the first summer break as a student: "As I lay awake a vision came to mind . . . a vision of the cross, but it was the cross spanning the space between heaven and earth, between ideals and present realities, and with arms that embraced the whole world."[1]

This crucial point in Newbigin's life shaped his understanding of the atonement and became the foundation of his experience of new life in Christ. For the next forty years, Newbigin served as a missionary, initially on university campuses, then in India. He then took on a strategic global missions role, followed by a further long stint in India. On his retirement in 1974, Lesslie and his wife returned from Madras to England with just two suitcases and a rucksack

---

1. Lesslie Newbigin, *Unfinished Agenda: An Autobiography* (Grand Rapids: Eerdmans, 1985), 11.

for luggage.[2] Newbigin took up a lectureship at the Selly Oak Colleges in Birmingham. He described his new ministry context as being "much harder than anything I met in India. There is a cold contempt for the Gospel which is harder to face than any opposition. . . . England is a pagan society and the development of a truly missionary encounter with this very tough form of paganism is the greatest intellectual and practical task facing the Church."[3]

It was this missionary reverse culture shock that prompted Newbigin at the age of sixty-five to undertake his most significant theological and missiological project—the "Gospel and Our Culture" (GOC) program—while also taking up an unsalaried position at a United Reformed Church with a declining congregation in a deprived area of Birmingham. He served there for eight years and then retired to London but was still an active speaker and author with the GOC movement.

Newbigin's experience as a parachurch staff worker, ecumenical advocate, missionary theologian, evangelist, pastor, and theological educator gives his writings a firm grounding in missionary praxis rather than purely academic speculation. Because Newbigin's theology was hammered out on the anvil of missional experience, he has so much to offer both practitioners and academics. His broad-ranging experiences of missions and evangelism and his participation in the global ecumenical movement, gave him a unique perspective on the communication of the gospel and on what apologetics might need to look like in increasingly pluralist contexts. This perspective, combined with Newbigin's experience as a returning missionary who no longer felt at home in his country of origin, provided the impetus for his missiological encounter with late-modern Western cultures and provides an excellent basis for exploring apologetics in the world today.

THEOLOGICAL CONTEXT

Newbigin was a bridge-builder in a time of great division in the church. He also lived during a strategic moment of the church's relationship with Western culture and a time of huge philosophical and cultural shift. To understand the significance of Newbigin's contribution, we need to understand both the ecclesiological and cultural moment in which he lived. He was an ecumenist to a divided church and an evangelist to a divided culture.

2. Dan Beeby, "Obituary: The Right Rev Lesslie Newbigin," *Independent*, February 4, 1998, http://www.independent.co.uk/news/obituaries/obituary-the-right-rev-lesslie-newbigin-1142813.html.
3. Newbigin, *Unfinished Agenda*, 249.

An Ecumenist to a Divided Church

Even in his youthful years, Newbigin was committed to unity and as a student regularly attended the evensong in the college chapel. He explained, "It was the only place where SCM [Student Christian Movement] and CICCU [Cambridge Inter Collegiate Christian Union] could pray together, for the official evangelical view was that the SCM members were unbelievers."[4] This commitment to unity was to become a defining feature of Newbigin's ministry. Newbigin invested a large part of his life to building unity, and a great deal of his writing centered on this issue, as Newbigin scholar Michael Goheen observes: "There is no other subject that he addressed more often in his writings."[5] Newbigin's career in ministry testifies to his commitment to the unity of the church, as he served tirelessly, and often thanklessly, in ecumenical contexts.[6] What is not widely acknowledged is the centrality of evangelism in motivating Newbigin's ecumenism.

"The Reunion of the Church" was Newbigin's theological defense of the 1947 Church of South India (CSI) unification scheme, in which Newbigin played a strategic role. Newbigin's motivation for his involvement in this large-scale church unity endeavor was clearly evangelistic: "It is not possible to account for the contentment with divisions of the church except upon the basis of a loss of the conviction that the church exists to bring all men to Christ."[7]

Indeed, Newbigin blamed the fragmentation of the church firstly on the failure of the church to live up to its missional calling and secondly on the fact that when the missionary societies sought to remedy the situation, they brought to the mission field an inadequate doctrine of the church.[8] Therefore, the church lost sight of the fact that it was she who was commissioned to represent Christ to people.[9] Driven by his evangelistic ecumenism, Newbigin was not afraid to challenge those who might describe their theological position as liberal or those who would describe themselves as evangelicals: "All seriously committed Christians presumably believe that the gospel is for the whole world. The *evangel* is

---

4. Ibid., 14. Newbigin was studying in Cambridge from 1928 to 1931. He found greater affinity with the Student Christian Movement than the Cambridge Inter Collegiate Christian Union. The CICCU had disassociated from the SCM because of a theological dispute about the nature of Christian confession a few years before Newbigin's time at Cambridge. But Newbigin was studying in Cambridge in 1928, the year that the Intervarsity Fellowship (now known as UCCF in the UK) was founded as a national evangelical alternative to the Student Christian Movement, which was perceived to be theologically liberal. Cambridge was thus the epicenter of the evangelical and liberal division in university ministry.

5. Michael Goheen, *"As the Father Has Sent Me, I Am Sending You": Lesslie Newbigin's Missionary Ecclesiology* (Amsterdam: Boekcentrum, 2000), 200.

6. Twelve years as bishop of Madurai with the CSI, six years as an administrator with IMC and WCC, and nine years as bishop of Madras with the CSI.

7. Lesslie Newbigin, *The Reunion of the Church: A Defence of the South India Scheme–Revised Edition.* (London: SCM, 1960), 3.

8. Ibid., 10.

9. Ibid.

for the *oikoumene*. It is therefore strange and sad that the adjectives 'evangelical' and 'ecumenical' should have come in our time to stand for mutually opposed positions.... Every Christian must be evangelical and ecumenical."[10]

Thus, Newbigin understood his own position as being both evangelical and ecumenical, both an advocate for unity and for truth, categories that both groups contest. Because these wings of the church are often so polarized, they rarely interact or engage with one another and therefore lack the challenge from the perspective of the other. By operating at the liminal space between ecumenicals and evangelicals[11] and between conservatives and liberals, Newbigin had an important prophetic role to both groups. Whatever the critiques levied against Newbigin, he does offer a challenging word in season to both sides of the theological continuum, and these ideas are worthy of engagement. In our increasingly polarized church, the different streams and traditions have become isolated confessional echo chambers. As we shall see, the health of the church and the apologetic task are intimately connected, and thus, a unified church finds increased credibility as an apologetic community.

AN EVANGELIST TO A DIVIDED CULTURE

Newbigin did more than bring unique insight to the internal theological disputes and tribal divisions within the church. Newbigin also lived at a time of major global cultural change and had a unique vantage point, which led to an incisive analysis that is instructive in navigating similar trends in our present context. In a short essay such as this, it is almost impossible to summarize Newbigin's wide-ranging thought leadership in the many fields he engaged with, particularly as his ministry spans several decades and hundreds of books, articles, and lectures. But for our purposes we will focus on two important cultural shifts with which Newbigin recognized and engaged.

The End of Christendom

When Lesslie and Helen Newbigin caught the bus home to the UK, their overland reentry to the West acted as a kind of cultural decompression chamber.

---

10. Lesslie Newbigin, "Cross-Currents in Ecumenical and Evangelical Understandings of Mission." *International Bulletin of Missionary Research* 6.4 (1982): 146.

11. Newbigin appears broadly evangelical by the most widely accepted standards. Newbigin's theological project gives the Bible a central place. He also has a strong theology of conversion as is apparent from his own conversion experience and writings. He has a strong emphasis on the atonement and the need for definite action as a result of faith. Newbigin also argues that the central revelatory moment in the gospel narrative is the cross of Christ. Newbigin was also clearly ecumenical in his practice; his ability to span this divide between ecumenicals and evangelicals is noteworthy and allows him to draw on a large corpus of theological tradition that lends eclectic and ecumenical breadth to his theologizing. See David Bebbington, *Evangelicalism in Modern Britain: from the 1730s to the 1980s* (London: Unwin Hyman, 1989), 1–19.

They realized there had been a radical change in the relationship between Christianity and Western culture.[12] A significant shift in the church's self-understanding took place with the conversion of the Roman Emperor Constantine. This was the beginning of Christendom. For over a millennium and a half, the church dominated the political and public life of European nations. Though there were many benefits of Christianity receiving official sanction, there were also negative implications. During much of this era, the church had a skewed sense of self-understanding and a skewed view of mission. Newbigin argues, "During the Christendom era, the church developed the self-understanding that it existed 'for the edification and sanctification of its own members rather than for witness and service to the world outside.'"[13]

Through his work both on the field as a missionary in India and as a global missionary statesman, Newbigin was one of the leading voices reflecting on the missiological and theological implications of the end of Christendom. His influential voice helped the church to see that mission is not to be restricted to outside the geographical boundaries of the Christendom of the West. Newbigin argued there needed to be a missionary encounter with Western culture itself. He was once described as "God's Missionary to Us,"[14] that we may assume a missionary "posture"[15] toward the West. Newbigin's celebrated essay "Can the West be converted?" can be read as a programmatic proposal of his post-India project:

> If one looks at the world scene from a missionary point of view, surely the most striking fact is that, while in great areas of Asia and Africa the Church is growing, often growing very rapidly, in the lands which were once called Christendom it is in decline; and moreover wherever the culture of the West, under the name of "modernization," penetrates, it carries with it what Lippman called "the acids of modernity," dissolving the most enduring of religious beliefs including the beliefs of Christians. Surely there can be no more crucial question for the world mission of the church than the one I have posed. Can there be an effective missionary encounter with *this* culture—this so powerful, persuasive, and confident culture

---

12. According to Oliver O'Donovan, Christendom is "the idea of a professedly Christian . . . political order." Oliver O'Donovan, *The Desire of the Nations: Rediscovering the Roots of Political Theology* (Cambridge: Cambridge University Press. 1996), 194–95.

13. Lesslie Newbigin, *A Faith for This One World?* (London: SCM, 1961), 111.

14. Tim Stafford, "God's Missionary to Us" *Christianity Today* 40.14 (1996): 24.

15. George Hunsberger, "Acquiring the Posture of a Missionary Church" in *The Church between Gospel and Culture: The Emerging Mission in North America*. eds George Hunsberger and Craig Van Gelder (Grand Rapids: Eerdmans, 1996), 289–97.

which (at least until very recently) simply regarded itself as "the coming world civilization." Can the West be converted?[16]

This crucial challenge of the conversion of the West came as a clarion call to the church to rethink its missionary posture.[17] Unlike many contemporary missiologists, Newbigin's estimation of Christendom[18] itself was not wholly negative.[19] Rather, Newbigin saw the unfortunate state of the church, which had either failed to recognize the end of Christendom or had maintained a futile and unhealthy "nostalgia for Christendom."[20]

Newbigin's insights are vital not just in Europe, where there has been a clear integration of church and state, but also in the US, where there is a clear legal distinction between church and state. The acceptance of the ending of Christendom provides an opportunity to reevaluate the church's identity as well as its ambitions and strategies. A flawed approach to public life makes the apologetic task of the church more complicated. If the church is seen to be politically partisan, it can be an obstacle for the commendation of the gospel. When the church colludes with secular powers or, even worse, provides legitimate ideological support for wickedness as in the case of apartheid South Africa, Nazi Germany, or genocidal Rwanda, it has a crippling effect on the church's witness.

The Advent of Postmodernity

In Newbigin's later writing, he focused much of his attention on the contested nature of truth. As the acceptance of pluralism rose, so did challenges to the truth claims of Christianity, which were increasingly seen as tyrannical. What became known as postmodernity involved a number of cultural, sociological, and epistemological shifts. Postmodernity is notoriously difficult to define as it involves such a wide range of interrelated and sometimes conflicting ideas. For our purposes, the change in approach to truth and knowledge are the most salient.

16. Lesslie Newbigin, *Foolishness to the Greeks: The Gospel and Western Culture* (London: SPCK, 1987), 25.

17. Though Newbigin had highlighted the implications of the end of Christendom for mission forty years. Lesslie Newbigin, *A Faith for This One World?* (London: SCM, 1961), 9; David Smith, *Mission After Christendom* (London: Dartman, Longman & Todd, 2003); Stuart Murray, *Post-Christendom: Church and Mission in a Strange New World* (Carlisle: Paternoster, 2004); Douglas John Hall, *The End of Christendom and the Future of Christianity* (Pennsylvania: Trinity International , 1997).

18. "We have to accept as matter of fact that the first great attempt to translate the universal claim of Christ into political terms was the Constantinian settlement." Lesslie Newbigin, *Sign of the Kingdom* (Grand Rapids: Eerdmans, 1980), 47.

19. "We cannot disown all that we have inherited from the thousand year experience of the medieval corpus Christianum." Lesslie Newbigin, *Foolishness to the Greeks: The Gospel and Western Culture* (London: SPCK, 1998), 130. For similar sentiments, see David Harvey, *The Condition of Post-Modernity* (Oxford: Blackwells, 1989), 80–81.

20. Lesslie Newbigin, *Truth to Tell: The Gospel as Public Truth* (Grand Rapids: Eerdmans, 1991), 68.

Under postmodernity, the concept of truth tends to be viewed through the lens of power relationships. The idea of unmediated access to reality and a simple correspondence theory of truth was brought into question. This left the church in a particularly vulnerable situation, in three distinct ways. First, her apologetics had not been written for such a conversation. Second, the church, in the wider culture, was perceived to be a marginalized minority with no right to claim any special status. And third, Christian claims to truth were often seen as bigoted and narrow-minded. During this period deconstruction, a trend that developed in the field of literary criticism thanks to the groundbreaking work of Jacques Derrida that denied that there is a fixed meaning in any text but instead a text will be understood differently by each reader.[21]

Deconstruction theory came to be applied far more widely than literary criticism as the slogan "everything is a text"[22]demonstrates. As the idea of an objective "view from nowhere" was found to be suspect, claims to truth are interpreted as claims from a particular perspective and are therefore subjective. Thus, postmodernity developed a relativistic streak.

Newbigin's response is not to lament the passing of modernity, which has been an approach taken by a number of contemporary apologists. Newbigin invested a great deal of energy dismantling some of the naive assumptions of modernity—for example, its rejection of the notion of divine revelation, its rejection of faith as means to knowledge,[23] and its naive empiricism and the bifurcation of truth and values.[24] He wants a fresh gospel engagement with our pluralist societies. It is into this cultural and epistemological context that Newbigin's work is especially valuable to apologetics.

APOLOGETIC METHODOLOGY AND RESPONSE

The church faces epochal changes with respect to its place in an increasingly pluralist and postmodern world. Some of our apologetic approaches have ignored these changes and tried to carry on with familiar and trusted techniques, or they have taken a fight-or-flight mentality. Many apologists have sought to fight off postmodernity and return to the safety of modernity to defend objectivity and

---

21. Roger Poole, "Deconstruction" in *New Fontana Dictionary of Modern Thought,* 3rd ed., eds. Alan Bullock and Stephen Trombley (London: Fontana, 1999), 202.

22. John Rawlings, "Jacques Derrida," 1999, https://prelectur.stanford.edu/lecturers/derrida/.

23. Lesslie Newbigin, "Truth and Authority in Modernity" in Philip Sampson, Vinnay Samuel, and Chris Sugden, *Faith and Modernity* (Oxford: Regnum, 1994), 61.

24. Lesslie Newbigin "Can the West be Converted?" *Princeton Seminary Bulletin* 6.1 (1985): 30.

epistemological confidence. At the other end of the scale, some have taken flight from historic Christian orthodoxy and sought to adapt to a relativistic account of Christianity. This is the classic tension of contextualization, the ongoing conversation between the gospel and culture,[25] a dialogue Newbigin pioneered especially when it came to understanding the way in which the gospel relates to Western cultures. There is a tension between seeking to utilize the language and thought forms of the culture you are seeking to evangelize and allowing the language or thought forms to compromise the gospel you are seeking to communicate. Newbigin argued that the gospel can be at home in modernity as there is common ground between the gospel and some of modernity's assumptions, but the gospel will also seek to challenge and transcend modernity as it will never ultimately be at home in any culture until the kingdom of God is established.

The question must be asked, How do we communicate the Christian faith without succumbing to the naive objectivity of modernity and without falling into the relativistic pluralism of postmodernity? Newbigin offers us some positive ways forward that avoid both extremes and provide powerful resources for a nuanced gospel focus that is biblically faithful and for the church.

THE GOSPEL AS PUBLIC TRUTH

One of Newbigin's biggest challenges to the assumptions of modernity was its bifurcation of truth into facts and values. Newbigin argued that the Enlightenment was the decisive moment in the division of Western thought into the public and private. Thus, a central element in Newbigin's apologetic approach was to tackle head-on this public-private dichotomy. He asks and answers,

> What in our culture is the meaning of the word "fact"? In its earliest use in the English language it is simply the Latin *factum*, the past participle of the verb "to do," something which has been done. But plainly it has acquired a much richer meaning. In ordinary use "fact" is contrasted with belief, opinion, value. Value-free facts are the most highly prized commodities in our culture. . . . Our values, our views of what is good and bad, are a matter of personal opinion, and everyone is free to have his own opinions. But on the facts we must all agree. Here is the core of our culture.[26]

This distinction between scientific truth and religious values continues on today despite the philosophical deconstructions of the myth of scientific

---

25. Lesslie Newbigin, "The Dialogue of Gospel and Culture: Reflections on the Conference of World Mission and Evangelism, Salvador, Brazil." *International Bulletin of Missionary Research* 21.2 (1997): 50–52.
26. Newbigin, "Truth and Authoriity in Modernity," 30.

objectivity by philosophers of science such as Karl Popper[27] and Thomas Kuhn.[28] Newbigin argues that this dualistic approach has "at least from the eighteenth century . . . been the public culture of Europe, and has—under the name of 'modernisation'—extended its power into every part of the world."[29] Objective facts are for the public realm, taught at school and presented without the need for the preface "I believe," while subjective values belong to the private world of religion and ethics. "With respect to what are called 'facts' a statement is either right or wrong, true or false. But with respect to values, and supremely with respect to the religious beliefs on which these values ultimately rest, one does not use this kind of language. . . . They are matters of personal choice."[30]

This fact-value dichotomy between science and religion became and would remain a prevailing characteristic of modernity. The reaction to the elevation of science at the expense of values was that every other discipline tried to justify their existence by claiming to be a science. Paul Hiebert shows how many of the systematic theologies produced in the first half of the twentieth century reformulated theology in scientific terms.[31] Being dismissed into the realm of the subjective, Christians reacted by defending the truth of Christianity through appealing to the objective facts of the resurrection or through arguing for the concrete existence of God through rational, self-evident proofs.

Newbigin's championing of the gospel as public truth is part of his challenge to both modernity and postmodernity. Newbigin is insistent that the gospel is not just a set of private values but truth to be debated and contested in the market place of ideas. Newbigin launched his "Gospel as Public Truth" project at a significant meeting of Christian leaders in Swanwick, England in 1992. The notion of "public truth" featured heavily in Newbigin's later writings and was his attempt to challenge the church to avoid both a relativistic acquiescence of denying the uniqueness of Christ or a pietistic retreat into a personal spirituality. In his opening comments, Newbigin explained that from the birth of Christianity, the gospel has always been proclaimed as public truth and that the church did not need to rely on social status or political recognition to proclaim it as such. The first communicators of the gospel were the eyewitnesses who could say: "We proclaim to you what we have seen and heard" (1 John 1:3). They were well aware that their story could be and would be rejected and that only the Holy Spirit

27. Karl Popper, *Conjectures and Refutations: The Growth of Scientific Knowledge* (London: Routledge & Kegan Paul, 1963).

28. Thomas Kuhn, *The Structure of Scientific Revolutions—Second Edition* (Chicago: University of Chicago Press, 1970).

29. Newbigin, "Truth and Authority in Modernity," 30.

30. Newbigin, *Foolishness to the Greeks*, 16–17.

31. Paul Hiebert, *Anthropological Reflections on Missiological Issues* (Grand Rapids: Baker, 1994), 19.

could convince people of its truth. But they did not draw the conclusion that its truth was a private matter for the individual. They did not avail themselves of the protection that Roman law provided for the exercise of religions of personal salvation. They affirmed that the message that had been entrusted to them was one that concerned the destiny of the whole human race. The one who had died and risen again was the Savior and Judge of the world. This news was of vital concern to every human being. It was public truth. Fidelity to it required the momentous decision to withhold acknowledgment of the emperor as supreme power. They accepted the price that had to be paid for this fidelity.[32]

Nevertheless, this public truth is not just the assertion of the facts of Christianity. It is the telling of God's story in the world. Thus, the gospel as public truth is both a challenge to the fact-value dichotomy of modernity, but as it is linked to the retelling of the human story, it is a challenge to the antimetanarrative stance of postmodernity. In the posthumously published book *A Walk through the Bible*,[33] Newbigin provides a nontechnical overview of the biblical story and particularly how Christ provides the hermeneutical key to the canon. Newbigin begins the book with a quotation from a Hindu friend: "I can't understand why you missionaries present the Bible to us in India as a book of religion. It is not a book of religion. . . . I find in your Bible a unique interpretation of human history."[34]

This is a significant quotation for Newbigin, and it appears in many of his writings. This statement was seminal for him because it led to the realization that Christ is not just the core of the biblical narrative or the provider of individualistic salvation; Christ is the organizing center of all human history. Thus, for Newbigin, the *gospel as public truth* is a story that needs to be shared, and it leads us to the next significant challenge Newbigin gives contemporary apologetics: we need to understand the gospel as narrative.

THE GOSPEL AS NARRATIVE

Presenting the truthfulness of the gospel in the face of skepticism toward claims to truth has been a major challenge, particularly since the onset of postmodernity. One common way to seek to legitimate the claims of Christianity was to use foundationalist apologetics,[35] which tried to justify the truthfulness of Christian beliefs by starting with a set of foundational indubitable beliefs

---

32. Lesslie Newbigin, *The Gospel and Our Culture Movement Supplement*, January (1992), 1–2.

33. Lesslie Newbigin, *A Walk Through the Bible* (London: SPCK, 1999).

34. Ibid., 4.

35. John Frame points to Augustine, Luther, and Calvin as exemplars to this approach in John Frame, *Apologetics to the Glory of God: An Introduction* (Philipsburg, PA: P&R, 1994), 221. Modern examples of this approach would be John Gerstner, R. C. Sproul, and Arthur Lindsey.

from which to infer God's existence.[36] Newbigin argues that this approach fails to recognize the extent to which cultures affect rationality. The most vehement critics of foundational apologetics have been the reformed presuppositional apologists who followed Cornelius Van Til's rejection of autonomous reason because of the noetic effects of sin. Presuppositional apologists argue that in commending the gospel to others, the "properly basic" belief in the existence of the God of the Bible must be first assumed, and then the rationality of the Christian faith will be evident.[37] Yet Newbigin's approach is different from both presuppositional and foundational apologetics, most notably in his use of narrative as a vital resource to communicate the gospel in a late-modern environment.

Newbigin draws on the work of Martin Buber[38] and his differentiation between acquiring "I-It" and "I-Thou" knowledge.[39] Newbigin implies that natural theology and, by implication, most forms of classical and foundational apologetics provide only "I-it" knowledge of God, and the "I-Thou" personal encounter with God is possible only when we surrender our sovereign autonomy and respond to God's self-disclosure of his character in the narrative of Scripture. Newbigin emphasizes the personal revelation of God, which provides support for divine sovereignty in revelation. This instinct, which is a dominant theme in Karl Barth's theology, dates back to Newbigin's earliest written work in this area, predating his primary engagement with Barthian theology.[40] It is Newbigin's contention that because God is personal and relational, he reveals himself through narrative. Newbigin provides the following illustration: "Consider what it means to get to know a person. One can read an account of his character and career such as might be embodied in an obituary notice. But in order to know a person one must see how she meets situations, relates to other people, acts in times of crisis and in times of peace. It is in narrative that character is revealed, and there is no substitute for this."[41]

Thus, we are given the narrative of Scripture to reveal God's character. For example, throughout God's long covenantal relationship with Israel, he reveals

---

36. Norman Geisler, *Christian Apologetics* (Grand Rapids: Baker, 1993).

37. This term was coined by the Christian philosopher and apologist Alvin Plantinga from Notre Dame University.

38. Martin Buber, *I and Thou*—a new translation with prologue and notes by Walter Kaufmann (New York: Scribner's Sons, 1970).

39. "I-it" knowledge is the knowledge we have of objects, it's the kind of knowledge a medical doctor has with the body of an unconscious patient—they know details such as weight, body temperature, and eye color. "I-Thou" knowledge is the kind of knowledge that a doctor can have with a conscious patient where, if the patient chooses to reveal it the doctor can know something of the character, the dreams, and the hopes of the person in front of them.

40. Newbigin's main exposure to Barthian theology occurred in the 1970s when on his return from India, Newbigin read *Church Dogmatics*, although he interacted with Barth through the WCC previously.

41. Lesslie Newbigin, *The Gospel in a Pluralist Society* (London: SPCK, 1989), 99.

himself not simply through a series of propositional statements but in the concrete realities of his historical dealings with his people. In the New Testament, this is even more clearly demonstrated as God's character is revealed through the incarnation and the narrative accounts of Jesus's life in the gospels.

> The dogma, the thing given for our acceptance in faith, is not a set of timeless propositions: it is a story. . . . Here I think the eighteenth century defenders of the faith were most wide of the mark. The Christian religion which they sought to defend was a system of timeless metaphysical truths about God, nature, and man. . . . Any defence of the Christian faith . . . must take a quite different route. The Christian faith, rooted in the Bible, is . . . primarily to be understood as an interpretation of the story—the human story set with the story of nature.[42]

Newbigin's rejection of an approach to apologetics that is simply a defense of timeless propositional truths resonates with the postmodern antipathy toward supposed objectivity. Thus, Newbigin's advocacy of narrative is timely. But at the same time, his description of the Christian faith as an interpretation of the entire human story also runs counter to the postmodern suspicion toward metanarratives.[43]

In an article where Newbigin has attributed the liberal-fundamentalist split to common acquiescence to modernity, Newbigin argues instead that "the true understanding of the Bible is that it tells a story of which my life is a part, the story of God's tireless, loving, wrathful, inexhaustible patience with the human family, and of our unbelief, blindness, disobedience. To accept this story as the truth of the human story (and so of my story) commits me personally to a life of discernment and obedience in the new circumstances of each day."[44]

Newbigin's narrative apologetic centers around locating an individual's story within the biblical story.

Newbigin is adamant that the biblical story is historically true. This is where he parts company with most postliberal-narrative theologians who argue that the Christian story is simply one story among many and that theology in general, and biblical theology in particular, is simply a second-order internal discipline for the Christian community. Newbigin uses the work of the Hungarian philosopher of

---

42. Ibid., 12–13.

43. But this suspicion toward metanarratives could be criticized as an attempt to provide a universal narrative of suspicion. Thus, rejection of metanarratives can be read as a covert attempt to replace current metanarratives with a new anti-metanarrative narrative!

44. Lesslie Newbigin, *A Word in Season: Perspectives on Christian World Missions*, ed. Eleanour Jackson (Grand Rapids: Eerdmans, 1994), 204.

science Michael Polanyi and his concept of "universal intent."[45] This is a significant step as it tries to provide a nonfoundationalist approach to the justification
of knowledge that also avoids relativism. Newbigin uses Polanyi's principal of
"universal intent" to argue for the universal truthfulness of the gospel story. The
concept of universal intent allows an evangelist to humbly assert that the gospel
has not been finally proved according to any modernist conception of objective
proof and thus the gospel is open to refutation.[46] But the gospel is held with
universal intent such that it is held to be the truth for all people everywhere.
Both Polanyi and Newbigin recognize the mediating function of interpretive
frameworks such that all truth claims are in some sense necessarily perspectival.
Newbigin is not offering a naive bypass to the effects of cultural context by
arguing that a narrative approach means direct access to the biblical text and
therefore to the pure unadulterated gospel. Instead, Newbigin shows awareness
of the existence of interpretive frameworks prior to the reading of any text and
understands the act of reading Scripture as an ongoing conversation between
a believer, with their imperfect worldview, and Scripture. "The person who
allows the biblical story to be the all-surrounding ambience of daily life and who
continually seeks to place all experiences in this context finds that daily life is a
continuous conversation with the one whose character is revealed in the biblical
story taken as a whole."[47]

Newbigin argues that the world should be interpreted through the lens of
the gospel, not the gospel through the lens of the world. This can be put technically in terms of a hermeneutical spiral, borne out in another citation, which
shows Newbigin's awareness of the process of reformation and the fallibility of
the interpretation of the world. He says, "The Christian community is invited
to indwell the story, tacitly aware of it as shaping the way we understand but
focally attending to the world we live in so we are able to confidently, though not
infallibly, to increase our understanding of it and our ability to cope with it."[48]

This narrative approach to biblical hermeneutics offers many resources for
apologetics in a postmodern context. Most apologetics texts ignore that the Bible
is a narrative book. If they quote the Bible at all, it is to deploy proof texts mainly
from the New Testament epistles or a few isolated historical nuggets gleaned

---

45. Michael Polanyi, *Personal Knowledge: Towards a Post-Critical Philosophy* (London: Routledge, 1962), 65.

46. Here objective proof is used within the definitional nuance expected by individuals such as Karl Popper who would demand objectivity as the qualifying criteria for a statement to be scientific. In Newbigin, "Truth and Authority in Modernity," 256, Popper explains that *falsifiabilty* should be the grounds of demarcation between science and metaphysics.

47. Lesslie Newbigin, *Proper Confidence: Faith, Doubt and Certainty in Christian Discipleship* (Grand Rapids: Eerdmans, 1995), 88.

48. Op Cit.(1861), 38.

from the gospel accounts of the resurrection. Much of our apologetic work seeks to transform the Bible into a philosophical textbook rather than allowing the givenness of Scripture to shape our apologetic method. While some argue that the truth claims of stories can be easily avoided by dismissing them simply as myths or limiting them to the personal sphere, stories provide an excellent resource for challenging the worldview of the hearer. Once heard, stories provide not just simple assertions but a whole network of ideas, values, and propositions that must be evaluated as a whole. This evaluation is nonconfrontational and yet subversive of the hearer's interpretative framework. The authority of a story is to a large extent internal, and therefore prior epistemological justification is unnecessary. Through borrowing from postliberal narrative theologians—the philosopher of science Michael Polanyi and the Jewish existential philosopher Martin Buber—and a close reading of Scripture, Newbigin provides the theoretical framework for using the biblical narrative to challenge the reigning metanarratives of postmodernity without appealing to modernist conceptions of truth.

THE GOSPEL AS A BIGGER STORY THAN WE HAVE BEEN USED TO TELLING

One of the dangers for apologetics is that we assume the gospel we are defending is the gospel as Scripture presents it. One of Newbigin's gifts to the church is his insistence that we understand the gospel in its fullness. He is very critical of escapist and reductionist evangelistic presentations. For example, Newbigin argues that "by concentrating on the fate of the individual soul after death, it abstracts the soul from the full reality of the human person as an actor and sufferer in the ongoing history of the world."[49] There are two concerns here. One is a docetic tendency to focus on the soul and ignore the body, and the second is that the eschatological dimension of salvation is overemphasized. Newbigin's first concern identifies a major flaw of much evangelical apologetics that has ignored the holistic nature of a robust biblical anthropology. Newbigin's fourfold understanding of the gospel is expressed in his short work *Sin and Salvation*.[50] In a chapter entitled "What is Salvation?", Newbigin provides a four-dimensional schema for understanding the alienation that sin has brought to humanity: (1) humanity is in a state of contradiction against the natural world, (2) humans are in a state of contradiction against their fellow human beings, (3) humanity is in a state of inner self-contradiction, and (4) humanity is in a state of contradiction against God.

---

49. Ibid., 178.
50. Lesslie Newbigin, *Sin and Salvation* (London: SCM, 1956).

The repairing of these four fractured relationships is salvation as Newbigin understands it. Newbigin describes salvation as "the restoration of creation to its original purpose."[51] This approach takes seriously the emotional, social, environmental, and spiritual consequences of the fall. Goheen comments, "The context of Newbigin's reflections on salvation was the rift between ecumenicals and evangelicals on social action produced by different understandings of salvation."[52] Newbigin's approach counteracts reductionist conceptions of salvation: the therapeutic gospel, the individualistic gospel, the social gospel, which are all exposed as, at best, half-truths.

Again, his insights are a helpful corrective to much of contemporary apologetics. One of the challenges for apologists is that in our desire to win the argument and the person with which we are communicating, we do not dilute the gospel we are seeking to share. This is where I have found his four-dimensional schema so helpful. It challenges the apologist to look for points of contact in all four of the relational dimensions and to look for what it means to call hearers to seek the Lordship of Jesus in all four of these dimensions. For example, Newbigin argues against overly-individualized conceptions of the gospel as the key to fulfillment, which were part of a Christian response to "secularization" more influenced by existentialism than Scripture. Newbigin argues vehemently that the "gospel is vastly more than an offer to men who care to accept it as a meaning for their personal lives. It is the declaration of God's cosmic purpose by which the whole public history of mankind is sustained and overruled, and by which all men without exception will be judged. It is the invitation to be fellow workers with God in the fulfilment of that purpose through the atoning work of Christ and through the witness of the Holy Spirit."[53]

THE CHURCH IS THE PLACE WHERE THE GOSPEL STORY MAKES BEST SENSE

One of the challenges for contemporary apologetics is the separation of apologetics from the life of the church. Apologetics is often seen as the purview of parachurch organizations and student ministries. Apologetic events and lectures often take place in nonecclesial settings, and the gospel presented often sees the church as an optional extra at best or a bit of an embarrassment at worst. Newbigin had a radically different approach. The church was not only an essential element of his apologetic method but a vital part of his apologetic message.

Newbigin's clearest exposition of the local congregation as an indispensable

51. Ibid., 124.
52. Goheen, "As the Father Has Sent Me," 292.
53. Lesslie Newbigin, *Honest Religion for Secular Man* (London: SCM, 1966), 47.

apologetic is contained in the chapter "Congregation as the Hermeneutic of the Gospel"[54] in his book *Gospel in a Pluralist Society*. It is significant that Newbigin has chosen the term *congregation* rather than church: the local congregation is a more concrete entity than the church universal. By refusing to argue that the church in general is the hermeneutic of the gospel, Newbigin forces reflection and evaluation of actual congregational life in terms of its missionary purpose. In Newbigin's missiology, the local congregation is the primary missionary entity. Newbigin argues that one must see the "local congregation as having a certain real primacy among the various units into which we may think of the church as being divided."[55] For Newbigin, evangelism must be seen as primarily the responsibility of the congregation. Newbigin's emphasis on the congregation as hermeneutic of the gospel is the direct outworking of his congregational approach to evangelism. This is a sober reminder to the individualism of much of contemporary apologetics. For many Christians, an apologist is a lone intellectual warrior taking on an atheist in debate while the packed auditorium watches on in wonder. For Newbigin, the basic unit of evangelism and apologetics is a local congregation. Congregations living out the gospel message as a community, modeling the values of the kingdom in its shared life as well as proclaiming the gospel through preaching, is the most effective evangelism.

Within the context of his thesis, Newbigin begins by exploring the nature of truth and by appropriating Polanyi's approach to personal knowledge. He challenges the myth of objective scientific neutrality that was promulgated under modernity, leading to the dichotomy between scientific truth and religious beliefs. Newbigin skillfully marshals Polanyi's critique of doubt to challenge skepticism toward the truth claims of the gospel, challenging rationalism and defending revelation using the problem of historiography as an apologetic for the necessity of revelation for understanding human history. Newbigin then goes on to unpack the doctrine of divine election as a way of understanding how the specific revelation of the gospel can have universal implications for humanity. Newbigin balances his argument for the universality of the gospel for world history with the need for (re)contextualization that takes other religions and cultures seriously. He then embarks on a deconstruction of the myth of secular, and therefore neutral, state. He then argues for the unique role of the congregation to act as the hermeneutic of the gospel. Newbigin offers the local congregation as the "primary reality of which we have to take into account in seeking for a

---

54. Op Cit (1861), 223.
55. Lesslie Newbigin, *The Household of God: Lectures on the Nature of the Church* (London: SCM, 1953), 106.

Christian impact on public life."[56] He gives the local congregation a crucial role in the apologetic task:

> How is it possible that the gospel should be credible, that people should come to believe that the power which has the last word in human affairs is represented by a man hanging on a cross? I am suggesting that the only answer, the only hermeneutic of the gospel, is a congregation of men and women who believe it and live by it. I am of course, not denying the importance of the many activities by which we seek to challenge public life with the gospel—evangelistic campaigns, distribution of Bibles and Christian literature, conferences and even books such as this one. But I am saying that these are all secondary, and that they have their power to accomplish their purpose only as they are rooted in and lead back to a believing community.[57]

This is such an important line of thought, pregnant with meaning for understanding Newbigin's missiological project. In this chapter we need to make just two cursory observations to encourage further exploration of Newbigin's apologetic ecclesiology.

First, the congregation can be the hermeneutic of the gospel only if empowered by the Spirit. By describing the congregation as the "hermeneutic of the gospel," Newbigin emphasizes the importance of the local congregation's participation in the mission of the triune God. But the tension between the above passage and Newbigin's pneumatological emphasis shows that there is a dual nature in a congregation's existence; the congregation is to be both an active participator in God's mission, and yet this participation is possible only because of the presence of the Spirit in the congregation as "empowering presence."[58] Newbigin's ecclesiology is centered on the twin foci of the congregation as a pneumatological and hermeneutical community.

Second, the congregation can be the hermeneutic of the gospel only if it moves beyond technique toward an authentic expression of the character of the coming kingdom of God. Instead of offering techniques or programs, Newbigin concentrates on the qualities of a congregation that enable it to function as the hermeneutic of the gospel. He includes in this that the congregation is sixfold: (1) a community of praise, (2) a community of truth, (3) a community that does

---

56. Op Cit. (1861), 227.
57. Ibid.
58. Gordon Fee, *God's Empowering Presence: The Holy Spirit in the Letters of Paul* (Exeter: Paternoster, 1994).

not live for itself but is deeply involved in the concerns of its neighborhood, (4) a community that prepares its membership for service in the world, (5) a community that models the new social order of the kingdom, and (6) a community of hope. Overall, communal life is emphasized in this description because, for Newbigin, the congregation is not primarily individual and secondarily communal as is so often the case with evangelical ecclesiologies. Newbigin's emphasis on the hermeneutical and thus apologetic impact of the life of the congregation is a challenge to the reductionistic and over-intellectualized approaches of much of contemporary apologetics.[59] It reads as a contemporary echo of the ancient Letter to Diognetus, which included an account of the radical nature of Christian obedience and the life of the church:

> "For the Christians are distinguished from other men neither by country, nor language, nor the customs which they observe. . . . They love all men, and are persecuted by all. They are unknown and condemned; they are put to death, and restored to life. They are poor, yet make many rich; they are in lack of all things, and yet abound in all; they are dishonoured, and yet in their very dishonour are glorified. They are evil spoken of, and yet are justified; they are reviled, and bless; they are insulted, and repay the insult with honour; they do good, yet are punished as evil-doers. When punished, they rejoice as if quickened into life; they are assailed by the Jews as foreigners, and are persecuted by the Greeks; yet those who hate them are unable to assign any reason for their hatred."[60]

CONTRIBUTIONS TO THE FIELD OF APOLOGETICS

Lesslie Newbigin's cross-cultural experience and his pan-denominational engagement shaped his missionary experience and reflection. A lifetime spent in cross-cultural mission and ecumenical community means Newbigin brings a unique perspective to the apologetic ministry. In our tribalized church contexts, where we run the risk of being locked into an echo chamber filled with people who agree with us, he brings a fresh and challenging voice. Newbigin offers the contemporary church some unique and powerful tools for the apologetic task we

---

59. Take for example the modern classic apologetics text books J. P. Moreland, *Scaling the Secular City* (Grand Rapids: Baker, 1987); William Lane Craig, *Apologetics: An Introduction* (Chicago: Moody, 1984); Norman Gesiler, *Christian Apologetics* (Grand Rapids: Baker Adademic, 1991). Not one of them make reference to the church.

60. Anonymous, A Letter to Diognetus, English Translation, James A. Kleist, ACW, 6:127–147 cited in Avery Dulles, *A History of Apologetics* (San Francisco: Ignatius, 1999), 35.

face today. Through studying his work, readers should be challenged to rethink their approach to evangelism and apologetics. First, readers should recognize the temptation to share a reductionist gospel and respond with a robust telling of the entire gospel. Second, readers should recognize the potential downfalls of a churchless and individualistic approach to apologetics and respond with an apologetic method that is congregational. Third, I hope readers begin consciously to evaluate the role that Scripture plays (or, sadly, does *not* play) in the way we do apologetics. It is often easier to present propositional statements about Christ rather than the storied gospel portraits that Scripture gives us. In each of these temptations, Newbigin can inspire new (or old!) apologists to rethink their methodologies and approach. Through his tutelage, I hope readers will reflect afresh on Scripture, the church, the gospel, and our mission. My prayer, and what I believe Newbigin's would be as well, is that this work will help us faithfully and relevantly fulfill God's missionary call on us, the church, in this generation.

BIBLIOGRAPHY
Primary Source Material
Newbigin, Lesslie. "Can the West be Converted?" *Princeton Seminary Bulletin* 6.1 (1985): 25–37.
———. "Cross-Currents in Ecumenical and Evangelical Understandings of Mission." *International Bulletin of Missionary Research* 6.4 (1982): 146–51.
———. "The Dialogue of Gospel and Culture: Reflections on the Conference of World Mission and Evangelism, Salvador, Brazil." *International Bulletin of Missionary Research* 21.2 (1997): 50–52.
———. *A Faith for This One World?* London: SCM, 1961.
———. *Foolishness to the Greeks: The Gospel and Western Culture.* London: SPCK, 1987.
———. *The Gospel in a Pluralist Society.* London: SPCK, 1989.
———. *Honest Religion for Secular Man.* London: SCM, 1966.
———. *The Household of God: Lectures on the Nature of the Church.* London: SCM, 1953.
———. *Proper Confidence: Faith, Doubt and Certainty in Christian Discipleship.* Grand Rapids: Eerdmans, 1995.
———. *The Reunion of the Church: A Defence of the South India Scheme–revised edition.* London: SCM, 1960.
———. *Sin and Salvation.* London: SCM, 1956.
———. *Truth and Authority in Modernity.* In *Faith and Modernity.* Ed. by P. Sampson, V. Samuel, and C. Sugden. Oxford: Regnum, 1994, 89–115.
———. *Truth to Tell: The Gospel as Public Truth.* Grand Rapids: Eerdmans, 1991.
———. *Unfinished Agenda: An Autobiography.* Grand Rapids: Eerdmans, 1985.
———. *A Word in Season: Perspectives on Christian World Missions.* Ed. by E. Jackson. Grand Rapids: Eerdmans, 1994.

Other Works Cited
Bebbington, D. W. *Evangelicalism in Modern Britain: From the 1730s to the 1980s.* London: Unwin Hyman, 1989.
Cahoone, Lawrence. *From Modernism to Post-Modernism: An Anthology.* Oxford: Blackwells, 1996.
Cox, Harvey. *Secular City: Secularization and Urbanization in Theological Perspective.* New York: Macmillan, 1966.
Craig, William Lane. *Apologetics: An Introduction.* Chicago: Moody, 1989.
Davie, Grace. *Religion in Britain since 1945: Believing without Belonging.* Oxford: Blackwell, 1994.
Dulles, Avery Cardinal. *A History of Apologetics.* San Francisco: Ignatius, 1999.

Fee, Gordon D. *God's Empowering Presence: The Holy Spirit in the Letters of Paul.* Exeter: Paternoster, 1994.

Foucault, Michael. *Politics, Philosophy, Culture: Interviews and Other Writings 1977–1984.* Ed. by Lawrence D. Kritzman. New York: Routledge, 1988.

Frame, John M. *Apologetics to the Glory of God: An Introduction.* Phillipsburg, NJ: P&R, 1994.

Geisler, Norman L. *Christian Apologetics.* Grand Rapids: Baker, 1993.

Gill, Robin. *The Myth of the Empty Church.* London: SPCK, 1993.

Goheen, Michael. *"As the Father has Sent me, I am Sending you": Lesslie Newbigin's Missionary Ecclesiology.* Amsterdam: Boekcentrum, 2000.

———. Review of "Bearing the Witness of the Spirit." *International Bulletin of Missionary Research* 23.2 (1999): 80.

Hall, Douglas John. *The End of Christendom and the Future of Christianity.* Pennsylvania: Trinity International, 1997.

Harvey, David. *The Condition of Postmodernity.* Oxford: Blackwells, 1989.

Hiebert, Paul G. *Anthropological Reflections on Missiological Issues.* Grand Rapids: Baker, 1994.

Hunsberger, George R. "Acquiring the Posture of a Missionary Church." Pages 289–97 in *The Church between Gospel and Culture: The Emerging Mission in North America.* Ed. by George R. Hunsberger and Craig Van Gelder. Grand Rapids: Eerdmans, 1996.

Kuhn, Thomas S. *The Structure of Scientific Revolutions—Second Edition.* Chicago: University of Chicago Press, 1970.

Lyotard, Jean-François. *The Postmodern Condition: A Report on Knowledge, Theory and History of Literature, Volume 10.* Manchester: Manchester University Press, 1997.

Moreland, J. P. *Scaling the Secular City.* Chicago: Moody, 1993.

Murray, Stuart. *Post-Christendom: Church and Mission in a Strange New World.* Carlisle: Paternoster, 2004.

O'Donnovan, Oliver. *The Desire of the Nations: Rediscovering the Roots of Political Theology.* Cambridge: Cambridge University Press, 1996.

Polanyi, Michael. *Personal Knowledge: Toward A Post-Critical Philosophy.* London: Routledge, 1962.

Popper, Karl. *Conjectures and Refutations: The Growth of Scientific Knowledge.* London: Routledge & Kegan Paul, 1963.

Rawlings, John. "Jacques Derrida," 1999, https://prelectur.stanford.edu/lecturers/derrida/.

Sire, James W. "On Being a Fool for Christ and an Idiot for Nobody." Pages 101–27 in *Christian Apologetics in the Post-modern World.* Ed. by Timothy R. Phillips and Dennis L. Okholm. Downers Grove, IL: InterVarsity Press, 1995.

Smith, David. *Mission After Christendom.* London: Dartman, Longman & Todd, 2003.

Stafford, Tim. "God's Missionary to Us." *Christianity Today* 40.14 (1996): 24.

Walls, Andrew F. *The Missionary Movement in Christian History: Studies in the Transmission of faith.* Edinburgh: T&T Clark, 1996.

Wright, N. T. "How Can the Bible Be Authoritative?" *Vox Evangelica* 21 (1991):7–32.

Zizioulas, John D. *Being as Communion: Studies in Personhood and the Church.* New York: St. Vladimir's Seminary Press, 2000.

Part Seven

CONTEMPORARY APOLOGISTS

In the last fifty years, interest in apologetics has increased significantly within Western Christianity, partly reflecting growing awareness of the need to respond to secular challenges to religious belief on the one hand and an increasing realization of its importance for Christian discipleship on the other. Where American apologetics of the second half of the twentieth century tended to be shaped by specific schools or methods, this has given way to a more diverse range of approaches, often developed by individual apologists with their own specific concerns and ministries in mind.

Two of the most important such ministries merit special note. **Ravi Zacharias** founded Ravi Zacharias International Ministries (RZIM) in 1984 to encourage the development of an international apologetic ministry, aiming to engage skeptics through publications such as *The End of Reason: A Response to the New Atheists* or regular radio shows such as *Let My People Think*. Zacharias's apologetic approach is not easily reduced to traditional categories. While emphasizing the importance of reason in reflecting on the meaning of life, Zacharias recognizes the role of the imagination, feelings, and experience in making sense of the world. Zacharias has made substantial contributions to the teaching of apologetics globally, most recently through the founding of the Zacharias Institute in 2017.

Timothy Keller, founding pastor of Redeemer Presbyterian Church, New York City, developed an apologetic ministry in response to the questions raised by members of his young professional congregation. His bestselling *Reason for God* represents a strongly relational, thoughtful response to these questions. Where earlier apologists may have sought to engage reason alone, Keller's strongly pastoral and relational approach engages the person as a whole, aiming to demonstrate that the Christian faith is both truthful and transformative. Once more, Keller does not easily map onto traditional apologetic categories.

Despite significant cultural shifts since the 1960s, evidentialism remains an important component of contemporary apologetics and can be seen in different forms in the writings of **John Warwick Montgomery** and **Gary R. Habermas**. Montgomery's evidential and fact-driven apologetic approach draws on his strengths as a legal theorist and is modeled on the approach of Simon Greenleaf, while safeguarding core theological insights through a strongly christological emphasis. While other apologists deal with probabilistic judgments through an appeal to Bayesian theory, Montgomery deals with such questions using classical legal probability reasoning, seen at its best in his discussion of the principle of the "burden of proof." Habermas's "minimal facts approach" retains a core element of traditional evidentialism, while adapting this for an envisaged audience that does not share a belief that the Bible is inerrant, inspired, or even reliable. Habermas's evidentialist approach emphasizes the grounding of the Christian faith in history rather than arguing for the logical consistency of faith.

The surge in fortunes of Christian philosophy since the 1970s, often seen as reflecting the work of **Alvin Plantinga**, did more than restore theism's legitimacy within the philosophical community; it also created a new interest in deploying philosophical defenses of faith in apologetics. Three of the most significant contemporary apologists are professional philosophers of religion with strong academic credentials. Alvin Plantinga's robust defense of the rationality of Christian faith remains significant in its own right, while having inspired others to explore the apologetic possibilities opened up by his approach. Plantinga's demonstration that belief in God can be justified in the absence of propositional evidence remains highly significant. His *God and Other Minds* argued for acknowledging a set of beliefs that we are strongly inclined to accept as epistemically appropriate yet for which compelling arguments or evidence is lacking.

British philosopher **Richard Swinburne** has also achieved wide recognition for his defense of the rationality of faith, particularly his argument that the simplicity of theistic belief is an indication of its plausibility. Swinburne's landmark works *The Coherence of Theism* and *The Existence of God* remain widely cited and have had a significant impact on many younger apologists.

William Lane Craig's wide-ranging defense of Christianity has been very influential, particularly in student circles. Perhaps his most significant achievement has been the revitalization and redirection of the *kalām* argument for the existence of God, which has arguably been given new significance through developments in scientific cosmology.

Two of the most significant—and possibly interconnected—forces in Western culture are secularism and the natural sciences. How should apologetics relate to these trends? Many have drawn on the work of Canadian social philosopher **Charles Taylor**, whose analysis of the nature and origins of secularism has been deeply influential. Taylor's *Secular Age* challenged the then-dominant model of secularization, which holds that religion has gradually diminished in social influence and significance, arguing instead that the modern world is not characterised by the disappearance of religion but rather by its diversification and in many places its growth. This clearly opens up new apologetic possibilities, which Taylor particularly links with recognizing the distinction between "seekers" and "dwellers."

The natural sciences continue to be apologetically significant, not least because of the persistence of the "warfare" narrative of the relation of science and faith, which lies at the heart of the "New Atheism" of writers such as Richard Dawkins and Sam Harris. Oxford apologist **Alister McGrath** is one of a number of writers to challenge this narrative, as well as the idea that the natural sciences are the sole source of reliable knowledge about our world and ourselves. McGrath argues for the possibility of science and faith enriching each other when both are rightly understood. Although McGrath's apologetic interests go beyond this specific issue, it remains an important element of his overall approach.

It is clear that the apologetic scene has changed significantly in the West in the last two generations, both in terms of the questions being asked and the manner in which answers are given. Many apologists have noted that traditional questions (such as those concerning the authority of the Bible) have given way to more relational or existential questions (such as how to live or the meaning of life). Further shifts are to be expected in the future. Yet the diversity of approaches and responses is clear evidence of the current vitality of apologetics. There is a growing realization that apologetics can help churches to engage and answer life's deepest questions in ways that are theologically faithful and culturally relevant.

JOHN WARWICK MONTGOMERY

Evangelical, Evidential, and Confessional Lutheran Apologist

CRAIG A. PARTON

Summarizing the contribution of any important apologist can be challenging, and the continued scope of John Warwick Montgomery's work in writing, lecturing, debating, and hosting tours for travelers visiting the International Academy of Apologetics, Evangelism, and Human Rights in the Alsace region of France makes it even more so. His expertise ranges from Wittgenstein[1] to Luther,[2] and from Tolkien[3] to Sherlock Holmes.[4] He is a rare American member of both an elite culinary academy in Paris[5] and wine society in the Alsace,[6] who founded the first Christian law school that integrated theology, law, and apologetics; is a member of the

---

1. See John Warwick Montgomery, *Tractatus Logico-Theologicus* (Bonn, Germany: Culture & Science, 2009). This theological magnum opus by Montgomery mirrors in structure what many consider the most important work of philosophy in modern times done by the great twentieth-century analytical philosopher Ludwig Wittgenstein. Elsewhere Montgomery's *Tractatus* has been described as the "apologetical equivalent of Bach's *Mass in B Minor.*" See Craig A. Parton, *The Defense Never Rests: A Lawyer Among the Theologians* (Saint Louis: Concordia, 2015), 177. Montgomery himself considers it his most comprehensive work.

2. Montgomery's commitment to the insights of the Lutheran Reformation are better known within evangelicalism than they are within his own Lutheran church, a fact that is discussed in more detail elsewhere in this article. Suffice it at this point to say that it is widely thought that his volume on the issue of Scripture's total reliability and authority (*Crisis in Lutheran Theology* Vols 1 & 2. 2d ed. [Minneapolis: Bethany, 1973]) was perhaps the single most important and comprehensive work that lanced the boil of doubt concerning Scriptural authority that lay festering within the Lutheran Church, Missouri Synod. His volume dedicated solely to the work of Martin Luther has such fascinating chapters as "Luther, Libraries and Learning." See John Warwick Montgomery, *In Defense of Martin Luther* (Milwaukee: Northwestern, 1970).

3. John Warwick Montgomery, *Myth, Allegory & Gospel* (Minneapolis: Bethany, 1974).

4. John Warwick Montgomery, *The Transcendent Holmes* (Ashcroft, British Columbia: Calabash, 2000). Here one learns of Holmes's evolving religious position, which includes a refutation of the popular notion—which Montgomery shows to be utterly unsupportable—that Holmes ended up in Tibetan Buddhism.

5. L'Académie Internationale des Gourmets et des Traditions Gastronomiques, where he has the rank of Académicien, seat number 41 of 50, dedicated to the French translator of Apicius, Bertrand Guégan. For his most recent work dealing with gastronomy and theology, see John Warwick Montgomery, *A Gastronomic Vade-Mecum: A Christian Field Guide to Eating, Drinking and Being Merry Now and Forever* (Irvine, CA: 1517 Legacy, 2018).

6. La Confrérie St-Etienne, where he has attained the highest rank of Master on the basis of three sets of blind taste tests. For a fuller discussion of the connection of gastronomy to metaphysics, see John Warwick Montgomery, "Transcendental Gastronomy" *Christianity Today*, November 22, 1974.

Sherlock Holmes Society of England; holds citizenship in three countries (US, UK, and France); argues cases of international import involving religious liberty and human rights before the European Court of Human Rights in Strasbourg;[7] has debated the likes of the infamous atheist Madalyn Murray O'Hair, death-of-God theologian Thomas J. J. Altizer, and liberal Bishop James Pike; and who, at last count, has twelve earned degrees (including advanced degrees in law, history, philosophy, and theology) from such diverse institutions as UC Berkeley, University of Chicago, Essex, Cardiff, and Strasbourg. He has published over seventy books and 250 articles in eight languages,[8] is the editor of an international journal of classical theology and apologetics,[9] has done the definitive treatment on the history of efforts to locate Noah's ark as well as personally led two expeditions up Mount Ararat in search of the ark.[10] With such an interesting and encompassing scholarly background and reputation for utterly engaging public lecturing, and with the honed polemical ability of an English barrister and American attorney licensed to practice in California, Virginia, and Washington and before the Supreme Court of the United States, John Warwick Montgomery (1931–) has had a colossal impact for the gospel of Jesus Christ in the modern secular era.

HISTORICAL BACKGROUND

John Warwick Montgomery was born on October 18, 1931, in Warsaw, New York, to Maurice Warwick and Harriet Smith Montgomery. John's father owned a retail feed company, so when they discovered that young John had severe, life-threatening allergies to farm animals, he was sent to live with his grandmother, who was a believing Christian. As a young adult, John attended Cornell University and majored in classics, and it was while at Cornell that he first encountered serious orthodox and evangelical theology. He was converted

---

7. Montgomery's critical work on the general topic of human rights and apologetics is *Human Rights and Human Dignity* (Grand Rapids: Zondervan, 1986). His legal role in the critical case vindicating the freedom to preach Christ crucified in Greece but outside the dominion of the Orthodox Church is chronicled in *The Repression of Evangelism in Greece* (Lanham, MA: University Press of America, 2001). That work, in addition to being dedicated to his son Jean-Marie and daughter-in-law Laurence, is inscribed as follows: "For My Lay Clients and Their Missionary Organizations Endeavoring, As Did Saint Paul, To Preach the Gospel in Greece."

8. For a catalog of the writings, debates, videotapes, film, and lectures of Dr. Montgomery through at least 2007, see "Bibliography of Dr. John Warwick Montgomery's Writings," in *Tough-Minded Christianity: Honoring the Legacy of John Warwick Montgomery* (Nashville: Broadman & Holman, 2008), 704–34. Many of Montgomery's books and lectures are now available at 1517 The Legacy Project.

9. See *Global Journal of Classical Theology*, published by Concordia University Wisconsin. The journal has a strong emphasis on apologetics and classical and Reformation theology.

10. John Warwick Montgomery, *The Quest for Noah's Ark* (Minneapolis: Bethany, 1972). The book is worth the price for the hilarious pictures of Montgomery and his particularly greasy mountain climbing guides.

to Christianity in 1949.[11] Montgomery immediately sought to determine which expression of Christianity most clearly mirrored the Scriptures, so he set the Greek text of the New Testament alongside the thirty-nine Articles of the Anglican Church of England, the Reformed Heidelberg Catechism, and the Lutheran Augsburg Confession. He concluded that Lutheranism adhered most closely to the biblical text and promptly became a confessional Lutheran operating within the conservative Lutheran Church, Missouri Synod. Montgomery appreciated how Lutheran theology emphasized the doctrine of justification as the central doctrine on which the church rises or falls, and early in his academic studies, he decided to focus on the defense and proclamation of the gospel of Jesus Christ while advocating for the reliability of the Scriptures.[12]

Montgomery finished his studies at Cornell University, graduating in 1952 with distinction and a degree in philosophy. His academic studies were far from over, as he later earned an additional eleven degrees, including: a BLS (1954) and MA (1958) from University of California-Berkeley, an MDiv (1958) and STM (1960) from Wittenberg University, a PhD (1962) from the University of Chicago, a ThD (1964) from the University of Strasbourg, an LLB (1977) from LaSalle University, a diploma (1978) from the International Institute of Human Rights in Strasbourg, France, an MPhil (1983) from the University of Essex, an honorary doctorate (1999) from the Institute for Religion and Law in Moscow, an LLM (2000) and LLD (2003) from Cardiff University in Wales.

Montgomery considers himself an evangelical, but his embrace of the evangelical label should not be confused with an acceptance of the *sociological* evangelicalism of the United States. Montgomery's formal theological commitment, training, and temperament mark him out clearly as a confessional Lutheran.[13] His theological roots are found in Luther's Reformation and the doctrine of the freedom of the Christian rather than the revivalistic Wesleyan Methodism or pietistic and moralistic Arminianism of American evangelicalism.

---

11. The impact of Herman John Eckelmann on Montgomery at Cornell is incalculable. Montgomery later edited a set of essays in honor of Eckelmann, all authored by Cornell graduates. See *Evidence for Faith: Deciding the God Question*, ed. J. W. Montgomery (Irvine, CA: New Reformation, 2016). The essays sprung out of The Cornell Symposium on Evidential Apologetics, which took place in Ithaca, New York, in 1986. For the complete story of Montgomery's time at Cornell and his conversion, see chapter 3 of his autobiography, *Fighting the Good Fight: A Life in Defense of the Faith* (Bonn, Germany: Culture & Science, 2015).

12. The titles of two of his works say it all: *Faith Founded on Fact: Essays in Evidential Apologetics* (Nashville: Nelson, 1978), n. 14 and *God's Inerrant Word*, *infra*, n. 25.

13. As a "confessional" Lutheran, Montgomery "holds to the validity of the Ecumenical Creeds of Christendom" and to the Reformation's commitment that "the Holy Scriptures, as originally given, are correct, reliable, and sufficient to provide the church and the world with perspicuous revelational truth" and that "the central answer to human need is a personal, living relationship with Jesus Christ." See Montgomery, *Christ Our Advocate: Studies in Polemical Theology, Jurisprudence and Canon Law* (Bonn, Germany: Culture & Science, 2002), 10. He is also an ordained clergyman in the Lutheran Church, Missouri Synod.

This partly explains why North American theologians have had something of a love-hate relationship with John Warwick Montgomery.[14] In North America he is best known in evangelical circles, having lectured in many of evangelicalism's best teaching institutions for the past fifty years. But with his Lutheran sacramental theological orientation grounded in the Reformation, he is often still seen (albeit wrongly) as an outsider looking in. And though his output has been prodigious over the past decades, many American Christians are still unaware of Montgomery's significant contributions to the field of apologetics. His three-decade residency in Europe has kept him off the radar of contemporary American Christianity, and even among those who are familiar with him, his unique apologetic approach as an historian, philosopher, theologian, and lawyer does not always fit neatly into the traditional apologetic camps of North American evangelicalism.

THEOLOGICAL CONTEXT

When there is no orthodoxy confessed, there is little left to defend.[15] This simple statement provides the context for many of Montgomery's theological and apologetical contributions. During the 1960s and 70s, theological liberalism had infiltrated many American denominations. Liberalism elevated humans and downgraded God and his Word, prioritizing a call to a new life and social action over objective, propositional statements of truth. The influence of liberalism was often accompanied by a growing atmosphere of pluralism, which led to little interest in rigorous theological reflection that took the claims of Scripture seriously.[16] At the same time, on the other theological side of American Christianity, there was a pull by many to embrace a faith focused on practical daily living while neglecting some of the more serious pursuits, such as apologetics or *"contending* for the faith."

---

14. One may find amusement in pondering what it was like at the charismatic Melodyland School of Theology in Anaheim when Dr. Montgomery taught there in the late 1970s along with now sainted and then highly polemical Walter Martin. Dr. Rod Rosenbladt, described by J. I. Packer as a "living embodiment of Luther," was also a member of the faculty at the time. We do know that because of Montgomery's influence, that school became the first theological seminary in the world to adapt a doctrinal statement with built-in hermeneutic commitments. Those commitments are a template for any modern-day seminary or college that wants to get its epistemology right from the get-go and desires that real teeth be set in place to combat the twin cancers of neoorthodox and postmodern deconstructionist hermeneutical approaches. For that doctrinal statement, see Montgomery, *Faith Founded on Fact*, 225ff. Virtually the same doctrinal statement became the foundation for the later Simon Greenleaf School of Law, for which Montgomery served as Dean in the 1980s.

15. For a fuller discussion of liberalism's devastating impact on American Christianity, see "Protestant Liberalism: A Christianity Without A Cross," in Parton, *The Defense Never Rests*, n. 1, 68ff.

16. See the devastation of Protestant liberalism in John Warwick Montgomery, *The Suicide of Christian Theology* (Minneapolis: Bethany, 1975), 180ff., entitled "Bibliographical Bigotry."

In the 1970s and 80s, Lutheranism (as did many denominations) went through a series of theological conflicts centered on opposing views on the authority and inerrancy of Scripture. During these debates, Montgomery, a Missouri Synod Lutheran (a very conservative branch of American Lutheranism) was a veritable menace to liberals but was also disliked by many so-called "moderating" Lutherans. During the 1970s, the Missouri Synod had a significant faction arguing that Scripture contained errors and contradictions, and in his distinctive fashion, Montgomery called out (by name) those he viewed as compromising while at the same time documenting the intellectual vacuity of their arguments (which in many cases had been articulated and refuted centuries earlier).[17]

As a French-speaking Lutheran without a German surname and lacking degrees from Synod-blessed schools,[18] Montgomery was regarded with a large dose of suspicion by many in old-line Lutheran circles. Oddly enough, the most frequent criticisms of Montgomery are accusations that he is either a liberal (because he is willing to teach all manner of Christians[19]) or an Arminian (because he values argument as a tool for communicating the Christian message and invites non-Christians to weigh the evidence for the truth of the claims of Christianity).[20] Even his own Lutheran church body has alternately ignored or been irritated with his work at a time when its rediscovery would be invaluable. It was largely due to thinkers such as Montgomery and Robert Preus in the late 1960s and early 70s that the Lutheran Church, Missouri Synod successfully steered its seminary away from the path of theological liberalism.[21] Yet despite

---

17. See John Warwick Montgomery, *Crisis in Lutheran Theology* Vols. 1 & 2, 2nd ed. (Minneapolis: Bethany, 1973), n. 17. Montgomery continues the fight within his own Synod, recently confronting the suspect textual critic Dr. Jeffrey Kloha and exposing Kloha's methodology and advocacy of a "plastic text." After their debate in Chicago in 2016, Kloha left his academic position at the Concordia Seminary in St. Louis and is now at the Bible Museum in Washington DC, where the implications of his methodology are unlikely to be understood by its corporate sponsors. See discussion of Kloha's article "Text and Authority: Theological and Hermeneutical Reflections on a Plastic Text" and Montgomery's response and the fallout from the debate all discussed in John Warwick Montgomery, *Defending the Gospel in Legal Style: Essays on Legal Apologetics & the Justification of Classical Christian Faith* (Bonn, Germany: Culture & Science, 2017), 227–72.

18. His master's in Sacred Theology from Wittenberg University apparently does not count.

19. Montgomery held faculty positions at the charismatic-oriented Melodyland School of Theology (appropriately located across the street from Disneyland) as well as at the Trinity Evangelical Divinity School in Illinois. In addition, he has taught for numerous campus evangelical groups at universities across the country, including Campus Crusade for Christ (now Cru), Inter-Varsity and The Navigators, even lecturing for the Veritas Forum at UCLA on "Why Human Rights Are Impossible Without Religion."

20. "Synergism does not come about when unbelievers are expected to accept persuasive, objective evidence for the truth of the Bible or its gospel message, any more than it is synergistic for evangelists to call for decisions for Christ. Apologists (and evangelists) operate outside the house of salvation; they are not pastors or systematic theologians interpreting the conversion experience after it has come about. Synergism exists only when, following conversion, the justified man is led to believe that in any way whatever (rational, moral, volitional) he contributed to his own salvation." John Warwick Montgomery, "The Holy Spirit and the Defense of the Faith," *Bibliotheca Sacra* 154.616 (October–December 1997), 387–95.

21. Montgomery, *Crisis in Lutheran Theology*. Happily, though, one of the best apologetical shows on

Montgomery's essential role in this theological turnaround, Lutherans by-and-large have never understood, let alone embraced, Montgomery as one of their own. Of course, that assumes Lutherans have heard of him. Most have not.

APOLOGETICAL RESPONSE AND METHODOLOGY

Montgomery's unique contributions to the apologetic task and his robust defense of the faith are best seen in his ability to integrate his training as a theologian, historian, philosopher, and lawyer with an unswerving commitment to the centrality of the saving message of Jesus Christ as it is contained in a totally reliable Scripture. His commitment to centering his apologetic on both the formal (Scripture and its reliability) and material (the gospel) principles arises directly from his Lutheran orthodoxy. Montgomery's evidential approach to apologetics is directly tied to the incarnational focus of Lutheran theology—that God became man at a specific time in history. In summary, John Warwick Montgomery's impact can be best understood by seeing him as an evangelical, evidential, and confessional Lutheran apologist.

EVANGELICAL APOLOGIST

John Warwick Montgomery's life and work is above all *evangelical*—that is, its sum and substance is a commitment to the intellectual defensibility of the gospel, the complete trustworthiness of the record in which that gospel is found, and the aggressive presentation of that saving gospel to all people by calling for their personal commitment to Jesus, who saves. The early Lutherans were called "evangelicals," a term that comes from the Greek word *evangelion*, or *evangel*, and simply means "good news" or "gospel." The Lutherans of sixteenth-century Germany were originally called "evangelicals" because of their emphasis on Christ's atoning death and resurrection, and this same gospel has been the focus of all Montgomery's writing, lecturing, and debating. He never fails to deliver a lecture on human rights, gastronomy, Sherlock Holmes, analytical philosophy, or the music of J. S. Bach without discussing the implications that topic has for the proclamation and defense of the gospel at the highest levels of scholarship.

Montgomery's evangelical focus is particularly evident in his public presentations. There are three things one can *always* be sure of when attending a Montgomery lecture. First, he is as prepared as a trial lawyer about to address a

---

radio is now produced by the Lutheran Church, Missouri Synod, and it has had Montgomery on as a guest on a regular basis. Recently, they devoted a series of one-hour programs to discussing each chapter of Montgomery's monumental *Tractatus Logico-Theologicus*. See www.issuesetc.org.

jury in a court of law. Montgomery has a keen awareness of his audience and can relate content to any level, whatever the topic might be and regardless of whether there are six hundred people, sixty people, or six people. Second, Montgomery ensures the case for the truth of the gospel of Jesus Christ (Christ's perfect life, atoning death, and verifiable resurrection) finds its way into his presentation in a way that is never contrived, always clear, unfailingly defensible, and emphasizes the *extra nos*[22] character of that case. Third, his presentation is at a high level of scholarship and has such academic rigor that one could confidently invite a skeptic without the least apprehension. One can advise someone to listen to Montgomery with the same confidence one has when recommending they read C. S. Lewis's *Mere Christianity*.[23] Any non-Christian in the audience will be respected, not talked down to, and not subjected to "in group" Christian lingo. Modern-day American evangelicalism could benefit from a rediscovery of this apologetic acumen, an approach that combines rigorous research, clarity in message, breadth of application, and upholds the utter centrality of the gospel [24] as the intellectually credible center in dialogue with unbelief.

The Reformers referred to the gospel as the "material principle of all theology."[25] Recognizing the centrality of this good news, Montgomery has been readily aware that a gospel contained in a text with errors and contradictions is intellectually indefensible. If the texts that give us the gospel (that is, the Holy Scripture, sometimes known as the "formal principle of all theology") cannot be trusted in what they say about what the Temple in Jerusalem looked like, how can they be trusted when they speak of the heavenly Jerusalem? Montgomery saw the logical landmines created by neoorthodox theologians and "mediating evangelicals" as they sought to maintain what Montgomery regarded as a hopelessly unbiblical contradiction—an *inerrant* gospel residing in an *errant* Scripture. Montgomery had no leniency for those who sought to undermine this theological foundation. He viewed those who replaced inerrancy with "infallibility" and

---

22. *Extra nos* simply means "outside of us," and it is Luther's characterization of the gospel. This is evidenced by Montgomery's debates, where he is often quick to make clear to the audience that the debate is not about the personalities of the debaters but about an objective and *extra nos* truth fully capable of being investigated by the serious inquirer.

23. Montgomery sent Lewis the monograph that became the basis for one of Montgomery's earliest (and still most popular) works, *History and Christianity* (Minneapolis: Bethany, 1964). Lewis, in a letter to Montgomery in August 1963, said that Montgomery's work "did me good and I shall constantly find them useful. . . . I don't think it could be bettered." Id. at 6–7. The consistently popular book is now reprinted as *History, Law and Christianity* (Irvine, CA: New Reformation, 2014). It is strongly recommended as a first read in Montgomery.

24. For how his entire apologetical effort has been christocentric, whether focusing on juridical apologetics, or literary or aesthetic apologetics, or human rights and apologetics, see his volume *Christ as Centre and Circumference: Essays Theological, Cultural and Polemic* (Bonn, Germany: Culture & Science, 2012).

25. Robert D. Preus, *The Theology of Post-Reformation Lutheranism* (St. Louis: Concordia, 1970), 270–71, 331.

"partial inerrancy" as existing on the same theological continuum with those willing to give up the faith altogether.[26] As an evangelical apologist, Montgomery encourages modern evangelicals to rediscover total confidence in the gospel[27] and to recover a vigorous and intellectually defensible ground for the gospel in a totally reliable Scripture.

EVIDENTIAL APOLOGIST

Montgomery utilized an evidential and fact-driven approach in his defense of the saving gospel and the record that contains it. His best-known work, *History, Law, and Christianity*, presents a "historical-legal" apologetic that sets him apart from other contemporary apologists.[28] This work sets forth several tests to determine the reliability of the New Testament gospels. Montgomery builds on these tests and presents a tight evidential progression that culminates by proving the case for Christianity under legal standards of evidential probability.[29]

The outline for the historical-legal argument progresses through a series of arguments. First, Montgomery asserts (1) the gospels are reliable historical documents or *primary source material*. Virtually all scholars (even non-Christians) admit that Matthew, Mark, and Luke were written within fifty years after Christ's death, and most agree that John was written within sixty-five years after Christ's death. Objectors can verify this in any credible biblical encyclopedia. In these gospels, (2) Christ claims to be God in human flesh (see Matt 11:27; John 12:45; John 10:30; Matt 16:13–17). In addition, (3) Christ's bodily resurrection is described in great detail in all four gospel accounts. Following this, (4) Christ's resurrection proves his claim to deity because (5) if Christ is God, whatever he says is true, and (6) Christ stated that the Old Testament was infallible

---

26. Montgomery's central articles on inerrancy and the complete reliability of Scripture are found in Montgomery, *The Suicide of Christian Theology*, n. 13, esp. the article "Inductive Inerrancy," 356 ff; Montgomery, *Crisis in Lutheran Theology*, vol. 1, n. 17, esp. "Inspiration and Inerrancy: A New Departure" and "Lutheran Hermeneutics and Hermeneutics Today," 15–77; *God's Inerrant Word: An International Symposium on the Trustworthiness of Scripture*, ed. J. W. Montgomery (Minneapolis: Bethany, 1974), esp. "Biblical Inerrancy: What is at Stake?" and "Lessons from Luther on the Inerrancy of Holy Writ,"15–42 and 63–94; *Ecumenicity, Evangelicals and Rome* (Grand Rapids: Zondervan, 1969), esp. "The Approach of New Shape Roman Catholicism to Scriptural Inerrancy: A Case Study for Evangelicals," 73–93; and Montgomery, *Faith Founded on Fact*, n. 23, esp. "The Fuzzification of Biblical Inerrancy," 215ff.

27. See Parton, "Whatever Happened to the Gospel?" in Parton, *Defense Never Rests*, n. 1, 13ff.

28. See Montgomery, *History, Law and Christianity*, n. 23. The three-part test for establishing the reliability of the gospel records are the *bibliographical test* (deals with how good the manuscript tradition is from which we get the present text), the *internal evidence test* (answers whether the authors had the means, motive, and opportunity to be accurate eyewitnesses of the events or not or whether they make factual errors), and the *external evidence test* (determines if any other historical materials confirm or deny the biblical material).

29. This material is a summary of the analysis found in John Warwick Montgomery, *The Shape of the Past: A Christian Response to Secular Philosophies of History* (Minneapolis: Bethany, 1975). See also John Warwick Montgomery, "The Jury Returns: A Juridical Defense of Christianity," in *Evidence for Faith: Deciding the God Question* (Dallas: Probe, 1991), 319 et seq. (repr by New Reformation Press in 2016).

(Matt 5:17–19) and that the coming New Testament (written by apostles or close associates of apostles) would be infallible as well (John 14:26–27; John 16:12–15).

The flow of Montgomery's legal defense of the faith reveals his training as an English barrister and an American attorney and is based on the groundbreaking work of professor Simon Greenleaf of the Harvard Law School. Following Greenleaf's approach, much of the juridical or legal apologetic presuppositions are kept to the absolute minimum in his argumentation. The least quantum of data is *assumed* (only presuppositions of form, such as assuming the objectivity of the external world, the inferential operations of induction and deduction, the meaningfulness of language, the validity of the law of noncontradiction) so that the maximum amount of data is capable of being *discovered*. In the historical-legal apologetic presented by Montgomery, inquirers are invited to investigate the claims of Christianity contained in the New Testament documents as they would any other work of antiquity and to apply probability reasoning and the widely accepted canons of legal evidence.

The importance of Montgomery's legal or juridical emphasis in apologetics can be seen in at least three applications. First, in the concept of probability reasoning; second, in his use of the principle of the "burden of proof;" and finally, in his insistence that a *verdict* be rendered and that the historical case elevates one beyond mere intellectual acknowledgment of the claims of Christ into the very presence of the transcendent God who has become man via the mystery of the incarnation.

Montgomery utilizes probability reasoning in his claim that the case for Christianity is ultimately based on establishing the facticity of certain events (as opposed to arguing that Christianity is true because it is necessarily the most "logical" system). This means that if certain central events did *not* occur, Christianity is both false and virulent. Because Christianity is fact centered, one must understand the general nature of factual assertions. Facts never rise to the level of didactic proof, and there is *always* the possibility of error. This leads Montgomery to conclude that the case for Christianity is never apodictically certain because 100 percent certainty comes only in matters of pure logic or pure mathematics. Instead, one weighs probabilities, looks at the evidence as a lawyer would in presenting evidence to a court or jury, and then renders a decision. One should never demand of religious claims a level of factual certainty not demanded in any other domain.[30]

---

30. For further work in this area, see the second and third propositions of Montgomery, *Tractatus Logico-Theologicus*, ft.1, 23–128.

Second, Montgomery stresses that the "burden of proof" is on the Christian to establish the case for Christianity. This assertion has several significant, practical implications. First, Christians should recognize the importance of bringing the case for Christ into the marketplace with arguments that can be checked out and verified. When talking about one of his numerous debates, Montgomery has publically remarked that his aim is to win the person in the audience who truly does not know which side they are on but is "sitting on the fence."[31] His belief that the burden of proof rests on the Christian has practically meant that Montgomery's apologetic is focused on positive, fact-driven arguments for the case for Christianity rather than tearing down the weaker arguments of other world religions.

As a trained trial lawyer, Montgomery knows that as a plaintiff with the burden of proof, the goal of his argument and presentation is the return of a favorable verdict. The law recognizes this since even an executive pardon must be "accepted" to be effective.[32] When one is confronted with the claims of Christianity, the mere acceptance of facts is not enough. If the factual case is solid—which, based on the overwhelmingly solid evidence trial lawyers have concluded for centuries is indeed the situation—then personal commitment to those facts is central. As our Lord himself said, "The one who believes in me will live, even though they die" (John 11:25).

Montgomery's point here helps us understand why lawyers have been more inclined to do apologetics than dentists or engineers. It's not becuase Scripture is so intertwined with law but because Christian truth claims cry out for verification. Montgomery has dedicated his energy to establishing that the testimony of biblical witnesses are not subject to the hearsay objection, but they stand up to the most rigorous cross-examination.[33] Whether he is applying the parol evidence rule or the principles of the ancient document rule, the biblical documents are, simply put, the best attested works of all antiquity.[34]

---

31. Dallas K. Miller, "The Role of Public Debate in Apologetics," in *Tough-Minded Christianity: Honoring the Legacy of John Warwick Montgomery*, eds. William Dembski and Thomas Schirrmacher (Nashville, TN: Broadman & Holman, 2008), 473.

32. *United States v. Wilson 32 U.S. 150, 161*(1833). ("Thus a prisoner cannot be forced to accept a pardon, whether conditional or not. The pardon recipient always has the choice of rejecting the offer of clemency and suffering the consequences of the judicially imposed sentence.... Either the prisoner accepts the pardon or commutation as conditioned or he rejects it. The choice is clear and there is no in-between.") For a more robust exposure to Montgomery's legal or juridical apologetic, see Montgomery *Defending the Gospel in Legal Style*, n. 17. See also Ross Clifford, *John Warwick Montgomery's Legal Apologetic: An Apologetic for All Seasons* (Bonn, Germany: Culture & Science, 2004).

33. John Warwick Montgomery, *The Law Above the Law* (Irvine, CA: New Reformation, 2015), see esp. 84ff. dealing with legal reasoning and Christian apologetics.

34. Montgomery's *The Law Above the Law* deals with these issues, as does his work *Law and Gospel: A Study in Jurisprudence* (Oak Park, IL: Christian Legal Society, 1978), esp. 34–37. For a current treatment,

CONFESSIONAL LUTHERAN APOLOGIST

Montgomery's apologetic is both evangelical and evidential *because* it is confessionally Lutheran. His apologetic efforts focus on the perfect life and atoning death of the Jesus who suffered under Pontius Pilate. As a confessional Lutheran, Montgomery and his approach is centered on the gospel of Jesus Christ, and from his earliest lectures in Lutheranism and the defense of the biblical gospel,[35] Montgomery has consistently spelled out an apologetical approach from which he has never wavered and which has, instead, grown and matured in quality. He has remained a faithful proclaimer of Christ crucified for all and has maintained an unfailing commitment to the truth of the Christian faith (as expressed in the confessional documents of the Lutheran Reformation), to Luther's freedom of the Christian in Christ (who has indeed set us free from the law of sin and death), and to the Lordship of Christ over all intellectual and cultural life. This sets him apart among the apologists of our present day. His apologetic work flows directly out of his commitment to the insights of the Lutheran Reformation. Yet what sets Montgomery apart from other serious confessional Lutherans is that he is not only an apologist and a contagiously zealous defender of the faith but also an *evangelist*. For Montgomery, there is ultimately no tension between being a serious follower of the insights of the Lutheran Reformation, a zealous advocate of Christ crucified for unbelievers, and a proclaimer of "many infallible proofs" that demand a personal verdict.

CONTRIBUTIONS TO THE FIELD OF APOLOGETICS

John Warwick Montgomery has consistently defended the total trustworthiness of Scripture and has utilized innovative techniques from other disciplines to do this. The insights of analytical philosophy and legal argumentation are present throughout his works defending the inerrancy of Scripture. Similarly, his defense of the gospel found in Scripture has also benefitted from his training in legal argumentation. His development of a legal-historical case for Christ, beginning with the factual assertion of the primary source quality and general reliability of the gospel records, is unique among apologists. His unrelentingly evidential

---

see Parton, *The Defense Never Rests*, n. 1, esp. "A Lawyer's Case for Christianity: An Apologetic for the Tough-Minded," 99ff.

35. This foundational and critical material is contained in a series of lectures delivered at Bethany College in Mankato, Minnesota, at a time when the sainted Robert Preus presided as president of the college. See John Warwick Montgomery, "Lutheranism and the Defense of the Christian Faith," *Lutheran Synod Quarterly* 9.1 (Fall, 1970): 1–56. For a contemporary discussion, see Parton, "Why Distrust of Evidential Apologetics is not Lutheran," *The Defense Never Rests*, n. 1, 79ff.

and legal approach to defending Christ crucified sets Montgomery apart from many modern apologists whose focus is on proving "mere theism." Montgomery was led to pursue his legal training later in life, and he has indicated that he did this for the explicit purpose of integrating legal reasoning with the defense of the central claims of the Christian faith. Today, his Academy of Apologetics, Evangelism & Human Rights in Strasbourg, France, has influenced a generation of lawyers and judges who have attended annual July lectures or have obtained fellow status from the academy.[36]

Montgomery's significant impact on apologetics has not prevented him from engaging in robust public debates with renowned secularists or from having an active career litigating some of the most influential human rights cases at the European Court of Human Rights. He has defended the freedom to preach the gospel in Greece (outside of the influence of the Orthodox Church), as well as more recently defending the practice of religious freedom by Christians in Moldova.

Montgomery's contributions can be generally characterized as focused on the gospel of Christ for both the tough- and the tender-minded. For the tough-minded individual, he offers an impressive body of legal, historical, philosophical, and evidential apologetical writings that will be of critical value for future defenders of the faith for generations to come. For the tender-minded—those perhaps more interested in literature, art, music, and aesthetics—he offers works that speak to how the gospel fulfills the deepest longings of the fractured human heart. His works on the power of compelling allegorical and mythical stories, such as those presented by C. S. Lewis, J. R. R. Tolkien, and Charles Williams and reflected in the "transcendent" life of Sherlock Holmes, highlight the apologetical possibilities inherent in the so-called "archetypes of the collective unconscious."

John Warwick Montgomery is an evangelical, evidential, and confessional apologist, a defender of the faith for all people and for all seasons. The *raison d'être* for the degrees, the books, the debates, and his tireless contribution to the defense of the faith is not the pursuit of an esoteric idea or an intellectual chess game to win human souls. Rather, it is a life lived *sub crucis*—under the cross—and dedicated to the aggressive defense and presentation of Christ crucified for sinners and raised again for our justification.

---

36. Attendees at past Academy sessions have included lawyers and trial court and appellate and high court judges from Singapore, Malta, Jamaica, Australia, Germany, France, Romania, Nigeria, Malaysia, England, Canada, and the United States to name but a few countries represented. The Academy is approaching its twenty-fifth year of training professionals and laity in the apologetic task. See www.apologeticsacademy.eu.

BIBLIOGRAPHY

Carnell, E. J. *Introduction to Christian Apologetics*. Grand Rapids: Eerdmans, 1948.

Clifford, Ross. *John Warwick Montgomery's Legal Apologetic: An Apologetic for All Seasons*. Bonn, Germany: Culture & Science, 2004.

Horton, Michael. "The New Gnosticism." *Modern Reformation* (July/August 1995): 4–12.

Kloha, Jeffery. "Text and Authority: Theological and Hermeneutical Reflections on a Plastic Text." Pages 33–34 in John Warwick Montgomery, *Crisis in Lutheran Theology*. Vol. 3. Irvine, CA: New Reformation, 2017.

Metzger, Will. *Tell the Truth*. Downers Grove, IL: InterVarsity Press, 1981.

Montgomery, John Warwick. *A Gastronomic Vade-Mecum: A Christian Field Guide to Eating, Drinking and Being Merry Now and Forever*. Irvine, CA: 1517 Legacy Publishers, 2018.

———. *Christ as Centre and Circumference: Essays Theological, Cultural and Polemic*. Bonn, Germany: Culture & Science, 2012.

———. *Christ Our Advocate: Studies in Polemical Theology, Jurisprudence and Canon Law*. Bonn, Germany: Culture & Science, 2002.

———. *Crisis in Lutheran Theology*. Vols 1 & 2. 2d ed. Minneapolis: Bethany, 1973.

———. *Defending the Gospel in Legal Style: Essays on Legal Apologetics & the Justification of Classical Christian Faith*. Bonn, Germany: Culture & Science, 2017.

———. *Ecumenicity, Evangelicals and Rome*. Grand Rapids: Zondervan, 1969.

———, ed. *Evidence for Faith: Deciding the God Question*. Irvine, CA: New Reformation, 2016.

———. *Faith Founded on Fact: Essays in Evidential Apologetics*. Nashville: Nelson, 1978.

———. *Fighting the Good Fight: A Life in Defense of the Faith*. Bonn, Germany: Culture & Science, 2015.

———, ed. *God's Inerrant Word: An International Symposium on the Trustworthiness of Scripture*. Minneapolis: Bethany, 1974.

———. *History and Christianity*. Minneapolis: Bethany, 1964. Repr. as *History, Law and Christianity*. Irvine, CA: New Reformation, 2014.

———. *Human Rights and Human Dignity*. Grand Rapids: Zondervan, 1986.

———. *In Defense of Martin Luther*. Milwaukee: Northwestern, 1970.

———. *Jurisprudence: A Book of Readings*. Strasbourg, France: International Scholarly, 1973.

———. *Law and Gospel: A Study in Jurisprudence*. Oak Park, IL: Christian Legal Society, 1978.

———. "Lutheranism and the Defense of the Christian Faith." *Lutheran Synod Quarterly* 9.1 (Fall 1970): 1–56.

———. *Myth, Allegory & Gospel*. Minneapolis: Bethany, 1974.

———. "The Holy Spirit and the Defense of the Faith." *Bibliotheca Sacra* 154.616 (October-December 1997): 387–95.

———. *The Law above the Law*. Irvine, CA: New Reformation, 2015.

———. *The Quest for Noah's Ark*. Minneapolis: Bethany, 1972.

———. *The Repression of Evangelism in Greece*. Lanham, MD: University Press of America, 2001.

———. *The Shape of the Past: a Christian Response to Secular Philosophies of History*. Minneapolis: Bethany, 1975.

———. *The Suicide of Christian Theology*. Minneapolis: Bethany, 1975.

———. *The Transcendent Holmes*. Ashcroft, British Columbia: Calabash, 2000.

———. *Tractatus Logico-Theologicus*. Bonn, Germany: Culture & Science, 2009.

———. "Transcendental Gastronomy." Pages 415–17 in John Warwick Montgomery, *Christ as Centre and Circumference*. Bonn, Germany: Culture & Science, 2012.

Moore, Will. "Bibliography of Dr. John Warwick Montgomery's Writings." Pages 704–34 in *Tough-Minded Christianity: Honoring the Legacy of John Warwick Montgomery*. Ed. by William Dembski and Thomas Schirrmacher. Nashville: Broadman & Holman, 2008.

Parton, Craig A. *The Defense Never Rests*. 2nd ed. Saint Louis: Concordia, 2015.

Rushdoony, R. J. *The Institutes of Biblical Law*. Nutley, NJ: Presbyterian & Reformed, 1973.

Smith, Wilbur. *Therefore Stand*. Boston: Wilde & Co., 1945.

CHARLES TAYLOR

Apologetics in a Secular Age

BRUCE RILEY ASHFORD

MATTHEW NG

Charles Margrave Taylor (1931–) is a Canadian philosopher and professor emeritus
of McGill University.[1] He is best known
for his contributions to political and social
philosophy, intellectual history, and philos-
ophy of language. Often overlooked are his contributions to late-twentieth century and early twenty-first century apologetics.[2] Although we have reservations
about some of Taylor's unorthodox interpretations of Christianity, Taylor remains
an important guide for countering the amnesia of our secular age.

HISTORICAL BACKGROUND

Charles Taylor was born on November 5, 1931, in Montreal, Quebec.[3] His
mother's side of the family spoke French, and his father's side English. Taylor
recounts how growing up bilingually influenced his intellectual views, in particular his attraction to Herder's expressivist theory of language and selfhood.[4] As
a child, Taylor observed two different approaches to language. On the one hand
were anglophones, who took an instrumentalist approach to language, seeing
English as a means to accomplish certain ends. On the other hand were fran-
cophones, who viewed French as constitutive or "expressive" of their identity.[5]
Taylor's fascination with the nexus of language, culture, and identity fostered his
philosophical interests and planted the seeds for his future work on the "politics
of recognition." Indeed, later in life, Taylor would become a tireless defender

---

1. Nicholas H. Smith, *Charles Taylor: Meaning, Morals, and Modernity* (Malden, MA: Polity, 2002), 12.

2. We would like to thank Kampen Theological University, who assisted with the research for this
chapter through their Advanced Theological Studies Fellowship.

3. Smith, *Charles Taylor*, 12.

4. Philippe de Lara and Charles Taylor, "From Philosophical Anthropology to the Politics of Recognition:
An Interview with Charles Taylor," *Thesis Eleven* 52 (1998): 109.

5. de Lara and Taylor, "From Philosophical Anthropology to the Politics of Recognition," 109.

of Quebec's right to be recognized as a distinct society while at the same time opposing secession from Canada.[6]

From an early age, Taylor showed an interest in political activism. As an undergraduate student at Oxford, he led a petition to ban the hydrogen bomb in Britain and became the first president of the Oxford University Campaign for Nuclear Disarmament.[7] When the Soviet Union invaded Hungary in October 1956, Taylor left Britain to spend six months living with Hungarian student refugees in Vienna.[8]

Later, as a postgraduate student under the supervision of Isaiah Berlin, Taylor bemoaned the "enormous gap between the discourse of science and political philosophy, and the reality of life and political passions."[9] He expressed disappointment in "the limits of the then dominant empiricist version of analytical philosophy at Oxford."[10] Dissatisfied with the reductionism and impracticality of the regnant paradigms of thought, Taylor formed a group of like-minded students to read books outside the curriculum, in particular those by the phenomenologist Maurice Merleau-Ponty.[11]

After completing postgraduate studies, Taylor ran for federal office in Canada four times between 1962 to 1968 but failed to win a seat.[12] In one of the elections, he received the support of the future prime minister of Canada, Pierre Elliot Trudeau, who, interestingly, would later become Taylor's political opponent.[13] At one point Taylor was considered the "number one policy consultant within the New Democratic Party."[14] Taylor's political activism profoundly shaped his philosophy: "The unity of theory and practice is true for me, in the sense that I have learnt enormously from my involvement in politics. There are things I have learnt that I never could have learnt in books."[15] In many ways, Taylor's philosophical interests have been driven by the practical political problems faced by Canada's cultural, religious, and linguistic pluralism.

Nevertheless, Taylor's career as a philosopher has been far more successful than his career in politics. Serving as a professor of social and political theory at the University of Oxford and a professor of political science and philosophy

---

6. Smith, *Charles Taylor*, 12.

7. Ibid., 12–13.

8. Ibid.

9. de Lara and Taylor, "From Philosophical Anthropology to the Politics of Recognition," 103.

10. Ibid., 104. Taylor's dissertation under Berlin became the basis of his first book, *The Explanation of Behavior* (New York: Routledge & Keegan Paul, 1964), which was an attack on naturalism and behaviorism.

11. Chris Bloor and Charles Taylor, "Interview with Charles Taylor," *Philosophy Now* 74 (2009), https://philosophynow.org/issues/74/Charles_Taylor.

12. Ruth Abbey, *Charles Taylor* (Princeton: Princeton University Press, 2000), 6.

13. Smith, *Charles Taylor*, 14; Abbey, *Charles Taylor*, 6.

14. Smith, *Charles Taylor*, 15.

15. Ibid., 16–17.

at McGill University, Taylor has earned widespread recognition, receiving many awards, including the Templeton Prize, the Kyoto Prize, and the Social Sciences and Humanities Research Council's Gold Medal for Achievement in Research. His books include *Hegel, Sources of the Self, The Malaise of Modernity*, and *A Secular Age*.[16]

Taylor's conversation partners throughout the years have often been philosophers and political scientists. As a result, the importance of his religious faith to his academic work is sometimes neglected. And yet, as James L. Heft has remarked, Taylor's Christian faith has been a "central, if mostly implicit, element in his philosophical writings."[17] Taylor admits that theistic/religious issues have "been at the center of my concern for decades. They have been reflected in my philosophical work . . . [implicitly] . . . because of the nature of philosophical discourse . . . , which has to try to persuade honest thinkers of any and all metaphysical or theological commitments."[18]

THEOLOGICAL CONTEXT

Taylor's project bears many similarities to that of British theologian and missiologist Lesslie Newbigin. After serving as a missionary in India for four decades, Newbigin returned to England to find that his home country had undergone a process of radical secularization. The culture shock prompted Newbigin to write that Christians must now approach Western culture the same way missionaries approached a foreign culture. Naively assuming that secular modernity was neutral and acultural, the Western church had failed to appreciate just how much it had accommodated to the reigning plausibility structures of modernity. Citing an old Chinese proverb, Newbigin once wrote that if you want to know what water is, "don't ask a fish."[19] In other words, because a fish has never lived on dry land, it has no outside perspective to describe its environment accurately. By analogy, Newbigin argued that the Western church had been "swimming" in the waters of secular modernity for so long that it had unwittingly assumed modernity's basic axioms and presuppositions.

Like Newbigin, Taylor also calls for a "missionary approach" to Western culture, an approach that does not assume modernity's plausibility structures but

---

16. For a complete bibliography of Taylor's works that is updated biannually, see https://www3.nd.edu/~rabbey1/index.html.

17. Charles Taylor, "A Catholic Modernity?," in *A Catholic Modernity? Charles Taylor's Marianist Award Lecture*, ed. James L. Heft (New York: Oxford University Press, 1999), 3.

18. Ibid., 13.

19. Lesslie Newbigin, *Foolishness to the Greeks: The Gospel and Western Culture* (Grand Rapids: Eerdmans, 1986), 21.

seeks to unearth and challenge its basic axioms. Taylor urges Western Christians to develop a "Ricci reading of modernity," referring to Matteo Ricci, the Catholic missionary known for his pathbreaking work in China.[20] According to Taylor, the modern world contains authentic fruits of the gospel but also much that negates the gospel. Because we are too immersed in modernity to see its problems clearly, Taylor argues that we need a "Ricci perspective" to create enough distance between ourselves and our culture to adequately diagnose its ailments. For Taylor, the standpoint from which to create this distance is history, and Taylor's corpus of writings serve to initiate the reader into this historical perspective.

APOLOGETIC RESPONSE

British philosopher Fergus Kerr rightly notes that Taylor's corpus must be read as a unified project, and a deeply apologetic one at that.[21] Among Taylor's many writings, three stand out as especially deserving of exploration—*A Secular Age*, *The Malaise of Modernity*, and *Sources of the Self*. This chapter will examine each book not only in respect to its unique focus but also as being organically related.

The Origins of Our Secular Age

Since *A Secular Age* stands at nearly eight hundred pages, it is easy to miss one of the central theses; namely, that the origins of secularism lie within Christian reform movements beginning in the Middle Ages.[22] In making this argument, Taylor rejects the standard view of the rise of secularism, so-called "subtraction" accounts.[23] In the subtraction account of secularism, religion is viewed as a social construction—a superficial residue that is shed or "subtracted," through science and reason, to reveal an inner core of secularity. In contrast, Taylor turns the tables on this narrative: it is the secular—*not* the religious—that is socially constructed. Furthermore, and even more significantly, Taylor argues that the secular could *only* have emerged from the religious.[24] In other words, exclusive humanism—the

---

20. Taylor, "A Catholic Modernity?," 16; Taylor, "Concluding Reflections and Comments," in *A Catholic Modernity?*, 106.

21. Fergus Kerr, "How Much Can a Philosopher Do?" *Modern Theology* 26:3 (July 2010): 321–26. Kerr, a Catholic friar, was pleased that Taylor wished to make an apologetic for the Christian faith but upbraided him for drawing on Christian spirituality and theology while claiming to do philosophy. Kerr went so far as to accuse him of "stage strutting." Taylor responded by arguing that he wanted his philosophical apologetic to be "substantive" and that substantive philosophy and apologetics cannot be accomplished "neutrally." Charles Taylor, "Challenging Issues About the Secular Age," *Modern Theology* 26:3 (July 2010): 404–16.

22. Charles Taylor, *A Secular Age* (Cambridge, MA: Belknap Press of Harvard University Press, 2007).

23. Ibid., 22.

24. By employing the term *social imaginary*, Taylor intends to go beyond "worldview" to include more than the cognitive aspect. "What I'm trying to get at with this term is something much broader and deeper than the intellectual schemes people may entertain when they think about social reality in a disengaged mode. I am

view that meaning and significance are found only within the immanent without appealing to the transcendent—could *only* have arisen from Christianity.

Taylor begins his work by laying out three different types of secularism.[25] Secular 1 refers to a situation where religion retreats from public life and plays less of a role in the common institutions of society. Secular 2 refers to an overall decline of belief in the supernatural, replaced by a belief that the immanent contains all the resources for a meaningful life. Secular 3, however, is the secularism that Taylor is more interested in. Secular 3 concerns itself with the following question: How is it that five hundred years ago, to deny the existence of God or the transcendent would have been unthinkable, whereas today, belief in God is simply one option among many? According to Taylor, the engine that drove these shifts in our social imaginary were reform movements within Latin Christendom itself. In contrast to subtraction accounts of secularism, Taylor calls his account the Reform Master Narrative.

The Drive to Reform

Taylor begins his discussion of the Reform Master Narrative by describing a tension that arose within postaxial spirituality.[26] Preaxial religions had been primarily focused on human flourishing—prosperity, health, long life, fertility, and protection from natural disasters.[27] But in the eighth century BC, the axial revolution swept the world, giving rise to such figures as Confucius, Gautama, Socrates, and the Hebrew prophets. In contrast to preaxial religions, postaxial religions (Buddhism, Confucianism, Judaism) taught that religious fullness and transcendence required a way of life distinct from the ordinary, mundane activities of everyday living. The asceticism of the Buddha or the radical teachings of Jesus seemed to be at odds with normal everyday existence. For postaxial religions, transcendence and fullness could only be achieved by religious virtuosi (for example, monks, gurus, philosophical sages) that required a separation or disembedding from the world of ordinary life. This tension gradually evolved, in Latin Christendom, into a sharp distinction between the supernatural and the

---

thinking rather of the ways in which they imagine their social existence, how they fit together with others, how things go on between them and their fellows, the expectations which are normally met, and the deeper normative notions and images which underlie these expectations." Taylor, *A Secular Age*, 171.

25. Ibid., 1–3.

26. The term *axial age*, first coined by the German philosopher Karl Jasper, refers to the massive religious and philosophical changes that occurred in Asia and Europe between 800 and 200 BC. Some of the thinkers who arose in this period include Siddartha Gautama (the founder of Buddhism), Laozi (Taoism), Confucius, Zoroaster, Homer, Plato, Socrates, Parmenides, Heraclitus, Elijah, Jeremiah, and Isaiah. See Charles E. Farhadian, *Introducing World Religions: A Christian Engagement* (Grand Rapids: Baker Academic, 2015), 260.

27. Taylor, *A Secular Age*, 147–53. For further discussion of Taylor's view of the axial age, see Charles Taylor, "What Was the Axial Revolution?," in *Dilemmas and Connections: Selected Essays* (Cambridge: Belknap Press of Harvard University Press, 2014), 367–79.

natural, which manifested, in medieval Roman Catholicism, into a distinction between the religious vocations and the laity. Only a few individuals—monks, nuns, and priests—had callings and could achieve a spiritually fulfilling life. The laity were unable to achieve a life of fullness.

This two-tiered system was eventually challenged by reform movements, which were themselves ironically responsible for the rise of secularism.[28] While the Reformation was the ultimate fruit of the reform spirit, the Reform Master Narrative is not confined to Protestantism. Taylor notes that the drive to reform started in the eleventh century under Hildebrand and carried on into the Catholic Counter-Reformation. Nevertheless, the Reformation is the example *par excellence* of the drive to reform and served as the main engine for the rise of the secular. According to Taylor, the Reformation contributed to the genesis of secularism in three ways.

First, the Reformation disenchanted the world by attacking the superstitious practices of the masses, which were seen as a holdover from paganism. For example, there was widespread belief in magic among the populace—evil spirits living in the woods or magic potions that could bring about an illness. Some of these practices were even Christianized in popular beliefs surrounding the purchasing of indulgences and the veneration of relics, which were repudiated by the Protestant Reformers.

Secondly, in addition to disenchanting the world, the Reformation contributed to the rise of secularism by sanctifying ordinary life.[29] For the Reformers, religious fullness is achievable by everyone, not just by spiritual elites. The butcher and the candlestick maker, not just priests or monks, has a God-given vocation. Thus, an ordinary person's attempt to flourish in the everyday world—by marrying, having children, and working—is compatible with our highest religious aspirations.

Finally, the Reformation also brought what Taylor calls the rise of the "disciplinary society" or the "rage for order"—a desire that everyone, not just the spiritual elite, live up to the demands of the gospel.[30] The asceticism, renunciation, and drive for holiness in medieval monasticism became democratized and transmuted into everyday life. To use Max Weber's words, an "inner-worldly asceticism" developed.[31] True godliness was thus equated with a bourgeois ethic, idealizing "orderly, sober, disciplined, productive ways of living."[32]

---

28. Taylor, *A Secular Age*, 61–66; Taylor, "What Was the Axial Revolution?," 377.
29. Taylor, *A Secular Age*, 179.
30. Ibid., 104.
31. Max Weber, *The Protestant Ethic and the Spirit of Capitalism*, trans. Talcott Parsons (New York: Scribner, 1958), 151.
32. Taylor, *A Secular Age*, 344.

By focusing on personal discipline, religious reformers hoped that societies could become "more peaceful, more ordered, more industrious."[33] Societies in premodern Europe were often uncivil environments. Taylor, for example, compares the English nobility's ethic during the War of the Roses with the nobility's ethic under the Tudors. The difference is striking: whereas the ancient English nobility were expected to prove their valor by living in a state of perpetual war and internecine conflict, under the Tudors, fighting was no longer considered a normal part of aristocratic life.[34] What accounts for this change? According to Taylor, it was the rage for order inspired by religious reformers that domesticated lingering elements of pagan culture that celebrated glory and honor in combat.

A critical part of bringing about a disciplined society was the rise of the "disengaged rational agent."[35] Disenchantment liberated the individual from the determinism of magical and external forces: the self became a free agent, no longer subject to the whims and caprices of different spirits. Individuals now were seen to be responsible for the cultivation of virtue and discipline through reason. In other words, disenchantment buffers the self, creates space between the individual and world, and this abstraction of the self from the world (disengagement) allows reason a greater role in remaking both the self and world to meet the demands of the gospel. In fact, as we will see shortly, it was disengaged reason that spurred the growth of scientific development.

The Rise of the Immanent Frame

According to Taylor, one of the great ironies of history is that so much of the "fruit of devotion and faith, prepares the way for an escape from faith, into a purely immanent world."[36] The Western march toward secularity, for Taylor, was intertwined from the start with the drive toward having a more personal, committed faith.[37] For example, in disenchanting the world through its attack on superstition, magic, and sacramentalism, the Reformation opened the door to naturalism and, eventually, to a world denuded of the supernatural. The buffered self allowed individuals to feel a greater sense of responsibility for the cultivation of personal virtue, but it inadvertently created a self that is closed off, not just from magical forces but from the transcendent as a whole. In sanctifying

---

33. Taylor, "What Was the Axial Revolution?," 377.

34. Taylor, *A Secular Age*, 101.

35. Ibid., 135–37. See also Abbey, *Charles Taylor*, 81–84, 205–7. Taylor also discusses disengaged reason in Charles Taylor, *Sources of the Self: The Making of the Modern Identity* (Cambridge: Harvard University Press, 1989). See chapter 8, "Descartes's Disengaged Reason," 143–58, and chapter 9, "Locke's Punctual Self," 159–76.

36. Taylor, *A Secular Age*, 145.

37. Charles Taylor, "Western Secularity," in *Rethinking Secularism*, eds. Craig J. Calhoun, Mark Juergensmeyer, and Jonathan VanAntwerpen (Oxford: Oxford University Press, 2011), 37–38.

ordinary life, the drive to reform unintentionally catalyzed an anthropocentric shift in which society focused on human flourishing almost exclusively from within the immanent frame. Finally, Taylor argues that the rage for order, when combined with the affirmation of ordinary life, mutated into a hyperrationalism that sought to control nature, leaving little room for God and grace.

As Taylor's story progresses, this drive to reform results in seeing more and more of our lives in an immanent and impersonal order of political, economic, and physical laws without reference to God. Disenchantment combined with philosophical nominalism, for example, to destroy the medieval idea of the Great Chain of Being, in which society was arranged hierarchically, in a neo-platonic fashion, from kings to nobles to clergy all the way down to peasants. With the destruction of the Great Chain of Being, a new basis for social order had to be created, resulting in what Taylor calls "modern moral order"—a social order in which society organizes itself on the basis of mutual self-interest.[38] The laws of politics and economics show that self-interest is the basis of organizing society, and thus John Locke's social contract theory and Adam Smith's "invisible hand" emerge.

For Taylor, it was primarily the ethical ideals of the drive to reform that brought about modern moral order. In other words, it was not simply that reason made the modern moral order persuasive, although reason certainly plays a role. But the force of modern moral order was just that, a *moral* force. We already saw how disenchantment destroys the Great Chain of Being, but other ideals from the drive to reform also come into play. For example, pursuing our self-interest in politics and economics enhances human flourishing and is thus consistent with the will of Providence in sanctifying ordinary life. Disengaged reason and the rage for order result in a Puritan work ethic that emphasizes thrift, industry, and punctuality that coheres well with the modern economy. Taylor further sees modern moral order as a secularized form of Christianity's call to love all humanity, a universal benevolence that contrasted sharply with the tribalism of paganism. He goes so far as to say that modern moral order would never have come about were it not for benevolence found in Christianity.[39] It took sacrifice to build a political and economic system that would allow for the harmony of self-interest, and those who made the sacrifice did so in the name of a love for humanity in general.

---

38. Taylor, *A Secular Age*, 159–71.
39. Taylor writes that modern humanism "innovated in relation to the ancients, drawing on the forms of Christian faith they emerged from: active re-ordering; instrumental rationality; universalism; benevolence. But of course, their aim was also to reject Christian aspirations to transcendence," Taylor, *A Secular Age*, 247. He later says, "It would probably not have been possible to make the transition to an exclusive humanism on any other basis," Taylor, *A Secular Age*, 247.

Similar to the rise of modern moral order, the rise of science and technology also came about through the drive to reform. In the disenchanted world of nominalism, the world becomes devoid of *telos* or purpose, and we look to science—with its mastery of efficient and material causes—to impose its will on bare, unformed reality. The sanctification of ordinary life and the rage for order drive us to seek greater rational control over nature in order to promote human flourishing.

When humanity relates to God primarily through an impersonal order, it becomes easier to drop the notion of God entirely, and so providential deism becomes a midwife for exclusive humanism. The irony is that Christianity itself helped to bring about this impersonal/immanent order: "My thesis here is that, although reformed Christianity (and not only its Protestant variants) was a large part of the motor behind [modernity], its successful advance creates a predicament—where we in fact do live in an immanent order, of law, ethics, and a universe governed by natural law—which can be read in terms of the anthropocentric shift. Indeed, in the absence of some strong sense of what is being excluded, it even could be said to invite this reading."[40] Taylor's narrative of secularism thus builds on the so called "grave digger" thesis of modernity, which states that one of the great ironies of history is that the fruits of Christianity (science, technology, liberal democracy, and so forth) actually serve to undermine the faith.[41]

Yet Taylor argues that it would be wrong to think that exclusive humanism came about because of *rational* arguments for disbelieving in God. To reiterate: it was for moral reasons that exclusive humanism became so powerful, and those moral reasons were derived from Christianity. According to the exclusive humanist, the affirmation of ordinary life, benevolence, active reordering, and instrumental reasoning could be better accomplished if the world were conceived in purely immanent terms.

The perceived moral power of modern humanism is what makes it different from ancient versions of humanism. While something like modern humanism was anticipated by ancient humanists such as Lucretius or Democritus, ancient humanism could never catalyze a mass movement because it could never capture the moral imagination of a people. Indeed, Taylor argues that Catholic bishops

---

40. Ibid., 291.

41. Peter L. Berger, *The Sacred Canopy: Elements of a Sociological Theory of Religion* (New York: Doubleday, 1969), 128–29. Berger takes this idea from Max Weber. For further discussion of the "grave digger thesis," see Craig M. Gay, *The Way of the (Modern) World: Or, Why It's Tempting to Live as If God Doesn't Exist* (Grand Rapids: Eerdmans, 1999). For a popular level treatment of this theme, see Os Guinness, *The Last Christian on Earth: Uncover the Enemy's Plot to Undermine the Church* (Ventura, CA: Regal, 2010). John G. Stackhouse mentions the "grave digger thesis" in his response to Charles Taylor's Laing Lecture given at Regent College. See Charles Taylor, "History, Secularity, and the Nova Effect" (presented at the Laing Lectures, Regent College, 2001), and John G. Stackhouse, "History Lessons for the Christian Church (Response by John G. Stackhouse)" (presented at the Laing Lectures, Regent College, 2001).

"could have slept peacefully in their beds" if all they had to deal with were Lucretian skeptics or Humean arguments against miracles.[42] Although ancient and modern humanism bear a family resemblance, modern humanism differs significantly from its ancient counterpart in its moral idealism. Modern humanism, writes Taylor, "incorporates an activist, interventionist stance, both towards nature and to human society. Both are to be re-ordered, in the light of instrumental reason, to suit human purposes."[43] Moreover, modern humanism "has taken over universalism from its Christian roots." In other words, "The good of everyone must be served in the re-ordering of things."[44]

The exclusive humanists of our secular age can hardly be compared to Lucretius. Modern humanists defend human rights, call for social justice in remote areas of the world, desire progress through science, and strive to make the world a better place. Taylor remarks with amazement at how extraordinary, in one sense, our moral culture is when measured against the norms of human history. Worldwide movements of sympathy and solidarity arise in the wake of natural disasters. Courageous humanitarian organizations such as Amnesty International and Doctors Without Borders arise in droves. All this is possible, Taylor concludes, because of the Christian social imaginary from which our secular age emerged.[45]

The Malaise of Modernity

Nevertheless, despite the immanent frame's perceived merits, Taylor writes that there is pervasive unease about whether the immanent frame has the resources to fund our deepest moral and spiritual aspirations. Attempting to manage life without reference to the transcendent results in what Taylor calls the "malaise of modernity"—a sense of flatness and meaninglessness, which suggests that something more than the immanent order is needed. In response to this malaise, Taylor notes the rise of the "immanent counter-enlightenment," represented by Nietzschean antihumanism, which rejects the transcendent but also rejects the spiritual anemia of modern moral order.

The malaise we feel from being constrained by the immanent frame triggers what Taylor calls the "nova effect"—an explosion of new religions, ideologies, moral codes, and spiritual options to fill the void left by the displacement of Christianity.[46] Disoriented and suffocated by the restrictions and spiritual-moral ambiguities of the immanent frame, the buffered self is "cross pressured"

---

42. Taylor, *A Secular Age*, 268.
43. Ibid., 246.
44. Ibid.
45. Taylor, "A Catholic Modernity?," 26.
46. Taylor, *A Secular Age*, 300.

and "fragilized." [47] We are "cross-pressured" in that we feel the twin gravitational pulls of immanence/disenchantment, on the one hand, and transcendence/ enchantment, on the other.[48] Because our "take" on life is simply one option among many, we find ourselves epistemologically vulnerable, or "fragile"— hauntingly aware that we could be wrong about our ultimate commitments. Thus, under the weight of the immanent order, doubt seeps into the mind of the believer. But fragilization works in the opposite direction as well: the beliefs of the exclusive humanist are also fragilized, and there is a sense in which the exclusive humanist is haunted by the transcendent. The combination of malaise, the nova effect, and fragilization leads to "a spiritual super-nova, a kind of galloping pluralism on the spiritual plane."[49]

THE MALAISE OF MODERNITY AND THE ETHICS OF AUTHENTICITY

In the *Malaise of Modernity*, subsequently published as the *Ethics of Authenticity*, Taylor further characterizes the malaise of our secular age by highlighting three afflictions of the modern world. First, a lack of meaning and significance due to the fading of a transcendent framework for understanding the world and our life within it. Second, a loss of purpose as a result of instrumental reasoning. And finally, the combination of the first and the second leads to a third affliction: a loss of freedom, which results from the "soft despotism" of large bureaucratic institutions.

Taylor sees the malaise of modernity arising from deviant versions of what he calls "the ethic of authenticity"—a moral ideal set forth by the German Romantic J. G. Herder, which posits that each individual has their own "measure," or original way of being human.[50] "[There is] a certain way of being human that is *my* way. I am called upon to live my life in this way, and not in imitation of anyone else's."[51] If I fail to give expression to my original way of being human, according to this ethic, I miss the point of my life. Hence, the importance in our culture on "listening to your inner voice" and "being true to yourself."

Part of Taylor's project in the *Malaise of Modernity* is to push back on those who see the ethic of authenticity as simply a form of relativism, subjectivism, and self-indulgence.[52] Rather than abandoning the ethic of authenticity, which

---

47. Ibid., 303–4.
48. Ibid., 302, 555.
49. Ibid., 300.
50. Charles Taylor, *The Ethics of Authenticity* (Cambridge: Harvard University Press, 1992), 28.
51. Ibid., 29.
52. Ibid., 14, 72. For Taylor's discussion of Bellah, see Taylor, *Sources of the Self*, 508–9. Taylor has in mind critics of the ethic of authenticity, such as Allan Bloom, Christopher Lasch, and Robert Bellah.

Taylor believes is a great moral achievement (and one that has Christian roots), he wants to rescue the ethic from its deviant and debased versions.

According to Taylor, these deviant versions arose, in part, through the loss of moral horizons—frameworks of meaning or backgrounds of intelligibility. Our secular disenchanted world, after all, emerged by breaking free of such horizons. This loss has been reinforced by the individualism created by our political and economic institutions and procedural views of ethics, which set aside comprehensive accounts of the good in public discourse. With the absence of horizons of significance, each individual must now choose their own pattern of meaning without conforming to a preexisting cosmic order. Hence, in the "age of authenticity," all patterns of meaning are worthy as long as they reflect one's own choice, for choice alone is what confers worth.[53]

Nevertheless, writes Taylor, moral choices always take place against horizons of significance. For example, Taylor avers, I can try to define myself—to state what makes me unique—by the fact that I have 3,732 hairs on my head or that I am as tall as some tree in the Siberian plane.[54] Yet we are immediately aware that such statements are absurd. Instead, we determine significance on the basis of what Taylor calls "strong evaluators" and "hypergoods." Strong evaluators are independent standards that make qualitative distinctions among our desires, and hypergoods are supreme goods that provide the standpoint by which all other goods are weighed.

Not only do debased versions of the ethic of authenticity ignore moral horizons, but they also operate under the false assumption that identity is *monologically* self-generated, independent of community. In contrast, Taylor argues that the self is *dialogical*: my identity is never a matter exclusively of personal choice but is always negotiated vis-à-vis, and sometimes in a struggle against, others.[55] In describing the dialogical self, Taylor draws upon Hegel. Although he finds Hegel's ontology incredulous and incompatible with Christianity, Taylor sees in Hegel's philosophy evidence that identity requires recognition by others.[56] In our secular age, this can be seen in the heightened importance our culture places on romantic relationships toward forging one's identity, as well as in the rise of identity politics, which has increasingly come to dominate our public life.[57]

Thus, the ethic of authenticity, in its ideal form, rightly presupposes horizons of meaning, strong evaluators, and a dialogical view of the self. Moreover,

---

53. Taylor, *The Ethics of Authenticity*, 37.
54. Ibid., 36.
55. Ibid., 47.
56. Charles Taylor, *Hegel* (Cambridge: Cambridge University Press, 2005), 494; Taylor, *The Ethics of Authenticity*, 49.
57. Taylor, *The Ethics of Authenticity*, 49.

according to Taylor, it was Christian theistic moral horizons that gave rise to the ethic of authenticity. Although Herder is the primary historical voice for the ethic of authenticity, the moral sources behind it are Christian. According to Taylor, our contemporary understanding of complementarity, "which can be traced back through Humboldt to Herder, have in the latter's work an explicitly Christian source, even if not explicitly rooted in Trinitarian theology."[58] Unlike the monological and homogenous identity of the modern tradition, which neglects the plurality and difference within humanity, Trinitarian doctrine posits that "human diversity is part of the way in which we are made in the image of God."[59] Thus, the Trinity's unity-in-diversity undergirds and reveals not only humanity's commonality but also our plural ways of being. This "unity-across-difference" as opposed to "unity-through-identity" is what allows for mutual enrichment and complementarity.[60]

THE AUGUSTINIAN SOURCES OF THE SELF

The necessity of retrieving theistic horizons of meaning to counter the malaise of modernity is more explicitly stated in *Sources of the Self*, which is Taylor's account of the rise of modern identity. Augustine is the hero of Taylor's narrative. Indeed, *Sources of the Self* can be read as an exposition of how Augustine's language of inwardness changes and mutates over time. For Taylor, the myriad of transpositions from Augustine can be placed on a spectrum from negative to positive, with most of them falling somewhere in between.

Augustine's major contribution to the rise of the modern self, Taylor argues, is the primacy he placed on turning to the self in the first-person dimension as fundamental to our search for truth.[61] Augustine was the first to introduce the notion of "radical reflexivity." Whereas simple reflexivity is the awareness that I am a being who thinks and experiences, radical reflexivity concerns not just our experience of the world but our experience *of our experience* of the world, or our awareness of our awareness.[62] For Taylor, Augustine's radically reflexive turn to the self was not a step toward subjectivism but a step toward God: the inward path leads toward the transcendent. For Augustine, when a person turns inward, they become aware of their own sensing and thinking and, in so doing, become aware of their "dependence on something beyond."[63] In other words, radical

---

58. Taylor, "Concluding Reflections and Comments," in *A Catholic Modernity: Charles Taylor's Marinist Lectures* (Oxford: Oxford University Press, 1999), 114.
59. Taylor, "A Catholic Modernity?," 14–15.
60. Ibid., 14.
61. Taylor, *Sources of the Self*, 133.
62. Ibid., 130–31.
63. Ibid., 134.

reflexivity presupposes something or somebody higher than the self to which we owe reverence.[64] My thinking puts me in contact with perfection, an "eternal, unchanging truth" that is "presupposed in our thinking and yet manifestly not our own product."[65] We are thus beings with inner depths, because "God is to be found not just in the world but also and more importantly at the very foundation of the person. . . . God is to be found in the intimacy of self-presence."[66]

Additionally, Taylor argues, Augustine appropriated the Platonic notion of memory but gives it a unique Christian twist. Whereas Plato argued that all knowledge comes from the recollection of knowledge from a previous life, Augustine rejects the idea of preexistent souls but argues that "deep within us is an implicit understanding, which we have to think hard to bring to explicit and conscious formulation. This is our *'memoria.'*"[67] The content of this implicit or tacitly held background knowledge is, for Augustine, "the Master within, the source of the light which lights every man coming into the world, God."[68] Hence, "at the very root of memory, the soul finds God. And so the soul can be said to 'remember God.'"[69]

Not only, however, has God been present, implicitly and pretheoretically, as the very foundation of our reasoning, but for Augustine, God is also the source, power, and *eros* that sustains us on our inward journey. Our self-knowledge, after all, is thwarted by self-deception and an imperfect will that darkens our ability to see truth. We need God's grace to guide us. Thus, writes Taylor, "At the end of this road we see that God's is the power sustaining and directing this activity. We grasp the intelligible not just because our soul's eye is directed to it, but primarily because we are directed by the Master within."[70] Behind our epistemological "eye" is the One whose ideas we attempt to discern.

Taylor sees the Augustinian notion of inwardness as essential to certain moral developments. Radical reflexivity is the precursor for disengaged reason, which is crucial to the development of science. In addition, radical reflexivity prepares the way for the "rage for disorder" and the disciplinary society, for the self becomes an "object" that we can refine and improve on. (Although in objectifying the self, Augustine does not exchange the first-person view for the third person, abstracted, perspective.)[71] Finally, it is Augustinian spirituality,

---

64. Ibid.
65. Ibid., 140.
66. Ibid., 134.
67. Ibid., 135.
68. Ibid.
69. Ibid.
70. Ibid., 136.
71. Ibid., 131.

channeled through the Reformers, that leads to the affirmation of ordinary life and the drive to reform.

Yet radical reflexivity can also spawn a deviant alternative: Cartesian disengagement. Although a superficial similarity exists between Augustine and Descartes—namely, both turn to the self, and both use an argument from perfection to argue for God's existence—Descartes's philosophy is an "aberration" of the Augustinian tradition.[72] Indeed, Descartes's deformation of Augustine's argument results in a radical revolution in which the source of morality migrates from the transcendent deity to the immanent self.

Whereas for Augustine the discovery of God within the self cannot be separated from devotion to God, for Descartes, the self's reasoning process is detached from the spiritual background.[73] Similarly, whereas in Augustine, inward reasoning heightens our sense of dependence on God, in Descartes, "God's existence has become a stage in *my* progress towards science through the methodical ordering of evident insight. God's existence is a theorem in *my* system of perfect science."[74] In other words, God becomes an inference based on my powers of reason, which are in turn based on standards of rationality that are self-generated.

For Augustine, the higher moral sources are located in our implicit understanding and buried under layers of self-deception and inordinate loves. In contrast, for Descartes, the self is completely transparent: the *cogito* has access to clear and distinct ideas. For Augustine, radical reflexivity still speaks in first person language—the vantage point, from which we think of the self, is embodied subjectivity. The path toward God embraces the particularities of Augustine's life as told in the *Confessions*. With Descartes, however, the self is objectified using third-person language. The vantage point is the "view from nowhere"—a disembodied self, abstracted from particularity. For Augustine, our identity is found in dialogue with the Master; with Descartes, our identity is the *cogito*, understood monologically. In short, instead of meeting God within the self, for Descartes, when I turn inward, I meet myself—the new moral source.

According to Taylor, it is Cartesian disengagement that starts the path toward modern subjectivism, which in turn gives rise to the deviant versions of the ethic of authenticity. Locke, for example, denied innate ideas of truth or morality, conceiving of the human mind as a *tabula rasa* that creatively

---

72. Ibid.

73. Charles Taylor, "Reply and Re-Articulation," in *Philosophy in an Age of Pluralism: The Philosophy of Charles Taylor in Question*, ed. James Tully (New York: Cambridge University Press, 1994), 216.

74. "Following Augustine's path, the thinker comes to sense more and more his lack of self-sufficiency, comes to see more and more that God acts within him," Taylor, *Sources of the Self*, 156–57.

synthesizes our beliefs and personalities. Rousseau's emphasis on the "inner voice" further disconnects moral values from strong evaluators, and this loss of external standards is given greater philosophical precision in Kant's radical autonomy. For Kant, neither instinct, desire, feeling, other people, and even God should influence my pursuit of the good, for they ultimately undermine my dignity as a rational agent. Moral action should be based only on the formal reasoning of the categorical imperative. By the time we get to the deconstructionism of the neo-Nietzscheans, we have deviated significantly from Augustine even though his language of inwardness is still present.

APOLOGETIC METHODOLOGY

Three aspects of Taylor's apologetic method emerge as especially significant: Taylor's method is presuppositional, historic-narratival, and existential.

Taylor's approach is, first and foremost, presuppositional.[75] He rejects an exclusively evidential methodology, arguing that Christian apologists who employed evidential methods reinforced the immanent frame, undermined belief in the transcendent, and aided the rise of exclusive humanism.[76] In *Philosophy in an Age of Pluralism*, he states, "My account doesn't leave much place for the five ways of proving the existence of God propounded by Aquinas, provided (which is by no means unproblematically given) that they are meant to convince us quite independently of our moral and spiritual experience, that one can take them as an unbeliever would, as showing the inescapable rational cogency of certain conclusions, regardless of their spiritual meaning to the thinker."[77] Thus, Taylor is not opposed to using the five ways, per se, but opposes using them in a way that implies or assumes "neutrality."

Taylor is skeptical of approaches that ignore that our rationality is shaped by our social imaginary. Epistemologically, he is indebted to Michael Polanyi, with his postcritical arguments against classical foundationalism and its commitment to neutral, abstract laws of logic.[78] Drawing upon Polanyi, Taylor argues that all reasoning takes place against tacitly held background beliefs (a view Taylor also ascribes to Heidegger and Wittgenstein).[79] Indeed, an important characteristic

75. By presuppositional, we mean that, similar to Francis Schaeffer, Taylor seeks to push secular humanity toward the logical—and existentially unsatisfying—conclusions of their presuppositions and that he employs transcendental arguments.

76. Taylor, *A Secular Age*, 225–26.

77. Taylor, "Reply and Re-Articulation," 228.

78. Charles W. Lowney II, ed., *Charles Taylor, Michael Polanyi and the Critique of Modernity: Pluralist and Emergentist Directions* (Cham, Switzerland: Palgrave Macmillan, 2017).

79. Charles Taylor, "Converging Roads Around Dilemmas of Modernity," in *Charles Taylor, Michael Polanyi and the Critique of Modernity*, 15–26.

of Taylor's work is his articulation of the background beliefs that are often unsaid or presupposed in our culture.[80]

Instead of evidentialist arguments, Taylor employs transcendental methods to argue for theism. Transcendental arguments take a certain truth or fact of experience and determine the necessary conditions or presuppositions, which make that experience possible to begin with. A transcendental argument can take a "positive" or a "negative" form, although some presuppositionalists argue that the two are ultimately inseparable.[81] For example, a "positive" transcendental argument would argue as follows: "If rationality, then God; rationality, therefore God." In contrast, a "negative" transcendental argument takes an indirect approach: it assumes a rival worldview's presuppositions and, through a *reductio ad absurdum*, shows how those presuppositions lead to contradictory and absurd conclusions.

Taylor has defended the validity of both positive and negative transcendental arguments; both forms play an important role in Taylor's work.[82] In *Sources of the Self*, for example, he offers a positive transcendental argument by showing how our moral values presuppose frameworks and horizons of meaning, strong evaluators, hypergoods, and ultimately theism. But he also employs a negative transcendental argument by stepping inside the pretheoretical commitments of the exclusive humanist, showing how they fail to undergird the high moral values they wish to affirm.

Taylor's argument is also historical-narratival in a manner reminiscent of Augustine's *City of God*. Augustine's immediate context was the sacking of Rome. In response to the pagan intellectual's charge that Christianity was responsible for Rome's fall, Augustine retells the narrative of Rome's rise and development, exposing its pretention to justice as a veil for Rome's lust for domination. Similarly, Taylor's immediate context is a secular age in which secular intellectuals, such as the "New Atheists," claim that the West's ills stem from its Christian roots. And like Augustine, Taylor writes a narrative of the rise of secularity that exposes exclusive humanism's self-identity by showing how the moral values used to critique theism are in fact parasitic on theistic roots.

Finally, Taylor seeks to reveal the existential unviability of the exclusive

---

80. Ruth Abbey and Charles Taylor, "The Articulated Life: An Interview with Charles Taylor," *Reason in Practice* 1.3 (2001): 3.

81. John M. Frame, *Apologetics to the Glory of God: An Introduction* (Phillipsburg, NJ: P&R, 1994), 75–77.

82. Charles Taylor, "The Validity of Transcendental Arguments," in *Philosophical Arguments* (Cambridge: Harvard University Press, 1997), 20–33; Deane-Peter Baker, "Charles Taylor's Sources of the Self: A Transcendental Apologetic?," *International Journal for Philosophy of Religion* 47 (2000): 155–74; Deane-Peter Baker, *Tayloring Reformed Epistemology: Charles Taylor, Alvin Plantinga and the De Jure Challenge to Christian Belief* (London: SCM, 2007).

humanism. This can be seen in his exploration of the malaise of modernity. On his account, exclusive humanism leaves one existentially "flat." Indeed, for Taylor, as for Augustine, humans are by nature *homo religious*.[83] The rise of our secular age demonstrates that human beings are intrinsically oriented toward transcendence: it was the yearning for fullness that sparked the drive for reform within Latin Christendom. And it was the yearning for fullness that sparked the immanent counter Enlightenment's reaction against the malaise of the modern world, resulting in the "nova effect"—an explosion of moral spiritual options.

CONTRIBUTIONS TO THE FIELD OF APOLOGETICS

Taylor's contribution to Christian apologetics is not insignificant, as seen by the increasing number of apologetic resources that draw heavily upon his work and the concession of some nontheistic critics that Taylor's arguments against naturalism have yet to be countered successfully.[84] Taylor once described his writings as "the work of a monomaniac" whose singular focus is the inadequacy of naturalism to make sense of humanity and its life in this world.[85] Finding naturalism "terribly implausible," he attacks it from a variety of angles, including not only those mentioned in this chapter but also from the perspective of agency, intentionality, and language.

One of the unique contributions of Taylor's apologetic against naturalism is found in his contention that naturalism's influence has less to do with epistemological and scientific reasonings, which are "extremely implausible," and more to do with moral aspirations. According to Taylor, materialistic anthropologies seduce us by presenting a certain image of ourselves that we accept as *morally* superior:

> I believe that they derive their force from the underlying image of the self, and that this exercises its hold on us because of the ideal of disengagement and the images of freedom, dignity, and power which attach to it.

83. Taylor, *A Secular Age*, 639; Ruth Abbey, "Theorizing Secularity 3: Authenticity, Ontology, Fragilization," in *Aspiring to Fullness in a Secular Age: Essays on Religion and Theology in the Work of Charles Taylor*, eds. Carlos D. Colorado and Justin D. Klassen (Notre Dame: University of Notre Dame, 2014), 114.

84. For examples of recent apologetic resources that draw heavily upon Taylor, see Timothy Keller, *Making Sense of God: An Invitation to the Skeptical* (New York: Viking, 2016); and Joshua D. Chatraw and Mark D. Allen, *Apologetics at the Cross: An Introduction for Christian Witness* (Grand Rapids: Zondervan, 2018). For an example of a noted nontheistic critic who concedes the power of Taylor's argument, see Smith, *Charles Taylor*, 242.

85. Charles Taylor, *Philosophical Papers, Vol. 1: Human Agency and Language* (New York: Cambridge University Press, 1985), 1.

More specifically, the claim is that the more we are led to interpret ourselves in the light of the disengaged picture, to define our identity by this, the more the connected epistemology of naturalism will seem right and proper to us. Or otherwise put, a commitment to this identity generates powerful resistances against any challenges to the naturalistic outlook. In short, its epistemological weaknesses are more than made up for by is moral appeal.[86]

In other words, the primary driving force for the rise of naturalism and exclusive humanism are moral and spiritual reasons, not epistemological ones: "through the whole course of the development of modern identity, the moral motivation has been intertwined with the epistemological, how the latter has never been a sufficient motive force but has always been seconded by the former, but how paradoxically the very nature of this modern identity has tended to make us reluctant to acknowledge this moral dimension. The very ideal of disengagement militates against it."[87]

According to Taylor, high moral standards require strong moral sources, and the crisis of modernity rests in the fact that, while in one sense, there is a remarkable degree of agreement on moral ideals, the original theistic vision that gave rise to the ideals has been shattered. Our moral sources are insufficient to fund our high ideals. And modernity's Cartesian epistemology and materialistic anthropology militate against even speaking of moral sources.

The scholarly reception of Taylor's reading of modernity has been mixed. Nonetheless, a broad array of philosophers and theologians have praised Taylor's account of the rise and development of secular modernity.[88] Although not persuaded by Taylor's case for theism, Nicholas H. Smith acknowledges the force of Taylor's argument: Can modernity build on moral sources that are nontheistic? Smith writes that for the nontheist this question "is troubling" but that it "is now up to secular humanists to meet Taylor's challenge."[89]

Augustine, as we noted above, turned to the self as the way to make explicit what was always implicit in the background; namely, God. Hence, "at the very

---

86. Taylor, *Philosophical Papers*, 1:6.
87. Ibid., 1:7.
88. A broad array of scholars have praised Taylor's narrative of the rise of our secular age. See, for example, Richard Amesbury, "Charles Taylor, 'A Secular Age'," *Philosophical Investigations* 33:1 (Jan 1, 2010): 67–74; Gregory Baum, "The Response of a Theologian to Charles Taylor's *A Secular Age*," *Modern Theology* 26:3 (July 2010): 363–81; Collin Hansen, ed., *Our Secular Age: Ten Years of Reading and Applying Charles Taylor* (Deerfield, IL: The Gospel Coalition, 2017); John Kinsey, "A Secular Age—By Charles Taylor," *Philosophical Investigations* 33:1 (Jan 1, 2010): 75–81; D. Stephen Long, "How to Read Charles Taylor: The Theological Significance of a Secular Age," *Pro Ecclesia* 18:1 (2009): 93–107; James K. A. Smith, *How (Not) To Be Secular: Reading Charles Taylor* (Grand Rapids: Eerdmans, 2014).
89. Smith, *Charles Taylor*, 242.

root of memory, the soul finds God. And so the soul can be said to 'remember God.'"[90] What Augustine does in his analysis of the self, Taylor does with his analysis of culture—helping us to remember and make explicit the theistic sources of modernity that have laid inarticulate in the background intelligibility of our culture.

While we appreciate Taylor's contributions to apologetics, we do have reservations about some of his unorthodox and idiosyncratic interpretations of Christian doctrine. Michael Horton, for example, notes several areas where Taylor quite significantly deviates from traditional teachings. For example, Taylor rejects penal substitution, divine impassibility, and immutability, approves of the decline in the belief in hell, and compares God to a tennis player who is always reacting to his creation.[91] Another concern with Taylor's project is the way he describes transcendence and fullness. It seems as if fullness can be achieved through a variety of religions, such as Buddhism, as well as through literature and poetry.[92] Colin Jager, in an essay on Taylor's Romanticism, notes that the "lines between scripture and literature fade in *Sources of the Self*."[93] Jager notes that in the latter half of *A Secular Age*, literature becomes a "privileged window—perhaps the privileged window—into the inner workings of the varieties of secularism."[94] Taylor, in his response to Jager, offers little to fend off this charge. With respect to Romanticism, Taylor writes, "I plead guilty as charged: I'm a hopeless German romantic of the 1790's."[95]

Nevertheless, Taylor remains an important guide for countering the amnesia of our secular age. We are sympathetic to Taylor's "Ricci reading of modernity." And Taylor's ethics of authenticity, rightly understood, can be seen as a modern day articulation of the Protestant notion of calling. Finally, Taylor is correct in arguing for a Christian Augustinian humanism, whose divine affirmation of the human is more total and complete than an exclusive humanism can ever hope to accomplish on its own.

Nevertheless, Taylor's narrative of secularism is incomplete unless it is set more explicitly within the context of Christian Scripture and its overarching narrative.[96] The place to stand to critique Western culture is not history alone

---

90. Taylor, *Sources of the Self*, 135.

91. Michael Horton, "The Enduring Power of the Christian Story: Reformation Theology for a Secular Age," in *Our Secular Age: Ten Years of Reading and Applying Charles Taylor*, 24–29.

92. Taylor, *A Secular Age*, 17.

93. Colin Jager, "The Detail, This History: Charles Taylor's Romanticism," in *Varieties of Secularism in A Secular Age* (Cambridge: Harvard University Press: 2010), 180.

94. Ibid, 181.

95. Charles Taylor, "Afterword: Apologia pro Libro suo," *Varieties of Secularism in A Secular Age*, 320.

96. Bruce Riley Ashford, "Politics and Public Life in a Secular Age," in *Our Secular Age: Ten Years of Reading and Applying Charles Taylor*, ed. Collin Hansen, 87–98.

but the world of the Bible, the true story of the world. We indwell the narrative of the Bible by indwelling the community that acts as the hermeneutic of that story—the church. The local congregation, as Newbigin once wrote, is a community "in which through constant remembering and rehearsing of the true story of human nature and destiny, an attitude of healthy skepticism can be sustained, a skepticism which enable some to take part in the life of society without being bemused and deluded by its own beliefs about itself."[97] In short, only by standing within the plausibility structure of the church will we be able to prophetically challenge our secular age to remember the God of Abraham, Isaac, and Jacob, the God who is present, as Taylor has shown, in the deepest recesses of the self.

BIBLIOGRAPHY

Abbey, Ruth. *Charles Taylor.* Princeton: Princeton University Press, 2000.
———. "Theorizing Secularity 3: Authenticity, Ontology, Fragilization." Pages 98–124 in *Aspiring to Fullness in a Secular Age: Essays on Religion and Theology in the Work of Charles Taylor.* Ed. by Carlos D. Colorado and Justin D. Klassen. Notre Dame: University of Notre Dame Press, 2014.
Abbey, Ruth, and Charles Taylor. "The Articulated Life: An Interview with Charles Taylor." *Reason in Practice* 1.3 (2001): 3–9.
Amesbury, Richard. "Charles Taylor, 'A Secular Age.'" *Philosophical Investigations* 33.1 (2010): 67–74.
Ashford, Bruce Riley. "Politics and Public Life in a Secular Age." Pages 87–98 in *Our Secular Age: Ten Years of Reading and Applying Charles Taylor.* Ed. by Collin Hansen. Deerfield, IL: The Gospel Coalition, 2017.
Baker, Deane-Peter. "Charles Taylor's Sources of the Self: A Transcendental Apologetic?" *International Journal for Philosophy of Religion* 47.3 (2000): 155–74.
———. *Tayloring Reformed Epistemology: Charles Taylor, Alvin Plantinga and the De Jure Challenge to Christian Belief.* London: SCM, 2007.
Baum, Gregory. "The Response of a Theologian to Charles Taylor's A Secular Age." *Modern Theology* 26.3 (2010): 363–81.
Berger, Peter L. *The Sacred Canopy: Elements of a Sociological Theory of Religion.* New York: Doubleday, 1969.
Bloor, Chris, and Charles Taylor. "Interview with Charles Taylor." *Philosophy Now* 74 (2009). https://philosophynow.org/issues/74/Charles_Taylor.
Chatraw, Joshua D., and Mark D. Allen. *Apologetics at the Cross: An Introduction for Christian Witness.* Grand Rapids: Zondervan Academic, 2018.
de Lara, Philippe, and Charles Taylor. "From Philosophical Anthropology to the Politics of Recognition: An Interview with Charles Taylor." *Thesis Eleven* 52 (1998): 103–12.
Farhadian, Charles E. *Introducing World Religions: A Christian Engagement.* Grand Rapids: Baker Academic, 2015.
Frame, John M. *Apologetics to the Glory of God: An Introduction.* Phillipsburg, NJ: P&R, 1994.
Gay, Craig M. *The Way of the (Modern) World: Or, Why It's Tempting to Live as If God Doesn't Exist.* Grand Rapids: Eerdmans, 1999.
Guinness, Os. *The Last Christian on Earth: Uncover the Enemy's Plot to Undermine the Church.* Ventura, CA: Regal, 2010.
Hansen, Collin, ed. *Our Secular Age: Ten Years of Reading and Applying Charles Taylor.* Deerfield, IL: The Gospel Coalition, 2017.
Horton, Michael S. "The Enduring Power of the Christian Story: Reformation Theology for a Secular Age." Pages 23–38 in *Our Secular Age: Ten Years of Reading and Applying Charles Taylor.* Ed. by Collin Hansen. Deerfield, IL: The Gospel Coalition, 2017.
Jager, Colin. "This Detail, This History: Charles Taylor's Romanticism." Pages 166–92 in *Varieties of*

---

97. Lesslie Newbigin, *The Gospel in a Pluralist Society* (Grand Rapids: Eerdmans, 1989), 228–29.

Secularism in a Secular Age. Ed. by Michael Warner, Jonathan VanAntwerpen, and Craig J. Calhoun. Cambridge: Harvard University Press, 2013.

Keller, Timothy. *Making Sense of God: An Invitation to the Skeptical*. New York: Viking, 2016.

Kerr, Fergus. "How Much Can a Philosopher Do?" *Modern Theology* 26.3 (2010): 321–36.

Kinsey, John. "A Secular Age—By Charles Taylor." *Philosophical Investigations* 33.1 (2010): 75–81.

Long, D. Stephen. "How to Read Charles Taylor: The Theological Significance of a Secular Age." *Pro Ecclesia* 18.1 (2009): 93–107.

Lowney, Charles W., II, ed. *Charles Taylor, Michael Polanyi and the Critique of Modernity: Pluralist and Emergentist Directions*. Cham, Switzerland: Palgrave Macmillan, 2017.

———, ed. "Converging Roads around Dilemmas of Modernity." Pages 15–26 in *Charles Taylor, Michael Polanyi and the Critique of Modernity: Pluralist and Emergentist Directions*. Cham, Switzerland: Palgrave Macmillan, 2017.

Newbigin, Lesslie. *Foolishness to the Greeks: The Gospel and Western Culture*. Grand Rapids: Eerdmans, 1986.

———. *The Gospel in a Pluralist Society*. Later Printing Used edition. Grand Rapids: Eerdmans, 1989.

Smith, James K. A. *How (Not) to Be Secular: Reading Charles Taylor*. Grand Rapids: Eerdmans, 2014.

Smith, Nicholas H. *Charles Taylor: Meaning, Morals and Modernity*. Malden, MA: Polity, 2002.

Stackhouse, John G. "History Lessons for the Christian Church (Response by John G. Stackhouse)" presented at the Laing Lectures, Regent College, 2001.

Taylor, Charles. "A Catholic Modernity?" Pages 13–38 in *A Catholic Modernity? Charles Taylor's Marianist Award Lecture*. Ed. by James L. Heft. New York: Oxford University Press, 1999.

———. "Afterword: Apologia pro Libro Suo." Pages 300–321 in *Varieties of Secularism in a Secular Age*. Edited by Michael Warner, Jonathan VanAntwerpen, and Craig J. Calhoun. Cambridge: Harvard University Press, 2013.

———. *A Secular Age*. Cambridge, MA: Belknap Press of Harvard University Press, 2009.

———. "Challenging Issues About the Secular Age." *Modern Theology* 26.3 (2010): 404–16.

———. "Concluding Reflections and Comments." Pages 105–26 in *A Catholic Modernity? Charles Taylor's Marianist Award Lecture*. Ed. by James L. Heft. New York: Oxford University Press, 1999.

———. *Hegel*. Cambridge: Cambridge University Press, 2005.

———. "History, Secularity, and the Nova Effect" presented at the Laing Lectures, Regent College, 2001.

———. *Philosophical Papers*. Vol. 1: Human Agency and Language. New York: Cambridge University Press, 1985.

———. "Reply and Re-Articulation." Pages 213–57 in *Philosophy in an Age of Pluralism: The Philosophy of Charles Taylor in Question*. Ed. by James Tully. New York: Cambridge University Press, 1994.

———. *Sources of the Self: The Making of the Modern Identity*. Cambridge: Cambridge University Press, 1989.

———. *The Ethics of Authenticity*. Cambridge: Harvard University Press, 1992.

———. *The Explanation of Behavior*. New York: Routledge, 1964.

———. "The Validity of Philosophical Arguments." Pages 20–33 in *Philosophical Arguments*. Cambridge: Harvard University Press, 1997.

———. "Western Secularity." Pages 31–53 in *Rethinking Secularism*. Ed. by Craig J. Calhoun, Mark Juergensmeyer, and Jonathan VanAntwerpen. Oxford: Oxford University Press, 2011.

———. "What Was the Axial Revolution?" Pages 367–79 in *Dilemmas and Connections: Selected Essays*. Cambridge: Belknap Press of Harvard University Press, 2014.

Weber, Max. *The Protestant Ethic and the Spirit of Capitalism*. Trans. by Talcott Parsons. New York: Scribner, 1958.

ALVIN PLANTINGA

Christian Philosophy as Apologetics

JAMES BEILBY

Alvin Plantinga (1932–) is a contemporary philosopher of religion working in the analytic tradition of philosophy whose contributions in the fields of metaphysics, epistemology, and philosophy of religion have been nothing short of ground-breaking. He is the author of seventeen books and well over 150 articles and essays; he is the past president of the American Philosophical Association and the Society of Christian Philosophers, a Guggenheim fellow, a fellow of the American Academy of Arts and Sciences. He has also been awarded a number of prestigious lectureships, including two Gifford Lectures (University of Aberdeen), the Wilde Lectures (Oxford University), and the Suarez Lecture (Fordham University). He has been granted honorary degrees from Valparaiso University, the Free University of Amsterdam, Brigham Young University, North Park College, and the University of Glasgow, and Calvin College named him a distinguished alumnus in 1986. Finally, and most recently, he is the 2017 Templeton Prize Laureate.

HISTORICAL BACKGROUND

Alvin Plantinga was born on November 15, 1932, in Ann Arbor, Michigan, into a Dutch Reformed family that took their faith and education very seriously.[1] After being introduced to Plato by his father, Plantinga decided that he wanted to be a philosopher, and to that end he enrolled at Calvin College in the spring of 1950. During his first semester, Plantinga applied for and was given a substantial

---

1. For greater detail on Plantinga's upbringing and academic training, see his two autobiographical essays, "Self-Profile" in *Alvin Plantinga*, eds. James Tomberlin and Peter van Inwagen (Dordrecht: Reidel, 1985), 3–97; and "A Christian Life Partly Lived," in *Philosophers Who Believe: The Spiritual Journeys of 11 Leading Thinkers*, ed. Kelly James Clark (Downers Grove, IL: InterVarsity Press, 1993), 47. See also James Beilby, *Epistemology as Theology* (Aldershot: Ashgate, 2005), 3–32.

scholarship to attend Harvard, so in the fall of 1950, he made the trip east. While not lengthy, Plantinga's time at Harvard was impactful for a pair of reasons. First, he encountered serious and thoughtful non-Christians for the first time and recounts being struck by "the enormous diversity of opinions about [religious] matters, some of them held by highly intelligent and accomplished people who had little but contempt for what I believed."[2] These contrary opinions caused him to evaluate and question his own beliefs, but as he did so, he wondered whether the objections to traditional Christian belief that many of his peers took for granted had the substance they appeared to have. Second, one evening on his way back to his dorm, Plantinga had a profound religious experience that has greatly affected his approach to belief in God. "Suddenly it was as if the heavens opened; I heard, so it seemed, music of overwhelming power and grandeur and sweetness; there was light of unimaginable splendor and beauty; it seemed I could see into heaven itself; and I suddenly saw or perhaps felt with great clarity and persuasion and conviction that the Lord was really there and was all that I thought."[3] Compared with this experience, the arguments for and against God's existence seemed "merely academic, of little existential concern."[4] While Plantinga greatly appreciated his time at Harvard, a trip home to visit his parents during the spring of 1951 changed his plans. While home, he visited the class of William Harry Jellema. Plantinga loved Jellema's teaching and was particularly impressed with the way he engaged objections to Christianity, and as a result Plantinga transferred from Harvard back to Calvin.

Following his graduation from Calvin, Plantinga completed an MA at Michigan under William Alston and a PhD at Yale under Paul Weiss and Brand Blanshard. Plantinga's first teaching job at Wayne State University was academically fruitful, largely because of the interaction of his departmental colleagues. Plantinga characterized the philosophy department at Wayne State as "less of a philosophy department than a loosely organized but extremely intense discussion society."[5] Despite the fertile intellectual soil at Wayne State, in 1963 Plantinga accepted an offer to replace Jellema at Calvin. The reasons behind such a move were not apparent to some of his colleagues but were undoubtedly very similar to the reasons Plantinga decided to leave Harvard for Calvin College—namely, his desire to do philosophy in community with those who shared his theistic and theological commitments. Plantinga flourished at Calvin for nineteen years. But in 1982 he surprised many by accepting a position at the University of Notre

---

2. Plantinga, "A Christian Life Partly Lived," 51.
3. Ibid.
4. Ibid., 51–52.
5. Plantinga, "Self-Profile," 23.

Dame as the John A. O'Brien professor of philosophy. His move to Notre Dame allowed him to teach high quality PhD students and to share with them some of what he had learned about philosophical theology and doing philosophy as a Christian and thus profoundly influence the next generation of students. He retired from Notre Dame in 2010, and to the surprise of nobody who knows him, Plantinga returned to Calvin as the inaugural holder of the William Harry Jellema chair in Christian philosophy.

THEOLOGICAL CONTEXT

Plantinga's apologetic work has been influenced by two significant contextual factors. The first was the widespread antireligious and antitheistic demeanor in the academic world and particularly in philosophical circles in the 1950s and 60s. Not only were there relatively few Christians doing philosophy in the 1950s, those philosophers that were Christians tended to avoid religious and theological topics to avoid being marginalized. Moreover, there was a widespread (even if poorly argued for) belief that the very idea of religious and metaphysical inquiry was of minimal use, or perhaps, fundamentally incoherent. As such, Plantinga's early philosophical training took place during, as he describes it, "the positivistic heyday of anti-metaphysical animus."[6] The influence of this antitheistic context can be seen most clearly in his description of his time at Wayne State University. While at Wayne State, Plantinga's colleagues (Hector Castañeda, Edmund Gettier, and George Nakhnikian especially) confronted Plantinga "with antitheistic arguments of a depth and philosophical sophistication and persistence [he] had never encountered before."[7] Being forced to deal with antitheistic arguments of such a level and caliber was, according to Plantinga, "a great stimulus to rigor and penetration in my own work."[8] Nevertheless, he suggests that it had another, less positive impact:

> I was never able to get beyond a sort of defensive posture. I concentrated on arguing (contrary to my colleague's claims) that theism was not *wholly irrational*. . . . I often felt beleaguered and, with respect to my Christianity, alone, isolated, nonstandard, a bit peculiar or weird, a somewhat strange specimen in which my colleagues displayed an interest that was friendly, and for the most part uncensorious, but also incredulous and

6. Ibid, 19.
7. Plantinga, "A Christian Life Partly Lived," 64.
8. Ibid.

uncomprehending. It wasn't that this atmosphere induced doubt about the central elements of Christianity; it was more that my philosophical horizons were heavily formed by my colleagues and friends at Wayne.[9]

Given this environment, Plantinga's interest in apologetics was strengthened, but his apologetic methodology was formed in a highly defensive, minimalist direction.

The second contextual factor influencing Plantinga's apologetics is Calvin College, a place he calls "the major intellectual influence in my life."[10] The impact of the community of Calvin College on Plantinga is undoubtedly complex and varied, but two broad lines of influence seem particularly important.[11] First, and most generally, Calvin provided a fertile community for the development of a full-orbed way of looking at the world as a Christian and understanding the task and nature of Christian scholarship. In Plantinga's own words: "I thought of scholarship in general and philosophy in particular as in large part a communal enterprise: promising insights, interesting connections, subtle difficulties— these come more easily and rapidly in a group of like-minded people than for the solitary thinker. The topics I most wanted to work on were the topics I'd been introduced to in college: the connection between Christian faith and philosophy (as well as the other disciplines) and the question of how best to be a Christian in philosophy."[12]

At Calvin, starting in 1964, "communal philosophical work" came in the form of the Tuesday colloquium, the most helpful members of which were Peter de Vos, Kenneth Konyndyk, Del Ratzsch, and Nicholas Wolterstorff.[13] A second, more specific line of influence of Calvin on Plantinga can be discerned. In all his academic interaction at Calvin, from his first class with Jellema to his discussion with his colleagues in the philosophy department, the idea that there is no such thing as a "serious, substantial and relatively complete intellectual endeavor that is religiously neutral" was continually emphasized.[14] This mindset gave Plantinga's apologetic work an independence that powerfully shaped both the content of his arguments and his apologetic methodology.

---

9. Ibid., 65; italics mine.
10. Plantinga, "Self-Profile," 9.
11. While Calvin College's influence on Plantinga is significant, it would be a mistake to infer that Plantinga is unequivocally theologically Calvinistic. His soteriology, for instance, is Arminian. And as an elder in the Christian Reformed Church, he signed the Belgic and Heidelberg Confessions but not the Canons of Dordt (personal correspondence).
12. Plantinga, "Self-Profile," 30.
13. Ibid., 31.
14. Ibid., 13; Plantinga, "A Christian Life Partly Lived," 47.

APOLOGETIC METHODOLOGY

In describing his work, Plantinga has said, "One of my chief interests over the years has been in philosophical theology and apologetics: the attempt to defend Christianity (or, more broadly, theism) against various sorts of attacks brought against it. . . . I can scarcely remember a time when I wasn't aware of and interested in objections to Christianity and arguments against it."[15]

His contribution to apologetics has spawned what many people view as a new apologetic methodology: Reformed epistemology.[16] But labeling Reformed epistemology as a distinct apologetic methodology is complicated. It seems better to say that Reformed epistemology is not a distinct apologetic method. Rather, it has a number of important implications for apologetics, for the nature of Christian philosophy, and for the task of religious epistemology and that those implications are crucially important for apologetics because they are a way of thinking about how religious beliefs are (and should be) related to arguments, evidence, and counterevidence.[17] But these insights are not usable only within a single apologetic methodology; even evidentialists could adopt at least some of the assertions of Reformed epistemology.

Even if Plantinga's Reformed epistemology is not best thought of as a distinct apologetic methodology, it certainly involves a set of assertions that are enormously important from an apologetic point of view. The first of these concerns the nature of Christian philosophy and Christian scholarship in general. Plantinga's work expresses the conviction that theists and nontheists have fundamental differences in their approach to important philosophical questions. What sorts of beliefs are possible objects of knowledge? Are there "truths" that are, by definition, beyond the ken of human beings? One's answer to these questions will be affected by many things: whether or not you think reality is solely materialistic, what sort of beings you think humans are, what kind of cognitive faculties they have, and what sorts of beliefs are properly thought of as arising from those cognitive faculties. And one's answer to these questions will affect one's appraisal of what counts as a suitable explanation of a given range of facts. Of course, philosophy is more than just expressing in philosophical form the content of one's theological convictions. The point is, rather, that one's philosophy is shaped by

---

15. Plantinga, "A Christian Life Partly Lived," 69.

16. Reformed epistemology is included as a separate methodology in Steven B. Cowan, ed. *Five Views on Apologetics* (Grand Rapids: Zondervan, 2000) and more recently in Brian K. Morley, *Mapping Apologetics* (Downers Grove, IL: InterVarsity Academic, 2015).

17. Nicholas Wolterstorff refers to Plantinga's work as addressing the "epistemology of philosophy." See his "Then, Now, and Al," in *Reason, Metaphysics, and Mind: New Essays on the Philosophy of Alvin Plantinga*, eds. Kelly James Clark and Michael Rea (New York: Oxford University Press, 2012) 213.

one's theological convictions, or by the lack of such—how you approach philosophy, what questions you think are worth answering, and what sorts of answers you deem to be adequate are all affected by your stance toward religious matters. Consequently, while Plantinga would vehemently reject the idea that theists and nontheists cannot engage in discussion on philosophical matters, he repeatedly avers that there is no real neutral territory from which these conversations can proceed. This is the main message of his "Advice to Christian Philosophers."[18] In this address, Plantinga issued a clarion call for Christian philosophers not to be content with reactionary philosophical sparring with the unbelieving academic majority. He also wanted Christian philosophers to cease to allow non-Christian and nontheistic assumptions to set the parameters and boundaries of their philosophical work but instead to feel free to explore the questions that motivate and interest Christians, regardless of whether the secular world finds those questions interesting, valuable, or even sensible.

Second, Reformed epistemology involves the rejection of the evidentialist requirement for belief in God. The evidentialist requirement is, stated simply, the idea that belief in God requires propositional arguments—like the theistic arguments produced by natural theology—if it is to have positive epistemic status (rationality, justification, warrant, etc.). Plantinga argues that the evidentialist requirement is flawed in a number of respects (more on this below) and that instead belief in God can be properly basic—it can be fully rational, justified, and warranted even if a person does not know of any good arguments for the existence of God. In other words, the epistemic status of belief in God can be similar to that of my memory belief that I had breakfast this morning or my perceptual belief that a steaming cup of coffee is on the table next to my laptop, both of which are held in the absence of propositional evidence. This claim is called the "parity thesis" and is one of the enduring aspects of Plantinga's Reformed epistemology.

While Plantinga does not believe that theistic arguments are necessary for grounding religious knowledge, that does not mean he thinks that such arguments are pointless. In fact, Plantinga has written a paper titled "2 Dozen (or so) Theistic Arguments."[19] These arguments might have a variety of benefits, including increasing the warrant a Christian has for their religious beliefs,

---

18. Alvin Plantinga, "Advice to Christian Philosophers," *Faith and Philosophy* 1/3 (July 1984): 253–71.

19. First developed in 1986 and circulated for many years as a handout. It was finally published as an appendix in *Alvin Plantinga*, ed. Deane-Peter Baker, Contemporary Philosophy in Focus series (New York: Cambridge, 2007). Recently, Jerry Walls and Trent Doherty have assembled an impressive team to undertake Plantinga's goal of showing a wide range of good arguments for God. See *Two Dozen (or so) Arguments for God: The Plantinga Project*, eds. Jerry Walls and Trent Doherty (New York: Oxford, 2018).

but they do not successfully establish the truth of beliefs about God.[20] "I don't know how to do something one could sensibly call 'showing' that either [theism and Christianity] *is* true. I believe that there are a large number (at least a couple dozen) good arguments for the existence of God; none, however, can really be thought of as a *showing* or *demonstration*. . . . Of course, this is nothing against either their truth or warrant; very little of what we believe can be 'demonstrated' or 'shown.'"[21]

Instead of grounding the positive epistemic status of Christian belief on propositional arguments, Plantinga argues for an experiential grounding paralleling my perfectly justified belief that I see a cup of coffee on the table. As such, if we simplify apologetic methodologies down to three—evidential, experiential, and presuppositional—Plantinga's Reformed epistemology is on the experiential-presuppositional wings of the apologetic enterprise.[22]

CONTRIBUTIONS TO THE FIELD OF APOLOGETICS

Plantinga is a philosopher par excellence, but his philosophical work has ultimately served a theological or apologetic purpose. In the broadest possible terms, Plantinga's apologetic efforts can be described as the attempt to excavate important philosophical issues and expose the philosophical assumptions that sit poorly with or run contrary to the Christian worldview. In fact, a single conceptual strand can be traced through the whole of Plantinga's work, which may be summarized as follows: "There is no plausible objection, set of objections, or epistemological theory that rules out theistic belief as a category of epistemically appropriate belief."[23] Plantinga has developed this claim in a number of significant ways; I will discuss four specific contributions and close with a brief discussion of Plantinga's broad impact on Christian apologetics.

RELIGIOUS LANGUAGE

Plantinga began his philosophical career during a time of hostility toward "Christian" philosophy. Logical positivism had a firm grip on many quarters of the western philosophical world, and their proposed way to think about language, the Verification Theory of Meaning, was widely influential. On this

---

20. Plantinga discusses a variety of benefits of theistic arguments in the preface to the appendix in Baker, *Alvin Plantinga*, 209.

21. Alvin Plantinga, *Warranted Christian Belief* (New York: Oxford, 2000), 170.

22. I argue for the appropriateness (and fruitfulness) of a threefold typology with numerous subcategories in *Thinking About Christian Apologetics* (Downers Grove, IL: InterVarsity Academic, 2011).

23. James Beilby, *Epistemology as Theology, 22.*

theory, a statement (or proposition) is meaningful if and only if it is empirically verifiable. By the lights of logical positivists, statements such as "God loves me" couldn't even be described as false; they were assertorically meaningless. And even in places where positivism was not entrenched (like Yale, where Plantinga did his PhD), the philosophy of religion focused on God-talk, not on God. Plantinga's book *God and Other Minds* was a radical affront to this entire approach to religious language. Not only did he argue that verificationism was self-referentially incoherent—after all, the statement "a proposition is meaningful only if it is empirically verifiable" isn't obviously empirically verifiable itself—he unapologetically talked about God and assumed that statements could meaningfully refer to God.[24] As a result (although undoubtedly with the help of others), logical positivism and verificationism "has retreated into the obscurity it so richly deserves."[25] And the philosophical world was provided a stunning example of what philosophy of religion could look like when it was not shackled by the fashionable but implausible strictures on what religious statements could and could not do.

PROBLEM OF EVIL

In apologetic circles Plantinga is arguably best known for his response to the problem of evil. His free will defense is a response to the logical problem of evil as typified by J. L. Mackie's 1955 article "Evil and Omnipotence," which claims that the coexistence of an all-powerful, perfectly good God and evil is a logical contradiction.[26] While Christians, going back at least to the early Augustine,[27] have sought to answer the problem of evil with reference to the free choices of human beings, the difficulty for such a response to Mackie's argument comes in explaining why an all-powerful God could not create people who always freely choose the good. This difficulty raises a series of thorny metaphysical questions about the nature of necessity (what must be) and possibility (what might be). But the antimetaphysical philosophical climate in the 1950s and 1960s did not provide a robust understanding of these concepts. In response, Plantinga gave the concepts of necessity and possibility sustained attention,[28] resulting in his ground-breaking book *The Nature of Necessity*.[29] The understanding of modality

---

24. Wolterstorff's story about the impact of *God and Other Minds* is powerful and instructive (Wolterstorff, "Then, Now, and Al," 204–08).

25. Plantinga, "Advice to Christian Philosophers," 258.

26. J. L. Mackie, "Evil and Omnipotence," *Mind* 64 (1955): 200–12.

27. See his *On Free Will*, book 1, xvi, 34 and *Conf.* VII, 5.

28. There were, of course, others engaging these questions, most notably Saul Kripke. See his *Naming and Necessity* (Cambridge: Harvard University Press, 1972).

29. Simultaneous with the publication of *The Nature of Necessity*, Plantinga published a somewhat simplified (though still quite dense) version of his free will defense in *God, Freedom, and Evil* (New York:

in this volume gave him the tools necessary to articulate his free will defense—an argument that uses possible worlds semantics, a Molinist account of God's foreknowledge, and a libertarian account of freedom to answer the logical problem of evil.[30] The central insight of the free will defense is that while there may be many possible worlds that have a better overall balance of good as compared with evil, because of the existence of significantly free creatures in at least some of those worlds, it is possible that even an omnipotent being could not create (or actualize) any of them. Plantinga's free will defense thus answers the objection that God's existence is logically incompatible with the existence of evil.

While some continue to argue that the logical problem of evil is unscathed (or somewhat less than fully scathed) by Plantinga's argument, the vast majority have accepted Plantinga's argument as successful. In the words of Richard Gale (who is not a theist), "It is generally conceded that the logical challenge of evil has been successfully neutralized by Plantinga and his cohorts."[31] Perhaps the best evidence for the success of Plantinga's free will defense is that since the publication of his argument, the vast majority of atheists who advance the problem of evil have shifted to the evidential problem of evil—evil is merely claimed to be evidence against God's existence; it does not render God's existence logically impossible.[32]

RELIGIOUS EPISTEMOLOGY

Other than his free will defense, Plantinga is best known in apologetics circles for his work on religious epistemology. His first contribution came in *God and Other Minds*, in which he argues that there are a set of beliefs that we are strongly inclined to accept as epistemically appropriate—the paradigm example of which is belief in the existence of other minds—for which compelling arguments or evidence is lacking. Since some of what we rationally believe, and even know, is held in the absence of propositional evidence or arguments—in fact,

---

Harper & Row, 1974; 2nd ed., Grand Rapids: Eerdmans, 1977). I do not mean to suggest that Plantinga's *only* purpose for thinking about the modal concepts of necessity and possibility was to develop his free will defense. The subjects were undoubtedly intrinsically interesting to him, and moreover, his work on modality allowed him to develop his modal version of the ontological argument. But it is difficult to deny that his philosophical work had an intentionally apologetic telos.

30. Plantinga developed his account of God's knowledge of counterfactuals of creaturely freedom independently, without knowledge of Luis de Molina's previous work (Plantinga, "Self-Profile," 50).

31. Richard Gale, "Evil and Alvin Plantinga," in Baker, *Alvin Plantinga*, 59. In addition, noted atheist William Rowe has defended Plantinga's free will defense against objections in his "In Defense of the Free Will Defense," *International Journal for Philosophy of Religion* 44/2 (October 1998): 115–20.

32. Plantinga has also written on the evidential problem of evil. For example, see his "On Being Evidentially Challenged" in *The Evidential Argument from Evil*, ed. Daniel Howard-Snyder (Bloomington, IN: Indiana University Press, 1996), 244–61 and "Degenerate Evidence and Rowe's New Evidential Argument From Evil" *Noûs* 32/4 (1998): 531–44.

in the absence of any clear idea of how to go about building an argument for such things—then what is wrong with the Christians treating their religious beliefs in a similar fashion? His controversial conclusion: "If my belief in other minds is rational, so is my belief in God. But obviously the former is rational; so, therefore, is the latter."[33] *God and Other Minds* set the basic direction of Plantinga's religious epistemology in two fundamental respects: religious beliefs enjoy epistemic parity with other widely accepted beliefs (such as belief in other minds), and like those beliefs, it does not require propositional evidence to be epistemically acceptable.

In the early 1980s, a flurry of articles and essays extended Plantinga's basic argument in *God and Other Minds*, the longest of which was "Reason and Belief in God."[34] In these works Plantinga returned to the argument originally laid out in *God and Other Minds*—that belief in God could be entirely rational even in the absence of propositional evidence. To bolster this claim, Plantinga sought to show that evidentialism—the supposition that beliefs require propositional evidence (usually given in the form of an argument) to be rational—was rooted in classical foundationalism and that classical foundationalism was untenable in that it was self-referentially incoherent. In the late 1980s, Plantinga published a series of works on epistemology and religious epistemology that signaled a transition in his approach to religious epistemology. Rather than merely defending the rationality or justification of religious belief, Plantinga asked a pair of prior questions: What is the nature of rationality or justification? And what is it that converts merely true beliefs into knowledge? "Justification and Theism" was Plantinga's first step on this journey.[35] In this article he outlined the structure of his new approach to religious epistemology. Central to this approach was the notion of *proper function*; belief in God, according to Plantinga, could count as knowledge if it was produced by properly functioning cognitive faculties. This approach represented a fundamental step away from his previous approach to epistemological questions. Before, Plantinga had discussed rationality and justification as deontological notions, involving the keeping of one's epistemic duties. But in Plantinga's new account, the concept of epistemic duties takes a back seat to the reliability of one's belief-producing mechanisms. Plantinga developed this

---

33. Plantinga, *God and Other Minds*, 271.

34. In *Faith and Rationality: Reason and Belief in God*, eds. Alvin Plantinga and Nicholas Wolterstorff (Notre Dame: University of Notre Dame Press, 1983). See also "Is Belief in God Rational?" in *Rationality and Religious Belief*, ed. C. F. Delaney (Notre Dame: University of Notre Dame Press, 1979), 7–27; "The Reformed Objection to Natural Theology." In *Proceedings of the American Catholic Philosophical Association*, 54, Philosophical Knowledge, eds. John B. Brough, Donald O. Dahlstrom and Henry B. Veatch, 49–62. Washington, DC: American Catholic Philosophical Assoc, 1980; and "Is Belief in God Properly Basic?" *Noûs* 15 (1981): 41–51.

35. Alvin Plantinga, "Justification and Theism," *Faith and Philosophy* 4 (October 1987): 403–26.

account of epistemology in a series of articles and most decisively in his Warrant trilogy: *Warrant: The Current Debate*, in which he critiqued the reigning epistemologies; *Warrant and Proper Function*, in which he laid out the details of his own theory of knowledge; and *Warranted Christian Belief*, in which he applies his account of knowledge to belief in God.[36]

In *Warranted Christian Belief*, Plantinga identifies two categories of objections to belief in God: the *de facto* objection and the *de jure* objection. A *de facto* objection is an objection to the *truth* of Christian belief, and a *de jure* objection involves the claim that Christian belief is flawed epistemically. In other words, a *de jure* objection is that even if it is true that God exists, there is not sufficient evidence, arguments, grounds, or reasons for a person to be rational, justified, or warranted in their belief that God exists. Plantinga develops two claims in *Warranted Christian Belief*. First, Plantinga argues that *de jure* objections are not independent of *de facto* concerns—that is, whether religious belief is warranted or not depends crucially on whether God exists and has created humans with a capacity for knowledge of him. Second, Plantinga offers a way Christians might think about the warrant of their religious beliefs. Warranted Christian beliefs, according to Plantinga, are not produced by humanity's original cognitive equipment. Rather, "they come instead by way of the work of the Holy Spirit, who gets us to accept, causes us to believe, these great truths of the gospel. These beliefs don't come by way of the normal operation of our noetic faculties; they are a supernatural gift."[37] These beliefs are produced in humans in a way that meets Plantinga's conditions for warrant—they are a product of a belief-producing process that is functioning properly in an appropriate cognitive environment (the one for which they were designed), according to a design plan successfully aimed at the production of true beliefs.[38]

While not all Christians will accept Plantinga's understanding of warrant or all the details of his model of the warrant of Christian belief, from an apologetic point of view, Plantinga's religious epistemology is significant in two respects. He describes a way in which Christian belief could have warrant, thus invalidating the claim that Christian beliefs cannot possess positive epistemic status, and he shows that atheists cannot simply advance *de jure* objections to Christian belief; they must argue that Christian belief is not true (a much more difficult task).

---

36. All three books of the Warrant trilogy were published by Oxford University Press. Recently, Plantinga has published a condensed version of *Warranted Christian Belief*, entitled *Knowledge and Christian Belief* (Grand Rapids: Eerdmans, 2015).

37. Plantinga, *Warranted Christian Belief*, 245.

38. Ibid, 246.

SCIENCE AND NATURALISM

Plantinga's consideration of the relationship between science and religious belief has produced a pair of apologetic contributions: his argument against methodological naturalism and his evolutionary argument against naturalism. Methodological naturalism, as Plantinga defines it, is "the idea that science, properly so-called, cannot involve religious belief or commitment."[39] It's not that a Christian cannot do science, but rather that as they do science, they must not allow their religious beliefs to affect the content of their scientific work. Plantinga's ruminations on methodological naturalism are directly connected to his perspective on the nature of scholarship and flow from his commitment to the idea that there is no reasonably complete important academic work that is religiously neutral. A Christian might want to see how a scientific question could be answered if they bracketed their religious beliefs, but—and this is Plantinga's main point—why should they have to? He says, "Isn't it perverse to limit yourself to only some of what you know, or only some sources of knowledge, if your aim is to reach the truth about the phenomenon in question?"[40] Instead, Christians should feel free to take into account all they know as they engage in science and in scholarship in general.

While an emphasis on negative apologetics had characterized Plantinga's apologetic career, in the final chapter of *Warrant and Proper Function*, Plantinga offers a bold and controversial piece of positive apologetics in the form of an argument against naturalism.[41] Plantinga argues that the conjunction of metaphysical naturalism (the view that only natural objects, kinds, and properties are real) and contemporary evolutionary theory is self-defeating. One who accepts both naturalism and evolution has a "defeater" for their belief that human belief-producing mechanisms, so evolved, are reliable. This defeater constitutes a defeater for any belief those mechanisms produce, including the beliefs that comprise naturalism and evolution. Therefore, even though metaphysical naturalism and evolution are typically thought of as very closely and comfortably connected, taken together, their conjunction cannot rationally be held. If this argument is correct, then some variety of supernaturalism must be true.

Misunderstandings of this argument abound, so some clarifications are important. First, Plantinga's argument should not be mistaken for an argument against contemporary evolutionary theory by itself but rather against *unguided*

---

39. Alvin Plantinga, "Methodological Naturalism," *Perspectives on Science and Christian Faith* 49 (September 1997): 143.

40. Alvin Plantinga, "Sheehen's Shenanigans: How Theology Becomes Tomfoolery," in *The Analytic Theist*, ed. James Sennett (Grand Rapids: Eerdmans, 1998), 326. Originally published in the *Reformed Journal* 37 (April 1987): 19–25.

41. Plantinga, *Warrant and Proper Function*, 216–37.

evolution; it is the conjunction of naturalism and evolution that is in the cross-hairs of Plantinga's argument. Second, Plantinga's argument in no way suggests that human belief-forming mechanisms are unreliable but rather that the naturalist is not justified in believing them to be reliable given the epistemological implications of their metaphysical commitments. Finally, Plantinga's proposed defeater for the naturalist's belief that their belief-producing mechanisms are reliable is of a special sort; it is a *purely alethic* defeater. A purely alethic rationality defeater specifies that the reasons a person might have for sustaining belief in cognitive reliability (and dismissing defeaters for that belief) must be "successfully aimed at truth (i.e., at the maximization of true belief and the minimization of false belief) and nothing more."[42]

Recently, Plantinga has engaged the broader apologetic question of whether there is a genuine conflict between Christianity and science, as commonly advanced by detractors of the Christian faith. In his *Where the Conflict Really Lies*, he argues: "There is superficial conflict, but deep concord between science and theistic religion, but superficial concord and deep conflict between science and naturalism."[43] The alleged conflicts between Christianity and science are either specious or superficial. Examples of specious conflict are the supposed conflict between Christianity and evolution and between Christian accounts of divine action only and science. The former becomes a conflict only if it is assumed that Scripture teaches that the earth is very young, and the latter becomes a genuine conflict only if it is assumed that nature is a closed system of cause and effect. And the alleged conflict between the disciplines of evolutionary psychology and historical biblical criticism, while real, are only superficial—that is, they do not necessarily give Christians a defeater for the core beliefs of the faith. Not only is there at best superficial conflict between Christianity and science, Plantinga finds deep concord between the two. He describes a number of ways in which human cognitive faculties match the world—an *adaequatio intellectus ad rem*, as the medievals termed it—and that this match allows us to know things about the world. This match is perfectly sensible given the Christian belief in human beings created in God's image but can be regarded only as blind luck given naturalism. From this, Plantinga urges that "it is theism, not naturalism, that deserves to be called 'the scientific worldview.'"[44] Finally, not only is there greater concord between theism and science than between natural-

---

42. For more on purely alethic defeaters, see *Warranted Christian Belief,* 363 and "Reply to Beilby's Cohorts," 209.

43. Alvin Plantinga, *Where the Conflict Really Lies: Science, Religion, and Naturalism* (New York: Oxford University Press, 2011), ix.

44. Ibid., 309.

ism and science, there is deep conflict between naturalism and science, a conflict that can be seen in the fact that the conjunction of naturalism and evolution is self-defeating—a conclusion demonstrated by his evolutionary argument against naturalism.

SYSTEMIC AND PERSONAL CONTRIBUTIONS

The final apologetic contribution to be discussed is of a different sort. As significant as the apologetic impact of Plantinga's various works has been, it can be argued that the whole of his impact has been greater than the sum of its parts. Plantinga did not just defend the Christian faith; he fundamentally changed the climate in academia with respect to belief in God and philosophy of religion. He did so by his willingness to talk about God himself, rather than just God-talk; his positive and substantive engagement with robust Christian faith, not just a watered-down or academically-palatable version of Christian belief; and his encouragement that Christians in the academic world should work unapologetically as Christians rather than addressing only subjects that the broader academic community found important or interesting. Speaking to Plantinga's influence, Kelly James Clark says, "In the 1950's there was not a single published defense of religious belief by a prominent philosopher; by the 1990's there were literally hundreds of books and articles, from Yale to UCLA and from Oxford to Heidelberg, defending and developing the spiritual dimension. The difference between 1950 and 1990 is, quite simply, Alvin Plantinga."[45] Likewise, Yoram Hazony, president of the Herzl Institute in Jerusalem, said of Plantinga's impact on academia: "Plantinga's Christianity hit the sleepy old atheism of the university philosophy departments like a tornado plowing into a haystack. Belief in God became an open possibility again. All of us who've come after him are in his debt."[46] Strikingly, the atheist philosopher Quentin Smith credits Plantinga's *God and Other Minds* with beginning the "unraveling of the secularization of mainstream academia."[47] He says, "It became apparent to the philosophical profession that this book displayed that realist theists were not outmatched by naturalists in terms of the most valued standards of analytic philosophy: conceptual precision, rigor of argumentation, technical erudition, and an in-depth defense of an original worldview. . . . This book, followed seven years later by Plantinga's

45. Kelly James Clark, "Alvin Plantinga and the Revival of Religious Philosophy," *Huffington Post*, May 8, 2017, https://www.huffingtonpost.com/entry/alvin-plantinga-and-the-revival-of-religious-philosophy_us_59107108e4b056aa2363d70e.

46. Announcement of 2017 Templeton Prize. https://www.templetonprize.org/pdfs/2017/20170924-templetonprize-ceremonypr.pdf.

47. Quentin Smith, "The Metaphilosophy of Naturalism," *Philo* 4/2 (2001): 2.

even more impressive book, *The Nature of Necessity*, made it manifest that a realist theist was writing at the highest qualitative level of analytic philosophy."[48]

Of course, Plantinga had help in changing the culture in Christian philosophy. Nicholas Wolterstorff, William Alston, Eleonore Stump, and others joined him in starting the Society of Christian Philosophers, and many other younger scholars have taken Plantinga's advice to heart and propelled the movement forward, but it is difficult to see how all of that happens in the absence of Plantinga's work and influence. Justifiably, as a recognition of his influence, Plantinga was given the 2017 Templeton Prize.

Plantinga's influence has also been manifest in a more personal way. He has intentionally taken an active interest in and encouraged an entire generation of younger scholars. Plantinga says:

> It is . . . hard to think of any task more important, for a Christian philosopher, than doing what one can to train and equip the next generation of Christian philosophers. This means seeing younger philosophers, fledgling philosophers and graduate students as of immense value. Their well-being and development as members of the community of Christian philosophers is a source of real concern: it requires our best efforts and any encouragement and help we can give. For it is they, after all, who will carry on this task of Christian philosophy after the current generation has left the scene.[49]

Because this aspect of Plantinga's influence has been deeply personal, it is fitting to close this essay on a more personal note. There is no more influential figure on my faith and academic development than Al Plantinga. Not only was his work profoundly instrumental in transforming the way a rebellious college student in the middle of a faith crisis looked at the life of the mind and belief in God, he has consistently gone above and beyond in encouraging my academic work, and this even though I was never formally his student. This included writing an encouraging three-page, single-spaced letter giving advice to a philosophical neophyte who had just recovered from a faith crisis, numerous life-shaping philosophical and personal conversations during disc-golf matches, and collaborating on academic projects. If I am now in a place where I can encourage the next generation, it is because of Al's investment in my academic career. And stories such as these are legion. Not only is Plantinga's apologetic contribution

---

48. Ibid., 2.
49. Plantinga, "A Christian Life Partly Lived," 81.

unparalleled in the contemporary world, but the way he has lived has been an apologetic for the faith his work has defended.[50]

BIBLIOGRAPHY

Baker, Deane-Peter, ed. *Alvin Plantinga*. Contemporary Philosophy in Focus series. New York: Cambridge, 2007.

Beilby, James. *Epistemology as Theology*. Aldershot: Ashgate, 2005.

———, ed. *Naturalism Defeated? Essays on Plantinga's Evolutionary Argument Against Naturalism*. Ithaca, NY: Cornell, 2002.

Clark, Kelly James. "Reformed Epistemology Apologetics." Pages 265–84 in *Five Views on Apologetics*. Ed. by Steven B. Cowan. Grand Rapids: Zondervan, 2000.

Clark, Kelly James, and Michael Rea. *Reason, Metaphysics, and Mind: New Essays on the Philosophy of Alvin Plantinga*. New York: Oxford, 2012.

Morley, Brian K. *Mapping Apologetics*. Downers Grove, IL: InterVarsity Academic, 2015.

Plantinga, Alvin. "A Christian Life Partly Lived." Pages 45–82 in *Philosophers Who Believe: The Spiritual Journeys of 11 Leading Thinkers*. Ed. by Kelly James Clark. Downers Grove, IL: InterVarsity, 1993.

———. "Advice to Christian Philosophers." *Faith and Philosophy* 1/3 (July 1984): 253–71.

———. "An Initial Statement of the Argument." Pages 1–12 in *Naturalism Defeated? Essays on Plantinga's Evolutionary Argument Against Naturalism*. Ed. by James Beilby. Ithaca, NY: Cornell University Press, 2002.

———. *God and Other Minds: A Study in the Rational Justification of Belief in God*. Ithaca, NY: Cornell University Press, 1967; 2nd ed., 1990.

———. *God, Freedom and Evil*. New York: Harper & Row, 1974; 2nd ed., Grand Rapids: Eerdmans, 1977.

———. "Justification and Theism." *Faith and Philosophy* 4 (October 1987): 403–26.

———. *The Nature of Necessity*. Oxford: Clarendon, 1974. 2nd ed., 1989.

———. "Reason and Belief in God." Pages 16–93 in *Faith and Rationality: Reason and Belief in God*. Ed. by Alvin Plantinga and Nicholas Wolterstorff. Notre Dame: University of Notre Dame Press, 1983.

———. "Reply to Beilby's Cohorts." Pages 204–75 in *Naturalism Defeated? Essays on Plantinga's Evolutionary Argument against Naturalism*. Ed. by James Beilby. Ithaca, NY: Cornell University Press, 2002.

———. "Self Profile." Pages 3–97 in *Alvin Plantinga*. Ed. by James Tomberlin and Peter van Inwagen. Dordrecht: D. Reidel, 1985.

———. *Warrant and Proper Function*. New York: Oxford University Press, 1993.

———. *Warrant: The Current Debate*. New York: Oxford University Press, 1993.

———. *Warranted Christian Belief*. New York: Oxford University Press, 2000.

———. *Where the Conflict Really Lies: Science Religion, and Naturalism*. New York: Oxford University Press, 2011.

Plantinga, Alvin, and Daniel C. Dennett. *Science and Religion: Are They Compatible?* Point/Counterpoint Series. New York: Oxford University Press, 2010.

Walls, Jerry L., and Trent Doherty, eds. *Two Dozen (or so) Arguments for God: The Plantinga Project*. New York: Oxford University Press, 2018.

---

50. This paper has benefitted from editing work by Sierra Beilby and from a course release provided by Bethel University. I am thankful for both.

RICHARD SWINBURNE

Pioneering Analytic Apologetics

GREG WELTY

Richard Swinburne (1934–) is one of the most influential philosophers of religion in the past fifty years. By persistently applying the tools of analytic philosophy to topics of perennial religious concern, Swinburne ended up accomplishing what virtually no other contemporary philosopher has even attempted: defending all the central doctrines of Christianity from the impressive array of philosophical criticisms currently launched against them. In doing so, he has significantly influenced the way all these matters are discussed in an intellectual context today. At a 2014 academic conference at Purdue University, many of the most distinguished philosophers of religion in the world gathered to celebrate Swinburne's work and to honor him on the occasion of his eightieth birthday.[1] As an observer, I was struck by how the papers that disagreed with him nevertheless displayed the deep influence of his method: clarity of expression and rigor of argument combined with appeal to philosophy, science, and history as tools for articulating and defending one's religious views. Many of these philosophers openly acknowledged their debt to his influence.

HISTORICAL BACKGROUND

Richard G. Swinburne was born on December 26, 1934, in Smethwick, Staffordshire, England, and studied philosophy, politics, and economics at Exeter College, University of Oxford (receiving a first-class BA in 1957). He received a graduate degree in philosophy (BPhil, 1959), a diploma in theology (University Diploma in Philosophy, St. Stephen's House, Oxford, 1960, in anticipation of ordination to Anglican ministry), and then studied the history of science for the next three years via two research fellowships. After this training, Swinburne became convinced

---

1. Purdue University, "Faith and Reason: Themes from Swinburne," conference held September 25–27, 2014. https://www.conf.purdue.edu/landing_pages/swinburne/.

that the best use of his gifts lay in an academic environment rather than being ordained in the Church of England. He became a lecturer in philosophy at the University of Hull (1963–72), a professor of philosophy at the University of Keele (1972–84), and then served as the successor to Basil Mitchell as the Nolloth Professor of the Philosophy of the Christian Religion at Oriel College, University of Oxford (1985–2002). Beyond these academic appointments and throughout his career, Swinburne has been a visiting professor or lecturer in at least twenty-four different academic institutions around the world, and he continues to maintain an international presence in lecturing and teaching. Swinburne was a lifelong Anglican before converting to Orthodoxy in 1995. The doctrines he sought to defend were those of "ecumenical Christianity" (of the early Christian creeds), and in this respect his project has some affinity with C. S. Lewis's "mere Christianity," although pursued with more philosophical rigor and less rhetorical and literary flair.

Starting in 1968 Swinburne's earliest books were on space and time (viewed in light of scientific theory such as relativity) and confirmation theory (how science uses probability theory to confirm its theses).[2] But soon his focus shifted to articulating and defending theism and Christian theology in an academic context, and a steady stream of substantive monographs on just about every important topic in the philosophy of religion and philosophical theology issued from his pen, including works defending the coherence of theism, the existence of God, the compatibility of faith and reason, the relation between body and soul, and the Christian doctrines of the Trinity, incarnation, atonement, resurrection, biblical revelation, and divine providence as the solution to the problem of evil. Indeed, since 1968 he has published eighteen monographs (fourteen with Oxford University Press), five edited volumes, and 172 articles in leading academic journals of philosophy. Swinburne remarked at the Purdue conference, "One difficulty I have in defending myself from criticisms is that I have written so much, and I sometimes forget exactly where I said something!"[3]

THEOLOGICAL CONTEXT

Swinburne's theological context at the time of his academic training posed two seemingly insuperable barriers to the defense of Christian theism. First, God-talk

2. Richard Swinburne, *Space and Time* (London: Macmillan, 1968), and Richard Swinburne, *An Introduction to Confirmation Theory* (London: Methuen, 1973).

3. Some of the dates in the preceding paragraphs were drawn from Richard Swinburne, "Short intellectual autobiography" (undated), http://users.ox.ac.uk/~orie0087/. Further material was adapted from Greg Welty, "Review of *Reason and Faith: Themes from Richard Swinburne*. Michael Bergmann and Jeffrey E. Brower, eds. New York: Oxford University Press, 2016," *Themelios* vol. 41, issue 2 (August 2016), http://themelios.thegospelcoalition.org/review/reason-and-faith-themes-from-richard-swinburne.

was argued by many to be unintelligible, and second, science was assumed to be the only, or at least premier, source for justified beliefs about the world, not religion. Because of these cultural factors that operated in a largely Anglo-American context, philosophy of religion and philosophical theology became largely moribund disciplines.[4] If religious belief is both nonsensical to contemplate and irrational to believe, Christian apologetics is stopped dead in its tracks. Philosophy has come to bury it, not aid it.

CONTENDING WITH LOGICAL POSITIVISM AS A THEORY OF MEANING

One reason the early days of analytic philosophy in the first half of the twentieth century did not bode well for productive philosophical reflection on the content of Christian theology was because quite a few philosophers were in the grip of a theory of knowledge known as "empiricism": roughly, the view that all our knowledge of the world must start from our sensory experience of the observable world. This view turned into a theory of meaning that seemed to preclude the meaningfulness of metaphysical and religious claims. Philosophers such as Rudolph Carnap and A. J. Ayer[5] were impressed by empiricism because it promised to protect logic, mathematics, and the natural sciences from pseudo-scientific nonsense. At the heart of this logical positivist movement in philosophy was its empiricist criteria for cognitive significance: unless a claim could be verified (confirmed, supported) or falsified (disconfirmed, disproven) by testing it against *empirical* observations of the world, that claim should be regarded as literally *meaningless*, a bit of language that doesn't even have the dignity of being capable of truth or falsity.

In his widely read 1950 essay "Theology and Falsification," British philosopher Antony Flew applied these insights to religious language. Flew argued that claims about God are typically not regarded by believers as empirically falsifiable, since believers would cling to their faith in God no matter how the world went. Flew concluded that talk about God is literally meaningless.[6] Philosophers of religion needed to come up with an alternative defense of the significance of their key religious terms. The "falsifiability criterion" at the heart of this cri-

---

4. At least among Protestant-influenced philosophers. Within Roman Catholic institutions of priestly training, the enormous and authoritative influence of medieval systematizers such as Augustine, Anselm, and Aquinas kept up lively and profitable academic discussion of these matters to a very great degree.

5. Rudolph Carnap, *Philosophy and Logical Syntax (Psyche Miniatures General Series, No. 70)* (London: Kegan Paul, Trench, Trubner & Co., Ltd., 1937). A. J. Ayer, *Language, Truth, and Logic* (London: Gollancz, 1936).

6. Antony Flew, R. M. Hare, and Basil Mitchell, "Theology and Falsification: A Symposium" (1950), repr. in pages 13–22 of Basil Mitchell, ed., *The Philosophy of Religion* (Oxford: Oxford University Press, 1971). Flew's critique is on pp. 13–15, 20–22 of the roundtable discussion.

tique had to be critiqued itself if philosophical theology was to be recovered as a viable discipline.

But at the very time Flew was touting his logical positivist critique of God-talk, secular philosophers were beginning to doubt its underpinnings.[7] Additionally, a group of Christian philosophers, including Swinburne, provided a variety of responses as well.[8] Eventually it became evident that the empiricist criterion was so strict that typical scientific claims otherwise acceptable would have to be excluded. Their criterion was also a bit of metaphysical theorizing; as Wolterstorff put it, "The faith which the positivists displayed in natural science was not itself arrived at scientifically."[9] In fact, it is often the case in the history of science that "scientists convinced of the truth of some scientific theory behave exactly the way Flew says religious believers do," that is, dogmatically.[10]

Once positivism was undermined in this way by the arguments of both secular and religious philosophers, Christian philosophers were free to use religious language and openly refer to a transcendent, nonempirical God without embarrassment. By moving forward and addressing objections to the Christian faith in a clear and systematic manner, these philosophers helped establish a solid foundation for contemporary progress in Christian apologetics, bequeathing to future generations a wealth of edifying, perceptive, and intellectually dazzling religious reflection.

CONTENDING WITH SCIENTISM AS A THEORY OF KNOWLEDGE

A second philosophical and cultural barrier to the defense of Christian theism in the twentieth century was created not by difficulties over religious language but instead by the triumph of nonreligious modes of thought. The enormous success of science in not only discovering truths about the world but in developing technology and medicine for human good seemed to dwarf the

---

7. Carl Hempel, "Problems and Changes in the Empiricist Criterion of Meaning," *Revue Internationale de Philosophie* Vol. 4.11 (January 1950): 41–63. Willard Van Orman Quine, "Two Dogmas of Empiricism," *The Philosophical Review* 60 (1951): 20–43.

8. See Basil Mitchell in Flew et. al., "Theology and Falsification," 18–20; William Alston "Are Positivists Metaphysicians?", *Philosophical Review* 63 (1954): 42–57 (cf. p. 52). William Alston, *Philosophy of Language* (Englewood Cliffs, NJ: Prentice-Hall, 1964), 62–83. William Alston, "Religious Language and Verificationism," in Paul Copan and Paul Moser, eds., *The Rationality of Theism* (New York: Routledge, 2003), 17–34; Alvin Plantinga, *God and Other Minds: A Study of the Rational Justification of Belief in God* (Ithaca, NY: Cornell University Press, 1967), 156–58; and Richard Swinburne, "Confirmability and Factual Meaningfulness," *Analysis* Vol. 33, Issue 3 (January 1973): 71–76. Richard Swinburne, *The Coherence of Theism* (Oxford: Oxford University Press, 1977) (2nd ed., 2016, 40–43).

9. Nicholas Wolterstorff, *Reason within the Bounds of Religion* (Grand Rapids: Eerdmans, 1976) (2nd ed., 1984, 16).

10. Wolterstorff, *Reason*, 20.

accomplishments of religion. Science was a way of knowing that *worked*, thus deserving to become our paradigm for acquiring knowledge. By comparison, religion looked like ill-informed guesswork at best.

In seeking to overcome this barrier, Swinburne made good use of his academic training in the history and philosophy of science to make several observations. First, scientists frequently make their theses accessible to each other and to the broader public not only by way of straightforward literal uses of words but occasionally by way of analogy and metaphor, in so doing explaining the unknown in light of the known. Scientists (as well as philosophers) also construct thought experiments in literal, analogical, and even metaphorical language to help others picture what scientific theories were claiming about the world, thus not only helping others picture the possible truth of scientific theories but also helping them to be open to any evidence that such theories are true. Why couldn't religious believers also do these things, clearly defining their terms but also utilizing analogy, metaphor, and thought experiment in religious discourse?[11]

Second, scientists regularly posit unobservable entities to explain observable effects. Chemists posited unobservable molecules to explain observed chemical behavior; physicists posited unobservable waves and fields to explain observed electromagnetic and gravitational behavior; astronomers posited unobservable planets (at the time) to explain observed perturbations in the orbits of other, nearby planets. The question must be asked: Why aren't these kinds of moves open to theists when they argue for God's existence from observed features of the world? Doesn't the success of chemistry, physics, and astronomy show that there is nothing intellectually impermissible in explaining the observable by way of the unobservable?[12]

Third, scientists do not support the truth of their theories by flipping a coin. Rather, they appeal to relevant criteria of the probability calculus. A scientific theory is said to be a good explanation of the data—and therefore *confirmed* or *supported* by the data—to the extent that it has predictive power (it leads us to expect the kinds of things we see), simplicity (positing fewer entities and kinds of entity relative to alternative theories), and fit with background knowledge (being consistent with and not contrary to the various things we already know about the world). Once again, perhaps theists can argue for God, Scripture, miracles,

---

11. Richard Swinburne, "Part I. Religious Language," in *The Coherence of Theism, 2nd ed.* (Oxford: Oxford University Press, 2016), 11–99.

12. Richard Swinburne, "The Argument from Design," *Philosophy*, vol. 43, no. 165 (July 1968): 208. Cf. Richard Swinburne, *The Existence of God, 2nd ed.* (Oxford: Oxford University Press, 2004), 57–58.

and even the resurrection by offering a carefully reasoned case that appeals to these same criteria.[13]

Finally, rarely do scientists support their theories by way of a single argument. Rather, a series of arguments from a disparate range of data are strung together to make a "cumulative case" for the truth of the theory, a case that would survive any later revisions to a significant degree. The greater the range of data (quantitatively), and the greater the difference between kinds of data (qualitatively) said to support the theory, the greater the likelihood that the theory *is* the best explanation of the available data. Even if one part of the case needs to be revised in light of later considerations, the total case for the theory doesn't collapse. Thus, probable truth—a theory being established as more likely than not, or at least more likely than its alternatives—rather than certainty is the goal.[14]

Thus, Swinburne saw that the success of science in the modern era is not a barrier to Christian apologetics but an important ally in making a full-orbed, robust case for faith. Swinburne's response to this second cultural barrier was largely unique to him. His extended argument for the coherence of theism by way of imaginative thought experiments and his cumulative case for God's existence from empirical data by way of the criteria of the probability calculus are probably his most influential achievements.[15]

APOLOGETIC METHODOLOGY

"First Philosophy, then Theology"

The preceding insights—faith in ordinary use of language to express religious claims and reliance on norms of rationality at home in the empirical sciences—were applied by Swinburne with a remarkable degree of thoroughness in a series of seven volumes written over twenty-one years. These are the "trilogy" (on the philosophy of theism) and "tetralogy" (on the philosophy of Christian doctrine), which taken together is his most influential body of work.

To read each of these volumes is to discover a single method repeated without deviation but applied with creativity, summed up in the slogan "first philosophy, then theology." This is the methodological skeleton key that unlocks the door to effective Christian apologetics for every topic under the sun. In an

---

13. Swinburne, *The Existence of God, 2nd ed.*, ch. 3 "The Justification of Explanation."
14. Swinburne, *The Existence of God, 2nd ed.*, ch. 14 "The Balance of Probability."
15. Arguably, Swinburne's "cumulative case" method was an extension of a style of religious argument pioneered by Swinburne's predecessor at Oxford, Basil Mitchell. Cf. Basil Mitchell, *The Justification of Religious Belief* (Oxford: Oxford University Press, 1981). It also applied insights articulated earlier by John Henry Newman. But neither of these earlier presentations approached the rigor and development that characterizes Swinburne's presentation.

illuminating autobiographical piece, Swinburne explains that the medieval philosopher Thomas Aquinas became for him his most influential model for how to pursue the defense of the Christian faith in the modern era.[16] In effect, figure out what are the best philosophy and science of your day and then show that your religious views are rational with respect to them. For Aquinas, that was Aristotle. For Swinburne, it was the best that ordinary language philosophy and inductive, empirical science of the twentieth century had to offer.

Accordingly, in each of the seven volumes that compose the trilogy and the tetralogy, Swinburne divides the book in half. The first half is always philosophy, setting out a case for his views in whatever subdiscipline in philosophy is most relevant to the forthcoming theological content of the book. The second half then makes a case for specific theological conclusions in light of the philosophy that has just been set out. To read the trilogy and tetralogy is to take a tour of philosophy in its entire breadth, with enough depth to get the job done on theological questions. The following sketch helps us see at a glance this twofold method at work.

Trilogy on the Philosophy of Theism[17]

- *The Coherence of Theism* (1977, revised 1993, second edition 2016)
  - First philosophy: philosophy of language
  - Then theology: philosophy of language helps us define the divine attributes without contradiction, and so it is possible that God exists.
- *The Existence of God* (1979, revised 1991, second edition 2004)
  - First philosophy: principles of the probability calculus used in empirical confirmation of theories
  - Then theology: principles of the probability calculus help us make a cumulative case argument that God's existence is more likely than not.
- *Faith and Reason* (1981, second edition 2005)
  - First philosophy: the epistemology of rational belief
  - Then theology: this epistemology of rational belief helps us see that the arguments for theism are more than enough to support a faith that seriously investigates and then commits itself to the Christian path.

16. Richard Swinburne, "Intellectual Autobiography," in Alan Padgett, ed., *Reason and the Christian Religion: Essays in Honour of Richard Swinburne* (Oxford: Clarendon, 1994), 1–18.
17. This trilogy is summarized at the popular level in Richard Swinburne, *Is There a God?* (Oxford: Oxford University Press, 1996).

Tetralogy on the Philosophy of Christian Doctrine[18]
- *Responsibility and Atonement* (1989)
  - First philosophy: moral philosophy of obligation, responsibility, and guilt
  - Then theology: moral philosophy helps us see that Christ's life and death are more than adequate as an offering to atone for the sins of human beings who are responsible to live their lives in obedience to God but have failed to do so.
- *Revelation* (1991, second edition 2007)
  - First philosophy: philosophy of semantics and hermeneutics pertaining to texts
  - Then theology: hermeneutics helps us see that we have good reason to think that the Christian Scriptures are the verbal revelation of God to humanity, communicating the message of salvation.
- *The Christian God* (1994)
  - First philosophy: metaphysics of substance, properties, causation, necessity, and time
  - Then theology: metaphysics helps us define the distinctively Christian doctrines of the Trinity and incarnation without contradiction, and it can even give us positive *a priori* reason for expecting these doctrines to be true.
- *Providence and the Problem of Evil* (1998)
  - First philosophy: moral philosophy of rights and obligations
  - Then theology: moral philosophy helps us argue from the broad range of deep goods available for God to pursue, and from the necessary conditions for pursuing them, that God has the right to providentially permit the amount and kinds of significant pain and suffering we see in the world for the sake of great goods.

APOLOGETIC RESPONSE

So what was Swinburne's apologetic response to the conflicts of his day? What follows is a survey of Swinburne's thought in ten different areas of philosophy of religion and Christian philosophical theology—which are Christian apologetics under different names.

---

18. This tetralogy is summarized at the popular level in Richard Swinburne, *Was Jesus God?* (Oxford: Oxford University Press, 2008).

THE COHERENCE OF THEISM

In *The Coherence of Theism*, Swinburne argued that the concept of God is subject to no obvious incoherence. In particular, he argued that there can be an omnipresent spirit who is perfectly free, the creator of the universe, omnipotent, omniscient, perfectly good, a source of moral obligation, eternal, immutable, necessarily existing, holy, and worthy of worship. At each stage of his argument he clearly defined the attribute under discussion, considered whether it is coherent on its own, and then whether it is coherent with the preceding attributes on the list. Swinburne appealed to the philosophy of language to show that the words of theology can be ordinary words with ordinary senses. But because God necessarily exists and has his attributes necessarily, he can only be a "person" in an analogical sense (since ordinary persons do not necessarily exist nor do they have their properties necessarily in the degree to which they have them).

THE EXISTENCE OF GOD

In *The Existence of God*, by far his most influential book, Swinburne sets forth the existence of God as the best explanation for a wide range of otherwise disparate empirical data: the existence of a complex physical universe subject to relatively simple laws of nature, the existence of embodied humans who have consciousness, freedom, awareness of moral truth, and providential opportunity to do good to others, occasional miracles (and "super-miracles" such as the resurrection), and religious experiences seemingly of God. By carefully applying contemporary probability theory, Swinburne argued that each of these things would be extremely improbable if there were no God, and when we string these arguments together, we have a powerful "cumulative case" for the existence of God. Swinburne's presentation repeatedly appealed to three criteria for a sound "inference to the best explanation": predictive power, simplicity, and fit with background knowledge (i.e., other things we know to be true).

THE COMPATIBILITY OF FAITH AND REASON

In *Faith and Reason*, Swinburne argued that the purpose of religion is to achieve salvation and to worship and obey God. Particular religious creeds, by explaining what this salvation consists in, explain how pursuing a particular religion will achieve the goals of that religion. Faith therefore involves a means-end belief that pursuing the religious way outlined in a creed is more likely to attain the goals of religion than pursuing the ways of any other creed. Acquiring this means-end belief involves investigating which creeds are most likely to be true (considering both moral plausibility and miraculous authentication by way of the resurrection of Jesus) and investigating which creeds offer the most worthwhile religious goals.

THE TRINITY

In *The Christian God*, Swinburne defended the coherence of the Christian doctrine of the Trinity by way of a moderate "social Trinitarianism." He developed a metaphysical framework according to which there can be substances (including individual souls) with "thisness," such that they can be distinct from other substances that have all the same properties. (Thus, the three persons of the Trinity having all the same divine properties does not preclude them from being distinct persons.) God's having "pure, limitless, intentional power" entails that he has perfect freedom, omnipotence, omniscience, and exists of metaphysical necessity.

The most discussed feature of his argument is his adaptation of Richard of Saint Victor's *a priori* argument from reason for the doctrine of the Trinity. "I believe that there is overriding reason for a first divine individual to bring about a second divine individual and with him to bring about a third divine individual, but no reason to go further."[19] This is because of the nature of love. "Love involves sharing, giving to the other what of one's own is good for him and receiving from the other what of his is good for one; and love involves co-operating with another to benefit third parties. This latter is crucial for worthwhile love."[20] So "the most probable kind of God is such that inevitably he becomes tripersonal."[21] Swinburne's argument here is an important example of his willingness to depart from Aquinas's conclusions when necessary, as Aquinas regarded the Trinity as an article of faith.

THE INCARNATION

Also in *The Christian God*, Swinburne argued that the incarnation is possible if we confess that Christ is one individual with two natures (divine and human), including two minds. This allows for the human mind to be less aware than the divine mind (thus explaining certain features of his humanity expressed in the Scriptures), while maintaining Christ's full omniscience. Swinburne defended his view as consistent with Chalcedonian orthodoxy, over and against various heretical Christologies. Of particular interest is his appeal to both Platonic and Aristotelian theories of the soul in order to avoid both Nestorianism and Apollinarianism. Finally, by arguing that God has some reason to become incarnate, Swinburne supplies a crucial premise for his historical argument for the resurrection of Christ, since God's reasons for becoming incarnate are part of the "general background evidence" that we bring to our study of the relevant

19. Richard Swinburne, *The Christian God* (Oxford: Oxford University Press, 1994), 176.
20. Ibid.
21. Ibid., 190.

historical material (see below). If God exists and he has good reason to become incarnate, then we would *expect* God to become incarnate and to seal his incarnation by way of a "super-miracle" such as the resurrection.

The Atonement

In *Responsibility and Atonement*, Swinburne situated the doctrine of Christ's atonement within the Christian scheme of salvation and within a broader theory of moral responsibility. Swinburne first clearly defined and defended the importance of morally significant concepts such as moral goodness, moral responsibility, free will, merit, guilt, praise, blame, reward, and punishment. These concepts already have application in everyday human life, and it is only in light of them that the Christian doctrines of atonement and forgiveness can be satisfactorily understood. Atonement involves wrongdoers expressing repentance and apology to those whom they have wronged, and typically involves them making reparation and penance as well. The guilt of wrongdoers can be removed when, after they make atonement, the victim forgives them. But in the absence of atonement, wrongdoers are justly liable to punishment. Since God exists and is our greatest benefactor, we have wronged him in many ways and owe atonement for our sins. But even if we repent and apologize to God, due to our actual sin and a proneness to sin inherited from Adam (original sin), it is very difficult if not impossible for us to do all that is required for atonement, especially making reparation and doing penance. But the perfect life and sacrificial death of the God-man Jesus Christ can be offered to God as the very reparation and penance that we owe to him. Whether we make use of the atonement God provides us in Christ makes a vital difference to whether we spend our afterlife in heaven or in hell.

The Resurrection

On Swinburne's view, Jesus's perfect life and miraculous resurrection is evidence that he was in fact God incarnate. Swinburne marshaled the available historical evidence into a powerful case for the resurrection in *The Resurrection of God Incarnate*, further applying the probability theory he employed in *The Existence of God*. First, we have two important pieces of "background evidence," argued for in other volumes: God exists, and he has at least some reason to become incarnate. Second, we have two kinds of "historical evidence." "Prior" historical evidence (evidence we investigate before we consider the resurrection) includes historical sources that indicate that Jesus's life and teaching point to his moral perfection, his divinity, his life and death as an atonement for sin, and his founding a church through apostles who would interpret his teaching to the world. "Posterior" historical evidence (more directly concerning the resurrection) includes the historical testimony to the appearances of the risen Jesus, the emptiness of Jesus's tomb, and the regarding of Sunday as a sacred day by the early disciples. Third, Swinburne asks, what are the chances that *both* the prior historical evidence *and* the posterior historical evidence would come together in the life of *one* person (Jesus), unless that person were God incarnate risen from the dead? While there are explanations of this historical evidence that do not appeal to the literal resurrection of Jesus, the balance of probability supports the resurrection over these rival theories, particularly once we respond to Hume's argument against miracles (a subject Swinburne first broached thirty-two years earlier in *The Concept of Miracle*).[22]

REVELATION

In *Revelation*, Swinburne argued that the Christian Bible—and in particular its doctrinal and moral teaching—constitutes revealed truth. First, he developed an account of "meaning" by way of concepts widely used in the philosophy of language, to explain the various ways that literature can communicate true claims: by history, allegory, parable, analogy, and metaphor. Swinburne then argued that if God exists, we would expect him to provide a verbal revelation of himself in order to give us moral knowledge and to meet our spiritual needs. There are four tests for judging whether a putative revelation is in fact from God: avoidance of intrinsic improbability, miraculous confirmation, having an interpretation that is plausibly from a church tracing back to the prophet behind the revelation, and having a plausible interpretation. Swinburne applied these tests to the Christian Scriptures—concluding that "the Christian Revelation is very probable"—and defended his case from Plantinga's "objection from dwindling probabilities."[23]

Swinburne stressed that the meaning of individual sentences in the Bible must be understood in terms of God's ultimate authorship of the whole Bible (rather than being understood merely in terms of what the individual human author would have intended). He also maintained that there is need for a church to both authenticate the Bible for us and interpret its teaching to us, and he considered principles by which we can identify that church in history.

Swinburne offered an extended defense of traditional Christian moral teaching in the second edition of *Revelation*, covering the topics of sexuality (adultery, divorce, fornication, homosexual acts, family headship, contraception, abortion), women priests, usury, and slavery.

---

22. Richard Swinburne, *The Resurrection of God Incarnate* (Oxford: Oxford University Press, 2003), 214. Even as Swinburne popularized his case for God in *Is There a God?*, so he provided a more popularized case for the Trinity, incarnation, atonement, and resurrection in *Was Jesus God?*.

23. Richard Swinburne, *Revelation, 2nd ed.* (Oxford: Oxford University Press, 2007), 337, 354–56.

THE PROBLEM OF EVIL

In *Providence and the Problem of Evil*, Swinburne eschewed any appeal to divine inscrutability (a strategy favored by William Alston and Alvin Plantinga), in favor of presenting free will and soul-building theodicies that he argued are sufficient to respond to the problem of evil. If God is to provide good things for humans, such as beauty, thought, feeling, action, and worship, he must allow the possibility of various bad things as well. Thus, God's permission of the *fact* of moral evils (i.e., significant cases of pain and suffering due to human abuse of free will, such as murder, rape, and genocide) is justified as presupposed in the greatest gift God has given to humans: their free will. God's permission of the *great range* of moral evils is presupposed in the *significant* responsibility he has given humans for themselves and others, a responsibility it is good to have. God's permission of natural evil (i.e., significant cases of pain and suffering not due to human abuse of free will, such as famine, plague, disease, and natural disasters) gives humans great scope for courageous and sympathetic response and for forming their characters by way of that response. In fact, the laws of nature, which make possible various natural evils, give humans the possibility of knowledge of how to exploit nature's processes for creatures' good.

SOUL-BODY SUBSTANCE DUALISM

In *The Evolution of the Soul*, Swinburne argued that the best understanding of the metaphysical nature of human beings is a modified form of Cartesian substance dualism, which is far superior to materialist theories and fits quite well with Christian beliefs about God and the afterlife. He argued in two follow-up volumes, *Mind, Brain, and Free Will* and *Are We Bodies or Souls?*, that a modified Cartesian dualism can be defended in light of the philosophy of language and the latest discoveries in neuroscience.

Swinburne's case here relates to his overall Christian apologetic in several ways. First, in both volumes he develops further a defense of libertarian free will as the kind of free will we both can and must have in order to be morally responsible. This view of free will is in turn crucial to his account of divine omniscience (in *The Coherence of Theism*), of the kind of choice needed to pursue Christian salvation (in *Faith and Reason*), of the kind of moral responsibility we must have for sins, which require atonement (in *Responsibility and Atonement*), of the nature of divine freedom (again in *The Coherence of Theism* and in *The Christian God*), and of the free will theodicy that is so central to his response to the problem of evil (in *Providence and the Problem of Evil*).

Arguing for a modified version of Cartesian body-soul substance dualism also helps defend the coherence of the Christian doctrine of postmortem survival and resurrection of human beings. Finally, it is a bulwark against the reductive materialism about human beings so fashionable today, while fitting the emergence of humans on the historical scene into an overall evolutionary scheme by the creative power of God. (Swinburne is a "theistic evolutionist.")

CONTRIBUTIONS TO THE FIELD OF APOLOGETICS

We've seen Swinburne's twofold response to his theological context, his twofold method for constructing a Christian apologetic, and ten areas of apologetic conflict he directly engaged. How shall we analyze the contribution of Richard Swinburne to the field of Christian apologetics for students and readers today? The preceding survey allows the following seven points of application to emerge.

First, it is possible to be a catalyst for great good in Christian apologetics, in your own time and place, far beyond what you ever anticipated. The "greats" in Christian apologetics are not restricted to the giants of a revered, unchanging past. Swinburne did not set out in 1954 (the year he entered Oxford as an undergraduate) to be a philosopher of religion celebrated on the global scene sixty years later in 2014. He did not set out to be a foundational influence for Anglo-American philosophy of religion from the late 1970s to the present. Rather, "being a Christian was, I claimed to myself, the most important thing in my life."[24] As part of that calling, "I came to believe it to be my Christian vocation to try to make a contribution to this process" of making "Christian theology again intellectually respectable."[25] The "modern world-view" of "modern theoretical science" was "supposed to count against the traditional Christian world-view."[26] So he studied the history of the question and went from there. His goal was modest—"To try to make a contribution"—but the accomplishment speaks for itself. We find here similar encouragement to any Christian philosopher or apologist who does not despise the day of small things.

Second, there is great value for Christian apologetics in planning, dedication, and persistence. The trilogy and tetralogy did not arise haphazardly. They were planned. After one has been equipped with the tools of argument and the sweep of history in one's own discipline, it is time to think. What do you really want to accomplish? What areas do you want to engage? Which aspects of philosophy or science or history will support which lines of reasoning? What are the alleged intellectual barriers to your even attempting to succeed in defending

---

24. Swinburne, "Intellectual Autobiography," 1.
25. Ibid., 4.
26. Ibid.

the Christian faith? How will you address them? Why do unbelievers come to the conclusions they do? Is there something right in their views? If so, how can you capitalize on it? Are there fundamental ways they go wrong? If so, how can you show it? When should you redirect their assumptions, and when should you challenge those assumptions? Swinburne gave attention to all these questions and applied his answers to articulate a sweeping vision of how the Christian worldview can compete against the modern worldview.

Third, the order in which we address topics in Christian apologetics can be highly significant. It will do no good to argue that God exists if your interlocuter isn't even convinced that he *can* exist! (Thus, *The Coherence of Theism* chronologically precedes *The Existence of God*.) It will do no good to commend faith in a God whom the mind rejects as impossible or highly implausible. (Thus, *The Coherence of Theism* and *The Existence of God* chronologically precedes *Faith and Reason*.) It will do no good to argue that theism is coherent if clarity of language isn't to be had when speaking of transcendent matters. (Thus, "Part I Religious Language" precedes "Part II" and "Part III" in *The Coherence of Theism*.) Given that Swinburne pursued his "philosophy first, then theology" method throughout his works, examples here could be multiplied. But effective Christian apologetics involves working out some idea of which answers depend on *previous* answers. Don't treat unbelievers like a random jumble of laundry that needs to be put away, giving no thought as to the order in which you proceed.

Fourth, don't be afraid to chart new ways in learning from and building on the apologetic accomplishments of the past. By Swinburne's own admission, Aquinas's general approach to apologetic ministry in a medieval context exerted incalculable influence on Swinburne's approach to the modern context. Yet he is not slavishly dependent on the details of that tradition. In fact, it is somewhat startling to see the kind of philosophical eclecticism that emerges when one considers the "philosophy first" halves of the trilogy and tetralogy. No one philosopher, historical or contemporary, would subscribe to the *entire* package of philosophical views worked out by Swinburne (except for Swinburne!). At times it seems as if he picks and chooses which argument from which philosopher he likes the most. But there is no arbitrariness here; it depends on whether the argument is any good. *Any* argument in history from *any* philosopher is a possible contender for being incorporated into your own Christian defense (subject to canons of consistency, of course). And why not? Only the Scriptures are inspired and ultimately authoritative; every other source of insight is hit-and-miss. Working out a consistent approach in Christian apologetics might lead you to be *selective* in following any noncanonical thinker of the past. In doing so, these uninspired-but-useful thinkers find their proper place—neither above you nor below you but by your side.

Fifth, be prepared to accept and make your peace with the deeply integrated nature of Christian apologetics. It often seems that any one thing leads to everything else! This is unavoidable in philosophy, so take a deep breath and come to grips with this reality, making the best use of it that you can. I often speak to my students about how philosophy of religion seeks to make keen use of whatever discoveries are made in every *other* subdiscipline of philosophy. We float on the accomplishments of others. Christian apologetics is a Swiss Army knife with a diverse and balanced set of borrowed blades. Earlier we saw how in the trilogy and tetralogy the one topic of free will was thoroughly integrated with a whole host of other topics so that the arguments of seven different volumes mutually reinforced one another. Examples could be multiplied. In *The Coherence of Theism*, Swinburne offers an extended argument for the objectivity of ethics, against various sorts of subjectivist theories, so that later in the same book, he can characterize God as perfectly good and a source of moral obligation. But the argument for objective ethics is also used in *Responsibility and Atonement* when Christ's atonement is said to be relevant precisely because we have *real*, objective guilt before God. The argument is presupposed again in *Revelation* when Swinburne argues that we need divine revelation as a source of moral teaching and (later in the same book) when he clarifies the nature and scope of biblical moral teaching on a number of topics. Arguing for "the objectivity of ethics" is quite relevant for a wide range of apologetic arguments! Or again, the *Introduction to Confirmation Theory* was first put to good use in arguing for the probability of theism (in *The Existence of God*), then used to argue the probability of the Christian revelation (in *Revelation*), and finally used to argue the probability of the resurrection (in *The Resurrection of God Incarnate*). And even as the account of each person of the Trinity as equally divine (in *The Christian God*) presupposes the earlier definition of the attributes of divinity (in *The Coherence of Theism*), so also the account of Jesus as both God and man (in *The Christian God*) presupposes the earlier account of human personhood (in *The Evolution of the Soul*). Finally, fundamental principles of epistemic justification—of "simplicity," "credulity," and "testimony"—are deeply integrated throughout Swinburne's body of work, serving to anchor his religious justifications in a set of clear principles that readers can evaluate for themselves. This integrative nature of Christian apologetics, the mutual interdependence of sets of arguments, might seem like a time-waster, for these connections take time to learn! But in practical deployment, it can be a time-saver. Swinburne's footnotes are filled with the equivalent of: "As I have argued elsewhere . . ."

Sixth, be willing to revise your apologetic work when the balance of argument truly suggests it. Publication dates are always being updated for Swinburne's books.

728   CONTEMPORARY APOLOGISTS

Which version of *The Coherence of Theism* are we talking about? The original version of 1977, the revised edition of 1993, or the largely rewritten second edition of 2016? What about *The Existence of God*, written in 1979, revised in 1991, and given a largely rewritten second edition in 2004? *Faith and Reason* gets similar treatment, written in 1981 and largely rewritten for a second edition in 2005. Ditto for *The Evolution of the Soul* (original 1986, revised 1997) and *Revelation* (original 1991, second edition 2007). What is the example being set here? Decade after decade, Swinburne has been in continuous interaction with his detractors, seeking to address and overcome their criticisms. Typically, this takes place in the journals first, and then his monographs and their revisions draw on the fruits of those earlier labors. This breadth of interaction with your peers can keep you from succumbing to the deadly, paralyzing disease of intellectual isolation.

Seventh, be someone who can benefit people even if they disagree with you. I disagree with quite a few of Swinburne's theses. I accept divine timelessness (he does not). I doubt both the value and existence of libertarian free will (he does not). I accept God's foreknowledge of everything that takes place in the universe (he does not). I accept the moral argument for God's existence (he does not). I think the ontological argument for God's existence may have some value (he does not). I think the divine inscrutability approach to the problem of evil has some value (he does not). I think there are abstract objects such as propositions, properties, and possible worlds (he does not). Given all this, at times he must have wondered why I traveled 5,430 miles to write tutorial essays against him and then spar with him in his office, during my MPhil and DPhil in philosophical theology.[27] Well, to be honest, I wasn't aware of half of these differences at the time I boarded the plane. But more importantly, Swinburne is the kind of thinker who benefits you *in* your disagreements with him.

He writes in such a way that he provokes thoughtful questions from his readers, precisely because he takes the time to *argue* his position and is careful to do so with clarity, charity, and thoroughness. The people we are trying to reach for God, people made in his image, deserve at least that. I think this is just as much a part of Swinburne's legacy as anything else. Useful Christian apologetics is incompatible with two kinds of people: the fearful and the over-confident. The fearful are too afraid to lay their cards on the table, while the over-confident engage in sleight-of-hand to effect a quick outcome when no one is looking. Both approaches hide the truth, though for different reasons, and so neither approach really makes a case. But anxious secrecy and cynical manipulation have a habit of

---

27. Typically, in these sessions, I was the sniper in the tower utterly crushed by the shells of the methodically-advancing German tank.

disappointing people who are really interested in the truth. Make a case! Have faith that you can do it (point 1 above), plan to be persistent in doing it (point 2 above), think hard about how to do it (points 3–5 above), and then do your best, being open to correction by others (point 6 above). This is the kind of work that can do a lot of good. When I read Swinburne, I find myself asking things such as "What's so special about *my* alternative? Why is it better?" "Aren't my principles more contested than his, now that I think about it?" "Have I examined the history of thought on this topic?" I find that I want to do apologetics in such a way that my readers ask these same questions. In Christian apologetics we leave the results with God. But be an apologist who can still produce good results even if you don't gain immediate acceptance of your ideas.

CONCLUSION

I close with five of the most important theses that emerge from Swinburne's body of work, which he defends with great rigor. First, the classic doctrine of God as the all-knowing, all-powerful, perfectly good, personal Creator of all that exists can be stated in literal terms and defended as free from obvious incoherence.

Second, distinctive Christian doctrines, including the Trinity, the incarnation, the atonement, the resurrection, and Scripture as divine speech can have the clarity of their statement and the strength of their defense enhanced through conceptual distinctions afforded by the tools of modern analytic philosophy.

Third, traditional arguments for God's existence can be reformulated in probabilistic, inductive, "cumulative case" terms so as to present a powerful contemporary case for theism. Many of these arguments dodge traditional objections while appealing to well-confirmed advances in scientific knowledge.

Fourth, the evidential argument against God from evil is not as successful as it might initially seem, once we address it by way of theodicy.

Fifth, philosophical reflection on central religious claims, so important to philosophy of religion and philosophical theology, can make use of the best theories philosophy has to offer about language, logic, modality, metaphysics, epistemology, science, and ethics. The full range of tools and insights offered by these philosophical subdisciplines can effectively serve the Christian apologetic task.

In all these ways and more, Swinburne left the disciplines of philosophy of religion, Christian philosophical theology, and Christian apologetics far healthier than he found them.[28]

---

28. Some of the material in this chapter was adapted from an earlier essay of mine that had much broader scope, surveying the thought of Alvin Plantinga and Nicholas Wolterstorff in addition to that of Swinburne: "Forerunners to Contemporary Philosophical Theology," in Greg Ganssle and Ben Arbour, eds., *Christian*

BIBLIOGRAPHY

Alston, William. "Are Positivists Metaphysicians?" *Philosophical Review* 63 (1954): 42–57.
———. *Philosophy of Language.* Englewood Cliffs, NJ: Prentice-Hall, 1964.
———. "Religious Language and Verificationism." Pages 17–34 in *The Rationality of Theism.* Ed. by Paul Copan and Paul Moser. New York: Routledge, 2003.
Ayer, A. J. *Language, Truth, and Logic.* London: Gollancz, 1936.
Carnap, Rudolph. *Philosophy and Logical Syntax (Psyche Miniatures General Series, No. 70).* London: Paul, Trench, Trubner & Co., Ltd., 1937.
Flew, Antony, R. M. Hare, and Basil Mitchell. "Theology and Falsification: A Symposium" (1950). Repr. in pages 13–22 of *The Philosophy of Religion.* Ed. by Basil Mitchell. Oxford: Oxford University Press, 1971.
Hempel, Carl. "Problems and Changes in the Empiricist Criterion of Meaning." *Revue Internationale de Philosophie* Vol. 4.11 (January 1950): 41–63.
Mitchell, Basil, ed. *The Justification of Religious Belief.* Oxford: Oxford University Press, 1981.
———. *The Philosophy of Religion.* Oxford: Oxford University Press, 1971.
Plantinga, Alvin. *God and Other Minds: A Study of the Rational Justification of Belief in God.* Ithaca, NY: Cornell University Press, 1967.
Purdue University. "Faith and Reason: Themes from Swinburne." Conference held on September 25–27, 2014. https://www.conf.purdue.edu/landing_pages/swinburne/.
Quine, Willard Van Orman. "Two Dogmas of Empiricism." *The Philosophical Review* 60 (1951): 20–43.
Shoemaker, Sydney, and Richard Swinburne. *Personal Identity.* Oxford: Blackwell, 1984.
Swinburne, Richard. *Are We Bodies or Souls?* Oxford: Oxford University Press, 2019.
———. "The Argument from Design." *Philosophy.* Vol. 43, no. 165 (July 1968): 199–212.
———. *The Christian God.* Oxford: Oxford University Press, 1994.
———. *The Coherence of Theism.* Oxford: Oxford University Press, 1977.
———. *The Coherence of Theism (rev. ed.).* Oxford: Oxford University Press, 1993.
———. *The Coherence of Theism (2nd ed).* Oxford: Oxford University Press, 2016.
———. *The Concept of Miracle (New Studies in the Philosophy of Religion).* London: Macmillan, 1970.
———. "Confirmability and Factual Meaningfulness." *Analysis* Vol. 33, issue 3 (January 1973): 71–76.
———. *Epistemic Justification.* Oxford: Oxford University Press, 2001.
———. *The Evolution of the Soul.* Oxford: Oxford University Press, 1986.
———. *The Evolution of the Soul (rev. ed.).* Oxford: Oxford University Press, 1997.
———. *The Existence of God.* Oxford: Oxford University Press, 1979.
———. *The Existence of God (rev. ed.).* Oxford: Oxford University Press, 1991.
———. *The Existence of God (2nd ed.).* Oxford: Oxford University Press, 2004.
———. *Faith and Reason.* Oxford: Oxford University Press, 1981.
———. *Faith and Reason (2nd ed.).* Oxford: Oxford University Press, 2005.
———. "Intellectual Autobiography." Pages 1–18 in *Reason and the Christian Religion: Essays in Honour of Richard Swinburne.* Ed. by Alan Padgett. Oxford: Clarendon, 1994.
———. *An Introduction to Confirmation Theory.* London: Methuen, 1973.
———. *Is There a God?* Oxford: Oxford University Press, 1996.
———. *Mind, Brain, and Free Will.* Oxford: Oxford University Press, 2013.
———. *Providence and the Problem of Evil.* Oxford: Oxford University Press, 1998.
———. *Responsibility and Atonement.* Oxford: Oxford University Press, 1989.
———. *The Resurrection of God Incarnate.* Oxford: Oxford University Press, 2003.
———. *Revelation.* Oxford: Oxford University Press, 1991.
———. *Revelation (2nd ed.).* Oxford: Oxford University Press, 2007.
———. "Short intellectual autobiography" (undated) http://users.ox.ac.uk/~orie0087/.
———. *Simplicity as Evidence of Truth.* Milwaukee: Marquette University Press, 1997.
———. *Space and Time.* London: Macmillan, 1968.
———. *Was Jesus God?* Oxford: Oxford University Press, 2008.
Welty, Greg. "Forerunners to Contemporary Philosophical Theology." In *Christian Theology and the Modern Philosophers.* Ed. by Greg Ganssle and Ben Arbour. Grand Rapids: Zondervan Academic, forthcoming.
———. "Review of *Reason and Faith: Themes from Richard Swinburne.* Michael Bergmann and Jeffrey E. Brower, eds. New York: Oxford University Press, 2016." *Themelios.* Vol. 41, Issue 2 (August 2016). http://themelios.thegospelcoalition.org/review/reason-and-faith-themes-from-richard-swinburne.
Wolterstorff, Nicholas. *Reason within the Bounds of Religion.* 2nd ed. Grand Rapids: Eerdmans, 1984).

Theology and the Modern Philosophers (Zondervan Academic, forthcoming). Focusing on Swinburne alone in this chapter allowed me to expand that earlier material.

RAVI ZACHARIAS

Evangelist as Apologist

JO VITALE
VINCE VITALE

Considering both his origins and the trajectory of his life, Ravi Zacharias (1946–) was truly born "for such a time as this" (Est 4:14). Growing up in Delhi, India, Zacharias was influenced by a plurality of religious traditions, which uniquely prepared him for the twentieth-century challenges of postmodernism. Likewise, his personal wrestling with questions of meaning and subsequent conversion as a teenager on a "bed of suicide" readied him to respond to the angst of existentialism. Raised in the storytelling East and trained in the philosophy of the West, the convergence of an eastern methodology with a western mind has enabled Zacharias to connect with audiences that span the globe and to bridge the distance between the head and the heart of his hearers. At a time when apologetics was considered a discipline for the academic and the evangelical church was losing its intellectual edge, Zacharias effectively combined apologetics and evangelism in a manner that continues to inspire the Christian and appeal to the skeptic. This culturally-rich combination of evangelism and apologetics has resulted in Zacharias becoming one of the foremost evangelistic apologists of the last century.

HISTORICAL BACKGROUND

On March 26, 1946, Frederick Antony Ravi Kumar Zacharias was born in the city of Madras (now Chennai), in the state of Tamil Nadu, South India. Ravi Zacharias was the third of five children born to Isabella and Oscar Zacharias, although Oscar, studying overseas, did not meet him until he was eight months old, a distance that contributed to the strained relationship between father and son.[1]

---

1. Ravi Zacharias and R. S. B. Sawyer, *Walking from East to West: God in the Shadows* (Grand Rapids: Zondervan, 2006), 39.

While Isabella's family hailed from Chennai, Oscar's side traced their roots to Kerala. Zacharias's grandfather Oliver, who worked at Madras Christian College, was the first Indian appointed by the British as an English professor. Despite these Southern roots, when Zacharias was a young child, his family relocated to Delhi for his father's promotion within the Indian government. This promotion was the first of several, eventually leading to Oscar's role as deputy secretary of India's Home Ministry (the equivalent of the US State Department).

A child of the South in name, coloring, and history, raised in the customs and languages of the North, Zacharias keenly felt this cultural dialectic, in which "[r]eligion, language, and ancestral indebtedness are carved into the consciousness of every child of the East."[2] Despite their move from a one-bedroom home in Chennai to a two-bedroom home in Delhi, the poverty and suffering that Zacharias saw on a daily basis had a lifelong impact on him. He has described the gap between the prosperous and the impoverished, saying, "India is a nation of polarities of incredible proportions . . . the raw reality of life stares you in the face."[3]

As for religion, although Zacharias's ancestors were Nambudiris—the highest caste of the Hindu priesthood—his family broke away from that lineage when Zacharias's paternal great-great-great-grandmother was converted to Christianity by German-Swiss missionaries. But by the time Zacharias was born, the family's faith had diluted to a form of nominal Anglicanism, putting them in the minority in the North, where the religious landscape is predominantly Hindu and Muslim. From the first time he saw a man lie down on his side to roll down a dirty street yelling out to God, Zacharias came to wonder whether religion was all "just superstition born out of fear, dressed up into a system, and embedded into a culture."[4]

As for "western" religion, as a child Zacharias found it equally incomprehensible. Despite the family's nominal Anglican faith, the only lasting impression that church attendance had on Zacharias was his memory of the priest yelling at him for eating communion wafers, which he had mistaken for biscuits. Likewise, despite being taught by Jehovah's Witnesses who visited his home for a year and a half, Zacharias ultimately concluded that a faith that offered paradise to only 144,000 people held no hope for him. The one notable exception from Zacharias's childhood was when his brother Ramesh recovered from a life-threatening bout of pneumonia and typhoid after a Pentecostal missionary, Mr. Dennis, interceded with the family before a picture of Jesus. Although that

2. Ibid., 36.
3. Ibid., 20–21.
4. Ibid., 23.

incident impacted Zacharias, it wasn't until several years later, at the age of fifteen, that he seriously began seeking for meaning. His questioning was instigated by an increasing sense of such purposelessness. He remarks, "There were nights I lay in bed wondering if I was going to make it."[5] The search became more urgent after a friend died, and when Zacharias asked the Hindu priest scattering her ashes, "Where is she now?," the priest responded, "Young man, that is a question you'll be asking all your life. And you will never find an answer."[6]

Zacharias discovered his first glimmer of an answer a year later when his sister became a Christian through the witness of Youth for Christ (YFC) and invited him to their rally. The second time Zacharias attended, although unclear on the message, he found himself drawn to the sincerity of the speaker, Sam Wolgemuth. At the end of that meeting, Zacharias walked forward to receive prayer. But while a seed had been planted, it was not enough to overcome Zacharias's escalating sense of despair. Although excelling at sports, Zacharias struggled to succeed academically. This displeased his father, who called him a "complete failure"[7] and violently berated Zacharias over his academic performance: "His fears of my failure and my fear of him met in some very painful memories."[8] This tension came to a head upon his father's discovery of Zacharias's repeated absences from his premed degree at the University of Delhi, when Oscar beat Zacharias until his mother intervened. Summarizing his feeling of hopelessness at that time, Zacharias writes, "If you have the idea that life is something random; that there is no point to it, no purpose; that you just happen to be here—in existential terms, that you are a useless being floating on a sea of nothing for whom in the end it all comes to nothing—then the idea of becoming *nothing* can seem better than that random *something*."[9]

To spare his family further shame, and himself further failure, Zacharias determined to take his life by swallowing poison that he had stolen from the university's chemistry laboratory. The chemicals were so toxic that Zacharias instinctively began throwing up. A house-servant overheard his cries for help and got him to Wellington Hospital. Unsure what the long-term damage from his suicide attempt might be, Zacharias was in the hospital with his mother for four days when Fred David, a director of YFC, brought a Bible with a verse highlighted for Zacharias's mother to read to him. Given that Zacharias's parents had kept the reason that he was in hospital a secret, Zacharias was shocked to hear his

5. Ibid., 71.
6. Ibid., 84.
7. Ibid., 82.
8. Ibid., 39.
9. Zacharias, *Walking from East To West*, 101.

mother read the verse David had chosen—words spoken to the apostle Thomas by Jesus: "Because I live, you also will live" (John 14:19).

Those seven words impacted Zacharias so profoundly that they became to him "the defining paradigm" for his life.[10] On that day he made a promise to God: "I will leave no stone unturned in my pursuit of truth."[11] In that moment, Zacharias experienced a renewed hope that drastically changed the course of his life.[12] From then on, YFC became very significant for Zacharias. Under their discipleship, Zacharias found his lackluster scholarship transformed into a passion for reading Christian literature, from the works of missionaries to Bible expositors to his first encounters with Christian apologetics through C. S. Lewis and the British journalist Malcolm Muggeridge. At the same time, Zacharias transferred to the Institute of Hotel Management in Delhi and excelled there. Zacharias explains this newfound dedication as the outcome of seeing life "through a window of meaning. . . . Jesus wasn't just the best option to me; He was the *only* option. He provided the skin of reason to the flesh and bones of reality. His answers to life's questions were both unique and true."[13]

YFC was also Zacharias's doorway into evangelism, particularly when at the age of nineteen he won the preaching prize at the 1965 YFC Youth Congress in Hyderabad. That same year, Zacharias and four others established a YFC teen preaching team and travelled from Delhi to Calcutta, Hyderabad, and Madras (Chennai) to share the gospel. During those ten days, Zacharias preached twenty-nine times, and to his astonishment they saw hundreds give their lives to Christ. Summing up those first experiences of evangelism, Zacharias notes, "I wasn't sure of myself, but I was very sure of my message."[14] Observing the rapidly escalating impact that Zacharias was having as an evangelist, John Teibe, YFC director of Asia, cautioned Zacharias, "You will either make a very profound impact with your life and God will use you mightily, or you will be a colossal wreck."[15]

In May 1966, Zacharias and his brother Ajit were sent to Toronto, Canada, to prepare the way for the remainder of the family to relocate. Arriving with fifty dollars in cash, Zacharias found work as the assistant to the banquet manager at the Westbury Hotel in downtown Toronto, and he began worshipping at the Yonge Street Alliance Tabernacle. It was at a Christian and Missionary Alliance (C&MA) youth symposium that Zacharias met Margie Reynolds, although on

---

10. Ibid., 105.
11. Ibid.
12. Ibid., 107.
13. Ibid., 118, 120.
14. Ibid., 133.
15. Margie Zacharias, personal interview by author, Alpharetta, GA, January 29, 2019. Zacharias, *Walking from East To West*, 134.

account of her family's initial resistance to the relationship, they did not date until two years later.

Forming another youth preaching team, Zacharias continued evangelizing across southern Ontario, as well as studying part time at Toronto Baptist Seminary. Eventually Zacharias moved into full-time theological study, beginning at Ontario Bible College in 1968. Although Zacharias's father initially struggled with this decision, not long after that, he also gave his life to Christ. While at theological college, Zacharias was approached by Ruth Jeffrey, a retired missionary, who arranged for him to go preach to the US troops fighting in Vietnam.

In May 1971 Zacharias landed in Saigon at the height of the Vietnam War and proceeded to travel across the country on the back of a motorcycle for three months through some of the most deadly warzones to preach the gospel to troops at military bases, the wounded in hospitals, the Vietcong in prisons, and to pastors and missionaries. For Zacharias, it was a disorientating experience of preaching to so many soldiers who were about to die and yet at the same time seeing the life-giving power of the gospel. Although "intensely aware I was unfit to be there,"[16] throughout those harrowing months, Zacharias and his translator Hien saw over three thousand people become Christians.[17] The impact of that experience on Zacharias is highlighted by the fervency of his tone in this 1971 article: "The need of the hour is an unleashing to God's demands in total commitment—the need for a hunger and thirst after Him—the disciplined prayer life—the willingness to bet their lives that Christ *is*—the call to give into His hands every area of their lives. This is what I shared with the youth as I traveled throughout South Vietnam. I found hungry hearts."[18]

This trip was definitive for Zacharias in confirming his calling: "I am an evangelist. I am called to do this—to be in places at risk, places where people are willing to hear."[19]

In April 1972, after graduating and getting married, Zacharias was invited by Reverend William B. Newell to be a district evangelist for the C&MA.[20] Soon after, Zacharias began studying for an MDiv at Trinity Evangelical Divinity School (TEDS), where he was most influenced by his mentors in philosophy and apologetics, John Warwick Montgomery and Norman Geisler.

16. Zacharias, *Walking from East To West*, 167.
17. Charlotte Stemple, *My Vietnam: Stories of the War Years from the Inside Out* (Maitland, FL: Xulon, 2010), 188, 192. For the remarkable testimony of Ravi's translator, Hien, during the Vietnam war years, see Ibid., 188–95.
18. Ravi Zacharias, "God's Justice Demands Total Commitment," *Vietnam Today: News Magazine of the Vietnam Field, Christian and Missionary Alliance* 10 (Winter 1971): 1.
19. Zacharias, *Walking from East to West*, 169.
20. Reverend William B. Newell was district superintendent of the Eastern and Central Canadian District of the C&MA.

Reflecting on Geisler, Zacharias notes that he "inspired me with the confidence to walk into any lions' den and believe I would come away victorious for the gospel. His best gift to me was his twin loves, the Bible and philosophy."[21] Zacharias's time at TEDS also overlapped with William Lane Craig, who lived just two doors down in the same block of student housing.

From his second year of study onwards, Zacharias spent most weekends preaching evangelistically. During the summer of 1974, he was invited on his second extended overseas trip for the C&MA—this time to Cambodia, where the team again saw many give their lives to Christ. That same summer, Zacharias's relationship with his father was also greatly restored after Oscar handed him a letter apologizing for the way he had treated him during his youth.

In 1977 Zacharias embarked on a forty-eight-week preaching tour around the world after graduating from TEDS, this time with Margie and his young daughter Sarah. In total, Zacharias preached 576 times on a trip that began in the UK and ended in Hong Kong. Despite being one of the most challenging years of their lives, [22] this trip confirmed Zacharias's calling as an evangelist to the nations.

After two years serving as their national evangelist in Canada, in 1980 Zacharias was ordained into the C&MA and reluctantly accepted a teaching post at the Alliance Theological Seminary in Nyack, New York. This took place at the behest of Dr. L. L. King, who forcefully told Zacharias that "the call of the church is the call of the Lord, and we as a church are calling you."[23] Overburdened with seminary classes while still preaching evangelistically on the weekends, Zacharias and his family describe that as one of the hardest seasons of their life.[24] In 1983 Zacharias was invited by Billy Graham to speak at a historic gathering of four thousand worldwide evangelists in Amsterdam. Not only did Zacharias's sermon "The Lostness of Man" leave a marked impression on his hearers, but the event proved to be catalytic for Zacharias as well.

Upon returning home, Zacharias was convinced that he needed to be in full-time evangelistic ministry and with great relief gave a year's notice for his teaching role at Nyack. At the same time, determining that it would take around $50,000 to launch an evangelistic ministry tailored toward the thinking skeptic, the Zachariases committed to tell no one about their desire to start a ministry, nor about the financial need, but instead to pray.[25] To their astonishment, a few months

---

21. Zacharias, *Walking from East to West*, 175.
22. Margie Zacharias, personal interview.
23. Ibid.
24. Ibid. Zacharias, *Walking from East to West*, 188.
25. Ibid., 196.

later at a conference, Zacharias was approached by a stranger named D. D. Davis, who shared that God had laid it on his heart to give Zacharias a gift of $50,000 for whatever purpose God was calling him to. Initially responding that he was uncomfortable taking such a large sum of money from a stranger, Zacharias suggested that they meet to discuss the vision before Davis decided whether to offer financial backing. Upon confirmation of Davis's support, Zacharias asked what he would like in return, to which Davis responded, "All I want is your integrity."[26] With the assistance of D. D. Davis and other ministry partners, in August 1984 Ravi Zacharias International Ministries (RZIM) was established.

THEOLOGICAL CONTEXT

Zacharias's theological framework was forged during an era in which truth was highly disputed both within the church and within the culture at large. As an evangelical seminarian during the 1960s and 1970s, Zacharias was strongly informed by what he describes as "the big break" taking place between liberal and conservative theology.[27] On the one hand, many in the mainline churches had shifted from the liberal Protestantism of the nineteenth century to the neoorthodoxy of Karl Barth and Reinhold Neibuhr.[28]

In conservative circles, on the other hand, a reactionary anti-intellectualism had become pervasive within evangelicalism. As Harry Blamires accurately predicted in 1963, "The bland assumption that the Church's life will continue to be fruitful so long as we go on praying and cultivating our souls, irrespective of whether we trouble to think and talk Christianly, and therefore theologically . . . may turn out to have dire results."[29] Reflecting on his student years in the early 1970s, Zacharias comments that "those were the days in which the evangelical church lost the universities."[30]

In place of critical thinking, there was a strong shift within evangelicalism toward the experiential. In Canada, Zacharias's own denomination was impacted by the 1971 revival led by the Sutera twins. Beginning in Saskatoon, Saskatchewan, it spread into Western Canada (including Ontario Bible College) and the northwestern United States.[31] As part of that revival, students began

26. Ibid., 217.

27. Ravi Zacharias, personal interview by author, Alpharetta, GA, June 5, 2019.

28. Reinhold Neibuhr, *The Nature and Destiny of Man: A Christian Interpretation* (New York: Scribner's Sons, 1941).

29. Harry Blamires, *The Christian Mind: How Should a Christian Think?* (Ann Arbor, MI: Servant, 1963), 77. See also Mark Noll, *The Scandal of the Evangelical Mind* (Grand Rapids: Eerdmans, 1994).

30. Ravi Zacharias, personal interview.

31. Ralph Sutera, "The Canadian Revival and Concepts of Revival," *Sermon Index*, February 2, 2008, https://www.img.sermonindex.net/modules/newbb/viewtopic_pdf.php?topic_id=22390&forum=40.

walking up to the microphone in church meetings and publicly repenting. While the spiritual renewal was genuine, what concerned Zacharias and some of his peers was that such confessions were required from their fellow seminarians in the first place, rather than keeping short accounts with God.[32]

Consequently, Zacharias felt caught in a tension between the assault of the mainline churches whom he saw as "hitting hard at the roots of our belief" and the evangelical churches who were abandoning their intellectual heritage to get "swept into some mode of the expressions."[33]

This struggle for theological truth and intellectual rigor within the church was compounded by the wave of postmodernism that arose in the West during that same era and which seeped into every facet of culture, from philosophy to the arts, through the latter part of the twentieth century. To Zacharias, whose homeland of India is a seedbed of religious diversity, postmodernism was hardly a new threat: "I came amid the thunderous cries of a culture that has 330 million deities. I remain with [Jesus] knowing that truth cannot be all-inclusive."[34] What concerned Zacharias was how the church, already caught in a "whirlwind of confusing signals, theologically and spiritually," would cope with the surge of relativism and pluralism.[35]

Zacharias's unease was only heightened by the state of evangelism at that time. Televangelism was a new phenomenon, with the *Jimmy Swaggart Telecast* launching in 1971 and *The PTL Club* with Jim and Tammy Bakker in 1974. To Zacharias, this form of evangelism seemed insufficient for combatting the tide of skepticism, disillusionment, and antiauthoritarianism that shaped US society in the 1970s.[36]

The turning point for Zacharias came at Billy Graham's International Conference for Itinerant Evangelists in Amsterdam, 1983. While speaking on "The Lostness of Man," Zacharias referenced Meursault, a character from Albert Camus's *L'Étranger* who, facing execution, informs the chaplain that although he does now know whether God exists, Meursault is indifferent to the question.[37] What disturbed Zacharias upon returning home from Amsterdam was the ques-

---

32. Ravi Zacharias, personal interview.

33. Ibid. Os Guinness was another author writing around that time who commented on the abandonment of the intellect for experience in the evangelical church (Os Guinness, *Fit Bodies, Fat Minds: Why Evangelicals Don't Think and What to Do About It* [Vancouver, BC: Hourglass, 1994]).

34. Ravi Zacharias, *Jesus Among Other Gods: The Absolute Claims of the Christian Message* (Nashville: W Publishing, 2000), 12.

35. Ravi Zacharias, personal interview.

36. Among other concerns, these cultural trends were brought on largely by the sexual revolution (1960s), US involvement in the war in Vietnam (1968–73), and the political tumult of the Watergate scandal (1972).

37. Albert Camus, *L'Étranger* (Paris: Éditions Gallimard,1942). Ravi Zacharias, *The Lostness of Man*, (Lecture at the International Evangelists Conference, Amsterdam, 1983).

tion of who was going to reach those, like Meursault, with a skeptical disposition of heart. Given that Zacharias had been asked to address his fellow evangelists at the conference as though he were preaching to twelve-year-olds,[38] the experience left him concerned that the church was ill-equipped to engage with the prevailing intellectual skepticism and spiritual apathy of the West. He noted that there were not many evangelists "who had the training or access to reach those opinion makers of society. The combination of a proclaimer and apologist was very rare, especially the cultural evangelist-apologist. . . . They weren't reaching upward."[39]

Therefore, motivated by what Zacharias perceived to be the inadequacies in contemporary evangelism to engage the cultural influencers of the day, RZIM was founded with a specific intent to reach, with the gospel, the "intellectuals, opinion-makers, and 'the happy pagan'" . . . a ministry that would communicate the gospel effectively within the context of the prevailing skepticism. It would seek to reach the thinker and to clear all obstacles in his path so that he or she could see the cross, clearly and unhindered."[40]

APOLOGETIC RESPONSE AND METHODOLOGY

THE APOLOGIST-EVANGELIST

To understand Ravi Zacharias the apologist, one must first understand him as Ravi Zacharias the evangelist. To Zacharias, the call of the evangelist is the primary task that God set before him since his earliest days in the faith. In seeking to reach the intellectual, however, Zacharias perceived the importance of apologetics in undergirding a more traditional form of proclamation evangelism. Noting the demand for a thoughtful apologetic in today's culture, Zacharias observes that "between intellectual attacks that pummel the mind and arts that provide immeasurable allurements, the idea of God in a pleasure-mad society is a hindrance."[41] Apologetics, as Zacharias envisions it, is an essential tool for overcoming that hindrance, "clearing the obstacles in someone's spiritual journey" in order that they might see Christ.[42] In order of priority, however, it is always the apologetic that serves the evangelism: "Apologetics is the seasoning, evangelism is the meal."[43]

When we situate the role of apologetics within Zacharias's broader evangelistic framework, it is clear how his methodology has been shaped around that

---

38. Margie Zacharias, personal interview.
39. Zacharias, *Walking from East to West*, 195.
40. Ibid., 198.
41. David Goetz, "Reaching the Happy Thinking Pagan," *The Leadership Journal* (*Christianity Today*, Spring 1995). https://www.christianitytoday.com/pastors/1995/spring/5l218.html.
42. Ravi Zacharias, *Beyond Opinion* (Nashville: Nelson, 2008), xvii.
43. Ravi Zacharias, personal interview.

singular purpose. In many ways, Zacharias has been richly influenced by those who have gone before him. For example, he admires Norman Geisler for exemplifying the best of classical apologetics, he credits C. S. Lewis for his ability to appeal to the "moral imagination," and he lauds the "prophetic" ability of Francis Schaeffer, as a cultural apologist, to foresee the trajectory of Western society.[44] But unlike these individuals, Zacharias resists categorization within one particular discipline of apologetics. Zacharias was intentional about developing his apologetic in that way because he believed that, for the evangelist, each apologetic tradition has a particular purpose and usefulness.

To demonstrate this point, Zacharias highlights the shifts in worldviews down through the centuries from the rationalism of the 1500s and 1600s, to the empiricism of the 1700s and 1800s, to the existentialism of the 1900s, and on to the postmodernism of the late twentieth century. Zacharias contends that for each philosophical predisposition, a different apologetic will have greater or less persuasive power. This holds true not only for the dominant worldview of a culture but also for that of an individual. For the apologist-evangelist, Zacharias argues that "apologetics is not to be a single-lane approach. Rather, just as a human being is a composite, so also should the approach be to that person."[45]

Just as Zacharias's evangelistic focus carved out a unique position for him among apologists, so too did his apologetic bent distinguish Zacharias among evangelists. Reflecting on his early days as an apologist-evangelist, Zacharias comments that he found himself "trying to break free from the straightjacketed approach to evangelistic preaching."[46] For example, Zacharias's yearning to bolster his preaching with deeper theological training concerned Dr. L. L. King, president of the C&MA, who cautioned him before he left to study for his MDiv at TEDS, "I am afraid you will lose your keen edge."[47] This theme continued in those early years, as there seemed to be an unspoken consensus that apologetics ought to be relegated to academic institutions rather than proclaimed from the pulpit.

In particular, Ravi recalls preaching at a church in Toronto during the early 1980s when a gentleman who disapproved of his apologetic content approached him afterward with the rebuke: "You're speaking to an audience that's not there."[48] Other times, criticism came in the form of disagreement over meth-

---

44. Zacharias, *Beyond Opinion*, 333. Ravi has also emphasized time and again what an enormous debt of gratitude he owes to G. K. Chesterton, Malcolm Muggeridge, and Fyodor Dostoevsky for influencing his thinking as a young man while he grappled with questions pertaining to the state of society and the purpose of the individual within it.
    45. Zacharias, *Beyond Opinion*, 333.
    46. Ravi Zacharias, personal interview.
    47. Ibid.
    48. Ibid.

odology, especially concerning Zacharias's use of academic terminology in his discourse. In response, Zacharias asserts that rather than preaching to the lowest common denominator, if you want to help people to grow in the knowledge of faith, "you don't just place things on the lowest shelf; you place them where people have to stand on their toes to reach for them, and they grow in the process."[49]

What motivated Zacharias during those early days was the experience of individuals approaching him with sincere gratitude that somebody at last dared to address the kind of intellectual doubts that they had secretly struggled with. Gradually, the invitations to speak began pouring in as Christians increasingly came to see the significance of partnering evangelism with apologetics, particularly in light of the impact that the liberal scholarship was having on the next generations of students.

This is by no means to imply that Zacharias was the first to utilize apologetics as a tool for evangelism. Two of his predecessors who were doing just that were Josh McDowell in the US and Michael Green in the UK, both of whose works Zacharias recalls reading as a young man and reflecting, "This is what I want to do."[50] But in terms of methodology, there were several distinctions between those already serving as apologist-evangelists, and Zacharias's own cross-cultural approach.

A CONVERGENCE OF CULTURES

The influence of Zacharias's eastern upbringing on his apologetic method cannot be overstated. As Zacharias himself has reflected, "There is no doubt that God prepared me for this life I now lead, connecting the varied and ironic threads of my experience into a beautiful tapestry as He would see fit."[51]

One of the primary areas in which we can see the eastern mindset at work is in Zacharias's use of storytelling both as an *external* bridge between the apologist and his audience and as a means of *internally* bridging the head and the heart of the listener. Zacharias often credits his frequent use of story to the impact of the writers that he was reading during his early years of ministry, in particular G. K. Chesterton, Malcolm Muggeridge, the Baptist preacher F. W. Boreham, and the novelist Fyodor Dostoevsky.

But long before that, Zacharias was captivated by the "wonder" of eastern mythologies at a young age,[52] and it was his culture's unique emphasis on folk-

---

49. Ibid.
50. In particular, Zacharias points to the influence of the following books: Josh McDowell, *Evidence that Demands a Verdict* (USA: Campus Crusade for Christ International, 1972); Michael Green, *Jesus Spells Freedom* (Downers Grove, IL: InterVarsity Press, 1972); Michael Green, *Man Alive!* (Downers Grove, IL: InterVarsity Press, 1967); Michael Green, *Runaway World* (Downers Grove, IL: InterVarsity Press, 1969).
51. Zacharias, *Walking from East to West*, 20.
52. Ibid., 23.

tales and conveying deep spiritual truths through stories—a practice that he saw paralleled in the parables of Jesus—that ultimately shaped the way Zacharias articulated the Christian faith. As an easterner, Zacharias grasped the significance of using story to stretch his hearer's thinking "in unexpected ways," by combining both argument and story to "take them in a radius of directions, like the spokes of a wheel. This is an easterner's natural way of thinking, while the typical westerner's way is more linear."[53]

Even more than a methodological device, storytelling, from Zacharias's perspective, is not just a means of delivery but the message itself, not simply a methodology but the very content of the apologetic. As Zacharias explains, "You see, the gospel is a story, a story that needs to be argued."[54] Zacharias's storytelling connects with the human longing to find a place in the unfolding narrative of reality, a longing that is typically overlooked in a postmodern era in which metanarrative is dismissed. This longing also accounts for the evangelistic effectiveness of Zacharias's presentation of four framing categories of worldview: origin, meaning, morality, and destiny.[55] Rather than offering a single "knock-down" argument, Zacharias instead sets forth an overarching apologetic framework—an ultimate story—in which to situate the whole of one's life.

Conversely, while Zacharias's use of storytelling has made a tremendous impact in the "linear" West, [56] his western philosophical outlook has likewise yielded fruit in the storytelling East. This has proven particularly useful when refuting a relativistic approach to truth, as Zacharias cuts against the grain of Eastern thought by applying the law of noncontradiction to demonstrate the exclusive nature of truth. This effective convergence of Western philosophical thinking and Eastern storytelling is evident in the following illustration, which Zacharias shared with a Hindu professor at a university in California: "I've got some shocking news for you, even in India you look both ways before you cross the street. It is either the bus or me, not both of us."[57]

REACHING THE INFLUENCER

While Zacharias's call as a cross-cultural apologist-evangelist is unusual, his methodology has also been unique on account of his deliberate focus on specific spheres of cultural influence—the marketplace, the political arena, the academy,

---

53. Ravi Zacharias, personal interview. Zacharias, *Walking from East to West*, 204.
54. Zacharias, *Beyond Opinion*, xvii.
55. For more on this, see the discussion on Zacharias's *3.4.5 Grid* (Lecture for the RZIM Online Academy) and Ravi Zacharias, *A Shattered Visage: The Real Face of Atheism* (Grand Rapids: Baker, 1993).
56. Ravi Zacharias, personal interview. Zacharias, *Walking from East to West*, 204.
57. Ravi Zacharias, *The Basis of Truth* (Lecture at The University of Utah, November 2004).

and the arts.[58] In directing his apologetic primarily at culture-shapers, Zacharias's vision is twofold: to reach the "happy pagan"—typically overlooked by mainstream evangelistic ministry—and to see those strategically placed individuals in turn leverage their influence to reach the broader culture for Christ.

This strategic approach has proven far more effective than Zacharias could ever have anticipated. Globally, Zacharias began receiving invitations from across the world after Billy Graham's invitation to share at Amsterdam '83. For instance, in 1989, not long after the fall of the Berlin Wall, Zacharias was invited to Russia to speak at both the Lenin Military Academy and the Center for Geopolitical Strategy. From that point on, Zacharias reflects that "God had begun to set a table for me to address the political world."[59] As for the academy, the event that opened the door wide into that arena was the first Veritas Forum at Harvard in 1993, during which Zacharias presented on the topics "Is Atheism Dead?" and "Is God Alive?"[60] Veritas '93 catalyzed Zacharias's ministry to college campuses, and to this day he regularly addresses audiences of thousands on university campuses.

Although Zacharias has at times been met with hostility by skeptical college students, [61] perhaps more surprising are the occasions when hostility has come from the church, as in 2004 when Zacharias preached at the Mormon Tabernacle on "Who Is the Truth? Defending Jesus Christ as The Way, The Truth and The Life."[62] Before then, the last evangelical invited to speak there had been D. L. Moody in 1899. Aware of the possible controversy in accepting the invitation, Ravi spoke with Chuck Colson, who encouraged him to accept even as he warned him, "Keep the shutters closed; it's going to be a cold winter!"[63] Zacharias's willingness to accept the invitation, despite the backlash, evidences his commitment to building bridges for the gospel rather than burning them.[64] As Zacharias explained while preaching at the Mormon Tabernacle, "We find a common ground on which to meet and talk, because conviction that is not undergirded by love makes the possessor of that conviction obnoxious."[65]

---

58. Zacharias, *Walking from East to West*, 198.

59. Ibid., 203.

60. It was Chuck Colson who encouraged Zacharias to use those talks to form the basis of his second book, *Can Man Live Without God?* (Nashville: W Publishing, 1994).

61. Jessica Washington, "Controversial Evangelist Zacharias Speaks at Penn," *The Daily Pennsylvanian*, February 11, 2014, https://www.thedp.com/article/2014/02/ravi-zacharias.

62. Ted Olson, "Ravi Zacharias to Speak at Mormon Tabernacle," *Christianity Today Magazine*, September 1, 2004, 04. https://www.christianitytoday.com/ct/2004/septemberweb-only/9-13-51.0.html.

63. Margie Zacharias, personal interview.

64. For a full statement from Ravi in defense of his decision, see Pauline J. Chang, "Evangelical Defends Decision to Speak at Mormon Tabernacle," *The Christian Post*, December 28, 2004, https://www.christianpost.com/news/evangelical-defends-decision-to-speak-at-mormon-tabernacle.html.

65. Ravi Zacharias, "Who is the Truth? Defending Jesus Christ as the Way, the Truth, and the Life" (Lecture at the Mormon Tabernacle, November 14, 2004).

THE 3.4.5 GRID

While Zacharias's decision to prioritize opinion-makers and skeptics proved to be an effective approach, the question remains as to *why* he has been given such a wide hearing both internationally and in secular arenas, where evangelists are not typically welcome. In short, the willingness of the listener to hear from Zacharias has largely been a result of both the *methodology* and the *manner* in which he has spoken.

Regarding the former, Zacharias emphasizes that before engaging an audience or an individual with the gospel, you first have to understand their worldview. To this end, Zacharias has created a methodological framework that he calls the 3.4.5 Grid.[66]

As a basic premise, Zacharias asserts that for any worldview to be credible, it must first measure up to *Two Theories of Truth*: the *Correspondence Theory* (that facts correspond to reality) and the *Coherence Theory* (that when all the facts are combined, they cohere with one another).[67] These two theories allow the apologist to assess any worldview by three tests, which Zacharias calls the *Three Levels of Philosophy*. The first of these tests is that of logical consistency. In other words, is this worldview rational?[68] The second test is that of empirical adequacy—is there a way to test these claims empirically? The third test is what Zacharias calls experiential relevance—essentially, the question of whether this worldview can meet an individual in their everyday life: is it *liveable*?

Once a worldview has been put to these three tests, Zacharias then deepens the examination by considering it through what he calls the four essential categories for life: origin—Where do I come from?; meaning—What does life really mean?; morality—How do I differentiate between good and evil?; destiny—What happens to a human being when he or she dies? According to Zacharias, most of the questions he has heard over five decades of ministry fall into one of these four categories, and taken together they expose the weaknesses of any worldview that may provide robust responses to the questions of some categories but lack with respect to others.

When evaluating a worldview, Zacharias keeps five academic disciplines in view. First, theology—because the apologist is talking about God; second, metaphysics—because these are questions concerning reality; third, epistemology

---

66. Zacharias, *The 3.4.5 Grid*; Zacharias, *A Shattered Visage: The Real Face of Atheism*; Zacharias, "Living an Apologetic Life," https://www.rzim.org/read/just-thinking-magazine/living-an-apologetic-life.

67. Zacharias, *The 3.4.5 Grid*. Zacharias credits Os Guinness as the person who first taught him the importance of clarifying truth claims as a starting point for apologetics (Ravi Zacharias and Norman Geisler, eds., *Is Your Church Ready; Motivating Leaders to Live an Apologetic Life* [Grand Rapids: Zondervan, 2003], 25).

68. For a more in-depth explanation, Zacharias directs his readers to Peter Kreeft's "Rules for Talking Back," in his book *Three Philosophies of Life* (San Francisco: Ignatius, 1989), 54.

—because the conversation deals with issues of what we can know to be true; fourth, ethics—because the discussion has profound moral implications; and last, anthropology—because this is ultimately a question of what it means to be human. Zacharias argues that if you sift a worldview through these threefold, fourfold, and fivefold grids, then the strength of Christianity is displayed because, uniquely among the worldviews, it "pulls together the convergence of disciplines."[69]

The comprehensive nature of Zacharias's 3.4.5 Grid provides an insight into what has made Zacharias such an effective apologist. Unsatisfied with addressing only the presenting issue or surface-level question, Zacharias is determined to thoroughly understand the underlying worldview that drives a person before attempting to make any kind of response. As Zacharias explains, "Apologetics is not just giving people answers to questions—it is questioning people's answers, and even questioning their questions. When you question someone's question, you compel him or her to open up about his or her own assumptions. Our assumptions must be examined."[70]

FROM THE HEAD TO THE HEART

Although Zacharias has developed an apologetic framework for thoroughly analyzing a worldview, ultimately what has made him effective as an apologist-evangelist is the *manner* in which he ministers. Zacharias's emphasis on the holistic needs of the person, coupled with his personal experience of growing up surrounded by extreme forms of suffering, led him to establish a humanitarian arm within the broader ministry of RZIM—Wellspring International. Serving women and children at risk, Wellspring is motivated by a belief that "love is the most powerful apologetic."[71]

This same compassionate tone characterizes Zacharias's communication, whether in spoken or written form. As committed as Zacharias may be to tearing down barriers to truth, he is even more committed to reaching "the questioner behind the question."[72] Desiring to reach not just the intellect but the whole person, Zacharias emphasizes the essentiality of engaging both the "head and the heart," often quoting the former archbishop of Canterbury, Donald Coggan: "The journey from head to heart is one of the longest and most difficult that we know."[73]

---

69. Zacharias, *The 3.4.5 Grid*. Zacharias also notes in this lecture that there are five sources of credibility through which truth can be tested: the pragmatic, the experiential, the metaphysical, the historical, and the community basis.

70. Zacharias, *Walking from East to West*, 204.

71. Ravi Zacharias, "Apologetics: Shadow or Reality?" RZIM, https://www.rzim.org/read/just-thinking-magazine/apologetics-shadow-or-reality.

72. Zacharias, personal interview.

73. Ibid. These words of Donald Coggan, 101st archbishop of Canterbury, are recalled by Alister McGrath in his article "Loving God with Heart and Mind," *Knowing & Doing* (C.S. Lewis Institute, Winter 2002): 1.

It is on account of this pastoral approach that Zacharias has become particularly well-regarded for his respectful Q&A forums, in which he models both how to speak directly to the individual and how to use story as a means of connecting the head and the heart of the listener. Having come to faith "on a bed of suicide," [74] Zacharias is also careful to emphasize that beneath any academic question there lies a hurt of one kind or another. As Zacharias reflects: "At every university where I've lectured, the intellectual questions eventually turn into questions of meaning. Often behind a difficult or angry question is a hurting heart; the intellect is intertwined with the heart. I always try to rescue a question from mere academic connotations."[75]

This attitude, more than any other, has led to Zacharias having such a profound impact on so many. As one woman commented to Zacharias upon meeting him on June 7, 2019, "When I began watching your videos, I did not always fully understand the arguments, but I was struck by your kindness."[76]

CONTRIBUTIONS TO THE FIELD OF APOLOGETICS

The contribution of Ravi Zacharias is perhaps best characterised by his oft-used description of RZIM's ministry: "Helping the thinker believe, helping the believer think."

In terms of evangelistic impact, few people have preached the gospel on so many international platforms and at so many college campuses as Zacharias has over the last five decades. As early as 1980, Zacharias had already been awarded an honorary doctorate from Houghton College, New York: "In recognition of [his] pioneering impact in international evangelism."[77] Several years later, Billy Graham introduced him to the crowd of ten thousand or so evangelists at Amsterdam '86 as "one of the most articulate young evangelists of our time."[78] From his first itinerant trip with YFC's teen preaching team in India, countless people have been persuaded to entrust their lives to Jesus through Zacharias's preaching, writing, radio shows, and one-on-one conversations.

Although best known for his public ministry of preaching and writing, Zacharias's impact may arguably be greater still among the cultural influencers

---

74. Zacharias, personal interview.
75. David Goetz, "Reaching the Happy Thinking Pagan," *The Leadership Journal* (*Christianity Today*, Spring 1995). https://www.christianitytoday.com/pastors/1995/spring/5l218.html.
76. Reported by Vince Vitale on a trip to Louisiana State Penitentiary, 06/07/2019.
77. Zacharias, *Walking from East to West*, 190.
78. Danielle DuRant, "Remarkable Evangelist: Ravi Zacharias," *Ambassadors For Christ*, ed. John D. Woodbridge (Chicago: Moody, 1994), 327.

of the world—whether in business, entertainment, politics, or the leadership of other religions—whom he is frequently asked to meet with in confidence to discuss Christianity. In this respect, Zacharias has stayed true to RZIM's calling to reach the opinion-makers of society, and this untraceable legacy has had far-reaching implications for the gospel, with many of these individuals going on to influence their respective spheres for Christ.

Now with a team of nearly one hundred itinerant apologist-evangelists, based out of offices in fifteen different countries worldwide, the global impact of RZIM continues to grow as the team members are able to more deeply influence their respective regions of the world with the gospel.

As for "helping the believer think," Zacharias has authored or coauthored twenty-eight books, over 2,200 English-speaking radio stations play his messages weekly around the world, and more than 2.8 million people have listened to his podcasts online in the last month alone.[79] For many Christians across the US, listening to Zacharias on Sunday morning radio on the drive to church has been a staple of their Christian discipleship. But what is striking about these figures is that they are not specific to the United States. With an itinerary that has always traversed the globe—and the help of social media—Zacharias has brought apologetics to an international audience in a way that has never been done before. With students from over 130 countries having enrolled in RZIM's online academy within its first five years of existence, the perception of apologetics as a western discipline is rapidly dwindling.

In light of the evangelical church's initial wariness toward apologetics when Zacharias started out as evangelist, he has also left a legacy of popularizing apologetics so that it is no longer confined to the academy nor viewed as an intellectual hobby but increasingly is being adopted by countless Christians as a vital tool for evangelism. As Josh Chatraw and Mark Allen comment, "In our contemporary setting, in many cases an unfortunate divide exists between apologists and evangelists, which would have been strange to both the New Testament authors and the early church. Among modern apologists, Ravi Zacharias (and his organization RZIM) has exemplified a way to reunite apologetics and evangelism."[80]

In the process of reuniting apologetics and evangelism, perhaps one of the most significant contributions Zacharias has made in this area has been not only to encourage believers that they can *do* apologetics but to model for them *how* to do apologetics: with kindness, by asking good questions, and always with the goal of winning the person rather than the argument.

---

79. These statistics were captured in June 2019 by the RZIM media team.
80. Josh D. Chatraw and Mark D. Allen, *Apologetics at the Cross: An Introduction For Christian Witness* (Grand Rapids: Zondervan, 2018), 137.

Furthermore, Zacharias has not only inspired believers toward evangelism, but in an era of intellectual confusion and societal division has given many doubting Christians a renewed confidence that the Christian faith is not just plausible but is the only worldview that is able to satisfactorily address the central and most important questions of life.

When asked what he hoped his lasting contribution would be, Zacharias shared a story about a man he met recently who was a missionary to China from the state of Georgia. This man asked Zacharias to sign three books: one for him, one for his mother, and one for his grandmother. What struck Zacharias was that his message had spanned three generations of the same family. Reflecting on this, Zacharias shared that he hoped to leave the church with the confidence and conviction that "truth is transgenerational, truth is transcultural, and if you present it the right way . . . and illustrate it with stories that are current, you will connect with every culture. If you can take the truth that is eternal and illustrate it with stories that are current, you reach every generation."[81]

BIBLIOGRAPHY

Blamires, Harry. *The Christian Mind: How Should a Christian Think?* Ann Arbor, MI: Servant, 1963.

Camus, Albert. *L'Étranger*. Paris: Éditions Gallimard, 1942.

Chang, Pauline, J. "Evangelical Defends Decision to Speak at Mormon Tabernacle." *The Christian Post*. December 28, 2004. https://www.christianpost.com/news/evangelical-defends-decision-to-speak-at-mormon-tabernacle.html.

Chatraw, Josh D., and Mark D. Allen. *Apologetics at the Cross: An Introduction For Christian Witness*. Grand Rapids: Zondervan, 2018.

DuRant, Danielle. "Remarkable Evangelist: Ravi Zacharias." *Ambassadors for Christ*. Ed. by John D. Woodbridge, Chicago: Moody, 1994.

Goetz, David. "Reaching the Happy Thinking Pagan." *The Leadership Journal, Christianity Today*. Spring 1995, https://www.christianitytoday.com/pastors/1995/spring/5l218.html.

Green, Michael. *Jesus Spells Freedom*. Downers Grove, IL: InterVarsity Press, 1972.

———. *Man Alive!* Downers Grove, IL: InterVarsity Press, 1967.

———. *Runaway World*. Downers Grove, IL: InterVarsity Press, 1969.

Guinness, Os. *Fit Bodies, Fat Minds: Why Evangelicals Don't Think and What to Do About It*. Vancouver, BC: Hourglass, 1994.

Kreeft, Peter. *Three Philosophies of Life*. San Francisco: Ignatius, 1989.

McDowell, Josh. *Evidence that Demands a Verdict*. San Bernardino, CA: Campus Crusade for Christ International, 1972.

McGrath, Alister. "Loving God with Heart and Mind." *Knowing & Doing*. C. S. Lewis Institute (Winter 2002): 6–7, 18, 21.

Neibuhr, Reinhold. *The Nature and Destiny of Man: A Christian Interpretation*. New York: Scribner's Sons, 1941.

Noll, Mark. *The Scandal of the Evangelical Mind*. Grand Rapids: Eerdmans, 1994.

Olson, Ted. "Ravi Zacharias to Speak at Mormon Tabernacle." *Christianity Today Magazine*. January 9, 2004. https://www.christianitytoday.com/ct/2004/septemberweb-only/9-13-51.0.html.

Stemple, Charlotte. *My Vietnam: Stories of the War Years from the Inside Out*. Maitland, FL: Xulon, 2010.

Sutera, Ralph. "The Canadian Revival and Concepts of Revival." *Sermon Index*. February 2, 2008. https://www.img.sermonindex.net/modules/newbb/viewtopic_pdf.php?topic_id=22390&forum=40.

---

81. Zacharias, personal interview.

Washington, Jessica. "Controversial Evangelist Zacharias Speaks at Penn." *The Daily Pennsylvanian*. February 11, 2014. https://www.thedp.com/article/2014/02/ravi-zacharias.

Zacharias, Ravi. *The 3.4.5 Grid*. Lecture for the RZIM Online Academy.

———. *The Basis of Truth*. Lecture at The University of Utah, November 2004.

———. *Beyond Opinion*. Nashville: Nelson, 2008.

———. *Can Man Live Without God?* Nashville: W Publishing, 1994.

———. "God's Justice Demands Total Commitment." *Viet Nam Today: News Magazine of the Viet Nam Field, Christian and Missionary Alliance* 10 (Winter 1971): 1.

———. *Jesus Among Other Gods: The Absolute Claims of the Christian Message*. Nashville: W Publishing, 2000.

———. "Living an Apologetic Life." https://www.rzim.org/read/just-thinking-magazine/living-an -apologetic-life.

———. *The Lostness of Man*. Lecture at the International Evangelists Conference, Amsterdam, 1983.

———. *A Shattered Visage: The Real Face of Atheism*. Grand Rapids: Baker, 1993.

Zacharias, Ravi, and Norman Geisler, eds. *Is Your Church Ready; Motivating Leaders to Live an Apologetic Life*. Grand Rapids: Zondervan, 2003.

Zacharias, Ravi, and R. S. B. Sawyer. *Walking from East to West: God in the Shadows*. Grand Rapids: Zondervan, 2006.

WILLIAM LANE CRAIG

Philosopher as Apologist

R. KEITH LOFTIN

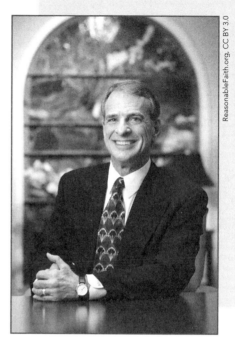

It has been suggested with good reason that William Lane Craig (1949–) may be the most important Christian apologist since the Oxford don C. S. Lewis. Craig has two earned doctorates, the heart of an evangelist, and an apologetics ministry that straddles the popular and scholarly divide. According to *The Chronicle of Higher Education*, Craig is "Christian philosophy's boldest apostle,"[1] and The Best Schools named Craig one of "The 50 Most Influential Living Philosophers."[2] A proponent of classical apologetics, Craig's influence on the substance and shape of contemporary discussions ranging from historical Jesus studies and the resurrection, to cosmological and moral evidence for God's existence, to the coherence of Christian theism is evident. Beyond his scholarly contributions, Craig is also a regular Sunday school teacher and the author of a series of children's books.

HISTORICAL BACKGROUND

William Lane Craig was born in Peoria, Illinois, on August 23, 1949. The second of three children born to Doris Irene (née Walker) Craig, a fulltime homemaker, and Mallory John Craig, an executive for the Toledo, Peoria, and Western railway, Craig was raised in a non–Christian albeit loving, middle-class home. Craig's boyhood sense of curiosity and love of learning were cultivated diligently by his mother. Desiring to be a zoo director someday, Craig was allowed to keep a menagerie of pets (provided he could catch them!) at home—from snakes, toads,

---

1. Nathan Schneider, "The New Theist: How William Lane Craig Became Christian Philosophy's Boldest Apostle," *The Chronicle of Higher Education* (01 July 2013), available at https://www.chronicle.com /article/The-New-Theist/140019.

2. https://thebestschools.org/features/most-influential-living-philosophers/.

and katydids to stray cats and dogs, rabbits, and a raccoon. With an eye toward stimulating her children's education, Mrs. Craig took her children on a variety of field trips, including to manufacturing facilities of all stripes, a dairy, a pig iron plant where scrap metal was melted down, and the enormous hydroelectric dam spanning the Mississippi River at Craig's boyhood home of Keokuk, Iowa, all of which instilled in Craig an early love of learning.

Though generally happy as a child, Craig suffered from Charcot-Marie-Tooth syndrome (CMT), a rare genetic neurological disorder affecting less than one-half of one percent of the American population and for which there is no cure. CMT affects the peripheral nerves in one's body, causing progressively worsening muscle weakness and atrophy. When Craig was a boy, this forced him to walk abnormally, constantly up on his toes, making him a target for mockery by other schoolchildren. CMT's debilitating effect on reflexes and balance denied Craig any athletic ability, which further alienated him from his peers.

Refused success at physical play, Craig turned to academics in search of self–worth. Finding in academia an arena wherein his CMT was inconsequential, he threw himself into his high school studies and became obsessively goal oriented and driven to succeed. As a teenager Craig asked the "big questions" of life—What is the meaning of my existence? Who am I? Why am I here? And Craig's search for answers, which included a period of church attendance, was in earnest. It was, however, unsatisfying. A diffident and somewhat embittered adolescent who "felt deeply the meaninglessness of life and the despair that it brings,"[3] Craig became socially hermetic. He became convinced, as he observed the phony, unctuous behavior of those around him (especially the students who claimed to be Christians), that all people are pretending to be something they're not. *Everyone*, he thought, *is a hypocrite.* "*They're all just a bunch of phonies, holding up a plastic mask to the world, while the real person is cowering down inside, afraid to come out and be real.*"[4]

It was only later that Craig realized *he* was the "phony," pretending to need no one while longing hypocritically for love and meaningful relationship with others. Amid this inner turmoil, Craig walked into his sophomore German class. It was the spring of 1965. Taking his seat behind classmate Sandy Tiffan, a radiantly happy Christian, Craig asked, "Sandy, what are you always so happy about, anyway?" She replied, "I know Jesus Christ as my personal Savior." Explaining God's love for him, Sandy prompted Craig to consider the gospel. Staggered that the creator of the universe would have any interest in—let alone *love*—him, Craig went home and for the first time read the New Testament,

---

3. William Lane Craig, *On Guard: Defending Your Faith with Reason and Precision* (Colorado Springs: Cook, 2010), 46.
4. Ibid., 47.

where he encountered the life and teachings of Jesus. Six months later, on September 11, 1965, Craig accepted Christ as his savior. "Finally I just came to the end of my rope and cried out to God. I cried out all the anger and bitterness that had built up inside me, and at the same time I felt this tremendous infusion of joy. . . . I remember I rushed outdoors—it was a clear Midwestern summer night, and you could see the Milky Way stretched from horizon to horizon. As I looked up at the stars, I thought, *God! I've come to know God!*"[5]

Craig's remaining time at East Peoria Community High School took on a different hue. His life now imbued with *meaning*, Craig knew immediately upon conversion that he was called to spend his life spreading the gospel.

VOCATIONAL INFLUENCES

On Sandy's recommendation, Craig matriculated into Wheaton College in 1967. His years at Wheaton proved formative to Craig's faith and vocation. Having participated on his high school's debate team for four years (being named to the all-state debate team), Craig continued honing his debate skills during college, participating for four years on Wheaton's debate team. Although debating would feature prominently in Craig's future ministry, it was at this time a sort of intellectual sport for him rather than conscious preparation for apologetic ministry.

Three vocational influences stand out from Craig's Wheaton years, beginning with Wheaton's intellectual culture of emphasizing the integration of faith and learning. Alongside the requirement to take courses across the broad liberal arts tradition as a Wheaton undergraduate, this emphasis on integrative thinking instilled in Craig an important framework within which his vocation would become defined.[6] Also impactful was Craig's reading of E. J. Carnell's *An Introduction to Christian Apologetics* as a senior at Wheaton.[7] Carnell, himself a Wheaton alumnus who went on to earn double doctorates (in theology and philosophy at Harvard Divinity School and Boston University, respectively), impressed Craig as an apologist who capably defended the faith philosophically. Having by this time grown convinced his would be an apologetics ministry concentrating on giving an intellectual defense of the faith, Craig was captivated by Carnell's discussion of the nature of truth and how one tests for truth—

---

5. Ibid., 48–49.
6. Fifty years later, in February 2018, in an address to the faculty at North Carolina State University, Craig would say: "All truth is God's truth, and somehow it all fits into an integrated whole, which is perfectly known to God alone. Our goal should be to seek to discover how our field of study fits into the whole scheme of God's truth" (https://tinyurl.com/y6v47e23). Cf. Craig's "Concluding Thoughts on the Two Tasks of the Christian Scholar," in *The Two Tasks of the Christian Scholar: Redeeming the Soul, Redeeming the Mind*, eds. William Lane Craig and Paul M. Gould (Wheaton, IL: Crossway, 2007), 185–87.
7. E. J. Carnell, *An Introduction to Christian Apologetics* (Grand Rapids: Eerdmans, 1948).

questions Craig himself had been asking—as well as with how Carnell brought that discussion to bear on the apologetic endeavor. Indeed, Carnell's work convinced Craig "that reason might be used to show the systematic consistency of Christian faith without thereby becoming the basis of that faith."[8]

Doubtlessly the most abiding influence from these years was Stuart Hackett. Having earned his doctorate in philosophy at Syracuse University, Hackett was at this time professor of philosophy at Wheaton. In those days, as Alvin Plantinga recalls, "there were few Christian philosophers in the United States, and even fewer Christian philosophers willing to identify themselves as such."[9] This was largely due, perhaps, to the dominance from the 1920s and into the 1960s of verificationism, one implication of which was the belief that talk about God (along with other metaphysical claims that are not "verifiable") was worse than false: it was *meaningless*. The 1967 publication of Plantinga's *God and Other Minds* is widely thought to represent the tipping point of Christian philosophers' rebuttal. Plantinga's work deserves its high praise, but worth noting is that Hackett's *The Resurrection of Theism* was published a full decade earlier.[10] Hackett's work is a full-scale defense of arguments for God's existence. Whereas Wheaton's theology faculty held a rather dim view of natural theology—Craig's theology professors denigrated the use of arguments for God as hopeless—Hackett was conspicuous as a champion of natural theology.

As a freshman at Wheaton, Craig enrolled in Hackett's Introduction to Philosophy course. Craig reflects: "I have to confess that I didn't particularly like the class. It was basically a course surveying the history of western philosophy. . . . With no background in philosophy, I was bewildered by the parade of thinkers—Plato, Aristotle, Descartes, Hume, Leibniz, and so forth—all spouting these weird, contradictory, and equally unsubstantiated opinions on things. Tragically, even though I got an 'A' in the class, I came away thinking that philosophy was just irrelevant."[11]

Craig admired and enjoyed Hackett nonetheless and continued to talk with him on a personal level. Shortly before graduating in 1971 with his BA in speech and communication, Craig noticed a copy of *The Resurrection of Theism* on the clearance table in the campus bookstore. Having heard others praise the book, Craig purchased it. Craig was "absolutely stunned by what I read. In contrast to what I had been taught at Wheaton, Hackett, with devastating logic,

8. William Lane Craig and Joseph E. Gorra, *A Reasonable Response* (Chicago: Moody, 2013), 314.
9. Alvin Plantinga, "A Christian Life Partly Lived," in *Philosophers Who Believe*, ed. Kelly James Clark (Downers Grove, IL: InterVarsity Press, 1993), 81.
10. Stuart C. Hackett, *The Resurrection of Theism: Prolegomena to Christian Apology* (Grand Rapids: Baker, 1957), now reprinted by Wipf & Stock.
11. Craig, "Stuart Hackett," https://tinyurl.com/ya6chbet.

was defending arguments for God's existence and providing further refutations of every conceivable objection to them."[12] This was momentous for Craig, not least because it galvanized him into studying philosophy. Upon reading Hackett's treatment of the argument for the impossibility of an infinite regress of temporal events, Craig knew this would be the topic of his dissertation were he ever to pursue doctoral studies. It was only later, in reading Frederick Copleston, that Craig learned this argument was not original to Hackett but has ancient roots.

To Seminary

Craig's ministry as an evangelist began on the campus of Northern Illinois University in the fall of 1971, where he served for roughly two years on staff with Campus Crusade for Christ (rechristened "Cru" in 2011), sharing the gospel with university students. In the spring term of 1972, Norman Geisler—then on faculty at Trinity Evangelical Divinity School (TEDS)—gave a talk in the NIU student union on God and evil. Impressed not only by Geisler's talk but also by the philosophy program he represented, Craig resolved to earn the MA in philosophy of religion at TEDS. In preparing for the required Graduate Record Exam in philosophy, Craig made a close study of Frederick Copleston's multivolume *A History of Western Philosophy*.[13] Significantly, Geisler was not the only person to impress Craig at NIU. It was here that Craig met Jan Coleman, a recent graduate of the University of North Dakota and fellow Crusade staff at NIU. The two were married on May 13, 1972.

Craig matriculated into TEDS in the summer term of 1973, immediately taking John Warwick Montgomery's apologetics course (along with classmates Ravi Zacharias and Tim Erdel). In addition to Montgomery's class, Craig took courses under Norman Geisler, Clark Pinnock, John Woodbridge, David Wolfe, Paul Feinberg, David Wells, J. I. Packer, and Murray Harris. While never taking Carl F. H. Henry for a class, Craig was able to engage in conversation with him on several occasions during his time at TEDS. Amazingly, in just two years Craig completed not only the MA in philosophy of religion but the MA in church history as well.[14]

Nearing graduation at TEDS, the Craigs sat one evening discussing their postseminary plans. "If money were no object," Jan asked, "what would you really *like* to do next?" At this time Craig did not anticipate his own fascination with philosophy. Although he recognized the relevance of doctoral studies

---

12. Craig, *On Guard*, 68.
13. Frederick Copleston, *A History of Western Philosophy*, 9 vols. (New York: Image Books, 1962).
14. These were completed concurrently, although rules then disallowed granting both degrees in June 1975. Hence the 1976 bestowal of the church history degree.

for apologetics and evangelism (his goal was the development of an argument for God to be used in such ministry), earning a PhD also would go far toward establishing credentials for his ministry. "If money were no object," Craig replied, "what I'd really like to do is go to England and do a doctorate under John Hick."[15]

To Birmingham

Hick was among the handful of philosophers worldwide then doing serious work on the arguments for God's existence. After Hick replied positively to Craig's proposal for a study of the cosmological argument, in August 1975 the Craigs relocated to the University of Birmingham in England. Although Hick was not a conservative Christian nor in agreement with Craig's thesis, Craig found in his supervisor something of a father figure.[16] Whereas Hick had a reputation as a somewhat formal, even aloof supervisor, Craig recalls him as warm and engaging, and the Craigs spent much personal time together with the Hicks. With the approval of Hick and Anthony Kenny, Craig's external reader, Craig was awarded the PhD in philosophy from the University of Birmingham in 1977.

Nearing completion of his time at Birmingham, Craig still believed his vocation was evangelism and apologetics, thinking this would take shape around a full-time faculty position. To that end he applied to several job openings at American universities, but to no avail. Somewhat discouraged, the Craigs once again found themselves sitting at the dinner table one autumn evening discussing their future. "If money were no object," Jan asked once more, "what would you really *like* to do next?" Craig recalls the moment well: "I laughed because I remembered how the Lord had used her question to guide us in the past. I had no trouble answering the question. 'If money were no object, what I'd really like to do is go to Germany and study under Wolfhart Pannenberg. . . . If I could study with him, I could develop a historical apologetic for the resurrection of Jesus.'"[17]

Ever enterprising, Jan discovered in the university's library literature about the Alexander von Humboldt-Stiftung, a foundation whose purpose "is to provide opportunities for highly-qualified young academics (. . .) to carry out research projects in the Federal Republic of Germany."[18] The foundation offered full funding to fellowship recipients. Given the Craigs' meager finances, this seemed almost too good to be true. As they gathered the required application materials, they said goodbye to Birmingham in November 1976.

---

15. Craig, *On Guard*, 69.
16. Notably, Hick's edited volume *The Myth of God Incarnate* (Philadelphia: Westminster, 1977) was completed while Craig was at Birmingham. For more on Hick's life, see his *John Hick: An Autobiography* (London: Oneworld, 2002), wherein he recalls his former student as "brilliant" and "very bright and energetic."
17. Craig, *On Guard*, 177.
18. https://www.humboldt-foundation.de/web/chronology.html.

To Munich

At Jan's suggestion the Craigs enrolled in the Centre Missionaire, a French language school nestled in the picturesque French Alps in Albertville, France. Beginning in January 1977, their training lasted nine months. Meantime, the Craigs were homeless for December 1976, so on a whim they made their way to Paris to improvise for the month. Unable to afford much of anything, they were allowed to stay at the Armée du Salut (then little more than an abandoned, unheated Salvation Army building), thanks to the intercession of a local pastor.

Soon after arriving in Albertville, the Craigs hastened to complete the Humboldt-Stiftung application. Having grown a beard to appear older in the required applicant photograph, Craig mailed the application materials. It would take the Humboldt-Stiftung some seven months to evaluate and reply to Craig's application, so in the meantime the Craigs set about learning French. In June, Craig received an invitation to speak at a Campus für Christus event in Munich, and it was in preparation for these talks that Craig "hit upon a scheme that has proved very helpful to me in illuminating the difference between faith and reason—namely, the distinction between *knowing* Christianity to be true and *showing* Christianity to be true."[19] Meanwhile, as their time in Albertville grew short, the Craigs had become proficient in French, with Craig himself "preaching in French at our small church," and Jan "had the joy of leading our French neighbors to faith in Christ."[20]

As June gave way to July 1977, the Humboldt-Stiftung wrote to inform Craig he'd been granted a fellowship to study Jesus's resurrection with Wolfhart Pannenberg, one of the twentieth century's most influential Protestant theologians. The fellowship covered all tuition and living expenses, including for the duration of their time in Munich the provision of a charming apartment directly across from the English Gardens, as well as occasional discretional money. The entirety of Craig's work at Munich—coursework, dissertation, *Rigorosum* (i.e., an oral examination broadly covering one's chosen field of study and two side disciplines)—was to be conducted in German, which Craig hadn't studied since high school. The Craigs therefore spent January through April at the Goethe-Institut in Göttingen before relocating in May 1978 several hundred miles south to Munich.

Although a student of Pannenberg from May 1978 till Christmas 1979, Craig had minimal personal interaction with the famous theologian. Indeed, Craig found his new supervisor condescending and impatient—a marked contrast with John Hick. Nonetheless, Craig attended Pannenberg's seminars and

---

19. Craig and Gorra, *A Reasonable Response*, 315. I talk more about this distinction in the methodology section below.

20. Craig, *On Guard*, 180.

lectures while pursuing his research diligently. Since the deist controversy of the seventeenth and eighteenth centuries was central to his resurrection studies, Craig spent the summer of 1978 at the University of Cambridge poring through the primary texts of that debate (a move that did not please Pannenberg).

By the end of 1979, Craig had a completed and approved dissertation, having added considerably to his project in response to Pannenberg's rejection of his biblical exegesis as excessively "fundamentalist." All that remained was to pass the *Rigorosum*, scheduled for late December. But Craig did not pass the exam.[21] Fortunately, earlier in the summer of 1979, Craig had been contacted by Warren Benson, then acting Dean at TEDS, and was offered a position as assistant professor of philosophy with generous terms, which Craig happily accepted. It was with mixed feelings, then, that the Craigs departed Germany for Deerfield, where from January 1980 through May 1986, Craig filled the faculty vacancy created by Norman Geisler's move to Dallas Theological Seminary.

The Craigs resettled in Deerfield, moving into their first home that September. A particular joy for Craig was reuniting with his former professor, Stuart Hackett, recently transitioned from Wheaton. Between preparing and delivering course lectures, revising his second dissertation for publication, publishing a half dozen professional articles and chapters, and running a Monday evening discipleship group for his students, Craig kept busy during his first two years at TEDS. Meanwhile, he was preparing to retake the *Rigorosum*. Having received helpful study aids while on a brief stay in Erlangen in summer 1981, the Craigs—including daughter Charity, born in May 1982—returned to Munich in summer 1982, this time for a successful *Rigorosum*. Since it was then a requirement at Munich that one's dissertation be published before one's degree was awarded, Craig's second doctorate was not awarded until 1984, when he secured a publisher.[22]

VOCATIONAL TRANSITIONS

Having completed his studies at Munich, Craig read Anthony Kenny's *The God of the Philosophers*, discovering in its pages an intriguing view of divine omniscience called "middle knowledge." This solidified his selection of the "coherence of theism" as his next major research topic (one that would occupy him for over three decades), beginning with the nature of omniscience. Upon returning stateside, Craig committed himself to researching divine foreknowledge and human freedom in the University of Arizona's library while on sabbatical with his family

---

21. Craig recounts this experience in various places, including his *Hard Questions, Real Answers* (Wheaton, IL: Crossway, 2003), 64–66.

22. William Lane Craig, *The Historical Evidence for the Resurrection of Jesus during the Deist Controversy* (Lewiston: Mellen, 1985).

in Tucson from September 1982 through summer 1983. It is worth noting that Craig's work on omniscience was completed well before the rise of "open theism" in the mid–1990s, although Craig drew heavily upon his research in critiquing the open view.[23]

After working for seven years on the doctrine of omniscience, Craig then spent eleven years studying the nature of time and divine eternality before spending thirteen years on the difficult doctrine of divine aseity. Indeed, the coherence of theism (not, as is frequently asserted, arguments for God's existence) is Craig's area of specialization.

Returning to TEDS in autumn 1983, Craig taught through the end of the spring quarter of 1985. Although he enjoyed teaching, Craig increasingly yearned for itinerant ministry; his vocation, he came to realize, was not full-time teaching. In late spring the Craigs—now also including son John, born May 1984—traveled to Paris for the remainder of what would prove to be a tumultuous year. Two events stand out, beginning with Craig's taking a train from Paris to Brussels to give a talk at the Belgian Bible Institute. While there, Craig's friend Bruce Benson toured him around the Université Catholique de Louvain. Craig was struck not only by the historic university's beauty but also by its impressive philosophy and theology libraries. Shortly thereafter the second event occurred: Craig traveled to Müllheim, West Germany, where he met Kalevi Lehtinen, the European director of Agape Europe (a branch of Campus Crusade for Christ), who invited Craig to join the Agape staff. Although such a position had much to commend it, Craig intended to continue teaching at TEDS. He would not discover until returning to Deerfield that Benson's successor had decided to close the philosophy of religion program and disband the department—namely, Craig and Hackett.

It was not until returning to campus and being summoned to meet with the new dean that Craig learned of this decision. He was stunned. "Stu was disgracefully shunted over to the undergraduate college and I found myself out of a job, now with two small children to support."[24] This circumstance precipitated Craig into accepting Lehtinen's invitation to join the Agape Europe staff, after all.

Upon deciding to join Agape, the Craigs promptly relocated to Santa Barbara, where Craig taught religious studies at Westmont College for the 1986–87 academic year while busily raising financial support. In July 1987 the Craigs moved to Brussels, Belgium—near the university town that had so impressed

---

23. See, e.g., Clark Pinnock et. al., *The Openness of God: A Biblical Challenge to the Traditional Understanding of God* (Downers Grove, IL: InterVarsity Press, 1994). Craig critiques and rejects open theism in *Divine Foreknowledge: Four Views*, eds. James K. Beilby and Paul R. Eddy (Downers Grove, IL: InterVarsity, 2009) and in *God Under Fire: Modern Scholarship Reinvents God*, eds. Douglas S. Huffman and Eric L. Johnson (Grand Rapids: Zondervan, 2002).

24. Craig, at https://tinyurl.com/ya6chbet.

Craig two years earlier—to help spread the gospel throughout Europe while pursuing Craig's research. The Craigs resided in Brussels for the next seven years, during which time Craig spoke all over eastern and western Europe, the former Soviet Union, and North America. In addition to itinerant speaking, Craig spent considerable time at the Université Catholique de Louvain researching and writing, completing his study of divine omniscience before shifting his attention to the complex issue of divine eternity.

Desiring an American education for their children, now twelve and ten years old, the Craigs moved in September 1994 to Atlanta, Georgia. Craig transitioned from Agape Europe to Christian Leadership Ministries (later renamed "Faculty Commons"), a stateside branch of Campus Crusade, where his ministry continued as before. Shortly after the Craigs' arrival in Atlanta, the second edition of Craig's *Apologetics: An Introduction*—now retitled *Reasonable Faith*—was published.[25] It was also about this time that Craig accepted a position in the nascent philosophy department at Talbot School of Theology—then consisting of only J. P. Moreland, Scott Rae, and Douglas Geivett—as research professor of philosophy, teaching only during January-terms. In 2014 he accepted a similar appointment as professor of philosophy at Houston Baptist University.

Between 1994 and 2004 Craig, still engaged full-time as Crusade staff, was remarkably productive. In addition to teaching at Talbot, speaking and participating in debates, and taking over as president of the Evangelical Philosophical Society (1996–2005), Craig published nearly twenty books and roughly sixty peer-reviewed journal articles—not to mention chapter contributions, book reviews, and popular pieces.

At the same time, Craig was frustrated by the Christian "spokespeople" in the public square. He was also dissatisfied with his own ministry's apparent lack of impact. Motivated by these concerns, Craig prayerfully reexamined his ministry strategy, becoming increasingly convinced of the need for a new, unique apologetics platform. He was still contemplating these matters in August 2005, when he participated as a speaker for Stand to Reason's apologetics cruise to Alaska. While aboard, Craig had a momentous conversation with Curt Swindoll, who convinced him to launch a *web*-based ministry (it must be remembered that, although the internet was invented in the mid-1980s, it wasn't popular and widely used until the early 2000s). Despite Craig's concerns that such a move seemed risky and expensive, Swindoll's advice proved prescient. In 2007 Craig founded Reasonable Faith (www.ReasonableFaith.org) as an independent 501(c)(3).

---

25. William Lane Craig, *Reasonable Faith: Christian Truth and Apologetics*, 3d ed. (Wheaton, IL: Crossway, 2008).

APOLOGETIC METHODOLOGY

William Lane Craig is fundamentally an evangelist. Craig believes it is possible and appropriate to offer an intellectually rigorous, positive case for Christian theism. He explains:

> As one reads the Acts of the Apostles, it's evident that it was the apostles' standard procedure to argue for the truth of the Christian worldview, both with Jews and pagans (e.g., Acts 17:2–3, 17; 19:8; 28:23–24). In dealing with Jewish audiences, the apostles appealed to fulfilled prophecy, Jesus' miracles, and especially Jesus' resurrection as evidence that he was the Messiah (Acts 2:22–32). When they confronted gentile audiences . . . the apostles appealed to God's handiwork in nature as evidence of the existence of the Creator (Acts 14:17). Then appeal was made to the eyewitness testimony to the resurrection of Jesus to show specifically that God had revealed himself in Jesus Christ (Acts 17:30–31; 1 Cor. 15:3–8).[26]

In this vein, Craig's apologetic methodology prioritizes establishing the existence of God and God's self-revelation in Jesus (especially as evidenced in the resurrection of Jesus) as the twin pillars of Christian faith, an approach commonly known as "classical apologetics."

Craig's approach to apologetics is informed by a certain religious epistemology.[27] Though rejecting theological rationalism, that is, the claim that arguments and evidence are necessary to ground faith, Craig is emphatic that faith *is* rational. Building on the work of Alvin Plantinga, Craig distinguishes between a Christian's *knowing* the faith is true and *showing* that Christianity is true.[28] The idea is that the former need not involve arguments at all; the inner testimony of the indwelling Holy Spirit "gives us an immediate and veridical assurance of the truth" of Christianity so that one's belief that Christianity is true is a properly basic belief.[29] "God is not," Craig points out, "the conclusion of a syllogism; he is the living God of Abraham, Isaac, and Jacob dwelling within us."[30] The Spirit's inner witness, therefore, provides perfectly rational grounds for faith. To be

---

26. Craig, *Reasonable Faith*, 21–22. Craig affirms a role for apologetics beyond evangelism as well (*Reasonable Faith*, 16–21, 86ff).

27. This is unpacked in Craig, "Classical Apologetics," in *Five Views on Apologetics*, ed. Steven B. Cowan (Grand Rapids: Zondervan, 2000), 26–55, as well as Craig, *Reasonable Faith*, 29–60.

28. See especially Plantinga, "Reason and Belief in God," in *Faith and Rationality*, eds. Alvin Plantinga and Nicholas Wolterstorff (Notre Dame: University of Notre Dame Press, 1983), 16–93 and Alvin Plantinga, *Warranted Christian Belief* (New York: Oxford University Press, 2000).

29. Craig, "Classical Apologetics," 28.

30. Craig *Reasonable Faith*, 46. Craig makes the case that there is ample biblical warrant for this claim.

clear: Craig is here talking only about the experience of a believer's reassurance that Christianity is true, *not* how an unbeliever comes to faith. There is a sense, then, in which a believer's "knowing" Christianity to be true is distinct from the apologetic task.

It is *showing* Christianity to be true that Craig regards as the true task of apologetics. Here, again, the role of the Holy Spirit is central, now in "opening the heart of the obdurate unbeliever to attend to and be persuaded by the argumentation."[31] Thus, "when a person refuses to come to Christ, it is . . . [because] he willingly ignores and rejects the drawing of God's Spirit on his heart. . . . But anyone who responds to the drawing of God's Spirit with an open mind and an open heart can know with assurance that Christianity is true, because God's Spirit will convict him that it is."[32] It is clear that Craig affirms the Spirit's essential role in apologetic circumstances alongside the prominent role of arguments and evidences, which ultimately are means the Spirit uses *through* believers, in showing Christianity to be true. The presentation of arguments or evidence is, on Craig's view, not to be regarded as in competition with or an alternative to the work of the Spirit. Recalling that Craig's own conversion to Christianity did not involve apologetics, it is not surprising that he readily acknowledges the contingency of apologetics for conversion. God, of course, sees fit to use various means of drawing people to himself. Yet there is much value for apologetics, in Craig's view, beyond personal evangelism: bolstering the faith of believers, for example, as well as helping "create and sustain a cultural milieu in which the gospel can be heard as an intellectually viable option for thinking men and women."[33]

It is evident that Craig has a high view of natural theology, which he defines as "that branch of theology that seeks to provide warrant for belief in God's existence apart from the resources of authoritative, propositional revelation."[34] Natural theology is not understood as identical with general revelation; the former develops out of humans' contemplation of the latter.[35] Craig considers an argument successful as a piece of natural theology if it is formally and informally (logically) valid and comprises premises that are both true and more plausible than their negations.

In constructing his positive case for Christianity, Craig appeals widely to

---

31. Craig, "Classical Apologetics," 38.
32. Craig, *Reasonable Faith*, 47 (cf. "Classical Apologetics," 53).
33. William Lane Craig, "Faith, Reason and the Necessity of Apologetics," in *To Everyone an Answer*, eds. Francis J. Beckwith, William Lane Craig, and J. P. Moreland (Downers Grove, IL: InterVarsity Press, 2004), 22.
34. William Lane Craig and J. P. Moreland, "Introduction," in *The Blackwell Companion to Natural Theology*, eds. William Lane Craig and J. P. Moreland (Oxford: Wiley–Blackwell, 2009), ix.
35. This is not unlike the view developed in C. Stephen Evans, *Natural Signs and Knowledge of God* (Oxford: Oxford University Press, 2010).

God's general revelation, taking this as the locus (or perhaps the inspiration) for his arguments. Craig's doctoral thesis at Birmingham, for example, developed and defended the *kalām* version of the cosmological argument. The *kalām* (derived from the Arabic term for "speech") cosmological argument can be stated as a simple syllogism:

(1) Everything that begins to exist has a cause of its existence.
(2) The universe began to exist.
(3) Therefore, the universe has a cause of its existence.[36]

Without launching into a full evaluation of this argument, it is noteworthy that beyond philosophical support Craig appeals as well to big bang cosmology in support of his argument. The central idea of the *kalām* is that if the universe began to exist a finite time ago and everything that begins to exist must have a cause of its existence, then there must be a cause of the universe's coming into existence.

In order to establish premise 2, Craig must show that the past series of temporal events must be finite; there must be a beginning of the universe in time. One way Craig does this is by arguing that an infinite temporal regress of events would be an actual infinite.[37] Now, history (the collection of prior events) is a determinate collection, that is, a set of discrete events which stretches back into the past. As members of the set of prior events, these temporal events are or have been actual; they have occurred in reality. This means that if history comprises an infinite collection of temporal events (e.g., days or years), then that collection will be an actual infinite. But, Craig continues, attempts to translate or posit the notion of an actual infinite into the real world can result only in absurdity. This is evident, Craig argues, when one tries to perform inverse operations on transfinite numbers (e.g., subtracting infinity from infinity yields conflicting answers: zero and infinity).[38] It follows, then, that the notion of history as an infinite collection of past events is logically absurd. In other words, the past collection of temporal events cannot be infinite; the universe must have had a beginning at some point in the finite past, and we are forced, then, to contemplate the *cause* of the universe's beginning. The best explanation, Craig argues,

---

36. William Lane Craig, *The Kalām Cosmological Argument* (New York: Macmillan, 1979), 63. Craig's formulation is nearly identical with that of eleventh-century Arabic philosopher Al-Ghāzalī (William Lane Craig, *The Cosmological Argument from Plato to Leibniz* [London: Macmillan, 1980], 103–04).

37. Craig, *The Kalām Cosmological Argument*, 65–66. To grasp this we must distinguish between the *potential* and the *actual* infinite. According to Craig, potential infinites are infinite not in any determinate sense but merely in the sense that we could ceaselessly go on counting them—regardless of how much time one spends counting—never reaching the end (imagine counting for years: "one, two, three . . . *infinity*!"). But actual infinites are defined as determinate totalities.

38. Craig, *The Kalām Cosmological Argument*, 80–82.

is that God exists as the personal agent who chose to bring the universe into existence. Craig's research at Birmingham on the *kalām* argument yielded three books: *The Kalām Cosmological Argument, The Existence of God and the Beginning of the Universe*, and *The Cosmological Argument from Plato to Leibniz*.

In establishing the second pillar of the Christian faith, the revelation of God in Jesus Christ, Craig emphasizes the historicity of the bodily resurrection of Jesus. Since he is here constructing a historical case, Craig's focus is on handling the relevant historical evidence in accordance with the standards of modern historiography. Specifically, Craig focuses on establishing certain minimal facts central to Christian belief in the resurrection of Jesus. Various evidences support each of these three facts, Craig argues. After establishing them, Craig's approach is—like that of a detective—to infer from these facts an explanation that best explains all three.[39]

The first fact is that Jesus's tomb was found empty after his death. There is, Craig explains, a variety of evidence supporting this fact. First, the empty tomb account is found in multiple independent sources, which provides corroboration of this claim. Further, the location of Jesus's burial tomb was well known, and the gospels report the "embarrassing fact" that it was several of Jesus's *women* followers who made the initial discovery. As Craig highlights, in first-century Jewish society, the testimony of women was not well regarded, and so the mere inclusion of this detail indicates truthfulness in the resurrection narratives.[40]

The fact of Jesus's postmortem appearances is, in Craig's estimation, very well-attested. In 1 Corinthians 15, Paul lists numerous witnesses to appearances of the Lord Jesus after his death on the cross, each of which enjoys independent attestation. After analyzing the plausibility of each appearance claim, Craig sums up: "The list of witnesses of postmortem appearances of Jesus which Paul transmits thus makes it indisputable that individuals and groups had such experiences."[41] Widening the scope of his analysis to include appearance accounts in the gospel narratives, Craig shows that these appearances were physical and bodily in nature.

Finally, that Jesus's disciples came ultimately to place their faith in him as the Messiah is significant. "It is difficult to overemphasize," Craig explains, "what a disaster the crucifixion was for the disciples' faith. Jesus' death on the cross spelled the humiliating end for any hopes they had that he was the Messiah."[42] Yet these same followers came boldly to preach (e.g., Acts 2:32–36) that Jesus is indeed the Messiah, often at great risk to their own well-being.

39. William Lane Craig, "Did Jesus Rise from the Dead?," in *Jesus Under Fire*, eds. Michael J. Wilkins and J. P. Moreland (Grand Rapids: Zondervan, 1995), 143–44.
40. Craig, *Reasonable Faith*, 367–69.
41. Ibid., 380.
42. Ibid., 388.

Having firmly established these core facts, Craig considers one after the other naturalistic attempt to explain them, in each case demonstrating their inadequacy.[43] The best explanation, he argues, is the supernatural explanation that God raised Jesus from the dead.

While it is true that Craig emphasizes these three facts, his apologetic approach here is not to be confused with the "minimal facts" approach. The hallmark of that approach is appealing only to facts that the majority of (both believing and skeptical) scholars accept, whereas Craig's work moves beyond this—including, indeed thoroughly defending, the reliability of the New Testament resurrection narratives. As before at Birmingham, Craig's research at Munich yielded three books: *The Son Rises, The Historical Evidence for the Resurrection of Jesus during the Deist Controversy,* and *Assessing the New Testament Evidence for the Historicity of the Resurrection of Jesus.*

CONTRIBUTIONS TO THE FIELD OF APOLOGETICS

Craig's apologetic contributions, both nonwritten and written, are considerable. Craig's success in leveraging the internet for his ministry is extraordinary. Functioning as both a virtual office and a clearinghouse for ministry materials, Craig's website features many of his writings (both popular and scholarly), replies to inquirers' "Question of the Week," and includes videos of interviews, lectures, and debates, as well as links to his regular podcast ("Reasonable Faith," also on iTunes) and the "Defenders" weekly Sunday school class he teaches. With some 83,300 visitors monthly, this platform makes Craig's work available to people around the world.[44]

Perhaps Craig's most recognizable contribution to apologetics is his participation in professional debates. In Spring 1982, Campus Crusade-Canada asked Craig to travel to the University of Calgary to debate atheist Kai Nielsen.[45] After eight years of competitive debate during his school years, this was Craig's first professional debate. The electric atmosphere and sizeable audience attracted by the debate impressed Craig. Indeed, "it became very clear to [him] that debating was really the forum for doing evangelism on the university campus today."[46]

Since then Craig has participated in more than 150 professional debates.

---

43. Craig, "Did Jesus Rise from the Dead?" 162–65.
44. This is alongside over 800,000 Facebook followers, just shy of 90,000 Twitter followers, and roughly 90,000 YouTube subscribers. These figures accurate as of 11 June 2018.
45. The audio of this debate was unfortunately ruined, but the two debated again in February 1991 (https://tinyurl.com/y9mshzj2).
46. Undated interview with "The Best Schools," https://thebestschools.org/features/william-lane-craig -interview/.

Notable among these are his February 18, 1998, debate with then atheist philosopher Antony Flew.[47] It was after this debate, in contemplating Craig's defense of the design argument, that Flew "found reason to think that an argument to Design does have substantial force" and ultimately rejected atheism.[48] On February 1, 2013, at Purdue University, Craig debated Alex Rosenberg, professor of philosophy at Duke University. Between the large in-house audience and those livestreaming, more than fourteen thousand people from over sixty countries watched this debate.[49] Most of Craig's debates, like the Flew and Rosenberg debates, are on the question of God's existence. But on April 11, 2011, Craig debated neuroscientist and prominent New Atheist Sam Harris at the University of Notre Dame on the question "Is the Foundation of Morality Natural or Supernatural?" During his opening speech, Harris quipped that Craig is "the one Christian apologist who seems to have put the fear of God into my fellow atheists"![50] What is compelling from these debates is Craig's consistency in appealing to the cosmological argument, the teleological argument, and the moral argument in establishing theism and then moving to a defense of the historicity of Jesus's resurrection to establish Christian theism.[51] Collectively, Craig's debates have amassed several million views on YouTube.

Notwithstanding the sheer number of people reached by his nonwritten work, Craig's most enduring contribution to the field of apologetics is his written work. Repudiating the tendency of some to equate "apologetic" with "nonscholarly" works, Craig's apologetic concerns have directed his scholarly research. With an eye toward reaching different audiences, his practice is to write scholarly level books and then a popular level distillation of the same research—including a series of children's books.[52] Craig has authored or edited some fifty books (not counting his over eighty chapter contributions) and has published over 125 peer-reviewed journal articles. His popular works are read by countless lay apologists, and Craig's scholarly publications are essential reading in many classrooms and continue to demand engagement at the highest levels of academia.

Reflecting his apologetic methodology, Craig's written work centers on two foci. The first, natural theology and historical evidence, is concerned with the

---

47. See Stan W. Wallace, ed., *Does God Exist? The Craig-Flew Debate* (Burlington, VT: Ashgate, 2003), which contains the full text of the debate.

48. Personal letter from Flew to Stan W. Wallace of December 8, 2000, https://tinyurl.com/y8ld7q8w. Cf. Gary Habermas and Antony Flew, "My Pilgrimage from Atheism to Theism: A Discussion between Antony Flew and Gary Habermas," *Philosophia Christi* 6.2 (2004): 197–211.

49. See Corey Miller and Paul Gould, eds. *Is Faith in God Reasonable?* (New York: Routledge, 2014), 5.

50. https://www.youtube.com/watch?v=yqaHXKLRKzg.

51. The transcripts for most of Craig's debates are available at www.reasonablefaith.org/media/debates.

52. The series, titled *What is God Like?*, comprises ten illustrated volumes, each introducing children to a different attribute of God. https://www.reasonablefaith.org/store/popular-books/.

existence of God and the revelation of God in Jesus. This includes, of course, Craig's work on the *kalām* cosmological argument and the resurrection of Jesus. It also includes his critiques of naturalism and his treatments of the ontological, teleological, and moral arguments for God's existence. The second focus, on philosophical theology, is discernable in Craig's development of the middle knowledge view of divine foreknowledge and human freedom, his extensive work on divine eternality alongside the philosophy of time, his work on divine aseity and the nature of abstract objects, and (most recently) his treatment of the doctrine of the atonement.[53]

BIBLIOGRAPHY

Craig, William Lane. *The Cosmological Argument from Plato to Leibniz*. London: Macmillan, 1980.
———. *Hard Questions, Real Answers*. Wheaton: Crossway, 2003.
———. *The Historical Evidence for the Resurrection of Jesus during the Deist Controversy*. Lewiston: Mellen, 1985.
———. *The Kalām Cosmological Argument*. New York: MacMillan, 1979.
———. *On Guard: Defending Your Faith with Reason and Precision*. Colorado Springs: David C. Cook, 2010.
———. *Reasonable Faith: Christian Truth and Apologetics*. 3d ed. Wheaton: Crossway, 2008.
Craig, William Lane and Paul Copan, eds. *The Kalām Cosmological Argument*, vol. 1: *Philosophical Arguments for the Finitude of the Past*. New York: Bloomsbury, 2018.
———, eds. *The Kalām Cosmological Argument*, vol. 2: *Scientific Evidence for the Beginning of the Universe*. New York: Bloomsbury, 2018.
Miller, Corey, and Paul M. Gould, eds. *Is Faith in God Reasonable? Debates in Philosophy, Science, and Rhetoric*. New York: Routledge, 2014.
Moreland, J. P., and William Lane Craig eds. *The Blackwell Companion to Natural Theology*. Oxford: Wiley-Blackwell, 2009.
Wallace, Stan W., ed. *Does God Exist? The Craig-Flew Debate*. Burlington, VT: Ashgate, 2003.

---

53. I should like to thank William Lane Craig for several interviews and answering numerous email inquiries regarding the opening section of this chapter. Thanks also to J.P. Moreland, Stephen Mizell, and Mark Janzen.

GARY R. HABERMAS

A Minimal Facts Ministry for Disciples and Doubters

W. DAVID BECK

BENJAMIN C. F. SHAW

Gary Habermas (1950–) is best known for his "minimal facts approach" to the historicity of Jesus's resurrection. This approach has been considered so influential that it is the one most often used in Christian apologetics for Jesus's resurrection. The minimal facts approach seeks to use (1) highly evidenced historical facts surrounding Jesus's resurrection that are (2) agreed upon by virtually all scholars from wide-ranging theological backgrounds, including skeptical ones. Naturalistic hypotheses have failed to adequately account for these "minimal facts," while Jesus's resurrection does so comfortably. Additionally, Habermas has contributed to several other areas of apologetics, such as philosophy, near-death experiences, doubt counseling, and the Shroud of Turin.

HISTORICAL BACKGROUND

Gary Robert Habermas was born in Detroit on June 18, 1950. His interest in apologetics started, as others' did, with an existential crisis in his childhood: the death of his grandmother. While the loss of a grandparent is difficult for any child, in Habermas's case it was especially challenging since she was his closest friend. Although he grew up in a German Baptist church, the loss of his grandmother planted various seeds of emotional doubt, the results of which eventually manifested in his teenage years in the form of factual doubts.

Habermas began to investigate the claims of Christianity, as well as other religions, more carefully. Importantly, he was interested in claims that had empirical components that could potentially be confirmed or disconfirmed. It was crucial for him that his beliefs be grounded, given that various religious claims were often made without any support. He also dialogued with Christians

768   CONTEMPORARY APOLOGISTS

and non-Christians regarding the empirical data for their beliefs. At one point during this period, Habermas contemplated Buddhism since he thought it was consistent with the models of physics of that period.

While he did see value in the classical arguments for theism, they were unable to anchor the truth of Christianity specifically. Similarly, while he viewed the reliability of the New Testament's arguments as strong, they seemed to stop just short of providing the type of confidence in the truth of Christianity he was seeking. Ultimately, it was the topic of Jesus's resurrection that Habermas viewed as the cornerstone of Christianity (1 Cor 15:13–19). He recognized that the truth of Christianity centered on Jesus's resurrection and examined the data in more detail.

Habermas used his time in college to pursue these various research interests. His undergraduate work was done at William Tyndale College, where he had three majors (Bible, social sciences, and Christian education) and three minors (Greek, Philosophy, and English and speech). He obtained an MA from the University of Detroit, a Jesuit school, where he studied philosophical theology and world religions. He then earned a PhD in history and philosophy of religion from Michigan State University in only two years and graduated in 1976. His dissertation, *The Resurrection of Jesus: A Rational Inquiry*, examined the resurrection from historical, philosophical, and theological perspectives.[1] Since his degree integrated these three fields, he had to satisfy three departments for his dissertation to pass successfully.

In preparing his dissertation, one of the members of his committee told him it was okay to use the Bible in his research as long as he used it critically. What this meant was that he could not simply say that something was true because the Bible said so. Rather, he had to use critical arguments that supported the veracity of a given text. Using these arguments, Habermas not only provided strong refutations of naturalistic theories but also compiled a list of facts that scholarship, including secular historians, has widely regarding as being historically reliable.[2] Habermas concluded that "it is not only the evidence from the elimination of all alternate theories which makes the resurrection plausible, but there are actual 'positive' facts which also demonstrate that this event is the most probable."[3]

His findings on the resurrection provided the firm anchor for Christianity that Habermas had sought. It secured the truth of Christianity with an actual

---

1. Gary R. Habermas, *The Resurrection of Jesus: A Rational Inquiry* (Ann Arbor, MI: University Microfilms, 1976).
2. Regarding the list of facts, he used the work of George Eldon Ladd, *I Believe in the Resurrection of Jesus* (Grand Rapids: Eerdmans, 1975), 93–94. See also 13, 132.
3. Habermas, *The Resurrection of Jesus*, 317. See also 320.

event that could be confirmed. The factual data surrounding Jesus's resurrection provided a substantial amount of emotional comfort for Habermas since other questions, doubts, and worries could be put in their proper perspective given the promise of eternal life.

After graduating from MSU, Habermas began teaching in Lewistown, Montana, at the Montana Institute of the Bible (later Big Sky Bible College), and then in 1979 he moved to a teaching position at William Tyndale College back home in Detroit. In 1981 he started working for Liberty University, which was then called Liberty Baptist College.[4] In addition to teaching, he coached the men's ice hockey team for almost a decade. He is currently a distinguished research professor and chair of the philosophy department.

Two losses of loved ones have shaped much of Habermas's apologetic understanding. The first loss started his apologetic journey, and the second challenged it. This second major loss in his life occurred when his wife of twenty-three years passed away in 1995. She initially went to the doctor because they thought she had the flu. Unfortunately, it was discovered that she had severe stomach cancer, and she passed away only four months later. This quick and unexpected tragedy deeply affected not only him but their four children as well. Habermas still describes it as "the worst thing that could have happened to me."[5]

Like the passing of his grandmother, the loss of his wife also led him to reflect on his Christianity. But unlike the passing of his grandmother, the apologetic work Habermas had done up to that point offered a way to minister to him. As we will see below, the ministry of apologetics contributed to the healing process by providing an anchor to the reality of Jesus's resurrection and promise of eternal life. Of course, this does not mean it was an easy process.

THEOLOGICAL CONTEXT

There were some notable changes in the theological aspects of philosophy, history, and apologetic method during Habermas's career. The shifts that occurred in the latter years of the twentieth century were, in many ways, shifts toward more conservative positions.

THEOLOGY AND PHILOSOPHY

Logical positivism (also known as logical empiricism or verificationism), for example, was a largely popular philosophical movement in the 1920s to 1950s

---

4. Habermas has also served as a visiting professor at over fifteen schools.
5. Gary R. Habermas, *The Risen Jesus and Future Hope* (Lanham, MD: Rowman & Littlefield, 2003), 187. For his full account, see 187–97.

and was similar to what many today would call "scientism." It viewed questions related to philosophy of religion (e.g., metaphysics, ontology, etc.) as meaningless since they could not be tested experimentally.[6] One of the flaws of this movement was that it failed its own criteria and was self-defeating. Logical positivism was itself unable to be tested experimentally. This, in part, caused this movement to decline in the 1960s and was virtually abandoned by the 1970s.

There was also a change in the landscape of philosophical theology: an explosive growth in the numbers of theistic and Christian philosophers. This led, for example, to the founding of both the Society of Christian Philosophers and the Evangelical Philosophical Society around 1978. Habermas was active in both. The impact of these philosophers in academia was recognized in 2001 by Quentin Smith in an article he wrote for *Philo*, the journal for the Society of Humanist Philosophers.[7] Incredibly, he writes that, not only did academia go through a process of "desecularization" that began in the late 1960s but that a majority of naturalist philosophers are unjustified in their beliefs that naturalism is true and also unjustified in their assertions that theism is false! One of the contributing factors to this was the scholarship of Christian philosophers such as Alvin Plantinga, Richard Swinburne, and many others.

THEOLOGY AND HISTORY

Historians during this same period were in many ways addressing the issue of faith and evidence. Throughout the eighteenth and nineteenth centuries, many historians tried to extract the "real" Jesus from the New Testament by developing a large variety of historical methods and tools.[8] In 1906 Albert Schweitzer famously pointed out that many historical descriptions of Jesus appeared to be made in the image of the historian (and their time) rather than Jesus![9] For this reason, along with the increasing realization that history was not as "objective" or "neutral" as generally supposed, the relationship between historical evidence and faith became increasingly fragmented.

This can be seen in the works of two highly influential theologians of the

---

6. One prominent English-speaking proponent of this view was A. J. Ayer (1910–1989). Although prior to the movement, Hume's famous line may be considered a forerunner of this type of thought. "If we take in our hand any volume; of divinity or school metaphysics, for instance; let us ask, *Does it contain any abstract reasoning concerning quantity or number?* No. *Does it contain any experimental reasoning concerning matter of act and existence?* No. Commit it then to the flames: For it can contain nothing but sophistry and illusion." David Hume, *Enquiry Concerning Human Understanding* (Chicago: Open Court, 1900), 176.

7. Quentin Smith, "The Metaphilosophy of Naturalism," *Philo* 4.2 (2001): 195–215.

8. Regarding the number of attempts to write a life of Jesus, Michael Grant writes that there "have been more of them than of any other man or woman in history; 60,000 were written in the nineteenth century alone." Michael Grant, *Jesus: An Historian's Review of the Gospels* (New York: Simon & Schuster, 1995), 197.

9. Albert Schweitzer, *The Quest of the Historical Jesus: A Critical Study of Its Progress from Reimarus to Wrede*, trans. W. Montgomery (New York: Macmillan, 1978 [1906]), 309.

early and middle of the twentieth century. Karl Barth and Rudolf Bultmann were both known for having approaches that were less interested in questions of history for Christian faith.[10] Bultmann is of particular importance since not only was he someone who Habermas read as a teenager but also because he held to various teachings from the *Religionsgeschichtliche Schule* (History of Religion School). This school argued for the influence of Hellenism and various mystery religions on the New Testament. Moreover, Bultmann maintained that modern man believed the world to be a closed system of cause-and-effect, which means biblical miracles are forms of myth, not history.[11] Faith was an existential decision toward authentic living in the continued significance of the gospel, not the result of the historical life, death, and resurrection of Jesus.

During the middle of the twentieth century, scholars recognized that the pendulum had swung too far away from the value of history for faith. While there were those, such as Oscar Cullmann, who had been arguing for increased attention on historical matters as they relate to faith, it was one of Bultmann's students, Ernst Käsemann, who many attribute to reviving the "quest" for the historical Jesus in 1953.[12] While there still remains a dichotomy between the historical evidence and faith for many, leading New Testament scholar N. T. Wright noted the importance of both history and faith and that such a dichotomy should be avoided because certain theologies, particularly Christian ones, require their integration.[13]

All of this was a crucial part of Habermas's education. He needed to conquer not only his own inner difficulties but a whole environment antagonistic to even the possibility of the historical reliability of the New Testament.

THEOLOGY AND APOLOGETIC METHODOLOGY

Finally, there were lengthy debates in the 1960s to 1980s on the propriety of different apologetic methods. The presuppositionalist approaches of Cornelius Van Til or Gordon Clark highlighted the potential limitations of evidence to the unbeliever who may suppress the evidence according to Romans 1. Evidentialists, such as Habermas or John Warwick Montgomery, believed the use of evidences

---

10. Stanley J. Grenz and Roger E. Olson, *20th-Century Theology: God and the World in a Transitional Age* (Downers Grove, IL: IVP Academic, 1993), 75 (Barth), 96–97 (Bultmann).

11. He famously wrote, "It is impossible to use electric light and the wireless and to avail ourselves of modern medical and surgical discoveries, and at the same time, to believe in the New Testament world of spirits and miracles." Rudolf Bultmann, "New Testament and Mythology: The Mythological Element in the Message of the New Testament and the Problem of Its Re-Interpretation," in *Kerygma and Myth: A Theological Debate*, ed. Hans Werner Bartsch, trans. Reginald H. Fuller, rev. ed. (New York: Harper & Row, 1966), 5.

12. For more information, see Stephen Neill and N. T. Wright, *The Interpretation of the New Testament, 1861–1986*, new ed. (Oxford: Oxford University Press, 1988).

13. N. T. Wright, *The New Testament and the People of God*, vol. 1 (Minneapolis: Fortress, 1992), 94–95.

were important in the defense of faith, appealing to Acts 17 or 1 Corinthians 15:3–8. These debates have appeared to become somewhat calmer over recent years, with the differing approaches seeming to find more common ground.[14]

APOLOGETIC AND THEOLOGICAL RESPONSE

THE MINIMAL FACTS APPROACH

In response to the surrounding historical, philosophical, and theological opposition of his day, Habermas developed what is called the "minimal facts approach" (MFA).[15] The MFA uses a list of "minimal facts" (MFs) that are agreed upon by virtually all historians, including the skeptical ones.[16] When this list of facts is examined, it becomes clear that naturalistic theories are unable to adequately account for them and, more importantly, that Jesus's resurrection appearances are the best explanation of the MFs.[17]

The list of MFs can vary depending on the context or skepticism of one's dialogue partner. So, for example, while Habermas lists twelve known facts in one situation, he can reduce the number to six, and even four, if needed for the sake of the discussion.[18] The reason for having the varying lists is so that one can avoid irrelevant questions or red herrings and start with the "lowest common denominator" of accepted critical facts.[19] A shortened list of MF may look like the following:

1. Jesus died by Roman crucifixion.
2. The disciples had experiences that they thought were actual appearances of the risen Jesus.

---

14. Steven B. Cowan, ed., *Five Views on Apologetics* (Grand Rapids: Zondervan, 2000).

15. Habermas technically started developing the minimal facts approach prior to the completion of his dissertation. Between 1970 and 1973, Habermas was seeking to address the legend theory using only data that critical scholars would allow. This began his interest in using data that was highly evidenced and granted by critical scholars.

16. While also in his dissertation (1976), Habermas discusses the MFA in Gary R. Habermas, *The Resurrection of Jesus: An Apologetic* (Grand Rapids: Baker, 1980). For more recent discussions, see Gary R. Habermas, "Evidential Apologetics," in *Five Views on Apologetics*, ed. Steven B. Cowan (Grand Rapids: Zondervan, 2000), 100, 115–21; Habermas, *Risen Jesus*, 8–31; Gary R. Habermas and Michael Licona, *The Case for the Resurrection of Jesus* (Grand Rapids: Kregel, 2004), 43–47; Gary Habermas, "Resurrection Research From 1975 to the Present: What Are Critical Scholars Saying?," *Journal for the Study of the Historical Jesus* 3.2 (January 1, 2005): 135–53; Gary R. Habermas, "The Minimal Facts Approach to the Resurrection of Jesus: The Role of Methodology as a Crucial Component in Establishing Historicity," *Southeastern Theological Review* 3.1 (2012): 15–18.

17. Habermas, *Risen Jesus*, 31–32.

18. Habermas, 9–10 (list of twelve), 26–27 (list of six). An even shorter list (four plus one) is the foundation for Habermas and Licona, *The Case for the Resurrection of Jesus*, 48–77.

19. Habermas, "The Minimal Facts Approach," 16–17.

3. The disciples were thoroughly transformed, even willing to die for this belief.
4. The apostolic proclamation of the resurrection began very early, when the church was in its infancy.
5. James, the brother of Jesus and a former skeptic, became a Christian because of an experience that he believed was an appearance of the risen Jesus.
6. Saul (Paul), the church persecutor, became a Christian because of an experience that he believed was an appearance of the risen Jesus.

Thus, even with only six core historical facts, the resurrection appearances of Jesus remain the most plausible explanation, while naturalistic theories fail.

Many scholars have presented lists of generally agreed-upon facts, such as George Eldon Ladd, Robert Funk, Geza Vermes, E. P. Sanders, et. al. But Habermas's contribution is to develop specific criteria that a fact must meet to be a MF. The fact must (1) be supported by multiple lines of evidence and (2) must be widely accepted by accepted scholars with expertise in the area. Of these two criteria, the first is the more crucial because it provides the supportive arguments. The second criterion is less significant since scholarly opinion can change or scholars could simply be mistaken. It is nevertheless important because "the chief thrust of the minimal facts approach is to argue whenever possible on more limited grounds, both to challenge a larger range of thinkers and to show that our basis is exceptionally firm."[20] It also mitigates against confirmation bias since it includes scholars from a wide range of theological backgrounds, from secular skeptics to believers.

A brief sketch is important here to give an example of what is meant by a MF meeting the first criterion. Jesus's death by crucifixion around AD 30 is highly evidenced as a historical fact in several ways.[21] First, it is multiply attested to in a number of sources (such as 1 Cor 15:3–5; Mark 15:20–47; Tacitus, *Annals* 15:44). Second, the reports are early (esp. the early creed in 1 Cor 15:3–5 as well as Mark, the earliest gospel). Third, it is an embarrassing admission that Jesus received death on a cross, a punishment reserved for those considered under a curse or for slaves (1 Cor 1:23). Fourth, the process of crucifixion was designed to kill its victims, and the executioners would have done their job. Many additional lines of evidence could be provided for this MF, but the point we want to emphasize here is that each of the MFs have multiple critically developed lines

---

20. Habermas, "Evidential Apologetics," 100.
21. Habermas, *Risen Jesus*, 16–17. For an in-depth study of arguments for Jesus's death, see Michael R. Licona, *The Resurrection of Jesus: A New Historiographical Approach* (Downers Grove, IL: IVP Academic, 2010), 303–18.

of argument that demonstrate their historicity.[22] These arguments, then, also explain why the majority of scholars from widely differing backgrounds affirm these historical details.[23]

Although some may be concerned that Habermas's approach gives up too much ground, one of its benefits is that, in doing so, it avoids a variety of discussions that can generally prevent someone from ever examining the evidence for the resurrection itself. His approach does not require that one prove God exists, and it does not require one to accept inerrancy or the inspiration of Scripture prior to examining the evidence. It does not even require one to believe that the Bible is a generally trustworthy or reliable collection of writings. In fact, in many lectures Habermas will begin by stating there are generally three groups of people: those who believe the Bible is inerrant and inspired, those who believe the Bible is errant but generally trustworthy, and those who believe the Bible is generally untrustworthy. Habermas will then point out that regardless of which group one falls into, the resurrection can still be demonstrated using the MFs. Habermas notes that the "most obvious advantage of using historically confirmed data is that there is little chance of it being rejected as unhistorical. The result of such a methodology is a potential case for the resurrection that is acceptable even by critical research procedures. There is no requirement that the New Testament be accepted as inspired. In fact, this ground work is not even based on the New Testament being a reliable text."[24]

Thus, the approach, much like his MSU dissertation, does not assume that the Bible is inerrant, inspired, or even reliable.

It is important to understand the significance of this point because all too often the discussion surrounding Jesus's resurrection becomes a discussion of alleged contradictions in the New Testament, inerrancy, or some other large-scope issue.[25] The MFA allows one to grant those points *for the sake of the argument* to focus on the historical facts.[26] Thus, whether there are contradictions,

---

22. Another argument would be David Strauss's famous critique of the apparent death theory in which he argues that if Jesus did not die on the cross, the disciples would have screamed to get a doctor instead of proclaiming the bloodied, beaten, and barely alive Jesus as Lord of Life and Conqueror of the grave!

23. The noted skeptical scholar Bart Ehrman provides an example of such a scholar when he writes, "The most certain element of the tradition about Jesus is that he was crucified on the orders of the Roman prefect of Judea, Pontius Pilate." Bart D. Ehrman, *The New Testament: A Historical Introduction to the Early Christian Writings*, 2nd ed. (New York: Oxford University Press, 2000), 233, 241, 247–50.

24. Habermas, *Risen Jesus*, 16.

25. Another common misconception is that one is not able to use the Bible at all, especially if it is considered "unreliable." Yet this is not how historians who view the Bible as unreliable do history. Skeptical historians use the Bible and apply historical-critical methods to better determine what they believe is a reliable event from an unreliable text. So if they will use it, so should believers!

26. Although Habermas's approach does not require a conservative position with the Bible, he nonetheless is quite conservative in his view of the Bible.

whether the Bible is inerrant, and so on, can be set aside for a separate discussion since none of the MFs are dependent on one's position of biblical inerrancy. Rather, the MFs are established by data that are so highly evidenced that scholars from wide-ranging backgrounds accept them. This approach, then, enables one to move directly to the facticity of the resurrection and its implications.

The approach has been remarkably influential in scholarship and ministry. Indeed, even those who think Habermas's approach is too restrictive have recognized its impact, with one such scholar even suggesting that the MFA has attained a "near-exclusive use in Christian apologetics."[27] By utilizing already agreed-upon historical data, with each having multiple lines of evidence, and providing a simple and straightforward model, Habermas's approach is both academically rigorous and apologetically practical. It avoids more difficult and sometimes technical questions while, more importantly, it keeps the focus on Jesus's resurrection as central to the gospel.

DEALING WITH DOUBT

A second aspect of Habermas's apologetic work has dealt with theological doubt. As noted above, it was doubt that contributed to Habermas's research into apologetic questions. While researching the factual questions, Habermas was also cognizant that other questions appeared to be following him. From early in his career, Habermas spent a lot of time talking with doubting Christians. He would frequently take notes regarding the types of questions they asked and discovered that there were different forms of doubt. These sorts of questions led Habermas to do some additional research in psychology, including a workshop with the renowned psychologist Albert Ellis, who specialized in Rational Emotive Behavioral Therapy (REBT). This led Habermas to eventually publish several insightful books that give suggestions, methods, and strategies for addressing doubt.[28]

Interestingly, Habermas admits that although the area of apologetics was his favorite topic and that a good dose of evidence would answer all his doubts, "What I found out, many years and thousands of books later, was that while having a firm foundation was helpful as a base, and certainly addressed certain sorts of questions, it was impotent against other forms of doubt. That was a shock."[29]

---

27. Lydia McGrew, *Hidden in Plain View: Undesigned Coincidences in the Gospels and Acts* (Chillicothe, OH: DeWard, 2017), 220–21.

28. Gary R. Habermas, *Dealing with Doubt* (Chicago: Moody, 1990); Gary R. Habermas, *The Thomas Factor: Using Your Doubts to Draw Closer to God* (Nashville: Broadman & Holman, 1999); Gary R. Habermas, *Why Is God Ignoring Me?: What to Do When It Feels Like He's Giving You the Silent Treatment* (Carol Stream, IL: Tyndale, 2010).

29. Habermas, *The Thomas Factor*, 6.

One may wonder what sort of doubts are not addressed by the evidences Habermas had studied. C. S. Lewis provides a helpful illustration of such doubts from everyday life. He writes, "My reason is perfectly convinced by good evidence that anaesthetics do not smother me and that properly trained surgeons do not start operating until I am unconscious. But that does not alter the fact that when they have me down on the table and clap their horrible mask over my face, a mere childish panic begins inside me. I start thinking I am going to choke, and I am afraid they will start cutting me up before I am properly under. In other words, I lose my faith in anaesthetics."[30]

Habermas noticed a similar feature in religious doubt. There were certain emotional doubts that were impervious to issues of matter-of-fact. He points out that emotional doubts "*do not constitute any evidence against Christianity.*"[31] Rather, they ask "What if" questions despite the data ("What if I'm wrong about Christianity?" or "What if I'm not saved?"). Frequently these fictional scenarios created by "What if" questions come to be believed as actual scenarios. In these situations, these misbeliefs can be the *cause* of intense anguish, pain, and suffering.[32]

In 1990 Habermas wrote *Dealing with Doubt*. In this book he identifies three varieties of doubt that would shape his approach over the next decades. Factual doubt deals with issues of evidence for Christianity. Second is emotional doubt, which is the most common and *most painful*. It arises from any number of subjective responses regarding the way an individual feels about a subject or situation.[33] Importantly, Habermas has observed that emotional doubt "most frequently masquerades as intellectual doubt and hence does not immediately reveal its disguised emotional basis."[34] Lastly, volitional doubt is associated with one's will and may be the least painful but the most dangerous.[35]

Habermas's first forays into exploring doubt came when he lost his grandmother. After having addressed those doubts, in 1995 Habermas endured the most devastating event in his life, the loss of his wife, the mother of their four children. This event was undoubtedly an emotionally and spiritually painful experience, but how would Habermas's earlier experience minister to him during this tragedy?

Habermas responded to this heartbreak by turning to biblical examples such as Job. Like Job, Habermas envisioned himself having a discussion with God. He

---

30. C. S. Lewis, *The Complete C.S. Lewis Signature Classics* (New York: HarperOne, 2007), 115–16.
31. Habermas, *The Thomas Factor*, 91 (emphasis in original).
32. A book by two Christian psychologists that is frequently referred to in Habermas's lectures is William Backus and Marie Chapian, *Telling Yourself the Truth: Find Your Way Out of Depression, Anxiety, Fear, Anger, and Other Common Problems by Applying the Principles of Misbelief Therapy* (Minneapolis: Bethany, 1980). Habermas notes his own experience with this as well. Habermas, *Risen Jesus*, 194.
33. Habermas notes the intense pain that this type of doubt causes. Habermas, *The Thomas Factor*, 48.
34. Habermas, *Dealing with Doubt*, 63; Habermas, *The Thomas Factor*, 48.
35. Habermas, *The Thomas Factor*, 44.

imagined God continually asking him whether Jesus was raised from the dead, to which Habermas constantly answered yes.[36] Habermas, the world's leading expert on the evidence for the resurrection, had to repeatedly remind himself of the fact of the resurrection to be assured of what follows from this fact. *The important thing was not just the reality of the resurrection but also what follows from it*, namely, the promise of eternal life for believers, including his wife. These internal conversations, according to Habermas, provided immense relief and caused him to trust God by persistently reminding himself that "He created the world, raised His Son from the dead, made a path of salvation for us, answered our prayers, and prepared heaven for us."[37]

This example highlights the reality that apologetical ministries have practical and personal significance in the lives of people who are hurting or asking questions. For Habermas, "not only is apologetics exceptionally useful with believers, it may even be its major value. This is an area where we need to apply theory to life in a variety of ways, and radically so. We need to be as committed to the practical, ministry task as we are to the scholarly pursuit."[38] It was what followed from facts of his historical apologetic of Jesus's resurrection that helped alleviate the pain and suffering that such doubting caused. The *application* of historical facts concerning Christianity provides help to those struggling with various doubts.

APOLOGETIC METHODOLOGY

Habermas is one of the best-known representatives of evidentialism.[39] In *Five Views on Apologetics*, Habermas was the chosen representative of the evidentialist position. Here he argued that evidentialism is a "one-step" approach in that "historical evidences can serve as a species of argument for God."[40] This is different from "two-step" approaches, such as that of William Lane Craig and others, which seek to demonstrate God's existence prior to examining specific evidences for Christianity.

As noted, Habermas has a definite concern for the practical applications in ministering to other believers with respect to the use of apologetics in helping to address doubts. He also views this method as one that could be "useful in witnessing to unbelievers by the power of the Holy Spirit. One advantage of the

---

36. Habermas, *Risen Jesus*, 192–94.
37. Habermas, 195.
38. Habermas, "Evidential Apologetics," 98. See also 121.
39. Brian K. Morley, *Mapping Apologetics: Comparing Contemporary Approaches* (Downers Grove, IL: IVP Academic, 2015), 334–50.
40. Habermas, "Evidential Apologetics," 92.

evidential method is in presenting the gospel. . . . Evidentialism specializes in the one-step approach, arriving at a more direct presentation of the gospel by using data that are still very persuasive."[41] Evidentialism, then, is two-pronged. It is able to address believers and unbelievers alike.

Habermas argues that there are several important principles of evidentialism that make it a significant and effective apologetic method.[42] Historical arguments are undoubtedly significant for Habermas. But history does not yield brute facts but always contains a subjective human factor. This does *not* mean history is relative or that we cannot have objectively true knowledge of the past, but it does remind us to be on guard since subjective prejudices can inappropriately intrude on historical investigation.

Evidentialism does not seek to coerce anyone into becoming a Christian. It recognizes the need to consider the effects of sin as well as the grace of God and the role of the Holy Spirit.[43] But there is common *epistemological* ground between believers and unbelievers such that both could agree, in principle, to certain facts about reality (historical, scientific, etc.).[44] Additionally, while evidentialists are in large part concerned with "positive" apologetics, it is able to function polemically as well. In doing so it can freely appeal to a variety of disciplines (philosophy, science, theology, etc.). "Evidential arguments," writes Habermas, "can profitably be utilized in strengthening believers who have questions or even factual doubts in laying a theological foundation on which to build (along with the application of additional, non-apologetic methods) for those who have certain emotional struggles concerning their beliefs."[45] The Holy Spirit can work through apologetics in bringing unbelievers to repentance, and he can also provide assurance to believers struggling with various forms of doubt.

The evidentialist method is one that is eclectic. Although Habermas is well known for his application of this method in the MFA, he has extended it into other areas as well. Given Habermas's expertise on the questions surrounding Jesus's death and resurrection, it is understandable that he would apply the same method to related areas such as near-death experiences (NDEs) or the Shroud of Turin.[46] For example, Habermas has recently contributed to some of the most

---

41. Ibid., 121.

42. For his full description see Habermas, 94–99.

43. See, for example, Gary R. Habermas, "The Personal Testimony of the Holy Spirit to the Believer and Christian Apologetics," *Journal of Christian Apologetics* 1.1 (1997): 49–64.

44. One could consider Pinchas Lapide, a Jewish historian, as an example here. He believed that Jesus resurrected but did not believe Jesus was the Messiah for the Jewish people. Pinchas Lapide, *The Resurrection of Jesus: A Jewish Perspective* (Eugene, OR: Wipf & Stock, 2002). Moreover, one may think of verses such as James 2:19 as being consistent with epistemological common ground but a will that refuses to worship God.

45. Habermas, "Evidential Apologetics," 121.

46. Although we have space only to discuss NDEs above, Habermas has done many lectures on the

advanced research on evidential NDEs.[47] Evidential NDEs occur when someone experiences medical death, comes back to life, and then reports various events or observations that took place while they were "dead" that can later be verified.

These evidential NDEs provide at least two positive contributions apologetically. First, they offer evidence that life continues after death. Not only does this add support to Jesus's resurrection, in that life continues after death, but Habermas has included NDEs in his discussions on doubt since they can be comforting to those who are struggling.[48] Second, it provides a polemic against materialist naturalistic worldviews. According to these worldviews, nothing should occur after one dies, but we have many documented cases of people who were "dead," came back, and later provided reports of their experiences that were corroborated. Thus, for Habermas, NDEs are a comfortable fit with both his primary area of expertise—Jesus's resurrection—but also for his evidentialist method when arguing against naturalism.

CONTRIBUTIONS TO THE FIELD OF APOLOGETICS

Habermas's main contribution to the field of apologetics has been the development and implementation of his MFA. As we saw above, it is widely used in apologetics.[49] The short list of facts is easy to remember, provides positive evidence for Jesus's resurrection, and highlights the failure of naturalistic theories. The approach avoids issues that are secondary to the resurrection and the established facts (e.g., alleged contradictions). The argument can be presented in a manner that grade-schoolers can grasp or in such a way that satisfies the rigors of an advanced academic setting.[50] This approach has also been used on other topics and been adopted by other historians.[51]

Shroud of Turin and coauthored a book with one of the leading scientist from the Shroud of Turin Research Project in 1978. Kenneth E. Stevenson and Gary R. Habermas, *Verdict on the Shroud: Evidence for the Death and Resurrection of Jesus Christ* (Ann Arbor, MI: Servant, 1981); Stevenson and Habermas, *The Shroud and the Controversy* (Nashville: Nelson, 1990).

47. In a recent article for *The Blackwell Companion to Substance Dualism*, Habermas argued that there are *many* evidenced NDEs, which fall into five categories. Gary R. Habermas, "Evidential Near-Death Experiences," in *The Blackwell Companion to Substance Dualism*, eds. Jonathan J. Loose, Angus J. L. Menuge, and J. P. Moreland (Oxford: Wiley-Blackwell, 2018), 227–46. For his earlier work, see Gary R. Habermas and J. P. Moreland, *Immortality: The Other Side of Death* (Nashville: Nelson, 1992).

48. Habermas, *The Thomas Factor*, 63; Habermas, *Why Is God Ignoring Me?*, 15–17.

49. Although, perhaps Habermas's biggest contribution has not occurred yet. For the past few years, he has been working on the culmination of his life's work on the resurrection to produce his magnum opus. This is expected to be a multivolume work focusing on Jesus's resurrection and addressing it from several angles.

50. This also applies to Habermas's "Timeline Argument," where Habermas describes the importance of the early creed in 1 Corinthians 15 with Galatians 1 and 2.

51. Habermas applies it to Jesus's deity and the veracity of the New Testament in Habermas, *Risen*

Another important consequence of the MFA is how it integrates into ministry. Habermas has helped many of those who have struggled with various forms of doubt by reminding them of the facts surrounding Jesus's resurrection as well as how the consequences of this event should impact their lives in the present. His work in this area has provided an immensely helpful example of the application of apologetics in the context of ministry.

Habermas has contributed a vast number of writings (over forty books, eighty chapters, and 150 articles and reviews) but is also well known for having done several debates, dialogues, interviews, and lectures, many of which are available on his website for free.[52] Among his many interlocutors, one of the most well-known was the former atheist philosopher Antony Flew.[53] Although Flew became a theist but not a Christian, these debates helped publicize Habermas's influential arguments for the resurrection as well as the shortcomings of naturalistic theories.[54] He has had subsequent debates or dialogues with other notable scholars, such as Thomas Sheehan, John Hick, James Crossley, Michael Ruse, Evan Fales, and others.

He is also well known for his work on NDEs. His interest here began early when he first read of such occurrences in Elisabeth Kübler-Ross. He saw here something that could be relevant to an understanding of the resurrection as well as our own death. He has made significant contributions to the study of NDEs, the result of which is that he is on the panel of editors of the *Journal of Near-Death Studies*. He has not only written a good deal on the subject but also often includes this kind of evidence in his public talks and lectures.

He presents NDEs as strong evidence that (1) there is empirical data for consciousness beyond measurable heart and brain death and that (2) the naturalistic view of consciousness as physical brain function must be false. Together this provides a powerful apologetic argument, not only for a Christian view of death but especially for the possibility of human resurrection.

Finally, he has made important contributions to the study and apologetic use of the Shroud of Turin. He has contributed, along with Ken Stevenson, two books and numerous articles and lectures on the topic. While he has said the evidence places the probability of the Shroud being Jesus's burial wrapping at

Jesus, 89–121, 213–24. It has also been applied to the Shroud of Turin. Tristan Casabianca, "The Shroud of Turin: A Historiographical Approach," *Heythrop Journal* 54.3 (May 2013): 414–23. A recent application of this method to the resurrection was used by Licona, *The Resurrection of Jesus*.

52. www.garyhabermas.com.

53. Their first debate, of three, occurred in 1985. Gary R. Habermas and Antony G. N. Flew, *Did Jesus Rise from the Dead?: The Resurrection Debate*, ed. Terry L. Miethe (San Francisco: HarperCollins, 1987).

54. Antony Flew and Roy Abraham Varghese, *There Is a God: How the World's Most Notorious Atheist Changed His Mind* (New York: HarperOne, 2007).

about 80 percent, the real importance and apologetic value is in arguing for the necessity of history and science to work hand in hand in doing the work of apologetics. The study of the Shroud itself places the resurrection clearly as an object of scientific and historical research and thus evidences that Christians must be involved in science and history, and it states clearly to skeptics that Christians do not avoid such scholarly research.

In conclusion, for Habermas, apologetics has two goals. It should not only minister to believers but, by the mercy and grace of the Holy Spirit, present the gospel to unbelievers.[55] His work on Jesus's resurrection, doubt, NDEs, naturalistic philosophy, and the Shroud of Turin have been geared toward helping believers and unbelievers alike.

BIBLIOGRAPHY

Backus, William, and Marie Chapian. *Telling Yourself the Truth: Find Your Way Out of Depression, Anxiety, Fear, Anger, and Other Common Problems by Applying the Principles of Misbelief Therapy.* Minneapolis: Bethany, 1980.

Bultmann, Rudolf. "New Testament and Mythology: The Mythological Element in the Message of the New Testament and the Problem of Its Re-Interpretation." Pages 1–44 in *Kerygma and Myth: A Theological Debate.* Ed. by Hans Werner Bartsch. Trans. by Reginald H. Fuller. Rev. ed. New York: Harper & Row, 1966.

Casabianca, Tristan. "The Shroud of Turin: A Historiographical Approach." *Heythrop Journal* 54.3 (May 2013): 414–23.

Cowan, Steven B., ed. *Five Views on Apologetics.* Grand Rapids: Zondervan, 2000.

Ehrman, Bart D. *The New Testament: A Historical Introduction to the Early Christian Writings.* 2nd ed. New York: Oxford University Press, 2000.

Flew, Antony, and Roy Abraham Varghese. *There Is a God: How the World's Most Notorious Atheist Changed His Mind.* New York: HarperOne, 2007.

Grant, Michael. *Jesus: An Historian's Review of the Gospels.* New York: Simon & Schuster, 1995.

Grenz, Stanley J., and Roger E. Olson. *20th-Century Theology: God and the World in a Transitional Age.* Downers Grove, IL: IVP Academic, 1993.

Habermas, Gary R. *Dealing with Doubt.* Chicago: Moody, 1990.

———. "Evidential Apologetics." Pages 92–121 in *Five Views on Apologetics.* Ed. by Steven B. Cowan. Grand Rapids: Zondervan, 2000.

———. "Evidential Near-Death Experiences." Pages 227–46 in *The Blackwell Companion to Substance Dualism.* Ed. by Jonathan J. Loose, Angus J. L. Menuge, and J. P. Moreland. Oxford: Wiley-Blackwell, 2018.

———. "The Minimal Facts Approach to the Resurrection of Jesus: The Role of Methodology as a Crucial Component in Establishing Historicity." *Southeastern Theological Review* 3.1 (2012): 15–26.

———. "The Personal Testimony of the Holy Spirit to the Believer and Christian Apologetics." *Journal of Christian Apologetics* 1.1 (1997): 49–64.

———. *The Resurrection of Jesus: A Rational Inquiry.* Ann Arbor, MI: University Microfilms, 1976.

———. *The Resurrection of Jesus: An Apologetic.* Grand Rapids: Baker, 1980.

———. "Resurrection Research From 1975 to the Present: What Are Critical Scholars Saying?" *Journal for the Study of the Historical Jesus* 3.2 (January 1, 2005): 135–53.

———. *The Risen Jesus and Future Hope.* Lanham, MD: Rowman & Littlefield, 2003.

———. *The Thomas Factor: Using Your Doubts to Draw Closer to God.* Nashville: Broadman & Holman, 1999.

---

55. Habermas, "Evidential Apologetics," 121.

————. *Why Is God Ignoring Me?: What to Do When It Feels Like He's Giving You the Silent Treatment.* Carol Stream, IL: Tyndale, 2010.

Habermas, Gary R., and Antony G. N. Flew. *Did Jesus Rise from the Dead?: The Resurrection Debate.* Ed. by Terry L. Miethe. San Francisco: HarperCollins, 1987.

Habermas, Gary R., and Michael Licona. *The Case for the Resurrection of Jesus.* Grand Rapids: Kregel, 2004.

Habermas, Gary R., and J. P. Moreland. *Immortality: The Other Side of Death.* Nashville: Nelson, 1992.

Habermas, Gary R., with Kenneth E. Stevenson. *The Shroud and the Controversy.* Nashville: Nelson, 1990.

Habermas, Gary R., with Kenneth E. Stevenson. *Verdict on the Shroud: Evidence for the Death and Resurrection of Jesus Christ.* Ann Arbor, MI: Servant, 1981.

Ladd, George Eldon. *I Believe in the Resurrection of Jesus.* Grand Rapids: Eerdmans, 1975.

Lapide, Pinchas. *The Resurrection of Jesus: A Jewish Perspective.* Eugene, OR: Wipf & Stock, 2002.

Lewis, C. S. *The Complete C.S. Lewis Signature Classics.* San Francisco: HarperOne, 2007.

Licona, Michael R. *The Resurrection of Jesus: A New Historiographical Approach.* Downers Grove, IL: IVP Academic, 2010.

McGrew, Lydia. *Hidden in Plain View: Undesigned Coincidences in the Gospels and Acts.* Chillicothe, OH: DeWard, 2017.

Morley, Brian K. *Mapping Apologetics: Comparing Contemporary Approaches.* Downers Grove, IL: IVP Academic, 2015.

Neill, Stephen, and N. T. Wright. *The Interpretation of the New Testament, 1861–1986.* New ed. Oxford: Oxford University Press, 1988.

Schweitzer, Albert. *The Quest of the Historical Jesus: A Critical Study of Its Progress from Reimarus to Wrede.* Trans. by W. Montgomery. New York: Macmillan, 1978.

Smith, Quentin. "The Metaphilosophy of Naturalism." *Philo* 4.2 (2001): 195–215.

Wright, N. T. *The New Testament and the People of God.* Vol. 1. 3 vols. Minneapolis: Fortress, 1992.

ALISTER E. MCGRATH

Scientist and Theologian
as Apologist

JAMES K. DEW JR.
JORDAN L. STEFFANIAK

Alister E. McGrath (1953–) is one of evangelicalism's foremost theological authorities on historical theology and the relationship between theology and science. Deeply committed to atheism and Marxism as a young man, McGrath came to faith in Christ while studying science at Oxford University, where he went on to earn a DPhil in molecular biophysics and then later two additional doctorates in historical theology (DD) and the intersection of science and theology (DLitt). McGrath's apologetic work, as he is one of the chief critics of "New Atheism," has focused on showing how theology and science can benefit from each other as dialogue partners. And his retrieval of natural theology offers a more historical, and potentially more promising, account of this important theological enterprise.[1]

HISTORICAL BACKGROUND

Alister E. McGrath was born on January 23, 1953 in Belfast, Ireland. He then grew up in Downpatrick, which he describes as "a market town of about 3,000 people in County Down, Northern Ireland."[2] During his high school years, he was a committed atheist who thought of Christianity as nothing more than "a relic of a past era, for which the future had no place."[3] Christianity was "to my youthful eyes, an inherently violent presence within Western culture,

---

1. Due to Alister McGrath's prominence in contemporary apologetics, we (Ben and Josh) decided this chapter was essential to this volume and commissioned it in the early stages of the project, before Alister was enlisted as a coeditor.

2. Alister E. McGrath, "Contributors: An Appreciation and Response," in *Alister E. McGrath & Evangelical Theology*, ed. Sung Wook Chung (Devon: Paternoster, Exeter, 2003), 333.

3. Alister E. McGrath, *A Scientific Theology* (Grand Rapids: Eerdmans, 2001), 1:xii.

whose elimination was only a matter of time."[4] His committed atheism was ardent. It was what he calls "a principled and informed decision to *reject* belief in God."[5] His rejection of God was encouraged in large part by Marxism and the works of A. J. Ayer and Bertrand Russell.[6] When McGrath began studying at Methodist College in Belfast, he was "convinced that the future lay with atheism, and that religion would either die of exhaustion or be eliminated by resentful humanity within [his] lifetime."[7] He even tried to found an Atheist Society during his time at Methodist College, but to no success.[8] It was the natural sciences, rather than religion, that could explain everything in the universe, according to McGrath. Therefore, he thought "religion was irrational superstition, which depended on blind faith on the part of very stupid people."[9] During this time the natural sciences were clearly his passion, which he recalls was stimulated by a great uncle who was a pathologist and gave him an old microscope that allowed him to begin serious study of biology.[10] So it was at Methodist College where McGrath began his first significant studying of pure and applied mathematics, physics, and chemistry from September 1966 until 1971.[11] During his final year at Methodist College, he studied history and the philosophy of science before beginning his studies at Oxford in the fall of 1971.[12] Oxford was where McGrath's life and career aspirations drastically changed. McGrath comments on this foundational time, saying, "By the end of my first term at Oxford, I was in a state of mental flux. I had suffered the immense inconvenience of discovering that Christianity could not be dismissed as easily as I had thought. In fact, it seemed to have rather a lot going for it."[13] Instead of trying to suppress his newfound respect for Christianity, he embraced it. He says:

> I began to discover that Christianity was much more exciting than I had realized. While I had been severely critical of Christianity as a young man, I had never extended that same critical evaluation to atheism, tending to assume that it was self-evidently correct, and was hence exempt from being assessed in this way. During October and November 1971, I began

4. Alister McGrath, *The Twilight of Atheism: The Rise and Fall of Disbelief in the Modern World* (New York: Doubleday, 2004), 176.
5. McGrath, *Twilight*, 175.
6. McGrath, *A Scientific Theology*, vol. 1, xii; McGrath, *Twilight*, 176.
7. Alister E. McGrath, *The Science of God* (Grand Rapids: Eerdmans, 2004), 3.
8. McGrath, *Twilight*, 176.
9. Ibid.
10. McGrath, *The Science of God*, 2.
11. McGrath, "Contributors: An Appreciation and Response," 334.
12. McGrath, *Science of God*, 3.
13. McGrath, *A Scientific Theology*, 1:xiv.

to discover that the intellectual case for atheism was rather insubstantial. Christianity, on the other hand, seemed rather more interesting. . . . I also discovered that I knew far less about Christianity than I had assumed. It gradually became clear to me that I had rejected a religious stereotype.[14]

Thus, by the end of his first full term at Oxford, McGrath had converted to Christianity, believing it to be "both intellectually persuasive and personally fulfilling."[15] He says, "I was converted to Christianity in November 1971, and found myself having to rethink countless questions, not least that of what I should do with the rest of my life."[16] After his conversion he considered dropping his studies in natural science to pursue Christian theology alone but was "dissuaded from this, and in the end completed [his] first degree in chemistry and went on to gain a doctorate from Oxford in molecular biophysics."[17] He says the "conclusion that I came to was quite simple. I would complete my studies in chemistry. In fact, I would do more than that: I would undertake research in some aspect of the natural sciences. And then I would switch to theology, and try to establish the connection between them."[18] So during this time, he would spend part of the day working on biochemistry while spending the remainder of his time "trying to master the basics of Christian theology."[19] By 1978 McGrath had received his DPhil in molecular biology as well as first class honors in theology.

Shortly after, in 1980, he was ordained as a deacon in the Church of England before being ordained as a priest in September 1981. As a result of this ministry, McGrath's commitment to the Christian faith—particularly evangelicalism—was significantly strengthened. He notes:

I found myself regaining confidence in the intellectual and spiritual vitality of evangelicalism as a result of my pastoral and preaching ministries. Preaching regularly to a suburban congregation, week by week, convinced me of the need to be able to interpret the Christian theological tradition in terms that ordinary people could understand, and in ways that conveyed its relevance to their lives. Like many others, I began to grow impatient with academic theology, which seemed at times to dismiss the questions and concerns of ordinary Christians, and speak a language that nobody could understand. My natural home is the world of the Christian community of

---

14. McGrath, *Science of God*, 4.
15. McGrath, *A Scientific Theology*, 1:xiv.
16. McGrath, "Contributors: An Appreciation and Response," 334.
17. McGrath, *A Scientific Theology*, 1:xiv.
18. McGrath, *Science of God*, 4.
19. Ibid., 7.

faith, rather than the dwindling ranks of academic theologians, and I have
to confess my concerns over the viability of the latter.[20]

Afterward, in 1983, he was appointed lecturer in Christian doctrine and ethics at Wycliffe Hall, Oxford. Then he was elected university research lecturer in
theology at Oxford University in 1993 and then served concurrently as research
professor of theology at Regent College, Vancouver, from 1993 to 1997. In 2001
he received his DD in historical and systematic theology, and in September 2004
he become the first director of the Oxford Centre for Christian Apologetics.
Then, in September 2008, McGrath took up the chair of theology, ministry, and
education at King's College, London. Most recently, in 2013, McGrath received
his DLitt from the division of humanities at Oxford for his research in science
and religion and accepted the Andreas Idreos Professorship in Science and Religion at the University of Oxford. He has not only three earned doctorates but
also has three honorary doctorates from Virginia Theological Seminary, Union
Theological Seminary, and Wycliffe College, which is a part of the University
of Toronto.

THEOLOGICAL CONTEXT

Given McGrath's background and interests, it is no surprise that his premier theological foes were atheism (particularly "New Atheism"), atheism's
twin sister—naturalism—and atheism's offspring of scientific and religious
incompatibility.

First, McGrath's premier challenger was atheism in general. He considered
atheism to be the chief "empire of the modern mind."[21] The empire of atheism
was supposed to capture the minds and loyalties of the masses if only given
enough time. As McGrath says, "the idea that there is no God captures human
minds and imaginations, offering intellectual liberation and spiritual inspiration
to generations that saw themselves as imprisoned, mentally and often (it must be
said) physically, by religious past."[22] Religion was oppressive, and atheism was
liberating. Indeed, even McGrath agreed with this early in his life, which is why
it is instructive to inquire as to his personal reasons for clinging so tightly to
atheism. Doing so will reveal to a significant degree his own opposing interlocutors. He found atheism appealing for four central reasons. First, it offered liberation from the religious past, which was full of strife, violence, and oppression.

20. McGrath, "Contributors: An Appreciation and Response," 336.
21. McGrath, *Twilight*, xi.
22. Ibid., xii.

Second, it made a certain degree of sense about the world. As he says, "If there was no God, then life was what we chose to make of it."[23] There was a great degree of black and white, with no shades of gray to complicate things.[24] Third, atheism offered hope and a future that could be changed and molded for the better.[25] Fourth, it was science that initially spurred much of his distaste for religion since science was considered the enemy of religion.[26] For these reasons, early on McGrath was inclined to think modern science had destroyed God. The scientific evidence proved that God could not exist, and atheism was the only serious alternative.[27] Therefore, these major tenets of atheism offered supple ground for apologetic interaction for McGrath.

The challenge of atheism was not just a general and vague phenomenon for McGrath to rebut. It also took shape in specific challengers, such as the "New Atheism."[28] The New Atheists were those in the twenty-first century who were militant in their quest to rid the world of alternative viewpoints—particularly those of religious persuasions. So his combat with atheism particularly looked to those such as Richard Dawkins and Daniel Dennett, whose Darwinian acid was supposed to erode through even the strongest of theistic foundations.[29] But it was Dawkins who was most vocal, causing McGrath to issue a book in response.[30] What is interesting about Dawkins is how similar he was to McGrath. As McGrath explains, "Dawkins and I have thus traveled in totally different directions, but for substantially the same reasons. We are both Oxford academics who love the natural sciences. Both of us believe passionately in evidence-based thinking and are critical of those who hold passionate beliefs for inadequate reasons. We would both like to think that we would change our minds about God if the evidence demanded it. Yet, based on our experience and analysis of the same world, we have reached radically different conclusions about God."[31]

Second, McGrath continually wrestled with the challenge of naturalism. Beginning in the seventeenth century, the idea that naturalistic explanations

23. Ibid., 177.
24. Ibid., 258.
25. Ibid., 177.
26. McGrath, *A Scientific Theology*, 1:xvi.
27. Alister McGrath and Joanna Collicutt McGrath, *The Dawkins Delusion? Atheist Fundamentalism and the Denial of the Divine* (Downers Grove, IL: InterVarsity Press, 2007), 33.
28. "New Atheism" was a movement in the early 2000s that brought a resurgence of atheistic thought. Unlike earlier atheistic movements that were largely in academic circles, "New Atheism" was grounded much more in popular culture. Specifically, thinkers such as Sam Harris, Daniel Dennett, Christopher Hitchens, and Richard Dawkins argued that religious belief in general—but Christian belief in particular—was (1) not only irrational but also (2) morally repugnant because of the negative effects it has had on the world.
29. Alister E. McGrath, *Darwinism and the Divine: Evolutionary Thought and Natural Theology* (Oxford: Blackwell, 2011), 281.
30. McGrath and McGrath, *The Dawkins Delusion?*
31. Ibid., 9.

were superior to all other explanations began to take root. Once this began, naturalism gained momentum, and intellectuals thought "the world could explain its properties with reference to itself, rather than require the invocation of God."[32] The full flower of naturalism required all reality to be fully and solely explainable by science as the only epistemological source of truth.[33] It required the elimination of metaphysics in philosophical and ethical reflection, building itself on pure materialism.[34] In sum, naturalism came to be the view that only scientific empirical methods were valid and that nature was only what these natural sciences could discover it to be and nothing more.[35] McGrath notes that the "result of this is entirely predictable. In that God cannot be observed by the methods of the natural sciences, God does not exist. Those who make statements which refer to God are therefore mistaken in doing so, and a purely natural explanation of those statements is to be sought."[36] Clearly naturalism was a challenge. If true, it would cut to the core of Christianity and theism in general. Without an epistemological method that can account for God, he quite simply cannot exist. If he does, he cannot be known.

Third, McGrath's final constant challenger was the presumed incompatibility of science and religion. Due to what McGrath calls the "warfare" school of interpretation, hostile barriers were erected between science and religion, so much so that dialogue was typically cut off completely.[37] Those such as Richard Dawkins found the antiscientific stance of American fundamentalism an easy target and portrayed it as a representation of all religion.[38] But this perspective remains only at the popular level—infecting the masses influenced by Dawkin's nontechnical thought. But at the academic level, it is what McGrath calls "the myth that an atheistic, fact-based science is permanently at war with a faith-based religion."[39] True scholarly consensus knew that these two areas were not incompatible. Despite the myth, even McGrath admitted to believing it for some time. He says, "Having previously thought, in rather uncritical terms which I now realize to have been shaped by Andrew Dickson White's hostile and inaccurate account of the relation of Christianity and the sciences, that the natural sciences were the enemy of religion, I now began to realize that the situation was rather more complex (and interesting), demanding a more nuanced and informed response."[40]

---

32. McGrath, *A Scientific Theology*, 1:100.
33. Ibid., 1:124–25.
34. Ibid., 1:125
35. Ibid., 1:126.
36. Ibid., 1:127.
37. Alister E. McGrath, *The Foundations of Dialogue in Science & Religion* (Oxford: Blackwell, 1998), 20.
38. Ibid., 21.
39. McGrath, *Twilight*, 87.
40. McGrath, *A Scientific Theology*, 1:xvi.

So, while the incompatibility of science and religion was *and is* a myth, it remained a significant challenge because of its popular appeal and strength. But McGrath could not sit idly by once he realized the myth was just that—a myth. During the summer of 1976, he came to an epiphany. He would explore the relation between Christian theology and the natural sciences. He would be faithful to the historic Christian tradition but would be open to science and scientific insights. This was to be a proposal for synergy.[41] Therefore, he directly engaged the challenge of faith and science, along with the challenges of atheism and naturalism.

APOLOGETIC RESPONSE

Unlike some Christian apologists who use rigid analytic arguments in support of Christian theism, McGrath focuses more on showing how Christianity makes sense of the world. As C. S. Lewis famously said, "I believe in Christianity as I believe that the sun has risen, not only because I see it but because by it, I see everything else."[42] McGrath's apologetic approach resonates deeply with this sentiment. Christianity, in response to all three theological challenges expanded above, provides a far more robust understanding of the world than the alternatives. Everything else in the world is made clear from the vantage point of Christianity. But how did McGrath specifically apply this insight to each of his challenges in particular?

First, he countered atheism through several books and debates, both popular and academic. The "New Atheism" put forth by those such as Richard Dawkins continually derided theism for being trapped in a delusion with no evidence. The only people committed to theism were blinded by faith. But McGrath strongly rejects this account of science and Christian theology. For example, he chastised the foundation of Dawkins's method: "How can Dawkins be so sure that his current beliefs are true, when history shows a persistent pattern of the abandonment of scientific theories as better approaches emerge? What historian of science can fail to note that what was once regarded as secure knowledge was eroded through the passage of time? Conveniently enough, Dawkins turns a blind eye to history. He also turns a blind eye (how many does he have?) to the philosophy of science."[43]

In this, McGrath's tactic is clear. He turns the tables on the atheist. Atheists, such as Dawkins, have failed to consider the limits of their own scientific

---

41. Ibid., 1:xi.
42. C. S. Lewis, *The Weight of Glory* (San Francisco: HarperOne, 2001), 140.
43. McGrath, *Twilight*, 95.

method. McGrath certainly has no intension of deriding the achievements of science, but he does intend to show its limits. Science simply cannot explain its ontological or epistemological foundations. Only something as expansive and deep as Christianity can explain the regularities and truths of science. That is, only Christianity can provide the proper foundation on which the natural sciences may operate.

Second, he countered naturalism by arguing for a robust Christian doctrine of creation. He began by offering the mutually agreed-upon reality of regularity and intelligibility in the universe. Both the natural sciences and Christian theology affirm their fundamental truth—the world is both ordered and rational. He then considered whether a thoroughgoing naturalism can offer a legitimate explanation. Can we "see everything else" through the narrow lens of naturalism alone? His conclusion is that naturalism fails because the whole of reality cannot be understood through the lens of the natural world alone. It does not have the resources to make sense of order and reason. It is bound to be circulatory in its reasoning since it privileges the natural sciences to explain all reality, which also happens to be nothing more than the natural world. While naturalism may offer internal coherence, which is necessary for any true theory, it is insufficient for justifying any true theory. There is no way to justify naturalism apart from naturalism itself. McGrath concludes, "From a naturalist point of view, there are no adequate grounds for asserting that naturalism is true."[44] Due to this, naturalism generally devolves into nothing more than "a posteriori validation of the existing notions and values of the allegedly neutral observer."[45] For example, he says, "There are no meaningful criteria by which a "Darwinian" view of the world can be proposed as an ultimate ideological system that is itself invulnerable to corrosion by its own universal acid. The ultimate circularity of the notion of the meme, especially when coupled with its notorious evidential under-determination, illustrates how the strategists of 'Universal Darwinism' have managed to declare themselves to occupy a privileged intellectual 'zone of invulnerability' from the corrosiveness of its own ideas."[46]

McGrath offers the Christian doctrine of creation in its place, which is fundamentally approaching nature from the vantage point of Christianity.[47] He explains its importance as follows: "The Christian doctrine of creation is thus of meta-traditional significance. The scientific tradition, for example, finds itself having to presuppose the uniformity and ordering of creation; Christian theol-

44. McGrath, *A Scientific Theology*, 1:131.
45. Ibid., 1:132.
46. McGrath, *Darwinism and the Divine*, 282.
47. McGrath, *A Scientific Theology*, 1:137.

ogy offers an account of this. The scientific tradition recognizes that the natural world has a rationality which human rationality can discern and systematize; Christian theology, however, offers an explanation of why this is the case."[48] Thus, Christianity offers an account for the common ground of order and rationality. Naturalism fails to do so.

Explicating the content of this doctrine of creation is at the heart of McGrath's entire apologetic enterprise. It is the engine that drives his work. Biblically speaking, creation is an act of *wisdom* that gives the reasoning behind its inherent rationality. God did not merely create the world; he created it "by wisdom" (Prov 3:19).[49] Further, the New Testament explicates a christological dimension to creation, where Christ as the *wisdom* of God is the fundamental ordering principle of creation *ex nihilo*.[50] It is through this christologically shaped creation that humans are created in his image as well—being inherently rational themselves.[51] Therefore, on the Christian understanding, rationality and order are explained by means of God's creative purpose. Rationality and order need not be mystical notions of pure chance as they are in naturalism.

But the Christian doctrine of creation is even more interesting since it offers room for both creation as act *and* process. It is generally clear that creation involves God's singular act, but what does he mean by creation as process? He retrieves the work of Augustine to a significant extent for this aspect. He comments as follows, "Implicit within Augustine's account of creation is the notion that creation entails the origination of a potentially multi-leveled reality, whose properties *emerge* under certain conditions that either did not exist, or were not considered appropriate for development, at the origins of the universe."[52] Therefore, the Christian doctrine of creation does not exclude new growth or emergence from the initial act of creation. Since it does not demand particular scientific theories, it is flexible enough to be compatible with whatever science may discover. Thus, the Christian doctrine of creation provides the proper foundation on which the natural sciences may operate—a foundation that naturalism lacks. McGrath explains this saying, "What the natural sciences are forced to assume—in that it cannot be formally demonstrated without falling into some form of circularity of argument or demonstration—the Christian understanding of 'wisdom' allows to be affirmed on the basis of divine revelation, and correlated

---

48. Alister E. McGrath, *The Order of Things: Explorations in Scientific Theology* (Oxford: Blackwell, 2006), 64.
49. McGrath, *A Scientific Theology*, 1:149.
50. Ibid., 1:155.
51. Ibid., 1:200.
52. McGrath, *Darwinism and the Divine*, 226.

with the existence of a transcendent creator God, responsible both for the order-ing of the world and the human ability to grasp and discern it."[53]

Creation grounds order and rationality, which are mutually agreed-upon principles. Naturalism is not up to the task. Rather than closing scientific inquiry, Christianity opens it up to far greater possibilities and understanding. McGrath comments, "A Christian natural theology is fundamentally hospitable toward a deeper engagement with reality."[54] It turns out that naturalism is the viewpoint that fails to engage reality with the deepest inquiry.

Third, he countered the unnatural bifurcation between science and religion. While the exact origin of this rift is not clear, McGrath locates it somewhere in the sixteenth century, potentially in the late Renaissance Aristotelian com-mentaries of those such as Jacopo Zabarella.[55] Whatever the exact origin of the warfare thesis, McGrath notes that "there is no doubt that precisely this perception remains deeply embedded in western academic life and culture."[56] But according to McGrath, such a thesis is an atheistic myth.[57] Science is not at war with religion. In fact, "Science is at its most interesting when it engages in dialogue with other disciplines—including theology, religion, and spirituality."[58] And religion, as shown in the Christian doctrine of creation, has all the tools necessary to engage science in a robust and useful manner, appropriating all matters of insight. But how does the mantra of Lewis—"I believe in Christianity as I believe that the sun has risen, not only because I see it but because by it, I see everything else"—apply here? McGrath counters the presumed warfare between science and theology by offering Christian theology as the sufficient basis for wedding the natural sciences and humanities (particularly religion).[59] The perceived divorce between the two subjects is not necessary since Christianity can provide a substantial foundation for both to be pursued together in dialogue and mutual enrichment.[60]

APOLOGETIC METHODOLOGY

McGrath's theological and apologetic methodology is on display in his interac-tions with his theological opponents. But it is helpful to systematize his methods to bring further clarity to their foundations. McGrath is a prolific author, so

53. McGrath, *A Scientific Theology*, 1:222.
54. McGrath, *Darwinism and the Divine*, 12.
55. McGrath, *A Scientific Theology*, 1:28.
56. Ibid., 1:33.
57. McGrath, *Twilight*, 87.
58. McGrath, *Darwinism and the Divine*, 2.
59. McGrath, *A Scientific Theology*, 1:34.
60. For those interested in a proposed synthesis of these two, we recommend McGrath's *A Scientific Theology*.

summarizing these methods and insights may appear daunting at first glance. But McGrath is a consistent thinker who offers several fundamental assumptions throughout his works, including: (1) his evangelical and orthodox commitments, (2) his critical realist epistemology and the way it undergirds much of his apologetic engagement, and (3) his understanding of the *ancilla theologiae* or handmaiden role of science in theological construction.

CREEDAL CHRISTIAN ORTHODOXY

First, McGrath is committed to evangelical and traditional creedal Christian orthodoxy. In his view, "Christian theology is under an obligation to pay respectful and obedient attention to the biblical testimony and allow itself to be shaped and reshaped by what it finds expressed there."[61] This evangelical approach is "an approach to theology which insists that theology must be nourished and governed at all points by Holy Scripture, and that it seeks to offer a faithful and coherent account of what it finds there."[62] So McGrath's apologetic method must conform to biblical revelation if it is to be both coherent and accurate. Any method or conclusion that conflicts with Scripture is to be rejected. By traditional creedal Christian orthodoxy, he means the most "authentic form of Christianity, representing the consensus of the Christian communities of faith over an extended period of time."[63] In pursuing a traditional Christianity, he rejects theological novelty and creativity. Anything that lacks significant historical grounding is to be suspected as a theological imposter. This does not mean that new insights cannot emerge and form, but it does mean that anything conflicting with the universal assent of the church throughout history is likely faulty. Therefore, his apologetic method requires historical grounding and cannot depart from the classical affirmations of the Christian church. Thus, authorities such as Augustine, Athanasius, Thomas Aquinas, and John Calvin all play significant roles as methodological tutors and guides. Within this manifold tradition, answers to most apologetic problems find their solution, or at least the resources from which to construct a contemporary solution.[64]

CRITICAL REALIST EPISTEMOLOGY

Second, McGrath affirms a critical realist epistemology. To best understand what this is and why he accepts it, it is useful to consider briefly the competing

---

61. Alister E. McGrath, "Engaging the Great Tradition: Evangelical Theology and the Role of Tradition," in *Evangelical Futures: A Conversation on Theological Method*, ed. John G. Stackhouse Jr. (Grand Rapids: Regent, 2000), 140.

62. McGrath, *A Scientific Theology*, 1:xix.

63. Ibid., 1:36.

64. McGrath, *Darwinism and the Divine*, 280.

theories that he rejects as inadequate. First, he denies classic foundationalism since its understanding and requirements for knowledge as infallible, incorrigible, and indubitable are too stringent.[65] Being required to base all knowledge on such a foundation leads to significant challenges for much of what Christians want to say. Second, he also denies coherentism since it is insufficient to determine truth. McGrath helpfully comments at length:

> The coherentist position, taken on its own, is perfectly capable of validating an internally consistent world-view which makes no significant point of contact with the real world, or which evades such contact altogether. Coherency does not guarantee truth—merely logical consistency. A belief can be consistent with all other beliefs within a system, and yet have no independent supporting evidence. A scientific theology affirms the critical importance of both extra-systemic reference and intra-systemic consistency, holding that a proper grasp of spiritual reality will ensure both.[66]

Finally, McGrath also denies postmodern antirealism since it fails to account for "the two most awkward stumbling-blocks" of the natural sciences and mathematics, which do not admit the relativism required by the postmodern project.[67] If postmodern antirrealism is about rejecting all objective norms, the acceptance of *any* objective norm is deadly for the overall project. But most are not willing to deny the objective status of the natural sciences.

With these views as a backdrop, how does critical realism fit into the methodological picture? Critical realism finds its way somewhere in the middle between the direct (naive) realism of the Enlightenment and the antirealism of postmodernity. Critical realism insists that there is an objective reality (hence realism rather than antirealism), but also maintains that this reality is apprehended by the human mind, which tries to understand, express, and accommodate that reality as best it can (hence critical rather than naive). To help distinguish critical realism for other epistemological perspectives, McGrath suggests the following:

1. Naive realism: reality impacts directly upon the human mind, without any reflection on the part of the human knower. An objective reality within the world directly determines the resulting knowledge.

65. McGrath, *The Science of God*, 97.
66. McGrath, *A Scientific Theology*, 2:19.
67. McGrath, *The Science of God*, 107.

2. Critical realism: reality is apprehended by the human mind which tries to express and accommodate that reality as best it can with the tools at its disposal—such as mathematical formulae or mental models.
3. Postmodern antirealism: the human mind freely constructs its ideas without any reference to an alleged external world.[68]

Thus, as McGrath explains it, critical realism recognizes "the active involvement of the knower in the process of knowing."[69] McGrath again gives further clarity to critical realism and its contrasting with other forms of epistemology when he says, "Against postmodernism, critical realism affirms that there is a reality, which may be known, and which we are under a moral and intellectual obligation to investigate and represent as best as we can. Against certain types of modernism, critical realism affirms that the human knower is involved in the process of knowing, thus raising immediately the possibility of the use of 'constructions'—such as analogies, models, and more specifically social constructs—as suitably adapted means for representing what is encountered."[70]

Knowledge is not a purely objective or a purely subjective pursuit. It requires both aspects in order to understand. This cashes out in his apologetic method, especially in his deconstruction of the "intellectually plastic notion" of nature.[71] While there is an objective reality of nature, it is significantly culturally conditioned and requires intellectual reflection. It is neither purely subjective nor purely objective.

ANCILLA THEOLOGIAE

Third, McGrath uses science as an *ancilla theologiae*—natural sources of knowledge that complement and serve theology as a dialogue partner. This is particularly true of the way he understands natural theology, which differs from other more contemporary versions of natural theology. First, unlike other contemporary models, McGrath's method does not focus on specific arguments for the existence of God (e.g., the cosmological, ontological, or teleological arguments). His view of natural theology suggests that nature and natural science serve in a confirmatory role for theological claims. Specifically, he understands natural theology to be "the enterprise of seeing nature as creation, which both presupposes and reinforces fundamental Christian theological affirmations."[72]

68. McGrath, *A Scientific Theology*, 2:195.
69. Ibid., 2:196.
70. McGrath, *The Science of God*, 142.
71. Alister E. McGrath, *The Open Secret: A New Vision for Natural Theology* (Malden, MA: Blackwell, 2008), 9.
72. McGrath, *The Science of God*, 113.

Second, he situates his natural theology within an assumed set of beliefs previously gleaned from special revelation. Nature is designed to function as a divinely given aid for understanding special revelation—as a useful dialogue partner—rather than as an authoritative master over special revelation. In this role, natural theology is limited. It is not allowed to function as the foundation for special revelation, though it is elevated to a privileged place of instruction.[73] McGrath explains this approach of limiting and yet promoting natural theology: "There is a long tradition within Christian theology of drawing on intellectual resources outside the Christian tradition as a means of developing a theological vision. This approach is often referred to by the Latin phrase *ancilla theologiae*, 'a handmaid of theology.' The basic idea is that philosophical systems can be a very helpful way of stimulating theological development and of enabling a dialogue to be opened up between Christian thinkers and their cultural environment. The two most important historical examples of this approach to theology are the dialogues with Platonism and Aristotelianism."[74] This means that all of God's creation offers helpful insights into understanding who he is and what the world is. Nothing should be cast off as irrelevant to understanding God and his world.

With this understanding of natural theology in hand, for McGrath, the natural sciences are an exceptionally useful handmaiden to explore and understand theology. McGrath says regarding this, "The natural sciences today offer to Christian theology today precisely the role that Platonism offered our patristic, and Aristotelianism our medieval forebears. A scientific theology will treat the working assumptions and methods of the natural sciences as offering a supportive and illuminative role for the Christian theological enterprise, both assisting theological reflection and identifying and allowing exploitation of apologetic possibilities and strategies."[75]

So natural theology is not antagonistic toward Christianity, nor is it antagonistic toward the supremacy of Scripture. It is designed to aid and supplement divine written revelation, just as the Platonic worldview aided the church fathers and the Aristotelian worldview aided Thomas Aquinas and the scholastics. As McGrath says, "Natural theology gains its plausibility and derives its intellectual foundations from within the Christian tradition. Its roots lie *intra muros ecclesiae*, even if its relevance extends *extra muros ecclesiae*."[76] Far from overtaking God's self-disclosure in the written word, it highlights it, resources it, and aids it. So, things such as science can function as a divinely given gift of understanding

---

73. McGrath, *A Scientific Theology*, 1:7–8.
74. McGrath, *The Science of God*, 18.
75. McGrath, *A Scientific Theology*, 1:7.
76. Ibid., 2:74.

for the Christian, rather than a sworn enemy of the faith. Thus, McGrath finds fertile grounds in the natural sciences to benefit the Christian faith. It ought to be plundered for its contributions to the Christian worldview rather than rejected or ignored.

CONTRIBUTIONS TO THE FIELD OF APOLOGETICS

The contributions McGrath offers to apologetics are numerous. Beyond his specific and practical works of engagement, there are several overall principles that can be gleaned. Eight of them will be offered here. First, McGrath consistently desires to offer a "public theology" that provides maximum common ground. He thinks the Christian doctrine of creation can provide such a foundation.[77] This is significant because it is an insight that serves all within the Christian world, not just a small sect or subgroup with their own theological idiosyncrasies. To be public in the true sense, apologetics must have wide support. All corners of the Christian church should be able to benefit from and use one's apologetic method. As with the apostle Paul in Acts 17, creation is McGrath's chief ground for apologetic engagement.

Second, theology and apologetics are deeply rooted in the life of the church for McGrath. All too often apologetics is divorced from the local church, making contact only through the occasional guest speaker to a youth group on the challenges of evolution. But for McGrath, his entire approach is rooted in the church. An example of this is the way he employs natural theology. He says, "Natural theology is not an individual undertaking; it is rooted in the life and ministry of the Christian community. Through faith, Christians develop habits of engagement with the natural world that allow it to be seen, understood, and evaluated in new ways."[78] These Christian "habits" are developed through the nurture of the church. The church is the source of intellectual and apologetic nurturing and imagination. More than the church being the source for strong apologetic thought, McGrath says, "the church is thus called to be an active interrogator, not a passive endorser, of secular and secularizing visions of the world. It is called upon to proclaim, exhibit, and embody its own 'social imaginary,' deeply rooted in the gospel on the one hand, and with the capacity to transform reflection and practice on the other."[79] The church is to be the chief herald of the good news of

---

77. McGrath, *Darwinism and the Divine*, 62.
78. Ibid., 285.
79. Ibid., 286.

creation and the gospel. Apologetics is not primarily the tool of the disenchanted and isolated academic but the vibrant and growing church.

Third, McGrath finds the intellectual requirements of apologetics to be pragmatically useful. He comments in one of his works that "all this seems to make writing books like this somewhat pointless. Except that once I too was an atheist and was awaked from my dogmatic slumber through reading books that challenged my rapidly petrifying worldview."[80] This is a reminder to all who fear or loath the rigorous and often lonely work of theological academia. Intellectual depth in academic writing is not simply an exercise of the mind but is intensely practical for many who are struggling and searching to find meaning in life and, as such, can be used mightily by God.

Fourth, McGrath continually promotes dialogue over warfare.[81] In the contemporary climate in which McGrath interacts, this is a rarity. The apostle Paul exhorts Timothy to correct his opponents with gentleness (2 Tim 2:25). Such a posture is exemplified throughout McGrath's works. McGrath provides something of a model and inspiration for those seeking to engage the world with their faith in gentleness and respect, as Christians ought.

Fifth, McGrath promotes the classical understanding of natural theology that does not require it to start from "objective" or "neutral" starting points, as the Enlightenment required it to do. As McGrath laments, natural theology has fallen on hard times in the contemporary milieu, not least of all because of the likes of Karl Barth and contemporary Reformed presuppositionalism. Yet he tries to retrieve its usefulness. He bridles it significantly from what many current models have done, which provides greater common ground for those suspicious of natural theology.

Sixth, McGrath's personal humility and determination to understand deeply should inspire people. At one point in McGrath's life, because of his scientific and theological accomplishments, he was asked to "consider writing a book on the theme of Christianity and the natural sciences, in particular to respond to Richard Dawkin's book *The Selfish Gene*. I gave this proposal very serious consideration. However, I came to the conclusion that I would need to immerse myself in the further study of religion, and especially the history of Christian theology, before I could make a positive and informed contribution to this field."[82] Such a response is rare within Christianity today. Far too often, Christians are quick to offer arguments for the sake of building their own platform, even when their grasp of philosophy or science is too limited to be of

---

80. McGrath and McGrath, *The Dawkins Delusion?*, 15.
81. McGrath, *Foundations of Dialogue*, 28.
82. McGrath, "Contributors: An Appreciation and Response," 335.

significant impact. Yet McGrath offers a different way—a way of humility, hard work, honesty, and clarity. Contending for the faith is not designed for those seeking fame and honor but those pursuing truth and the honor of Christ.

Seventh, in recent years McGrath has also championed narrative approaches to apologetics, pointing out the apologetic potential of biblical narratives, as well as highlighting the role of storytelling in the apologetics of C. S. Lewis and J. R. R. Tolkien.[83] Such an approach offers significant benefit for the current cultural milieu entranced by both narrative and storytelling. Stories have unique power over the minds and imaginations of the current culture at large, and McGrath's approach is both nuanced and accessible to nearly anyone. This gives it power and pragmatic value for apologetics at large.

Eighth and finally, McGrath offers helpful reminders regarding the wariness of transient theological trends. He offers wise caution for those considering such a departure from the classical orthodoxy of Christianity. He states, "Historically, alternatives to Christian orthodoxy tend to be transient developments, often linked with specific historical situations whose passing leads to an erosion of plausibility of the variant of Christian theology being proposed."[84] In reality, it is often just a cultural mood of restlessness with the past and with the perceived institution of power rather than rigorous theological argument that leads one to depart from the historical path.[85] To withdraw from the great tradition leads only to an impoverished Christianity, lacking the many resources developed throughout the ages. For these reasons, McGrath's work is extremely valuable for evangelical apologetics.

BIBLIOGRAPHY

Lewis, C. S. *The Weight of Glory*. New York: HarperOne, 2001.
McGrath, Alister E. "Contributors: An Appreciation and Response." Pages 333–64 in *Alister E. McGrath & Evangelical Theology*. Ed. by Sung Wook Chung. Devon: Paternoster, Exeter, 2003.
———. *Darwinism and the Divine: Evolutionary Thought and Natural Theology*. Oxford: Blackwell, 2011.
———. "Engaging the Great Tradition: Evangelical Theology and the Role of Tradition." Pages 139–58 in *Evangelical Futures: A Conversation on Theological Method*. Ed. by John G. Stackhouse Jr. Grand Rapids: Regent, 2000.
———. *The Foundations of Dialogue in Science & Religion*. Oxford: Blackwell, 1998.
———. *Narrative Apologetics: Sharing the Relevance, Joy, and Wonder of the Christian Faith*. Grand Rapids: Baker, 2019.
———. *The Order of Things: Explorations in Scientific Theology*. Oxford: Blackwell, 2006.
———. *The Science of God*. Grand Rapids: Eerdmans, 2004.
———. *A Scientific Theology*. Grand Rapids: Eerdmans, 2001.
———. *The Twilight of Atheism: The Rise and Fall of Disbelief in the Modern World*. New York: Doubleday, 2004.
McGrath, Alister, and Joanna Collicutt McGrath. *The Dawkins Delusion? Atheist Fundamentalism and the Denial of the Divine*. Downers Grove, IL: InterVarsity Press, 2007.

---

83. See Alister E. McGrath, *Narrative Apologetics: Sharing the Relevance, Joy, and Wonder of the Christian Faith* (Grand Rapids: Baker, 2019).
84. McGrath, *A Scientific Theology*, 1:36.
85. Ibid., 1:37.

TIMOTHY KELLER

The Pastor as Apologist

JOSHUA D. CHATRAW

© Nathan Troester

Rarely does one meet a person who is a skilled practitioner as well as an insightful intellectual, but Timothy Keller (1950–) is clearly both. It is this unique combination, which has garnered him acclaim as a leading apologist for the Christian faith, with *Newsweek* even declaring that Keller is "pitching" himself as "a C. S. Lewis for the 21st century."[1] To the contrary, Keller has been hesitant to embrace this comparison between himself and the celebrated British apologist.[2] This, however, has not stopped reviewers from drawing parallels—and it is not hard to see why. Both men represent significant bodies of their own writings, communicate in styles that are both erudite and understandable, appeal to both the head and the heart, and continue to make a global impact. Yet despite these similarities as well as Keller's own deep appreciation for Lewis's work, a straight-line analogy might conceal more than it reveals. The comparison proves more instructive if some significant contrasts are also underscored.

Lewis was a literature professor who taught at Oxford and Cambridge. Undoubtedly, his vocation and setting in the academy were formative in how he approached apologetics. Lewis's writings include a wide range of genres and, for the most part, were first envisioned and formulated as writing projects or lectures.[3] In short, Lewis was an author and a don.

Tim Keller is a pastor, and he is quick to remind people of this. He is certainly an apologist and a writer, but he is, foremost, a pastor. Keller, unlike Lewis, is not writing imaginative novels or spending his days tutoring students in the finer elements of medieval literature. Keller's major books were all written in the later

---

1. Lisa Miller, "The Smart Shepherd," *Newsweek*, February 9, 2008, http://www.newsweek.com/smart-shepherd-93595.

2. Anthony Sacramone, "An Interview with Timothy Keller," First Things, February 25, 2008, https://www.firstthings.com/web-exclusives/2008/02/an-interview-with-timothy-kell. In this interview, Keller explains, "I don't even deserve to be mentioned in the same sentence as a writer like C.S. Lewis. And yet everybody's doing that, and I take it as a compliment, but it's pretty unjustified. However, he's the benchmark, so everybody's going to be compared."

3. Of course, *Mere Christianity* is an exception to this, as the content were first delivered as a series of radio addresses.

part of his pastorate and have been developed from the sermons and day-to-day conversations in his roughly thirty-year New York City ministry. As he himself says, "I'm just a practitioner."[4]

Indeed, "just" a practitioner who has read Charles Taylor's massive and—for many—impenetrable eight-hundred-page tome, *A Secular Age*, three times and regularly interjects references to high-level academics into the normal course of a conversation. Keller is no typical practitioner.[5] But he does have a point. His books are molded from within a pastor's study—where he also counselled congregants, lamented with grieving parents, celebrated over new converts, and prepared his weekly sermons. And this social context matters. The weekly formative duties and routines of any person should not be overlooked. In other words, Keller's vocational setting and self-identity should not be quickly bypassed to get to how he does it. Essential to understanding Keller's apologetic approach is to understand who he is (his story and his formative influences) and his ministry (his mission and his vocational identity).

HISTORICAL BACKGROUND

Timothy J. Keller was born in 1950 in Lehigh Valley, Pennsylvania. It was here where Keller grew up—about one hundred miles west of New York City and the metropolitan church he would later plant and pastor. He was raised in a traditional northeastern Protestant home and as a teenager went through two years of confirmation class at the Lutheran church he attended with his parents and two siblings. But as he left for Bucknell University, Keller describes himself as not feeling "very rooted in anything."[6] He transitioned to college in 1967 and felt the revolutionary moral changes that were occurring across American campuses in the 1960s and 70s.[7]

It was in the early part of the 1970s, through an InterVarsity Fellowship, that Keller came to faith. Keller went from being a "garden-variety nerd, filled with self-doubt and angst" to a true follower of Christ.[8] In his book *Encounters*

4. Timothy Keller, Interview by author, New York, December 11, 2017.
5. Timothy Keller, *Making Sense of God: An Invitation to the Skeptical* (New York: Viking, 2016); Timothy Keller, *Walking with God Through Pain and Suffering* (New York: Dutton, 2013).
6. Timothy Keller, "Life, Ministry, and Books with Tim Keller—Part 1: Life," Interview with Mark Dever, *9 Marks*, February 9, 2015, https://www.9marks.org/interview/life-ministry-and-books-with-tim-keller-part-1-life/.
7. "It was a big, big, big change right there. The sex in the rooms and the drugs and all that was a real departure ... [and] ... most of the administration and the faculty ... did think that there was some kind of real revolution going on." Ibid.
8. Joseph Hooper, "Tim Keller Wants to Save Your Yuppie Soul," *NYMag*, November 29, 2009, http://nymag.com/nymag/features/62374/index1.html.

with Jesus, Keller describes how he was thrust into leadership with InterVarsity Bible study groups even before he was quite sure where he stood with his own faith. As he led these studies, he explains, "I began to sense more than ever that the Bible was not an ordinary book. Yes, it carried the strange beauty of literature from the remote past; but there was something else. It was through these studies of encounters with Jesus that I began to sense an inexplicable life and power in the text. These conversations from centuries ago were uncannily relevant and incisive to *me—right now*. I began to search the Scriptures not just for intellectual stimulation but in order to find God."[9]

Amid the turmoil of the early seventies, Keller describes how his small fellowship of Christians attended Bucknell student strikes. The protests included a speaker's corner, and as Keller explains, "Our small group got radical at a certain point, and we put out a sign on the square. I still remember what it said, 'The resurrection of Jesus Christ is intellectually credible and existentially satisfying.'"[10] Here we see glimmers of Tim Keller the apologist emerging: "We sat at a booth because it was a free-for-all. . . . We had dozens and dozens of people right there at the quad just come by and talk to us about why Christianity is relevant to you and so on. The following September, 120 or 130 people showed up at our first meeting. Before that the average attendance had been 15."[11]

Later, as Keller became a prominent minister, he became known for graciously engaging with other traditions and incorporating insights from a variety of perspectives. It's this Lewisian perspective—which has been attractive to so many—that can be traced back to his early days at Bucknell's InterVarsity Fellowship, when he began to voraciously read theology and apologetics books, particularly works by C. S. Lewis and Francis Schaeffer. Schaeffer and Lewis proved pivotal for Keller's early apologetics and had an abiding influence, even though, as we will see, other thinkers would exert significant influence as Keller developed his approach.[12]

Keller explains how his early reading selections—during a time when evangelical scholarship in America was still largely dormant—had a long-term effect on him: "Up until about 1975 if you were a college educated evangelical in America you really had almost no American authors to read. . . . Everyone you read was British. . . . I must say the early books you read and the early stuff you

9. Timothy Keller, *Encounters with Jesus: Unexpected Answers to Life's Biggest Questions* (New York: Penguin, 2013), xvi.

10. Timothy Keller and James K. A. Smith, "Catechesis for a Secular Age: What if the Common Good Just Might Depend on Conversions?" *Comment* 35.3 (Fall 2017): 58.

11. Ibid., 58.

12. Keller, interview by author, 2017.

immerse yourself in creates a foundational layer that I'm not sure ever goes away, and so I'm not very American in my sensibilities."[13]

Keller alludes here to the fact that evangelicals in the UK are often less tribal, partly stemming from the impact of secularization that has encouraged interaction and teamwork among different Christian traditions. By depending so much on British authors in these early days of his Christian pilgrimage, he became a "little less sectarian," explaining in part why he doesn't "have a problem mixing it up with evangelicals from other traditions."[14]

An Unlikely Apologist

After graduating from Bucknell in 1972, Keller matriculated at Gordon-Conwell Theological Seminary in Boston, Massachusetts, to pursue a master of divinity. During his three years in Boston, he also began as an associate staff member with InterVarsity. While at Gordon-Conwell, Keller credits professors such as Richard Lovelace and Roger Nicole for their godly influence and instruction. He was also impacted by the homiletic approach of Edmund Clowney and the works of the Reformed theologian of the Great Awakening, Jonathan Edwards. Unusual as it might seem for someone now recognized as a leading Christian apologist, Keller did not invest heavily into learning apologetics during his time in seminary. Instead, this early training was dedicated to establishing a theological, biblical, and historical foundation for pastoral ministry, which would only later serve as a broader framework for his apologetics.

It was during seminary that he met Kathy, whom he married just before graduation in 1975. Kathy would impact Keller's apologetic approach in some significant ways. For one, Kathy was an avid reader of C. S. Lewis. As a young girl, she traded letters with the famous British author, and her love for Lewis seems to have spurred on her husband's appreciation for his work. Tim and Kathy also have formally collaborated on three books, though Kathy has served as a sounding board during many of his writing projects.[15]

At the age of twenty-five, Keller moved to Hopewell, Virginia, a rural town south of Richmond, to pastor West Hopewell Presbyterian Church. During this time, Keller also served as a director of church planting for the Presbyterian Church in America (PCA) and earned his doctor of ministry at Westminster (1979–1982). In the course of nine years of serving at West Hopewell, Keller had the responsibilities that accompany a typical pastor in a rural town: counseling, organizing, preaching three times weekly, performing weddings, officiating

---

13. Keller, "Part 1: Life," interview with Mark Dever, 2015.
14. Ibid.
15. Sacramone, "An Interview with Timothy Keller," 2008; Timothy Keller, interview with author, 2017.

funerals, and visiting with families. This was not a large church, where tasks could be divided up and left to specialists in different areas; he had to be a jack-of-all-trades.

During his years in Hopewell, Keller spent little to no time in apologetics. In this rural town in the 1970s and 80s, most people confessed some kind of Christian belief. Most of his older congregants had never attended high school, and a fair number of them were illiterate. Few could have identified this as a training ground for one of late modern's leading apologists. But then again, upon closer inspection, this turns out to have been just the type of formative experience that was essential in shaping Keller as a pastor-apologist.

Later, Keller would become known for his holistic approach to ministry and persuasion. We see the roots of this emphasis in his early formative days, laboring in Hopewell and learning from his congregants about practical mercy ministry: "If you just set them loose on a family that had some kind of practical problem, some family that was in need, they needed childcare, and they needed training, some—they just knew what to do. And so I was forced to get interested in the deeds side of how a church cared for its members and, to some degree, for its neighbors . . . when I showed up there I had no concept of it."[16]

In 1984 the Kellers moved to Philadelphia for Tim to serve as an associate professor of practical theology and director of the Doctor of Ministry program at Westminster Theological Seminary. During this time he and Kathy became involved in urban ministry, and he served as the director of Mercy Ministries for the PCA.

In 1989, now with three boys, the Kellers made the transition to Manhattan, New York, to plant Redeemer Presbyterian Church. The idea to plant a church in New York City was first initiated by Keller's denomination, and Keller was asked to help select the lead pastor for the new church. After his first two choices declined, Keller accepted the position himself. "I just felt it would be cowardly of me not to," he explains, "But we had a kind of 'sick in the pit of our stomach' feeling every day."[17] The first service in April 1989 had about seventy-five people in attendance, but by the fall of the same year, the church was holding two weekly Sunday services of up to 250 people.[18] Upon Keller's retirement from the pastorate in 2017, Redeemer had eight Sunday services with over five thousand in attendance.[19]

---

16. Keller, "Part 1: Life," interview with Mark Dever, 2015.
17. Hooper, "Tim Keller Wants to Save Your Yuppie Soul."
18. Ibid.
19. Kate Shellnutt, "Tim Keller Stepping Down as Redeemer Senior Pastor," *Christianity Today*, February 26, 2017, http://www.christianitytoday.com/news/2017/february/tim-keller-stepping-down-nyc-redeemer-senior-pastor.html.

After a fifteen-year hiatus from apologetics—at least from it occupying the forefront of his mind—church-planting in New York City forced Keller to return to apologetics afresh.[20] Again, considering his current reputation as an apologist, this large gap will likely surprise many. And yet, as we have already suggested, it seems this unconventional path uniquely prepared him for his success as an apologist.

Keller had long been an avid reader and possessed a keen intellect, along with a remarkable memory. Studying at Gordon-Conwell, pastoring in a rural setting, and then leading a practical ministry program at Westminster were all seedbeds that helped foster several apologetic distinctives. First, his background equipped him with a firm theological base that had been honed for practical ministry. In serving as a pastor in Hopewell, preaching over 1,500 sermons in nine years and tending to the everyday trials and concerns of his congregants, Keller developed as an applied theologian, learning how to appeal to both the head and the heart. Second, Keller's apologetic books display a keen sensitivity to others and a high level of emotional intelligence, which must surely be due in some measure to his years in pastoral ministry. Third, Keller's ministry has also balanced apologetic arguments with "embodied apologetics." This refers to a Christian community that is consistent with the emphasis in the New Testament (for example, consider 1 Peter), embodying a type of apologetic by the way it serves and cares for those around it. This emphasis was not only born out of his pastoral ministry in Hopewell but also his leadership in mercy ministries while teaching in Philadelphia.

As Keller began his new church in New York, to his surprise, he discovered that there were far more skeptics in Redeemer's regular worship services than he had seen in churches in other parts of the country. He estimated that 15 to 20 percent of his Sunday audiences were nonbelievers, and many of them were eager to talk one-on-one. He also began to be invited to present Christianity on university campuses in New York City, such as Columbia, New York University, and Juilliard. Practical necessity had propelled Keller back to apologetics.

Along with his background in Lewis and Schaeffer, in the early nineties, Keller engaged with the works of contemporary philosophers such as Alvin Plantinga, Nicholas Wolterstorff, and George Mavrodes.[21] Appropriating Christian academics for nonspecialists along with the writings of C. S. Lewis were both important for his day-to-day apologetic and eventually for his book *The Reason for God.*

---

20. "My apologetics and evangelism interest from college just kind of went to sleep and it wasn't until I came here in '89 that suddenly I realized, yeah, I can do this. So, I kind of lost my interest in it." Keller, interview with author, 2017.

21. Keller, interview with author, 2017.

APOLOGETIC METHODOLOGY AND RESPONSE

THE REASON FOR GOD: APOLOGETICS
MOLDED BY MINISTRY IN THE CITY

With the *New York Times* bestseller *The Reason for God*, Tim Keller emerged on the national map as a Christian apologist.[22] And yet, for those who knew Keller personally, the success of the book was no surprise. *The Reason for God* was an extension of years of teaching and evangelism in New York City. He worked on the book for six years, mostly during summers and vacations. The idea was encouraged by people in his church who had come from non-Christian backgrounds asking for him to make his teaching, which had helped them justify their beliefs, more readily available to family and friends. He had avoided writing books at the beginning of his ministry because he had found himself evolving, but as he reached his fifties, he decided it was time to put some of his teachings into print. His patience also meant he had plenty of material to draw on.[23]

Keller refers to *The Reason for God* as his more traditional apologetic. It is arranged into two general sections. Part one offers responses to seven common reasons people reject Christianity. The responses display an understanding of the underlying concerns behind these objections. He often asks the reader to consider how they might be approaching Christianity with overly narrow cultural assumptions, and in doing so, he uses Western culture's own disdain of ethnocentrism to open the door for deeper reflection on the Christian doctrine in question. After all, if God is God, he transcends culture and will challenge different cultures at different points. The aim of this first section is to clear away the common objections so readers will be willing to consider the case for Christianity in the second section of the book.

Part two builds a positive case for Christianity using historical evidence, logic, science, sociology, philosophy, and theology. Keller is careful to set the stage by emphasizing the limits to such arguments. He is not trying to "prove" Christianity in the traditional, hardline sense of the term. Instead, Keller proposes that, analogous to scientific theories, Christianity can be tested by contrasting it with its chief rivals to see whether it offers the best account for what we see in the world. Summarizing arguments by such contemporary thinkers as Alvin Plantinga, Francis Collins, and N. T. Wright, as well as older luminaries such as Søren Kierkegaard, Flannery O'Connor, and of course C. S. Lewis, Keller not only builds a case for Christianity but also explains how the gospel

---

22. Timothy Keller, *The Reason for God: Belief in an Age of Skepticism* (New York: Dutton, 2008).
23. Sacramone, "An Interview with Timothy Keller," 2008.

makes sense of the world. Again, Keller's pastoral sensitivity and winsome tone contribute to the book's appeal.

Even though *The Reason for God* is often compared to Lewis's *Mere Christianity*, Keller has explained a key difference. On the one hand,

> Lewis definitely lived at a time in which people were more certain across the board that empirical, straight-line rationality was the way you decided what truth was, and there's just not as much of a certainty now. Also, when Lewis was writing, people were able to follow sustained arguments that had a number of points that built on one another. I guess I should say we actually have a kind of rationality-attention-deficit disorder now. You can make a reasonable argument, you can use logic, but it really has to be relatively transparent. You have to get to your point pretty quickly.[24]

On the other hand, he explains that in his modern context in New York City,

> These are pretty smart people, very educated people, but even by the mid-nineties I had found . . . *Mere Christianity* . . . didn't keep their attention, because they really couldn't follow the arguments. They took too long. This long chain of syllogistic reasoning wasn't something that they were trained in doing. I don't think they're irrational, they are as rational [as people in Lewis' context], but they want something of a mixture of logic and personal appeal. . . . One of the reasons I started doing this was I thought I needed something that gave them shorter, simpler, more accessible arguments.[25]

In Keller's explanation, his contextual approach to apologetics is evident. He is not simply theorizing about apologetics for hypothetical people, but rather, his apologetic is built for the real people he interacts with daily in his own context. For Keller, non-Christians are "not abstractions, they're either Greek non-Christians, or Jewish non-Christians, or Buddhist non-Christians or something. And so, apologetics is automatically contextualization."[26]

WHEN "REASON" ISN'T ENOUGH

Despite the popularity of *The Reason for God*, Keller did not rest on his apologetic laurels. Two things caused Keller to develop another layer to his apologetic. First, ministry caused him to further consider how to interact with those

---

24. Ibid.
25. Ibid.
26. Keller, interview with author, 2017.

uninterested in the type of arguments found in *The Reason for God*. Through a series of outreach events his church hosted for nonbelievers, Keller realized that while *The Reason for God* and its general approach proved effective for non-Christians who were already interested in Christianity, it was less persuasive for those who were more skeptical.[27] So Keller started working on how to engage the more cynical by interacting with functional beliefs—baseline assumptions concerning essential aspects of life, such as meaning, value, purpose, and morality. Second, in the early 2010s, an additional group of authors influenced his apologetic. Heading up the list was Charles Taylor and his *A Secular Age*, which Keller refers to as "one of the most important books I have ever read in my life."[28] Both of these events led him to write *Making Sense of God*, which Keller refers to as his prequel to *The Reason for God*.

Where do you begin with someone who believes Christianity is irrelevant, "Which is, after all, why religion is dying out" or, even worse, believes organized religion is suppressive—"Just look at religion's track record"? Offering purpose and fulfillment through religion can seem pretty strange to the late twenty-something Wall Street broker who has quickly risen up through the ranks of the Manhattan meritocracy—"My life is pretty good, thank you." Christian morality feels stifling to the modern hedonist seeking self-actualization; arguments designed for the head can seem pretty lame when modern idols have captivated the heart. If you are interacting with a secular humanist whose cultural plausibility structures make Christianity seem *prima facie* irrational, childish, and exploitive, you will be lucky to get a passing glance if you lead off by listing evidences for the resurrection or offering logical syllogisms in support of a Creator.[29]

For these reasons, Keller recognizes the need to challenge what traditional apologetics has often failed to sufficiently address: the culture that tacitly provides a grid of plausibility and cultivates hearts toward a vision of the "good." This modern "social imaginary" works under the radar of most people's intellectual reflections—making Christianity less plausible. The "social imaginary" itself needs to be challenged. In his book *Preaching*, Keller foreshadowed an approach that is on display in *Making Sense of God* by emphasizing the need to expand how Christian apologetics is undertaken: "Secularity is not simply

---

27. Ibid.

28. Ibid. Keller also mentioned the impact of Alasdair MacIntyre, Jonathan Haidt, and Phillip Rieff in his intellectual development.

29. *Cultural plausibility structure* is a term coined by Peter Berger and corresponds with what a variety of authors from different fields of study describe as the inherited assumptions about the world that people take for granted, the "preunderstandings" or the "tacit knowledge," or what Charles Taylor refers to as the "modern social imaginary." Peter L. Berger and Thomas Luckmann, *The Social Construction of Reality: A Treatise in the Sociology of Knowledge* (1966; repr., New York: Anchor, 1967); Charles Taylor, *A Secular Age* (Cambridge: Harvard University Press, 2007).

an absence of belief. Christians often accept this claim and respond by getting out their proofs and other rational bona fides. Not so fast. . . . Secularism is its own web of beliefs that should be open to examination."[30] For more traditional apologetic appeals to receive a serious hearing, Keller first comes alongside his secular readers, helping them articulate their own beliefs and assumptions. The first step is to help them see that they indeed have faith—beliefs not provable by simple logic or empirical observation.

MAKING SENSE OF GOD: THE NEED TO START FURTHER BACK

In the first section of *Making Sense of God*, Keller sets out to expose what Charles Taylor refers to as a "subtraction story" of late modernism.[31] In this story, secularism is what happens when the religious myths of the past are negated and the neutral facts about the world are left to be discovered through science and reason. The emergence of this enlightened society, as the story is often told, will lead to a less religious world and one that is more just and free. This is the secular coming-of-age narrative Keller ventures to unmask. Using a variety of sources, Keller outlines what has been a surprising development to many theorists who first predicted the fall of religion with increased modernization. Broadly speaking, conservative religious faith seems to be growing.

Next, Keller argues that "every person embraces his own worldview for a variety of rational, emotional, cultural, and social factors."[32] Lest Keller should be misunderstood, he is not trying to create some kind of "neutral" field for apologetic arguments to be played out on. Instead, following the philosopher Alasdair MacIntyre, the philosopher-scientist Michael Polanyi, as well as a host of other thinkers (and it's safe to say, intuitions from his Reformed tradition), Keller denies there are any "'standards of truth and rational justification' that are independent and can be used to judge all viewpoints, because any standards you come up with will come from and already assume one of these worldviews and therefore the wrongness of all the others."[33]

Keller levels the field so the modern secularist is not allowed to get away with assuming they are just using common sense and reason to come to conclusions. We all—religious and irreligious—assume fiduciary frameworks, which our reasoning operates within. Keller stresses the impossibility of anyone being

---

30. Timothy Keller, *Preaching: Communicating Faith in an Age of Skepticism* (New York: Penguin, 2015), 126.

31. Because *Making Sense of God* departs from more traditional approaches to apologetics, we have reserved more space in this section to provide a fuller explanation.

32. Timothy Keller, *Making Sense of God: An Invitation to the Skeptical* (New York: Viking, 2016), 4.

33. Ibid., 280.

able to *just look at the facts* while also trying to deflate the false caricature of religion as simply resting on blind faith.[34] Both the religious and the irreligious embrace their worldview for both objective and subjective reasons. We all use "reason" and "faith," so religious beliefs can't be written off so quickly.

After Keller alerts readers of their own assumptions and the inescapabilty of some kind of "faith," part two proceeds to make a case for Christianity. But his approach does not start from some kind of theoretical or logical ground floor that can be built upon, one brick of logic at a time, to prove Christianity. In the footnotes, Keller argues that when someone is evaluating the classical proofs for God, these rational judgments are not happening in a vacuum, sealed off from various traditions of rationality that must be assumed when making critical evaluations. This means that simply starting with classical apologetic proofs and assuming "they either work or they don't" takes for granted a universal *agreement* concerning frameworks for rationality that does not exist.[35]

In an important footnote, which provides a peek into the philosophical framework behind his approach, Keller outlines Alasdair MacIntyre's proposal for *respecting* how philosophical and moral traditions provide different frameworks for rationality *without giving up* on the prospect of converting someone from a rival worldview.

> First they must 'come to understand what it is to think in the terms prescribed by that particular rival tradition.' They must do everything they can to sympathetically put themselves in the shoes of the other viewpoint. . . . Second, in both their own worldview and the one they are assessing, they should identify 'unresolved issues and unsolved problems—unresolved and unsolved *by the standards of that tradition*.' One kind of problem is inconsistency, so that some beliefs of the worldview contradict others. Another kind of problem is unlivability, so that some beliefs are impossible for the bearer to actually practice.[36]

A crucial step in identifying unlivable and inconsistent beliefs is "when adherents of one worldview are found smuggling in ideas and values from other worldviews in order to deal with their own tradition's contradictions and inconsistencies."[37] This is the metaapproach of *Making Sense of God*. Modern

34. Derek Rishmawy, host, "With Tim Keller, on 'Making Sense of God,'" *Mere Fidelity*, podcast audio, December 13, 2016, https://mere orthodoxy.com/mere-fidelity-tim-keller-making-sense-god/.
35. Keller, *Making Sense of God*, 280.
36. Ibid.
37. Ibid.

secularists claim a set of beliefs that are inconsistent and unlivable. Thus, and normally unwittingly, they have to borrow from Christianity, which supports the conclusion that Christianity makes better "emotional, cultural, and rational" sense than its chief Western rival. [38]

This philosophical framework for his approach is most fully articulated in the footnotes, while in the main body of his work, Keller first affirms the human search for meaning, satisfaction, freedom, identity, morality, and hope and then deconstructs how each of these essential aspects of the human experience are undermined by secular assumptions and better explained by Christianity.

Outlining how Keller addresses the subject of identity in chapters six and seven, as just one example, further illuminates his overall approach. Keller explains that identity formation is normally invisibly pushed on us by the cultures we inhabit. In traditional cultures, sense of self is developed as individuals assume roles in family and community. Conversely, in the West, we are taught to be "true to yourself," "not to worry about what anyone thinks," and "detach and leave to find your own way." The hero story that is absorbed through the popular imagination is one of self-assertion rather than the ancient story of self-sacrifice.

While the modern identity has major problems that Keller will challenge, he first affirms aspects of the culture's aspirations. In traditional societies, social status was tethered to hierarchal orders with little hope for advancement. People were to "know their place," and those on the lower end of the social stratus were often exploited. Today Western individualism challenges this hierarchal and oppressive order; most of us could not imagine a "good" society today functioning in any other way. In other words, the development of the modern identity carries with it some advancements and aspirations that our theology (e.g., humans made in the image of God and *agape*) calls on us to affirm.

And yet, Keller shows this new view of identity ultimately cannot deliver what it promises. It is (1) *incoherent* because the modern self is supposed to be built on personal desires, but our internal desires often contradict each other, change, and are elusive. It is (2) *illusory* in that we cannot help but care about what others think. "No one can affirm or bless themselves."[39] Someone else has to affirm our worth. It is (3) *crushing* because our quest to create our own identity, prove our significance, and be validated will often result in overwhelming anxiety and stress. And finally, modern identity is (4) *fracturing*, as relationships and community are undermined when other people are treated instrumentaly for achieving our own personal actualization. Keller has stepped into the

---

38. Ibid., 281.
39. Ibid., 134.

late-modern view of identity, explained it, and then deconstructed it to show that it cannot ultimately stand.

Next he turns to show how Christianity better fits with our deepest aspirations and leads to human flourishing. Instead of primarily looking outward (traditional views) or inward (new view), Christianity calls us to look upward to God for our identity. What matters ultimately is what God thinks, and his approval cannot be earned; this is an identity that must be received. Here Keller asks the reader to "imagine" and "consider" what it would be like to believe in the gospel and embrace the promises Jesus made—unconditional acceptance and living a life full of meaning and service to others out of a love for God. Keller asks the nonbeliever, who now sees the problems of their current cultural approach to identity, to imagine how Christ would change their life:

> Now, for example, you pursue a career not to get a self and achieve self-worth. You do it to serve God and the common good. Your work is still part of your identity, as are your family, your nationality, and so on. But they are all relieved of the terrible burden of being the ultimate source of yourself and value. They no longer can distort your life as they do when they are forced into that role. . . . Work is no longer something you use desperately to feel good about yourself. It becomes just another good gift from God that you can use to serve others.[40]

His argument, which space constrains us from fully tracing out, goes on to explain how the modern self establishes identity by exclusion of others (think, for example, of identity politics). Christianity, in contrast, offers a unique identity that enables people to live in peace with each other: "To forgive and embrace, rather than exclude or subjugate, requires a self-image that does strengthen itself through drawing such contrasts."[41] This requires, paradoxically, both radical humility and an undergirding confidence, which is available only at the cross of Christ. Accepting that the Son died for your sins leads to profound humility (it was my sins that required such a sacrifice) and confidence (he died for me). In contrast to self-assertion, Christianity thus provides the resources for forgiveness, reconciliation, and stable self.

This example of how he compares the Christian view on identity with its secular counterpart serves to illustrate Keller's approach throughout these core chapters:

---

40. Ibid., 137–38.
41. Ibid., 146.

1. Articulate late-modern cultural aspirations and values
2. Affirm elements that overlap with Christianity
3. Point out where the secular position is inconsistent, undermines its deepest aspiration, and is unlivable
4. Explain how Christianity offers a more consistent, livable, and rational way to live

Part three surveys arguments for the reasonableness of Christianity—the case for God (chapter 11) and Jesus (chapter 12)—what he calls the thirty-thousand feet view of the positive case for faith. This section functions as a compressed version of *The Reason for God*, which even though was written prior to *Making Sense of God*, functions as a sequel logically. Due to the summary of *The Reason for God* in the previous section, there is little need to rehearse his approach in these final chapters. One way to put this is that part one and part two of *Making Sense of God* argue that Christianity makes more "emotional and cultural sense," while part 3, or in its more expanded form *The Reason for God*, makes the rational case for Christianity.

OTHER RELEVANT BOOKS

In addition to his two general apologetic works, *The Reason for God* and *Making Sense of God*, Keller has written several other books that either function apologetically or train Christians how to engage with nonbelievers. In view of space constraints, only a brief summary of each book can be included here.

The Prodigal God

In a secular culture, part of the role of apologetics is to clear up misunderstandings and clarify the central message of the gospel. In *The Prodigal God*, using the biblical story of the prodigal son, Keller explains "the essentials of the Christian message" as an "introduction to the Christian faith for those who are unfamiliar with its teachings or who may have been away from it for some time."[42]

Counterfeit Gods

In *Counterfeit Gods*, Keller takes aim at the idols that have led to what Alexis de Tocqueville referred to as a "strange melancholy" found in America. Following the theology of Saint Augustine, *Counterfeit Gods* observes how this

---

42. Timothy Keller, *The Prodigal God: Recovering the Heart of the Christian Faith* (New York: Riverhead, 2008), xi.

deep despair and unrest is palpable in the West and points readers to the "only Lord who, if you find him, can truly fulfill you, and if you fail him can truly forgive you."[43]

Center Church

Center Church is the only textbook Keller has written. The book, undergirded by a theological vision, serves as a practical guide for ministry. "Part 3: Gospel Contextualization" develops a biblical approach to contextualization and instructs readers how to interact with the skeptical assumptions of late moderns.

Walking with God through Pain and Suffering

The first part of *Walking with God through Pain and Suffering* serves as a defense of and case for experiential and logical rationality for the Christian understanding of evil and suffering. By first exploring the phenomenon of suffering, Keller outlines the various ways different cultures—both ancient and modern—have understood and sought to live with the universal experience of pain. Christianity, he argues, offers the best resource to live with suffering. Moreover, incorporating what philosophers refer to as "skeptical theism" but perhaps more aptly labeled "humble theism,"[44] Keller argues that if one assumes the God of the Bible exists, it is consistent to conclude that humans are not epistemologically in a position to understand most of the reasons God allows suffering.

Encounters with Jesus

Encounters with Jesus began as two sets of apologetic talks. The first half began as a series of talks delivered in 2012 in Oxford Town Hall in Oxford, England, to a group of students, most of whom were skeptical about Christianity. The second half of the book is based on a series Keller taught at the Harvard Club of New York City, in which he addressed a group of city leaders. In *Encounters with Jesus*, Keller surveys the biblical accounts in which Jesus is in conversations concerning key universal, fundamental questions of life and displays the relevance of Jesus's life and teaching to modern aspirations.

Preaching

While *Preaching* does not focus on apologetics, chapters 4 ("Preaching Christ to Culture") and 5 ("Preaching and the [Late] Modern Mind") outline

---

43. Timothy Keller, *Counterfeit Gods: The Empty Promises of Money, Sex, and Power and the Only Hope that Matters* (New York: Penguin, 2009), xxiv.

44. Stephen Wykstra, "A Skeptical Theist View," in *God and the Problem of Evil: Five Views*, eds. Chad Meister and James K. Dew Jr. (Downers Grove, IL: InterVarsity Press, 2017), 111.

how to do apologetics from the pulpit. Both chapters are filled with practical instructions as well as a guide to the implications of Charles Taylor's *A Secular Age* for apologetic preaching.

CONTRIBUTIONS TO THE FIELD OF APOLOGETICS

THE PASTOR APOLOGIST PAR EXCELLENCE

Keller's teaching and writings are chock-full of examples from culture, literature, intellectuals, and popular periodicals. A leading apologist, well-known in his own right, once commented to me in an aside, "I don't know how Keller has been able to read and retain that much. It's amazing." Considering that Keller has spent his career as a minister, with all the responsibilities and demands that come with planting and leading a church, his encyclopedic endnotes are a testimony to his disciplined reading schedule, deep learning, and sharp memory. Yet it is not just that Keller is intelligent. He is also perceptive and wise, known widely for his sensitivity to context and his pastoral intuitions. By learning to contextualize to the features of his Manhattan community, Keller has honed the ability to encapsulate the most incisive and relevant points of high-level thinkers and translate them in the service of conversations, sermons, and books. And he does this while avoiding arid intellectualism that challenges only ideas, because as he often emphasizes, people "change not by merely changing their thinking but by changing what they love most. Such a shift requires nothing *less* than changing their thinking, but it entails more."[45]

LEADING A WORLDWIDE MOVEMENT

In 2017 Keller stepped down from the pastorate but remains the pastor emeritus at Redeemer Presbyterian Church and functions as a "teacher-trainer" for church leaders.[46] His focus in ministry is to build a movement of Reformed evangelical churches in the major cities of the world. With this goal at the fore, he continues to serve as the vice president of the Gospel Coalition, "a fellowship of evangelical churches in the Reformed tradition deeply committed to renewing our faith in the gospel of Christ and to reforming our ministry practices to conform fully to the Scriptures."[47] He also founded and serves as the chairman of the board for Redeemer City to City, a leadership development organization,

45. Ibid., 159.
46. Shellnutt, "Tim Keller Stepping Down as Redeemer Senior Pastor."
47. "Foundation Documents," The Gospel Coalition, https://www.thegospelcoalition.org/about/foundation-documents/.

"to help leaders build gospel movements in cities."[48] At the time this chapter was written, City to City had helped start 632 churches in 75 cities across the world. In addition to providing leadership to these organizations, Keller concentrates on writing books needed to train and do ministry in the major cities of the world, helping "church planters give people a vision" for ministry and serving readers well beyond his immediate reach.[49]

FROM MILAN TO MANHATTAN

In the opening of this chapter, we suggested that while the common comparison with C. S. Lewis is understandable, it can cloud one's perception of Tim Keller if the two are not also contrasted. If a historical analogy is to be made that corresponds to Keller's vocation and setting, perhaps a better fit is Ambrose, the bishop who contextualized sermons for the intellectually sophisticated city of Milan and profoundly impacted the prodigious young Augustine.[50]

With characteristics mirroring Keller, Augustine recounts Ambrose's reputation for service to others, deep learning, being a voracious reader, and his eloquence as a preacher. "At Milan I came to Bishop Ambrose, who had a worldwide reputation, was a devout servant of yours and a man whose eloquence in those days gave abundantly. . . . Often when we came to him . . . we found him reading. . . ." And when he listened to him preach, before Augustine was converted, he recounts how Ambrose's teaching impacted him,

> Together with the language, which I admired, the subject matter also, to which I was indifferent, began to enter into my mind. Indeed I could not separate the one from the other. And as I opened my heart in order to recognize how eloquently he was speaking it occurred to me at the same time (though this idea came gradually) how truly he was speaking. First I began to see that the points which he made were capable of being defended. . . . it now appeared to me that this faith could be maintained on reasonable grounds.[51]

One can easily imagine a modern Manhattanite describing Keller in such terms.

Yet Ambrose is best known for serving as an exemplar and a pastoral influence for Augustine, the most important theologian in the Western tradition.

48. "About," Redeemer City to City, https://www.redeemercitytocity.com/about/.
49. Timothy Keller, "Life, Ministry, and Books with Tim Keller—Part 2," interview with Mark Dever, 2015.
50. Thanks to James K. A. Smith for bringing this comparison to my attention.
51. Augustine, *Confessions* 5.13.23, 5.14.24.

What can we say about Keller's lasting legacy? Wisdom calls for patience before trying to articulate all it will entail, for Keller's story is not yet finished. Nevertheless, it very well could be that if a vibrant movement of Reformed evangelical churches arise in the world's major cities with pastors leading as apologists in the coming years, the church will be praising the Lord for raising up Timothy Keller as the exemplary pastor-apologist who forged the way. And who knows, maybe—just maybe—another epoch-shaping leader will emerge, first convinced by Keller that "this faith could be maintained on reasonable grounds."[52]

BIBLIOGRAPHY

"About." Redeemer City to City. https://www.redeemercitytocity.com/about/.

Berger, Peter L., and Thomas Luckmann. *The Social Construction of Reality: A Treatise in the Sociology of Knowledge.* 1966. Repr., New York: Anchor, 1967.

"Foundation Documents." The Gospel Coalition. https://www.thegospelcoalition.org /about/foundation -documents/.

Hooper, Joseph. "Tim Keller Wants to Save Your Yuppie Soul." *NYMag.* November 29, 2009. http://nymag .com/nymag/features/62374/index1.html.

Keller, Timothy. *Center Church: Doing Balanced, Gospel Centered Ministry in Your City.* Grand Rapids: Zondervan, 2012.

———. *Counterfeit Gods: The Empty Promises of Money, Sex, and Power and the Only Hope that Matters.* New York: Penguin, 2009.

———. *Encounters with Jesus: Unexpected Answers to Life's Biggest Questions.* New York: Penguin, 2013.

———. Interview with Joshua Chatraw. Personal interview. New York, December 11, 2017.

———. "Life, Ministry, and Books with Tim Keller—Part 1: Life." Interview with Mark Dever. *9 Marks.* February 9, 2015. https://www.9marks.org/interview/life-ministry-and-books-with-tim-keller-part-1-life/.

———. "Life, Ministry, and Books with Tim Keller—Part 2: Ministry." Interview with Mark Dever. *9 Marks.* February 17, 2015. https://www.9marks.org/interview/life-ministry-and-books-with-tim -keller-part-2-ministry/.

———. *Making Sense of God: An Invitation to the Skeptical.* New York: Viking, 2016.

———. *Preaching: Communicating Faith in an Age of Skepticism.* New York: Penguin, 2015.

———. *The Prodigal God: Recovering the Heart of the Christian Faith.* New York: Riverhead, 2008.

———. *The Reason for God: Belief in an Age of Skepticism.* New York: Dutton, 2008.

———. *Walking with God Through Pain and Suffering.* New York: Dutton, 2013.

Keller, Timothy, and James K. A. Smith. "Catechesis for a Secular Age: What if the Common Good Just Might Depend on Conversions?" *Comment* 35.3 (Fall 2017): 54–61.

Miller, Lisa. "The Smart Shepherd." *Newsweek.* February 9, 2008. http://www.newsweek.com/smart -shepherd-93595.

Rishmawy, Derek. "With Tim Keller, on 'Making Sense of God.'" *Mere Fidelity.* Podcast audio, December 13, 2016. https://mere orthodoxy.com/mere-fidelity-tim-keller-making-sense-god/.

Sacramone, Anthony. "An Interview with Timothy Keller." *First Things.* February 25, 2008. https://www .firstthings.com/web-exclusives/2008/02/an-interview-with-timothy-kell.

Shellnutt, Kate. "Tim Keller Stepping Down as Redeemer Senior Pastor." *Christianity Today.* February 26, 2017. http://www.christianitytoday.com/news/2017/february/tim-keller-stepping-down-nyc -redeemer-senior-pastor.html.

Taylor, Charles. *A Secular Age.* Cambridge: Harvard University Press, 2007.

Wykstra, Stephen. "A Skeptical Theist View." Chapter 5 in Kindle edition of *God and the Problem of Evil: Five Views.* Ed. by Chad Meister and James K. Dew Jr. Downers Grove, IL: InterVarsity Press, 2017.

---

52. Ibid.

SUBJECT INDEX

A Legacy of Preaching, Volume One

Apostles to the Revivalists

A Legacy of Preaching, Volume Two

Enlightenment to the
Present Day

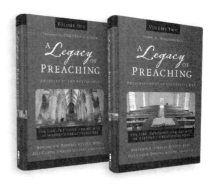

A Legacy of Preaching explores the history and development of preaching through a biographical and theological examination of its most important preachers. Instead of teaching the history of preaching from the perspective of movements and eras, each contributor tells the story of a particular preacher in history, allowing the preachers from the past to come alive and instruct us through their lives, theologies, and methods of preaching.

Each chapter introduces readers to a key figure in the history of preaching, followed by an analysis of the theological views that shaped their preaching, their methodology of sermon preparation and delivery, and an appraisal of the significant contributions they have made to the history of preaching. This diverse collection of familiar and lesser-known individuals provides a detailed and fascinating look at what it has meant to communicate the gospel over the past two thousand years. By looking at how the gospel has been communicated over time and across different cultures, pastors, scholars, and homiletics students can enrich their own understanding and practice of preaching for application today.

Volume One covers the period from the apostles to the Puritans and profiles thirty preachers, including Paul, Origen of Alexandria, Augustine of Hippo, Francis of Assisi, Martin Luther, Jonathan Edwards, John Wesley, George Whitefield, and more.

Volume Two covers the period from the Enlightenment to the present day and profiles thirty-one preachers, including Charles Haddon Spurgeon, Karl Barth, John Stott, Martin Luther King Jr., Billy Graham, and more.

ZONDERVAN
ACADEMIC